商品归类及申报要素速查手册（汉英、英汉对照）

HANDBOOK FOR CUSTOMS CLASSIFICATION AND DECLARATION REQUIREMENTS

(CHINESE-ENGLISH & ENGLISH-CHINESE)

王　雯◎著

WRITED BY WANG WEN

中国海关出版社

CHINA CUSTOMS PRESS

图书在版编目（CIP）数据

商品归类及申报要素速查手册/王雯著．—北京：中国海关出版社，2010.7

ISBN 978-7-80165-756-5

Ⅰ.①商…　Ⅱ.①王…　Ⅲ.①商品-分类-手册　Ⅳ.①F760.2-62

中国版本图书馆 CIP 数据核字（2010）第 126263 号

商品归类及申报要素速查手册

SHANGPIN GUILEI JI SHENBAO YAOSU SUCHA SHOUCE

作　　者：王　雯
责任编辑：沈楚铃
助理编辑：冯　伟　刘　贞
出版发行：中国海关出版社
社　　址：北京市朝阳区东四环南路甲 1 号　　邮政编码：100023
网　　址：www.hgcbs.com.cn　www.hgbookvip.com
编 辑 部：01065194242-7532（电话）　01065194231（传真）
发 行 部：01065194242-7540/42/44/45（电话）　01065194233（传真）
社办书店：01065195616（电话）　01065195127（传真）
北京市建国门内大街 6 号海关总署东配楼一层
印　　刷：北京市白帆印务有限公司　　经　　销：新华书店
开　　本：880mm×1230mm　1/16
印　　张：58.25　　字　　数：1800 千字
版　　次：2010 年 7 月第 1 版
印　　次：2010 年 7 月第 1 次印刷
书　　号：ISBN 978-7-80165-756-5
定　　价：300.00 元

前　　言

《商品归类及申报要素速查手册》是一本根据商品名称关键字快速查找商品编码的工具书。

随着国际贸易的发展和政府管理的需要，商品分类技术在19世纪中期就已经出现，20世纪初期出现了国际公认的商品分类统计目录。发展到今天，由海关合作理事会（1995年更名为世界海关组织）编制的《商品名称及编码协调制度》（以下简称HS）已经成为最权威的商品分类目录，被200多个国家和地区使用。联合国统计署、世界贸易组织等国际组织均以HS为政策制定和实施的基础工具。世界海关组织将HS称为“国际贸易的语言”，作为缔约方海关税则的基本框架。

商品编码是海关进出口管理的基础工具，是实施税率计征、贸易管制、加工贸易管理、出口退税、商品检验等管理措施的载体，商品编码承载了国家对进出口商品各项管理政策的信息，是海关管理中重点关注的事项。

法律规定，正确申报商品编码是进出口经营单位的法定义务。然而，由于商品归类工作具有规则性强、技术特征明显、条文复杂等原因，一直是进出口企业申报的难点。错误申报商品编码将导致漏征税款及违反国家进出口管制措施，给国家和进出口企业带来损失。

作者根据多年来从事商品归类工作的经验，试图以一种简便的思路解决目前存在的难题，使进出口企业能够通过便捷的查询方式得到正确的商品分类编码信息，避免因商品归类差错而引发的行政复议、诉讼等后续法律问题。

《商品归类及申报要素速查手册》将进出口商品的品名按照关键词排序，并通过逐级确定修饰语、限定语缩小商品范围，读者可据此查到相应的商品编码。该方法简单直接、快速有效，适合所有层面的使用者，即使是没有任何进出口商品分类经验的读者，也能很快掌握查询的方法。本书分汉英、英汉两大部分，并针对海关的管理要求，添加了主要的申报要素，为读者填报商品信息提供参考。

另外，我们还计划在本书的基础上，引入商品的分类层级，出版《简明商品归类法》。《简明商品归类法》将商品按照税则的层级分成大类，逐渐细分类别，然后配合词条索引，确定商品编码。这种分类方法较本书复杂，但可查询商品的范围更广、准确性更高，对于专门从事进出口商品归类的读者将是一本得力的工具书。

本书选取的关键词参考了以往商品申报的统计信息，可能与部分读者对商品的理解存在差异，遇有此问题，请读者尝试其他关键词。同时为了方便检索，本书将一些商品名称中的“其他”要素置于商品名称末尾，如“百合，其他”，意指除种用百合以外的其他百合。

本书按照现行海关法规编写，为简便起见，申报要素采用了代码的方式进行编写（见“申报要素代码表”），读者可自行进行对照，权威申报要素的规定请以海关总署发布的最新内容为准。

本书为初次出版，内容繁多，可能存在差错，请读者指正。

作　者

2010年6月

Preface

"Handbook for customs classification and declaration requirements" is a book by which readers can find the commodity classification code quickly.

With the development of trade and manage needs of government authorities, commodity classification has set up in the mid-19th century. Then the International Convention on Commodity classification and statistics established in the early 20th century. By this time, "Commodity Description and Coding System" (Compiled by Customs cooperation council, which renamed the World Customs Organization in 1995. as the HS) has become the most authoritative nomenclature, which has been applied in more than 200 countries and regions. The international organizations, such as United Nations Statistics Department, WTO, all take the HS as the basis platform for policy formulation and implementation. World Customs Organization entitles the HS as "the language of international trade", and carry on it as the basic framework for customs of contracting parties.

Import and export commodity classification is based instrument for Customs and other government authorities to implement duty collection, trade controls, bonding trade management, tax refund, commodity inspection and relative measures. Classification codes carry the administrative policy information of national importation and exportation, and have been fundamentally concerned in Customs administration.

Importer and export have been legally obliged to declare the correct commodity classification. But the classification is still a tough task for them to apply legal text accurately owing to the complexity of classification rules and comprehensive technical features. Incorrecting classification declaration will result in violation of state levied taxes regulations and import and export control provisions, and brings loss for state revenue and for import and export enterprises.

With many years of working experience on the customs classification, the author is trying to find an effective approach to help import and export enterprises solve the classification difficulties and to aim to get an efficiency guidance of classification, so that they can avoid the legal issues such as administrative review, litigation raised by the incorrect declaration classification of commodities.

This book arranges commodities description by keywords and attributive words based on both Chinese and English literal habits. Product Codes come out eventually by limiting the scope with adding attributive words gradually. The method is understandable and effective, which is suitable for all levels of users. Readers without any experience on classification can quickly grasp and make use of it. Taking readers' declaration need into account, this book also attaches declaration requirements information in the main body according to the Customs management regulation.

"Shortcut for commodity classification" will be published in succession. That book will introduce classification method with systematic categories. With the commodity categories expanding according to the tariff schedule, the classification code will be found with entry index. That book will be more complicated than this book, but it can broaden inquiries with high accuracy. Specialized readers will have another effective tool on commodity classification.

The keywords are selected from former declaration statistical data. They may have difference with a few readers' understanding in some case. And readers can change other keywords for new tries. For the sake of brevity, the book use abbreviation for declaration requirements. In addition to mention, the "nes" of Commodity Description is commonly put on the last place. Such as "lily, nes", which meas lilies not elsewhere specified other than lilies of seedlings.

This book is compiled with the present version of customs regulations. The declaration elements are descrided in numbers for convieniece (see The Abbreviation for Declaration Requirements). In case of policy changes, readers are requested to refer the latest version published by General Administration of Customs. This book is a debut publication which may have some mistakes or omissions. Suggestion for improvements will be gratefully received.

Author

June, 2010

申报要素代码表
The Abbreviation for Declaration Requirements

代码 Abbreviation	申报要素	Declaration Requirements
1	状态或外观	Status or appearance
2	品牌或型号	Brand or specification
3	用途或通用性	Usage or versatility
4	工艺或来源	Process or source
5	式样或种类	Form or type
6	成分或含量（包括材质）	Composition or content（including materials）
7	原理或功能	Principle or function
8	重量或体积（包括尺寸）	Weight or volume（including size）
9	其他	Other

目　　录

Contents

汉英对照

Chinese—English

English—Chinese

英汉对照

汉英对照

Chinese—English

A

商品名称	Article Description	税则号列	申报要素①
a			
阿芬太尼(INN)以及盐	Alfentanil(INN);salts thereof	2933.3300	36
阿拉伯胶	Gum arabic	1301.2000	3
阿拉伯裤,非针织或钩编的,男式,合成纤维制	Arabian trousers,not knitted or crocheted,for men or boys,of synthetic fibres	6203.4310	2456
阿拉伯裤,非针织或钩编的,男式,棉制	Arabian trousers,not knitted or crocheted,for men or boys,of cotton	6203.4210	2456
阿拉伯裤,非针织或钩编的,男式,其他纺织材料制	Arabian trousers,not knitted or crocheted,for men or boys,of other textile material	6203.4910	2456
阿拉伯袍,非针织或钩编的,男式,化学纤维制	Arabian robes, not knitted or crocheted, for men or boys,of man-made fibres	6211.3310	2456
阿拉伯袍,非针织或钩编的,男式,棉制	Arabian robes, not knitted or crocheted, for men or boys,of cotton	6211.3210	2456
阿洛巴比妥(INN)以及盐	Allobarbital (INN);salts thereof	2933.5300	36
阿米雷司(INN)及盐	Aminorex(INN);salts thereof	2934.9100	36
阿尼利定(INN)以及盐	Anileridine(INN);salts thereof	2933.3300	36
阿普唑仑(INN)以及盐	Alprazolam (INN);salts thereof	2933.9100	36
阿斯匹林	Acetylsalicylic acid	2918.2210	36
阿魏	Asafoetida	1301.9030	
阿月浑子果(开心果)	Pistachios	0802.5000	134
ai			
埃托啡 (INN) 及盐	Etorphine(INN) and salts	2939.1100	34
艾克辛	Ecaussine	2515.2000	148
艾氏剂(ISO)	Aldrin (ISO)	2903.5200	36
艾司唑仑(INN)以及盐	Estazolam (INN);salts thereof	2933.9100	36
an			
安瓿	Ampoules	7010.1000	8
安非拉酮以及它们的盐	Amfepramone (INN) and salts thereof	2922.3100	36
安非他明(INN)以及它们的盐	Amfetamine (INN),salts thereof	2921.4600	36
安乃近	Analgin	2933.1920	36
安全别针,钢铁制的	Safety pins,of iron or steel	7319.2000	
安全带	Life-belts	6307.2000	346
安全刀片,包括未分开的刀片条	Safety razor blades, including razor blade blanks in strips	8212.2000	256
安全导火索	Safety fuses	3603.0000	
安全阀	Safety valves	8481.4000	

① 本栏所列为主要申报要素,权威申报要素以海关总署发布的相关规定为准。

A

商品名称	Article Description	税则号列	申报要素
安全帽	Safety headgear	6506.1000	26
安全设备,电气的,道路的	Safety electrical equipment for roads	8530.8000	
安全设备,电气的,电车道的	Safety electrical equipment for tramways	8530.1000	
安全设备,电气的,港口的	Safety electrical equipment for port installations	8530.8000	
安全设备,电气的,机场的	Safety electrical equipment for airfields	8530.8000	
安全设备,电气的,内河航道的	Safety electrical equipment for inland waterways	8530.8000	
安全设备,电气的,铁道的	Safety electrical equipment for railways	8530.1000	
安全设备,电气的,停车场的	Safety electrical equipment for parking facilities	8530.8000	
安全设备的零件	Safety electrical equipment parts	8530.9000	3
安全设备及其零件,机械的,道路用	Safety equipment and parts, for roads	8608.0090	3
安全设备及其零件,机械的,电车道用	Safety equipment and parts, for tramways	8608.0090	3
安全设备及其零件,机械的,港口用	Safety equipment and parts, for port installations	8608.0090	3
安全设备及其零件,机械的,机场用	Safety equipment and parts, for airfields	8608.0090	3
安全设备及其零件,机械的,内河航道用	Safety equipment and parts, for inland water-ways	8608.0090	3
安全设备及其零件,机械的,铁道用	Safety equipment and parts, for railways	8608.0090	3
安全设备及其零件,机械的,停车场用	Safety equipment and parts, for parking facilities	8608.0090	3
安替比林及其衍生物	Antipyrin and its derivatives	2933.1100	36
安装玻璃用油灰	Glaziers' putty	3214.1090	3
桉叶油	Essential oils of eucalyptus	3301.2960	34
氨,水溶液的	Ammonia, in aqueous solution	2814.2000	6
氨,无水的	Ammonia, anhydrous	2814.1000	6
氨苄青霉素	Ampicillin	2941.1011	
氨苄青霉素及其盐,其他	Ampicillin and its salts, nes	2941.1019	
氨苄青霉素三水酸	Ampicillin trihydrate	2941.1012	
氨苄青霉素药品,混合或未混合的,配定剂量或制成零售包装	Ampicillin medicaments, mixed or unmixed, put up in measured doses or in forms or packings for retail sale	3004.1011	368
氨苄青霉素药品,两种或两种以上成分混合而成的,未配定剂量或制成零售包装	Ampicillin medicaments, consisting of two or more constituents which have been mixed together, not put up in measured doses or in forms or packings for retail sale	3003.1011	368
氨茶碱及其衍生物以及它们的盐,其他	Aminophylline (theophylline-ethylenediamine) and their derivatives; salts thereof, nes	2939.5900	34
氨基醇(但含有一种以上含氧基的除外)及其醚和酯,以及它们的盐,其他	Amino-alcohols, other than those containing more than one kind of oxygen function, their ethers and esters; salts thereof, nes	2922.1990	36
氨基醇酚	Amino-alcohol-phenols	2922.5000	36
氨基酚(但含有一种以上含氧基的除外)及其醚和酯,以及它们的盐,其他	Amino-phenols, other than those containing more than one kind of oxygen function, their ethers and esters; salts thereof, nes	2922.2990	36
氨基钾	Potassium amide	2853.0090	

商品名称	Article Description	税则号列	申报要素
氨基醌,但含有一种以上含氧基的除外,以及它们的盐,其他	Amino-quinones, other than those containing more than one kind of oxygen function; salts thereof, nes	2922.3900	36
氨基钠	Sodamide	2853.0090	
氨基萘酚(但含有一种以上含氧基的除外)及其醚和酯,以及它们的盐,其他	Amino-naphthols, other than those containing more than one kind of oxygen function, their ethers and esters; salts thereof, nes	2922.2990	36
氨基脲	Semicarbazide	2928.0000	36
氨基羟基萘磺酸及其盐	Aminohydroxynaphthalenesulphonic acid and their salts	2922.2100	36
氨基醛,但含有一种以上含氧基的除外,以及它们的盐,其他	Amino-aldehydes, other than those containing more than one kind of oxygen function; salts thereof, nes	2922.3900	36
氨基树脂,初级形状的,其他	Amino-resins, in primary forms, nes	3909.3090	1256
氨基酸,其他	Amino acids, nes	2922.4910	36
氨基酸酚	Amino-acidphenols	2922.5000	36
氨基酸及其酯,但含有一种以上含氧基的除外,以及它们的盐,其他	Amino-acids, other than those containing more than one kind of oxygen function, and their esters; salts thereof, nes	2922.4999	36
氨基酸衍生物(用作激素)	Amino-acid derivatives(as hormones)	2937.4000	36
氨基酮,但含有一种以上含氧基的除外,以及它们的盐,其他	Amino-ketones, other than those containing more than one kind of oxygen function; salts thereof, nes	2922.3900	36
氨纶弹性单纱,未加捻或捻度每米不超过50转,非供零售用	Polyurethane elastomeric single yarn, untwisted or with a twist not exceeding 50 turns per metre, not put up for retail sale	5402.4410	3468
氨纶多股纱线或缆线,非供零售用	Polyurethane multiple or cabled yarn, not put up for retail sale	5402.6920	3468
氨水	Ammonia, in aqueous solution	2814.2000	6
鹌鹑,改良种用	Quail, pure-bred breeding	0106.3910	34
鹌鹑,食用	Quail, for human consumption	0106.3929	34
鞍具,适合各种动物用,各种材料制成的	Saddlery for any animal, of any material	4201.0000	1458
鞍褥,适合各种动物用	Saddle cloths for any animal, of any material	4201.0000	1458
鞍座,摩托车(包括机器脚踏两用车)用	Saddles, of motorcycles (including mopeds)	8714.1100	3
鞍座,自行车及脚踏车	Saddles, of bicycles and other cycles	8714.9500	3
铵的碳酸盐,其他	Ammonium carbonates, nes	2836.9940	
按摩器具	Massage apparatus	9019.1010	
ao			
凹版印刷机	Gravure printing machinery	8443.1700	57
奥步生及类似式样的手织装饰毯	Aubusson type hand-woven tapestries	5805.0090	468
奥沙西泮(INN)以及盐	Oxazepam(INN); salts thereof	2933.9100	36

B

B

商品名称	Article Description	税则号列	申报要素
ba			
八氟异丁烯	Isobutylene octafluoride	2903. 3910	36
八角茴香	Seeds of badian	0909. 1010	
八音盒	Musical boxes	9208. 1000	5
巴巴苏棕榈果油及其分离品,初榨的	Babassu oil and fractions thereof, crude oil	1513. 2100	4
巴巴苏棕榈果油及其分离品,其他	Babassu oil and fractions thereof, nes	1513. 2900	4
巴比土酸及其盐	Barbituric acid and its salts	2933. 5200	36
巴比土酸衍生物以及它们的盐,其他	Barbituric acid derivatives; salts thereof, nes	2933. 5400	36
巴比妥(INN)以及盐	Barbital (INN); salts thereof	2933. 5300	36
巴旦杏,去壳	Almonds, shelled	0802. 1200	134
巴旦杏,未去壳	Almonds, in shell	0802. 1100	134
巴拉圭茶	Paraguay tea	0903. 0000	
巴拉塔胶	Balata gums	4001. 3000	12
巴厘纱,玻璃纤维制	Voiles, of glass fibres	7019. 3200	56
巴西果,去壳	Brazil nuts, shelled	0801. 2200	134
巴西果,未去壳	Brazil nuts, in shell	0801. 2100	134
芭蕉,鲜或干的	Plantains, fresh or dried	0803. 0000	1245
拔管机,冷拔的,300 吨及以下,金属或金属陶瓷用,非切削	Drawing tube benches, cold drawing, with 300t or less, for working metal or cermets, without removing material	8463. 1011	7
拔管机,冷拔的,金属或金属陶瓷用,非切削,其他	Drawing tube benches, cold drawing, for working metal or cermets, without removing material, nes	8463. 1019	7
拔丝机,金属或金属陶瓷用,非切削	Drawing machines for wire, for working metal or cermets, without removing material	8463. 1020	7
拔丝机,金属或金属陶瓷用,非切削	Wire drawing machines, for working metal or cermets, without removing material	8463. 1020	7
拔桩机	Pile-extractors	8430. 1000	5
拔桩机零件	Pile-extractors parts	8431. 4990	3
钯,板、片	Palladium, plates and sheets	7110. 2910	46
钯,其他	Palladium, nes	7110. 2990	46
钯,未锻造或粉末状	Palladium, unwrought or in powder form	7110. 2100	46
bai			
白安矿	Cervantite	2617. 1090	146
白蛋白,卵清蛋白,干的	Albumin from egg, dried	3502. 1100	13
白蛋白,卵清蛋白,其他	Albumin from egg, nes	3502. 1900	13
白蛋白,乳白蛋白,包括两种或两种以上的乳清蛋白浓缩物	Albumin from milk, including concentrates of two or more whey proteins	3502. 2000	13

商品名称	Article Description	税则号列	申报要素
白蛋白盐	Albuminates	3502.9000	13
白蛋白衍生物,其他	Albumin derivatives, nes	3502.9000	13
白垩	Chalk	2509.0000	
白果	Gingko nuts	0802.9020	134
白酒	Spirits, chinese distilled	2208.9020	2468
白蜡	Chinese wax	1521.9090	
白兰地酒	Brandy	2208.2000	2468
白磷	Phosphorus, white	2804.7010	6
白榴石	Leucite	2529.3000	13
白蘑菇,盐水的,暂时保藏,但不适合直接使用的	White mushroom, in brine, provisionally preserved, but unsuitable in that state for immediate consumption	0711.5112	34
白柠檬油	Essential oils of lime	3301.1910	34
白铅矿	Cerussite	2607.0000	146
白巧克力	White chocolate	1704.9000	258
白阮化汞	Mercury albuminate	2852.0000	
白芍	Radix paeoniae lactiflorae	1211.9021	34
白术	Rhizoma atractylodis macrocephalae	1211.9025	34
白水泥,不论是否人工着色	White cement, whether or not artificially coloured	2523.2100	3
白铁剪及类似工具	Metal cutting shears and similar tools, hand tools	8203.3000	256
白铜	Cupronickel	7403.2900	146
白钨矿	Scheelite	2611.0000	146
白细胞三烯及其衍生物和结构类似物	Leukotrienes, their derivatives and structural analogues	2937.5000	36
白香肠,有天然肠衣	White puddings, with a natural casing	1601.0010	348
白药	Bai yao	3004.9053	368
白云石,夯混	Dolomite ramming mix	2518.3000	14
白云石,未煅烧或烧结的	Dolomite, not calcinecd or sintered	2518.1000	14
白云石,已煅烧或烧结的	Dolomite, calcined or sintered dolomite	2518.2000	14
百合,其他	Lily, nes	0602.9094	
百合,种用	Lily, seedlings	0602.9091	3
百合花,鲜的,制花束或装饰用的	Lily, fresh, suitable for bouquets or for ornamental purposes	0603.1910	34
百合球茎,其他,休眠的	Lily corms, dormant, nes	0601.1029	135
百合球茎,种用,休眠的	Lily corms, dormant, seed	0601.1021	135
百科全书及其连续出版的分册	Encyclopaedias, and serial instalments thereof	4901.9100	15
百里酚蓝	Thymol blue	2934.9910	36
百里香酚	Thymol	2907.1990	36
百叶窗(包括威尼斯式百叶窗)或类似制品及其零件,塑料的	Blinds (including venetian blinds) and similar articles and parts thereof, of plastics	3925.3000	23

B

商品名称	Article Description	税则号列	申报要素
百叶窗扇,包括风机,本身装有一个输出功率不超过125瓦的电动机	Repeating front louver fan, with a self-contained electric motor of an output not exceeding 125W	8414.5130	23
百音盒	Musical boxes	9208.1000	5
百音盒的机械装置	Mechanisms for musical boxes	9209.9920	3
ban			
扳手及扳钳,手动,固定的	Spanners and wrenches, hand-operated, non-adjustable	8204.1100	256
扳手及扳钳,手动,可调的	Spanners and wrenches, hand-operated, adjustable	8204.1200	256
扳手套筒,可互换的,不论是否带手柄	Spanner sockets, interchangeable, with or without handles, hand tools	8204.2000	256
斑点叉尾鮰鱼,制作或保藏的,整条或切块,但未绞碎	Channel catfish (ictalurus punctatus), prepared or preserved, whole or in pieces, but not minced	1604.1931	48
斑蝥	Cantharides	0510.0040	14
斑铜矿	Bornite (erubescite)	2603.0000	146
斑岩	Porphyry	2516.9000	148
搬运机器,自动的,集成电路工厂用的	Handling machines, automated, solely or principally of a kind used in the electronic integrated circuits factories	8486.4031	7
板及类似品,用水泥、石膏及其他矿物粘合材料粘合植物纤维、稻草、刨花、木片屑、木粉、锯末或木废料制成	Boards and similar articles of vegetable fibre, of straw or of shavings, chips, particles, sawdust or other waste, of wood, agglomerated with cement, plaster or other mineral binders	6808.0000	456
板,硬质合金制,以焊剂涂面或以焊剂为芯,用于焊接或沉积金属、硬质合金	Plates, of metal carbides, coated or cored with flux material, of a kind used for soldering, brazing, welding or deposition of metal or of metal carbides	8311.9000	56
板,超过0.2毫米的箔,铅制	Plates, foil exceeding 0.2mm, of lead	7804.1900	16
板、杆、角材、型材、异型材、管子及类似品,结构体用,钢铁的,已加工	Plates, rods, angles, shapes, sections, tubes and the like, prepared for use in structures, of iron or steel, worked	7308.9000	6
板、片、带,非海绵橡胶制	Plates, sheets and strip of non-cellular rubber	4008.2100	18
板、片、带,海绵橡胶制	Plates, sheets and strip of cellular rubber	4008.1100	18
板、片、带、箔,非合金镍制	Plates, sheets, strip and foil, of nickel, not alloyed	7506.1000	46
板、片、带、箔,镍合金制	Plates, sheets, strip and foil, of nickel alloys	7506.2000	46
板、片、带、箔,钛的,厚度不超过0.8毫米	Plates, sheets, strap, foil, of titanium, of a thickness not more than 0.8mm	8108.9031	16
板、片、带、箔,钛的,厚度超过0.8毫米	Plates, sheets, strap, foil, of titanium, of a thickness more than 0.8mm	8108.9032	16
板、片、带、箔,锌的	Plates, sheets, strip and foil, of zinc	7905.0000	16
板、片及带,非合金铝制,矩形(包括正方形),铝厚度超过0.2毫米,其他	Plates, sheets and strip, of aluminium, not alloyed, rectangular (including square), of a thickness exceeding 0.2mm, nes	7606.1190	246

商品名称	Article Description	税则号列	申报要素
板、片及带,非合金铝制,矩形(包括正方形),厚度在0.30毫米及以上,但不超过0.36毫米	Plates, sheets and strip, of aluminium, not alloyed, rectangular(including square), of a thickness of 0.30mm or more but not exceeding 0.36mm	7606.1120	246
板、片及带,非合金铝制,铝厚度超过0.2毫米,其他	Plates, sheets and strip, of aluminium, not alloyed, of a thickness exceeding 0.2mm, nes	7606.9100	246
板、片及带,厚度超过0.2毫米,锡制	Plates, sheets and strip, of a thickness exceeding 0.2mm, of tin	8007.0020	16
板、片及带,精炼铜制,厚度超过0.15毫米,其他	Plates, sheets and strip, of refined copper, of a thickness exceeding 0.15mm, nes	7409.1900	16
板、片及带,精炼铜制,盘卷的,厚度超过0.15毫米,含氧量不超过10PPM的	Plates, sheets and strip, of refined copper, in coils, of a thickness exceeding 0.15mm, containing oxygen not exceeding 10PPM	7409.1110	16
板、片及带,精炼铜制,盘卷的,厚度超过0.15毫米,其他	Plates, sheets and strip, of refined copper, in coils, of a thickness exceeding 0.15mm, nes	7409.1190	16
板、片及带,铝合金制,矩形(包括正方形),铝厚度超过0.2毫米,其他	Plates, sheets and strip, of aluminium alloys, rectangular(including square), of a thickness exceeding 0.2mm, nes	7606.1290	246
板、片及带,铝合金制,矩形(包括正方形),厚度小于0.28毫米,铝厚度超过0.2毫米	Plates, sheets and strip, of aluminium alloys, rectangular(including square), of a thickness less than 0.28mm, of a thickness exceeding 0.2mm	7606.1220	246
板、片及带,铝合金制,矩形(包括正方形),厚度在0.28毫米及以上,但不超过0.35毫米	Plates, sheets and strip, of aluminium alloys, rectangular(including square), of a thickness of 0.28mm or more but not exceeding 0.35mm	7606.1230	246
板、片及带,铝合金制,矩形(包括正方形),厚度在0.35毫米以上,但不超过4毫米	Plates, sheets and strip, of aluminium alloys, rectangular(including square), of a thickness more than 0.35mm but not exceeding 4mm	7606.1250	246
板、片及带,铝合金制,铝厚度超过0.2毫米,其他	Plates, sheets and strip, of aluminium alloys, of a thickness exceeding 0.2mm, nes	7606.9200	246
板、片及带,镍锌合金(德银)制,厚度超过0.15毫米,	Plates, sheets and strip, of copper-nickel-zinc base alloys (nickel silver), of a thickness exceeding 0.15mm	7409.4000	16
板、片及带,其他铜合金制厚度超过0.15毫米,	Plates, sheets and strip, of other copper alloys, of a thickness exceeding 0.15mm	7409.9000	16
板、片及带,铜镍合金(白铜),厚度超过0.15毫米,	Plates, sheets and strip, of copper-nickel base alloys (cupronickel), of a thickness exceeding 0.15mm	7409.4000	16
板、片及带,铜锡合金(青铜)制,厚度超过0.15毫米,其他	Plates, sheets and strip, of copper-tin base alloys (bronze), of a thickness exceeding 0.15mm, nes	7409.3900	16
板、片及带,铜锡合金(青铜)制,盘卷的厚度超过0.15毫米,	Plates, sheets and strip, of copper-tin base alloys (bronze), in coils, of a thickness exceeding 0.15mm	7409.3100	16
板、片及带,铜锌合金(黄铜)制,厚度超过0.15毫米,其他	Plates, sheets and strip, of copper-zinc base alloys (brass), of a thickness exceeding 0.15mm, nes	7409.2900	16

B

商品名称	Article Description	税则号列	申报要素
板、片及带，铜锌合金（黄铜）制，盘卷的，厚度超过0.15毫米，	Plates, sheets and strip, of copper-zinc base alloys (brass), in coils, of a thickness exceeding 0.15mm	7409.2100	16
板材冷轧机	Sheet mills, cold-rolled	8455.2210	7
板材热轧机	Sheet mills, hot-rolled	8455.2110	7
板带横剪机，加工金属用，其他	Shearing transverse, for working metal, nes	8462.3920	7
板带横剪机，数控的，加工金属用	Shearing transverse, numerically controlled, for working metal	8462.3120	7
板带纵剪机，加工金属用，其他	Shearing lengthwise, for working metal, nes	8462.3910	7
板带纵剪机，数控的，加工金属用	Shearing lengthwise, numerically controlled, for working metal	8462.3110	7
板栗	Chestnuts	0802.4010	134
板坯连铸机	Ingot slab continuous casting machines	8454.3022	
板钛矿	Brookite	2614.0000	146
板岩	Slate	2514.0000	
板岩的制品	Slate articles	6803.0010	4
板岩的制品，粘聚的	Slate articles, agglomerated	6803.0090	4
办公室或学校用品，塑料的	Plastic articles, for office or school supplies	3926.1000	236
办公室用机器，其他	Office machines, nes	8472.9090	
办公室用机器的零件、附件，其他	Office machines' parts and accessories, nes	8473.4090	3
办公用具，贱金属制，办公室家具除外	Office or desk equipment, of base metal, other than office furniture	8304.0000	256
办公用品，其他，贱金属制	Office articles, of base metal, nes	8305.9000	256
半导体晶片或器件用测试或检验仪器及装置	Semiconductor wafers or devices measuring or checking instruments and apparatus	9030.8200	
半导体开关元件，但光敏器件除外	Thyristors, other than photosensitive devices	8541.3000	5
半导体媒体，未录制，其他	Semiconductor media, unrecorded, nes	8523.5910	37
半导体媒体，已录制，其他	Semiconductor media, recorded, nes	8523.5920	37
半导体模块，具有变流功能的	Semiconductor modules with converting function	8504.4091	
半导体器件，其他	Semiconductor devices, nes	8541.5000	5
半导体器件封装材料	Encapsulation material for semiconductor devices	3214.1010	3
半导体器件零件	Semiconductor devices parts	8541.9000	3
半发酵茶，内包装每件净重不超过3千克，其他	Partly fermented tea, in immediate packings of a content not exceeding 3kg, nes	0902.3090	248
半发酵茶，其他	Partly fermented tea, nes	0902.4090	248
半化学浆，从回收（废碎）纸或纸板提取的	Semi-chemical pulp, derived from recovered (waste and scrap) paper or paperboard	4706.9300	46
半精米或精米，其他	Semimilled or wholly milled rice, nes	1006.3090	35
半乳糖	Galactose	2940.0000	6
半缩醛，不论是否含有其他含氧基，及其卤化、磺化、硝化或亚硝化衍生物	Hemiacetals, whether or not with other oxygen function, and their haogenated, sulphonated, nitrated or nitrosated derivatives	2911.0000	36
半夏	Rhizoma pinelliae	1211.9019	34

商品名称	Article Description	税则号列	申报要素
bang			
棒糖,冰的	Lollipops, iced	2105.0000	28
bao			
包、袋或信封的制造机器,纸浆、纸或纸板制的	Machines for making bags, sacks or envelopes, of paper pulp, paper or paperboard	8441.2000	
包缝机	Overlock machines	8452.2120	
包贵金属表壳	Precious metal clad watch cases	9111.1000	6
包馅面食,其他,不论是否烹煮或经其他方法制作	Pasta, stuffed, nes, whether or not cooked or otherwise prepared	1902.2000	46
包心生菜,鲜或冷藏的	Head lettuce, fresh or chilled	0705.1100	1
包扎用绳,聚乙烯或聚丙烯制	Binder or baler twine, of polyethylene or polypropylene	5607.4100	368
包扎用绳,西沙尔麻或其他纺织用龙舌兰类纤维制	Binder or baler twine, of sisal or other textile fibres of the genus agave	5607.2100	368
包装板条箱,木制的	Crates packings, of wood	4415.1000	56
包装袋,黄麻或其他韧皮纺织纤维制	Sacks and bags, for packing, of jute or of other textile bast fibres	6305.1000	346
包装袋,棉制	Sacks and bags, for packing, of cotton	6305.2000	346
包装袋,其他,聚乙烯、聚丙烯扁条或类似材料制	Sacks and bags, for packing, of polyethylene or polypropylene strip or the like	6305.3300	346
包装袋,其他纺织材料制	Sacks and bags, for packing, of other textile materials	6305.9000	346
包装袋,其他化学纤维材料制	Sacks and bags, for packing, of man-made textile materials, nes	6305.3900	346
包装盒,木制的	Boxes packings, of wood	4415.1000	56
包装或打包机器,其他	Packing or wrapping machinery, nes	8422.4000	
包装机,瓶、罐、箱、袋或其他容器的	Packing machines, for bottles, cans, boxes, bags or other containers	8422.3030	
包装机零件	Packing machines parts	8422.9090	
包装容器,纸制的,其他	Packing containers, of paper, nes	4819.5000	68
包装箱,木制的	Cases packings, of wood	4415.1000	56
包装圆桶及类似的包装容器,木制的	Drums and similar packing containers, of wood	4415.1000	56
包装纸,亚硫酸盐浆的,未经涂布的	Wrapping paper, sulphite, uncoated	4805.3000	458
刨床,加工木材、软木、骨、硬质橡胶、硬质塑料或类似硬质材料的	Planing machines, for working wood, cork, bone, hard rubber, hard plastics or similar hard materials	8465.9200	7
刨床,龙门式,切削金属或金属陶瓷用	Planing machines, double column, for removing metal or cermets	8461.9011	7
刨床,切削金属或金属陶瓷用,其他	Planing machines, for removing metal or cermets, nes	8461.9019	7
刨子,木工用	Planes, for working wood	8205.3000	256
胞嘧啶	Cytosine	2933.5910	36
宝石(钻石除外)或半宝石,加工的,其他	Precious stones (other than diamonds) and semi-precious stones, worked, nes	7103.9990	145

B

商品名称	Article Description	税则号列	申报要素
宝石(钻石除外)或半宝石,未加工或经简单锯开或粗制成形	Precious stones (other than diamonds) and semi-precious stones, unworked or simply sawn or roughly shaped	7103.1000	145
宝石或半宝石,合成或再造的,工业用,其他	Precious or semiprecious stones, synthetic or reconstructed, for technical use, nes	7104.9019	145
宝石或半宝石,合成或再造的,其他	Precious or semiprecious stones, synthetic or reconstructed, nes	7104.9099	145
宝石或半宝石,合成或再造的,未加工或经简单锯开或粗制成形,其他	Precious or semiprecious stones, synthetic or reconstructed, unworked or simply sawn or roughly shaped, nes	7104.2090	145
宝石或半宝石的粉末,天然或合成的其他	Precious or semi-precious stones dust and powder, natural or synthetic, nes	7105.9000	145
宝石轴承,钟、表的	Jewel bearings, of clock or watch	9114.2000	6
饱和无环一元羧酸及其酸酐、酰卤化物、过氧化物和过氧酸以及它们的卤化、磺化、硝化或亚硝化衍生物,其他	Saturated acyclic monocarboxylic acids and their anhydrides, halides, peroxides and peroxyacids; their halogenated, sulphonated, nitrated or nitrosated derivatives, nes	2915.9000	36
饱和一元醇,其他	Saturated monohydric alcohols, nes	2905.1990	36
保管箱,保险库用,带锁,贱金属制	Safe deposit lockers for strong rooms, of base metal	8303.0000	256
保龄球	Bowling balls	9504.9022	
保龄球瓶	Bowling pins	9504.9023	
保龄球自动分瓶机	Bowling pin distributing machines, automatic	9504.9021	
保龄球自动球道设备及器具,其他	Bowling alley equipments and appliances, automatic, nes	9504.9029	5
保温瓶,带壳的	Vacuum flasks, complete with case	9617.0010	
保温瓶或其他保温容器用的玻璃胆	Glass inners for vacuum flasks or for other vacuum vessels	7020.0091	6
保险杠及其零件	Bumpers and parts thereof	8708.1000	3
保险柜,装甲或加强的,贱金属制	Strong boxes, armoured or reinforced, of base metal	8303.0000	256
保险库的门,贱金属制	Strong boxes doors, of base metal	8303.0000	256
保险箱,装甲或加强的,贱金属制	Safes, armoured or reinforced, of base metal	8303.0000	256
报纸、杂志及期刊,每周至少出版四次	Newspapers, journals and periodicals, appearing at least four times a week	4902.1000	
报纸、杂志及期刊,其他	Newspapers, journals and periodicals, nes	4902.9000	
抱子甘蓝,鲜或冷藏的	Brussels sprouts, fresh or chilled	0704.2000	1
鲍鱼,冻、干、盐腌或盐渍的	Abalone, frozen, dried, salted or in brine	0307.9910	14
鲍鱼,活、鲜或冷的	Abalone, live, fresh or chilled	0307.9191	1
爆竹	Fireworks	3604.1000	
曝光表	Exposure meters	9027.8091	
曝光装置及设备,自动将已冲洗胶卷曝光到成卷感光纸上的,彩色胶卷用	Exposing apparatus and equipment, automatically, for developed film to rolls of photographic paper, for the colour photographic film in rolls	9010.1091	7

商品名称	Article Description	税则号列	申报要素
曝光装置及设备,自动将已冲洗胶卷曝光到成卷感光纸上的,电影用	Exposing apparatus and equipment, automatically, for developed film to rolls of photographic paper, of a kind used in cinematographic film	9010. 1010	7
曝光装置及设备,自动将已冲洗胶卷曝光到成卷感光纸上的,其他	Exposing apparatus and equipment, automatically, for developed film to rolls of photographic paper, nes	9010. 1099	7
曝光装置及设备,自动将已冲洗胶卷曝光到成卷感光纸上的,特种照相用	Exposing apparatus and equipment, automatically, for developed film to rolls of photographic paper, of a kind used in special photographic film or paper	9010. 1020	7
bei			
碑石或建筑用石及其制品,简单切削或锯开并具有一个平面的,其他	Monumental or building stone and articles thereof, simply cut or sawn, with a flat or even surface, nes	6802. 2990	3468
碑用或建筑用石,其他	Monumental or building stone, nes	2516. 9000	148
碑用或建筑用石,石灰质,其他	Monumental or building stone, ecaussine and other calcareous, nes	2515. 2000	148
北方长额虾,冻的	Northem pandalus(pandalus), frozen	0306. 1312	18
贝母	Bulbs fritillariae thunbergii	1211. 9017	34
贝母,药用	Fritillaria, used in pharmacy	1211. 9017	34
背心,针织或钩编的,丝及绢丝制	Vests, knitted or crocheted, of silk or silk waste	6109. 9010	2456
背心,针织或钩编的,棉制	Vests, knitted or crocheted, of cotton	6109. 1000	2456
背心,针织或钩编的,其他	Vests, knitted or crocheted, nes	6109. 9090	2456
背心及类似品,针织或钩编的,化学纤维制	Waistcoats and similar articles, knitted or crocheted, of man-made fibres	6110. 3000	2456
背心及类似品,针织或钩编的,喀什米尔山羊细毛制	Waistcoats and similar articles, knitted or crocheted, of kashmir(cashmere) goats	6110. 1200	2456
背心及类似品,针织或钩编的,毛制	Waistcoats and similar articles, knitted or crocheted, of wool	6110. 1100	2456
背心及类似品,针织或钩编的,棉制	Waistcoats and similar articles, knitted or crocheted, of cotton	6110. 2000	2456
背心及类似品,针织或钩编的,其他	Waistcoats and similar articles, knitted or crocheted, nes	6110. 9090	2456
背心及类似品,针织或钩编的,其他动物细毛制	Waistcoats and similar articles, knitted or crocheted, of fine animal hair	6110. 1990	2456
背心及类似品,针织或钩编的,其他山羊细毛制	Waistcoats and similar articles, knitted or crocheted, of other goats	6110. 1910	2456
背心及类似品,针织或钩编的,丝及绢丝制	Waistcoats and similar articles, knitted or crocheted, of silk or silk waste	6110. 9010	2456
背心及类似品,针织或钩编的,兔毛制	Waistcoats and similar articles, knitted or crocheted, of rabbit and hare	6110. 1920	2456
背心及其他内衣,非针织或钩编的,男式,化学纤维制	Singlets and other vests, not knitted or crocheted, for men or boys, of man-made fibres	6207. 9920	2456
背心及其他内衣,非针织或钩编的,男式,棉制	Singlets and other vests, not knitted or crocheted, for men or boys, of cotton	6207. 9100	2456

B

商品名称	Article Description	税则号列	申报要素
背心及其他内衣,非针织或钩编的,男式,其他	Singlets and other vests, not knitted or crocheted, for men or boys, nes	6207. 9990	2456
背心及其他内衣,非针织或钩编的,男式,丝及绢丝制	Singlets and other vests, not knitted or crocheted, for men or boys, of silk or silk waste	6207. 9910	2456
背心及其他内衣,非针织或钩编的,女式,化学纤维制	Singlets and other vests, not knitted or crocheted, for women or girls, of man-made fibres	6208. 9200	2456
背心及其他内衣,非针织或钩编的,女式,棉制	Singlets and other vests, not knitted or crocheted, for women or girls, of cotton	6208. 9100	2456
背心及其他内衣,非针织或钩编的,女式,其他	Singlets and other vests, not knitted or crocheted, for women or girls, nes	6208. 9990	2456
背心及其他内衣,非针织或钩编的,女式,丝及绢丝制	Singlets and other vests, not knitted or crocheted, for women or girls, of silk or silk waste	6208. 9910	2456
钡的氧化物、氢氧化物及过氧化物	Barium, oxides, hydroxides and peroxides	2816. 4000	
被褥块状纺织品,化学纤维制	Quilted textile products in the piece, of man-made fibres	5811. 0040	
被褥块状纺织品,棉制	Quilted textile products in the piece, of cotton	5811. 0030	
被褥块状纺织品,其他	Quilted textile products in the piece, nes	5811. 0090	
被褥块状纺织品,丝及绢丝制	Quilted textile products in the piece, of silk or silk waste	5811. 0010	
被褥块状纺织品,羊毛或动物细毛制	Quilted textile products in the piece, of wool or fine animal hair	5811. 0020	
被子,化纤棉填充的	Quilts, stuffed with man-made fibres	9404. 9040	6
被子,其他	Quilts, nes	9404. 9090	6
被子,兽毛填充的	Quilts, stuffed with animal hair	9404. 9020	6
被子,丝棉填充的	Quilts, stuffed with silk wadding	9404. 9030	6
被子,羽毛或羽绒填充的,其他	Quilts, stuffed with feathers or down, nes	9404. 9010	6
焙烧黄铁矿	Roasted iron pyrites	2601. 2000	1346
ben			
本芴醇	Benflumetol	2922. 1950	36
苯	Benzene	2902. 2000	6
苯胺	Aniline	2921. 4110	36
苯胺黑	Nigrosines, as synthetic organic colouring matter	3204. 1300	345
苯胺盐	Aniline salts	2921. 4190	36
苯胺衍生物及其盐	Aniline derivatives and their salts	2921. 4200	36
苯胺印刷机	Flexographic printing machinery	8443. 1600	57
苯巴比妥(INN)以及盐	Phenobarbital (INN); salts thereof	2933. 5300	36
苯巴曲嗪(INN)及盐	Phendimet razine (INN); salts thereof	2934. 9100	36
苯丙酮	Propiophenone	2914. 3100	36
苯并呋喃树脂,初级形状的	Coumarone, in primary forms	3911. 1000	16
苯并呋喃一茚树脂,初级形状的	Coumarone-indene resins and polyterpenes, in primary forms	3911. 1000	16

商品名称	Article Description	税则号列	申报要素
苯并噻唑环系化合物,结构上含有,未经进一步稠合的,不论是否氢化	Benzothiazole ring-system compounds, not further fused in the structure, whether or not hydrogenated	2934.2000	36
苯丁胺(INN)以及它们的盐	Phentermine(INN);salts thereof	2921.4600	36
苯酚	Phenol	2907.1110	36
苯酚盐	Phenol salts	2907.1190	36
苯环利定(INN)以及盐	Phencyclidine (INN) (pcp);salts thereof	2933.3300	36
苯基丙-2-酮	Phenyl propan-2-one	2914.3100	36
苯甲醛	Benzaldehyde	2912.2100	36
苯甲酸及其盐和酯	Benzoic acid, its salts and esters	2916.3100	36
苯哌利定(INN)以及盐	Phenoperidine (INN);salts thereof	2933.3300	36
苯氰米特(INN)以及盐	Bezitramide (INN);salts thereof	2933.3300	36
苯乙酸及其盐	Phenylacetic acid and its salts	2916.3400	36
苯乙酸酯	Esters of phenylacetic acid	2916.3500	36
苯乙酮	Acetophenone	2914.3910	36
苯乙烯	Styrene	2902.5000	6
苯乙烯-丙烯腈(SAN)共聚物,初级形状的	Styrene-acrylonitrile (SAN) copolymers, in primary forms	3903.2000	1256
苯乙烯聚合物,初级形状的,其他	Styrene polymers, in primary forms, nes	3903.9000	1256
beng			
绷带,供医疗、外科、牙科或兽医用	Bandages for medical, surgical, dental or veterinary purposes	3005.9010	1346
绷缝机	Interlock machines	8452.2130	
泵,分装燃料或润滑油的,用于加油站或车库	Pumps for dispensing fuel or lubricants, of the type used in filling-stations or in garages	8413.1100	23
泵,混凝土用	Pumps for concrete	8413.4000	23
泵,冷却剂用	Pumps for cooling medium	8413.3090	23
泵,离心式,电动潜油泵及潜水电泵	Pumps of centrifugal, electric submersible oil pumps and electric submersible pumps	8413.7091	27
泵,离心式,其他	Pumps of centrifugal, nes	8413.7099	27
泵,离心式,转速在10000转/分及以上	Pumps of centrifugal, rotational speed no less than 10000r/min	8413.7010	27
泵,排液泵,往复式,电动式	Pumps, positive displacement pumps, reciprocating, electric	8413.5020	23
泵,排液泵,往复式,其他	Pumps, positive displacement pumps, reciprocating, nes	8413.5090	23
泵,排液泵,往复式,气动式	Pumps, positive displacement pumps, reciprocating, pneumatic	8413.5010	23
泵,排液泵,往复式,液压式,其他	Pumps, positive displacement pumps, reciprocating, hydraulic, nes	8413.5039	23
泵,排液泵,往复式,柱塞泵	Pumps, positive displacement pumps, reciprocating, plunger pumps	8413.5031	23

B

商品名称	Article Description	税则号列	申报要素
泵,排液回转式,齿轮的,电动式	Pumps, for positive displacement, rotary, gear, electric	8413.6021	27
泵,排液回转式,齿轮的,其他	Pumps, for positive displacement, rotary, gear, nes	8413.6029	27
泵,排液回转式,齿轮的,液压式	Pumps, for positive displacement, rotary, gear, hydraulic	8413.6022	27
泵,排液回转式,径向柱塞泵	Pumps, for positive displacement, rotary, radial plunger	8413.6050	27
泵,排液回转式,螺杆泵	Pumps, for positive displacement, rotary, helicoida	8413.6040	27
泵,排液回转式,其他	Pumps, for positive displacement, rotary, nes	8413.6090	27
泵,排液回转式,叶片的,电动式	Pumps, for positive displacement, rotary, vane, electric	8413.6031	27
泵,排液回转式,叶片的,其他	Pumps, for positive displacement, rotary, vane, nes	8413.6039	27
泵,排液回转式,叶片的,液压式	Pumps, for positive displacement, rotary, vane, hydraulic	8413.6032	27
泵,排液回转式,轴向柱塞泵	Pumps, for positive displacement, rotary, axial plunger	8413.6060	27
泵,其他	Pumps, nes	8413.8100	27
泵,燃油用,其他	Pumps for fuel, nes	8413.3029	23
泵,燃油用,输出功率在132.39千瓦(180马力)及以上的发动机用	Pumps for fuel, for engines of an output of 132.39kW (180hp) or more	8413.3021	23
泵,润滑油用	Pumps for lubricating oil	8413.3030	23
泵,手用,但子目号8413.11或8413.19的货品除外	Pumps for hand, other than those of subheading No. 8413.11 or 8413.19	8413.2000	23
泵,装有或可装计量装置的,其他	Pumps fitted or designed to be fitted with a measuring device, nes	8413.1900	23
泵压式咖啡机,电热的	Pump espresso makers, electro-thermic	8516.7130	7
泵用零件	Pumps parts	8413.9100	27
bi			
荸荠	Water chestnut	0714.9010	34
比较照相机,法庭或犯罪学用的	Comparison cameras for forensic or criminological purposes	9006.3000	7
比例缩放仪	Pantographs	9017.8000	7
比目鱼,其他,冻的	Flatfish, nes, frozen	0303.3900	18
比目鱼,其他,鲜或冷的,	Flat fish, nes, fresh or chilled	0302.2900	18
吡啶环化合物,结构上含有一个喹啉或异喹啉体系,非稠合,不论是否氢化,其他	Pyridine ring compounds, containing a quinoline or isoquinoline ring-systern, unfused in the structure, whether or not hydrogenated, nes	2933.3990	36
吡啶及其盐	Pyridine and its salts	2933.3100	36
吡哆醇	Adermin	2936.2500	36
吡咯戊酮(INN)以及盐	Pyrovalerone(INN); salts thereof	2933.9100	36
吡唑环化合物,结构上含有一个非稠合咪唑环,非稠合的,不论是否氢化,其他	Pyrazole ring compounds, containing an unfused imidazole ring, unfused in the structure, whether or not hydrogenated, nes	2933.1990	36
笔,成套的,由上述两个或多个组成的	Pen, in sets of two or more pens	9608.5000	

商品名称	Article Description	税则号列	申报要素
笔,钢笔,其他	Pens,nes	9608.3990	3
笔,活动铅笔	Pens,propelling or sliding pencils	9608.4000	
笔,机器、仪器用	Pen of a kind used on machines or instruments	9608.9910	
笔,记号笔	Pens,markers	9608.2000	
笔,蜡纸铁笔	Pens,duplicating stylos	9608.9920	
笔,唛头笔	Pens,markers	9608.2000	
笔,墨汁画笔	Pens,indian ink drawing pens	9608.3100	
笔,渗水式笔	Pens,porous-tipped pens	9608.2000	
笔,圆珠笔	Pens,ball point pens	9608.1000	
笔,毡尖笔	Pens,felt tipped pens	9608.2000	
笔,自来水笔	Pens,fountain pens	9608.3910	
笔的零件	Pen or pencil parts	9608.9990	3
笔记本,纸或纸板制的	Note books,of paper or paperboard	4820.1000	
笔盘,贱金属制,办公室家具除外	Pen trays,of base metal,other than office furniture	8304.0000	256
笔套	Pen-holders,pencil-holders and similar holders	9608.9920	
笔头及笔尖粒,钢笔的	Pen nibs and nib points	9608.9100	
笔芯,圆珠笔的	Pens refills of ball point pens	9608.6000	
荜拨,调味料	Long pepper	0904.1100	4
荜拨,医药级	Long pepper,used in pharmacy	1211.9039	34
铋,未锻轧	Bismuth,unwrought	8106.0010	16
铋粉末	Bismuth powders	8106.0010	16
铋华	Bismite	2617.9090	146
铋制品,其他	Bismuth articles,nes	8106.0090	16
蓖麻毒素	Ricitoxin	3002.9020	34
蓖麻油及其分离品	Castor oil and its fractions	1515.3000	4
蓖麻籽	Castor oil seeds	1207.9993	3
壁扇,包括风机,本身装有一个输出功率不超过125瓦的电动机	Wall fans,with a self-contained electric motor of an output not exceeding 125W	8414.5193	23
壁玄岩	Lydite	2530.9099	13456
壁玄岩制品	Lydite	6815.9990	6
壁纸,用木粒或草粒等饰面的	Ingrain paper	4814.1000	4
壁纸,用木粒或草粒等饰面的	Wallpaper of “ingrain”	4814.1000	4
壁纸及类似品,用塑料涂面或盖面的,起纹、压花、着色、印刷图案或经其他装饰	Wallpaper and similar wall coverings, consisting of paper coated or covered, on the face side, with a grained, embossed, coloured, design-printed or otherwise decorated layer of plastics	4814.2000	4
壁纸原纸	Wallpaper base	4802.4000	3458
避雷器,用于电压超过1000伏的线路	Lightning arresters,for a voltage exceeding 1000V	8535.4000	8
避孕套	Sheath contraceptives	4014.1000	23
避孕药,以激素为基本成分的	Contraceptive preparations based on hormones	3006.6010	36

B

商品名称	Article Description	税则号列	申报要素
bian			
编带、吊索及类似品,非绝缘钢铁的	Plaited bands, slings and the like, of iron or steel, not electrically insulated	7312.9000	36
编号戳,手用	Numbering stamps, designed for operating in the hand	9611.0000	
编织带机	Braid making machines	8447.9090	7
编织网机	Net making machines	8447.9090	7
编织针,钢铁制的,手工用	Knitting needles, for use in the hand, of iron or steel	7319.9000	
鞭条及类似产品,不论是否缝合成宽条,其他	Plaits and similar products of plaiting materials, whether or not assembled into strips, nes	4601.9910	6
鞭子	Whips	6602.0000	
鞭子的零件	Whips parts	6603.9000	
扁豆,其他,脱荚的,干的	Lentils, nes, dried, shelled	0713.4090	34
扁豆,种用,脱荚的,干的	Lentils, seed, dried, shelled	0713.4010	34
扁平石,天然石料(不包括板岩)制的	Flagstones, of natural stone(except slate)	6801.0000	46
扁条及类似品,表观宽度不超过5毫米,合成纤维纺织材料制	Strip and the like of synthetic textile materials of an apparent width not exceeding 5mm	5404.9000	568
扁条及类似品,表观宽度不超过5毫米,人造纤维纺织材料制	Strip and the like of artificial textile materials of an apparent width not exceeding 5mm	5405.0000	568
扁条及类似品的机织物	Strip or the like woven fabrics	5407.2000	2468
苄醇	Benzyl alcohol	2906.2100	36
苄非他明(INN)以及它们的盐	Benzfetamine (INN), salts thereof	2921.4600	36
便服套装,非针织或钩编的,男式,合成纤维制	Ensembles, not knitted or crocheted, for men or boys, of synthetic fibres	6203.2300	2456
便服套装,非针织或钩编的,男式,棉制	Ensembles, not knitted or crocheted, for men or boys, of cotton	6203.2200	2456
便服套装,非针织或钩编的,男式,其他	Ensembles, not knitted or crocheted, for men or boys, nes	6203.2990	2456
便服套装,非针织或钩编的,男式,丝及绢丝制	Ensembles, not knitted or crocheted, for men or boys, of silk or silk waste	6203.2910	2456
便服套装,非针织或钩编的,男式,羊毛或动物细毛制	Ensembles, not knitted or crocheted, for men or boys, of wool or fine animal hair	6203.2920	2456
便服套装,非针织或钩编的,女式,合成纤维制	Ensembles, not knitted or crocheted, for women or girls, of synthetic fibres	6204.2300	2456
便服套装,非针织或钩编的,女式,棉制	Ensembles, not knitted or crocheted, for women or girls, of cotton	6204.2200	2456
便服套装,非针织或钩编的,女式,其他	Ensembles, not knitted or crocheted, for women or girls, nes	6204.2990	2456
便服套装,非针织或钩编的,女式,丝及绢丝制	Ensembles, not knitted or crocheted, for women or girls, of silk or silk waste	6204.2910	2456
便服套装,非针织或钩编的,女式,羊毛或动物细毛制	Ensembles, not knitted or crocheted, for women or girls, of wool or fine animal hair	6204.2100	2456

商品名称	Article Description	税则号列	申报要素
便服套装,针织或钩编的,男式,合成纤维制	Ensembles, knitted or crocheted, of men or boys, of synthetic fibres	6103.2300	2456
便服套装,针织或钩编的,男式,棉制	Ensembles, knitted or crocheted, of men or boys, of cotton	6103.2200	2456
便服套装,针织或钩编的,男式,其他纺织材料制	Ensembles, knitted or crocheted, of men or boys, of other textile materials	6103.2990	2456
便服套装,针织或钩编的,男式,羊毛或动物细毛制	Ensembles, knitted or crocheted, of men or boys, of wool or fine animal hair	6103.2910	2456
便服套装,针织或钩编的,女式,合成纤维制	Ensembles, knitted or crocheted, of women or girls, of synthetic fibres	6104.2300	2456
便服套装,针织或钩编的,女式,棉制	Ensembles, knitted or crocheted, of women or girls, of cotton	6104.2200	2456
便服套装,针织或钩编的,女式,其他	Ensembles, knitted or crocheted, of women or girls, nes	6104.2990	2456
便服套装,针织或钩编的,女式,羊毛或动物细毛制	Ensembles, knitted or crocheted, of women or girls, of wool or fine animal hair	6104.2910	2456
便盆,塑料的	Lavatory pans, of plastics	3922.9000	236
变流机,旋转式	Converters, electric rotary	8502.4000	8
变色镜	Photochromic spectacles	9004.9010	
变色镜片,玻璃制	Photochromic spectacle lenses, of glass	9001.4010	
变色镜片,其他材料制	Photochromic spectacle lenses, of other materials	9001.5010	
变速箱及其零件,30 座及以上客运机动车辆用	Gear boxes and parts of motor vehicles with 30 seats or more	8708.4020	3
变速箱及其零件,其他	Gear boxes and parts, nes	8708.4099	3
变速箱及其零件,特种车辆用	Gear boxes and parts of motor vehicles with special purpose	8708.4060	3
变速箱及其零件,拖拉机的	Gear boxes and parts of tractors	8708.4010	3
变速箱及其零件,小轿车用	Gear boxes and parts of saloon cars	8708.4040	3
变速箱及其零件,越野车(4 轮驱动)用	Gear boxes and parts of cross-country cars(4WD)	8708.4050	3
变速箱及其零件,自卸车用	Gear boxes and parts of dumpers	8708.4030	3
变像管	Image converters	8540.2090	35
变形机,化学纤维的	Crimping machinery for man-made filaments	8444.0040	
变形机的辅助机器,化学纤维的	Crimping machinery auxiliary, for man-made filaments	8448.1900	3
变形纱线,非供零售用,其他	Textured yarn, not put up for retail sale, nes	5402.3900	3468
变压器,额定容量不超过 1 千伏安,其他	Transformers, having a power handling capacity not exceeding 1kVA	8504.3190	78
变压器,额定容量超过 16 千伏安,但不超过 500 千伏安	Transformers, having a power handling capacity exceeding 16kVA but not exceeding 500kVA	8504.3300	78
变压器,额定容量超过 1 千伏安,但不超过 16 千伏安,其他	Transformers, having a power handling capacity exceeding 1kVA but not exceeding 16kVA	8504.3290	78

B

商品名称	Article Description	税则号列	申报要素
变压器,额定容量超过 500 千伏安	Transformers, having a power handling capacity exceeding 500kVA	8504.3400	78
变压器,液体介质,额定容量不超过 650 千伏安	Transformers, liquid dielectric, having a power handling capacity not exceeding 650kVA	8504.2100	78
变压器,液体介质,额定容量超过 10 兆伏安,但小于 220 兆伏安	Transformers, liquid dielectric, having a power handing capacity exceeding 10MVA but less than 220MVA	8504.2311	78
变压器,液体介质,额定容量超过 650 千伏安,但不超过 10 兆伏安	Transformers, liquid dielectric, having a power handling capacity exceeding 650kVA but not exceeding 10MVA	8504.2200	78
变压器,液体介质,额定容量在 220 兆伏安及以上,但小于 330 兆伏安	Transformers, liquid dielectric, having a power handling capacity exceeding 220MVA but less than 330MVA	8504.2312	78
变压器,液体介质,额定容量在 330 兆伏安及以上,但小于 400 兆伏安	Transformers, liquid dielectric, having a power handling capacity exceeding 330MVA but less than 400MVA	8504.2313	78
变压器,液体介质,额定容量在 400 兆伏安及以上,但小于 500 兆伏安	Transformers, liquid dielectric, having a power handling capacity exceeding 400MVA but less than 500MVA	8504.2321	78
变压器,液体介质,其他	Transformers, liquid dielectric, nes	8504.2329	78
变压器用零件,其他	Transformers parts, nes	8504.9019	3
变压器用零件,液体介质,额定容量在 400 兆伏安及以上,但小于 500 兆伏安	Transformers parts, liquid dielectric, having a power handling capacity exceeding 400MVA but less than 500MVA	8504.9011	3
变压器用零件,液体介质,其他	Transformers parts, liquid dielectric, nes	8504.9011	3
变阻器,可变的	Rheostats and potentiometers, variable	8533.4000	58
变阻器,线绕可变,额定功率不超过 20 瓦	Rheostats, wirewound variable, for a power handling capacity not exceeding 20W	8533.3100	58
变阻器,线绕可变,其他	Rheostats, wirewound variable, nes	8533.3900	58
缏条(绳),稻草制的	Plaits of straw	4601.9411	6
缏条及类似产品,不论是否缝合成宽条,其他植物材料制的	Plaits and similar products of plaiting meterials, whether or not assembled into strips, of other vegetable materials	4601.9491	6
缏条及类似产品,不论是否缝合成宽条,藤制的	Plaits and similar products of plaiting meterials, whether or not assembled into strips, of rattan	4601.9310	6
缏条及类似产品,不论是否缝合成宽条,竹制的	Plaits and similar products of plaiting meterials, whether or not assembled into strips, of bamboo	4601.9210	6
biao			
标签,纸或纸板制的,其他	Labels of all kinds, of paper or paperboard, nes	4821.9000	4
标签,纸或纸板制的,印制	Labels of all kinds, of paper or paperboard, printed	4821.1000	4

商品名称	Article Description	税则号列	申报要素
标签、徽章及类似品,纺织材料制,成匹、成条或裁成一定形状或尺寸,非绣制,机织	Labels, badges and similar articles of textile materials, in the piece, in strips or cut to shape or size, not embroidered, woven	5807.1000	468
标签、徽章及类似品,纺织材料制,成匹、成条或裁成一定形状或尺寸,非绣制,其他	Labels, badges and similar articles of textile materials, in the piece, in strips or cut to shape or size, not embroidered, nes	5807.9000	468
标志牌,贱金属制,税号94.05的货品除外	Sign-plates, of base metal, excluding those of heading No. 94.05	8310.0000	256
表,表壳用贵金属或包贵金属制成的,其他	Watches, with case of precious metal or of metal clad with precious metal, nes	9101.9900	56
表,电力驱动的,表壳用贵金属或包贵金属制成的,其他	Watches, electrically operated, with case of precious metal or of metal clad with precious metal, nes	9101.9100	56
表,电力驱动的,其他	Watches, electrically operated, nes	9102.9100	56
表,其他	Watches, nes	9102.9900	56
表带及其零件,贵金属或包贵金属制	Watch straps, watch bands and watch bracelets, and parts thereof, of precious metal or of metal clad with precious metal	9113.1000	
表带及其零件,贱金属制,不论是否镀金或镀银	Watch straps, watch bands and watch bracelets, and parts thereof, of base metal, whether or not gold-plated or silver-plated	9113.2000	6
表带及其零件,其他	Watch straps, watch bands and watch bracelets, and parts thereof, nes	9113.9000	6
表壳,贵金属或包贵金属的	Watch cases, of precious metal or of metal clad with precious metal	9111.1000	6
表壳,贱金属的,不论是否镀金或镀银	Watch cases, of base metal, whether or not gold-plated or silver-plated	9111.2000	6
表壳,其他	Watch cases, nes	9111.8000	6
表壳零件	Watch cases parts	9111.9000	6
表氯醇	Epichlorohydrin	2910.3000	36
表面回火机器及装置,气体推动的	Surface tempering machines and appliances, gas-operated	8468.2000	57
表芯,不完整的,未组装	Rough movements, of watches	9110.1900	1
表芯,不完整的,未组装	Watch movements, incomplete, unassembled	9110.1900	1
表芯,不完整的,已组装	Watch movements, incomplete, assembled	9110.1200	1
表芯,完整的,未组装或部分组装(机芯套装件)	Watch movements, complete, unassembled or partly assembled (movement sets)	9110.1100	1
表芯,已组装完整的,表面尺寸在33.8毫米及以下	Watch movements, complete and assembled, measuring 33.8mm or less	9108.9010	58
表芯,已组装完整的,电力驱动的,仅有光电显示器的	Watch movements, complete and assembled, electrically operated, with optoelectronic display only	9108.1200	58

B

商品名称	Article Description	税则号列	申报要素
表芯,已组装完整的,电力驱动的,仅有机械指示器或有可装机械指示器的装置的	Watch movements, complete and assembled, electrically operated, with mechanical display only or with a device to which a mechanical display can be incorporated	9108.1100	58
表芯,已组装完整的,电力驱动的,其他	Watch movements, complete and assembled, electrically operated, nes	9108.1900	58
表芯,已组装完整的,其他	Watch movements, complete and assembled, nes	9108.9090	58
表芯,已组装完整的,自动上弦的	Watch movements, complete and assembled, automatic winding	9108.2000	58
bie			
别特酒	Aromatic bitters	2103.9020	268
别针,钢铁制的,其他	Other pins, of iron or steel, nes	7319.3000	
bin			
槟榔,冷冻的	Betel nuts, frozen	0811.9090	1
槟榔,鲜的或干的	Betel nuts, fresh or dried	0802.9010	134
槟榔罐头	Betel nuts, in airtight containers	2008.1920	248
bing			
冰	Ice	2201.9090	248
冰果棒及类似一次性制品,木制	Popsicle sticks and the like, of wood	4421.9021	56
冰果棒及类似一次性制品,其他	Popsicle sticks and the like, nes	4421.9029	56
冰果棒及类似一次性制品,竹制	Popsicle sticks and the like, of bamboo	4421.9022	56
冰片	Borneol	2906.1990	36
冰淇淋及其他冰制食品,不论是否含可可	Ice cream and other edible ice, whether or not containing cocoa	2105.0000	28
冰糖	Candies, not containing cocoa	1702.9000	
冰乙酸,其他	Acetic acid, glacial, nes	2915.2119	36
冰乙酸,食品级	Acetic acid, glacial, food grade	2915.2111	36
冰洲石	Calcite	2530.9099	13456
冰洲石	Iceland spar (calcite)	2530.9099	13456
丙醇	Propan-1-ol (propyl alcohol)	2905.1210	36
丙二烯	Allene	2901.2990	368
丙二酰脲及其盐	Malonylurea and its salts	2933.5200	36
丙二酰脲衍生物以及它们的盐,其他	Malonylurea derivatives; salts thereof, nes	2933.5400	36
丙三醇(甘油),单独有化学定义的	Glycerol, separate chemically defined	2905.4500	36
丙酸	Propionic acid	2915.5010	36
丙酸盐和酯	Propionic acid salts and esters	2915.5090	36
丙酮	Acetone	2914.1100	36
丙酮肟	Acetoxime	2928.0000	36
丙烷,液化的	Propane, liquefied	2711.1200	1468
丙烯	Propene (propylene)	2901.2200	368

B

商品名称	Article Description	税则号列	申报要素
丙烯,液化的	Propylene, liquefied	2711.1400	1468
丙烯共聚物,其他	Propylene copolymers, nes	3902.3090	1256
丙烯或其他烯烃聚合物,初级形状的,其他	Propylene or of other olefins polymers, in primary forms, nes	3902.9000	1256
丙烯腈	Acrylonitrile	2926.1000	36
丙烯腈-丁二烯-苯乙烯(ABS)共聚物,初级形状的,其他	Acrylonitrile-butadiene-styrene(ABS) copolymers, in primary forms, nes	3903.3090	1256
丙烯腈-丁二烯-苯乙烯(ABS)共聚物,改性的,初级形状的	Acrylonitrile-butadiene-styrene (ABS) copolymers, modified, in primary forms	3903.3010	1256
丙烯酸丁酯	Butyl acrylate	2916.1230	36
丙烯酸及其盐	Acrylic acid and its salts	2916.1100	36
丙烯酸甲酯	Methyl acrylate	2916.1210	36
丙烯酸聚合物,初级形状的,其他	Acrylic polymers, in primary forms, nes	3906.9090	1256
丙烯酸乙酯	Ethyl acrylate	2916.1220	36
丙烯酸异辛酯	Isooctyl acrylate	2916.1240	36
丙烯酸酯,其他	Esters of acrylic acid, nes	2916.1290	36
饼干	Biscuits	1905.9000	28
并线机	Textile doubling machines	8445.3000	7
并线机的辅助机器	Textile doubling machines auxiliary	8448.1900	3
病床,带机械装置的	Hospital beds with mechanical fittings	9402.9000	3
病员监护仪	Patient monitors	9018.1930	
bo			
拨弦古钢琴	Harpsichords	9201.9000	5
波分复用光传输设备	Optical transmission equipments for wave-division multiplexing	8517.6222	7
"波威"及类似式样的手织装饰毯	Beauvais type hand-woven tapestries	5805.0090	468
波纹钉,钢铁制的	Corrugated nails, of iron or steel	7317.0000	36
玻璃,废的	Glass waste and scrap	7001.0000	13
玻璃,经弯曲、磨边、镂刻、钻孔、涂珐琅或其他加工的,但未用其他材料镶框或装配	Glass, bent, edge-worked, engraved, drilled, enamelled or otherwise worked, but not framed or fitted with other materials	7006.0000	134
玻璃,视力矫正眼镜用,未经光学加工的,玻璃制,其他	Glasses for corrective spectacles, not optically worked, of glass, nes	7015.1090	1345
玻璃,碎的	Cullet	7001.0000	13
玻璃板片,表面研磨或抛光,非夹丝玻璃,其他	Glass, surface ground or polished, non-wired, nes	7005.2900	134
玻璃板片,表面研磨或抛光,夹丝玻璃	Glass, surface ground or polished, wired	7005.3000	134
玻璃板片,表面研磨或抛光,具有吸收、反射或非反射层的非夹丝玻璃	Glass, surface ground or polished, non-wired glass, having an absorbent, reflecting or non-reflecting layer	7005.1000	134

B

商品名称	Article Description	税则号列	申报要素
玻璃板片,表面研磨或抛光,整块着色、不透明、镶色或仅表面研磨的非夹丝玻璃,其他	Glass, surface ground or polished, coloured throughout the mass (body tinted), opacified, flashed or merely surface ground, non-wired, nes	7005. 2100	134
玻璃板片,非夹丝的,铸制或轧制的,其他	Glass sheets, non-wired, cast and rolled, nes	7003. 1900	134
玻璃板片,非夹丝的,铸制或轧制的,整块着色、不透明、镶色或具有吸收、反射或非反射层的	Glass sheets, non-wired, cast and rolled, coloured throughout the mass (body tinted), opacified, flashed or having an absorbent, or non-reflecting reflecting layer	7003. 1200	134
玻璃板片,浮法工艺制造,非夹丝玻璃,其他	Glass, by float process, non-wired, nes	7005. 2900	134
玻璃板片,浮法工艺制造,夹丝玻璃	Glass, by float process, wired	7005. 3000	134
玻璃板片,浮法工艺制造,具有吸收、反射或非反射层的非夹丝玻璃	Glass, by float process, non-wired glass, having an absorbent, reflecting or non-reflecting layer	7005. 1000	134
玻璃板片,浮法工艺制造,整块着色、不透明、镶色或仅表面研磨的非夹丝玻璃,其他	Glass, by float process, coloured throughout the mass (body tinted), opacified, flashed or merely surface ground, nes	7005. 2100	134
玻璃板片,夹丝的,铸制或轧制的	Glass sheets, wired, cast and rolled	7003. 2000	134
玻璃板片,拉制或吹制的,其他	Glass sheets, drawn and blown, nes	7004. 9000	134
玻璃板片,拉制或吹制的,整块着色、不透明、镶色或具有吸收、反射或非反射层的	Glass sheets, drawn and blown, coloured throughout the mass (body tinted), opacified, flashed or having an absorbent, reflecting or non-reflecting layer	7004. 2000	134
玻璃棒,未加工的,其他	Glass in rods, unworked, nes	7002. 2090	238
玻璃杯子,但玻璃陶瓷制的除外,其他	Drinking glasses, other than of glass ceramics, nes	7013. 3700	356
玻璃杯子,但玻璃陶瓷制的除外,铅晶质玻璃制	Drinking glasses, other than of glass ceramics, of lead crystal	7013. 3300	356
玻璃粗纱	Glass rovings	7019. 1200	568
玻璃刀,家用	Glaziers' diamonds for household	8205. 5100	256
玻璃的热加工设备,其他	Glass or glasswares hot working equipments, nes	8475. 2919	3
玻璃短切纤维,长度不超过 50 毫米的	Glass chopped strands, of a length of not more than 50mm	7019. 1100	568
玻璃管,其他	Glass tubes, nes	7002. 3900	238
玻璃管,熔融石英或其他熔融硅石制,其他	Glass tubes, of fused quartz or other fused silica, nes	7002. 3190	238
玻璃管,石英的,光导纤维用,波导级	Glass tubes for optical fibres use, of quartz, waveguide grade	7002. 3110	238
玻璃管,温度在 0℃ 至 300℃ 时线膨胀系数不超过 5×10^{-6}/开尔文的其他玻璃制	Glass tubes, of other glass having a linear coefficient of expansion not exceeding 5×10^{-6} per Kelvin within a temperature range of 0℃ to 300℃	7002. 3200	238
玻璃或玻璃制品的制造或热加工机器,其他	Glass or glassware hot working or manufacturing machines, nes	8475. 2990	3
玻璃或玻璃制品的制造或热加工机器的零件,其他	Glass or glassware hot working or manufacturing machines parts, nes	8475. 9000	3

商品名称	Article Description	税则号列	申报要素
玻璃假眼,但医用假眼除外	Glass eyes other than prosthetic articles	7018.9000	3458
玻璃镜,未镶框	Glass mirrors, unframed	7009.9100	4
玻璃镜,已镶框	Glass mirrors, framed	7009.9200	4
玻璃块、板、片及类似品,压制或模制的,多孔或泡沫	Glass in blocks, panels, plates, shells or similar forms, pressed or moulded, multicellular or foam	7016.9090	345
玻璃块、砖、片、瓦及其他制品,建筑用,压制或模制的,其他	Glass pavingblocks, slabs, bricks, squares, tiles and other articles of a kind used for building or construction purposes, pressed or moulded, nes	7016.9090	345
玻璃块料	Glass in the mass	7001.0000	13
玻璃马赛克及其他小件玻璃品,供镶嵌或类似装饰用的,压制或模制的	Glass cubes and other glass smallwares, for mosaics or similar decorative purposes, pressed or moulded	7016.1000	345
玻璃抛光机床	Glass or glassware polishing machines	8464.2010	7
玻璃器,其他	Glassware, nes	7013.9900	356
玻璃器,铅晶质玻璃制,其他	Glassware of lead crystal, nes	7013.9100	356
玻璃器,实验室、卫生及配药用,不论有无刻度或标量,其他	Glassware, for laboratory, hygienic or pharmaceutical, whether or not graduated or calibrated, nes	7017.9000	356
玻璃器,实验室、卫生及配药用,不论有无刻度或标量,熔融石英或其他熔融硅石制	Glassware, for laboratory, hygienic or pharmaceutical, whether or not graduated or calibrated, of fused quartz or other fused silica	7017.1000	356
玻璃器,实验室、卫生及配药用,不论有无刻度或标量,温度在0℃至300℃时线膨胀系数不超过5×10^{-6}/开尔文的其他玻璃制	Glassware, for laboratory, hygienic or pharmaceutical, whether or not graduated or calibrated, of other glass having a linear coefficient of expansion not exceeding 5×10^{-6} per Kelvin within a temperature range of 0℃ to 300℃	7017.2000	356
玻璃器,装饰或类似用途,玻璃陶瓷制	Glassware of a kind used for decoration or similar purposes, of glass-ceramics	7013.1000	356
玻璃器皿(不包括杯子),餐桌或厨房用,但玻璃陶瓷制的除外,其他	Glassware of a kind used for table (other than drinking glasses) or kitchen purposes, other than of glass-ceramics, nes	7013.4900	356
玻璃器皿(不包括杯子),餐桌或厨房用,但玻璃陶瓷制的除外,铅晶质玻璃制	Glassware of a kind used for table (other than drinking glasses) or kitchen purposes, other than of glass-ceramics, of lead crystal	7013.4100	356
玻璃器皿(不包括杯子),餐桌或厨房用,但玻璃陶瓷制的除外,温度在0℃至300℃时线膨胀系数不超过5×10^{-6}/开尔文的其他玻璃制	Glassware of a kind used for table (other than drinking glasses) or kitchen purposes, other than of glass-ceramics, of glass having a linear coefficient of expansion not exceeding 5×10^{-6} per Kelvin within a temperature range of 0℃ to 300℃	7013.4200	356
玻璃球,微型的,直径不超过1毫米	Glass microspheres, not exceeding 1mm in diameter	7018.2000	3458
玻璃球,未加工的	Glass in balls, unworked	7002.1000	3
玻璃容器,不超过0.15升	Glass containers, not exceeding 0.15L	7010.9090	8
玻璃容器,超过0.15升,但不超过0.33升	Glass containers, exceeding 0.15L but not exceeding 0.33L	7010.9030	8

B

商品名称	Article Description	税则号列	申报要素
玻璃容器,超过 0.33 升,但不超过 1 升	Glass containers, exceeding 0.33L but not exceeding 1L	7010.9020	8
玻璃容器,超过 1 升	Glass containers, exceeding 1L	7010.9010	8
玻璃塞、盖及类似的封口器	Glass stoppers, lids and other closures	7010.2000	8
玻璃梳条、纱线	Glass slivers, yarn	7019.1900	568
玻璃塑像,灯工方法制作的,以及其他玻璃装饰品,但仿首饰除外	Statuettes and other ornaments of lampworked glass, other than imitation jewellery	7018.9000	3458
玻璃外壳及其玻璃零件,电子管用(阴极射线管用的除外),未封口,未装有配件	Glass envelopes and glass parts thereof, for electronic tubes and valves (other than cathode-ray tubes), open, without fittings	7011.9010	4
玻璃外壳及其玻璃零件,未封口,未装有配件,其他	Glass envelopes and glass parts thereof, open, without fittings, nes	7011.9090	4
玻璃外壳及其玻璃零件,制电灯用,未封口,未装有配件	Glass envelopes and glass parts thereof, for electric lighting, open, without fittings	7011.1000	4
玻璃外壳及其玻璃零件,制阴极射线管用,未封口,未装有配件,其他	Glass envelopes and glass parts thereof, for cathode-ray tubes, open, without fittings, nes	7011.2090	4
玻璃纤维拉丝机(光纤拉丝机除外)	Fiber glass winder (excluding opticaefiber winder)	8475.2912	
玻璃纤维制品,其他	Glass fibres articles, nes	7019.9000	6
玻璃型材及异型材,铸制或轧制的	Glass profiles, cast and rolled	7003.3000	134
玻璃研磨机床	Glass or glassware grinding machines	8464.2010	7
玻璃用型模	Moulds for glass	8480.5000	7
玻璃制品,工业用,其他	Glass articles, for technical use, nes	7020.0019	6
玻璃制品,其他	Glass articles, nes	7020.0099	6
玻璃珠	Glass beads	7018.1000	3458
剥离装置,平板显示器的制造机器及装置,其他	Stripping apparatus, flat panel displays manufacture machines and apparatus, nes	8486.3049	7
菠菜,冷冻的	Spinach, New Zealand spinach and orache spinach (garden spinach), frozen	0710.3000	1
菠菜,鲜或冷藏的	Spinach, New Zealand spinach and orache spinach (garden spinach), fresh or chilled	0709.7000	1
菠萝	Pineapples	0804.3000	145
菠萝,罐头	Pineapples, in airtight containers	2008.2010	248
菠萝,其他,用其他方法制作或保藏的	Pineapples, nes, otherwise prepared, or preserved	2008.2090	248
菠萝汁,白利糖度值不超过 20 的	Pineapple juice, of a brix value not exceeding 20	2009.4100	2468
菠萝汁,其他	Pineapple juice, nes	2009.4900	2468
播种机,农业、园艺及林业用	Seeders, for agricultural, horticultural or forestry use	8432.3000	
铂,板、片	Platinum, plates and sheets	7110.1910	46
铂,其他	Platinum, nes	7110.1990	46
铂,未锻造或粉末状	Platinum, unwrought or in powder form	7110.1100	46
铂包覆材料,以贱金属、银或金为底的,未加工成半成品的	Platinum clothing base metals, silver or gold, not further worked than semi-manufactured	7111.0000	46
铂矿砂及其精矿	Platinum ores and concentrates	2616.9000	146

商品名称	Article Description	税则号列	申报要素
薄荷醇	Menthol	2906. 1100	36
薄膜沉积设备,制造半导体器件或集成电路的机器及装置,其他	Film deposition equipment, semiconductor devices or of electronic integrated circuits manufacture machines and apparatus, nes	8486. 2029	7
薄膜沉积设备,制造平板显示器用的机器及装置,其他	Film deposition equipment, flat panel displays manufacture machines and apparatus, nes	8486. 3029	7
薄膜沉积设备零件及附件,制造半导体器件、集成电路、平板显示器的机器及装置	Film deposition equipment parts and accessories, semiconductor devices or of electronic integrated circuits or flat panel displays manufacture machines and apparatus	8486. 9090	3
薄片,玻璃纤维制	Thin sheets, of glass fibres	7019. 3200	56
bu			
哺乳动物,改良种用	Mammals, pure-bred breeding, nes	0106. 1910	34
哺乳动物,其他	Mammals, nes	0106. 1990	48
哺乳动物,食用	Mammals, for human consumption, nes	0106. 1920	48
捕蝶网	Butterfly nets	9507. 9000	5
捕鸟用品及类似的狩猎用品	Decoy birds and similar hunting or shooting requisites	9507. 9000	5
捕蝇纸,零售包装	Fly-papers, put up for retail sale	3808. 9910	36
捕鱼船,非机动船舶	Fishing vessels, not-motorized vessels	8902. 0090	5
捕鱼船,机动船舶	Fishing vessels, motor vessels	8902. 0010	5
不饱和无环一元羧酸及其酸酐、酰卤化物、过氧化物和过氧酸以及它们的衍生物,其他	Unsaturated acyclic monocarboxylic acids, their anhydrides, halides, peroxides, peroxyacids and their derivatives, nes	2916. 1900	36
不饱和一元醇,其他	Unsaturated monohydric alcohols, nes	2905. 2900	36
不间断供电电源	Uninterrupted power suppliers	8504. 4020	8
不间断供电电源用零件	Uninterrupted power suppliers parts	8504. 9020	3
不锈钢,锭状及其他初级形状	Stainless steel ingots and other primary forms	7218. 1000	468
不锈钢,矩形(正方形除外)截面的	Stainless steel of rectangular (other than square) crosssection	7218. 9100	468
不锈钢半制成品,其他	Stainless steel semi-finished products, nes	7218. 9900	468
不锈钢丝	Stainless steel wire	7223. 0000	468
布,镍丝制	Cloth, of nickel wire	7508. 1010	6
布,铜丝制	Cloth, of copper wire	7419. 9930	4
布、网、篱及格栅,铝丝制的	Cloth, grill, netting and fencing, of aluminium wire	7616. 9100	36
布里乳酪,未加工	Brie cheese, unworked	0406. 9000	2468
布洛芬	Brufen(Ibuprofen)	2916. 3920	36
布他比妥(INN)以及盐	Butalbital (INN); salts thereof	2933. 5300	36
布线组,机动车辆点火用	Wiring sets, for motor vehicles ignition	8544. 3020	35
布线组,机动车辆用,其他	Wiring sets, for motor vehicles, nes	8544. 3020	35
布线组,其他	Wiring sets, nes	8544. 3090	35

B

商品名称	Article Description	税则号列	申报要素
步进光刻机，制造半导体器件或集成电路的机器及装置	Step and repeat alignersw, semiconductor devices or of electronic integrated circuits manufacture machines and apparatus	8486. 2031	7
步进光刻机零件及附件，制造半导体器件、集成电路、平板显示器的机器及装置	Step and repeat alignersw parts and accessories, semiconductor devices or of electronic integrated circuits or flat panel displays manufacture machines and apparatus	8486. 9090	3
步枪	Rifles	9303. 3000	
步枪用零件、附件	Rifles parts and accessories	9305. 2900	3
步数计及类似仪表	Pedometers and the like	9029. 1090	7
步数计零件、附件	Pedometers parts and accessories	9029. 9000	3
钚及其化合物	Plutonium and its compounds	2844. 2000	

C

商品名称	Article Description	税则号列	申报要素
ca			
擦地布及类似擦拭用布	Floor-cloths and similar cleaning cloths	6307.1000	346
擦锅器及类似品	Pot scourers and the like	7323.1000	24
擦锅器及类似品,铝制	Pot scourers and the like,of aluminium	7615.1100	36
擦锅器及类似品,铜制	Pot scourers and the like,of copper	7418.1100	56
擦碗布及类似擦拭用布	Dish-cloths and similar cleaning cloths	6307.1000	346
擦洗膏及类似制品	Scouring pastes and other scouring preparations	3405.4000	36
cai			
裁缝划粉	Tailors chalks	9609.9000	3
裁缝剪刀及类似品、剪刀片	Tailors shears and similar shears,and blades therefor	8213.0000	256
裁纸刀及其刀片	Paper knives and blades therefor	8214.1000	256
采矿钻机,自推进的,其他	Mining drills,self-propelled,nes	8430.5039	5
采矿钻机,自推进的,牙轮直径380毫米及以上	Mining drills, self-propelled, gear wheel diameter more than 380mm	8430.5031	5
采油机械,自推进的,其他	Oil production machinery,self-propelled,nes	8430.5010	5
彩色超声波诊断仪	Chromoscope ultrasonic diagnostic equipment	9018.1291	
彩色滤光片	Color filters	9001.9010	
彩色相纸用双面涂塑纸,漂白的,每平方米重量超过150克	Paper coated on both sides with plastics for colour photography, bleached, weighing more than $150g/m^2$	4811.5110	458
菜豆,鲜或冷藏的	Beans(phaseolus spp.),fresh or chilled	0708.2000	1
菜花,鲜或冷藏的	Cauliflowers,fresh or chilled	0704.1000	1
菜子油,其他,初榨的	Rape oil,nes,crude	1514.9110	4
菜子油及其分离品,低芥子酸的,初榨的	Colza oil and its fractions,low erucic acid,crude oil	1514.1100	46
菜子油及其分离品,低芥子酸的,初榨的	Rape oil and its fractions,low erucic acid,crude oil	1514.1100	46
菜子油及其分离品,低芥子酸的,其他	Colza oil and its fractions,low erucic acid,nes	1514.1900	46
菜子油及其分离品,低芥子酸的,其他	Rape oil and its fractions,low erucic acid,nes	1514.1900	46
菜子油及其分离品,其他	Colza oil and fractions thereof,nes	1514.9900	4
菜子油及其分离品,其他	Rape oil and fractions thereof,nes	1514.9900	4
can			
餐叉,镀贵金属的,厨房或餐桌用具	Forks, plated with precious metal, kitchen or tableware	8215.9100	256
餐叉,非镀贵金属的,厨房或餐桌用具	Forks,other than plated with precious metal,kitchen or tableware	8215.9900	256

C

商品名称	Article Description	税则号列	申报要素
餐匙,镀贵金属的	Spoons, plated with precious metal	8215.9100	256
餐匙,非镀贵金属的	Spoons, other than plated with precious metal	8215.9900	256
餐匙,非镀贵金属的	Spoons, other than plated with precious metal	8215.9900	256
餐刀,刃面固定的	Table knives having fixed blades	8211.9100	256
餐巾纸,纸浆、纸、纤维素絮纸或纤维素纤维网纸制的	Serviettes, of paper pulp, paper, cellulose wadding or webs of cellulose fibres	4818.3000	568
餐巾纸以及家庭或卫生用的类似纸,成卷或成张的	Towel or napkin stock and similar paper of a kind used for household or sanitary purposes, in rolls or sheets	4803.0000	58
餐具,瓷制	Tableware, of porcelain	6911.1010	268
餐具,塑料的	Tableware, of plastics	3924.1000	23
餐具,陶制	Tableware, of pottery	6912.0010	268
餐具及厨房用具,竹制,其他	Tableware and kitchenware, of bamboo, nes	4419.0091	6
餐具及厨房用具,其他木制	Tableware and kitchenware, of other wood	4419.0099	6
餐桌、厨房或家用器具及其零件,铜制,其他	Table, kitchen or other household articles and parts thereof, of copper, nes	7418.1990	56
餐桌、厨房家用器具及其零件,铝制,其他	Table, kitchen or household articles and parts thereof, of aluminium, nes	7615.1900	36
餐桌、厨房器具及其零件,钢铁制,家用,其他	Table, kitchen or other household articles and parts thereof, for household, of iron or steel, nes	7323.9900	24
餐桌、厨房器具及其零件,钢铁制,家用,已搪瓷,其他	Table, kitchen or other household articles and parts thereof, of iron or steel, for household, enamelled, nes	7323.9490	24
餐桌、厨房器具及其零件,家用,不锈钢制	Table, kitchen or other household articles and parts theref, for household, of stainless steel	7323.9300	24
餐桌、厨房器具及其零件,铸铁制,家用,未搪瓷	Table, kitchen or other household articles and parts theref, for household, of cast iron, not enamelled	7323.9100	24
餐桌、厨房器具及其零件,铸铁制,家用,已搪瓷	Table, kitchen or other household articles and parts theref, for household, of cast iron, enamelled	7323.9200	24
餐桌用具,成套货品,其他	Tableware, in sets of assorted articles, nes	8215.2000	256
餐桌用具,成套货品,至少其中一件物品是镀贵金属的	Tableware, in sets of assorted articles containing at least one article plated with precious metal	8215.1000	256
餐桌用具,镀贵金属的	Tableware, plated with precious metal	8215.9100	256
餐桌用具,其他	Tableware, nes	8215.9900	256
餐桌用织物制品,刺绣的,化学纤维制	Table linen, embroidered, of man-made fibres	6302.5310	346
餐桌用织物制品,刺绣的,棉制	Table linen, embroidered, of cotton	6302.5110	346
餐桌用织物制品,刺绣的,亚麻制	Table linen, embroidered, of flax	6302.5911	346
餐桌用织物制品,棉制,其他	Table linen, of cotton, nes	6302.5190	346
餐桌用织物制品,亚麻制,其他	Table linen, of flax, nes	6302.5919	346
餐桌用织物制品,化学纤维制,其他	Table linen, of man-made fibres, nes	6302.5390	346
餐桌用织物制品,其他纺织材料制	Table linen, of other textile materials	6302.5990	346
餐桌用织物制品,针织或钩编的,其他	Table linen, knitted or crocheted, nes	6302.4090	346

C

商品名称	Article Description	税则号列	申报要素
餐桌用织物制品,针织或钩编的,手工制	Table linen, knitted or crocheted, hand-worked	6302.4010	346
残疾人车,非机械驱动	Disabled persons carriages, not mechanically propelled	8713.1000	7
残疾人车,其他	Disabled persons carriages, nes	8713.9000	7
残疾人车辆用零件、附件	Disabled persons carriages parts and accessoris	8714.2000	3
残疾人用车,非机械驱动	Carriages for disabled persons, not mechanically propelled	8713.1000	7
残疾人用车,其他	Carriages for disabled persons, nes	8713.9000	7
残渣,加工处理油脂物质及动植物蜡所剩的	Residues resulting from the treatment of fatty substances of animal or vegetable waxes	1522.0000	4
残渣,其他,石油或从沥青矿物提取的油类的	Residues, nes, of petroleum oils or of oils obtained from bituminous minerals	2713.9000	134
蚕豆,其他,脱荚的,干的	Broad beans (vicia fabavar major) and horse beans (viciafaba var. Equina, vicia fabavar. minor, nes, dried, shelled	0713.5090	34
蚕豆,种用,脱荚的,干的	Broad beans (vicia fabavar major) and horse beans (viciafaba var. Equina, vicia fabavar. minor, seed, dried, shelled	0713.5010	34
蚕豆罐头,用醋或醋酸以外的其他方法制作或保藏的,未冷冻	Broad beans, in airtight containers, prepared or preserved otherwise than by vinegar or acetic acid, not frozen	2005.9920	1248
蚕茧,适于缫丝的,其他	Silk-worm cocoons, suitable for reeling, nes	5001.0090	45
蚕胶丝	Silk-worm gut	5006.0000	356
蚕蛹	Silkworm eggs	0511.9930	
蚕种	Silkworm graine	0511.9930	
cao			
糙米,其他	Husked (brown) rice, nes	1006.2090	35
槽钢,除热轧、热拉拔或热挤压外未经进一步加工,截面高度低于80毫米	U sections, not further worked than hot-rolled, hot-drawn or extruded, of a height of less than 80mm	7216.1090	468
槽钢,除热轧、热拉拔或热挤压外未经进一步加工,截面高度在80毫米及以上	U sections, not further worked than hot-rolled, hot-drawn or extruded, of a height of 80mm or more	7216.3100	468
草本花卉植物种子	Seeds of herbaceous plants cultivated principally for their flowers	1209.3000	358
草地网球	Lawn-tennis balls	9506.6100	
草地网球拍,不论是否装弦	Lawn-tennis rackets, whether or not strung	9506.5100	
草地早熟禾子,饲料植物用的	Kentucky blue grass (poa pratensis L.) Seed, forage plants	1209.2400	358
草菇,干的	Paddy straw mushroom, dried	0712.3930	4
草菇,鲜或冷藏的	Paddy straw mushroom, fresh or chilled	0709.5940	1
草料打包机,包括收集打包机	Straw or fodder balers, including pickup balers	8433.4000	

C

C

商品名称	Article Description	税则号列	申报要素
草料打包机零件	Straw or fodder balers parts	8433.9090	
草料根,饲料用	Fodder roots, forage products	1214.9000	
草莓,冷冻的	Strawberries, frozen	0811.1000	1
草莓,鲜的	Strawberries, fresh	0810.1000	1
草莓,用其他方法制作或保藏的	Strawberries, otherwise prepared or preserved	2008.8000	248
草坪及运动场地滚压机	Lawn or sports-ground rollers	8432.8010	
草酸	Oxalic acid	2917.1110	36
草酸钴	Cobalt oxalate	2917.1120	36
草酸盐和酯,其他	Oxalic acid salts and esters, nes	2917.1190	36
ce			
侧铲推土机,履带式,其他	Angledozers, track laying, nes	8429.1190	57
侧铲推土机,其他	Angledozers, nes	8429.1990	57
侧铲推土机用铲	Angledozer blades	8431.4200	3
侧围,机动车辆的	Side appearance of bodies, of the motor vehicles	8708.2951	3
测距仪	Rangefinders	9015.1000	
测量或检验仪器、器具及机器,其他	Measuring or checking instruments, appliances and machines, nes	9031.8090	7
测量或检验仪器、器具及机器零件、附件,其他	Measuring or checking instruments, appliances and machines parts and accessories, nes	9031.9000	3
测量仪器及装置,海洋的,其他	Surveying instruments and appliances, oceanographic, nes	9015.8000	7
测量仪器及装置,其他	Surveying instruments and appliances, nes	9015.8000	7
测量仪器及装置,气象的,其他	Surveying instruments and appliances, meteorological, nes	9015.8000	7
测量仪器及装置,摄影用	Surveying instruments and appliances for photogrammetrical	9015.4000	
测量仪器及装置,水文的,其他	Surveying instruments and appliances, hydrological, nes	9015.8000	7
测量仪器及装置的零件、附件	Surveying instruments and appliances parts and accessories	9015.9000	3
ceng			
层压安全玻璃,车辆用	Laminated safety glass, of size and shape suitable for vehicles	7007.2190	234
层压安全玻璃,航空器、航天器及船舶用	Laminated safety glass, for aircraft, spacecraft or vessels	7007.2110	234
层压安全玻璃,其他	Laminated safety glass, nes	7007.2900	234
cha			
叉尾鮰鱼,其他,制作或保藏的,整条或切块,但未绞碎	Ictalurus, nes, prepared or preserved, whole or in pieces, but not minced	1604.1939	48

商品名称	Article Description	税则号列	申报要素
叉子,农业、园艺、林业用手工工具	Forks, hand tools of a kind used in agriculture, horticulture or foresty	8201.2000	256
插床,切削金属或金属陶瓷用	Slotting machines, for removing metal or cermets	8461.2020	7
插管及类似品,医疗、外科、牙科或兽医用	Cannulae and the like, used in medical, surgical, dental or veterinary sciences	9018.3900	3
插花及花蕾,其他,制花束或装饰用的	Cut flowers and flower buds, nes, suitable for bouquets or for ornamental purposes	0603.9000	34
插花及花蕾,鲜的,制花束或装饰用的,其他	Cut flowers and flower buds, fresh, suitable for bouquets or for ornamental purposes, nes	0603.1990	34
插头及插座,用于电压不超过1000伏的线路	Plugs and sockets, for a voltage not exceeding 1000V	8536.6900	8
插头及其他连接器,用于电压超过1000伏的线路	Plugs and other connectors, for a voltage exceeding 1000V	8535.9000	8
茶壶,电热的	Tea makers, electro-thermic	8516.7190	7
茶碱及其衍生物以及它们的盐,其他	Theophylline and their derivatives; salts thereof, nes	2939.5900	34
茶浓缩精汁,包括马黛茶浓缩精汁	Tea extracts, essences and concentrates, including tea or maté extracts, essences and concentrates	2101.2000	268
茶浓缩精汁为基本成分的制品,包括马黛茶浓缩精汁为基本成分的制品	Tea preparations with a basis of extracts, essences and concentrates, including maté preparations with a basis of extracts, essences and concentrates	2101.2000	268
茶为基本成分的制品,包括马黛茶为基本成分的制品	Tea preparations with abasis of tea, including tea preparations with abasis of maté	2101.2000	268
chai			
柴油机曲轴,船舶用	Crank shafts of diesel engine, for ships	8483.1010	
柴油及其他燃料油,其他	Diesel oils and other fuel oils, nes	2710.1929	6
chan			
产量计数器	Production counters	9029.1090	7
产量计数器零件、附件	Production counters parts and accessories	9029.9000	3
铲,侧铲推土机用	Blades for angledozer	8431.4200	3
铲,推土机用	Blades for bulldozer	8431.4200	3
铲斗,推土机或起重机零件	Shovels, parts of bulldozer or cranes	8431.4100	3
铲运机,斗容量超过10立方米的	Scrapers, having a capacity of shovel exceeding $10m^3$	8429.3010	57
铲运机,非自推进的	Scrapers, not self-propelled	8430.6920	5
铲运机,其他	Scrapers, nes	8429.3090	57
铲运机零件	Scrapers parts	8431.4990	3
铲运机械,对泥土、矿物或矿石的,非自推进的,其他	Scraping machinery, for earth, minerals or ores, not self-propelled, nes	8430.6990	5
铲运机械,对泥土、矿物或矿石的,自推进的,其他	Scraping machinery, for earth, minerals or ores, self-propelled, nes	8430.5090	5
铲子	Shovels	8201.1000	256

商品名称	Article Description	税则号列	申报要素
chang			
鲳鱼,冻的	Butterfish(pampus) ,frozen	0303. 7930	18
鲳鱼,鲜或冷的	Butterfish(pamus) ,fresh or chilled	0302. 6930	18
鲳鱼,盐腌及盐渍的	Butterfish(pampus) ,salted or in brine	0305. 6930	4
长柄勺,镀贵金属的,厨房或餐桌用具	Ladles, plated with precious metal, kitchen or tableware	8215. 9100	256
长柄勺,非镀贵金属的,厨房或餐桌用具	Ladles,other than plated with precious metal,kitchen or tableware	8215. 9900	256
长衬裙及衬裙,非针织或钩编的,女式,化学纤维制	Slips and petticoats, not knitted or crocheted, for women or girls,of man-made fibres	6208. 1100	2456
长衬裙及衬裙,非针织或钩编的,女式,棉制	Slips and petticoats, not knitted or crocheted, for women or girls,of cotton	6208. 1920	2456
长衬裙及衬裙,非针织或钩编的,女式,其他	Slips and petticoats, not knitted or crocheted, for women or girls,nes	6208. 1990	2456
长衬裙及衬裙,非针织或钩编的,女式,丝及绢丝制	Slips and petticoats, not knitted or crocheted, for women or girls,of silk or silk waste	6208. 1910	2456
长衬裙及衬裙,针织或钩编的,女式,化学纤维制	Slips and petticoats,knitted or crocheted,for women or girls,of man-made fibres	6108. 1100	2456
长衬裙及衬裙,针织或钩编的,女式,棉制	Slips and petticoats,knitted or crocheted,for women or girls,of cotton	6108. 1910	2456
长衬裙及衬裙,针织或钩编的,女式,其他	Slips and petticoats,knitted or crocheted,for women or girls,nes	6108. 1990	2456
长衬裙及衬裙,针织或钩编的,女式,丝及绢丝制	Slips and petticoats,knitted or crocheted,for women or girls,of silk or silk waste	6108. 1920	2456
长方砌石,天然石料(不包括板岩)制的	Setts,of natural stone(except slate)	6801. 0000	46
长裤,非针织或钩编的,男式,合成纤维制	Trousers,not knitted or crocheted,for men or boys,of synthetic fibres	6203. 4390	2456
长裤,非针织或钩编的,男式,棉制	Trousers,not knitted or crocheted,for men or boys,of cotton	6203. 4290	2456
长裤,非针织或钩编的,男式,其他纺织材料制	Trousers,not knitted or crocheted,for men or boys,of other textile material	6203. 4990	2456
长裤,非针织或钩编的,男式,羊毛或动物细毛制	Trousers,not knitted or crocheted,for men or boys,of wool or fine animal hair	6203. 4100	2456
长裤,非针织或钩编的,女式,棉制	Trousers,not knitted or crocheted,for women or girls,of cotton	6204. 6200	2456
长裤,非针织或钩编的,女式,合成纤维制	Trousers,not knitted or crocheted,for women or girls,of synthetic fibres	6204. 6300	2456
长裤,非针织或钩编的,女式,其他纺织材料制	Trousers,not knitted or crocheted,for women or girls,of other textile materials	6204. 6900	2456
长裤,非针织或钩编的,女式,羊毛或动物细毛制	Trousers,not knitted or crocheted,for women or girls,of fine animal hair	6204. 6100	2456

C

商品名称	Article Description	税则号列	申报要素
长裤,针织或钩编的,男式,合成纤维制	Trousers, knitted or crocheted, for men or boys, of synthetic fibres	6103.4300	2456
长裤,针织或钩编的,男式,棉制	Trousers, knitted or crocheted, for men or boys, of cotton	6103.4200	2456
长裤,针织或钩编的,男式,其他纺织材料制	Trousers, knitted or crocheted, for men or boys, of other textile materials	6103.4900	2456
长裤,针织或钩编的,男式,羊毛或动物细毛制	Trousers, knitted or crocheted, for men or boys, of wool or fine animal hair	6103.4100	2456
长裤,针织或钩编的,女式,合成纤维制	Trousers, knitted or crocheted, for women or girls, of synthetic fibres	6104.6300	2456
长裤,针织或钩编的,女式,棉制	Trousers, knitted or crocheted, for women for girls, of cotton	6104.6200	2456
长裤,针织或钩编的,女式,其他纺织材料制	Trousers, knitted or crocheted, for women or girls, of other textile materials	6104.6900	2456
长裤,针织或钩编的,女式,羊毛或动物细毛制	Trousers, knitted or crocheted, for women or girls, of wool or fine animal hair	6104.6100	2456
长毛绒织物	Long pilefabrics, knitted or crocheted	6001.1000	46
长矛及其零件	Lances and parts	9307.0000	
长鳍金枪鱼,冻的	Albacore tunas (thunnus alalunga), frozen	0303.4100	18
长鳍金枪鱼,冻的	Longfinned tunas (thunnus alalunga), frozen	0303.4100	18
长鳍金枪鱼,鲜或冷的,	Albacore or longfinned tunas (thunnus alalunga), fresh or chilled	0302.3100	18
长鳍金枪鱼,鲜或冷的,	Longfinned tunas (thunnus alalunga)	0302.3100	18
长石	Felspar	2529.1000	13
长睡衣及睡衣裤,非针织或钩编的,男式,化学纤维制	Nightshirts and pyjamas, not knitted or crocheted, for men or boys, of man-made fibres	6207.2200	2456
长睡衣及睡衣裤,非针织或钩编的,男式,棉制	Nightshirts and pyjamas, not knitted or crocheted, for men or boys, of cotton	6207.2100	2456
长睡衣及睡衣裤,非针织或钩编的,男式,其他	Nightshirts and pyjamas, not knitted or crocheted, for men or boys, nes	6207.2990	2456
长睡衣及睡衣裤,非针织或钩编的,男式,丝及绢丝制	Nightshirts and pyjamas, not knitted or crocheted, for men or boys, of silk or silk waste	6207.2910	2456
长睡衣及睡衣裤,针织或钩编的男式,化学纤维制	Nightshirts and pyjamas, knitted or crocheted, for men or boys, of man-made fibres	6107.2200	2456
长睡衣及睡衣裤,针织或钩编的男式,棉制	Nightshirts and pyjamas, knitted or crocheted, for men or boys, of cotton	6107.2100	2456
长睡衣及睡衣裤,针织或钩编的男式,其他	Nightshirts and pyjamas, knitted or crocheted, for men or boys, nes	6107.2990	2456
长睡衣及睡衣裤,针织或钩编的男式,丝及绢丝制	Nightshirts and pyjamas, knitted or crocheted, for men or boys, of silk or silk waste	6107.2910	2456
长统袜或中统袜,针织或钩编的,每根单丝细度在 67 分特以下,女式,其他	Full-length or knee-length hosiery, knitted or crocheted, measuring per single yarn less than 67 decitex, for women or girls, nes	6115.3000	2456

商品名称	Article Description	税则号列	申报要素
长途电话交换机	Toll telephonic switching apparatus	8517.6211	
长尾鹦鹉,改良种用	Parakeets, pure-bred breeding	0106.3210	3
肠,动物的(鱼除外)	Guts of animals (other than fish)	0504.0090	14
肠线(蚕胶丝除外)、肠膜、膀胱或筋腱制品	Articles of gut (other than silkwormgut), of goldbeater's skin, of bladders or of tendons	4206.0000	
肠线,外科用无菌	Catgut, for surgical sterile	3006.1000	3
肠衣,其他	Casings, nes	0504.0019	14
唱机,不带录制装置的,不论是否带有扬声器,其他	Record-players, not incorporating a sound recording device, with or without loudspeakers, nes	8519.8910	5
唱片,其他	Gramophone records, nes	8523.8019	37
唱片,已录制	Gramophone records, recorded	8523.8011	37
唱片套,纸制的,其他	Record sleeves, of paper, paperboard, nes	4819.5000	68
chao			
钞票	Banknotes	4907.0020	1
超声波清洗装置,平板显示器的制造机器及装置	Ultrasonic apparatus for cleaning, flat panel displays manufacture machines and apparatus	8486.3041	7
超声波清洗装置零件及附件,平板显示器的制造机器及装置	Ultrasonic apparatus parts and accessories for cleaning, flat panel displays manufacture machines and apparatus	8486.9090	3
超声波扫描装置,其他	Ultrasonic scanning apparatus, nes	9018.1299	7
超声波探伤检测仪	Ultrasonic examinations apparatus	9031.8031	
超声波诊断仪,B 型	Ultrasonic diagnostic equipment, B-type	9018.1210	
超声波诊断仪,彩色	Ultrasonic diagnostic equipment, chromoscope	9018.1291	
巢菜,饲料用	Vetches, forage products	1214.9000	
che			
车窗玻璃升降器	Windowpane raiser	8708.2930	3
车床,切削金属的,其他	Lathes, for removing metal, nes	8458.9900	7
车床,数控的,切削金属的,其他	Lathes, numerically controlled, for removing metal, nes	8458.9100	7
车床,卧式,切削金属的,其他	Lathes, horizontal, for removing metal, nes	8458.1900	7
车床,卧式,数控的,切削金属的	Lathes, horizontal, numerically controlled, for removing metal	8458.1100	7
车达乳酪,粉化	Cheddar cheese, powdered	0406.2000	24
车达乳酪,未加工	Cheddar cheese, not processed	0406.9000	2468
车费计	Taximeters	9029.1020	
车费计零件、附件	Taximeters parts and accessories	9029.9000	3
车架,30 座及以上客运机动车辆用	Frames, of motor vehicles with 30 seats or more	8708.9921	3
车架,机动车辆用,其他	Frames, of motor vehicles, nes	8708.9991	3
车架,小轿车用	Frames, of saloon cars	8708.9941	3
车架,越野车(4 轮驱动)用	Frames, of cross-country cars (4WD)	8708.9951	3

商品名称	Article Description	税则号列	申报要素
车架,自卸车用	Frames, of dumpers	8708. 9931	3
车架、轮叉及其零件,自行车及脚踏车的	Frames and forks, and parts thereof, of bicycles and other cycles	8714. 9100	3
车辆发动机,压燃式,其他	Engines vehicles, compression-ignition, nes	8408. 2090	123
车辆发动机,压燃式,输出功率在132. 39 千瓦(180 马力)及以上	Engines for vehicles, compression-ignition, of an output of 132. 39kW (180hp) or more	8408. 2010	123
车辆后视镜	Rear-view mirrors for vehicles	7009. 1000	4
车轮及其零件、附件,30 座及以上客运机动车辆用	Road wheels and parts and accessories of motor vehicles with 30 seats or more	8708. 7020	3
车轮及其零件、附件,其他	Road wheels and parts and accessories of motor vehicles, nes	8708. 7090	3
车轮及其零件、附件,特种车辆用	Road wheels and parts and accessories of motor vehicles with special purpose	8708. 7060	3
车轮及其零件、附件,拖拉机的	Road wheels and parts and accessories of tractors	8708. 7010	3
车轮及其零件、附件,小轿车用	Road wheels and parts and accessories of saloon cars	8708. 7040	3
车轮及其零件、附件,越野车(4 轮驱动)用	Road wheels and parts and accessories of cross-country cars(4WD)	8708. 7050	3
车轮及其零件、附件,自卸车用	Road wheels and parts and accessories of dumpers	8708. 7030	3
车门,机动车辆的	Doors, of the motor vehicles	8708. 2952	3
车身(包括驾驶室),10 座以上客车用	Bodies(including cabs), for the motor vehicles, with 10 seats or more	8707. 9010	7
车身(包括驾驶室),10 座以下客车用	Bodies(including cabs), for the motor vehicles, with seats less than 10	8707. 1000	7
车身(包括驾驶室),特种车辆用	Bodies (including cabs), for motor vehicles with special purpose	8707. 9090	7
车身(包括驾驶室)的其他零件、附件,其他	Bodies parts and accessories, of the motor vehicles, nes	8708. 2990	3
车身覆盖件,机动车辆的,其他	Bodies covered parts, of the motor vehicles, nes	8708. 2959	3
车厢或类似品的附件,塑料的	Fittings for coachwork or the like, of plastics	3926. 3000	236
车削用工具,可互换,带有金刚石等工作部件的	Turning tools, interchangeable, with working part of diamonds etc.	8207. 8010	256
车削用工具,可互换,其他	Turning tools, interchangeable, nes	8207. 8090	256
车削中心,切削金属的,其他	Turning centres, for removing metal, nes	8458. 9900	7
车削中心,数控的,切削金属的,其他	Turning centres, numerically controlled, for removing metal, nes	8458. 9100	7
车削中心,卧式,切削金属的,其他	Turning centres, horizontal, for removing metal, nes	8458. 1900	7
车削中心,卧式,数控的,切削金属的	Turning centres, horizontal, numerically controlled, for removing metal	8458. 1100	7
车用汽油	Motor gasoline	2710. 1110	6
车载音频转播器或发射器	Tone converters or transmission apparatus of a kind used for vehicles	8522. 9091	3

C

商品名称	Article Description	税则号列	申报要素
chen			
沉淀硫磺	Sulphur, precipitated	2802.0000	
沉积铜	Cement copper	7401.0000	46
沉降片,针织机的	Sinkers for knitting machines	8448.5190	3
沉香	Aloes wood	1211.9033	34
辰砂	Cinnabar	2617.9010	146
衬衫,非针织或钩编的,男式,化学纤维制	Shirts, not knitted or crocheted, for men or boys, of man-made fibres	6205.3000	2456
衬衫,非针织或钩编的,男式,棉制	Shirts, not knitted or crocheted, for men or boys, of cotton	6205.2000	2456
衬衫,非针织或钩编的,男式,其他	Shirts, not knitted or crocheted, for men or boys, nes	6205.9090	2456
衬衫,非针织或钩编的,男式,丝及绢丝制	Shirts, not knitted or crocheted, for men or boys, of silk or silk waste	6205.9010	2456
衬衫,非针织或钩编的,男式,羊毛或动物细毛制	Shirts, not knitted or crocheted, for men or boys, of wool or fine animal hair	6205.9020	2456
衬衫,非针织或钩编的,女式,化学纤维制	Shirts and shirtblouses, not knitted or crocheted, for women or girls, of man-made fibres	6206.4000	2456
衬衫,非针织或钩编的,女式,棉制	Shirts and shirtblouses, not knitted or crocheted, for women or girls, of cotton	6206.3000	2456
衬衫,非针织或钩编的,女式,其他纺织材料制	Shirts and shirtblouses, not knitted or crocheted, for women or girls, of other textile materials	6206.9000	2456
衬衫,非针织或钩编的,女式,丝及绢丝制	Shirts and shirtblouses, not knitted or crocheted, for women or girls, of silk or silk waste	6206.1000	2456
衬衫,非针织或钩编的,女式,羊毛或动物细毛制	Shirts and shirtblouses, not knitted or crocheted, for women or girls, of wool or fine animal hair	6206.2000	2456
衬衫,针织或钩编的,男式,化学纤维制	Shirts, knitted or crocheted, for men or boys, for man-made fibres	6105.2000	2456
衬衫,针织或钩编的,男式,棉制	Shirts, knitted or crocheted, for men or boys, of cotton	6105.1000	2456
衬衫,针织或钩编的,男式,其他纺织材料制	Shirts, knitted or crocheted, for men or boys, of other textile materials	6105.9000	2456
衬衫,针织或钩编的,女式,化学纤维制	Shirts, knitted or crocheted, for women or girls, of man-made fibres	6106.2000	2456
衬衫,针织或钩编的,女式,棉制	Shirts, knitted or crocheted, for women or girls, of cotton	6106.1000	2456
衬衫,针织或钩编的,女式,其他纺织材料制	Shirts, knitted or crocheted, for women or girls, of other textile materials	6106.9000	2456
cheng			
成匹的编带	Braids in the piece	5808.1000	468
成匹装饰带,非绣制的其他	Ornamental trimmings in the piece, without embroidery	5808.9000	468

商品名称	Article Description	税则号列	申报要素
成品油船,载重量不超过10万吨	Finished oil tanker ships, loading not exceeding 100000t	8901.2011	8
成品油船,载重量超过10万吨,但不超过30万吨	Finished oil tanker ships, loading exceeding 100000t, but not exceeding 300000t	8901.2012	8
成品油船,载重量超过30万吨	Finished oil tanker ships, loading exceeding 300000t	8901.2013	8
成圈机件,针织机的	Stitches forming articles for knitting machines	8448.5190	3
成束或成簇的材料,供制帚、刷用的	Knots and tufts for broom or brush making, prepared	9603.9090	3
成套餐桌用具,其他	Sets of assorted tableware articles, nes	8215.2000	256
成套厨房用具,其他	Sets of assorted kitchenware articles, nes	8215.2000	256
成套刀及刀片,不论是否有锯齿(包括整枝刀),税号82.08的刀除外	Sets of assorted knives with cutting blades, serrated or not (including pruning knives), other than knives of heading No. 82.08, and blades therefor	8211.1000	256
成套的笔,由上述两个或多个组成的	Sets of two or more pens	9608.5000	
成套灯具,圣诞树用	Sets of christmas trees lighting	9405.3000	5
成套工具,由两个或多个子目所列手工工具组成的	Sets of tools, of two or more of other subheadings of hand tools	8205.9000	256
成套工具,由税号82.02至82.05中两个或多个税号所列组成的,零售包装	Sets of tools, of two or more of the headings No. 82.02 to 82.05, put up for retail sale	8206.0000	256
成套或全套的组装玩具,其他	Sets or outfits of toys, nes	9503.0081	5
成套旅行用具,个人梳妆、缝纫或清洁鞋靴、衣服用	Sets for personal travel toilet, sewing or shoe or clothes cleaning	9605.0000	6
成套玩具,缩小(按比例缩小)的建筑的	Sets of toys, of constructional toys	9503.0040	5
成套物品,密封垫的	Sets of gaskets	8484.9000	56
成套物品,由机织物及纱线构成的,不论是否带附件,用以制作小地毯、装饰毯、绣花台布、餐巾或类似的纺织物品,零售包装	Sets consisting of woven fabric and yarn, whether or not with accessories, for making up into rugs, tapestries, embroidered table cloths or serviettes, or similar textile articles, put up in packings for retail sale	6308.0000	3
成套颜料	Sets of colours	3213.1000	3
成形机器的零件	Forming machines parts	8474.9000	3
城市垃圾	Municipal waste	3825.1000	34
橙	Oranges	0805.1000	1245
橙油	Essential oils of orange	3301.1200	34
橙汁,非冷冻的,白利糖度值不超过20	Orange juice, not frozen, of a brix value not exceeding 20	2009.1200	2468
橙汁,冷冻的	Orange juice, frozen	2009.1100	2468
橙汁,其他	Orange juice, nes	2009.1900	2468
橙汁饮料	Orangeade	2202.1000	248
秤,输送带上连续称货的,其他	Scales for continuous weighing of goods on conveyors, nes	8423.2090	

商品名称	Article Description	税则号列	申报要素
秤砣,衡器用	Weighing machine weights of all kinds, for weighing machine	8423.9000	
chi			
齿轮泵,排液回转式,电动式	Gear pumps, for positive displacement, rotary, electric	8413.6021	27
齿轮泵,排液回转式,其他	Gear pumps, for positive displacement, rotary, nes	8413.6029	27
齿轮泵,排液回转式,液压式	Gear pumps, for positive displacement, rotary, hydraulic	8413.6022	27
齿轮及齿轮传动装置,其他	Gears and gearing, nes	8483.4090	7
齿轮及齿轮传动装置零件	Gears and gearing parts	8483.9000	3
齿轮精加工机床,切削金属或金属陶瓷用,其他	Gear finishing machines, for removing metal or cermets, nes	8461.4090	7
齿轮精加工机床,数控的,切削金属或金属陶瓷用	Gear finishing machines, numerically controlled, for removing metal or cermets	8461.4010	7
齿轮磨床,切削金属或金属陶瓷用,其他	Gear grinding machines, for removing metal or cermets, nes	8461.4090	7
齿轮磨床,数控的,切削金属或金属陶瓷用	Gear grinding machines, numerically controlled, for removing metal or cermets	8461.4010	7
齿轮箱及其他变速装置	Gear boxes and other speed changers	8483.4090	7
赤豆,其他,脱荚的,干的	Small red (adzuki) beans (phaseolus or vigna angularis), nes, shelled, dried	0713.3290	34
赤豆,种用,其他,脱荚的,干的	Small red (adzuki) beans (phaseolus or vigna angularis), seed, nes, shelled, dried	0713.3219	34
赤豆馅,用醋或醋酸以外的其他方法制作或保藏的,未冷冻,其他	Red bean paste, prepared or preserved otherwise than by vinegar or acetic acid, not frozen, nes	2005.5191	148
赤豆馅罐头	Red bean paste, in airtight containers	2005.5111	148
赤铁矿,已烧结	Brown haematite, agglomerated	2601.1200	1346
赤铁矿,已烧结	Red haematite, agglomerated	2601.1200	1346
赤铜矿	Cuprite	2603.0000	146
chong			
充气筏	Inflatable rafts	8907.1000	5
充气筏	Rafts, inflatable	8907.1000	5
充气褥垫,化学纤维制	Pneumatic mattresses, of man-made fibres	6306.4020	346
充气褥垫,棉制	Pneumatic mattresses, of cotton	6302.5990	346
充气褥垫,其他	Pneumatic mattresses, nes	6306.4090	346
充气橡胶轮胎,翻新的,航空器用	Pneumatic tyres, retreaded, of a kind used on aircratr	4012.1300	234
充气橡胶轮胎,翻新的,机动大客车或货运机动车辆用	Pneumatic tyres, retreaded, of a kind used on buses or corries	4012.1200	234
充气橡胶轮胎,翻新的,机动小客车(包括旅行小客车及赛车)用	Pneumatic tyres, retreaded, of a kind used on motor cars (including station wagons and racing cars)	4012.1100	234
充气橡胶轮胎,翻新的,其他	Pneumatic tyres, retreaded, nes	4012.1900	234
充气橡胶轮胎,旧的,其他	Pneumatic tyres, used, nes	4012.2090	234

商品名称	Article Description	税则号列	申报要素
充气橡胶轮胎,旧的,汽车用	Pneumatic tyres, used, of a kind used on motor cars, buses or lorries	4012.2010	234
充气橡胶轮胎,新的,航空器用	Pneumatic tyres, new, of rubber of a kind used on aircraft	4011.3000	1238
充气橡胶轮胎,新的,机动小客车(包括旅行小客车及赛车)用	Pneumatic tyres, new, of rubber of a kind used on motor cars (including station wagons and racing cars)	4011.1000	1238
充气橡胶轮胎,新的,建筑业或工业搬运车辆及机器用,辋圈尺寸不超过61厘米	Pneumatic tyres, new, of rubber, of a kind used on construction or industrial handling vehicles and machines and having a rim size not exceeding 61cm, nes	4011.9300	1238
充气橡胶轮胎,新的,建筑业或工业搬运车辆及机器用,辋圈尺寸超过61厘米	Pneumatic tyres, new, of rubber, of a kind used on construction or industrial handling vehicles and machines and having a rim size exceeding 61cm, nes	4011.9400	1238
充气橡胶轮胎,新的,客运机动车辆或货运机动车辆用	Pneumatic tyres, new, of rubber of a kind used on buses or lorries	4011.2000	1238
充气橡胶轮胎,新的,摩托车用	Pneumatic tyres, new, of rubber of a kind used on motorcycles	4011.4000	1238
充气橡胶轮胎,新的,农业或林业车辆及机器用	Pneumatic tyres, new, of rubber, of a kind used on agricultural or forestry vehicles and machines	4011.9200	1238
充气橡胶轮胎,新的,其他	Pneumatic tyres, new, of rubber, nes	4011.9900	
充气橡胶轮胎,新的,人字形胎面或类似胎面的,建筑业或工业搬运车辆及机器用,辋圈尺寸不超过61厘米	Pneumatic tyres, new, of rubber, having a "herring-bone" or similar tread, of a kind used on construction or industrial handling vehicles and machines and having a rim size not exceeding 61cm	4011.6200	1238
充气橡胶轮胎,新的,人字形胎面或类似胎面的,建筑业或工业搬运车辆及机器用,辋圈尺寸超过61厘米	Pneumatic tyres, new, of rubber, having a "herring-bone" or similar tread, of a kind used on construction or industrial handling vehicles and machines and having a rim size exceeding 61cm	4011.6300	1238
充气橡胶轮胎,新的,人字形胎面或类似胎面的,农业或林业车辆及机器用	Pneumatic tyres, new, of rubber, having a "herring-bone" or similar tread, of a kind used on agricultural or forestry vehicles and machines	4011.6100	1238
充气橡胶轮胎,新的,人字形胎面或类似胎面的,其他	Pneumatic tyres, new, of rubber, having a "herring-bone" or similar tread, nes	4011.6900	1238
充气橡胶轮胎,新的,自行车用	Pneumatic tyres, new, of rubber of a kind used on bicycles	4011.5000	1238
冲床,加工金属用,其他	Punch press, for working metal, nes	8462.4900	7
冲床,数控的,加工金属用,其他	Punch press, numerically controlled, for working metal	8462.4119	7
冲剪两用机,加工金属用	Combined punching and shearing machines, for working metal	8462.4900	7

C

商品名称	Article Description	税则号列	申报要素
冲剪两用机,加工金属用	Punching and shearing combined machines, for working metal	8462.4900	7
冲剪两用机,数控的,加工金属用	Combined punching and shearing machines, numerically controlled, for working metal	8462.4190	7
冲剪两用机,数控的,加工金属用	Punching and shearing combined machines, numerically controlled, for working metal	8462.4190	7
冲浪板	Surf-boards	9506.2900	5
冲压机床,加工金属用,其他	Die-stamping machines, for working metal, nes	8462.1090	7
冲压机床,数控的,加工金属用	Die-stamping machines, numerically controlled, for working metal	8462.1010	7
虫胶	Lac	1301.9090	
虫蜡,其他	Insect waxes, nes	1521.9090	
chou			
抽水马桶,陶制	Water closet pans, of pottery	6910.9000	268
抽水马桶,瓷制	Water closet pans, of porcelain or china	6910.1000	268
抽提溶剂油	Rubber solvent, paint solvent, extractive solvent	2710.1130	6
抽油烟机,罩的平面最大边长不超过120厘米	Range hoods, hoods having a maximum horizontal side not exceeding 120cm	8414.6010	23
臭氧治疗器	Ozone therapy apparatus	9019.2000	
chu			
初级形状的,其他	Polyacetals, in primary forms, nes	3907.1090	1256
除草机,农业、园艺及林业用,其他	Weeders, for agricultural, horticultural or forestry use, nes	8432.2900	
除草剂,零售包装	Herbicides, put up for retail sale	3808.9311	36
除草剂,其他	Herbicides, nes	3808.9319	36
除尘器,工业用,袋式	Dust collectors for industry uses, baghoused	8421.3922	7
除尘器,工业用,其他	Dust collectors for industry uses, nes	8421.3929	7
除尘器,工业用,静电式	Dust collectors for industry uses, electrostatic	8421.3921	7
除尘器,工业用,旋风式	Dust collectors for industry uses, cyclone	8421.3923	7
除臭剂,人体用	Deodorants, for personal use	3307.2000	23
除虫菊	Pyrethrum	1211.9091	34
除灰器,过热水锅炉的辅助设备	Soot removers, auxiliary plant for use with super-heated water boilers	8404.1010	3
除灰器,集中供暖用的热水锅炉的辅助设备	Soot removers, auxiliary plant for use with central heating boilers	8404.1020	3
除灰器,蒸汽锅炉的辅助设备	Soot removers, auxiliary plant for use with steam or other vapour generating watertube boilers	8404.1010	3
除墨剂及类似品	Ink-removers and the like	3824.9020	36
除霜器,机动车辆用	Defrosters for motor vehicles	8512.4000	7
厨房废物处理器,家用电动器具	Kitchen waste disposers, electro-mechanical domestic appliances	8509.8020	

商品名称	Article Description	税则号列	申报要素
厨房器具,瓷制	Kitchenware, of porcelain	6911.1020	268
厨房器具,陶制	Kitchenware, of pottery	6912.0090	268
厨房用具,成套货品,其他	Kitchenware sets of assorted articles, nes	8215.2000	256
厨房用具,成套货品,至少其中一件物品是镀贵金属的	Kitchenware sets of assorted articles containing at least one article plated with precious metal	8215.1000	256
厨房用具,镀贵金属的	Kitchenware plated with precious metal	8215.9100	256
厨房用具,其他	Kitchenware, nes	8215.9900	256
厨房用具,塑料的	Kitchenware, of plastics	3924.1000	23
厨房用制品,化学纤维制,其他	Kitchen linen, of man-made fibres, nes	6302.9300	346
厨房用制品,毛巾织物或类似的毛圈织物的,棉制	Kitchen linen, of terry towelling or similar terry fabrics, of cotton	6302.6090	346
厨房用制品,棉制,其他	Kitchen linen, of cotton, nes	6302.9100	346
厨房用制品,其他	Kitchen linen, nes	6302.5990	346
厨房用制品,亚麻制,其他	Kitchen linen, of flax, nes	6302.9910	346
锄	Picks	8201.3000	256
储存保管箱,带锁,贱金属制	Safe deposit lockers for cash boxes and the like, of base metal	8303.0000	256
储存式电热水器	Electric storage waterheaters	8516.1010	7
储存式电散热器	Electric storage heating radiators	8516.2100	7
处理纺织纱线的机器,其他	Machines for preparing textile yarns, nes	8445.9090	7
处理器,集成电路,不论是否带有存储器、转换器、逻辑电路、放大器、时钟及时序电路或其他电路	Processors, electronic integrated circuits, whether or not combined with memories, converters, logic circuits, amplifiers, clock and timing circuits, or other circuits	8542.3100	37
chuan			
川芎	Rhizoma ligustici	1211.9018	34
穿戴器具,弥补生理缺陷或残疾的	Worn appliances, to compensate for a defect or disability	9021.9000	3
传动带或输送带及带料,纺织材料制的,不论是否用塑料浸渍、涂布、包覆或压层,也不论是否用金属或其他材料加强	Transmission or conveyor belts or belting, of textile material, whether or not impregnated, coated, covered or laminated with plastics, or reinforced with metal or other material	5910.0000	
传动带及带料,硫化橡胶制的,其他	Transmission belts or belting, of vulcanized rubber, nes	4010.3900	1368
传动阀,气压的	Transmissions valves, for pneumatic	8481.2020	
传动阀,油压的	Transmissions valves, for oleohydraulic	8481.2010	
传动元件,单独报验的带齿的轮、链轮及其他	Toothed wheels, chain sprockets and other transmission elements presented separately	8483.9000	3
传动元件零件	Toothed wheels parts	8483.9000	3
传动轴,船舶用,其他	Transmission shafts, for ships, nes	8483.1010	
传动轴,机动车辆用,其他	Transmission shafts, of motor vehicles, nes	8709.9992	3

C

商品名称	Article Description	税则号列	申报要素
传动轴,其他	Transmission shafts,nes	8483.1090	
传动轴零件	Transmission shafts parts	8483.9000	3
船舶,不以航行为主要功能,其他	Vessels, the navigability of which is subsidiary to their main function,nes	8905.9090	37
船舶,非机动的,其他	Vessels, with non-motor,nes	8901.9090	8
船舶,供拆卸的	Vessels,for breaking up	8908.0000	5
船舶,机动的,多用途的	Vessels,motor powered,multi-purposes	8901.9050	8
船舶,机动的,其他	Vessels,motor powered,nes	8901.9080	8
船舶,未制成或不完整的	Vessels,unfinished or incomplete	8906.9030	5
船舶,娱乐或运动用,其他	Vessels,for pleasure or sports,nes	8903.9900	58
船舶发动机,点燃往复式或旋转式,其他	Marine propulsion engines, spark-ignition reciprocating or rotary,nes	8407.2900	3
船舶发动机,压燃式	Marine propulsion engines,compression-ignition	8408.1000	
船舶分段	Vessels segments	8906.9030	5
船舶或码头的碰垫,不论是否可充气	Boat or dock fenders,whether or not inflatable	4016.9400	236
船舶舷外发动机,点燃往复式或旋转式	Marine outboard motors, spark-ignition reciprocating or rotary	8407.2100	3
船桨叶	Ships or boats blades	8487.1000	3
船用推进器及桨叶	Ships or boats propellers and blades therefor	8487.1000	3
船用洗舱机,喷雾喷射机械器具	Marine cabinet washer, spraying mechanical appliances	8424.8991	7
串音测试器,通讯专用的	Cross-talk meters, specially designed for telecommunications	9030.4090	7
chuang			
窗、法兰西式(落地)窗及其框架,辐射松制的	Windows,French-windows and their frames,of radiata pine	4418.1010	58
窗、法兰西式(落地)窗及其框架,辐射松制的,其他木制的	Windows,French-windows and their frames,of radiata pine,of other wood	4418.1090	58
窗板或类似制品及其零件,塑料的	Shutters and similar articles and parts thereof, of plastics	3925.3000	23
窗及其框架,塑料的	Windows and their frames,of plastics	3925.2000	23
窗帘,钩编的,合成纤维制	Curtains,crocheted,of synthetic fibres	6303.1220	346
窗帘,钩编的,棉制	Curtains,crocheted,of cotton	6303.1932	346
窗帘,钩编的,其他纺织材料制	Curtains,crocheted,of other textile materials	6303.1992	346
窗帘,合成纤维制,其他	Curtains,of synthetic fibres,nes	6303.9200	346
窗帘,棉制,其他	Curtains,of cotton,nes	6303.9100	346
窗帘,其他纺织材料制	Curtains,of other textile materials	6303.9900	346
窗帘,针织的,合成纤维制	Curtains,knitted,of synthetic fibres	6303.1210	346
窗帘,针织的,棉制	Curtains,knitted,of cotton	6303.1931	346
窗帘,针织的,其他纺织材料制	Curtains,knitted,of other textile materials	6303.1991	346
窗用透明纸	Window transparencies of paper	4814.9000	4

商品名称	Article Description	税则号列	申报要素
床单,棉制,其他	Bed sheets, of cotton, nes	6302.3191	346
床单,印花的,化学纤维制	Bed sheets, printed, of man-made fibres	6302.2210	346
床单,印花的,棉制	Bed sheets, printed, of cotton	6302.2110	346
床垫,海绵橡胶或泡沫塑料制,不论是否包面	Mattresses, of cellular rubber or plastics, whether or not covered	9404.2100	6
床垫,其他材料制	Mattresses, of other materials	9404.2900	6
床垫支架	Mattress supports	9404.1000	
床上用织物制品,刺绣的,化学纤维制	Bed linen, embroidered, of man-made fibres	6302.3210	346
床上用织物制品,刺绣的,麻制,其他	Bed linen, embroidered, of bast fibres, nes	6302.3921	346
床上用织物制品,刺绣的,棉制	Bed linen, embroidered, of cotton	6302.3110	346
床上用织物制品,刺绣的,其他	Bed linen, embroidered, nes	6302.3991	346
床上用织物制品,化学纤维制,其他	Bed linen, of man-made fibres, nes	6302.3290	346
床上用织物制品,麻制,其他	Bed linen, of bast fibres, nes	6302.3929	346
床上用织物制品,棉制,其他	Bed linen, embroidered, of cotton, nes	6302.3199	346
床上用织物制品,其他	Bed linen, nes	6302.3999	346
床上用织物制品,丝及绢丝制,其他	Bed linen, of silk or silk waste, nes	6302.3910	346
床上用织物制品,印花的,化学纤维制,其他	Bed linen, printed, of man-made fibres, nes	6302.2290	346
床上用织物制品,印花的,麻制	Bed linen, printed, of bast fibres	6302.2920	346
床上用织物制品,印花的,棉制,其他	Bed linen, printed, of cotton, nes	6302.2190	346
床上用织物制品,印花的,其他纺织材料制	Bed linen, printed, of other textile materials	6302.2990	346
床上用织物制品,印花的,丝及绢丝制	Bed linen, printed, of silk or silk waste	6302.2910	346
床上用织物制品,针织或钩编的,棉制	Bed linen, knitted or crocheted, of cotton	6302.1010	346
床上用织物制品,针织或钩编的,其他纺织材料制	Bed linen, knitted or crocheted, of other textile materials	6302.1090	346
床头灯,电气的	Bedside lamps, electric	9405.2000	5
床帷,钩编的,合成纤维制	Bed valances, crocheted, of synthetic fibres	6303.1220	346
床帷,钩编的,棉制	Bed valances, crocheted, of cotton	6303.1932	346
床帷,钩编的,其他纺织材料制	Bed valances, crocheted, of other textile materials	6303.1992	346
床帷,合成纤维制,其他	Bed valances, of synthetic fibres, nes	6303.9200	346
床帷,棉制,其他	Bed valances, of cotton, nes	6303.9100	346
床帷,其他纺织材料制	Bed valances, of other textile materials	6303.9900	346
床帷,针织的,合成纤维制	Bed valances, knitted, of synthetic fibres	6303.1210	346
床帷,针织的,棉制	Bed valances, knitted, of cotton	6303.1931	346
床帷,针织的,其他纺织材料制	Bed valances, knitted, of other textile materials	6303.1991	346
床罩,刺绣的,化学纤维制	Bedspreads, embroidered, of man-made fibres	6304.1931	346
床罩,刺绣的,棉或麻制	Bedspreads, embroidered, of cotton or bast fibres	6304.1921	346
床罩,刺绣的,其他纺织材料制	Bedspreads, embroidered, of other textile materials	6304.1991	346
床罩,钩编的,其他	Bedspreads, crocheted, nes	6304.1139	346
床罩,钩编的,手工制	Bedspreads, crocheted, hand-worked	6304.1131	346

C

商品名称	Article Description	税则号列	申报要素
床罩,化学纤维制,其他	Bedspreads, of man-made fibres, nes	6304. 1939	346
床罩,棉或麻制,其他	Bedspreads, of cotton or bast fibres, nes	6304. 1929	346
床罩,其他纺织材料制,其他	Bedspreads, of other textile materials, nes	6304. 1999	346
床罩,丝及绢丝制	Bedspreads, of silk or silk waste	6304. 1910	346
床罩,针织的,其他	Bedspreads, knitted, nes	6304. 1129	346
床罩,针织的,手工制	Bedspreads, knitted, hand-worked	6304. 1121	346
chui			
吹风机,理发器具,电热的	Hair dryers, hair-dressing apparatus, electro-thermic	8516. 3100	7
吹塑机	Blow moulding machines, for working plastics	8477. 3000	7
吹雪机	Snow-blowers	8430. 2000	5
吹雪机零件	Snow-blowers parts	8431. 4990	3
锤子	Hammers and sledge hammers	8205. 2000	256
chun			
纯 MDI	Diphenylmethane diisocyanate	2929. 1030	36
纯碱	Disodium carbonate	2836. 2000	
醇酸树脂,初级形状的	Alkyd resins, in primary forms	3907. 5000	1256
ci			
瓷器,实验室、化学或其他专门技术用途的	Porcelain wares for laboratory, chemical or other technical uses	6909. 1100	5
瓷制品,其他	Porcelain articles, nes	6914. 1000	36
瓷砖,建筑用	Ceramic bricks for building	6904. 1000	5
磁带,其他	Magnetic tapes, nes	8523. 2990	37
磁带,未录制的宽度不超过4毫米的	Magnetic tapes, of a width not exceeding 4mm, unrecorded	8523. 2921	37
磁带,未录制的宽度超过4毫米,但不超过6.5毫米的	Magnetic tapes, of a width exceeding 4mm, but not exceeding 6.5mm, unrecorded	8523. 2922	37
磁带,未录制的宽度超过6.5毫米的	Magnetic tapes, of a width exceeding 6.5mm, unrecorded	8523. 2923	37
磁带,已录制的,其他	Magnetic tapes, recorded, nes	8523. 2929	37
磁带,重放声音或图像信息的	Magnetic tapes, for reproducing sound or image phenomena	8523. 2928	37
磁飞轮,点燃式或压燃式内燃发动机用的,其他	Magnetic flywheels, for electrical ignition or starting equipment, nes	8511. 2090	7
磁飞轮,机车、航空器及船舶用,点燃式或压燃式内燃发动机用的	Magnetic flywheels, for locomotives, aircraft or ships, for electrical ignition or starting equipment	8511. 2010	7
磁粉探伤检测仪	Magnetic examinations apparatus	9031. 8032	
磁化后准备制永磁铁的物品	Articles intended to become permanent magnets after magnetization	8505. 1900	48
磁黄铁矿,含镍	Pyrrhotite, nickeliferous	2604. 0000	146
磁控管	Magnetrons	8540. 7100	35

商品名称	Article Description	税则号列	申报要素
磁盘,其他	Magnetic discs, nes	8523.2919	37
磁盘,未录制	Magnetic discs, unrecorded	8523.2911	37
磁条卡,未录制	Magnetic stripe cards, unrecorded	8523.2110	37
磁条卡,已录制	Magnetic stripe cards, recorded	8523.2120	37
磁头,盒式磁带录音机或放声机用	Magnetic heads, of cassette magnetic tape recorders or reproducers	8522.9022	3
磁头零件,盒式磁带录音机或放声机用	Parts of magnetic heads, of cassette magnetic tape recorders or reproducers	8522.9023	3
雌(甾)激素	Oestrogens	2937.2300	36
次磷酸盐,无机的	Phosphinates (hypophosphites), inorganic	2835.1000	
次硫酸盐,其他,无机的	Sulphoxylates, nes, inorganic	2831.9000	
次氯酸钙,商品级	Calcium hypochlorite, commercial	2828.1000	
次氯酸盐,其他,无机的	Hypochlorites, nes, inorganic	2828.9000	
次溴酸盐,无机的	Hypobromites, inorganic	2828.9000	
刺刀及其零件	Bayonets and parts	9307.0000	
刺槐豆,包括刺槐豆子	Locust beans, including locust bean seeds	1212.9920	134
刺绣穿孔锥及类似制品,手工用	Embroidery stilettos and similar articles, for use in the hand	7319.9000	
刺绣品,成匹、成条或成小块图案的,不见底布的	Embroidery in the piece, in strips or in motifs, without visible ground	5810.1000	46
刺绣品,成匹、成条或成小块图案的,化学纤维制	Embroidery in the piece, in strips or in motifs, of man-made fibres	5810.9200	46
刺绣品,成匹、成条或成小块图案的,棉制	Embroidery in the piece, in strips or in motifs, of cotton	5810.9100	46
刺绣品,成匹、成条或成小块图案的,其他	Embroidery in the piece, in strips or in motifs, nes	5810.9900	46
cong			
从油类提取的油膏	Factice derived from oils	4002.9990	136
葱属蔬菜,其他,鲜或冷藏的	Alliaceous vegetables, nes, fresh or chilled	0703.9090	1
cu			
粗苯	Benzole	2707.1000	6
粗二甲苯	Xylole	2707.3000	6
粗甘油	Glycerol, crude	1520.0000	6
粗甲苯	Toluole	2707.2000	6
粗酒石	Argol	2307.0000	
粗粒及粗粉,其他谷物的	Groats and meal of cereal, nes	1103.1990	4
粗粒及粗粉,其他米的	Groats and meal of rice, nes	1103.1929	4
粗粒及粗粉,籼米的	Groats and meal of long grain	1103.1921	4
粗粒及粗粉,小麦的	Groats and meal of wheat	1103.1100	4
粗粒及粗粉,燕麦的	Groats and meal of oats	1103.1910	4
粗粒及粗粉,玉米的	Groats and meal of maize(corn)	1103.1300	4

C

C

商品名称	Article Description	税则号列	申报要素
粗木精	Wood naphtha	3807.0000	3
粗萘	Naphthalene, crude	2707.4000	6
粗纱机,毛纺的	Roving machines, for worsted	8445.1322	7
粗纱机,棉纺的	Roving frames, for cotton	8445.1321	7
粗纱机,其他	Roving machines, nes	8445.1329	7
粗纱机织物,玻璃纤维制	woven fabrics of rovings, of glass fibres	7019.4000	46
粗筛,手用	Hand sieves	9604.0000	
粗松螺旋花线,扁条及类似品制的螺旋花线	Gimped yarn, and strip and the like, gimped	5606.0000	
粗制二聚戊烯	Crude dipentene	3805.9090	36
醋	Vinegar	2209.0000	268
醋代用品,用醋酸制得的	Substitutes for vinegar, obtained from acetic acid	2209.0000	268
醋栗,黑、白或红的,冷冻的	Currants, black, white or red, frozen	0811.2000	1
醋栗,黑、白或红的,鲜的	Currants, black, white or red, fresh	0810.9020	1
醋氢可酮(INN)及盐	Thebacon (INN) and salts	2939.1100	34
醋酸纤维单纱,非供零售用,其他	Viscose rayon single yarn, not put up for retail sale, nes	5403.3390	3468
醋酸纤维多股纱线或缆线	Cellulose acetate multiple or cabled yarn	5403.4200	3468
醋纤纤维制机织物,按重量计人造纤维长丝、扁条或类似品含量在85%及以上,染色	Cellulose acetate woven fabrics, containing 85% or more by weight of artificial filament or strip or the like, dyed	5408.2220	2468
醋纤纤维制机织物,按重量计人造纤维长丝、扁条或类似品含量在85%及以上,色织	Cellulose acetate woven fabrics, containing 85% or more by weight of artificial filament or strip or the like, of yarns of different colours	5408.2320	2468
醋纤纤维制机织物,按重量计人造纤维长丝、扁条或类似品含量在85%及以上,未漂白或漂白	Cellulose acetate woven fabrics, containing 85% or more by weight of artificial filament or strip or the like, unbleached or bleached	5408.2120	2468
醋纤纤维制机织物,按重量计人造纤维长丝、扁条或类似品含量在85%及以上,印花	Cellulose acetate woven fabrics, containing 85% or more by weight of artificial filament or strip or the like, printed	5408.2420	2468
簇绒机,地毯织机	Tufting machines, for making carpets or rugs	8447.9011	7
簇绒机,其他	Tufting machines, nes	8447.9019	7
簇绒机的辅助机器	Tufting machines auxiliary, for making carpets or rugs	8448.1900	3
簇绒织物,纺织材料制,其他	Tufted textile fabrics of textile materials, nes	5802.3090	468
簇绒织物,化学纤维制	Tufted textile fabrics of man-made fibres	5802.3040	468
簇绒织物,棉或麻制	Tufted textile fabrics of cotton or bast fibres	5802.3030	468
簇绒织物,丝及绢丝制	Tufted textile fabrics of silk or silk waste	5802.3010	468
簇绒织物,羊毛或动物细毛制	Tufted textile fabrics of wool or fine animal hair	5802.3020	468
cui			
催干剂,配制的,油漆及清漆用	Driers, prepared, for paints and varnishes	3211.0000	36
脆银矿	Stephanite	2616.1000	146

商品名称	Article Description	税则号列	申报要素
cun			
存储盒及类似品，办公室、商店及类似场所使用的，纸制的	Storage boxes and similar articles, of a kind used in offices, shops or the like, of paper, paperboard,	4819.6000	68
存储器，集成电路	Memories, electronic integrated circuits	8542.3200	37
cuo			
锉屑、车屑及颗粒，已按规格分级的，镁的	Raspings, turnings and granules, graded according to size, of magnesium	8104.3000	16

D

商品名称	Article Description	税则号列	申报要素
da			
打靶用步枪,其他	Target shooting rifles, nes	9303.3000	
打靶用猎枪,包括组合式滑膛来复枪	Target shooting shotguns, including combination shotgun rifles	9303.2000	
打火机,其他	Lighters, nes	9613.8000	5
打火机,袖珍型,可充气的	Lighters, pocket, gas fuelled, refillable	9613.2000	
打火机,一次性袖珍型气体的	Lighters, pocket, gas fuelled, non refillable	9613.1000	
打火机芯或类似品,用纺织材料机织、编结或针织而成的	Wicks, of woven textile, plaited or knitted, for lighters or the like	5908.0000	
打击乐器,其他	Percussion musical instruments, nes	9206.0000	5
打孔冲子及类似工具	Perforating punches and similar tools	8203.4000	256
打孔机,装订用	Perforator, for stapling	8472.9021	
打印机,激光的,专用于自动数据处理设备的	Printers, laser, of a kind solely used for automatic data processing machine	8443.3212	57
打印机,可与网络连接的	Printers, capable of connecting to a network	8443.3290	57
打印机,喷墨的,专用于自动数据处理设备的	Printers, ink-jet, of a kind solely used for automatic data processing machine	8443.3213	57
打印机,热敏的,专用于自动数据处理设备的	Printers, thermal, of a kind solely used for automatic data processing machine	8443.3214	57
打印机,针式,专用于自动数据处理设备的	Printers of stylus, of a kind solely used for automatic data processing machine	8443.3211	57
打印机,专用于自动数据处理设备的,其他	Printers, of a kind solely used for automatic data processing machine, nes	8443.3219	57
打印纸卷、纸张及纸盘,已印制的,自动记录器用	Rolls, sheets and dials, printed for self-recording apparatus	4823.4000	68
打桩机	Pile-drivers	8430.1000	5
打桩机零件	Pile-drivers parts	8431.4990	3
打字机,电动的,其他	Typewriters, electric, nes	8469.0020	
打字机,非电动,其他	Typewriters, non-electric, nes	8469.0030	
打字机,自动的	Typewriters, automatic	8469.0012	
打字机的零件、附件	Parts and accessories of the type writer	8473.1000	3
大螯虾,冻的	Lobsters (homarus spp.), frozen	0306.1200	1
大螯虾,其他,未冻的	Lobsters (homarus spp.), nes, not frozen	0306.2290	14
大螯虾种苗	Lobsters (homarus spp.), for cultivation	0306.2210	3
大葱,鲜或冷藏的	Scallion, fresh or chilled	0703.9020	1
大豆,黄色	Soya beans, yellow	1201.0091	3
大豆,黑色	Soya beans, black	1201.0092	3
大豆,其他	Soya beans, nes	1201.0099	3

商品名称	Article Description	税则号列	申报要素
大豆,青色	Soya beans,green	1201.0093	3
大豆,种用	Soya beans,seed	1201.0010	3
大豆粉	Flours and meals,of soya beans	1208.1000	4
大钢琴	Grand pianos	9201.2000	5
大海子	Bantaroi seeds	1211.9032	34
大黄	Rhubarb	1211.9024	34
大理石,用锯或其他方法切割成矩形,包括正方形	Marble, merely cut, by sawing or otherwise, into blocks or slabs of a rectangular (including square) shape	2515.1200	148
大理石,原状或粗加修整	Marble,crude or roughly trimmed	2515.1100	148
大理石碑石或建筑用石及其制品,简单切削或锯开并具有一个平面的	Marble monumental or building stone and articles thereof, simply cut or sawn, with a flat or even surface	6802.2110	3468
大理石及其制品,已加工的,其他	Marble and articles thereof,worked,nes	6802.9190	3468
大理石经人工染色的石粒、石片及石粉	Marble artificially coloured granules, chippings and powder	6802.1010	3468
大理石石刻	Marble carvings	6802.9110	3468
大理石碎粒、碎屑及粉末,不论是否热处理	Marble granules, chippings and powder, whether or not heat treated	2517.4100	1
大理石砖、瓦、方块及类似品,不论是否为矩形(包括正方形),其最大表面以可置入边长小于7厘米的方格为限	Marble tiles, cubes and similar articles, whether or not rectangular (including square), the largest surface area of which is capable of being enclosed in a square the side of which is less than 7cm	6802.1010	3468
大丽花,种用,休眠的	Dahlia,seed,dormant	0601.1091	135
大麻,生的或经沤制的	True hemp,raw or retted	5302.1000	4
大麻短纤	True hemp tow	5302.9000	4
大麻废麻	True hemp waste	5302.9000	4
大麻机织物	True hemp woven fabrics	5311.0030	2468
大麻纱线	True hemp yarn	5308.2000	568
大马哈鱼,其他,冻的	Pacific salmon,nes,frozen	0303.1900	18
大马哈鱼,鲜或冷的,	Pacific salmon (oncorhynchus nerka, oncorhynchus gorbuscha, oncorhynchus keta, oncorhynchus tschawytscha, oncorhynchus kisutch, oncorhynchus masou and oncorhynchus rhodurus), fresh or chilled	0302.1220	18
大麦,滚压或制片的	Barley,rolled or flaked	1104.1910	4
大麦,其他	Barley,nes	1003.0090	3
大麦,其他加工的	Barley,other worked	1104.2910	4
大麦,种用	Barley,seed	1003.0010	3
大蒜,干的	Garlic,dried	0712.9050	4
大蒜,其他	Garlic,nes	0703.2090	1

D

商品名称	Article Description	税则号列	申报要素
大蒜,盐水的,暂时保藏,但不适合直接使用的	Garlic, in brine, provisionally preserved, but unsuitable in that state for immediate consumption	0711.9034	34
大蒜,用醋或醋酸制作或保藏的	Garlic, prepared or preserved by vinegar or acetic acid	2001.9010	48
大桶,辐射松制的	Casks, of radiata pine	4416.0010	56
大桶,其他木制的	Casks, of other wood	4416.0090	56
大西洋鲑鱼,冻的	Atlantic salmon(salmo salar), frozen	0303.2210	18
大西洋鲑鱼,鲜或冷的,	Atlantic salmon, fresh or chilled	0302.1210	18
大西洋鲑鱼,制作或保藏的,其他	Atlantic salmon, prepared or preserved, nes	1604.1190	48
大西洋鲑鱼,制作或保藏的,整条或切块,但未绞碎	Atlantic salmon, prepared or preserved, whole or in pieces, but not minced	1604.1110	48
大型机(计算机)	Mainframe	8471.4110	26
大型机(计算机),以系统形式进口或出口的	Mainframe, presented in the form of systems	8471.4910	26
大型机处理部件	Mainframes processing units	8471.5010	26
大眼金枪鱼,冻的	Bigeye tunas(thunnus obesus), frozen	0303.4400	18
大眼金枪鱼,鲜或冷的,	Bigeye tunas(thunnus obesus), fresh or chilled	0302.3400	18
大衣,非针织或钩编的,男式,充绒,化学纤维制	Overcoats, not knitted or crocheted, for men or boys, padded with feathers or down, of man-made fibres	6201.1390	2456
大衣,非针织或钩编的,男式,棉制,其他	Overcoats, not knitted or crocheted, for men or boys, of cotton, nes	6201.1290	2456
大衣,非针织或钩编的,男式,其他纺织材料制	Overcoats, not knitted or crocheted, for men or boys, of other textile materials	6201.1900	2456
大衣,非针织或钩编的,男式,羊毛或动物细毛制	Overcoats, not knitted or crocheted, for men or boys, of wool or fine animal hair	6201.1100	2456
大衣,非针织或钩编的,男式,羊毛或动物细毛制	Overcoats, not knitted or crocheted, for women or girls, of wool or fine animal hair	6202.1100	2456
大衣,非针织或钩编的,女式,充绒,化学纤维制	Overcoats, not knitted or crocheted, for women or girls, padded with feathers or down, of man-made fibres	6202.1390	2456
大衣,非针织或钩编的,女式,棉制,其他	Overcoats, not knitted or crocheted, for women or girls, of cotton, nes	6202.1290	2456
大衣,非针织或钩编的,女式,其他纺织材料制	Overcoats, not knitted or crocheted, for women or girls, of other textile materials	6202.1900	2456
大衣及类似品,针织或钩编的,男式,化学纤维制	Overcoats and similar articles, knitted or crocheted, for men or boys, for man-made fibres	6101.3000	2456
大衣及类似品,针织或钩编的,男式,棉制	Overcoats and similar articles, knitted or crocheted, for men or boys, of cotton	6101.2000	2456
大衣及类似品,针织或钩编的,男式,其他	Overcoats and similar articles, knitted or crocheted, for men or boys, of other textile materials	6101.9090	2456
大衣及类似品,针织或钩编的,男式,羊毛或动物细毛制	Overcoats and similar articles, knitted or crocheted, for men or boys, of wool or fine animal hair	6101.9010	2456

商品名称	Article Description	税则号列	申报要素
大衣及类似品,针织或钩编的,女式,化学纤维制	Overcoats and similar articles, knitted or crocheted, for women or girls, for man-made fibres	6102.3000	2456
大衣及类似品,针织或钩编的,女式,棉制	Overcoats and similar articles, knitted or crocheted, for women or girls, of cotton	6102.2000	2456
大衣及类似品,针织或钩编的,女式,其他	Overcoats and similar articles, knitted or crocheted, for women or girls, of other textile materials	6102.9000	2456
大衣及类似品,针织或钩编的,女式,羊毛或动物细毛制	Overcoats and similar articles, knitted or crocheted, for women or girls, of wool or fine animal hair	6102.1000	2456
dai			
带充气系统的安全气囊及其零件	Safety airbags with inflater system; parts thereof	8708.9500	3
带刺钢铁丝	Barbed wire of iron or steel	7313.0000	36
带风帽的防寒短上衣(包括滑雪短上衣),非针织或钩编的,男式,化学纤维制	Anoraks (including skijackets), not knitted or crocheted, for men or boys, of man-made fibres	6201.9390	2456
带风帽的防寒短上衣(包括滑雪短上衣),非针织或钩编的,男式,棉制	Anoraks (including skijackets), not knitted or crocheted, for men or boys, of cotton	6201.9290	2456
带风帽的防寒短上衣(包括滑雪短上衣),非针织或钩编的,男式,其他纺织材料制	Anoraks (including skijackets), not knitted or crocheted, for men or boys, of other textile materials	6201.9900	2456
带风帽的防寒短上衣(包括滑雪短上衣),非针织或钩编的,女式,化学纤维制	Anoraks (including skijackets), not knitted or crocheted, for women or girls, of man-made fibres	6202.9390	2456
带风帽的防寒短上衣(包括滑雪短上衣),非针织或钩编的,女式,棉制	Anoraks (including skijackets), not knitted or crocheted, for women or girls, of cotton	6202.9290	2456
带风帽的防寒短上衣(包括滑雪短上衣),非针织或钩编的,女式,其他纺织材料制	Anoraks (including skijackets), not knitted or crocheted, for women or girls, of other textile materials	6202.9900	2456
带风帽的防寒短上衣(包括滑雪短上衣),男式,羊毛或动物细毛制非针织或钩编的	Anoraks (including skijackets), not knitted or crocheted, for men or boys, of wool or fine animal hair	6201.9100	2456
带风帽的防寒短上衣(包括滑雪短上衣),女式,羊毛或动物细毛制非针织或钩编的	Anoraks (including skijackets), not knitted or crocheted, for women or girls, of wool or fine animal hair	6202.9100	2456
带风帽的防寒短上衣(包括滑雪短上衣)及类似品,针织或钩编的,男式,化学纤维制	Anoraks (including ski-jackets) and similar articles, knitted or crocheted, for men or boys, of man-made fibres	6101.3000	2456
带风帽的防寒短上衣(包括滑雪短上衣)及类似品,针织或钩编的,男式,棉制	Anoraks (including ski-jackets) and similar articles, knitted or crocheted, for men or boys, of cotton	6101.2000	2456
带风帽的防寒短上衣(包括滑雪短上衣)及类似品,针织或钩编的,男式,其他	Anoraks (including ski-jackets) and similar articles, knitted or crocheted, for men or boys, of other textile materials	6101.9090	2456

D

商品名称	Article Description	税则号列	申报要素
带风帽的防寒短上衣(包括滑雪短上衣)及类似品,针织或钩编的,男式,羊毛或动物细毛制	Anoraks (including ski-jackets) and similar articles, knitted or crocheted, for men or boys, of wool or fine animal hair	6101.9010	2456
带风帽的防寒短上衣(包括滑雪短上衣)及类似品,针织或钩编的,女式,化学纤维制	Anoraks (including ski-jackets) and similar articles, knitted or crocheted, for women or girls, of man-made fibres	6102.3000	2456
带风帽的防寒短上衣(包括滑雪短上衣)及类似品,针织或钩编的,女式,棉制	Anoraks (including ski-jackets) and similar articles, knitted or crocheted, for women or girls, of cotton	6102.2000	2456
带风帽的防寒短上衣(包括滑雪短上衣)及类似品,针织或钩编的,女式,其他	Anoraks (including ski-jackets) and similar articles, knitted or crocheted, for women or girls, of other textile materials	6102.9000	2456
带风帽的防寒短上衣(包括滑雪短上衣)及类似品,针织或钩编的,女式,羊毛或动物细毛制	Anoraks (including ski-jackets) and similar articles, knitted or crocheted, for women or girls, of wool or fine animal hair	6102.1000	2456
带锯片	Band saw blades	8202.2000	256
带鱼,冻的	Scabber fish (trichurius), frozen	0303.7910	18
带鱼,鲜或冷的	Scabber fish (trichurius), fresh or chilled	0302.6910	18
带鱼,盐腌及盐渍的	Scabber fish (trichurius), or in brine	0305.6910	4
带座手杖	Seat-sticks	6602.0000	
玳瑁壳,已加工的	Tortoise-shell, worked	9601.9000	5
袋及包(包括锥形的),其他塑料制	Sacks and bags (including cones), of other plastics	3923.2900	23
袋及包(包括锥形的),乙烯聚合物制	Sacks and bags (including cones), of polymers of ethylene	3923.2100	23
袋式除尘器	Baghoused dust collectors, for industry uses	8421.3922	7
袋用牛皮纸,起皱的,不论是否压花或穿孔	Sack kraft paper, creped or crinkled, whether or not embossed or perforated	4808.2000	58
袋用牛皮纸,未经涂布的,其他	Sack kraft paper, uncoated, nes	4804.2900	24568
袋用牛皮纸,未经涂布的,未漂白	Sack kraft paper, uncoated, unbleached	4804.2100	24568
dan			
单板,厚度不超过6毫米,红柳桉木,其他	Veneer sheets, of a thickness not exceeding 6mm, of tropical wood, nes	4408.3990	458
单板,厚度不超过6毫米,红柳桉木,制胶合板用	Veneer sheets, of a thickness not exceeding 6mm, of meranti (Dark Red, Light Red and Bakau), for plywood	4408.3120	458
单板,厚度不超过6毫米,红柳桉木的,其他	Veneer sheets, of a thickness not exceeding 6mm, of meranti (Dark Red, Light Red and Bakau), nes	4408.3119	458
单板,厚度不超过6毫米,红柳桉木的,其他	Veneer sheets, of a thickness not exceeding 6mm, of meranti (Dark Red, Light Red and Bakau), nes	4408.3190	458
单板,厚度不超过6毫米,红柳桉木的,用多层板制的	Veneer sheets, of a thickness not exceeding 6mm, of meranti (Dark Red, Light Red and Bakau), of laminated plywood	4408.3111	458

商品名称	Article Description	税则号列	申报要素
单板,厚度不超过6毫米,其他	Veneer sheets, of a thickness not exceeding 6mm, nes	4408. 9019	458
单板,厚度不超过6毫米,其他	Veneer sheets, of a thickness not exceeding 6mm, nes	4408. 9099	458
单板,厚度不超过6毫米,热带木,制胶合板用	Veneer sheets, of a thickness not exceeding 6mm, of tropical wood, for plywood	4408. 3920	458
单板,厚度不超过6毫米,热带木的,其他	Veneer sheets, of a thickness not exceeding 6mm, of tropical wood, nes	4408. 3919	458
单板,厚度不超过6毫米,热带木的,用多层板制的	Veneer sheets, of a thickness not exceeding 6mm, of tropical wood, of laminated plywood	4408. 3911	458
单板,厚度不超过6毫米,温带非针叶木制,其他	Veneer sheets, of a thickness not exceeding 6mm, of temperate non-coniferous wood, nes	4408. 9091	458
单板,厚度不超过6毫米,温带非针叶木制,用多层板制的	Veneer sheets, of a thickness not exceeding 6mm, of temperate non-coniferous wood, of laminated plywood	4408. 9012	458
单板,厚度不超过6毫米,温带非针叶木制,制胶合板用	Veneer sheets, of a thickness not exceeding 6mm, of temperate non-coniferous wood, of laminated plywood	4408. 9021	458
单板,厚度不超过6毫米,用多层板制的,其他	Veneer sheets, of a thickness not exceeding 6mm, of laminated plywood, nes	4408. 9011	458
单板,厚度不超过6毫米,针叶木,制类似多层板用,其他	Veneer sheets, of a thickness not exceeding 6mm, coniferous, nes	4408. 1090	458
单板,厚度不超过6毫米,针叶木,制胶合板用	Veneer sheets, of a thickness not exceeding 6mm, coniferous, for plywood	4408. 1020	458
单板,厚度不超过6毫米,针叶木的,其他	Veneer sheets, of a thickness not exceeding 6mm, coniferous, nes	4408. 1019	458
单板,厚度不超过6毫米,针叶木的,用多层板制的	Veneer sheets, of a thickness not exceeding 6mm, coniferous, of laminated plywood	4408. 1011	458
单板,厚度不超过6毫米,制胶合板用,其他	Veneer sheets, of a thickness not exceeding 6mm, of laminated plywood, nes	4408. 9029	458
单反相机镜头	Cameras lens for single lens reflex	9002. 1131	3
单工位组合机床,加工金属的	Unit construction machines (single station), for working metal	8457. 2000	7
单股扁丝,不论是否带刺,钢铁的,围篱用的	Single flat wire, barbed or not, of a kind used for fencing, of iron or steel	7313. 0000	36
单簧管	Clarinets	9205. 9090	5
单晶硅棒,按重量计含硅量不少于99.99%,经掺杂用于电子工业的,其他	Monocrystals doped for use in electronics, containing by weight not less than 99.99% of silicon, in the form of cylinders or rods, nes	2804. 6120	3468
单晶硅棒,按重量计含硅量不少于99.99%,经掺杂用于电子工业的,直径在30厘米及以上的	Monocrystals doped for use in electronics, containing by weight not less than 99.99% of silicon, in the form of cylinders or rods, 30cm or more in diameter	2804. 6117	3468

D

商品名称	Article Description	税则号列	申报要素
单晶硅棒,按重量计含硅量不少于99.99%,经掺杂用于电子工业的,直径在7.5厘米及以上但小于30厘米的	Monocrystals doped for use in electronics, containing by weight not less than 99.99% of silicon, in the form of cylinders or rods, 7.5cm or more in diameter, less than 30cm	2804.6119	3468
单晶硅切片,直径在15.24厘米及以上的,掺杂的	Monocrystalline sillicon, diameter exceeding 15.24cm, doped	3818.0019	13468
单晶硅切片,直径在15.24厘米及以下的,掺杂的	Monocrystalline sillicon, diameter not exceeding 15.24cm, doped	3818.0011	13468
单晶硅切片,直径在7.5厘米及以下的,掺杂的	Monocrystalline sillicon, diameter not exceeding 7.5cm, doped	3818.0090	13468
单晶硅柱或硅晶片的制造机器及装置,化学机械抛光设备(CMP)	Boules or wafers manufacture machines and apparatus, chemical mechanical polishers (CMP)	8486.1040	7
单晶硅柱或硅晶片的制造机器及装置,利用温度变化处理单晶硅的机器及装置	Boules or wafers manufacture machines and apparatus, for the treatment of monocrystalline sillicon by a process involving a change of temperature	8486.1010	7
单晶硅柱或硅晶片的制造机器及装置,其他	Boules or wafers manufacture machines and apparatus, nes	8486.1090	7
单晶硅柱或硅晶片的制造机器及装置,切割设备	Boules or wafers manufacture machines and apparatus, sawing machines	8486.1030	7
单晶硅柱或硅晶片的制造机器及装置,研磨设备	Boules or wafers manufacture machines and apparatus, grinding machines	8486.1020	7
单宁酸汞	Mercury tannate	2852.0000	
单纱,捻度每米超过50转,非供零售用,其他	Single yarn, with a twist exceeding 50 turns per metre, not put up for retail sale, nes	5402.5990	3468
单纱,未加捻或捻度每米不超过50转,非供零售用,其他	Single yarn, untwisted or with a twist not exceeding 50 turns per metre, not put up for retail sale, nes	5402.4900	3468
单丝、条、杆、型材及异型材,聚酰胺制	Monofilament rods, sticks and profile shapes, of polyamides	3916.9010	168
单丝、条、杆、型材及异型材,氯乙烯聚合物制	Monofilament rods, sticks and profile shapes, of polymers of vinyl chloride	3916.2000	168
单丝、条、杆、型材及异型材,其他塑料制	Monofilament rods, sticks and profile shapes, of other plastics	3916.9090	168
单丝、条、杆、型材及异型材,乙烯聚合物制	Monofilament rods, sticks and profile shapes, of polymers of ethylene	3916.1000	168
单筒望远镜	Monoculars	9005.8090	5
单筒望远镜零件、附件(包括座架),其他	Monoculars parts and accessories (including mountings), nes	9005.9090	3
单细胞微生物,已死的,其他	Single-cell microorganisms, dead, nes	2102.2000	28
单乙醇胺及其盐,其他	Monoethanolamine and its salts, nes	2922.1190	36
胆固醇	Cholesterol	2906.1310	36
胆碱及其盐	Choline and its salts	2923.1000	36
胆汁,不论是否干制;	Bile, whether of not dried	0510.0090	14

商品名称	Article Description	税则号列	申报要素
弹簧,铜制	Springs of copper	7419.9920	4
弹簧秤,最大称量不超过30千克	Spring balances, having a maximum weighing capacity not exceeding 30kg	8423.8120	
弹簧垫圈,钢铁制的	Spring washers, of iron or steel	7318.2100	268
弹簧及弹簧片,钢铁制,其他	Springs and leaves for springs, of iron or steel, nes	7320.9090	36
弹簧及弹簧片,钢铁制,铁道车辆用	Springs and leaves for springs, of iron or steel, for railway locomotives and rollingstock	7320.9010	36
弹簧枪	Spring guns	9304.0000	
弹簧针,针织机用28号以下的	Barbered needles for knitting machines, smaler than gauge No. 28	8448.5120	3
弹球机	Pintables	9504.9090	5
弹丸,气枪的	Pellets for air gun	9306.2900	3
弹性单纱,未加捻或捻度每米不超过50转,非供零售用,其他	Elastomeric single yarn, untwisted or with a twist not exceeding 50 turns per metre, not put up for retail sale, nes	5402.4490	3468
弹性单丝,合成纤维,截面尺寸不超过1毫米,细度在67分特及以上	Elastomeric monofilament, synthetic, of 67 decitex or more and of which no cross-sectional dimension exceeding 1mm	5404.1100	568
淡红银矿	Proustite	2616.1000	146
淡水小龙虾,其他	Freshwater crawfish, nes	0306.1919	1
淡水小龙虾,其他,制作或保藏的	Freshwater crawfish, nes, prepared or preserved	1605.4019	48
淡水小龙虾,虾仁,制作或保藏的	Freshwater crawfish, shelled, prepared or preserved	1605.4011	48
蛋,禽的,其他,带壳的,鲜的	Eggs, of birds, nes, in shell, fresh	0407.0029	1
蛋,禽的,其他,带壳的、腌制或煮过的	Eggs, of birds, nes, in shell, fresh, preserved or cooked	0407.0099	14
蛋,禽的,去壳的,干的	Eggs, of birds, not in shell, dried	0408.9100	14
蛋,禽的,去壳的,其他	Eggs, of birds, not in shell, nes	0408.9900	14
蛋氨酸	Methionine	2930.4000	36
蛋白胨	Peptones	3504.0010	1346
蛋白胨衍生物	Peptones derivatives	3504.0090	1346
蛋白激素及其衍生物和结构类似物,其他	Protein hormones, their derivatives and structural analogues, nes	2937.1900	36
蛋白质,浓缩的	Protein concentrates	2106.1000	268
蛋白质,人组织化的	Protein substances, textured	2106.1000	268
蛋白质及其衍生物	Protein substances and their derivatives	3504.0090	1346
蛋黄,干的	Egg yolks, dried	0408.1100	14
蛋黄,其他	Egg yolks, nes	0408.1900	14
蛋黄酱	Bearnaise (sauce)	2103.9090	268
蛋黄酱	Mayonnaise	2103.9090	268
氮	Nitrogen	2804.3000	
氮化物,不论是否已有化学定义	Nitrides, whether or not chemically defined	2850.0000	

D

商品名称	Article Description	税则号列	申报要素
dang			
当归	Radix angelicae sinensis	1211.9011	34
挡风镜	Goggles	9004.9090	5
党参	Radix codonopsitis	1211.9013	34
档案柜,贱金属制,办公室家具除外	Filing cabinets, of base metal, other than office furniture	8304.0000	256
dao			
刀,刃面不固定的	Knives having other than fixed blades	8211.9300	256
刀,刃面固定的,其他	Knives having fixed blades, nes	8211.9200	256
刀,屠刀	Butchers cleavers	8214.9000	256
刀柄,贱金属制的	Knives handles of base metal	8211.9500	256
刀及刀片,不论是否有锯齿(包括整枝刀),成套货品,税号 82.08 的刀除外	Knives with cutting blades, serrated or not (including pruning knives), sets of assorted articles, other than knives of heading No. 82.08, and blades therefor	8211.1000	256
刀及刀片,厨房器具或食品工业机器用	Knives and cutting blades, for kitchen appliances or for machines used by the food industry	8208.3000	256
刀及刀片,机器或机械器具的,金属加工用,其他	Knives and cutting blades, for machines or for mechanical appliances, for metal working, nes	8208.1090	256
刀及刀片,机器或机械器具的,金属加工用,硬质合金制的,经镀或涂层的	Knives and cutting blades, for machines or for mechanical appliances, for metal working, of metal carbides, plated or coated	8208.1011	256
刀及刀片,机器或机械器具的,金属加工用,硬质合金制的,其他	Knives and cutting blades, for machines or for mechanical appliances, for metal working, of metal carbides, nes	8208.1019	256
刀及刀片,机器或机械器具的,其他	Knives and cutting blades, for machines or for mechanical appliances, nes	8208.9000	256
刀及刀片,木器加工机械用	Knives and cutting blades, for wood working machines	8208.2000	256
刀及刀片,农业、园艺或林业机器用	Knives and cutting blades, for agricultural, horticultural or forestry machines	8208.4000	256
刀及刀片成套货品,不论是否有锯齿	Knives with cutting blades, sets of assorted articles, serrated or not	8211.1000	256
刀片,税号 82.08 的刀除外	Blades, other than knives of heading No. 82.08, and blades therefor	8211.9400	256
刀鞘	Scabbards and parts	9307.0000	
导爆索	Detonating fuses	3603.0000	
导弹及其零件	Missiles and parts	9306.9000	3
导电玻璃,工业用	Conductivity glass, for technical use	7020.0011	6
导电水	Conductivity water	2853.0090	
导管及类似品,医疗、外科、牙科或兽医用	Catheters and the like, used in medical, surgical, dental or veterinary sciences	9018.3900	3

商品名称	Article Description	税则号列	申报要素
导航仪器及装置(罗盘除外),航空或航天用,其他	Navigation instruments and appliances (other than compasses), for aeronautical or space, nes	9014.2090	7
导航仪器及装置(罗盘除外),其他	Navigation instruments and appliances (other than compasses), nes	9014.8000	7
导航仪器及装置的零件、附件,其他	Navigation instruments and appliances parts and accessories, nes	9014.9090	3
倒轮制动毂及其零件,自行车及脚踏车的	Coaster braking hubs and parts, of bicycles and other cycles	8714.9400	3
倒水塞,贱金属制	Pouring stoppers, of base metal	8309.9000	256
倒卸式起重机的零件	Skip hoists parts	8431.3100	3
捣固机零件	Tamping machines parts	8431.4990	3
捣固机械,对泥土、矿物或矿石的,自推进的,其他	Tamping machinery, for earth, minerals or ores, self-propelled, nes	8430.5090	5
捣固机械,非自推进的	Tamping machinery, not self-propelled	8430.6100	5
捣固机械,其他	Tamping machines, nes	8429.4090	57
道碴捣固车,铁道及电车道用	Ballast tampers, for railway or tramway maintenance or service	8604.0099	37
道岔尖轨、辙叉、尖轨拉杆及其他叉道段体	Switch blades, crossing frogs, point rods and other crossing pieces	7302.3000	6
稻草的茎杆,其他的	Cereal straw, nes	1213.0090	4
稻草的茎杆,未经处理的	Cereal straw, unprepared	1213.0010	4
稻谷,其他	Rice in husk (paddy or rough), nes	1006.1099	35
稻谷,其他,种用	Rice in husk (paddy or rough), nes, seed	1006.1019	35
de			
德银	Nickel silver	7403.2900	146
deng			
灯,不包括紫外线灯或红外线灯,12伏及以下的	Filament lamps, excluding ultraviolet or infra-red lamps, of a voltage 12V or less	8539.2991	35
灯,不包括紫外线灯或红外线灯,火车、航空器及船舶用	Filament lamps, excluding ultraviolet or infra-red lamps, for locomotives and roiling-stock, aircraft or ships	8539.2920	35
灯,不包括紫外线灯或红外线灯,机动车辆用	Filament lamps, excluding ultraviolet or infra-red lamps, for motor vehicles	8539.2930	35
灯,不包括紫外线灯或红外线灯,科研、医疗专用	Filament lamps, excluding ultraviolet or infra-red lamps, for scientific or medical uses only	8539.2910	35
灯,不包括紫外线灯或红外线灯,其他	Filament lamps, excluding ultraviolet or infra-red lamps, nes	8539.2999	35
灯,功率不超过200瓦,但额定电压超过100伏,不包括紫外线灯或红外线灯,科研、医疗专用	Filament lamps, of a power not exceeding 200W and for a voltage exceeding 100V, excluding ultraviolet or infra-red lamps, for scientific or medical uses only	8539.2210	35

D

商品名称	Article Description	税则号列	申报要素
灯,功率不超过200瓦,但额定电压超过100伏,不包括紫外线灯或红外线灯,其他	Filament lamps, of a power not exceeding 200W and for a voltage exceeding 100V, excluding ultraviolet or infra-red lamps, nes	8539.2290	35
灯船	Light-vessels	8905.9090	37
灯的零件	Lamps parts	8539.9000	3
灯管,其他	Valves and tubes, nes	8540.8900	35
灯具,成套的,圣诞树用	Lighting sets of a kind used for christmas trees	9405.3000	5
灯具零件,玻璃制	Lamps parts, of glass	9405.9100	36
灯具零件,其他	Lamps parts, nes	9405.9900	36
灯具零件,塑料制	Lamps parts, of plastics	9405.9200	36
灯碳棒	Lamp carbons	8545.9000	3
灯芯或类似品,用纺织材料机织、编结或针织而成的	Wicks, of woven textile, plaited or knitted, for stoves or the like	5908.0000	
灯用煤油	Lamp-kerosene	2710.1912	6
灯座,用于电压不超过1000伏的线路	Lamp-holders, for a voltage not exceeding 1000V	8536.6100	8
登记本,纸或纸板制的	Registers, of paper or paperboard	4820.1000	
等离子弧焊接机器及装置,全自动或半自动的,其他	Plasma arc welding of metals machines and apparatus, fully or partly automatic, nes	8515.3190	
等离子弧焊接机器及装置零件	Plasma arc welding of metals machines and apparatus parts	8515.9000	3
等离子切割机	Cutting machines of plasma arc	8456.9010	7
等离子体干法刻蚀机,制造半导体器件或集成电路的机器及装置	Dry plasma etching equipment, semiconductor devices or of electronic integrated circuits manufacture machines and apparatus	8486.2041	7
等离子体干法刻蚀机零件及附件,制造半导体器件或集成电路的机器及装置	Dry plasma etching equipment parts and accessories, semiconductor devices or of electronic integrated circuits manufacture machines and apparatus	8486.9090	3
等离子显像组件及其零件电视接收机用零件	Plasma display modules and part thereof, television receivers parts	8529.9082	3
di			
低剂量X射线安全检查设备	Low dosage X-ray security inspecting equipment	9022.1910	
滴滴涕(ISO,INN)	DDT (ISO,INN)	2903.6200	36
滴液式咖啡机,电热的	Drip coffee makers, electro-thermic	8516.7110	7
镝	Dysprosium	2805.3012	56
狄氏剂(ISO,INN)	Dieldrin (ISO,INN)	2910.4000	36
敌菌丹(ISO)	Captafol (ISO)	2930.5000	36
底盘,大型客车的,装有发动机的	Chassis for passenger motor vehicles with 30 seats or more, fitted with engines	8706.0030	7
底盘,非公路用自卸车用,装有发动机的	Chassis for off-road dumpers, fitted with engines	8706.0010	7

商品名称	Article Description	税则号列	申报要素
底盘,货车的,车辆总重量在 14 吨及以上的,装有发动机的	Chassis for motor vehicles of goods transportation, for vehicles g. v. w of 14 tons or more, fitted with engines	8706.0021	7
底盘,货车的,车辆总重量在 14 吨以下的,装有发动机的	Chassis for motor vehicles of goods transportation, for vehicles g. v. w less than 14 tons, fitted with engines	8706.0022	7
底盘,汽车起重机的,装有发动机的	Chassis for crane lorries, fitted with engines	8706.0040	7
底盘,装有发动机的机动车辆用,其他	Chassis fitted with engines, for the motor vehicles, nes	8706.0090	7
地板,已装拼的,多层的,其他	Flooring panels, assembled, multilayer, nes	4418.7290	58
地板,已装拼的,多层的,竹制	Flooring panels, assembled, multilayer, of bamboo	4418.7210	58
地板,已装拼的,马赛克地板用,木制的	Flooring panels, assembled, for mosaic floors, of wood	4418.7100	58
地板,已装拼的,其他	Flooring panels, assembled, nes	4418.7990	58
地板,已装拼的,竹制	Flooring panels, assembled, of bamboo	4418.7910	58
地板打蜡机,家用电动器具	Floor polishers, electro-mechanical domestic appliances	8509.8010	
地板清扫器,手工操作的,机械的	Floor sweepers, hand-operated, mechanical	9603.9090	3
地板条(块),非针叶木	Floor board strips, non-coniferous	4409.2910	158
地板条(块),针叶木	Floor board strips, coniferous	4409.1010	158
地板条(块),竹的	Floor board strips, of bamboo	4409.2110	158
地达诺新及它们的盐	Didanosine and their salts	2938.9010	34
地芬诺新 (INN)以及盐	Difenoxin(INN); salts thereof	2933.3300	36
地芬诺酯 (INN)以及盐	Diphenoxylate(INN); salts thereof	2933.3300	36
地黄	Radix rehmanniae	1211.9026	34
地蜡	Ozokerite	2712.9090	6
地乐酚(ISO)及其盐	Dinoseb (ISO) and its salts	2908.9100	36
地乐酚(ISO)乙酸酯	Dinoseb (ISO) acetate	2915.3600	36
地雷及其零件	Mines and parts	9306.9000	3
地洛西泮(INN)以及盐	Delorazepam(INN); salts thereof	2933.9100	36
地面飞行训练器及其零件,其他	Ground flying trainers and parts, nes	8805.2900	3
地名牌,贱金属制,税号 94.05 的货品除外	Address- plates, of base metal, excluding those of heading No. 94.05	8310.0000	256
地匹哌酮(INN)以及盐	Dipipanone (INN); salts thereof	2933.3300	36
地球仪,印制的	Globes, printed	4905.1000	
地塞米松	Dexamethasone	2937.2210	36
地毯,"苏麦克"及类似手织的	Rugs, schumacks and similar handwoven	5702.1000	468
地毯及铺地制品,纺织材料结织栽绒的,化学纤维制	Carpets and other textile floor coverings knotted of man-made textile materials	5701.9010	468
地毯及铺地制品,纺织材料结织栽绒的,其他	Carpets and other textile floor coverings knotted, nes	5701.9090	468
地毯及铺地制品,纺织材料结织栽绒的,丝制	Carpets and other textile floor coverings knotted, of silk	5701.9020	468

D

商品名称	Article Description	税则号列	申报要素
地毯及铺地制品,纺织材料结织栽绒的,羊毛或动物细毛制	Carpets and other textile floor coverings knotted, of wool or fine animal hair	5701.1000	468
地毯及铺地制品,纺织材料制,簇绒纺织材料的,其他	Carpets and other textile floor coverings, of other textile materials, tufted, nes	5703.9000	468
地毯及铺地制品,化学纤维制,其他	Carpets and textile floor coverings, of man-made textile materials, nes	5705.0020	468
地毯及铺地制品,尼龙或聚酰胺制,簇绒纺织材料的	Carpets and other textile floor coverings, of nylon or other polyamides, tufted	5703.2000	468
地毯及铺地制品,其他	Carpets and textile floor coverings, nes	5705.0090	468
地毯及铺地制品,其他化学纤维制,簇绒纺织材料的	Carpets and other textile floor coverings, of other man-made textile materials, tufted	5703.3000	468
地毯及铺地制品,羊毛或动物细毛制,簇绒纺织材料的	Carpets and other textile floor coverings, of wool or fine animal hair, tufted	5703.1000	468
地毯及铺地制品,羊毛或动物细毛制,其他	Carpets and textile floor coverings, of wool or fine animal hair, nes	5705.0010	468
地毯及铺地制品,毡呢纺织材料的,其他	Carpets and other textile floor coverings, of felt, nes	5704.9000	468
地毯及铺地制品,毡呢纺织材料的,最大铺装表面面积不超过0.3平方米	Carpets and other textile floor coverings, of felt, tiles, having a maximum surface area of 0.3m^2	5704.1000	468
地毯织机	Carpets or rugs making machines	8447.9011	7
地毯织机,动力的,所织织物宽度超过30厘米的梭织机	For making carpets or rugs, powered, for weaving fabrics of width exceeding 30cm, shuttle type	8446.2110	7
地毯织机的辅助机器	Carpets or rugs making machines auxiliary	8448.1900	3
地图册,印制的,成册的	Maps, printed, in book form	4905.9100	1
地图挂图,印制的	Maps for wall, printed	4905.9900	1
地图盒、瓶盒、刀叉餐具盒及类似容器,其他	Map-cases, bottle-cases, cutlery cases and similar containers, nes	4202.9900	256
地图盒、瓶盒、刀叉餐具盒及类似容器,以皮革、再生皮革或漆皮作面	Map-cases, bottle-cases, cutlery cases and similar containers, with outer surface of leather, of composition leather or of patent leather	4202.9100	256
地图盒、瓶盒、刀叉餐具盒及类似容器,以塑料片或纺织材料作面	Map-cases, bottle-cases, cutlery cases and similar containers, with outer surface of plastic sheeting or of textile materials	4202.9200	256
地西泮(INN)以及盐	Diazepam (INN); salts thereof	2933.9100	36
地形或类似用途的设计图纸,手绘的	Topographical or similar purposes plans and drawings, being originals drawn by hand	4906.0000	
地形图,印制的	Topographical plans, printed	4905.9900	1
地址铭牌压印机	Address plate embossing machines	8472.9040	
地址印写机	Addressing machines	8472.9040	
地质钻管、套管,无缝的,合金钢的,圆形截面管,冷拔或冷轧的,其他	Geological casing and drill pipes, seamless, of alloy steel, of circular cross-section, cold-drawn or cold-rolled, nes	7304.5120	6

商品名称	Article Description	税则号列	申报要素
地质钻管、套管,无缝的,合金钢的,圆形截面管,其他	Geological casing and drill pipes, seamless, of alloy steel, of circular cross-section, nes	7304.5920	6
地质钻管、套管,无缝的,铁或非合金钢的,圆形截面,冷拔或冷轧的	Geological casing and drill pipes, seamless, of iron or non-alloysteel, of circular cross-section, cold-drawn or cold-rolled	7304.3120	6
地质钻管、套管,无缝的,铁或非合金钢的,圆形截面,其他	Geological casing and drill pipes, seamless, of iron or non-alloysteel, of circular cross-section, nes	7304.3920	6
地中衡,其他	Weigh bridges, nes	8423.8910	
地中衡,最大称量超过30千克,但不超过5000千克	Weigh bridges, having a maximum weighing capacity exceeding 30kg but not exceeding 5000kg	8423.8210	
地砖,建筑用	Flooring blocks for building	6904.1000	5
第纳斯土	Dinas earths	2508.7000	134
蒂巴因及盐	Thebaine and salts	2939.1100	34
碲	Tellurium	2804.5000	
碲化镉	Cadmium telluride	2842.9020	
碲金矿	Calaverite	2616.9000	146
dian			
点火布线组,机动车辆用	Ignition wiring sets, for motor vehicles	8544.3020	35
点火布线组,其他	Ignition wiring sets, nes	8544.3090	35
点火磁电机,点燃式或压燃式内燃发动机用的,其他	Ignition magnetos, for electrical ignition or starting equipment, nes	8511.2090	7
点火磁电机,机车、航空器及船舶用,点燃式或压燃式内燃发动机用的	Ignition magnetos, for locomotives, aircraft or ships, for electrical ignition or starting equipment	8511.2010	7
点火线圈,点燃式或压燃式内燃发动机用的,其他	Ignition coils, for electrical ignition or starting equipment, nes	8511.3090	7
点火线圈,机车、航空器及船舶用,点燃式或压燃式内燃发动机用的	Ignition coils, for locomotives, aircraft or ships, for electrical ignition or starting equipment	8511.3010	7
碘	Iodine	2801.2000	
碘化物及碘氧化物	Iodides and iodide oxides	2827.6000	
碘酸盐,无机的	Iodates, inorganic	2829.9000	
电报交换机	Telegraphic switching apparatus	8517.6211	
电报交换机用零件	Telegraphic switching apparatus parts	8517.7010	3
电炒锅	Electric frying pans	8516.6040	7
电池隔膜,丙烯聚合物制,非泡沫,未用其他材料强化、层压、支撑或用类似方法合制	Battery separator, of polymers of propylene, non-cellular and not reinforced, laminated, supported or similarly combined with other materials	3920.2010	16
电池隔膜,乙烯聚合物制,非泡沫,未用其他材料强化、层压、支撑或用类似方法合制	Battery separator, of polymers of ethylene, non-cellular and not reinforced, laminated, supported or similarly combined with other materials	3920.1010	16
电池壳体坯料,锌制	Cellpacking blanks(zinc biscuits), of zinc	7907.0030	16
电池壳体坯料,锌制	Zinc biscuits	7907.0030	16
电池碳棒	Battery carbons	8545.9000	3

D

商品名称	Article Description	税则号列	申报要素
电磁离合器	Electro-magnetic clutches	8505.2000	
电磁联轴节	Electro-magnetic couplings	8505.2000	
电磁炉	Electromagnetic ovens	8516.6010	7
电磁起重吸盘	Electro-magnetic lifting heads	8505.9010	3
电磁铁	Electro-magnets	8505.9090	3
电磁铁或永磁铁夹具及类似的工件夹具	Electro-magnetic or permanent magnet clamps and similar holding devices	8505.9090	3
电磁铁或永磁铁卡盘	Electro-magnetic or permanent magnet chucks	8505.9090	3
电磁制动器	Electro-magnetic brakes	8505.2000	
电导体,绝缘的,额定电压不超过 80 伏,其他	Electric conductors, insulated, for a voltage not exceeding 80V, nes	8544.4919	35
电导体,绝缘的,额定电压超过 1000 伏,其他	Electric conductors, insulated, for a voltage exceeding 1000V, nes	8544.6090	35
电导体,绝缘的,额定电压超过 80 伏,但不超过 1000 伏,其他	Electric conductors, insulated, for a voltage exceeding 80V but not exceeding 1000V, nes	8544.4929	35
电导体,绝缘的,额定电压超过 80 伏,但不超过 1000 伏,有接头,其他	Electric conductors, insulated, fitted with connectors, for a voltage exceeding 80V but not exceeding 1000V, nes	8544.4229	35
电导体,绝缘的,有接头,额定电压不超过 80 伏,其他	Electric conductors, insulated, fitted with connectors, for a voltage not exceeding 80V, nes	8544.4219	35
电笛,电气的	Sirens, electric	8531.8090	3
电笛零件,电气的	Sirens parts, electric	8531.9090	3
电点火及电起动装置零件,点燃式或压燃式内燃发动机用的,其他	Electrical ignition or starting equipment parts, for electrical ignition or starting equipment, nes	8511.9090	3
电点火及电起动装置零件,供机车、航空器及船舶用,点燃式或压燃式内燃发动机用的	Electrical ignition or starting equipment parts, for locomotives, aircraft or ships, for electrical ignition or starting equipment	8511.9010	3
电动火车,缩小(按比例缩小)的成套模型组件	Electric trains, reduced-size (" scale ") model assembly kits	9503.0031	5
电动机,单相交流,其他	Motors, AC, single-phase, nes	8501.4000	8
电动机,输出功率不超过 37.5 瓦的,其他	Motors of an output not exceeding 37.5W, nes	8501.1099	8
电动机,输出功率不超过 37.5 瓦的,玩具用	Motors of an output not exceeding 37.5W, for use in toys	8501.1010	8
电动机,输出功率不超过 37.5 瓦的,微电机,机座尺寸在 20 毫米及以上,但不超过 39 毫米	Motors of an output not exceeding 37.5W, micromotors with a housing size of 20mm or more but not exceeding 39mm	8501.1091	8
电动机,输出功率不超过 750 瓦,多相交流	Motors of an output not exceeding 750W, AC, multi-phase	8501.5100	8
电动机,输出功率不超过 750 瓦,直流	Motors of an output not exceeding 750W, DC	8501.3100	8
电动机,输出功率超过 37.5 瓦,交直流两用	Motors of an output exceeding 37.5W, universal AC/DC	8501.2000	8
电动机,输出功率超过 375 千瓦,直流	Motors of an output exceeding 375kW, DC	8501.3400	8

商品名称	Article Description	税则号列	申报要素
电动机,输出功率超过750瓦,但不超过75千瓦,多相交流	Motors of an output exceeding 750W but not exceeding 75kW, AC, multi-phase	8501.5200	8
电动机,输出功率超过750瓦,但不超过75千瓦,直流	Motors of an output exceeding 750W but not exceeding 75kW, DC	8501.3200	8
电动机,输出功率超过75千瓦,但不超过375千瓦,直流	Motors of an output exceeding 75kW but not exceeding 375kW, DC	8501.3300	8
电动机,输出功率超过75千瓦,多相交流	Motors of an output exceeding 75kW, AC, multi-phase	8501.5300	8
电动机的零件,其他	Motors parts, nes	8503.0090	3
电动机的零件,输出功率不超过37.5瓦的,玩具用	Motors parts, of an output not exceeding 37.5W, for use in toys	8503.0010	3
电动机的零件,输出功率不超过37.5瓦的,微电机,机座尺寸在20毫米及以上,但不超过39毫米	Motors parts, of an output not exceeding 37.5W, micromotors with a housing size of 20mm or more but not exceeding 39mm	8503.0010	3
电度表,单相电子式(静止式)	Watt-hour meter, single-phase electronic types (static)	9028.3013	
电度表,单相感应式	Watt-hour meter, single-phase induction types	9028.3011	
电度表,其他	Watt-hour meter, nes	9028.3019	7
电度表,三相电子式(静止式)	Watt-hour meter, three-phase electronic types (static)	9028.3014	
电度表,三相感应式	Watt-hour meter, three-phase induction types	9028.3012	
电度表零件、附件,工业用	Watt-hour meter parts and accessories, for industrial use	9028.9010	3
电度表零件、附件,其他	Watt-hour meter parts and accessories, nes	9028.9090	3
电镀设备及装置	Electroplating machines and apparatus	8543.3000	37
电饭锅	Electric rice cookers	8516.6030	7
电感测试仪,带记录装置	Inductances measuring instruments and apparatus, with a recording device	9030.8410	
电感测试仪,其他	Inductances measuring instruments and apparatus, nes	9030.8910	
电感器,其他	Inductors, nes	8504.5000	
电感器零件	Inductors parts	8504.9090	3
电话机,其他	Telephone sets, nes	8517.1800	
电话机,用于蜂窝网络或其他无线网络的,其他	Telephones for cellular networks or for other wireless networks, nes	8517.1290	
电话交换机,数字式程控,其他	Telegraphic switching apparatus, digital program-controlled, nes	8517.6219	
电话设备用零件,数字式程控的	Telephonic apparatus parts, digital program-controlled	8517.7010	3
电话应答机	Telephone answering machines	8519.5000	
电极,贱金属制,以焊剂涂面,电弧焊用	Electrodes of base metal, coated with flux material, for electric arc-welding	8311.1000	56
电极,硬质合金制,以焊剂涂面或以焊剂为芯,用于焊接或沉积金属、硬质合金	Electrodes of metal carbides, coated or cored with flux material, of a kind used for soldering, brazing, welding or deposition of metal or of metal carbides	8311.9000	56

D

商品名称	Article Description	税则号列	申报要素
电加热器,对流式,充液式	Space heating apparatus, oil-filled types, electric convection	8516.2932	7
电加热器,对流式,风扇式	Space heating apparatus, electric convection, fan type	8516.2931	7
电加热器,对流式,其他	Space heating apparatus, electric convection, nes	8516.2939	7
电加热器,辐射式	Space heating apparatus, electric, radiant	8516.2920	7
电加热器,空间的,其他	Electric space heating apparatus, nes	8516.2990	7
电加热器,土壤的	Heating apparatus for soil, electric	8516.2910	7
电解电容器原纸,每平方米重量在150克及以下	Paper for electrolytic capacitor, weighing 150g/m^2 or less	4805.9110	458
电解设备及装置	Electrolysis machines and apparatus	8543.3000	37
电烤箱	Electric roaster oven	8516.6050	7
电控燃油喷射装置	Electric fuel injection devices	8409.9191	2
电缆,绝缘的,额定电压不超过35千伏	Electric cable, insulated, for a voltage not exceeding 35kV	8544.6012	35
电缆,绝缘的,额定电压不超过80伏,其他	Electric cable, insulated, for a voltage not exceeding 80V, nes	8544.4911	35
电缆,绝缘的,额定电压超过1000伏,其他	Electric cable, insulated, for a voltage exceeding 1000V	8544.6019	35
电缆,绝缘的,额定电压超过110千伏,但不超过220千伏	Electric cable, insulated, for a voltage exceeding 110kV but not exceeding 220kV	8544.6014	35
电缆,绝缘的,额定电压超过35千伏,但不超过110千伏	Electric cable, insulated, for a voltage exceeding 35kV but not exceeding 110kV	8544.6013	35
电缆,绝缘的,额定电压超过80伏,但不超过1000伏,其他	Electric cable, insulated, for a voltage exceeding 80V but not exceeding 1000V, nes	8544.4921	35
电缆,绝缘的,额定电压超过80伏,但不超过1000伏,有接头	Electric cable, insulated, fitted with connectors, for a voltage exceeding 80V but not exceeding 1000V	8544.4221	35
电缆,绝缘的,有接头,额定电压不超过80伏	Electric cable, insulated, fitted with connectors, for a voltage not exceeding 80V	8544.4211	35
电缆卷筒,木制的	Cable-drums, of wood	4415.1000	56
电雷管	Electric detonators	3603.0000	
电篱网激发器	Electric fence energizers	8543.7093	37
电力	Electrical energy	2716.0000	
电力分配盘、板、台、柜及其他基座,用于电压不超过1000伏的线路,装有两个或多个开关、保护或连接用的电器装置,其他	Electricity distribution boards, panels, consoles, desks, cabinets and other bases, for a voltage not exceeding 1000V, equipped with two or more switching or protecting or connecting apparatus, nes	8537.1090	78
电力分配盘、板、台、柜及其他基座,用于电压超过1000伏的线路,装有两个或多个开关、保护或连接用的电器装置,其他	Electricity distribution boards, panels, consoles, desks, cabinets and other bases, for a voltage exceeding 1000V, equipped with two or more switching or protecting or connecting apparatus, nes	8537.2090	78

商品名称	Article Description	税则号列	申报要素
电力分配盘、板、台、柜及其他基座的零件,用于电压超过1000伏的线路,但未装有关装置	Electricity distribution boards, panels, consoles, desks, cabinets and other bases' parts, for a voltage exceeding 1000V, not equipped with their apparatus	8538.1090	3
电量测量或检验的仪器和装置,带记录装置,其他	Electrical quantities measuring or checking instruments and apparatus, with a recording device, nes	9030.8490	7
电量测量或检验的仪器和装置,其他	Electrical quantities measuring or checking instruments and apparatus, nes	9030.8990	7
电量测量或检验的仪器和装置的零件、附件,其他	Electrical quantities measuring or checking instruments and apparatus parts and accessories, nes	9030.9000	3
电量计,生产或供应计量仪表,其他	Electricity meters, supply or production meters, nes	9028.3090	7
电量计零件、附件,工业用	Electricity meters parts and accessories, for industrial use	9028.9010	3
电量计零件、附件,其他	Electricity meters parts and accessories, nes	9028.9090	3
电铃,电气的	Bells, electric	8531.8090	3
电铃零件,电气的	Bells parts, electric	8531.9090	3
电流表,带记录装置	Ammeters, with a recording device	9030.3900	7
电流表,量程在五位半及以下的,数字的,不带记录装置	Ammeters, of measuring range of 5.5 or less, digital, without a recording device	9030.3310	
电路保护装置,用于电压不超过1000伏的线路,其他	Protecting electrical circuits apparatus, for a voltage not exceeding 1000V	8536.3000	8
电路的保护装置,用于电压不超过1000伏的线路	Electrical apparatus for protecting electrical circuits, for a voltage not exceeding 1000V	8536.9000	8
电路的保护装置,用于电压超过1000伏的线路	Electrical apparatus for protecting electrical circuits, for a voltage exceeding 1000V	8535.9000	8
电路的保护装置的零件	Electrical apparatus parts for protecting electrical circuits	8538.9000	3
电路的开关装置,用于电压不超过1000伏的线路	Electrical apparatus for switching electrical circuits, for a voltage not exceeding 1000V	8536.9000	8
电路的开关装置,用于电压超过1000伏的线路	Electrical apparatus for switching electrical circuits, for a voltage exceeding 1000V	8535.9000	8
电路的开关装置的零件	Electrical apparatus parts for switching electrical circuits	8538.9000	3
电路的连接用电气装置,用于电压超过1000伏的线路	Electrical apparatus for making connections to or in electrical circuits, for a voltage exceeding 1000V	8535.9000	8
电路的连接用电气装置的零件	Electrical apparatus parts for making connections to or in electrical circuits	8538.9000	3
电暖毯	Electric blankets	6301.1000	56
电刨,手提式	Planings, hand tools, with self-contained electric motor	8467.2920	57

D

商品名称	Article Description	税则号列	申报要素
电气化接触网架线机(轨行式),铁道及电车道用	Installing vehicles for suspension of contact wire (running on rails), for railway or tramway maintenance or service	8604. 0091	37
电气空间电加热器,其他	Electric space heating apparatus, nes	8516. 2990	7
电气控制盘、板、台、柜及其他基座,用于电压不超过1000伏的线路,装有两个或多个开关、保护或连接用的电器装置,其他	Electric control boards, panels, consoles, desks, cabinets and other bases, for a voltage not exceeding 1000V, equipped with two or more switching or protecting or connecting apparatus, nes	8537. 1090	78
电气控制盘、板、台、柜及其他基座,用于电压超过1000伏的线路,装有两个或多个开关、保护或连接用的电器装置,其他	Electric control boards, panels, consoles, desks, cabinets and other bases, for a voltage exceeding 1000V, equipped with two or more switching or protecting or connecting apparatus, nes	8537. 2090	78
电气控制盘、板、台、柜及其他基座的零件,用于电压超过1000伏的线路,但未装有关装置	Electric control boards, panels, consoles, desks, cabinets and other bases' parts, for a voltage exceeding 1000V, not equipped with their apparatus	8538. 1090	3
电气扩音机组	Electric sound amplifier sets	8518. 5000	5
电气扩音机组零件	Electric sound amplifier sets parts	8518. 9000	3
电气零件,其他	Electrical parts of machinery or apparatus, nes	8548. 9000	3
电气设备及装置,具有独立功能的,其他	Electrical machines and apparatus, having individual functions, nes	8543. 7099	37
电气设备及装置的零件,其他	Electrical machines and apparatus parts, nes	8543. 9090	3
电热板	Electric cooking plates	8516. 6090	7
电热的理发器具用零件	Electro-thermichair-dressing apparatus parts	8516. 9090	3
电热器具,其他	Electro-thermic appliances, nes	8516. 7990	7
电热器具用零件,家用	Electro-thermic appliances parts, of a kind used for domestic purposes	8516. 9090	3
电热塞,点燃式或压燃式内燃发动机用的	Glow plugs, for electrical ignition or starting equipment	8511. 8000	7
电热水器,储存式	Waterheaters, storage, electric	8516. 1010	7
电热水器,即热式	Waterheaters, instantaneous, electric	8516. 1020	7
电热水器,浸入式	Waterheaters heaters, immersion, electric	8516. 1090	7
电容测试仪,带记录装置	Capacitances measuring instruments and apparatus, with a recording device	9030. 8410	
电容测试仪,其他	Capacitances measuring instruments and apparatus, nes	9030. 8910	
电容器,单层瓷介的	Capacitors, ceramic dielectric, single layer	8532. 2300	56
电容器,多层瓷介,片式	Capacitors, ceramic dielectric, multilayer, laminate	8532. 2410	56
电容器,多层瓷介,其他	Capacitors, ceramic dielectric, multilayer, nes	8532. 2490	56
电容器,固定式,其他	Capacitors, fixed, nes	8532. 2900	56

商品名称	Article Description	税则号列	申报要素
电容器,固定式,用于50/60赫兹电路,其额定无功功率不低于0.5千瓦(电力电容器)	Capacitors, fixed, designed for use in 50/60Hz circuits and having a reactive power handling capacity of not less than 0.5kVar (power capacitors)	8532.1000	56
电容器,可变或可调(微调)	Capacitors, variable or adjustable (pre-set)	8532.3000	56
电容器,铝电解式,片式	Capacitors, of aluminium electrolytic, laminate	8532.2210	56
电容器,铝电解式,其他	Capacitors, of aluminium electrolytic, nes	8532.2290	56
电容器,钽的,片式	Capacitors, of tantalum, laminate	8532.2110	56
电容器,钽的,其他	Capacitors, of tantalum, fixed, nes	8532.2190	56
电容器,纸介质或塑料介质,片式	Capacitors, dielectric of paper or plastics, laminate	8532.2510	56
电容器,纸介质或塑料介质,其他	Capacitors, dielectric of paper or plastics,	8532.2590	56
电容器零件,固定式,用于50/60赫兹电路,其额定无功功率不低于0.5千瓦(电力电容器)	Capacitors parts, fixed, designed for use in 50/60Hz circuits and having a reactive power handling capacity of not less than 0.5kVar (power capacitors)	8532.9010	3
电容器零件,其他	Capacitors parts, nes	8532.9090	3
电散热器,储存式	Storage heating radiators, electric	8516.2100	7
电视发送、差转设备用零件	Television transmission or translation apparatus parts	8529.9010	3
电视接收机用零件(等离子显像组件及其零件除外)彩色的	Television receivers parts, of colour television receivers (other than plasma display modules or parts thereof)	8529.9081	3
电视接收机用零件,等离子显像组件及其零件	Television receivers parts, plasma display modules and part thereof	8529.9082	3
电视接收机用零件,其他	Television receivers parts, nes	8529.9089	3
电视接收装置,彩色的,模拟的	Television reception apparatus, colour, analogue	8528.7291	135
电视接收装置,彩色的,其他	Television reception apparatus, colour, nes	8528.7299	135
电视接收装置,彩色的,数字的	Television reception apparatus, colour, digital	8528.7292	135
电视接收装置,彩色的,液晶显示器的,模拟的,其他	Television reception apparatus, colour, of LCD, analogue, nes	8528.7221	135
电视接收装置,彩色的,液晶显示器的,其他	Television reception apparatus, colour, of LCD, nes	8528.7229	135
电视接收装置,彩色的,液晶显示器的,数字的,其他	Television reception apparatus, colour, of LCD, digital	8528.7222	135
电视接收装置,彩色的,阴极射线显像管的,模拟的	Television reception apparatus, colour, of CRT, analogue	8528.7211	135
电视接收装置,彩色的,阴极射线显像管的,其他	Television reception apparatus, colour, of CRT, nes	8528.7219	135
电视接收装置,彩色的,阴极射线显像管的,数字的	Television reception apparatus, colour, of CRT, digital	8528.7212	135
电视接收装置,彩色的等离子显示器的,模拟的	Television reception apparatus, colour, of plasma, analogue	8528.7231	135
电视接收装置,彩色的等离子显示器的,其他	Television reception apparatus, colour, of plasma, nes	8528.7239	135

D

商品名称	Article Description	税则号列	申报要素
电视接收装置,彩色的等离子显示器的,数字的	Television reception apparatus, colour, of plasma, digital	8528.7232	135
电视接收装置,其他黑白或单色的	Television reception apparatus, black and white or other monochrome, nes	8528.7300	135
电视接收装置,在设计上不带有视频显示器或屏幕的,彩色的,其他	Television reception apparatus, not designed to incorporate a video display or screen, colour, nes	8528.7180	135
电视接收装置,在设计上不带有视频显示器或屏幕的,黑白的或其他单色的	Television reception apparatus, not designed to incorporate a video display or screen, black and white or other monochrome	8528.7190	135
电视摄像管	Television camera tubes	8540.2010	35
电视摄像管用零件	Television camera tubes parts	8540.9910	3
电视摄像机用零件,非特种用途的取像模块	Television cameras parts, camera modules without special purposes	8529.9042	3
电视摄像机用零件,其他	Television cameras parts, nes	8529.9049	3
电视摄像机用零件,特种用途的	Television cameras parts, of special purposes	8529.9041	3
电视显像管用零件	Television picture tubes parts	8540.9110	3
电梯,载客用	Lifts, designed for the transport of persons	8428.1010	
电位器,可变的	Rheostats and potentiometers, variable	8533.4000	58
电位器,线绕可变,额定功率不超过 20 瓦	Potentiometers, wirewound variable, for a power handling capacity not exceeding 20W	8533.3100	58
电位器,线绕可变,其他	Potentiometers, wirewound variable, nes	8533.3900	58
电压表,不带记录装置,其他	Voltmeters, without a recording device, nes	9030.3390	
电压表,带记录装置	Voltmeters, with a recording device	9030.3900	
电压表,量程在五位半及以下的,数字的,不带记录装置	Voltmeters, of measuring range of 5.5 or less, digital, without a recording device	9030.3310	
电压限幅器,用于电压超过 1000 伏的线路	Voltage limiters, for a voltage exceeding 1000V	8535.4000	8
电影胶片,未曝光的,彩色摄影用的,宽度超过 16 毫米,但不超过 35 毫米,长度超过 30 米	Cinematographic film, unexposed, for colour photography, of a width exceeding 16mm but not exceeding 35mm and of a length exceeding 30m	3702.5520	12368
电影胶片,未曝光的,彩色摄影用的,宽度超过 35 毫米	Cinematographic film, unexposed, for colour photography, of a width exceeding 35mm	3702.5620	12368
电影胶片,未曝光的,宽度超过 16 毫米,但不超过 35 毫米,长度超过 30 米,其他	Cinematographic film, unexposed, of a width exceeding 16mm but not exceeding 35mm and of a length exceeding 30m, nes	3702.9420	12368
电影胶片,未曝光的,宽度超过 35 毫米,其他	Cinematographic film, unexposed, of a width exceeding 35mm, nes	3702.9520	12368
电影胶片,已曝光未冲洗的	Cinematographic film, exposed but not developed	3704.0010	1238
电影胶片,已曝光已冲洗的,教学专用,其他	Cinematographic film, exposed and developed, for educational use only, nes	3706.9010	1238
电影胶片,已曝光已冲洗的,宽度在 35 毫米及以上,教学专用	Cinematographic film, exposed and developed, of a width of 35mm or more, for educational use only	3706.1010	1238

商品名称	Article Description	税则号列	申报要素
电影胶片,已曝光已冲洗的,宽度在35毫米及以上,其他	Cinematographic film, exposed and developed, of a width of 35mm or more, nes	3706. 1090	1238
电影胶片,已曝光已冲洗的,其他	Cinematographic film, exposed and developed, nes	3706. 9090	1238
电影用装置及设备的零件、附件	Cinematographic apparatus and equipment parts and accessories	9010. 9010	3
电泳设备及装置	Electrophoresis machines and apparatus	8543. 3000	37
电泳仪	Electrophoresis instruments	9027. 2020	
电泳仪零件、附件	Electrophoresis instruments parts and accessories	9027. 9000	3
电涌抑制器,用于电压超过1000伏的线路	Surge suppressors, for a voltage exceeding 1000V	8535. 4000	8
电源车(频率为400赫兹),航空用	Charging vehicles (frequency 400Hz) for airplane	8705. 9051	7
电源车,其他	Charging vehicles, nes	8705. 9059	7
电源车,其他	Mobile electric generator sets, nes	8705. 9059	7
电熨斗	Electric smoothing irons	8516. 4000	7
电子分色机	Electronic colour scanners	9006. 1010	7
电子计算器,不需外接电源的	Electronic calculators capable of operation without an external source of electric power	8470. 1000	
电子计算器的零件、附件	Electronic calculating machines parts and accessories	8473. 2100	3
电子膨胀阀	Electronic expansion valves	8481. 8031	
电子皮带秤	Electronic belt weighing machines	8423. 2010	
电子清纱器	Electronic yarn clearers	8448. 3920	3
电子万能试验机,金属材料试验用	Electric multitesting machines, for testing metals	9024. 1010	
电子镇流器,放电灯或放电管用	Electronic ballats, for discharge lamps or tubes	8504. 1010	
电阻测试仪,不带记录装置	Resistance measuring instruments, without a recording device	9030. 3320	
电阻测试仪,带记录装置	Resistance measuring instruments, with a recording device	9030. 3900	7
电阻焊接机器及装置,其他	Resistance welding of metals machines and apparatus, nes	8515. 2900	
电阻焊接机器及装置,全自动或半自动的,其他	Resistance welding of metals machines and apparatus, fully or partly automatic, nes	8515. 2190	
电阻焊接机器及装置零件	Resistance welding of metals machines and apparatus	8515. 9000	3
电阻器,固定,额定功率不超过20瓦,片式	Resistors, fixed, for a power handling capacity not exceeding 20W, laminate	8533. 2110	5
电阻器,固定,额定功率不超过20瓦,其他	Resistors, fixed, for a power handling capacity not exceeding 20W, nes	8533. 2190	5
电阻器,固定,其他	Resistors, fixed, nes	8533. 2900	5
电阻器,固定碳质,合成或薄膜式	Resistors, fixed carbon, composition or film types	8533. 1000	56
电阻器,可变的,包括变阻器及电位器	Resistors, variable, including rheostats and potentiometers	8533. 4000	58
电阻器,线绕可变,额定功率不超过20瓦	Resistors, wirewourd variable, for a power handling capacity not exceeding 20W	8533. 3100	58

D

商品名称	Article Description	税则号列	申报要素
电阻器,线绕可变,其他	Resisters, wirewound variable, nes	8533. 3900	58
电阻器零件	Resistors parts	8533. 9000	3
垫片、垫圈及其他密封垫,机器及仪器用,硫化橡胶(硬质橡胶除外)的	Gaskets, washers and other seals of a kind used in machines or instruments, of vulcanized rubber other than hard rubber	4016. 9310	236
垫片、垫圈及其他密封垫,硫化橡胶(硬质橡胶除外)的,其他	Gaskets, washers and other seals, of vulcanized rubber other than hard rubber, nes	4016. 9390	236
垫圈(包括弹簧垫圈),铜制	Washers (including spring washers), of copper	7415. 2100	56
垫圈,钢铁制的,其他	Washers, of iron or steel, nes	7318. 2200	268
垫圈及类似品,铝制	Washers and similar articles, of aluminium	7616. 1000	36
淀粉,马铃薯的	Starch of potato	1108. 1300	
淀粉,木薯的	Starch of manioc (cassava)	1108. 1400	
淀粉,其他	Starches, nes	1108. 1900	
淀粉,玉米的	Starch, of maize(corn)	1108. 1200	
淀粉,预凝化的	Starches, pregelatinized	3505. 1000	36
淀粉,酯化的	Starches, esterified	3505. 1000	36
淀粉胶	Starche glues	3505. 2000	36
靛蓝,合成的	Indigo, synthetic	3204. 1510	345
靛蓝,还原型	Indigo, reductive	3204. 1510	345
靛蓝及以其为基本成分的制品,天然的	Indigo and preparations based thereon, natural	3203. 0011	34
靛铜矿	Covellite	2603. 0000	146
diao			
貂,改良种用	Mink, pure-bred breeding	0106. 1910	34
貂,其他	Mink, live, nes	0106. 1990	48
貂,食用	Mink, for human consumption	0106. 1920	48
雕版画的原本	Engravings, original	9702. 0000	
雕刻材料及其制品,动物质的,已加工的	Carving material and articles of animal, worked	9601. 9000	5
雕刻材料及其制品,矿物质的,已加工的	Carving material and articles of mineral, worked	9602. 0090	5
雕刻材料及其制品,植物质的,已加工的	Carving material and articles of vegetable, worked	9602. 0090	5
雕刻或模塑制品,其他	Carved or moulded articles, nes	9602. 0090	5
雕刻模塑或制品,蜡的	Carved or moulded articles of wax	9602. 0090	5
雕刻模塑或制品,塑型膏制成的	Carved or moulded articles of modelling pastes	9602. 0090	5
雕刻模塑或制品,天然树胶的	Carved or moulded articles of natural gums	9602. 0090	5
雕刻模塑或制品,天然树脂的	Carved or moulded articles of natural resins	9602. 0090	5
雕刻模塑或制品,硬脂的	Carved or moulded articles of stearin	9602. 0090	5
雕塑品原件,各种材料制的	Sculptures and statuary, in any material, original	9703. 0000	

商品名称	Article Description	税则号列	申报要素
雕塑像及其他装饰品,贱金属制,镀贵金属的	Statuettes and other ornaments of base metal, plated with precious metal	8306. 2100	256
雕塑像及其他装饰品,贱金属制,景泰蓝的	Statuettes and other ornaments of base metal, cloisonne	8306. 2910	256
雕塑像及其他装饰品,贱金属制,其他	Statuettes and other ornaments of base metal, nes	8306. 2990	256
雕像及装饰品,木制,其他	Statuettes and ornaments, of wood, nes	4420. 1090	56
吊秤	Hanging scales	8423. 8930	
吊裤带,化学纤维制	Braces, of man-made fibres	6212. 9010	2456
吊裤带,其他纺织材料制	Braces, of other textile materials	6212. 9090	2456
吊扇,包括风机,本身装有一个输出功率不超过125瓦的电动机	Ceiling or roof fans, with a self-contained electric motor of an output not exceeding 125W	8414. 5110	23
吊扇,其他	Ceiling or roof fans, nes	8414. 5910	23
吊袜带,化学纤维制	Suspenders, of man-made fibres	6212. 9010	2456
吊袜带,其他纺织材料制	Suspenders, of other textile materials	6212. 9090	2456
钓线轮	Fishing reels	9507. 3000	
钓鱼钩,不论有无系钩丝	Fish-hooks, whether or not snelled	9507. 2000	
调味香料,混合的	Mixtures spices	0910. 9100	6
调味汁及其制品	Sauces and preparations therefor	2103. 9090	268
调心球轴承	Self-aligning ball bearings	8482. 1010	5
调制解调器,有线数字通信设备	Modem, telecommunication apparatus for digital line system	8517. 6234	7
die			
叠氮化物,不论是否已有化学定义	Azides, whether or not chemically defined	2850. 0000	
叠氮化铅	Lead azide	2850. 0000	
鲽鱼,冻的	Plaice(pleuronectes platessa), frozen	0303. 3200	18
鲽鱼,鲜或冷的,	Plaice(pleuronectes platessa), fresh or chilled	0302. 2200	18
ding			
丁苯橡胶(SBR),其他	SBR, nes	4002. 1990	1346
丁苯橡胶(SBR)胶乳,	SBR latex	4002. 1190	12
丁苯橡胶,充油的	SBR, oil-filled	4002. 1912	1346
丁苯橡胶,充油热塑的	SBR, oil-filled and thermo-plasticated	4002. 1914	1346
丁苯橡胶,其他,初级形状的	SBR, in primary forms, nes	4002. 1919	1346
丁苯橡胶,热塑的	SBR, thermo-plasticated	4002. 1913	1346
丁苯橡胶,未经任何加工的	SBR, not worked	4002. 1911	1346
丁丙诺啡(INN) 及盐	Buprenorphine (INN) and salts	2939. 1100	34
丁二烯,液化的	Butadiene, liquefied	2711. 1400	1468
丁二烯橡胶(BR),初级形状的	Butadiene rubber(BR), in primary forms	4002. 2010	136
丁二烯橡胶(BR),其他	Butadiene rubber(BR), nesr	4002. 2090	136
丁腈橡胶(NBR),初级形状的	Acrylonitrile-butadient rubber (NBR), in primary forms	4002. 5910	136

D

商品名称	Article Description	税则号列	申报要素
丁腈橡胶(NBR),其他	Acrylonitrile-butadient rubber (NBR), nes	4002.5990	136
丁腈橡胶(NBR)胶乳	Acrylonitrile-butadient rubber (NBR) latex	4002.5100	136
丁酸及其盐和酯	Butanoic, their salts and esters	2915.6000	36
丁酮	Butanone	2914.1200	36
丁烷,液化的,其他	Butanes, liquefied, nes	2711.1390	1468
丁烷,液化的,直接灌注香烟打火机及类似打火器用,其包装容器的容积超过300立方厘米	Butanes, liquefied, in containers of a kind used for filling or refilling cigarette or similar lighters and of a capacity exceeding $300cm^3$	2711.1310	1468
丁烯,液化的	Butylene, liquefied	2711.1400	1468
丁香(母丁香、公丁香及丁香梗)	Cloves(whole fruit, cloves and stems)	0907.0000	
丁字钢,除热轧、热拉拔或热挤压外未经进一步加工,截面高度低于80毫米	T sections, not further worked than hot-rolled, hot-drawn or extruded, of a height of less than 80mm	7216.2200	468
丁字钢,除热轧、热拉拔或热挤压外未经进一步加工,截面高度在80毫米及以上	T sections, not further worked than hot-rolled, hot-drawn or extruded, of a height of 80mm or more	7216.4020	468
钉,铝制	Nails, of aluminium	7616.1000	36
钉及类似品,铜制或钢铁制带铜头的	Nails and similar articles, of copper or of iron or steel with heads of copper	7415.1000	56
顶推船	Pusher craft	8904.0000	
订书钉,成条的	Staples in strips	8305.2000	256
订书机,锁线式	Book sewing binders	8440.1010	
订书机,装订用	Stapler	8472.9022	
订书机零件,锁线式	Book sewing binders parts	8440.9000	3
定货本,纸或纸板制的	Order books, of paper or paperboard	4820.1000	
定减径轧管机	Fixed and reduced tube mills	8455.1030	7
定量包装秤	Rationed packing scales	8423.3010	
定量分选秤	Rationed sorting scales	8423.3020	
定时开关,装有钟、表机芯或同步电动机的	Time switches with clock or watch movement or with synchronous motor	9107.0000	5
定向罗盘	Direction finding compasses	9014.1000	
定向刨花板	Oriented strand board (osb) of wood	4410.1200	6
定向刨花板	Oriented strand board (osb), of ligneous materials	4410.9090	6
定型剂	Hair lacquers	3305.3000	23
定音管	Pitch pipes	9209.9910	3
锭模	Ingot moulds	8454.2090	
dong			
冬虫夏草	Cordyceps sinensis	1211.9016	34
动臂式装卸桥,其他	Derrick loading and unloading bridges, nes	8426.1943	7
动力织机,所织织物宽度超过30厘米的梭织机,其他	Power looms, for weaving fabrics of width exceeding 30cm, shuttle type, nes	8446.2190	7

商品名称	Article Description	税则号列	申报要素
动物,活的,改良种用,其他	Living animals, pure-bred breeding, nes	0106.9019	4
动物,活的,其他	Living animals, nes	0106.9090	4
动物,活的,食用,其他	Living animals, for human consumption, nes	0106.9020	34
动物,死的,第三章的,不适合供人食用的	Animals of Chapter 3, dead, unfit for human consumption	0511.9190	34
动物,死的,第一章的,不适合供人食用的	Animals of Chapter 1, dead, unfit for human consumption	0511.9990	34
动物产品,其他	Animal products, nes	0511.9990	34
动物产品,其他,供配制药用的,鲜、冷、冻或用其他方法暂时保藏的	Products, of animal, used in the preparation of pharmaceutical products, fresh, chilled, frozen or otherwise provisionally preserved	0510.0090	14
动物产品,食用,其他税号未列名的	Products of animal origin, edible, nes	0410.0090	34
动物粗毛,未梳的	Coarse animal hair, not carded orcombed	5102.2000	48
动物粗毛,已梳的	Coarse animal hair, carded or combed	5105.4000	5
动物粗毛的回收纤维	Garnetted stock of coarse animal hair	5104.0090	5
动物粗毛的机织物	Woven fabrics of coarse animal hair	5113.0000	4568
动物粗毛废料	Waste of coarse animal hair	5103.3000	5
动物粗毛纱线,不论是否供零售用	Yarn of coarse animal hair, whether or not put up for retail sale	5110.0000	56
动物肝,制作或保藏的	Liver of any animal, prepared or preserved	1602.2000	48
动物或植物肥料,其他	Animal or vegetable fertilizers, nes	3101.0090	1346
动物或植物肥料,未经化学处理	Animal or vegetable fertilizers, not chemically treated	3101.0019	1346
动物胶,其他,但不包括税号35.01的酪蛋白胶	Glues of animal origin, nes, excluding casein glues of heading No. 35.01	3503.0090	13
动物精液(牛的精液除外)	Animal semen, other than bovine semen	0511.9910	4
动物胚胎	Animal embryo	0511.9920	4
动物饲料,配制的,其他	Preparations of a kind used in animal feeding, nes	2309.9090	2468
动物饲料用的其他税号未列名的植物原料、废料、残渣及副产品,不论是否制成团粒	Vegetable materials and veget-able waste, vegetable residues and by-products, whether or not in the form of pellets, of a kind used in animal feeding, not elsewhere specified or included	2308.0000	36
动物炭黑	Animal black	3802.9000	34
动物炭黑,废的	Animal black, spent	3802.9000	34
动物细毛,未梳的,喀什米尔山羊的	Fine animal hair, not carded or combed, of kashmir goats	5102.1100	48
动物细毛,未梳的,骆驼毛、骆驼绒	Fine animal hair, not carded or combed, of camel	5102.1930	48
动物细毛,未梳的,其他	Fine animal hair, not carded or combed, nes	5102.1990	48
动物细毛,未梳的,山羊绒,其他	Fine animal hair, not carded or combed, of goats, nes	5102.1920	48
动物细毛,未梳的,兔毛	Fine animal hair, not carded or combed, of rabbit and hare	5102.1910	48
动物细毛,已梳的,喀什米尔山羊的	Fine animal hair, carded or combed, of kashmir goats	5105.3100	5
动物细毛,已梳的,其他	Fine animal hair, carded or combed, nes	5105.3990	5

D

商品名称	Article Description	税则号列	申报要素
动物细毛,已梳的,山羊绒,其他	Fine animal hair, carded or combed, of goats, nes	5105.3929	5
动物细毛,已梳的,兔毛	Fine animal hair, carded or combed, of rabbit and hare	5105.3910	5
动物细毛,已梳的,无毛山羊绒	Fine animal hair, carded or combed, of dehaired goats	5105.3921	5
动物细毛的回收纤维	Garnetted stock of fine animal hair	5104.0090	5
动物细毛的机织物,粗梳的,按重量计羊毛或动物细毛含量在85%及以上,每平方米重量不超过300克,其他动物细毛的	Woven fabrics of carded fine animal hair, containing 85% or more by weight of wool or of fine animal hair, of a weight not exceeding 300g/m^2, of fine animal hair, nes	5111.1119	4568
动物细毛的机织物,粗梳的,按重量计羊毛或动物细毛含量在85%及以上,每平方米重量不超过300克,山羊绒的	Woven fabrics of carded fine animal hair, containing 85% or more by weight of wool or of fine animal hair, of a weight not exceeding 300g/m^2, of goats	5111.1111	4568
动物细毛的机织物,粗梳的,按重量计羊毛或动物细毛含量在85%及以上,其他动物细毛的	Woven fabrics of carded fine animal hair, containing 85% or more by weight of wool or of fine animal hair, of fine animal hair	5111.1919	4568
动物细毛的机织物,粗梳的,按重量计羊毛或动物细毛含量在85%及以上,山羊绒的	Woven fabrics of carded fine animal hair, containing 85% or more by weight of wool or of fine animal hair, of goats	5111.1911	4568
动物细毛的机织物,粗梳的,其他	Woven fabrics of carded fine animal hair, nes	5111.9000	4568
动物细毛的机织物,粗梳的,主要或仅与化学纤维长丝混纺	Woven fabrics of carded fine animal hair, mixed mainly or solely with man-made filaments	5111.2000	4568
动物细毛的机织物,粗梳的,主要或仅与化学纤维短纤混纺	Woven fabrics of carded fine animal hair, mixed mainly or solely with man-made staple fibres	5111.3000	4568
动物细毛的机织物,精梳的,按重量计羊毛或动物细毛含量在85%及以上,其他	Woven fabrics of combed fine animal hair, containing 85% or more by weight of wool or of fine animal hair, nes	5112.1900	4568
动物细毛的机织物,精梳的,其他	Woven fabrics of combed fine animal hair, nes	5112.9000	4568
动物细毛的机织物,精梳的,主要或仅与化学纤维长丝混纺	Woven fabrics of combed fine animal hair, mixed mainly or solely with man-made filaments	5112.2000	4568
动物细毛的机织物,精梳的,主要或仅与化学纤维短纤混纺	Woven fabrics of combed fine animal hair, mixed mainly or solely with man-made staple fibres	5112.3000	4568
动物细毛的机织物,精梳的按重量计羊毛或动物细毛含量在85%及以上,每平方米重量不超过200克	Woven fabrics of combed fine animal hair, containing 85% or more by weight of wool or of fine animal hair, of a weight not exceeding 200g/m^2	5112.1100	4568
动物细毛废料	Waste of fine animal hair	5103.2090	5
动物细毛落毛	Noils of fine animal hair	5103.1090	5
动物细毛纱线,粗梳的,非供零售用,按重量计动物细毛含量在85%及以上的,其他	Yarn of fine animal hair, carded, not put up for retail sale, containing 85% or more by weight of fine animal hair, nes	5108.1019	346
动物细毛纱线,粗梳的,非供零售用,按重量计动物细毛含量在85%及以上的,山羊绒的	Yarn of fine animal hair, carded, not put up for retail sale, containing 85% or more by weight of fine animal hair, of goats	5108.1011	346

商品名称	Article Description	税则号列	申报要素
动物细毛纱线,粗梳的,非供零售用,其他	Yarn of fine animal hair, carded, not put up for retail sale, nes	5108.1090	346
动物细毛纱线,供零售用,按重量计羊毛或动物细毛含量在85%及以上,其他动物细毛的	Yarn of fine animal hair, put up for retail sale, containing 85% or more by weight of wool or of fine animal hair, of fine animal hair, nes	5109.1019	346
动物细毛纱线,供零售用,按重量计羊毛或动物细毛含量在85%及以上,山羊绒的	Yarn of fine animal hair, put up for retail sale, containing 85% or more by weight of wool or of fine animal hair, of goats	5109.1011	346
动物细毛纱线,供零售用,其他	Yarn of fine animal hair, put up for retail sale, nes	5109.1090	346
动物细毛纱线,供零售用,其他动物细毛的	Yarn of fine animal hair, put up for retail sale, of fine animal hair, nes	5109.9019	346
动物细毛纱线,供零售用,山羊绒的	Yarn of fine animal hair, put up for retail sale, of goats	5109.9011	346
动物细毛纱线,精梳的,非供零售用,按重量计动物细毛含量在85%及以上的,其他	Yarn of fine animal hair, combed, not put up for retail sale, containing 85% or more by weight of fine animal hair, nes	5108.2019	346
动物细毛纱线,精梳的,非供零售用,按重量计动物细毛含量在85%及以上的,山羊绒的	Yarn of fine animal hair, combed, not put up for retail sale, containing 85% or more by weight of fine animal hair, of goats	5108.2011	346
动物细毛纱线,精梳的,非供零售用,其他	Yarn of fine animal hair, combed, not put up for retail sale, nes	5108.2090	346
动物血制品,治病、防病或诊断用的	Animal blood prepared for therapeutic, prophylactic or diagnostic uses	3002.9090	34
动物油脂及其分离品	Animal fats and oil and fractions thereof	1516.1000	
动物油脂及其分离品,其他	Animal fats and oils and fractions thereof, nes	1518.0000	46
动物油脂加工的机器	Animal fats or oils preparation machinery	8479.2000	7
动物油脂提取的机器	Animal fats or oils extraction machinery	8479.2000	7
动物质海绵,天然的	Sponges of animal origin, natural	0511.9990	34
冻石,未破碎及未研粉	Natural steatite, not crushed, not powdered	2526.1010	4
冻石,已破碎或已研粉	Natural steatite, crushed or powdered	2526.2010	4
dou			
斗篷,非针织或钩编的,男式,化学纤维制	Capes, not knitted or crocheted, for men or boys, of man-made fibres	6201.1390	2456
斗篷,非针织或钩编的,男式,棉制	Capes, not knitted or crocheted, for men or boys, of cotton	6201.1290	2456
斗篷,非针织或钩编的,男式,其他纺织材料制	Capes, not knitted or crocheted, for men or boys, of other textile materials	6201.1900	2456
斗篷,非针织或钩编的,男式,羊毛或动物细毛制	Capes, not knitted or crocheted, for men or boys, of wool or fine animal hair	6201.1100	2456
斗篷,非针织或钩编的,女式,化学纤维制	Capes, not knitted or crocheted, for women or girls, of man-made fibres	6202.1390	2456

D

商品名称	Article Description	税则号列	申报要素
斗篷,非针织或钩编的,女式,棉制	Capes,not knitted or crocheted,for women or girls,of cotton	6202.1290	2456
斗篷,非针织或钩编的,女式,其他纺织材料制	Capes,not knitted or crocheted,for women or girls,of other textile materials	6202.1900	2456
斗篷,非针织或钩编的,女式,羊毛或动物细毛制	Capes,not knitted or crocheted,for women or girls,of wool or fine animal hair	6202.1100	2456
斗篷及类似品,针织或钩编的,男式,化学纤维制	Capes and similar articles, knitted or crocheted, for men or boys,for man-made fibres	6101.3000	2456
斗篷及类似品,针织或钩编的,男式,棉制	Capes and similar articles, knitted or crocheted, for men or boys,of cotton	6101.2000	2456
斗篷及类似品,针织或钩编的,男式,其他	Capes and similar articles, knitted or crocheted, for men or boys,nes	6101.9090	2456
斗篷及类似品,针织或钩编的,男式,羊毛或动物细毛制	Capes and similar articles, knitted or crocheted, for men or boys,of wool or fine animal hair	6101.9010	2456
斗篷及类似品,针织或钩编的,女式,化学纤维制	Capes and similar articles, knitted or crocheted, for women or girls,of man-made fibres	6102.3000	2456
斗篷及类似品,针织或钩编的,女式,棉制	Capes and similar articles, knitted or crocheted, for women or girls,of cotton	6102.2000	2456
斗篷及类似品,针织或钩编的,女式,其他	Capes and similar articles, knitted or crocheted, for women or girls,nes	6102.9000	2456
斗篷及类似品,针织或钩编的,女式,羊毛或动物细毛制	Capes and similar articles, knitted or crocheted, for women or girls,of wool or fine animal hair	6102.1000	2456
豆蔻	Cardamoms	0908.3000	
豆类,其他,脱荚的,干的	Leguminous vegetables,nes,shelled,dried	0713.9090	34
豆类,其他,种用,脱荚的,干的	Leguminous vegetables,nes,seed,shelled,dried	0713.9010	34
豆类蔬菜,其他,冷冻的	Leguminous vegetables,nes,frozen	0710.2900	1
豆类蔬菜,其他,鲜或冷藏的	Leguminous vegetables,nes,fresh or chilled	0708.9000	1
豆油及其分离品,初榨的,不论是否脱胶	Soyabean oil and its fractions, crude oil, whether or not degummed	1507.1000	4
豆油及其分离品,其他	Soyabean oil and its fractions,nes	1507.9000	4
du			
毒重石	Witherite	2511.2000	4
独居石	Monazites	2612.2000	146
杜鹃(植),不论是否嫁接,其他	Rhododendrons and azaleas,grafted or not,nes	0602.3090	
杜鹃(植),不论是否嫁接,种用	Rhododendrons and azaleas,grafted or not,seedlings	0602.3010	3
杜松果	Juniper berries	0909.5000	
杜松子酒	Geneva	2208.5000	2468
杜松子酒	Gin	2208.5000	2468
杜仲	Cortex eucommiae	1211.9028	34
渡船,非机动船舶	Ferryboats,nes	8901.1090	5
渡船,机动船舶	Ferryboats,motor vessels	8901.1010	5
镀金属皮革	Metallised leather	4114.2000	1458

商品名称	Article Description	税则号列	申报要素
duan			
短大衣,非针织或钩编的,男式,化学纤维制	Car-coats, not knitted or crocheted, for men or boys, of man-made fibres	6201.1390	2456
短大衣,非针织或钩编的,男式,棉制	Car-coats, not knitted or crocheted, for men or boys, of cotton	6201.1290	2456
短大衣,非针织或钩编的,男式,其他纺织材料制	Car-coats, not knitted or crocheted, for men or boys, of other textile materials	6201.1900	2456
短大衣,非针织或钩编的,男式,羊毛或动物细毛制	Car-coats, not knitted or crocheted, for men or boys, of wool or fine animal hair	6201.1100	2456
短大衣,非针织或钩编的,女式,化学纤维制	Car-coats, not knitted or crocheted, for women or girls, of man-made fibres	6202.1390	2456
短大衣,非针织或钩编的,女式,棉制	Car-coats, not knitted or crocheted, for women or girls, of cotton	6202.1290	2456
短大衣,非针织或钩编的,女式,其他纺织材料制	Car-coats, not knitted or crocheted, for women or girls, of other textile materials	6202.1900	2456
短大衣,非针织或钩编的,女式,羊毛或动物细毛制	Car-coats, not knitted or crocheted, for women or girls, of wool or fine animal hair	6202.1100	2456
短大衣及类似品,针织或钩编的,男式,化学纤维制	Car-coats and similar articles, knitted or crocheted, for men or boys, for man-made fibres	6101.3000	2456
短大衣及类似品,针织或钩编的,男式,棉制	Car-coats and similar articles, knitted or crocheted, for men or boys, of cotton	6101.2000	2456
短大衣及类似品,针织或钩编的,男式,其他	Car-coats and similar articles, knitted or crocheted, for men or boys, nes	6101.9090	2456
短大衣及类似品,针织或钩编的,男式,羊毛或动物细毛制	Car-coats and similar articles, knitted or crocheted, for men or boys, of wool or fine animal hair	6101.9010	2456
短大衣及类似品,针织或钩编的,女式,化学纤维制	Car-coats and similar articles, knitted or crocheted, for women or girls, of man-made fibres	6102.3000	2456
短大衣及类似品,针织或钩编的,女式,棉制	Car-coats and similar articles, knitted or crocheted, for women or girls, of cotton	6102.2000	2456
短大衣及类似品,针织或钩编的,女式,其他	Car-coats and similar articles, knitted or crocheted, for women or girls, nes	6102.9000	2456
短大衣及类似品,针织或钩编的,女式,羊毛或动物细毛制	Car-coats and similar articles, knitted or crocheted, for women or girls, of wool or fine animal hair	6102.1000	2456
短斗篷及类似品,非针织或钩编的,男式,化学纤维制	Cloaks and similar articles not knitted or crocheted, for men or boys, for man-made fibres	6201.1390	2456
短斗篷及类似品,非针织或钩编的,男式,棉制	Cloaks and similar articles, not knitted or crocheted, for men or boys, of cotton	6201.1290	2456
短斗篷及类似品,非针织或钩编的,男式,其他纺织材料制	Cloaks and similar articles not knitted or crocheted, for men or boys, of other textile materials	6201.1900	2456
短斗篷及类似品,非针织或钩编的,男式,羊毛或动物细毛制	Cloaks and similar articles not knitted or crocheted, for men or boys, of wool or fine animal hair	6201.1100	2456
短斗篷及类似品,非针织或钩编的,女式,化学纤维制	Cloaks and similar articles not knitted or crocheted, for women or girls, of man-made fibres	6202.1390	2456

商品名称	Article Description	税则号列	申报要素
短斗篷及类似品,非针织或钩编的,女式,棉制	Cloaks and similar articles,not knitted or crocheted, for women or girls,of cotton	6202. 1290	2456
短斗篷及类似品,非针织或钩编的,女式,其他纺织材料制	Cloaks and similar articles not knitted or crocheted, for women or girls,of other textile materials	6202. 1900	2456
短斗篷及类似品,非针织或钩编的,女式,羊毛或动物细毛制	Cloaks and similar articles not knitted or crocheted, for women or girls,of wool or fine animal hair	6202. 1100	2456
短斗篷及类似品,针织或钩编的,男式,化学纤维制	Cloaks and similar articles,knitted or crocheted,for men or boys,for man-made fibres	6101. 3000	2456
短斗篷及类似品,针织或钩编的,男式,棉制	Cloaks and similar articles,knitted or crocheted,for men or boys,of cotton	6101. 2000	2456
短斗篷及类似品,针织或钩编的,男式,其他	Cloaks and similar articles,knitted or crocheted,for men or boys,of other textile materials	6101. 9090	2456
短斗篷及类似品,针织或钩编的,男式,羊毛或动物细毛制	Cloaks and similar articles,knitted or crocheted,for men or boys,of wool or fine animal hair	6101. 9010	2456
短斗篷及类似品,针织或钩编的,女式,化学纤维制	Cloaks and similar articles,knitted or crocheted,for women or girls,of man-made fibres	6102. 3000	2456
短斗篷及类似品,针织或钩编的,女式,棉制	Cloaks and similar articles,knitted or crocheted,for women or girls,of cotton	6102. 2000	2456
短斗篷及类似品,针织或钩编的,女式,其他	Cloaks and similar articles,knitted or crocheted,for women or girls,of other textile materials	6102. 9000	2456
短斗篷及类似品,针织或钩编的,女式,羊毛或动物细毛制	Cloaks and similar articles,knitted or crocheted,for women or girls,of wool or fine animal hair	6102. 1000	2456
短裤,非针织或钩编的,男式,合成纤维制	Shorts,not knitted or crocheted,for men or boys,of synthetic fibres	6203. 4390	2456
短裤,非针织或钩编的,男式,棉制	Shorts,not knitted or crocheted,for men or boys,of cotton	6203. 4290	2456
短裤,非针织或钩编的,男式,其他纺织材料制	Shorts,not knitted or crocheted,for men or boys,of other textile material	6203. 4990	2456
短裤,非针织或钩编的,男式,羊毛或动物细毛制	Shorts,not knitted or crocheted,for men or boys,of wool or fine animal hair	6203. 4100	2456
短裤,非针织或钩编的,女式,合成纤维制	Shorts,not knitted or crocheted,for women or girls,of synthetic fibres	6204. 6300	2456
短裤,非针织或钩编的,女式,棉制	Shorts,not knitted or crocheted,for women or girls,of cotton	6204. 6200	2456
短裤,非针织或钩编的,女式,其他纺织材料制	Shorts,not knitted or crocheted,for women or girls,of other textile materials	6204. 6900	2456
短裤,非针织或钩编的,女式,羊毛或动物细毛制	Shorts,not knitted or crocheted,for women or girls,of wool or fine animal hair	6204. 6100	2456
短裤,针织或钩编的,男式,合成纤维制	Shorts, knitted or crocheted, for men or boys, of synthetic fibres	6103. 4300	2456
短裤,针织或钩编的,男式,棉制	Shorts,knitted or crocheted,for men or boys,of cotton	6103. 4200	2456
短裤,针织或钩编的,男式,其他纺织材料制	Shorts,knitted or crocheted,for men or boys,of other textile materials	6103. 4900	2456

商品名称	Article Description	税则号列	申报要素
短裤,针织或钩编的,男式,羊毛或动物细毛制	Shorts, knitted or crocheted, for men or boys, of wool or fine animal hair	6103. 4100	2456
短裤,针织或钩编的,女式,合成纤维制	Shorts, knitted or crocheted, for women or girls, of synthetic fibres	6104. 6300	2456
短裤,针织或钩编的,女式,棉制	Shorts, knitted or crocheted, for women or girls, of cotton	6104. 6200	2456
短裤,针织或钩编的,女式,其他纺织材料制	Shorts, knitted or crocheted, for women or girls, of other textile materials	6104. 6900	2456
短裤,针织或钩编的,女式,羊毛或动物细毛制	Shorts, knitted or crocheted, for women or girls, of wool or fine animal hair	6104. 6100	2456
短统靴(过踝),但低于小腿的,内底长度小于24厘米的,皮革制外底的,皮革制鞋面的	Footwear, covering the ankle but not covering the calf, length of inner soles less than 24cm, with outer soles of leather and upers of leather	6403. 5111	26
短统靴(过踝),但低于小腿的,内底长度小于24厘米的,橡胶、塑料、皮革或再生皮革制外底,皮革制鞋面的	Footwear, covering the ankle but not covering the calf, length of inner soles less than 24cm, with outer soles of rubber, plastics, leather or composition leather and upers of leather	6403. 9111	26
短统靴(过踝),但低于小腿的,皮革制外底的,皮革制鞋面的,其他	Footwear, covering the ankle but not covering the calf, with outer soles of leather and upers of leather, nes	6403. 5119	26
短统靴(过踝),但低于小腿的,橡胶、塑料、皮革或再生皮革制外底,皮革制鞋面的,其他	Footwear, covering the ankle but not covering the calf, with outer soles of rubber, plastics, leather or composition leather and upers of leather, nes	6403. 9119	26
短统靴(过踝),内底长度小于24厘米的,皮革制外底的,皮革制鞋面的,其他	Footwear, covering the ankle, length of inner soles less than 24cm, with outer soles of leather and upers of leather, nes	6403. 5191	26
短统靴(过踝),内底长度小于24厘米的,橡胶、塑料、皮革或再生皮革制外底,皮革制鞋面的,其他	Footwear, covering the ankle, length of inner soles less than 24cm, with outer soles of rubber, plastics, leather or composition leather and upers of leather, nes	6403. 9191	26
短统靴(过踝),皮革制外底的,皮革制鞋面的,其他	Footwear, covering the ankle, with outer soles of leather and upers of leather, nes	6403. 5199	26
短统靴(过踝),橡胶、塑料、皮革或再生皮革制外底,皮革制鞋面的,其他	Footwear, covering the ankle, with outer soles of rubber, plastics, leather or composition leather and upers of leather, nes	6403. 9199	26
短统靴(过踝),橡胶或塑料制外底及鞋面的其他鞋靴	Footwear with outer soles and uppers of rubber or plastics, covering the ankle	6402. 9100	26
短弯刀及其零件	Cutlasses and parts	9307. 0000	
断层检查仪,X射线的	Tomography apparatus, X-rays computed	9022. 1200	
断流器,点燃式或压燃式内燃发动机用的	Cutouts, for electrical ignition or starting equipment	8511. 8000	7
断续开关,用于电压超过1000伏的线路	Make-and-break switches, for a voltage exceeding 1000V	8535. 3000	8

D

商品名称	Article Description	税则号列	申报要素
椴树皮	Lime bark	1401. 9090	3
锻锤,锻造或冲压机床用,加工金属用	Hammers, for forging or die-stamping machines, for working metal	8462. 1090	7
锻压或冲压用工具,可互换	Pressing, stamping or punching tools, interchangeable	8207. 3000	256
锻造机床,加工金属用,其他	Forging machines, for working metal, nes	8462. 1090	7
锻造机床,数控的,加工金属用	Forging machines, numerically controlled, for working metal	8462. 1010	7
dui			
堆垛机,无轨的,电动的	Stackers of trackless alleyway, powered by an electric motor	8427. 1020	7
堆垛机,有轨的,电动的	Stackers of track alleyway, powered by an electric motor	8427. 1010	7
堆垛机的零件	Stackers parts	8431. 2000	3
对苯二酚	Hydroquinone	2907. 2210	36
对苯二酚盐	P-dihydroxybenzene salts	2907. 2290	36
对苯二甲酸,其他	Terephthalic acid, nes	2917. 3619	36
对苯二甲酸二甲酯	Dimethyl terephthalate	2917. 3700	36
对苯二甲酸盐	Terephthalie acid salts	2917. 3690	36
对二甲苯	P-xylene	2902. 4300	6
对二氯苯	P-dichlorobenzene:	2903. 6190	36
对焊件,不锈钢制	Butt welding fittings, of stainless steel	7307. 2300	6
对焊件,钢铁的,其他	Butt welding fittings, of iron or steel, nes	7307. 9300	6
对讲机	Walkie-talkie	8517. 1220	
对讲机用零件(天线除外)	Walkie-talkie parts, other than aerials	8517. 7040	3
对流式空间电加热器,充液式	Electric convection space heating apparatus, oil-filled types	8516. 2932	7
对流式空间电加热器,风扇式	Electric convection space heating apparatus, fan type	8516. 2931	7
对流式空间电加热器,其他	Electric convection space heating apparatus, nes	8516. 2939	7
对硫磷(ISO)	Parathion (ISO)	2920. 1100	36
对氯苯酚	P-chlorophenol	2908. 1910	36
对氯甲苯	P-chlorotoluene	2903. 6910	36
对氯氰苄	P-chlorobenzyl cyanide	2926. 9010	36
对叔丁基-α-甲基-氧化肉桂醛	P-tert-butyl-α-methyl-oxocinn amaldehyde	2912. 2910	36
对虾,冻的,其他	Prawns, frozen, nes	0306. 1329	18
对虾,未冻的,其他	Prawns, not frozen, nes	0306. 2399	14
对虾,鲜或冷的	Prawns, fresh or chilled	0306. 2391	1
对虾种苗	Prawns, for cultivation	0306. 2310	3
对硝基酚	P-nitrophenol	2908. 9910	36
对硝基酚钠	Sodium p-nitro-phenolate	2908. 9910	36
对硝基氯化苯	P-nitrochlorobenzene	2904. 9013	36
对乙酰氨基苯乙醚	Phenacetin	2924. 2910	36

商品名称	Article Description	税则号列	申报要素
对乙酰氨基酚	P-acetaminophenol	2924.2920	36
对异丙基苯胺	P-isopropyl-aniline	2921.4910	36
dun			
囤、柜、罐、桶及类似容器,钢铁的,容积超过300升,不论是否衬里或隔热,但无机械或热力装置,盛装物料用的(装压缩气体或液化气体的除外)	Reservoirs, tanks, vats and similar containers for any material, of iron or steel, of a capacity exceeding 300L, whether or not lined or heat-insulated, but not fitted with mechanical or thermal equipment (other than compressed or liquefied gas)	7309.0000	36
囤、柜、罐、桶及类似容器,铝制,容积超过300升,不论是否衬里或隔热,但无机械可热力装置,盛装物料用的(装压缩气体或液化气体的除外)	Reservoirs, tanks, vats and similar containersfor any material, of aluminium, of a capacity exceeding 300L, whether or not lined or heat-insulated, but not fitted with mechanical or thermal equipment (other than compressed or liquefied gas)	7611.0000	68
囤、柜、罐、桶及类似容器,铝制,容积超过300升,不论是否衬里或隔热,但无机械可热力装置,盛装物料用的(装压缩气体或液化气体的除外),其他	Reservoirs, tanks, vats and similar containersfor any material, of aluminium, of a capacity not exceeding 300L, whether or not lined or heat-insulated, but not fitted with mechanical or thermal equipment (other than compressed or liquefied gas), nes	7612.9090	368
囤及类似容器,容积超过300升,建筑用	Reservoirs, of plastics, of a capacity exceeding 300L, for builders	3925.1000	23
duo			
多臂机及其所用的卡片缩小、复制、穿孔或汇编机器	Dobbies and card reducing, copying, punching or assembling machines for use there with	8448.1100	3
多层隔温、隔音玻璃组件,其他	Multiplewalled insulating units of glass, nes	7008.0090	234
多工位组合机床,加工金属的	Multi-station transfer machines, for working metal	8457.3000	7
多股纱线或缆线,按重量计聚丙烯腈或变性聚丙烯腈短纤含量在85%及以上	Synthetic staple fibres multiple or cabled yarn, containing 85% or more by weight of acrylic or modacrylic staple fibres	5509.3200	68
多股纱线或缆线,非供零售用,其他	Multiple or cabled yarn, not put up for retail sale, nes	5402.6990	3468
多聚甲醛	Paraformaldehyde	2912.6000	136
多联商业表格纸,纸或纸板制的	Manifold business forms, of paper or paperboard	4820.4000	
多磷酸,其他	Polyphosphoric acids, nes	2809.2090	6
多磷酸盐,其他,无机的	Polyphosphates, nes, inorganic	2835.3990	3
多硫化物,初级形状的	Polysulphides, in primary forms	3911.9000	16
多硫化物,其他,无论是否已有化学定义	Polysulphides, nes, whether or not chemically defined	2830.9090	
多瑙哲罗鱼,冻的	Danube salmon, frozen	0303.2220	18
多瑙哲罗鱼,鲜或冷的	Danube salmon (hucho hucho), fresh or chilled	0302.1220	18
多士炉	Toasters, slice pop-up	8516.7220	7
多肽激素及其衍生物和结构类似物	Polypeptide hormones, their derivatives and structural analogues	2937.1900	36
多萜树脂,初级形状的	Polyterpenes, in primary forms	3911.1000	16

D

商品名称	Article Description	税则号列	申报要素
多元醇,其他	Polyhydric alcohols,nes	2905.4990	36
多元酚,其他	Polyphenols,nes	2907.2990	36
多爪锚及其零件,钢铁的	Grapnels and parts thereof,of iron or steel	7316.0000	36
舵机,船舶用	Steering and rudder equipment for ships	8479.8910	7
舵机零件,船舶用	Steering and rudder equipment parts,for ships	8479.9010	3

D

E

商品名称	Article Description	税则号列	申报要素
e			
锇,板、片	Osmium,plates and sheets	7110.4910	46
锇,其他	Osmium,nes	7110.4990	46
锇,未锻造或粉末状	Osmium,unwrought or in powder form	7110.4100	46
鹅,改良种用,重量不超过185克	Geese, pure-bred breeding, weighing not more than 185g	0105.1910	48
鹅,改良种用,重量超过185克	Geese,pure-bred breeding,weighing more than 185g	0105.9910	48
鹅,改良种用除外,重量超过185克	Geese, ex. pure-bred breeding, weighing more than 185g	0105.9992	48
鹅,整只,冻的	Geese,not cut in pieces,frozen	0207.3320	1
鹅,整只,鲜或冷的	Geese,not cut in pieces,fresh or chilled	0207.3220	1
鹅蛋,鲜的、带壳	Eggs,of geese,in shell,fresh	0407.0023	1
鹅块,冻的	Cuts of geese,frozen	0207.3620	1
鹅块,鲜或冷的	Cuts of geese,fresh or chilled	0207.3520	1
鹅卵石,不论是否热处理	Shingle,whether or not bead-treated	2517.1000	13
鹅莓,冷冻的	Gooseberries,frozen	0811.2000	1
鹅莓,鲜的	Gooseberries,fresh	0810.9020	1
苊	Acenaphthene	2902.9090	6
恶唑仑(INN)及盐	Oxazolam(INN);salts thereof	2934.9100	36
鳄梨	Avocados	0804.4000	14
鳄鱼苗	Crocodiles for cultivation,pure-bred breeding	0106.2011	3
蒽醌	Anthraquinone	2914.6100	36
er			
儿茶酚胺激素及其衍生物和结构类似物,其他	Catecholamine hormones, their derivatives and structural analogues,nes	2937.3900	36
儿童图画书、绘画或涂色书	Children's picture,drawing or colouring books	4903.0000	35
耳机、耳塞机,其他	Headphones and earphones,nes	8518.3090	5
耳机零件	Headphones parts	8518.9000	3
二苯胺及其衍生物以及它们的盐	Diphenylamine and its derivatives;salts thereof	2921.4400	36
二苯基酚丙烷及其盐	Diphenylolpropane and its salts	2907.2300	36
二苯基甲烷二异氰酸酯	Diphenylmethane diisocyanate	2929.1030	36
二苯羟乙酸	Ahydroxydiphenylacetic acid	2918.1910	36
二苯乙醇酸	Benzilic acid	2918.1910	36
二苯乙醇酸-3-奎宁环脂	Benzilic acid-3-quinuclidinate	2933.3910	36
二醋酸纤维单纱,非供零售用	Cellulose diacetate single yarn,not put up for retail sale	5403.3310	3468
二醋酸纤维丝束	Cellulose diacetate filament tow	5502.0010	68

E

商品名称	Article Description	税则号列	申报要素
二甘醇	Diethylene glycol, digol	2909. 4100	36
二极管,但光敏二极管或发光二极管除外	Diodes, other than photosensitive or light emitting diodes	8541. 1000	
二甲氨基乙醇及其质子化盐	N, N-dimethylaminoethanol and corresponding protonated salts	2922. 1921	36
二甲胺及其盐	Dimethylamine and their salts	2921. 1100	36
二甲苯二异氰酸酯	o-Xylene diisocyanate	2929. 1020	36
二甲基苯胺	Dimethylanilines	2921. 4920	36
二甲基苯基吡唑酮及其衍生物	Phenazone and its derivatives	2933. 1100	36
二甲基环己醇	Dimethylcyctohexanols	2906. 1200	36
二甲基甲酰胺	N, N-dimetheylformamide	2924. 1910	36
二硫代氨基甲酸盐	Dithiocarbamates	2930. 2000	36
二硫代碳酸酯(或盐)	Dithiocarbonates	2930. 9020	36
二硫化二烃氨基硫羰	Thiuram disulphide	2930. 3000	36
二硫化碳	Carbon disulphide	2813. 1000	
二氯二氟甲烷	Dichlorodifluoromethane	2903. 4200	36
二氯化硫	Sulfur dichloride	2812. 1042	
二氯甲烷	Dichloromethane (methylene chloride)	2903. 1200	36
二氯六氟丙烷	Dichlorohexafluoropropane	2903. 4591	36
二氯四氟乙烷	Dichlorotetrafluoroethanes	2903. 4400	36
二氯乙酸或三氯乙酸及其盐和酯	Di-chloroacetic acids, their salts and esters	2915. 4000	36
二氯异氰脲酸	Dichloroisooyanurate acid	2933. 6921	36
二烷(甲、乙、正丙或异丙)氨基膦酸二烷(甲、乙、正丙或异丙)酯	Dialkyl (me, et, n-pr or i-pr) N, N-dialkyl (me, et, n-pr or i-pr)-phosphoramidates	2929. 9030	36
二烷(甲、乙、正丙或异丙)氨基膦酰二卤	N, N-dialkyl (me, et, n-pr or i-pr) phosphoramidic dihalides	2929. 9020	36
二烷(甲、乙、正丙或异丙)氨基乙-2-醇及其质子化盐,其他	N, N-dialkyl-(me, et, n-pr or i-pr) aminoethane-2-ols and corresponding protonated salts, nes	2922. 1929	36
二烷(甲、乙、正丙或异丙)氨基乙基-2-氯及其质子化盐	N, N-dialkyl (me, et, n-pr or i-pr) aminoethyl-2-chlorides and corresponding protonated salts	2921. 1960	36
二硝基甲苯	Dinitrotoluene and dinitrochlorobenzene	2904. 2030	36
二硝基氯化苯	Dinitrochlorobenzene	2904. 9020	36
二溴菊酸	Dibromochrysanthermic acid	2916. 2010	36
二溴四氟乙烷	Dibromotetraf luoroethane	2903. 4600	36
二氧化锆	Zirconium dioxide	2825. 6000	
二氧化硅	Silicon dioxide	2811. 2200	1346
二氧化锰	Manganese dioxide	2820. 1000	6
二氧化钛	Titanic anhydride	2823. 0000	4
二氧化碳	Carbon dioxide	2811. 2100	36
二氧化碳压缩机	CO_2 compressors	8414. 8020	23
二乙氨基乙醇及其质子化盐	N, N-diethylaminoethanol and corresponding protonated salts	2922. 1922	36

E

商品名称	Article Description	税则号列	申报要素
二乙醇胺及其盐	Diethanolamine and its salts	2922. 1200	36
二元醇,其他	Diols, nes	2905. 3990	36
二正丙胺	Di-n-propylamine	2921. 1910	36

F

商品名称	Article Description	税则号列	申报要素
fa			
发菜	Black moss	1212.2020	14
发电机,点燃式或压燃式内燃发动机用的,其他	Generators, for electrical ignition or starting equipment, nes	8511.5090	7
发电机,机车、航空器及船舶用,点燃式或压燃式内燃发动机用的,其他	Generators, for locomotives, aircraft or ships, for electrical ignition or starting equipment, nes	8511.5010	7
发电机,输出功率不超过750瓦,直流	Generators of an output not exceeding 750W, DC	8501.3100	8
发电机,输出功率不超过75千伏安,交流	Generators of an output not exceeding 75kVA, AC	8501.6100	8
发电机,输出功率超过350兆伏安,但不超过665兆伏安,交流	Generators of an output exceeding 350MVA but not exceeding 665MVA, AC	8501.6420	8
发电机,输出功率超过375千伏安,但不超过750千伏安,交流	Generators of an output exceeding 375kVA but not exceeding 750kVA, AC	8501.6300	8
发电机,输出功率超过375千瓦,直流	Generators of an output exceeding 375kW, DC	8501.3400	8
发电机,输出功率超过665兆伏安,交流	Generators of an output exceeding 665MVA, AC	8501.6430	8
发电机,输出功率超过750千伏安,但不超过350兆伏安,交流	Generators of an output exceeding 750kVA but not exceeding 350MVA, AC	8501.6410	8
发电机,输出功率超过750瓦,但不超过75千瓦,直流	Generators of an output exceeding 750W but not exceeding 75kW, DC	8501.3200	8
发电机,输出功率超过75千伏安,但不超过375千伏安,交流	Generators of an output exceeding 75kVA but not exceeding 375kVA, AC	8501.6200	8
发电机,输出功率超过75千瓦,但不超过375千瓦,直流	Generators of an output exceeding 75kW but not exceeding 375kW, DC	8501.3300	8
发电机的零件,其他	Generators parts, nes	8503.0090	3
发电机的零件,输出功率超过350兆伏安,但不超过665兆伏安,交流	Generators parts, of an output exceeding 350MVA but not exceeding 665MVA, AC	8503.0020	3
发电机零件,点燃式或压燃式内燃发动机用的,其他	Generators parts, for electrical ignition or starting equipment, nes	8511.9090	3
发电机零件,供机车、航空器及船舶用,点燃式或压燃式内燃发动机用的	Generators parts, for locomotives, aircraft or ships, for electrical ignition or starting equipment	8511.9010	3
发电机组,风力驱动的	Generating sets, wind-powered	8502.3100	8
发电机组,其他	Generating sets, nes	8502.3900	8
发电机组,装有点燃式活塞内燃发动机的	Generating sets with spark-ignition internal combustion piston engines	8502.2000	8
发电机组,装有压燃式活塞内燃发动机(柴油或半柴油发动机)的,输出功率不超过75千伏安	Generating sets with compression-ignition internal combustion piston engines (diesel or semi-diesel engines), of an output not exceeding 75kVA	8502.1100	8

商品名称	Article Description	税则号列	申报要素
发电机组,装有压燃式活塞内燃发动机(柴油或半柴油发动机)的,输出功率超过2兆伏安	Generating sets with compression-ignition internal combustion piston engines (diesel or semi-diesel engines) of an output exceeding 2MVA	8502.1320	8
发电机组,装有压燃式活塞内燃发动机(柴油或半柴油发动机)的,输出功率超过375千伏安,但不超过2兆伏安	Generating sets with compression-ignition internal combustion piston engines (diesel or semi-diesel engines) of an output exceeding 375kVA but not exceeding 2MVA	8502.1310	8
发电机组,装有压燃式活塞内燃发动机(柴油或半柴油发动机)的,输出功率超过75千伏安,但不超过375千伏安	Generating sets with compression-ignition internal combustion piston engines (diesel or semi-diesel engines), of an output exceeding 75kVA but not exceeding 375kVA	8502.1200	8
发电机组的零件,风力驱动的	Generating sets parts, wind-powered	8503.0030	3
发电机组的零件,其他	Generating sets parts, nes	8503.0090	3
发动机,车辆用,往复式,气缸容量(排气量)超过1000毫升,但不超过3000毫升	Engines for vehicles, reciprocating, of a cylinder capacity exceeding1000cc but not exceeding 3000cc	8407.3410	123
发动机,车辆用,往复式,气缸容量(排气量)不超过50毫升	Engines for vehicles, reciprocating, of a cylinder capacity not exceeding 50cc	8407.3100	123
发动机,车辆用,往复式,气缸容量(排气量)超过250毫升,但不超过1000毫升	Engines for vehicles, reciprocating, of a cylinder capacity exceeding 250cc but not exceeding 1000cc	8407.3300	123
发动机,车辆用,往复式,气缸容量(排气量)超过3000毫升	Engines for vehicles, reciprocating, of a cylinder capacity exceeding 3000cc	8407.3420	123
发动机,车辆用,往复式,气缸容量(排气量)超过50毫升,但不超过250毫升	Engines for vehicles, reciprocating, of a cylinder capacity exceeding 50cc but not exceeding 250cc	8407.3200	123
发动机,车辆用,压燃式,其他	Engines for vehicles, compression-ignition, nes	8408.2090	123
发动机,车辆用,压燃式,输出功率在132.39千瓦(180马力)及以上	Engines for vehicles, compression-ignition, of an output of 132.39kW (180hp) or more	8408.2010	123
发动机,船舶舷外用,活塞内燃发动机,点燃往复式或旋转式,	Engines for marine outboard, spark-ignition reciprocating or rotary	8407.2100	3
发动机,船舶用,活塞内燃发动机,点燃往复式或旋转式,其他	Engines for marine, spark-ignition reciprocating or rotary, nes	8407.2900	3
发动机,船舶用,压燃式	Engines for marine, compression-ignition	8408.1000	
发动机,点燃往复式或旋转式,其他	Engines, spark-ignition reciprocating or rotary, nes	8407.9090	25
发动机,航空器用,点燃往复式或旋转式,输出功率不超过298千瓦	Engines for aircraft, spark-ignition reciprocating or rotary, of an output not exceeding 298kW	8407.1010	3
发动机,航空器用,点燃往复式或旋转式,输出功率超过298千瓦	Engines for aircraft, spark-ignition reciprocating or rotary, of an output exceeding 298kW	8407.1020	3
发动机,机车用,压燃式	Engines for locomotive, compression-ignition	8408.9010	2
发动机,喷气的,但涡轮喷气发动机除外,航空器及航天器用	Engines of jet other than turbo-jets, for aircraft or spacecraft	8412.1010	27

F

商品名称	Article Description	税则号列	申报要素
发动机,喷气的,但涡轮喷气发动机除外,其他	Engines of jet other than turbo-jets, nes	8412.1090	27
发动机,涡轮风扇的,推力不超过25千牛顿	Engines of turbo fan, of a thrust not exceeding 25kN	8411.1110	27
发动机,涡轮风扇的,推力超过25千牛顿	Engines of turbo fan, of a thrust exceeding 25kN	8411.1210	27
发动机,涡轮螺桨的,功率不超过1100千瓦	Engines of turbo-propellers, of a power not exceeding 1100kW	8411.2100	27
发动机,涡轮螺桨的,功率超过1100千瓦,但不超过2238千瓦	Engines of turbo-propellers, of a power exceeding 1100kW but not exceeding 2238kW	8411.2210	27
发动机,涡轮螺桨的,功率超过2238千瓦,但不超过3730千瓦	Engines of turbo-propellers, of a power exceeding 2238kW but not exceeding 3730kW	8411.2220	27
发动机,涡轮螺桨的,功率超过3730千瓦	Engines of turbo-propellers, of a power exceeding 3730kW	8411.2230	27
发动机,涡轮喷气的,推力不超过25千牛顿,其他	Engines of turbo-jets, of a thrust not exceeding 25kN, nes	8411.1190	27
发动机,涡轮喷气的,推力超过25千牛顿,其他	Engines of turbo-jets, of a thrust exceeding 25kN, nes	8411.1290	27
发动机,压燃式,输出功率不超过14千瓦,其他	Engines, compression-ignition, of an output not exceeding 14kW, nes	8408.9091	2
发动机,压燃式,输出功率超过14千瓦,但小于132.39千瓦(180马力),其他	Engines, compression-ignition, of an output exceeding 14kw but not exceeding 132.39kW (180hp), nes	8408.9092	2
发动机,压燃式,输出功率在132.39千瓦(180马力)及以上,其他	Engines, compression-ignition, of an output of 132.39kW (180hp) or more, nes	8408.9093	2
发动机,用沼气的,活塞内燃发动机,点燃往复式或旋转式	Engines of firedamp, internal combustion piston engines, spark-ignition reciprocating or rotary	8407.9010	25
发动机及动力装置,其他	Engines and motors, nes	8412.8000	27
发动机及动力装置的零件,其他	Engines and motors parts, nes	8412.9090	
发动机零件,船舶发动机用,专用于或主要用于点燃式活塞内燃发动机的	Engines parts, for marine propulsion engines, suitable for use solely or principally with spark-ignition internal combustion piston engines	8409.9110	2
发动机零件,船舶发动机用,其他	Engines parts, for marine propulsion engines, nes	8409.9910	2
发动机零件,航空器发动机用	Engines parts, for aircraft engines	8409.1000	2
发动机零件,机车发动机用	Engines parts, for locomotive engines	8409.9920	2
发动机零件,喷气的,但涡轮喷气发动机除外,航空器及航天器用的	Engines parts of jet other than turbo-jets, for aircraft or spacecraft	8412.9010	23
发动机零件,其他	Engines parts, nes	8409.9999	2
发动机零件,输出功率在132.39千瓦(180马力)及以上的发动机用	Engines parts, for engines with an output of 132.39kW (180hp) or more	8409.9991	2
发动机零件,涡轮螺桨发动机的	Engines parts of turbo-propellers	8411.9100	27
发动机零件,涡轮喷气发动机的	Engines parts of turbo-jets	8411.9100	27
发动机零件,涡轮轴发动机的	Engines parts of turboshaft engines	8411.9910	27

F

商品名称	Article Description	税则号列	申报要素
发动机零件,专用于或主要用于点燃式活塞内燃发动机的,其他	Engines parts, suitable for use solely or principally with spark-ignition internal combustion piston engines, nes	8409.9199	2
发动机用启动电机,输出功率在132.39千瓦(180马力)及以上的,点燃式或压燃式内燃发动机用的	Starter motors for engines of an output of 132.39kW (180hp) or more, for electrical ignition or starting equipment	8511.4091	7
发动机罩盖,机动车辆的	Bonnets, of the motor vehicles	8708.2953	3
发光标志及类似品,装有固定光源的	Illuminated signs and the like, having a permanently fixed light source	9405.6000	5
发光二极管,光敏半导体器件	Light emitting diodes (LED), photosensitive semiconductor devices	8541.4010	5
发光铭牌及类似品,装有固定光源的	Illuminated nameplates and the like, having a permanently fixed light source	9405.6000	5
发光体,无机产品	Luminophores, inorganic products	3206.5000	2368
发夹,其他	Hair-slide, nes	9615.1900	6
发夹,硬质橡胶或塑料制	Hair-slide, of hard rubber or plastics	9615.1100	6
发酵粉	Baking powders, prepared	2102.3000	28
发酵饮料,其他	Fermented beverages, nes	2206.0090	2468
发卡	Hair-pins	9615.9000	
发面酵母	Bakers' yeast	2102.1000	28
发射药	Propellent powders	3601.0000	6
发刷	Hair brushes	9603.2900	
发送设备,无线电广播、电视用	Transmission apparatus for radio-broadcasting or television	8525.5000	7
发送设备,无线电广播、电视用,装有接收装置的,其他	Transmission apparatus for radio-broadcasting or television, incorporating reception apparatus, nes	8525.6090	7
发条,包括游丝,钟、表的	Springs, including hairsprings, of clock or watch	9114.1000	6
发网	Hair-nets	6505.1000	26
发烟硫酸	Oleum	2807.0000	346
伐木楔子	Timber wedges	8201.9000	256
阀门,其他	Valves, nes	8481.8040	
阀门用零件	Valves parts	8481.9010	3
法兰,塑料的	Flanges, of plastics	3917.4000	
法兰,不锈钢制	Flanges, of stainless steel	7307.2100	6
法兰,钢铁的,其他	Flanges, of iron or steel, nes	7307.9100	6
砝码,衡器用	Weighing machine weights of all kinds, for weighing machine	8423.9000	
珐琅及类似制品,陶瓷、搪瓷及玻璃工业用	Enamels and similar preparations, vitrifiable, of a kind used in the ceramic, enamelling or glass industry	3207.2000	13
fan			
帆板	Sailboards	9506.2100	

F

商品名称	Article Description	税则号列	申报要素
帆船,不论是否装有辅助发动机,娱乐或运动用	Sailboats, with or without auxiliary motor for pleasure or sports	8903. 9100	58
番红花	Saffron	0910. 2000	
番红花球茎,休眠的	Stigma croci corms, dormant	0601. 1010	135
番荔枝,罐头	Sweetsops, in airtight containers	2008. 9990	248
番荔枝,鲜的	Sugar apple, fresh	0810. 9050	1
番木鳖碱及其盐	Strychnine and its salts	2939. 9920	34
番茄,其他,用醋或醋酸以外的其他方法制作或保藏的	Tomatoes, nes, prepared or preserved otherwise than by vinegar or acetic acid	2002. 9090	48
番茄,鲜或冷藏的	Tomatoes, fresh or chilled	0702. 0000	1
番茄,整个或切片,其他,用醋或醋酸以外的其他方法制作或保藏的	Tomatoes, whole or in pieces, nes, prepared or preserved otherwise than by vinegar or acetic acid	2002. 1090	248
番茄酱罐头,重量不超过5kg的番茄酱罐头	Tomato paste, in airtight containers, weighing not more than 5kg	2002. 9011	28
番茄酱罐头,重量大于5kg的番茄酱罐头	Tomato paste, in airtight containers, weighing more than 5kg	2002. 9019	28
番茄沙司及其他番茄调味汁	Ketchup, of tomato and other tomato sauces	2103. 2000	268
番茄汁	Tomato juice	2009. 5000	2468
番石榴	Guavas	0804. 5010	14
番石榴果汁	Guva juice	2009. 8014	2468
凡士林	Petroleum jelly	2712. 1000	
矾,其他	Alums, nes	2833. 3090	
矾土水泥	Aluminous cement	2523. 3000	3
钒,未锻轧	Vanadium, unwrought	8112. 9220	16
钒的氧化物及氢氧化物,其他	Vanadium oxides and hydroxides, nes	2825. 3090	
钒粉末	Vanadium powders	8112. 9220	16
钒矿砂及其精矿	Vanadium ores and concentrates	2615. 9090	146
钒铅矿	Vanadinite	2615. 9090	146
钒铅锌矿	Descloizite	2615. 9090	146
钒铁合金,按重量计含钒量在75%及以上	Ferro-vanadium alloys, containing by weight more than 75% of vanadium	7202. 9210	6
钒铁合金,其他	Ferro-vanadium alloys, nes	7202. 9290	6
钒云母	Roscoelite	2615. 9090	146
钒制品	Vanadium articles	8112. 9920	16
反射镜,未装配的各种材料制	Mirrors and other optical elements, of any material, unmounted	9001. 9090	5
反射镜,已装配的各种材料制,照相机用	Mirrors, of any material, mounted, for cameras	9002. 9010	3
反射镜,已装配的各种材料制,作为仪器或装置的零件、配件	Mirrors, of any material, mounted, being parts of or fittings for instruments or apparatus	9002. 9090	3
反应促进剂,其他	Reaction accelerators, nes	3815. 9000	36
反应引发剂,其他	Reaction initiators, nes	3815. 9000	36

商品名称	Article Description	税则号列	申报要素
返波管	Carcinotrons	8540. 7900	35
fang			
方坯连铸机	Ingot block continuous casting machines	8454. 3021	
方铅矿	Galena	2607. 0000	146
方锑矿	Senarmontite	2617. 1090	146
方头螺钉,钢铁制的	Coach screws, of iron of steel	7318. 1100	268
方铀钍石	Uranothorianite	2612. 1000	146
芳烃混合物,其他,温度在250℃时蒸馏量以体积计(包括损耗)在65%及以上(以美国标准试验法D86为准)	Aromatic hydrocarbon mixtures of which 65% or more by volume (including losses) distils at 250℃ by the ASTM D86 method, nes	2707. 5000	6
芳烃卤化衍生物,其他	Halogenated derivatives of aromatic hydrocarbons, nes	2903. 6990	36
芳香醇	Cyclic alcohols, aromatic	2906. 2990	36
芳香单胺及其衍生物以及它们的盐,其他	Aromatic monoamines and their derivatives; salts thereof, nes	2921. 4990	36
芳香多胺及其衍生物以及它们的盐,其他	Aromatic polyamines and their derivatives; salts thereof, nes	2921. 5900	36
芳香多元羧酸及其酸酐、酰卤化物、过氧化物和过氧酸以及它们的衍生物,其他	Aromatic polycarboxylic acids, their anhydrides, halides, peroxides, peroxyacids and their derivatives, nes	2917. 3990	36
芳香料制品及化妆盥洗品,其他	Perfumery, cosmetic or toilet preparations, nes	3307. 9000	23
芳香醚及其卤化、磺化、硝化或亚硝化衍生物	Aromatic ethers and their halogenated, sulphonated, nitrated or nitrosated derivatives	2909. 3000	36
芳香酮,不含其他含氧基的,其他	Aromatic ketones without other oxygen function, nes	2914. 3990	36
芳香一元羧酸及其酸酐、酰卤化物、过氧化物和过氧酸以及它们的衍生物,其他	Aromatic monocarboxylic acids, their anhydrides, halides, peroxides, peroxyacids and their derivatives, nes	2916. 3990	36
芳樟醇	Linalool	2905. 2230	36
防抱死制动系统(ABS),其他	Anti-slid brake system (ABS), nes	8708. 3029	3
防抱死制动系统(ABS),拖拉机的	Anti-slid brake system (ABS), of tractors	8708. 3021	3
防抱死制动系统(ABS),自卸车的	Anti-slid brake system (ABS), of dumpers	8708. 3021	3
防盗报警器,机动车辆用	Burglar alarm for motor vehicles	8512. 3012	7
防盗报警器及类似装置	Burglar alarms and similar apparatus	8531. 1000	3
防盗报警器及类似装置用零件	Burglar alarms parts	8531. 9010	3
防冻剂	Anti-freezing preparations	3820. 0000	36
防毒面具,不包括既无机械零件又无可互换过滤器的防护面具	Gas masks, excluding protective masks having neither mechanical parts nor replaceable filters	9020. 0000	
防风短上衣及类似品,非针织或钩编的,男式,化学纤维制	Wind-jackets and similar articles, not knitted or crocheted, for men or boys, of man-made fibres	6201. 9390	2456
防风短上衣及类似品,非针织或钩编的,男式,棉制	Wind-jackets and similar articles, not knitted or crocheted, for men or boys, of cotton	6201. 9290	2456
防风短上衣及类似品,非针织或钩编的,男式,其他纺织材料制	Wind-jackets and similar articles, not knitted or crocheted, for men or boys, of other textile materials	6201. 9900	2456

F

商品名称	Article Description	税则号列	申报要素
防风短上衣及类似品,非针织或钩编的,男式,羊毛或动物细毛制	Wind-jackets and similar articles, not knitted or crocheted, for men or boys, of wool or fine animal hair	6201.9100	2456
防风短上衣及类似品,非针织或钩编的,女式,化学纤维制	Wind-jackets and similar articles, not knitted or crocheted, for women or girls, of man-made fibres	6202.9390	2456
防风短上衣及类似品,非针织或钩编的,女式,棉制	Wind-jackets and similar articles, not knitted or crocheted, for women or girls, of cotton	6202.9290	2456
防风短上衣及类似品,非针织或钩编的,女式,其他纺织材料制	Wind-jackets and similar articles, not knitted or crocheted, for women or girls, of other textile materials	6202.9900	2456
防风短上衣及类似品,非针织或钩编的,女式,羊毛或动物细毛制	Wind-jackets and similar articles, not knitted or crocheted, for women or girls, of wool or fine animal hair	6202.9100	2456
防风短上衣及类似品,针织或钩编的,男式,化学纤维制	Wind-jackets and similar articles, knitted or crocheted, for men or boys, of man-made fibres	6101.3000	2456
防风短上衣及类似品,针织或钩编的,男式,棉制	Wind-jackets and similar articles, knitted or crocheted, for men or boys, of cotton	6101.2000	2456
防风短上衣及类似品,针织或钩编的,男式,其他	Wind-jackets and similar articles, knitted or crocheted, for men or boys, of other textile materials, nes	6101.9090	2456
防风短上衣及类似品,针织或钩编的,男式,其他	Wind-jackets and similar articles, knitted or crocheted, for women or girls, of other textile materials, nes	6102.9000	2456
防风短上衣及类似品,针织或钩编的,男式,羊毛或动物细毛制	Wind-jackets and similar articles, knitted or crocheted, for men or boys, of wool or fine animal hair	6101.9010	2456
防风短上衣及类似品,针织或钩编的,女式,化学纤维制	Wind-jackets and similar articles, knitted or crocheted, for women or girls, of man-made fibres	6102.3000	2456
防风短上衣及类似品,针织或钩编的,女式,棉制	Wind-jackets and similar articles, knitted or crocheted, for women or girls, of cotton	6102.2000	2456
防风短上衣及类似品,针织或钩编的,女式,羊毛或动物细毛制	Wind-jackets and similar articles, knitted or crocheted, for women or girls, of wool or fine animal hair	6102.1000	2456
防风衣,非针织或钩编的,男式,化学纤维制	Wind-cheaters, not knitted or crocheted, for men or boys, for man-made fibres	6201.9390	2456
防风衣,非针织或钩编的,男式,棉制	Wind-cheaters, not knitted or crocheted, for men or boys, of cotton	6201.9290	2456
防风衣,非针织或钩编的,男式,其他纺织材料制	Wind-cheaters, not knitted or crocheted, for men or boys, of other textile materials	6201.9900	2456
防风衣,非针织或钩编的,男式,羊毛或动物细毛制	Wind-cheaters, not knitted or crocheted, for men or boys, of wool or fine animal hair	6201.9100	2456
防风衣,非针织或钩编的,女式,化学纤维制	Wind-cheaters, not knitted or crocheted, for women or girls, of man-made fibres	6202.9390	2456

F

商品名称	Article Description	税则号列	申报要素
防风衣,非针织或钩编的,女式,棉制	Wind-cheaters, not knitted or crocheted, for women or girls, of cotton	6202.9290	2456
防风衣,非针织或钩编的,女式,其他纺织材料制	Wind-cheaters, not knitted or crocheted, for women or girls, of other textile materials	6202.9900	2456
防风衣,非针织或钩编的,女式,羊毛或动物细毛制	Wind-cheaters, not knitted or crocheted, for women or girls, of wool or fine animal hair	6202.9100	2456
防腐蚀制剂,用于矿物油及类似液体	Anti-corrosive preparations, for mineral oils and alike	3811.9000	236
防滑链,钢铁的	Skid chain, of iron or steel	7315.2000	36
防火报警器及类似装置	Fire alarms and similar apparatus	8531.1000	3
防火报警器及类似装置用零件	Fire alarms parts and parts of similar apparatus	8531.9010	3
防胶剂,用于矿物油及类似液体	Gum inhibitors, for mineral oils and alike	3811.9000	236
防晒油	Sunscreen preparations	3304.9900	23
防水鞋靴,其鞋面不是用缝、铆、钉、旋、塞或类似方法固定在鞋底上的,橡胶或塑料制外底,塑料制鞋面的,中、短统靴(过踝但未到膝)	Waterproof footwear, the uppers of which are neither fixed to the sole nor assembled by stitching, riveting, nailing, screwing, plugging or similar processes, with outer soles of rubber or of plastics and uppers of plastics, covering the ankle but not covering the knee	6401.9290	26
防水鞋靴,其鞋面不是用缝、铆、钉、旋、塞或类似方法固定在鞋底上的,橡胶或塑料制外底,橡胶制鞋面的,中、短统靴(过踝但未到膝)	Waterproof footwear, the uppers of which are neither fixed to the sole nor assembled by stitching, riveting, nailing, screwing, plugging or similar processes, with outer soles of rubber or of plastics and uppers of rubber, covering the ankle but not covering the knee	6401.9210	26
防水鞋靴,其鞋面不是用缝、铆、钉、旋、塞或类似方法固定在鞋底上的,橡胶或塑料制外底及鞋面的,其他	Waterproof footwear, the uppers of which are neither fixed to the sole nor assembled by stitching, riveting, nailing, screwing, plugging or similar processes, with outer soles and uppers of rubber or of plastics, nes	6401.9900	26
防水鞋靴,装有金属防护鞋头,其鞋面不是用缝、铆、钉、旋、塞或类似方法固定在鞋底上的,橡胶或塑料制外底,塑料制鞋面的	Waterproof footwear, incorporating a protective metal toe-cap, the uppers of which are neither fixed to the sole nor assembled by stitching, riveting, nailing, screwing, plugging or similar processes, with outer soles of rubber or of plastics and uppers of rubber and uppers of plastics	6401.1090	26
防水鞋靴,装有金属防护鞋头,其鞋面不是用缝、铆、钉、旋、塞或类似方法固定在鞋底上的,橡胶或塑料制外底,橡胶制鞋面的	Waterproof footwear, incorporating a protective metal toe-cap, the uppers of which are neither fixed to the sole nor assembled by stitching, riveting, nailing, screwing, plugging or similar processes, with outer soles of rubber or of plastics and uppers of rubber	6401.1010	26
防松垫圈,钢铁制的,其他	Lock washers, of iron or steel, nes	7318.2100	268

F

商品名称	Article Description	税则号列	申报要素
防锈或防腐蚀制剂,以润滑剂为基本成分的,含有石油或从沥青矿物提取的油类	Anti-rust or anticorrosion preparations, based on lubricants, containing petroleum oils or oils obtained from bituminous minerals	3403.1900	2368
防锈或防腐蚀制剂,以润滑剂为基本成分的,其他	Anti-rust or anticorrosion preparations, based on lubricants, nes	3403.9900	2368
防油纸	Greaseproof papers	4806.2000	58
仿宝石或仿半宝石及类似小件玻璃品	Imitation precious or semi-precious stones and similar glass smallwares	7018.1000	3458
仿首饰,贱金属制,不论是否镀贵金属,其他	Imitation jewellery, of base metal, whether or not plated with precious metal, nes	7117.1900	46
仿首饰,其他	Imitation jewellery, nes	7117.9000	46
仿珍珠	Imitation pearls, of glass	7018.1000	3458
纺纱机,喷气式	Spinner machine, jet	8445.2032	7
纺纱机,其他	Textile spinning machines, nes	8445.2090	7
纺纱机,转杯式	Spinning machine, rotor	8445.2031	7
纺纱机,自由端的,其他	Spinner machine, open-end, nes	8445.2039	7
纺纱机的辅助机器	Spinner machine auxiliary	8448.1900	3
纺纱机及其辅助机器的零件、附件,其他	Spinner machine or of their auxiliary machines' parts and accessories, nes	8448.3990	3
纺丝环	Spinning rings	8448.3390	3
纺丝机,合成纤维长丝的	Spinning jets for synthetic filaments	8444.0010	
纺丝机,合成纤维短纤的	Spinning jets for synthetic staple fibres	8444.0020	
纺丝机,人造纤维的	Spinning jets for artificial fibres	8444.0030	
纺丝机的辅助机器,人造纤维的	Spinning jets auxiliary, for artificial fibres	8448.1900	3
纺丝机及其辅助机器的零件、附件,其他	Spinning jets machines or of their auxiliary machines's parts and accessories, nes	8448.2090	3
纺织产品及制品,作专门技术用途的,其他	Textile products and articles, for technical uses, nes	5911.9000	
纺织纱线、扁条及类似品,用橡胶或塑料浸渍、涂布、包覆或套裹的	Textile yarn, and strip and the like, impregnated, coated, covered or sheathed with rubber or plastics	5604.9000	46
纺织物,浸渍、涂布或包覆的,其他	Textile fabrics, impregnated, coated or covered, nes	5907.0090	4
纺织物,用胶或淀粉物质涂布的,作书籍封面及类似用途的,化学纤维制	Textile fabrics coated with gum or amylaceous substances, of a kind used for the outer covers of books or the like, of man-made fibres	5901.1020	
纺织物,用胶或淀粉物质涂布的,作书籍封面及类似用途的,棉或麻制	Textile fabrics coated with gum or amylaceous substances, of a kind used for the outer covers of books or the like, of cotton or bast fibres	5901.1010	
纺织物,用胶或淀粉物质涂布的,作书籍封面及类似用途的,其他	Textile fabrics coated with gum or amylaceous substances, of a kind used for the outer covers of books or the like, nes	5901.1090	
纺织物,用聚氨基甲酸酯浸渍、涂布、包覆或层压的,其他	Textile fabrics, impregnated, coated, covered or laminated with polyurethane, nes	5903.2090	

商品名称	Article Description	税则号列	申报要素
纺织物,用聚氯乙烯浸渍、涂布包覆或层压的,其他	Textile fabrics, impregnated, coated, covered or laminated with poly(vinyl chloride), nes	5903.1090	
纺织物,用塑料浸渍、涂布、包覆或层压的,其他	Textile fabrics, impregnated, coated, covered or laminated with plastics, nes	5903.9090	
纺织物,用橡胶处理的,其他	Textile fabrics, rubberized, nes	5906.9990	48
纺织物,针织或钩编的,用橡胶处理的	Textile fabrics, knitted or crocheted, rubberized	5906.9100	48
纺织物、毡呢及毡呢衬里机织物,用橡胶、皮革或其他材料涂布、包覆或层压的,作针布用以及作专门技术用途的类似织物,其他	Textile fabrics, felt and felt-lined woven fabrics, coated, covered or laminated with rubber, leather or other material, of a kind used for card clothing, and similar fabrics of a kind used for other technical purposes, nes	5911.1090	
纺织物及毡呢,环状或装有连接装置的,用于造纸机器或类似机器,每平方米重量在650克及以上	Textile fabrics and felts, endless or fitted with linking devices, of a kind used in paper-making or similar machines, weighing 650g/m² or more	5911.3200	
纺织物及毡呢,环状或装有连接装置的,用于造纸机器或类似机器,每平方米重量在650克以下	Textile fabrics and felts, endless or fitted with linking devices, of a kind used in paper-making or similar machines, weighing less than 650g/m²	5911.3100	
纺织纤维预处理机器的零件、附件,其他	Textile fibres preparing auxiliary machines's parts and accessories, nes	8448.3200	3
纺织用韧皮纤维(不包括亚麻、大麻及苎麻),生的或经沤制的	Textile bast fibres (excluding flax, true hemp and ramie), raw or retted	5303.1000	4
纺织制成品,其他	Textiles articles, made up, nes	6307.9000	346
放大管	Amplifier valves and tubes	8540.8100	35
放大镜	Hand magnifying glasses	9013.8010	
放大器,集成电路	Amplifiers, electronic integrated circuits	8542.3300	37
放电灯,但紫外线灯除外,火车、航空器及船舶用	Discharge lamps, other than ultra-violet lamps, for locomotives and rolling-stock, aircraft or ships	8539.3920	35
放电灯,但紫外线灯除外,其他	Discharge lamps, other than ultra-violet lamps, nes	8539.3990	35
放电灯,但紫外线灯管除外,科研、医疗专用	Discharge lamps, other than ultra-violet lamps, for scientific or medical uses only	8539.3910	35
放射线检查车	Mobile radiological units	8705.9020	7
放射性废物用压实机	Radioactive waste material presses	8479.8950	7
放像机,磁带型	Video tape reproducers, magnetic tape-type	8521.1020	5
放映机,其他	Projectors, nes	9007.2090	8
放映机,数字式	Projectors, digital	9007.2010	8
放映机用零件、附件	Projectors parts and accessories	9007.9200	3
fei			
飞机除冰车	Mobile vehicles for aircraft deicing	8705.9060	7
飞机的零件,其他	Aeroplanes parts, nes	8803.3000	3
飞机调温车	Mobile vehicles for aircraft air-conditioning	8705.9060	7
飞机及其他航空器,空载重量不超过2000千克	Aeroplanes and other aircraft, of an unladen weight not exceeding 2000kg	8802.2000	

商品名称	Article Description	税则号列	申报要素
飞机及其他航空器,空载重量超过15000千克,但不超过45000千克	Aeroplanes and other aircraft, of an unladen weight exceeding 15000kg but not exceeding 45000kg	8802.4010	
飞机及其他航空器,空载重量超过2000千克,但不超过15000千克	Aeroplanes and other aircraft, of an unladen weight exceeding 2000kg but not exceeding 15000kg	8802.3000	
飞机及其他航空器,空载重量超过45000千克	Aeroplanes and other aircraft, of an unladen weight exceeding 45000kg	8802.4020	
飞机加油车	Mobile vehicles for aircraft refuelling	8705.9060	7
飞轮	Flywheels	8483.5000	
飞轮,自行车及脚踏车的	Free wheel, of bicycles and other cycles	8714.9320	3
飞轮零件	Flywheels parts	8483.9000	3
飞艇	Dirigibles	8801.0090	
非机械驱动车辆,其他	Vehicles, not mechanically propelled, nes	8716.8000	
非机械驱动车辆零件	Vehicles parts, not mechanically propelled	8716.9000	3
非金属硫化物,其他	Sulphides of non-metals, nes	2813.9000	
非金属卤化物及卤氧化物,其他	Halides and halide oxides of non-metals, nes	2812.9000	
非金属氯化物,其他	Chlorides of non-metals, nes	2812.1049	
非金属无机酸酯(不包括卤化氢的酯)及其盐以及它们的卤化、磺化、硝化或亚硝化衍生物,其他	Esters of inorganic acids of nonmetals (excluding esters of hydrogen halides) and their salts; their halogenated, sulphonated, nitrated or nitrosated derivatives, nes	2920.9090	36
非金属无机氧化物,其他	Inorganic oxygen compounds of nonmetals, nes	2811.2900	
非那西丁	Phenacetin	2924.2910	36
非耐火涂面制剂,涂门面、内墙、地板、天花板等用	Non-refractory surfacing preparations for facades, indoor walls, floors, ceilings or the like	3214.9000	36
非片状粉末,铝的	Powders of non-lamellar structure, of aluminium	7603.1000	6
非驱动的桥及其零件,30座及以上客运机动车辆用	Non-driving axles and parts of motor vehicles with 30 seats or more	8708.5082	3
非驱动的桥及其零件,其他	Non-driving axles and parts, nes	8708.5089	3
非驱动的桥及其零件,特种车辆用	Non-driving axles and parts of motor vehicles with special purpose	8708.5086	3
非驱动的桥及其零件,拖拉机的	Non-driving axles and parts of tractors	8708.5081	3
非驱动的桥及其零件,小轿车用	Non-driving axles and parts of saloon cars	8708.5084	3
非驱动的桥及其零件,越野车(4轮驱动)用	Non-driving axles and parts of cross-country cars (4WD)	8708.5085	3
非驱动的桥及其零件,自卸车用	Non-driving axles and parts of dumpers	8708.5083	3
非食用脂油,未经乳化、混合或其他方法制作	Tallow oil, not emulsified or mixed or otherwise prepared	1503.0000	4
鲱鱼(大西洋鲱鱼、太平洋鲱鱼),但鱼肝及鱼卵除外,鲜或冷的	Herrings (clupea harengus, clupea pallasii), excluding livers and roes, fresh or chilled	0302.4000	18
鲱鱼(大西洋鲱鱼、太平洋鲱鱼),盐腌及盐渍的	Herrings (clupea harengus, clupea pallasii), salted or in brine	0305.6100	4

F

商品名称	Article Description	税则号列	申报要素
鲱鱼,制作或保藏的,整条或切块,但未绞碎	Herrings, prepared or preserved, whole or in pieces, but not minced	1604.1200	48
肥肝,鲜或冷的	Fatty livers (foie gras), fresh or chilled	0207.3400	1
肥料,毛重不超过10千克的,	Fertilizers in packages of a gross weight not exceeding 10kg	3105.1000	68
肥料,其他	Fertilizers, nes	3105.9000	68
肥皂,其他形状的	Soap in other form	3401.2000	123
肥料,制成片及类似形状的	Fertilizers in tablets or similar forms	3105.1000	68
肥皂,条状、块状或模制形状的,盥洗用	Soap, in the form of bars, cakes, moulded pieces or shapes, for toilet use	3401.1100	123
肥皂,洗衣用	Soap for laundry	3401.1910	123
肥皂及有机表面活性产品,其他	Soap and organic surface-active products and preparations, nes	3401.1990	123
肥皂浸渍 、涂面或包覆的纸、絮胎、毡呢及无纺织物,盥洗用	Soap impregnated (coated or covered) paper (wadding, felt and Non-wovens), for toilet use	3401.1100	123
翡翠,加工的	Jadeite, worked	7103.9910	145
翡翠,未加工	Jadeite, unworked	7103.1000	145
翡翠的粉末	Jadeite dust and powder	7105.9000	145
废玻璃	Waste and scrap of glass	7001.0000	13
废的防冻液	Wastes of antifreeze fluids	3825.5000	34
废的金属酸液	Wastes of metal pickling liquors	3825.5000	34
废的液压油	Wastes of hydraulic fluids	3825.5000	34
废的制动油	Wastes of brake fluids	3825.5000	34
废料,钢铁的,车、刨、铣、磨、锯、锉、剪、冲加工过程中产生的不论是否成捆	Waste, ferrous, from turnings, shavings, chips, milling sawdust, filings, trimmings and stampings, whether or not in bundles	7204.4100	46
废料,兽毛,制刷用,其他	Waste of bristles or hair, for making brush, nes	0502.9020	3
废料,猪毛的	Waste of pigs' hair	0502.1030	
废料,猪鬃的	Waste of pigs' bristles	0502.1030	
废棉,其他	Cotton waste, nes	5202.9900	46
废棉回收纤维	Cotton garnetted stock	5202.9100	46
废棉纱线	Cotton yarn waste	5202.1000	46
废棉线	Cotton thread waste	5202.1000	46
废丝,回收纤维,未梳	Silk waste, garnetted stock, not carded or combed	5003.0010	145
废丝,茧衣,未梳	Silk waste, cocoon outer floss, not carded or combed	5003.0010	145
废丝,锦球,其他	Silk waste, silk top, nes	5003.0091	145
废丝,其他	Silk waste, nes	5003.0099	145
废丝,未梳	Silk waste, not carded or combed	5003.0010	145
废碎料,铋的	Waste and scrap of bismuth	8106.0010	16
废碎料,铂及包铂的,但含有其他贵金属的除外	Waste and scrap of platinum, including metal clad with platinum but excluding sweepings containing other precious metals	7112.9210	46

F

商品名称	Article Description	税则号列	申报要素
废碎料,不锈钢的	Waste and scrap of stainless steel	7204.2100	46
废碎料,镀锡钢铁的	Waste and scrap of tinned iron or steel	7204.3000	46
废碎料,钒的	Waste and scrap of vanadium	8112.9220	16
废碎料,钢铁的,其他	Waste and scrap, ferrous, nes	7204.4900	46
废碎料,锆的	Waste and scrap of zirconium	8109.3000	16
废碎料,镉的	Waste and scrap of cadmium	8107.3000	16
废碎料,铬的	Waste and scrap of chromium	8112.2200	16
废碎料,钴的	Waste and scrap of cobalt	8105.3000	16
废碎料,铪的	Waste and scrap of hafnium	8112.9290	16
废碎料,含有铂或铂化合物的,但含有其他贵金属的除外	Wasted and scrap with platinum, but excluding sweepings containing other precious metals	7112.9220	46
废碎料,含有金或金化合物的	Waste and scrap with gold or gold compounds	7112.9120	46
废碎料,合金钢的,其他	Waste and scrap of alloy steel, nes	7204.2900	46
废碎料,镓的	Waste and scrap of gallium	8112.9290	16
废碎料,金及包金的,但含有其他贵金属的除外	Waste and scrap of gold or gold compounds, including metal clad with gold but excluding swee-pings containing other precious metals	7112.9110	46
废碎料,金属陶瓷及其制品的	Waste and scrap of cermets and articles thereof	8113.0090	16
废碎料,铼的	Waste and scrap of rhenium	8112.9290	16
废碎料,铝的	Waste and scrap of aluminium	7602.0000	46
废碎料,镁的	Waste and scrap of magnesium	8104.2000	16
废碎料,锰的	Waste and scrap of manganese	8111.0010	16
废碎料,钼的	Waste and scrap, of molybdenum	8102.9700	16
废碎料,铌的	Waste and scrap of niobium	8112.9240	16
废碎料,镍的	Waste and scrap of nickel	7503.0000	46
废碎料,铍的	Waste and scrap of beryllium	8112.1300	16
废碎料,铅的	Waste and scrap of lead	7802.0000	46
废碎料,铊的	Waste and scrap of thallium	8112.5200	16
废碎料,钛的	Waste and scrap, of titanium	8108.9090	16
废碎料,钽的	Waste and scrap of tantalum	8103.3000	16
废碎料,锑的	Waste and scrap of antimony	8110.2000	16
废碎料,铜的	Waste and scrap of copper	7404.0000	46
废碎料,钨的	Waste and scrap of tungsten	8101.9700	16
废碎料,锡的	Waste and scrap of tin	8002.0000	16
废碎料,铟的	Waste and scrap of indium	8112.9230	16
废碎料,原电池、原电池组及蓄电池的	Waste and scrap of primary cells, primary batteries and electric accumulators	8548.1000	3
废碎料,锗的	Waste and scrap of germanium	8112.9210	16
废碎料,铸铁的	Waste and scrap of cast iron	7204.1000	46

F

商品名称	Article Description	税则号列	申报要素
废碎料、下脚料及其粉、粒,橡胶(硬质橡胶的除外)的	Waste, parings and scrap of rubber (other than hard rubber) and powders and granules obtained therefrom	4004.0000	146
废物,化学工业及相关工业的,其他	Wastes from chemical or allied industries, nes	3825.6900	34
废物,化学工业及相关工业的,主要含有有机成分的	Wastes from chemical or allied industries, mainly containing organic constituents	3825.6100	34
废线、绳、索、缆及其制品,纺织材料的,经分拣的	Scrap twine, cordage, rope and cables and worn out articles thereof, sorted	6310.1000	146
废线、绳、索、缆及其制品,纺织材料的,其他	Scrap twine, cordage, rope and cables and worn out articles thereof, nes	6310.9000	146
废药物	Waste pharmaceuticals	3006.9200	3
废油,含多氯联苯(PCBs)、多氯三联(PCTs)或多溴联苯(PBBs)的	Waste oils, containing poly chlorinated biphenyls (PCBs), polychlorinated terphenyls (PCTs) or polybrominated biphenyls (PBBs)	2710.9100	4
废油,其他	Waste oils, nes	2710.9900	4
废有机溶剂,卤化物的	Waste organic solvents, halogenated	3825.4100	34
废有机溶剂,其他	Waste organic solvents, nes	3825.4900	34
fen			
分步重复光刻机(步进光刻机),制造半导体器件或集成电路的机器及装置	Step and repeat alignersw, semiconductor devices or of electronic integrated circuits manufacture machines and apparatus	8486.2031	7
分步重复光刻机(步进光刻机)零件及附件,制造半导体器件、集成电路、平板显示器的机器及装置	Step and repeat alignersw parts and accessories, semiconductor devices or of electronic integrated circuits or flat panel displays manufacture machines and apparatus	8486.9090	3
分步重复光刻机,平板显示器的制造机器及装置	Step and repeat alignersw, flat panel displays manufacture machines and apparatus	8486.3031	7
分电器,点燃式或压燃式内燃发动机用的,其他	Distributors, for electrical ignition or starting equipment, nes	8511.3090	7
分电器,机车、航空器及船舶用,点燃式或压燃式内燃发动机用的	Distributors, for locomotives, aircraft or ships, for electrical ignition or starting equipment	8511.3010	7
分度规	Protractors	9017.8000	7
分度头,机床的附件	Dividing heads for machine-tools	8466.3000	3
分光光度计,使用光学射线(紫外线、可见光、红外线)的	Spectrophotometers, using optical radiations (UV, visible, IR)	9027.3000	
分光光度计零件、附件	Spectrophotometers parts and accessories	9027.9000	3
分光仪,使用光学射线(紫外线、可见光、红外线)的	Spectrometers, using optical radiations (UV, visible, IR)	9027.3000	
分光仪零件、附件	Spectrometers parts and accessories	9027.9000	3
分级机器,对蛋类、水果或其他农产品的	Grading machines for eggs, fruit or other agricultural produce	8433.6000	

F

商品名称	Article Description	税则号列	申报要素
分级机器,种子、谷物或干豆用	Grading machines for seed, grain or dried leguminous vegetables	8437. 1090	3
分级机器零件,对蛋类、水果或其他农产品的	Grading machines parts, for gees, furits or other agricultural products	8433. 9090	
分级机器零件,种子、谷物或干豆用	Grading machines parts, for seed, grain or dried leguminous vegetables	8437. 9000	3
分拣及封装信件设备,邮政用	Sorting or banding mail machines	8472. 3010	
分拣设备,邮政用	Sorting machines, used in post offices	8479. 8940	7
分类、计数及包装机,硬币的	Sorting, counting or wrapping machines, for coin	8472. 9090	
分类机器,泥土、石料、矿石或其他固体矿物质的	Sorting machines, for earth, stone, ores or other mineral substances	8474. 1000	
分离机器,泥土、石料、矿石或其他固体矿物质的	Separating machines, for earth, stone, ores or other mineral substances	8474. 1000	
分散型工业过程控制设备,以系统形式进口或出口的	Processing machines for the distributed control system, presented in the form of systems	8471. 4991	26
分析仪零件、附件	Analysis apparatus parts and accessories	9027. 9000	3
分选机器,对蛋类、水果或其他农产品的	Sorting machines for eggs, fruit or other agricultural produce	8433. 6000	
分选机器,种子、谷物或干豆用	Sorting machines for seed, grain or dried leguminous vegetables	8437. 1090	3
分选机器零件,对蛋类、水果或其他农产品的	Sorting machines parts for eggs, fruits or other agricuture products	8433. 9090	
分选机器零件,种子、谷物或干豆用	Sorting machines parts, for seed, grain or dried leguminous vegetables	8437. 9000	3
分指手套、连指手套及露指手套,非针织或钩编的	Gloves, mittens and mitts, not knitted or crocheted	6216. 0000	2456
分指手套、连指手套及露指手套,针织或钩编的,合成纤维制	Gloves, mittens and mitts, knitted or crocheted, of synthetic fibres	6116. 9300	2456
分指手套、连指手套及露指手套,针织或钩编的,棉制	Gloves, mittens and mitts, knitted or crocheted, of cotton	6116. 9200	2456
分指手套、连指手套及露指手套,针织或钩编的,其他纺织材料制	Gloves, mittens and mitts, knitted or crocheted, of other textile materials	6116. 9900	2456
分指手套、连指手套及露指手套,针织或钩编的,羊毛或动物细毛制	Gloves, mittens and mitts, knitted or crocheted, of wool of fine animal hair	6116. 9100	2456
分指手套、连指手套及露指手套,针织或钩编的,用塑料或橡胶浸渍、涂布或包覆的	Gloves, mittens and mitts, impregnated, coated or covered with plastics or rubber	6116. 1000	2456
吩噻嗪环系化合物,结构上含有,未经进一步稠合的,不论是否氢化	Phenothiazine ring-system compounds, not further fused in the structure, whether or not hydrogenated	2934. 3000	36
芬坎法明(INN)以及它们的盐	Fencamfamin (INN); salts thereof	2921. 4600	36
芬美曲嗪(INN) 及盐	Phenmetrazine (INN) ; salts thereof	2934. 9100	36
芬普雷司(INN)及其盐	Fenproporex (INN) and its salts	2926. 3000	36
芬太尼(INN)以及盐	Fentanyl (INN); salts thereof	2933. 3300	36

商品名称	Article Description	税则号列	申报要素
芬乙茶碱(INN)及其盐	Fenetylline(INN) and its salts	2939.5100	34
酚,蒸馏高温煤焦油所得的	Phenols, of the distillation of high temperature coal tar	2707.9910	6
酚醇	Phenol-alcohols	2907.2990	36
酚及酚醇,仅含卤素取代基的衍生物及其盐,其他	Phenols or phenol alcohols, derivatives containing only halogen substituents and their salts, nes	2908.1990	36
酚及酚醇的卤化、磺化、硝化或亚硝化衍生物,其他	Phenols or phenolalcohols, halogenated, sulphonated, nitrated ornitrosated derivatives of, nes	2908.9990	36
酚醛树脂	Phenolic resins	3909.4000	1256
焚烧炉,放射性废物	Burn furnaces for radioactive waste	8417.8020	7
粉笔	Chalks	9609.9000	3
粉盒,以皮革、再生皮革或漆皮作面	Powder-boxes, with outer surface of leather, of composition leather or of patent leather	4202.3100	256
粉盒,以塑料片或纺织材料作面	Powder-boxes, with outer surface of plastic sheeting or of textile materials	4202.3200	256
粉及片状粉末,非合金镍的	Powders and flakes, of nickel, not alloyed	7504.0010	46
粉及片状粉末,合金镍的	Powders and flakes, of nickel alloys	7504.0020	
粉及片状粉末,锡制	Powders and flakes of tin	8007.0030	16
粉及片状粉末,锌的,其他	Powders and flakes, of zinc, nes	7903.9000	16
粉末,铋的	Powders, of bismuth	8106.0010	16
粉末,钒的	Powders of vanadium	8112.9220	16
粉末,锆的	Powders of zirconium	8109.2000	16
粉末,镉的	Powders of cadmium	8107.2000	16
粉末,铬的	Powders of chromium	8112.2100	16
粉末,钴的	Powders of cobalt	8105.2090	16
粉末,铪的	Powders of hafnium	8112.9290	16
粉末,合金钢的,其他	Powders of alloy steel, nes	7205.2100	6
粉末,镓的	Powders of gallium	8112.9290	16
粉末,铼的	Powders of rhenium	8112.9290	16
粉末,镁的	Powders of magnesium	8104.3000	16
粉末,锰的	Powders of manganese	8111.0010	16
粉末,钼的	Powders of molybdenum	8102.1000	16
粉末,铌的	Powders of niobium	8112.9240	16
粉末,钕铁硼磁粉	Powders, Nd-Fe-B magnetic powder	7202.9912	6
粉末,铍的	Powders of beryllium	8112.1200	16
粉末,生铁、镜铁及钢铁的,其他	Powders, of pig iron, spiegeleisen, iron or steel, nes	7205.2900	6
粉末,铊的	Powders of thallium	8112.5100	16
粉末,钛的	Powder of titanium	8108.2030	16
粉末,钽的,其他	Powders of tantalum, nes	8103.2019	16
粉末,锑的	Powders of antimony	8110.1020	16
粉末,钨的	Powders of tungsten (wolfram)	8101.1000	16
粉末,铟的	Powders of indium	8112.9230	16

F

商品名称	Article Description	税则号列	申报要素
粉末,锗的	Powders of germanium	8112.9210	16
粉末及废料,棘皮动物壳	Powder and waste, shells of echinoderms	0508.0010	14
粉末及废料,甲壳动物壳	Powder and waste, shells of crustaceans	0508.0010	14
粉末及废料,墨鱼骨	Powder and waste, cuttlebone	0508.0010	14
粉末及废料,软体动物壳	Powder and waste, shells of molluscs	0508.0010	14
粉末及废料,珊瑚及类似品,	Powder and waste, coral and similar materials	0508.0010	14
粉末及片状粉末,铅制	Powders and flakes, of lead	7804.2000	16
粉扑及粉拍,施敷脂粉或化妆品用	Powder puffs and pads for the application of cosmetics or toilet preparations	9616.2000	
粉扑及粉拍,施敷脂粉或化妆品用	Puffs and pads for the application powder of cosmetics or toilet preparations	9616.2000	
粉丝	Bean vermicelli, cooked	1902.3020	46
feng			
风挡刮水器,机动车辆用	Windscreen wipers for motor vehicles	8512.4000	7
风挡刮水器,自行车用	Windscreen wipers for bicycles	8512.4000	7
风笛	Bag pipes	9205.9090	5
风帆,合成纤维制	Sails, of synthetic fibres	6306.3010	346
风帆,其他纺织材料制	Sails, of other textile materials	6306.3090	346
风机、风扇,包括风机,本身装有一个输出功率不超过125瓦的电动机,其他	Fans, with a self-contained electric motor of an output not exceeding 125W, nes	8414.5199	23
风机、风扇,其他	Fans, nes	8414.5990	23
风衣及类似品,针织或钩编的,男式,化学纤维制	Wind-cheaters and similar articles, knitted or crocheted, for men or boys, of man-made fibres	6101.3000	2456
风衣及类似品,针织或钩编的,男式,棉制	Wind-cheaters and similar articles, knitted or crocheted, for men or boys, of cotton	6101.2000	2456
风衣及类似品,针织或钩编的,男式,其他纺织材料制	Wind-cheaters and similar articles, knitted or crocheted, for men or boys, of other texitile materials	6101.9090	2456
风衣及类似品,针织或钩编的,男式,羊毛或动物细毛制	Wind-cheaters and similar articles, knitted or crocheted, for men or boys, of wool or fine animal hair	6101.9010	2456
风衣及类似品,针织或钩编的,女式,化学纤维制	Wind-cheaters and similar articles, knitted or crocheted, for women or girls, of man-made fibres	6102.3000	2456
风衣及类似品,针织或钩编的,女式,棉制	Wind-cheaters and similar articles, knitted or crocheted, for women or girls, of cotton	6102.2000	2456
风衣及类似品,针织或钩编的,女式,其他纺织材料制	Wind-cheaters and similar articles, knitted or crocheted, for women or girls, of other textile materials	6102.9000	2456
风衣及类似品,针织或钩编的,女式,羊毛或动物细毛制	Wind-cheaters and similar articles, knitted or crocheted, for women or girls, of wool or fine animal hair	6102.1000	2456

商品名称	Article Description	税则号列	申报要素
封闭式聚光灯	Sealed beam lamp units	8539.1000	35
封缄戳,手用	Sealing stamps, designed for operating in the hand	9611.0000	
封缄信片,纸或纸板制的	Letter cards of paper or paperboard	4817.2000	6
封碱	Sealing wafers	1905.9000	28
封口机器,瓶、罐、箱、袋或其他容器的	Sealing machines, for bottles, cans, boxes, bags or other containers	8422.3090	
封志及其他包装用附件,贱金属制	Seals and other packing accessories, of base metal	8309.9000	256
封装半导体器件或集成电路的设备,其他	Encapsulating machines for semiconductor devices, nes	8486.4029	7
封装机器,电灯泡、灯管、电子管、闪光灯泡及类似品的	Assembling machines for electric or electronic lamps, tubes or valves or flashbulbs, in glass envelopes	8475.1000	
封装机器的零件,灯泡的	Assembling machines parts, for electric lamps	8475.9000	3
葑酮	Fenchone	2914.2900	36
蜂产品,其他	Bee products, nes	0410.0049	12
蜂花粉	Bee pollen	0410.0043	12
蜂蜡	Beeswax	1521.9010	
蜂蜜,天然的	Honey, natural	0409.0000	24
蜂蜜酒	Mead	2206.0090	2468
蜂鸣器,电气的	Buzzers, electric	8531.8010	3
蜂鸣器,机动车辆用	Buzzers, for motor vehicles	8512.3011	7
蜂鸣器零件,电气的	Buzzers parts, electric	8531.9090	3
蜂鸟,改良种用	Humming birds, pure-bred breeding	0106.3910	34
蜂王浆制剂	Royal jelly, put up as tonic essences	2106.9030	268
蜂窝结构木镶板	Cellular wood panels	4418.9000	
缝编机	Stitch-bonding machines	8447.2030	7
缝编机的辅助机器	Stitch-bonding machines auxiliary	8448.1900	3
缝合材料,无菌	Suture materials, sterile	3006.1000	3
缝合用针	Needles for sutures	9018.3220	
缝纫机,家用型,多功能	Sewing machines of household type, multifunctional	8452.1010	
缝纫机,家用型,其他	Sewing machines of household type, nes	8452.1099	
缝纫机,家用型,手动式	Sewing machines of household type, hand operated	8452.1091	
缝纫机,平缝机	Sewing machines, flat seam	8452.2110	
缝纫机,其他	Sewing machines, nes	8452.2900	
缝纫机,自动的,其他	Sewing machines, automatic units, nes	8452.2190	
缝纫机零件,家用型缝纫机用,其他	Sewing machines parts, of the household type sewing machines, nes	8452.9019	3
缝纫机零件,其他	Sewing machines parts, nes	8452.9099	3
缝纫机针	Sewing machine needles	8452.3000	
缝纫机专用的特制底座及其零件	Sewing machines bases and parts thereof	8452.4000	3
缝纫机专用的特制家具及其零件	Sewing machines furniture and parts thereof	8452.4000	3
缝纫机专用的特制罩盖及其零件	Sewing machines covers and parts thereof	8452.4000	3

F

商品名称	Article Description	税则号列	申报要素
缝纫线,合成纤维长丝纺制,非供零售用	Sewing thread of synthetic filaments, not put up for retail sale	5401.1010	3468
缝纫线,合成纤维长丝纺制,供零售用	Sewing thread of synthetic filaments, put up for retail sale	5401.1020	3468
缝纫线,人造纤维长丝纺制,非供零售用	Sewing thread of artificial filaments, not put up for retail sale	5401.2010	3468
缝纫线,人造纤维长丝纺制,供零售用	Sewing thread of artificial filaments, put up for retail sale	5401.2020	3468
缝线,无菌,可吸收的	Dental yarns, for surgical sterile, absorbable	3006.1000	3
缝针,钢铁制的,手工用	Sewing needles, for use in the hand, of iron or steel	7319.9000	
fu			
佛尔酮	Phorones	2914.1900	36
呋喃酚	Furan phenol	2932.9910	36
呋喃环化合物,结构上含有,非稠合的,不论是否氢化,其他	Furan ring compounds, unfused in the structure, whether or not hydrogenated, nes	2932.1900	36
呋喃唑酮	Furazolidone	2934.9920	36
呋咱	Furazan	2934.9990	36
孵卵器,家禽用	Incubators for poultry	8436.2100	
敷料,供医疗、外科、牙科或兽医用	Dressings, medical, surgical, dental or veterinary purposes	3005.9090	1346
弗朗德及类似式样的手织装饰毯	Flanders type hand-woven tapestries	5805.0090	468
伏特加酒	Vodka	2208.6000	2468
服装,非针织或钩编的,男式,化学纤维制,其他	Garments, not knitted or crocheted, for men or boys, of man-made fibres, nes	6211.3390	2456
服装,非针织或钩编的,男式,棉制,其他	Garments, not knitted or crocheted, for men or boys, of cotton, nes	6211.3290	2456
服装,非针织或钩编的,男式,其他纺织材料制	Garments, not knitted or crocheted, for men or boys, of other textile materials	6211.3990	2456
服装,非针织或钩编的,男式,丝及绢丝制,其他	Garments, not knitted or crocheted, for men or boys, of silk or silk waste, nes	6211.3910	2456
服装,非针织或钩编的,男式,羊毛或动物细毛制,其他	Garments, not knitted or crocheted, for men or boys, of wool or fine animal hair, nes	6211.3920	2456
服装,非针织或钩编的,女式,化学纤维制,其他	Garments, not knitted or crocheted, for women or girls, of man-made fibres, nes	6211.4390	2456
服装,非针织或钩编的,女式,棉制,其他	Garments, not knitted or crocheted, for women or girls, of cotton, nes	6211.4290	2456
服装,非针织或钩编的,女式,其他纺织材料制	Garments, not knitted or crocheted, for women or girls, of other textile materials	6211.4990	2456
服装,非针织或钩编的,女式,丝及绢丝制,其他	Garments, not knitted or crocheted, for women or girls, of silk or silk waste, nes	6211.4910	2456
服装,非针织或钩编的,女式,羊毛或动物细毛制,其他	Garments, not knitted or crocheted, for women or girls, of wool or fine animal hair, nes	6211.4100	2456

商品名称	Article Description	税则号列	申报要素
服装,男式,织物经处理的,其他	Garments, for men or boys, fabrics treated, nes	6210.4000	2456
服装,女式,织物经处理的,其他	Garments, for women or girls, fabrics treated, nes	6210.5000	2456
服装,用毡呢或无纺织物制成的,织物经处理的,化学纤维制	Garments, made up of felt or Non-wovens treated, of man-made fibres	6210.1030	2456
服装,用毡呢或无纺织物制成的,织物经处理的,棉或麻制	Garments, made up of felt or Non-wovens treated, of cotton or bast fibres	6210.1020	2456
服装,用毡呢或无纺织物制成的,织物经处理的,其他纺织材料制	Garments, made up of felt or Non-wovens treated, of other textile materials	6210.1090	2456
服装,用毡呢或无纺织物制成的,织物经处理的,羊毛或动物细毛制	Garments, made up of felt or Non-wovens treated, of wool or fine animal hair	6210.1010	2456
服装,针织或钩编的,化学纤维制	Garments, knitted or crocheted, of man-made fibres	6114.3000	2456
服装,针织或钩编的,棉制	Garments, knitted or crocheted, of cotton	6114.2000	2456
服装,针织或钩编的,其他	Garments, knitted or crocheted, nes	6114.9090	2456
服装,针织或钩编的,羊毛或动物细毛制	Garments, knitted or crocheted, of wool or fine animal hair	6114.9010	2456
服装,针织物或钩编织物制成的,织物经处理的	Garments, made up of knitted or crocheted fabrics treated	6113.0000	2456
服装,子目号 6201.11 至 6201.19 所列类型的,织物经处理的	Garments, of the type described in subheadings 6201.11 to 6201.19, fabrics treated	6210.2000	2456
服装,子目号 6202.11 至 6202.19 所列类型的,织物经处理的	Garments, of the type described in subheadings 6202.11 to 6202.19, fabrics treated	6210.3000	2456
服装裁剪样	Dress patterns	6307.9000	346
服装的零件,非针织或钩编的	Garments parts, not knitted or crocheted	6217.9000	2456
服装附件的零件,针织或钩编的	Garments accessories parts	6117.9000	2456
服装及衣着附件,非针织或钩编的,婴儿的,合成纤维制	Garments and clothing accessories, not knitted or crocheted, for babies, of synthetic fibres	6209.3000	2456
服装及衣着附件,非针织或钩编的,婴儿的,棉制,其他	Garments and clothing accessories, not knitted or crocheted, for babies, of cotton, nes	6209.2090	2456
服装及衣着附件,非针织或钩编的,婴儿的,其他纺织材料制	Garments and clothing accessories, not knitted or crocheted, for babies, of other textile materials	6209.9090	2456
服装及衣着附件,非针织或钩编的,婴儿的,羊毛或动物细毛制	Garments and clothing accessories, not knitted or crocheted, for babies, of wool or fine animal hair	6209.9010	2456
氟	Fluorine	2801.3010	
氟地西泮(INN)以及盐	Fludiazepam (INN); salts thereof	2933.9100	36
氟硅酸盐	Fluorosilicates	2826.9010	
氟化铵	Ammonium fluorides	2826.1910	
氟化铝,其他	Aluminium fluorides, nes	2826.1290	
氟化铝,无水的	Aluminium fluorides, anhydrous	2826.1210	
氟化钠	Sodium fluorides	2826.1920	
氟化氢	Hydrofluorid	2811.1100	6
氟化物,其他,无机的	Fluorides, nes, inorganic	2826.1990	
氟化稀土	Rareearth fluorides	2846.9030	6

商品名称	Article Description	税则号列	申报要素
氟聚合物，初级形状的，其他	Fluoro-polymers, in primary forms, nes	3904.6900	1256
氟铝酸盐	Fluoroaluminates	2826.9090	
氟络盐，其他	Complex fluorine salts, nes	2826.9090	
氟西泮（INN），以及盐	Flurazepam (INN); salts thereof	2933.9100	36
氟硝西泮（INN）以及盐	Flunitrazepam (INN); salts thereof	2933.9100	36
氟乙酰胺（ISO）	Fluoroacetamide (ISO)	2924.1200	36
茯苓	Poria	1211.9029	34
浮船坞	Floating docks	8905.9010	
浮动结构体，供拆卸的	Floating structures for breaking up	8908.0000	5
浮动结构体，其他	Floating structures, nes	8907.9000	5
浮动式钻探或生产平台	Floating drilling or production platforms	8905.2000	
浮法玻璃板片，非夹丝玻璃，其他	Float glass, non-wired, nes	7005.2900	134
浮法玻璃板片，夹丝玻璃	Float glass, wired	7005.3000	134
浮法玻璃板片，具有吸收、反射或非反射层的非夹丝玻璃	Float glass, non-wired glass, having an absorbent, reflecting or non-reflecting layer	7005.1000	134
浮法玻璃板片，整块着色、不透明、镶色或仅表面研磨的非夹丝玻璃，其他	Float glass, coloured throughout the mass (body tinted), opacified, flashed or merely surface ground	7005.2100	134
浮码头	Landing stages	8907.9000	5
浮石	Pumice stone	2513.1000	14
浮筒	Buoys	8907.9000	5
浮渣（粒状熔渣除外），冶炼钢铁所产生的	Dross (other than granulated slag), from the manufacture of iron or steel	2619.0000	134
福尔可定（INN）及盐	Pholcodine (INN) and salts	2939.1100	34
辐射式空间电加热器	Electric radiant space heating apparatus	8516.2920	7
斧子及类似砍伐工具	Axes and similar hewing tools	8201.4000	256
腐叶土	Leaf moulds	2530.9099	13456
负片显示器	Negatoscopes	9010.5010	7
附件及架座，建筑用，贱金属制	Mountings, fittings and similar articles, suitable for buildings, of base metal	8302.4100	256
附件及架座，贱金属制，机动车辆用	Mountings, fittings and similar articles suitable for motor vehicles	8302.3000	256
附件及架座，贱金属制，家具用	Mountings, fittings and similar articles, of base metal, suitable for furniture	8302.4200	256
附件及架座，贱金属制，其他	Mountings, fittings and similar articles, of base metal, nes	8302.4900	256
复合肥，含氮、磷、钾三种肥效元素的矿物肥料或化学肥料	Fertilizers containing the three fertilizing elements nitrogen, phosphorus and potassium, mineral or chemical	3105.2000	68
复合肥，含磷、钾两种肥效元素的矿物肥料或化学肥料	Fertilizers containing the two fertilizing elements phosphorus and potassium, mineral or chemical fertilizers	3105.6000	68

F

商品名称	Article Description	税则号列	申报要素
复合肥,含有硝酸盐及磷酸盐	Fertilizers containing nitrates and phosphates	3105.5100	68
复合肥,其他,含氮、磷两种肥效元素的矿物肥料或化学肥料	Fertilizers, nes, containing the two fertilizing elements nitrogen and phosphorus, mineral or chemical	3105.5900	68
复合罐生产设备,纸塑铝的	Composite can manufacture machines for paper, plastic and aluminium	8441.3010	
复合罐生产设备零件,纸塑铝的	Composite can manufacture machines parts, for paper, plastic and aluminium	8441.9090	
复合橡胶,未硫化的,板、片、带	Compounded rubber, unvulcanized, in plates, sheets and strip	4005.9100	16
复合橡胶,未硫化的,初级形状的	Compounded rubber, unvulcanized, in primary forms	4005.9900	16
复合橡胶,未硫化的,与碳黑或硅石混合	Compounded rubber, unvulcanized, compounded with carbon black or silica	4005.1000	16
复合橡胶溶液,未硫化的	Compounded rubber solutions, unvulcanized	4005.2000	16
复合增塑剂,橡胶或塑料用	Compound plasticizers for rubber or plastics	3812.2000	36
复合针,针织机用28号以下的	Complex needles for knitting machines, smaler than gauge No. 28	8448.5120	3
复合纸及纸板,成卷或成张的,未经表面涂布或未浸渍,不论内层是否有加强材料	Composite paper and paperboard, in rolls or sheets, not surface-coated or impregnated, whether or not internally reinforced	4807.0000	48
复写本,页间夹有纸的,纸或纸板制的	Interleaved carbon sets, of paper or paperboard	4820.4000	
复写纸,成卷或成张的,卷宽度超过36厘米,或长超过36厘米且宽超过15厘米	Carbon paper, in rolls or sheets, of width exceeding 36cm or in roll or one side exceeding 36cm and other side exceeding 15cm in rectangular sheets	4809.9000	458
复写纸,其他	Carbon paper, nes	4816.9090	58
复印机,胶版的	Duplicating machines of hectograph	8472.1000	
复印设备,感光的,带有光学系统的	Copying apparatus, photocopying, incorporating an optical system	8443.3921	57
复印设备,感光的,接触式的	Copying apparatus, photocopying, of the contact type	8443.3922	57
复印设备,静电感光的,将原件通过中间体转印的(间接法)	Copying apparatus, electrostatic photocopying, operating by reproducing the original image via an intermediate onto the copy (indirect process)	8443.3912	57
复印设备,静电感光的,将原件直接复印的(直接法)	Copying apparatus, electrostatic photocopying, operating by reproducing the original image directly onto the copy (direct process)	8443.3911	57
复印设备,其他	Copying machines, nes	8443.3990	57
复印设备,热敏的	Copying apparatus, thermocopying	8443.3923	57
复印设备,热升华的	Copying apparatus, thermo-sublime	8443.3924	57
复印设备零件及附件,其他	Copying machines parts and accessories, nes	8443.9990	3
富硫酸盐水泥	Supersulphate cement	2523.9000	3
富铝红柱石	Mullite	2508.6000	134
腹肉(五花肉),猪的,干、熏、盐腌或盐渍的	Bellies (streaky) and cuts thereof, of pig salted, in brine, dried or smoked	0210.1200	14
覆盆子酮	Raspberry ketone	2914.5011	36

G

商品名称	Article Description	税则号列	申报要素
ga			
咖喱	Curry	0910.9900	6
gai			
改错刀及其刀片	Erasing knives and blades thereof	8214.1000	256
改性淀粉,其他	Starches, modified, nes	3505.1000	36
改性乳清,不论是否浓缩、加糖或其他甜物质	Whey, modified, whether or not concentrated or containing added sugar or other sweetening matter	0404.1000	248
改性天然聚合物,初级形状的	Natural polymers, modified, in primary forms	3913.9000	146
钙	Calcium	2805.1200	6
钙的次氯酸盐,其他	Calcium hypochlorites, nes	2828.1000	
盖销邮票机	Cancelling postage stamps machines	8472.3090	
盖子,贱金属制	Caps, of base metal	8309.9000	256
盖子,贱金属制	Lids, of base metal	8309.9000	256
gan			
干草,饲料用	Hay, forage products	1214.9000	
干草加工机器,其他	Haymaking machinery, nes	8433.3000	
干果,其他	Nuts, nes	0813.4090	34
干腊肠,有天然肠衣	Saveloys, with a natural casing	1601.0010	348
干瓶机	Bottles drying machinery	8422.2000	
干湿球温度计	Psychrometers	9025.8000	3
干湿球温度计零件、附件	Psychrometers parts and accessories	9025.9000	7
干手器,电热的	Hand-drying apparatus, electro-thermic	8516.3300	7
干洗机	Dry-cleaning machines	8451.1000	
干洗机零件	Dry-cleaning machines parts	8451.9000	
干小麦,碾碎的	Bulgur wheet	1904.3000	48
干椰子肉	Copra	1203.0000	3
干衣机,离心式,干衣量不超过 10 千克	Clothes-dryers of a dry linen capacity not exceeding 10kg, centrifuges	8421.1210	7
干衣机,离心式,其他	Clothes-dryers, centrifuges, nes	8421.1290	
干衣机用零件,干衣量不超过 10 千克的	Clothes-dryers parts, of a dry linen capacity not exceeding 10kg	8421.9110	3
干鱼,其他	Dried fish, nes	0305.5990	4
干鱼,鳕鱼的	Dried fish, cod (gadus morhua, gadus ogac, gadus macrocephalus)	0305.5100	4
干燥机,干衣量不超过 10 千克	Drying machines, each of a dry linen capacity not exceeding 10kg	8451.2100	

商品名称	Article Description	税则号列	申报要素
干燥机,干衣量超过 10 千克	Drying machines, each of a dry linen capacity exceeding 10kg	8451.2900	
干燥机零件	Drying machines parts	8451.9000	
干燥器,利用温度变化处理,木材、纸浆、纸或纸板干燥用	Dryers, with a process involving a change of temperature, for wood, paper pulp, paper or paperboard	8419.3200	57
干燥器,利用温度变化处理,农产品干燥用	Dryers, with a process involving a change of temperature, for agricultural products	8419.3100	57
干燥器,利用温度变化处理,其他	Dryers, with a process involving a change of temperature, nes	8419.3990	57
干燥器,利用温度变化处理,微空气流动陶瓷坯件用	Dryers, with a process involving a change of temperature, for breeze pottery blanks use	8419.3910	57
甘草	Liquorice roots	1211.9036	34
甘露,冷冻的	Chinese artichokes, frozen	0710.8090	1
甘露,冷冻的,用醋或醋酸以外的其他方法制作或保藏的	Chinese artichokes, frozen, prepared or preserved, not by vinegar or acetic acid	2004.9000	48
甘露,鲜或冷藏的	Chinese artichokes, fresh or chilled	0706.9000	1
甘露,用醋或醋酸以外的其他方法制作或保藏的,其他	Chinese artichokes, prepared or preserved otherwise than by vinegar or acetic acid, nes	2005.9999	148
甘露糖醇	Mannitol	2905.4300	36
甘薯,干的	Sweet potatoes, dried	0714.2020	34
甘薯,冷或冻的	Sweet potatoes, chilled or frozen	0714.2030	34
甘薯,其他,鲜的	Sweet potatoes, nes, fresh	0714.2019	34
甘薯,种用,鲜的	Sweet potatoes, for cultivation, fresh	0714.2011	34
甘油碱液	Glycerol lyes	1520.0000	6
甘油水	Glycerol waters	1520.0000	6
甘蔗	Sugar cane	1212.9995	134
甘蔗收获机	Harvesting machines for sugarcane	8433.5910	
杆或型材及异型材,非海绵橡胶制	Rods and profile shapes of non-cellular rubber	4008.2900	18
杆或型材及异型材,海绵橡胶制	Rods and profile shapes of cellular rubber	4008.1900	18
肝素及其盐	Heparin and its salts	3001.9010	34
坩埚,含有按重量计超过 50% 的三氧化二铝或三氧化二铝和二氧化硅的混合物或化合物	Crucibles, containing by weight more than 50% of alumina(Ai_2O_3) or of a mixture of compound of alumina and of silica(SiO_2)	6903.2000	6
坩埚,含有按重量计超过 50% 的石墨、其他碳或其混合物	Crucibles, containing by weight more than 50% of graphite or other carbon or of a mixture of these products	6903.1000	6
苷(配糖物)及其盐、醚、酯和其他衍生物,天然或合成再制的,其他	Glycosides, natural or reproduced bysynthesis, and their salts, ethers, esters and other derivatives, nes	2938.9090	34
柑橘,其他	Mandarins (including tangerines and satsumas), nes	0805.2090	14
柑橘,杂交,其他	Clementines, wilkings and similar citrus hybrids, nes	0805.2090	14
柑橘酱,烹煮的	Marmalades, being cooked preparations	2007.9100	248

G

商品名称	Article Description	税则号列	申报要素
柑橘属果实的精油,其他	Essential oils of citrus fruit, nes	3301.1990	34
柑橘属水果,罐头	Citrus fruit, in airtight containers	2008.3010	248
柑橘属水果,其他,用其他方法制作或保藏的	Citrus fruit, nes, otherwise prepared, or preserved	2008.3090	248
柑橘属水果汁,其他	Juice of any other single citrus fruit, nes	2009.3990	2468
柑橘属水果汁,其他,白利糖度值不超过 20 的	Juice of any other single citrus fruit, nes, of a brix value not exceeding 20	2009.3190	2468
感光纺织物,未曝光的,彩色摄影用	Photographic textiles, unexposed, for colour photography	3703.2090	1238
感光纺织物,未曝光的,成卷,宽度超过 610 毫米	Photographic textiles, unexposed, in rolls of a width exceeding 610mm	3703.1090	1238
感光纺织物,未曝光的,其他	Photographic textiles, unexposed, nes	3703.9090	1238
感光复印设备,带有光学系统的	Photocopying apparatus, incorporating an optical system	8443.3921	57
感光复印设备,接触式的	Photocopying apparatus, of the contact type	8443.3922	57
感光卷片,未曝光的,X 光用	Photographic film in rolls, sensitized, unexposed, for X-ray	3702.1000	12368
感光卷片,未曝光的,彩色摄影用的,非幻灯片用,宽度超过 16 毫米,但不超过 35 毫米,长度不超过 30 米,其他	Photographic film in rolls, unexposed, for colour photography, of a width exceeding 16mm but not exceeding 35mm and of a length not exceeding 30m, other than for slides, nes	3702.5490	12368
感光卷片,未曝光的,彩色摄影用的,非幻灯片用,宽度为 35 毫米,长度不超过 2 米	Photographic film in rolls, unexposed, for colour photography, other than for slides, of a width 34mm and of a length not exceeding 2m	3702.5410	12368
感光卷片,未曝光的,彩色摄影用的,幻灯片用,宽度超过 16 毫米,但不超过 35 毫米,长度不超过 30 米	Photographic film in rolls, unexposed, for colour photography, of a width exceeding 16mm but not exceeding 35mm and of a length not exceeding 30m, for slides	3702.5300	12368
感光卷片,未曝光的,彩色摄影用的,宽度不超过 16 毫米,长度不超过 14 米	Photographic film in rolls, unexposed, for colour photography, of a width not exceeding 16mm and of a length not exceeding 14m	3702.5100	12368
感光卷片,未曝光的,彩色摄影用的,宽度不超过 16 毫米,长度超过 14 米	Photographic film in rolls, unexposed, for colour photography, of a width not exceeding 16mm and of a length exceeding 14m	3702.5200	12368
感光卷片,未曝光的,彩色摄影用的,宽度超过 16 毫米,但不超过 35 毫米,长度超过 30 米,其他	Photographic film in rolls, unexposed, for colour photography, of a width exceeding 16mm but not exceeding 35mm and of a length exceeding 30m, nes	3702.5590	12368
感光卷片,未曝光的,彩色摄影用的,宽度超过 35 毫米,其他	Photographic film in rolls, unexposed, for colour photography, of a width exceeding 35mm, nes	3702.5690	12368
感光卷片,未曝光的,宽度不超过 16 毫米,其他	Photographic film in rolls, unexposed, of a width not exceeding 16mm, nes	3702.9100	12368

商品名称	Article Description	税则号列	申报要素
感光卷片,未曝光的,宽度超过16毫米,但不超过35毫米,长度不超过30米,其他	Photographic film in rolls, unexposed, of a width exceeding 16mm but not exceeding 35mm and of a length not exceeding 30m, nes	3702.9390	12368
感光卷片,未曝光的,宽度超过16毫米,但不超过35毫米,长度超过30米,其他	Photographic film in rolls, unexposed, of a width exceeding 16mm but not exceeding 35mm and of a length exceeding 30m, nes	3702.9490	12368
感光卷片,未曝光的,宽度超过35毫米,其他	Photographic film in rolls, unexposed, of a width exceeding 35mm, nes	3702.9590	12368
感光卷片,未曝光的,宽度为35毫米,长度不超过2米	Photographic film in rolls, unexposed, of a width 35mm and of a length not exceeding 2m	3702.9310	12368
感光卷片,未曝光的,无齿孔的,彩色摄影用,宽度超过610毫米,长度超过200米	Photographic film in rolls, sensitized, unexposed, without perforations, of a width exceeding 610mm and of a length exceeding 200 m, for colour photography	3702.4100	12368
感光卷片,未曝光的,无齿孔的,非彩色摄影用,宽度超过610毫米,长度超过200米,其他	Photographic film in rolls, unexposed, without perforations, of a width exceeding 610mm and of a length exceeding 200 m, other than for colour photography, nes	3702.4299	12368
感光卷片,未曝光的,无齿孔的,宽度不超过105毫米,彩色摄影用,其他	Photographic film in rolls, sensitized, unexposed, without perforations, of a width not exceeding 105mm, for colour photography, nes	3702.3190	12368
感光卷片,未曝光的,无齿孔的,宽度不超过105毫米,其他	Photographic film in rolls, sensitized, unexposed, without perforations, of a width not exceeding 105mm, nes	3702.3990	12368
感光卷片,未曝光的,无齿孔的,宽度不超过105毫米,涂卤化银乳液的,其他	Photographic film in rolls, sensitized, unexposed, without perforations, of a width not exceeding 105mm, with silver halide emulsion, nes	3702.3290	12368
感光卷片,未曝光的,无齿孔的,宽度不超过105毫米,照相制版用,其他	Photographic film in rolls, sensitized, unexposed, without perforations,, of a width not exceeding 105mm, for preparing printing plates or cylinders, nes	3702.3920	12368
感光卷片,未曝光的,无齿孔的,宽度不超过105毫米,照相制版用,涂卤化银乳液的	Photographic film in rolls, sensitized, unexposed, without perforations, of a width not exceeding 105mm, for preparing printing plates or cylinders, with silver halide emulsion	3702.3220	12368
感光卷片,未曝光的,无齿孔的,宽度超过105毫米,但不超过610毫米,其他	Photographic film in rolls, unexposed, without perforations, of a width exceeding 105mm but not exceeding 610mm, nes	3702.4490	12368
感光卷片,未曝光的,无齿孔的,宽度超过610毫米,长度不超过200米,其他	Photographic film in rolls, unexposed, without perforations, of a width exceeding 610mm and of a length not exceeding 200m, nes	3702.4390	12368

G

商品名称	Article Description	税则号列	申报要素
感光卷片,未曝光的,无齿孔的,照相制版用,宽度超过105毫米,但不超过610毫米,其他	Photographic film in rolls, unexposed, without perforations, for preparing printing plates or cylinders, of a width exceeding 105mm but not exceeding 610mm, nes	3702.4429	12368
感光卷片,未曝光的,无齿孔的,照相制版用,宽度超过610毫米,长度不超过200米,其他	Photographic film in rolls, unexposed, without perforations, for preparing printing plates or cylinders, of a width exceeding 610mm and of a length not exceeding 200m, nes	3702.4329	12368
感光卷片,未曝光的,无齿孔的,照相制版用,宽度超过610毫米,长度超过200米,其他	Photographic film in rolls, sensitized, unexposed, without perforations, for preparing printing plates or cylinders, of a width exceeding 610mm and of a length exceeding 200m, nes	3702.4229	12368
感光乳液	Sensitizing emulsions	3707.1000	36
感光硬片及平面软片,未曝光的,X光用	Photographic plates and film in the flat, sensitized, unexposed, for X-ray	3701.1000	12368
感光硬片及平面软片,未曝光的,彩色摄影用	Photographic plates and film in the flat, sensitized, unexposed, for colour photography (polychrome)	3701.9100	12368
感光硬片及平面软片,未曝光的,其他	Photographic plates and film in the flat, sensitized, unexposed, nes	3701.9990	12368
感光硬片及平面软片,未曝光的,任何一边超过255毫米,其他	Photographic plates and film in the flat, sensitized, unexposed, with any side exceeding 255mm, nes	3701.3090	12368
感光硬片及平面软片,未曝光的,任何一边超过255毫米,照相制版用,其他	Photographic plates and film in the flat, sensitized, unexposed, with any side exceeding 255mm, for preparing printing plates or cylinders, nes	3701.3029	12368
感光硬片及平面软片,未曝光的,照相制版用,其他	Photographic plates and film in the flat, sensitized, unexposed, for preparing printing plates or cylinders, nes	3701.9920	12368
感光用化学制剂,复印机用	Sensitizing chemical preparations, for use in photo-copying apparatus	3707.9020	36
感光纸及纸板,未曝光的,彩色摄影用	Photographic paper and paperboard, unexposed, for colour photography	3703.2010	1238
感光纸及纸板,未曝光的,成卷,宽度超过610毫米	Photographic paper and paperboard, unexposed, in rolls of a width exceeding 610mm	3703.1010	1238
感光纸及纸板,未曝光的,其他	Photographic paper and paperboard, unexposed, nes	3703.9010	1238
橄榄,糖渍的	Preserved olives by sugar (drained, glace or crystallized)	2006.0020	48
橄榄油及其分离品,其他,不论是否精制,但未经化学改性,包括掺有税号15.09的油或分离品的混合物	Oils and their fractions, nes, obtained solely from olives, whether or not refined, but not chemically modified, including blends of these oils or fractions with oils or fractions of heading No. 15.09	1510.0000	24
gang			
刚玉,人造的,其他	Corundum, artificial, nes, whether or not chemically defined	2818.1090	136

G

商品名称	Article Description	税则号列	申报要素
刚玉砂,天然	Corundum, natural	2513.2000	
刚玉岩	Emery	2513.2000	
钢笔,其他	Pens, nes	9608.3990	3
钢笔套、铅笔套及类似的笔套	Pen-holders, pencil-holders and similar holders	9608.9920	
钢笔头及笔尖粒	Pen nibs and nib points	9608.9100	
钢锉及类似工具	Files and similar tools	8203.1000	256
钢轨	Rails	7302.1000	6
钢轨夹、底板、固定板及其他专门用于连接或加固路轨的材料	Rail clips, bedplates, ties and other material specialized for jointing or fixing rails	7302.9090	6
钢轨在线打磨列车,铁道及电车道用	Sanding vehicles for on-line rails, for railway or tramway maintenance or service	8604.0012	37
钢化安全玻璃,车辆用	Toughened(tempered) safety glass, of size and shape suitable for vehicles	7007.1190	234
钢化安全玻璃,航空器、航天器及船舶用	Toughened (tempered) safety glass, for aircraft, spacecraft or vessels	7007.1110	234
钢化安全玻璃,其他	Toughened(tempered) safety glass, nes	7007.1900	234
钢筋混凝土管、杆、板、桩等	Reinforced concrete, pipes, rods, plates, piles and similar articles, reinforced by steel	6810.9110	56
钢坯连铸机,其他	Ingot continuous casting machines, nes	8454.3029	
钢琴,大钢琴	Pianos, grand	9201.2000	5
钢琴,平台式	Pianos, grand	9201.2000	5
钢琴,竖式的	Pianos, upright	9201.1000	5
钢琴,自动的	Pianos, automatic	9201.9000	5
钢琴的零件、附件	Pianos parts and accessories	9209.9100	3
钢丝锯,加工石料、陶瓷、混凝土、石棉水泥或类似矿物材料的	Scroll sawing machines, for working stone, ceramics, concrete, asbestos-cement or like mineral materials	8464.1020	7
钢丝圈	Ring travellers	8448.3390	3
钢丝针布	Card clothing	8448.3100	3
钢铁板桩	Sheet piling of iron or steel	7301.1000	6
钢铁丝,带刺的	Wire of iron or steel, barbed	7313.0000	36
钢铁丝绒	Iron or steel wool	7323.1000	24
钢铁丝制品,工业用	Iron or steel wire articles, for technical use	7326.2010	346
钢铁丝制品,其他	Iron or steel wire articles, nes	7326.2090	346
钢铁桶及类似容器,容积超过300升,不论是否衬里或隔热,但无机械或热力装置,盛装物料用的	Iron vats and similar containers for any material, of a capacity exceeding 300L, whether or not lined or heat-insulated, but not fitted with mechanical or thermal equipment	7309.0000	36
钢铁制的钉及类似品,不论钉头是否用其他材料制成,但不包括铜头钉	Nails and similar articles, of iron or steel, whether or not with heads of other material, but excluding such articles with heads of copper	7317.0000	36
钢铁制品,工业用,其他	Iron or steel articles, for technical use, nes	7326.9010	346

商品名称	Article Description	税则号列	申报要素
钢铁制品,经锻造或冲压,但未经进一步加工,工业用	Iron or steel articles, forged or stamped, but not further worked, for technical use	7326.1910	346
钢铁制品,经锻造或冲压,但未经进一步加工,其他	Iron or steel articles, forged or stamped, but not further worked, nes	7326.1990	346
钢铁制品,其他	Iron or steel articles, nes	7326.9090	346
gao			
羔羊毛皮,整张的,不论是否带头、尾或爪(阿斯特拉罕、喀拉科尔、波斯羔羊及类似羔羊、印度、中国或蒙古羔羊)	Raw furskins of lamb (astrakhan, broadtail, caracul, persian and similar lamb, indian, chinese, mongolian or tibetan lamb, whole, with or without head, tail or paws)	4301.3000	15
羔羊肉,冻的,整头及半头	Meat of lamb, frozen, carcasses and half carcasses	0204.3000	14
羔羊肉,鲜或冷的,整头及半头	Meat of lamb, fresh or chilled, carcasses and half carcasses	0204.1000	14
高碘酸盐,无机的	Periodates, inorganic	2829.9000	
高尔夫球	Golf balls	9506.3200	
高尔夫球车及类似车辆,其他	Golf cars and similar vehicles, nes	8703.1019	58
高尔夫球棍,全套	Golf clubs, complete	9506.3100	
高尔夫球用具,其他	Golf equipment, nes	9506.3900	5
高光泽透明或半透明纸	Glassine and other glazed transparent or translucent papers	4806.4000	58
高脚杯,但玻璃陶瓷制的除外,其他	Stemware drinking glasses, other than of glass-ceramics, nes	7013.2800	356
高脚杯,但玻璃陶瓷制的除外,铅晶质玻璃制	Stemware drinking glasses, other than of glass-ceramics, of lead crystal	7013.2200	356
高粱,其他	Grain sorghum, nes	1007.0090	35
高粱,种用	Grain sorghum, seed	1007.0010	35
高岭类似土	Kaolinic clays	2507.0090	1346
高岭土	Kaolin clays	2507.0010	1346
高氯酸盐,无机的	Perchlorates, inorganic	2829.9000	
高锰酸钾	Potassium permanganate	2841.6100	1
高锰酸盐,其他	Permanganates, nes	2841.6900	1
高频放大器	High frequency amplifiers	8543.7092	37
高频放大器用零件	High frequency amplifiers parts	8543.9040	3
高速摄影机	High speed cameras	9007.1910	8
高效减水剂	High efficiency water reducing agent	3824.4010	36
高压开关装置,全封闭组合式,用于电压在 500 千伏及以上的线路	Insulated switch gear of gas, for a voltage of 500kV or more	8537.2010	78
高压开关装置零件,全封闭组合式,用于电压在 500 千伏及以上的线路	Insulated switch gear parts of gas, for a voltage of 500kV or more	8538.1010	3
糕饼	Cakes	1905.9000	28
糕点	Pastry	1905.9000	28

G

商品名称	Article Description	税则号列	申报要素
糕点加工机器	Bakery machinery	8438.1000	
糕点加工机器的零件	Bakery machinery parts	8438.9000	3
糕点夹,镀贵金属的	Cake servers, plated with precious metal	8215.9100	256
糕点夹,非镀贵金属的	Cake servers, other than plated with precious metal	8215.9900	256
镐	Mattocks	8201.3000	256
锆,未锻轧	Zirconium, unwrought	8109.2000	16
锆的氯氧化物及氢氧基氯化物	Zirconium chloride oxides and chloride hydroxides	2827.4910	
锆粉末	Zirconium powders	8109.2000	16
锆矿砂及其精矿	Zirconium ores and concentrates	2615.1000	1346
锆英石	Zircon sands	2615.1000	1346
锆制品,其他	Zirconium articles, nes	8109.9000	16
ge			
哥白林及类似式样的手织装饰毯	Gobelins type hand-woven tapestries	5805.0090	468
割草机,包括牵引装置用的刀具杆,其他	Mowers, including cutter bars for tractor mounting, nes	8433.2000	
割草机,草坪、公园或运动场地用,机动的,切割装置在同一水平面上旋转的	Mowers for lawns, parks or sports grounds, powered, with the cutting device rotating in a horizontal plane	8433.1100	7
割草机,草坪、公园或运动场地用,其他	Mowers for lawns, parks or sports grounds, nes	8433.1900	7
割草机零件	Mowers parts	8433.9090	
格陵兰庸鲽鱼,冻的	Greenland halibut, frozen	0303.3110	18
格鲁米特(INN)	Glutethimide(INN)	2925.1200	36
蛤,冻、干、盐腌或盐渍的	Clam, frozen, dried, salted or in brine	0307.9930	14
蛤,活、鲜或冷的	Clam, live, fresh or chilled	0307.9193	1
蛤,制作或保藏的	Clam, prepared or preserved	1605.9020	48
隔离开关,用于电压超过1000伏的线路	Isolating switches, for a voltage exceeding 1000V	8535.3000	8
隔热的矿物材料的混合物及制品,其他	Heat-insulating mineral materials, mixtures and articles, nes	6806.9000	68
隔音的矿物材料的混合物及制品,其他	Sound insula-ting mineral materials, mixtures and articles, nes	6806.9000	68
镉,未锻轧	Cadmium, unwrought	8107.2000	16
镉粉末	Cadmium powders	8107.2000	16
镉制品,其他	Cadmium articles, nes	8107.9000	16
铬,未锻轧	Chromium, unwrought	8112.2100	16
铬的硫酸盐	Chromium sulphates	2833.2920	
铬的氢氧化物,其他	Chromium hydroxides, nes	2819.9000	
铬的氧化物,其他	Chromium oxides, nes	2819.9000	
铬粉末	Chromium powders	8112.2100	16
铬矿砂及其精矿	Chromium ores and concentrates	2610.0000	1346

G

商品名称	Article Description	税则号列	申报要素
铬酸盐	Chromates	2841. 5000	1
铬铁合金,按重量计含碳量在 4% 以上	Ferro-chromium alloys, containing by weight more than 4% of carbon	7202. 4100	6
铬铁合金,其他	Ferro-chromium alloys, nes	7202. 4900	6
铬铁矿	Chromite	2610. 0000	1346
铬制品,其他	Chromium articles, nes	8112. 2900	16
geng			
根茎,其他,休眠的	Rhizomes, nes, dormant	0601. 1099	135
根茎,生长或开花的	Rhizomes, in growth or in flower	0601. 2000	
根茎,食用,其他,鲜或冷藏的	Roots, edible, nes, fresh or chilled	0706. 9000	1
根茎,种用,休眠的	Rhizomes, seed, dormant	0601. 1091	135
根茎,其他,休眠的	Crowns, nes, dormant	0601. 1099	135
根茎,生长或开花的	Crowns, in growth or in flower	0601. 2000	
根茎,种用,休眠的	Crowns, seed, dormant	0601. 1091	135
耕耘机,农业、园艺及林业用,其他	Hoes, for agricultural, horticultural or forestry use, nes	8432. 2900	
gong			
工场车,铁道及电车道用	Workshops, for railway or tramway maintenance or service	8604. 0099	37
工程钻机,非自推进的,其他	Engineering drills, not self-propelled, nes	8430. 6919	5
工程钻机,非自推进的,钻筒直径 3 米及以上	Engineering drills, not self-propelled, boring casing diameter more than 3m	8430. 6911	5
工件夹具	Work holders	8466. 2000	3
工具,辐射松制的	Tools, of radiata pine	4417. 0010	56
工具,其他木制的	Tools, of other wood	4417. 0090	56
工具柄,辐射松制的	Tool handles, of radiata pine	4417. 0010	56
工具柄,其他木制的	Tool handles, of other wood	4417. 0090	56
工具成套货品,由两个或多个子目所列手工工具组成的	Tools sets, of two or more of other subheadings of hand tools	8205. 9000	256
工具成套货品,由税号 82. 02 至 82. 05 中两个或多个税号所列组成的,零售包装	Tools sets, of two or more of the headings No. 82. 02 to 82. 05, put up for retail sale	8206. 0000	256
工具夹具	Tool holders	8466. 1000	3
工具支架,辐射松制的	Tool bodies, of radiata pine	4417. 0010	56
工具支架,其他木制的	Tool bodies, of other wood	4417. 0090	56
工业机器人,多功能的	Industrial robots for multiple uses	8479. 5010	7
工业机器人,其他	Industrial robots, nes	8479. 5090	7
工业用除尘器,其他	Dust collectors for industry uses, nes	8421. 3929	7
工字钢,除热轧、热拉拔或热挤压外未经进一步加工,截面高度低于 80 毫米	I sections, not further worked than hot-rolled, hot-drawn or extruded, of a height of less than 80mm	7216. 1020	468

G

商品名称	Article Description	税则号列	申报要素
工字钢,除热轧、热拉拔或热挤压外未经进一步加工,截面高度在200毫米以上	I sections, not further worked than hot-rolled, hot-drawn or extruded of a height	7216.3210	468
工字钢,除热轧、热拉拔或热挤压外未经进一步加工,截面高度在80毫米及以上,且不超过200毫米	I sections, not further worked than hot-rolled, hot-drawn or extruded of a height of 80mm or more, and not exceeding 200mm	7216.3290	468
工作车,电动的,短距离运输货物的,未装有提升或搬运设备,其他	Works trucks, electrical, not fitted with lifting or handling equipment, for short distance transport of goods, nes	8709.1190	
工作车,装有升降或搬运装置的,其他	Works trucks fitted with lifting or handing equipment, nes	8427.9000	7
工作车,自驱动的,短距离运输货物的,未装有提升或搬运设备,其他	Works trucks, self-propelled, not fitted with lifting or handling equipment, for short distance transport of goods, nes	8709.1990	
工作车零件,自驱动工作车的,短距离运输货物的,未装有提升或搬运设备	Works trucks parts, of self-propelled works trucks, not fitted with lifting or handling equipment, for short distance transport of goods	8709.9000	3
弓弦乐器	Bow string musical instruments	9202.1000	5
公共工程用机器,其他	Public works or building machinery, nes	8479.1090	7
公路牵引车,半挂车用的	Road tractors for semi-trailers	8701.2000	
公文包,以皮革、再生皮革或漆皮作面	Briefcases, with outer surface of leather, of composition leather or of patent leather	4202.1190	1458
公文包,以塑料或纺织材料作面	Briefcases, with outer surface of plastics or of textile materials	4202.1290	256
公文箱,以皮革、再生皮革或漆皮作面	Executive-cases, with outer surface of leather, of composition leather or of patent leather	4202.1190	1458
公文箱,以塑料或纺织材料作面	Executive-cases, with outer surface of plastics or of textile materials	4202.1290	256
公章架及类似的办公用具,贱金属制,办公室家具除外	Office-stamp stands and similar office or desk equipment, of base metal, other than office furniture	8304.0000	256
功率检测仪器及装置,不带记录装置	Power measuring or checking instruments and apparatus, without a recording device	9030.3390	7
功率检测仪器及装置,带记录装置	Power measuring or checking instruments and apparatus, with a recording device	9030.3900	7
攻丝工具	Threading or tapping tools, hand tools	8205.1000	256
攻丝机床,切削金属的,其他	Threading or tapping machines, for removing metal, nes	8459.7000	7
攻丝工具,可互换	Threading or tapping tools, interchangeable	8207.4000	256
供暖器具及其零件,铜制,非电热的,家用	Heating apparatus of a kind used for domestic purposes, non-electric, and parts thereof, of copper	7419.9950	4
宫内节育器	Intrauterine contraceptive device	9018.9080	
汞	Mercury	2805.4000	

商品名称	Article Description	税则号列	申报要素
汞的无机或有机化合物,汞齐除外	Mercury compounds, inorganic or organic, excluding amalgams	2852.0000	
汞齐,非贵金属的	Amalgams, other than amalgams of precious metals	2853.0090	
汞齐,贵金属的	Amalgams of precious metals	2843.9000	
汞蒸汽灯	Mercury vapour lamps	8539.3240	35
gou			
钩,贱金属制,用于衣着、鞋靴、天篷、提包、旅行用品或其他制成品	Hooks, of base metal, of a kind used for clothing, footwear, awnings, handbags, travel goods or other made up articles	8308.1000	256
钩,铁道及电车道机车或其他车辆的	Hooks, of railway or tramway locomotives or rolling-stock	8607.3000	3
钩刀及类似砍伐工具	Bill hooks and similar hewing tools	8201.4000	256
钩头螺钉,钢铁制的	Screw hooks, of iron of steel	7318.1300	268
钩头螺钉,铝制	Screw hooks, of aluminium	7616.1000	36
钩鱼竿	Fishing rods	9507.1000	
钩针,钢铁制的,手工用	Crochet hooks, for use in the hand, of iron or steel	7319.9000	
钩针,针织机用28号以下的	Crotchet hooks for knitting machines, smaler than gauge No. 28	8448.5120	3
狗外套及类似品	Dog coats and the like	4201.0000	1458
狗鳕鱼(无须鳕鱼、长鳍鳕鱼),冻的	Hake(merluccius spp. Urophycis spp.), frozen	0303.7800	18
枸杞	Fructus lycii	1211.9031	34
枸橼酸铁	Iron citrate	2918.1500	36
购物袋,其他	Shopping-bags, nes	4202.9900	256
购物袋,以皮革、再生皮革或漆皮作面	Shopping-bags, with outer surface of leather, of composition leather or of patent leather	4202.9100	256
购物袋,以塑料片或纺织材料作面	Shopping-bags, with outer surface of plastic sheeting or of textile materials	4202.9200	256
毂闸及其零件,自行车及脚踏车的	Hub brakes and parts, of bicycles and other cycles	8714.9400	3
gu			
箍木,非针叶木的	Hoopwood, non-coniferous	4404.2000	15
箍木,针叶木的	Hoopwood, coniferous	4404.1000	15
箍桶及其零件,包括桶板,辐射松制的	Tubs and other coopers products and parts thereof, of wood, including staves, of radiata pine	4416.0010	56
箍桶及其零件,包括桶板,其他木制的	Tubs and other coopers products and parts thereof, of wood, including staves, of other wood	4416.0090	56
古柯叶	Coca leaf	1211.3000	34
古斯古斯面食	Couscous	1902.4000	46
古塔波胶	Gutta-percha gums	4001.3000	12
古物,超过100年的	Antiques of an age exceeding one hundred years	9706.0000	5
谷氨酸	Glutamic acid	2922.4210	36
谷氨酸钠	Sodium glutamate	2922.4220	36

商品名称	Article Description	税则号列	申报要素
谷氨酸盐,其他	Glutamic acid salts,nes	2922.4290	36
谷壳,未经处理的	Cereal husks,unprepared	1213.0090	4
谷类植物的茎秆(麦秸除外)	Cereal straw(other than wheat straw)	1401.9010	3
谷粒(玉米除外)或谷物片,预煮或经其他方法制作的,细粉及粗粉除外	Cereals (other than maize (corn)) in grain form or in the form of flakes or other worked grains (except flour, groats and meal), precooked or otherwise prepared,not elsewhere specified or included	1904.9000	48
谷物,其他	Cereals,nes	1008.9090	3
谷物,其他,滚压或制片的	Cereal grains,rolled or flaked	1104.1990	4
谷物,其他,其他加工的	Cereal grains,other worked	1104.2990	4
谷物,其他,种用	Cereals,nes,seed	1008.9010	3
谷物胚芽,整粒、滚压、制片或磨碎的	Germ of cereals,whole,rolled,flaked or ground	1104.3000	4
谷子	Millet	1008.2000	3
股票、债券及类似所有权凭证	Stock, share or bond certificates and similar documents of title	4907.0030	5
骨,经酸处理的	Bones treated with acid	0506.1000	4
骨,其他	Bones,nes	0506.9090	146
骨废料,含牛羊成分的	Bones,waste,of bovine and sheep	0506.9011	146
骨废料,其他	Bones,waste,nes	0506.9019	14
骨粉,含牛羊成分的	Bones,powder,of bovine and sheep	0506.9011	146
骨粉,其他	Bones,powder,nes	0506.9019	14
骨骼粘固剂	Bone reconstruction cements	3006.4000	36
骨胶原,经酸处理的	Ossein treated with acid	0506.1000	4
骨折用器具	Fracture appliances	9021.1000	
钴,未锻轧	Cobalt,unwrought	8105.2090	16
钴胺素	Cobalamins	2936.2600	36
钴的氧化物及氢氧化物,其他	Cobalt oxides and hydroxides,nes	2822.0090	
钴粉末	Cobalt powders	8105.2090	16
钴及钴盐,放射性的	Cobalt and its salts	2844.4020	
钴矿砂及其精矿	Cobalt ores and concentrates	2605.0000	146
钴锍	Cobalt mattes	8105.2090	16
钴湿法冶炼中间品	Intermediate products of cobalt metallurgy by wet process	8105.2010	16
钴冶炼时所得的中间产品,其他	Intermediate products of cobalt matallurgy,nes	8105.2090	16
钴制品,其他	Cobalt articles,nes	8105.9000	16
鼓	Drums	9206.0000	5
鼓形滚子轴承	Spherical roller bearings	8482.3000	5
固醇	Sterol	2906.1310	36
固定植物油脂及其分离品,其他	Fixed vegetable fats and oils and fractions thereof,nes	1515.9090	
固体残渣,其他,提炼豆油所得的	Solid residues, resulting from the extraction of soyabean oil	2304.0090	46

G

商品名称	Article Description	税则号列	申报要素
固体残渣,其他,提炼花生油所得的	Solid residues, resulting from the extraction of groundnut oil	2305.0000	46
固液分离机,离心式	Solid-liquor separators, centrifuges	8421.1920	7
gua			
瓜子,黑的	Black watermelon seeds	1212.9991	134
瓜子,白的	Pumpkin seeds	1212.9993	134
瓜子,红的	Red watermelon seeds	1212.9992	134
刮削机器,加工木材、软木、骨、硬质橡胶、硬质塑料或类似硬质材料的	Paring machines, for working wood, cork, bone, hard rubber, hard plastics or similar hard materials	8465.9600	7
挂车及半挂车,供居住或野营用厢式	Trailers and semi-trailers of the caravan type, for housing or camping	8716.1000	
挂车及半挂车,罐式货运,其他	Trailers and tanker semi-trailer of tanker, nes	8716.3190	
挂车及半挂车,货柜的	Trailers and semi-trailers, van type	8716.3910	
挂车及半挂车,货运用,其他	Trailers and semi-trailers for the transport of goods, nes	8716.3990	
挂车及半挂车,农用自装或自卸式	Trailers and semi-trailers for agricultural purposes, self-loading or self-unloading	8716.2000	
挂车及半挂车,其他	Trailers and semi-trailers, nes	8716.4000	
挂车及半挂车,油罐的	Trailers and semi-trailers of oil tanker	8716.3110	
挂车及半挂车零件	Trailers and semi-trailers parts	8716.9000	3
挂锁,贱金属制	Padlocks, of base metal	8301.1000	256
挂钟,电力驱动的	Wall clocks, electrically operated	9105.2100	5
挂钟,其他	Wall clocks, nes	9105.2900	5
guan			
观赏鱼	Ornamental fish	0301.1000	15
冠形瓶塞,贱金属制	Crown corks, of base metal	8309.1000	256
管,非合金铝制	Tubes and pipes, of aluminium, not alloyed	7608.1000	68
管,非合金镍制	Tubes and pipes of nickel, not alloyed	7507.1100	6
管,钢铁的,圆形截面的,焊接的,外径超过406.4毫米,其他	Tubes and pipes, of iron or steel, having circular cross-sections, the external diameter of which exceeds 406.4mm, welded, nes	7305.3900	6
管,钢铁的,圆形截面的,外径超过406.4毫米,其他	Tubes and pipes, of iron or steel, having circular cross-sections, the external diameter of which exceeds 406.4mm, nes	7305.9000	6
管,钢铁的,圆形截面的,纵向焊接的,外径超过406.4毫米	Tubes and pipes, of iron or steel, having circular cross-sections, longitudinally welded, the external diameter of which exceeds 406.4mm	7305.3100	6
管,精炼铜制,其他	Tubes and pipes of refined copper, nes	7411.1090	6
管,精炼铜制,外径不超过25毫米的,带有螺纹或翅片的	Tubes and pipes of refined copper, having an outside diameter not exceeding 25mm, threaded or with fins	7411.1011	6

G

商品名称	Article Description	税则号列	申报要素
管,精炼铜制,外径不超过25毫米的,其他	Tubes and pipes of refined copper, having an outside diameter not exceeding 25mm, nes	7411.1019	6
管,精炼铜制,外径超过70毫米的	Tubes and pipes of refined copper, having an outside diameter exceeding 70mm	7411.1020	6
管,铝合金制,壁厚不超过25毫米	Tubes and pipes, of aluminium alloys, having a wall thickness not exceeding 25mm	7608.2091	68
管,铝合金制,其他	Tubes and pipes, of aluminium alloys, nes	7608.2099	68
管,铝合金制,外径不超过10厘米的	Tubes and pipes, of aluminium alloys, having an outside diameter not exceeding 10cm	7608.2010	68
管,镍合金制	Tubes and pipes of nickel alloys	7507.1200	6
管,钛的	Tubes or pipes, of titanium	8108.9040	16
管,铜合金制,其他	Tubes and pipes of copper alloys, nes	7411.2900	6
管,铜镍合金(白铜)制	Tubes and pipes of copper-nickel base alloys (cupronickel)	7411.2200	6
管,铜镍锌合金(德银)制	Tubes and pipes of copper-nickel-zinc base alloys (nickel silver)	7411.2200	6
管,铜锌合金(黄铜)制,盘卷的	Tubes and pipes of copper-zinc base alloys (brass), in coils	7411.2110	6
管,铜锌合金(黄铜)制,其他	Tubes and pipes of copper-zinc base alloys (brass), nes	7411.2190	6
管,硬质合金制,以焊剂涂面或以焊剂为芯,用于焊接或沉积金属、硬质合金	Tubes, of metal carbides, coated or cored with flux material, of a kind used for soldering, brazing, welding or deposition of metal or of metal carbides	8311.9000	56
管道管,石油或天然气用,外径超过406.4毫米,其他	Line pipe of a kind used for oil or gas pipelines, the external diameter of which exceeds 406.4mm, nes	7305.1900	6
管道管,石油或天然气用,其他纵向焊接的,外径超过406.4毫米	Line pipe of a kind used for oil or gas pipelines, longitudinally welded, the external diameter of which exceeds 406.4mm	7305.1200	6
管道管,石油或天然气用,无缝的,不锈钢制,其他	Line pipe of a kind used for oil or gas pipelines, seamless, of stainless steel, nes	7304.1190	6
管道管,石油或天然气用,无缝的,不锈钢制,外径不超过114.3毫米	Line pipe of a kind used for oil or gas pipelines, seamless, of stainless steel, having an outside diament not exceeding 114.3mm	7304.1130	6
管道管,石油或天然气用,无缝的,不锈钢制,外径超过114.3毫米,但小于215.9毫米	Line pipe of a kind used for oil or gas pipelines, seamless, of stainless steel, having an outside diameter exceeding 114.3mm but less than 215.9mm	7304.1120	6
管道管,石油或天然气用,无缝的,不锈钢制,外径大于等于215.9毫米,但不超过406.4毫米	Line pipe of a kind used for oil or gas pipelines, seamless, of stainless steel, having an outside diameter of 215.9mm or more but not exceeding 406.4mm	7304.1110	6
管道管,石油或天然气用,无缝的,其他	Line pipe of a kind used for oil or gas pipelines, seamless, nes	7304.1990	6

G

商品名称	Article Description	税则号列	申报要素
管道管,石油或天然气用,无缝的,外径不超过114.3毫米	Line pipe of a kind used for oil or gas pipelines, seamless, having an outside diament not exceeding 114.3mm	7304.1930	6
管道管,石油或天然气用,无缝的,外径超过114.3毫米,但小于215.9毫米	Line pipe of a kind used for oil or gas pipelines, seamless, having an outside diameter exceeding 114.3mm but less than 215.9mm	7304.1920	6
管道管,石油或天然气用,无缝的,外径大于等于215.9毫米,但不超过406.4毫米	Line pipe of a kind used for oil or gas pipelines, seamless, having an outside diameter of 215.9mm or more but not exceeding 406.4mm	7304.1910	6
管道管,石油或天然气用,纵向埋弧焊接的,外径超过406.4毫米	Line pipe of a kind used for oil or gas pipelines, longitudinally submerged arc welded, the external diameter of which exceeds 406.4mm	7305.1100	6
管道管,石油及天然气用,焊接的,不锈钢的,其他	Line pipe of a kind used for oil or gas pipelines, of stainless steel, welded, nes	7306.1100	6
管道管,石油及天然气用,其他	Line pipe of a kind used for oil or gas pipelines, nes	7306.1900	6
管及管子附件(例如,接头、肘管、管套),锌制	Tubes, pipes and tube or pipe fittings (for example couplings, elbows, sleeves) of zinc	7907.0020	16
管及管子附件(例如,接头、肘管、管套),锡制	Tubes, pipes and tube or pipe fittings (for example, couplings, elbows, sleeves) of tin	8007.0040	16
管及空心异型材,不锈钢的,圆形截面,焊接的,其他	Tubes, pipes and hollow profiles, of stainless steel, of circular cross-section, welded, nes	7306.4000	6
管及空心异型材,合金钢的圆形截面,焊接的,其他	Tubes, pipes and hollow profiles, of alloy steel, of circular cross-section, welded, nes	7306.5000	6
管及空心异型材,矩形或正方形截面的,焊接的	Tubes, pipes and hollow profiles, of square or rectangular cross-section, welded	7306.6100	6
管及空心异型材,其他	Tubes, pipes and hollow profiles, nes	7306.9000	6
管及空心异型材,其他非圆形截面的,焊接的	Tubes, pipes and hollow profiles, of other non-circular cross-section, welded	7306.6900	6
管及空心异型材,铁或非合金钢的,圆形截面,焊接的,其他	Tubes, pipes and hollow profiles, of iron or non-alloy steel, of circular cross-section, welded, nes	7306.3090	6
管及空心异型材,铁或非合金钢的,圆形截面,焊接的,外径不超过10毫米的,壁厚在0.7毫米及以下	Tubes, pipes and hollow profiles, of iron or non-alloy steel, of circular cross-section, welded, having an outside diameter not exceeding 10mm, and having a wall thickness of 0.7mm or less	7306.3011	6
管及空心异型材,铁或非合金钢的,圆形截面,焊接的,外径不超过10毫米的,其他	Tubes, pipes and hollow profiles, of iron or non-alloy steel, of circular cross-section, welded, having an outside diameter not exceeding 10mm, nes	7306.3019	6
管及空心异型材,无缝的,不锈钢的,圆形截面,冷拔或冷轧的,其他	Tubes, pipes and hollow profiles, seamless, of stainless steel, of circular cross-section, cold-drawn or cold-rolled, nes	7304.4190	6
管及空心异型材,无缝的,不锈钢的,圆形截面,其他	Tubes, pipes and hollow profiles, seamless, of circular cross-section, of stainless steel, nes	7304.4990	6

商品名称	Article Description	税则号列	申报要素
管及空心异型材,无缝的,钢铁的,其他	Tubes, pipes and hollow profiles, seamless, of iron or steel, nes	7304.9000	6
管及空心异型材,无缝的,合金钢的,圆形截面管,冷拔或冷轧的,其他	Tubes, pipes and hollow profiles, seamless, of alloy steel, of circular cross-section, cold-drawn or cold-rolled, nes	7304.5190	6
管及空心异型材,无缝的,合金钢的,圆形截面管,其他	Tubes, pipes and hollow profiles, seamless, of alloy steel, of circular cross-section, nes	7304.5990	6
管及空心异型材,无缝的,铁或非合金钢的,圆形截面,冷拔或冷轧的,其他	Tubes, pipes and hollow profiles, seamless, of iron or non-alloysteel, of circular cross-section, cold-drawn or cold-rolled, nes	7304.3190	6
管及空心异型材,无缝的,铁或非合金钢的,圆形截面,其他	Tubes, pipes and hollow profiles, seamless, of iron or non-alloysteel, of circular cross-section, nes	7304.3990	6
管及空心异型材,铸铁的,内径在500毫米及以上的圆形截面管	Tubes and pipes of circular cross-section, of the internal diameter of 500mm or more	7303.0010	6
管及空心异型材,铸铁的,其他	Tubes, pipes and hollow profiles, of cast iron, nes	7303.0090	6
管形铆钉,贱金属制,	Tubular rivets, of base metal	8308.2000	256
管状金属针头,医疗、外科、牙科或兽医用	Tubular metal needles, used in medical, surgical, dental or veterinary sciences	9018.3210	
管子,硫化橡胶(硬质橡胶除外)制的,未经加强或未与其他材料合制,未装有附件	Tubes, pipes and hoses, of vulcanized rubber other than hard rubber, not reinforced or otherwise combined with other materials, without fittings	4009.1100	136
管子,硫化橡胶(硬质橡胶除外)制的,未经加强或未与其他材料合制,装有附件	Tubes, pipes and hoses, of vulcanized rubber other than hard rubber, not reinforced or otherwise combined with other materials, with fittings	4009.1200	136
管子,硫化橡胶(硬质橡胶除外)制的,用纺织材料加强或只与纺织材料合制,未装有附件	Tubes, pipes and hoses, of vulcanized rubber other than hard rubber, reinforced or otherwise combined only with textile materials, without fittings	4009.3100	136
管子,硫化橡胶(硬质橡胶除外)制的,用纺织材料加强或只与纺织材料合制,装有附件	Tubes, pipes and hoses, of vulcanized rubber other than hard rubber, reinforced or otherwise combined only with textile materials, with fittings	4009.3200	136
管子,硫化橡胶(硬质橡胶除外)制的,用金属加强或只与金属合制,装有附件	Tubes, pipes and hoses, of vulcanized rubber other than hard rubber, reinforced or otherwise combined only with metal, with fittings	4009.2200	136
管子,硫化橡胶(硬质橡胶除外)制的,用金属加强或只与金属合制,未装有附件	Tubes, pipes and hoses, of vulcanized rubber other than hard rubber, reinforced or otherwise combined only with metal, without fittings	4009.2100	136
管子,硫化橡胶(硬质橡胶除外)制的,用其他材料加强或与其他材料合制,未装有附件	Tubes, pipes and hoses, of vulcanized rubber other than hard rubber, reinforced or otherwise combined with other materials, without fittings	4009.4100	136
管子,硫化橡胶(硬质橡胶除外)制的,用其他材料加强或与其他材料合制,装有附件	Tubes, pipes and hoses, of vulcanized rubber other than hard rubber, reinforced or otherwise combined with other materials, with fittings	4009.4200	136
管子附件,塑料的	Fittings of plastics	3917.4000	

G

商品名称	Article Description	税则号列	申报要素
管子附件,不锈钢制,其他	Tube or pipe fittings, of stainless steel, nes	7307.2900	6
管子附件,钢铁的,其他	Tube or pipe fittings, of iron or steel, nes	7307.9900	6
管子附件,钢铁铸件,其他	Tube or pipe fittings, of iron or steel, cast fittings, nes	7307.1900	6
管子附件,精炼铜制	Tube or pipe fittings, of refined copper	7412.1000	6
管子附件,铝制	Tube or pipe fittings, of aluminium	7609.0000	6
管子附件,镍制	Tube or pipe fittings of nickel	7507.2000	6
管子附件,铜合金制,其他	Tube or pipe fittings, of copper alloys, nes	7412.2090	6
管子附件,铜镍合金(白铜)制	Tube or pipe fittings, of copper-nickel base alloys (cupronickel)	7412.2010	6
管子附件,铜镍锌合金(德银)制	Tube or pipe fittings, of copper-nickel-zinc base alloys (nickel silver)	7412.2010	6
管子附件,无可锻性铸铁制	Tube or pipe fittings, of non-malleable cast iron	7307.1100	6
盥洗盆,塑料的	Wash-basins, of plastics	3922.1000	236
盥洗用具,塑料的	Toilet articles, of plastics	3924.9000	23
盥洗用制品,化学纤维制,其他	Toilet linen, of man-made fibres, nes	6302.9300	346
盥洗用制品,毛巾织物或类似的毛圈织物的,棉制,其他	Toilet linen, of terry towelling or similar terry fabrics, of cotton, nes	6302.6090	346
盥洗用制品,棉制,其他	Toilet linen, of cotton, nes	6302.9100	346
盥洗用制品,其他	Toilet linen, nes	6302.5990	346
盥洗用制品,亚麻制,其他	Toilet linen, of flax, nes	6302.9910	346
灌装设备,饮料及液体用	Bottling or canning machinery for beverages or liquid food	8422.3010	
罐,钢铁的,盛装物料用,容积在50升以下,焊边或卷边接合的,不论是否衬里或隔热,但无机械或热力装置	Cans, of iron or steel, for any material, of a capacity of less than 50L, closed by soldering or crimping, whether or not lined or heat-insulated, but not fitted with mechanical or thermal equipment	7310.2100	36
罐及类似容器,容积超过300升,建筑用	Vats, of plastics, of a capacity exceeding 300L, for builders	3925.1000	23
罐式挂车及半挂车,货运,其他	Tanker trailers and tanker semi-trailer, nes	8716.3190	
罐头,番茄的,整个或切片	Airtight containers, of tomatoes, whole or in pieces	2002.1010	248
罐头,鸡的	Airtight containers, of fowls of the species gallus domesticus	1602.3210	48
罐头,蘑菇,伞菌属	Mushrooms, of agaricus, in airtight containers	2003.1090	248
罐头,蘑菇,伞菌属,其他	Mushrooms, of agaricus, in airtight containers, nes	2003.1019	248
罐头,蘑菇及块菌,其他	Mushrooms and truffles, in airtight containers, nes	2003.9010	248
罐头,牛的	Airtight containers of bovine animals	1602.5010	248
罐头,其他	Airtight containers, of any animal, nes	1602.9010	248
罐头,其他,蔬菜及什锦蔬菜	Vegetables and mixtures of vegetables, in airtight containers	2005.9991	148
罐头,其他家禽的	Airtight containers, of poultry of heading 01.05, nes	1602.3910	248
罐头,其他鱼的	Fish, nes, in airtight containers	1604.2019	48
罐头,小白蘑菇	Small white agaric, in airtight containers	2003.1011	248

商品名称	Article Description	税则号列	申报要素
罐头,鱼翅的	Shark's fin, in airtight containers	1604. 2011	48
罐头,猪的	Airtight containers of swine	1602. 4910	248
guang			
光传输设备,波分复用的	Optical transmission equipments for wave-division multiplexing	8517. 6222	7
光瓷釉及类似制品,陶瓷、搪瓷及玻璃工业用	Liquid lustres and similar preparations, of a kind used in the ceramic, enamelling or glass industry	3207. 3000	13
光导纤维	Optical fibres	9001. 1000	6
光导纤维及其预制棒的制造机器	Optical fibres and preforms making machines	8475. 2100	6
光导纤维束	Optical fibre bundles	9001. 1000	6
光导纤维束用连接器,用于电压不超过1000伏的线路	Optical fibre bundles connectors, for a voltage not exceeding 1000V	8536. 7000	8
光导纤维用连接器,用于电压不超过1000伏的线路	Optical fibres connectors, for a voltage not exceeding 1000V	8536. 7000	8
光导纤维预制棒	Preformed bars for drawing optical fibre	7002. 2010	238
光端机	Optical line terminal equipments	8517. 6221	7
光端机用零件	Optical line terminal equipments parts	8517. 7020	3
光洁剂及类似制品,其他	Polishes and creams, nes	3405. 9000	36
光缆,其他	Optical fibre cables, nes	9001. 1000	6
光缆,单根被覆的	Optical fibre cables, made up of individually sheathed fibres	8544. 7000	35
光缆用连接器,用于电压不超过1000伏的线路	Optical fibre cables connectors, for a voltage not exceeding 1000V	8536. 7000	8
光卤石	Carnallite	3104. 9010	68
光敏半导体器件,其他	Photosensitive semiconductor devices, nes	8541. 4090	5
光盘,仅用于重放声音信息的,已录制	Optical disks, for reproducing sound only, recorded	8523. 4010	37
光盘驱动器	CD drivers	8471. 7030	
光气	Phosgene	2812. 1030	
光通信设备的激光收发模块	Laser transmitting and receiving unit of optical communication equipments	8517. 7060	3
光通讯设备,其他	Optical communication equipments, nes	8517. 6229	7
光纤通信及光纤性能测试仪	Optical telecommunication and optical fibre performance testing instruments	9031. 8010	
光学测量或检验仪器及器具,其他	Optical measuring or checking instruments and appliances, nes	9031. 4990	7
光学测量或检验仪器及器具,制造半导体器件时检验半导体晶片、器件或检测光掩模或光栅用	Optical measuring or checking instruments and appliances, for inspecting semiconductor wafers or devices or for inspecting photomasks or reticles used in manufacturing semiconductor devices	9031. 4100	
光学媒体,其他	Optical media, nes	8523. 4099	37
光学媒体,未录制	Optical media, unrecorded	8523. 4091	37

G

商品名称	Article Description	税则号列	申报要素
光学媒体,用于重放声音、图像以外信息的,税号 84.71 所列机器用	Optical media, for reproducing phenomena other than sound or image, for the machines of heading 84.71	8523.4020	37
光学元件,玻璃制,未经光学加工的	Glass optical elements, not optically worked	7014.0090	345
光学元件,其他	Optical elements, nes	9001.9090	5
光学元件,已装配的各种材料制,照相机用	Optical elements, of any material, mounted, for cameras	9002.9010	3
光学元件,已装配的各种材料制,作为仪器或装置的零件、配件	Optical elements, of any material, mounted, being parts of or fittings for instruments or apparatus	9002.9090	3
光学元件毛坯,光学仪器用,玻璃制,未经光学加工的	Blanks of optical elements, for optical instruments	7014.0010	345
光学装置、仪器及器具,其他	Optical devices, appliances and instruments, nes	9013.8090	
光学装置、仪器及器具的零件、附件,其他	Optical devices (or appliances and instruments) parts and accessories, nes	9013.9090	3
光阴极管,其他	Photocathode tubes, nes	8540.2090	35
光阴极管零件,其他	Photocathode parts, nes	8540.9990	3
胱氨酸	Cystine	2930.9010	36
gui			
龟壳及其粉末	Tortoiseshell and powder thereof	0507.9090	14
硅,按重量计含硅量不少于 99.99%,其他	Silicon, containing by weight not less than 99.99%, nes	2804.6190	1346
硅,其他	Silicon, nes	2804.6900	346
硅铬铁合金	Ferro-silico-chromium alloys	7202.5000	6
硅化物,不论是否已有化学定义,但可归入税号 28.49 的碳化物除外	Silicides, whether or not chemically defined but other than the carbon compounds classified to 28.49	2850.0000	
硅灰石	Wollastonite	2530.9091	13456
硅铝酸盐,不论是否已有化学定义的	Aluminosilicates whether or not chemically defined	2842.1000	
硅镁镍矿	Garnierite	2604.0000	146
硅锰铁合金	Ferro-silico-manganese alloys	7202.3000	6
硅铍钇矿	Gadolinite	2530.9020	13456
硅砂	Silica sands	2505.1000	34
硅酸复盐	Silicates, double	2842.1000	
硅酸络盐	Silicates, complex	2842.1000	
硅酸钍矿	Thorite	2612.2000	146
硅酸盐,其他	Silicates, nes	2839.9000	
硅酸盐水泥,其他	Portland cement, nes	2523.2900	3
硅钛铁合金	Ferro-silico-titanium alloys	7202.9100	6
硅铁合金,按重量计含硅量在 55% 以上	Ferro-silicon alloys, containing by weight more than 55% of silicon	7202.2100	6
硅铁合金,其他	Ferro-silicon alloys, nes	7202.2900	6
硅土制的砖、块、瓦及其他陶瓷制品	Siliceous earths bricks, blocks, tiles and other ceramic goods	6901.0000	6

G

商品名称	Article Description	税则号列	申报要素
硅钨铁合金	Ferro-silico-tungsten alloys	7202.8020	6
硅线石	Sillimanite	2508.5000	134
硅藻土	Kieselguhr	2512.0010	1234568
硅质化粗粉,其他	Siliceous fossil meals, nes	2512.0090	1234568
硅质化石粉制的砖、块、瓦及其他陶瓷制品	Siliceous fossil meals bricks, blocks, tiles and other ceramic goods	6901.0000	6
硅质土	Siliceous earths	2512.0090	1234568
鲑鱼,其他,冻的	Salmonidae, nes, frozen	0303.2900	18
鲑鱼,其他,鲜或冷的,	Salmonidae, nes, fresh or chilled	0302.1900	18
轨道衡	Track scales	8423.8920	
轨道校正车,铁道及电车道用	Trackliners, for railway or tramway maintenance or service	8604.0099	37
轨道自动计轴设备	Rail automatic axle counting equipments	8608.0010	3
轨枕,钢铁制,铁道用	Sleepers (cross-ties), for railway or tramway track construction, of iron or steel	7302.9010	6
轨座、轨座楔	Chairs, chair wedges, specialized for jointing or fixing rails	7302.9090	6
癸二酸及其盐和酯	Sebacic acid, its salts and esters	2917.1310	36
柜、桶、罐、听、盒及类似容器,钢铁的,盛装物料用,容积在 50 升及以上,不论是否衬里或隔热,但无机械或热力装置(装压缩气体或液化气体的除外)	Tanks, casks, drums, cans, boxes and similar containers, for any material, of iron or steel, of a capacity of 50L or more, whether or not lined or heat-insulated, but not fitted with mechanical or thermal equipment (other than compressed or liquefied gas)	7310.1000	36
柜、桶、罐、听、盒及类似容器,钢铁的,盛装物料用,容积在 50 升以下,不论是否衬里或隔热,但无机械或热力装置(装压缩气体或液化气体的除外),其他	Tanks, casks, drums, cans, boxes and similar containers, for any material, of iron or steel, Of a capacity of less than 50L, whether or not lined or heat-insulated, but not fitted with mechanical or thermal equipment (other than compressed or liquefied gas), nes	7310.2900	36
柜及类似容器,容积超过 300 升,建筑用	Tanks, of plastics, of a capacity exceeding 300L, for builders	3925.1000	23
柜式冷冻箱,容积不超过 800 升,制冷温度在 -40℃及以下	Freezers of the chest type, not exceeding 800L capacity, of a refrigerating temperature of -40℃ or lower	8418.3010	57
柜式冷冻箱,容积不超过 800 升,制冷温度在 -40℃以上,其他	Freezers of the chest type, not exceeding 800l capacity, of a refrigerating temperature higher than -40℃, nes	8418.3029	57
柜式冷冻箱,容积超过 500 升,制冷温度在 -40℃以上	Freezers of the chest type, of a capacity exceeding 500l, of a refrigerating temperature higher than -40℃	8418.3021	57
贵金属,汞齐	Precious metals amalgams	2843.9000	
贵金属,胶态的	Precious metals, colloidal	2843.1000	

G

商品名称	Article Description	税则号列	申报要素
贵金属表壳	Precious metal watch cases	9111.1000	6
贵金属化合物,其他	Precious metals compounds, nes	2843.9000	
贵金属或包贵金属制品,工业或实验室用	Precious metal articles or articles of metal clad with precious metal for technical or laboratory use	7115.9010	46
贵金属或包贵金属制品,其他	Precious metal articles or articles of metal clad with precious metal, nes	7115.9090	46
贵金属或金属化合物的灰,其他	Precious metal or precious metal compounds ash, nes	7112.3090	46
贵金属矿砂及其精矿,其他	Precious metal ores and concentrates, nes	2616.9000	146
桂油	Essential oils of cassia	3301.2940	34
gun			
辊压成型机,固体矿物燃料、陶瓷坯泥、未硬化水泥、石膏材料或其他粉状、浆状矿产品的粘聚或成形用	Rolling forming machines, for agglomerating, shaping or moulding solid mineral fuels, ceramic paste, unhardened cements, plastering materials or other mineral products in powder or paste form	8474.8010	7
滚筒,滚压机用	Cylinders for rolling machines	8420.9100	3
滚筒,研光机用	Cylinders for calendering machines	8420.9100	3
滚筒的制造机器、器具及设备,其他	Cylinders preparing or making machinery, nes	8442.3090	
滚筒制造机器零件	Cylinders making machinery parts	8442.4000	3
滚压机滚筒	Rolling machines cylinders	8420.9100	3
滚压机零件,其他	Rolling machines parts, nes	8420.9900	3
滚压机器,加工金属或玻璃用的除外	Rolling machines, other than for metals or glass	8420.1000	
滚针轴承	Needle roller bearings	8482.4000	5
滚针轴承零件	Needles bearings parts	8482.9100	3
滚珠轴承,其他	Ball bearings, nes	8482.1090	5
滚珠轴承零件	Balls bearings parts	8482.9100	3
滚柱轴承零件	Rollers bearings parts	8482.9100	3
滚装船,机动的,载重量在2万吨及以下	Ro-Ro ships, motor powered, loading with 20000t or less	8901.9031	8
滚装船,机动的,载重量在2万吨以上	Ro-Ro ships, motor powered, loading more than 20000t	8901.9032	8
滚子链,钢铁的,摩托车用	Roller chain, of iron or steel, for motorcycles	7315.1120	36
滚子链,钢铁的,其他	Roller chain, of iron or steel, nes	7315.1190	36
滚子链,钢铁的,自行车用	Roller chain, of iron or steel, for bicycles	7315.1110	36
滚子螺杆传动装置	Roller screws	8483.4010	7
guo			
锅炉管,无缝的,不锈钢的,圆形截面,冷拔或冷轧的	Boiler tubes and pipes, seamless, of stainless steel, of circular cross-section, cold-drawn or cold-rolled	7304.4110	6
锅炉管,无缝的,不锈钢的,圆形截面,其他	Boiler tubes and pipes, seamless, of stainless steel, of circular cross-section, nes	7304.4910	6

商品名称	Article Description	税则号列	申报要素
锅炉管,无缝的,合金钢的,圆形截面管,冷拔或冷轧的,其他	Boiler tubes and pipes, seamless, of alloy steel, of circular cross-section, cold-drawn or cold-rolled, nes	7304.5110	6
锅炉管,无缝的,合金钢的,圆形截面管,其他	Boiler tubes and pipes, seamless, of alloy steel, of circular cross-section, nes	7304.5910	6
锅炉管,无缝的,铁或非合金钢的,圆形截面,冷拔或冷轧的	Boiler tubes and pipes, seamless, of iron or non-alloysteel, of circular cross-section, cold-drawn or cold-rolled	7304.3110	6
锅炉管,无缝的,铁或非合金钢的,圆形截面,其他	Boiler tubes and pipes, seamless, of iron or non-alloysteel, of circular cross-section, nes	7304.3910	6
国际象棋等棋类用品	International chess and other board games	9504.9030	
果冻,不含可可,糖食	Fruit jellies, sweets, not containing cocoa	1704.9000	258
果冻,烹煮的,柑橘属水果的	Fruit jellies, citrus fruit, being cooked preparations	2007.9100	248
果冻,烹煮的,柑橘属水果的,罐头	Fruit jellies, citrus fruit, being cooked preparations, in airtight containers	2007.9910	248
果冻,烹煮的,其他	Fruit jellies, being cooked preparations, nes	2007.9990	248
果膏,烹煮的,柑橘属水果的	Pastes, citrus fruit, being cooked preparations	2007.9100	248
果膏,烹煮的,柑橘属水果的,罐头	Pastes, citrus fruit, being cooked preparations, in airtight containers	2007.9910	248
果膏,烹煮的,其他	Pastes, being cooked preparations, nes	2007.9990	248
果核、果仁及植物产品,主要供人食用的	Fruit stones and kernels and other vegetable products, of a kind used primarily for human consumption	1212.9999	134
果酱,烹煮的,柑橘属水果的	Jams, citrus fruit, being cooked preparations	2007.9100	248
果酱,烹煮的,柑橘属水果的,罐头	Jams, citrus fruit, being cooked preparations, in airtight containers	2007.9910	248
果酱,烹煮的,其他	Jams, being cooked preparations, nes	2007.9990	248
果胶	Pectic substances	1302.2000	3
果胶酸盐	Pectinates and pectates	1302.2000	3
果胶酸酯	Pectates	1302.2000	3
果酒	Ratafias	2208.7000	2468
果泥,不含可可,糖食	Fruit pastes sweets not containing cocoa	1704.9000	258
果泥,烹煮的,柑橘属水果的	Puree, citrus fruit, being cooked preparations	2007.9100	248
果泥,烹煮的,柑橘属水果的,罐头	Puree, citrus fruit, being cooked preparations, in airtight containers	2007.9910	248
果泥,烹煮的,其他	Puree, being cooked preparations, nes	2007.9990	248
果皮,柑橘属水果或甜瓜(包括西瓜)的,鲜、冻、干或用盐水、亚硫酸水或其他防腐液暂时保藏的	Peel of citrus fruit or melons (including watermelons), fresh, frozen, dried or provisionally preserved in brine, in sulphur water or in other preservative solutions	0814.0000	14
果仁,其他,罐头	Nuts, nes, in airtight containers	2008.1920	248
果仁,其他,用其他方法制作或保藏的	Nuts, nes, otherwise prepared, or preserved	2008.1999	248

G

商品名称	Article Description	税则号列	申报要素
果糖,化学纯	Fructose, chemically pure	1702.5000	6
果糖及果糖浆,其他,按重量计干燥状态的果糖含量在50%以上	Fructose and fructose syrup, nes, containing in the dry state more than 50% by weight of fructose	1702.6000	356
过铬酸盐	Peroxochromates	2841.5000	1
过金属酸盐,其他	Peroxometallicacids salts, nes	2841.9000	1
过磷酸钙,其他	Superphosphates, nes	3103.1090	68
过硫酸盐,无机的	Peroxosulphates, inorganic	2833.4000	
过硫酸盐,无机的	Persulphates, inorganic	2833.4000	
过滤机器及装置,过滤或净化水用,其他	Filtering machinery and apparatus, for filtering or purifying water, nes	8421.2190	7
过滤机器及装置,过滤或净化饮料(水除外)用	Filtering machinery and apparatus, for filtering or purifying beverages other than water	8421.2200	7
过滤机器及装置,家用型,过滤或净化水用	Filtering machinery and apparatus, of the household type, for filtering or purifying water	8421.2110	7
过滤机器及装置,家用型,气体用	Filtering machinery and apparatus, of the household type, for gases	8421.3910	7
过滤机器及装置,液体用,其他	Filtering machinery and apparatus, for liquids, nes	8421.2990	7
过滤器,内燃发动机进气用	Intake air filters for internal combustion engines	8421.3100	7
过滤装置,内燃发动机排气用	Filtering apparatus for exhaust air, for internal combustion engines	8421.3930	7
过滤装置,气体用,其他	Filtering apparatus for gases, nes	8421.3990	7
过滤装置用零件,家用型	Filtering machines parts, of household-type	8421.9910	3
过滤装置用零件,其他	Filtering machines parts, nes	8421.9990	3
过硼酸盐	Peroxoborates (perborates)	2840.3000	
过热器,过热水锅炉的辅助设备	Super-heaters, auxiliary plant for use with boilers	8404.1010	3
过热器,集中供暖用的热水锅炉的辅助设备	Super-heaters, auxiliary plant for use with central heating boilers	8404.1020	3
过热器,蒸汽锅炉的辅助设备	Super-heaters, auxiliary plant for use with steam or other vapour generating watertube boilers	8404.1010	3
过热水锅炉	Super-heated water boilers	8402.2000	27
过热水锅炉的辅助设备	Super-heated water boilers auxiliary plant	8404.1010	3
过热水锅炉的辅助设备的零件	Super-heated water boilers auxiliary plant parts	8404.9090	3
过热水锅炉零件	Super-heated water boilers parts	8402.9000	27
过碳酸盐	Peroxocarbonates (percarbonates)	2836.9990	
过溴酸盐,无机的	Perbromates, inorganic	2829.9000	
过氧化苯甲酰及苯甲酰氯	Benzoyl peroxied and benzoyl chloride	2916.3200	36
过氧化醇及其卤化、磺化、硝化或亚硝化衍生物	Alcohol peroxides and their halogenated, sulphonated, nitrated or nitrosated derivatives	2909.6000	36
过氧化钾	Potassium peroxides	2815.3000	136
过氧化镁	Magnesium peroxide	2816.1000	
过氧化醚及其卤化、磺化、硝化或亚硝化衍生物	Ether peroxides and their halogenated, sulphonated, nitrated or nitrosated derivatives	2909.6000	36

G

商品名称	Article Description	税则号列	申报要素
过氧化钠	Sodium peroxides	2815.3000	136
过氧化氢,不论是否用尿素固化	Hydrogen peroxide, whether or not solidified with urea	2847.0000	6
过氧化酮及其卤化、磺化、硝化或亚硝化衍生物	Ketone peroxides and their halogenated, sulphonated, nitrated or nitrosated derivatives	2909.6000	36
过氧化锌	Zinc peroxide	2817.0090	34

H

商品名称	Article Description	税则号列	申报要素
ha			
铪,未锻轧	Hafnium, unwrought	8112.9290	16
铪粉末	Hafnium powders	8112.9290	16
铪制品	Hafnium articles	8112.9990	16
哈拉西泮(INN)以及盐	Halazepam (INN); salts thereof	2933.9100	36
哈蜜瓜,鲜的	Hami melons, fresh	0807.1910	1
hai			
海参,冻、干、盐腌或盐渍的	Sea cucumbers (bechesdemer), frozen, dried, salted or in brine	0307.9920	14
海草及其他藻类	Seaweeds and other algae	1212.2090	14
海草及其他藻类制品,其他	Preparations of seaweeds and other algar, nes	2008.9939	248
海带	Sea tangle	1212.2010	14
海带,盐腌的	Sea tangle, salted	2008.9932	248
海龟蛋	Turtles' eggs	0410.0090	34
海狸香	Castoreum	0510.0020	14
海马,干的	Hippocampi, dried	0305.5910	4
海龙,干的	Pipefish, dried	0305.5910	4
海洛因及盐	Heroin and salts	2939.1100	34
海绵,天然的,动物质	Sponges of animal origin, natural	0511.9990	34
海绵,天然的,植物质	Sponges of vegetable origin, natural	1404.9090	
海绵钛	Titanium sponge	8108.2021	16
海绵铁产品,块、团、团粒及类似形状,其他	Spongy ferrous products, in lumps, pellets or similar forms, nes	7203.9000	6
海绵铁回转窑用零件	Sponge iron rotary kiln parts	8417.9010	3
海牛	Manatees	0106.1200	
海牛肉,鲜或冷或冻的	Meat of manatees, fresh, chilled or frozen	0208.4000	15
海牛肉粉,食用	Flours and meals of meat of manatees, edible	0210.9200	14
海水	Brine	2501.0030	1368
海水	Sea water	2501.0030	1368
海豚	Dolphins	0106.1200	
海豚肉,鲜或冷或冻的	Meat of dolphins, fresh, chilled or frozen	0208.4000	15
海豚肉粉,食用	Flours and meals of meat of dolphins, edible	0210.9200	14
海盐	Sea salt	2501.0020	1368
海藻灰(海草灰)	Seaweed ash (kelp)	2621.9000	134
海藻糖	Fucose	2940.0000	6
海藻糖,茧蜜糖	Trehalose	2940.0000	6

商品名称	Article Description	税则号列	申报要素
海蜇,制作或保藏的	Jelly fish, prepared or preserved	1605.9010	48
胲(羟胺)的有机衍生物	Organic derivatives of hydroxylamine	2928.0000	36
胲(羟胺)及其无机盐	Hydroxylamine and their inorganic salts	2825.1090	
han			
含醇基但不含其他含氧基的羧酸及其酸酐、酰卤化物、过氧化物和过氧酸以及它们的衍生物,其他	Carboxylic acids with alcohol function but without other oxygen function, their anhydrides, halides, peroxides, peroxyacids and their derivatives, nes	2918.1990	36
含氮基化合物,其他	Compounds with other nitrogen function, nes	2929.9090	36
含酚基但不含其他含氧基的羧酸及其酸酐、酰卤化物、过氧化物和过氧酸以及它们的衍生物,其他	Carboxylic acids with phenol function but without other oxygen function, their anhydrides, halides, peroxides, peroxyacids and their derivatives, nes	2918.2900	36
含附加含氧基的羧酸及其酸酐、酰卤化物、过氧化物和过氧酸以及它们的卤化、磺化、硝化或亚硝化衍生物,其他	Carboxylic acids with additional oxygen function and their anhydrides, halides, peroxides and peroxyacids; their halogenated, sulphonated, nitrated or nitrosated derivatives, nes	2918.9900	36
含金属纱线,不论是否螺旋花线,由纺织纱线或扁条及类似品与金属线、扁条或粉末混合制得或用金属包覆制得	Metallized yarn, whether or not gimped, being textile yarn, or strip or the like, combined with metal in the form of thread, strip or powder or covered with metal	5605.0000	6
含咖啡的咖啡代用品	Coffee substitutes containing coffee	0901.9020	6
含浓缩精油的脂肪、固定油、蜡及类似品,用花香吸取法或浸渍法制成的	Concentrates of essential oils in fats, in fixedoils, in waxes or the like, obtained by enfleurage or maceration	3301.9090	34
含铅抗震化合物的淤渣	Leaded anti-knock compound sludges	2620.2100	134
含铅汽油的淤渣	Leaded gasoline sludges	2620.2100	134
含醛基或酮基但不含其他含氧基的羧酸及其酸酐、酰卤化物、过氧化物和过氧酸以及它们的衍生物	Carboxylic acids with aldehyde or ketone function but without other oxygen function, their anhydrides, halides, peroxides, peroxyacids and their derivatives	2918.3000	36
含天然乳的产品,其他税号未列名的,不论是否加糖或其他甜物质	Products consisting of natural milk constituents, whether or not containing added sugar or other sweetening matter, nes	0404.9000	6
含油子仁及果实,其他	Oil seeds and oleaginous fruits, nes	1207.9999	3
含油子仁及果实,其他,种用	Oil seeds and oleaginous fruits, nes, seed	1207.9910	3
含有奎宁或其盐药品,混合或未混合的,配定剂量或制成零售包装	Quinine or its salts medicaments, mixed or unmixed, put up in measured doses or in forms or packings for retail sale	3004.4010	368
含有奎宁或其盐药品,两种或两种以上成分混合而成的,未配定剂量或制成零售包装	Quinine or its salts medicaments, consisting of two or more constituents which have been mixed together, not put up in measured doses or in forms or packings for retail sale	3003.4010	368

商品名称	Article Description	税则号列	申报要素
含有两种或两种以上不同卤素的无环烃卤化衍生物,其他	Halogenated derivatives of acyclic hydrocarbons containing two or more different halogens, nes	2903.4990	36
含有其他贵金属或贵金属化合物的废碎料,其他	Waste and scrap with other precious metals, nes	7112.9990	46
含有其他贵金属或贵金属化合物的废碎料,主要用于回收贵金属	Waste and scrap with other precious metals, of a kind used principally for the recoverey of precious metal	7112.9920	46
含有银或银化合物的废碎料	Waste and scrap with silver or silver compounds	7112.9910	46
汗衫,针织或钩编的,丝及绢丝制	Singlets, knitted or crocheted, of silk or silk waste	6109.9010	2456
汗衫,针织或钩编的,棉制	Singlets, knitted or crocheted, of cotton	6109.1000	2456
汗衫,针织或钩编的,其他	Singlets, knitted or crocheted, nes	6109.9090	2456
旱冰鞋及用品	Roller skates and articles	9506.7020	
焊粉,金属及其他材料制成的	Soldering, brazing or welding pastes consisting of metal and other materials	3810.1000	36
焊膏,金属及其他材料制成的	Soldering, brazing or welding powders consisting of metal and other materials	3810.1000	36
焊剂,其他	Soldering, brazing or welding preparations, nes	3810.9000	36
焊接机器及装置,其他	Welding machinery and apparatus, nes	8468.8000	57
焊接机器及装置,电弧的	Welding machines and apparatus of metals, with arc, nes	8515.3900	
焊接机器及装置,气体推动的	Welding machinery and apparatus, gas-operated	8468.2000	57
焊接机器及装置,全自动或半自动的,其他	Welding of metals machines and apparatus, fully or partly automatic, nes	8515.3190	
焊接机器及装置的零件	Welding machinery and apparatus parts	8468.9000	3
焊接链,钢铁的,其他	Welded link, of iron or steel, nes	7315.8200	36
焊接用辅助剂,其他	Soldering, brazing or welding fluxes and other auxiliary preparations, nes	3810.9000	36
焊枪	Soldering guns	8515.1100	
焊丝,贱金属制,以焊剂为芯,电弧焊用	Cored wire of base metal, for electric arcwelding	8311.2000	56
焊锡,按重量计含铅量在 0.1% 以下的	Solder, containing by weight less than 0.1% of lead	8001.2021	16
hang			
航标,浮动结构体	Beacons, floating structures	8907.9000	5
航空煤油	Aviation kerosene	2710.1911	6
航空汽油	Aviation gasoline	2710.1110	6
航空器,无动力的	Aircraft, non-powered	8801.0090	
航空器的发射装置及其零件	Aircraft launching gear and parts thereof	8805.1000	3
航空器的零件,其他	Aircraft parts, nes	8803.9000	3
航空器发动机,点燃往复式或旋转式,输出功率不超过 298 千瓦	Aircraft engines, spark-ignition reciprocating or rotary, of an output not exceeding 298kW	8407.1010	3
航空器发动机,点燃往复式或旋转式,输出功率超过 298 千瓦	Aircraft engines, spark-ignition reciprocating or rotary, of an output exceeding 298kW	8407.1020	3

商品名称	Article Description	税则号列	申报要素
航天器(包括卫星)及其运载工具、亚轨道运载工具	Spacecraft (including satellites) and suborbital and spacecraft launch vehicles	8802.6000	
hao			
蚝,其他	Oysters, nes	0307.1090	14
蚝,种苗	Oysters, for cultivation	0307.1010	3
号角	Call horns	9208.9000	5
号码,贱金属制,税号94.05的货品除外	Numbers, of base metal, excluding those of heading No. 94.05	8310.0000	256
he			
合成纤维长丝机织物,染色,其他	Synthetic filament yarn woven fabrics, dyed, nes	5407.9200	2468
合成纤维长丝机织物,色织,其他	Synthetic filament yarn woven fabrics, of yarns of different colours, nes	5407.9300	2468
合成纤维长丝机织物,未漂白或漂白,其他	Synthetic filament yarn woven fabrics, unbleached or bleached, nes	5407.9100	2468
合成纤维长丝机织物,印花,其他	Synthetic filament yarn woven fabrics, printed, nes	5407.9400	2468
合成纤维长丝纱线,供零售用	Synthetic filament yarn, put up for retail sale	5406.0010	
合成纤维长丝丝束,其他	Synthetic filament tow, nes	5501.9000	68
合成纤维单丝,截面尺寸不超过1毫米,细度在67分特及以上,其他	Synthetic monofilament of 67 decitex or more and of which no cross-sectional dimension exceeding 1mm, nes	5404.1900	568
合成纤维的废料	Synthetic fibres waste	5505.1000	68
合成纤维短纤,未梳或未经其他纺前加工,其他	Synthetic staple fibres, not carded, combed or otherwise processed for spinning, nes	5503.9000	68
合成纤维短纤,已梳或经其他纺前加工,其他	Synthetic staple fibres, carded, combed or otherwise processed for spinning, nes	5506.9000	68
合成纤维短纤单纱,按重量计合成纤维短纤含量在85%及以上,其他	Synthetic staple fibres single yarn, containing 85% or more by weight of synthetic staple fibres, nes	5509.4100	68
合成纤维短纤单纱,按重量计聚丙烯腈或变性聚丙烯腈短纤含量在85%及以上	Synthetic staple fibres single yarn, containing 85% or more by weight of acrylic or modacrylic staple fibres	5509.3100	68
合成纤维短纤单纱,按重量计聚酯短纤含量在85%及以上	Synthetic staple fibres single yarn, containing 85% or more by weight of polyester staple fibres	5509.2100	68
合成纤维短纤单纱,按重量计尼龙或其他聚酰胺短纤含量在85%及以上	Synthetic staple fibres single yarn, containing 85% or more by weight of staple fibres of nylon or other polyamides	5509.1100	68
合成纤维短纤多股纱线或缆线,按重量计合成纤维短纤含量在85%及以上,其他	Synthetic staple fibres multiple or cabled yarn, containing 85% or more by weight of synthetic staple fibres, nes	5509.4200	68
合成纤维短纤多股纱线或缆线,按重量计聚酯短纤含量在85%及以上	Synthetic staple fibres multiple or cabled yarn, containing 85% or more by weight of polyester staple fibres	5509.2200	68

H

商品名称	Article Description	税则号列	申报要素
合成纤维短纤多股纱线或缆线，按重量计尼龙或其他聚酰胺短纤含量在85%及以上	Synthetic staple fibres multiple or cabled yarn, containing 85% or more by weight of staple fibres of nylon or other polyamides	5509.1200	68
合成纤维短纤缝纫线，不论是否供零售用	Synthetic staple fibres sewing thread, whether or not put up for retail sale	5508.1000	68
合成纤维短纤机织物，按重量计合成纤维短纤含量在85%以下，主要或仅与棉混纺，每平方米重量不超过170克，染色，其他	Synthetic staple fibres woven fabrics, containing less than 85% by weight of such fibres, mixed mainly or solely with cotton, of a weight not exceeding $170g/m^2$, dyed, nes	5513.2900	2468
合成纤维短纤机织物，按重量计合成纤维短纤含量在85%以下，主要或仅与棉混纺，每平方米重量不超过170克，色织，其他	Synthetic staple fibres woven fabrics, containing less than 85% by weight of such fibres, mixed mainly or solely with cotton, of a weight not exceeding $170g/m^2$, of yarns of different colours, nes	5513.3990	2468
合成纤维短纤机织物，按重量计合成纤维短纤含量在85%以下，主要或仅与棉混纺，每平方米重量不超过170克，未漂白或漂白的，其他	Synthetic staple fibres woven fabrics, containing less than 85% by weight of such fibres, mixed mainly or solely with cotton, of a weight not exceeding $170g/m^2$, unbleached or bleached, nes	5513.1900	2468
合成纤维短纤机织物，按重量计合成纤维短纤含量在85%以下，主要或仅与棉混纺，每平方米重量不超过170克，印花，其他	Synthetic staple fibres woven fabrics, containing less than 85% by weight of such fibres, mixed mainly or solely with cotton, of a weight not exceeding $170g/m^2$, printed, nes	5513.4990	2468
合成纤维短纤机织物，按重量计合成纤维短纤含量在85%以下，主要或仅与棉混纺，每平方米重量超过170克，染色，其他	Synthetic staple fibres woven fabrics, containing less than 85% by weight of such fibres, mixed mainly or solely with cotton, of a weight exceeding $170g/m^2$, dyed, nes	5514.2900	2468
合成纤维短纤机织物，按重量计合成纤维短纤含量在85%以下，主要或仅与棉混纺，每平方米重量超过170克，色织，其他	Synthetic staple fibres woven fabrics, containing less than 85% by weight of such fibres, mixed mainly or solely with cotton, of a weight exceeding $170g/m^2$, of yarns of different colours, nes	5514.3090	2468
合成纤维短纤机织物，按重量计合成纤维短纤含量在85%以下，主要或仅与棉混纺，每平方米重量超过170克，未漂白或漂白，其他	Synthetic staple fibres woven fabrics, containing less than 85% by weight of such fibres, mixed mainly or solely with cotton, of a weight exceeding $170g/m^2$, unbleached or bleached, nes	5514.1990	2468
合成纤维短纤机织物，按重量计合成纤维短纤含量在85%以下，主要或仅与棉混纺，每平方米重量超过170克，印花，其他	Synthetic staple fibres woven fabrics, containing less than 85% by weight of such fibres, mixed mainly or solely with cotton, of a weight exceeding $170g/m^2$, printed, nes	5514.4900	2468
合成纤维短纤机织物，按重量计聚丙烯腈或变性聚丙烯腈短纤含量在85%及以上，其他	Synthetic staple fibres woven fabrics, containing 85% or more by weight of acrylic or modacrylic staple fibres, nes	5512.2900	2468
合成纤维短纤机织物，按重量计聚丙烯腈或变性聚丙烯腈短纤含量在85%及以上，未漂白或漂白	Synthetic staple fibres woven fabrics, containing 85% or more by weight of acrylic or modacrylic staple fibres, unbleached or bleached	5512.2100	2468

H

商品名称	Article Description	税则号列	申报要素
合成纤维短纤机织物,按重量计聚酯短纤含量在85%及以上,其他	Synthetic staple fibres woven fabrics, containing 85% or more by weight of polyester staple fibres, nes	5512.1900	2468
合成纤维短纤机织物,按重量计聚酯短纤含量在85%及以上,未漂白或漂白	Synthetic staple fibres woven fabrics, containing 85% or more by weight of polyester staple fibres, unbleached or bleached	5512.1100	2468
合成纤维短纤机织物,按重量计合成纤维短纤含量在85%以上,其他	Synthetic staple fibres woven fabrics, containing 85% or more by weight of synthetic staple fibres, nes	5512.9900	2468
合成纤维短纤机织物,其他	Synthetic staple fibres woven fabrics, nes	5515.9900	2468
合成纤维短纤机织物,未漂白或漂白	Synthetic staple fibres woven fabrics, unbleached or bleached	5512.9100	2468
合成纤维短纤机织物,主要或仅与化学纤维长丝混纺,其他	Synthetic staple fibres woven fabrics, mixed mainly or solely with man-made filaments, nes	5515.9100	2468
合成纤维短纤纱线,按重量计合成纤维短纤含量在85%及以上,供零售用	Synthetic staple fibres yarn, containing 85% or more by weight of such fibres, put up for retail sale	5511.1000	68
合成纤维短纤纱线,按重量计合成纤维短纤含量在85%以下,供零售用	Synthetic staple fibres yarn, containing less than 85% by weight of such fibres, put up for retail sale	5511.2000	68
合成纤维短纤纱线,其他	Synthetic staple fibres yarn, nes	5509.9900	68
合成纤维短纤纱线,主要或仅与棉混纺	Synthetic staple fibres yarn, mixed mainly or solely with cotton	5509.9200	68
合成纤维短纤纱线,主要或仅与羊毛或动物细毛混纺	Synthetic staple fibres yarn, mixed mainly or solely with wool or fine animal hair	5509.9100	68
合成纤维机织物,按重量计长丝含量在85%及以上,染色	Synthetic filaments woven fabrics, containing 85% or more by weight, dyed	5407.7200	2468
合成纤维机织物,按重量计长丝含量在85%及以上,色织	Synthetic filaments woven fabrics, containing 85% or more by weight, of yarns of different colours	5407.7300	2468
合成纤维机织物,按重量计长丝含量在85%及以上,未漂白或漂白	Synthetic filaments woven fabrics, containing 85% or more by weight, unbleached or bleached	5407.7100	2468
合成纤维机织物,按重量计长丝含量在85%及以上,印花	Synthetic filaments woven fabrics, containing 85% or more by weight, printed	5407.7400	2468
合成纤维机织物,按重量计长丝含量在85%以下,主要或仅与棉混纺,染色	Synthetic filaments woven fabrics, containing less than 85% by weight, mixed mainly or solely with cotton, dyed	5407.8200	2468
合成纤维机织物,按重量计长丝含量在85%以下,主要或仅与棉混纺,色织	Synthetic filaments woven fabrics, containing less than 85% by weight, mixed mainly or solely with cotton, of yarns of different colours	5407.8300	2468
合成纤维机织物,按重量计长丝含量在85%以下,主要或仅与棉混纺,未漂白或漂白	Synthetic filaments woven fabrics, containing less than 85% by weight, mixed mainly or solely with cotton, unbleached or bleached	5407.8100	2468
合成纤维机织物,按重量计长丝含量在85%以下,主要或仅与棉混纺,印花	Synthetic filaments woven fabrics, containing less than 85% by weight, mixed mainly or solely with cotton, printed	5407.8400	2468

H

商品名称	Article Description	税则号列	申报要素
合成橡胶(含胶乳)与天然橡胶(含胶乳)的混合物	Synthetic rubber (including latex) mixtures with natural rubber(including latex)	4002.8000	136
合成橡胶,初级形状的,其他	Synthetic rubber, in primary forms, nes	4002.9911	136
合成橡胶,其他	Synthetic rubber, nes	4002.9919	136
合成橡胶胶乳,其他	Synthetic rubber latex, nes	4002.9100	136
合金、分散体(包括金属陶瓷)、陶瓷产品及混合物,含U235浓缩铀、钚或它们的化合物的	Alloys dispersion (including cermets), ceramic products and mixtures containing uranium enriched in U235, plutonium or compounds of these products	2844.2000	
合金、分散体(包括金属陶瓷)、陶瓷产品及混合物,含U235贫化铀、钍或它们的化合物的	Alloys, dispersions (including cermets), ceramic products and mixtures containing uranium depleted in U235, thorium or compounds of these products	2844.3000	
合金、分散体(包括金属陶瓷)、陶瓷产品及混合物,含天然铀或天然铀化合物的	Aloys, dispersions (including cermets), ceramic products and mixtures containing natural uranium or natural uranium compouds	2844.1000	
合金钢,锭状及其他初级形状,其他	Alloy steel in ingots and other primary forms, nes	7224.1000	468
合金钢粉末,其他	Alloy steel powders, nes	7205.2100	6
合金钢制的半制成品,单件重量在10吨及以上的粗铸锻件坯	Alloy steel semi-finished products, raw casting forging stocks, individual piece weight of 10t or more, nes	7224.9010	468
合金钢制的半制成品,其他	Alloy steel semi-finished products, nes	7224.9090	468
和服腰带,非针织或钩编的	Kimono belts, not knitted or crocheted	6217.1020	2456
和纤维素纤维网纸,成卷或成张的	Webs of cellulose fibres, in rolls or sheets	4803.0000	58
核磁共振成像装置,医疗、外科、牙科或兽医用	Magnetic resonance imaging apparatus, used in medical, surgical, dental or veterinary sciences	9018.1300	
核反应堆	Nuclear reactors	8401.1000	2
核反应堆的堆内构件	Nuclear reactor internals	8401.4020	2
核反应堆的相关组件,未辐照	Nuclear reactors associated assembly, non-irradiated	8401.4010	2
核反应堆零件,其他	Nuclear reactors parts, nes	8401.4090	2
核反应堆燃料元件,未辐照	Nuclear reactors fuel elements, non-irradiated	8401.3010	2
核反应堆燃料元件的零件,未辐照	Nuclear reactors fuel elements parts, non-irradiated	8401.3090	2
核反应堆释热元件,的未辐照	Nuclear reactors cartridges, non-irradiated	8401.3010	2
核反应堆已耗尽(已辐照)的燃料元件(释热元件)	Spent (irradiated) fuel elements (cartridges) of nuclear reactors	2844.5000	
核黄素	Lactoflavine (vitamin B_2)	2936.2300	36
核及核仁,杏、桃(包括油桃)、梅或李的,其他	Stones and kernels, apricot, peach (including nectarine) or plum, nes	1212.9919	134
核酸及其盐	Nucleic acids and their salts	2934.9930	36
核桃,去壳	Walnuts, shelled	0802.3200	134
核桃,未去壳	Walnuts, in shell	0802.3100	134
核桃仁,罐头	Walnut meats, in airtight containers	2008.1910	248
盒、箱(包括板条箱)及类似品,塑料的	Boxes, cases, crates and similar articles, of plastics	3923.1000	23

H

商品名称	Article Description	税则号列	申报要素
盒式磁带录音机或放声机用零件、附件,其他	Cassette magnetic tape recorders or reproducers parts and accessories, nes	8522.9029	3
盒子和匣子及类似品,装珠宝或刀具用的,木制	Caskets and cases for jewellery or cutlery, and similar articles, of wood	4420.9090	56
褐煤,不论是否粉化,但未制成型	Lignite, whether or not pulverized, but not agglomerated	2702.1000	1
褐煤,制成型的	Lignite, agglomerated	2702.2000	1
褐煤蜡	Lignite wax	2712.9090	6
褐锰矿	Braunite	2602.0000	1346
褐铁矿,已烧结	Limonite, agglomerated	2601.1200	1346
褐藻胶	Algin	1302.3912	3
hei			
黑板,不论是否镶框	Black boards, whether or not framed	9610.0000	
黑板,具有书写或绘画面的	Boards, with writing or drawing surfaces	9610.0000	
黑麦,其他	Rye, nes	1002.0090	3
黑麦,种用	Rye, seed	1002.0010	3
黑麦草种子,饲料植物用的	Rye grass (lolium multiflorum lam., lolium perenne L.) Seed, forage plants	1209.2500	358
黑莓,冷冻的	Blackberries, frozen	0811.2000	1
黑莓,鲜的	Blackberries, fresh	0810.2000	1
黑锰矿	Hausmannite	2602.0000	1346
黑铜矿	Tenorite	2603.0000	146
黑线鳕鱼,冻的	Haddock (melanogrammus aeglefinus), frozen	0303.7200	18
黑线鳕鱼,鲜或冷的	Haddock (melanogrammus aeglefinus), fresh or chilled	0302.6200	18
黑珍珠,天然的,其他	Tahitian pearls, natural, nes	7101.1091	145
黑珍珠,天然的,未分级	Tahitian pearls, natural, ungraded	7101.1011	145
heng			
恒定秤,定量包装用	Constant weight scales, for rationed packing	8423.3010	
恒定秤,定量分选用	Constant weight scales, for rationed sorting	8423.3020	
恒温控制阀	Thermostatically controlled valves	8481.8040	
恒温器	Thermostats	9032.1000	
恒压器	Manostats	9032.2000	
桁架桥式起重机	Transporter cranes	8426.1990	7
珩磨机床,加工金属或金属陶瓷用	Honing machines, for metal or cermets	8460.4010	7
横担(过桥),钟、表的	Bridges, of clock or watch	9114.4000	6
衡器,其他	Weighing machinery, nes	8423.8990	
衡器,最大称量不超过 30 千克,其他	Weighing machinery, having a maximum weighing capacity not exceeding 30kg, nes	8423.8190	

H

商品名称	Article Description	税则号列	申报要素
衡器,最大称量超过 30 千克,但不超过 5000 千克,其他	Weighing machinery, having a maximum weighing capacity exceeding 30kg but not exceeding 5000kg, nes	8423. 8290	
衡器的零件	Weighing machinery parts	8423. 9000	
衡器用的各种砝码、秤砣	Weighing machine weights of all kinds	8423. 9000	
hong			
烘焙糕饼	Bakers wares	1905. 9000	28
烘炒食品,谷物或谷物产品的	Prepared foods obtained by the roasting of cereals or cereal products	1904. 1000	48
烘箱,电阻加热的,工业或实验室用,其他	Ovens, resistance heated, for industrial or laboratory use, electric, nes	8514. 1090	7
烘箱,工业或实验室用,电的,其他	Ovens, for industrial or laboratory use, electric, nes	8514. 3000	7
烘箱,面包房用及包括做饼干用的	Bakery ovens, including biscuit ovens	8417. 2000	7
烘箱,通过感应或介质损耗工作的,工业或实验室用	Ovens functioning by induction or dielectric loss, for industrial or laboratory use, electric	8514. 2000	7
烘箱及炉,焙烧熔化或其他热处理矿砂、黄铁矿或金属用	Furnaces and ovens for the roasting, melting or other heat-treatment of ores, pyrites or of metals	8417. 1000	7
烘箱及炉,非电热的工业或实验室用,其他	Furnaces and ovens for industrial or laboratory, non-electric, nes	8417. 8090	7
烘箱及炉零件,非电热的工业或实验室用,其他	Furnaces and ovens parts, for industrial or laboratory, non-electric, nes	8417. 9090	3
红宝石,加工的	Rubies, worked	7103. 9100	145
红宝石,未加工	Rubies, unworked	7103. 1000	145
红宝石的粉末	Rubies dust and powder	7105. 9000	145
红茶(已发酵),内包装每件净重不超过 3 千克,其他	Black tea (fermented), nes, in immediate packings of a content not exceeding 3kg	0902. 3090	248
红茶(已发酵),其他	Black tea (fermented), nes	0902. 4090	248
红大马哈鱼,冻的	Sockeye salmon (red salmon) (on corhynchus nerka), frozen	0303. 1100	18
红花油及其分离品,初榨的	Safflower oil and fractions thereof, crude oil	1512. 1100	4
红花油及其分离品,其他	Safflower oil and fractions thereof, nes	1512. 1900	4
红花籽	Safflower seeds	1207. 9994	3
红毛丹,鲜的	Rambutan, fresh	0810. 9040	1
红霉素及其衍生物以及它们的盐	Erythromycin and its derivatives, salts thereof	2941. 5000	
红砷镍矿	Niccolite	2604. 0000	146
红锑矿	Kermesite	2617. 1090	146
红外或氦氖激光胶片,未曝光的,无齿孔的,宽度超过 610 毫米,长度超过 200 米	Infra-res or helium-neon laser film, unexposed, without perforations, of a width exceeding 610mm and of a length exceeding 200 m	3702. 4291	12368
红外线灯	Infra-red lamps	8539. 4900	35
红外线分光仪、分光光度计及摄谱仪	IR spectrometers, spectrophotometers and spectrographs	9027. 3000	

H

商品名称	Article Description	税则号列	申报要素
红外线装置,医疗、外科、牙科或兽医用	Infra-red ray apparatus, used in medical, surgical, dental or veterinary sciences	9018. 2000	
红小豆,冷冻的	Small red (Adzuki) beans (Phaseolus or Vigna angularis), frozen	0710. 2210	1
红小豆,种用,脱荚的,干的	Small red(Adzuri) beans, seed, shelled, dried	0713. 3211	34
红锌矿	Zincite	2608. 0000	146
红枣,干的	Red jujubes, dried	0813. 4030	34
红柱石	Andalusite	2508. 5000	134
hou			
后腿及其肉块,猪的,冻的,带骨	Hams, shoulders and cuts thereof, with bone in, of swine, frozen	0203. 2200	14
后腿及其肉块,猪的,鲜或冷的,带骨	Hams and cuts thereof, with bone in, of swine, fresh or chilled	0203. 1200	14
后腿及其肉块,猪的,制作或保藏的	Hams and cuts thereof, of swine	1602. 4100	48
后围,机动车辆的	Rear appearance of bodies, of the motor vehicles	8708. 2956	3
hu			
呼吸器具,不包括既无机械零件又无可互换过滤器的防护面具	Breathing appliances, excluding protective masks having neither mechanical parts nor replaceable filters	9020. 0000	
呼吸器具,治疗用,其他	Therapeutic respiration apparatus, nes	9019. 2000	
弧光灯	Arc-lamps	8539. 4100	35
狐皮,整张的,不论是否带头、尾或爪	Raw furskins of fox, whole, with or without head, tail or paws	4301. 6000	15
胡椒,未磨	Pepper, neither crushed nor ground	0904. 1100	4
胡椒,已磨	Pepper, crushed or ground	0904. 1200	4
胡椒薄荷油	Essential oils of mentha piperita	3301. 2400	34
胡椒薄荷油	Essential oils of peppermint	3301. 2400	34
胡椒醛	Piperonal	2932. 9300	36
胡萝卜,鲜或冷藏的	Carrots, fresh or chilled	0706. 1000	1
胡萝卜素,合成有机着色料	B- carotene, sythetic orgaric colouring	3204. 1700	345
胡萝卜素,天然 α 型	A- carotene	3203. 0019	34
胡萝卜素,天然 γ 型	Γ- carotene	3203. 0019	34
糊精	Dextrins	3505. 1000	36
糊墙品,氯乙烯聚合物制	Wall or ceiling coverings, of polymers of vinyl chloride	3918. 1010	36
糊墙品,其他塑料制	Wall or ceiling coverings, of other plastics	3918. 9010	36
糊墙织物	Textile wall coverings	5905. 0000	8
琥珀	Ambroid (agglomerated amber)	2530. 9099	13456
琥珀酰亚胺	Succinimide	2925. 1900	36
互感器,额定容量不超过 1 千伏安	Mutual inductor, having a power handling capacity not exceeding 1kVA	8504. 3110	78

H

商品名称	Article Description	税则号列	申报要素
互感器,额定容量超过1千伏安,但不超过16千伏安	Mutual inductor, having a power handling capacity exceeding 1kVA but not exceeding 16kVA	8504.3210	78
护发品,其他	Hair use preparations, nes	3305.9000	23
护肤品,粉状,不论是否压紧	Skin care preparations, in powders, whether or not compressed	3304.9100	23
护肤品,其他	Skin care preparations, nes	3304.9900	23
护轨、齿轨	Check-rails and rack rails	7302.9090	6
护腿、裹腿和类似品及其零件,木制	Gaiters, leggings and similar articles, and parts thereof, of wood	6406.9100	6
护腿、裹腿和类似品及其零件,其他材料制	Gaiters, leggings and similar articles, and parts thereof, of other materials	6406.9900	6
护膝垫,适合各种动物用	Knee pads for any animal, of any material	4201.0000	1458
护胸背带工装裤,非针织或钩编的,男式,合成纤维制	Bib and brace overalls, not knitted or crocheted, for men or boys, of synthetic fibres	6203.4390	2456
护胸背带工装裤,非针织或钩编的,男式,棉制	Bib and brace overalls, not knitted or crocheted, for men or boys, of cotton	6203.4290	2456
护胸背带工装裤,非针织或钩编的,男式,其他纺织材料制	Bib and brace overalls, not knitted or crocheted, for men or boys, of other textile material	6203.4990	2456
护胸背带工装裤,非针织或钩编的,男式,羊毛或动物细毛制	Bib and brace overalls, not knitted or crocheted, for men or boys, of wool or fine animal hair	6203.4100	2456
护胸背带工装裤,非针织或钩编的,女式,合成纤维制	Bib and brace overalls, not knitted or crocheted, for women or girls, of synthetic fibres	6204.6300	2456
护胸背带工装裤,非针织或钩编的,女式,棉制	Bib and brace overalls, not knitted or crocheted, for women or girls, of cotton	6204.6200	2456
护胸背带工装裤,非针织或钩编的,女式,其他纺织材料制	Bib and brace overalls, not knitted or crocheted, for women or girls, of other textile materials	6204.6900	2456
护胸背带工装裤,非针织或钩编的,女式,羊毛或动物细毛制	Bib and brace overalls, not knitted or crocheted, for women or girls, of wool or fine animal hair	6204.6100	2456
护胸背带工装裤,针织或钩编的,男式,合成纤维制	Bib and brace overalls, knitted or crocheted, of men or boys, of synthetic fibres	6103.4300	2456
护胸背带工装裤,针织或钩编的,男式,棉制	Bib and brace overalls, knitted or crocheted, of men or boys, of cotton	6103.4200	2456
护胸背带工装裤,针织或钩编的,男式,其他纺织材料制	Bib and brace overalls, knitted or crocheted, of men or boys, of other textile materials	6103.4900	2456
护胸背带工装裤,针织或钩编的,男式,羊毛或动物细毛制	Bib and brace overalls, knitted or crocheted, of men or boys, of wool or fine animal hair	6103.4100	2456
护胸背带工装裤,针织或钩编的,女式,合成纤维制	Bib and brace overalls, knitted or crocheted, of women or girls, of synthetic fibres	6104.6300	2456
护胸背带工装裤,针织或钩编的,女式,棉制	Bib and brace overalls, knitted or crocheted, of women or girls, of cotton	6104.6200	2456
护胸背带工装裤,针织或钩编的,女式,其他纺织材料制	Bib and brace overalls, knitted or crocheted, of women or girls, of other textile materials	6104.6900	2456

商品名称	Article Description	税则号列	申报要素
护胸背带工装裤,针织或钩编的,女式,羊毛或动物细毛制	Bib and brace overalls, knitted or crocheted, of women or girls, of wool or fine animal hair	6104.6100	2456
戽斗,推土机或起重机零件	Buckets, parts of bulldozer or cranes	8431.4100	3
hua			
花边,机制,化学纤维制	Lace, mechanically made, of man-made fibres	5804.2100	468
花边,机制,棉制	Lace, mechanically made, of cotton	5804.2920	468
花边,机制,其他	Lace, mechanically made, nes	5804.2990	468
花边,机制,丝及绢丝制	Lace, mechanically made, of silk or silk waste	5804.2910	468
花边,手工制	Lace, hand-made	5804.3000	468
花边薄纱机	Tulle lace making machines	8447.9090	7
花茶,内包装每件净重不超过3千克	Green tea (not fermented), flavoured, in immediate packings of a content not exceeding 3kg	0902.1010	248
花茶,其他	Green tea (not fermented), flavoured, nes	0902.2010	248
花岗岩,仅用锯或其他方法切割成矩形,包括正方形	Granite, merely cut, by sawing or otherwise, into blocks or slabs of a rectangular (including square) shape	2516.1200	148
花岗岩,原状或粗加修整	Granite, crude or roughly trimmed	2516.1100	148
花岗岩碑石或建筑用石及其制品,简单切削或锯开并具有一个平面的	Granite monumental or building stone and articles thereof, simply cut or sawn, with a flat or even surface	6802.2300	3468
花岗岩及其制品,已加工的,其他	Granite and articles thereof, worked, nes	6802.9390	3468
花岗岩石刻	Granite carvings	6802.9310	3468
花露水	Toilet waters	3303.0000	2
花生,烘焙的	Groundnuts, roasted	2008.1120	248
花生,其他,未去壳,未焙炒或未烹煮的	Groundnuts, nes, in shell, not roasted or otherwise cooked	1202.1090	34
花生,其他,用其他方法制作或保藏的	Groundnuts, nes, otherwise prepared, or preserved	2008.1190	248
花生,去壳的,未焙炒或未烹煮的,不论是否破碎	Groundnuts, shelled, not roasted or otherwise cooked, whether or not broken	1202.2000	34
花生,种用	Groundnuts, seed	1202.1010	34
花生酱	Groundnut butter	2008.1130	248
花生酱	Peanut butter	2008.1130	248
花生米,罐头	Groundnut kernels, in airtight containers	2008.1110	248
花生油及其分离品,初榨的	Groundnut oil and its fractions, crude oil	1508.1000	
花生油及其分离品,其他	Groundnut oil and its fractions, nes	1508.9000	
花饰铅条窗玻璃及类似品,压制或模制的	Leaded lights and the like, pressed or moulded	7016.9010	345
华夫板	Waferboard of wood	4410.1900	6
华夫饼	Waffles	1905.3200	28
滑板	Skateboards	9506.9120	
滑车的零件	Pulley tackle parts	8431.1000	3

H

商品名称	Article Description	税则号列	申报要素
滑车及提升机,倒卸式提升机及提升车辆用的提升机除外,其他	Pulley tackle and hoists other than skip hoists or hoists of a kind used for raising vehicles, nes	8425. 1900	78
滑车及提升机,电动的,倒卸式提升机及提升车辆用的提升机除外	Pulley tackle and hoists powered by electric motor, other than skip hoists or hoists of a kind used for raising vehicles	8425. 1100	78
滑动轴承	Plain shaft bearings	8483. 3000	
滑轮,包括滑轮组	Pulleys, including pulley blocks	8483. 5000	
滑轮零件	Pulleys parts	8483. 9000	3
滑石,未破碎及未研粉	Talc, not crushed, not powdered	2526. 1020	4
滑石,已破碎或已研粉	Talc, crushed or powdered	2526. 2020	4
滑水板	Water-skis	9506. 2900	5
滑翔机	Gliders	8801. 0010	
滑翔伞及其零件、附件	Paragliders parts and accessories	8804. 0000	3
滑雪板靴,橡胶、塑料、皮革或再生皮革制外底,皮革制鞋面的	Snowboard boots, with outer soles of rubber, plastics, leather or composition leather and upers of leather	6403. 1200	26
滑雪板靴,橡胶或塑料制外底及鞋面的	Snowboard boots, with outer soles and uppers of rubber or plastics	6402. 1200	26
滑雪服,非针织或钩编的,棉制	Ski suits, not knitted or crocheted, of cotton	6211. 2010	2456
滑雪服,非针织或钩编的,其他纺织材料制	Ski suits, not knitted or crocheted, of other textile materials	6211. 2090	2456
滑雪服,针织或钩编的,棉制	Ski suits, knitted or crocheted, of cotton	6112. 2010	2456
滑雪服,针织或钩编的,其他	Ski suits, knitted or crocheted, nes	6112. 2090	2456
滑雪屐	Skis	9506. 1100	
滑雪屐	Snow skis	9506. 1100	
滑雪屐扣件(滑雪屐带)	Ski-fastenings(ski-bindings)	9506. 1200	
滑雪屐扣件(滑雪屐带)	Snow ski-fastenings(ski-bindings)	9506. 1200	
滑雪拉索,其他	Ski-draglines, nes	8428. 6090	
滑雪靴,橡胶、塑料、皮革或再生皮革制外底,皮革制鞋面的	Ski-boots, with outer soles of rubber, plastics, leather or composition leather and upers of leather	6403. 1200	26
滑雪靴,橡胶或塑料制外底及鞋面的	Ski-boots, with outer soles and uppers of rubber or plastics	6402. 1200	26
滑雪用具,其他	Snow-ski equipmen, nes	9506. 1900	5
化学纯糖,但蔗糖、乳糖、麦芽糖、葡萄糖及果糖除外	Sugars, chemically pure, other than sucrose, lactose, maltose, glucose and fructose	2940. 0000	6
化学工业及其相关工业的副产品,其他	Residual products of the chemical or allied industries, nes	3825. 9000	34
化学工业及其相关工业的化学产品及配制品,其他	Chemical products and preparations of the chemical or allied industries, nes	3824. 9099	36
化学机械抛光设备(CMP),单晶硅柱或硅晶片的制造机器及装置	Chemical mechanical polishers (CMP), boules or wafers manufacture machines and apparatus	8486. 1040	7

商品名称	Article Description	税则号列	申报要素
化学机械抛光设备(CMP)零件及附件,制造半导体器件或集成电路的机器及装置	Chemical mechanical polishers (CMP) parts and accessories, semiconductor devices or of electronic integrated circuits manufacture machines and apparatus	8486.9090	3
化学浆,从回收(废碎)纸或纸板提取的	Chemical pulp, derived from recovered (waste and scrap) paper or paperboard	4706.9200	46
化学木浆,溶解级	Chemical wood pulp, dissolving grades	4702.0000	
化学气相沉积设备(CVD),平板显示器的制造机器及装置	Chemical vapour deposition (CVD) equipment, flat panel displays manufacture machines and apparatus	8486.3021	7
化学气相沉积装置(CVD)零件及附件,制造半导体器件、集成电路、平板显示器的机器及装置	Chemical vapour deposition (CVD) equipment parts and accessories, semiconductor devices or of electronic integrated circuits or flat panel displays manufacture machines and apparatus	8486.9090	3
化学气相沉积装置(CVD),制造半导体器件或集成电路的机器及装置	Chemical vapour deposition (CVD) equipment, semiconductor devices or of electronic integrated circuits manufacture machines and apparatus	8486.2021	7
化学元素,放射性的,其他	Elements, radioactive, nes	2844.4090	
化妆包,以皮革、再生皮革或漆皮作面	Toilet bags, with outer surface of leather, of composition leather or of patent leather	4202.3100	256
化妆包,以塑料片或纺织材料作面	Toilet bags, with outer surface of plastic sheeting or of textile materials	4202.3200	256
化妆品,唇用	Make-up preparations for lip	3304.1000	23
化妆品,其他,粉状,不论是否压紧	Make-up preparations, nes, in powders, whether or not compressed	3304.9100	23
化妆品,眼用	Make-up preparations for eye	3304.2000	23
化妆品,指(趾)甲用	Manicture or pedicure preparations	3304.3000	23
化妆用笔,其他	Brushes for the application of cosmetics, nes	9603.3090	3
化妆用喷雾器及其座架、喷头	Toilet sprays, and mounts and heads thereof	9616.1000	
化妆用刷,其他	Toilet brushes for use on the person, nes	9603.2900	
划艇,充气的	Rowing boats, inflatable	8903.1000	58
划艇,其他	Rowing boats, nes	8903.9900	58
划线器具	Marking-out instruments	9017.2000	
划线器具的零件、附件	Marking-out instruments parts and accessories	9017.9000	3
画笔	Artists brushes	9603.3010	
画框及类似框架,贱金属制	Picture or similar frames, of base metal	8306.3000	256
画框及类似品,辐射松制的	Frames for paintings or similar objects, of radiata pine	4414.0010	56
画框及类似品,其他木制的	Frames for paintings or similar objects, of other wood	4414.0090	56
huai			
怀表,表壳用贵金属或包贵金属制成的,其他	Pocket-watches, with case of precious metal or of metal clad with precious metal, nes	9101.9900	56

H

商品名称	Article Description	税则号列	申报要素
怀表,电力驱动的,表壳用贵金属或包贵金属制成的	Pocket-watches, electrically operated, with case of precious metal or of metal clad with precious metal	9101. 9100	56
怀表,电力驱动的,其他	Pocket-watches, electrically operated, nes	9102. 9100	56
怀表,其他	Pocket-watches, nes	9102. 9900	56
槐米	Flos sophorae	1211. 9027	34
huan			
獾毛	Badger hair	0502. 9019	3
环,贱金属制,用于衣着、鞋靴、天篷、提包、旅行用品或其他制成品	Eyelets, of base metal, of a kind used for clothing, footwear, awnings, handbags, travel goods or other made up articles	8308. 1000	256
环丙氟哌酸	Ciprofloxacin	2933. 4910	36
环定细纱机紧密纺装置	Compact set of ring spinning frames	8448. 3940	3
环锭细纱机,其他	Ring spinning frames, nes	8445. 2049	7
环已巴比妥(INN)以及盐	Cyclobarbital (INN); salts thereof	2933. 5300	36
环已醇	Cyclohexanol	2906. 1200	36
环已酮	Cyclohexanone	2914. 2200	36
环已烷	Cyclohexane	2902. 1100	6
环境监测车	Mobile environmental monitoring units	8705. 9030	7
环聚醛	Cyclic polymers of aldehydes	2912. 5000	36
环醛,不含其他含氧基的,其他	Cyclic aldehydes without other oxygen function, nes	2912. 2990	36
环萜烯醚,其他	Cycloterpenic ethers, nes	2909. 2089	36
环萜烯酮,不含其他含氧基的,其他	Cycloterpenic ketones without other oxygen function, nes	2914. 2900	36
环烃,其他	Cyclic hydrocarbons, nes	2902. 9090	6
环头螺钉,钢铁制的	Screw rings, of iron or steel	7318. 1300	268
环烷醇、环烯醇及环萜烯醇,其他	Cyclanic, cyclenic or cycloterpenic alcohols, nes	2906. 1990	36
环烷单胺或多胺、环烯单胺或多胺、环萜烯单胺或多胺及其衍生物以及它们的盐	Cyclanic, cyclenic or cycloterpenic monoor polyamines, and their derivatives; salts thereof	2921. 3000	36
环烷多元羧酸、环烯多元羧酸、环萜烯多元羧酸及其酸酐、酰卤化物、过氧化物和过氧酸以及它们的衍生物,其他	Cyclanic, eyclenic or cycloterpenic polycarboxylic acids, their anhydrides, halides, peroxides, peroxyacids and their derivatives, nes	2917. 2090	36
环烷醚、环烯醚或环萜烯醚及其卤化、磺化、硝化或亚硝化衍生物,其他	Cyclanic, cyclenic or cycloterpenic ethers and their halogenated, sulphonated, nitrated or nitrosated derivatives, nes	2909. 2090	36
环烷烃、环烯及环萜烯,其他	Cyclanes, cyclenes and cycloterpenes, nes	2902. 1990	6
环烷烃、环烯烃或萜烯烃的卤化衍生物,其他	Halogenated derivatives of cyclanic, cyclenic or cycloter penic hydrocarbons, nes	2903. 5900	36
环烷酮,不含其他含氧基的,其他	Cyclanic ketones, without other oxygen function, nes	2914. 2900	36

商品名称	Article Description	税则号列	申报要素
环烷一元羧酸、环烯一元羧酸或环萜烯一元羧酸及其酸酐、酰卤化物、过氧化物和过氧酸以及它们的衍生物,其他	Cyclanic, cyclenic or cycloterpenic monocarboxylic acids, their anhydrides, halides, peroxides, peroxyacids and their derivatives, nes	2916.2090	36
环烯酮,不含其他含氧基的,其他	Cyclenic ketones without other oxygen function, nes	2914.2900	36
环酰胺(包括环氨基甲酸酯)及其衍生物以及它们的盐,其他	Cyclic amides (including cyclic carbamates) and their derivatives; salts thereof, nes	2924.2990	36
环形传动带(三角带),梯形截面的,V形肋状的,外周长超过180厘米,但不超过240厘米	Endless transmission belts of trapezoidal cross-section (V-belts), V-ribbed, of an outside circumference exceeding 180cm but not exceeding 240cm	4010.3300	1368
环形传动带(三角带),梯形截面的,V形肋状的,外周长超过60厘米,但不超过180厘米	Endless transmission belts of trapezoidal cross-section (V-belts), V-ribbed, whether or not grooved, of a circumference exceeding 60cm but not exceeding 180cm	4010.3100	1368
环形传动带(三角带),梯形截面的,V形肋状的除外外周长超过60厘米,但不超过180厘米	Endless transmission belts of trapezoidal cross-section (V-belts), other than V-ribbed, of an outside circumference exceeding 60cm but not exceeding 180cm	4010.3200	1368
环形传动带(三角带),梯形截面的,外周长超过180厘米,但不超过240厘米,V形肋状的除外	Endless transmission belts of trapezoidal cross-section (V-belts), V-ribbed, of an outside circumference exceeding 180cm but not exceeding 240cm	4010.3400	1368
环形带,机器用,不锈钢丝制	Endless bands for machinery, of stainless steel wire	7314.1200	36
环形带,铜丝制	Endless hands, of copper wire	7419.9930	4
环形同步带,外周长超过150厘米,但不超过198厘米	Endless synchronous belts, of an outside circumference exceeding 150cm but not exceeding 198cm	4010.3600	1368
环形同步带,外周长超过60厘米,但不超过150厘米	Endless synchronous belts, of an outside circumference exceeding 60cm but notexceeding 150cm	4010.3500	1368
环氧醇,三节环	Epoxyalcohols, with a three-membered ring	2910.9000	36
环氧酚,三节环	Epoxyphenols, with a three-membered ring	2910.9000	36
环氧化物,三节环	Epoxides, with a three-membered ring	2910.9000	36
环氧醚,三节环	Epoxyethers, with a three-membered ring	2910.9000	36
环氧树脂,初级形状的	Epoxide resins, in primary forms	3907.3000	1256
环氧乙烷	Oxirane	2910.1000	36
环已基氨基磺酸钠	Sodium cyclamate	2929.9010	36
缓冲器及其零件,铁道及电车道机车或其他车辆的	Buffers and parts, of railway or tramway locomotives or rolling-stock	8607.3000	3
幻灯机	Slide projectors	9008.1000	
幻灯机零件、附件	Slide projectors parts and accessories	9008.9090	3
换气扇,包括风机,本身装有一个输出功率不超过125瓦的电动机	Window fans, with a self-contained electric motor of an output not exceeding 125W	8414.5120	23

H

商品名称	Article Description	税则号列	申报要素
换气扇,其他	Window fans, nes	8414.5920	23
换梭装置,织机的辅助机器	Shuttle changing mechanisms, weaving auxiliary machines	8448.1900	3
换向阀,电磁式	Directional control valves, electromagnetic	8481.8021	
换向阀,其他	Directional control valves, nes	8481.8029	
huang			
黄丹	Massicot	2824.1000	
黄瓜,用醋或醋酸保存或制作的	Cucumbers, prepared or preserved by vinegar or acetic acid	2001.1000	48
黄瓜,鲜或冷藏的	Cucumbers, fresh or chilled	0707.0000	1
黄瓜,暂时保藏,但不适合直接使用的	Cucumbers, provisionally preserved, but unsuitable in that state for immediate consumption	0711.4000	34
黄花菜,干的	Day lily flowers, dried	0712.9030	4
黄酒	Yellow rice wine	2206.0010	248
黄连	Rhizoma coptidis	1211.9014	34
黄磷	Phosphorus, yellow	2804.7010	6
黄麻,生的或经沤制的	Jute, raw or retted	5303.1000	4
黄麻或纺织用韧皮纤维机织物,其他	Jute or textilebast fibres woven fabrics, nes	5310.9000	2468
黄麻或纺织用韧皮纤维机织物,未漂白	Jute or textilebast fibres woven fabrics, unbleached	5310.1000	2468
黄麻及纺织用韧皮纤维短纤	Jute and other textile bast fibres tow	5303.9000	4
黄麻及纺织用韧皮纤维废麻	Jute and other textile bast fibres waste	5303.9000	4
黄麻纱线或纺织用韧皮纤维纱线,单纱	Jute yarn or textile bast fibres yarn, single	5307.1000	58
黄麻纱线或纺织用韧皮纤维纱线,多股纱线或缆线	Jute yarn or textile bast fibres yarn, multiple(folded) or cabled	5307.2000	58
黄芪	Radix astragali	1211.9023	34
黄鳍金枪鱼,冻的	Yellowfin tunas(thunnus albacares), frozen	0303.4200	18
黄鳍金枪鱼,鲜或冷的	Yellowfin tunas(thunnus albacares), fresh or chilled	0302.3200	18
黄鼠狼尾	Weasel tails	4301.9010	15
黄鼠狼尾毛	Weasel tail hair	0502.9012	3
黄铁矿,未焙烧的	Iron pyrites, unroasted	2502.0000	4
黄铜	Brass	7403.2100	146
黄铜矿	Chalcopyrite	2603.0000	146
黄药	Bezoar	0510.0010	14
黄油	Butter	0405.1000	268
黄油刀,镀贵金属的	Butter knives, plated with precious metal	8215.9100	256
黄油刀,非镀贵金属的	Butter knives, other than plated with precious metal	8215.9900	256
黄鱼,冻的	Yellow croaker(pseudosicaena), frozen	0303.7920	18
黄鱼,鲜或冷的	Yellow croaker(pseudosicaena), fresh or chilled	0302.6920	18
黄鱼,盐腌及盐渍的	Yellow croaker(pseudosicaena), salted or in brine	0305.6920	4

H

商品名称	Article Description	税则号列	申报要素
黄原酸酯(或盐)	Xanthates	2930.9020	36
黄樟脑	Safrole	2932.9400	36
磺(酰)胺,其他	Sulphonamides, nes	2935.0090	36
磺胺甲噁唑	Sulfamethoxazole	2935.0030	36
磺胺类药品,混合或未混合的,配定剂量或制成零售包装	Sulfa drugs medicaments, mixed or unmixed, put up in measured doses or in forms or packings for retail sale	3004.9010	368
磺胺类药品,两种或两种以上成分混合而成的,未配定剂量或制成零售包装	Sulfa drugs medicaments, consisting of two or more constituents which have been mixed together, not put up in measured doses or in forms or packings for retail sale	3003.9010	368
磺胺嘧啶	Sulphadiazine	2935.0010	36
磺胺双甲基嘧啶	Sulfadimidine	2935.0020	36
磺苄青霉素	Sulfobenzylpenicillin	2941.1095	
磺内酰胺	Sultams	2934.9910	36
磺内酯	Sultones	2934.9910	36
磺硝酸	Sulphonitric acids	2808.0000	6
簧风琴及类似的游离金属簧片键盘乐器	Harmoniums and similar keyboard instruments with free metal reeds	9205.9010	5
hui			
灰、渣,焚化城市垃圾所产生的	Ash and residues from the incineration of municipal waste	2621.1000	134
灰泥,非耐火的	Mortars, non-refractory	3824.5000	36
灰泥,耐火的	Mortars for refractory	3816.0000	36
辉铋矿	Bismuth glance	2617.9090	146
辉钴矿	Cobaltite	2605.0000	146
辉钼矿,非冶金用途	Molybdenite, non-metallurgical uses	2530.9099	13456
辉钼矿,已焙烧	Molybdenite, roasted	2613.1000	146
辉锑矿	Antimonite	2617.1090	146
辉锑矿	Stibnite	2617.1090	146
辉铜矿	Chalcocite	2603.0000	146
辉银矿	Argentite	2616.1000	146
回收(废碎)纸或纸板,包括未分选的废碎品,其他	Recovered (waste and scrap) paper or paperboard, including unsorted waste and scrap, nes	4707.9000	125
茴芹子	Seeds of anise	0909.1090	
茴香胺、二茴香胺、氨基苯乙醚及其盐	Anisidines, dianisidines, phenetidines, and their salts	2922.2910	36
茴香酒	Anisette	2208.7000	2468
茴香脑	Anethole	2909.3000	36
茴香醛	Anisaldehyde	2912.4900	36
茴香醛	Aubepine	2912.4900	36
茴香油	Essential oils of aniseed	3301.2930	34

H

商品名称	Article Description	税则号列	申报要素
绘图器具,其他	Drawing instruments,nes	9017.2000	
绘图器具的零件、附件	Drawing instruments parts and accessories	9017.9000	3
绘图台及绘图机,不论是否自动	Drafting tables and machines, whether or not automatic	9017.1000	
喙及其粉末	Beaks and powder thereof	0507.9090	14
hun			
馄饨,不论是否烹煮或经其他方法制作	Ravioli,whether or not cooked or otherwise prepared	1902.2000	46
混合调味品	Condiments,mixed	2103.9090	268
混合调味品	Seasonings,mixed	2103.9090	268
混合二甲苯异构体	Mixed xylene isomers	2902.4400	6
混合机,其他	Mixing machines,nes	8479.8200	7
混合机器,泥土、石料、矿石或其他固体矿物质的,其他	Mixing machines, for earth, stone, ores or other mineral substances,nes	8474.3900	
混合氯化稀土	Mixture of rare-earth chlorides	2846.9028	6
混合麦	Maslin	1001.9090	356
混合食品,未烘炒的谷物片与烘炒的谷物片或膨化的谷物混合而成	Prepared foods obtained from mixtures of unroasted cereal flakes and roasted cereal flakes or swelled cereals	1904.2000	48
混合碳酸稀土	Mixture of rare-earth carbonate	2846.9048	6
混合烷基苯,烷基化制得	Alkylbenzenes,mixed,from alkylation process	3817.0000	36
混合烷基萘,烷基化制得	Alkylnaphthalenes,mixed,from alkylation process	3817.0000	36
混合物,按重量计含滑石50%以上的	Mixtures containing more than 50% by weight of talc	3824.9091	36
混合物,按重量计含氧化镁70%以上的	Mixtures containing more than 70% by weight of magnesium oxide	3824.9092	36
混合物,含1,1,1-三氯乙烷(甲基氯仿)的	Mixtures containing 1,1,1-trichloroethane (methyl chloroform)	3824.7600	36
混合物,含氢氯氟烃(HCFCs)的,不论是否含全氟烃(PFCs)或氢氟烃(HFCs),但不含全氯氟烃(CFCs)	Mixtures containing hydrochlorofluorocarbons (HCFCs), whether or not containing perfluorocarbons (PFCs) or hydrofluorocarbons (HFCs), but not containing chlorofluorocarbons (CFCs)	3824.7400	36
混合物,含氢溴氟烃(HBFCs)的	Mixtures containing hydrobromofluorocarbons (HBFCs)	3824.7300	36
混合物,含全氟烃(PFCs)或氢氟烃(HFCs)的,但不含全氯氟烃(CFCs)或氢氯氟烃(HCFCs)的	Mixtures containing perfluorocarbons (PFCs) or hydrofluorocarbons (HFCs), but not containing chlorofluorocarbons (CFCs) or hydrochlorofluorocarbons (HCFCs)	3824.7800	36

H

商品名称	Article Description	税则号列	申报要素
混合物,含全氯氟烃(CFCs)的,不论是否含氢氯氟烃(HCFCs)、全氟烃(PFCs)或氢氟烃(HFCs)	Mixturescontaining chlorofluorocarbons (CFCs), whether or not containing hydrochlorofluorocarbons (HCFCs), perfluorocarbons (PFCs) or hydrofluorocarbons (HFCs)	3824.7100	36
混合物,含四氯化碳的	Mixtures containing carbon tetrachloride	3824.7500	36
混合物,含溴化甲烷(甲基溴)或溴氯甲烷的	Mixtures containing bromomethane (methyl bromide) or bromochloro methane	3824.7700	36
混合物,含溴氯二氟甲烷、溴三氟甲烷或二溴四氟乙烷的	Mixtures containing bromochlorodifluoromethane, bromotrifluoromethane or dibromotetrafluoroethanes	3824.7200	36
混合物,含有甲烷、乙烷或丙烷的卤化衍生物的混合物,其他	Mixtures containing halogenated derivatives of methane, ethane or propane, nes	3824.7900	36
混合物及制品,含多氯联苯(PCBs)、多氯三联苯(PCTs)或多溴联苯(PBBs)的	Mixtures and preparations containing polychlorinated biphenyls (PCBs), polychlorinated terphenyls (PCTs) or polybrominated biphenyls (PBBs)	3824.8200	36
混合物及制品,含环氧乙烷(氧化乙烯)的	Mixtures and preparations containing oxirane (ethylene oxide)	3824.8100	36
混合物及制品,含三(2,3-二溴丙基)磷酸酯的	Mixtures and preparations containing tris (2, 3-dibromopropyl) phosphate	3824.8300	36
混合油脂或制品,其他,食用,但税号15.16的食用油脂及其分离品除外	Mixtures or preparations of fats or oils of this chapter, nes, edible, other than edible fats or oils or their fracitions of heading No. 15.16	1517.9090	24
混合汁	Juice, mixtures, nes	2009.9090	2468
混凝土,非耐火的	Concretes, non-refractory	3824.5000	36
混凝土泵	Concrete pumps	8413.4000	23
混凝土扁平石及类似品	Concrete flagstones and similar articles	6810.1990	56
混凝土管、杆、板、桩等,钢筋加强的	Concrete tubes, pipes, rods, plates, piles and similar articles, reinforced by steel	6810.9110	56
混凝土管、杆、板、桩等,预应力的	Concrete tubes, pipes, rods, plates, piles and similar articles, prestressed	6810.9110	56
混凝土混合机器	Concrete mixers	8474.3100	
混凝土及类似耐火混合制品	Concretes and similar compositions for refractory	3816.0000	36
混凝土搅拌车	Concrete mixer lorries	8705.4000	7
混凝土瓦及类似品	Concrete tiles and similar articles	6810.1990	56
混凝土制品,其他	Concrete articles, nes	6810.9990	56
混凝土砖及块,建筑用	Concrete blocks and bricks, for building	6810.1100	56
huo			
活动陈列品,橱窗装饰用的	Animated displays used for shop window dressing	9618.0000	
活动房屋	Prefabricated buildings	9406.0000	
活动封面(书籍封面除外),纸或纸板制的	Binders (other than book covers), of paper or paperboard	4820.3000	
活动铅笔	Propelling pencils	9608.4000	
活动铅笔	Sliding pencils	9608.4000	

H

商品名称	Article Description	税则号列	申报要素
活动式鞋内底、跟垫及类似品,木制	Removable in-soles, heel cushions and similar articles, of wood	6406.9100	6
活动式鞋内底、跟垫及类似品,其他材料制	Removable in-soles, heel cushions and similar articles, of other materials	6406.9900	6
活塞内燃发动机,点燃往复式或旋转式,船舶发动机,其他	Internal combustion piston engines, spark-ignition reciprocating or rotary, for marine, nes	8407.2900	3
活塞内燃发动机,点燃往复式或旋转式,船舶舷外发动机	Internal combustion piston engines, spark-ignition reciprocating or rotary, for marine, outboard motors	8407.2100	3
活塞内燃发动机,点燃往复式或旋转式,航空器用,输出功率不超过298千瓦	Internal combustion piston engines, spark-ignition reciprocating or rotary, for aircraft, of an output not exceeding 298kW	8407.1010	3
活塞内燃发动机,点燃往复式或旋转式,航空器用,输出功率超过298千瓦	Internal combustion piston engines, spark-ignition reciprocating or rotary, for aircraft, of an output exceeding 298kW	8407.1020	3
活塞内燃发动机,点燃往复式或旋转式,其他	Internal combustion piston engines, spark-ignition reciprocating or rotary, nes	8407.9090	25
活性碳,木质的	Activated carbon, wood based	3802.1010	34
活性碳,其他	Activated carbon, nes	3802.1090	34
活性天然矿产品	Activated natural mineral products	3802.9000	34
活页夹的附件	Fittings for loose-leaf binders	8305.1000	256
活植物(包括其根),其他	Live plants (including their roots), nes	0602.9099	
火柴,但烟火制品除外	Matches, other than pyrotechnic articles	3605.0000	
火花塞,点燃式或压燃式内燃发动机用的	Sparking plugs, for electrical ignition or starting equipment	8511.1000	
火鸡,改良种用,重量不超过185克	Turkeys, pure-bred breeding, weighing not more than 185g	0105.1210	48
火鸡,改良种用,重量超过185克	Turkeys, pure-bred breeding, weighing more than 185g	0105.9910	48
火鸡,改良种用除外,重量不超过185克	Turkeys, ex. pure-bred breeding, weighing not more than 185g	0105.1290	48
火鸡,改良种用除外,重量超过185克	Turkeys, ex. pure-bred breeding, weighing more than 185g	0105.9994	48
火鸡,制作或保藏的	Turkeys, prepared or preserved	1602.3100	48
火鸡块,冻的	Cuts of turkeys, frozen	0207.2700	1
火鸡块,鲜或冷的	Cuts of turkeys, fresh or chilled	0207.2600	1
火箭发射装置	Rocket launchers	9301.2000	
火龙果,鲜的	Dragon fruit, fresh	0810.9080	1
火帽或雷管	Percussion or detonating caps	3603.0000	
火泥	Chamotte	2508.7000	134
火炮武器,其他	Artillery weapons, nes	9301.1900	7
火炮武器,自推进的,其他	Artillery weapons, self-propelled, nes	9301.1100	7
火炮武器用零件、附件	Artillery weapons parts and accessories	9305.9100	3

商品名称	Article Description	税则号列	申报要素
火山灰	Pozzolana earth	2530.9099	13456
火山土	Trass earth	2530.9099	13456
火焰喷射器	Flame-throwers	9301.2000	
货车,敞篷的,厢壁固定且高度超过60厘米,铁道及电车道用的,非机动	Goods vans and wagons, open, with non-removable sides of a height exceeding 60cm, for railway or tramway, not self-propelled	8606.9200	37
货车,带篷及封闭的,铁道及电车道用的,非机动	Goods vans and wagons, covered and closed, for railway or tramway, not self-propelled	8606.9100	37
货车,铁道及电车道用的非机动,其他	Goods vans and wagons, for railway or tramway, not self-propelled, nes	8606.9900	37
货车倾卸装置	Wagon tippers	8428.9010	
货柜挂车及半挂车	Van trailers and semi-trailers	8716.3910	
货运架空索道	Cargo aerial cableways	8428.6010	
霍霍巴油及其分离品	Jojoba oil and its fractions	1515.9010	

J

商品名称	Article Description	税则号列	申报要素
ji			
机铲装载机	Shovel loaders	8429.5900	57
机场用旅客登机桥	Passenger boarding bridge used at airport	8479.8991	7
机车发动机,压燃式	Locomotive engines, compression-ignition	8408.9010	2
机车煤水车	Locomot-ive tenders	8602.9000	37
机车用零件	Locomotives parts	8607.9100	3
机床专用附件	Machine-tools special attachments	8466.3000	3
机动车辆,货运,车辆总重量不超过5吨,装有压燃式活塞内燃发动机	Motor vehicles for the transport of goods, with compression-ignition internal combustion piston engine, g. v. w. not exceeding 5 tons	8704.2100	58
机动车辆,货运,车辆总重量不超过5吨,装有点燃式活塞内燃发动机的其他货车	Motor vehicles for the transport of goods, with spark-ignition internal combustion piston engine, g. v. w. not exceeding 5 tons	8704.3100	58
机动车辆,货运,车辆总重量超过20吨,装有压燃式活塞内燃发动机	Motor vehicles for the transport of goods, with compression-ignition internal combustion piston engine, g. v. w. Exceeding 20 tons	8704.2300	58
机动车辆,货运,车辆总重量超过5吨,但小于14吨,装有压燃式活塞内燃发动机	Motor vehicles for the transport of goods, with compression-ignition internal combustion piston engine, g. v. w. exceeding 5 tons but not exceeding 14 tons	8704.2230	58
机动车辆,货运,车辆总重量超过5吨,但不超过8吨,装有点燃式活塞内燃发动机的其他货车	Motor vehicles for the transport of goods, with spark-ignition internal combustion piston engine, g. v. w. exceeding 5 tons, but not exceeding 8 tons.	8704.3230	58
机动车辆,货运,车辆总重量超过8吨,装有点燃式活塞内燃发动机的其他货车	Motor vehicles for the transport of goods, with spark-ignition internal combustion piston engine, g. v. w. exceeding 8 tons	8704.3240	58
机动车辆,货运,车辆总重量在14吨及以上,但不超过20吨,装有压燃式活塞内燃发动机	Motor vehicles for the transport of goods, with compression-ignition internal combustion piston engine, g. v. w. of 14 tons or more but not exceeding 20 tons	8704.2240	58
机动车辆,货运,装有点燃式活塞内燃发动机的其他货车,其他	Motor vehicles for the transport of goods, with spark-ignition internal combustion piston engine, nes	8704.9000	58
机动车辆,客运,10座及以上,但不超过19座,其他	Motor vehicles for the transport of persons, with 10 seats or more, but not exceeding 19 seats, nes	8702.9030	58
机动车辆,客运,10座及以上,但不超过19座,装有压燃式活塞内燃发动机的	Motor vehicles for the transport of persons, with 10 seats or more, but not exceeding 19 seats, with compression-ignition internal combustion piston engine	8702.1093	58

商品名称	Article Description	税则号列	申报要素
机动车辆,客运,20座及以上,但不超过29座,其他	Motor vehicles for the transport of persons, with 20 seats or more, but not exceeding 29 seats, nes	8702. 9020	58
机动车辆,客运,20座及以上,但不超过29座,装有压燃式活塞内燃发动机的	Motor vehicles for the transport of persons, with 20 seats or more, but not exceeding 29 seats, with compression-ignition internal combustion piston engine	8702. 1092	58
机动车辆,客运,30座及以上(大型客车),装有压燃式活塞内燃发动机的	Motor vehicles for the transport of persons, with 30 seats or more, with compression-ignition internal combustion piston engine	8702. 1091	58
机动车辆,客运,30座及以上,其他	Motor vehicles for the transport of persons, with 30 seats or more, nes	8702. 9010	58
机动车辆,客运,气缸容量(排气量)不超过1000毫升,装有点燃往复式活塞内燃发动机的,其他	Motor cars, of a cylinder capacity not exceeding 1000cc, with spark-ignition internal combustion reciprocating piston engine, for the transport of persons, nes	8703. 2190	58
机动车辆,客运,气缸容量(排气量)不超过1000毫升,装有压燃式活塞内燃发动机的,其他	Motor cars, of a cylinder capacity not exceeding 1000cc, with compression-ignition internal combustion piston engine, for the transport of persons, nes	8703. 3119	58
机动车辆,客运,气缸容量(排气量)超过1000毫升,但不超过1500毫升,装有点燃往复式活塞内燃发动机的,其他	Motor cars, of a cylinder capacity exceeding 1000cc but not exceeding 1500cc, with spark-ignition internal combustion reciprocating piston, for the transport of persons, nes	8703. 2290	58
机动车辆,客运,气缸容量(排气量)超过1000毫升,但不超过1500毫升,装有压燃式活塞内燃发动机的,其他	Motor cars, of a cylinder capacity exceeding 1500cc but not exceeding 2500cc, with compression-ignition internal combustion piston engine, for the transport of persons, nes	8703. 3129	58
机动车辆,客运,气缸容量(排气量)超过1500毫升,但不超过2000毫升,装有点燃往复式活塞内燃发动机的,其他	Motor cars, of a cylinder capacity exceeding 1500cc but not exceeding 2000cc, with spark-ignition internal combustion reciprocating piston, for the transport of persons, nes	8703. 2349	58
机动车辆,客运,气缸容量(排气量)超过1500毫升,但不超过2000毫升,装有压燃式活塞内燃发动机的,其他	Motor cars, of a cylinder capacity exceeding 1500cc but not exceeding 2000cc, with compression-ignition internal combustion piston engine, for the transport of persons, nes	8703. 3219	58
机动车辆,客运,气缸容量(排气量)超过2000毫升,但不超过2500毫升,装有点燃往复式活塞内燃发动机的,其他	Motor cars, of a cylinder capacity exceeding 2000cc but not exceeding 2500cc, with spark-ignition internal combustion reciprocating piston, for the transport of persons, nes	8703. 2359	58
机动车辆,客运,气缸容量(排气量)超过2000毫升,但不超过2500毫升,装有压燃式活塞内燃发动机的,其他	Motor cars, of a cylinder capacity exceeding 2000cc but not exceeding 2500cc, with compression-ignition internal combustion piston engine, for the transport of persons, nes	8703. 3229	58

J

商品名称	Article Description	税则号列	申报要素
机动车辆,客运,气缸容量(排气量)超过2500毫升,但不超过3000毫升,装有点燃往复式活塞内燃发动机的,其他	Motor cars, of a cylinder capacity exceeding 2500cc but not exceeding 3000cc, with spark-ignition internal combustion reciprocating piston, for the transport of persons, nes	8703. 2369	58
机动车辆,客运,气缸容量(排气量)超过2500毫升,但不超过3000毫升,装有压燃式活塞内燃发动机的,其他	Motor cars, of a cylinder capacity exceeding 2500cc, but not exceeding 3000cc, with compression-ignition internal combustion piston engine, for the transport of persons, nes	8703. 3319	58
机动车辆,客运,气缸容量(排气量)超过3000毫升,但不超过4000毫升,装有点燃往复式活塞内燃发动机的,其他	Motor cars, of a cylinder capacity exceeding 3000cc, but not exceeding 4000cc, with spark-ignition internal combustion reciprocating piston, for the transport of persons, nes	8703. 2419	58
机动车辆,客运,气缸容量(排气量)超过3000毫升,但不超过4000毫升,装有压燃式活塞内燃发动机的,其他	Motor cars, of a cylinder capacity exceeding 3000cc, but not exceeding 4000cc, with compression-ignition internal combustion piston engine, for the transport of persons, nes	8703. 3329	58
机动车辆,客运,气缸容量(排气量)超过4000毫升,装有点燃往复式活塞内燃发动机的,其他	Motor cars, of a cylinder capacity exceeding 3000cc, but not exceeding 4000cc, with spark-ignition internal combustion reciprocating piston, for the transport of persons, nes	8703. 2429	58
机动车辆,客运,气缸容量(排气量)超过4000毫升,装有压燃式活塞内燃发动机的,其他	Motor cars, of a cylinder capacity exceeding 4000cc, with compression-ignition internal combustion piston engine, for the transport of persons, nes	8703. 3369	58
机动车辆,特殊用途的,其他	Motor vehicles, special purpose, nes	8705. 9090	7
机动车辆,主要用于载人的,其他	Motor cars, principally designed for the transport of persons, nes	8703. 9000	58
机动车辆用散热器零件、附件,其他	Radiators parts and accessories, nes	8708. 9190	3
机动车辆用零件、附件,其他	Motor vehicles parts and accessories, nes	8708. 9999	3
机动车辆用视觉信号装置	Motor vehicles visual signalling equipment	8512. 2090	7
机动车辆用照明装置	Motor vehicles lighting equipment	8512. 2010	57
机坪客车,装有压燃式活塞内燃发动机的	Buses for transport passengers at airport, with compression-ignition internal combustion piston engine	8702. 1020	58
机器、器具、仪器或装置用的零件、附件,其他	Machines, appliances, instruments or apparatus parts and accessories, nes	9033. 0000	3
机器及机械器具,其他	Machines and mechanical appliances, nes	8479. 8999	7
机器及仪器用零件,海绵橡胶制	Articles of a kind used in machines or instruments, of cellular rubber	4016. 1010	236
机器及仪器用零件,硫化橡胶(硬质橡胶除外)的,其他	Articles of a kind used in machines or instruments of vulcanized rubber other than hard rubber, nes	4016. 9910	236
机器及仪器用零件,海绵橡胶制	Articles of a kind used in machines or instruments, of cellular rubber, nes	4016. 1090	236

商品名称	Article Description	税则号列	申报要素
机器及仪器用零件,塑料的	Plastic articles, of a kind for used in machines or instruments, of plastics	3926.9010	236
机器零件,不具有电气接插件、绝缘体、线圈、触点或其他电气器材特征的,其他	Machinery parts, not containing electrical connectors, insulators, coils, contacts or other electrical features, nes	8487.9000	3
机器设备,加工热饮料或烹调、加热食品用	Machinery, plant and equipment, for making hot drinks of for cooking or heating food	8419.8100	57
机器设备,利用温度变化处理,其他	Machinery, with a process involving a change of temperature, nes	8419.8990	57
机器设备零件,利用温度变化处理,其他	Machinery parts, with a process involving a change of temperature, nes	8419.9090	3
机械,农业、园艺及林业用,其他	Machinery for agricultural, horticultural or forestry use, nes	8432.8090	
机械,上部结构可旋转360度的,其他	Machinery with a 360° revolving superstructure, nes	8429.5290	57
机械铲	Mechanical shovels	8429.5900	57
机械加煤机	Mechanical stokers	8416.3000	
机械加煤机出灰器	Mechanical stokers ash dischargers and similar appliances	8416.3000	
机械加煤机零件	Mechanical stokers parts	8416.9000	
机械加煤机炉篦	Mechanical stokers grates	8416.3000	
机械浆,从回收(废碎)纸或纸板提取的	Mechanical pulp, derived from recovered (waste and scrap) paper or paperboard	4706.9100	46
机械疗法器具	Mechano-therapy appliances	9019.1090	7
机械零件,农业、园艺及林业用	Machinery parts, for agricultural, horticultural or forestry use	8432.9000	
机械零件平衡试验机	Machines for balancing mechanical parts	9031.1000	
机械密封件	Mechanical seals	8484.2000	56
机械鸣禽	Mechanical singing birds	9208.9000	5
机械木浆	Mechanical wood pulp	4701.0000	
机械性能试验机器及器具,非金属材料试验用	Mechanical properties testing machines and appliances	9024.8000	7
机械性能试验机器及器具,金属材料试验用,其他	Mechanical properties testing machines and appliances, for testing metals, nes	9024.1090	7
机械性能试验机器及器具的零件、附件	Mechanical properties testing machines and appliances parts and accessories	9024.9000	7
机械压力机,加工金属或硬质合金用	Mechanical presses, for working metal or metal carbides	8462.9910	7
机芯套装件,表的	Movement sets, of watches	9110.1100	1
机芯套装件,钟的	Movement sets, of clock	9110.9090	1
机油冷却器,机动车辆用	Oil coolers, of motor vehicles	8708.9120	3
机织品,不锈钢丝制,其他	Woven cloth, of stainless steel wire, nes	7314.1400	36
机织品,钢铁丝制,其他	Woven cloth, of iron or steel wire, nes	7314.1900	36

商品名称	Article Description	税则号列	申报要素
机织物,玻璃纤维制,其他	Woven fabrics, of glass fibres, nes	7019.5900	468
机织物,第十一类注释九所列的	Fabrics specified in Note 9 to section XI	5407.3000	2468
机织物,宽度不超过 30 厘米的,玻璃纤维制	Woven fabrics of a width not exceeding 30cm, of glass fibres	7019.5100	468
机织物,宽度超过 30 厘米的长丝平纹织物,每平方米重量不超过 250 克,单根纱线细度不超过 136 特克斯,玻璃纤维制	Woven fabrics of a width exceeding 30cm, plain weave, weighing less than $250g/m^2$, of filaments measuring per single yarn not more than 136 tex, of glass fibres	7019.5200	468
肌氨酸	Sarcosine	2922.4910	36
肌醇	Inositol	2906.1320	36
鸡,改良种用,重量不超过 185 克	Fowls of the species gallus domesticus, pure-bred breeding, weighing not more than 185g	0105.1110	48
鸡,改良种用,重量超过 185 克	Fowls of the species gallus domesticus, pure-bred breeding, weighing more than 185g	0105.9410	48
鸡,改良种用除外,重量不超过 185 克	Fowls of the species gallus domesticus, ex. pure-bred breeding, weighing not more than 185g	0105.1190	48
鸡,改良种用除外,重量超过 185 克	Fowls of the species gallus domesticus, ex. pure-bred breeding, weighing more than 185g	0105.9490	48
鸡,整只,冻的	Fowls of the species gallus domesticus, not cut in pieces, frozen	0207.1200	1
鸡,整只,鲜或冷的	Fowls of the species gallus domesticus, not cut in pieces, fresh or chilled	0207.1100	1
鸡蛋,带壳的,鲜的	Eggs, of hens, in shell, fresh	0407.0021	1
鸡块,带骨的,冻的	Cut of fowls of the species gallus domesticus, with bone, frozen	0207.1411	1
鸡块,带骨的,鲜或冷的	Cut of fowls of the species gallus domesticus, with bone, fresh or chilled	0207.1311	1
鸡块,其他,冻的	Cut of fowls of the species gallus domesticus, nes, frozen	0207.1419	1
鸡块,其他,鲜或冷的	Cut of fowls of the species gallus domesticus, nes, fresh or chilled	0207.1319	1
鸡腿肉,制作或保藏的,其他	Chicken leg meat, prepared or preserved, nes	1602.3292	48
鸡胸肉,制作或保藏的,其他	Chicken breast filets, prepared or preserved, nes	1602.3291	48
鸡翼(不包括翼尖),冻的	Midjoint wing of fowls of the species gallus domesticus, frozen	0207.1421	1
鸡翼(不包括翼尖),鲜或冷的	Midjoint wing of fowls of the species gallus domesticus, fresh or chilled	0207.1321	1
鸡胗,冷、冻的	Gizzard, of chicken, cold, frozen	0504.0021	14
鸡爪,冻的	Claw of fowls of the species gallus domesticus, frozen	0207.1422	1
基站,移动通信用	Base stations for mobile communication	8517.6110	
基站,有线或无线网络的,其他	Base stations, for wired or wireless network, nes	8517.6190	
激光唱机,未装有声音录制装置,使用光学媒体的	Compact disc players, not incorporating a sound recording device, using optical media	8519.8121	5

J

商品名称	Article Description	税则号列	申报要素
激光打印机,专用于自动数据处理设备的	Laser printers, of a kind solely used for automatic data processing machine	8443.3212	57
激光器,激光二极管除外	Lasers, other than laser diodes	9013.2000	
激光器的零件、附件,激光二极管除外	Lasers parts and accessories, other than laser diodes	9013.9010	3
激光视盘机,其他	Laser video compact disk player, nes	8521.9019	5
激光视盘机的机芯	Movements for laser video compact disk player, of video recording or reproducing apparatus	8522.9031	3
激光印刷机,数字式	Laser printing machines, digital	8443.3222	57
激光照排片,未曝光的	Laser phototypesetting film, unexposed	3701.3021	12368
激光照排片,未曝光的,无齿孔的,宽度超过105毫米,但不超过610毫米	Laser phototypesetting film, unexposed, without perforations, of a width exceeding 105mm but not exceeding 610mm	3702.4421	12368
激光照排片,未曝光的,无齿孔的,宽度超过610毫米,长度不超过200米	Laser phototypesetting film, unexposed, without perforations, of a width exceeding 610mm and of a length not exceeding 200 m	3702.4321	12368
激光照相排版设备	Laser photo typesetting equipments	9006.5910	7
激素药品,其他,混合或未混合的,配定剂量或制成零售包装	Hormones medicaments, nes, mixed or unmixed, put up in measured doses or in forms or packings for retail sale	3004.3900	368
激素药品,其他,两种或两种以上成分混合而成的,未配定剂量或制成零售包装	Hormones medicaments, nes, consisting of two or more constituents which have been mixed together, not put up in measured doses or in forms or packings for retail sale	3003.3900	368
吉他	Guitars	9202.9000	5
吉他的零件、附件	Guitars parts and accessories	9209.9200	3
即热式电热水器	Electric instantaneous waterheaters	8516.1020	7
即食或快熟面条	Instant noodle	1902.3030	2468
急救药箱、药包	First-aid boxes and kits	3006.5000	36
棘皮动物壳	Echinoderms	0508.0090	14
集成电路,其他	Electronic integrated circuits, nes	8542.3900	37
集成电路零件	Electronic integrated circuits parts	8542.9000	37
集线器,有线数字通信设备	Hubs, telecommunication apparatus for digital line system	8517.6235	7
集中供暖用的热水锅炉,家用型	Central heating boilers, household type	8403.1010	27
集中供暖用的热水锅炉,其他	Central heating boilers, nes	8403.1090	27
集中供暖用的热水锅炉辅助设备	Central heating boilers auxiliary plant	8404.1020	3
集中供暖用的热水锅炉辅助设备的零件	Central heating boilers auxiliary plant parts	8404.9010	3
集中供暖用的热水锅炉零件	Central heating boilers parts	8403.9000	27
集装箱,20英尺的,保温式	Containers, of 20 feet, insulated	8609.0011	58
集装箱,20英尺的,罐式	Containers, of 20 feet, tank type	8609.0012	58
集装箱,20英尺的,其他	Containers, of 20 feet, nes	8609.0019	58

J

商品名称	Article Description	税则号列	申报要素
集装箱,40 英尺的,保温式	Containers, of 40 feet, insulated	8609. 0021	58
集装箱,40 英尺的,罐式	Containers, of 40 feet, tank type	8609. 0022	58
集装箱,40 英尺的,其他	Containers, of 40 feet, nes	8609. 0029	58
集装箱,45、48、53 英尺的	Containers, of 45, 48, 53 feet	8609. 0030	58
集装箱,其他	Containers, nes	8609. 0090	58
集装箱叉车,自推进的	Fork-lift trucks, for lifting or handing containers, self-propelled	8427. 2010	7
集装箱船,机动的,可载标准集装箱在 6000 箱及以下	Container vessels, motor powered, capable loading standard containers with 6000 or less	8901. 9021	8
集装箱船,机动的,可载标准集装箱在 6000 箱以上	Container vessels, motor powered, capable loading standard containers more than 6000	8901. 9022	8
集装箱装卸桥	Container loading and unloading bridges	8426. 1942	7
己二酸及其盐和酯	Adipic acid, its salts and esters	2917. 1200	36
己二酸己二胺盐	Nylon-66 salt	2921. 2210	36
挤出机,加工橡胶或塑料及其产品用,其他	Extruders, for working rubber or plastics or for the manufacture of products from these materials, nes	8477. 2090	7
挤奶机	Milking machines	8434. 1000	
挤奶机零件	Milking machines parts	8434. 9000	3
挤压机,化学纺织纤维的	Extruding machinery for man-made textile materials	8444. 0090	
挤压机,纱线、织物及纺织制品用	Presses machines, for textile yarns, fabrics or made up textile articles	8451. 3000	
挤压机的辅助机器,化学纺织纤维的	Extruding machinery auxiliary, for man-made textile materials	8448. 1900	3
挤压机零件,纱线、织物及纺织制品用	Presses machines parts, for textile yarns, fabrics or made up textile articles	8451. 9000	
计价秤,最大称量不超过 30 千克	Account balances, having a maximum weighing capacity not exceeding 30kg	8423. 8110	
计算机器,其他	Calculating machines, nes	8470. 3000	
计算机直接制版设备	CTP plates preparing machines	8442. 3021	
计算器,电子式,不需外接电源的	Calculators, electronic, capable of operation without an external source of electric power	8470. 1000	
计算器,电子式,其他	Calculating machines, electronic, nes	8470. 2900	
计算器,电子式,装有打印装置的	Calculating machines, electronic, incorporating a printing device	8470. 2100	
计算器具的零件、附件,其他	Calculating machines parts and accessories, nes	8473. 2900	3
记号笔	Markers	9608. 2000	
记事本,纸或纸板制的	Memorandum pads, of paper or paperboard	4820. 1000	
季铵碱,无论是否已有化学定义	Quaternary ammonium hydroxides, whether or not chemically defined	2923. 9000	36
季铵盐,无论是否已有化学定义	Quaternary ammonium salts, whether or not chemically defined	2923. 9000	36
季戊四醇	Pentaerythritol	2905. 4200	36

商品名称	Article Description	税则号列	申报要素
继电器,用于电压不超过1000伏的线路,其他	Relays, for a voltage not exceeding 1000V, nes	8536.4900	8
继电器,用于电压不超过60伏的线路	Relays, for a voltage not exceeding 60V	8536.4100	8
jia			
加工船,非机动船舶,加工保藏鱼类产品的	Factory ships, not-motorized vessels, for processing or preserving fishery products	8902.0090	5
加工船,机动船舶,加工保藏鱼类产品的	Factory ships, motor vessels, for processing or preserving fishery products	8902.0010	5
加工机床,玻璃冷加工用,其他	Machines for cold-working glass or glassware, nes	8464.9019	7
加工机床,加工木材、软木、骨、硬质橡胶、硬质塑料或类似硬质材料的,不需更换工具即可进行不同机械加工的机器	Machine-tools for working wood, cork, bone, hard rubber, hard plastics or similar hard materials, which can carry out different types of machining operations without tool change between such operations	8465.1000	7
加工机床,加工木材、软木、骨、硬质橡胶、硬质塑料或类似硬质材料的,其他	Achine-tools for working wood, cork, bone, hard rubber, hard plastics or similar hard materials, nes	8465.9900	7
加工机床,加工石料、陶瓷、混凝土、石棉水泥或类似矿物材料的,其他	Machine-tools for working stone, ceramics, concrete, asbestos-cement or like mineral materials, nes	8464.9090	7
加工机床,金属或金属陶瓷用,非切削的,其他	Machine-tools for working metal or cermets, without removing material, nes	8463.9000	7
加工机床,其他	Machine-tools, nes	8456.9090	7
加工机床,用超声波处理的	Machine-tools, operated by ultrasonic processes	8456.2000	7
加工机床,用放电处理的,其他	Machine-tools, operated by electro-discharge processes, nes	8456.3090	7
加工机床,用放电处理的,数控的	Machine-tools, operated by electro-discharge processes, numerically controlled	8456.3010	7
加工机床,用激光、其他光或光子束处理的	Machine-tools, operated by laser or other light or photon beam processes	8456.1000	7
加工机床的零件及附件,非切削加工金属或其他材料的	Machine-tools parts and accessories, without removing metal or other materials	8466.9400	3
加工机床的零件及附件,加工木材、软木、骨、硬质橡胶、硬质塑料或类似硬质材料的	Machine-tools parts and accessories, for working wood, cork, bone, hard rubber, hard plastics or similar hard materials	8466.9200	3
加工机床的零件及附件,加工石料、陶瓷、混凝土、石棉水泥或类似矿物材料的	Machine-tools parts and accessories, for working stone, ceramics, concrete, asbestos-cement or like mineral materials	8466.9100	3
加工机床的零件及附件,切削加工金属或其他材料的	Machine-tools parts and accessories, for removing metal or other materials	8466.9300	3
加工机器,谷物、干豆用,农业用机器除外	Working machinery of cereals or dried leguminous vegetables, other than farm-type machinery	8437.8000	3

商品名称	Article Description	税则号列	申报要素
加工机器零件,谷物、干豆用,农业用机器除外	Working machinery parts, of cereals or dried leguminous vegetables, other than farm-type machinery	8437. 9000	3
加工中心,加工金属的,其他	Machining centres, for working metal, nes	8457. 1090	7
加工中心,立式,加工金属的	Machining centres, vertical, for working metal	8457. 1010	7
加工中心,龙门式,加工金属的	Machining centres, plano, for working metal	8457. 1030	7
加工中心,卧式,加工金属的	Machining centres, horizontal, for working metal	8457. 1020	7
加勒比甜瓜,鲜的	Calia melons, fresh	0807. 1920	1
加仑子,黑、白或红的,冷冻的	Currants, black, white or red, frozen	0811. 2000	1
加仑子,黑、白或红的,鲜的	Currants, black, white or red, fresh	0810. 9020	1
加那利草子	Canary seed	1008. 3000	3
加捻机	Textile twisting machines	8445. 3000	7
加捻机的辅助机器	Textile twisting machines auxiliary	8448. 1900	3
加氢反应器,利用温度变化处理	Hydroformer vessels, with a process involving a change of temperature	8419. 8910	57
加热电阻器	Electric heating resistors	8516. 8000	3
加热电阻器用零件	Electric heating resistors parts	8516. 9010	3
夹板,钟、表的	Plates, of clock or watch	9114. 4000	6
夹斗,推土机或起重机零件	Grips, parts of bulldozer or cranes	8431. 4100	3
夹钳及类似品	Clamps and the like	8205. 7000	256
家具,办公室用,金属的	Furniture of a kind used in offices, of metal	9403. 1000	6
家具,办公室用,木的	Furniture of a kind used in offices, wooden	9403. 3000	6
家具,厨房用,木的	Furniture of a kind used in the kitchen, wooden	9403. 4000	6
家具,红木制,其他	Furniture of rose wood, nes	9403. 6010	6
家具,金属的,其他	Furniture, of metal, nes	9403. 2000	6
家具,柳条及类似材料制的	Furniture of osier or similar materials	9403. 8910	6
家具,木的,其他	Furniture of wood, nes	9403. 6099	6
家具,漆木的,其他	Furniture of lacquered wood, nes	9403. 6091	6
家具,其他	Furniture, nes	9403. 8990	6
家具,石制的	Furniture of stone	9403. 8920	6
家具,塑料的	Furniture of plastics	9403. 7000	6
家具,卧室用,红木制	Furniture of a kind used in the bedroom, of rose wood	9403. 5010	6
家具,卧室用,漆木的	Furniture of a kind used in the bedroom, of lacquered wood	9403. 5091	6
家具,卧室用,木制,其他	Furniture of a kind used in the bedroom, of wood, nes	9403. 5099	6
家具,竹制或藤制的	Furniture of bamboo or rattan	9403. 8100	6
家具或类似品的附件,塑料的	Fittings for furniture, or the like, of plastics	3926. 3000	236
家具零件	Furniture parts	9403. 9000	3
家禽,其他,重量不超过 185 克	Poultry Live, nes, weighing not more than 185g	0105. 1990	48
家禽孵卵器及育雏器	Poultry incubators and brooders	8436. 2100	
家禽孵卵器及育雏器的零件	Poultry incubators and brooders parts	8436. 9100	

商品名称	Article Description	税则号列	申报要素
家禽加工机器	Poultry preparation machinery	8438.5000	
家禽加工机器的零件	Poultry preparation machinery parts	8438.9000	3
家禽剪及类似的单手操作剪刀	Poultry shears and similar one-handed pruners and shears	8201.5000	256
家禽饲养用的机器	Poultry-keeping machinery	8436.2900	
家禽饲养用机器的零件	Poultry-keeping machinery parts	8436.9100	
家禽脂肪,但税号02.09及15.03的货品除外	Poultry fat, other than that of heading No. 02.09 or 15.03	1501.0000	
家禽脂肪,未炼制或用其他方法提取的不带瘦肉的,鲜、冷、冻、干、熏、盐腌或盐渍的	Poultry fat, not rendered or otherwise extracted, fresh, chilled, frozen, salted, in brine, dried or smoked	0209.0000	14
家庭、卫生或医院用品,纸浆、纸、纤维素絮纸或纤维素纤维网纸制的,其他	Articles of household, sanitary or hospital, of paper pulp, paper, cellulose wadding or webs of cellulose fibres, nes	4818.9000	568
家庭用具,塑料的	Household articles, of plastics	3924.9000	23
家用电动器具,其他	Electro-mechanical domestic appliances, nes	8509.8090	
家用电动器具零件	Electro-mechanical domestic appliances parts	8509.9000	3
家用电热器具用零件	Electro-thermic appliances parts, of a kind used for domestic purposes	8516.9090	3
家用或盥洗用器,瓷制,其他	Household articles and toilet articles, of porcelain, nes	6911.9000	268
家用或盥洗用器,陶制,其他	Household articles and toilet articles, of pottery, nes	6912.0090	268
家用器具,非电热的家用,其他,包括使用固体燃料的	Domestic appliances, of iron or steel, non-electric, nes, including appliances for solid fuel	7321.8900	7
家用器具,非电热的家用,使用气体燃料或可使用气体燃料及其他燃料的	Domestic appliances, of iron or steel, non-electric, for gas fuel or for both gas and other fuels	7321.8100	7
家用器具,非电热的家用,使用液体燃料的	Domestic appliances, of iron or steel, non-electric, for liquid fuel	7321.8200	7
家用器具零件,非电热的家用	Domestic appliances parts, of iron or steel, non-electric	7321.9000	7
家用自动面包机	Household automated bread makers	8516.7210	7
镓,未锻轧	Gallium, unwrought	8112.9290	16
镓粉末	Gallium powders	8112.9290	16
镓制品	Gallium articles	8112.9990	16
甲胺及其盐	Methylamine and their salts	2921.1100	36
甲胺磷(ISO)	Methamidophos (ISO)	2930.5000	36
甲板停机装置或类似装置及其零件	Deck-arrestor or similar gear and parts thereof	8805.1000	3
甲苯	Toluene	2902.3000	6
甲苯胺及其衍生物以及它们的盐	Toluidines and their derivatives; salts thereof	2921.4300	36
甲苯巴比妥(INN)以及盐	Methylphenobarbital(INN); salts thereof	2933.5300	36
甲苯二异氰酸酯TDI	Toluene diisocyanate	2929.1010	36
甲苯肼	Tolylhydrazine	2928.0000	36

J

商品名称	Article Description	税则号列	申报要素
甲丙氨酯(INN)	Meprobamate(INN)	2924.1100	36
甲醇	Methanol(methyl alcohol)	2905.1100	36
甲酚,其他	Cresol,nes	2907.1219	36
甲酚的盐	Cresol salts	2907.1290	36
甲基丙烯酸及其盐	Methacrylie acid and its salts	2916.1300	36
甲基丙烯酸酯	Methacrylie acid esters	2916.1400	36
甲基对硫磷(ISO)	Parathion-methyl(ISO)(methyl-parathion)	2920.1100	36
甲基二乙醇胺	Methyldiethanolamine	2922.1940	36
甲基环已醇	Methylcyclohexanols	2906.1200	36
甲基环已酮	Methylcyclohexanone	2914.2200	36
甲基环氧乙烷	Methyloxirane	2910.2000	36
甲基香豆素	Methylcoumarins	2932.2100	36
甲基乙基(甲) 酮	Methyl ethyl ketone	2914.1200	36
甲基异丁基(甲)酮	Isobutylmethyl ketone	2914.1300	36
甲基芷香酮	Methylionones	2914.2300	36
甲及其粉末	Nails and powder thereof	0507.9090	14
甲壳动物,其他,冻的	Crustaceans,nes,frozen	0306.1990	1
甲壳动物,其他,未冻的	Crustaceans,nes,not frozen	0306.2990	14
甲壳动物,其他,制作或保藏的	Crustaceans,nes,prepared or preserved	1605.4090	48
甲壳动物、软体动物、其他水生无脊椎动物的产品	Products of fish or crustaceans, molluscs or other aquatic invertebrates,nes	0511.9190	34
甲壳动物壳	Shells of crustaceans	0508.0090	14
甲喹酮 (INN)以及盐	Methaqualone (INN);salts thereof	2933.5500	36
甲硫氨酸	Methionine	2930.4000	36
甲氯喹酮(INN)以及盐	Mecloqualone (INN);salts thereof	2933.5500	36
甲醛	Formaldehyde	2912.1100	36
甲醛	Methanal	2912.1100	36
甲酸	Formic acid	2915.1100	36
甲酸盐	Salts of formic acid	2915.1200	36
甲酸酯	Esters of formic acid	2915.1300	36
甲乙哌酮(INN)	Methyprylon(INN)	2933.7200	36
钾的磷酸盐	Potassium phosphates	2835.2400	
钾碱液	Potash lye	2815.2000	136
钾铝矾	Potassium aluminum sulfate	2833.3010	
钾盐	Sylvite	3104.9010	68
驾驶转向架及轴,铁道及电车道机车或其他车辆的	Driving bogies and bissel-bogies, of railway or tramway locomotives or rolling-stock	8607.1100	3
假辫子及类似品,动物毛或纺织材料制的,其他	Switches and the like, of animal hair or textile materials,nes	6704.9000	4
假辫子及类似品,合成纤维纺织材料制,其他	Switches and the like,of synthetic textile materials, nes	6704.1900	4

J

商品名称	Article Description	税则号列	申报要素
假辫子及类似品,人发制	Switches and the like, of human hair	6704.2000	4
假发及类似品,动物毛或纺织材料制的,其他	Wigs and the like, of animal hair or textile materials, nes	6704.9000	4
假发及类似品,合成纤维纺织材料制,其他	Wigs and the like, of synthetic textile materials, nes	6704.1900	4
假发及类似品,人发制	Wigs and the like, of human hair	6704.2000	4
假胡须及类似品,合成纤维纺织材料制,其他	False beards and the like, of synthetic textile materials, nes	6704.1900	4
假胡须及类似品,人发制	False beards and the like, of human hair	6704.2000	4
假胡须类似品,动物毛或纺织材料制的,其他	False beards and the like, of animal hair or textile materials, nes	6704.9000	4
假睫毛及类似品,动物毛或纺织材料制的,其他	False eyelashes and the like, of animal hair or textile materials, nes	6704.9000	4
假睫毛及类似品,人发制	False eyelashes and the like, of human hair	6704.2000	4
假麻黄碱及其盐	Pseudoephedrine(INN) and its salts	2939.4200	34
假眉毛及类似品,动物毛或纺织材料制的,其他	False eyebrows and the like, of animal hair or textile materials, nes	6704.9000	4
假眉毛及类似品,合成纤维纺织材料制,其他	False eyebrows and the like, of synthetic textile materials, nes	6704.1900	4
假眉毛及类似品,人发制	False eyebrows and the like, of human hair	6704.2000	4
假牙	Artificial teeth	9021.2100	
假牙模膏及粉	Denture fixative pastes and powders	3306.9000	23
jian			
尖吻鲈鱼,冻的	Sea bass (Dicentrarchus labrax, Dicentrarchus punctatus), frozen	0303.7700	18
坚果,其他,冷冻的	Nuts, nes, frozen	0811.9090	1
坚果,其他,鲜或干的	Nuts, nes, fresh or dried	0802.9090	134
坚果,其他,暂时保藏,但不适于直接食用的	Nuts, nes, provisionally preserved, but unsuitable in that state for immediate consumption	0812.9000	34
坚果加工机器	Nuts preparation machinery	8438.6000	
坚果加工机器的零件	Nuts preparation machinery parts	8438.9000	3
坚木浸膏	Quebracho extract	3201.1000	34
间苯二酚及其盐	M-dihydroxybenzene (resorcinol) and its salts	2907.2100	36
间苯二甲腈	M-phthalonitrile	2926.9020	36
间苯二甲酸	M-phthalic acid	2917.3910	36
间苯氧基苄醇	M-phenoxy benzalcohol	2909.4910	36
间二甲苯	M-xylene	2902.4200	6
间甲酚	M-cresol	2907.1211	36
间硝基氯化苯	M-nitrochlorobenzene	2904.9012	36
监视器,彩色的,其他	Monitors, colour, nes	8528.5910	135
监视器,黑白或单色的,其他	Monitors, black and white or other monochrome, nes	8528.5990	135

J

商品名称	Article Description	税则号列	申报要素
监视器,液晶的,专用于或主要用于税号 84.71 的自动数据处理系统的	Monitors of lcd, of a kind solely or principally used in an automatic data processing system of heading 84.71, nes	8528.5110	135
监视器,阴极射线管的,彩色的	Monitors of cathode-ray tube, colour	8528.4910	135
监视器,阴极射线管的,黑白或其他单色的	Monitors of cathode-ray tube, black and white or other monochrome	8528.4990	135
监视器,阴极射线管的,专用于或主要用于税号 84.71 的自动数据处理系统的	Monitors of cathode-ray tube, of a kind solely or principally used in an automatic data processing system of heading 84.71	8528.4100	135
监视器,专用于或主要用于税号 84.71 的自动数据处理系统的,其他	Monitors, of a kind solely or principally used in an automatic data processing system of heading 84.71, nes	8528.5190	135
监视器零件,其他	Monitor parts, nes	8529.9090	3
鲣鱼,冻的	Skipjack or stripebellied bonito, frozen	0303.4300	18
鲣鱼,鲜或冷的	Skipjack or stripe-bellied bonito [Euthynnus (Katsuwonus) pelamis], fresh or chilled	0302.3300	18
鲣鱼,制作或保藏的,整条或切块,但未绞碎	Skipjack and bonito (Sarda spp.), prepared or preserved, whole or in pieces, but not minced	1604.1400	48
减湿器,空气的	Dehumidifiers for air	8479.8920	7
减湿器用零件,空气的	Dehumidifiers parts, for air	8479.9020	3
减压阀	Pressure-reducing valves	8481.1000	
剪齿边机器,纺织物的	Pinking machines for textile fabrics	8451.5000	
剪齿边机器零件,纺织物的	Pinking machines parts, for textile fabrics	8451.9000	
剪刀,白铁剪	Shears for cutting metal, hand tools	8203.3000	256
剪刀,单手操作的	Shears for one-handed pruning	8201.5000	256
剪刀,家禽剪,单手操作的	Shears for poultry	8201.5000	256
剪刀,双手操作的	Shears for two-handed pruning	8201.6000	256
剪刀,修枝剪,单手操作的	Secateurs, one-handed pruners and shears	8201.5000	256
剪刀及类似品、刀片	Scissors and similar shears, and blades thereof	8213.0000	256
剪刀片,剪刀、裁缝剪刀用	Blades for scissors, tailors' shears and similar shears	8213.0000	256
剪钳及类似工具	Cutting pliers and similar tools	8203.2000	256
剪切机床,加工金属用,其他	Shearing machines, for working metal, nes	8462.3990	7
剪切机床,数控的,加工金属用,其他	Shearing machines, numerically controlled, for working metal, nes	8462.3190	7
剪切机器,纺织物的	Cutting machines for textile fabrics	8451.5000	
剪切机器零件,纺织物的	Cutting machines parts for textile fabrics	8451.9000	
检查台,医疗、外科、牙科或兽医用	Examination tables, for medical, surgical, dental or veterinary usages	9402.9000	3
检定参照物	Certified reference materials	3822.0090	36
检镜切片机	Microtomes	9027.9000	3
检验车及查道车,铁道及电车道用,其他	Testing coaches and track inspection vehicles, for railway or tramway maintenance or service, nes	8604.0019	37

商品名称	Article Description	税则号列	申报要素
碱金属,其他	Alkali metals, nes	2805.1900	
碱木浆,但溶解级的除外,半漂白或漂白,非针叶木的	Chemical wood pulp, soda, other than dissolving grades, semi-bleached or bleached, non-coniferous	4703.2900	46
碱木浆,但溶解级的除外,半漂白或漂白,针叶木的	Chemical wood pulp, soda, other than dissolving grades, semi-bleached or bleached, coniferous	4703.2100	46
碱木浆,但溶解级的除外,未漂白,非针叶木的	Chemical wood pulp, soda, other than dissolving grades, unbleached, non-coniferous	4703.1900	46
碱木浆,但溶解级的除外,未漂白,针叶木的	Chemical wood pulp, soda, other than dissolving grades, unbleached, coniferous	4703.1100	
碱土金属,其他	Alkaline-earth metals, nes	2805.1900	
碱性蛋白酶	Basic proteinase	3507.9010	35
碱性脂肪酶	Basic lipase	3507.9020	35
建筑玩具,缩小(按比例缩小)的,成套的	Model assembly kits, of constructional toys	9503.0040	5
建筑玩具套件,缩小(按比例缩小)的,成套的	Model assembly kits, of construction toys sets	9503.0040	5
建筑装饰物,陶瓷制	Architectural ornaments, ceramic	6905.9000	5
剑杆织机,所织织物宽度超过30厘米的无梭织机	Rapier looms, for weaving fabrics of a with exceeding 30cm, shuttleless type	8446.3020	7
剑及其零件	Swords and parts	9307.0000	
剑鞘	Sheaths and parts	9307.0000	
剑鱼,冻的	Swordfish (Xiphias gladius), frozen	0303.6100	18
剑鱼,鲜或冷的	Swordfish (Xiphias gladius), fresh or chilled	0302.6700	18
健身及康复器械	Exercise and recovery equipments	9506.9110	
渐紧压袜类(例如,用以治疗静脉曲张的长统袜)	Graduated compression hosiery (for example, stockings for varicose veins)	6115.1000	2456
键盘	Keyboards	8471.6071	
键盘管风琴	Keyboard pipe organs	9205.9010	5
键盘乐器,手风琴除外,通过电产生或扩大声音的	Keyboard musical instruments, other than accordions, the sound of which is produced or must be amplified electrically	9207.1000	5
键盘乐器零件、附件	Keyboard musical instruments parts and accessories	9209.9400	3
键盘弦乐器,其他	Keyboard string musical instruments, nes	9201.9000	5
jiang			
江蓠,干的	Gracilaria, dried	1212.2071	14
江蓠,其他	Gracilaria, nes	1212.2079	14
姜	Ginger	0910.1000	
姜饼及类似品	Gingerbread and the like	1905.2000	28
姜黄	Turmric (curcuma)	0910.3000	

J

商品名称	Article Description	税则号列	申报要素
将电路图投影或绘制到感光半导体材料上的装置,平板显示器的制造机器及装置,其他	Apparatus for the projection or drawing of circuit patterns on sensitized semiconductor materials, flat panel displays manufacture machines and apparatus, nes	8486. 3039	7
将电路图投影或绘制到感光半导体材料上的装置,制造半导体器件或集成电路的机器及装置,其他	Apparatus for the projection or drawing of circuit patterns on sensitized semiconductor materials, semiconductor devices or of electronic integrated circuits manufacture machines and apparatus, nes	8486. 2039	7
浆料涂布机器,涂布铺地制品的布基或其他底布用	Paste applying machines for the base fabric or other support used in the manufacture of floor coverings	8451. 8000	
浆料涂布机器零件	Paste applying machines parts	8451. 9000	
浆纱机	Sizing machines	8445. 9020	7
浆纱机的辅助机器	Sizing machines auxiliary	8448. 1900	3
豇豆,鲜或冷藏的	Beans(Vigna spp.),fresh or chilled	0708. 2000	1
豇豆及菜豆,其他,脱荚的,干的	Beans (Vigna spp., Phaseolus spp.), nes, dried, shelled	0713. 3900	34
豇豆及菜豆,脱荚的,用醋或醋酸以外的其他方法制作或保藏的,未冷冻,其他	Bean, shelled, prepared or preserved otherwise than by vinegar or acetic acid, not frozen, nes	2005. 5199	148
豇豆及菜豆,用醋或醋酸以外的其他方法制作或保藏的,未冷冻,其他	Bean, prepared or preserved otherwise than by vinegar or acetic acid, not frozen, nes	2005. 5990	148
豇豆及菜豆罐头,其他	Bean, in airtight containers, nes	2005. 5910	148
豇豆及菜豆罐头,脱荚的,其他	Bean, in airtight containers, shelled, nes	2005. 5119	148
缰绳,适合各种动物用	Traces for any animal, of any material	4201. 0000	1458
桨叶,船用	Blades for ships or boats	8487. 1000	3
降落伞(包括可操纵降落伞)及其零件、附件	Parachutes (including dirigible parachutes), parts and accessories	8804. 0000	3
降雨火箭及其他	Rain rockets, nes	3604. 9000	
酱油	Soya sauce	2103. 1000	268
jiao			
交换机,长途电话的	Switching apparatus for toll telephonic	8517. 6211	
交换机,电报的	Switching apparatus for telegraphic	8517. 6211	
交换机,局用电话的	Switching apparatus for public telephonic	8517. 6211	
交换机,数字式程控电话用,其他	Switching apparatus, telegraphic, digital program-controlled, nes	8517. 6219	
交换机,移动通信的	Switching system for mobile communication	8517. 6212	
交流稳压电源,功率小于10千瓦,精度低于千分之一,其他	Ac voltage-stabilized suppliers, of a power of less than 10kW and an accuracy of not better than 0. 001, nes	8504. 4015	78
交通管理设备,电气的,道路的	Traffic control electrical equipment for roads	8530. 8000	
交通管理设备,电气的,电车道的	Traffic control electrical equipment for tramways	8530. 1000	

商品名称	Article Description	税则号列	申报要素
交通管理设备,电气的,港口的	Traffic control electrical equipment for port installations	8530.8000	
交通管理设备,电气的,机场的	Traffic control electrical equipment for airfields	8530.8000	
交通管理设备,电气的,内河航道的	Traffic control electrical equipment for inland waterways	8530.8000	
交通管理设备,电气的,铁道的	Traffic control electrical equipment for railways	8530.1000	
交通管理设备,电气的,停车场的	Traffic control electrical equipment for parking facilities	8530.8000	
交通管理设备的零件	Traffic control electrical equipment parts	8530.9000	3
交通管理设备及其零件,机械的,道路用	Traffic control equipment and parts,for roads	8608.0090	3
交通管理设备及其零件,机械的,电车道用	Traffic control equipment and parts,for tramways	8608.0090	3
交通管理设备及其零件,机械的,港口用	Traffic control equipment and parts, for port installations	8608.0090	3
交通管理设备及其零件,机械的,机场用	Traffic control equipment and parts,for airfields	8608.0090	3
交通管理设备及其零件,机械的,内河航道用	Traffic control equipment and parts,for inland waterways	8608.0090	3
交通管理设备及其零件,机械的,铁道用	Traffic control equipment and parts,for railways	8608.0090	3
交通管理设备及其零件,机械的,停车场用	Traffic control equipment and parts, for parking facilities	8608.0090	3
浇包	Ladles	8454.2090	
胶,调制的,其他	Glues,prepared,nes	3506.9900	36
胶,以淀粉、糊精或其他改性淀粉为基本成分的	Glues, based on starches, or on dextrins or other modified starches	3505.2000	36
胶版复印机	Hectograph duplicating machines	8472.1000	
胶带,宽度不超过20厘米的,用橡胶处理的,其他	Adhesive tape of a width not exceeding 20cm, rubberized,nes	5906.1090	48
胶订机	Glueing binders,for book	8440.1020	
胶订机零件	Glueing binders parts,for book	8440.9000	3
胶合板,仅由薄板制的,竹制的,每层厚度不超过6毫米,其他	Plywood consisting solely of sheets of wood, of bamboo, each ply not exceeding 6mm thickness, nes	4412.1019	48
胶合板,仅由薄板制的,竹制的,每层厚度不超过6毫米,至少有一表层是本章子目注释所列的热带木	Plywood consisting solely of sheets of wood, of bamboo, each ply not exceeding 6mm thickness, with at least one outer ply of tropical wood specified in subheading note to this chapter	4412.1011	48
胶合板,仅由薄木板制的(竹制除外),每层厚度不超过6毫米,其他	Plywood, consisting solely of sheets of wood (other than bamboo), each ply not exceeding 6mm thickness,nes	4412.3900	48

J

商品名称	Article Description	税则号列	申报要素
胶合板,仅由薄木板制的(竹制除外),每层厚度不超过6毫米,至少有一表层是本章子目注释所列的热带木	Plywood, consisting solely of sheets of wood (other than bamboo), each ply not exceeding 6mm thickness, with at least one outer ply of tropical wood specified in subheading note to this chapter	4412. 3100	48
胶合板,仅由薄木板制的(竹制除外),每层厚度不超过6毫米,至少有一表层是非针叶木,其他	Plywood, consisting solely of sheets of wood (other than bamboo), each ply not exceeding 6mm thickness, with at least one outer ply of non-coniferous wood, nes	4412. 3290	48
胶合板,仅由薄木板制的(竹制除外),每层厚度不超过6毫米,至少有一表层是温带非针叶木	Plywood, consisting solely of sheets of wood (other than bamboo), each ply not exceeding 6mm thickness, with at least one outer ply of temperate non-coniferous wood	4412. 3210	48
胶合板、单板饰面板及类似的多层板,其他	Plywood, veneered panels and similar laminated wood, nes	4412. 9999	48
胶合板、单板饰面板及类似的多层板,至少含有一层木碎料板,其他	Plywood, veneered panels and similar laminated wood, containing at least one layer of particle board, nes	4412. 9992	48
胶合板、单板饰面板及类似的多层板,至少有一表层是非针叶木,其他	Plywood, veneered panels and similar laminated wood, with at least one outer ply of non-coniferous wood, nes	4412. 9910	48
胶合板、单板饰面板及类似的多层板,至少有一层是热带木,其他	Plywood, veneered panels and similar laminated wood, with at least one outer ply of tropical wood, nes	4412. 9991	48
胶合板、单板饰面板及类似的多层板,竹制的,其他	Plywood, veneered panels and similar laminated wood, of bamboo, nes	4412. 1099	48
胶合板、单板饰面板及类似的多层板,竹制的,至少含有一层木碎料板,其他	Plywood, veneered panels and similar laminated wood, of bamboo, containing at least one layer of particle board, nes	4412. 1092	48
胶合板、单板饰面板及类似的多层板,竹制的,至少有一表层是非针叶木,其他	Plywood, veneered panels and similar laminated wood, of bamboo, with at least one outer ply of non-coniferous wood, nes	4412. 1020	48
胶合板、单板饰面板及类似的多层板,竹制的,至少有一层是热带木,其他	Plywood, veneered panels and similar laminated wood, of bamboo, with at least one outer ply of tropical wood, nes	4412. 1091	48
胶黄耆树胶	Gum tragacanth	1301. 9010	
胶或粘合剂,零售包装每件净重不超过1千克	Glues or adhesives, put up for retail sale, not exceeding a net weight, of 1 kg	3506. 1000	36
胶棉,初级形状的	Collodions, in primary forms	3912. 2000	16
胶囊,装药用	Capsules, pharmaceutical	9602. 0010	
胶囊型反光膜,成卷,自粘的,宽度不超过20厘米	Encapsulant reflective film, in rolls, self-adhesive plates, of a width not exceeding 20cm	3919. 1091	16
胶囊型反光膜,自粘的,其他	Encapsulant reflective film, self-adhesive plates, nes	3919. 9010	16
胶态硫磺	Colloidal sulphur	2802. 0000	

J

商品名称	Article Description	税则号列	申报要素
胶液及增稠剂,从刺槐豆、刺槐豆子或瓜尔豆制得的,不论是否改性	Mucilages and thickeners, whether or not modified, derived from locust beans, locust bean seeds or guar seeds	1302.3200	4
胶液及增稠剂,海草及其他藻类制品	Mucilages and thickeners, preparations of seaweeds and other algae	1302.3919	3
胶液及增稠剂,其他	Mucilages and thickeners, nes	1302.3990	34
胶印版纸,成卷或成张的,卷宽度超过36厘米,或长超过36厘米且宽超过15厘米	Offset plates, in rolls or sheets, of width exceeding 36cm or in roll or one side exceeding 36cm and other side exceeding 15cm in rectangular sheets	4809.9000	458
胶印版纸,其他	Offset plates, nes	4816.9090	58
胶印机,卷取进料式	Offset printing machinery, reel-fed	8443.1100	57
胶印机,片取进料式,办公室用(以未折叠计,片尺寸一边长不超过22cm,另一边长不超过36cm)	Offset printing machinery, sheet-fed, office type (using sheets with one side not exceeding 22cm and the other side not exceeding 36cm in the unfolded state)	8443.1200	57
胶印机,平张纸进料式,单色机	Offset printing machinery, sheet fed, single color	8443.1311	57
胶印机,平张纸进料式,其他	Offset printing machinery, sheet fed, nes	8443.1319	57
胶印机,平张纸进料式,双色机	Offset printing machinery, sheet fed, two colors	8443.1312	57
胶印机,平张纸进料式,四色机	Offset printing machinery, sheet fed, four colors	8443.1313	57
胶印机,其他	Offset printing machinery, nes	8443.1390	57
胶粘敷料	Adhesive dressings	3005.1090	1346
椒盐卷饼	Pretzels	1905.9000	28
焦磷酸	Pyrophosphoric acid	2809.2019	6
焦宁,派若宁(一种染料)	Pyronine (as synthetic organic colouring matter)	3204.9090	345
焦炭及半焦炭,煤、褐煤或泥煤制成的	Coke and semi-coke, of lignite or of peat, whether or not agglomerated	2704.0010	34
焦糖	Caramel	1702.9000	
焦糖	Caramelised sugars	1702.9000	
焦油,再造的	Tars, reconstituted	2706.0000	146
焦油及其他矿物焦油,从煤、褐煤或泥煤蒸馏所得的,不论是否脱水或部分蒸馏	Tar distilled from coal, from lignite or from peat, and other mineral tars, whether or not dehydrated or partially distilled	2706.0000	146
焦油砂	Tar sands	2714.1000	1346
焦油纸及纸板	Tarred paper and paperboard	4811.1000	458
蕉柑	Chiaokan	0805.2010	14
蕉麻	Abaca	5305.0020	4
角,已加工的	Horn, worked	9601.9000	5
角材、型材及异型材,不锈钢的	Angles, shapes and sections of stainless steel	7222.4000	468
角材、型材及异型材,除热轧、热拉拔或热挤压外未经进一步加工,其他	Angles, shapes and sections, not further worked than hot-rolled, hot-drawn or extruded, nes	7216.5090	468
角材、型材及异型材,钢铁的,焊接的	Angles, shapes and sections, of iron or steel, welded	7301.2000	6
角材、型材及异型材,合金钢,其他	Angles, shapes and sections, nes	7228.7090	468

J

商品名称	Article Description	税则号列	申报要素
角材、型材及异型材,履带板型钢	Angles, shapes and sections, shapes of crawler tread	7228. 7010	468
角材、型材及异型材,铁或非合金钢的,除冷成形或冷加工外未经进一步加工,其他	Angles, shapes and sections, of iron or non-alloy steel, not further worked than cold-formed or cold-finished, nes	7216. 6900	468
角材、型材及异型材,铁或非合金钢的,平板轧材经冷成形或冷加工制的	Angles, shapes and sections of iron or nonalloy steel, cold-formed or cold-finished from flatrolled products	7216. 9100	468
角材、型材及异型材,铁或非合金钢的,其他	Angles, shapes and sections of iron or nonalloy steel, nes	7216. 9900	468
角材、型材及异型材,铁或非合金钢的平板轧材制的,除冷成形或冷加工外未经进一步加工	Angles, shapes and sections, of flat-rolled iron or non-alloy steel, not further worked than cold-formed or cold-finished	7216. 6100	468
角蛋白	Keratins	3504. 0090	1346
角钢,除热轧、热拉拔或热挤压外未经进一步加工,截面高度低于 80 毫米	L sections, not further worked than hot-rolled, hot-drawn or extruded, of a height of less than 80mm	7216. 2100	468
角钢,除热轧、热拉拔或热挤压外未经进一步加工,截面高度在 80 毫米及以上	L sections, not further worked than hot-rolled, hot-drawn or extruded, of a height of 80mm or more	7216. 4010	468
角黄素	Canthaxanthin	3204. 1700	345
角及其粉末	Horns and powder thereof	0507. 9090	14
角接触轴承	Angular contact bearings	8482. 1030	5
角鲨,冻的	Dogfish, frozen	0303. 7500	18
角鲨,鲜或冷的	Dogfish, fresh or chilled	0302. 6500	18
角银矿	Cerargyrites	2616. 1000	146
角柱,其他	Horncores, nes	0506. 9090	146
绞带,不论是否带刺,钢铁的,围篱用的	Twisted hoop, barbed or not, of a kind used for fencing, of iron or steel	7313. 0000	36
绞股线、缆、编带及类似品,非绝缘的铜丝	Stranded wire, cables plaited bands and the like, of copper, not electrically insulated	7413. 0000	6
绞股线、缆、编带及类似品,铝制,非绝缘的,带钢芯的	Stranded wire, cables, plaited bands and the like, of aluminium, not electrically insulated, with steel core	7614. 1000	6
绞股线、缆、编带及类似品,铝制,非绝缘的,其他	Stranded wire, cables, plaited bands and the like, of aluminium, not electrically insulated, nes	7614. 9000	6
绞股线、绳、缆,非绝缘钢铁的	Stranded wire, ropes and cables, of iron or steel, not electrically insulated	7312. 1000	36
绞盘,电动的,矿井口用	Capstans, pit-head winding gear, powered by electric motor	8425. 3110	78
绞盘,电动的,其他	Capstans, powered by electric motor, nes	8425. 3190	78
绞盘,电动的,专为井下使用设计的	Capstans, powered by electric motor, specially designed for use underground	8425. 3110	78
绞盘,其他	Capstans, nes	8425. 3990	78

J

商品名称	Article Description	税则号列	申报要素
饺子,不论是否烹煮或经其他方法制作	Ravioli, whether or not cooked or otherwise prepared	1902.2000	46
矫形器具	Orthopaedic appliances	9021.1000	
矫直或矫平机,加工金属用,其他	Straightening machines, for working metal, nes	8462.2910	7
矫直或矫平机,数控的,加工金属用	Straightening or flattening machines, numerically controlled, for working metal	8462.2110	7
脚蹬及其零件,自行车及脚踏车的	Pedals and parts thereof, of bicycles and other cycles	8714.9610	3
脚手架、模板或坑道支撑用的支柱及类似设备,钢铁的	Equipment for scaffolding, shuttering, propping or pit-propping, of iron or steel	7308.4000	6
脚踏车,非机动	Cycles, not motorized	8712.0090	8
铰接链,钢铁的,其他	Articulated link chain, of iron or steel, nes	7315.1200	36
铰接链零件,钢铁的	Articulated link chain parts, of iron or steel	7315.1900	36
铰链(折叶),贱金属制,用于家具、门窗、楼梯、百叶窗、车厢、鞍具、衣箱、盒子及类似品的	Hinges, of base metal, suitable for furniture, doors, staircases, windows, blinds, coachwork, saddlery, trunks, chests, caskets, or the like	8302.1000	256
搅拌机,其他	Kneading machines, nes	8479.8200	7
搅拌机器,泥土、石料、矿石或其他固体矿物质的,其他	Kneading machines, for earth, stone, ores or other mineral substances, nes	8474.3900	
搅拌器,食品用,家用电动器具	Mixers for food, electro-mechanical domestic appliances	8509.4090	
教学示范而无其他用途的仪器、装置及模型	Education instruments, designed for demonstrational purposes, unsuitable for other uses	9023.0000	
教学专用幻灯片,已曝光已冲洗的	Lantern slides, for educational use only, exposed and developed	3705.9010	1238
酵母,非活性	Inactive yeasts	2102.2000	28
酵母,活性	Active yeasts	2102.1000	28
jie			
接缝用油灰	Grafting putty	3214.1090	3
接合衬垫,各种不同材料制	Joints assortments, dissimilar in composition	8484.9000	56
接合衬垫,用金属片与其他材料制成或用双层或多层金属片制成	Joints of metal sheeting combined with other material or of two or more layers of metal	8484.1000	56
接收管	Receiver valves and tubes	8540.8100	35
接穗,活植物的	Slips, for live plants	0602.1000	3
接梭箱,织机用	Catching shuttle boxes for looms	8448.4910	3
接头,塑料的	Joints, of plastics	3917.4000	
接线盒,用于电压不超过1000伏的线路	Junction boxes, for a voltage not exceeding 1000V	8536.9000	8
接线盒,用于电压超过1000伏的线路	Junction boxes, for a voltage exceeding 1000V	8535.9000	8
节拍器	Metronomes	9209.9910	3
节热器,过热水锅炉的辅助设备	Economizers, auxiliary plant for use with super-heated water boilers	8404.1010	3

J

商品名称	Article Description	税则号列	申报要素
节热器,集中供暖用的热水锅炉的辅助设备	Economizers, auxiliary plant for use with central heating boilers	8404.1020	3
节热器,蒸汽锅炉的辅助设备	Economizers, auxiliary plant for use with steam or other vapour generating watertube boilers	8404.1010	3
节日用品	Festive entertainment articles	9505.9000	5
洁齿品,其他	Dentifrices, nes	3306.1090	23
结构体及其部件,钢铁的,其他	Structures and parts of structures, of iron or steel, nes	7308.9000	6
结晶器,钢坯连铸机用	Crystallizers, for ingot continuous casting machines	8454.9021	3
结球莴苣,鲜或冷藏的	Cabbage lettuce, fresh or chilled	0705.1100	1
睫毛刷	Eyelash brushes	9603.2900	
截煤机,其他	Coal cutters, nes	8430.3900	5
截煤机,自推进的	Coal cutters, self-propelled	8430.3100	5
截煤机零件	Coal cutters parts	8431.4990	3
解冻剂	De-icing fluids, prepared	3820.0000	36
芥菜类蔬菜,食用,鲜或冷藏的,其他	Brassicas, edible, fresh or chilled, nes	0704.9090	1
芥菜籽,其他	Mustard seeds, nes	1207.5090	3
芥菜籽,种用	Mustard seeds for cultivation	1207.5010	3
芥子粉及其调制品	Mustard flour and meal and prepared mustard	2103.3000	268
芥子油,其他,初榨的	Mustard oil, crude, nes	1514.9190	4
芥子油及其分离品,其他	Mustard oil and frac tions thereof, nes	1514.9900	4
jin			
金(包括镀铂的金),半制成形状,非货币用,其他	Gold (including gold plated with platinum), non-monetary, semi-manufactured forms, non-monetary, nes	7108.1300	46
金(包括镀铂的金),货币用	Gold (including gold plated with platinum), monetary	7108.2000	46
金(包括镀铂的金),未锻造形状,非货币用,其他	Gold (including gold plated with platinum), unwrought forms, non-monetary, nes	7108.1200	46
金包覆材料,以贱金属或银为底的,未加工成半成品的	Gold clothing base metals or silver, not further worked than semi-manufactured	7109.0000	46
金币	Coin of gold	7108.2000	46
金粉,非货币用	Gold powder, non-monetary	7108.1100	46
金刚鹦鹉,改良种用	Macaws, pure-bred breeding	0106.3210	3
金红石	Rutile	2614.0000	146
金化合物	Gold compounds	2843.3000	
金鸡纳生物碱及其衍生物以及它们的盐	Cinchona alkaloids and their derivatives; salts thereof	2939.2000	34
金橘	Kumquats, frozen	0811.9090	1
金橘,鲜或干的	Kumquats, fresh or dried	0805.9000	14
金橘,制作的	Kumquats, prepared or preserved	2008.3010	248
金橘果酱	Kumquats marmalade	2007.9100	248

J

商品名称	Article Description	税则号列	申报要素
金矿砂及其精矿	Gold ores and concentrates	2616. 9000	146
金枪鱼(蓝鳍金枪鱼),冻的	Bluefin tunas(thunnus thynnus),frozen	0303. 4500	18
金枪鱼,其他,冻的	Tunas,nes,frozen	0303. 4900	18
金枪鱼,其他,鲜或冷的	Tunas,nes,fresh or chilled	0302. 3900	18
金枪鱼,制作或保藏的,整条或切块,但未绞碎	Tunas,prepared or preserved,whole or in pieces,but not minced	1604. 1400	48
金丝燕窝	Nests,salanganes	0410. 0010	3
金银器及其零件,贵金属制,不论是否包、镀贵金属,其他	Goldsmiths or silversmiths' wares and parts thereof,of precious metal,whether or not plated or clad with precious metal,nes	7114. 1900	46
金银器及其零件,以贱金属为底的包贵金属制	Goldsmiths or silversmiths' wares and parts thereof,of base metal clad with precious metal	7114. 2000	46
金银器及其零件,银制,不论是否包、镀其他贵金属	Goldsmiths or silversmiths' wares and parts thereof,of silver,whether or not pla-ted or clad with other precious metal	7114. 1100	46
金针菜,干的	Day lily flowers,dried	0712. 9030	4
金针菇,干的	Flammulina Velutipes,dried	0712. 3920	4
金针菇,鲜或冷藏的	Flammulina Velutipes,fresh or chilled	0709. 5930	1
金属、硬质合金用型模,其他	Moulds for metal or metal carbides,nes	8480. 4900	7
金属表面酸洗剂	Pickling preparations for metal surfaces	3810. 1000	36
金属处理的机械,其他	Metal treating machines and mechanical appliances,nes	8479. 8190	7
金属拉拔或挤压用模,带有天然或合成金刚石、立方氮化硼制的工作部件,可互换	Dies for drawing or extruding metal,with working part of natural or synthetic diamonds or cubic boron nitride,interchangeable	8207. 2010	256
金属拉拔或挤压用模,其他	Dies for drawing or extruding metal,interchangeable,nes	8207. 2090	256
金属卤化物灯	Metal halide lamps	8539. 3290	35
金属密封垫	Metal gaskets	8484. 1000	56
金属纱线的机织物,用于衣着、装饰及类似用途,其他	Woven fabrics of metal thread, of a kind used in apparel, as furnishing fabrics or for similar purposes,nes	5809. 0090	468
金属纱线的机织物,与化学纤维混制,用于衣着、装饰及类似用途	Woven fabrics of Metal thread ,combined with man-made fibres, of a kind used in apparel, as furnishing fabrics or for similar purposes	5809. 0020	468
金属纱线的机织物,与棉混制,用于衣着、装饰及类似用途	Woven fabrics of metal thread,combined with cotton,of a kind used in apparel,as furnishing fabrics or for similar purposes	5809. 0010	468
金属丝布或格栅形状的铂催化剂	Catalysts in the form of wire cloth or grill,of platinum	7115. 1000	46
金属丝加工机,非切削	Wire working machines,for working metal or cermets,without removing material	8463. 3000	7
金属丝刷,其他	Brushes of metal wire,nes	9603. 5019	3

J

商品名称	Article Description	税则号列	申报要素
金属丝刷,作为机器、器具零件的	Brushes of metal wire, constituting parts of machines or appliances	9603.5011	3
金属酸盐,其他	Oxometanic salts, nes	2841.9000	1
金属探测器	Metal detectors	8543.7091	37
金属探测器用零件	Metal detectors parts	8543.9030	3
金属碳化物,混合的,未烧结	Metal carbides, mixed, non-agglomerated	3824.3000	36
金属碳化物,与金属粘合剂混合的,未烧结	Metal carbides mixed with metallic binders, non-agglomerated	3824.3000	36
金属陶瓷,颗粒或粉末	Cermets, in granules or powder	8113.0010	16
金属陶瓷,其他	Cermets, nes	8113.0090	16
金属陶瓷板,未装配的工具用	Cermets plates for tools, unmounted	8209.0010	256
金属陶瓷刀头,未装配的工具用	Cermets tips for tools, unmounted	8209.0030	256
金属陶瓷杆,未装配的工具用	Cermets sticks for tools, unmounted	8209.0020	256
金属陶瓷制品,颗粒或粉末	Cermets articles, in granules or powder	8113.0010	16
金属陶瓷制品,其他	Cermets articles, nes	8113.0090	16
金属陶瓷制品,未装配的工具用,其他	Cermets for tools, unmounted, nes	8209.0090	256
金属线机织物,用于衣着、装饰及类似用途,其他	Metal thread woven fabrics, of a kind used in apparel, as furnishing fabrics or for similar purposes, nes	5809.0090	468
金属线机织物,与化学纤维混制,用于衣着、装饰及类似用途	Metal thread woven fabrics, combined with man-made fibres, of a kind used in apparel, as furnishing fabrics or for similar purposes	5809.0020	468
金属线机织物,与棉混制,用于衣着、装饰及类似用途	Metal thread woven fabrics, combined with cotton, of a kind used in apparel, as furnishing fabrics or for similar purposes	5809.0010	468
金属型材挤压机	Metal section squeezing machine	8462.9110	7
金属氧化物、氢氧化物及过氧化物,其他	Inorganic bases, metal oxides, hydroxides and peroxides, nes	2825.9090	
金属铸造用型箱	Moulding boxes for metal foundry	8480.1000	7
仅含氟和氯的甲烷、乙烷及丙烷的卤化衍生物,其他	Methane, ethane and propane halogenated derivatives only with fluorine and chlorine, nes	2903.4910	36
仅含氟和氯的全卤化衍生物,其他	Derivatives perhalogenated only with fluorine and chloirine, nes	2903.4599	36
仅含氟和溴的甲烷、乙烷及丙烷的卤化衍生物,其他	Methane, ethane and propane halogenated derivatives with fluorine and bromine, nes	2903.4920	36
仅含磺基的衍生物及其盐和乙酯	Derivatives containing only sulpho groups, their salts and ethyl esters	2904.1000	36
仅含硝基或亚硝基的衍生物	Derivatives containing only nitro or nitroso groups, their salts and ethyl esters	2904.2090	36
仅含有氮杂原子的杂环化合物,其他	Heterocyclic compounds with nitrogen hetero-atom (s) only, nes	2933.9900	36
仅含有氧杂原子的杂环化合物,其他	Heterocyclic compounds with oxygen hetero-atom (s) only, nes	2932.9990	36

J

商品名称	Article Description	税则号列	申报要素
浸入式液体加热器,电热的	Electric immersion heaters	8516.1090	7
浸渍机器,纺织物的	Impregnating machines for textile fabrics	8451.8000	
浸渍机器零件,纺织物的	Impregnating machines parts for textile fabrics	8451.9000	
jing			
经编机,拉舍尔式	Warp knitting machines, rashel machines	8447.2012	7
经编机,其他	Warp knitting machines, nes	8447.2019	7
经编机,特里科式	Warp knitting machines, tricot machines	8447.2011	7
经编机的辅助机器	Warp knitting machines auxiliary	8448.1900	3
经编织物,合成纤维制,染色	Warp knit fabrics, of synthetic fibres, dyed	6005.3200	46
经编织物,合成纤维制,色织	Warp knit fabrics, of synthetic fibres, of yarns of different colours	6005.3300	46
经编织物,合成纤维制,未漂白或漂白	Warp knit fabrics, of synthetic fibres, unbleached or bleached	6005.3100	46
经编织物,合成纤维制,印花	Warp knit fabrics, of synthetic fibres, printed	6005.3400	46
经编织物,棉制,染色	Warp knit fabrics, of cotton, dyed	6005.2200	46
经编织物,棉制,色织	Warp knit fabrics, of cotton, of yarns of different colours	6005.2300	46
经编织物,棉制,未漂白或漂白	Warp knit fabrics, of cotton, unbleached or bleached	6005.2100	46
经编织物,棉制,印花	Warp knit fabrics, of cotton, printed	6005.2400	46
经编织物,其他	Warp knit fabrics, nes	6005.9090	46
经编织物,人造纤维制,染色	Warp knit fabrics, of artificial fibres, dyed	6005.4200	46
经编织物,人造纤维制,色织	Warp knit fabrics, of artificial fibres, of yarns of different colours	6005.4300	46
经编织物,人造纤维制,未漂白或漂白	Warp knit fabrics, of artificial fibres, unbleached or bleached	6005.4100	46
经编织物,人造纤维制,印花	Warp knit fabrics, of artificial fibres, printed	6005.4400	46
经编织物,羊毛或动物细毛制,其他	Warp knit fabrics, of wool or fine animal hair	6005.9010	46
经纬仪	Theodolites	9015.2000	
荆树皮浸膏	Wattle extract	3201.2000	34
晶体管,但光敏晶体管除外,耗散功率小于1瓦的	Transistors, other than photosensitive transistors, with a dissipation rate of less than 1W	8541.2100	5
晶体管,但光敏晶体管除外,其他	Transistors, other than photosensitive transistors, nes	8541.2900	5
腈基化合物,其他	Nitrile-function compounds, nes	2926.9090	36
精对苯二甲酸	Pta(purified terephthalic acid)	2917.3611	36
精加工的机床,加工金属或金属陶瓷用,其他	Finishing machine-tools, for metal or cermets, nes	8460.9090	7
精加工机床,齿轮的,切削金属或金属陶瓷用,其他	Finishing machines of gear, for removing metal or cermets, nes	8461.4090	7
精加工机床,齿轮的,数控的,切削金属或金属陶瓷用	Finishing machines of gear, numerically controlled, for removing metal or cermets	8461.4010	7
精炼硼砂,其他	Refined borax, nes	2840.1900	

J

商品名称	Article Description	税则号列	申报要素
精炼硼砂,无水的	Refined borax, anhydrous	2840.1100	
精馏塔	Rectifying towers	8419.4020	57
精萘	Naphthalene, refined	2902.9020	6
精梳机,毛的	Combing machines, for worsted	8445.1220	7
精梳机,棉的	Combing machines, for cotton	8445.1210	7
精梳机,其他	Combing machines, nes	8445.1290	7
精油,柑橘属果实的,其他	Essential oils other than those of citrus fruit, nes	3301.2999	34
精油水馏液及水溶液	Essential oils aqueous distillates and aqueous solutions	3301.9090	34
精汁,肉、鱼、甲壳动物、软体动物或其他水生无脊椎动物的	Extracts and juices of meat, fish or crustaceans, molluscs or other aquatic invertebrates	1603.0000	48
精制木焦油	Wood tar oils	3807.0000	3
鲸	Whales	0106.1200	
鲸蜡	Spermaceti	1521.9090	
鲸肉,鲜或冷或冻的	Meat of whales, fresh, chilled or frozen	0208.4000	15
鲸肉粉,食用	Flours and meals of meat of whales, edible	0210.9200	14
鲸须及其粉末	Whalebone and powder thereof	0507.9090	14
鲸须毛及其粉末	Whalebone hair and powder thereof	0507.9090	14
鲸油	Whale oil	1504.3000	4
肼(联氨)的有机衍生物	Organic derivatives of hydrazine	2928.0000	36
肼(联氨)及其无机盐	Hydrazine and their inorganic salts	2825.1090	
景泰蓝雕塑像及其他装饰品,贱金属制	Cloisonne statuettes and other ornaments of base metal	8306.2910	256
警棍	Truncheons	9304.0000	
净化机器及装置,过滤或净化水用,其他	Purifying machinery and apparatus, for filtering or purifying water, nes	8421.2190	7
净化机器及装置,过滤或净化饮料(水除外)用	Purifying machinery and apparatus, for filtering or purifying beverages other than water	8421.2200	7
净化机器及装置,家用型,过滤或净化水用	Purifying machinery and apparatus, of the household type, for filtering or purifying water	8421.2110	7
净化机器及装置,家用型,气体用	Purifying machinery and apparatus, of the household type, for gases	8421.3910	7
净化机器及装置,液体用,其他	Purifying machinery and apparatus, for liquids, nes	8421.2990	7
净化装置,内燃发动机排气用	Purifying apparatus for exhaust air, for internal combustion engines	8421.3930	7
净化装置,气体用,其他	Purifying apparatus for gases, nes	8421.3990	7
净化装置用零件,家用型	Purifying machines parts, of household-type	8421.9910	3
净化装置用零件,其他	Purifying machines parts, nes	8421.9990	3
径向柱塞泵,排液回转式	Radial plunger pump, for positive displacement, rotary	8413.6050	27
静电除尘器	Electrostatic dust collectors for industry uses	8421.3921	7

商品名称	Article Description	税则号列	申报要素
静电感光复印设备,将原件通过中间体转印的(间接法)	Electrostatic photocopying apparatus, operating by reproducing the original image via an intermediate onto the copy (indirect process)	8443.3912	57
静电感光复印设备,将原件直接复印的(直接法)	Electrostatic photocopying apparatus, operating by reproducing the original image directly onto the copy (direct process)	8443.3911	57
静电照相印刷机(激光印刷机),数字式,可与自动数据处理设备或网络连接的	Electrostatic photographic printing machines (laser printing machines), digital, capable of connecting to an ADP machine or to a network	8443.3222	57
静电照相印刷机(激光印刷机),数字式	Electrostatic photographic printing machines (laser printing machines), digital	8443.3932	57
静像视频摄像机用零件,非特种用途的取像模块	Still image video cameras parts, camera modules without special purposes	8529.9042	3
静像视频摄像机用零件,其他	Still image video cameras parts, nes	8529.9049	3
静像视频摄像机用零件,特种用途的	Still image video cameras parts, of special purposes	8529.9041	3
静止式变流器,其他	Static converters, nes	8504.4099	
静止式变流器零件	Static converters parts	8504.9090	3
镜框及类似品,辐射松制的	Frames for mirrors or similar objects, of radiata pine	4414.0010	56
镜框及类似品,其他木制的	Frames for mirrors or similar objects, of other wood	4414.0090	56
镜片坯件,变色眼镜用,未经光学加工的,玻璃制	Blanks for photochromic spectacles, of glass	7015.1010	13457
镜片坯件,平光变色眼镜用,未经光学加工的,玻璃制	Blanks for plane photochromic spectacles, of glass	7015.9020	13457
镜铁	Spiegeleisen	7201.5000	6
镜子,贱金属制	Mirrors of base metal	8306.3000	256
jiu			
久效磷(ISO)	Monocrotophos (ISO)	2924.1200	36
韭葱,鲜或冷藏的	Leeks, fresh or chilled	0703.9010	1
酒精制品,制造饮料用,复合的	Alcoholic preparations of a kind used for the manufacture of beverages, compound	2106.9020	268
酒石酸	Tartaric acid	2918.1200	36
酒石酸盐及酒石酸酯	Salts and esters of tartaric acid	2918.1300	36
酒椰叶	Raffia	1401.9090	3
旧衣物	Worn clothing and other worn articles	6309.0000	1
救火车,其他	Fire fighting vehicles, nes	8705.3090	7
救火车,装有云梯的	Fire fighting vehicles, mounted with scaling ladder	8705.3010	7
救生船,非机动船舶	Lifeboats, not-motorized vessels	8906.9020	5
救生船,机动船舶	Lifeboats, motor vessels	8906.9010	5
救生衣	Life-jackets	6307.2000	346
ju			
局用电话交换机	Public telephonic switching apparatus	8517.6211	

J

商品名称	Article Description	税则号列	申报要素
菊粉	Inulin	1108.2000	
菊花	Flos chrysanthemi	1211.9015	34
菊花,其他	Chrysathemum, nes	0602.9093	
菊花,鲜的,制花束或装饰用的	Chrysanthemums, fresh, suitable for bouquets or for ornamental purposes	0603.1400	34
菊花,种用	Chrysathemum, seedlings	0602.9091	3
菊苣,烘焙的	Chicory, roasted	2101.3000	268
菊苣,其他,鲜或冷藏的	Chicory, nes, fresh or chilled	0705.2900	1
菊苣根,未焙制的	Chicory roots of the variety cichorium intybus sativum, unroasted	1212.9999	134
菊苣植物及其根	Chicory plants and roots	0601.2000	
菊芋	Jerusalem artichokes	0714.9090	34
巨型机(计算机)	Supercomputer	8471.4110	26
巨型机(计算机),以系统形式进口或出口的	Supercomputer, presented in the form of systems	8471.4910	26
巨型机、大型机、中型机及小型机及其处理部件的零件、附件	Supercomputer, mainframes, mid-sized computer machine, mini-computers and their processing units's parts and accessories	8473.3010	3
巨型机处理部件	Supercomputer, processing units	8471.5010	26
具有独立功能的机器及机械器具,其他	Machines and mechanical appliances having individual functions, nes	8479.9090	3
具有旋转导风轮的风扇,包括风机,本身装有一个输出功率不超过125瓦的电动机	Repeating front louver fan, with a self-contained electric motor of an output not exceeding 125W	8414.5130	23
锯床,钢丝的,加工石料、陶瓷、混凝土、石棉水泥或类似矿物材料的	Sawing machines of scroll saw, for working stone, ceramics, concrete, asbestos-cement or like mineral materials	8464.1020	7
锯床,加工木材、软木、骨、硬质橡胶、硬质塑料或类似硬质材料的	Sawing machines, for working wood, cork, bone, hard rubber, hard plastics or similar hard materials	8465.9100	7
锯床,加工石料、陶瓷、混凝土、石棉水泥或类似矿物材料的,其他	Sawing machines for working stone, ceramics, concrete, asbestos-cement or like mineral materials, nes	8464.1090	7
锯床,切削金属或金属陶瓷用	Sawing machines, for removing metal or cermets	8461.5000	7
锯床,圆盘的,加工石料、陶瓷、混凝土、石棉水泥或类似矿物材料的	Sawing machines of disk saw, for working stone, ceramics, concrete, asbestos-cement or like mineral materials	8464.1010	7
锯末,不论是否粘结成圆木段、块、片或类似形状	Sawdust, whether or not agglomerated in logs, briquettes, pellets or similar forms	4401.3000	15
锯片,带状	Saw blades, band	8202.2000	256
锯片,机械锯用	Saw blades for sawing machines	8202.9910	256
锯片,链状	Saw blades, chain	8202.4000	256
锯片,其他	Saw blades, nes	8202.9990	256

商品名称	Article Description	税则号列	申报要素
锯片,圆状,包括部件,其他	Saw blades,circular,including parts,nes	8202.3900	256
锯片,圆状,带有钢制工作部件	Saw blades,circular,with working part of steel	8202.3100	256
锯片,直的,机械锯用	Straight saw blades,for sawing machines	8202.9110	256
锯片,直的,加工金属用,其他	Saw blades,straight,for working metal,nes	8202.9190	256
聚(亚甲基苯基异氰酸酯)	Poly(methylene phenyl isocyanate)	3909.3010	1256
聚氨基甲酸酯	Polyurethanes	3909.5000	1256
聚苯乙烯(含苯乙烯聚合物)的废碎料及下脚料	Polystyrene(including polymers of styrene) waste, parings and scrap	3915.2000	146
聚苯乙烯,初级形状的,其他	Polystyrene,in primary forms,nes	3903.1990	1256
聚苯乙烯,改性的,初级形状的	Polystyrene,modified,in primary forms	3903.1910	1256
聚苯乙烯,可发性的,初级形状的	Polystyrene,expansible,in primary forms	3903.1100	1256
聚丙烯	Polypropylene	3902.1000	1256
聚丙烯变形纱线,非供零售用	Polypropylene textured yarn,not put up for retail sale	5402.3400	3468
聚丙烯长丝丝束	Polypropylene filament tow	5501.4000	68
聚丙烯单纱,捻度每米超过50转,非供零售用	Polypropylene single yarn,with a twist exceeding 50 turns per metre,not put up for retail sale	5402.5910	3468
聚丙烯单纱,未加捻或捻度每米不超过50转,非供零售用	Polypropylenes single yarn,untwisted or with a twist not exceeding 50 turns per metre,not put up for retail sale	5402.4800	3468
聚丙烯单丝,截面尺寸不超过1毫米,细度在67分特及以上	Polypropylene monofilament of 67 decitex or more and of which no cross-sectional dimension exceeding 1mm	5404.1200	568
聚丙烯短纤,未梳或未经其他纺前加工	Polypropylene staple fibres,not carded,combed or otherwise processed for spinning	5503.4000	68
聚丙烯多股纱线或缆线,非供零售用	Polypropylene multiple or cabled yarn,not put up for retail sale	5402.6910	3468
聚丙烯腈或变性聚丙烯腈长丝丝束	Acrylic or modacrylic filament tow	5501.3000	68
聚丙烯腈或变性聚丙烯腈短机织物,其他	Acrylic or modacrylic staple fibres woven fabrics,nes	5515.2900	2468
聚丙烯腈或变性聚丙烯腈短机织物,主要或仅与化学纤维长丝混纺	Acrylic or modacrylic staple fibres woven fabrics, mixed mainly or solely with man-made filaments, nes	5515.2100	2468
聚丙烯腈或变性聚丙烯腈短机织物,主要或仅与羊毛或动物细毛混纺	Acrylic or modacrylic staple fibres woven fabrics, mixed mainly or solely with wool or fine animal hair,nes	5515.2200	2468
聚丙烯腈或变性聚丙烯腈短纤,未梳或未经其他纺前加工	Acrylic or modacrylie staple fibres, not carded, combed or otherwise processed for spinning	5503.3000	68
聚丙烯腈或变性聚丙烯腈短纤,已梳或经其他纺前加工	Acrylic or modacrylic staple fibres,carded,combed or otherwise processed for spinning	5506.3000	68
聚丙烯腈或变性聚丙烯腈短纤纱线,其他	Acrylic or modacrylic staple fibres yarn,nes	5509.6900	68
聚丙烯腈或变性聚丙烯腈短纤纱线,主要或仅与棉混纺	Acrylic or modacrylic staple fibres yarn,mixed mainly or solely with cotton	5509.6200	68

商品名称	Article Description	税则号列	申报要素
聚丙烯腈或变性聚丙烯腈短纤纱线，主要或仅与羊毛或动物细毛混纺	Acrylic or modacrylic staple fibres yarn, mixed mainly or solely with wool or fine animal hair	5509.6100	68
聚丙烯酰胺	Polyacrylamide	3906.9010	1256
聚对苯二甲酸丁二酯，初级形状的	PBT(Polybutylene terephthalate), in primary forms	3907.9910	1256
聚对苯二甲酸乙二酯，初级形状的，其他	Poly(ethylene terephthalate), in primary forms, nes	3907.6090	1256
聚对苯二甲酸乙二酯的废碎料及下脚料	Pdyethylene glycol tevephthalate waste, parings and scrap	3915.9010	146
聚对苯二甲酸乙二酯切片，高粘度	Poly(ethylene terephthalate) slices or chips, high viscosity	3907.6011	1256
聚对苯二甲酸乙二酯切片，其他	Poly(ethylene terephthalate) slices or chips, nes	3907.6019	1256
聚砜，初级形状的	Polysulphones, in primary forms	3911.9000	16
聚光灯	Spot lights	9405.4020	5
聚硅氧烷，初级形状的	Silicones in primary forms	3910.0000	136
聚甲基丙烯酸甲酯	Poly(methyl methacrylate)	3906.1000	1256
聚甲醛，初级形状的	Polyoxymethylene(POM), in primary forms	3907.1010	1256
聚氯乙烯(含氯乙烯聚合物)的废碎料及下脚料	Poly(vinyl chloride)(including polymers of vinyl chloride) waste, parings and scrap	3915.3000	146
聚氯乙烯，未掺其他物质，初级形状的，其他	Poly (vinyl chloride), not mixed with any other substances, in primary forms, nes	3904.1090	1256
聚氯乙烯，未掺其他物质，糊树脂	Poly (vinyl chloride), not mixed with any other substances, paste resins	3904.1010	1256
聚氯乙烯，未塑化，初级形状的	Poly (vinyl chloride), non-plasticized, in primary forms	3904.2100	1256
聚氯乙烯，已塑化，初级形状的	Poly(vinyl chloride), plasticized, in primary forms	3904.2200	1256
聚醚，初级形状的，其他	Polyethers, in primary forms, nes	3907.2090	1256
聚乳酸，初级形状的	Poly(lactic acid), in primary forms	3907.7000	1256
聚四氟乙烯，初级形状的	Polytetrafluoroethylene, in primary forms	3904.6100	1256
聚四亚甲基醚二醇	Polytetramethylene ether glycol (PTMEG)	3907.2010	1256
聚碳酸酯，初级形状的	Polycarbonates, in primary forms	3907.4000	1256
聚碳酸酯，初级形状的，其他	Polycarbonates, in primary forms, nes	3907.9990	1256
聚烯丙基酯，初级形状的	Polyallyl esters, in primary forms	3907.9990	1256
聚酰胺(芳香族)单纱，捻度每米超过50转，非供零售用	Aramides single yarn, with a twist exceeding 50 turns per metre, not put up for retail sale	5402.5130	3468
聚酰胺(芳香族)单纱，未加捻或捻度每米不超过50转，非供零售用	Aramides single yarn, untwisted or with a twist not exceeding 50 turns per metre, not put up for retail sale	5402.4530	3468
聚酰胺(芳香族)弹力丝，每根单纱细度不超过50特，非供零售用	Aramides elastic filament, measuring per single yarn not more than 50 rex, not put up for retail sale	5402.3113	3468
聚酰胺(芳香族)弹力丝，每根单纱细度超过50特，芳香族聚酰胺纺制，非供零售用	Aramides elastic filament, measuring per single yarn more than 50 tex, not put up for retail sale	5402.3213	3468

J

商品名称	Article Description	税则号列	申报要素
聚酰胺(芳香族)多股纱线或缆线,非供零售用	Aramides multiple or cabled yarn, not put up for retail sale	5402. 6130	3468
聚酰胺(芳香族)高强力纱,非供零售用,其他	Aramids high tenacity yarn, not put up for retail sale, nes	5402. 1190	3468
聚酰胺(芳香族)高强力纱,聚对苯二甲酰对苯二胺,非供零售用	Aramids high tenacity yarn, of poly-p-phenylene terephthamide, not put up for retail sale	5402. 1120	3468
聚酰胺(芳香族)高强力纱,聚间苯二甲酰间苯二胺,非供零售用	Aramids high tenacity yarn, of poly isophthaloyl metaphenylene daimine, not put up for retail sale	5402. 1110	3468
聚酰胺(芳族)短纤,聚对苯二甲酰对苯二胺,未梳或未经其他纺前加工	Aramids staple fibres, of poly-p-phenylene terephthamide, not carded, combed or otherwise processed for spinning	5503. 1190	68
聚酰胺(芳族)短纤,聚间苯二甲酰间苯二胺,未梳或未经其他纺前加工	Aramids staple fibres, of poly isophthaloyl metaphenylene daimine, not carded, combed or otherwise processed for spinning	5503. 1110	68
聚酰胺,初级形状的,其他	Polyamides in primary forms, nes	3908. 9000	1256
聚酰胺-6,6 切片	Polyamide -6,6 slices or chips	3908. 1011	1256
聚酰胺-6、-11、-12、-6,6、-6,9、-6,10或-6,12,初级形状的,其他	Polyamide-6, -11, -12, -6, 6, -6, 9, -6, 10 or -6, 12, in primary forms, nes	3908. 1090	1256
聚酰胺切片,其他	Polyamide slices or chips, nes	3908. 1019	1256
聚乙酸乙烯酯,初级形状的,其他	Poly(vinyl acetate), in primary forms, nes	3905. 1900	1256
聚乙酸乙烯酯,水分散体,初级形状的	Poly (vinyl acetate), in aqueous dispersion, in primary forms	3905. 1200	1256
聚乙烯(含乙烯聚合物)的废碎料及下脚料	Polyethylene(including polymers of ethylene) waste, parings and scrap	3915. 1000	146
聚乙烯,比重小于0.94,初级形状的	Polyethylene having a specific gravity of less than 0.94, in primary forms	3901. 1000	1256
聚乙烯,比重在0.94及以上,初级形状的	Polyethylene having a specific gravity of 0.94 or more, in primary forms	3901. 2000	1256
聚乙烯,线型低密度,初级形状的	Polyethylene, linearity low density, in primary forms	3901. 9020	1256
聚乙烯醇,不论是否含有未水解的乙酸酯基,初级形状的	Poly (vinyl alcohol), whether or not containing unhydrolyzed acetate groups, in primary forms	3905. 3000	1256
聚异丁烯	Polyisobutylene	3902. 2000	1256
聚酯,不饱和,初级形状的,其他	Polyesters, unsaturated, in primary forms, nes	3907. 9100	1256
聚酯,初级形状的,其他	Polyesters, in primary forms, nes	3907. 9990	1256
聚酯变形纱线,非供零售用,其他	Polyesters textured yarn, not put up for retail sale, nes	5402. 3390	3468
聚酯长丝丝束	Polyesters filament tow	5501. 2000	68
聚酯单纱,部分定向的,未加捻或捻度每米不超过50转,非供零售用	Polyesters single yarn, partially oriented, untwisted or with a twist not exceeding 50 turns per metre, not put up for retail sale	5402. 4600	3468
聚酯单纱,捻度每米超过50转,非供零售用	Polyesters single yarn, with a twist exceeding 50 turns per metre, not put up for retail sale	5402. 5200	3468

商品名称	Article Description	税则号列	申报要素
聚酯单纱,未加捻或捻度每米不超过50转,非供零售用	Polyesters single yarn, untwisted or with a twist not exceeding 50 turns per metre, not put up for retail sale	5402.4700	3468
聚酯弹力丝,非供零售用	Polyesters elastic filament, not put up for retail sale	5402.3310	3468
聚酯短纤,未梳或未经其他纺前加工	Polyesters staple fibres, not carded, combed or otherwise processed for spinning	5503.2000	68
聚酯短纤,已梳或经其他纺前加工	Polyesters staple fibres, carded, combed or otherwise processed for spinning	5506.2000	68
聚酯短纤纺制的平纹机织物,按重量计合成纤维短纤含量在85%以下,主要或仅与棉混纺,每平方米重量不超过170克,印花	Polyester staple fibres plain weave, containing less than 85% by weight of such fibres, mixed mainly or solely with cotton, of a weight not exceeding 170g/m^2, printed	5513.4100	2468
聚酯短纤机织物,按重量计合成纤维短纤含量在85%以下,主要或仅与棉混纺,每平方米重量不超过170克,印花,其他	Polyester staple fibres woven fabrics, containing less than 85% by weight of such fibres, mixed mainly or solely with cotton, of a weight not exceeding 170g/m^2, printed, nes	5513.4920	2468
聚酯短纤机织物,按重量计合成纤维短纤含量在85%以下,主要或仅与棉混纺,每平方米重量不超过170克,漂白	Polyester staple fibres woven fabrics, containing less than 85% by weight of such fibres, mixed mainly or solely with cotton, of a weight not exceeding 170g/m^2, bleached	5513.1320	2468
聚酯短纤机织物,按重量计合成纤维短纤含量在85%以下,主要或仅与棉混纺,每平方米重量不超过170克,染色,其他	Polyester staple fibres woven fabrics, containing less than 85% by weight of such fibres, mixed mainly or solely with cotton, of a weight not exceeding 170g/m^2, dyed, nes	5513.2390	2468
聚酯短纤机织物,按重量计合成纤维短纤含量在85%以下,主要或仅与棉混纺,每平方米重量不超过170克,色织,其他	Polyester staple fibres woven fabrics, containing less than 85% by weight of such fibres, mixed mainly or solely with cotton, of a weight not exceeding 170g/m^2, of yarns of different colours, nes	5513.3920	2468
聚酯短纤机织物,按重量计合成纤维短纤含量在85%以下,主要或仅与棉混纺,每平方米重量不超过170克,未漂白	Polyester staple fibres woven fabrics, containing less than 85% by weight of such fibres, mixed mainly or solely with cotton, of a weight not exceeding 170g/m^2, unbleached	5513.1310	2468
聚酯短纤机织物,按重量计合成纤维短纤含量在85%以下,主要或仅与棉混纺,每平方米重量超过170克,漂白,其他	Polyester staple fibres woven fabrics, containing less than 85% by weight of such fibres, mixed mainly or solely with cotton, of a weight exceeding 170g/m^2, bleached, nes	5514.1912	2468
聚酯短纤机织物,按重量计合成纤维短纤含量在85%以下,主要或仅与棉混纺,每平方米重量超过170克,染色,其他	Polyester staple fibres woven fabrics, containing less than 85% by weight of such fibres, mixed mainly or solely with cotton, of a weight exceeding 170g/m^2, dyed, nes	5514.2300	2468

商品名称	Article Description	税则号列	申报要素
聚酯短纤机织物,按重量计合成纤维短纤含量在85%以下,主要或仅与棉混纺,每平方米重量超过170克,色织,其他	Polyester staple fibres woven fabrics, containing less than 85% by weight of such fibres, mixed mainly or solely with cotton, of a weight exceeding $170g/m^2$, of yarns of different colours, nes	5514. 3030	2468
聚酯短纤机织物,按重量计合成纤维短纤含量在85%以下,主要或仅与棉混纺,每平方米重量超过170克,未漂白,其他	Polyester staple fibres woven fabrics, containing less than 85% by weight of such fibres, mixed mainly or solely with cotton, of a weight exceeding $170g/m^2$, unbleached, nes	5514. 1911	2468
聚酯短纤机织物,按重量计合成纤维短纤含量在85%以下,主要或仅与棉混纺,每平方米重量超过170克,印花,其他	Polyester staple fibres woven fabrics, containing less than 85% by weight of such fibres, mixed mainly or solely with cotton, of a weight exceeding $170g/m^2$, printed, nes	5514. 4300	2468
聚酯短纤机织物,其他	Polyester staple fibres woven fabrics, nes	5515. 1900	2468
聚酯短纤机织物,主要或仅与化学纤维长丝混纺	Polyester staple fibres woven fabrics, mixed mainly or solely with man-made filaments	5515. 1200	2468
聚酯短纤机织物,主要或仅与羊毛或动物细毛混纺	Polyester staple fibres woven fabrics, mixed mainly or solely with wool or fine animal hair	5515. 1300	2468
聚酯短纤机织物,主要或仅与粘胶纤维短纤混纺	Polyester staple fibres woven fabrics, mixed mainly or solely with viscose rayon staple fibres	5515. 1100	2468
聚酯短纤平纹机织物,按重量计合成纤维短纤含量在85%以下,主要或仅与棉混纺,每平方米重量不超过170克,漂白	Polyester staple fibres plain weave, containing less than 85% by weight of such fibres, mixed mainly or solely with cotton, of a weight not exceeding $170g/m^2$, bleached	5513. 1120	2468
聚酯短纤平纹机织物,按重量计合成纤维短纤含量在85%以下,主要或仅与棉混纺,每平方米重量不超过170克,染色	Polyester staple fibres plain weave, containing less than 85% by weight of such fibres, mixed mainly or solely with cotton, of a weight not exceeding $170g/m^2$, dyed	5513. 2100	2468
聚酯短纤平纹机织物,按重量计合成纤维短纤含量在85%以下,主要或仅与棉混纺,每平方米重量不超过170克,色织	Polyester staple fibres plain weave, containing less than 85% by weight of such fibres, mixed mainly or solely with cotton, of a weight not exceeding $170g/m^2$, of yarns of different colours	5513. 3100	2468
聚酯短纤平纹机织物,按重量计合成纤维短纤含量在85%以下,主要或仅与棉混纺,每平方米重量不超过170克,未漂白	Polyester staple fibres plain weave, ontaining less than 85% by weight of such fibres, mixed mainly or solely with cotton, of a weight not exceeding $170g/m^2$, unbleached	5513. 1110	2468
聚酯短纤平纹机织物,按重量计合成纤维短纤含量在85%以下,主要或仅与棉混纺,每平方米重量超过170克,漂白	Polyester staple fibres plain weave, containing less than 85% by weight of such fibres, mixed mainly or solely with cotton, of a weight exceeding $170g/m^2$, bleached	5514. 1120	2468
聚酯短纤平纹机织物,按重量计合成纤维短纤含量在85%以下,主要或仅与棉混纺,每平方米重量超过170克,染色	Polyester staple fibres plain weave, containing less than 85% by weight of such fibres, mixed mainly or solely with cotton, of a weight exceeding $170g/m^2$, dyed	5514. 2100	2468

J

商品名称	Article Description	税则号列	申报要素
聚酯短纤平纹机织物,按重量计合成纤维短纤含量在85%以下,主要或仅与棉混纺,每平方米重量超过170克,色织	Polyester staple fibres plain weave, containing less than 85% by weight of such fibres, mixed mainly or solely with cotton, of a weight exceeding 170g/m^2, of yarns of different colours	5514.3010	2468
聚酯短纤平纹机织物,按重量计合成纤维短纤含量在85%以下,主要或仅与棉混纺,每平方米重量超过170克,未漂白	Polyester staple fibres plain weave, containing less than 85% by weight of such fibres, mixed mainly or solely with cotton, of a weight exceeding 170g/m^2, unbleached	5514.1110	2468
聚酯短纤平纹机织物,按重量计合成纤维短纤含量在85%以下,主要或仅与棉混纺,每平方米重量超过170克,印花	Polyester staple fibres plain weave, containing less than 85% by weight of such fibres, mixed mainly or solely with cotton, of a weight exceeding 170g/m^2, printed	5514.4100	2468
聚酯短纤三线或四线斜纹机织物,包括双面斜纹机织物,按重量计合成纤维短纤含量在85%以下,主要或仅与棉混纺,每平方米重量不超过170克,印花	Polyester staple fibres 3-thread or 4-thread twill, including cross twill, containing less than 85% by weight of such fibres, mixed mainly or solely with cotton, of a weight not exceeding 170g/m^2, printed	5513.4910	2468
聚酯短纤三线或四线斜纹机织物,包括双面斜纹机织物,按重量计合成纤维短纤含量在85%以下,主要或仅与棉混纺,每平方米重量不超过170克,漂白	Polyester staple fibres 3-thread or 4-thread twill, including cross twill, containing less than 85% by weight of such fibres, mixed mainly or solely with cotton, of a weight not exceeding 170g/m^2, bleached	5513.1220	2468
聚酯短纤三线或四线斜纹机织物,包括双面斜纹机织物,按重量计合成纤维短纤含量在85%以下,主要或仅与棉混纺,每平方米重量不超过170克,染色	Polyester staple fibres 3-thread or 4-thread twill, including cross twill, containing less than 85% by weight of such fibres, mixed mainly or solely with cotton, of a weight not exceeding 170g/m^2, dyed	5513.2310	2468
聚酯短纤三线或四线斜纹机织物,包括双面斜纹机织物,按重量计合成纤维短纤含量在85%以下,主要或仅与棉混纺,每平方米重量不超过170克,色织	Polyester staple fibres 3-thread or 4-thread twill, including cross twill, containing less than 85% by weight of such fibres, mixed mainly or solely with cotton, of a weight not exceeding 170g/m^2, of yarns of different colours	5513.3910	2468
聚酯短纤三线或四线斜纹机织物,包括双面斜纹机织物,按重量计合成纤维短纤含量在85%以下,主要或仅与棉混纺,每平方米重量不超过170克,未漂白	Polyester staple fibres 3-thread or 4-thread twill, including cross twill, containing less than 85% by weight of such fibres, mixed mainly or solely with cotton, of a weight not exceeding 170g/m^2, unbleached	5513.1210	2468
聚酯短纤三线或四线斜纹机织物,包括双面斜纹机织物,按重量计合成纤维短纤含量在85%以下,主要或仅与棉混纺,每平方米重量超过170克,漂白	Polyester staple fibres 3-thread or 4-thread twill, including cross twill, containing less than 85% by weight of such fibres, mixed mainly or solely with cotton, of a weight exceeding 170g/m^2, bleached	5514.1220	2468

商品名称	Article Description	税则号列	申报要素
聚酯短纤三线或四线斜纹机织物,包括双面斜纹机织物,按重量计合成纤维短纤含量在85%以下,主要或仅与棉混纺,每平方米重量超过170克,染色	Polyester staple fibres 3-thread or 4-thread twill, including cross twill, containing less than 85% by weight of such fibres, mixed mainly or solely with cotton, of a weight exceeding $170g/m^2$, dyed	5514.2200	2468
聚酯短纤三线或四线斜纹机织物,包括双面斜纹机织物,按重量计合成纤维短纤含量在85%以下,主要或仅与棉混纺,每平方米重量超过170克,色织	Polyester staple fibres 3-thread or 4-thread twill, including cross twill, containing less than 85% by weight of such fibres, mixed mainly or solely with cotton, of a weight exceeding $170g/m^2$, of yarns of different colours	5514.3020	2468
聚酯短纤三线或四线斜纹机织物,包括双面斜纹机织物,按重量计合成纤维短纤含量在85%以下,主要或仅与棉混纺,每平方米重量超过170克,未漂白	Polyester staple fibres 3-thread or 4-thread twill, including cross twill, containing less than 85% by weight of such fibres, mixed mainly or solely with cotton, of a weight exceeding $170g/m^2$, unbleached	5514.1210	2468
聚酯短纤三线或四线斜纹机织物,包括双面斜纹机织物,按重量计合成纤维短纤含量在85%以下,主要或仅与棉混纺,每平方米重量超过170克,印花	Polyester staple fibres 3-thread or 4-thread twill, including cross twill, containing less than 85% by weight of such fibres, mixed mainly or solely with cotton, of a weight exceeding $170g/m^2$, printed	5514.4200	2468
聚酯短纤纱线,其他	Polyester staple fibres yarn, nes	5509.5900	68
聚酯短纤纱线,主要或仅与棉混纺	Polyester staple fibres yarn, mixed mainly or solely with cotton	5509.5300	68
聚酯短纤纱线,主要或仅与人造纤维短纤混纺	Polyester staple fibres yarn, mixed mainly or solely with artificial staple fibres	5509.5100	68
聚酯短纤纱线,主要或仅与羊毛或动物细毛混纺	Polyester staple fibres yarn, mixed mainly or solely with wool or fine animal hair	5509.5200	68
聚酯多股纱线或缆线,非供零售用	Polyesters multiple or cabled yarn, not put up for retail sale	5402.6200	3468
聚酯高强力纱,非供零售用	Polyesters high tenacity yarn, not put up for retail sale	5402.2000	3468
聚酯高强力纱纺制的机织物	Polyesters high tenacity yarn woven fabrics	5407.1020	2468
聚酯机织物,按重量计变形长丝含量在85%及以上,染色	Polyester woven fabrics, containing 85% or more by weight of textured filaments, dyed	5407.5200	2468
聚酯机织物,按重量计变形长丝含量在85%及以上,色织	Polyester woven fabrics, containing 85% or more by weight of textured filaments, of yarns of different colours	5407.5300	2468
聚酯机织物,按重量计变形长丝含量在85%及以上,未漂白或漂白	Polyester woven fabrics, containing 85% or more by weight of textured filaments, unbleached or bleached	5407.5100	2468
聚酯机织物,按重量计变形长丝含量在85%及以上,印花	Polyester woven fabrics, containing 85% or more by weight of textured filaments, printed	5407.5400	2468
聚酯机织物,按重量计长丝含量在85%及以上,其他	Polyester woven fabrics, containing 85% or more by weight of filaments, nes	5407.6900	2468

J

商品名称	Article Description	税则号列	申报要素
聚酯机织物,按重量计聚酯非变形长丝含量在85%及以上	Polyester woven fabrics, containing 85% or more by weight of non-textured polyester filaments	5407.6100	2468
juan			
卷发夹	Haircurlers or curling pins	9615.9000	
卷发器	Curling grips	9615.9000	
卷发器、电热的	Hair curlers, electro-thermic	8516.3300	7
卷绕机器,纺织物的	Reeling machines for textile fabrics	8451.5000	
卷绕机器零件,纺织物的	Reeling machines parts for textile fabrics	8451.9000	
卷纬机	Weft-winding machines	8445.4090	7
卷纬机的辅助机器	Weft-winding machines auxiliary	8448.1900	3
卷心菜,鲜或冷藏的	Cabbages (brassica oleracea var. Capitata), fresh or chilled	0704.9010	1
卷烟,烟草代用品制成的	Cigarettes, of tobacco substitutes	2402.9000	245
卷烟,烟草制的	Cigarettes containing tobacco	2402.2000	245
卷烟滤嘴	Cigarette filter tips	5601.2210	6
卷扬机,电动的,其他	Winches, powered by electric motor, nes	8425.3190	78
卷扬机,电动的,专为井下使用设计的	Winches, powered by electric motor, specially designed for use underground	8425.3110	78
卷扬机,其他	Winches, nes	8425.3990	78
卷扬机,专为井下使用设计的	Winches specially designed for use underground, nes	8425.3910	78
卷扬装置,电动的,矿井口用	Pit-head winding gear, powered by electric motor	8425.3110	78
卷扬装置,矿井口用	Pit-head winding gear	8425.3910	78
卷轴、纡子、筒管及类似品,塑料的	Spools, cops, bobbins and similar supports, of plastics	3923.4000	23
卷轴及类似品,木制	Spools and the like, of wood	4421.9010	56
卷宗盒类似品,办公室、商店及类似场所使用的,纸制的	Box files and similar articles, of a kind used in offices, shops or the like, of paper, paperboard,	4819.6000	68
卷宗夹的附件	Fittings for loose-leaf files	8305.1000	256
卷宗皮,纸或纸板制的	File covers, of paper or paperboard	4820.3000	
绢纺纱线,非供零售用,其他	Yarn spun from silk waste, not put up for retail sale, nes	5005.0090	356
绢丝机织物,按重量计丝或绢丝含量在85%及以上,其他	Silk waste fabrics, containing 85% or more by weight of silk or of silk waste, nes	5007.2039	4568
绢丝机织物,按重量计丝或绢丝含量在85%及以上,未漂白或漂白	Silk waste fabrics, unbleached or bleached, containing 85% or more by weight of silk or of silk waste	5007.2031	4568
jue			
绝缘布或带,浸渍、涂布或包覆的,其他	Insulating cloth or tape, impregnated, coated or covered, nes	5907.0010	4
绝缘布或带,用聚氨基甲酸酯浸渍、涂布、包覆或层压的	Insulating cloth or tape, impregnated, coated, covered or laminated with polyurethane	5903.2010	
绝缘布或带,用聚氯乙烯浸渍、涂布包覆或层压的	Insulating cloth or tape, impregnated, coated, covered or laminated with poly (vinyl chloride)	5903.1010	

商品名称	Article Description	税则号列	申报要素
绝缘布或带,用塑料浸渍、涂布、包覆或层压的,其他	Insulating cloth or tape, impregnated, coated, covered or laminated with plastics, nes	5903. 9010	
绝缘布或带,用橡胶处理的	Insulating cloth or tape, rubberized	5906. 9910	48
绝缘带,宽度不超过 20 厘米的,用橡胶处理的	Insulating tape, of a width not exceeding 20cm, rubberized	5906. 1010	48
绝缘零件,电气机器、器具或设备用,全部用绝缘材料制成	Insulating fittings for electrical machines, appliances or equipment, being fittings wholly of insulating material	8547. 9090	3
绝缘零件,塑料制	Insulating fittings of plastics	8547. 2000	3
绝缘零件,陶瓷制	Insulating fittings of ceramics	8547. 1000	3
绝缘纸及纸板,用蜡、石蜡、硬脂精、油或甘油涂布、浸渍、覆盖的	Insulating paper and paperboard, coated, impregnated or covered with wax, paraffin wax, stearin, oil or glyecrol	4811. 6010	458
绝缘纸及纸板,用塑料(不包括粘合剂)涂布、浸渍或覆盖的	Insulating paper and paperboard, coated, impregnated or covered with plastics(excluding adhesives)	4811. 5910	458
绝缘子,玻璃制	Electrical insulators of glass	8546. 1000	3
绝缘子,其他	Electrical insulators, nes	8546. 9000	3
绝缘子,陶瓷制,其他	Electrical insulators of ceramics, nes	8546. 2090	3
绝缘子,陶瓷制,输变电线路绝缘瓷套管	Electrical insulators of ceramics, power transmission and converting ceramic bushings	8546. 2010	3
绝缘子用玻璃伞盘,工业用	Glass umbrella for insulator, for technical use	7020. 0012	6
掘头	Hoes	8201. 3000	256
蕨莱,干的	Wild brake, dried	0712. 9040	4
嚼烟	Chewing tobacco	2403. 9900	
jun			
军舰	Warships	8906. 1000	
军用武器,手枪除外,其他	Military weapons, other than revolvers, pistols, nes	9301. 9000	7
均化混合食品	Homogenized composite food preparations	2104. 2000	28
均化机,其他	Homogenizing machines, nes	8479. 8200	7
均化食品,烹煮的	Homogenized preparations, being cooked preparations	2007. 1000	248
均化食品,制作或保藏的	Homogenized preparations, prepared or preserved	1602. 1000	48
均化蔬菜,用醋或醋酸以外的其他方法制作或保藏的,未冷冻	Homogenized vegetables, prepared or preserved otherwise than by vinegar or acetic acid, not frozen	2005. 1000	48
均化烟草	Homogenized tobacco	2403. 9100	

J

K

商品名称	Article Description	税则号列	申报要素
ka			
咖啡,未焙炒的,未浸除咖啡碱	Coffee, not roasted, not decaffeinated	0901.1100	14
咖啡,未焙炒的,已浸除咖啡碱	Coffee, not roasted, decaffeinated	0901.1200	14
咖啡,已焙炒的,未浸除咖啡碱	Coffee, roasted, not decaffeinated	0901.2100	14
咖啡,已焙炒的,已浸除咖啡碱	Coffee, roasted, decaffeinated	0901.2200	14
咖啡代用品及其浓缩精汁	Coffee substitutes, and extracts, essences and concentrates thereof	2101.3000	268
咖啡豆荚	Coffee husks	0901.9010	5
咖啡豆皮	Coffee skins	0901.9010	5
咖啡壶,电热的,其他	Coffee makers, electro-thermic, nes	8516.7190	7
咖啡机,电热的,泵压式	Coffee makers, electro-thermic, pump espresso	8516.7130	7
咖啡机,电热的,滴液式	Coffee makers, electro-thermic, drip	8516.7110	7
咖啡机,电热的,蒸馏渗滤式	Coffee makers, electro-thermic, steam espresso	8516.7120	7
咖啡浓缩精汁	Coffee extracts, essences and concentrates	2101.1100	268
咖啡浓缩精汁为基本成分的制品	Coffee preparations with a basis of extracts, essences or concentrates or with a basis of coffee	2101.1200	268
咖啡因及其盐	Caffeine and its salts	2939.3000	34
卡尺	Callipers	9017.3000	
卡拉胶	Carrageenan	1302.3911	35
卡拉马尼及类似的手织地毯	Karamanieand and similar handwoven rugs	5702.1000	468
卡喇杆胶	Gum tragacanth	1301.9010	
卡马西泮(INN)以及盐	Camazepam(INN); salts thereof	2933.9100	36
卡那霉素及其衍生物以及它们的盐	Kanamycin and its derivatives; salts thereof	2941.9020	
卡片,印有个人问候、祝贺、通告的	Printed cards bearing personal greetings, messages or announcements	4909.0090	4
卡片、盘及带卷,机械乐器用的	Cards, discs and rolls for mechanical instruments	9209.9990	3
卡片索引柜,贱金属制,办公室家具除外	Card-index cabinets, of base metal, other than office furniture	8304.0000	256
胩	Isocyanides	2929.9090	36
kai			
开槽机床,加工金属用,其他	Notching machines, for working metal, nes	8462.4900	7
开槽机床,数控的,加工金属用,其他	Notching machines, numerically controlled, for working metal	8462.4190	7
开封或闭封机,信件用	Opening or closing mail machines	8472.3090	
开关,用于电压不超过 1000 伏的线路,其他	Switches, for a voltage not exceeding 1000V, nes	8536.5000	8
开襟衫,针织或钩编的,化学纤维制	Cardigans, knitted or crocheted, of man-made fibres	6110.3000	2456

商品名称	Article Description	税则号列	申报要素
开襟衫,针织或钩编的,喀什米尔山羊细毛制	Cardigans, knitted or crocheted, of kashmir (cashmere) goats	6110.1200	2456
开襟衫,针织或钩编的,毛制	Cardigans, knitted or crocheted, of wool	6110.1100	2456
开襟衫,针织或钩编的,棉制	Cardigans, knitted or crocheted, of cotton	6110.2000	2456
开襟衫,针织或钩编的,其他	Cardigans, knitted or crocheted, nes	6110.9090	2456
开襟衫,针织或钩编的,其他动物细毛制	Cardigans, knitted or crocheted, of fine animal hair	6110.1990	2456
开襟衫,针织或钩编的,其他山羊细毛制	Cardigans, knitted or crocheted, of other goats	6110.1910	2456
开襟衫,针织或钩编的,丝及绢丝制	Cardigans, knitted or crocheted, of silk or silk waste	6110.9010	2456
开襟衫,针织或钩编的,兔毛制	Cardigans, knitted or crocheted, of rabbit and hare	6110.1920	2456
开口铆钉,贱金属制,	Bifurcated rivets, of base metal	8308.2000	256
开来姆及类似的手织地毯	Kelem and similar handwoven rugs	5702.1000	468
开尾销,铝制	Cotter-pins, of aluminium	7616.1000	36
开信刀及其刀片	Letter openers and blades thereof	8214.1000	256
凯他唑仑(INN)及盐	Ketazolam(INN); salts thereof	2934.9100	36
凯托米酮(INN)及盐	Ketobemidone (INN); salts thereof	2933.3300	36
kan			
砍骨刀	Kitchen cleavers	8214.9000	256
莰烯	Camphene	2902.1990	6
kang			
康乃馨,其他	Carnation, nes	0602.9095	
康乃馨,鲜的,制花束或装饰用的	Carnations, fresh, suitable for bouquets or for ornamental purposes	0603.1200	34
康乃馨,种用	Carnation, seedlings	0602.9091	3
糠、麸及其他残渣,豆类植物的	Bran, sharps and other residues, of leguminous plants	2302.5000	56
糠、麸及其他残渣,其他谷物的	Bran, sharps and other residues, of other cereals	2302.4000	56
糠、麸及其他残渣,小麦的	Bran, sharps and other residues, of wheat	2302.3000	56
糠、麸及其他残渣,玉米的	Bran, sharps and other residues, of maize (corn)	2302.1000	56
糠醇及四氢糠醇	Furfuryl alcohol and tetrahydrofurfuryl alcohol	2932.1300	36
抗菌素,其他	Antibiotics, nes	2941.9090	
抗菌素药品,其他,混合或未混合的,配定剂量或制成零售包装	Antibiotics medicaments, nes, mixed or unmixed, put up in measured doses or in forms or packings for retail sale	3004.2090	368
抗菌素药品,其他,两种或两种以上成分混合而成的,未配定剂量或制成零售包装	Antibiotics medicaments, nes, consisting of two or more constituents which have been mixed together, not put up in measured doses or in forms or packings for retail sale	3003.2090	368
抗萌剂,零售包装	Anti-sprouting products, put up for retail sale	3808.9391	36
抗萌剂,其他	Anti-sprouting products, nes	3808.9399	36
抗血清	Antisera	3002.1000	34

商品名称	Article Description	税则号列	申报要素
抗氧剂,用于矿物油及类似液体	Oxidation inhibitors, for mineral oils and alike	3811.9000	236
抗氧制剂及其他复合稳定剂,橡胶或塑料用,其他	Anti-oxidizing preparations and other compound stabilizers for rubber or plastics, nes	3812.3090	36
抗粘连阻隔材料,外科或牙科用,无菌,不论是否可吸收	Adhesion barriers, for surgical or dental use, sterile, whether or not absorbable	3006.1000	3
抗震剂,用于矿物油及类似液体,其他	Anti-knock preparations, for mineral oils and alike, nes	3811.1900	236
抗震剂,用于矿物油及类似液体,以铅化合物为基本成分	Anti-knock preparations, for mineral oils and alike, based on lead compounds	3811.1100	236
钪	Scandium	2805.3019	56
钪,与稀土相互混合或相互熔合,电池级	Scandium, inuermixed or interalloyed with rare-earth metals, battery grade	2805.3021	56
钪,与稀土相互混合或相互熔合,其他	Scandium, inuermixed or interalloyed with rare-earth metals, nes	2805.3029	56
kao			
考勤钟	Time-registers	9106.1000	5
拷贝或转印纸,其他	Copying or transfer papers, nes	4816.9090	58
拷贝纸,成卷或成张的,卷宽度超过36厘米,或长超过36厘米且宽超过15厘米	Copying papers, in rolls or sheets, of width exceeding 36cm or in roll or one side exceeding 36cm and other side exceeding 15cm in rectangular sheets	4809.9000	458
烤宽面条,生的,含蛋的	Lasagne, uncooked, containing eggs	1902.1100	46
烤宽面条,生的,其他	Lasagne, uncooked, nes	1902.1900	46
烤炉,钢铁制,非电热的家用,其他,包括使用固体燃料的	Braziers, of iron or steel, non-electric domestic appliances, nes, including appliances for solid fuel	7321.1900	7
烤炉,钢铁制,非电热的家用,使用气体燃料或可使用气体燃料及其他燃料的	Braziers, of iron or steel, non-electric domestic appliances, for gas fuel or for both gas and other fuels	7321.1100	7
烤炉,钢铁制,非电热的家用,使用液体燃料的	Braziers, of iron or steel, non-electric domestic appliances, for liquid fuel	7321.1290	7
烤炉,面包房用及包括做饼干用的	Bakery ovens, including biscuit ovens	8417.2000	7
烤面包器,其他	Toasters, nes	8516.7290	7
烤肉架,钢铁制,非电热的家用,其他,包括使用固体燃料的	Barbecues, of iron or steel, non-electric domestic appliances, nes, including appliances for solid fuel	7321.1900	7
烤肉架,钢铁制,非电热的家用,使用气体燃料或可使用气体燃料及其他燃料的	Barbecues, of iron or steel, non-electric domestic appliances, for gas fuel or for both gas and other fuels	7321.1100	7
烤肉架,钢铁制,非电热的家用,使用液体燃料的	Barbecues, of iron or steel, non-electric domestic appliances, for liquid fuel	7321.1290	7
烤烟,部分或全部去梗的	Tobacco, partly or wholly stemmed/stripped, flue-cured	2401.2010	4
烤烟,未去梗的	Tobacco, not stemmed/stripped, flue-cured	2401.1010	4
靠垫,化纤棉填充的	Cushions, stuffed with man-made fibres	9404.9040	6

商品名称	Article Description	税则号列	申报要素
靠垫,其他	Cushions, nes	9404.9090	6
靠垫,兽毛填充的	Cushions, stuffed with animal hair	9404.9020	6
靠垫,丝棉填充的	Cushions, stuffed with silk wadding	9404.9030	6
靠垫,羽毛或羽绒填充的	Cushions, stuffed with feathers or down	9404.9010	6
ke			
苛性钾	Caustic potash	2815.2000	136
柯迪尔酒	Cordials	2208.7000	2468
颗粒,生铁、镜铁及钢铁的	Granules, of pig iron, spiegeleisen, iron or steel	7205.1000	6
可编程序控制器,用于电压不超过1000伏的线路,装有两个或多个开关、保护或连接用的电器装置	Programmable logic controller (PLC), for a voltage not exceeding 1000V, equipped with two or more switching or protecting or connecting apparatus	8537.1011	78
可充气的球,体育用品,其他	Balls, inflatable, sports articles, nes	9506.6290	5
可充气制品,硫化橡胶(硬质橡胶除外)的,其他	Inflatable articles of vulcanized rubber other than hard rubber, nes	4016.9500	236
可待因及盐	Codeine and salts	2939.1100	34
可的松	Cortisone	2937.2100	36
可互换工具,带有天然或合成金刚石、立方氮化硼制的工作部件	Interchangeable tools, with working part of natural or synthetic diamonds or cubic boron nitride	8207.9010	256
可互换工具,其他	Interchangeable tools, nes	8207.9090	256
可见光分光仪、分光光度计及摄谱仪	Visible spectrometers, spectrophotometers and spectrographs	9027.3000	
可卡因及其盐	Cocaine and its salts	2939.9110	34
可可豆,整颗或破碎的,生的或焙炒的	Cocoa beans, whole or broken, raw or roasted	1801.0000	4
可可粉,加糖或其他甜物质的	Cocoa powder, containing added sugar or other sweetening matter	1806.1000	248
可可粉,未加糖或其他甜物质的	Cocoa powder, not containing added sugar or other sweetening matter	1805.0000	468
可可粉生产机器	Cocoa manufacture machinery	8438.2000	
可可粉生产机器的零件	Cocoa manufacture machinery parts	8438.9000	3
可可膏,全脱脂或部分脱脂	Cocoa paste, wholly or partly defatted	1803.2000	6
可可膏,未脱脂	Cocoa paste, not defatted	1803.1000	6
可可荚、壳、皮及废料	Cocoa shells, husks, skins and other cocoa waste	1802.0000	4
可可食品,其他	Chocolate and other food preparations containing cocoa, nes	1806.9000	268
可可食品,其他,不夹心,块状或条状的	Chocolate and other food preparations containing cocoa, not filled, in blocks, slabs or bars	1806.3200	12468
可可食品,其他,夹心,块状或条状的	Chocolate and other food preparations containing cocoa, filled, in blocks, slabs or bars	1806.3100	12468
可可油	Cocoa oil	1804.0000	
可可脂	Cocoa butter, fat	1804.0000	
克拉维酸及其盐	Clavulanic acid and its salts	2934.9950	36

商品名称	Article Description	税则号列	申报要素
刻花机,玻璃冷加工用	Carving machines, for cold-working glass or glassware	8464. 9012	7
刻蚀及剥离设备,制造半导体器件或集成电路的机器及装置,其他	Etching and stripping equipment, semiconductor devices or of electronic integrated circuits manufacture machines and apparatus, nes	8486. 2049	7
刻蚀及剥离设备零件及附件,制造半导体器件或集成电路的机器及装置	Etching and stripping equipment parts and accessories, semiconductor devices or of electronic integrated circuits manufacture machines and apparatus	8486. 9090	3
客运船舶,非机动船舶	Vessels for the transport of persons, not-motorized vessels	8901. 1090	5
客运船舶,机动船舶	Vessels for the transport of persons, motor vessels	8901. 1010	5
客运架空索道,单线循环式	Passanger aerial cableways, monocable endless	8428. 6021	
客运架空索道,其他	Passanger aerial cableways, nes	8428. 6029	
kong			
空包弹发射的左轮手枪和其他手枪	Blank ammunition firing pistols and revolvers	9303. 9000	
空气,压缩的	Air, compressed	2853. 0090	
空气,液态的	Air, liquid	2853. 0090	
空气泵,手动或脚踏式	Air pumps, hand-operated or foot-operated	8414. 2000	27
空气泵零件	Air pumps parts	8414. 9090	23
空气调节器,窗式或壁式,独立式	Air conditioning machines, window or wall types, self-contained	8415. 1010	25
空气调节器,窗式或壁式,分体式,制冷量不超过4000大卡/时	Air conditioning machines, window or wall types, split systerm, of a refrigerating effect not exceeding 4000Cal per hour	8415. 1021	25
空气调节器,窗式或壁式,分体式,制冷量超过4000大卡/时	Air conditioning machines, window or wall types, split systerm, of a refrigerating effect exceeding 4000Cal per hour	8415. 1022	25
空气调节器,机动车辆上供人使用的	Air conditioning machines, of a kind used for persons, in motor vehicles	8415. 2000	25
空气调节器,未装有制冷装置的	Air conditioning machines, not incorporating a refrigerating unit	8415. 8300	25
空气调节器,装有制冷装置的,制冷量不超过4000大卡/时	Air conditioning machines, incorporating a refrigerating unit, of a refrigerating effect not exceeding 4000Cal per hour	8415. 8210	25
空气调节器,装有制冷装置的,制冷量超过4000大卡/时	Air conditioning machines, incorporating a refrigerating unit, of a refrigerating effect exceeding 4000Cal per hour	8415. 8220	25
空气调节器,装有制冷装置及一个冷热循环换向阀的(可逆式热泵),制冷量不超过4000大卡/时	Air conditioning machines, incorporating a refrigerating unit and a valve for reversal of the cooling/heat cycle (reversible heat pumps), of a refrigerating effect not exceeding 4000Cal per hour	8415. 8110	25

K

商品名称	Article Description	税则号列	申报要素
空气调节器,装有制冷装置及一个冷热循环换向阀的(可逆式热泵),制冷量超过4000大卡/时	Air conditioning machines, incorporating a refrigerating unit and a valve for reversal of the cooling/heat cycle (reversible heat pumps), of a refrigerating effect exceeding 4000Cal per hour	8415. 8120	25
空气调节器零件,非机动车辆上供人使用的	Air conditioning machines parts, other than a kind used for persons, in motor vehicles	8415. 9010	23
空气调节器零件,机动车辆上供人使用的	Air conditioning machines parts, of a kind used for persons, in motor vehicles	8415. 9090	23
空气加热器及其零件,钢铁制,非电热的,装有电动风扇或鼓风机	Air heaters and parts thereof, of iron or steel, not electrically heated, incorporating a motor-dirven fan or blower	7322. 9000	7
空气减湿器	Air dehumidifiers	8479. 8920	7
空气冷却器,蒸发式的	Air coolers, evaporative	8479. 6000	7
空气捻接器	Air twisting devices	8448. 3930	3
空气压缩机,装在拖车底盘上的	Air compressors mounted on a wheeled chassis for towing	8414. 4000	23
空气增湿器	Air humidifiers	8479. 8920	7
空气制动器及其零件,铁道及电车道机车或其他车辆的	Air brakes and parts, of railway or tramway locomotives or rolling-stock	8607. 2100	3
空心玻璃球面及片段,制造钟表玻璃及眼镜用玻璃的凹面用	Hollow glass spheres and their segments, for the manufacture of clock, watch or spectacles glasses	7015. 9090	1345
空心异型材,铝合金制	Hollow profiles of aluminium alloys	7604. 2100	16
空心钻钢,合金钢或非合金钢制的	Hollow drill bars and rods, of alloy or non-alloy steel	7228. 8000	468
空战模拟器及其零件	Air combat simulators and parts thereof	8805. 2100	3
控制阀,恒温的	Controlled valves, thermostatically	8481. 8040	
控制器,集成电路,不论是否带有存储器、转换器、逻辑电路、放大器、时钟及时序电路或其他电路	Controllers, electronic integrated circuits, whether or not combined with memories, converters, logic circuits, amplifiers, clock and timing circuits, or other circuits	8542. 3100	37
kou			
口吹音响信号器	Mouth-blown sound signalling instruments	9208. 9000	5
口蘑,干的	Tricholoma mongolicum imai, dried	0712. 3940	4
口蘑,鲜或冷藏的	Tricholoma mongolicum imai, fresh or chilled	0709. 5950	1
口琴	Mouth organs	9205. 9030	5
口套,适合各种动物用	Muzzles for any animal, of any material	4201. 0000	1458
口香糖	Cachous	1704. 1000	268
口香糖,不论是否裹糖	Chewing gum, whether or not sugarcoated, not containing cocoa	1704. 1000	268
扣,带栓的,贱金属制,用于衣着、鞋靴、天篷、提包、旅行用品或其他制成品	Buckle-clasps, of base metal, of a kind used for clothing, footwear, awnings, handbags, travel goods or other made up articles	8308. 9000	256

K

商品名称	Article Description	税则号列	申报要素
扣,贱金属制,用于衣着、鞋靴、天篷、提包、旅行用品或其他制成品	Buckles, of base metal, of a kind used for clothing, footwear, awnings, handbags, travel goods or other made up articles	8308.9000	256
扣环及扣环框架,带锁的,贱金属制	Clasps and frames with clasps, incorporating locks, of base metal	8301.5000	256
扣式原电池及原电池组,碱性锌锰的	Button shape primary cells and primary batteries, alkaline zinc-manganese dioxide	8506.1011	68
扣眼,贱金属制,用于衣着	Clothing eyes, of base metal	8308.1000	256
筘,织机用	Reeds for looms	8448.4200	3
ku			
枯茗子	Seeds of cumin	0909.3000	
苦艾酒	Absinth	2208.9090	2468
苦杏仁	Bitter apricot kernels	1212.9911	134
库秤	Hopper scales	8423.3090	
kuai			
块、板、片及条,任何形状的砖、瓦,压制软木制	Blocks, plates, sheets and strip, tiles of any shape, of agglomerated cork	4504.1000	16
块根,其他,休眠的	Tuberous roots, nes, dormant	0601.1099	135
块根,生长或开花的	Tuberous roots, in growth or in flower	0601.2000	
块根,种用,休眠的	Tuberous roots, seed, dormant	0601.1091	135
块根芹,鲜或冷藏的	Celeriac, fresh or chilled	0706.9000	1
块茎,其他,休眠的	Tubers, nes, dormant	0601.1099	135
块茎,生长或开花的	Tubers, in growth or in flower	0601.2000	
块茎,种用,休眠的	Tubers, seed, dormant	0601.1091	135
块菌	Truffles	2003.2000	248
块菌,鲜或冷藏的	Truffle, fresh or chilled	0709.5960	1
快门组件,照相机用	Shutter units for cameras	9006.9192	3
快艇,充气的,娱乐或运动用	Yachts, inflatable, for pleasure or sports	8903.1000	58
筷子,一次性的,木制	Chopsticks, for one-time use, of wood	4419.0031	6
筷子,一次性的,其他木质材料制	Chopsticks, for one-time use, of other wooden materials	4419.0039	6
筷子,一次性的,竹制	Chopsticks, for one-time use, of bamboo	4419.0032	6
会计计算机,装有计算装置的	Accounting machines	8470.3000	
kuang			
狂欢节用品	Carnival entertainment articles	9505.9000	5
矿藏探测器	Mine detectors	8543.7091	37
矿藏探测器用零件	Mine detectors parts	8543.9030	3
矿产品,其他	Mineral substances, nes	2530.9099	13456
矿车推动机	Mine wagon pushers	8428.9010	
矿泉水,加味、加糖或其他甜物质的	Mineral waters, containing added sugar or other sweetening matter or flavoured	2202.1000	248

商品名称	Article Description	税则号列	申报要素
矿泉水,未加糖或其他甜物质及未加味的	Mineral waters, not containing added sugar or other sweetening matter or flavoured	2201.1010	28
矿砂及其精矿,其他	Ores and concentrates, nes	2617.9090	146
矿物材料用型模	Moulds for mineral materials	8480.6000	7
矿物氮肥及化学氮肥,其他	Mineral or chemical fertilizers, nitrogenous, nes	3102.9090	68
矿物钾肥及化学钾肥,其他	Mineral or chemical fertilizers, potassic, nes	3104.9090	68
矿物蜡,其他	Mineral waxes, nes	2712.9090	6
矿物磷肥及化学磷肥,其他	Mineral or chemical fertilizers, phosphatic, nes	3103.9000	68
矿物性药材	Mineral medicinal substances	2530.9010	13456
矿物与沥青的混合机器	Mineral substances with bitumen mixing machines	8474.3200	
矿物质或纤维素为基本成分的未装配摩擦材料及其制品,适于作制动器、离合器及类似品,不含石棉的,其他	Mineral substances or cellulose friction material and articles thereof, not mpunted, for brakes, for clutches or the like, not containing asbestos	6813.8900	6
矿用电铲,自推进的	Mining power shovels, self-propelled	8430.5020	5
矿用电铲用零件	Mining power shovels parts	8431.4910	3
矿渣、矿灰及残渣(冶炼钢铁所产生的灰、渣除外),含砷、汞、铊及其混合物,用于提取或生产砷、汞、铊及其化合物	Slag, ash and residues (other than from the manufacture of iron or steel) containing arsenic, mercury, thallium or their mixtures, of a kind used for the extraction of arsenic or those metals or for the manufacture of their chemical compounds	2620.6000	134
矿渣、矿灰及残渣(冶炼钢铁所产生的灰、渣除外),含锑、铍、镉、铬及其混合物	Slag, ash and residues (other than from the manufacture of iron or steel) containing antimony, beryllinm, cadmium, chromium or their mixtures	2620.9100	134
矿渣、矿灰及残渣(冶炼钢铁所产生的灰、渣除外),含硬锌	Slag, ash and residues (other than from the manufacture of iron or steel) containing hard zinc spelter	2620.1100	134
矿渣、矿灰及残渣(冶炼钢铁所产生的灰、渣除外),含有金属及其化合物的,其他	Slag, ash and residues (other than from the manufacture of iron or steel) containing metals or their compounds, nes	2620.9990	134
矿渣、矿灰及残渣(冶炼钢铁所产生的灰、渣除外),主要含铝	Slag, ash and residues (other than from the manufacture of iron or steel) containing mainly aluminium	2620.4000	134
矿渣、矿灰及残渣(冶炼钢铁所产生的灰、渣除外),主要含铅,其他	Slag, ash and residues (other than from the manufacture of iron or steel) containing mainly lead, nes	2620.2900	134
矿渣、矿灰及残渣(冶炼钢铁所产生的灰、渣除外),主要含铜	Slag, ash and residues (other than from the manufacture of iron or steel) containing mainly copper	2620.3000	134
矿渣、矿灰及残渣(冶炼钢铁所产生的灰、渣除外),主要含钨	Slag, ash and residues (other than from the manufacture of iron or steel) containing mainly tungsten	2620.9910	134

K

商品名称	Article Description	税则号列	申报要素
矿渣、矿灰及残渣(冶炼钢铁所产生的灰、渣除外),主要含锌,其他	Slag, ash and residues (other than from the manufacture of iron or steel) containing mainly zinc, nes	2620. 1900	134
矿渣及矿灰,其他	Slag and ash, nes	2621. 9000	134
矿渣棉、岩石棉及类似的矿质棉(包括其相互混合物),块状、成片或成卷	Slag wool, rock wool and similar mineral wools (including intermixtures thereof), in bulk, sheets or rolls	6806. 1000	68
矿渣水泥	Slag cement	2523. 9000	3
框,带栓的,贱金属制,用于衣着、鞋靴、天篷、提包、旅行用品或其他制成品	Frames with clasps, of base metal, of a kind used for clothing, footwear, awnings, handbags, travel goods or other made up articles	8308. 9000	256
kui			
奎宁环-3-醇	Quinuclidine-3-ol	2933. 3920	36
喹啉环系化合物,结构上含有,未经进一步稠合的,不论是否氢化,其他	Quinoline ring-system compounds, not further fused in the structure, whether or not hydrogenated, nes	2933. 4990	36
葵花油及其分离品,初榨的	Sunflowerseed oil and fractions thereof, crude oil	1512. 1100	4
葵花油及其分离品,其他	Sunflowerseed or safflower oil and fractions thereof, nes	1512. 1900	4
葵花籽,其他	Sunflower seed, nes	1206. 0090	3
葵花籽,种用	Sunflower seed, seedlings	1206. 0010	3
kun			
昆布及无菌昆布塞条,无菌	Laminaria and sterile laminaria tents, sterile	3006. 1000	3
醌,卤化、磺化、硝化或亚硝化衍生物	Quinones, halogenated, sulphonated, nitrated or nitrosated derivatives of	2914. 7000	36
醌,其他	Quinones, nes	2914. 6900	36
醌茜	Quinizarin	2914. 6900	36
kuo			
扩散处理设备,平板显示器的制造机器及装置	Oxidation treatment equipment, flat panel displays manufacture machines and apparatus	8486. 3010	7
扩散处理设备,制造半导体器件或集成电路的机器及装置	Diffusion treatment equipment, semiconductor devices or of electronic integrated circuits manufacture machines and apparatus	8486. 2010	7
阔叶柑橘	Latifolia citrus	0805. 2020	14

L

商品名称	Article Description	税则号列	申报要素
la			
拉拔机,金属或金属陶瓷用,非切削,其他	Drawing benches, for working metal or cermets, without removing material, nes	8463.1090	7
拉床,切削金属或金属陶瓷用	Broaching machines, for removing metal or cermets	8461.3000	7
拉链,零件	Slide fasteners, parts	9607.2000	3
拉链,其他	Slide fasteners, nes	9607.1900	5
拉链,装有贱金属制咪牙齿的	Slide fasteners, fitted with chain scoops of base metal	9607.1100	5
拉米夫定及它们的盐	Lamivudine and their salts	2938.9010	34
拉舍尔经编机	Rashel machines	8447.2012	7
拉伸机,纺织纤维的	Drawing machines, for textile fibres	8445.1310	7
拉伸机,化学纺织纤维的	Drawing machinery for man-made textile materials	8444.0090	
拉伸机的辅助机器,化学纺织纤维的	Drawing machinery auxiliary, for man-made textile materials	8448.1900	3
喇叭,机动车辆用	Loudspeaker for motor vehicles	8512.3011	7
腊肠,有天然肠衣	Bolognas, with a natural casing	1601.0010	348
蜡,聚氧乙烯制	Wax of poly-oxyethylene	3404.2000	136
蜡,聚乙二醇制	Wax of poly-ethyleneglycol	3404.2000	136
蜡,人造及调制的,其他	Waxes, artificial and prepared, nes	3404.9000	136
蜡笔(粉)	Pastels	9609.9000	3
蜡石	Alabaster	2515.2000	148
蜡石碑石或建筑用石及其制品,简单切削或锯开并具有一个平面的	Alabaster monumental or building stone and articles thereof, simply cut or sawn, with a flat or even surface	6802.2190	3468
蜡石及其制品,已加工的,其他	Alabaster and articles thereof, worked, nes	6802.9190	3468
蜡石石刻	Alabaster carvings	6802.9110	3468
蜡纸改正液及类似品	Stencil correctors and the like	3824.9020	36
蜡纸铁笔	Duplicating stylos	9608.9920	
蜡烛	Candles and the like	3406.0000	
蜡烛,细长的	Tapers and the like	3406.0000	
辣根,冷冻的	Horseradish, frozen	0710.8090	1
辣根,鲜或冷藏的	Horseradish, fresh or chilled	0706.9000	1
辣根,用醋或醋酸以外的其他方法制作或保藏的	Horseradish, prepared or preserved otherwise than by vinegar or acetic acid	2005.9999	148
辣椒,鲜或冷藏的	Fruits of the genus capsicum, fresh or chilled	0709.6000	1
辣椒粉	Fruits of the genus capsicum or of the genus pimenta, in powder	0904.2020	4
辣椒干	Fruits of the genus capsicum or of the genus pimenta, dried	0904.2010	4

商品名称	Article Description	税则号列	申报要素
lai			
莱克多巴胺和盐酸莱克多巴胺	Ractopamine and ractopamine hydrochloride	2922. 1110	36
铼,未锻轧	Rhenium, unwrought	8112. 9290	16
铼粉末	Rhenium powders	8112. 9290	16
铼制品	Rhenium articles, nes	8112. 9990	16
赖氨酸	Lysine	2922. 4110	36
赖氨酸酯以及它们的盐	Lysine esters; salts thereof	2922. 4190	36
lan			
兰花,其他	Orchid, nes	0602. 9092	
兰花,鲜的,制花束或装饰用的	Orchids, fresh, suitable for bouquets or for ornamental purposes	0603. 1300	34
兰花,种用	Orchid, seedlings	0602. 9091	3
兰科植物块茎	Salep	0714. 9090	34
蓝宝石,加工的	Sapphires, worked	7103. 9100	145
蓝宝石,未加工	Sapphires, unworked	7103. 1000	145
蓝宝石的粉末	Sapphires dust and powder	7105. 9000	145
蓝晶石	Kyanite	2508. 5000	134
蓝鳍金枪鱼,其他,活的	Bluefin tunas, nes, living	0301. 9490	15
蓝鳍金枪鱼,其他	Thunnus thynnus, nes, living	0301. 9490	15
蓝鳍金枪鱼,鲜或冷的,	Bluefin tunas(thunnus thynnus), fresh or chilled	0302. 3500	18
蓝鳍金枪鱼苗	Fry, bluefin tunas	0301. 9410	15
蓝鳍金枪鱼苗	Fry, thunnus thynnus	0301. 9410	15
蓝纹乳酪	Blueveined cheese	0406. 4000	2468
蓝纹乳酪和娄地青霉生产的带有纹理的其他乳酪	Blueveined cheese and other cheese containing veins produced by penicillium roqueforti	0406. 4000	2468
蓝牙耳机	Bluetooth headphones	8518. 3010	5
篮筐,用编结材料直接编成,草制的	Basketwork, made directly to shape from plaiting materials or made up from goods, of grass or straw	4602. 1910	6
篮筐,用编结材料直接编成,其他植物材料制	Basketwork, made directly to shape from plaiting materials or made up from goods, of other vegetable materials	4602. 1990	6
篮筐,用编结材料直接编成,藤制的	Basketwork, made directly to shape from plaiting materials or made up from goods, of rattan	4602. 1200	6
篮筐,用编结材料直接编成,玉米皮制的	Basketwork, made directly to shape from plaiting materials or made up from goods, of maize-shuck	4602. 1920	6
篮筐,用编结材料直接编成,竹制的	Basketwork, made directly to shape from plaiting materials or made up from goods, of bamboo	4602. 1100	6
篮球	Basketballs	9506. 6210	
缆车,其他	Teleferics, nes	8428. 6090	
缆车零件	Teleferics parts	8431. 3900	3
缆的制造机器	Cable making machines	8479. 4000	7

商品名称	Article Description	税则号列	申报要素
lang			
朗姆酒及蒸馏已发酵甘蔗产品制得的其他烈性酒	Rum and other spirits obtained by distilling fermented sugar-caneproducts	2208.4000	2468
lao			
捞鱼网	Fish landing nets	9507.9000	5
劳保手套,皮革或再生皮革制的	Gloves, mittens and mitts, working gloves, of leather or of composition leather	4203.2910	456
劳动布(棉机织物,按重量计含棉量在85%及以上,每平方米重量超过200克,色织)	Denim (woven fabrics of cotton, containing 85% or more by weight of cotton, weighing more than 200g/m², of yarns of different colours)	5209.4200	468
劳动布(棉机织物,按重量计含棉量在85%以下,主要或仅与化学纤维混纺,每平方米重量超过200克,色织,粗斜纹布)	Denim (woven fabrics of cotton, containing less than 85% by weight of cotton, mixed mainly or solely with man-made fibres, weighing more than 200g/m², of yarns of different colours)	5211.4200	468
劳拉西泮(INN)以及盐	Lorazepam (INN); salts thereof	2933.9100	36
老鹳草油	Essential oils of geranium	3301.2991	34
铑,其他	Rhodium, nes	7110.3990	46
铑,未锻造或粉末状	Rhodium, unwrought or in powder form	7110.3100	46
铑,板、片	Rhodium, plates and sheets	7110.3910	46
烙铁	Soldering irons	8515.1100	
酪氨酸	Tyrosine	2922.5000	36
酪蛋白	Casein	3501.1000	
酪蛋白胶	Casein glues	3501.9000	
酪蛋白酸盐	Caseinates	3501.9000	
酪蛋白衍生物,其他	Casein derivatives, nes	3501.9000	
酪乳	Buttermilk	0403.9000	248
le			
乐杀螨(ISO)	Binapacryl (ISO)	2916.3600	36
lei			
雷达设备,导航用	Radar apparatus, for navigational aid	8526.1010	
雷达设备,其他	Radar apparatus, nes	8526.1090	
雷达设备用零件	Radar apparatus parts	8529.9050	3
雷达显示管,阴极射线管	Radar display tubes, cathode-ray tubes	8540.6010	35
雷达显示管用零件	Radar display tubes parts	8540.9120	3
雷酸汞	Mercury fulminate	2852.0000	
雷酸盐	Fulminates	2842.9010	
镭及镭盐,放射性的	Radium and its salts	2844.4010	
类毒素	Toxoids	3002.9090	34

L

商品名称	Article Description	税则号列	申报要素
leng			
棱镜,未装配的各种材料制	Prisms, of any material, unmounted	9001.9090	5
棱镜,已装配的各种材料制,照相机用	Prisms, of any material, mounted, for cameras	9002.9010	3
棱镜,已装配的各种材料制,作为仪器或装置的零件、配件	Prisms, of any material, mounted, being parts of or fittings for instruments or apparatus	9002.9090	3
冷拔管机,300吨及以下,金属或金属陶瓷用,非切削	Cold-drawing tube benches, with 300t or less, for working metal or cermets, without removing material	8463.1011	7
冷拔管机,金属或金属陶瓷用,非切削,其他	Cold-drawing tube benches, for working metal or cermets, without removing material, nes	8463.1019	7
冷藏船,液货船除外	Refrigerated vessels, other than tanker ships	8901.3000	8
冷藏或冷冻设备专用设备零件	Furniture parts, designed to receive refrigerating or freezing equipment	8418.9100	3
冷藏-冷冻组合机,各自装有单独外门的,容积不超过200升	Refrigerator-freezers, combined, fitted with separate external doors, of a capacity not exceeding 200L	8418.1030	57
冷藏-冷冻组合机,各自装有单独外门的,容积超过200升,但不超过500升	Refrigerator-freezers, combined, fitted with separate external doors, of a capacity exceeding 200L, not exceeding 500L	8418.1020	57
冷藏-冷冻组合机,各自装有单独外门的,容积超过500升	Refrigerator-freezers, combined, fitted with separate external doors, of a capacity exceeding 500L	8418.1010	57
冷藏箱,家用型,半导体制冷式	Refrigerators, household type, semiconductor freezing type	8418.2910	57
冷藏箱,家用型,电气吸收式	Refrigerators, household type, absorption-type, electrical	8418.2920	57
冷藏箱,家用型,其他	Refrigerators, household type, nes	8418.2990	57
冷藏箱,家用型,压缩式,容积不超过50升	Refrigerators, household type, compression-type, of a capacity not exceeding 50L	8418.2130	57
冷藏箱,家用型,压缩式,容积超过150升	Refrigerators, household type, compression-type, of a capacity exceeding 150L	8418.2110	57
冷藏箱,家用型,压缩式,容积超过50升,但不超过150升	Refrigerators, household type, compression-type, of a capacity exceeding 50L, not exceeding 150L	8418.2120	57
冷凝器,水蒸气或其他蒸汽动力装置的	Condensers for steam or other vapour power units	8404.2000	3
冷凝器零件,水蒸气或其他蒸汽动力装置的	Condensers for steam or other vapour power units parts	8404.9090	3
冷却剂泵,活塞式内燃发动机用	Cooling medium pumps for internal combustion piston engines	8413.3090	23
冷热联合轧机	Rolling mills, combination hot and cold-rolled	8455.2190	7
冷室压铸机	Cold chamber die-casting machines	8454.3010	
冷阴极管零件,其他	Cold cathode parts, nes	8540.9990	3
冷轧管机	Tube mills for cold-rolled	8455.1020	7
冷轧机,其他	Rolling mills, cold-rolled, nes	8455.2290	7

商品名称	Article Description	税则号列	申报要素
冷轧机零件	Rolling mills parts, cold-rolled	8455.9000	3
li			
梨,罐头	Pears, in airtight containers	2008.4010	248
梨,其他,鲜的	Pears, nes, fresh	0808.2019	1
梨,其他,用其他方法制作或保藏的	Pears, nes, otherwise prepared, or preserved	2008.4090	248
梨酒	Perry	2206.0090	2468
离合器	Clutches	8483.6000	
离合器及其零件,30 座及以上客运机动车辆用	Clutches and parts of motor vehicles with 30 seats or more	8708.9320	3
离合器及其零件,其他	Clutches and parts, nes	8708.9390	3
离合器及其零件,特种车辆用	Clutches and parts of motor vehicles with special purpose	8708.9360	3
离合器及其零件,拖拉机的	Clutches and parts of tractors	8708.9310	3
离合器及其零件,小轿车用	Clutches and parts of saloon cars	8708.9340	3
离合器及其零件,越野车(4 轮驱动)用	Clutches and parts of cross-country cars(4WD)	8708.9350	3
离合器及其零件,自卸车用	Clutches and parts of dumpers	8708.9330	3
离合器零件	Clutches parts	8483.9000	3
离心泵,电动潜油泵及潜水电泵	Centrifugal pumps, electric submersible oil pumps and electric submersible pumps	8413.7091	27
离心泵,其他	Centrifugal pumps, nes	8413.7099	27
离心泵,转速在 10000 转/分及以上	Centrifugal pumps, rotational speed no less than 10000r/min	8413.7010	27
离心机,其他	Centrifugal dryers, nes	8421.1990	7
离心机零件,其他	Other	8421.9190	3
离心通风机,其他	Centrifugal ventilation fans, nes	8414.5930	23
离子交换剂,以聚合物为基本成分的,初级形状的	Ion-exchangers based on polymers, in primary forms	3914.0000	136
离子射线的测量或检验仪器及装置	Ionizing radiations measuring or detecting instruments and apparatus	9030.1000	
离子注入机,制造半导体器件或集成电路的机器及装置	Ion implanters, semiconductor devices or of electronic integrated circuits manufacture machines and apparatus	8486.2050	7
离子注入机零件及附件,制造半导体器件或集成电路的机器及装置	Ion implanters parts and accessories, semiconductor devices or of electronic integrated circuits manufacture machines and apparatus	8486.9090	3
犁,农业、园艺及林业用	Ploughs, for agricultural, horticultural or forestry use	8432.1000	
李,鲜的	Sloes, fresh	0809.4000	1
里程计	Mileometers	9029.1020	
里程计零件、附件	Mileometers parts and accessories	9029.9000	3
理发器具,电热的,其他	Hair-dressing apparatus, electro-thermic, nes	8516.3200	7

商品名称	Article Description	税则号列	申报要素
理发器具用零件,电热的	Hair-dressing apparatus implements, electro-thermic	8516.9090	3
理发推剪	Hair clippers	8214.9000	256
理发用椅及其零件	Barbers chairs and parts thereof	9402.1010	3
理化分析仪器及装置,其他	Physical or chemical analysis instruments and apparatus, nes	9027.8099	7
理化分析仪器及装置,使用光学射线(紫外线、可见光、红外线)的,其他	Physical or chemical analysis instruments and apparatus, using optical radiations (UV, visible, IR), nes	9027.5000	
理化分析仪器及装置零件、附件	Physical or chemical analysis instruments and apparatus parts and accessories	9027.9000	3
锂的碳酸盐	Lithium carbonates	2836.9100	
锂的氧化物和氢氧化物,其他	Lithium oxide and hydroxide, nes	2825.2090	
锂离子蓄电池	Lithium ion accumulators	8507.8020	68
锂云母	Lepidolite	2530.9099	13456
锂云母	Lithium mica	2530.9099	13456
鲤鱼,其他	Carp, nes, living	0301.9390	15
鲤鱼苗	Fry, of carp	0301.9310	15
立式冷冻箱,容积不超过900升,制冷温度在-40℃及以下	Freezers of the upright type, of a refrigerating temperature of -40°c or lower	8418.4010	57
立式冷冻箱,容积不超过900升,制冷温度在-40℃以上,其他	Freezers of the upright type, not exceeding 900L capacity, of a refrigerating temperature higher than -40℃, nes	8418.4029	57
立式冷冻箱,容积超过500升,制冷温度在-40℃以上	Freezers of the upright type, of a capacity exceeding 500L, of a refrigerating temperature higher than -40℃	8418.4021	57
立体显微镜,光学的	Stereoscopic microscopes, optical	9011.1000	
利非他明以及它们的盐	Lefetamine (INN); salts thereof	2921.4600	36
利福平及其衍生物以及它们的盐	Rifampicin (RFP) and its derivatives; salts thereof	2941.9030	
利口酒	Liqueurs	2208.7000	2468
利口器,其他	Cutlery articles, nes	8214.9000	256
利马豆,鲜或冷藏的	Lima beans or butter beans, fresh or chilled	0708.9000	1
利托那韦及盐	Ritonavir and their salts	2934.9940	36
沥青	Pitch	2708.1000	14
沥青混合物,以沥青为基本成分的	Bituminous mixtures based on asphalt or bitumen	2715.0000	1346
沥青混凝土摊铺机	Bituminous concrete spreading machines	8479.1021	7
沥青或类似原料的制品,成卷	Asphalt or of similar material articles, in rolls	6807.1000	
沥青或类似原料的制品,其他	Asphalt or of similar material articles, nes	6807.9000	
沥青胶粘剂,以沥青为基本成分的	Bituminous mastics, based on asphalt or bitumen	2715.0000	1346
沥青焦	Pitch coke	2708.2000	14
沥青碎石	Tarred macadam	2517.3000	13
沥青岩	Asphaltites and asphaltic rocks	2714.9090	1346
沥青页岩	Bituminous shale	2714.1000	1346

商品名称	Article Description	税则号列	申报要素
沥青纸及纸板	Bituminised or asphalted paper and paperboard	4811.1000	458
荔枝,鲜的	Lychee,fresh	0810.9010	1
荔枝干	Preserved litchi,dried	0813.4040	34
荔枝罐头	Lychee can	2008.9910	248
栗仁,用其他方法制作或保藏的	Chestnut seed,otherwise prepared,or preserved	2008.1991	248
栗子,其他	Chestnuts(Castanea spp.),nes	0802.4090	134
栗子,未去壳,冷冻的	Chestnuts,in shell,frozen	0811.9010	14
砾石,通常作混凝土粒料、铺路、铁道路基或其他路基用的	Gravel, of a kind commonly used for concrete aggregates,for road metalling or for railway	2517.1000	13
粒子加速器	Particle accelerators	8543.1000	37
粒子加速器用零件	Particle accelerators parts	8543.9010	3
lian			
连二亚硫酸盐,其他,无机的	Dithionites,nes,inorganic	2831.9000	
连裤袜及紧身裤袜,针织或钩编的,每根单丝细度在67分特及以上的合成纤维制	Panty hose and tights, knitted or crocheted, of synthetic fibres, measuring per single yarn 67 decitex or more	6115.2200	2456
连裤袜及紧身裤袜,针织或钩编的,每根单丝细度在67分特以下的合成纤维制	Panty hose and tights, knitted or crocheted, of synthetic fibres,measuring per single yarn less than 67 decitex	6115.2100	2456
连裤袜及紧身裤袜,针织或钩编的,棉制	Panty hose and tights,knitted or crocheted,of cotton	6115.2910	2456
连裤袜及紧身裤袜,针织或钩编的,其他	Panty hose and tights,knitted or crocheted,nes	6115.2990	2456
连续式玻璃热弯炉	Continuous hot bending furnaces, for hot working glass or glasswares	8475.2911	
连衣裙,非针织或钩编的,女式,合成纤维制	Dresses,not knitted or crocheted,for women or girls, of synthetic fibres	6204.4300	2456
连衣裙,非针织或钩编的,女式,棉制	Dresses,not knitted or crocheted,for women or girls, of cotton	6204.4200	2456
连衣裙,非针织或钩编的,女式,其他	Dresses,not knitted or crocheted,for women or girls, nes	6204.4990	2456
连衣裙,非针织或钩编的,女式,人造纤维制	Dresses,not knitted or crocheted,for women or girls, of artificial fibres	6204.4400	2456
连衣裙,非针织或钩编的,女式,丝及绢丝制	Dresses,not knitted or crocheted,for women or girls, of silk or silk waste	6204.4910	2456
连衣裙,非针织或钩编的,女式,羊毛或动物细毛制	Dresses,not knitted or crocheted,for women or girls, of wool or fine animal hair	6204.4100	2456
连衣裙,针织或钩编的,女式,合成纤维制	Dresses, knitted or crocheted, of women or girls, of synthetic fibres	6104.4300	2456
连衣裙,针织或钩编的,女式,棉制	Dresses, knitted or crocheted, of women or girls, of cotton	6104.4200	2456

商品名称	Article Description	税则号列	申报要素
连衣裙,针织或钩编的,女式,其他纺织材料制	Dresses, knitted or crocheted, of women or girls, of other textile materials	6104.4900	2456
连衣裙,针织或钩编的,女式,人造纤维制	Dresses, knitted or crocheted, of women or girls, of artificial fibres	6104.4400	2456
连衣裙,针织或钩编的,女式,羊毛或动物细毛制	Dresses, knitted or crocheted, of women or girls, of wool or fine animal hair	6104.4100	2456
连铸机,板坯的	Casting machines for ingot slab, continuous	8454.3022	
连铸机,方坯的	Casting machines for ingot block, continuous	8454.3021	
连铸机,钢坯,其他	Casting machines for ingot, continuous, nes	8454.3029	
连铸机用零件,钢坯的,其他	Casting machines parts, for ingot continuous casting machines, nes	8454.9029	3
连铸机用零件,其他	Casting machines parts, nes	8454.9090	3
帘子布,聚酯高强力纱制	Tyre cord fabric of high tenacity yarn of polyesters	5902.2000	
帘子布,尼龙-6,6 高强力纱制	Tyre cord fabric of high tenacity yarn of nylon-6,6	5902.1020	
帘子布,尼龙-6 高强力纱制	Tyre cord fabric of high tenacity yarn of nylon-6	5902.1010	
帘子布,尼龙或聚酰胺制高强力纱,其他	Tyre cord fabric of high tenacity yarn of nylon or polyamides, nes	5902.1090	
帘子布,粘胶纤维高强力纱制	Tyre cord fabric of high tenacity yarn of viscose rayon	5902.9000	
莲雾,鲜的	Wax apple, fresh	0810.9070	1
莲子	Lotus seeds (Semen Nelurnbinis)	1212.9994	134
联苯	Biphenyl	2902.9090	6
联苯酚	Diphenols	2907.1990	36
联苯双酯	Bifendate	2932.9920	36
联苯双酯类药品,混合或未混合的,配定剂量或制成零售包装	Biphenyl dicarbxybte medicaments, mixed or unmixed, put up in measured doses or in forms or packings for retail sale	3004.9020	368
联合收割机	Combine harvester-threshers	8433.5100	
联合收割机用零件	Combine harvester-threshers parts	8433.9010	
联结器及其零件,铁道及电车道机车或其他车辆的	Coupling devices and parts, of railway or tramway locomotives or rolling-stock	8607.3000	3
联轴器	Shaft couplings	8483.6000	
联轴器零件	Shaft couplings parts	8483.9000	3
镰刀	Scythes	8201.9000	256
脸盆,陶制	Wash basins, of pottery	6910.9000	268
脸盆,瓷制	Wash basins, of porcelain	6910.1000	268
脸盆座,陶制	Wash basin pedestals, of pottery	6910.9000	268
脸盆座,瓷制	Wash basin pedestals, of porcelain or china	6910.1000	268
练习本,纸或纸板制的	Exercise books, of paper or paperboard	4820.2000	
炼钢电炉用零件	Steel making electric furnaces parts	8514.9010	3
炼焦炉	Coke ovens	8417.8010	7
炼焦炉用零件	Coke ovens parts	8417.9020	3
炼焦煤	Coking coal	2701.1210	156

L

商品名称	Article Description	税则号列	申报要素
链,钢铁的,其他	Chain, of iron or steel, nes	7315.8900	36
链多肽,改性的,主要用作激素的	Polypeptides, chain modified, used pri-marily as hormones	2937.9000	36
链锯,手提式,本身装有电动动力装置的	Chain saws, hand tools, with self-contained electric motor	8467.2210	57
链锯,手提式,其他	Chain saws, hand tools, nes	8467.8100	57
链锯零件,电动的,手提式	Chain saws parts, with self-contained electric motor, for hand tools	8467.9110	3
链锯零件,手提式,其他	Chain saws parts, for hand tools, nes	8467.9190	3
链锯片	Chain saw blades	8202.4000	256
链零件,钢铁的	Chain parts, of iron or steel	7315.9000	36
链轮,自行车及脚踏车的	Sprocket wheels, of bicycles and other cycles	8714.9390	3
链霉素及其衍生物以及它们的盐	Streptomycins and their derivatives; salts thereof	2941.2000	
链条及其零件,铜制	Chain and parts thereof, of copper	7419.1000	4
liang			
两端交流开关元件,但光敏器件除外	Diacs, other than photosensitive devices	8541.3000	5
两用启动发电机,点燃式或压燃式内燃发动机用的,其他	Dual purpose starter generators, for electrical ignition or starting equipment, nes	8511.4099	7
两用启动发电机,机车、航空器及船舶用,点燃式或压燃式内燃发动机用的	Dual purpose starter generators, for locomotives, aircraft or ships, for electrical ignition or starting equipment	8511.4010	7
两用椅,能做床用的,庭园坐具或野营设备除外,皮革或再生皮革面的	Seats other than garden seats or camping equipment, convertible into beds, with outer surface of leather or composition leather	9401.4010	6
两用椅,能做床用的,庭园坐具或野营设备除外,其他	Seats other than garden seats or camping equipment, convertible into beds, nes	9401.4090	6
亮晶片,贱金属制	Spangles, of base metal	8308.9000	256
量尺、量带	Measuring rods and tapes	9017.8000	7
量规	Gauges	9017.3000	
liao			
钌,板、片	Ruthenium, plates and sheets	7110.4910	46
钌,其他	Ruthenium, nes	7110.4990	46
钌,未锻造或粉末状	Ruthenium, unwrought or in powder form	7110.4100	46
lie			
列诺伦	Linoleum	5904.1000	
烈性酒,蒸馏葡萄酒制得的	Spirits obtained by distilling grape wine or grape marc	2208.2000	2468
猎枪	Shotguns	9303.2000	
猎枪筒	Shotgun barrels	9305.2100	3
猎枪用零件、附件	Shotguns parts and accessories	9305.2900	3
猎枪子弹	Shotgun cartridges	9306.2100	

商品名称	Article Description	税则号列	申报要素
猎枪子弹零件	Shotgun cartridges parts	9306.2900	3
lin			
邻-、间-、对-二氨基甲苯及其衍生物以及它们的盐,其他	O-, m-, p-diaminotoluener and their derivatives; salts thereof, nes	2921.5190	36
邻-、间-、对-苯二胺及其衍生物以及它们的盐,其他	O-, m-, p-phenylenediamine and their derivatives; salts thereof, nes	2921.5190	36
邻氨基苯甲酸(氨茴酸)	Anthranilic acid	2922.4310	36
邻氨基苯甲酸(氨茴酸)盐	Anthranilic acid salts	2922.4390	36
邻苯二胺	O-phenylenediamine	2921.5110	36
邻苯二酚	Catechol, pyrocatechol	2907.2910	36
邻苯二酚	O-dihydroxybenzene(catechol, pyrocatechol)	2907.2910	36
邻苯二甲酸二丁酯	Dibutyl orthophthalates	2917.3410	36
邻苯二甲酸二癸酯	Didecyl orthophthalates	2917.3300	36
邻苯二甲酸二壬酯	Dinonyl orthophthalates	2917.3300	36
邻苯二甲酸二辛酯	Dioctyl orthophthalates	2917.3200	36
邻苯二甲酸酐	Phthalic anhydride	2917.3500	36
邻苯二甲酸酯,其他	Esters of orthophthalic acid, nes	2917.3490	36
邻二甲苯	O-xylene	2902.4100	6
邻二氯苯	O-dichlorobenzene	2903.6110	36
邻甲酚	O-cresol	2907.1212	36
邻甲基苯甲酸	M-methylbenzoic acid	2916.3910	36
邻氯青霉素	Cloxacillin	2941.1096	
邻硝基氯化苯	O-nitrochlorobenzene	2904.9011	36
邻乙酰水杨酸	Acetylsalicylic acid	2918.2210	36
邻乙酰水杨酸盐和酯,其他	O-acetylsalicylic acid salts and esters, nes	2918.2290	36
邻异丙基酚	O-isopropyl phenol	2907.1910	36
邻仲丁基酚	O-sec-butyl phenol	2907.1910	36
林丹(ISO, INN)	Lindane(ISO, INN)	2903.5100	36
林可霉素及其衍生物以及它们的盐	Lincomycin and its derivatives; salts thereof	2941.9040	
林业用机器,包括装有机械或热力装置的催芽设备,其他	Forestry machinery, including germination plant fitted with mechanical or thermal equipment, nes	8436.8000	
林业用机器零件,其他	Forestry machinery parts, nes	8436.9900	3
淋浴盘,塑料的	Shower-baths, of plastics	3922.1000	236
磷,其他	Phosphorus, nes	2804.7090	6
磷氨基类脂,其他	Phosphoam-inolipids, nes	2923.2000	36
磷胺(ISO)	Phosphamidon (ISO)	2924.1200	36
磷化物,不论是否已有化学定义,但不包括磷铁	Phosphides, whether or not chemically defined, excluding ferrophophorus	2848.0000	6
磷灰石,未碾磨	Apatite, unground	2510.1010	46
磷灰石,已碾磨	Apatite, ground	2510.2010	46
磷绿铅矿	Pyromorphite	2607.0000	146

商品名称	Article Description	税则号列	申报要素
磷酸,其他	Phosphoric acid, nes	2809.2019	6
磷酸,食品级	Phosphoric acid, food grade	2809.2011	6
磷酸二氨铵与磷酸氢二铵的混合物	Ammonium dihydrogenorthophosphate (monoammonium phosphate) mixtures with diammonium hydrogenorthophosphate (diammonium phosphate)	3105.4000	68
磷酸二钠	Disodium phosphates	2835.2200	
磷酸二氢铵	Ammonium dihydrogenorthophosphate (monoammonium phosphate)	3105.4000	68
磷酸钙,其他	Phosphates of calcium, nes	2835.2600	
磷酸铝钙,天然的,碾磨	Aluminium calcium phosphates, natural, ground	2510.2090	46
磷酸铝钙,天然的,未碾磨	Aluminium calcium phosphates, natural, unground	2510.1090	46
磷酸氢二铵	Diammonium hydrogenorthophosphate (diammonium phosphate)	3105.3000	68
磷酸三钠	Trisodium phosphate	2835.2910	
磷酸盐,其他,无机的	Phosphates, nes, inorganic	2835.2990	
磷酸盐白垩,碾磨	Phosphatic chalk, ground	2510.2090	46
磷酸盐白垩,未碾磨	Phosphatic chalk, unground	2510.1090	46
磷酸一钠	Mono-sodium phosphates	2835.2200	
磷酸酯及其盐,以及它们的卤化、磺化、硝化或亚硝化衍生物	Phosphoric esters and their salts, their halogenated, sulphonated, nitrated or nitrosated derivatives	2919.9000	36
磷酰氯	Phosphoryl monochloride	2812.1020	
磷钇矿	Xenotime	2530.9020	13456
鳞茎,其他,休眠的	Bulbs, nes, dormant	0601.1099	135
鳞茎,生长或开花的	Bulbs, in growth or in flower	0601.2000	
鳞茎,种用,休眠的	Bulbs, seed, dormant	0601.1091	135
蔺草	Mat rush	1401.9031	3
ling			
灵长目,改良种用	Primates, pure-bred breeding	0106.1110	3
灵长目,改良种用除外	Primates, ex. pure-bred breeding	0106.1190	
灵猫香	Civet	0510.0020	14
铃及类似品,贱金属制,非电动的	Bells and the like, of base metal, non-electric	8306.1000	256
铃兰醛	Lilial	2912.2910	36
羚羊,改良种用	Antelopes, pure-bred breeding	0106.1910	34
羚羊角及其粉末和废料	Antelope horns and powder or waste thereof	0507.9010	14
菱角	Water chestnut (trapa natas)	0802.9090	134
菱镁矿	Magnesite	2519.1000	146
菱锰矿	Dialogite (rhodocrosite)	2602.0000	1346
菱铁矿,已烧结	Siderite, agglomerated	2601.1200	1346
菱锌矿	Calamine (hemimorphite)	2608.0000	146
菱锌矿	Smithsonite	2608.0000	146

商品名称	Article Description	税则号列	申报要素
零件,风机、风扇或循环气罩的	Parts, for fans or ventilating or recycling hoods	8414. 9020	23
零件,冷藏箱、冷冻箱用或空气调节器的,其他	Parts, for refrigerators or freezers or air conditioning machines	8414. 9019	23
零件、附件,同样适用于税号 84. 69 至 84. 72 中两个或两个以上税号所列机器的	Parts and accessories equally suitable for use with machines of two or more of the headings No. 84. 69 to 84. 72	8473. 5000	3
零件及附件,税号 84. 56 至 84. 61 所列机器用	Parts and accessories, for machines of headings No. 84. 56 to 84. 61	8466. 9300	3
零件及附件,税号 84. 62 或 84. 63 所列机器用	Parts and accessories, for machines of heading No. 84. 62 or 84. 63	8466. 9400	3
零件及附件,税号 84. 64 所列机器用	Parts and accessories, for machines of heading No. 84. 64	8466. 9100	3
零件及附件,税号 84. 65 所列机器用	Parts and accessories, for machines of heading No. 84. 65	8466. 9200	3
零售包装的狗食或猫食,罐头	Dog or cat food, put up for retail sale, in airtight containers	2309. 1010	23468
零售包装的狗食或猫食,其他	Dog or cat food, put up for retail sale, nes	2309. 1090	23468
领带及领结,非针织或钩编的,化学纤维制	Ties, bow ties and cravats, not knitted or crocheted, of man-made fibres	6215. 2000	2456
领带及领结,非针织或钩编的,其他纺织材料制	Ties, bow ties and cravats, not knitted or crocheted, of other textile materials	6215. 9000	2456
领带及领结,非针织或钩编的,丝或绢丝制	Ties, bow ties and cravats, not knitted or crocheted, of silk or silk waste	6215. 1000	2456
领带及领结,针织或钩编的	Ties, bow ties and cravats knitted or crocheted	6117. 8010	2456
领巾,非针织或钩编的,合成纤维制	Scarves, not knitted or crocheted, of synthetic fibres	6214. 3000	2456
领巾,非针织或钩编的,其他动物细毛制	Scarves, not knitted or crocheted, of other fine animal hair	6214. 2090	2456
领巾,非针织或钩编的,其他纺织材料制	Scarves, not knitted or crocheted, of other textile materials	6214. 9000	2456
领巾,非针织或钩编的,人造纤维制	Scarves, not knitted or crocheted, of artificial fibres	6214. 4000	2456
领巾,非针织或钩编的,山羊绒制	Scarves, not knitted or crocheted, of goats fine animal hair	6214. 2020	2456
领巾,非针织或钩编的,丝或绢丝制	Scarves, not knitted or crocheted, of silk or silk waste	6214. 1000	2456
领巾,非针织或钩编的,羊毛制	Scarves, not knitted or crocheted, of wool	6214. 2010	2456
领巾,针织或钩编的,其他	Scarves, knitted or crocheted, nes	6117. 1090	2456
领巾,针织或钩编的,其他动物细毛制	Scarves, knitted or crocheted, of fine animal hair, nes	6117. 1019	2456
领巾,针织或钩编的,山羊绒制	Scarves, knitted or crocheted, of goats fine animal hair	6117. 1011	2456
领巾,针织或钩编的,羊毛制	Scarves, knitted or crocheted, of wool	6117. 1020	2456
领纸机	Web feeder	8443. 9111	3
liu			
溜冰鞋及用品	Ice skates and articles	9506. 7010	
流动动物园	Travelling menageries	9508. 1000	

商品名称	Article Description	税则号列	申报要素
流动工场车	Mobile workshops	8705.9090	7
流动剧团	Travelling theatres	9508.9000	5
流动马戏团	Travelling circuses	9508.1000	
流量阀,其他	Flow control valves, nes	8481.8039	
流量计,测量或检验液体变化量的	Flow, measuring or checking variables of liquids or gases	9026.1000	7
流量计零件、附件	Flow meter parts and accessories	9026.9000	3
流苏、绒球及类似品	Tassels, pompons and similar articles	5808.9000	468
流速仪	Hydrometers	9025.8000	3
流速仪零件、附件	Hydrometers parts and accessories	9025.9000	7
硫胺	Thiamin (Vitamin B_1)	2936.2200	36
硫醇	Mercaptans	2930.9090	36
硫醇	Thiols	2930.9090	36
硫代氨基甲酸盐(或酯)	Thiocarbamates	2930.2000	36
硫代磷酸酯及其盐以及它们的卤化、磺化、硝化或亚硝化衍生物,其他	Thiophosphoric esters (phosphorothioates) and their salts; their halogenated, sulphonated, nitrated or nitrosated derivatives, nes	2920.1900	36
硫代硫酸盐,无机的	Thiosulphates, inorganic	2832.3000	
硫钴矿	Linnaeite	2605.0000	146
硫光气	Thiophosgene	2853.0090	
硫化钴	Cobalt sulphide	2830.9030	
硫化黑(硫化青)及以其为基本成分的制品	Sulphur black and preparations based thereon	3204.1911	345
硫化钠	Sodium sulphide	2830.1010	
硫化染料及以其为基本成分的制品,其他	Dyes and preparations based thereon, sulphur type, nes	3204.1919	345
硫化锑	Antimony sulphide	2830.9020	
硫化物,其他,无论是否已有化学定义	Sulphides, nes, whether or not chemically defined	2830.9090	
硫化橡胶线及绳	Vulcanized rubber thread and cord	4007.0000	18
硫磺,沉淀的	Sulphur, precipitated	2802.0000	
硫磺,但升华硫磺、沉淀硫磺及胶态硫磺除外	Sulphur of all kinds, other than sublimed sulphur, precipitated sulphur and colloidal sulphur	2503.0000	1468
硫磺,胶态的	Sulphur, of colloidal	2802.0000	
硫磺,升华的	Sulphur, sublimed	2802.0000	
硫镁矾矿	Kieserite	2530.2000	13456
硫尿树脂,初级形状的	Thiourea resins, in primary forms	3909.1000	1256
硫氰酸汞	Mercuric thiocyanate	2852.0000	
硫氰酸盐	Thiocyanates	2842.9010	
硫酸	Sulphuric acid	2807.0000	346
硫酸铵	Ammonium sulphate	3102.2100	68
硫酸铵和硝酸铵的复盐及混合物	Ammonium sulphate and ammonium nitrate, double salts or mixtures	3102.2900	68

L

商品名称	Article Description	税则号列	申报要素
硫酸钡	Barium sulphates	2833.2700	
硫酸钾	Potassium sulphate	3104.3000	68
硫酸铝	Aluminium sulphates	2833.2200	
硫酸镁	Magnesium, sulphates	2833.2100	
硫酸钠	Disodium sulphate	2833.1100	
硫酸铅矿	Anglesite	2607.0000	146
硫酸羟胺	Hydroxylamine sulfate	2825.1020	
硫酸锌	Zine sulphate	2833.2930	
硫酸亚铁	Ferrous sulphate	2833.2910	
硫酸盐,其他,无机的	Sulphates, nes, inorganic	2833.2990	
硫酸盐木浆,但溶解级的除外,半漂白或漂白,非针叶木的	Chemical wood pulp, sul-phate, other than dissolving grades, semi-bleached or bleached, non-coniferous	4703.2900	46
硫酸盐木浆,但溶解级的除外,半漂白或漂白,针叶木的	Chemical wood pulp, sul-phate, other than dissolving grades, semi-bleached or bleached, coniferous	4703.2100	46
硫酸盐木浆,但溶解级的除外,未漂白,非针叶木的	Chemical wood pulp, sul-phate, other than dissolving grades, unbleached, non-coniferous	4703.1900	46
硫酸盐木浆,但溶解级的除外,未漂白,针叶木的	Chemical wood pulp, sul-phate, other than dissolving grades, unbleached, coniferous	4703.1100	
硫酸盐松节油	Sulphate turpentine oils	3805.1000	36
硫锑铜银矿	Polybasite	2616.1000	146
榴弹炮,其他	Howitzers, nes	9301.1900	7
榴弹炮,自推进的	Howitzers, self-propelled	9301.1100	7
榴莲,鲜的	Durian, fresh	0810.6000	12
柳条	Osier	1401.9090	3
柳条编结品及其他制品,用编结材料直接编成	Wickerwork and other articles, made directly to shape from plaiting materials or made up from goods	4602.1930	6
六氟铝酸钠	Sodium hexafluoroaluminate	2826.3000	
六六六(ISO)	HCH (ISO)	2903.5100	36
六氯苯(ISO)	Hexachlorobenzene (ISO)	2903.6200	36
六氯二氟丙烷	Hexachlorodifluoropropane	2903.4550	36
六偏磷酸钠,其他	Sodium hexametaphosphate, nes	2835.3919	3
六偏磷酸钠,食品级的	Sodium hexametaphosphate, food grade	2835.3911	
六氢吡啶	Hexahydropyridine	2933.3210	36
六氢吡啶盐	Isoniazidum	2933.3220	36
六亚甲基二胺及其盐,其他	Hexamethylenediamine and its salts, nes	2921.2290	36
六亚甲基二异氰酸酯	Hexamethelene diisocyanate	2929.1040	36
long			
龙门刨床,切削金属或金属陶瓷用	Double column planing machines, for removing metal or cermets	8461.9011	7
龙门式起重机	Gantry cranes	8426.1930	7
龙门铣床,切削金属的,其他	Planomilling machines, for removing metal, nes	8459.6910	7

商品名称	Article Description	税则号列	申报要素
龙门铣床,数控的,切削金属的	Planomilling machines, numerically controlled, for removing metal	8459.6110	7
龙舌兰酒	Tequila, mezcal	2208.9010	2468
龙头,用于管道、锅炉、罐、桶或类似品的	Taps, for pipes, boiler shells, tanks, vats or the like	8481.8090	
龙头用零件	Taps parts	8481.9090	3
龙虾,冻的	Rock lobster and other sea crawfish (Palinurus spp., Panulirus spp., Jasus spp.), frozen	0306.1100	1
龙虾,其他,未冻的	Rock lobster and other sea crawfish (Palinurus spp., Panulirus spp., Jasus spp.), nes, not frozen	0306.2190	14
龙虾,制作或保藏的	Lobster, prepared or preserved	1605.3000	48
龙虾种苗	Rock lobster and other sea crawfish (Palinurus spp., Panulirus spp., Jasus spp.), for cultivation,	0306.2110	3
龙涎香	Ambergris	0510.0020	14
龙眼,鲜的	Longan, fresh	0810.9030	1
龙眼干	Longans, dried	0813.4010	345
龙眼罐头	Longan can	2008.9920	248
龙眼肉,干的	Longan pulps, dried	0813.4010	345
lou			
漏勺,镀贵金属的	Skimmers, plated with precious metal	8215.9100	256
漏勺,非镀贵金属的	Skimmers, other than plated with precious metal	8215.9900	256
lu			
芦笋,鲜或冷藏的	Asparagus, fresh or chilled	0709.2000	1
芦笋,用醋或醋酸以外的其他方法制作或保藏的,未冷冻	Asparagus, prepared or preserved otherwise than by vinegar or acetic acid, not frozen, nes	2005.6090	148
芦笋,种用,休眠的	Asparagus crowns, seed, dormant	0601.1091	135
芦笋罐头	Asparagus, in airtight containers	2005.6010	148
芦苇	Reeds	1401.9020	3
炉,电阻加热的,工业或实验室用,其他	Furnaces, resistance heated, for industrial or laboratory use, electric, nes	8514.1090	7
炉,工业或实验室用,电的,其他	Furnaces, for industrial or laboratory use, electric, nes	8514.3000	7
炉,通过感应或介质损耗工作的,工业或实验室用	Furnaces functioning by induction or dielectric loss, for industrial or laboratory use, electric	8514.2000	7
炉煤气	Producer gas	2705.0000	4
炉外精炼设备	Fining equipments outside converters	8454.2010	
炉外精炼设备用零件	Fining equipments outside converters parts	8454.9010	3
炉用燃烧器,包括复式燃烧器,其他	Furnace burners, including combination burners, nes	8416.2090	5
炉用燃烧器,使用气体的,其他	Furnace burners, for gas, nes	8416.2019	5
炉用燃烧器,使用天然气的	Furnace burners, of using natural gas	8416.2011	5
炉用燃烧器,使用液体燃料的	Furnace burners for liquid fuel	8416.1000	5

商品名称	Article Description	税则号列	申报要素
炉用燃烧器零件	Furnace burners parts	8416.9000	
鲈鱼苗	Fry, of perches	0301.9911	15
卤代丁基橡胶(CIIR 或 BIIR),初级形状的	Halo-isobutene-iso prene rubber(CIIR or BIIR), in pimary forms	4002.3910	136
卤代丁基橡胶(CIIR 或 BIIR),其他	Halo-isobutene-iso prene rubber(CIIR or BIIR), nes	4002.3990	136
卤恶唑仑(INN)及盐	Haloxazolam (INN); salts thereof	2934.9100	36
卤钨灯,火车、航空器及船舶用	Tungsten halogen, for locomotives and rolling-stock, aircraft or ships	8539.2120	35
卤钨灯,机动车辆用	Tungsten halogen, for motor vehicles	8539.2130	35
卤钨灯,科研、医疗专用	Tungsten halogen, for scientific or medical uses only	8539.2110	35
卤钨灯,其他	Tungsten halogen, other	8539.2190	35
录像机,磁带型,广播级	Video tape recorders, magnetic tape-type, broadcast quality	8521.1011	5
录像机,磁带型,其他	Video tape recorders, magnetic tape-type, nes	8521.1019	5
录音机,装有声音重放装置的,盒带型	Cassette-type recorders, incorporating sound reproducing apparatus	8519.8112	5
鹿角,已加工的	Antlers, worked	9601.9000	5
鹿茸及其粉末	Pilose antlers and powder thereof	0507.9020	14
路由器,有线数字通信设备	Routers, telecommunication apparatus for digital line system	8517.6236	7
路缘石,天然石料(不包括板岩)制的	Curbstones, of natural stone(except slate)	6801.0000	46
卤化烯烃聚合物,初级形状的,其他	Halogenated olefins polymers, in primary forms, nes	3904.9000	1256
lü			
滤布,用于榨油机器或类似机器的,包括人发制滤布	Straining cloth of a kind used in oil presses or the like, including that of human hair	5911.4000	
滤块、滤板及滤片,纸浆制的	Filter blocks, slabs and plates, of paper pulp	4812.0000	16
滤色镜,其他	Filters, nes	9002.2090	3
滤色镜,照相机用	Filters, for cameras	9002.2010	3
滤油器,内燃发动机的	Oil or petrol-filters for internal combustion engines	8421.2300	7
滤纸及纸板	Filter paper and paperboard	4805.4000	458
滤纸及纸板,成卷或成张的,卷宽度不超过36 厘米,或任何一边不超过36 厘米	Filter paper and paperboard, of width not exceeding 36cm or in roll or no side exceeding 36cm in unfoled state	4823.2000	68
驴,改良种用	Asses, pure-bred breeding	0101.1020	34
驴,改良种用除外	Asses, ex. pure-bred breeding	0101.9090	34
驴肉,鲜或冷或冻的	Meat of asses, fresh, chilled or frozen	0205.0000	14
驴喜草子	Sainfoin seeds	1209.2990	358
驴喜豆,饲料用	Sainfoin, forage products	1214.9000	
旅客登机桥,机场用	Passenger boarding bridge used at airport	8479.8991	7
旅行包、帆布包、工具包、运动包、食品或饮料保温包,其他	Travelling-bags, ruck-sacks, tool bags, sports bags, insulated food or beverages bags, nes	4202.9900	256

L

商品名称	Article Description	税则号列	申报要素
旅行包、帆布包、工具包、运动包、食品或饮料保温包,以皮革、再生皮革或漆皮作面	Travelling-bags, ruck-sacks, tool bags, sports bags, insulated food or beverages bags, with outer surface of leather, of composition leather or of patent leather	4202.9100	256
旅行包、帆布包、工具包、运动包、食品或饮料保温包,以塑料片或纺织材料作面	Travelling-bags, ruck-sacks, tool bags, sports bags, insulated food or beverages bags, with outer surface of plastic sheeting or of textile materials	4202.9200	256
旅行用具,成套的,个人梳妆、缝纫或清洁鞋靴、衣服用	Travel sets for personal toilet, sewing or shoe or clothes cleaning	9605.0000	6
铝,非合金的,按重量计含铝量在99.95%及以上	Aluminium, not alloyed, containing by weight 99.95% or more of aluminium	7601.1010	6
铝,非合金的,其他	Aluminium, not alloyed, nes	7601.1090	6
铝板、杆、型材、异型材、管子及类似品,结构体用的,已加工	Aluminium plates, rods profiles, tubes and the like, prepared for use in structures, worked	7610.9000	56
铝箔,无衬背,厚度不超过0.2毫米,其他	Aluminium foil, not backed, of a thickness not exceeding 0.2mm, nes	7607.1900	68
铝箔,无衬背,轧制后未经进一步加工的,厚度不超过0.007毫米	Aluminium foil, not backed, rolled but not further worked, of a thickness not exceeding 0.007mm	7607.1110	68
铝箔,无衬背,轧制后未经进一步加工的,厚度不超过0.2毫米,其他	Aluminium foil, not backed, rolled but not further worked, of a thickness not exceeding 0.2mm, nes	7607.1190	68
铝箔,无衬背,轧制后未经进一步加工的,厚度大于0.007毫米,但不超过0.01毫米	Aluminium foil, not backed, rolled but not further worked, of a thickness exceeding 0.007mm but not exceeding 0.01mm	7607.1120	68
铝箔,有衬背,铝厚度不超过0.2毫米	Aluminium foil, backed, of a thickness not exceeding 0.2mm	7607.2000	68
铝合金	Aluminium alloys	7601.2000	6
铝合金条、杆,铝合金制	Bars and rods of aluminium alloys	7604.2910	16
铝矿砂及其精矿	Aluminium ores and concentrates	2606.0000	146
铝制结构体,其他	Aluminium structures, nes	7610.9000	56
铝制品,其他	Aluminium articles, nes	7616.9990	36
铝制品,工业用	Aluminium articles for technical use	7616.9910	36
履带式起重机	Crawler cranes	8426.4910	7
履带式牵引车、拖拉机	Track-laying tractors	8701.3000	
绿宝石,加工的	Emeralds, worked	7103.9100	145
绿宝石,未加工	Emeralds, unworked	7103.1000	145
绿宝石的粉末	Emeralds dust and powder	7105.9000	145
绿茶(未发酵),内包装每件净重不超过3千克	Green tea (not fermented), nes, in immediate packings of a content not exceeding 3kg	0902.1090	248
绿茶(未发酵),其他	Green tea (not fermented), nes	0902.2090	248
绿豆,其他,脱荚的,干的	Beans of the species vigna mungo (L.) hepper or vigna radiata (L.) Wilczek, nes, dried, shelled	0713.3190	34
绿豆,种用,脱荚的,干的	Beans of the species vigna mungo (L.) hepper or vigna radiata (L.) Wilczek, seed, dried, shelled	0713.3110	34

商品名称	Article Description	税则号列	申报要素
绿泥石,未膨胀的	Chlorites, unexpanded	2530. 1010	13456
绿青鳕鱼,冻的	Coalfish(pollachius virens), frozen	0303. 7300	18
绿青鳕鱼,鲜或冷的	Coalfish(pollachius virens), fresh or chilled	0302. 6300	18
绿铜矿	Dioptase	2603. 0000	146
氯	Chlorine	2801. 1000	
氯巴占(INN)	Clobazam (INN)	2933. 7200	36
氯苯	Chlorobenzene	2903. 6190	36
氯丙烯	Chloro propene	2903. 2910	36
氯丹(ISO)	Chlordane (ISO)	2903. 5200	36
氯氮卓(INN)以及盐	Chlordiazepoxide (INN); salts thereof	2933. 9100	36
氯丁二烯(氯丁)橡胶(CR),初级形状的	Chloroprene (ehlorobutadiene) rubber (CR) in primary forms	4002. 4910	136
氯丁二烯(氯丁)橡胶(CR),其他	Chloroprene (ehlorobutadiene) rubber(CR), nes	4002. 4990	136
氯丁二烯(氯丁)橡胶(CR)胶乳	Chloroprene (ehlorobutadiene) rubber(CR) latex	4002. 4100	136
氯恶唑仑(INN)及盐	Cloxazolam(INN); salts thereof	2934. 9100	36
氯仿(三氯甲烷)	Chloroform(trichloromethane)	2903. 1300	36
氯氟卓乙酯(INN)以及盐	Ethyl loflazepate(INN); salts thereof	2933. 9100	36
氯化铵,肥料用	Ammonium chloride, for use as fertilizer	2827. 1010	13
氯化铵,其他	Ammonium chloride, nes	2827. 1090	13
氯化钡	Barium chloride	2827. 3920	
氯化镝	Dysprosium chloride	2846. 9022	
氯化钙	Calcium chloride	2827. 2000	
氯化钴	Cobalt chloride	2827. 3930	
氯化钾,分析纯的	Potassium chloride, analytically pure	3104. 2010	68
氯化钾,其他	Potassium chloride, nes	3104. 2090	68
氯化苦	Chloropicrin	2904. 9030	36
氯化苦	Trichloronitromethane(chloropicrin, nitrochloroform)	2904. 9030	36
氯化锂	Lithium chloride	2827. 3910	
氯化铝	Aluminium chlorides	2827. 3200	
氯化镁	Magnesium chlorides	2827. 3100	
氯化钠,纯的	Sodium chloride, pure	2501. 0020	1368
氯化钠的盐,其他	Salt, of sodium chloride, nes	2501. 0019	1368
氯化镍	Nickel chlorides	2827. 3500	
氯化氢	Hydrogen chloride	2806. 1000	6
氯化氰	Chlorocyanogen, cyanogen chloride	2853. 0020	3
氯化铽	Terbium chloride	2846. 9021	
氯化物,其他,无机的	Chlorides, nes, inorganic	2827. 3990	
氯化物及氯氧化物,其他	Chlorides and chloride oxides, nes	2812. 1090	
氯化稀土,其他	Rareearth chlorides, nes	2846. 9029	6
氯化亚砜	Sulphoxide chloride	2812. 1010	
氯磺酸	Chlorosulphuric acid	2806. 2000	6

商品名称	Article Description	税则号列	申报要素
氯甲西泮(INN)以及盐	Lormetazepam (INN);salts thereof	2933.9100	36
氯拉卓酸以及盐	Clorazepate;salts thereof	2933.9100	36
氯霉素及其衍生物以及它们的盐	Chloramphenicol and its derivatives;salts thereof	2941.4000	
氯普唑仑(INN)以及盐	Loprazolam (INN);salts thereof	2933.5500	36
氯七氟丙烷	Chloroheptafluoropropane	2903.4592	36
氯噻西泮(INN)及盐	Clotiazepam (INN);salts thereof	2934.9100	36
氯三氟甲烷	Chlorotrifluoromethane	2903.4510	36
氯酸钾(洋硝)	Potassium chlorate	2829.1910	
氯酸钠	Sodium chlorates	2829.1100	
氯酸盐,其他	Chlorates,nes	2829.1990	
氯五氟乙烷	Chloropenta-fluoroethane	2903.4400	36
氯硝西泮(INN)以及盐	Clonazepam (INN);salts thereof	2933.9100	36
氯氧化物及氢氧基氯化物,其他,无机的	Chloride oxides and chloride hydroxides, inorganic, nes	2827.4990	
氯乙烷	Chloroethane(ethyl chloride)	2903.1100	36
氯乙烯	Vinyl chloride(chloroethylene)	2903.2100	36
氯乙烯共聚物,初级形状的,其他	Vinyl chloride copolymers,in primary forms,nes	3904.4000	1256
氯乙烯-乙酸乙烯酯共聚物,初级形状的	Vinyl chloride-vinyl acetate copolymers, in primary forms	3904.3000	1256
luan			
卵磷脂	Lecithins	2923.2000	36
卵石,通常作混凝土粒料、铺路、铁道路基或其他路基用的	Pebbles, of a kind commonly used for concrete aggregates,for road metalling or for railway	2517.1000	13
lun			
轮,铁道及电车道机车或其他车辆的	Wheels,of railway or tramway locomotives or rolling-stock	8607.1990	3
轮毂(倒轮制动毂及毂闸除外),自行车及脚踏车的	Hubs,of bicycles and other cycles,other than coaster braking hubs and hub brakes	8714.9310	3
轮廓投影仪	Profile projectors	9031.4910	
轮圈及辐条,自行车及脚踏车的	Wheel rims and spokes,of bicycles and other cycles	8714.9200	3
轮胎式起重机,自推进的	Wheel mounted cranes,self-propelled	8426.4110	7
luo			
罗非鱼	Tilapia,living	0301.9991	15
罗非鱼,冻的	Tilapia,frozen	0303.7940	18
罗非鱼,鲜或冷的	Tilapia,fresh or chilled	0302.6940	18
罗非鱼,盐腌及盐渍的	Tilapia,salted or in brine	0305.6940	4
罗非鱼,制作或保藏的,整条或切块,但未绞碎	Tilapia,prepared or preserved,whole or in pieces,but not minced	1604.1920	48
罗甘莓,冷冻的	Loganberries,frozen	0811.2000	1
罗甘莓,鲜的	Loganberries,fresh	0810.2000	1

商品名称	Article Description	税则号列	申报要素
罗马甜瓜,鲜的	Cantaloupe melons, fresh	0807.1920	1
罗盘,定向用	Compasses, for direction finding	9014.1000	
罗盘零件、附件,其他	Compasses parts and accessories	9014.9090	3
萝卜,鲜或冷藏的	Turnips, fresh or chilled	0706.1000	1
锣及类似品,贱金属制,非电动的	Gongs and the like, of base metal, non-electric	8306.1000	256
骡	Hinnies	0101.9090	34
骡	Mules	0101.9090	34
骡肉,鲜或冷或冻的	Meat of mules or hinnies, fresh, chilled or frozen	0205.0000	14
螺,种苗	Snails, other than sea snails, for cultivation	0307.6010	8
螺钉,不论是否带有螺母或垫圈,钢铁制的,其他	Screws, whether or not with their nuts or washers, of iron of steel, nes	7318.1500	268
螺钉,铝制	Screws, of aluminium	7616.1000	36
螺钉,铜制,其他	Screws, of copper, nes	7415.3390	56
螺口盖,贱金属制	Screw caps, of base metal	8309.9000	256
螺口塞	Threaded bungs, of base metal	8309.9000	256
螺母,钢铁制的	Nuts, of iron of steel	7318.1600	268
螺母,铝制	Nuts, of aluminium	7616.1000	36
螺母,铜制	Nuts, of copper	7415.3390	56
螺栓,不论是否带有螺母或垫圈,钢铁制的,其他	Bolts, whether or not with their nuts or washers, of iron of steel, nes	7318.1500	268
螺栓,铝制	Bolts, of aluminium	7616.1000	36
螺栓,铜制	Bolts, of copper	7415.3390	56
螺栓或螺母松开剂,以润滑剂为基本成分的,含有石油或从沥青矿物提取的油类	Bolt or nut release preparations, based on lubricants, containing petroleum oils or oils obtained from bituminous minerals	3403.1900	2368
螺栓或螺母松开剂,以润滑剂为基本成分的,其他	Bolt or nut release preparations, based on lubricants, nes	3403.9900	2368
螺栓切头器	Bolt croppers, hand tools	8203.4000	256
螺丝刀	Screwdrivers	8205.4000	256
螺纹滚轧机,金属或金属陶瓷用,非切削	Thread rolling machines, for working metal or cermets, without removing material	8463.2000	7
螺纹制品,钢铁制的,其他	Threaded articles, of iron of steel, nes	7318.1900	268
螺纹制品,铜制,其他	Articles, threaded, of copper, nes	7415.3900	56
螺纹肘管、弯管及管套,不锈钢制	Threaded elbows, bends and sleeves, of stainless steel	7307.2200	6
螺纹肘管、弯管及管套,钢铁的,其他	Threaded elbows, bends and sleeves, of iron or steel, nes	7307.9200	6
螺旋弹簧,钢铁制,其他	Helical springs, of iron or steel, nes	7320.2090	36
螺旋弹簧,钢铁制,铁道车辆用	Helical springs, of iron or steel, for railway locomotives and rollingstock	7320.2010	36
螺旋焊管机,全自动或半自动的	Spiralling tube welding machines, fully or partly automatic	8515.3110	
螺旋花线机	Gimped yarn making machines	8447.9090	7

商品名称	Article Description	税则号列	申报要素
络纱机,其他	Textile winding machines, nes	8445.4090	7
络纱机的辅助机器	Textile winding machines auxiliary	8448.1900	3
络筒锭	Winding spindle	8448.3310	3
络筒锭壳	Winding spindle flyers	8448.3390	3
落地灯,电气的	Floorstanding lamps, electric	9405.2000	5
落地扇,包括风机,本身装有一个输出功率不超过125瓦的电动机	Floor fans, with a self-contained electric motor of an output not exceeding 125W	8414.5192	23

M

商品名称	Article Description	税则号列	申报要素
ma			
麻黄碱及其盐	Ephedrine and its salts	2939.4100	34
麻黄碱类及其盐,其他	Ephedrines and their salts,nes	2939.4900	34
麻将及类似桌上游戏用品	Mahjong and similiar table games	9504.9040	
麻醉设备	Anaesthetic apparatus and instruments	9018.9070	
马,改良种用	Horses,pure-bred breeding	0101.1010	34
马,改良种用除外	Horese,ex. pure-bred breeding	0101.9010	34
马鞭及类似品	Ridingcrops and the like	6602.0000	
马褡裢,适合各种动物用	Saddle bags for any animal,of any material	4201.0000	1458
马黛茶	Mate	0903.0000	
马弗罩,含有按重量计超过50%的三氧化二铝或三氧化二铝和二氧化硅的混合物或化合物	Muffles, containing by weight more than 50% of alumina(Al_2O_3) or of a mixture of compound of alumina and of silica(SiO_2)	6903.2000	6
马弗罩,含有按重量计超过50%的石墨、其他碳或其混合物	Muffles, containing by weight more than 50% of graphite or other carbon or of a mixture of these products	6903.1000	6
马卡达姆坚果,其他	Macadamia nuts,nes	0802.6090	134
马卡达姆坚果,种用	Macadamia nuts,seed	0802.6010	134
马裤,非针织或钩编的,男式,合成纤维制	Breeches,not knitted or crocheted,for men or boys,of synthetic fibres	6203.4390	2456
马裤,非针织或钩编的,男式,棉制	Breeches,not knitted or crocheted,for men or boys,of cotton	6203.4290	2456
马裤,非针织或钩编的,男式,其他纺织材料制	Breeches,not knitted or crocheted,for men or boys,of other textile material	6203.4990	2456
马裤,非针织或钩编的,男式,羊毛或动物细毛制	Breeches,not knitted or crocheted,for men or boys,of wool or fine animal hair	6203.4100	2456
马裤,非针织或钩编的,女式,合成纤维制	Breeches, not knitted or crocheted, for women or girls,of synthetic fibres	6204.6300	2456
马裤,非针织或钩编的,女式,棉制	Breeches, not knitted or crocheted, for women or girls,of cotton	6204.6200	2456
马裤,非针织或钩编的,女式,其他纺织材料制	Breeches, not knitted or crocheted, for women or girls,of other textile materials	6204.6900	2456
马裤,非针织或钩编的,女式,羊毛或动物细毛制	Breeches, not knitted or crocheted, for women or girls,of wool or fine animal hair	6204.6100	2456
马裤,针织或钩编的,男式,合成纤维制	Breeches, knitted or crocheted, for men or boys, of synthetic fibres	6103.4300	2456
马裤,针织或钩编的,男式,棉制	Breeches, knitted or crocheted, for men or boys, of cotton	6103.4200	2456

商品名称	Article Description	税则号列	申报要素
马裤,针织或钩编的,男式,其他纺织材料制	Breeches, knitted or crocheted, for men or boys, of other textile materials	6103.4900	2456
马裤,针织或钩编的,男式,羊毛或动物细毛制	Breeches, knitted or crocheted, for men or boys, of wool or fine animal hair	6103.4100	2456
马裤,针织或钩编的,女式,合成纤维制	Breeches, knitted or crocheted, for women or girls, of synthetic fibres	6104.6300	2456
马裤,针织或钩编的,女式,棉制	Breeches, knitted or crocheted, for women or girls, of cotton	6104.6200	2456
马裤,针织或钩编的,女式,其他纺织材料制	Breeches, knitted or crocheted, for women or girls, of other textile materials	6104.6900	2456
马裤,针织或钩编的,女式,羊毛或动物细毛制	Breeches, knitted or crocheted, for women or girls, of wool or fine animal hair	6104.6100	2456
马来酐	Maleic anhydride	2917.1400	36
马铃薯,冷冻的	Potatoes, frozen	0710.1000	1
马铃薯,用醋或醋酸以外的其他方法制作或保藏的,冷冻的	Potatoes, prepared or preserved otherwise than by vinegar or acetic acid, frozen	2004.1000	48
马铃薯,粉片、颗粒及团粒	Potatoes, flakes, granules and pellets	1105.2000	4
马铃薯,其他,鲜或冷藏的	Potatoes, nes, fresh or chilled	0701.9000	13
马铃薯,细粉、粗粉及粉末	Potatoes, flour, meal and powder	1105.1000	4
马铃薯,用醋或醋酸以外的其他方法制作或保藏的,未冷冻	Potatoes, prepared or preserved otherwise than by vinegar or acetic acid, not frozen	2005.2000	48
马铃薯,种用	Potatoes, seeds	0701.1000	13
马毛粗松螺旋花线,不论是否供零售用	Gimped horsehair yarn, whether or not put up for retail sale	5110.0000	56
马毛的机织物	Woven fabrics of horsehair	5113.0000	4568
马毛及废马毛,不论是否制成有或无衬垫的毛片	Horsehair and horsehair waste, whether or not put up as a layer with or without supporting material	0511.9940	
马毛纱线,不论是否供零售用	Yarn of horse hair, whether or not put up for retail sale	5110.0000	56
马肉,鲜或冷或冻的	Meat of horses, fresh, chilled or frozen	0205.0000	14
马赛克及类似品,陶瓷的,上釉的,其最大表面以可置入边长小于7厘米的方格为限	Mosaic cubes and the like, ceramic, glazed, the largest surface area of which is capable of being enclosed in a square the side of which is less than 7cm	6908.1000	5
马赛克及类似品,陶瓷的,未上釉的,其最大表面以可置入边长小于7厘米的方格为限	Mosaic cubes and the like, ceramic, unglazed, the largest surface area of which is capable of being enclosed in a square the side of which is less than 7cm	6907.1000	5
马赛克及类似品,天然石料(包括板岩)制的,不论是否有衬背,其最大表面以可置入边长小于7厘米的方格为限	Mosaic cubes and the like, of natural stone (including slate), whether or not on a backing, the largest surface area of which is capable of being enclosed in a square the side of which is less than 7cm	6802.1090	3468

M

商品名称	Article Description	税则号列	申报要素
马赛克及其他小件玻璃品,供镶嵌或类似装饰用,压制或模制的	Mosaic cubes of glass and other glass smallwares, for decorative or similar purposes, pressed or moulded	7016.1000	345
马桶座圈及盖,塑料的	Lavatory seats and covers, of plastics	3922.2000	236
马吲哚(INN)以及盐	Mazindol(INN) ; salts thereof	2933.9100	36
mai			
唛头笔	Markers	9608.2000	
吗啡及盐	Morphine and salts	2939.1100	34
麦迪霉素及其衍生物以及它们的盐	Midecamycin and its derivatives; salts thereof	2941.9060	
麦角胺及其盐	Ergotamine(INN) and its salts	2939.6200	34
麦角生物碱及其衍生物以及它们的盐,其他	Rye ergot alkaloids and their derivatives; salts thereof, nes	2939.6900	34
麦角酸及其盐	Lysergic acid and its salts	2939.6300	34
麦角新碱及其盐	Ergometrine(INN) and its salts	2939.6100	34
麦精	Malt extract	1901.9000	68
麦克风及其座架	Microphones and stands thereof	8518.1000	
麦克风零件	Microphones parts	8518.9000	3
麦乳精,非幼儿食品	Malted milk, other than for infant use	1901.9000	68
麦芽,未焙制	Malt, not roasted	1107.1000	4
麦芽,已焙制	Malt, roasted	1107.2000	4
麦芽糖及糖浆	Maltose and maltose syrup	1702.9000	
脉冲编码调制设备(PCM)	Pulse code modulation equipments	8517.6221	7
脉冲编码调制设备(PCM)用零件	Pulse code modulation equipments parts	8517.7020	3
man			
鳗鱼,冻的	Eels(Anguilla spp.), frozen	0303.7600	18
鳗鱼,其他,活的	Eels(Anguilla spp.), nes, living	0301.9290	15
鳗鱼,鲜或冷的	Eels(Anguilla spp.), fresh or chilled	0302.6600	18
鳗鱼,制作或保藏的,整条或切块,但未绞碎	Eels, prepared or preserved, whole or in pieces, but not minced	1604.1910	48
鳗鱼苗	Fry, eels(Anguilla spp.)	0301.9210	15
鳗鱼苗	Eel fry	0301.9210	15
蔓越桔,鲜的	Cranberries, fresh	0810.4000	1
mang			
芒果	Mangoes	0804.5020	14
芒果汁	Mango juice	2009.8012	2468
mao			
毛笔	Writing brushes	9603.3020	
毛掸	Feather dusters	9603.9010	
毛发推剪,电动的	Hair clippers, with self-contained electric motor	8510.2000	
毛发推剪零件,电动的	Hair clippers parts, with self-contained electric motor	8510.9000	3

商品名称	Article Description	税则号列	申报要素
毛纺粗纱机	Worsted roving machines	8445.1322	7
毛巾被,棉制,其他	Towelling coverlets, of cotton, nes	6302.3192	346
毛巾及毛圈织物,狭幅织物除外,化学纤维制	Terry towelling and terry fabrics, of man-made fibres	5802.2030	468
毛巾及毛圈织物,狭幅织物除外,棉制,其他	Terry towelling and terry fabrics, of cotton, nes	5802.1900	468
毛巾及毛圈织物,狭幅织物除外,棉制,未漂白	Terry towelling and terry fabrics, of cotton, unbleached	5802.1100	468
毛巾及毛圈织物,狭幅织物除外,其他	Terry towelling and terry fabrics, nes	5802.2090	468
毛巾及毛圈织物,狭幅织物除外,丝及绢丝制	Terry towelling and terry fabrics, of silk or silk waste	5802.2010	468
毛巾及毛圈织物,狭幅织物除外,羊毛或动物细毛制	Terry towelling and terry fabrics, of wool or fine animal hair	5802.2020	468
毛精梳机	Worsted comber	8445.1220	7
毛皮,适合加工皮货用的头、尾、爪及块、片,其他	Raw furskins, heads, tails, paws and pieces or cuttings, suitable for furriers use, nes	4301.9090	15
毛皮,整张的,其他不论是否带头、尾或爪	Raw furskins, whole, with or without head, tall or paws, nes	4301.8090	15
毛皮制物品,其他	Furskin articles, nes	4303.9000	456
毛圈绒织物,纺织材料制,针织或钩编的,其他	Looped pile fabrics of textile materials, knitted or crocheted, nes	6001.2900	46
毛圈绒织物,化学纤维制,针织或钩编的	Looped pile fabrics of man-made fibres, knitted or crocheted	6001.2200	46
毛圈绒织物,棉制,针织或钩编的	Looped pile fabrics of cotton, knitted or crocheted	6001.2100	46
毛细纱机	Worsted ring spinning frame	8445.2042	7
锚及其零件,钢铁的	Anchors and parts thereof, of iron or steel	7316.0000	36
铆钉,钢铁制的	Rivets, of iron or steel	7318.2300	268
铆钉,铝制	Rivets, of aluminium	7616.1000	36
铆接机或类似工具用子弹及其零件	Cartridges for riveting or similar tools, and parts thereof	9306.3080	3
帽钩及类似品,贱金属制	Hat-pegs and similar fixtures, of base metal	8302.5000	256
帽架及类似品,贱金属制	Hat-racks and similar fixtures, of base metal	8302.5000	256
帽类,不论有无衬里或装饰物,编结帽或用任何材料的条带拼制而成的	Hats and other headgear, plaited or made by assembling strips of any material, whether or not lined or trimmed	6504.0000	24
帽类,钩编的	Hats and other headgear, knitted or crocheted	6505.9010	26
帽类,毛皮制,其他	Headgear, of furskin, nes	6506.9920	26
帽类,皮革制,其他	Headgear, of leather, nes	6506.9910	26
帽类,其他	Headgear, nes	6506.9990	26
帽类,橡胶或塑料制,其他	Headgear, of rubber or of plastics, nes	6506.9100	26

商品名称	Article Description	税则号列	申报要素
帽类,用毡呢帽身、帽兜或圆帽片制成的,不论有无衬里或装饰物	Hats and other headgear of felt, made from the hat bodies, hoods or plateaux of felt, whether or not lined or trimmed	6302. 5990	346
帽类,针织的	Hats and other headgear, knitted	6505. 9090	26
帽坯,未楦制成形,也未加帽边、衬里或装饰物,用任何材料的条带拼制而成或编结的	Hat-shapes, plaited or made by assembling strips of any material, neither blocked to shape, nor with made brims, nor lined, nor trimmed	6502. 0000	246
帽坯、帽身及帽兜,未楦制成形,也未加帽边,毡呢制的	Hat-forms, hat bodies and hoods of felt, neither blocked to shape nor with made brims	6501. 0000	26
帽圈、帽衬、帽套、帽帮、帽骨架、帽舌及帽颏带	Head-bands, linings, covers, hat foundations, hat frames, peaks and chinstraps, for headgear	6507. 0000	
mei			
玫瑰,不论是否嫁接,其他	Roses, grafted or not, nes	0602. 4090	
玫瑰,不论是否嫁接,种用	Roses, grafted or not, seedlings	0602. 4010	3
玫瑰,鲜的,制花束或装饰用的	Roses, fresh, suitable for bouquets or for ornamental purposes	0603. 1100	34
梅,鲜的	Plums, fresh	0809. 4000	1
媒体,其他	Media, nes	8523. 8099	37
媒体,税号 84. 71 所列机器用,其他	Media, for the machines of heading 84. 71, nes	8523. 8029	37
媒体,未录制	Media, unrecorded	8523. 8091	37
媒体,未录制,税号 84. 71 所列机器用	Media, unrecorded, for the machines of heading 84. 71	8523. 8021	37
媒诱音响器	Decoy calls	9208. 9000	5
煤,其他,不论是否粉化,但未制成型	Coal, nes, whether or not pulverized, but not agglomerated	2701. 1900	156
煤气	Coal gas	2705. 0000	4
煤气表	Coal gas meters	9028. 1010	
煤气表零件、附件,工业用	Coal gas meters parts and accessories, for industrial use	9028. 9010	3
煤气表零件、附件,其他	Coal gas meters parts and accessories, nes	9028. 9090	3
煤气灯纱筒及纱罩,不论是否浸渍	Incandescent gas mantles and tubular knitted gas mantle fabric therefor, whether or not impregnated	5908. 0000	
煤气发生器,不论有无净化器	Gas producer or generators, with or without their purifiers	8405. 1000	3
煤气发生器的零件	Gas producer or generators parts	8405. 9000	3
煤气灶,钢铁制,非电热的家用,其他,包括使用固体燃料的	Gas-rings, of iron or steel, non-electric domestic appliances, nes, including appliances for solid fuel	7321. 1900	7
煤气灶,钢铁制,非电热的家用,使用气体燃料或可使用气体燃料及其他燃料的	Gas-rings, of iron or steel, non-electric domestic appliances, for gas fuel or for both gas and other fuels	7321. 1100	7
煤气灶,钢铁制,非电热的家用,使用液体燃料的	Gas-rings, of iron or steel, non-electric domestic appliances, for liquid fuel	7321. 1290	7

商品名称	Article Description	税则号列	申报要素
煤球	Ovoids manufactured from coal	2701. 2000	156
煤油馏分,其他	Kerosene distillages, nes	2710. 1919	6
煤油炉,钢铁制,家用	Kerosene cooking stoves, of iron or steel, domestic appliances	7321. 1210	7
煤制成的固体燃料,其他	Solid fuels manufactured from coal, nes	2701. 2000	156
煤砖	Briquettes manufactured from coal	2701. 2000	156
酶及酶制品,其他	Enzymes and prepared enzymes, nes	3507. 9090	35
酶制剂,预鞣用	Enzymatic preparations for pre-tanning	3202. 9000	68
美达西泮(INN)以及盐	Medazepam (INN); salts thereof	2933. 9100	36
美芬雷司(INN)以及它们的盐	Mefenorex (INN); salts thereof	2921. 4600	36
美冠鹦鹉,改良种用	Cockatoos, pure-bred breeding	0106. 3210	3
美人蕉,种用,休眠的	Canna bulbs, seed, dormant	0601. 1091	135
美沙酮以及它们的盐	Methadone (INN) and salts thereof	2922. 3100	36
美沙酮中间体	Methadone (INN) intermediate	2926. 3000	36
美索卡(INN)及盐	Mesocarb (INN); salts thereof	2934. 9100	36
镁,未锻轧,按重量计含镁量至少为99. 8%	Magnesium, unwrought, containing at least 99. 8% by weight of magnesium	8104. 1100	16
镁,未锻轧,其他	Magnesium, unwrought, nes	8104. 1900	16
镁,已锻轧	Magnesium, wrought	8104. 9010	16
镁粉末	Powders, of magnesium	8104. 3000	16
镁氧矿,熔凝的	Magnesia, fused	2519. 9010	146
镁制品	Magnesium articles	8104. 9020	16
men			
门窗及其框架、门槛,钢铁的	Doors, windows and their frames and thresholds for doors, of iron or steel	7308. 3000	6
门窗及其框架、门槛,铝制	Doors, windows and their frames and thresholds for doors, of aluminium	7610. 1000	56
门及其框架,塑料的	Doors and their frames, of plastics	3925. 2000	23
门及其框架和门槛,木制的	Doors and their frames and thresholds, wooden	4418. 2000	58
门槛,塑料的	Doors thresholds, of plastics	3925. 2000	23
门式装卸桥	Frame loading and unloading bridges	8426. 1941	7
门眼,光学的	Door eyes, optical	9013. 8020	
门座式起重机	Portal cranes	8426. 3000	7
meng			
猛禽,改良种用	Birds of prey, pure-bred breeding	0106. 3110	3
猛禽,其他	Birds of prey, nes	0106. 3190	
锰,未锻轧	Manganese, unwrought	8111. 0010	16
锰的氧化物,其他	Manganese oxide, nes	2820. 9000	6
锰粉末	Powders of manganese	8111. 0010	16

商品名称	Article Description	税则号列	申报要素
锰矿砂及其精矿,包括以干重计含锰量在20%及以上的锰铁矿及其精矿	Manganese ores and concentrates, including ferruginous manganese ores and concentrates with a manganese content of 20% or more, calculated on the dry weight	2602.0000	1346
锰酸盐	Manganates	2841.6900	1
锰铁合金,按重量计含碳量在2%以上	Ferro-manganese alloys, containing by weight more than 2% of carbon	7202.1100	6
锰铁合金,其他	Ferro-manganese alloys, nes	7202.1900	6
锰渣,粒状	Manganese granulated slag, from the manufacture of iron or steel	2618.0010	146
锰制品,其他	Manganese articles, nes	8111.0090	16
mi			
咪达唑仑(INN)以及盐	Midazolam(INN); salts thereof	2933.9100	36
咪唑环化合物,结构上含有,非稠合的,不论是否氢化,其他	Imidazole ring compounds, unfused in the structure, whether or not hydrogenated, nes	2933.2900	36
猕猴桃,鲜的	Kiwifruit, fresh	0810.5000	15
醚醇酚及其卤化、磺化、硝化或亚硝化衍生物	Ether-alcohol-phenols and their halogenated, sulphonated, nitrated or nitrosated derivatives	2909.5000	36
醚醇及其卤化、磺化、硝化或亚硝化衍生物,其他	Ether-alcohols and their halogenated, sulphonated, nitrated or nitrosated derivatives, nes	2909.4990	36
醚酚及其卤化、磺化、硝化或亚硝化衍生物	Ether-phenols and their halogenated, sulphonated, nitrated or nitrosated derivatives	2909.5000	36
米粉干	Rice vermicelli, cooked	1902.3010	46
脒,其他	Amidines, nes	2925.2900	36
密封垫,用金属片与其他材料制成或用双层或多层金属片制成	Gaskets of metal sheeting combined with other material or of two or more layers of metal	8484.1000	56
密封垫成套物品	Gaskets sets	8484.9000	56
密封机器,瓶、罐、箱、袋或其他容器的	Closing machines, for bottles, cans, boxes, bags or other containers, nes	8422.3090	
嘧啶环化合物,结构上含有,不论是否氢化,其他	Pyrimidine ring compounds, in the structure, whether or not hydrogenated, nes	2933.5990	36
蜜胺	Melamine	2933.6100	36
蜜胺树脂,初级形状的	Melamine resins, in primary forms	3909.2000	1256
蜜蜂,改良种用	Bees, pure-bred breeding	0106.9019	4
蜜蜂,其他	Bees, live, nes	0106.9090	4
蜜饯	Sweetmeats	1704.9000	258
蜜枣,糖渍的	Preserved jujubes by sugar (drained, glace or crystallized)	2006.0010	48
mian			
绵羊,改良种用	Sheep, live, pure-bred breeding	0104.1010	3
绵羊,改良种用除外	Sheep, live, ex. pure-bred breeding	0104.1090	3

商品名称	Article Description	税则号列	申报要素
绵羊肉,冻的,其他,带骨	Meat of sheep, frozen, nes, other cuts with bone in	0204.4200	14
绵羊肉,冻的,其他,去骨	Meat of sheep, frozen, nes, boneless	0204.4300	14
绵羊肉,冻的,整头及半头	Meat of sheep, frozen, carcasses and halfcarcasses	0204.4100	14
绵羊肉,鲜或冷的,其他,带骨	Meat of sheep, fresh or chilled, nes, other cuts with bone in	0204.2200	14
绵羊肉,鲜或冷的,其他,去骨	Meat of sheep, fresh or chilled, nes, boneless	0204.2300	14
绵羊肉,鲜或冷的,整头及半头	Meat of sheep, fresh or chilled, carcasses and halfcarcasses	0204.2100	14
棉短绒	Cotton linters	1404.2000	6
棉短绒纸浆	Cotton linters pulp	4706.1000	5
棉纺粗纱机	Cotton roving frames	8445.1321	7
棉花,未梳的	Cotton, not carded or combed	5201.0000	48
棉花,已梳的	Cotton, carded or combed	5203.0000	48
棉花采摘机	Cotton picker	8433.5920	
棉机织物,按重量计含棉量在85%及以上,每平方米重量不超过200克,漂白,平纹机织物,每平方米重量不超过100克	Woven fabrics of cotton, containing 85% or more by weight of cotton, weighing not more than 200g/m², bleached, plain weave, weighing not more than 100g/m²	5208.2100	468
棉机织物,按重量计含棉量在85%及以上,每平方米重量不超过200克,漂白,平纹机织物,每平方米重量超过100克	Woven fabrics of cotton, containing 85% or more by weight of cotton, weighing not more than 200g/m², bleached, plain weave, weighing more than 100g/m²	5208.2200	468
棉机织物,按重量计含棉量在85%及以上,每平方米重量不超过200克,漂白,其他机织物	Woven fabrics of cotton, containing 85% or more by weight of cotton, weighing not more than 200g/m², bleached, other fabrics	5208.2900	468
棉机织物,按重量计含棉量在85%及以上,每平方米重量不超过200克,漂白,三线或四线斜纹机织物,包括双面斜纹机织物	Woven fabrics of cotton, containing 85% or more by weight of cotton, weighing not more than 200g/m², bleached, 3-thread or 4-thread twill, inluding cross twill	5208.2300	468
棉机织物,按重量计含棉量在85%及以上,每平方米重量不超过200克,染色,平纹机织物,每平方米重量不超过100克	Woven fabrics of cotton, containing 85% or more by weight of cotton, weighing not more than 200g/m², dyed, plain weave, weighing not more than 100g/m²	5208.3100	468
棉机织物,按重量计含棉量在85%及以上,每平方米重量不超过200克,染色,平纹机织物,每平方米重量超过100克	Woven fabrics of cotton, containing 85% or more by weight of cotton, weighing not more than 200g/m², dyed, plain weave, weighing more than 100g/m²	5208.3200	468
棉机织物,按重量计含棉量在85%及以上,每平方米重量不超过200克,染色,其他机织物	Woven fabrics of cotton, containing 85% or more by weight of cotton, weighing not more than 200g/m², dyed, other fabrics	5208.3900	468

商品名称	Article Description	税则号列	申报要素
棉机织物,按重量计含棉量在 85% 及以上,每平方米重量不超过 200 克,染色,三线或四线斜纹机织物,包括双面斜纹机织物	Woven fabrics of cotton, containing 85% or more by weight of cotton, weighing not more than $200g/m^2$, dyed, 3-thread or 4-thread twill, including cross twill	5208. 3300	468
棉机织物,按重量计含棉量在 85% 及以上,每平方米重量不超过 200 克,色织,平纹机织物,每平方米重量不超过 100 克	Woven fabrics of cotton, containing 85% or more by weight of cotton, weighing not more than $200g/m^2$, of yarns of different colours, plain weave, weighing not more than $100g/m^2$	5208. 4100	468
棉机织物,按重量计含棉量在 85% 及以上,每平方米重量不超过 200 克,色织,平纹机织物,每平方米重量超过 100 克	Woven fabrics of cotton, containing 85% or more by weight of cotton, weighing not more than $200g/m^2$, of yarns of different colours, plain weave, weighing more than $100g/m^2$	5208. 4200	468
棉机织物,按重量计含棉量在 85% 及以上,每平方米重量不超过 200 克,色织,其他机织物	Woven fabrics of cotton, containing 85% or more by weight of cotton, weighing not more than $200g/m^2$, of yarns of different colours, other fabrics	5208. 4900	468
棉机织物,按重量计含棉量在 85% 及以上,每平方米重量不超过 200 克,色织,三线或四线斜纹机织物,包括双面斜纹机织物	Woven fabrics of cotton, containing 85% or more by weight of cotton, weighing not more than $200g/m^2$, of yarns of different colours, 3-thread or 4-thread twill, including cross twill	5208. 4300	468
棉机织物,按重量计含棉量在 85% 及以上,每平方米重量不超过 200 克,未漂白,平纹机织物,每平方米重量不超过 100 克	Woven fabrics of cotton, containing 85% or more by weight of cotton, weighing not more than $200g/m^2$, unbleached, plain weave, weighing not more than $100g/m^2$	5208. 1100	468
棉机织物,按重量计含棉量在 85% 及以上,每平方米重量不超过 200 克,未漂白,平纹机织物,每平方米重量超过 100 克	Woven fabrics of cotton, containing 85% or more by weight of cotton, weighing not more than $200g/m^2$, unbleached, plain weave, weighing more than $100g/m^2$	5208. 1200	468
棉机织物,按重量计含棉量在 85% 及以上,每平方米重量不超过 200 克,未漂白,其他机织物	Woven fabrics of cotton, containing 85% or more by weight of cotton, weighing not more than $200g/m^2$, unbleached, other fabrics	5208. 1900	468
棉机织物,按重量计含棉量在 85% 及以上,每平方米重量不超过 200 克,未漂白,三线或四线斜纹机织物,包括双面斜纹机织物	Woven fabrics of cotton, containing 85% or more by weight of cotton, weighing not more than $200g/m^2$, unbleached, 3-thread or 4-thread twill, including cross twill	5208. 1300	468
棉机织物,按重量计含棉量在 85% 及以上,每平方米重量不超过 200 克,印花,平纹机织物,每平方米重量不超过 100 克	Woven fabrics of cotton, containing 85% or more by weight of cotton, weighing not more than $200g/m^2$, printed, plain weave, weighing not more than $100g/m^2$	5208. 5100	468
棉机织物,按重量计含棉量在 85% 及以上,每平方米重量不超过 200 克,印花,平纹机织物,每平方米重量超过 100 克	Woven fabrics of cotton, containing 85% or more by weight of cotton, weighing not more than $200g/m^2$, printed, plain weave, weighing more than $100g/m^2$	5208. 5200	468

商品名称	Article Description	税则号列	申报要素
棉机织物,按重量计含棉量在 85% 及以上,每平方米重量不超过 200 克,印花,其他机织物	Woven fabrics of cotton, containing 85% or more by weight of cotton, weighing not more than 200g/m^2, printed, other fabrics	5208.5990	468
棉机织物,按重量计含棉量在 85% 及以上,每平方米重量不超过 200 克,印花,三线或四线斜纹机织物,包括双面斜纹机织物	Woven fabrics of cotton, containing 85% or more by weight of cotton, weighing not more than 200g/m^2, printed, 3-thread or 4-thread twill, including cross twill	5208.5910	468
棉机织物,按重量计含棉量在 85% 及以上,每平方米重量超过 200 克,漂白,平纹机织物	Woven fabrics of cotton, containing 85% or more by weight of cotton, weighing more than 200g/m^2, bleached, plain weave	5209.2100	468
棉机织物,按重量计含棉量在 85% 及以上,每平方米重量超过 200 克,漂白,其他机织物	Woven fabrics of cotton, containing 85% or more by weight of cotton, weighing more than 200g/m^2, bleached, other fabrics	5209.2900	468
棉机织物,按重量计含棉量在 85% 及以上,每平方米重量超过 200 克,漂白,三线或四线斜纹机织物,包括双面斜纹机织物	Woven fabrics of cotton, containing 85% or more by weight of cotton, weighing more than 200g/m^2, bleached, 3-thread or 4-thread twill, including cross twill	5209.2200	468
棉机织物,按重量计含棉量在 85% 及以上,每平方米重量超过 200 克,染色,平纹机织物	Woven fabrics of cotton, containing 85% or more by weight of cotton, weighing more than 200g/m^2, dyed, plain weave	5209.3100	468
棉机织物,按重量计含棉量在 85% 及以上,每平方米重量超过 200 克,染色,其他机织物	Woven fabrics of cotton, containing 85% or more by weight of cotton, weighing more than 200g/m^2, dyed, other fabrics	5209.3900	468
棉机织物,按重量计含棉量在 85% 及以上,每平方米重量超过 200 克,染色,三线或四线斜纹机织物,包括双面斜纹机织物	Woven fabrics of cotton, containing 85% or more by weight of cotton, weighing more than 200g/m^2, dyed, 3-thread or 4-thread twill, including cross twill	5209.3200	468
棉机织物,按重量计含棉量在 85% 及以上,每平方米重量超过 200 克,色织,粗斜纹布	Woven fabrics of cotton, containing 85% or more by weight of cotton, weighing more than 200g/m^2, of yarns of different colours, denim	5209.4200	468
棉机织物,按重量计含棉量在 85% 及以上,每平方米重量超过 200 克,色织,平纹机织物	Woven fabrics of cotton, containing 85% or more by weight of cotton, weighing more than 200g/m^2, of yarns of different colours, plain weave	5209.4100	468
棉机织物,按重量计含棉量在 85% 及以上,每平方米重量超过 200 克,色织,其他机织物	Woven fabrics of cotton, containing 85% or more by weight of cotton, weighing more than 200g/m^2, of yarns of different colours, other fabrics	5209.4900	468
棉机织物,按重量计含棉量在 85% 及以上,每平方米重量超过 200 克,色织,三线或四线斜纹机织物,包括双面斜纹机织物	Woven fabrics of cotton, containing 85% or more by weight of cotton, weighing more than 200g/m^2, of yarns of different colours, other fabrics of 3-thread or 4-thread twill, including cross twill	5209.4300	468
棉机织物,按重量计含棉量在 85% 及以上,每平方米重量超过 200 克,未漂白,平纹机织物	Woven fabrics of cotton, containing 85% or more by weight of cotton, weighing more than 200g/m^2, unbleached, plain weave	5209.1100	468

商品名称	Article Description	税则号列	申报要素
棉机织物,按重量计含棉量在85%及以上,每平方米重量超过200克,未漂白,其他机织物	Woven fabrics of cotton, containing 85% or more by weight of cotton, weighing more than 200g/m², unbleached, other fabrics	5209.1900	468
棉机织物,按重量计含棉量在85%及以上,每平方米重量超过200克,未漂白,三线或四线斜纹机织物,包括双面斜纹机织物	Woven fabrics of cotton, containing 85% or more by weight of cotton, weighing more than 200g/m², unbleached, 3-thread or 4-thread twill, including cross twill	5209.1200	468
棉机织物,按重量计含棉量在85%及以上,每平方米重量超过200克,印花,平纹机织物	Woven fabrics of cotton, containing 85% or more by weight of cotton, weighing more than 200g/m², printed, plain weave	5209.5100	468
棉机织物,按重量计含棉量在85%及以上,每平方米重量超过200克,印花,其他机织物	Woven fabrics of cotton, containing 85% or more by weight of cotton, weighing more than 200g/m², printed, other fabrics	5209.5900	468
棉机织物,按重量计含棉量在85%及以上,每平方米重量超过200克,印花,三线或四线斜纹机织物,包括双面斜纹机织物	Woven fabrics of cotton, containing 85% or more by weight of cotton, weighing more than 200g/m², printed, 3-thread or 4-thread twill, including cross twill	5209.5200	468
棉机织物,按重量计含棉量在85%以下,主要或仅与化学纤维混纺,每平方米重量不超过200克,漂白,平纹机织物	Woven fabrics of cotton, containing less than 85% by weight of cotton, mixed mainly or solely with man-made fibres, weighing not more than 200g/m², bleached, plain weave	5210.2100	468
棉机织物,按重量计含棉量在85%以下,主要或仅与化学纤维混纺,每平方米重量不超过200克,漂白,其他机织物	Woven fabrics of cotton, containing less than 85% by weight of cotton, mixed mainly or solely with man-made fibres, weighing not more than 200g/m², bleached, other fabrics	5210.2990	468
棉机织物,按重量计含棉量在85%以下,主要或仅与化学纤维混纺,每平方米重量不超过200克,漂白,三线或四线斜纹机织物,包括双面斜纹机织物	Woven fabrics of cotton, containing less than 85% by weight of cotton, mixed mainly or solely with man-made fibres, weighing not more than 200g/m², bleached, 3-thread or 4-thread twill, including cross twill	5210.2910	468
棉机织物,按重量计含棉量在85%以下,主要或仅与化学纤维混纺,每平方米重量不超过200克,染色,平纹机织物	Woven fabrics of cotton, containing less than 85% by weight of cotton, mixed mainly or solely with man-made fibres, weighing not more than 200g/m², dyed, plain weave	5210.3100	468
棉机织物,按重量计含棉量在85%以下,主要或仅与化学纤维混纺,每平方米重量不超过200克,染色,其他机织物	Woven fabrics of cotton, containing less than 85% by weight of cotton, mixed mainly or solely with man-made fibres, weighing not more than 200g/m², dyed, other fabrics	5210.3900	468
棉机织物,按重量计含棉量在85%以下,主要或仅与化学纤维混纺,每平方米重量不超过200克,染色,三线或四线斜纹机织物,包括双面斜纹机织物	Woven fabrics of cotton, containing less than 85% by weight of cotton, mixed mainly or solely with man-made fibres, weighing not more than 200g/m², dyed, 3-thread or 4-thread twill, including cross twill	5210.3200	468

商品名称	Article Description	税则号列	申报要素
棉机织物,按重量计含棉量在85%以下,主要或仅与化学纤维混纺,每平方米重量不超过200克,色织,平纹机织物	Woven fabrics of cotton, containing less than 85% by weight of cotton, mixed mainly or solely with man-made fibres, weighing not more than $200g/m^2$, of yarns of different colours, plain weave	5210.4100	468
棉机织物,按重量计含棉量在85%以下,主要或仅与化学纤维混纺,每平方米重量不超过200克,色织,其他	Woven fabrics of cotton, containing less than 85% by weight of cotton, mixed mainly or solely with man-made fibres, weighing not more than $200g/m^2$, of yarns of different colours, other fabrics	5210.4990	468
棉机织物,按重量计含棉量在85%以下,主要或仅与化学纤维混纺,每平方米重量不超过200克,色织,三线或四线斜纹机织物,包括双面斜纹机织物	Woven fabrics of cotton, containing less than 85% by weight of cotton, mixed mainly or solely with man-made fibres, weighing not more than $200g/m^2$, of yarns of different colours, 3-thread or 4-thread twill, including cross twill	5210.4910	468
棉机织物,按重量计含棉量在85%以下,主要或仅与化学纤维混纺,每平方米重量不超过200克,未漂白,平纹机织物	Woven fabrics of cotton, containing less than 85% by weight of cotton, mixed mainly or solely with man-made fibres, weighing not more than $200g/m^2$, unbleached, plain weave	5210.1100	468
棉机织物,按重量计含棉量在85%以下,主要或仅与化学纤维混纺,每平方米重量不超过200克,未漂白,其他机织物	Woven fabrics of cotton, containing less than 85% by weight of cotton, mixed mainly or solely with man-made fibres, weighing not more than $200g/m^2$, unbleached, other fabrics	5210.1990	468
棉机织物,按重量计含棉量在85%以下,主要或仅与化学纤维混纺,每平方米重量不超过200克,未漂白,三线或四线斜纹机织物,包括双面斜纹机织物	Woven fabrics of cotton, containing less than 85% by weight of cotton, mixed mainly or solely with man-made fibres, weighing not more than $200g/m^2$, unbleached, 3-thread or 4-thread twill, including cross twill	5210.1910	468
棉机织物,按重量计含棉量在85%以下,主要或仅与化学纤维混纺,每平方米重量不超过200克,印花,平纹机织物	Woven fabrics of cotton, containing less than 85% by weight of cotton, mixed mainly or solely with man-made fibres, weighing not more than $200g/m^2$, printed, plain weave	5210.5100	468
棉机织物,按重量计含棉量在85%以下,主要或仅与化学纤维混纺,每平方米重量不超过200克,印花,其他机织物	Woven fabrics of cotton, containing less than 85% by weight of cotton, mixed mainly or solely with man-made fibres, weighing not more than $200g/m^2$, printed, other fabrics	5210.5990	468
棉机织物,按重量计含棉量在85%以下,主要或仅与化学纤维混纺,每平方米重量不超过200克,印花,三线或四线斜纹机织物,包括双面斜纹机织物	Woven fabrics of cotton, containing less than 85% by weight of cotton, mixed mainly or solely with man-made fibres, weighing not more than $200g/m^2$, printed, 3-thread or 4-thread twill, including cross twill	5210.5910	468
棉机织物,按重量计含棉量在85%以下,主要或仅与化学纤维混纺,每平方米重量超过200克,漂白	Woven fabrics of cotton, containing less than 85% by weight of cotton, mixed mainly or solely with man-made fibres, weighing more than $200g/m^2$, bleached	5211.2000	468

M

商品名称	Article Description	税则号列	申报要素
棉机织物,按重量计含棉量在 85% 以下,主要或仅与化学纤维混纺,每平方米重量超过 200 克,染色,平纹机织物	Woven fabrics of cotton, containing less than 85% by weight of cotton, mixed mainly or solely with man-made fibres, weighing more than $200g/m^2$, dyed, plain weave	5211.3100	468
棉机织物,按重量计含棉量在 85% 以下,主要或仅与化学纤维混纺,每平方米重量超过 200 克,染色,其他机织物	Woven fabrics of cotton, containing less than 85% by weight of cotton, mixed mainly or solely with man-made fibres, weighing more than $200g/m^2$, dyed, other fabrics	5211.3900	468
棉机织物,按重量计含棉量在 85% 以下,主要或仅与化学纤维混纺,每平方米重量超过 200 克,染色,三线或四线斜纹机织物,包括双面斜纹机织物	Woven fabrics of cotton, containing less than 85% by weight of cotton, mixed mainly or solely with man-made fibres, weighing more than $200g/m^2$, dyed, 3-thread or 4-thread twill, including cross twill	5211.3200	468
棉机织物,按重量计含棉量在 85% 以下,主要或仅与化学纤维混纺,每平方米重量超过 200 克,色织,粗斜纹布	Woven fabrics of cotton, containing less than 85% by weight of cotton, mixed mainly or solely with man-made fibres, weighing more than $200g/m^2$, of yarns of different colours, denim	5211.4200	468
棉机织物,按重量计含棉量在 85% 以下,主要或仅与化学纤维混纺,每平方米重量超过 200 克,色织,平纹机织物	Woven fabrics of cotton, containing less than 85% by weight of cotton, mixed mainly or solely with man-made fibres, weighing more than $200g/m^2$, of yarns of different colours, plainweave	5211.4100	468
棉机织物,按重量计含棉量在 85% 以下,主要或仅与化学纤维混纺,每平方米重量超过 200 克,色织,其他机织物	Woven fabrics of cotton, containing less than 85% by weight of cotton, mixed mainly or solely with man-made fibres, weighing more than $200g/m^2$, of yarns of different colours, other fabrics	5211.4900	468
棉机织物,按重量计含棉量在 85% 以下,主要或仅与化学纤维混纺,每平方米重量超过 200 克,色织,三线或四线斜纹机织物,包括双面斜纹机织物	Woven fabrics of cotton, containing less than 85% by weight of cotton, mixed mainly or solely with man-made fibres, weighing more than $200g/m^2$, of yarns of different colours, other fabrics of 3-thread or 4-thread twill, including cross twill	5211.4300	468
棉机织物,按重量计含棉量在 85% 以下,主要或仅与化学纤维混纺,每平方米重量超过 200 克,未漂白,平纹机织物	Woven fabrics of cotton, containing less than 85% by weight of cotton, mixed mainly or solely with man-made fibres, weighing more than $200g/m^2$, unbleached, plain weave	5211.1100	468
棉机织物,按重量计含棉量在 85% 以下,主要或仅与化学纤维混纺,每平方米重量超过 200 克,未漂白,其他机织物	Woven fabrics of cotton, containing less than 85% by weight of cotton, mixed mainly or solely with man-made fibres, weighing more than $200g/m^2$, unbleached, other fabrics	5211.1900	468
棉机织物,按重量计含棉量在 85% 以下,主要或仅与化学纤维混纺,每平方米重量超过 200 克,未漂白,三线或四线斜纹机织物,包括双面斜纹机织物	Woven fabrics of cotton, containing less than 85% by weight of cotton, mixed mainly or solely with man-made fibres, weighing more than $200g/m^2$, unbleached, 3-thread or 4-thread twill, including cross twill	5211.1200	468

商品名称	Article Description	税则号列	申报要素
棉机织物,按重量计含棉量在85%以下,主要或仅与化学纤维混纺,每平方米重量超过200克,印花,平纹机织物	Woven fabrics of cotton, containing less than 85% by weight of cotton, mixed mainly or solely with man-made fibres, weighing more than 200g/m^2, printed, plain weave	5211.5100	468
棉机织物,按重量计含棉量在85%以下,主要或仅与化学纤维混纺,每平方米重量超过200克,印花,其他机织物	Woven fabrics of cotton, containing less than 85% by weight of cotton, mixed mainly or solely with man-made fibres, weighing more than 200g/m^2, printed, other fabrics	5211.5900	468
棉机织物,按重量计含棉量在85%以下,主要或仅与化学纤维混纺,每平方米重量超过200克,印花,三线或四线斜纹机织物,包括双面斜纹机织物	Woven fabrics of cotton, containing less than 85% by weight of cotton, mixed mainly or solely with man-made fibres, weighing more than 200g/m^2, printed, 3-thread or 4-thread twill, including cross twill	5211.5200	468
棉机织物,每平方米重量不超过200克,漂白,其他	Woven fabrics of cotton, weighing not more than 200g/m^2, bleached, nes	5212.1200	468
棉机织物,每平方米重量不超过200克,染色,其他	Woven fabrics of cotton, weighing not more than 200g/m^2, dyed, nes	5212.1300	468
棉机织物,每平方米重量不超过200克,色织,其他	Woven fabrics of cotton, weighing not more than 200g/m^2, of yarns of different colours, nes	5212.1400	468
棉机织物,每平方米重量不超过200克,未漂白,其他	Woven fabrics of cotton, weighing not more than 200g/m^2, unbleached, nes	5212.1100	468
棉机织物,每平方米重量不超过200克,印花,其他	Woven fabrics of cotton, weighing not more than 200g/m^2, printed, nes	5212.1500	468
棉机织物,每平方米重量超过200克,漂白,其他	Woven fabrics of cotton, weighing more than 200g/m^2, bleached, nes	5212.2200	468
棉机织物,每平方米重量超过200克,染色,其他	Woven fabrics of cotton, weighing more than 200g/m^2, dyed, nes	5212.2300	468
棉机织物,每平方米重量超过200克,色织,其他	Woven fabrics of cotton, weighing more than 200g/m^2, of yarns of different colours, nes	5212.2400	468
棉机织物,每平方米重量超过200克,未漂白,其他	Woven fabrics of cotton, weighing more than 200g/m^2, unbleached, nes	5212.2100	468
棉机织物,每平方米重量超过200克,印花,其他	Woven fabrics of cotton, weighing more than 200g/m^2, printed, nes	5212.2500	468
棉精梳机	Cotton comber	8445.1210	7
棉蜡	Cotton wax [see also wax(es)]	1521.1000	6
棉纱线,按重量计含棉量在85%及以上,非供零售用,精梳纤维纺制的单纱,细度在106.38分特以下,但不细于83.33分特(超过94公支,但不超过120公支)	Cotton yarn, containing 85% or more by weight of cotton, not put up for retail sale, single yarn, of combed fibres, measuring less than 106.38 decitex but not less than 83.33 decitex (exceeding 94 metric number but not exceeding 120 metric number)	5205.2700	3468

M

商品名称	Article Description	税则号列	申报要素
棉纱线,按重量计含棉量在 85% 及以上,非供零售用,精梳纤维纺制的单纱,细度在 125 分特以下,但不细于 106.38 分特(超过 80 公支,但不超过 94 公支)	Cotton yarn, containing 85% or more by weight of cotton, not put up for retail sale, single yarn, of combed fibres, measuring less than 125 decitex but not less than 106.38 decitex (exceeding 80 metric number but not exceeding 94 metric number)	5205.2600	3468
棉纱线,按重量计含棉量在 85% 及以上,非供零售用,精梳纤维纺制的单纱,细度在 192.31 分特以下,但不细于 125 分特(超过 52 公支,但不超过 80 公支)	Cotton yarn, containing 85% or more by weight of cotton, not put up for retail sale, single yarn, of combed fibres, measuring less than 192.31 decitex but not less than 125 decitex (exceeding 52 metric number but not exceeding 80 metric number)	5205.2400	3468
棉纱线,按重量计含棉量在 85% 及以上,非供零售用,精梳纤维纺制的单纱,细度在 232.56 分特以下,但不细于 192.31 分特(超过 43 公支,但不超过 52 公支)	Cotton yarn, containing 85% or more by weight of cotton, not put up for retail sale, single yarn, of combed fibres, measuring less than 232.56 decitex but not less than 192.31 decitex (exceeding 43 metric number but not exceeding 52 metric number)	5205.2300	3468
棉纱线,按重量计含棉量在 85% 及以上,非供零售用,精梳纤维纺制的单纱,细度在 714.29 分特及以上(不超过 14 公支)	Cotton yarn, containing 85% or more by weight of cotton, not put up for retail sale, single yarn, of combed fibres, measuring 714.29 decitex or more (not exceeding 14 metric number)	5205.2100	3468
棉纱线,按重量计含棉量在 85% 及以上,非供零售用,精梳纤维纺制的单纱,细度在 714.29 分特以下,但不细于 232.56 分特(超过 14 公支,但不超过 43 公支)	Cotton yarn, containing 85% or more by weight of cotton, not put up for retail sale, single yarn, of combed fibres, measuring less than 714.29 decitex but not less than 232.56 decitex (exceeding 14 metric number but not exceeding 43 metric number)	5205.2200	3468
棉纱线,按重量计含棉量在 85% 及以上,非供零售用,精梳纤维纺制的单纱,细度在 83.33 分特以下(超过 120 公支)	Cotton yarn, containing 85% or more by weight of cotton, not put up for retail sale, single yarn, of combed fibres, measuring less than 83.33 decitex (exceeding 120 metric number)	5205.2800	3468
棉纱线,按重量计含棉量在 85% 及以上,非供零售用,精梳纤维纺制的多股纱线或缆线,每根单纱细度在 106.38 分特以下,但不细于 83.33 分特(每根单纱超过 94 公支,但不超过 120 公支)	Cotton yarn, containing 85% or more by weight of cotton, not put up for retail sale, multiple (folded) or cabled yarn, of combed fibres, measuring per singleyarn less than 106.38 decitex but not less than 83.33 decitex (exceeding 94 metric number but not exceeding 120 metric number per single yarn)	5205.4700	3468
棉纱线,按重量计含棉量在 85% 及以上,非供零售用,精梳纤维纺制的多股纱线或缆线,每根单纱细度在 125 分特以下,但不细于 106.38 分特(每根单纱超过 80 公支,但不超过 94 公支)	Cotton yarn, containing 85% or more by weight of cotton, not put up for retail sale, multiple (folded) or cabled yarn, of combed fibres, measuring per single yarn less than 125 decitex but not less than 106.38 decitex (exceeding 80 metric number but not exceeding 94 metric number per single yarn)	5205.4600	3468

商品名称	Article Description	税则号列	申报要素
棉纱线，按重量计含棉量在85%及以上，非供零售用，精梳纤维纺制的多股纱线或缆线，每根单纱细度在192.31分特以下，但不细于125分特（每根单纱超过52公支，但不超过80公支）	Cotton yarn, containing 85% or more by weight of cotton, not put up for retail sale, multiple (folded) or cabled yarn, of combed fibres, measuring per single yarn less than 192.31 decitex but not less than 125 decitex (exceeding 52 metric number but not exceeding 80 metric number per single yarn)	5205.4400	3468
棉纱线，按重量计含棉量在85%及以上，非供零售用，精梳纤维纺制的多股纱线或缆线，每根单纱细度在232.56分特以下，但不细于192.31分特（每根单纱超过43公支，但不超过52公支）	Cotton yarn, containing 85% or more by weight of cotton, not put up for retail sale, multiple (folded) or cabled yarn, of combed fibres, measuring per singleyarn less than 232.56 decitex but not less than 192.31 decitex (exceeding 43 metric number but not exceeding 52 metric number per single yarn)	5205.4300	3468
棉纱线，按重量计含棉量在85%及以上，非供零售用，精梳纤维纺制的多股纱线或缆线，每根单纱细度在714.29分特及以上（每根单纱不超过14公支）	Cotton yarn, containing 85% or more by weight of cotton, not put up for retail sale, multiple (folded) or cabled yarn, of combed fibres, measuring per single yarn 714.29 decitex or more (not exceeding 14 metric number per single yarn)	5205.4100	3468
棉纱线，按重量计含棉量在85%及以上，非供零售用，精梳纤维纺制的多股纱线或缆线，每根单纱细度在714.29分特以下，但不细于232.56分特（每根单纱超过14公支，但不超过43公支）	Cotton yarn, containing 85% or more by weight of cotton, not put up for retail sale, multiple (folded) or cabled yarn, of combed fibres, measuring per single yarn less than 714.29 decitex but not less than 232.56 decitex (exceeding 14 metric number but not exceeding 43 metric number per single yarn)	5205.4200	3468
棉纱线，按重量计含棉量在85%及以上，非供零售用，精梳纤维纺制的多股纱线或缆线，每根单纱细度在83.33分特以下（每根单纱超过120公支）	Cotton yarn, containing 85% or more by weight of cotton, not put up for retail sale, multiple (folded) or cabled yarn, of combed fibres, measuring per single yarn less than 83.33 decitex (exceeding 120 metric number per single yarn)	5205.4800	3468
棉纱线，按重量计含棉量在85%及以上，非供零售用，未精梳纤维纺制的单纱，细度在125分特以下（超过80公支）	Cotton yarn, containing 85% or more by weight of cotton, not put up for retail sale, single yarn, of uncombed fibres, measuring less than 125 decitex (exceeding 80 metric number)	5205.1500	3468
棉纱线，按重量计含棉量在85%及以上，非供零售用，未精梳纤维纺制的单纱，细度在192.31分特以下，但不细于125分特（超过52公支，但不超过80公支）	Cotton yarn, containing 85% or more by weight of cotton, not put up for retail sale, single yarn, of uncombed fibres, measuring less than 192.31 decitex but not less than 125 decitex (exceeding 52 metric number but not exceeding 80 metric number)	5205.1400	3468

商品名称	Article Description	税则号列	申报要素
棉纱线,按重量计含棉量在85%及以上,非供零售用,未精梳纤维纺制的单纱,细度在232.56分特以下,但不细于192.31分特(超过43公支,但不超过52公支)	Cotton yarn, containing 85% or more by weight of cotton, not put up for retail sale, single yarn, of uncombed fibres, measuring less than 232.56 decitex but not less than 192.31 decitex (exceeding 43 metric number but not exceeding 52 metric number)	5205.1300	3468
棉纱线,按重量计含棉量在85%及以上,非供零售用,未精梳纤维纺制的单纱,细度在714.29分特及以上(不超过14公支)	Cotton yarn, containing 85% or more by weight of cotton, not put up for retail sale, single yarn, of uncombed fibres, measuring 714.29 decitex or more (not exceeding 14 metric number)	5205.1100	3468
棉纱线,按重量计含棉量在85%及以上,非供零售用,未精梳纤维纺制的单纱,细度在714.29分特以下,但不细于232.56分特(超过14公支,但不超过43公支)	Cotton yarn, containing 85% or more by weight of cotton, not put up for retail sale, single yarn, of uncombed fibres, measuring less than 714.29 decitex but not less than 232.56 decitex (exceeding 14 metric number but not exceeding 43 metric number)	5205.1200	3468
棉纱线,按重量计含棉量在85%及以上,非供零售用,未精梳纤维纺制的多股纱线或缆线,每根单纱细度在125分特以下(每根单纱超过80公支)	Cotton yarn, containing 85% or more by weight of cotton, not put up for retail sale, multiple (folded) or cabled yarn, of uncombed fibres, measuring per single yarn less than 125 decitex (exceeding 80metric number per single yarn)	5205.3500	3468
棉纱线,按重量计含棉量在85%及以上,非供零售用,未精梳纤维纺制的多股纱线或缆线,每根单纱细度在192.31分特以下,但不细于125分特(每根单纱超过52公支,但不超过80公支)	Cotton yarn, containing 85% or more by weight of cotton, not put up for retail sale, multiple (folded) or cabled yarn, of uncombed fibres, measuring per single yarn less than 192.31 decitex but not less than 125 decitex (exceeding 52 metric number but not exceeding 80 metric number per single yarn)	5205.3400	3468
棉纱线,按重量计含棉量在85%及以上,非供零售用,未精梳纤维纺制的多股纱线或缆线,每根单纱细度在232.56分特以下,但不细于192.31分特(每根单纱超过43公支,但不超过52公支)	Cotton yarn, containing 85% or more by weight of cotton, not put up for retail sale, multiple (folded) or cabled yarn, of uncombed fibres, measuring per single yarn less than 232.56 decitex but not less than 192.31 decitex (exceeding 43 metric number but not exceeding 52 metric number per single yarn)	5205.3300	3468
棉纱线,按重量计含棉量在85%及以上,非供零售用,未精梳纤维纺制的多股纱线或缆线,每根单纱细度在714.29分特及以上(每根单纱不超过14公支)	Cotton yarn, containing 85% or more by weight of cotton, not put up for retail sale, multiple (folded) or cabled yarn, of uncombed fibres, measuring per single yarn 714.29 decitex or more (not exceeding 14 metric number per single yarn)	5205.3100	3468
棉纱线,按重量计含棉量在85%及以上,非供零售用,未精梳纤维纺制的多股纱线或缆线,每根单纱细度在714.29分特以下,但不细于232.56分特(每根单纱超过14公支,但不超过43公支)	Cotton yarn, containing 85% or more by weight of cotton, not put up for retail sale, multiple (folded) or cabled yarn, of uncombed fibres, measuring per single yarn less than 714.29 decitex but not less than 232.56 decitex (exceeding 14 metric number but not exceeding 43 metric number per single yarn)	5205.3200	3468

商品名称	Article Description	税则号列	申报要素
棉纱线,按重量计含棉量在85%以下,非供零售用,精梳纤维纺制的单纱,细度在125分特以下(超过80公支)	Cotton yarn, containing less than 85% by weight of cotton, not put up for retail sale, single yarn, of combed fibres, measuring less than 125 decitex (exceeding 80 metric number)	5206.2500	3468
棉纱线,按重量计含棉量在85%以下,非供零售用,精梳纤维纺制的单纱,细度在192.31分特以下,但不细于125分特(超过52公支,但不超过80公支)	Cotton yarn, containing less than 85% by weight of cotton, not put up for retail sale, single yarn, of combed fibres, measuring less than 192.31 decitex but not less than 125 decitex (exceeding 52 metric number but not exceeding 80 metric number)	5206.2400	3468
棉纱线,按重量计含棉量在85%以下,非供零售用,精梳纤维纺制的单纱,细度在232.56分特以下,但不细于192.31分特(超过43公支,但不超过52公支)	Cotton yarn, containing less than 85% by weight of cotton, not put up for retail sale, single yarn, of combed fibres, measuring less than 232.56 decitex but not less than 192.31 decitex (exceeding 43 metric number but not exceeding 52 metric number)	5206.2300	3468
棉纱线,按重量计含棉量在85%以下,非供零售用,精梳纤维纺制的单纱,细度在714.29分特及以上(不超过14公支)	Cotton yarn, containing less than 85% by weight of cotton, not put up for retail sale, single yarn, of combed fibres, measuring 714.29 decitex or more (not exceeding 14 metric number)	5206.2100	3468
棉纱线,按重量计含棉量在85%以下,非供零售用,精梳纤维纺制的单纱,细度在714.29分特以下,但不细于232.56分特(超过14公支,但不超过43公支)	Cotton yarn, containing less than 85% by weight of cotton, not put up for retail sale, single yarn, of combed fibres, measuring less than 714.29 decitex but not less than 232.56 decitex (exceeding 14 metric number but not exceeding 43 metric number)	5206.2200	3468
棉纱线,按重量计含棉量在85%以下,非供零售用,精梳纤维纺制的多股纱线或缆线,每根单纱细度在125分特以下(每根单纱超过80公支)	Cotton yarn, containing less than 85% by weight of cotton, not put up for retail sale, multiple (folded) or cabled yarn, of combed fibres, measuring per single yarn less than 125 decitex (exceeding 80 metric number per single yarn)	5206.4500	3468
棉纱线,按重量计含棉量在85%以下,非供零售用,精梳纤维纺制的多股纱线或缆线,每根单纱细度在192.31分特以下,但不细于125分特(每根单纱超过52公支,但不超过80公支)	Cotton yarn, containing less than 85% by weight of cotton, not put up for retail sale, multiple (folded) or cabled yarn, of combed fibres, measuring per single yarn less than 192.31 decitex but not less than 125 decitex (exceeding 52 metric number but not exceeding 80 metric number per single yarn)	5206.4400	3468
棉纱线,按重量计含棉量在85%以下,非供零售用,精梳纤维纺制的多股纱线或缆线,每根单纱细度在232.56分特以下,但不细于192.31分特(每根单纱超过43公支,但不超过52公支)	Cotton yarn, containing less than 85% by weight of cotton, not put up for retail sale, multiple (folded) or cabled yarn, of combed fibres, measuring per single yarn less than 232.56 decitex but not less then 192.31 decitex (exceeding 43 metric number but not exceeding 52 metric number per single yarn)	5206.4300	3468

商品名称	Article Description	税则号列	申报要素
棉纱线,按重量计含棉量在85%以下,非供零售用,精梳纤维纺制的多股纱线或缆线,每根单纱细度在714.29分特及以上(每根单纱不超过14公支)	Cotton yarn, containing less than 85% by weight of cotton, not put up for retail sale, multiple (folded) or cabled yarn, of combed fibres, measuring per single yarn 714.29 decitex or more (not exceeding 14 metric number per single yarn)	5206.4100	3468
棉纱线,按重量计含棉量在85%以下,非供零售用,精梳纤维纺制的多股纱线或缆线,每根单纱细度在714.29分特以下,但不细于232.56分特(每根单纱超过14公支,但不超过43公支)	Cotton yarn, containing less than 85% by weight of cotton, not put up for retail sale, multiple (folded) or cabled yarn, of combed fibres, measuring per single yarn less than 714.29 deeitex but not less than 232.56 decitex (exceeding 14 metric number but not exceeding 43 metric number per single yarn)	5206.4200	3468
棉纱线,按重量计含棉量在85%以下,非供零售用,未精梳纤维纺制的单纱,细度在125分特以下(超过80公支)	Cotton yarn, containing less than 85% by weight of cotton, not put up for retail sale, single yarn, of uncombed fibres, measuring less than 125 decitex (exceeding 80 metric number)	5206.1500	3468
棉纱线,按重量计含棉量在85%以下,非供零售用,未精梳纤维纺制的单纱,细度在192.31分特以下,但不细于125分特(超过52公支,但不超过80公支)	Cotton yarn, containing less than 85% by weight of cotton, not put up for retail sale, single yarn, of uncombed fibres, measuring less than 192.31 decitex but not less than 125 decitex (exceeding 52 metric number but not exceeding 80 metric number)	5206.1400	3468
棉纱线,按重量计含棉量在85%以下,非供零售用,未精梳纤维纺制的单纱,细度在232.56分特以下,但不细于192.31分特(超过43公支,但不超过52公支)	Cotton yarn, containing less than 85% by weight of cotton, not put up for retail sale, single yarn, of uncombed fibres, measuring less than 232.56 decitex but not less than 192.31 decitex (exceeding 43 metric number but not exceeding 52 metric number)	5206.1300	3468
棉纱线,按重量计含棉量在85%以下,非供零售用,未精梳纤维纺制的单纱,细度在714.29分特及以上(不超过14公支)	Cotton yarn, containing less than 85% by weight of cotton, not put up for retail sale, single yarn, of uncombed fibres, measuring 714.29 decitex or more (not exceeding 14 metric number)	5206.1100	3468
棉纱线,按重量计含棉量在85%以下,非供零售用,未精梳纤维纺制的单纱,细度在714.29分特以下,但不细于232.56分特(超过14公支,但不超过43公支)	Cotton yarn, containing less than 85% by weight of cotton, not put up for retail sale, single yarn, of uncombed fibres, measuring less than 714.29 decitex but not less than 232.56 decitex (exceeding 14 metric number but not exceeding 43 metric number)	5206.1200	3468
棉纱线,按重量计含棉量在85%以下,非供零售用,未精梳纤维纺制的多股纱线或缆线,每根单纱细度在125分特以下(每根单纱超过80公支)	Cotton yarn, containing less than 85% by weight of cotton, not put up for retail sale, multiple (folded) or cabled yarn, of uncombed fibres, measuring per single yarn less than 125 decitex (exceeding 80 metric number per single yarn)	5206.3500	3468

商品名称	Article Description	税则号列	申报要素
棉纱线,按重量计含棉量在85%以下,非供零售用,未精梳纤维纺制的多股纱线或缆线,每根单纱细度在192.31分特以下,但不细于125分特(每根单纱超过52公支,但不超过80公支)	Cotton yarn, containing less than 85% by weight of cotton, not put up for retail sale, multiple (folded) or cabled yarn, of uncombed fibres, measuring per single yarn less than 192.31 decitex but not less than 125 decitex (exceeding 52 metric number but not exceeding 80 metric number per single yarn)	5206.3400	3468
棉纱线,按重量计含棉量在85%以下,非供零售用,未精梳纤维纺制的多股纱线或缆线,每根单纱细度在232.56分特以下,但不细于192.31分特(每根单纱超过43公支,但不超过52公支)	Cotton yarn, containing less than 85% by weight of cotton, not put up for retail sale, multiple (folded) or cabled yarn, of uncombed fibres, measuring per single yarn less than 714.29 decitex but not less than 232.56 decitex (exceeding 14 metric number but not exceeding 43 metric number per single yarn)	5206.3300	3468
棉纱线,按重量计含棉量在85%以下,非供零售用,未精梳纤维纺制的多股纱线或缆线,每根单纱细度在714.29分特及以上,(每根单纱不超过14公支)	Cotton yarn, containing less than 85% by weight of cotton, not put up for retail sale, multiple (folded) or cabled yarn, of uncombed fibres, measuring per single yarn 714.29 decitex or more (not exceeding 14 metric number per single yarn)	5206.3100	3468
棉纱线,按重量计含棉量在85%以下,非供零售用,未精梳纤维纺制的多股纱线或缆线,每根单纱细度在714.29分特以下,但不细于232.56分特(每根单纱超过14公支,但不超过43公支)	Cotton yarn, containing less than 85% by weight of cotton, not put up for retail sale, multiple (folded) or cabled yarn, of uncombed fibres, measuring per single yarn less than 714.29 decitex but not less than 232.56 decitex (exceeding 14 metric number but not exceeding 43 metric number per single yarn)	5206.3200	3468
棉纱线,供零售用,按重量计含棉量在85%及以上	Cotton yarn, put up for retail sale, containing 85% or more by weight of cotton	5207.1000	36
棉纱线,供零售用,其他	Cotton yarn, put up for retail sale, nes	5207.9000	36
棉细纱机	Cotton ring spinning frame	8445.2041	7
棉制缝纫线,非供零售用,按重量计含棉量在85%及以上	Cotton sewing thread, not put up for retail sale, containing 85% or more by weight of cotton	5204.1100	3468
棉制缝纫线,非供零售用,其他	Cotton sewing thread, not put up for retail sale, nes	5204.1900	3468
棉制缝纫线,供零售用	Cotton sewing thread, put up for retail sale	5204.2000	3468
棉籽,其他	Cotton seeds, nes	1207.2090	3
棉籽,种用	Cotton seeds, for cultivation	1207.2010	3
棉子油及其分离品,初榨的,不论是否去除棉子酚	Cottonseed oil and fractions thereof, crued, whether or not gossypol has been removed	1512.2100	4
棉子油及其分离品,其他	Cottonseed oil and its fractions, nes	1512.2900	4
面包干	Rusks	1905.4000	28
面包机,家用自动的	Bread makers, household automated	8516.7210	7
面包片,脆的	Crispbread	1905.1000	28
面肥	Leaven, alsatian	2102.3000	28
面巾纸,成卷或成张的	Facial tissue stock, in rolls or sheets	4803.0000	58

商品名称	Article Description	税则号列	申报要素
面巾纸,纸浆、纸、纤维素絮纸或纤维素纤维网纸制的	Facial tissues, of paper pulp, paper, cellulose wadding or webs of cellulose fibres	4818. 2000	568
面筋,不论是否干制	Wheat gluten, whether or not dried	1109. 0000	
面盆及其零件,钢铁制,家用,已搪瓷	Basin and parts thereof, of iron or steel, for household, enamelled	7323. 9410	24
面纱及类似品,非针织或钩编的,合成纤维制	Veils and the like, not knitted or crocheted, of synthetic fibres	6214. 3000	2456
面纱及类似品,非针织或钩编的,其他动物细毛制	Veils and the like, not knitted or crocheted, of other fine animal hair	6214. 2090	2456
面纱及类似品,非针织或钩编的,其他纺织材料制	Veils and the like, not knitted or crocheted, of other textile materials	6214. 9000	2456
面纱及类似品,非针织或钩编的,人造纤维制	Veils and the like, not knitted or crocheted, of artificial fibres	6214. 4000	2456
面纱及类似品,非针织或钩编的,山羊绒制	Veils and the like, not knitted or crocheted, of goats fine animal hair	6214. 2020	2456
面纱及类似品,非针织或钩编的,丝或绢丝制	Veils and the like, not knitted or crocheted, of silk or silk waste	6214. 1000	2456
面纱及类似品,非针织或钩编的,羊毛制	Veils and the like, not knitted or crocheted, of wool	6214. 2010	2456
面纱及类似品,针织或钩编的,其他	Veils and the like, knitted or crocheted, nes	6117. 1090	2456
面纱及类似品,针织或钩编的,其他动物细毛制	Veils and the like, knitted or crocheted, of fine animal hair, nes	6117. 1019	2456
面纱及类似品,针织或钩编的,山羊绒制	Veils and the like, knitted or crocheted, of goats fine animal hair	6117. 1011	2456
面纱及类似品,针织或钩编的,羊毛制	Veils and the like, knitted or crocheted, of wool	6117. 1020	2456
面食,其他	Pasta, nes	1902. 3090	246
面食,其他,生的,未包馅或未经其他方法制作	Pasta, uncooked, nes, not stuffed or other wise prepared	1902. 1900	46
面条,生的,含蛋的	Noodles, uncooked, containing eggs	1902. 1100	46
面条,生的,其他	Noodles, uncooked, nes	1902. 1900	46
面条生产机器	Spaghetti manufacture machinery	8438. 1000	
面条生产机器的零件	Spaghetti manufacture machinery parts	8438. 9000	3
面团及调制品,供烘焙税号 19. 05 所列面包糕饼用的	Mixes and doughs for the preparation of bakers' wares of heading No. 19. 05	1901. 2000	368
miao			
苗木,种用的,食用水果或食用坚果的树、灌木,不论是否嫁接	Trees, shrubs and bushes, grafted or not, of kinds which bear edible fruit or nuts, seedlings	0602. 2010	3
描图布,化学纤维制	Tracing cloth of man-made fibres	5901. 9092	
描图布,棉或麻制	Tracing cloth of cotton or bast fibres	5901. 9091	
描图布,其他	Tracing cloth, nes	5901. 9099	
描图纸	Tracing papers	4806. 3000	58

商品名称	Article Description	税则号列	申报要素
秒表,表壳用贵金属或包贵金属制成的,其他	Stop-watches, with case of precious metal or of metal clad with precious metal, nes	9101. 9900	56
秒表,电力驱动的,表壳用贵金属或包贵金属制成的	Stop-watches, electrically operated, with case of precious metal or of metal clad with precious metal	9101. 9100	56
秒表,电力驱动的,其他	Stop-watches, electrically operated, nes	9102. 9100	56
秒表,其他	Stop-watches, nes	9102. 9900	56
mie			
灭火弹,已装药的	Fire-extinguishing grenades, charged	3813. 0020	36
灭火器,不论是否装药	Fire-extinguishers, whether or not charged	8424. 1000	
灭火器的装配药	Fire-extinguishers charges	3813. 0010	36
灭火器零件	Fire-extinguishers parts	8424. 9010	
ming			
明矾石	Alumstone	2530. 9099	13456
明胶,未硬化的,已加工的	Gelatin, unhardened, worked	9602. 0090	5
明胶及其衍生物	Gelatin and gelatin derivatives	3503. 0010	13
明胶制品,未硬化	Gelatin articles, unhardened	9602. 0090	5
明信片,印刷或有图画的	Postcards, printed or illustrated	4909. 0010	4
明信片,纸或纸板制的,素色的	Postcards of paper or paperboard, plain	4817. 2000	6
铭牌,贱金属制,税号 94. 05 的货品除外	Name-plates, of base metal, excluding those of heading No. 94. 05	8310. 0000	256
mo			
模板,水泥构件用的,木制的	Shuttering for concrete constructional work, of wood	4418. 4000	58
模塑或成型的机器,用于充气轮胎模塑或翻新的机器及内胎的	Moulding or forming machinery, for moulding or retreading pneumatic tyres or for moulding or otherwise forming inner tubes	8477. 5100	7
模塑或成型机器,其他	Moulding or forming machinery, nes	8477. 5900	7
模型组件,缩小(按比例缩小)的,成套的,其他	Model assembly kits, reduced-size ("scale"), nes	9503. 0039	5
模压成型机,固体矿物燃料、陶瓷坯泥、未硬化水泥、石膏材料或其他粉状、浆状矿产品的粘聚或成形用	Moulding forming machines, for agglomerating, shaping or moulding solid mineral fuels, ceramic paste, unhardened cements, plastering materials or other mineral products in powder or paste form	8474. 8020	7
摩托车(包括机器脚踏两用车)及装有辅助发动机的脚踏车,电动及电动助力的	Motorcycles (including mopeds) and cycles fitted with an auxiliary motor, electric or with electrical assistant	8711. 9010	58
摩托车(包括机器脚踏两用车)及装有辅助发动机的脚踏车,其他	Motorcycles (including mopeds) and cycles fitted with an auxiliary motor, nes	8711. 9090	58
摩托车(包括机器脚踏两用车)及装有辅助发动机的脚踏车,装有往复式活塞内燃发动机,气缸容量(排气量)不超过 50 毫升	Motorcycles (including mopeds) and cycles fitted with an auxiliary motor, with reciprocating internal combustion piston engine of a cylinder capacity not exceeding 50cc	8711. 1000	58

M

商品名称	Article Description	税则号列	申报要素
摩托车(包括机器脚踏两用车)及装有辅助发动机的脚踏车,装有往复式活塞内燃发动机,气缸容量(排气量)超过500毫升,但不超过800毫升	Motorcycles (including mopeds) and cycles fitted with an auxiliary motor, with reciprocating internal combustion piston engine of a cylinder capacity exceeding 500cc but not exceeding 800cc	8711.4000	58
摩托车(包括机器脚踏两用车)及装有辅助发动机的脚踏车,装有往复式活塞内燃发动机,气缸容量(排气量)超过800毫升	Motorcycles (including mopeds) and cycles fitted with an auxiliary motor, with reciprocating internal combustion piston engine of a cylinder capacity exceeding 800cc	8711.5000	58
摩托车(包括机器脚踏两用车)及装有辅助发动机的脚踏车,装有往复式活塞内燃发动机,气缸容量超过100毫升,但不超过125毫升	Motorcycles (including mopeds) and cycles fitted with an auxiliary motor, with reciprocating internal combustion piston engine of a cylinder capacity exceeding 100cc but not exceeding 125cc	8711.2020	58
摩托车(包括机器脚踏两用车)及装有辅助发动机的脚踏车,装有往复式活塞内燃发动机,气缸容量超过125毫升,但不超过150毫升	Motorcycles (including mopeds) and cycles fitted with an auxiliary motor, with reciprocating internal combustion piston engine of a cylinder capacity exceeding 125cc but not exceeding 150cc	8711.2030	58
摩托车(包括机器脚踏两用车)及装有辅助发动机的脚踏车,装有往复式活塞内燃发动机,气缸容量超过150毫升,但不超过200毫升	Motorcycles (including mopeds) and cycles fitted with an auxiliary motor, with reciprocating internal combustion piston engine of a cylinder capacity exceeding 150cc but not exceeding 200cc	8711.2040	58
摩托车(包括机器脚踏两用车)及装有辅助发动机的脚踏车,装有往复式活塞内燃发动机,气缸容量超过200毫升,但不超过250毫升	Motorcycles (including mopeds) and cycles fitted with an auxiliary motor, with reciprocating internal combustion piston engine of a cylinder capacity exceeding 200cc but not exceeding 250cc	8711.2050	58
摩托车(包括机器脚踏两用车)及装有辅助发动机的脚踏车,装有往复式活塞内燃发动机,气缸容量超过250毫升,但不超过400毫升	Motorcycles (including mopeds) and cycles fitted with an auxiliary motor, with reciprocating internal combustion piston engine of a cylinder capacity exceeding 250cc but not exceeding 400cc	8711.3010	58
摩托车(包括机器脚踏两用车)及装有辅助发动机的脚踏车,装有往复式活塞内燃发动机,气缸容量超过400毫升,但不超过500毫升	Motorcycles (including mopeds) and cycles fitted with an auxiliary motor, with reciprocating internal combustion piston engine of a cylinder capacity exceeding 400cc but not exceeding 500cc	8711.3020	58
摩托车(包括机器脚踏两用车)及装有辅助发动机的脚踏车,装有往复式活塞内燃发动机,气缸容量超过50毫升,但不超过100毫升	Motorcycles (including mopeds) and cycles fitted with an auxiliary motor, with reciprocating internal combustion piston engine of a cylinder capacity exceeding 50cc but not exceeding 100cc	8711.2010	58
摩托车(包括机器脚踏两用车)用零件、附件,其他	Motorcycles (including mopeds) parts and accessoris, nes	8714.1900	3
磨床,齿轮的,切削金属或金属陶瓷用,其他	Grinding machines of gear, for removing metal or cermets, nes	8461.4090	7
磨床,齿轮的,数控的,切削金属或金属陶瓷用	Grinding machines of gear, numerically controlled, for removing metal or cermets	8461.4010	7

商品名称	Article Description	税则号列	申报要素
磨床,内圆的,在任一坐标的定位精度至少是0.01毫米,加工金属或金属陶瓷用,其他	Grinding machines, internal, in which the positioning in any one axis can be set up to an accuracy of at least 0.01mm, for metal or cermets, nes	8460.2920	7
磨床,内圆的,在任一坐标的定位精度至少是0.01毫米,数控的,加工金属或金属陶瓷用	Grinding machines, internal, in which the positioning in any one axis can be set up to an accuracy of at least 0.01mm, numerically controlled, for metal or cermets	8460.2120	7
磨床,平面的,在任一坐标的定位精度至少是0.01毫米,加工金属或金属陶瓷用,其他	Grinding machines, flat-surface, in which the positioning in any one axis can be set up to an accuracy of at least 0.01mm, for metal or cermets, nes	8460.1900	7
磨床,平面的,在任一坐标的定位精度至少是0.01毫米,数控的,加工金属或金属陶瓷用	Grinding machines, flat-surface, in which the positioning in any one axis can be set up to an accuracy of at least 0.01mm, numerically controlled, for metal or cermets	8460.1100	7
磨床,外圆的,在任一坐标的定位精度至少是0.01毫米,加工金属或金属陶瓷用,其他	Grinding machines, cylindrical, in which the positioning in any one axis can be set up to an accuracy of at least 0.01mm, for metal or cermets, nes	8460.2910	7
磨床,外圆的,在任一坐标的定位精度至少是0.01毫米,数控的,加工金属或金属陶瓷用	Grinding machines, cylindrical, in which the positioning in any one axis can be set up to an accuracy of at least 0.01mm, numerically controlled, for metal or cermets	8460.2110	7
磨床,在任一坐标的定位精度至少是0.01毫米,加工金属或金属陶瓷用,其他	Grinding machines, in which the positioning in any one axis can be set up to an accuracy of at least 0.01mm, for metal or cermets, nes	8460.2990	7
磨床,在任一坐标的定位精度至少是0.01毫米,数控的,加工金属或金属陶瓷用,其他	Grinding machines, in which the positioning in any one axis can be set up to an accuracy of at least 0.01mm, numerically controlled, for metal or cermets, nes	8460.2190	7
磨床,轧辊的,在任一坐标的定位精度至少是0.01毫米,加工金属或金属陶瓷用,其他	Grinding machines of roll, in which the positioning in any one axis can be set up to an accuracy of at least 0.01mm, for metal or cermets, nes	8460.2930	7
磨粉机器,球磨式,泥土、石料、矿石或其他固体矿物质的	Grinding machines, em-peters type, for earth, stone, ores or other mineral substances	8474.2010	7
磨粉机器,齿辊式,泥土、石料、矿石或其他固体矿物质的	Grinding machines, toothing roller type, for earth, stone, ores or other mineral substances	8474.2010	7
磨粉机器,泥土、石料、矿石或其他固体矿物质的,其他	Grinding machines, for earth, stone, ores or other mineral substances, nes	8474.2090	7
磨粉业加工机器	Milling machinery used in the industry	8437.8000	3
磨粉业加工机器零件	Milling machinery parts, used in the industry	8437.9000	3
磨菇酱油	Mushroom sauce	2103.9090	268

商品名称	Article Description	税则号列	申报要素
磨光机,手提式,本身装有电动动力装置的	Burnisher, hand tools, with self-contained electric motor	8467. 2910	57
磨料,天然,其他	Abrasives, natural, nes	2513. 2000	
磨料或颗粒,天然或人造的,以纺织材料为底的	Abrasive powder or grain, natural or artificial, on a base of woven textile fabric only	6805. 1000	246
磨料或颗粒,天然或人造的,以其他材料为底的	Abrasive powder or grain, natural or artificial, on a base of other materials	6805. 3000	246
磨料或颗粒,天然或人造的,以纸为底的	Natural or artificial abrasive powder or grain, on a base of paper or paperboard only	6805. 2000	246
磨石,手用,其他	Sharpening stones, hand used, nes	6804. 3090	36
蘑菇,其他	Mushrooms, nes	0709. 5990	1
蘑菇及块菌,其他,干的	Mushrooms and truffles, dried, nes	0712. 3990	4
蘑菇及块菌,其他,盐水的,暂时保藏,但不适合直接使用的	Mushrooms and truffles, nes, in brine, provisionally preserved, but unsuitable in that state for immediate consumption	0711. 5919	34
蘑菇及块菌,其他,用醋或醋酸以外的其他方法制作或保藏的	Mushrooms and truffles, nes, prepared or preserved otherwise than by vinegar or acetic acid	2003. 9090	248
蘑菇及块菌,其他,暂时保藏,但不适合直接使用的	Mushrooms and truffles, nes, provisionally preserved, but unsuitable in that state for immediate consumption	0711. 5990	34
蘑菇菌丝	Mushroom spawn	0602. 9010	
魔术道具	Conjuring tricks	9505. 9000	5
抹布及类似擦拭用布	Dusters and similar cleaning cloths	6307. 1000	346
茉莉酮	Jasmone	2914. 2900	36
秣刀	Hay knives	8201. 9000	256
墨类,其他,不论是否固体或浓缩	Inks, nes, whether or not concentrated or solid	3215. 9090	3
墨水,书写或绘图用	Inks for writing or drawing	3215. 9010	3
墨鱼,其他,冻、干、盐腌或盐渍的	Cuttle fish (Sepia of ficinalis, Rossia macrosoma, Sepiola spp.), frozen, dried, salted or in brine	0307. 4900	148
墨鱼,其他,活、鲜或冷的	Cuttle fish (Sepia of ficinalis, Rossia macrosoma, Sepiola spp.), live, fresh or chilled	0307. 4190	18
墨鱼,制作的	Cuttle fish, prepared	1605. 9090	48
墨鱼,种苗	Cuttle fish (Sepia of ficinalis, Rossia macrosoma, Sepiola spp.), for cultivation	0307. 4110	3
墨鱼粉,食用	Cuttle fish meal, fit for human consumption	0307. 9990	14
墨鱼骨	Cuttlebone	0508. 0090	14
墨鱼骨粉	Cuttle fish bone powder	0508. 0010	14
墨汁画笔	Indian ink drawing pens	9608. 3100	
没药	Myrrh	1301. 9020	
mu			
牡蛎,其他	Oysters, nes	0307. 1090	14
牡蛎,制作或保藏的	Oysters, prepared or preserved	1605. 9090	48

商品名称	Article Description	税则号列	申报要素
牡蛎,种苗	Oysters,for cultivation	0307.1010	3
牡蛎粉,食用	Oyster flour,fit for human consumption	0307.9990	14
牡蛎壳,碎的	Oyster shells,crushed	0508.0010	14
牡蛎提取物	Oyster extract	1603.0000	48
木棒,适合制手杖、伞柄、工具把柄及类似品,非针叶木的	Wooden sticks, suitable for the manufacture of walking-sticks,umbrellas,tool handles or the like, non-coniferous	4404.2000	15
木棒,适合制手杖、伞柄、工具把柄及类似品,针叶木的	Wooden sticks, suitable for the manufacture of walking-sticks,umbrellas,tool handles or the like, coniferous	4404.1000	15
木材,经纵锯、纵切、刨切或旋切的,厚度超过6毫米,巴西胡桃木	Wood sawn or chipped lengthwise,sliced or peeled,of a thickness exceeding 6mm,Imbuia	4407.2200	458
木材,经纵锯、纵切、刨切或旋切的,厚度超过6毫米,白蜡木	Wood sawn or chipped lengthwise,sliced or peeled,of a thickness exceeding 6mm, of ash (Fraxinus spp.)	4407.9500	458
木材,经纵锯、纵切、刨切或旋切的,厚度超过6毫米,白柳安木、白色红柳桉木、白色柳安木、黄色红柳桉木及阿兰木	Wood sawn or chipped lengthwise,sliced or peeled,of a thickness exceeding 6mm, White Lauan, White Meranti,White Seraya,Yellow Meranti and Alan	4407.2600	458
木材,经纵锯、纵切、刨切或旋切的,厚度超过6毫米,白松(云杉和冷杉)	Wood sawn or chipped lengthwise,sliced or peeled,of a thickness exceeding 6mm,white pine(spruce and fir)	4407.1020	458
木材,经纵锯、纵切、刨切或旋切的,厚度超过6毫米,北美硬阔叶材(含黑胡桃木)	Wood sawn or chipped lengthwise,sliced or peeled,of a thickness exceeding 6mm, north american hard wood (including walnut)	4407.9930	458
木材,经纵锯、纵切、刨切或旋切的,厚度超过6毫米,波罗格	Wood sawn or chipped lengthwise,sliced or peeled,of a thickness exceeding 6mm,Merban	4407.2930	458
木材,经纵锯、纵切、刨切或旋切的,厚度超过6毫米,非洲桃花心木	Wood sawn or chipped lengthwise,sliced or peeled,of a thickness exceeding 6mm,Acajou	4407.2920	458
木材,经纵锯、纵切、刨切或旋切的,厚度超过6毫米,枫木	Wood sawn or chipped lengthwise,sliced or peeled,of a thickness exceeding 6mm,of maple (Acer spp.)	4407.9300	458
木材,经纵锯、纵切、刨切或旋切的,厚度超过6毫米,辐射松	Wood sawn or chipped lengthwise,sliced or peeled,of a thickness exceeding 6mm,of rediata pine	4407.1030	458
木材,经纵锯、纵切、刨切或旋切的,厚度超过6毫米,红木	Wood sawn or chipped lengthwise,sliced or peeled,of a thickness exceeding 6mm,of rosewood	4407.9910	458
木材,经纵锯、纵切、刨切或旋切的,厚度超过6毫米,红松和樟子松	Wood sawn or chipped lengthwise,sliced or peeled,of a thickness exceeding 6mm, of korean pine and mongolian scotch pine	4407.1010	458
木材,经纵锯、纵切、刨切或旋切的,厚度超过6毫米,花旗松	Wood sawn or chipped lengthwise,sliced or peeled,of a thickness exceeding 6mm,of douglas fir	4407.1040	458
木材,经纵锯、纵切、刨切或旋切的,厚度超过6毫米,栎木(橡木)	Wood sawn or chipped lengthwise,sliced or peeled,of a thickness exceeding 6mm,of oak(Ouercus spp.)	4407.9100	458

商品名称	Article Description	税则号列	申报要素
木材,经纵锯、纵切、刨切或旋切的,厚度超过6毫米,柳安木(深红、浅红、巴栲红)	Wood sawn or chipped lengthwise, sliced or peeled, of a thickness exceeding 6mm, meranti (Dark Red Meranti, Light Red Metanti and Meranti Bakau)	4407.2500	458
木材,经纵锯、纵切、刨切或旋切的,厚度超过6毫米,美洲轻木	Wood sawn or chipped lengthwise, sliced or peeled, of a thickness exceeding 6mm, Balsa	4407.2200	458
木材,经纵锯、纵切、刨切或旋切的,厚度超过6毫米,美洲桃花心木	Wood sawn or chipped lengthwise, sliced or peeled, of a thickness exceeding 6mm, mahogany (Swietenia spp.)	4407.2100	458
木材,经纵锯、纵切、刨切或旋切的,厚度超过6毫米,楠木	Wood sawn or chipped lengthwise, sliced or peeled, of a thickness exceeding 6mm, of nanmu	4407.9910	458
木材,经纵锯、纵切、刨切或旋切的,厚度超过6毫米,泡桐木	Wood sawn or chipped lengthwise, sliced or peeled, of a thickness exceeding 6mm, of Paulownia	4407.9920	458
木材,经纵锯、纵切、刨切或旋切的,厚度超过6毫米,其他	Wood sawn or chipped lengthwise, sliced or peeled, of a thickness exceeding 6mm, nes	4407.9990	458
木材,经纵锯、纵切、刨切或旋切的,厚度超过6毫米,热带木,其他	Wood sawn or chipped lengthwise, sliced or peeled, of a thickness exceeding 6mm, of tropical wood, nes	4407.2990	458
木材,经纵锯、纵切、刨切或旋切的,厚度超过6毫米,沙比利	Wood sawn or chipped lengthwise, sliced or peeled, of a thickness exceeding 6mm, Sapelli	4407.2700	458
木材,经纵锯、纵切、刨切或旋切的,厚度超过6毫米,山毛榉木	Wood sawn or chipped lengthwise, sliced or peeled, of a thickness exceeding 6mm, of beech (Fagus spp.)	4407.9200	458
木材,经纵锯、纵切、刨切或旋切的,厚度超过6毫米,苏里南肉豆蔻木	Wood sawn or chipped lengthwise, sliced or peeled, of a thickness exceeding 6mm, Virola	4407.2200	458
木材,经纵锯、纵切、刨切或旋切的,厚度超过6毫米,温带非针叶材,其他	Wood sawn or chipped lengthwise, sliced or peeled, of a thickness exceeding 6mm, temperate non-coniferous wood, nes	4407.9980	458
木材,经纵锯、纵切、刨切或旋切的,厚度超过6毫米,伊罗科木	Wood sawn or chipped lengthwise, sliced or peeled, of a thickness exceeding 6mm, Iroko	4407.2800	458
木材,经纵锯、纵切、刨切或旋切的,厚度超过6毫米,樱桃木	Wood sawn or chipped lengthwise, sliced or peeled, of a thickness exceeding 6mm, of cherry (Prunus spp.)	4407.9400	458
木材,经纵锯、纵切、刨切或旋切的,厚度超过6毫米,柚木	Wood sawn or chipped lengthwise, sliced or peeled, of a thickness exceeding 6mm, teak	4407.2910	458
木材,经纵锯、纵切、刨切或旋切的,厚度超过6毫米,樟木	Wood sawn or chipped lengthwise, sliced or peeled, of a thickness exceeding 6mm, of camphor-wood	4407.9910	458
木材,经纵锯、纵切、刨切或旋切的,厚度超过6毫米,针叶木,其他	Wood sawn or chipped lengthwise, sliced or peeled, of a thickness exceeding 6mm, coniferous, nes	4407.1090	458
木材,任何一边端或面制成连续形状的,非针叶木,其他	Wood continuously shaped along any of its edges, ends or faces, non-coniferous	4409.2990	158
木材,任何一边端或面制成连续形状的,针叶木,其他	Wood continuously shaped along any of its edges, ends or faces, coniferous, nes	4409.1090	158
木材,任何一边端或面制成连续形状的,竹的,其他	Wood continuously shaped along any of its edges, ends or faces, of bamboo	4409.2190	158
木材处理机	Wood treating machinery	8479.3000	7

商品名称	Article Description	税则号列	申报要素
木锉及类似工具	Rasps and similar tools	8203.1000	256
木耳,干的	Wood ears (Auricularia spp.),dried	0712.3200	4
木废料及碎片,不论是否粘结成圆木段、块、片或类似形状	Wood waste and scrap,whether or not agglomerated in logs,briquettes,pellets or similar forms	4401.3000	15
木粉	Wood flour	4405.0000	
木工制品,建筑用,其他	Builders joinery and carpentry of wood,nes	4418.9000	
木瓜,冷冻的	Pawpaws,frozen	0811.9090	1
木瓜,食用的,用其他方法制作或保藏的	Pawpaws,edible,otherwise prepared,or preserved	2008.9990	248
木瓜,鲜的	Papaws(Papayas),fresh	0807.2000	12
木瓜,鲜的	Pawpaws,fresh	0810.9090	1
木瓜,暂时保藏,但不适于直接食用的	Pawpaws, provisionally preserved, unsuitable for immediate consumption	0812.9000	34
木瓜蛋白酶	Papain	3507.9090	35
木浆,用机械与化学联合制浆法制得的	Wood pulp obtained by a combination of mechanical and chemical pulping processes	4705.0000	46
木浆残余碱液,不论是否浓缩、脱糖或经化学处理	Residual lyes from the manufacture of wood pulp, whether or not concentrated, desugared or chemically treated	3804.0000	
木焦油	Wood tar	3807.0000	3
木刻	Wood carvings	4420.1011	56
木块芯胶合板,侧板条芯胶合板及板条芯胶合板,其他	Blockboard,laminboard and battenboard,nes	4412.9499	48
木块芯胶合板,侧板条芯胶合板及板条芯胶合板,至少含有一层木碎料板	Blockboard, laminboard and battenboard, containing at least one layer of particle board	4412.9492	48
木块芯胶合板,侧板条芯胶合板及板条芯胶合板,至少有一表层是非针叶木	Blockboard,laminboard and battenboard,with at least one outer ply of non-coniferous wood	4412.9410	48
木块芯胶合板,侧板条芯胶合板及板条芯胶合板,至少有一层是本章子目注释所列的热带木	Blockboard,laminboard and battenboard,with at least one outer ply of tropical wood specified in Subheading Note to this Chapter	4412.9491	48
木螺钉,钢铁制的,其他	Wood screws,of iron or steel,nes	7318.1200	268
木螺钉,铜制	Screws for wood,of copper	7415.3310	56
木莓,冷冻的	Raspberries,frozen	0811.2000	1
木莓,鲜的	Raspberries,fresh	0810.2000	1
木棉子	Kapok seeds	1207.9999	3
木劈条,非针叶木的	Split poles,non-coniferous	4404.2000	15
木劈条,针叶木的	Split poles,coniferous	4404.1000	15
木片或木粒,非针叶木	Wood in chips or particles,non-coniferous	4401.2200	15
木片或木粒,针叶木	Wood in chips or particles,coniferous	4401.2100	15
木片条及类似品,非针叶木的	Chipwood and the like,non-coniferous	4404.2000	15

商品名称	Article Description	税则号列	申报要素
木片条及类似品,针叶木的	Chipwood and the like, coniferous	4404.1000	15
木琴	Xylophones	9206.0000	5
木扇	Wooden fans	4420.1020	56
木薯,干的	Manioc(cassava), dried	0714.1020	34
木薯,冷或冻的	Manioc(cassava), chilled or frozen	0714.1030	34
木薯,鲜的	Manioc(cassava), fresh	0714.1010	34
木丝	Wood wool	4405.0000	
木松节油	Wood turpentine oils	3805.1000	36
木素磺酸盐,但不包括妥尔油	Lignin sulphonates, but excluding tall oil	3804.0000	
木碎料板挤压机	Particle board manufacture presses	8479.3000	7
木糖醇	Xylitol	2905.4910	36
木托板木,辐射松制的	Pallets, of radiata pine	4415.2010	56
木托板木,其他木制的	Pallets, of other wood	4415.2090	56
木纤维板或其他木质材料纤维板,密度超过每立方厘米0.35克,但未超过每立方厘米0.5克	Fibreboard of wood or other ligneous materials, of a density exceeding 0.35g/cm³ but not exceeding 0.5g/cm³	4411.9410	48
木纤维板或其他木质材料纤维板,密度超过每立方厘米0.5克,但未超过每立方厘米0.8克,辐射松制的	Fibreboard of wood or other ligneous materials, of a density exceeding 0.5g/cm³ but not exceeding 0.8g/cm³, of radiata pine	4411.9310	48
木纤维板或其他木质材料纤维板,密度超过每立方厘米0.5克,但未超过每立方厘米0.8克,其他	Fibreboard of wood or other ligneous materials, of a density exceeding 0.5g/cm³ but not exceeding 0.8g/cm³, nes	4411.9390	48
木纤维板或其他木质材料纤维板,密度超过每立方厘米0.8克,其他	Fibreboard of wood or other ligneous materials, of a density exceeding 0.8g/cm³, not mechanically worked or surface covered, nes	4411.9290	48
木纤维板或其他木质材料纤维板,密度超过每立方厘米0.8克,未经机械加工或盖面的	Fibreboard of wood or other ligneous materials, of a density exceeding 0.8g/cm³, not mechanically worked or surface covered	4411.9210	48
木纤维板或其他木质材料纤维板,密度未超过每立方厘米0.35克,未经机械加工或盖面的	Fibreboard of wood or other ligneous materials, of a density not exceeding 0.35g/cm³, not mechanically worked or surface covered	4411.9421	48
木纤维板或其他木质材料纤维板,其他	Fibreboard of wood or other ligneous materials, nes	4411.9429	48
木纤维板挤压机	Fibre building board manufacture presses	8479.3000	7
木杂酚油	Wood creosote	3807.0000	3
木制品,其他	Articles of wood, nes	4421.9090	56
木制人造纤维短纤,未梳或未经其他纺前加工	Wood artificial staple fibres, not carded, combed or otherwise processed for spinning	5504.1020	
木制鞋靴楦及楦头,辐射松制的	Boot or shoe lasts and trees, of radiata pine	4417.0010	56
木制鞋靴楦及楦头,其他木制的	Boot or shoe lasts and trees, of other wood	4417.0090	56
木桩,已削尖但未经纵锯的木桩,非针叶木的	Piles, pickets and stakes of wood, pointed but not sawn lengthwise, non-coniferous	4404.2000	15

商品名称	Article Description	税则号列	申报要素
木桩,已削尖但未经纵锯的木桩,针叶木的	Piles, pickets and stakes of wood, pointed but not sawn lengthwise, coniferous	4404.1000	15
钼,未锻轧,包括简单烧结而成的条、杆	Molybdenum, unwrought, including bars and rods obtained simply by sintering	8102.9400	16
钼的氧化物及氢氧化物	Molybdenum oxides and hydroxides	2825.7000	
钼粉末	Molybdenum powders	8102.1000	16
钼矿砂及其精矿,其他	Molybdenum ores and concentrates, nes	2613.9000	146
钼矿砂及其精矿,已焙烧	Molybdenum ores and concentrates, roasted	2613.1000	146
钼铅矿,已焙烧	Wulfenite, roasted	2613.1000	146
钼丝	Molybdenum wire	8102.9600	16
钼酸铵	Ammonium molybdates	2841.7010	1
钼酸盐,其他	Molybdates, nes	2841.7090	1
钼铁合金	Ferro-molybdenum alloys	7202.7000	6
钼制品,其他	Molybdenum articles, nes	8102.9900	16

N

商品名称	Article Description	税则号列	申报要素
nei			
内裤及三角裤,非针织或钩编的,男式,化学纤维制	Underpants and briefs, not knitted or crocheted, for men or boys, of man-made fibres	6207.1920	2456
内裤及三角裤,非针织或钩编的,男式,棉制	Underpants and briefs, not knitted or crocheted, for men or boys, of cotton	6207.1100	2456
内裤及三角裤,非针织或钩编的,男式,其他	Underpants and briefs, not knitted or crocheted, for men or boys, nes	6207.1990	2456
内裤及三角裤,非针织或钩编的,男式,丝及绢丝制	Underpants and briefs, not knitted or crocheted, for men or boys, of silk or silk waste	6207.1910	2456
内裤及三角裤,针织或钩编的男式,化学纤维制	Underpants and briefs, knitted or crocheted, for men or boys, of man-made fibres	6107.1200	2456
内裤及三角裤,针织或钩编的男式,棉制	Underpants and briefs, knitted or crocheted, for men or boys, of cotton	6107.1100	2456
内裤及三角裤,针织或钩编的男式,其他	Underpants and briefs, knitted or crocheted, for men or boys, nes	6107.1990	2456
内裤及三角裤,针织或钩编的男式,丝及绢丝制	Underpants and briefs, knitted or crocheted, for men or boys, of silk or silk waste	6107.1910	2456
内窥镜	Endoscopes	9018.9030	
内酰胺,其他	Lactams, nes	2933.7900	36
内圆磨床,在任一坐标的定位精度至少是0.01毫米,加工金属或金属陶瓷用,其他	Internal grinding machines, in which the positioning in any one axis can be set up to an accuracy of at least 0.01mm, for metal or cermets, nes	8460.2920	7
内圆磨床,在任一坐标的定位精度至少是0.01毫米,数控的,加工金属或金属陶瓷用	Internal grinding machines, in which the positioning in any one axis can be set up to an accuracy of at least 0.01mm, numerically controlled, for metal or cermets	8460.2120	7
内酯,其他	Lactones, nes	2932.2900	36
na			
钠	Sodium	2805.1100	
钠的次硫酸盐	Sodium sulphoxylates	2831.1020	
钠的硅酸盐,其他	Sodium silicates	2839.1900	
钠的连二亚硫酸盐	Sodium dithionites	2831.1010	
钠的硫化物,其他	Sodium sulphides, nes	2830.1090	
钠的硫酸盐,其他	Sodium sulphates, nes	2833.1900	
钠的亚硫酸盐	Sodium sulphites	2832.1000	
钠蒸汽灯	Sodium vapour lamps	8539.3230	35

商品名称	Article Description	税则号列	申报要素
nai			
奶油,按重量计脂肪含量不超过1%,未浓缩及未加糖或其他甜物质的	Cream, of a fat content, by weight, not exceeding 1%, not concentrated nor containing added sugar or other sweetening matter	0401.1000	12468
奶油,按重量计脂肪含量超过1%,但不超过6%,未浓缩及未加糖或其他甜物质的	Cream, of a fat content, by weight, exceeding 1% but not exceeding 6%, not concentrated nor containing added sugar or other sweetening matter	0401.2000	12468
奶油,按重量计脂肪含量超过6%,未浓缩及未加糖或其他甜物质的	Cream, of a fat content, by weight, exceeding 6%, not concentrated nor containing added sugar or other sweetening matter	0401.3000	12468
奶油,发酵或酸化的,其他	Cream, fermented or acidified, nes	0403.9000	248
奶油,非固体形状,加糖或其他甜物质	Cream, not in solid forms, containing added sugar or other sweetening matter	0402.9900	12468
奶油,非固体形状,未加糖或其他甜物质	Cream, not in solid forms, not containing added sugar or other sweetening matter	0402.9100	12468
奶油,粉状、粒状或其他固体形状,按重量计脂肪含量不超过1.5%	Cream, in powder, granules or other solid forms, of a fat content, by weight, not exceeding 1.5%	0402.1000	12468
奶油,粉状、粒状或其他固体形状,按重量计脂肪含量超过1.5%,加糖或其他甜物质	Cream, in powder, granules or other solid forms, of a fat content, by weight, exceeding 1.5%, containing added sugar or other sweetening matter	0402.2900	12468
奶油,粉状、粒状或其他固体形状,按重量计脂肪含量超过1.5%,未加糖或其他甜物质	Cream, in powder, granules or other solid forms, of a fat content, by weight, exceeding 1.5%, not containing added sugar or other sweetening matter	0402.2100	12468
奶油,凝固的	Cream, curdled	0403.9000	248
奶油分离器,离心式	Cream separators, centrifuges	8421.1100	7
奶油面卷,不论是否烹煮或经其他方法制作	Cannelloni, whether or not cooked or otherwise prepared	1902.2000	46
奶嘴	Teats	4014.9000	23
奈韦拉平及盐	Nevirapine and their salts	2934.9940	36
耐火陶瓷制品,含有按重量计超过50%的三氧化二铝或三氧化二铝和二氧化硅的混合物或化合物	Refractory ceramic goods, containing by weight more than 50% of alumina (Al_2O_3) or of a mixture of compound of alumina and of silica (SiO_2)	6903.2000	6
耐火陶瓷制品,含有按重量计超过50%的石墨、其他碳或其混合物	Refractory ceramic goods, containing by weight more than 50% of graphite or other carbon or of a mixture of these pro-ducts	6903.1000	6
耐火陶瓷制品,其他	Refractory ceramic goods, nes	6903.9000	6
耐火粘土	Fire-clay	2508.3000	145
耐火砖、块、瓦及类似耐火陶瓷建材制品,单独或同时含有按重量计超过50%的镁、钙或铬(分别以氧化镁、氧化钙及三氧化二铬的含量计)	Refractory bricks, blocks, tiles and similar refractory ceramic constructional goods, containing by weight, singly or together, more than 50% of the elements Mg, Ca or Cr, expressed as MgO, CaO or Ca_2O_3	6902.1000	6

商品名称	Article Description	税则号列	申报要素
耐火砖、块、瓦及类似耐火陶瓷建材制品,含有按重量计超过50%的三氧化二铝、二氧化硅或其混合物或化合物	Refractory bricks, blocks, tiles and similar refractory ceramic constructional goods, containing by weight more than 50% of alumina (Al_2O_3), of silica (SiO_2) or of a mixture or compound of these products	6902.2000	6
耐火砖、块、瓦及类似耐火陶瓷建材制品,其他	Refractory bricks, blocks, tiles and similar refractory ceramic constructional goods, nes	6902.9000	6
萘,粗萘	Naphthalene, crude	2707.4000	6
萘,精萘	Naphthalene, refined	2902.9020	6
萘酚,其他	Naphthols, nes	2907.1590	36
萘酚盐	Naphthols salts	2907.1590	36
萘烷	Decahydronaphthalene	2902.1990	6
nan			
南方蓝鳍金枪鱼,其他	Southern bluefin tunas, nes, living	0301.9590	15
南方蓝鳍金枪鱼,其他	Thunnus maccoyii, nes, living	0301.9590	15
南方蓝鳍金枪鱼苗	Fry, southern bluefin tunas	0301.9510	15
南方蓝鳍金枪鱼苗	Fry, thunnus maccoyii	0301.9510	15
南极犬牙鱼(Dissostichus spp.),冻的	Toothfish (Dissostichus spp.), frozen	0303.6200	18
南极犬牙鱼(Dissostichus spp.),鲜或冷的	Toothfish (Dissostichus spp.), fresh or chilled	0302.6800	18
南金枪鱼(南方蓝鳍金枪鱼),冻的	Southern bluefin tunas (Thunnus maccoyii), frozen	0303.4600	18
南金枪鱼,鲜或冷的	Southern bluefin tunas (Thunnus maccoyii), fresh or chilled	0302.3600	18
nao			
铙钹	Cymbals	9206.0000	5
闹钟,电力驱动的	Alarm clocks, electrically operated	9105.1100	5
闹钟,其他	Alarm clocks, nes	9105.1900	5
闹钟芯,已组装完整的,电力驱动的	Alarm clocks movements, complete and assembled, elcetrically operated	9109.1100	5
ni			
尼可吗啡(INN)及盐	Nicomorphine (INN) and salts	2939.1100	34
尼龙-6,6单纱,捻度每米超过50转,非供零售用	Nylon-6,6 single yarn, with a twist exceeding 50 turns per metre, not put up for retail sale	5402.5120	3468
尼龙-6,6单纱,未加捻或捻度每米不超过50转,非供零售用	Nylon-6,6single yarn, untwisted or with a twist not exceeding 50 turns per metre, not put up for retail sale	5402.4520	3468
尼龙-6,6弹力丝,每根单纱细度不超过50特,非供零售用	Nylon-6,6 elastic filament, measuring per single yarn not more than 50 tex, not put up for retail sale	5402.3112	3468
尼龙-6,6弹力丝,每根单纱细度超过50特,非供零售用	Nylon-6,6 elastic filament, measuring per single yarn more than 50 tex, not put up for retail sale	5402.3212	3468

商品名称	Article Description	税则号列	申报要素
尼龙-6,6多股纱线或缆线,非供零售用	Nylon-6,6 multiple or cabled yarn, not put up for retail sale	5402.6120	3468
尼龙-6,6高强力纱,非供零售用	Nylon-6,6high tenacity yarn, not put up for retail sale	5402.1920	3468
尼龙-66盐	Nylon-66 salt	2921.2210	36
尼龙-6单纱,捻度每米超过50转,非供零售用	Nylon-6 single yarn, with a twist exceeding 50 turns per metre, not put up for retail sale	5402.5110	3468
尼龙-6单纱,未加捻或捻度每米不超过50转,非供零售用	Nylon-6 single yarn, untwisted or with a twist not exceeding 50 turns per metre, not put up for retail sale	5402.4510	3468
尼龙-6弹力丝,每根单纱细度不超过50特,非供零售用	Nylon-6 elastic filament, measuring per single yarn not more than 50 tex, not put up for retail sale	5402.3111	3468
尼龙-6弹力丝,每根单纱细度超过50特,非供零售用	Nylon-6 elastic filament, measuring per single yarn more than 50 tex, not put up for retail sale	5402.3211	3468
尼龙-6多股纱线或缆线,非供零售用	Nylon-6 multiple or cabled yarn, not put up for retail sale	5402.6110	3468
尼龙-6高强力纱,非供零售用	Nylon-6 high tenacity yarn, not put up for retail sale	5402.1910	3468
尼龙或聚酰胺变形纱线,每根单纱细度不超过50特,非供零售用,其他	Nylon or polyamides textured yarn, measuring per single yarn not more than 50 tex, not put up for retail sale, nes	5402.3190	3468
尼龙或聚酰胺变形纱线,每根单纱细度超过50特,非供零售用,其他	Nylon or polyamides textured yarn of measuring per single yarn more than 50 tex, not put up for retail sale, nes	5402.3290	3468
尼龙或聚酰胺长丝丝束	Nylon or other polyamides filament tow	5501.1000	68
尼龙或聚酰胺单纱,捻度每米超过50转,非供零售用,其他	Nylon or polyamides single yarn, with a twist exceeding 50 turns per metre, not put up for retail sale, nes	5402.5190	3468
尼龙或聚酰胺单纱,未加捻或捻度每米不超过50转,非供零售用,其他	Nylon or polyamides single yarn, untwisted or with a twist not exceeding 50 turns per metre, not put up for retail sale, nes	5402.4590	3468
尼龙或聚酰胺弹力丝,每根单纱细度不超过50特,非供零售用,其他	Nylon or polyamides elastic filament, measuring per single yarn not more than 50 tex, not put up for retail sale, nes	5402.3119	3468
尼龙或聚酰胺弹力丝,每根单纱细度超过50特,非供零售用,其他	Nylon or polyamides elastic filament, measuring per single yarn more than 50 tex, not put up for retail sale	5402.3219	3468
尼龙或聚酰胺短纤,未梳或未经其他纺前加工,其他	Nylon or polyamides staple fibres, not carded, combed or otherwise processed for spinning, nes	5503.1900	68
尼龙或聚酰胺短纤,已梳或经其他纺前加工	Nylon or other polyamides staple fibres, carded, combed or otherwise processed for spinning	5506.1000	68
尼龙或聚酰胺多股纱线或缆线,非供零售用,其他	Nylon or polyamides multiple or cabled yarn, not put up for retail sale, nes	5402.6190	3468

N

商品名称	Article Description	税则号列	申报要素
尼龙或聚酰胺高强力纱,非供零售用,其他	Nylon or polyamides high tenacity yarn, not put up for retail sale, nes	5402. 1990	3468
尼龙或聚酰胺高强力纱纺制的机织物	Nylon or other polyamides high tenacity yarn woven fabrics	5407. 1010	2468
尼龙或聚酰胺机织物,按重量计长丝含量在85%及以上,染色	Nylon or other polyamides woven fabrics, containing 85% or more by weight of filaments, dyed	5407. 4200	2468
尼龙或聚酰胺机织物,按重量计长丝含量在85%及以上,色织	Nylon or other polyamides woven fabrics, containing 85% or more by weight of filaments, of yarns of different colours	5407. 4300	2468
尼龙或聚酰胺机织物,按重量计长丝含量在85%及以上,未漂白或漂白	Nylon or other polyamides woven fabrics, containing 85% or more by weight of filaments, unbleached or bleached	5407. 4100	2468
尼龙或聚酰胺机织物,按重量计长丝含量在85%及以上,印花	Nylon or other polyamides woven fabrics, containing 85% or more by weight of filaments, printed	5407. 4400	2468
泥煤(包括肥料用泥煤),不论是否制成型	Peat (including peat litter), whether or not agglomerated	2703. 0000	14
泥煤蜡	Peat wax	2712. 9090	6
泥煤制品	Peat articles	6815. 2000	6
泥铜	Precipitated copper	7401. 0000	46
泥罨剂,供医疗、外科、牙科或兽医用	Poultices, medical, surgical, dental or veterinary purposes	3005. 9090	1346
泥釉及类似制品,陶瓷、搪瓷及玻璃工业用	Slips and similar preparations, of a kind used in the ceramic, enamelling or glass industry	3207. 2000	13
铌,未锻轧	Niobium, unwrought	8112. 9240	16
铌粉末	Niobium powders	8112. 9240	16
铌矿富集物	Enriched materials from niobium ore	2615. 9010	146
铌矿砂及其精矿	Niobium ores and concentrates	2615. 9010	146
铌铁合金	Ferro-niobium alloys	7202. 9300	6
铌铁矿	Columbite	2615. 9090	146
铌铁矿	Niobite	2615. 9090	146
铌制品	Niobium articles, nes	8112. 9940	16
逆变器	Inverter	8504. 4030	
nian			
粘度改良剂,用于矿物油及类似液体	Viscosity improvers, for mineral oils and alike	3811. 9000	236
粘合剂,调制的,其他	Adhesives, prepared, nes	3506. 9900	36
粘合剂,以环氧树脂为基本成分的	Adhesives based on epoxy resin	3506. 9120	36
粘合剂,以聚酰胺为基本成分的	Adhesives based on polyamide	3506. 9110	36
粘合剂,以橡胶或聚合物为基本成分的,其他	Adhesives, adhesives based on polymers or on rubber, nes	3506. 9190	36
粘合剂,铸模用	Binders for foundry moulds, prepared	3824. 1000	36
粘合剂,铸芯用	Binders for foundry cores, prepared	3824. 1000	36
粘合胶布,外伤创口闭合用的,无菌	Tissue adhesives for surgical wound closure, sterile	3006. 1000	3

N

商品名称	Article Description	税则号列	申报要素
粘胶纤维单纱，捻度每米超过120转，非供零售用，其他	Viscose rayon single yarn, with a twist exceeding 120 turns per rnette, not put up for retail sale, nes	5403.3290	3468
粘胶纤维单纱，未加捻或捻度每米不超过120转，非供零售用，其他	Viscose rayon single yarn, untwisted or with a twist not exceeding 120 turns per metre, not put up for retail sale, nes	5403.3190	3468
粘胶纤维短纤，未梳或未经其他纺前加工，其他	Viscose rayon staple fibres, not carded, combed or otherwise processed for spinning, nes	5504.1090	68
粘胶纤维多股纱线或缆线	Viscose rayon multiple or cabled yarn	5403.4100	3468
粘胶纤维高强力纱，非供零售用	Viscose rayon high tenacity yarn, not put up for retail sale	5403.1000	3468
粘胶纤维高强力纱的机织物	Viscose rayon high tenacity yarn woven fabrics	5408.1000	2468
粘胶纤维制机织物，按重量计人造纤维长丝、扁条或类似品含量在85%及以上，染色	Viscose rayon woven fabrics, containing 85% or more by weight of artificial filament or strip or the like, dyed	5408.2210	2468
粘胶纤维制机织物，按重量计人造纤维长丝、扁条或类似品含量在85%及以上，色织	Viscose rayon woven fabrics, containing 85% or more by weight of artificial filament or strip or the like, of yarns of different colours	5408.2310	2468
粘胶纤维制机织物，按重量计人造纤维长丝、扁条或类似品含量在85%及以上，未漂白或漂白	Viscose rayon woven fabrics, containing 85% or more by weight of artificial filament or strip or the like, unbleached or bleached	5408.2110	2468
粘胶纤维制机织物，按重量计人造纤维长丝、扁条或类似品含量在85%及以上，印花	Viscose rayon woven fabrics, containing 85% or more by weight of artificial filament or strip or the like, printed	5408.2410	2468
粘土，其他	Clays, nes	2508.4000	145
粘土砂	Clayey sands	2505.9000	
niang			
酿酒机器	Brewery machinery	8438.4000	
酿酒机器的零件	Brewery machinery parts	8438.9000	3
酿酒葡萄汁	Grape must, with fermentation prevented or arrested by the addition of alcohol	2204.3000	268
酿造及蒸馏过程中的糟粕及残渣	Brewing or distilling dregs and waste	2303.3000	56
niao			
鸟，改良种用，其他	Birs, pure-bred breeding, nes	0106.3910	34
鸟，其他	Birs, nes	0106.3990	34
鸟，食用，其他	Birs, for human consumption, nes	0106.3929	34
鸟粪，未经化学处理	Guano, not chemically treated	3101.0011	1346
鸟皮，带有羽毛或羽绒的	Skins of birds, with their feathers or down	0505.9090	34
鸟体，其他	Parts of birds, nes	0505.9090	34
尿布，非针织或钩编的，婴儿的，棉制，	Napkins(diapers), for babies, of cotton	6209.2010	2456
尿素，不论是否水溶液	Urea, whether or not in aqueous solution	3102.1000	68

商品名称	Article Description	税则号列	申报要素
尿素及硝酸铵混合物的水溶液或氨水溶液	Mixtures of urea and ammonium nitrate in aqueous or ammoniacal solution	3102.8000	68
尿素树脂,初级形状的	Urea resins,in primary forms	3909.1000	1256
nie			
镊子及类似工具	Tweezers and similar tools	8203.2000	256
镍,非合金的,按重量计镍、钴总量在99.99%及以上的,但钴含量不超过0.005%	Nickel,not alloyed,containing 99.99% or more by total weight of nickel and cobalt,but containing cobalt not exceeding 0.005%	7502.1010	46
镍,非合金的,其他	Nickel,not alloyed,nes	7502.1090	46
镍的硫酸盐	Nickel sulphates	2833.2400	
镍的氧化物及氢氧化物	Nickel oxides and hydroxides	2825.4000	
镍粉及片状粉末,非合金的	Nickel powders and flakes, not alloyed	7504.0010	46
镍粉及片状粉末,合金的	Nickel powders and flakes, of alloys	7504.0020	
镍镉蓄电池	Nickel-cadmium accumulators	8507.3000	68
镍合金,未锻轧的	Nickel, alloys,unwrought	7502.2000	46
镍黄铁矿	Pentlandite	2604.0000	146
镍矿砂及其精矿	Nickel ores and concentrates	2604.0000	146
镍锍	Nickel mattes	7501.1000	4
镍氢蓄电池	Nickel-hydrogen accumulators	8507.8010	68
镍湿法冶炼中间品	Intermediate products of nickel metallurgy by wet process	7501.2010	4
镍铁合金	Ferro-nickel alloys	7202.6000	6
镍铁蓄电池	Nickel-iron accumulators	8507.4000	68
镍阳极,电镀用	Nickel anodes for electroplating	7508.9010	6
镍制品,工业用,其他	Nickel articles, for technical use	7508.9080	6
镍制品,其他	Nickel articles,nes	7508.9090	6
ning			
柠檬	Lemons(Citrus limon, Citrus limonum)	0805.5000	124
柠檬汽水	Lemonade	2202.1000	248
柠檬醛	Citral	2912.1900	36
柠檬酸	Citric acid	2918.1400	36
柠檬酸铁	Iron citrate	2918.1500	36
柠檬酸盐及柠檬酸酯	Salts and esters of citric acid	2918.1500	36
柠檬油	Essential oils of lemon	3301.1300	34
柠檬汁,白利糖度值不超过20的	Lemon juice,of a brix value not exceeding 20	2009.3110	2468
柠檬汁,其他	Lemon juice,nes	2009.3910	2468
凝胶制品,专用于人类或作兽药用的	Gel preparations designed to be used in human or veterinary medicine	3006.7000	36
凝乳	Curd	0406.1000	24
凝乳酶及其浓缩物,粗制	Rennet and concentrates thereof	3507.1000	35

商品名称	Article Description	税则号列	申报要素
niu			
牛,改良种用	Bovine animals, live, pure-bred breeding	0102.1000	34
牛,改良种用除外	Bovine animals, live, ex. pure-bred breeding	0102.9000	34
牛的精液	Semen, of bovine	0511.1000	4
牛肚	Tripe	0504.0029	14
牛肚,罐头	Tripe, in airtight container	1602.5010	248
牛肝,冻的,可食用的	Livers of bovine animals, frozen, edible	0206.2200	15
牛肝菌,干的	Boletus, dried	0712.3950	4
牛皮挂面纸,其他	Kraftliner, nes	4804.1900	24568
牛皮挂面纸,未漂白	Kraftliner, unbleached	4804.1100	24568
牛皮纸,起皱的,不论是否压花或穿孔,其他	Kraft paper, creped or crinkled, whether or not embossed or perforated, nes	4808.3000	58
牛皮纸或纸板及瓦楞纸或纸板,未漂白的	Kraft paper or paperboard or of corrugated paper or paperboard, unbleached	4707.1000	125
牛皮纸及纸板,本体均匀漂白,但书写、印刷或类似用途的除外,所含用化学方法制得的木纤维超过全部纤维重量的95%,每平方米重量不超过150克,单面或双面涂布高岭土或其他无机物质的	Kraft paper and paperboard, bleached uniformly throughout the mass, other than that of a kind used for writing, printing or other graphic purposes, of which more than 95% by weight of the total fibre content consists of wood fibres obtained by a chemical process, and weighing 150 g/m² or less, coated on one or both sides with kaolin or other inorganic substances	4810.3100	14568
牛皮纸及纸板,本体均匀漂白,但书写、印刷或类似用途的除外,所含用化学方法制得的木纤维超过全部纤维重量的95%,每平方米重量超过150克,单面或双面涂布高岭土或其他无机物质的	Kraft paper and paperboard, bleached uniformly throughout the mass, other than that of a kind used for writing, printing or other graphic purposes, of which more than 95% by weight of the total fibre content consists of wood fibres obtained by a chemical process, and weighing more than 150 g/m², coated on one or both sides with kaolin or other inorganic substances	4810.3200	14568
牛皮纸及纸板,本体均匀漂白,未经涂布的,每平方米重量超过150克,但小于225克,所含用化学方法制得的木纤维超过全部纤维重量的95%	Kraft paper and paperboard, bleached uniformly throughout the mass, uncoated, weighing more than 150 g/m² but less than 225 g/m², of which more than 95% by weight of the total fibre content consists of wood fibres obtained by a chemical process	4804.4200	24568
牛皮纸及纸板,但书写、印刷或类似用途的除外,单面或双面涂布高岭土或其他无机物质的,其他	Kraft paper and paperboard, other than that of a kind used for writing, printing or other graphic purposes, coated on one or both sides with kaolin or other inorganic substances, nes	4810.3900	14568

商品名称	Article Description	税则号列	申报要素
牛皮纸及纸板,未经涂布的,本体均匀漂白,每平方米重量在225克及以上,所含用化学方法制得的木纤维超过全部纤维重量的95%	Kraft paper and paperboard, bleached uniformly throughout the mass, uncoated, weighing 225 g/m^2 or more, of which more than 95% by weight of the total fibre content consists of wood fibres obtained by a chemical process	4804.5200	24568
牛皮纸及纸板,未经涂布的,未漂白,每平方米重量超过150克,但小于225克	Kraft paper and paperboard, unbleached, uncoated, weighing more than 150g/m^2 but less than 225 g/m^2	4804.4100	24568
牛皮纸及纸板,未经涂布的,未漂白,每平方米重量在225克及以上	Kraft paper and paperboard, unbleached, uncoated, weighing 225g/m^2 or more	4804.5100	24568
牛皮纸及纸板,未经涂布的,每平方米重量不超过150克,其他	Kraft paper and paperboard, uncoated, weighing 150g/m^2 or less	4804.3900	24568
牛皮纸及纸板,未经涂布的,每平方米重量超过150克,但小于225克,其他	Kraft paper and paperboard, uncoated, weighing more than 150g/m^2 but less than 225g/m^2, nes	4804.4900	24568
牛皮纸及纸板,未经涂布的,每平方米重量在225克及以上,其他	Kraft paper and paperboard, uncoated, weighing 225g/m^2 or more, nes	4804.5900	24568
牛皮纸及纸板,未经涂布的,未漂白,每平方米重量不超过150克	Kraft paper and paperboard, uncoated, unbleached, weighing 150g/m^2 or less	4804.3100	24568
牛肉,冻的,带骨	Meat of bovine animals, frozen, other cuts with bone in	0202.2000	14
牛肉,冻的,去骨	Meat of bovine animals, frozen, boneless	0202.3000	14
牛肉,冻的,整头及半头	Meat of bovine animals, frozen, carcasses and halfcarcasses	0202.1000	14
牛肉,干、熏、盐腌或盐渍的	Meat of bovine animals, salted, in brine, dried or smoked	0210.2000	14
牛肉,鲜或冷的,带骨	Meat of bovine animals, fresh of chilled, other cuts with bone in	0201.2000	14
牛肉,鲜或冷的,去骨	Meat of bovine animals, fresh of chilled, boneless	0201.3000	14
牛肉,鲜或冷的,整头及半头	Meat of bovine animals, fresh of chilled, carcasses and halfcarcasses	0201.1000	14
牛舌,冻的	Tongues of bovine animals, frozen, edible	0206.2100	15
牛油树果	Karite nuts	1207.9991	3
牛油树果	Shea nuts	1207.9991	3
牛脂肪,其他	Fats of bovine animals, nes	1502.0090	4
牛脂肪,未炼制的	Fats of bovine animals, raw	1502.0010	4
扭矩变换器	Torque converters	8483.4090	7
钮扣,金属制,未用纺织材料包裹	Buttons, of base metal, not covered with textile material	9606.2200	5
钮扣,其他	Buttons, nes	9606.2900	5
钮扣,塑料制,未用纺织材料包裹	Buttons, of plastics, not covered with textile material	9606.2100	5
钮扣坯	Button blanks	9606.3000	5

商品名称	Article Description	税则号列	申报要素
钮扣芯及钮扣的其他零件	Button moulds and other parts of buttons	9606. 3000	5
nong			
农业用机器,包括装有机械或热力装置的催芽设备,其他	Agricultural machinery, including germination plant fitted with mechanical or thermal equipment, nes	8436. 8000	
农业用机器零件,其他	Agricultural machinery parts, nes	8436. 9900	3
浓雾信号弹	Fog signals	3604. 9000	
nu			
弩枪式人道捕杀器	Captive-bolt humane killers	9303. 9000	
弩枪式人道捕杀器用子弹及其零件	Cartridges for captive-bolt humane killers, and parts thereof	9306. 3080	3
钕	Neodymium	2805. 3011	56
钕铁硼磁粉	Nd-Fe-B magnetic powder	7202. 9912	6
钕铁硼合金,其他	Nd-Fe-B alloy, nes	7202. 9919	
钕铁硼速凝永磁片	Nd-Fe-B rapidly solidified permenent megnetic powder	7202. 9911	6
nuan			
暖气分布器(包括可分布新鲜空气或调节空气的)及其零件,钢铁制,非电热的,装有电动风扇或鼓风机	Hot air distributors (including distributors which can also distribute fresh or con-ditioned air) and parts thereof, of iron or steel, not electrically heated, incorporating a motor-dirven fan or blower	7322. 9000	7
nuo			
糯米纸	Rice paper	1905. 9000	28

N

O

商品名称	Article Description	税则号列	申报要素
ou			
偶氮化合物	Azo-compounds	2927.0000	36
偶合剂,躯体和医疗器械之间用的	Coupling agent between the body and medical instruments	3006.7000	36
藕,其他	Lotus (Nelumbo nucifera) rootstock, nes	0714.9029	34
藕,种用	Lotus (Nelumbo nucifera) rootstock, for cultivation	0714.9021	34

P

商品名称	Article Description	税则号列	申报要素
pa			
爬行动物(包括蛇及龟鳖),改良种用,其他	Reptiles (including snakes and turtles), pure-bred breeding, nes	0106.2019	3
爬行动物(包括蛇及龟鳖),其他	Reptiles (including snakes and turtles), nes	0106.2090	
爬行动物(包括蛇及龟鳖),食用	Reptiles (including snakes and turtles), for human consumption	0106.2020	48
爬行动物(包括蛇及龟鳖)的肉	Meat of reptiles (including snakes and turtles), fresh, chilled or frozen	0208.5000	15
耙	Rakes	8201.3000	256
耙,农业、园艺及林业用耕作机械,其他	Harrows, machinary for agricultural, horticultural or forestry use, nes	8432.2900	
pai			
排球	Volleyballs	9506.6210	
排液泵,回转式,齿轮的,电动式	Positive displacement pumps, rotary, gear, electric	8413.6021	27
排液泵,回转式,齿轮的,其他	Positive displacement pumps, rotary, gear, nes	8413.6029	27
排液泵,回转式,齿轮的,液压式	Positive displacement pumps, rotary, gear, hydraulic	8413.6022	27
排液泵,回转式,径向柱塞泵	Positive displacement pumps, rotary, radial plunger pump	8413.6050	27
排液泵,回转式,螺杆泵	Positive displacement pumps, rotary, screw pump	8413.6040	27
排液泵,回转式,其他	Positive displacement pumps, rotary, nes	8413.6090	27
排液泵,回转式,叶片的,电动式	Positive displacement pumps, rotary, vane, electric	8413.6031	27
排液泵,回转式,叶片的,其他	Positive displacement pumps, rotary, vane, nes	8413.6039	27
排液泵,回转式,叶片的,液压式	Positive displacement pumps, rotary, vane, hydraulic	8413.6032	27
排液泵,回转式,轴向柱塞泵	Positive displacement pumps, rotary, axial plunger pump	8413.6060	27
排液泵,往复式,电动式	Positive displacement pumps, reciprocating, electric	8413.5020	23
排液泵,往复式,其他	Positive displacement pumps, reciprocating, nes	8413.5090	23
排液泵,往复式,气动式	Positive displacement pumps, reciprocating, pneumatic	8413.5010	23
排液泵,往复式,液压式,其他	Positive displacement pumps, reciprocating, hydraulic, nes	8413.5039	23
排液泵,往复式,柱塞泵	Positive displacement pumps, reciprocating, plunger pumps	8413.5031	23
排字盘,手工操作的	Composing sticks, hand-operated	9611.0000	
哌苯甲醇(INN)以及盐	Pipradrol (INN); salts thereof	2933.3300	36
哌丙吡胺(INN)以及盐	Propiram (INN); salts thereof	2933.3300	36
哌醋甲酯(INN)以及盐	Methylphenidate (INN); salts thereof	2933.3300	36

商品名称	Article Description	税则号列	申报要素
哌啶	Piperidine	2933.3210	36
哌嗪环化合物,结构上含有,其他	Piperazine ring compounds, in the structure, whether or not hydrogenated, nes	2933.5990	36
哌氰米特(INN)以及盐	Piritramide (INN); salts thereof	2933.3300	36
哌替啶(INN)以及盐	Pethidine (INN); salts thereof	2933.3300	36
哌替啶中间体A(INN)以及盐	Pethidine (INN) intermediate A; salts thereof	2933.3300	36
蒎烯	Pinene	2902.1910	6
pan			
盘、碟、盆、杯及类似品,纸或纸板制的,其他	Trays, dishes, plates, cups and the like, of paper or paperboard, nes	4823.6900	68
盘、碟、盆、杯及类似品,竹浆纸制	Trays, dishes, plates, cups and the like, of bamboo	4823.6100	68
pang			
膀胱,动物的(鱼除外)	Bladders of animals (other than fish)	0504.0090	14
pao			
抛光机床,玻璃用	Polishing machines for glass or glassware	8464.2010	7
抛光机床,加工金属或金属陶瓷用	Polishing machines, for metal or cermets	8460.9020	7
抛光机床,加工石料、陶瓷、混凝土、石棉水泥或类似矿物材料的,其他	Polishing machines for working stone, ceramics, concrete, asbestos-cement or like mineral materials, nes	8464.2090	7
抛光机器,加工木材、软木、骨、硬质橡胶、硬质塑料或类似硬质材料的	Polishing machines, for working wood, cork, bone, hard rubber, hard plastics or similar hard materials	8465.9300	7
抛光石,手用	Polishing stones, hand used	6804.3090	36
抛缆枪	Line throwing guns	9303.9000	
泡铋矿	Bismutite	2617.9090	146
泡沫矿渣	Foamed slag	6806.2000	68
pei			
培养基,制成的供微生物(包括病毒及类似品)或植物、人体、动物细胞生长或维持用的	Culture media, prepared for the development or maintenance of micro-organisms (including viruses and the like) or of plant, human or animal cells	3821.0000	36
培养酵母	Culture yeast	2102.1000	28
培养微生物(不包括酵母)及类似产品	Cultures of micro-organisms (excluding yeasts) and similar products	3002.9090	34
配料秤	Proporating scales	8423.3030	
配制炸药,其他,但发射药除外	Explosives, prepared, nes, other than propellent powders	3602.0090	6
pen			
喷灯	Blow lamps	8205.6000	256
喷焊器,手提式	Blow pipes, hand-held	8468.1000	57

商品名称	Article Description	税则号列	申报要素
喷墨打印机,专用于自动数据处理设备的	Ink-jet printers, of a kind solely used for automatic data processing machine	8443.3213	57
喷墨印刷机,数字式,可与自动数据处理设备或网络连接	Ink-jet printing machines, digital, capable of connecting to an APP machine or to a network	8443.3221	57
喷墨印刷机,数字式	Ink-jet printing machines, digital	8443.3931	57
喷气纺纱机	Jet spinner	8445.2032	7
喷气织机,所织织物宽度超过30厘米的无梭织机	Air jet looms, for weaving fabrics of a with exceeding 30cm, shuttleless type	8446.3050	7
喷汽机及类似的喷射机器	Steam blasting machines and similar jet projecting machines	8424.3000	7
喷枪及类似器具	Spray guns and similar appliances	8424.2000	7
喷洒车	Spraying lorries	8705.9090	7
喷砂机及类似的喷射机器	Sand blasting machines and similar jet projecting machines	8424.3000	7
喷水织机,所织织物宽度超过30厘米的无梭织机	Water jet looms, for weaving fabrics of a with exceeding 30cm, shuttleless type	8446.3040	7
喷丝头或喷丝板	Extruding nipples or spinnerets	8448.2020	3
喷他左辛(INN)以及盐	Pentazocine (INN); salts thereof	2933.3300	36
喷雾喷射机械器具,家用型	Spraying mechanical appliances, of the household type	8424.8910	7
喷雾喷射机械器具,农业或园艺用	Spraying mechanical appliances, agricultural or horticultural	8424.8100	7
喷雾喷射机械器具零件,其他	Spraying mechanical appliances parts, nes	8424.9090	
喷雾喷射机械器具,其他	Spraying mechanical appliances, nes	8424.8999	7
喷雾喷射机械器具零件,家用型	Spraying mechanical appliances parts, of the household type	8424.9020	
喷雾治疗器	Aerosol therapy apparatus	9019.2000	
盆,辐射松制的	Vats, of radiata pine	4416.0010	56
盆,其他木制的	Vats, of other wood	4416.0090	56
peng			
烹饪器具及加热板,钢铁制,非电热的家用,其他,包括使用固体燃料的	Cooking appliances and plate warmers, of iron or steel, non-electric domestic appliances, nes, including appliances for solid fuel	7321.1900	7
烹饪器具及加热板,钢铁制,非电热的家用,使用气体燃料或可使用气体燃料及其他燃料的	Cooking appliances and plate warmers, of iron or steel, non-electric domestic appliances, for gas fuel or for both gas and other fuels	7321.1100	7
烹饪器具及加热板,钢铁制,非电热的家用,使用液体燃料的,其他	Cooking appliances and plate warmers, of iron or steel, non-electric domestic appliances, for liquid fuel, nes	7321.1290	7
烹饪器具及其零件,铜制,非电热的,家用	Cooking apparatus, of copper, of a kind used for domestic purposes, non-electric, and parts thereof, of copper	7418.1910	56

P

商品名称	Article Description	税则号列	申报要素
硼	Boron	2804. 5000	
硼的氧化物	Boron, oxides thereof	2810. 0010	6
硼化物,不论是否已有化学定义	Borides, whether or not chemically defined	2850. 0000	
硼酸	Boric acids	2810. 0020	6
硼酸盐,其他	Borates, nes	2840. 2000	
膨化食品,谷物或谷物产品的	Prepared foods obtained by the swelling of cereals or cereal products	1904. 1000	48
膨润土	Bentonite	2508. 1000	1345
膨胀粘土	Expanded clays	6806. 2000	68
pi			
披巾,非针织或钩编的,合成纤维制	Shawls, not knitted or crocheted, of other synthetic fibres	6214. 3000	2456
披巾,非针织或钩编的,其他动物细毛制	Shawls, not knitted or crocheted, of other fine animal hair	6214. 2090	2456
披巾,非针织或钩编的,其他纺织材料制	Shawls, not knitted or crocheted, of other textile materials	6214. 9000	2456
披巾,非针织或钩编的,人造纤维制	Shawls, not knitted or crocheted, of artificial fibres	6214. 4000	2456
披巾,非针织或钩编的,山羊绒制	Shawls, not knitted or crocheted, of goats fine animal hair	6214. 2020	2456
披巾,非针织或钩编的,丝或绢丝制	Shawls, not knitted or crocheted, of silk or silk waste	6214. 1000	2456
披巾,非针织或钩编的,羊毛制	Shawls, not knitted or crocheted, of wool	6214. 2010	2456
披巾,针织或钩编的,其他	Shawls, knitted or crocheted, nes	6117. 1090	2456
披巾,针织或钩编的,其他动物细毛制	Shawls, knitted or crocheted, of other fine animal hair, nes	6117. 1019	2456
披巾,针织或钩编的,山羊绒制	Shawls, knitted or crocheted, of goats fine animal hair	6117. 1011	2456
披巾,针织或钩编的,羊毛制	Shawls, knitted or crocheted, of wool	6117. 1020	2456
披纱,非针织或钩编的,合成纤维制	Mantillas, not knitted or crocheted, of synthetic fibres	6214. 3000	2456
披纱,非针织或钩编的,其他动物细毛制	Mantillas, not knitted or crocheted, of other fine animal hair	6214. 2090	2456
披纱,非针织或钩编的,其他纺织材料制	Mantillas, not knitted or crocheted, of other textile materials	6214. 9000	2456
披纱,非针织或钩编的,人造纤维制	Mantillas, not knitted or crocheted, of artificial fibres	6214. 4000	2456
披纱,非针织或钩编的,山羊绒制	Mantillas, not knitted or crocheted, of goats fine animal hair	6214. 2020	2456
披纱,非针织或钩编的,丝或绢丝制	Mantillas, not knitted or crocheted, of silk or silk waste	6214. 1000	2456
披纱,非针织或钩编的,羊毛制	Mantillas, not knitted or crocheted, of wool	6214. 2010	2456
披纱,针织或钩编的,其他	Mantillas, knitted or crocheted, nes	6117. 1090	2456
披纱,针织或钩编的,其他动物细毛制	Mantillas, knitted or crocheted, of fine animal hair, nes	6117. 1019	2456
披纱,针织或钩编的,山羊绒制	Mantillas, knitted or crocheted, of goats fine animal hair	6117. 1011	2456

商品名称	Article Description	税则号列	申报要素
披纱,针织或钩编的,羊毛制	Mantillas, knitted or crocheted, of wool	6117.1020	2456
铍,未锻轧	Beryllium, unwrought	8112.1200	16
铍粉末	Beryllium powders	8112.1200	16
铍制品,其他	Beryllium articles, nes	8112.1900	16
皮,马的,鞣制的,不带毛,湿革,其他	Hides and skins of equine animals, tanned, without hair on, in the wet state, nes	4104.1920	1458
皮,马的,鞣制的,不带毛,湿革,全粒面未剖层革;粒面剖层革	Hides and skins of equine animals, tanned, without hair on, in the wet state, full grains, unsplit; grain splits	4104.1120	1458
皮,马的,整张的,经鞣制或半硝处理后进一步加工的,不带毛的,整张的,粒面剖层革	Leather of equine animals, further prepared after tanning or crusting, without hair on, whole, grain splits	4107.1220	1458
皮,马的,整张的,经鞣制或半硝处理后进一步加工的,不带毛的,整张的,全粒面未剖层革	Leather of equine animals, further prepared after tanning or crusting, without hair on, whole, full grains, unsplit	4107.1120	1458
皮,牛的,经鞣制或半硝处理后进一步加工的,不带毛的,整张的,粒面剖层革	Leather of bovine animals, further prepared after tanning or crusting, without hair on, whole, grain splits	4107.1210	1458
皮,牛的,经鞣制或半硝处理后进一步加工的,不带毛的,整张的,全粒面未剖层革	Leather of bovine animals, further prepared after tanning or crusting, without hair on, whole, full grains, unsplit	4107.1110	1458
皮,牛的,鞣制的,不带毛,蓝湿的,其他	Hides and skins of bovine animals, tanned, without hair on, wet-blue, nes	4104.1911	1458
皮,牛的,鞣制的,不带毛,蓝湿的,全粒面未剖层革;粒面剖层革	Hides and skins of bovine animals, tanned, without hair on, wet-blue, full grains, unsplit; grain splits	4104.1111	1458
皮,牛的,鞣制的,不带毛,其他	Hides and skins of bovine animals, tanned, without hair on, nes	4104.1919	1458
皮,牛的,鞣制的,不带毛,全粒面未剖层革;粒面剖层革,其他	Hides and skins of bovine animals, tanned, without hair on, full grains, unsplit; grain splits, nes	4104.1119	1458
皮,牛或马的,干革,全粒面末剖层革粒面剖层革的	Hides and skins of bovine or equine animals, in the dry state, full grain, unsplit; grain splits	4104.4100	1458
皮,牛或马的,机器带用	Hides and skins of bovine or equine animals, for machinery belting	4104.4910	1458
皮,牛或马的,经鞣制或半硝处理后进一步加工的,不带毛的,机器带用,其他,包括半张的	Leather of bovine or quine animals, further prepared after tanning or crusting, without hair on, for machinery belting, nes, including sides	4107.9910	1458
皮,牛或马的,经鞣制或半硝处理后进一步加工的,不带毛的,粒面剖层革,其他,包括半张的	Leather of bovine or quine animals, further prepared after tanning or crusting, without hair on, grain splits, nes, including sides	4107.9200	1458
皮,牛或马的,经鞣制或半硝处理后进一步加工的,不带毛的,其他,包括半张的	Leather of bovine or quine animals, further prepared after tanning or crusting, without hair on, nes, including sides	4107.9990	1458

P

商品名称	Article Description	税则号列	申报要素
皮,牛或马的,经鞣制或半硝处理后进一步加工的,不带毛的,全粒面未剖层革,其他,包括半张的	Leather of bovine or quine animals, further prepared after tanning or crusting, without hair on, full grains, unsplit, nes, including sides	4107.9100	1458
皮,牛或马的,其他	Hides and skins of bovine or equine animals, nes	4104.4990	1458
皮,牛或马的,整张的,经鞣制或半硝处理后进一步加工的,不带毛的,机器带用	Leather of bovine or quine animals, further prepared after tanning or crusting, without hair on, whole, for machinery belting	4107.1910	1458
皮,牛或马的,整张的,经鞣制或半硝处理后进一步加工的,不带毛的,其他	Leather of bovine or quine animals, further prepared after tanning or crusting, without hair on, whole, nes	4107.1990	1458
皮蛋	Eggs, limepreserved	0407.0092	14
皮粉,不论是否加入铬矾	Hide powder, whether or not chromed	3504.0090	1346
皮革,经鞣制或半硝处理后进一步加工的,不带毛的,其他	Leather, further prepared after tanning or crusting, without wool on, nes	4113.9000	1458
皮革,绵羊或羔羊的,经鞣制或半硝处理后进一步加工的,不带毛的	Leather of sheep or lamb, further prepared after tanning or crusting, without wool on	4112.0000	1458
皮革,爬行动物皮的,经鞣制或半硝处理后进一步加工的,不带毛的	Leather of reptiles, further prepared after tanning or crusting, without wool on	4113.3000	1458
皮革,山羊或小山羊皮的,经鞣制或半硝处理后进一步加工的,不带毛的	Leather of goats or kids, further prepared after tanning or crusting, without wool on	4113.1000	1458
皮革,猪的,经鞣制或半硝处理后进一步加工的,不带毛的	Leather of swine, further prepared after tanning or crusting, without wool on	4113.2000	1458
皮革粉末	Leather dust, powder and flour	4115.2000	1458
皮革或再生皮革的边角废料,不适宜作皮革制品用	Leather or of composition leather's parings and other waste o, not suitable for the manufacture of leather articles	4115.2000	1458
皮革或再生皮革的制品,机器、机械器具或其他专门技术用途的	Leather articles of a kind used in machinery or mechanical appliances or for other technical uses	4205.0020	456
皮革或再生皮革的制品,其他	Leather articles or composition leather articles, nes	4205.0090	456
皮革加工机器零件	Skins or leather working machinery parts	8453.9000	3
皮革鞣制机器零件	Skins or leather tanning machinery parts	8453.9000	3
皮及其坯革,绵羊或者羔羊的,鞣制的不带毛,干革	Skins of sheep or lambs, tanned or crust, without wool on, in the dry state	4105.3000	1458
皮及其坯革,绵羊或者羔羊的,鞣制的不带毛,蓝湿的	Skins of sheep or lambs, tanned or crust, without wool on, wet -blue	4105.1010	1458
皮及其坯革,绵羊或者羔羊的,鞣制的不带毛,湿革,其他	Skins of sheep or lambs, tanned or crust, without wool on, in the wet state, nes	4105.1090	1458
皮及其坯革,爬行动物的,鞣制的,不带毛	Hides and skins of reptiles, tanned or crust, without wool or hair on	4106.4000	1458
皮及其坯革,鞣制的,不带毛,干革(坯革),其他	Hides and skins, tanned or crust, without wool or hair on, in the dry state (crust), nes	4106.9200	1458
皮及其坯革,鞣制的,不带毛,湿革,其他	Hides and skins, tanned or crust, without wool or hair on, in the wet state, nes	4106.9100	1458

P

商品名称	Article Description	税则号列	申报要素
皮及其坯革,山羊或小山羊的,鞣制的,不带毛,干革	Hides and skins of goats or kids, tanned or crust, without wool or hair on, in the dry state	4106.2200	1458
皮及其坯革,山羊或小山羊的,鞣制的,不带毛,湿革	Hides and skins of goats or kids, tanned or crust, without wool or hair on, in the wet state	4106.2100	1458
皮及其坯革,猪的,鞣制的,不带毛,干革(坯革)	Hides and skins of swine, tanned or crust, without wool or hair on, in the dry state (crust)	4106.3200	1458
皮及其坯革,猪的,鞣制的,不带毛,蓝湿的	Hides and skins of swine, tanned or crust, without wool or hair on, wet-blue	4106.3110	1458
皮及其坯革,猪的,鞣制的,不带毛,其他	Hides and skins of swine, tanned or crust, without wool or hair on, nes	4106.3190	1458
皮质(甾)类激素的卤化衍生物,其他	Halogenated derivatives of corticosteroidal hormones, nes	2937.2290	36
皮质甾类激素及其衍生物或结构类似物药品,其他,混合或未混合的,配定剂量或制成零售包装	Corticosteroid hormones, their derivatives and structural analogues medicaments, nes, mixed or unmixed, put up in measured doses or in forms or packings for retail sale	3004.3200	368
啤酒,麦芽酿造的	Beer made from malt	2203.0000	268
啤酒花,经研磨或制成团粒	Hop cones, ground, powdered or in the form of pellets	1210.2000	14
啤酒花,未经研磨也未制成团粒	Hop cones, neither ground nor powdered nor in the form of pellets	1210.1000	14
啤酒酵母	Brewery yeast	2102.1000	28
啤酒桶沥青及类似制品,以松香、树脂酸或植物沥青为基本成分的	Brewers'pitch and similar preparations based on rosin, resin acids or on vegetable pitch	3807.0000	3
琵琶桶,辐射松制的	Barrels, of radiata pine	4416.0010	56
琵琶桶,其他木制的	Barrels, of other wood	4416.0090	56
匹莫林(INN)盐	Pemoline (INN); salts thereof	2934.9100	36
匹那西泮(INN)以及盐	Pinazepam(INN); salts thereof	2933.9100	36
pian			
片、带及厚度(衬背除外)不超过0.2毫米的箔,铅制	Sheets, strip and foil of a thickness (excluding any backing) not exceeding 0.2mm, of lead	7804.1100	16
片簧及簧片,钢铁制,其他	Leaf-springs and leaves thereof, of iron or steel, nes	7320.1090	36
片簧及簧片,钢铁制,汽车用	Leaf-springs and leaves thereof, of iron or steel, for motor vehicles	7320.1020	36
片簧及簧片,钢铁制,铁道车辆用	Leaf-springs and leaves thereof, of iron or steel, for railway locomotives and rollingstock	7320.1010	36
片式烤面包机(多士炉)	Slice pop-up toasters	8516.7220	7
片式烤面包机(多士炉)	Toasters, slice pop-up	8516.7220	7
片梭织机,所织织物宽度超过30厘米的无梭织机	Carrier looms, for weaving fabrics of a with exceeding 30cm, shuttleless type	8446.3030	7
片状粉末,铝的	Powders of lamellar structure; flakes, of aluminium	7603.2000	6
片仔癀	Pien tzu huang	3004.9052	368

P

商品名称	Article Description	税则号列	申报要素
偏二氯乙烯聚合物,初级形状的	Vinylidene chloride polymers, in primary forms	3904.5000	1256
偏硅酸钠	Sodium metasilicates	2839.1100	
偏磷酸	Metaphosphoric acid	2809.2019	6
偏钨酸铵	Ammonium metatungstate	2841.8040	1
偏振材料制的片及板	Polarizing material sheets and plates	9001.2000	6
piao			
漂白机器,纱线、织物及纺织制品用	Bleaching machines, for textile yarns, fabrics or made up textile articles	8451.4000	
漂白机器零件,纱线、织物及纺织制品用	Bleaching machines parts, for textile yarns, fabrics or made up textile articles	8451.9000	
pin			
拼贴画及类似装饰板	Collages and similar decorative plaques	9701.9000	5
频率计,测试频率在12.4吉赫兹以下的,数字式	Frequency meters, of test frequency less than 12.4 GHz, digital	9030.4010	
频率计,其他	Frequency meters, nes	9030.4090	7
频闪观测仪	Stroboscopes	9029.2090	7
频闪观测仪零件、附件	Stroboscopes parts and accessories	9029.9000	3
品红,洋红	Fuchsine as synthetic organic colouring matter	3204.1300	345
ping			
乒乓球	Table-tennis balls	9506.4010	
乒乓球运动用品及器械,其他	Table-tennis articles and equipment, nes	9506.4090	5
平板显示器的制造机器及装置,扩散、氧化、退火及其他热处理设备	Flat panel displays manufacture machines and apparatus, oxidation, diffusion, annealing and other heat treatment equipment	8486.3010	7
平板显示器的制造机器及装置,其他	Flat panel displays manufacture machines and apparatus, nes	8486.3090	7
平板轧材,不锈钢的,宽度小于600毫米,除冷轧外未经进一步加工,厚度在0.35毫米及以下	Flat-rolled products stainless steel, of a width of less than 600mm, not further worked than cold-rolled, of a thickness of 0.35mm or less	7220.2020	468
平板轧材,不锈钢的,宽度小于600毫米,除冷轧外未经进一步加工,厚度在0.35毫米以上但小于3毫米	Flat-rolled products stainless steel, of a width of less than 600mm, not further worked than cold-rolled, of a thickness of more than 0.35mm but less than 3mm	7220.2030	468
平板轧材,不锈钢的,宽度小于600毫米,除冷轧外未经进一步加工,厚度在3毫米及以上	Flat-rolled products stainless steel, of a width of less than 600mm, not further worked than cold-rolled, nes	7220.2040	468
平板轧材,不锈钢的,宽度小于600毫米,除热轧外未经进一步加工,厚度小于4.75毫米	Flat-rolled products stainless steel, of a width of less than 600mm, not further worked than hot-rolled, of a thickness of less than 4.75mm	7220.1200	468

商品名称	Article Description	税则号列	申报要素
平板轧材,不锈钢的,宽度小于 600 毫米,除热轧外未经进一步加工,厚度在 4.75 毫米及以上	Flat-rolled products stainless steel, of a width of less than 600mm, not further worked than hot-rolled, of a thickness of 4.75mm or more	7220.1100	468
平板轧材,不锈钢的,宽度小于 600 毫米,其他	Flat-rolled products stainless steel, of a width of less than 600mm, nes	7220.9000	468
平板轧材,不锈钢的,宽度在 600 毫米及以上,除冷轧外未经进一步加工,厚度超过 1 毫米,但小于 3 毫米	Flat-rolled products of stainless steel, of a width of 600mm or more, not further worked than than cold-rolled, of a thickness exceeding 1mm but less than 3mm	7219.3300	468
平板轧材,不锈钢的,宽度在 600 毫米及以上,除冷轧外未经进一步加工,厚度小于 0.5 毫米	Flat-rolled products of stainless steel, of a width of 600mm or more, not further worked than than cold-rolled, of a thickness of less than 0.5mm	7219.3500	468
平板轧材,不锈钢的,宽度在 600 毫米及以上,除冷轧外未经进一步加工,厚度在 0.5 毫米及以上,但不超过 1 毫米	Flat-rolled products of stainless steel, of a width of 600mm or more, not further worked than than cold-rolled, of a thickness of 0.5mm or more but not exceeding 1mm	7219.3400	468
平板轧材,不锈钢的,宽度在 600 毫米及以上,除冷轧外未经进一步加工,厚度在 3 毫米及以上,但小于 4.75 毫米	Flat-rolled products of stainless steel, of a width of 600mm or more, not further worked than than cold-rolled, of a thickness of 3mm or more but less than 4.75mm	7219.3200	468
平板轧材,不锈钢的,宽度在 600 毫米及以上,除冷轧外未经进一步加工,厚度在 4.75 毫米及以上	Flat-rolled products of stainless steel, of a width of 600mm or more, not further worked than than cold-rolled, of a thickness of 4.75mm or more	7219.3100	468
平板轧材,不锈钢的,宽度在 600 毫米及以上,除热轧外未经进一步加工的非卷材,厚度超过 1 毫米但小于 3 毫米	Flat-rolled products of stainless steel, of a width of 600mm or more, not further worked than hot-rolled, not in coils, of a thickness exceeding 1mm but less than 3mm	7219.2410	468
平板轧材,不锈钢的,宽度在 600 毫米及以上,除热轧外未经进一步加工的非卷材,厚度超过 10 毫米	Flat-rolled products of stainless steel, of a width of 600mm or more, not further worked than hot-rolled, not in coils, of a thickness exceeding 10mm	7219.2100	468
平板轧材,不锈钢的,宽度在 600 毫米及以上,除热轧外未经进一步加工的非卷材,厚度小于 0.5 毫米	Flat-rolled products of stainless steel, of a width of 600mm or more, not further worked than hot-rolled, not in coils, of a thickness of less than 0.5mm	7219.2430	468
平板轧材,不锈钢的,宽度在 600 毫米及以上,除热轧外未经进一步加工的非卷材,厚度在 0.5 毫米及以上,但不超过 1 毫米	Flat-rolled products of stainless steel, of a width of 600mm or more, not further worked than hot-rolled, not in coils, of a thickness of 0.5mm or more but not exceeding 1mm	7219.2420	468
平板轧材,不锈钢的,宽度在 600 毫米及以上,除热轧外未经进一步加工的非卷材,厚度在 3 毫米及以上,但小于 4.75 毫米	Flat-rolled products of stainless steel, of a width of 600mm or more, not further worked than hot-rolled, not in coils, of a thickness of 3mm or more but less than 4.75mm	7219.2300	468

商品名称	Article Description	税则号列	申报要素
平板轧材,不锈钢的,宽度在 600 毫米及以上,除热轧外未经进一步加工的非卷材,厚度在 4.75 毫米及以上,但不超过 10 毫米	Flat-rolled products of stainless steel, of a width of 600mm or more, not further worked than hot-rolled, not in coils, of a thickness of 4.75mm or more but not exceeding 10mm	7219.2200	468
平板轧材,不锈钢的,宽度在 600 毫米及以上,除热轧外未经进一步加工的卷材,厚度超过 10 毫米	Flat-rolled products of stainless steel, of a width of 600mm or more, not further worked than hot-rolled, in coils, of a thickness exceeding 10mm	7219.1100	468
平板轧材,不锈钢的,宽度在 600 毫米及以上,除热轧外未经进一步加工的卷材,厚度在 3 毫米及以上,但小于 4.75 毫米,经酸洗的,按重量计含锰量在 5.5% 及以上的铬锰系不锈钢	Flat-rolled products of stainless steel, of a width of 600mm or more, Not further worked than hot-rolled, in coils, Of a thickness of 3mm or more but less than 4.75mm, Acid pickled, Containing more than 5.5% by weight of manganese of Ferro-chromium-manganese steel	7219.1322	468
平板轧材,不锈钢的,宽度在 600 毫米及以上,除热轧外未经进一步加工的卷材,厚度在 3 毫米及以上,但小于 4.75 毫米,经酸洗的,其他	Flat-rolled products of stainless steel, of a width of 600mm or more, not further worked than hot-rolled, in coils, of a thickness of 3mm or more but less than 4.75mm, acid pickled, nes	7219.1329	468
平板轧材,不锈钢的,宽度在 600 毫米及以上,除热轧外未经进一步加工的卷材,厚度在 3 毫米及以上,但小于 4.75 毫米,未经酸洗的,按重量计含锰量在 5.5% 及以上的铬锰系不锈钢	Flat-rolled products of stainless steel, of a width of 600mm or more, Not further worked than hot-rolled, in coils, Of a thickness of 3mm or more but less than 4.75mm, Not acid picked, Containing more than 5.5% by weight of manganese of Ferro-chromium-manganese steel	7219.1312	468
平板轧材,不锈钢的,宽度在 600 毫米及以上,除热轧外未经进一步加工的卷材,厚度在 3 毫米及以上,但小于 4.75 毫米,未经酸洗的,其他	Flat-rolled products of stainless steel, of a width of 600mm or more, not further worked than hot-rolled, in coils, of a thickness of 3mm or more but less than 4.75mm, not acid picked, nes	7219.1319	468
平板轧材,不锈钢的,宽度在 600 毫米及以上,除热轧外未经进一步加工的卷材,厚度在 3 毫米及以下,经酸洗的,按重量计含锰量在 5.5% 及以上的铬锰系不锈钢	Flat-rolled products of stainless steel, of a width of 600mm or more, not further worked than hot-rolled, in coils, of a thickness of 3mm or less, acid pickled, containing more than 5.5% by weight of manganese of ferro-chromium-manganese steel	7219.1422	468
平板轧材,不锈钢的,宽度在 600 毫米及以上,除热轧外未经进一步加工的卷材,厚度在 3 毫米及以下,经酸洗的,其他	Flat-rolled products of stainless steel, of a width of 600mm or more, not further worked than hot-rolled, in coils, of a thickness of 3mm or less, acid pickled, nes	7219.1429	468
平板轧材,不锈钢的,宽度在 600 毫米及以上,除热轧外未经进一步加工的卷材,厚度在 3 毫米及以下,未经酸洗的,按重量计含锰量在 5.5% 及以上的铬锰系不锈钢	Flat-rolled products of stainless steel, of a width of 600mm or more, not further worked than hot-rolled, in coils, of a thickness of 3mm or less, not acid pickled, containing more than 5.5% by weight of manganese of ferro-chromium-manganese steel	7219.1412	468

商品名称	Article Description	税则号列	申报要素
平板轧材,不锈钢的,宽度在 600 毫米及以上,除热轧外未经进一步加工的卷材,厚度在 3 毫米及以下,未经酸洗的,其他	Flat-rolled products of stainless steel, of a width of 600mm or more, not further worked than hot-rolled, in coils, of a thickness of 3mm or less, not acid pickled, nes	7219.1419	468
平板轧材,不锈钢的,宽度在 600 毫米及以上,除热轧外未经进一步加工的卷材,厚度在 4.75 毫米及以上,但不超过 10 毫米	Flat-rolled products of stainless steel, of a width of 600mm or more, not further worked than hot-rolled, in coils, of a thickness of 4.75mm or more but not exceeding 10mm	7219.1200	468
平板轧材,不锈钢的,宽度在 600 毫米及以上,其他	Flat-rolled products of stainless steel, of a width of 600mm or more, nes	7219.9000	468
平板轧材,高速钢制,宽度小于 600 毫米	Flat-rolled products of high speed steel, of a width of 600mm or less	7226.2000	468
平板轧材,高速钢制,宽度在 600 毫米及以上	Flat-rolled products of high speed steel, of a width of 600mm or more	7225.9910	468
平板轧材,硅电钢制,宽度小于 600 毫米,其他	Flat-rolled products of silicon-electrical steel, of a width of less than 600mm	7226.1900	468
平板轧材,硅电钢制,宽度在 600 毫米及以上,其他	Flat-rolled products of silicon-electrical steel, of a width of 600mm or more, nes	7225.1900	468
平板轧材,合金钢,宽度小于 600 毫米,除冷轧外未经进一步加工,其他	Flat-rolled products of other alloy steel, of a width of less than 600mm, not further worked than cold-rolled, nes	7226.9200	468
平板轧材,合金钢,宽度小于 600 毫米,除热轧外未经进一步加工,其他	Flat-rolled products of other alloy steel, of a width of less than 600mm, not further worked than hot-rolled, nes	7226.9100	468
平板轧材,合金钢,宽度小于 600 毫米,电镀锌的,其他	Flat-rolled products of other alloy steel, of a width of less than 600mm, electrolytically plated or coated with zinc, nes	7226.9910	468
平板轧材,合金钢,宽度小于 600 毫米,其他	Flat-rolled products of other alloy steel, of a width of less than 600mm, nes	7226.9990	468
平板轧材,合金钢,宽度小于 600 毫米,用其他方法镀或涂锌的,其他	Flat-rolled products of other alloy steel, of a width of less than 600mm, otherwise plated or coated with zinc, nes	7226.9920	468
平板轧材,合金钢的,宽度在 600 毫米及以上,除冷轧外未经进一步加工,其他	Flat-rolled products of other alloy steel, of a width of 600mm or more, not further worked than cold-rolled, nes	7225.5000	468
平板轧材,合金钢的,宽度在 600 毫米及以上,电镀或涂锌的,其他	Flat-rolled products of other alloy steel, of a width of 600mm or more, electrolytically plated or coated with zinc, nes	7225.9100	468
平板轧材,合金钢的,宽度在 600 毫米及以上,非卷材,除热轧外未经进一步加工,其他	Flat-rolled products of other alloy steel, of a width of 600mm or more, not further worked than hot-rolled, not in coils, nes	7225.4000	468
平板轧材,合金钢的,宽度在 600 毫米及以上,卷材,除热轧外未经进一步加工,其他	Flat-rolled products of other alloy steel, of a width of 600mm or more, not further worked than hot-rolled, in coils, nes	7225.3000	468

商品名称	Article Description	税则号列	申报要素
平板轧材,合金钢的,宽度在 600 毫米及以上,其他	Flat-rolled products of other alloy steel, of a width of 600mm or more, nes	7225.9990	468
平板轧材,合金钢的,宽度在 600 毫米及以上,用其他方法镀或涂锌的,其他	Flat-rolled products of other alloy steel, of a width of 600mm or more, otherwise plated or coated with zinc, nes	7225.9200	468
平板轧材,取向性硅电钢,宽度小于 600 毫米	Flat-rolled products of grain-oriented silicon-electrical steel, of a width of less than 600mm	7226.1100	468
平板轧材,取向性硅电钢,宽度在 600 毫米及以上	Flat-rolled products of grain-oriented silicon-electrical steel, of a width of 600mm or more	7225.1100	468
平板轧材,铁或非合金钢的,宽度在 600 毫米及以上的,经冷轧,但未经包覆、镀层或涂层,卷材,除冷轧外未经进一步加工,厚度超过 1 毫米,但小于 3 毫米,其他	Flat-rolled products of iron or non-alloy steel, of a width of 600mm or more, cold rolled, not clad, plated or coated, in coils, not further worked than cold-rolled, of a thickness exceeding 1mm but less than 3mm, nes	7209.1690	468
平板轧材,铁或非合金钢的,宽度在 600 毫米及以上的,经冷轧,但未经包覆、镀层或涂层,卷材,除冷轧外未经进一步加工,厚度超过 1 毫米,但小于 3 毫米,屈服强度大于 275 牛顿/平方毫米	Flat-rolled products of iron or non-alloy steel, of a width of 600mm or more, cold rolled, not clad, plated or coated, in coils, not further worked than cold-rolled, of a thickness exceeding 1mm but less than 3mm, of a yield strength exceeding 275N/mm^2	7209.1610	468
平板轧材,铁或非合金钢的,宽度在 600 毫米及以上的,经冷轧,但未经包覆、镀层或涂层,卷材,除冷轧外未经进一步加工,厚度在 3 毫米及以上,其他	Flat-rolled products of iron or non-alloy steel, of a width of 600mm or more, cold rolled, not clad, plated or coated, in coils, not further worked than cold-rolled, of a thickness of 3mm or more, nes	7209.1590	468
平板轧材,铁或非合金钢的,宽度在 600 毫米及以上的,经冷轧,但未经包覆、镀层或涂层,卷材,除冷轧外未经进一步加工,厚度在 3 毫米及以上,屈服强度大于 355 牛顿/平方毫米	Flat-rolled products of iron or non-alloy steel, of a width of 600mm or more, cold rolled, not clad, plated or coated, in coils, not further worked than cold-rolled, of a thickness of 3mm or more, of a yield strength exceeding 355N/mm^2	7209.1510	468
平板轧材,铁或非合金钢的,宽度在 600 毫米及以上的,经热轧,但未经包覆、镀层或涂层,非卷材,除热轧外未经进一步加工,厚度超过 10 毫米,其他	Flat-rolled products of iron or non-alloy steel of a width of 600mm or more, hot-rolled, not clad, plated or coated, not in coils, not further worked than hot-rolled, of a thickness exceeding 10mm, nes	7208.5190	468
平板轧材,铁或非合金钢的,宽度在 600 毫米及以上的,经热轧,但未经包覆、镀层或涂层,非卷材,除热轧外未经进一步加工,厚度超过 50 毫米	Flat-rolled products of iron or non-alloy steel of a width of 600mm or more, hot-rolled, not clad, plated or coated, not in coils, not further worked than hot-rolled, of a thickness exceeding 50mm	7208.5110	468

P

商品名称	Article Description	税则号列	申报要素
平板轧材,铁或非合金钢的,宽度在600毫米及以上的,经热轧,但未经包覆、镀层或涂层,非卷材,除热轧外未经进一步加工,厚度小于3毫米,厚度小于1.5毫米	Flat-rolled products of iron or non-alloy steel of a width of 600mm or more, hot-rolled, not clad, plated or coated, not in coils, not further worked than hot-rolled, of a thickness of less than 3mm, of a thickness of less than 1.5mm	7208.5410	468
平板轧材,铁或非合金钢的,宽度在600毫米及以上的,经热轧,但未经包覆、镀层或涂层,非卷材,除热轧外未经进一步加工,厚度小于3毫米,其他	Flat-rolled products of iron or non-alloy steel of a width of 600mm or more, hot-rolled, not clad, plated or coated, not in coils, not further worked than hot-rolled, of a thickness of less than 3mm, nes	7208.5490	468
平板轧材,铁或非合金钢的,宽度在600毫米及以上的,经热轧,但未经包覆、镀层或涂层,非卷材,除热轧外未经进一步加工,厚度在20毫米以上,但不超过50毫米	Flat-rolled products of iron or non-alloy steel of a width of 600mm or more, hot-rolled, not clad, plated or coated, not in coils, not further worked than hot-rolled, of a thickness exceeding 20mm but not exceeding 50mm	7208.5120	468
平板轧材,铁或非合金钢的,宽度在600毫米及以上的,经热轧,但未经包覆、镀层或涂层,非卷材,除热轧外未经进一步加工,厚度在3毫米及以上,但小于4.75毫米,其他	Flat-rolled products of iron or non-alloy steel of a width of 600mm or more, hot-rolled, not clad, plated or coated, not in coils, not further worked than hot-rolled, of a thickness of 3mm or more but less than 4.75mm, nes	7208.5390	468
平板轧材,铁或非合金钢的,宽度在600毫米及以上的,经热轧,但未经包覆、镀层或涂层,非卷材,除热轧外未经进一步加工,厚度在3毫米及以上,但小于4.75毫米,屈服强度大于355牛顿/平方毫米	Flat-rolled products of iron or non-alloy steel of a width of 600mm or more, hot-rolled, not clad, plated or coated, not in coils, not further worked than hot-rolled, of a thickness of 3mm or more but less than 4.75mm, of a yield strength exceeding $355N/mm^2$	7208.5310	468
平板轧材,铁或非合金钢的,宽度在600毫米及以上的,经热轧,但未经包覆、镀层或涂层,非卷材,除热轧外未经进一步加工,厚度在4.75毫米及以上,但不超过10毫米	Flat-rolled products of iron or non-alloy steel of a width of 600mm or more, hot-rolled, not clad, plated or coated, not in coils, not further worked than hot-rolled, of a thickness of 4.75mm or more but not exceeding 10mm	7208.5200	468
平板轧材,铁或非合金钢的,宽度在600毫米及以上的,经热轧,但未经包覆、镀层或涂层,经酸洗的卷材,除热轧外未经进一步加工,厚度小于3毫米,厚度小于1.5毫米	Flat-rolled products of iron or non-alloy steel of a width of 600mm or more, hot-rolled, not clad, plated or coated, pickled, in coils, not further worked than hot-rolled, of a thickness of less than 3mm, of a thickness of less than 1.5mm	7208.2710	468
平板轧材,铁或非合金钢的,宽度在600毫米及以上的,经热轧,但未经包覆、镀层或涂层,经酸洗的卷材,除热轧外未经进一步加工,厚度小于3毫米,其他	Flat-rolled products of iron or non-alloy steel of a width of 600mm or more, hot-rolled, not clad, plated or coated, pickled in coils, not further worked than hot-rolled, of a thickness of less than 3mm, nes	7208.2790	468

商品名称	Article Description	税则号列	申报要素
平板轧材,铁或非合金钢的,宽度在600毫米及以上的,经热轧,但未经包覆、镀层或涂层,经酸洗的卷材,除热轧外未经进一步加工,厚度在3毫米及以上,但小于4.75毫米,其他	Flat-rolled products of iron or non-alloy steel of a width of 600mm or more, hot-rolled, not clad, plated or coated, pickled, in coils, not further worked than hot-rolled, of a thickness of 3mm or more but less than 4.75mm, nes	7208.2690	468
平板轧材,铁或非合金钢的,宽度在600毫米及以上的,经热轧,但未经包覆、镀层或涂层,经酸洗的卷材,除热轧外未经进一步加工,厚度在3毫米及以上,但小于4.75毫米,屈服强度大于355牛顿/平方毫米	Flat-rolled products of iron or non-alloy steel of a width of 600mm or more, hot-rolled, not clad, plated or coated, pickled, in coils, not further worked than hot-rolled, of a thickness of 3mm or more but less than 4.75mm, of a yield strength exceeding $355N/mm^2$	7208.2610	468
平板轧材,铁或非合金钢的,宽度在600毫米及以上的,经热轧,但未经包覆、镀层或涂层,经酸洗的卷材,除热轧外未经进一步加工,厚度在4.75毫米及以上	Flat-rolled products of iron or non-alloy steel of a width of 600mm or more, hot-rolled, not clad, plated or coated, in coils, not further worked than hot-rolled, pickled, of a thickness of 4.75mm or more	7208.2500	468
平板轧材,铁或非合金钢的,宽度在600毫米及以上的,经热轧,但未经包覆、镀层或涂层,卷材,除热轧外未经进一步加工,厚度超过10毫米	Flat-rolled products of iron or non-alloy steel of a width of 600mm or more, hot-rolled, not clad, plated or coated, in coils, not further worked than hot-rolled, of a thickness exceeding 10mm	7208.3600	468
平板轧材,铁或非合金钢的,宽度在600毫米及以上的,经热轧,但未经包覆、镀层或涂层,卷材,除热轧外未经进一步加工,厚度小于1.5毫米	Flat-rolled products of iron or non-alloy steel of a width of 600mm or more, hot-rolled, not clad, plated or coated, in coils, not further worked than hot-rolled, of a thickness of less than 1.5mm	7208.3910	468
平板轧材,铁或非合金钢的,宽度在600毫米及以上的,经热轧,但未经包覆、镀层或涂层,卷材,除热轧外未经进一步加工,厚度在3毫米及以上,但小于4.75毫米,其他	Flat-rolled products of iron or non-alloy steel of a width of 600mm or more, hot-rolled, not clad, plated or coated, in coils, not further worked than hot-rolled, of a thickness of 3mm or more but less than 4.75mm, nes	7208.3890	468
平板轧材,铁或非合金钢的,宽度在600毫米及以上的,经热轧,但未经包覆、镀层或涂层,卷材,除热轧外未经进一步加工,厚度在3毫米及以上,但小于4.75毫米,屈服强度大于355牛顿/平方毫米	Flat-rolled products of iron or non-alloy steel of a width of 600mm or more, hot-rolled, not clad, plated or coated, in coils, not further worked than hot-rolled, of a thickness of 3mm or more but less than 4.75mm, of a yield strength exceeding 355 N/mm^2	7208.3810	468
平板轧材,铁或非合金钢的,宽度在600毫米及以上的,经热轧,但未经包覆、镀层或涂层,卷材,除热轧外未经进一步加工,厚度在4.75毫米及以上,但不超过10毫米	Flat-rolled products of iron or non-alloy steel of a width of 600mm or more, hot-rolled, not clad, plated or coated, in coils, not further worked than hot-rolled, of a thickness of 4.75mm or more but not exceeding 10mm	7208.3700	468

P

商品名称	Article Description	税则号列	申报要素
平板轧材,铁或非合金钢的,宽度在600毫米及以上的,经热轧,但未经包覆、镀层或涂层,卷材,除热轧外未经进一步加工,其他	Flat-rolled products of iron or non-alloy steel of a width of 600mm or more, hot-rolled, not clad, plated or coated, in coils, not further worked than hot-rolled, nes	7208.3990	468
平板轧材,铁或非合金钢的,宽度在600毫米及以上的,经热轧,但未经包覆、镀层或涂层,其他	Flat-rolled products of iron or non-alloy steel of a width of 600mm or more, hot-rolled, not clad, plated or coated, nes	7208.9000	468
平板轧材,铁或非合金钢的,宽度在600毫米及以上的,经热轧,但未经包覆、镀层或涂层,已轧压花纹,卷状,除热轧外未经进一步加工的	Flat-rolled products of iron or non-alloy steel of a width of 600mm or more, hot-rolled, not clad, plated or coated, in coils, with patterns in relief, not further worked than hot rolled	7208.1000	468
平板轧材,铁或非合金钢的,宽度在600毫米及以上的,经热轧,但未经包覆、镀层或涂层,已轧压花纹的非卷材,除热轧外未经进一步加工	Flat-rolled products of iron or non-alloy steel of a width of 600mm or more, hot-rolled, not clad, plated or coated, not in coils, not further worked than hotrolled, with patterns in relief	7208.4000	468
平板轧材,铁或非合金钢的宽度小于600毫米的,但未经包覆、镀层或涂层,除冷轧外未经进一步加工,按重量计含碳量低于0.25%	Flat-rolled products of iron or non-alloy steel, of a width of less than 600mm, not clad, plated or coated, not further worked than cold-rolled, containing by weight less than 0.25% of carbon	7211.2300	468
平板轧材,铁或非合金钢的宽度小于600毫米的,但未经包覆、镀层或涂层,除冷轧外未经进一步加工,其他	Flat-rolled products of iron or non-alloy steel, of a width of less than 600mm, not clad, plated or coated, not further worked than cold-rolled, nes	7211.2900	468
平板轧材,铁或非合金钢的宽度小于600毫米的,但未经包覆、镀层或涂层,除热轧外未经进一步加工,厚度在4.75毫米及以上,其他	Flat-rolled products of iron or non-alloy steel, of a width of less than 600mm, not clad, plated or coated, not further worked than hot-rolled, of a thickness of 4.75mm or more, nes	7211.1400	468
平板轧材,铁或非合金钢的宽度小于600毫米的,但未经包覆、镀层或涂层,除热轧外未经进一步加工,经四面轧制或在闭合匣内轧制的非卷材,宽度超过150毫米,厚度不小于4毫米,未轧压花纹	Flat-rolled products of iron or non-alloy steel, of a width of less than 600mm, not clad, plated or coated, not further worked than hot-rolled, rolled on four faces or in a closed box pass, of a width exceeding 150mm and a thickness of not less than 4mm, not in coils and without patterns in relief	7211.1300	468
平板轧材,铁或非合金钢的宽度小于600毫米的,但未经包覆、镀层或涂层,除热轧外未经进一步加工,其他	Flat-rolled products of iron or non-alloy steel, of a width of less than 600mm, not clad, plated or coated, not further worked than hot-rolled, nes	7211.1900	468
平板轧材,铁或非合金钢的宽度小于600毫米的,但未经包覆、镀层或涂层,其他	Flat-rolled products of iron or non-alloy steel, of a width of less than 600mm, not clad, plated or coated, nes	7211.9000	468
平板轧材,铁或非合金钢的宽度小于600毫米的,电镀锌的	Flat-rolled products of iron or non-alloy steel, of a width of less than 600mm, electrolytically plated or coated with zinc	7212.2000	468
平板轧材,铁或非合金钢的宽度小于600毫米的,镀或涂其他材料的	Flat-rolled products of iron or non-alloy steel, of a width of less than 600mm, otherwise plated or coated	7212.5000	468

商品名称	Article Description	税则号列	申报要素
平板轧材,铁或非合金钢的宽度小于600毫米的,镀或涂锡的	Flat-rolled products of iron or non-alloy steel, of a width of less than 600mm, plated or coated with tin	7212.1000	468
平板轧材,铁或非合金钢的宽度小于600毫米的,经包覆的	Flat-rolled products of iron or non-alloy steel, of a width of less than 600mm, clad	7212.6000	468
平板轧材,铁或非合金钢的宽度小于600毫米的,涂漆或涂塑的	Flat-rolled products of iron or non-alloy steel, of a width of less than 600mm, painted, varnished or coated with plastics	7212.4000	468
平板轧材,铁或非合金钢的宽度小于600毫米的,用其他方法镀或涂锌的	Flat-rolled products of iron or non-alloy steel, of a width of less than 600mm, otherwise plated or coated with zinc	7212.3000	468
平板轧材,铁或非合金钢的宽度在600毫米及以上的,电镀锌的	Flat-rolled products of iron or non-alloy steel, of a width of 600mm of more, electrolytically plated or coated with zinc	7210.3000	468
平板轧材,铁或非合金钢的宽度在600毫米及以上的,镀或涂铝的,镀或涂铝锌合金的	Flat-rolled products of iron or non-alloy steel, of a width of 600mm of more, plated or coated with aluminium, plated or coated with aluminium-zinc alloys	7210.6100	468
平板轧材,铁或非合金钢的宽度在600毫米及以上的,镀或涂铝的,其他	Flat-rolled products of iron or non-alloy steel, of a width of 600mm of more, plated or coated with aluminium, nes	7210.6900	468
平板轧材,铁或非合金钢的宽度在600毫米及以上的,镀或涂铅的,包括镀铅锡钢板	Flat-rolled products of iron or non-alloy steel, of a width of 600mm of more, plated or coated with lead, including terneplate	7210.2000	468
平板轧材,铁或非合金钢的宽度在600毫米及以上的,镀或涂锡的,厚度小于0.5毫米	Flat-rolled products of iron or non-alloy steel, of a width of 600mm of more, plated or coated with tin, of a thickness of less than 0.5mm	7210.1200	468
平板轧材,铁或非合金钢的宽度在600毫米及以上的,镀或涂锡的,厚度在0.5毫米及以上	Flat-rolled products of iron or non-alloy steel, of a width of 600mm of more, plated or coated with tin, of a thickness of 0.5mm or more	7210.1100	468
平板轧材,铁或非合金钢的宽度在600毫米及以上的,镀或涂氧化铬或铬及氧化铬的	Flat-rolled products of iron or non-alloy steel, of a width of 600mm of more, plated or coated with chromium oxides or with chromium and chromium oxides	7210.5000	468
平板轧材,铁或非合金钢的宽度在600毫米及以上的,经包覆、镀层或涂层,其他	Flat-rolled products of iron or non-alloy steel, of a width of 600mm of more, nes	7210.9000	468
平板轧材,铁或非合金钢的宽度在600毫米及以上的,经冷轧,但未经包覆、镀层或涂层,非卷材,除冷轧外未经进一步加工,厚度超过1毫米,但小于3毫米	Flat-rolled products of iron or non-alloy steel, of a width of 600mm or more, cold rolled, not clad, plated or coated, not in coils, not further worked than cold-rolled, of a thickness exceeding 1mm but less than 3mm	7209.2600	468

P

商品名称	Article Description	税则号列	申报要素
平板轧材,铁或非合金钢的宽度在600毫米及以上的,经冷轧,但未经包覆、镀层或涂层,非卷材,除冷轧外未经进一步加工,厚度小于0.5毫米	Flat-rolled products of iron or non-alloy steel, of a width of 600mm or more, cold rolled, not clad, plated or coated, not in coils, not further worked than cold-rolled, of a thickness of less than 0.5mm	7209.2800	468
平板轧材,铁或非合金钢的宽度在600毫米及以上的,经冷轧,但未经包覆、镀层或涂层,非卷材,除冷轧外未经进一步加工,厚度在0.5毫米及以上,但不超过1毫米	Flat-rolled products of iron or non-alloy steel, of a width of 600mm or more, cold rolled, not clad, plated or coated, not in coils, not further worked than cold-rolled, of a thickness of 0.5mm or more but not exceeding 1mm	7209.2700	468
平板轧材,铁或非合金钢的宽度在600毫米及以上的,经冷轧,但未经包覆、镀层或涂层,非卷材,除冷轧外未经进一步加工,厚度在3毫米及以上	Flat-rolled products of iron or non-alloy steel, of a width of 600mm or more, cold rolled, not clad, plated or coated, not in coils, not further worked than cold-rolled, of a thickness of 3mm or more	7209.2500	468
平板轧材,铁或非合金钢的宽度在600毫米及以上的,经冷轧,但未经包覆、镀层或涂层,卷材,除冷轧外未经进一步加工,厚度小于0.3毫米	Flat-rolled products of iron or non-alloy steel, of a width of 600mm or more, cold rolled, not clad, plated or coated, in coils, not further worked than cold-rolled, of a thickness less than 0.3mm	7209.1810	468
平板轧材,铁或非合金钢的宽度在600毫米及以上的,经冷轧,但未经包覆、镀层或涂层,卷材,除冷轧外未经进一步加工,厚度小于0.5毫米但等于或大于0.3毫米,其他	Flat-rolled products of iron or non-alloy steel, of a width of 600mm or more, cold rolled, not clad, plated or coated, in coils, not further worked than cold-rolled, of a thickness of less than 0.5mm but of 0.3mm or exceeding 0.3mm, nes	7209.1890	468
平板轧材,铁或非合金钢的宽度在600毫米及以上的,经冷轧,但未经包覆、镀层或涂层,卷材,除冷轧外未经进一步加工,厚度在0.5毫米及以上,但不超过1毫米,其他	Flat-rolled products of iron or non-alloy steel, of a width of 600mm or more, cold rolled, not clad, plated or coated, in coils, not further worked than cold-rolled, of a thickness of 0.5mm or more but not exceeding 1mm, nes	7209.1790	468
平板轧材,铁或非合金钢的宽度在600毫米及以上的,经冷轧,但未经包覆、镀层或涂层,卷材,除冷轧外未经进一步加工,厚度在0.5毫米及以上,但不超过1毫米,屈服强度大于275牛顿/平方毫米	Flat-rolled products of iron or non-alloy steel, of a width of 600mm or more, cold rolled, not clad, plated or coated, in coils, not further worked than cold-rolled, of a thickness of 0.5mm or more but not exceeding 1mm, of a yield strength exceeding 275N/mm^2	7209.1710	468
平板轧材,铁或非合金钢的宽度在600毫米及以上的,经冷轧,但未经包覆、镀层或涂层,其他	Flat-rolled products of iron or non-alloy steel, of a width of 600mm or more, cold rolled, not clad, plated or coated, nes	7209.9000	468
平板轧材,铁或非合金钢的宽度在600毫米及以上的,涂漆或涂塑的	Flat-rolled products of iron or non-alloy steel, of a width of 600mm of more, painted, varnished or coated with plastics	7210.7000	468

P

商品名称	Article Description	税则号列	申报要素
平板轧材,铁或非合金钢的宽度在600毫米及以上的,用其他方法镀或涂锌的,其他	Flat-rolled products of iron or non-alloy steel, of a width of 600mm of more, plated or coated with zinc, nes	7210.4900	468
平板轧材,铁或非合金钢的宽度在600毫米及以上的,用其他方法镀或涂锌的,瓦楞形	Flat-rolled products of iron or non-alloy steel, of a width of 600mm of more, plated or coated with zinc, corrugated	7210.4100	468
平地机,发动机输出功率超过235.36千瓦(320马力)的	Levellers, with an engine of an output exceeding 235.36kW(320hp)	8429.2010	57
平地机,其他	Levellers, nes	8429.2090	57
平地机零件	Levellers parts	8431.4990	3
平缝机	Flat seam machines	8452.2110	
平面磨床,在任一坐标的定位精度至少是0.01毫米,加工金属或金属陶瓷用,其他	Flat-surface grinding machines, in which the positioning in any one axis can be set up to an accuracy of at least 0.01mm, for metal or cermets, nes	8460.1900	7
平面磨床,在任一坐标的定位精度至少是0.01毫米,数控的,加工金属或金属陶瓷用	Flat-surface grinding machines, in which the positioning in any one axis can be set up to an accuracy of at least 0.01mm, numerically controlled, for metal or cermets	8460.1100	7
平台式钢琴	Grand pianos	9201.2000	5
平头钉,钢铁制的	Tacks, of iron or steel	7317.0000	36
平头钉,铝制	Tacks, of aluminium	7616.1000	36
平头钉及类似品,铜制或钢铁制带铜头的	Tacks and similar articles, of copper or of iron or steel with heads of copper	7415.1000	56
平网印刷机	Platen screen press	8443.1922	57
平行连结或编结的成片材料、缏条或类似的编结材料产品,稻草制的,其他	Plaiting materials, plaits and similar products of plaiting materials, bound together in parallel strands or woven, in sheet form, of straw, nes	4601.9419	6
平行连结或编结的成片材料、缏条或类似的编结材料产品,其他	Plaiting materials, plaits and similar products of plaiting materials, bound together in parallel strands or woven, in sheet form, nes	4601.9990	6
平行连结或编结的成片材料、缏条或类似的编结材料产品,其他植物材料制的	Plaiting materials, plaits and similar products of plaiting materials, bound together in parallel strands or woven, in sheet form, of other vegetable materials	4601.9499	6
平行连结或编结的成片材料、缏条或类似的编结材料产品,藤制的	Plaiting materials, plaits and similar products of plaiting materials, bound together in parallel strands or woven, in sheet form, of rattan	4601.9390	6
平行连结或编结的成片材料、缏条或类似的编结材料产品,竹制的	Plaiting materials, plaits and similar products of plaiting materials, bound together in parallel strands or woven, in sheet form, of bamboo	4601.9290	6
平型纬编机	Flat weft knitting machines	8447.2020	7
苹果,干的	Apples, dried	0813.3000	34

商品名称	Article Description	税则号列	申报要素
苹果,鲜的	Apples, fresh	0808.1000	125
苹果酒	Cider	2206.0090	2468
苹果汁,白利糖度值不超过20的	Apple juice, of a brix value not exceeding 20	2009.7100	2468
苹果汁,其他	Apple juice, nes	2009.7900	2468
瓶帽,贱金属制	Capsules for bottles, of base metal	8309.9000	256
瓶子或其他容器的洗涤或干燥机器	Bottles or other containers cleaning or drying machinery	8422.2000	
po			
婆罗门参,鲜或冷藏的	Salsify, fresh or chilled	0706.9000	1
破碎机器,齿辊式,泥土、石料、矿石或其他固体矿物质的	Crushing machines, toothing roller type, for earth, stone, ores or other mineral substances	8474.2010	7
破碎机器,泥土、石料、矿石或其他固体矿物质的,其他	Crushing machines, for earth, stone, ores or other mineral substances, nes	8474.2090	7
破碎机器,球磨式,泥土、石料、矿石或其他固体矿物质的	Crushing machines, em-peters type, for earth, stone, ores or other mineral substances	8474.2020	7
pou			
剖开机器,加工木材、软木、骨、硬质橡胶、硬质塑料或类似硬质材料的	Splitting machines, for working wood, cork, bone, hard rubber, hard plastics or similar hard materials	8465.9600	7
pu			
扑克牌	Playing cards	9504.4000	
扑热息痛	Paracetanol	2924.2920	36
铺地制品,纺织材料制,起绒结构的,未制成的,其他	Floor coverings of textile materials, of pile construction, not made up, nes	5702.3900	468
铺地制品,纺织材料制,起绒结构的,制成的,其他	Floor coverings of textile materials, of pile construction, made up, nes	5702.4900	468
铺地制品,化学纤维制,非起绒结构的,未制成的	Floor coverings of man-made textile materials, not of pile construction, not made up	5702.5020	468
铺地制品,化学纤维制,非起绒结构的铺地制品,制成的	Floor coverings of man-made textile materials, not of pile construction, made up	5702.9200	468
铺地制品,化学纤维制,起绒结构的,未制成的	Floor coverings of man-made textile materials, of pile construction, not made up	5702.3200	468
铺地制品,化学纤维制,起绒结构的,制成的	Floor coverings of man-made textile materials, of pile construction, made up	5702.4200	468
铺地制品,其他纺织材料制,非起绒结构的,未制成的,其他	Floor coverings of other textile materials, not of pile construction, not made up, nes	5702.5090	468
铺地制品,其他纺织材料制,非起绒结构的铺地制品,制成的,其他	Floor coverings of other textile materials, not of pile construction, made up, nes	5702.9900	468
铺地制品,塑料的,不论是否胶粘,氯乙烯聚合物制	Floor coverings of plastics, whether or not self-adhesive, of polymers of vinyl chloride	3918.1090	36
铺地制品,塑料的,不论是否胶粘,其他	Floor coverings of plastics, whether or not self-adhesive, nes	3918.9090	36

P

商品名称	Article Description	税则号列	申报要素
铺地制品,羊毛或动物细毛制,非起绒结构的,未制成的	Floor coverings of wool or fine animal hair, not of pile construction, not made up	5702.5010	468
铺地制品,羊毛或动物细毛制,非起绒结构的铺地制品,制成的	Floor coverings of wool or fine animal hair, not of pile construction, made up	5702.9100	468
铺地制品,羊毛或动物细毛制,起绒结构的,未制成的	Floor coverings of wool or fine animal hair, of pile construction, not made up	5702.3100	468
铺地制品,羊毛或动物细毛制,起绒结构的,制成的	Floor coverings of wool or fine animal hair, of pile construction, made up	5702.4100	468
铺地制品,椰壳纤维制的	Floor coverings of coconut fibres(coir)	5702.2000	468
铺地制品,以织物为底布经涂布或覆面的	Floor coverings consisting of a coating or covering applied on a textile backing	5904.9000	
铺地制品,以纸或纸板为底制成的	Floor coverings on a base of paper or of paperboard, whether or not cut to size	4823.9010	68
铺地制品及门垫,硫化橡胶(硬质橡胶除外)的	Floor coverings and mats of vulcanized rubber other than hard rubber	4016.9100	
铺地砖,建筑用	Flooring blocks for building	6904.1000	5
铺面砖,陶瓷的,上釉的,其最大表面以可置入边长小于7厘米的方格为限	Ceramic paving, glazed, the largest surface area of which is capable of being enclosed in a square the side of which is less than 7cm	6908.1000	5
铺面砖,陶瓷的,未上釉的,其最大表面以可置入边长小于7厘米的方格为限	Ceramic paving, unglazed, the largest surface area of which is capable of being enclosed in a square the side of which is less than 7cm	6907.1000	5
葡糖酸及其盐和酯	Gluconic acid, its salts and esters	2918.1600	36
葡萄,干的	Grapes, dried	0806.2000	24
葡萄,鲜的	Grapes, fresh	0806.1000	1245
葡萄酒,鲜葡萄酿造的,其他	Wine of fresh grapes, nes	2204.2900	24568
葡萄酒,鲜葡萄酿造的,其他,加植物或香料的	Wine of fresh grapes, nes, flavoured with plants or aromatic substances	2205.9000	248
葡萄酒,鲜葡萄酿造的,装入2升及以下容器的	Wine of fresh grapes, nes, in containers holding 2L or less	2204.2100	24568
葡萄酒,鲜葡萄酿造的,装入2升及以下容器的,加植物或香料的	Wine of fresh grapes, in containers holding 2L or less, flavoured with plants or aromatic substances	2205.1000	248
葡萄酒渣	Wine lees	2307.0000	
葡萄糖,按重量计干燥状态的果糖含量在20%及以上,但在50%以下	Glucose, containing in the dry state at least 20% but less than 50% by weight of fructose	1702.4000	6
葡萄糖,不含果糖或按重量计干燥状态的果糖含量在20% 以下	Glucose, not containing fructose or containing in the dry state less than 20% by weight of fructose	1702.3000	36
葡萄糖浆,按重量计干燥状态的果糖含量在20%及以上,但在50%以下	Glucose syrup, containing in the dry state at least 20% but less than 50% by weight of fructose	1702.4000	6
葡萄糖浆,不含果糖或按重量计干燥状态的果糖含量在20% 以下	Glucose syrup, not containing fructose or containing in the dry state less than 20% by weight of fructose	1702.3000	36
葡萄柚	Grapefruit	0805.4000	14

P

商品名称	Article Description	税则号列	申报要素
葡萄柚(包括柚)汁,白利糖度值不超过20的	Grapefruit(including pomelo) juice, of a brix value not exceeding 20	2009.2100	2468
葡萄柚(包括柚)汁,其他	Grapefruit(including pomelo) juice, nes	2009.2900	2468
葡萄汁,包括酿酒葡萄汁,白利糖度值不超过20的	Grape juice(including grape must), of a brix value not exceeding 20	2009.6100	2468
葡萄汁,包括酿酒葡萄汁,其他	Grape juice, nes	2009.6900	2468
普洱茶,内包装每件净重不超过3千克	Puer tea, in immediate packings of a content not exceeding 3kg	0902.3020	248
普洱茶,其他	Puer tea, nes	0902.4020	248
普拉西泮(INN),以及盐	Prazepam (INN); salts thereof	2933.9100	36
普鲁卡因	Procaine	2922.4991	36

P

Q

商品名称	Article Description	税则号列	申报要素
qi			
七氯(ISO)	Heptachlor (ISO)	2903.5200	36
七氯氟丙烷	Heptachlorofluoropropane	2903.4540	36
漆工用填料	Painters'fillings	3214.1090	3
漆皮及层压漆皮	Patent leather and patent laminated leather	4114.2000	1458
齐多夫定及它们的盐	Zidovudine and their salts	2938.9010	34
齐培丙醇(INN)以及盐	Zipeprol(INN);salts thereof	2933.5500	36
麒麟菜,干的	Eucheuma,dried	1212.2061	14
麒麟菜,其他	Eucheuma,nes	1212.2069	14
起动电机,点燃式或压燃式内燃发动机用的,其他	Starter motors, for electrical ignition or starting equipment,nes	8511.4099	7
起动电机,机车、航空器及船舶用,点燃式或压燃式内燃发动机用的	Starter motors,for locomotives, aircraft or ships,for electrical ignition or starting equipment	8511.4010	7
起落架及其零件	Under-carriages and parts thereof,of aircraft	8803.2000	3
起绒及绳绒织物,毛圈及狭幅织物除外,化学纤维制,不割绒的经起绒织物(棱纹绸)	Pile and chenille woven fabrics, other than terry or narrow fabrics, of man-made fibres, warp pile fabrics,èpinglè(uncut)	5801.3400	468
起绒及绳绒织物,毛圈及狭幅织物除外,化学纤维制,不割绒的纬起绒织物	Pile and chenille woven fabrics, other than terry or narrow fabrics,of man-made fibres,uncut weft pile fabrics	5801.3100	468
起绒及绳绒织物,毛圈及狭幅织物除外,化学纤维制,割绒的灯芯绒	Pile and chenille woven fabrics, other than terry or narrow fabrics,of man-made fibres,cut corduroy	5801.3200	468
起绒及绳绒织物,毛圈及狭幅织物除外,化学纤维制,割绒的经起绒织物	Pile and chenille woven fabrics, other than terry or narrow fabrics, of man-made fibres, warp pile fabrics, cut	5801.3500	468
起绒及绳绒织物,毛圈及狭幅织物除外,化学纤维制,绳绒织物	Pile and chenille woven fabrics, other than terry or narrow fabrics,of man-made fibres,chenille fabrics	5801.3600	468
起绒及绳绒织物,毛圈及狭幅织物除外,化学纤维制,纬起绒织物,其他	Pile and chenille woven fabrics, other than terry or narrow fabrics, of man-made fibres, weft pile fabrics,nes	5801.3300	468
起绒及绳绒织物,毛圈及狭幅织物除外,棉制,不割绒的经起绒织物(棱纹绸)	Pile and chenille woven fabrics, other than terry or narrow fabrics,of cotton,warp pile fabrics,èpinglè (uncut)	5801.2400	468
起绒及绳绒织物,毛圈及狭幅织物除外,棉制,不割绒的纬起绒织物	Pile and chenille woven fabrics, other than terry or narrow fabrics,of cotton,uncut weft pile fabrics	5801.2100	468
起绒及绳绒织物,毛圈及狭幅织物除外,棉制,割绒的灯芯绒	Pile and chenille woven fabrics, other than terry or narrow fabrics,of cotton,cut corduroy	5801.2200	468

商品名称	Article Description	税则号列	申报要素
起绒及绳绒织物,毛圈及狭幅织物除外,棉制,割绒的经起绒织物	Pile and chenille woven fabrics, other than terry or narrow fabrics, of cotton, warp pile fabrics, cut	5801.2500	468
起绒及绳绒织物,毛圈及狭幅织物除外,棉制,绳绒织物	Pile and chenille woven fabrics, other than terry or narrow fabrics, of cotton, chenille fabrics	5801.2600	468
起绒及绳绒织物,毛圈及狭幅织物除外,棉制,纬起绒织物,其他	Pile and chenille woven fabrics, other than terry or narrow fabrics, of cotton, weft pile fabrics, nes	5801.2300	468
起绒及绳绒织物,毛圈及狭幅织物除外,其他	Pile and chenille woven fabrics, other than terry or narrow fabrics, nes	5801.9090	468
起绒及绳绒织物,毛圈及狭幅织物除外,丝及绢丝制	Pile and chenille woven fabrics, other than terry or narrow fabrics, of silk or silk waste	5801.9010	468
起绒及绳绒织物,毛圈及狭幅织物除外,羊毛或动物细毛制	Pile and chenille woven fabrics, other than terry or narrow fabrics, of wool or fine animal hair	5801.1000	468
起绒织物,针织或钩编的,化学纤维制	Pile fabrics, of man-made fibres, knitted or crocheted	6001.9200	46
起绒织物,针织或钩编的,棉制	Pile fabrics, of cotton, knitted or crocheted	6001.9100	46
起绒织物,针织或钩编的,其他纺织材料制	Pile fabrics, of textile materials, knitted or crocheted, nes	6001.9900	46
起酥油	Shortening oil	1517.9010	246
起重车,全路面,最大起重重量不超过50吨	Crane lorries of all-road, of maxium lifting capacity not more than 50 tons	8705.1021	7
起重车,全路面,最大起重重量超过100吨	Crane lorries of all-road, of a maxium lifting capacity exceeding 100 tons	8705.1023	7
起重车,全路面,最大起重重量超过50吨,但不超过100吨	Crane lorries of all-road, of a maxium lifting capacity exceeding 50 tons but not exceeding 100 tons	8705.1022	7
起重车,最大起重重量不超过50吨,其他	Crane lorries, of maxium lifting capacity not more than 50 tons, nes	8705.1091	7
起重车,最大起重重量超过100吨,其他	Crane lorries, of a maxium lifting capacity exceeding 100 tons, nes	8705.1093	7
起重车,最大起重重量超过50吨,但不超过100吨,其他	Crane lorries, of a maxium lifting capacity exceeding 50 tons but not exceeding 100 tons, nes	8705.1092	7
起重船	Floating cranes	8905.9090	37
起重机,供装于公路车辆的	Cranes, designed for mounting on road vehicles	8426.9100	7
起重机,固定支架的高架移动式,其他	Cranes on fixed support, overhead travelling, nes	8426.1190	7
起重机,桁架桥式	Cranes, transporter cranes	8426.1990	7
起重机,龙门式	Cranes, gantry cranes	8426.1930	7
起重机,履带式	Cranes, crawler cranes	8426.4910	7
起重机,门座式	Cranes, portal cranes	8426.3000	7
起重机,其他	Cranes, nes	8426.9900	7
起重机,塔式	Cranes, tower cranes	8426.2000	7
起重机,通用型,桥式	Cranes, bridge cranes, all-purpose	8426.1120	7
起重机,自推进的,带胶轮的,其他	Cranes, self-propelled, on tyres, nes	8426.4190	7
起重机,自推进的,轮胎式	Cranes, self-propelled, wheel mounted	8426.4110	7
起重机,自推进的,其他	Cranes, self-propelled, nes	8426.4990	7

商品名称	Article Description	税则号列	申报要素
起重机,座式旋臂的	Cranes,pedestal jib cranes	8426.3000	7
起重机车,铁道及电车道用	Cranes,for railway or tramway maintenance or service	8604.0099	37
起重机的零件,倒卸式的	Skip hoists parts	8431.3100	3
起重机零件	Cranes parts	8431.4990	3
气动工具,手提式,其他	Pneumatic tools,working in the hand,nes	8467.1900	57
气动工具,手提式,旋转式(包括旋转冲击式的)	Pneumatic tools, working in the hand, rotary type (including combined rotarypercussion)	8467.1100	57
气动工具用零件,手提式	Pneumatic tools parts,for hand tools	8467.9200	3
气量计,生产或供应计量仪表,其他	Gas meters,supply or production meters,nes	9028.1090	7
气量计零件、附件,工业用	Gas meter parts and accessories,for industrial use	9028.9010	3
气量计零件、附件,其他	Gas meter parts and accessories,nes	9028.9090	3
气流杯	Open-end rotors	8448.3910	3
气枪	Air or gas guns	9304.0000	
气枪弹丸	Air gun pellets	9306.2900	3
气球	Balloons	8801.0090	
气手枪	Air or gas pistols	9304.0000	
气体分析仪	Gas analysis apparatus	9027.1000	
气体回收器,过热水锅炉的辅助设备	Gas recoverers, auxiliary plant for use with superheated water boilers	8404.1010	3
气体回收器,集中供暖用的热水锅炉的辅助设备	Gas recoverers, auxiliary plant for use with central heating boilers	8404.1020	3
气体回收器,蒸汽锅炉的辅助设备	Gas recoverers,auxiliary plant for use with steam or other vapour generating watertube boilers	8404.1010	3
气体压缩机零件	Gas compressors parts	8414.9090	23
气体压缩机,其他	Gas compressors,nes	8414.8090	23
气相色谱仪	Gas chromatographs instruments	9027.2011	
气压的自动调节或控制仪器及装置,其他	Pneumatic automatic regulating or controlling instruments and apparatus,nes	9032.8100	7
气压动力装置,其他	Pneumatic power engines and motors,nes	8412.3900	27
气压计	Barometers	9025.8000	3
气压计零件、附件	Barometers parts and accessories	9025.9000	7
气压升降机及输送机	Pneumatic elevators and conveyors	8428.2000	7
汽酒	Wine of fresh grapes,sparkling	2204.1000	24568
汽轮机,船舶动力用	Steam or vapour turbines for marine propulsion	8406.1000	3
汽轮机,船舶动力用	Turbines for marine propulsion	8406.1000	3
汽轮机,输出功率不超过40兆瓦的	Steam or vapour turbines,of an output not exceeding 40 MW	8406.8200	3
汽轮机,输出功率不超过40兆瓦的	Turbines,of an output not exceeding 40 MW	8406.8200	3
汽轮机,输出功率超过100兆瓦,但不超过350兆瓦的	Steam or vapour turbines,of an output exceeding 100 MW but not exceeding 350 MW	8406.8120	3
汽轮机,输出功率超过100兆瓦,但不超过350兆瓦的	Turbines, of an output exceeding 100 MW but not exceeding 350 MW	8406.8120	3

Q

商品名称	Article Description	税则号列	申报要素
汽轮机,输出功率超过350兆瓦的	Steam or vapour turbines, of an output exceeding 350 MW	8406.8130	3
汽轮机,输出功率超过350兆瓦的	Turbines, of an output exceeding 350 MW	8406.8130	3
汽轮机,输出功率超过40兆瓦,但不超过100兆瓦的	Steam or vapour turbines, of an output exceeding 40 MW but not exceeding 100MW	8406.8110	3
汽轮机,输出功率超过40兆瓦,但不超过100兆瓦的	Turbines, of an output exceeding 40 MW but not exceeding 100 MW	8406.8110	3
汽轮机零件	Steam or vapour turbines parts	8406.9000	3
汽轮机零件	Turbines parts	8406.9000	3
汽水,加味、加糖或其他甜物质的	Aerated waters, containing added sugar or other sweetening matter or flavoured	2202.1000	248
汽水,未加糖或其他甜物质及未加味的	Aerated waters, not containing added sugar or other sweetening matter or flavoured	2201.1020	28
汽艇,但装有舷外发动机的除外,娱乐或运动用	Motorboats, other than outboard motorboats for pleasure or sports	8903.9200	58
槭糖	Maple sugar	1702.2000	
槭糖浆	Maple syrup	1702.2000	
契约保管箱及类似品,带锁,贱金属制	Safe deposit lockers for deed boxes and the like, of base metal	8303.0000	256
器官及其分泌物的提取物	Organs extracts and secretions	3001.2000	34
qian			
千分尺	Micrometers	9017.3000	
千斤顶,其他	Jacks, nes	8425.4910	78
千斤顶,液压的	Jacks, hydraulic	8425.4210	78
千斤顶系统,车库中固定使用的	Jacking systems of a type used in garages, built-in	8425.4100	78
钎焊机器及装置,其他	Brazing or soldering machines and apparatus, nes	8515.1900	
钎焊机器及装置零件	Brazing or soldering machines and apparatus	8515.9000	3
牵引车,电动的,短距离运输货物的,未装有提升或搬运设备	Tractors, electrical, not fitted with lifting or handling equipment, for short distance transport of goods	8709.1110	
牵引车,其他	Tractors, nes	8701.9090	5
牵引车,自驱动的,短距离运输货物的,未装有提升或搬运设备	Tractors, self-propelled, not fitted with lifting or handling equipment, for short distance transport of goods	8709.1910	
铅,精炼的	Lead, refined	7801.1000	46
铅,未锻轧,按重量计所含其他元素是以锑为主的	Lead unwrought, containing by weight antimony as the principal other element	7801.9100	46
铅,未锻轧,其他	Lead unwrought, nes	7801.9900	46
铅笔	Pencils	9609.1010	
铅笔,活动铅笔	Pencils, propelling or sliding	9608.4000	
铅笔刀及其刀片	Pencil sharpeners and blades there of	8214.1000	256
铅笔套	Pencil-holders	9608.9920	
铅笔芯,黑的或其他颜色的	Pencil leads, black or other colour	9609.2000	

商品名称	Article Description	税则号列	申报要素
铅橙	Orange lead	2824.9010	
铅丹	Red lead	2824.9010	
铅的氧化物,其他	Lead oxides, nes	2824.9090	
铅黄	Litharge	2824.1000	
铅矿砂及其精矿	Lead ores and concentrates	2607.0000	146
铅酸蓄电池,其他	Lead-acid accumulators, nes	8507.2000	68
铅酸蓄电池,用于起动活塞式发动机	Lead-acid accumulators, of a kind used for starting piston engines	8507.1000	68
铅酸蓄电池用零件	Lead-acid accumulators parts	8507.9010	3
铅制品,其他	Lead articles of lead, nes	7806.0090	16
前铲装载机	Front-end shovel loaders	8429.5100	57
前列腺素及其衍生物和结构类似物	Prostaglandins, their derivatives and structural analogues	2937.5000	36
前腿及其肉块,猪的,冻的,带骨	Shoulders and cuts thereof, with bone in, of swine, frozen	0203.2200	14
前腿及其肉块,猪的,鲜或冷的,带骨	Shoulders and cuts thereof, with bone in, of swine, fresh or chilled	0203.1200	14
前腿及其肉块,猪的,制作或保藏的	Shoulders and cuts thereof, of swine, prepared or preserved	1602.4200	48
前围,机动车辆的	Frontal appearance of bodies, of the motor vehicles	8708.2954	3
前装枪	Muzzle-loading firearms	9303.1000	
钱包、钱夹,以皮革、再生皮革或漆皮作面	Wallets, purses, with outer surface of leather, of composition leather or of patent leather	4202.3100	256
钱包、钱夹,以塑料片或纺织材料作面	Wallets, purses, with outer surface of plastic sheeting or of textile materials	4202.3200	256
钱币兑换机	Money-changing machines	8476.8900	5
钳子及类似工具	Pincers and similar tools	8203.2000	256
钳子及类似工具	Pliers and similar tools	8203.2000	256
潜水式钻探或生产平台	Submersible drilling or production platforms	8905.2000	
潜水箱	Coffer-dams	8907.9000	5
潜望镜式望远镜	Periscopes	9013.1000	
茜素	Alizarin	3204.1200	345
嵌缝胶及其他类似胶粘剂	Caulking compounds and other mastics	3214.1090	3
qiang			
强化木,成块、板、条或异型的	Densified wood, in blocks, plates, strips or profile shapes	4413.0000	14
强韧箱纸板(再生挂面纸板),未经涂布的,每平方米重量超过150克	Testliner (recycled liner board), uncoated, weighing more than $150g/m^2$	4805.2500	
强韧箱纸板(再生挂面纸板),未经涂布的,每平方米重量在150克及以下	Testliner (recycled liner board), uncoated, weighing $150g/m^2$ or less	4805.2400	
抢修车	Breakdown lorries	8705.9090	7

Q

商品名称	Article Description	税则号列	申报要素
羟氨苄青霉素	Amoxycillin	2941.1091	
羟氨苄青霉素三水酸	Amoxycillin trihydrate	2941.1092	
羟氨苄青霉素药品，混合或未混合的，配定剂量或制成零售包装	Amoxycillin medicaments, mixed or unmixed, put up in measured doses or in forms or packings for retail sale	3004.1012	368
羟氨苄青霉素药品，两种或两种以上成分混合而成的，未配定剂量或制成零售包装	Amoxycillin medicaments, consisting of two or more constituents which have been mixed together, not put up in measured doses or in forms or packings for retail sale	3003.1012	368
羟考酮(INN)及盐	Oxycodone(INN) and salts	2939.1100	34
羟吗啡酮(INN)及盐	Oxymorphone(INN) and salts	2939.1100	34
羟硅铍石	Bertrandite	2617.9090	146
qiao			
锹	Spades	8201.1000	256
荞麦	Buckwheat	1008.1000	3
桥梁及桥梁体段，钢铁的	Bridges and bridge-sections, of iron or steel	7308.1000	6
桥梁及桥梁体段，铝制	Bridges and bridge-sections, of aluminium	7610.9000	56
桥式起重机，通用型	Bridge cranes, all-purpose	8426.1120	7
巧克力，白色的	Chocolate, white	1704.9000	258
巧克力，不夹心，块状或条状的	Chocolate, Not filled, in blocks, slabs or bars	1806.3200	12468
巧克力，夹心，块状或条状的	Chocolate, filled, in blocks, slabs or bars	1806.3100	12468
巧克力，其他	Chocolate, nes	1806.9000	268
巧克力及其他含可可的食品，其他，重量超过2千克的块状或条状含可可食品，或液状、膏状、粉状、粒状或其他散装形状的含可可食品，容器包装或内包装每件净重超过2千克的	Chocolate and other food preparations containing cocoa, nes, in blocks, slabs or bars weighing more than 2kg or in liquid, paste, powder, granular or other bulk form in containers or immediate packings, of a content exceeding 2kg	1806.2000	1268
巧克力酱，重量小于2kg	Chocolate spreads, of a weight less than 2kg	1806.9000	268
巧克力生产机器	Chocolate manufacture machinery	8438.2000	
巧克力生产机器的零件	Chocolate manufacture machinery parts	8438.9000	3
qie			
切菜刀	Mincing knives	8214.9000	256
切齿机，切削金属或金属陶瓷用，其他	Gear cutting machines, for removing metal or cermets, nes	8461.4090	7
切齿机，数控的，切削金属或金属陶瓷用	Gear cutting machines, numerically controlled, for removing metal or cermets	8461.4010	7
切断机，化学纤维的	Cutting machinery, for man-made filaments	8444.0050	
切断机，切削金属或金属陶瓷用	Cutting-off machines, for removing metal or cermets	8461.5000	7
切断机的辅助机器，化学纤维的	Cutting machinery auxiliary, for man-made filaments	8448.1900	3
切割机，玻璃冷加工用	Cutting-off machines, for cold-working glass or glassware	8464.9011	7

Q

商品名称	Article Description	税则号列	申报要素
切割设备,单晶硅柱或硅晶片的制造机器及装置	Sawing machines, boules or wafers manufacture machines and apparatus	8486.1030	7
切管器	Pipe-cutters, hand tools	8203.4000	256
切片机器,加工木材、软木、骨、硬质橡胶、硬质塑料或类似硬质材料的	Slicing machines, for working wood, cork, bone, hard rubber, hard plastics or similar hard materials	8465.9600	7
切肉刀	Choppers	8214.9000	256
切削成形机器,加工木材、软木、骨、硬质橡胶、硬质塑料或类似硬质材料的	Moulding machines, for working wood, cork, bone, hard rubber, hard plastics or similar hard materials	8465.9200	7
切削机床,切削金属或金属陶瓷用,其他	Removing machine-tools, for metal or cermets, nes	8461.9090	7
切削油制剂,以润滑剂为基本成分的,含有石油或从沥青矿物提取的油类	Cutting-oil preparations, based on lubricants, containing petroleum oils or oils obtained from bituminous minerals	3403.1900	2368
切削油制剂,以润滑剂为基本成分的,其他	Cutting-oil preparations, based on lubricants, nes	3403.9900	2368
切纸机	Cutting machines for making up paper pulp, paper or paperboard	8441.1000	
切纸机	Paper cutting machines	8441.1000	
切纸机用零件	Cutting machines parts	8441.9010	
茄子,鲜或冷藏的	Aubergines (eggplants), fresh or chilled	0709.3000	1
qin			
芹菜,但块根芹除外,鲜或冷藏的	Celery other than celeriac, fresh or chilled	0709.4000	1
芹盐	Celery salt	2103.9090	268
揿扣	Fasteners for pressing or snapping	9606.1000	5
揿扣及其零件	Press-fasteners, snap-fasteners and press-studs and parts thereof	9606.1000	5
qing			
青葱,鲜或冷藏的	Shallots, fresh or chilled	0703.1020	1
青蒿	Southernwood	1211.9035	34
青蒿素及其衍生物药品,混合或未混合的,配定剂量或制成零售包装	Artemisinins and their derivatives medicaments, mixed or unmixed, put up in measured doses or in forms or packings for retail sale	3004.9060	368
青蒿素及其衍生物药品,两种或两种以上成分混合而成的,未配定剂量或制成零售包装	Artemisinins and their derivatives medicaments, consisting of two or more constituents which have been mixed together, not put up in measured doses or in forms or packings for retail sale	3003.9020	368
青霉素 V	Penicillin V	2941.1094	
青霉素 V 药品,混合或未混合的,配定剂量或制成零售包装	Penicillin V medicaments, mixed or unmixed, put up in measured doses or in forms of packings for retail sale	3004.1013	368

商品名称	Article Description	税则号列	申报要素
青霉素V药品,两种或两种以上成分混合而成的,未配定剂量或制成零售包装	Penicillin V medicaments, consisting of two or more constituents which have been mixed together, not put up in measured doses or in forms of packings for retail sale	3003.1013	368
青霉素和具有青霉烷酸结构的青霉素衍生物及其盐,其他	Penicillins and their derivatives with a penicillanic acid structure; salts thereof, nes	2941.1099	
青霉素及其衍生物药品,其他,混合或未混合的,配定剂量或制成零售包装	Penicillins and their derivatives medicaments, nes, mixed or unmixed, put up in measured doses or in forms of packings for retail sale	3004.1019	368
青霉素及其衍生物药品,其他,两种或两种以上成分混合而成的,未配定剂量或制成零售包装	Penicillins and their derivatives medicaments, nes, consisting of two or more constituents which have been mixed together, not put up in measured doses or in forms of packings for retail sale	3003.1019	368
青霉烷酸结构的青霉素衍生物或链霉素及其衍生物的药品,混合或未混合的,配定剂量或制成零售包装	Penicillanic acid structure, or streptomycins or their derivatives medicaments, mixed or unmixed, put up in measured doses or in forms of packings for retail sale	3004.1090	368
青霉烷酸结构的青霉素衍生物或链霉素及其衍生物的药品,两种或两种以上成分混合而成的,未配定剂量或制成零售包装	Penicillanic acid structure, or streptomycins or their derivatives medicaments, consisting of two or more constituents which have been mixed together, not put up in measured doses or in forms of packings for retail sale	3003.1090	368
青石棉	Crocidolite	2524.1000	148
青石棉为基本成分或以石棉和碳酸镁为基本成分的混合物	Crocidolite mixtures with a basis of crocidoliteor with a basis of crocidolite and magnesium carbonate	6812.8000	56
青石棉纤维,已加工的	Crocidolite fibres, fabricated	6812.8000	56
青石棉制品,以青石棉为基本成分或以青石棉和碳酸镁混合物为基本成分的	Crocidolite articles of mixtures with a basis of crocidolite or with a basis of crocidolite and magnesium carbonate	6812.8000	56
青铜	Bronze	7403.2200	146
氢	Hydrogen	2804.1000	
氢氟酸	Hydrofluoric acid	2811.1100	6
氢化可的松	Hydrocortisone	2937.2100	36
氢化物,不论是否已有化学定义	Hydrides, whether or not chemically defined	2850.0000	
氢可酮(INN)及盐	Hydrocodone(INN) and salts	2939.1100	34
氢吗啡酮(INN)及盐	Hydromorphone(INN) and salts	2939.1100	34
氢氰酸	Hydrocyanic acid	2811.1910	6
氢氧化钾	Potassium hydroxide	2815.2000	136
氢氧化锂	Lithium hydroxide	2825.2010	
氢氧化铝	Aluminium hydroxide	2818.3000	26
氢氧化镁	Magnesium hydroxide	2816.1000	
氢氧化钠,固体	Sodium hydroxide, solid	2815.1100	136

商品名称	Article Description	税则号列	申报要素
氢氧化钠,水溶液	Sodium hydroxide, in aqueous solution	2815. 1200	136
氢氧化钠浓溶液	Soda lye	2815. 1200	136
氢氧化铈	Cerium hydroxide	2846. 1020	
轻便锻炉	Portable forges	8205. 8000	256
轻柴油	Light diesel oil	2710. 1921	6
轻烧镁	Magnesia, light-burned	2519. 9030	146
轻油及其制品,其他	Light oils and preparations, nes	2710. 1199	6
轻质涂布纸,书写、印刷或类似用途的纸及纸板,所含用机械或化学-机械方法制得的纤维超过全部纤维重量的10%,单面或双面涂布高岭土或其他无机物质的	Light-weight coated paper, of a kind used for writing, printing or other graphic purposes, of which more than 10% by weight of the total fibre content consists of fibres obtained by a mechanical or chemi-mechanical process, coated on one or both sides with kaolin or other inorganic substances	4810. 2200	14568
轻舟,充气的	Canoes, inflatable	8903. 1000	58
轻舟,其他	Canoes, nes	8903. 9900	58
清洁机器,对蛋类、水果或其他农产品的	Cleaning machines for eggs, fruit or other agricultural produce	8433. 6000	
清洁机器,种子、谷物或干豆用	Cleaning machines for seed, grain or dried leguminous vegetables	8437. 1090	3
清洁机器零件,对蛋类、水果或其他农产品的	Cleaning machines parts, for egg, fruit or other agricultural produce	8433. 9090	
清洁机器零件,种子、谷物或干豆用	Cleaning machines parts, for seed, grain or dried leguminous vegetables	8437. 9000	3
清凉油	Essential balm	3004. 9054	368
清梳联合机	Blowing-carding machinery, for cotton type fibres	8445. 1111	7
清水马蹄罐头,用醋或醋酸以外的其他方法制作或保藏的,未冷冻	Water chestnut, in airtight containers, prepared or preserved otherwise than by vinegar or acetic acid, not frozen	2005. 9910	1248
清洗装置,平板显示器的制造机器及装置,其他	Cleaning apparatus, flat panel displays manufacture machines and apparatus, nes	8486. 3049	7
鲭鱼,冻的	Mackerel (Scomber scombrus, Scomber australasicus, scomber japonicus), frozen	0303. 7400	18
鲭鱼,鲜或冷的	Mackerel (Scomber scombrus, Scomber australasicus, Scomber japonicus), fresh or chilled	0302. 6400	18
鲭鱼,制作或保藏的,整条或切块,但未绞碎	Mackerel, prepared or preserved, whole or in pieces, but not minced	1604. 1500	48
氰氨化钙	Calcium cyanamide	3102. 9010	68
氰化汞	Mercuric cyanide	2852. 0000	
氰化钾	Potassium cyanide	2837. 1910	6
氰化钠	Sodium cyanide	2837. 1110	6
氰化物及氧氰化物,其他,无机的	Cyanides and cyanide oxides, nes, inorganic	2837. 1990	6
氰络合物	Complex cyanides	2837. 2000	6

Q

商品名称	Article Description	税则号列	申报要素
氰酸盐	Cyanates	2842.9010	
庆大霉素及其衍生物以及它们的盐	Gentamycin and its derivatives; salts thereof	2941.9010	
qiong			
琼脂	Agaragar	1302.3100	5
qiu			
秋千	Swings	9508.9000	5
球,体育用品,其他	Balls, sports articles, nes	9506.6900	5
球茎,其他,休眠的	Corms, nes, dormant	0601.1099	135
球茎,生长或开花的	Corms, in growth or in flower	0601.2000	
球茎,种用,休眠的	Corms, seed, dormant	0601.1091	135
球茎甘蓝,鲜或冷藏的	Kohlrabi, fresh or chilled	0704.9090	1
球衣,针织或钩编的,化学纤维制	Jerseys, knitted or crocheted, of man-made fibres	6110.3000	2456
球衣,针织或钩编的,喀什米尔山羊细毛制	Jerseys, knitted or crocheted, of kashmir (cashmere) fine goats hair	6110.1200	2456
球衣,针织或钩编的,毛制	Jerseys, knitted or crocheted, of wool	6110.1100	2456
球衣,针织或钩编的,棉制	Jerseys, knitted or crocheted, of cotton	6110.2000	2456
球衣,针织或钩编的,其他	Jerseys, knitted or crocheted, nes	6110.9090	2456
球衣,针织或钩编的,其他动物细毛制	Jerseys, knitted or crocheted, of other fine animal hair	6110.1990	2456
球衣,针织或钩编的,其他山羊细毛制	Jerseys, knitted or crocheted, of other fine goats hair	6110.1910	2456
球衣,针织或钩编的,丝及绢丝制	Jerseys, knitted or crocheted, of silk or silk waste	6110.9010	2456
球衣,针织或钩编的,兔毛制	Jerseys, knitted or crocheted, of rabbit and hare	6110.1920	2456
球柱混合轴承	Combined ball/roller bearings	8482.8000	5
qu			
曲柄	Cranks	8483.1090	
曲柄链轮及其零件,自行车及脚踏车的	Crank-gear and parts thereof, of bicycles and other cycles	8714.9620	3
曲柄零件	Cranks parts	8483.9000	3
驱动桥及其零件,装有差速器的,30座及以上客运机动车辆用	Drive-axles with differential and parts of motor vehicles with 30 seats or more	8708.5072	3
驱动桥及其零件,装有差速器的,其他	Drive-axles with differential and parts of motor vehicles, nes	8708.5079	3
驱动桥及其零件,装有差速器的,特种车辆用	Drive-axles with differential and parts of motor vehicles with special purpose	8708.5076	3
驱动桥及其零件,装有差速器的,拖拉机的	Drive-axles with differential and parts of tractors	8708.5071	3
驱动桥及其零件,装有差速器的,小轿车用	Drive-axles with differential and parts of saloon cars	8708.5074	3
驱动桥及其零件,装有差速器的,越野车(4轮驱动)用	Drive-axles with differential and parts of cross-country cars (4WD)	8708.5075	3

商品名称	Article Description	税则号列	申报要素
驱动桥及其零件,装有差速器的,自卸车用	Drive-axles with differential and parts of dumpers	8708.5073	3
去甲美沙酮以及它们的盐	Normethadone (INN) and salts thereof	2922.3100	36
去甲西泮(INN)以及盐	Nordazepam(INN);salts thereof	2933.9100	36
去污粉及类似制品	Scouring powders and other scouring preparations	3405.4000	36
去雾器,机动车辆用	Demisters,for motor vehicles	8512.4000	7
去氧麻黄碱(INN),它的盐、酯及其他衍生物	Metamfetamine (INN); salts, esters and other derivatives thereof	2939.9190	34
去氧麻黄碱外消旋体,它们的盐、酯及其他衍生物	Metamfetamine racemate; salts, esters and other derivatives thereof	2939.9190	34
quan			
全地形车	All terrain vehicles	8703.1011	58
全封闭组合式高压开关装置,用于电压在500千伏及以上的线路	Gas insulated switch gear,for a voltage of 500kV or more	8537.2010	78
全封闭组合式高压开关装置零件,用于电压在500千伏及以上的线路	Gas insulated switch gear parts, for a voltage of 500kV or more	8538.1010	3
全氟异丁烯	Perfluorolisobutylene	2903.3910	36
全卤化衍生物,其他	Perhalogenated derivatives,nes	2903.4700	36
全氯乙烯	Perchloroethylene	2903.2300	36
醛,含氧基的,其他	Aldehydes with other oxygen function,nes	2912.4900	36
醛醇	Aldehyde-alcohols	2912.3000	36
醛的卤化、磺化、硝化或亚硝化衍生物	Halogenated, sulphonated, nitrated or nitrosated derivatives of Aldehydes	2913.0000	36
que			
炔已蚁胺(INN)	Ethinamate(INN)	2924.2400	36
qun			
裙带菜,干的	Pinnatifida,dried	1212.2031	14
裙带菜,其他	Pinnatifida,nes	1212.2039	14
裙带菜,鲜的	Pinnatifida,fresh	1212.2032	14
裙带菜,盐腌的	Pinnatifida,salted	2008.9933	248
裙子及裙裤,非针织或钩编的,女式,合成纤维制	Skirts and divided skirts,not knitted or crocheted,for women or girls,of synthetic fibres	6204.5300	2456
裙子及裙裤,非针织或钩编的,女式,棉制	Skirts and divided skirts,not knitted or crocheted,for women or girls,of cotton	6204.5200	2456
裙子及裙裤,非针织或钩编的,女式,其他	Skirts and divided skirts,not knitted or crocheted,for women or girls,nes	6204.5990	2456
裙子及裙裤,非针织或钩编的,女式,丝及绢丝制	Skirts and divided skirts,not knitted or crocheted,for women or girls,of silk or silk waste	6204.5910	2456
裙子及裙裤,非针织或钩编的,女式,羊毛或动物细毛制	Skirts and divided skirts,not knitted or crocheted,for women or girls,of wool or fine animal hair	6204.5100	2456

商品名称	Article Description	税则号列	申报要素
裙子及裙裤,针织或钩编的,女式,合成纤维制	Skirts and divided skirts, knitted or crocheted, for women or girls, of synthetic fibres	6104.5300	2456
裙子及裙裤,针织或钩编的,女式,棉制	Skirts and divided skirts, knitted or crocheted, for women or girls, of cotton	6104.5200	2456
裙子及裙裤,针织或钩编的,女式,其他纺织材料制	Skirts and divided skirts, knitted or crocheted, for women or girls, of other textile materials	6104.5900	2456
裙子及裙裤,针织或钩编的,女式,羊毛或动物细毛制	Skirts and divided skirts, knitted or crocheted, for women or girls, of wool or fine animal hair	6104.5100	2456
群青及以其为基本成分的制品	Ultramarine and preparations based thereon	3206.4100	2368

Q

R

商品名称	Article Description	税则号列	申报要素
ran			
燃料元件,核反应堆的,未辐照	Fuel elements, for nuclear reactors, non-irradiated	8401. 3010	2
燃料元件的零件,核反应堆的,未辐照	Fuel elements parts, for nuclear reactors, non-irradiated	8401. 3090	2
燃料油 5 ~7 号	Fuel oils, No. 5 ~7	2917. 1922	6
燃料油,其他	Fuel oils, nes	2917. 1929	6
燃气轮机,功率不超过 5000 千瓦,其他	Gas turbines, of a power not exceeding 5000kW, nes	8411. 8100	27
燃气轮机,功率超过 5000 千瓦,其他	Gas turbines, of a power exceeding 5000kW, nes	8411. 8200	27
燃气轮机零件,其他	Gas turbines parts, nes	8411. 9990	27
燃油泵,活塞式内燃发动机用的,其他	Fuel pumps for internal combustion piston engines, nes	8413. 3029	23
燃油泵,活塞式内燃发动机用的,输出功率在 132. 39 千瓦(180 马力)及以上的发动机用	Fuel pumps for internal combustion piston engines, for engines of an output of 132. 39kW (180hp) or more	8413. 3021	23
染料(包括颜料用的)及以其为基本成分的制品,其他,瓮染料或还原染料	Dyes (including those usable in that state as pigments) and preparations based thereon, vat dyes or reductive dyes, nes	3204. 1590	345
染料(不论是否预金属络合)及以其为基本成分的制品,酸性型	Dyes, whether or not premetallized, and preparations based thereon acid type	3204. 1200	345
染料或着色料,零售形状及零售包装的	Dyes and colouring matter put up in forms or packings for retail sale	3212. 9000	136
染料及以其为基本成分的制品, 活性的	Dyes and preparations based thereon, reactive	3204. 1600	345
染料及以其为基本成分的制品,分散型	Dyes and preparations based thereon, disperse type	3204. 1100	345
染料及以其为基本成分的制品,碱性型	Dyes and preparations based thereon, basic type	3204. 1300	345
染料及以其为基本成分的制品,媒染型	Dyes and preparations based thereon, mordant type	3204. 1200	345
染料及以其为基本成分的制品,直接型	Dyes and preparations based thereon, direct type	3204. 1400	345
染料加速着色或固色助剂,纺织工业及类似工业用,其他	Dye carriers to accelerate the dyeing or fixing of dye-stuffs, of a kind used in the textile or like industries, nes	3809. 9100	236
染料加速着色或固色助剂,以淀粉物质为基本成分	Dye carriers to accelerate the dyeing or fixing of dye-stuffs, with a basis of amylaceous substances	3809. 1000	236

商品名称	Article Description	税则号列	申报要素
染料加速着色或固色助剂,造纸工业及类似工业用,其他	Dye carriers to accelerate the dyeing or fixing of dye-stuffs, of a kind used in the paper or like industries, nes	3809. 9200	236
染料加速着色或固色助剂,制革工业及类似工业用,其他	Dye carriers to accelerate the dyeing or fixing of dye-stuffs, of a kind used in the leather or like industries, nes	3809. 9300	236
染料浸膏,但动物炭黑除外	Dyeing extracts, but excluding animal black	3203. 0020	34
染料浸膏,植物质的	Dyeing extracts, of vegetable origin	3203. 0019	34
染料指示剂	Dye indicators	3204. 9010	345
染色机器,纱线、织物及纺织制品用	Dyeing machines, for textile yarns, fabrics or made up textile articles	8451. 4000	7
染色机器零件,纱线、织物及纺织制品用	Dyeing machines parts, for textile yarns, fabrics or made up textile articles	8451. 9000	7
rao			
绕线机	Filament winding machines	8479. 8110	7
绕组电线,其他	Winding wire, nes	8544. 1900	35
绕组电线,铜制	Winding wire, of copper	8544. 1100	35
re			
热泵,空气调节器除外,其他	Heat pumps other than air conditioning machines, nes	8418. 6190	57
热泵,空气调节器除外,压缩式	Heat pumps other than air conditioning machines, compression-type	8418. 6120	57
热成型机器,加工橡胶或塑料及其产品用,其他	Hermoforming machines, for working rubber or plastics or for the manufacture of products from these materials, nes	8477. 4090	7
热处理炉,可控气氛的,工业或实验室用,电的	Heat treatment furnaces, atmosphere controllable, for industrial or laboratory use, electric	8514. 1010	7
热处理设备,平板显示器的制造机器及装置	Heat treatment equipment, flat panel displays manufacture machines and apparatus	8486. 3010	7
热处理设备,通过感应进行的,工业或实验室用,电的	Heat treatment equipment, by induction, for industrial or laboratory use, electric	8514. 4000	7
热处理设备,通过介质损耗进行的,工业或实验室用,电的	Heat treatment equipment, by dielectric loss, for industrial or laboratory use, electric	8514. 4000	7
热处理设备,制造半导体器件或集成电路的机器及装置	Heat treatment equipment, semiconductor devices or of electronic integrated circuits manufacture machines and apparatus	8486. 2010	7
热处理设备零件,工业或实验室用,电的,其他	Heat treatment equipment parts, for industrial or laboratory use, electric, nes	8514. 9090	3
热电子管零件,其他	Thermionic valves and tubes parts, nes	8540. 9990	3
热发钳,电热的	Curling tong heaters, electro-thermic	8516. 3300	7
热交换装置	Heat exchange units	8419. 5000	57
热量计	Heat meters	9026. 8000	7

R

商品名称	Article Description	税则号列	申报要素
热量计零件、附件	Heat meters parts and accessories	9026.9000	3
热敏打印机,专用于自动数据处理设备的	Thermal printers, of a kind solely used for automatic data processing machine	8443.3214	57
热敏打印头	Thermal print heads	8443.9921	3
热敏复印设备	Thermocopying apparatus	8443.3923	57
热敏转印纸	Heat transfer paper	4816.9010	58
热喷金属或金属陶瓷的电气机器及装置	Electric machines and apparatus for hot spraying of metals or cermets	8515.8000	
热升华复印设备	Thermo-sublime copying apparatus	8443.3924	57
热水器,电的,储存式	Waterheaters, storage, electric	8516.1010	7
热水器,电的,即热式	Waterheaters, electric instantaneous	8516.1020	7
热水器,电的,浸入式	Waterheaters heaters, immersion, electric	8516.1090	7
热水器,非电热的,燃气速热的	Water heaters, non-electric, instantaneous, gas type	8419.1100	57
热水器,非电热的,速热的,其他	Water heaters, non-electric, instantaneous, nes	8419.1990	57
热水器,非电热的,贮备式,其他	Water heaters, non-electric, instantaneous, storage type, nes	8419.1990	57
热水器,太阳能的	Water heaters, of solar enengy	8419.1910	57
热水器用零件	Water heaters parts	8419.9010	3
热缩包装机器	Heat-shrink wrapping machinery	8422.4000	
热阴极荧光灯,火车、航空器及船舶用	Fluorescent, hot cathode, for locomotives and rolling-stock, aircraft or ships	8539.3120	35
热阴极荧光灯,紧凑型	Fluorescent, hot cathode, compact type	8539.3191	35
热阴极荧光灯,科研、医疗专用	Fluorescent, hot cathode, for scientific or medical uses only	8539.3110	35
热阴极荧光灯,其他	Fluorescent, hot cathode, nes	8539.3199	35
热轧管机	Tube mills, for hot-rolled	8455.1010	7
热轧机,其他	Rolling mills, hot-rolled, nes	8455.2190	7
热轧机零件	Rolling mills parts, hot-rolled	8455.9000	3
ren			
人参,其他	Ginseng roots, nes	1211.2099	34
人参,鲜的	Ginseng roots, fresh	1211.2091	34
人发,未经加工的,不论是否洗涤	Human hair, unworked, whether or not washed or scoured	0501.0000	4
人发,废的	Human hair, wasted	0501.0000	4
人发,经梳理、稀疏、脱色或其他方法加工的	Human hair, dressed, thinned, bleached or otherwise worked	6703.0000	4
人工呼吸器	Artificial respiration apparatus	9019.2000	
人工肾	Dialysis	9018.9040	
人体除臭剂及止汗剂	Personal deodorants and antiperspirants	3307.2000	23

R

商品名称	Article Description	税则号列	申报要素
人体或动物制品,供治疗或预防疾病用的,其他税号未列名的	Human or animal substances, prepared for therapeutic or prophylactic uses, not elsewhere specified or included	3001.9090	34
人体模型及其他人体活动模型,裁缝用	Tailors dummies and other lay figures	9618.0000	
人血	Human blood	3002.9090	34
人用疫苗	Vaccines for human medicine	3002.2000	34
人造扁平石及类似品	Artificial stone flagstones and similar articles	6810.1910	56
人造冰晶石	Synthetic cryolite	2826.3000	
人造草,表观宽度不超过5毫米,合成纤维纺织材料制	Artificial straw, of synthetic textile materials of an apparent width not exceeding 5mm	5404.9000	568
人造草,表观宽度不超过5毫米的人造纤维纺织材料制	Artificial straw, of artificial textile materials of an apparent width not exceeding 5mm	5405.0000	568
人造肠衣,硬化蛋白或纤维素材料制的	Artificial guts, of hardened protein or of cellulosic materials	3917.1000	6
人造的人体部分,其他	Artificial parts of the body, nes	9021.3900	3
人造蜂蜜,不论是否含有天然蜂蜜	Honey, artificial, whether or not mixed with natural honey	1702.9000	
人造革,用聚氨基甲酸酯浸渍、涂布、包覆或层压的	Imitation leather, impregnated, coated, covered or laminated with polyurethane	5903.2020	
人造革,用聚氯乙烯浸渍、涂布、包覆或层压的	Imitation leather, impregnated, coated, covered or laminated with poly(vinyl chloride)	5903.1020	
人造革,用塑料浸渍、涂布、包覆或层压的,其他	Imitation leather, impregnated, coated, covered or laminated with plastics, nes	5903.9020	
人造革及合成革,泡沫塑料的,氯乙烯聚合物制	Man-made or synthetic leather, of polymers, of vinyl chloride	3921.1210	16
人造革及合成革,泡沫塑料的,氨酯聚合物制	Man-made or synthetic leather, of polyurethanes	3921.1310	16
人造革及合成革,其他	Man-made or synthetic leather, nes	3921.1910	16
人造关节	Artificial joints	9021.3100	
人造花、叶、果实及其零件,化学纤维制	Artificial flowers, foliage and fruit and parts thereof, of man-made fibres	6702.9030	
人造花、叶、果实及其零件,其他	Artificial flowers, foliage and fruit and parts thereof, nes	6702.9090	
人造花、叶、果实及其零件,丝及绢丝制	Artificial flowers, foliage and fruit and parts thereof, of silk or silk waste	6702.9020	
人造花、叶、果实及其零件,塑料制	Artificial flowers, foliage and fruit and parts thereof, of plastics	6702.1000	
人造花、叶、果实及其零件,羽毛制	Artificial flowers, foliage and fruit and parts thereof, of feathers or down	6702.9010	
人造花、叶或果实制成的物品,化学纤维制	Artificial flowers, foliage or fruit articles, of man-made fibres	6702.9030	
人造花、叶或果实制成的物品,其他	Artificial flowers, foliage or fruit articles, nes	6702.9090	

R

商品名称	Article Description	税则号列	申报要素
人造花、叶或果实制成的物品，丝及绢丝制	Artificial flowers, foliage or fruit articles, of silk or silk waste	6702.9020	
人造花、叶或果实制成的物品，塑料制	Artificial flowers, foliage or fruit articles, of plastics	6702.1000	
人造花、叶或果实制成的物品，羽毛制	Artificial flowers, foliage or fruit articles, of feathers or down	6702.9010	
人造黄油，但不包括液态的	Margarine, excluding liquid margarine	1517.1000	24
人造毛皮	Artificial fur	4304.0010	6
人造毛皮制品	Articles of artificial fur	4304.0020	6
人造石瓦	Artificial stone tiles	6810.1910	56
人造石制品，其他	Artificial stone articles, nes	6810.9990	56
人造石砖及块，建筑用	Artificial stone blocks and bricks, for building	6810.1100	56
人造纤维长丝纱线，供零售用	Artificial filament yarn, put up for retail sale	5406.0020	
人造纤维长丝纱线机织物，按重量计人造纤维长丝、扁条或类似品含量在85%及以上，染色，其他	Artificial filament yarn woven fabrics, containing 85% or more by weight of artificial filament or strip or the like, dyed, nes	5408.2290	2468
人造纤维长丝纱线机织物，按重量计人造纤维长丝、扁条或类似品含量在85%及以上，色织，其他	Artificial filament yarn woven fabrics, containing 85% or more by weight of artificial filament or strip or the like, of yarns of different colours, nes	5408.2390	2468
人造纤维长丝纱线机织物，按重量计人造纤维长丝、扁条或类似品含量在85%及以上，色织，印花，其他	Artificial filament yarn woven fabrics, containing 85% or more by weight of artificial filament or strip or the like, of yarns of different colours, printed, nes	5408.2490	2468
人造纤维长丝纱线机织物，按重量计人造纤维长丝、扁条或类似品含量在85%及以上，未漂白或漂白	Artificial filament yarn woven fabrics, containing 85% or more by weight of artificial filament or strip or the like, unbleached or bleached	5408.2190	2468
人造纤维长丝纱线机织物，染色	Artificial filament yarn woven fabrics, dyed	5408.3200	2468
人造纤维长丝纱线机织物，色织	Artificial filament yarn woven fabrics, of yarns of different colours	5408.3300	2468
人造纤维长丝纱线机织物，未漂白或漂白	Artificial filament yarn woven fabrics, unbleached or bleached	5408.3100	2468
人造纤维长丝纱线机织物，印花	Artificial filament yarn woven fabrics, printed	5408.3400	2468
人造纤维长丝丝束，其他	Artificial filament tow, nes	5502.0090	68
人造纤维单纱，非供零售用，其他	Artificial single yarn, not put up for retail sale, nes	5403.3900	3468
人造纤维单丝，截面尺寸不超过1毫米，细度在67分特及以上	Artificial monofilament of 67 decitex or more and of which no cross-sectional dimension exceeds 1mm	5405.0000	568
人造纤维的废料	Artificial fibres waste	5505.2000	68
人造纤维短机织物，按重量计人造纤维短纤含量在85%及以上，染色	Artificial staple fibres woven fabrics, containing 85% or more by weight of artificial staple fibres, dyed	5516.1200	2468
人造纤维短机织物，按重量计人造纤维短纤含量在85%及以上，色织	Artificial staple fibres woven fabrics, containing 85% or more by weight of artificial staple fibres, of yarns of different colours	5516.1300	2468

R

商品名称	Article Description	税则号列	申报要素
人造纤维短机织物,按重量计人造纤维短纤含量在85%及以上,未漂白或漂白	Artificial staple fibres woven fabrics, containing 85% or more by weight of artificial staple fibres, unbleached or bleached	5516.1100	2468
人造纤维短机织物,按重量计人造纤维短纤含量在85%及以上,印花	Artificial staple fibres woven fabrics, containing 85% or more by weight of artificial staple fibres, printed	5516.1400	2468
人造纤维短机织物,按重量计人造纤维短纤含量在85%以下,主要或仅与化学纤维长丝混纺,染色	Artificial staple fibres woven fabrics, containing less than 85% by weight of artificial staple fibres, mixed mainly or solely with man-made filaments, dyed	5516.2200	2468
人造纤维短机织物,按重量计人造纤维短纤含量在85%以下,主要或仅与化学纤维长丝混纺,色织	Artificial staple fibres woven fabrics, containing less than 85% by weight of artificial staple fibres, mixed mainly or solely with man-made filaments, of yarns of different colours	5516.2300	2468
人造纤维短机织物,按重量计人造纤维短纤含量在85%以下,主要或仅与化学纤维长丝混纺,未漂白或漂白	Artificial staple fibres woven fabrics, containing less than 85% by weight of artificial staple fibres, mixed mainly or solely with man-made filaments, unbleached or bleached	5516.2100	2468
人造纤维短机织物,按重量计人造纤维短纤含量在85%以下,主要或仅与化学纤维长丝混纺,印花	Artificial staple fibres woven fabrics, containing less than 85% by weight of artificial staple fibres, mixed mainly or solely with man-made filaments, printed	5516.2400	2468
人造纤维短机织物,按重量计人造纤维短纤含量在85%以下,主要或仅与棉混纺,染色	Artificial staple fibres woven fabrics, containing less than 85% by weight of artificial staple fibres, mixed mainly or solely with cotton, dyed	5516.4200	2468
人造纤维短机织物,按重量计人造纤维短纤含量在85%以下,主要或仅与棉混纺,色织	Artificial staple fibres woven fabrics, containing less than 85% by weight of artificial staple fibres, mixed mainly or solely with cotton, of yarns of different colours	5516.4300	2468
人造纤维短机织物,按重量计人造纤维短纤含量在85%以下,主要或仅与棉混纺,未漂白或漂白	Artificial staple fibres woven fabrics, containing less than 85% by weight of artificial staple fibres, mixed mainly or solely with cotton, unbleached or bleached	5516.4100	2468
人造纤维短机织物,按重量计人造纤维短纤含量在85%以下,主要或仅与棉混纺,印花	Artificial staple fibres woven fabrics, containing less than 85% by weight of artificial staple fibres, mixed mainly or solely with cotton, printed	5516.4400	2468
人造纤维短机织物,按重量计人造纤维短纤含量在85%以下,主要或仅与羊毛或动物细毛混纺,染色	Artificial staple fibres woven fabrics, containing less than 85% by weight of artificial staple fibres, mixed mainly or solely with wool or fine animal hair, dyed	5516.3200	2468
人造纤维短机织物,按重量计人造纤维短纤含量在85%以下,主要或仅与羊毛或动物细毛混纺,色织	Artificial staple fibres woven fabrics, containing less than 85% by weight of artificial staple fibres, mixed mainly or solely with wool or fine animal hair, of yarns of different colours	5516.3300	2468

R

商品名称	Article Description	税则号列	申报要素
人造纤维短机织物,按重量计人造纤维短纤含量在85%以下,主要或仅与羊毛或动物细毛混纺,未漂白或漂白	Artificial staple fibres woven fabrics, containing less than 85% by weight of artificial staple fibres, mixed mainly or solely with wool or fine animal hair, unbleached or bleached	5516.3100	2468
人造纤维短机织物,按重量计人造纤维短纤含量在85%以下,主要或仅与羊毛或动物细毛混纺,印花	Artificial staple fibres woven fabrics, containing less than 85% by weight of artificial staple fibres, mixed mainly or solely with wool or fine animal hair, printed	5516.3400	2468
人造纤维短机织物,染色,其他	Artificial staple fibres woven fabrics, dyed, nes	5516.9200	2468
人造纤维短机织物,色织,其他	Artificial staple fibres woven fabrics, of yarns of different colours, nes	5516.9300	2468
人造纤维短机织物,未漂白或漂白,其他	Artificial staple fibres woven fabrics, unbleached or bleached, nes	5516.9100	2468
人造纤维短机织物,印花,其他	Artificial staple fibres woven fabrics, printed, nes	5516.9400	2468
人造纤维短纤,未梳或未经其他纺前加工,其他	Artificial staple fibres, not carded, combed or otherwise processed for spinning, nes	5504.9000	68
人造纤维短纤,已梳或经其他纺前加工	Artificial staple fibres, carded, combed or otherwise processed for spinning	5507.0000	68
人造纤维短纤单纱,按重量计人造纤维短纤含量在85%及以上,非供零售用	Artificial staple fibres single yarn, containing 85% or more by weight of artificial staple fibres, not put up for retail sale	5510.1100	68
人造纤维短纤多股纱线或缆线,按重量计人造纤维短纤含量在85%及以上,非供零售用	Artificial staple fibres multiple or cabled yarn, containing 85% or more by weight of artificial staple fibres, not put up for retail sale	5510.1200	68
人造纤维短纤缝纫线,不论是否供零售用	Artificial staple fibres sewing thread, whether or not put up for retail sale	5508.2000	68
人造纤维短纤纱线,非供零售用,其他	Artificial staple fibres yarn, not put up for retail sale, nes	5510.9000	68
人造纤维短纤纱线,供零售用	Artificial staple fibres yarn, put up for retail sale	5511.3000	68
人造纤维短纤纱线,主要或仅与棉混纺,非供零售用,其他	Artificial staple fibres yarn, mixed mainly or solely with cotton, not put up for retail sale, nes	5510.3000	68
人造纤维短纤纱线,主要或仅与羊毛或动物细毛混纺,非供零售用,其他	Artificial staple fibres yarn, mixed mainly or solely with wool or fine animal hair, not put up for retail sale, nes	5510.2000	68
人造纤维多股纱线或缆线,其他	Artificial multiple or cabled yarn, nes	5403.4900	3468
壬二酸及其盐和酯	Azelaic acid, its salts and esters	2917.1390	36
壬基酚	Nonylphenol	2907.1310	36
壬烯,轻油	Nonene, light oils	2710.1191	6
刃磨机床,加工金属或金属陶瓷用,其他	Sharpening machines, for metal or cermets, nes	8460.3900	7
刃磨机床,数控的,加工金属或金属陶瓷用	Sharpening machines, numerically controlled, for metal or cermets	8460.3100	7

R

商品名称	Article Description	税则号列	申报要素
ri			
日记本及类似品,纸或纸板制的	Diaries and similar articles, of paper or paperboard	4820. 1000	
日历,包括日历芯,印刷的	Calendars of any kind, printed, including calendar blocks	4910. 0000	
日期戳,手用	Date stamps, designed for operating in the hand	9611. 0000	
日字环节链,钢铁的	Stud-link, of iron or steel	7315. 8100	36
rong			
容器,钢铁的,装压缩气体或液化气体用的,零售包装用	Containers for compressed or liquefied gas, of iron or steel, for retail packing	7311. 0010	36
容器,钢铁的,装压缩气体或液化气体用的,其他	Containers for compressed or liquefied gas, of iron or steel, nes	7311. 0090	36
容器,铝制,装压缩气体或液化气体用的,零售包装用	Containers of aluminium, for compressed or liquefied gas, for retail packing	7613. 0010	368
容器,铝制,装压缩气体或液化气体用的,其他	Containers of aluminium, for compressed or liquefied gas, nes	7613. 0090	368
熔断器,用于电压不超过1000伏的线路	Fuses, for a voltage not exceeding 1000V	8536. 1000	8
熔断器,用于电压超过1000伏的线路	Fuses, for a voltage exceeding 1000V	8535. 1000	8
熔压机,纱线、织物及纺织制品用	Fusing presses machines, for textile yarns, fabrics or made up textile articles	8451. 3000	
熔压机零件,纱线、织物及纺织制品用	Fusing presses machines parts, for textile yarns, fabrics or made up textile articles	8451. 9000	
熔渣(粒状熔渣除外),冶炼钢铁所产生的	Slag, other than granulated slag, from the manufacture of iron or steel	2619. 0000	134
熔渣,粒状,其他,冶炼钢铁所产生的	Granulated slag, nes, from the manufacture of iron or steel	2618. 0090	146
熔渣砂,其他,冶炼钢铁所产生的	Slag sand, nes, from the manufacture of iron or steel	2618. 0090	146
rou			
鞣料,无机的	Tanning substances, inorganic	3202. 9000	68
鞣料,有机合成的	Tanning substances, synthetic organic	3202. 1000	68
鞣料浸膏,其他	Tanning extracts, nes	3201. 9010	34
鞣料制剂,不论是否含有天然鞣料	Tanning preparations, whether or not containing natural tanning substances	3202. 9000	68
鞣酸及其盐、醚、酯和其他衍生物	Tannins and their salts, ethers, esters and other derivatives	3201. 9090	34
肉,灵长目的,鲜或冷或冻的	Meat, of primatesand, fresh, chilled or frozen	0208. 3000	15
肉,其他,鲜或冷或冻的	Meat, nes, fresh, chilled or frozen	0208. 9090	145
肉、杂碎及血,鸡的,制作或保藏的	Meat, offal and blood of fowls of the species gallus domesticus, prepared or preserved	1602. 3299	48
肉、杂碎及血,牛的,制作或保藏的	Meat, offal and blood of bovine animals, prepared or preserved	1602. 5090	48

R

商品名称	Article Description	税则号列	申报要素
肉、杂碎及血,其他,制作或保藏的	Meat, offal and blood of any animals, prepared or preserved, nes	1602.9090	48
肉、杂碎及血,鸭的,制作或保藏的	Meat, offal and blood of duck, prepared or preserved	1602.3991	248
肉、杂碎及血,猪的,制作或保藏的	Meat, offal and blood of swine, prepared or preserved	1602.4990	48
肉豆蔻	Nutmeg	0908.1000	
肉豆蔻衣	Mace	0908.2000	
肉粉,灵长目的,食用	Flours and meals of meat, of primates, edible	0210.9100	14
肉粉,爬行动物(包括蛇及龟鳖)的,食用	Flours and meals of meat, of reptiles (including snakes and turtles), edible	0210.9300	14
肉粉,食用,其他	Flours and meals of meat, edible, nes	0210.9900	14
肉骨粉,含牛羊成分的,不适于供人食用的	Flours and meals, of meat bones, of bovine and sheep unfit for human consumption	2301.1011	136
肉骨粉,其他,不适于供人食用的	Flours and meals, of meat bones, nes, unfit for human consumption	2301.1019	136
肉桂,其他,未磨	Cinnamon, nes, neither crushed nor ground	0906.1900	4
肉桂,锡兰,未磨	Cinnamon, cinnamomum zeylanicum blume, neither crushed nor ground	0906.1100	4
肉桂,已磨	Cinnamon, crushed or ground	0906.2000	4
肉桂花,未磨	Cinnamontree flowers, neither crushed nor ground	0906.1900	4
肉桂花,已磨	Cinnamontree flowers, crushed or ground	0906.2000	4
肉块,猪的,带骨的,干、熏、盐腌或盐渍的	Cuts of swine, with bone in, salted, in brine, dried or smoked	0210.1190	14
肉类加工机器	Meat preparation machinery	8438.5000	
肉类加工机器的零件	Meat preparation machinery parts	8438.9000	3
ru			
儒艮(海牛目哺乳动物)	Dugongs (mammals of the order sirenia)	0106.1200	
儒艮(海牛目哺乳动物)的肉	Meat of dugongs (mammals of the order sirenia)	0208.4000	15
儒艮(海牛目哺乳动物)的肉粉,食用	Flours and meals of meat of dugongs (mammals of the order sirenia), edible	0210.9200	14
乳,按重量计脂肪含量不超过1%,未浓缩及未加糖或其他甜物质的	Milk, of a fat content, by weight, not exceeding 1%, not concentrated nor containing added sugar or other sweetening matter	0401.1000	12468
乳,按重量计脂肪含量超过1%,但不超过6%,未浓缩及未加糖或其他甜物质的	Milk, of a fat content, by weight, exceeding 1% but not exceeding 6%, not concentrated nor containing added sugar or other sweetening matter	0401.2000	12468
乳,按重量计脂肪含量超过6%,未浓缩及未加糖或其他甜物质的	Milk, of a fat content, by weight, exceeding 6%, not concentrated nor containing added sugar or other sweetening matter	0401.3000	12468
乳,发酵或酸化的,其他	Milk, fermented or acidified, nes	0403.9000	248
乳,非固体形状,加糖或其他甜物质	Milk, not in solid forms, containing added sugar or other sweetening matter	0402.9900	12468
乳,非固体形状,未加糖或其他甜物质	Milk, not in solid forms, not containing added sugar or other sweetening matter	0402.9100	12468

R

商品名称	Article Description	税则号列	申报要素
乳,粉状、粒状或其他固体形状,按重量计脂肪含量不超过1.5%	Milk, in powder, granules or other solid forms, of a fat content, by weight, not exceeding 1.5%	0402.1000	12468
乳,粉状、粒状或其他固体形状,按重量计脂肪含量超过1.5%,加糖或其他甜物质	Milk, in powder, granules or other solid forms, of a fat content, by weight, exceeding 1.5%, containing added sugar or other sweetening matter	0402.2900	12468
乳,粉状、粒状或其他固体形状,按重量计脂肪含量超过1.5%,未加糖或其他甜物质	Milk, in powder, granules or other solid forms, of a fat content, by weight, exceeding 1.5%, not containing added sugar or other sweetening matter	0402.2100	12468
乳,凝固的	Milk, curdled	0403.9000	248
乳蛋饼	Quiche	1905.9000	28
乳鸽	Squabs	0106.3921	3
乳鸽肉,鲜或冷或冻的,	Meat of squabs, fresh, chilled or frozen	0208.9010	15
乳化机,其他	Emulsifying machines, nes	8479.8200	7
乳化沥青	Bitumen and asphalt, emulsified	2714.9020	1346
乳酱	Dairy spreads	0405.2000	268
乳酪,各种磨碎或粉化的	Cheese, grated or powdered, of all kinds	0406.2000	24
乳酪,经加工的乳酪,但磨碎或粉化的除外	Cheese, processed, not grated or powdered	0406.3000	24
乳酪,其他	Cheese, nes	0406.9000	2468
乳酪,其他,娄地青霉生产的带有纹理的乳酪	Cheese, nes, containing veins. produced by penicillium roqueforti	0406.4000	2468
乳磷酸盐,以及它们的卤化、磺化、硝化或亚硝化衍生物	Lactophosphates, their halogenated, sulphonated, nitrated or nitrosated derivatives	2919.9000	36
乳品加工机器	Dairy machinery	8434.2000	
乳品加工机器零件	Dairy machinery parts	8434.9000	3
乳清,不论是否浓缩、加糖或其他甜物质	Whey, whether or not concentrated or containing added sugar or other sweetening matter	0404.1000	248
乳清干酪	Ricotta	0406.1000	24
乳清乳酪	Whey cheese	0406.1000	24
乳球蛋白	Lactoglobulins	3504.0090	1346
乳酸汞	Mercury lactate	2852.0000	
乳酸及其盐和酯	Lactic acid, its salts and esters	2918.1100	36
乳糖,按重量计干燥无水乳糖含量在99%及以上	Lactose, containing by weight 99% or more lactose, expressed as anhydrous lactose, calculated on the dry matter	1702.1100	68
乳糖浆,按重量计干燥无水乳糖含量在99%及以上	Lactose syrup, containing by weight 99% or more lactose, expressed as anhydrous lactose, calculated on the dry matter	1702.1100	68
乳香	Olibanum	1301.9020	
乳猪	Sucking pig	0203.2110	14
乳猪,鲜或冷的,整头及半头	Sucking pig, fresh or chilled, carcasses and half-carcasses	0203.1110	14

R

商品名称	Article Description	税则号列	申报要素
ruan			
软包装生产设备,纸塑铝的	Flexible packaging manufacture machines, for paper plastic and aluminium	8441.8010	
软包装生产设备零件,纸塑铝的	Flexible packaging manufacture machines parts, for paper plastic and aluminium	8441.9090	
软管,钢铁制,不论是否有附件	Flexible tubing of iron or steel, with or without fittings	8307.1000	256
软管,贱金属制,不论是否有附件,其他	Flexible tubing of other base metal, with or without fittings, nes	8307.9000	256
软管,塑料制的,爆破压力不低于27.6兆帕斯卡	Tubes, pipes and hoses, flexible, of plastics, having a minimum burst pressure of 27.6 MPa	3917.3100	36
软管容器,铝制,容积不超过300升,不论是否衬里或隔热,但无机械或热力装置	Collapsible tubular containers, of aluminium, of a capacity not exceeding 300L, whether or not lined or heat-insulated, but not fitted with mechanical or thermal equipment	7612.1000	368
软木,碎的、粒状的或粉状的	Cork, crushed, granulated or ground	4501.9020	
软木,天然的,除去表皮或粗切成方形,或成长方块、正方块、板、片或条状	Cork, natural, debarked or roughly squared, or in rectangular (including square) blocks, plates, sheets or strip	4502.0000	146
软木,天然的,未加工或简单加工的	Cork, natrual, raw or simply prepared	4501.1000	46
软木处理机	Cork treating machinery	8479.3000	7
软木方块坯料,作塞子用的	Cork blanks, sharp-edged for corks or stoppers	4502.0000	146
软木废料	Cork waste	4501.9010	
软木制品,天然的,其他	Cork articles of natural, nes	4503.9000	568
软盘驱动器	Floppy disk drivers	8471.7020	
软糖	Fondants and fondant pastes	1704.9000	258
软体动物,其他,制作或保藏的	Molluscs, nes, prepared or preserved	1605.9090	48
软体动物和水生无脊椎动物(甲壳动物除外),冻、干、盐腌或盐渍的	Aquatic invertebrates and molluscs (other than crustaceans), frozen, dried, salted or in brine	0307.9990	14
软体动物和水生无脊椎动物(甲壳动物除外),其他	Aquatic invertebrates and molluscs (other than crustaceans), nes	0307.9199	1
软体动物壳	Shells of molluscs	0508.0090	14
rui			
锐钛矿	Anatase	2614.0000	146
run			
润滑剂(包括以润滑剂为基本成分的切削油制剂、螺栓或螺母松开剂、防锈或防腐蚀制剂及脱模剂),含有石油或从沥青矿物提取的油类	Lubricating preparations (including cutting-oil preparations, bolt or nutrelease preparations, anti-rust or anticorrosion preparations and mould release preparations, based on lubricants), containing petroleum oils or oils obtained from bituminous minerals	3403.1900	2368

商品名称	Article Description	税则号列	申报要素
润滑剂(包括以润滑剂为基本成分的切削油制剂、螺栓或螺母松开剂、防锈或防腐蚀制剂及脱模剂),其他	Lubricating preparations (including cutting-oil preparations, bolt or nutrelease preparations, anti-rust or anticorrosion preparations and mould release preparations, based on lubricants), nes	3403.9900	2368
润滑剂,外科手术或体检时躯体部位用	Lubricant for parts of the body for surgical operations or physical examinations	3006.7000	36
润滑油	Lubricating grease	2710.1991	2368
润滑油泵,活塞式内燃发动机用	Lubricating pumps for internal combustion piston engines	8413.3030	23
润滑油基础油	Basic oils for lubricating oils	2710.1993	238
润滑油添加剂,用于矿物油及类似液体,其他	Additives for lubricating oils, for mineral oils and alike, nes	3811.2900	236
润滑油添加剂,含有石油或从沥青矿物提取的油类	Additives for lubricating oils, containing petroleum oils or oils obtained from bituminous minerals	3811.2100	236
润滑脂	Lubricating oils	2710.1992	2368

R

S

商品名称	Article Description	税则号列	申报要素
sa			
萨罗芬	Acetanilide	2924. 2990	36
sai			
塞子,贱金属制	Stoppers, of base metal	8309. 9000	256
塞子,天然软木制	Stoppers of natural corks	4503. 1000	568
塞子、盖及类似的封口器,玻璃制	Stoppers, lids and other similiar closures, of glass	7010. 2000	8
塞子、盖子及类似品,塑料的	Stoppers, lids, caps and other similiar closures, of plastics	3923. 5000	23
塞子帽,贱金属制	Bung covers, of base metal	8309. 9000	256
噻唑环化合物,结构上含有,非稠合的,不论是否氢化	Thiazole ring compounds, unfused in the structure, whether or not hydrogenated	2934. 1000	36
san			
三(2,3-二溴丙基)磷酸酯	Tris(2,3-dibromopropyl) phosphate	2919. 1000	36
三(2-氯乙基)胺	Tri-(2-chloroethyl) amine	2921. 1950	36
三端双向可控硅开关元件,但光敏器件除外	Triacs, other than photosensitive devices	8541. 3000	5
三甲胺及其盐	Trimethylamine and their salts	2921. 1100	36
三甲利定(INN)以及盐	Trimeperidine(INN); salts thereof	2933. 3300	36
三角裤、短衬裤,非针织或钩编的,女式,化学纤维制	Briefs, panties, not knitted or crocheted, for women or girls, of man-made fibres	6208. 9200	2456
三角裤、短衬裤,非针织或钩编的,女式,棉制	Briefs, panties, not knitted or crocheted, for women or girls, of cotton	6208. 9100	2456
三角裤、短衬裤,非针织或钩编的,女式,其他	Briefs, panties, not knitted or crocheted, for women or girls, nes	6208. 9990	2456
三角裤、短衬裤,非针织或钩编的,女式,丝及绢丝制	Briefs, panties, not knitted or crocheted, for women or girls, of silk or silk waste	6208. 9910	2456
三角裤及短衬裤,针织或钩编的,女式,化学纤维制	Briefs and panties, knitted or crocheted, for women or girls, of man-made fibres	6108. 2200	2456
三角裤及短衬裤,针织或钩编的,女式,棉制	Briefs and panties, knitted or crocheted, for women or girls, of cotton	6108. 2100	2456
三角裤及短衬裤,针织或钩编的,女式,其他	Briefs and panties, knitted or crocheted, for women or girls, nes	6108. 2990	2456
三角裤及短衬裤,针织或钩编的,女式,丝及绢丝制	Briefs and panties, knitted or crocheted, for women or girls, of silk or silk waste	6108. 2910	2456
三聚磷酸钠,其他	Sodium tripolyphosphate, nes	2835. 3190	3
三聚磷酸钠,食品级的	Sodium tripolyphosphate, food grade	2835. 3110	
三聚氰胺	Melamine	2933. 6100	36

S

商品名称	Article Description	税则号列	申报要素
三聚氰氯	Cyanuric chloride	2933.6910	36
三联苯	Terphenyls	2902.9090	6
三磷酸钠,其他	Sodium triphosphate,nes	2835.3190	3
三磷酸钠,食品级的	Sodium triphosphate,food grade	2835.3110	
三硫化二磷,商品级	Phosphorus trisuiphides,commercial type	2813.9000	
三氯氟甲烷	Trichlorofluoromethane	2903.4100	36
三氯化磷	Phosphorus trichloride	2812.1043	
三氯化砷	Arsenic trichloride	2812.1044	
三氯三氟乙烷	Tichlorotrifluoroethanes	2903.4300	36
三氯五氟丙烷	Trichloropentafluoropropane	2903.4580	36
三氯硝基甲烷	Trichloronitromethane(chloropicrin,nitrochloroform)	2904.9030	36
三氯氧磷	Phosphorus oxytrichloride	2812.1020	
三氯乙酸及其盐和酯	Tri-chloroacetic acids,their salts and esters	2915.4000	36
三氯乙烯	Trichloroethylene	2903.2200	36
三氯异氰脲酸	Trichloroisocyanurate acid	2933.6922	36
三轮车及类似的带轮玩具	Tricycles and similar wheeled toys	9503.0010	
三轮脚踏车,运货用	Tricycles for delivery	8712.0090	8
三嗪环化合物,结构上含有,非稠合的,不论是否氢化,其他	Triazine ring compounds, unfused in the structure, whether or not hydrogenated,nes	2933.6990	36
三硝基甲苯(TNT)	Trinitrotoluene(TNT)	2904.2040	36
三氧化铬	Chromium trioxide	2819.1000	6
三氧化钨	Tungstic oxide	2825.9012	
三叶草,饲料用	Clover,forage products	1214.9000	
三叶草子,饲料植物用的	Clover(Trifblium spp.)seed,forage plants	1209.2200	358
三乙醇胺	Triethanolamine	2922.1310	36
三乙醇胺盐	Salts of triethanolamine	2922.1320	36
三唑仑(INN)以及盐	Triazolam (INN);salts thereof	2933.9100	36
伞的零件,其他	Umbrellas parts,nes	6603.9000	
伞骨,包括装在伞柄上的伞骨	Umbrella frames, including frames mounted on shafts (sticks)	6603.2000	
伞及类似伞,庭园用	Umbrellas,for garden or similar usage	6601.1000	
伞菌属蘑菇,鲜或冷藏的	Mushrooms of the genus agaricus,fresh or chilled	0709.5100	1
伞菌属蘑菇,干的	Mushrooms of the genus agaricus,dried	0712.3100	4
伞菌属蘑菇,其他,盐水的,暂时保藏,但不适合直接使用的	Mushrooms of the genus agaricus, nes, in brine, provisionally preserved,but unsuitable in that state for immediate consumption	0711.5119	34
伞菌属蘑菇,其他,暂时保藏,但不适合直接使用的	Mushrooms of the genus agaricus,nes,provisionally preserved, but unsuitable in that state for immediate consumption	0711.5190	34
散货船,机动的,载重量不超过15万吨	Bulk ships, motor powered, loading not exceeding 150000t	8901.9041	8

S

商品名称	Article Description	税则号列	申报要素
散货船,机动的,载重量超过 15 万吨,但不超过 30 万吨	Bulk ships, motor powered, loading exceeding 150000t, not exceeding 300000t	8901.9042	8
散货船,机动的,载重量超过 30 万吨	Bulk ships, motor powered, loading exceeding 300000t	8901.9043	8
散热器及其零件,钢铁制,非电热的,集中供暖用,其他	Radiators for central heating and parts thereof, of iron or steel, not electrically heated, nes	7322.1900	7
散热器及其零件,铸铁制,非电热的,集中供暖用	Radiators for central heating and parts thereof, of cast iron, not electrically heated	7322.1100	7
散页印刷品及类似印刷品,单张的,不论是否折叠	Leaflets and similar printed matter, in single sheets, whether or not folded	4901.1000	15
散装货物储运软袋,化学纤维材料制	Flexible intermediate bulk containers, of man-made textile materials	6305.3200	346
sang			
桑蚕茧,适于缫丝的	Silk-worm cocoons, mulberry feeding	5001.0010	45
桑蚕丝,厂丝	Mulberry silk-worm silk, plant reeled (filature silk)	5002.0011	45
桑蚕丝,其他	Mulberry silk-worm silk, nes	5002.0019	45
桑蚕丝,双宫丝	Mulberry silk-worm silk, doupion	5002.0013	45
桑蚕丝,土丝	Mulberry silk-worm silk, home reeled	5002.0012	45
桑蚕丝机织物,按重量计丝或绢丝含量在 85% 及以上,其他	Mulberry silk-worm silk fabrics, containing 85% or more by weight of silk or silk waste, nes	5007.2019	4568
桑蚕丝机织物,未漂白或漂白,按重量计丝或绢丝含量在 85% 及以上	Mulberry silk-worm silk fabrics, unbleached (unscoured or scoured) or bleached, containing 85% or more by weight of silk or silk waste	5007.2011	4568
桑椹,冷冻的	Mulberries, frozen	0811.2000	1
桑椹,鲜的	Mulberries, fresh	0810.2000	1
sao			
扫描仪	Scanner	8471.6050	
扫雪车	Snow sweep vehicles for cleansing streets or airfield runways	8705.9070	7
扫雪机	Snow-ploughs	8430.2000	5
扫雪机零件	Snow-ploughs parts	8431.4990	3
扫帚及刷子的身及柄, 辐射松制的	Broom or brush bodies and handles, of radiata pine	4417.0010	56
扫帚及刷子的身及柄,其他木制的	Broom or brush bodies and handles, of other wood	4417.0090	56
se			
色带, 已上油着色的	Ribbons, inked	9612.1000	
色淀	Colour lakes	3205.0000	
色淀制品	Colour lakes preparations	3205.0000	
色拉调味料	Salad dressings	2103.9090	268
色拉甜菜根,鲜或冷藏的	Salad beetroot, fresh or chilled	0706.9000	1
色谱仪,其他	Chromatographs instruments, nes	9027.2019	7

S

商品名称	Article Description	税则号列	申报要素
色谱仪零件、附件	Chromatographs instruments parts and accessories	9027.9000	3
色选机器,种子、谷物或干豆用	Sorting machines with color, for seed, grain or dried leguminous vegetables	8437.1010	3
sha			
杀虫灯芯、蜡烛,零售包装	Wicks and candles, put up for retail sale	3808.9910	36
杀虫剂,零售包装,其他	Insecticides, put up for retail sale, nes	3808.9119	36
杀虫剂,其他	Insecticides, nes	3808.9190	36
杀虫脒(ISO)	Chlordimeform (ISO)	2925.2100	36
杀菌剂,零售包装	Fungicides, put up for retail sale	3808.9210	36
杀菌剂,其他	Fungicides, nes	3808.9290	36
杀鼠剂,零售包装	Rodenticides, put up for retail sale	3808.9910	36
杀鼠剂,其他	Rodenticides, nes	3808.9990	36
沙参	Adenophora axilliflora	1211.9034	34
沙蚕,活、鲜或冷的	Clamworm, live, fresh or chilled	0307.9192	1
沙丁鱼,冻的	Sardines (Sardina pilchardus, Sardinops spp.), frozen	0303.7100	18
沙丁鱼,鲜或冷的	Sardines (Sardina pilchardus, Sardinops spp.), fresh or chilled	0302.6100	18
沙丁鱼,制作或保藏的,整条或切块,但未绞碎	Sardines and brisling or sprats, prepared or preserved, whole or in pieces, but not minced	1604.1300	48
沙球	Maracas	9206.0000	5
沙石,不论是否热处理	Ballast, whether or not bead-treated	2517.1000	13
纱布,供医疗、外科、牙科或兽医用	Gauze, medical, surgical, dental or veterinary purposes	3005.9010	1346
纱罗,狭幅织物除外,其他	Gauze, other than narrow fabrics, nes	5803.0090	468
纱罗,狭幅织物除外,化学纤维制	Gauze, other than narrow fabrics, of man-made fibres	5803.0030	468
纱罗,狭幅织物除外,棉制	Gauze, other than narrow fabrics, of cotton	5803.0010	468
纱罗,狭幅织物除外,丝及绢丝制	Gauze, other than narrow fabrics, of silk or silk waste	5803.0020	468
砂布	Abrasive powder or grain, natural or artificial, on a base of woven textile fabric only	6805.1000	246
砂光机,手提式,本身装有电动动力装置的	Belt sander, hand tools, with self-contained electric motor	8467.2910	57
砂浆混合机器	Mortar mixers	8474.3100	
砂轮,带支架的手摇或脚踏	Grindding wheels, hand or pedal operated, with frameworks	8205.8000	256
砂轮,其他粘聚磨料制或陶瓷制	Grinding wheels, of other agglomerated abrasives or of ceramics	6804.2210	236
砂轮,天然石料制	Grinding wheels, of natural stone	6804.2310	236
砂轮机,加工金属或金属陶瓷用	Grinding wheel machines, for metal or cermets	8460.9010	7
砂轮机,手提式,本身装有电动动力装置的	Wheel-sander, hand tools with self-contained electric motor	8467.2910	57

商品名称	Article Description	税则号列	申报要素
砂轮及类似品,粘聚合成或天然金刚石制	Grinding wheels and the like, of agglomerated synthetic or natural diamond	6804. 2100	236
砂磨机器,加工木材、软木、骨、硬质橡胶、硬质塑料或类似硬质材料的	Sanding machines, for working wood, cork, bone, hard rubber, hard plastics or similar hard materials	8465. 9300	7
砂岩	Sandstone	2516. 2000	148
砂纸	Natural or artificial abrasive powder or grain, on a base of paper or paperboard only	6805. 2000	246
鲨鱼,其他,冻的	Sharks, nes, frozen	0303. 7500	18
鲨鱼,其他,鲜或冷的	Sharks, nes, fresh or chilled	0302. 6500	18
shai			
筛布,不论是否制成的	Bolting cloth, whether or not made up	5911. 2000	
筛选机,其他	Screening machines, nes	8479. 8200	7
筛选机器,泥土、石料、矿石或其他固体矿物质的	Screening machines, for earth, stone, ores or other mineral substances	8474. 1000	
晒黑油	Sun tan preparations	3304. 9900	23
shan			
山苍子油	Essential oils of litsea cubeba	3301. 2950	34
山地自行车	Mountain bicycle	8712. 0030	8
山核桃,鲜或干的	Pecan nuts, fresh or dried	0802. 9090	134
山葵,鲜或冷藏的	Horseradish, fresh or chilled	0706. 9000	1
山梨醇,单独有化学定义的	D-glucitol(sorbitol), separate chemically defined	2905. 4400	36
山梨醇,其他	Sorbitol, nes	3824. 6000	1346
山羊,活的,改良种用	Goats, live, pure-bred breeding	0104. 2010	3
山羊,活的,改良种用除外	Goats, live, ex. pure-bred breeding	0104. 2090	3
山羊毛	Goat hair	0502. 9011	3
山羊肉	Meat of goats	0204. 5000	14
山竹果	Mangosteens	0804. 5030	14
珊瑚,已加工的	Coral, worked	9601. 9000	5
珊瑚及类似品	Coral and similar materials	0508. 0090	14
闪光灯,放电式(电子式),照相用	Flashlight, discharge lamp(electronic), photographic	9006. 6100	7
闪光灯,照相用,其他	Flashlight, photographic, nes	9006. 6990	7
闪光灯泡,照相用	Flash bulbs, photographic	9006. 6910	7
闪光灯装置及闪光灯泡的零件、附件,照相用,其他	Flashlight apparatus and flashbulbs parts and accessories, photographic, nes	9006. 9900	3
闪烁扫描装置,医疗、外科、牙科或兽医用	Scintigraphic apparatus, used in medical, surgical, dental or veterinary sciences	9018. 1400	
闪速存储器,未录制	Flash memory cards, unrecorded	8523. 5110	37
闪速存储器,已录制	Flash memory cards, recorded	8523. 5120	37
闪锌矿	Blende	2608. 0000	146

S

商品名称	Article Description	税则号列	申报要素
扇贝,包括海扇,冻、干、盐腌或盐渍的	Scallops, including queen scallops, of the genera pecten, chlamys or placopecte, frozen, dried, salted or in brine	0307. 2900	14
扇贝,包括海扇,其他,活或鲜或冷的	Scallops, including queen scallops, of the genera pecten, chlamys or placopecte, nes, live, fresh or chilled	0307. 2190	1
扇贝,包括海扇,种苗	Scallops, including queen scallops, of the genera pecten, chlamys or placopecte, for cultivation	0307. 2110	3
shang			
商业广告品、商品目录及类似印刷品,其他	Trade advertising material, commercial catalogues and the like, nes	4911. 1090	3
商业广告品、商品目录及类似印刷品,无商业价值的	Trade advertising material, commercial catalogues and the like, no commercial value	4911. 1010	3
上光剂及类似制品,保养木制家具、地板或其他木制品用的	Polishes, creams and similar preparations for the maintenance of wooden furniture, floors or other woodwork	3405. 2000	36
上光剂及类似制品,车身用的,但金属用的光洁剂除外	Polishes and similar preparations for coachwork, other than metal polishes	3405. 3000	36
上光剂及类似制品,鞋靴或皮革用的	Polishes, creams and similar preparations for footwear or leather	3405. 1000	36
上浆机器,纺织物的	Dressing machines for textile fabrics	8451. 8000	
上浆机器零件,纺织物的	Dressing machines parts for textile fabrics	8451. 9000	
上衣,非针织或钩编的,男式,合成纤维制	Jackets and blazers, not knitted or crocheted, for men or boys, of synthetic fibres	6203. 3300	2456
上衣,非针织或钩编的,男式,棉制	Jackets and blazers, not knitted or crocheted, for men or boys, of cotton	6203. 3200	2456
上衣,非针织或钩编的,男式,其他	Jackets and blazers, not knitted or crocheted, for men or boys, nes	6203. 3990	2456
上衣,非针织或钩编的,男式,丝及绢丝制	Jackets and blazers, not knitted or crocheted, for men or boys, of silk or silk waste	6203. 3910	2456
上衣,非针织或钩编的,男式,羊毛或动物细毛制	Jackets and blazers, not knitted or crocheted, for men or boys, of wool or fine animal hair	6203. 3100	2456
上衣,非针织或钩编的,女式,合成纤维制	Jackets and blazers, not knitted or crocheted, for women or girls, of synthetic fibres	6204. 3300	2456
上衣,非针织或钩编的,女式,棉制	Jackets and blazers, not knitted or crocheted, for women or girls, of cotton	6204. 3200	2456
上衣,非针织或钩编的,女式,其他	Jackets and blazers, not knitted or crocheted, for women or girls, nes	6204. 3990	2456
上衣,非针织或钩编的,女式,丝及绢丝制	Jackets and blazers, not knitted or crocheted, for women or girls, of silk or silk waste	6204. 3910	2456
上衣,非针织或钩编的,女式,羊毛或动物细毛制	Jackets and blazers, not knitted or crocheted, for women or girls, of wool or fine animal hair	6204. 3100	2456

商品名称	Article Description	税则号列	申报要素
上衣,针织或钩编的,男式,合成纤维制	Jackets and blazers, knitted or crocheted, for men or boys, of synthetic fibres	6103.3300	2456
上衣,针织或钩编的,男式,棉制	Jackets and blazers, knitted or crocheted, for men or boys, of cotton	6103.3200	2456
上衣,针织或钩编的,男式,其他纺织材料制	Jackets and blazers, knitted or crocheted, for men or boys, of other textile materials	6103.3900	2456
上衣,针织或钩编的,男式,羊毛或动物细毛制	Jackets and blazers, knitted or crocheted, for men or boys, of wool or fine animal hair	6103.3100	2456
上衣,针织或钩编的,女式,合成纤维制	Jackets and blazers, knitted or crocheted, for women or girls, of synthetic fibres	6104.3300	2456
上衣,针织或钩编的,女式,棉制	Jackets and blazers, knitted or crocheted, for women or girls, of cotton	6104.3200	2456
上衣,针织或钩编的,女式,其他纺织材料制	Jackets and blazers, knitted or crocheted, for women or girls, of other textile materials	6104.3900	2456
上衣,针织或钩编的,女式,羊毛或动物细毛制	Jackets and blazers, knitted or crocheted, for women or girls, of wool or fine animal hair	6104.3100	2456
shao			
烧锅及其零件,钢铁制,家用,已搪瓷	Casserole and parts thereof, of iron or steel, for household, enamelled	7323.9420	24
烧碱,固体	Caustic soda, solid	2815.1100	136
烧碱,水溶液	Caustic soda, in aqueous solution	2815.1200	136
烧碱,液体	Soda, liquid	2815.1200	136
烧烤炉及其零件,钢铁制,家用,使用固体燃料的	Barbecue and parts thereof, of iron or steel, for household, for solid fuel	7321.8900	7
哨子	Whistles	9208.9000	5
she			
蛇麻腺	Lupulin	1210.2000	14
设计图纸复制件,用感兴纸照相复印或用复写纸誊写的	Plans and drawings copies, photographic reqrodued on sensitized paper and carbon	4906.0000	
设计图纸原稿,手绘的,建筑、工程、工业、商业、地形或类似用途的	Plans and drawings for architectural, engineering, industrial, commercial topographical or similar purposes, being originals drawn by hand	4906.0000	
射击用靶	Shooting galleries	9508.9000	5
射线应用设备,医疗、外科、牙科或兽医用	Radiations apparatus, for medical, surgical, dental or veterinary uses	9022.2100	
射线照相设备的零件、附件	Radiography apparatus parts and accessories	9022.9090	3
射线治疗设备的零件、附件	Radiotherapy apparatus parts and accessories	9022.9090	3
摄谱仪,使用光学射线(紫外线、可见光、红外线)的	Spectrographs, using optical radiations (UV, visible, IR)	9027.3000	
摄谱仪零件、附件	Spectrographs parts and accessories	9027.9000	3
摄影机,高速的	Cameras, high speed	9007.1910	8

商品名称	Article Description	税则号列	申报要素
摄影机,胶片宽度小于16毫米或双8毫米	Cameras, for film of less than 16mm width or for double-8mm film	9007.1100	8
摄影机,其他	Cameras, nes	9007.1990	8
摄影机用零件、附件	Cameras parts and accessories	9007.9100	3
摄影硬片、软片、纸、纸板及纺织物,已曝光未冲洗的,其他	Photographic plates, film, paper, paperboard and textiles, exposed but not developed, nes	3704.0090	1238
摄影硬片及软片,供复制胶版用,已曝光已冲洗的	Photographic plates and film, for offset reproduction, exposed and developed	3705.1000	1238
摄影硬片及软片,已曝光已冲洗的,电影胶片除外,其他	Photographic plates and film, exposed and developed, other than cinematographic film, nes	3705.9090	1238
摄影用化学制剂,冲洗照相胶卷及相片用	Chemical preparations for photographic uses, for use in developing photographic film and photographs	3707.9010	36
摄影用化学制剂,其他	Chemical preparations for photographic uses, nes	3707.9090	36
麝香	Musk	0510.0030	14
麝香草	Thyme	0910.9900	6
shen			
砷	Arsenic	2804.8000	
深沟球轴承	Deep groove ball bearings	8482.1020	5
深红银矿	Pyrargyrite	2616.1000	146
神香	Agarbatti	3307.4100	23
神纸及类似用品	Joss paper and the like	4823.9020	68
肾上腺素	Epinephrine	2937.3100	36
肾脏透析设备(人工肾)	Artificial kidney (dialysis) apparatus	9018.9040	
渗水式笔	Porous-tipped pens	9608.2000	
sheng			
升华硫磺	Sulphur, sublimed	2802.0000	
升降、搬运、装卸机械,其他	Lifting, handling, loading or unloading machinery, nes	8428.9090	
升降机的零件	Lifts parts	8431.3100	3
升降机及倒卸式起重机,其他	Lifts and skip hoists, nes	8428.1090	
升降机及输送机,气压式	Elevators and conveyors, pneumatic type	8428.2000	7
升降机及输送机,用于连续运送货物或材料的,带式	Elevators and conveyors, continuous-action for goods or materials, belt type	8428.3300	57
升降机及输送机,用于连续运送货物或材料的,地下专用的	Elevators and conveyors, continuous-action for goods or materials, specially designed for underground use	8428.3100	57
升降机及输送机,用于连续运送货物或材料的,斗式	Elevators and conveyors, continuous-action for goods or materials, bucket type	8428.3200	57
升降机及输送机,用于连续运送货物或材料的,辊式	Elevators and conveyors, continuous-action for goods or materials, roller type	8428.3920	57

S

商品名称	Article Description	税则号列	申报要素
升降机及输送机,用于连续运送货物或材料的,链式	Elevators and conveyors, continuous-action for goods or materials, chain type	8428.3910	57
升降机及输送机,用于连续运送货物或材料的,其他	Elevators and conveyors, continuous-action for goods or materials, nes	8428.3990	57
生长激素及其衍生物和结构类似物	Somatotropin, its derivatives and structural analogues	2937.1100	36
生皮,马的,其他	Raw hides and skins, of equine animals, nes	4101.9020	1458
生皮,马的,整张的,完全干燥的每张重量不超过8千克,干盐腌的不超过10千克,鲜的、湿盐腌的或以其他方法保藏的不超过16千克	Raw hides and skins, of equine animals, whole, of a weight per skin not exceeding 8kg when simply dried, 10kg when dry-salted, or 16kg when fresh, wet-salted or otherwise preserved	4101.2020	1458
生皮,马的,整张的,重量超过16千克	Raw hides and skins, of equine animals, of a weight exceeding 16kg	4101.5020	1458
生皮,绵羊或羔羊的,不带毛的,经逆鞣处理的	Raw skins of sheep or lambs without wool on, have undergone a reversible tanning process	4102.2910	1458
生皮,绵羊或羔羊的,不带毛的,其他	Raw skins of sheep or lambs without wool on, nes	4102.2990	1458
生皮,绵羊或羔羊的,不带毛浸酸的,经逆鞣处理的	Raw skins of sheep or lambs without wool on, pickled, have undergone a reversible tanning process	4102.2110	1458
生皮,绵羊或羔羊的,不带毛浸酸的,其他	Raw skins of sheep or lambs without wool on, pickled, nes	4102.2190	1458
生皮,绵羊或羔羊的,带毛	Raw skins of sheep or lambs with wool on	4102.1000	1458
生皮,牛的,其他	Raw hides and skins, of bovine animals, nes	4101.9019	1458
生皮,牛的,经逆鞣处理的	Raw hides and skins, of bovine animals, have undergone a reversible tanning process	4101.9011	1458
生皮,牛的,整张的,完全干燥的每张重量不超过8千克,干盐腌的不超过10千克,鲜的、湿盐腌的或以其他方法保藏的不超过16千克,经逆鞣处理的	Raw hides and skins, of bovine animals, whole, of a weight per skin not exceeding 8kg when simply dried, 10kg when dry-salted, or 16kg when fresh, wet-salted or otherwise preserved, have undergone a reversible tanning process	4101.2011	1458
生皮,牛的,整张的,完全干燥的每张重量不超过8千克,干盐腌的不超过10千克,鲜的、湿盐腌的或以其他方法保藏的不超过16千克,其他	Raw hides and skins, of bovine animals, whole, of a weight per skin not exceeding 8kg when simply dried, 10kg when dry-salted, or 16kg when fresh, wet-salted or otherwise preserved, nes	4101.2019	1458
生皮,牛的,整张的,重量超过16千克,经逆鞣处理的	Raw hides and skins, whole, of a weight exceeding 16kg, have undergone a reversible tanning process	4101.5011	1458
生皮,牛的,整张的,重量超过16千克其他	Raw hides and skins, whole, of a weight exceeding 16kg, nes	4101.5019	1458
生皮,爬行动物的	Raw hides and skins of reptiles	4103.2000	1458
生皮,其他	Raw hides and skins, nes	4103.9090	1458
生皮,山羊板皮,经逆鞣处理的	Raw hides and skins of goats, have undergone a reversible tanning process	4103.9011	1458
生皮,山羊板皮,其他	Raw hides and skins of goats, nes	4103.9019	1458

商品名称	Article Description	税则号列	申报要素
生皮,小山羊皮,经逆鞣处理的	Raw hides and skins of goats kids, have undergone a reversible tanning process	4103.9021	1458
生皮,小山羊皮,其他	Raw hides and skins of goats kids, nes	4103.9029	1458
生皮,猪的	Raw hides and skins of swine	4103.3000	1458
生皮、皮革的处理机器	Skins or leather preparing machinery	8453.1000	
生皮、皮革的加工机器	Skins or leather working machinery	8453.1000	
生皮、皮革的鞣制机器	Skins or leather tanning machinery	8453.1000	
生皮、皮革的修理机器	Skins or leather repairing machinery	8453.8000	
生石膏	Gypsum	2520.1000	34
生石灰	Quicklime	2522.1000	
生丝,其他	Raw silk, nes	5002.0090	45
生锑	Crude antimony	2617.1010	146
生铁,非合金,按重量计含磷量在0.5%及以下	Pig iron, non-alloy, containing by weight 0.5% or less of phosphorus	7201.1000	6
生铁,非合金,按重量计含磷量在0.5%以上	Pig iron, non-alloy, containing by weight more than 0.5% of phosphorus	7201.2000	6
生铁,合金的	Pig iron, alloy	7201.5000	6
生铁、镜铁及钢铁的粉末,其他	Pig iron powders, spiegeleisen powders, iron or steel powders, nes	7205.2900	6
生物碱及其盐、醚、酯和其他衍生物,天然或合成再制的	Alkaloids, natural or reproduced by synthesis, and their salts, ethers, esters and other derivatives, nes	2939.9990	34
生物碱及其衍生物药品,其他,混合或未混合的,配定剂量或制成零售包装	Alkaloids or derivatives medicaments, nes, mixed or unmixed, put up in measured doses or in forms or packings for retail sale	3004.4090	368
生物碱及其衍生物药品,其他,两种或两种以上成分混合而成的,未配定剂量或制成零售包装	Alkaloids or derivatives medicaments, nes, consisting of two or more constituents which have been mixed together, not put up in measured doses or in forms or packings for retail sale	3003.4090	368
生物染色剂	Biological stains	3204.9010	345
声音录制或重放设备,其他	Sound recording or reproducing apparatus, nes	8519.8990	5
声音录制或重放设备,使用半导体媒体的,其他	Sound recording or reproducing apparatus, using semiconductor media, nes	8519.8139	5
声音录制或重放设备,使用磁性媒体的,其他	Sound recording or reproducing apparatus, using magnetic media, nes	8519.8119	5
声音录制或重放设备,使用光学媒体的,其他	Sound recording or reproducing apparatus, using optical media, nes	8519.8129	5
声音录制或重放设备,用硬币、钞票、银行卡、代币或其他支付方式使其工作的设备	Sound recording or reproducing apparatus, operated by coins, banknotes, bank cards, tokens or by other means of payment	8519.2000	5
声音录制或重放设备用零件、附件,其他	Sound recording or reproducing apparatus parts and accessories, nes	8522.9099	3

S

商品名称	Article Description	税则号列	申报要素
声音录制设备,装有声音重放装置的,闪速存储器型	Sound recorders, flash memory type, incorporating sound reproducing apparatus	8519. 8131	5
声音重放装置,未装有声音录制装置的,盒带型,编辑节目用放声机除外	Sound reproducing apparatus, cassette-type, not incorporating a sound recording device, other than transcribing machines	8519. 8111	5
绳的制造机器	Rope making machines	8479. 4000	7
绳绒线	Chenille yarn	5606. 0000	
圣餐饼	Wafers	1905. 3200	28
圣诞节用品	Christmas festivities articles	9505. 1000	5
圣诞树用成套灯具	Christmas trees lighting sets	9405. 3000	5
shi			
失真度表,通讯专用的	Distortion factor meters, specially designed for telecommunications	9030. 4090	7
施肥机,农业、园艺及林业用	Manure spreaders and fertilizer distributors, used in agriaulture, horticulture and forestry	8432. 4000	
湿度计	Hygrometers	9025. 8000	3
湿度计零件、附件	Hygrometers parts and accessories	9025. 9000	7
湿法蚀刻装置,平板显示器的制造机器及装置	For wet etching apparatus, flat panel displays manufacture machines and apparatus	8486. 3049	7
十二醇、十六醇及十八醇	Dodecan-1-ol(lauryl alcohol), hexade can-1-ol(cetyl alcohol) and octadecan-1-ol(stearyl alcohol)	2905. 1700	36
十二烷基苯	Dodecylbenzene	2902. 9030	6
什锦干果	Mixtures of nuts	0813. 5000	345
什锦果仁	Mixtures of nuts	2008. 1999	248
什锦坚果,干的	Mixtures of nuts, dried	0813. 5000	345
什锦蔬菜,冷冻的	Mixtures of vegetables, frozen	0710. 9000	16
什锦蔬菜,干的	Mixtures of vegetables, dried	0712. 9090	4
什锦蔬菜,用醋或醋酸以外的其他方法制作或保藏的	Mixtures of vegetables, prepared or preserved otherwise than by vinegar or acetic acid	2004. 9000	48
什锦蔬菜,暂时保藏,但不适合直接使用的	Mixtures of vegetables, provisionally preserved, but unsuitable in that state for immediate consumption	0711. 9090	34
什锦植物部分,食用的	Mixtures of parts of plants, edible	2008. 9200	248
石板,具有书写或绘画面的	Slates, with writing or drawing surfaces	9610. 0000	
石板,制成供印刷用	Lithographic stones, prepared for printing purposes	8442. 5000	
石房蛤毒素	Saxitoxin	3002. 9010	34
石膏板,未经装饰的,仅用纸、纸板贴面或加强的	Plaster boards, not ornamented, faced or reinforced with paper or paper board only	6809. 1100	46
石膏瓦及类似品,未经装饰的,仅用纸、纸板贴面或加强的	Plaster tiles and similar articles, not ornamented, faced or reinforced with paper or paper board only	6809. 1100	46
石膏镶板,未经装饰的,仅用纸、纸板贴面或加强的	Plaster panels, not ornamented, faced or reinforced with paper or paper board only	6809. 1100	46

S

商品名称	Article Description	税则号列	申报要素
石膏制品及以石膏为基本成分的混合材料制品,其他	Plaster articles or articles of compositions based on plaster, nes	6809. 9000	46
石膏制品及以石膏为基本成分的混合材料制品,未经装饰的,仅用纸、纸板贴面或加强的,其他	Plaster articles or articles of compositions based on plaster, not ornamented, faced or reinforced with paper or paper board only	6809. 1900	46
石灰华,用锯或其他方法切割成矩形,包括正方形	Travertine, merely cut, by sawing or otherwise, into blocks or slabs of a rectangular (including square) shape	2515. 1200	148
石灰华,原状或粗加修整	Travertine, crude or roughly trimmed	2515. 1100	148
石灰华碑石或建筑用石及其制品,简单切削或锯开并具有一个平面的	Travertine monumental or building stone and articles thereof, simply cut or sawn, with a flat or even surface	6802. 2120	3468
石灰华及其制品,已加工的,其他	Travertine and articles thereof, worked, nes	6802. 9190	3468
石灰华石刻	Travertine carvings	6802. 9110	3468
石灰石碑石或建筑用石及其制品,简单切削或锯开并具有一个平面的,其他	Calcareous stone monumental or building stone and articles thereof, simply cut or sawn, with a flat or even surface, nes	6802. 2910	3468
石灰石分解炉	Limestone decomposition furnace	8417. 8040	7
石灰石及其他钙质石,通常用于制造石灰或水泥的	Limestone and other calcareous stone, of a kind used for the manufacture of lime or cement	2521. 0000	3
石灰石及其制品,已加工的,其他	Calcareous stone and articles thereof, worked, nes	6802. 9290	3468
石灰石石刻,其他	Calcareous stone carvings, nes	6802. 9210	3468
石灰石助熔剂	Limestone flux	2521. 0000	3
石灰质碑用或建筑用石,其他	Calcareous monumental or building stone, nes	2515. 2000	148
石蜡,按重量计含油量小于0.75%	Paraffin wax, containing by weight less than 0.75% of oil	2712. 2000	146
石蜡,其他	Paraffin wax, nes	2712. 9090	6
石料的碎粒、碎屑及粉末,不论是否热处理,税号25.15及25.16所列,其他	Granules, chippings and powder, stones of heading No. 25.15 or 25.16, nes, whether or not heat-treated	2517. 4900	1
石榴石,天然	Garnet, natural	2513. 2000	
石棉,长纤维的,青石棉除外	Asbestos of long staple, ex. crocidolite	2524. 9010	148
石棉,其他	Asbestos, nes	2524. 9090	148
石棉、矿物质或纤维素为基本成分的未装配摩擦材料及其制品,适于作制动器、离合器及类似品,含石棉的,其他	Asbestos, mineral substances or cellulose friction material and articles thereof, not mpunted, for brakes, for clutches or the like, containing asbestos, nes	6813. 2090	6
石棉服装、衣着附件、帽类及鞋靴,以石棉为基本成分或以石棉和碳酸镁混合物为基本成分的	Asbestos clothing, clothing accessories, footwear and headgear, with a basis of asbestos or with a basis of asbestos and magnesium carbonate	6812. 9100	56
石棉摩擦材料及其制品,未装配,适于作制动器、离合器及类似品,其他	Asbestos friction material and articles thereof, not mpunted, for brakes, for clutches or the like, nes	6813. 2090	6
石棉水泥管子及附件	Asbestos tubes, pipes and fittings	6811. 4030	56

商品名称	Article Description	税则号列	申报要素
石棉水泥或类似材料制品,其他	Asbestos-cement articles or the like,nes	6811.4090	56
石棉水泥片、板、砖、瓦及类似制品	Asbestos-cement sheets, panels, tiles and similar articles	6302.5990	346
石棉瓦楞板	Asbestos corrugated sheets	6811.4010	56
石棉为基本成分或以石棉和碳酸镁混合物为基本成分的制品,其他	Asbestos articles of mixtures with a basis of crocidolite or with a basis of crocidolite and magnesium carbonate,nes	6812.9900	56
石棉纤维接合材料,成片或成卷的,压缩的	Asbestos fibre jointing, in sheets or rolls,compressed	6812.9300	56
石棉闸衬	Asbestos brake linings	6813.2010	6
石棉闸垫	Asbestos brake pads	6813.2010	6
石棉纸、麻丝板及毡子,以石棉为基本成分或以石棉和碳酸镁混合物为基本成分的	Asbestos paper, millboard and felt, with a basis of asbestos or with a basis of asbestos and magnesium carbonate	6812.9200	56
石磨、石碾,碾磨或磨浆用,未装支架的	Millstones and grindstones, for milling, grinding or pulping, without frameworks	6804.1000	36
石磨、石碾及类似品,其他粘聚磨料制或陶瓷制	Millstones and grindstones and the like, of other agglomerated abrasives or ceramics	6804.2290	236
石磨、石碾及类似品,天然石料制,其他	Millstones and grindstones and the like, of natural stone,nes	6804.2390	236
石磨、石碾及类似品,粘聚合成或天然金刚石制,其他	Millstones and grindstones and the like, of agglomerated synthetic or natural diamond,nes	6804.2100	236
石墨,胶态或半胶态	Graphite,colloidal or semi-colloidal	3801.2000	134
石墨,人造的	Graphite,artificial	3801.1000	134
石墨,天然的,粉末	Graphite,natural,in powder	2504.1099	13468
石墨,天然的,粉片	Graphite,natural,in flakes	2504.1010	13468
石墨,天然的,其他	Graphite,natural,nes	2504.9000	13468
石墨,天然的,球化的	Graphite,natural,spheroidized	2504.1091	13468
石墨或碳精制品,电气设备用,其他	Graphite or other carbon articles of a kind used for electrical purposes,nes	8545.9000	3
石墨制品,非电气的	Graphite articles,non-electrical	6815.1000	6
石墨制品或半制品,糊状、块状、板状	Graphite preparations or semi-manufactures, in the form of pastes,blocks,plates	3801.9000	134
石脑油	Naphtha	2710.1120	6
石印画的原本	Lithographs, original	9702.0000	
石英	Quartz	2506.1000	14
石英,压电,合成或再造的	Quartz,piezo-electric,synthetic or reconstructed	7104.1000	145
石英玻璃管,光导纤维用,波导级	Quartz tubes for optical fibres use,waveguide grade	7002.3110	238
石英砂	Quartz sands	2505.1000	34
石英岩	Quartzite	2506.2000	14
石油测井车	Petroleum well logging trucks	8705.9080	7
石油混沙车	Petroleum mixing sand trucks	8705.9080	7

S

商品名称	Article Description	税则号列	申报要素
石油及天然气钻探机,自推进的,其他	Oil and natural gas drilling machinery, self-propelled, nes	8430.4119	5
石油及天然气钻探机,自推进的,钻探深度在6000米及以上的	Oil and natural gas drilling machinery, self-propelled, of drilling depth of 6000m or more	8430.4111	5
石油焦,未煅烧,硫的重量百分比小于3%的	Petroleum coke, not calcined, containing by weight less than 3% of sulphur	2713.1110	134
石油焦,未煅烧,其他	Petroleum coke, not calcined, nes	2713.1190	134
石油焦,已煅烧,硫的重量百分比小于0.8%的	Petroleum coke, calcined, containing by weight less than 0.8% of sulphur	2713.1210	134
石油焦,已煅烧,其他	Petroleum coke, calcined, nes	2713.1290	134
石油沥青	Petroleum bitumen	2713.2000	12348
石油气及烃类气,其他,液态的	Petroleum gases and gaseous hydrocarbons, nes, liquid	2711.1990	1468
石油气及烃类气,其他,气态的	Petroleum gases and gaseous hydrocarbons, nes, in gaseous state	2711.2900	1468
石油树脂,初级形状的	Petroleum resins, in primary forms	3911.1000	16
石油压裂车	Petroleum fracturing unit trucks	8705.9080	7
石油原油	Petroleum oils, crude	2709.0000	56
石制品及矿物制品,其他	Stone or of other mineral articles, nes	6815.9990	6
石制品及矿物制品含有,菱镁矿、白云石或铬铁矿的	Stone or of other mineral articles, containing magnesite, dolomite or chromite	6815.9100	6
时间记录器,装有钟、表机芯或同步电动机的	Time of day recording apparatus, with clock or watch movement or with synchronous motor	9106.9000	5
时间间隔指示装置,装有钟、表机芯或同步电动机的	Time intervals indicating apparatus, with clock or watch movement or with synchronous motor	9106.9000	5
时刻记录器	Time-recorders	9106.1000	5
实心或半实心橡胶轮胎,航空器用	Solid or cushion tyres, of a kind used on aircraft	4012.9010	234
实心或半实心橡胶轮胎,其他	Solid or cushion tyres, nes	4012.9090	234
实心或半实心橡胶轮胎,汽车用	Solid or cushion tyres, of a kind used on motor cars, buses or lorries	4012.9020	234
实心圆柱体,包括圆片,压制软木制	Solid cylinders, including discs, of agglomerated cork	4504.1000	16
拾音头	Pick-up cartridges	8522.1000	3
食品,其他	Food preparations, nes	2106.9090	268
食品灌装设备用零件,饮料及液体用	Bottling machinery parts, for beverages or liquid food	8422.9020	
食品搅拌器,家用电动器具	Food mixers, electro-mechanical domestic appliances	8509.4090	
食品生产或加工机器	Food preparation or manufacture machinery	8438.8000	
食品生产或加工机器的零件	Food preparation or manufacture machinery parts	8438.9000	3
食品研磨机,家用电动器具	Food grinders, electro-mechanical domestic appliances	8509.4090	
食用水果或食用坚果的树、灌木,不论是否嫁接,其他	Trees, shrubs and bushes, grafted or not, of kinds which bear edible fruit or nuts, nes	0602.2090	
食用盐	Salt, edible	2501.0011	1368

商品名称	Article Description	税则号列	申报要素
食用脂油,未经乳化、混合或其他方法制作	Oleooil, not emulsified or mixed or otherwise prepared	1503.0000	4
莳萝,冷冻的	Dill, frozen	0710.8090	1
莳萝,鲜或冷藏的	Dill, fresh or chilled	0709.9090	1
莳萝粉	Dill powder	0910.9900	6
士的年及其盐	Strychnine and its salts	2939.9920	34
示波器,其他	Oscilloscopes and oscillographs, nes	9030.2090	7
示波器,通用的,测试频率在300兆赫兹以下的	Oscilloscopes and oscillographs, for general use, of test frequency less than 300 MHz	9030.2010	
示波器的零件、附件	Oscilloscopes and oscillographs parts and accessories	9030.9000	3
视距仪	Tachymeters(tacheometers)	9015.2000	
视觉信号装置,机动车辆用	Visual signalling equipment of a kind used for motor vehicles	8512.2090	7
视觉信号装置,自行车或机动车辆用	Visual signalling equipment parts for cycles or motor vehicles	8512.9000	3
视觉信号装置,自行车用	Visual signalling equipment of a kind used on bicycles	8512.1000	7
视频高密光盘(VCD)播放机	Video compact disc player	8521.9011	5
视频摄录一体机,非特种用途的广播极	Video camera recorders, broadcast quality, not for special purposes	8525.8032	7
视频摄录一体机,非特种用途的家用型	Video camera recorders, household-type, not for special purposes	8525.8033	7
视频摄录一体机,非特种用途的其他类型	Video camera recorders, not for special purposes	8525.8039	7
视频摄录一体机,特种用途的	Video camera recorders, for special purposes	8525.8031	7
视频摄录一体机用零件,非特种用途的取像模块	Video camera recorders parts, camera modules without special purposes	8529.9042	3
视频摄录一体机用零件,其他	Video camera recorders parts, nes	8529.9049	3
视频摄录一体机用零件,特种用途的	Video camera recorders parts, of special purposes	8529.9041	3
视频信号录制或重放设备,不论是否装有高频调谐器,其他	Video recording or reproducing apparatus, whether or not incorporating a video tuner, nes	8521.9090	5
视频信号录制或重放设备用零件、附件,其他	Video recording or reproducing apparatus parts and accessories, nes	8522.9039	3
视摄像机,非特种用途的广播级	Television cameras, broadcast quality, not for special purposes	8525.8012	7
视摄像机,非特种用途的其他类型	Television cameras, not for special purposes	8525.8013	7
视摄像机,特种用途的	Television cameras, for special purposes	8525.8011	7
试验台	Test benches	9031.2000	
饰扣,仿首饰,贱金属制,不论是否镀贵金属	Studs, imitation jewellery, of base metal, whether or not plated with precious metal	7117.1100	46
室内散香或除臭制品,其他	Perfuming or deodorizing preparations for rooms, nes	3307.4900	23
柿饼,干的	Persimmons, dried	0813.4020	34

商品名称	Article Description	税则号列	申报要素
柿子,食用的,用其他方法制作或保藏的	Persimmons, edible, otherwise prepared or preserved	2008.9990	248
柿子,鲜的	Kakis, fresh	0810.9090	1
柿子,鲜的	Persimmons, fresh	0810.9090	1
铈的化合物,其他	Ceric compounds, nes	2846.1090	
铈铁合金,其他	Ferro-cerium alloys, nes	3606.9019	13
铈铁合金,已切成形,可直接使用	Ferro-cerium alloys, cut to shape, for immediate use	3606.9011	13
释热元件,核反应堆的,未辐照	Cartridges, for nuclear reactors, non-irradiated	8401.3010	2
shou			
收割机,联合脱粒式	Harvesting machinery, combine type	8433.5990	
收割机,其他	Harvesting machinery, nes	8433.5990	
收割机,收获甘蔗用	Harvesting machinery, for sugarcane	8433.5990	
收割机,收获根茎或块茎用	Harvesting machinery, for root or tuber	8433.5990	
收割机零件	Harvesting machinery parts	8433.9090	
收获机,收获根茎或块茎用	Harvesting machines for root or tuber	8433.5300	
收集品及珍藏品,具有动物学、植物学、矿物学、解剖学、历史学、考古学、古生物学、人种学或钱币学意义的	Collections and collectors pieces of zoological, botanical, mineralogical, anatomical, historical, archaeolohical, palaeontological, ethnographic or numismatic interest	9705.0000	5
收据本,纸或纸板制的	Receipt books, of paper or paperboard	4820.1000	
手泵,但子目号 8413.11 或 8413.19 的货品除外	Hand pumps, other than those of subheading No. 8413.11 or 8413.19	8413.2000	23
手表,不论是否附有秒表装置,表壳用贵金属或包贵金属制成的,其他	Wrist-watches, whether or not incorporating a stop-watch facility, with case of precious metal or of metal clad with precious metal, nes	9101.2900	56
手表,不论是否附有秒表装置,其他	Wrist-watches, whether or not incorporating a stop-watch facility, nes	9102.2900	56
手表,不论是否附有秒表装置,自动上弦的,表壳用贵金属或包贵金属制成的	Wrist-watches, whether or not incorporating a stop-watch facility, automatic winding, with case of precious metal or of metal clad with precious metal	9101.2100	56
手表,不论是否附有秒表装置,自动上弦的,其他	Wrist-watches, whether or not incorporating a stop-watch facility, automatic winding, nes	9102.2100	56
手表,电力驱动的,不论是否附有秒表装置,表壳用贵金属或包贵金属制成的,其他	Wrist-watches, electrically operated whether or not incorporating a stop-watch faciiity, with case of precious metal or of metal clad with precious metal, nes	9101.1990	56
手表,电力驱动的,不论是否附有秒表装置,仅有光电显示器的,表壳用贵金属或包贵金属制成的	Wrist-watches, electrically operated whether or not incorporating a stop-watch facility, with optoelectronic display only, with case of precious metal or of metal clad with precious metal	9101.1910	56

S

商品名称	Article Description	税则号列	申报要素
手表,电力驱动的,不论是否附有秒表装置,仅有光电显示器的,其他	Wrist-watches, electrically operated whether or not incorporating a stop-watch facility, with optoelectronic display only, nes	9102. 1200	56
手表,电力驱动的,不论是否附有秒表装置,仅有机械指示器的,表壳用贵金属或包贵金属制成的	Wrist-watches, electrically operated whether or not incorporating a stop-watch facility, with mechanical display only, with case of precious metal or of metal clad with precious metal	9101. 1100	56
手表,电力驱动的,不论是否附有秒表装置,仅有机械指示器的,其他	Wrist-watches, electrically operated whether or not incorporating a stop-watch facility, with mechanical display only, nes	9102. 1100	56
手表,电力驱动的,不论是否附有秒表装置,其他	Wrist-watches, electrically operated whether or not incorporating a stop-watch facility, nes	9102. 1900	56
手电筒,自供能源的	Portable electric torches, designed to function by dry batteries	8513. 1010	5
手电筒用零件,自供能源的	Portable electric torches parts, designed to function by dry batteries	8513. 9010	3
手动机械器具,重量不超过 10 千克,用于加工或调制食品或饮料的	Hand-operated mechanical appliances, weighing 10kg or less, used in the preparation, conditioning or serving of food or drink	8210. 0000	256
手风琴及类似乐器	Accordions and similar instruments	9205. 9020	5
手扶拖拉机	Pedestrian controlled tractors	8701. 1000	
手稿	Hand-written text	4906. 0000	
手稿复制件,用感兴纸照相复印或用复写纸眷写的	Hand-written text copies, photographic reproduced on sensitized paper and carbon	4906. 0000	
手工工具,家用,其他	Hand tools for household, nes	8205. 5100	256
手工工具,其他	Hand tools, nes	8205. 5900	256
手工工具,用于农业、园艺或林业的,其他	Hand tools of a kind used in agriculture, horticulture or forestry, nes	8201. 9000	256
手工锯	Hand saws	8202. 1000	256
手工针绣嵌花装饰毯	Needle-worked tapestries	5805. 0010	468
手榴弹发射器	Grenade launchers	9301. 2000	
手榴弹及其零件	Grenades and parts	9306. 9000	3
手帕,非针织或钩编的,刺绣的,棉制	Handkerchiefs, not knitted or crocheted, embroidered, of cotton	6213. 2010	2456
手帕,非针织或钩编的,刺绣的,其他	Handkerchiefs, not knitted or crocheted, embroidered, nes	6213. 9020	2456
手帕,非针织或钩编的,棉制,其他	Handkerchiefs, not knitted or crocheted, of cotton, nes	6213. 2090	2456
手帕,非针织或钩编的,其他	Handkerchiefs, not knitted or crocheted, nes	6213. 9090	2456
手帕纸,纸浆、纸、纤维素絮纸或纤维素纤维网纸制的	Handkerchiefs, of paper pulp, paper, cellulose wadding or webs of cellulose fibres	4818. 2000	568
手枪,其他	Pistols, nes	9302. 0000	
手枪用零件、附件,其他	Pistols parts and accessories, nes	9305. 1000	3

S

商品名称	Article Description	税则号列	申报要素
手术台,医疗、外科、牙科或兽医用	Operating tables, for medical, surgical, dental or veterinary usages	9402.9000	3
手套,包括连指或露指的,皮革或再生皮革制的,其他	Gloves, mittens and mitts, of leather or composition leather, nes	4203.2990	456
手套,包括连指或露指的,专供运动用,皮革或再生皮革制的	Gloves, mittens and mitts, specially designed for use in sports, of leather or composition leather	4203.2100	456
手套,聚氯乙烯制	Gloves of poly(vinyl chloride)	3926.2011	236
手套,硫化橡胶(硬质橡胶除外)制的,其他	Gloves, of vulcanized rubber other than hard rubber, nes	4015.1900	23
手套,其他塑料的	Gloves of other plastics	3926.2019	236
手套,外科用	Gloves for surgical	4015.1100	23
手提包,其他	Handbags, nes	4202.2900	256
手提包,以皮革、再生皮革或漆皮作面	Handbags, with outer surface of leather, composition leather or patent leather	4202.2100	256
手提包,以塑料片或纺织材料作面	Handbags, with outer surface of plastic sheeting or textile materials	4202.2200	256
手提式电灯,自供能源的,其他	Portable electric lamps, designed to function by their own source of energy, nes	8513.1090	5
手提式电灯零件,自供能源的,其他	Portable electric lamps parts, designed to function by their own source of energy, nes	8513.9090	3
手提式工具,锯,本身装有电动动力装置的,其他	Hand tools, saws, with self-contained electric motor, nes	8467.2290	57
手提式工具,本身装有电动动力装置的,其他	Hand tools, with self-contained electric motor, nes	8467.2990	57
手提式工具,电刨,本身装有电动动力装置的	Hand tools, planings, with self-contained electric motor	8467.2920	57
手提式工具,各种钻,本身装有电动动力装置的	Hand tools, drills of all kinds, with self-contained electric motor	8467.2100	57
手提式工具,链锯	Hand tools, chain saws	8467.8100	57
手提式工具,链锯,本身装有电动动力装置的	Hand tools, chain saws, with self-contained electric motor	8467.2210	57
手提式工具,其他	Hand tools, nes	8467.8900	57
手提式工具,气动的,其他	Hand tools, pneumatic, nes	8467.1900	57
手提式工具,气动的,旋转式(包括旋转冲击式的)	Hand tools, pneumatic, rotary type (including combined rotarypercussion)	8467.1100	57
手提式工具,砂磨工具(包括磨光机,砂光机,砂轮机等),本身装有电动动力装置的	Hand tools, grinding tools (including burnisher, belt sander, wheel-sander)	8467.2910	57
手提式工具用零件,电动工具的,其他	Hand tools parts, for self-contained electric motor tools, nes	8467.9910	3
手提式工具用零件,其他	Hand tools parts, nes	8467.9990	3
手摇风琴	Mechanical street organs	9208.9000	5

S

商品名称	Article Description	税则号列	申报要素
手印器,带有排字盘的	Hand printing sets incorporating such composing sticks	9611.0000	
手杖	Walking-sticks	6602.0000	
手杖的零件	Walking-sticks parts	6603.9000	
首日封	First-day covers	9704.0090	5
首饰盒,其他	Jewellery boxes, nes	4202.9900	256
首饰盒,以皮革、再生皮革或漆皮作面	Jewellery boxes, with outer surface of leather, composition leather or patent leather	4202.9100	256
首饰盒,以塑料片或纺织材料作面	Jewellery boxes, with outer surface of plastic sheeting or textile materials	4202.9200	256
首饰及其零件,铂制,不论是否包、镀贵金属,其他	Jewellery articles and parts thereof, of platinium, whether or not plated or clad with precious metal, nes	7113.1929	46
首饰及其零件,铂制,不论是否包、镀贵金属,镶嵌钻石的	Jewellery articles and parts thereof, of platinium, whether or not plated or clad with precious metal, diamond mounted or set	7113.1921	46
首饰及其零件,贵金属制,不论是否包、镀贵金属,其他	Jewellery articles and parts thereof, of precious metal, whether or not plated or clad with precious metal, nes	7113.1999	46
首饰及其零件,贵金属制,不论是否包、镀贵金属,镶嵌钻石的	Jewellery articles and parts thereof, of precious metal, whether or not plated or clad with precious metal, diamond mounted or set, nes	7113.1991	46
首饰及其零件,黄金制,不论是否包、镀贵金属,其他	Jewellery articles and parts thereof, of gold, whether or not plated or clad with precious metal, nes	7113.1919	46
首饰及其零件,黄金制,不论是否包、镀贵金属,镶嵌钻石的	Jewellery articles and parts thereof, of gold, whether or not plated or clad with precious metal, diamond mounted	7113.1911	46
首饰及其零件,以贱金属为底的包贵金属制,其他	Jewellery articles and parts thereof, of base metal clad with precious metal, nes	7113.2090	46
首饰及其零件,以贱金属为底的包贵金属制,镶嵌钻石的	Jewellery articles and parts thereof, of base metal clad with precious metal, diamond mounted or set, nes	7113.2010	46
首饰及其零件,银制,不论是否包、镀其他贵金属,其他	Jewellery articles and parts thereof, of silver, whether or not plated or clad with other precious metal, nes	7113.1190	46
首饰及其零件,银制,不论是否包、镀其他贵金属,镶嵌钻石的	Jewellery articles and parts thereof, of silver, whether or not plated or clad with other precious metal, diamond mounted or set	7113.1110	46
受精鱼卵	Fertilized fish eggs	0511.9111	4
狩猎用步枪,其他	Hunting rifles, nes	9303.3000	
狩猎用猎枪,包括组合式滑膛来复枪	Hunting shotguns, including combination shotgun rifles	9303.2000	
兽骨,已加工的	Bone, worked	9601.9000	5
兽毛,其他,制刷用	Bristles and hair, nes, for brush making	0502.9019	3

商品名称	Article Description	税则号列	申报要素
兽牙	Ivory	0507.1000	14
兽牙废料	Ivory waste	0507.1000	14
兽牙粉末	Ivory powder	0507.1000	14
兽牙及其制品,已加工的	Ivory and articles of ivory, worked	9601.1000	
兽医用仪器及器具,其他	Veterinary sciences instruments and appliances, nes	9018.9090	7
兽用疫苗	Vaccines for veterinary medicine	3002.3000	34
售票机	Ticket issuing machines	8470.9000	
shu			
书包及类似容器,以皮革、再生皮革或漆皮作面	School satchels and similar containers, with outer surface of leather, of composition leather or patent leather	4202.1190	1458
书包及类似容器,以塑料或纺织材料作面	School satchels and similar containers, with outer surface of plastics or textile materials	4202.1290	256
书本装订机器,其他	Book binding machinery, nes	8440.1090	
书本装订机器零件,其他	Book binding machinery parts, nes	8440.9000	3
书籍、小册子	Printed books, brochures	4901.9900	15
书籍封面,纸或纸板制的	Book covers, of paper or paperboard	4820.9000	
书写、印刷或类似用途的纸及纸板,所含用机械或化学-机械方法制得的纤维超过全部纤维重量的10%,单面或双面涂布高岭土或其他无机物质的,其他	Paper and paperboard of a kind used for writing, printing or other graphic purposes, of which more than 10% by weight of the total fibre content, consists of fibres obtained by a mechanical or chemi-mechanical process, coated on one or both sides with kaolin or other inorganic substances, nes	4810.2900	14568
书写册子,内装各种纸制文具	Writing compendiums of paper or paperboard, containing an assortment of paper stationery	4817.3000	6
叔丁醇	Tertiary butanol	2905.1430	36
梳理机,毛纤维型	Carding machines, for wool type fibres	8445.1120	7
梳理机,棉纤维型,其他	Carding machines, for cotton type fibres, nes	8445.1119	7
梳理机,其他	Carding machines, nes	8445.1190	7
梳棉机	Card or carding machine, for cotton type fibres	8445.1113	7
梳子,其他	Combs, nes	9615.1900	6
梳子,硬质橡胶或塑料制	Combs, of hard rubber or plastics	9615.1100	6
疏松石蜡	Slack wax	2712.9090	6
舒芬太尼(INN)及盐	Sufentanil(INN); salts thereof	2934.9100	36
输送带及带料,硫化橡胶制的,仅用纺织材料加强的	Conveyor belts or belting, of vulcanized rubber, reinforced only with textile materials	4010.1200	1368
输送带及带料,硫化橡胶制的,仅用金属加强的	Conveyor belts or belting, of vulcanized rubber, reinforced only with metal	4010.1100	1368
输送带及带料,硫化橡胶制的,其他	Conveyor belts or belting, of vulcanized rubber, nes	4010.1900	1368
输送机零件	Conveyors parts	8431.3900	3
输血设备	Blood transfusion apparatus	9018.9060	

S

商品名称	Article Description	税则号列	申报要素
蔬菜,其他,冷冻的	Vegetables, nes, frozen	0710. 8090	1
蔬菜,其他,干的	Vegetables, nes, dried	0712. 9090	4
蔬菜,其他,鲜或冷藏的	Vegetables, nes, fresh or chilled	0709. 9090	1
蔬菜,其他,盐水的,暂时保藏,但不适合直接使用的	Vegetables, nes, in brine, provisionally preserved, but unsuitable in that state for immediate consumption	0711. 9039	34
蔬菜,其他,用醋或醋酸以外的其他方法制作或保藏的	Vegetables, nes, prepared or preserved otherwise than by vinegar or acetic acid	2004. 9000	48
蔬菜,其他,暂时保藏,但不适合直接使用的	Vegetables, nes, provisionally preserved, but unsuitable in that state for immediate consumption	0711. 9090	34
蔬菜及什锦蔬菜,其他	Vegetables and mixtures of vegetables, nes	2005. 9999	148
蔬菜加工机器	Vegetables preparation machinery	8438. 6000	
蔬菜加工机器的零件	Vegetables preparation machinery parts	8438. 9000	3
蔬菜榨汁机,家用电动器具	Vegetable juice extractors, electro-mechanical domestic appliances	8509. 4010	
蔬菜汁,其他单一蔬菜的	Vegetable juice, of any other single vegetable	2009. 8020	2468
蔬菜种子,种植用的	Vegetable seeds	1209. 9100	358
熟石膏,其他	Plasters, nes	2520. 2090	34
熟石膏,牙科用	Plasters, for dental use	2520. 2010	34
熟石灰	Slaked lime	2522. 2000	
黍鲱鱼,冻的	Brisling or sprats(Sprattus), frozen	0303. 7100	18
黍鲱鱼,鲜或冷的	Brisling or sprats(Sprattus), fresh or chilled	0302. 6100	18
黍鲱鱼,制作或保藏的,整条或切块,但未绞碎	Sardinella and Brisling or Sprats, prepared or preserved, whole or in pieces, but not minced	1604. 1300	48
鼠标器	Mouses	8471. 6072	
鼠海豚(鲸目哺乳动物)	Porpoises (mammals of the order cetacea)	0106. 1200	
鼠海豚(鲸目哺乳动物)的肉,鲜或冷或冻的	Meat of porpoises(mammals of the order cetacea), fresh, chilled or frozen	0208. 4000	15
鼠海豚(鲸目哺乳动物)肉粉,食用	Flours and meals of meat of porpoises(mammals of the order cetacea), edible	0210. 9200	14
鼠李糖	Rhamnose	2940. 0000	6
曙红	Eosins (as synthetic organic colouring matter)	3204. 1200	345
束袜带和类似品,化学纤维制	Arters and similar articles, of man-made fibres	6212. 9010	2456
束袜带和类似品,其他纺织材料制	Arters and similar articles, of other textile materials	6212. 9090	2456
束腰带及腹带,化学纤维制	Girdles and panty-girdles, of man-made fibres	6212. 2010	2456
束腰带及腹带,其他纺织材料制	Girdles and panty-girdles, of other textile materials	6212. 2090	2456
束腰胸衣,化学纤维制	Corselettes of man-made fibres	6212. 3010	2456
束腰胸衣,其他纺织材料制	Corselettes of other textile materials	6212. 3090	2456
树胶脂	Gumresins	1301. 9090	
树篱剪	Hedge shears	8201. 6000	256
树脂	Resins	1301. 9090	
树脂胶泥	Resin cements	3214. 1090	3
树脂酸	Resin acides	3806. 1020	4

S

商品名称	Article Description	税则号列	申报要素
树脂酸盐	Resin acids	3806.2010	4
竖琴	Harps	9202.9000	5
竖琴的零件、附件	Harps parts and accessories	9209.9200	3
竖式钢琴	Upright pianos	9201.1000	5
数据/图形显示管,彩色的,屏幕荧光点间距小于0.4毫米	Data/graphic display tubes, colour, with a phosphor dot screen pitch smaller than 0.4mm	8540.4000	35
数据/图形显示管,黑白的或其他单色的	Data/graphic display tubes, black and white or other monochrome	8540.5000	35
数据记录、重现及显示机器,具有计算功能的,袖珍式	Data recording, reproducing and displaying machines with calculating functions, pocket-size	8470.1000	
数控装置,用于电压不超过1000伏的线路,装有两个或多个开关、保护或连接用的电器装置,其他	Numerical control panels, for a voltage not exceeding 1000V, equipped with two or more switching or protecting or connecting apparatus, nes	8537.1019	78
数学计算器具	Mathematical calculating instruments	9017.2000	
数学计算器具的零件、附件	Mathematical calculating instruments parts and accessories	9017.9000	3
数字化视频光盘(DVD)播放机	Digital video disc player	8521.9012	5
数字化仪	Digitizer	8471.6060	
数字照相机,非特种用途的单镜头反光型	Digital cameras, single lens reflex, not for special purposes	8525.8022	7
数字照相机,非特种用途的其他类型	Digital cameras, not for special purposes	8525.8029	7
数字照相机,特种用途的	Digital cameras, for special purposes	8525.8021	7
数字照相机用零件,非特种用途的取像模块	Digital cameras parts, camera modules without special purposes	8529.9042	3
数字照相机用零件,其他	Digital cameras parts, nes	8529.9049	3
数字照相机用零件,特种用途的	Digital cameras parts, of special purposes	8529.9041	3
shua			
刷,其他	Brushes, nes	9603.5099	3
刷,作为机器、器具零件的	Brushes, constituting parts of machines or appliances	9603.5091	3
shuan			
栓,贱金属制,用于衣着、鞋靴、天篷、提包、旅行用品或其他制成品	Clasps, of base metal, of a kind used for clothing, footwear, awnings, handbags, travel goods or other made up articles	8308.9000	256
shuang			
双酚A及其盐	Bisphenol A and its salts	2907.2300	36
双氢可待因(INN)及盐	Dihydrocodeine (INN) and salts	2939.1100	34
双氰胺	Dicyandiamide	2926.2000	36
双巯丙氨酸	Cystine	2930.9010	36
双手修枝剪及类似的双手操作剪刀	Two-handed pruning shears and similar two-handed shears	8201.6000	256

S

商品名称	Article Description	税则号列	申报要素
双筒望远镜	Binoculars	9005. 1000	
双筒望远镜零件、附件(包括座架),其他	Binoculars parts and accessories (including mountings), nes	9005. 9090	3
shui			
水,加味、加糖或其他甜物质的	Waters, containing added sugar or other sweetening matter or flavoured	2202. 1000	248
水表	Water meters	9028. 2010	
水表零件、附件,工业用	Water meters parts and accessories, for industrial use	9028. 9010	3
水表零件、附件,其他	Water meters parts and accessories, nes	9028. 9090	3
水刺设备,毡呢或无纺织物制造用	Spunlaced equipment, for the manufacture of felt or non-wovens	8449. 0020	7
水道图及类似图表,印制的	Hydrographic or similar charts of all kinds, printed	4905. 9900	1
水貂皮,整张的,不论是否带头、尾或爪	Raw furskins of mink, whole, with or without head, tail or paws	4301. 1000	15
水钴矿	Heterogenite	2605. 0000	146
水硅铀矿	Coffinite	2612. 1000	146
水果,柑橘属,其他	Fruit, citrus, nes	0805. 9000	14
水果,其他,冷冻的	Fruits, nes, frozen	0811. 9090	1
水果,其他,鲜的	Fruits, nes, fresh	0810. 9090	1
水果,其他,暂时保藏,但不适于直接食用的	Fruits, nes, provisionally preserved, but unsuitable in that state for immediate consumption	0812. 9000	34
水果加工机器	Fruits preparation machinery	8438. 6000	
水果加工机器的零件	Fruits preparation machinery parts	8438. 9000	3
水果榨汁机,家用电动器具	Fruit juice extractors, electro-mechanical domestic appliances	8509. 4010	
水果汁,混合汁	Fruit juices, mixtures	2009. 9010	2468
水果汁,其他单一水果的	Fruit juice, of any other single fruit	2009. 8019	2468
水合肼	Hydrazine hydrate	2825. 1010	
水合钽铌原料	Hydrated tantalum/niobium materials	2615. 9010	146
水解气体发生器,不论有无净化器	Water process gas generators, with or without their purifiers	8405. 1000	3
水解气体发生器的零件	Water process gas generators parts	8405. 9000	3
水龙软管及类似的管子,纺织材料制的,不论有无其他材料作衬里、护套或附件	Hosepiping and similar tubing, of textile, with or without lining, armour or accessories of other materials	5909. 0000	
水轮机及水轮,功率不超过 1000 千瓦	Hydraulic turbines and water wheels, of a power not exceeding 1000kW	8410. 1100	2
水轮机及水轮,功率超过 10000 千瓦,其他	Hydraulic turbines and water wheels, of a power exceeding 10000kW	8410. 1390	
水轮机及水轮,功率超过 1000 千瓦,但不超过 10000 千瓦	Hydraulic turbines and water wheels, of a power exceeding 1000kW but not exceeding 10000kW	8410. 1200	2

S

商品名称	Article Description	税则号列	申报要素
水轮机及水轮,功率超过 200000 千瓦,水泵的	Hydraulic turbines and water wheels of a power exceeding 200000kW, pumping	8410.1330	27
水轮机及水轮,功率超过 30000 千瓦,冲击式的	Hydraulic turbines and water wheels of a power exceeding 30000kW, impulse	8410.1310	27
水轮机及水轮,功率超过 35000 千瓦,贯流式的	Hydraulic turbines and water wheels of a power exceeding 35000kW, radial	8410.1320	27
水轮机及水轮调节器	Hydraulic turbines and water wheels regulators	8410.9010	27
水轮机及水轮零件,其他	Hydraulic turbines and water wheels parts, nes	8410.9090	27
水煤气	Water gas	2705.0000	4
水煤气发生器,不论有无净化器	Water gas generators, with or without their purifiers	8405.1000	3
水煤气发生器的零件	Water gas generators parts	8405.9000	3
水泥,耐火的	Cements, for refractory	3816.0000	36
水泥、灰泥及混凝土用添加剂,其他	Cements, mortars or concretes additives, nes	3824.4090	36
水泥包装机,其他	Cement packing machinery, nes	8422.3029	
水泥包装机,全自动灌包机	Cement packing machinery, automatic filling and sacking machines	8422.3021	
水泥包装机零件	Cement packing machinery parts	8422.9090	
水泥扁平石及类似品	Cement flagstones and similar articles	6810.1990	56
水泥回转窑	Cement rotary kilns	8417.8030	7
水泥熟料	Cement clinkers	2523.1000	3
水泥瓦及类似品	Cement tiles and similar articles	6810.1990	56
水泥制品,其他	Cement articles, nes	6810.9990	56
水泥砖及块,建筑用	Cement blocks and bricks, for building	6810.1100	56
水凝水泥,其他	Hydraulic cements, nes	2523.9000	3
水平旋翼及其零件,航空器用	Rotors and parts thereof, of aircraft	8803.1000	3
水平仪	Levels	9015.3000	
水上运动用具,其他	Water-sport equipment, nes	9506.2900	5
水生无脊椎动物(甲壳动物除外)的细粉、粗粉及团粒,适合供人食用的	Flours, meals and pellets of aquatic invertebrates, fit for human consumption	0307.9990	14
水生无脊椎动物,其他,制作或保藏的	Aquatic invertebrates, nes, prepared or preserved	1605.9090	48
水箱, 陶制	Flushing cisterns, of pottery	6910.9000	268
水箱,瓷制	Flushing cisterns, of porcelain or china	6910.1000	268
水箱散热器,机动车辆用	Water tank radiators, of motor vehicles	8708.9110	3
水杨醇	Salicylic alcohol	2907.1990	36
水杨酸	Salicylic acid	2918.2110	36
水杨酸的其他酯及其盐	Esters of salicylic acid and their salts, nes	2918.2300	36
水杨酸钠	Sodium salicylate	2918.2110	36
水杨酸盐,其他	Salicylic acid salts, nes	2918.2190	36
水硬石灰	Hydraulic lime	2522.3000	
睡袋,其他	Sleeping bags, nes	9404.3090	6
睡袋,羽毛或羽绒填充的	Sleeping bags, stuffed with feathers or down	9404.3010	6

S

商品名称	Article Description	税则号列	申报要素
睡衣及睡衣裤,非针织或钩编的,女式,化学纤维制	Nightdresses and pyjamas, not knitted or crocheted, for women or girls, of man-made fibres	6208.2200	2456
睡衣及睡衣裤,非针织或钩编的,女式,棉制	Nightdresses and pyjamas, not knitted or crocheted, for women or girls, of cotton	6208.2100	2456
睡衣及睡衣裤,非针织或钩编的,女式,其他	Nightdresses and pyjamas, not knitted or crocheted, for women or girls, nes	6208.2990	2456
睡衣及睡衣裤,非针织或钩编的,女式,丝及绢丝制	Nightdresses and pyjamas, not knitted or crocheted, for women or girls, of silk or silk waste	6208.2910	2456
睡衣及睡衣裤,针织或钩编的,女式,化学纤维制	Nightdresses and pyjamas, knitted or crocheted, for women or girls, of man-made fibres	6108.3200	2456
睡衣及睡衣裤,针织或钩编的,女式,棉制	Nightdresses and pyjamas, knitted or crocheted, for women or girls, of cotton	6108.3100	2456
睡衣及睡衣裤,针织或钩编的,女式,其他	Nightdresses and pyjamas, knitted or crocheted, for women or girls, nes	6108.3990	2456
睡衣及睡衣裤,针织或钩编的,女式,丝及绢丝制	Nightdresses and pyjamas, knitted or crocheted, for women or girls, of silk or silk waste	6108.3910	2456
si			
丝,不锈钢的	Wire, of stainless steel	7223.0000	468
丝,非合金铝制,其他	Wire, of aluminium, not alloyed, nes	7605.1900	16
丝,非合金铝制,最大截面尺寸超过7毫米	Wire, of aluminium, not alloyed, of which the maximum cross-sectional dimension exceeding 7mm	7605.1100	16
丝,非合金镍制	Wire, of nickel, not alloyed	7505.2100	46
丝,高速钢制	Wire of high speed steel	7229.9010	6
丝,硅锰钢制	Wire of silico-manganese steel	7229.2000	6
丝,合金钢的,其他	Wire of other alloy steel, nes	7229.9090	6
丝,贱金属制,以焊剂涂面或以焊剂为芯,钎焊或气焊用	Wire, coated with flux material, of base metal, for soldering, brazing or welding by flame	8311.3000	56
丝,精炼铜制,其他	Wire, of refined copper, nes	7408.1900	16
丝,精炼铜制,最大截面尺寸超过6毫米	Wire, of refined copper, of which the maximum cross-sectional dimension exceeding 6mm	7408.1100	16
丝,铝合金制,其他	Wire, of aluminium alloys, nes	7605.2900	16
丝,铝合金制,最大截面尺寸超过7毫米	Wire, of aluminium alloys, of which the maximum cross-sectional dimension exceeding 7mm	7605.2100	16
丝,钼的	Wire, of molybdenum	8102.9600	16
丝,镍合金制	Wire, of nickel alloys	7505.2200	46
丝,钛的	Wire of titanium	8108.9020	16
丝,钽的,其他	Tantalum wire, nes	8103.9019	16
丝,钨的	Wire of tungsten	8101.9600	16
丝,硬质合金制,以焊剂涂面或以焊剂为芯,用于焊接或沉积金属、硬质合金	Wire, of metal carbides, coated or cored with flux material, of a kind used for soldering, brazing, welding or deposition of metal or of metal carbides	8311.9000	56

S

商品名称	Article Description	税则号列	申报要素
丝氨酸	Serine	2922.5000	36
丝瓜络制品	Loofah articles	4602.9000	6
丝或绢丝机织物,按重量计丝或绢丝含量在85%及以上,其他	Silk or of silk waste fabrics, containing 85% or more by weight of silk or of silk waste other than noil silk, nes	5007.2090	4568
丝或绢丝机织物,其他	Silk or of silk waste fabrics, nes	5007.9090	4568
丝或绢丝机织物,未漂白或漂白	Silk or of silk waste fabrics, unbleached or bleached	5007.9010	4568
丝或条,贱金属粉粘聚而成的,供金属喷镀用	Wire and rods, of agglomerated basemetal powder, used for metal spraying	8311.9000	56
丝纱线,非供零售用	Silk yarn, not put up for retail sale	5004.0000	3
丝纱线,供零售用	Silk yarn, put up for retail sale	5006.0000	356
丝袜、短袜及其他袜类,针织或钩编的,合成纤维制	Stockings, socks and other hosiery, knitted or crocheted, of synthetic fibres	6115.9600	2456
丝袜、短袜及其他袜类,针织或钩编的,棉制	Stockings, socks and other hosiery, knitted or crocheted, of cotton	6115.9500	2456
丝袜、短袜及其他袜类,针织或钩编的,其他纺织材料制	Stockings, socks and other hosiery, knitted or crocheted, of other textile materials	6115.9900	2456
丝袜、短袜及其他袜类,针织或钩编的,羊毛或动物细毛制	Stockings, socks and other hosiery, knitted or crocheted, of wool or fine animal hair	6115.9400	2456
丝纱钱及绢纺纱线,供零售用	Yarn spun from silk waste, put up for retail sale	5006.0000	356
司可巴比妥(INN)以及盐	Secobarbital(INN); salts thereof	2933.5300	36
司他夫定及它们的盐	Stavudine and their salts	2938.9010	34
锶的碳酸盐	Strontium carbonate	2836.9200	
锶的氧化物、氢氧化物及过氧化物	Strontium oxides, hydroxides and peroxides	2816.4000	
四环素	Tetracyclines	2941.3011	
四环素盐	Tetracyclines salts	2941.3012	
四环素衍生物及其盐	Tetracyclines derivatives and their salts	2941.3020	
四硫化二烃氨基硫羰	Thiuram tetrasulphide	2930.3000	36
四氯二氟乙烷	Tetrachlorodifluoroethane	2903.4530	36
四氯化碳	Carbon tetrachloride	2903.1400	36
四氯四氟丙烷	Tetrachlorotetrafluoropropane	2903.4570	36
四氯乙烯	Tetrachloroethylene	2903.2300	36
四硼酸钠,其他	Disodium tetraborate, nes	2840.1900	
四硼酸钠,无水的	Disodium tetraborate, anhydrous	2840.1100	
四氢苯酐	Tetrahydrobenzoic anhydride	2917.2010	36
四氢大麻酚(所有的异构体)	Tetrahydrocannabinols(all is omers)	2932.9500	36
四氢呋喃	Tetrahydrofuran	2932.1100	36
四氢萘	Tetrahydronaphthalene(tetralin)	2902.9010	6
四氢西泮(INN)和三唑仑(INN)以及盐	Tetrazepam (INN) and triazdam(INN); salts thereof	2933.9100	36
四氧化三钴	Cobalt tetroxide	2822.0010	
饲料,植物的,其他	Feeds stuffs of plants, nes	1214.9000	

S

商品名称	Article Description	税则号列	申报要素
饲料配制机,动物用	Feeding stuffs preparing machinery for animal	8436.1000	
饲料添加剂,制成的	Feeding stuffs preparations for use in making the complete feeds or supplementary feeds	2309.9010	2468
饲料甜菜,饲料用	Manigolds, forage products	1214.9000	
饲料羽衣甘蓝	Kale, forage products	1214.9000	
song			
松鸡,改良种用	Foxes, pure-bred breeding	0106.1910	34
松鸡,食用	Foxes, for human consumption	0106.1920	48
松绞双股丝,钢铁的,围篱用的	Loosely twisted double wire, of a kind used for fencing, of iron or steel	7313.0000	36
松茸,冷冻的	Sungmo, frozen	0710.8010	1
松茸,鲜或冷藏的	Sungmo, fresh or chilled	0709.5910	1
松茸,盐水的,暂时保藏,但不适合直接使用的	Sungmo, in brine, provisionally preserved, but unsuitable in that state for immediate consumption	0711.5911	34
松土机,农业、园艺及林业用,其他	Scarifiers, for agricultural, horticultural or forestry use, nes	8432.2900	
松香	Rosin	3806.1010	4
松香或树脂酸衍生物的盐	Rosin or resin acids derivatives	3806.2090	4
松香精	Rosin spirit	3806.9000	4
松香盐	Rosin salts	3806.2010	4
松香油	Rosin oils	3806.9000	4
松油	Pine oil	3805.9010	36
松脂	Pineresin	1301.9040	
松子仁	Pinenuts, shelled	0802.9030	134
送经装置,织机用	Let-off motions for looms	8448.4920	3
su			
苏打水	Soda water	2201.1020	28
苏麦克及类似的手织地毯	Schumacks and similar handwoven rugs	5702.1000	468
苏木红,正铁血红素	Haematein	3203.0019	34
酥油	Ghee	0405.9000	268
速调管	Klystrons	8540.7200	35
速度计,车辆用	Speed indicators for motor vehicles	9029.2010	
速度计,其他	Speed indicators, nes	9029.2090	7
速度计零件、附件	Speed indicators parts and accessories	9029.9000	3
塑封机,主要用于或专用于装配与封装半导体器件或集成电路	Plastics encapsulating machines, solely or principally of a kind used for assembling or encapsulating semiconductor devices	8486.4021	7
塑封机零件及附件,主要用于或专用于装配与封装半导体器件或集成电路	Plastics encapsulating machines parts and accessories, solely or principally of a kind used for assembling or encapsulating semiconductor devices	8486.9090	3

S

商品名称	Article Description	税则号列	申报要素
塑料板、片,聚乙烯制,嵌有玻璃纤维的	Plates, sheets of polyethylene with glass fibres	3921.9020	16
塑料板、片、卷材,聚异丁烯为基本成分的,附有人造毛毡的	Plates, sheets, coils of poly-isobutylene with man-made felt	3921.9030	16
塑料板、片、膜,箔、带、扁条及其他扁平形状材料,不论是否成卷,自粘的,其他	Sheets, film, foil, tape, strip and other flat shapes, of plastics, whether or not in rolls, self-adhesive plates, nes	3919.9090	16
塑料板、片、膜,箔、带、扁条及其他扁平形状材料,成卷,自粘的,宽度不超过20厘米,丙烯酸树脂类为基本成分	Sheets, film, foil, tape, strip and other flat shapes, of plastics, in rolls, self-adhesive plates, of a width not exceeding 20cm, based on acrylic resin	3919.1010	16
塑料板、片、膜,箔、带、扁条及其他扁平形状材料,成卷,自粘的,宽度不超过20厘米,其他	Sheets, film, foil, tape, strip and other flat shapes, of plastics, in rolls, self-adhesive plates, of a width not exceeding 20cm, nes	3919.1099	16
塑料板、片、膜、箔、扁条,泡沫塑料的,氨酯聚合物制,其他	Plates, sheets, film, foil and strip, of plastics, cellular, of polyurethanes, nes	3921.1390	16
塑料板、片、膜、箔、扁条,泡沫塑料的,苯乙烯聚合物制	Plates, sheets, film, foil and strip, of plastics, cellular, of polymers of styrene	3921.1100	16
塑料板、片、膜、箔、扁条,泡沫塑料的,氯乙烯聚合物制,其他	Plates, sheets, film, foil and strip, of plastics, cellular, of polymers of vingl chloride, nes	3921.1290	16
塑料板、片、膜、箔、扁条,泡沫塑料的,其他	Plates, sheets, film, foil and strip, of plastics, cellular, nes	3921.1990	16
塑料板、片、膜、箔、扁条,泡沫塑料的,再生纤维素制	Plates, sheets, film, foil and strip, of plastics, cellular, of regenerated cellulose	3921.1400	16
塑料板、片、膜、箔、扁条,其他	Plates, sheets, film, foil and strip, of plastics, nes	3921.9090	16
塑料板、片、膜、箔及扁条,非泡沫,未用其他材料强化、层压、支撑或用类似方法合制,氨基树脂制	Plates, sheets, film, foil and strip, of plastics, non-cellular and not reinforced, laminated, supported or similarly combined with other materials, of amino-resins	3920.9300	16
塑料板、片、膜、箔及扁条,非泡沫,未用其他材料强化、层压、支撑或用类似方法合制,苯乙烯聚合物制	Plates, sheets, film, foil and strip, of plastics, non-cellular and not reinforced, laminated, supported or similarly combined with other materials, of polymers of styrene	3920.3000	16
塑料板、片、膜、箔及扁条,非泡沫,未用其他材料强化、层压、支撑或用类似方法合制,丙烯酸聚合物制,其他	Plates, sheets, film, foil and strip, of plastics, non-cellular and not reinforced, laminated, supported or similarly combined with other materials, of acrylic polymers, nes	3920.5900	16
塑料板、片、膜、箔及扁条,非泡沫,未用其他材料强化、层压、支撑或用类似方法合制,不饱和聚酯制	Plates, sheets, film, foil and strip, of plastics, non-cellular and not reinforced, laminated, supported or similarly combined with other materials, of unsaturated polyesters	3920.6300	16

S

商品名称	Article Description	税则号列	申报要素
塑料板、片、膜、箔及扁条,非泡沫,未用其他材料强化、层压、支撑或用类似方法合制,酚醛树脂制	Plates, sheets, film, foil and strip, of plastics, non-cellular and not reinforced, laminated, supported or similarly combined with other materials, of phenolic resins	3920.9400	16
塑料板、片、膜、箔及扁条,非泡沫,未用其他材料强化、层压、支撑或用类似方法合制,聚对苯二甲酸乙二酯制	Plates, sheets, film, foil and strip, of plastics, non-cellular and not reinforced, laminated, supported or similarly combined with other materials, of poly (ethylene terephthalate)	3920.6200	16
塑料板、片、膜、箔及扁条,非泡沫,未用其他材料强化、层压、支撑或用类似方法合制,聚甲基丙烯酸甲酯制	Plates, sheets, film, foil and strip, of plastics, non-cellular and not reinforced, laminated, supported or similarly combined with other materials, of poly (methyl methacrylate)	3920.5100	16
塑料板、片、膜、箔及扁条,非泡沫,未用其他材料强化、层压、支撑或用类似方法合制,聚四氟乙烯制	Plates, sheets, film, foil and strip, of plastics, non-cellular and not reinforced, laminated, supported or similarly combined with other materials, of potytetrafluoroethylene	3920.9910	16
塑料板、片、膜、箔及扁条,非泡沫,未用其他材料强化、层压、支撑或用类似方法合制,聚碳酸酯制	Plates, sheets, film, foil and strip, of plastics, non-cellular and not reinforced, laminated, supported or similarly combined with other materials, of polycarbonates	3920.6100	16
塑料板、片、膜、箔及扁条,非泡沫,未用其他材料强化、层压、支撑或用类似方法合制,聚酰胺制	Plates, sheets, film, foil and strip, of plastics, non-cellular and not reinforced, laminated, supported or similarly combined with other materials, of polyamides	3920.9200	16
塑料板、片、膜、箔及扁条,非泡沫,未用其他材料强化、层压、支撑或用类似方法合制,聚乙烯醇缩丁醛制	Plates, sheets, film, foil and strip, of plastics, non-cellular and not reinforced, laminated, supported or similarly combined with other materials, of poly (vinyl butyral)	3920.9100	16
塑料板、片、膜、箔及扁条,非泡沫,未用其他材料强化、层压、支撑或用类似方法合制,氯乙烯聚合物制,按重量计增塑剂含量不小于6%	Plates, sheets, film, foil and strip, of plastics, non-cellular and not reinforced, laminated, supported or similarly combined with other materials, of polymers of vinyl chloride, containing by weight not less than 6% of plasticisers	3920.4300	16
塑料板、片、膜、箔及扁条,非泡沫,未用其他材料强化、层压、支撑或用类似方法合制,氯乙烯聚合物制,其他	Plates, sheets, film, foil and strip, of plastics, non-cellular and not reinforced, laminated, supported or similarly combined with other materials, of polymers of vinyl chloride, nes	3920.4900	16
塑料板、片、膜、箔及扁条,非泡沫,未用其他材料强化、层压、支撑或用类似方法合制,丙烯聚合物制,其他	Plates, sheets, film, foil and strip, of plastics, non-cellular and not reinforced, laminated, supported or similarly combined with other materials, of polymers of propylene, nes	3920.2090	16

商品名称	Article Description	税则号列	申报要素
塑料板、片、膜、箔及扁条,非泡沫,未用其他材料强化、层压、支撑或用类似方法合制,其他聚酯制	Plates, sheets, film, foil and strip, of plastics, non-cellular and not reinforced, laminated, supported or similarly combined with other materials, of other polyesters	3920.6900	16
塑料板、片、膜、箔及扁条,非泡沫,未用其他材料强化、层压、支撑或用类似方法合制,其他塑料制	Plates, sheets, film, foil and strip, of plastics, non-cellular and not reinforced, laminated, supported or similarly combined with other materials, of other plastics	3920.9990	16
塑料板、片、膜、箔及扁条,非泡沫,未用其他材料强化、层压、支撑或用类似方法合制,其他纤维素衍生物制	Plates, sheets, film, foil and strip, of plastics, non-cellular and not reinforced, laminated, supported or similarly combined with other materials, of other cellulose derivatives	3920.7900	16
塑料板、片、膜、箔及扁条,非泡沫,未用其他材料强化、层压、支撑或用类似方法合制,乙酸纤维素制	Plates, sheets, film, foil and strip, of plastics, non-cellular and not reinforced, laminated, supported or similarly combined with other materials, of cellulose acetate	3920.7300	16
塑料板、片、膜、箔及扁条,非泡沫,未用其他材料强化、层压、支撑或用类似方法合制,乙烯聚合物制,其他	Plates, sheets, film, foil and strip, of plastics, non-cellular and not reinforced, laminated, supported or similarly combined with other materials, of polymers of ethylene, nes	3920.1090	16
塑料板、片、膜、箔及扁条,非泡沫,未用其他材料强化、层压、支撑或用类似方法合制,再生纤维素制	Plates, sheets, film, foil and strip, of plastics, non-cellular and not reinforced, laminated, supported or similarly combined with other materials, of regenerated cellulose	3920.7100	16
塑料袋,乙烯聚合物制	Plastic bags, of polymers of ethylene	3923.2100	23
塑料的废碎料及下脚料,其他	Plastics waste, parings and scrap, nes	3915.9090	146
塑料盖	Plastic lids	3923.5000	23
塑料管,其他	Tubes, pipes and hoses, of plastics, nes	3917.3900	36
塑料管,未装有附件的,未经加强也未与其他材料合制	Tubes, pipes and hoses, of plastics, not reinforced or otherwise combined with other materials, without fittings	3917.3200	36
塑料管子,装有附件的,未经加强也未与其他材料合制	Tubes, pipes and hoses, of plastics, not reinforced or otherwise combined with other materials, with fittings	3917.3300	36
塑料或橡胶用,其他	Moulds for rubber or plastics, nes	8480.7900	7
塑料瓶	Plastic bottles	3923.3000	23
塑料压延成型机	Plastics calender-forming machines	8477.4020	7
塑料造粒机	Plastic pelletizers	8477.2010	7
塑料制品,供运输或包装货物用的,其他	Plastic articles for the conveyance or packing of goods, nes	3923.9000	23
塑料制品,建筑用,其他	Builders ware of plastics, nes	3925.9000	23
塑料制品,其他	Plastic articles, nes	3926.9090	236
塑料中空成型机	Plastics brideg-die-forming machines	8477.4010	7

S

商品名称	Article Description	税则号列	申报要素
塑像及其他装饰用品,瓷制	Tatuettesa and other ornamental ceramic articles, of porcelain or china	6913.1000	36
塑像及其他装饰用品,陶制	Tatuettesa and other ornamental ceramic articles, of pottery	6913.9000	36
塑型用膏,包括供儿童娱乐用的在内	Modelling pastes, including those put up for children's amusement	3407.0090	13
suan			
酸菜	Mustard pickles	2001.9090	48
酸橙	Limes (citrus aurantifolia)	0805.5000	124
酸橙油	Essential oils of lime	3301.1910	34
酸乳	Yogurt	0403.1000	
酸乳酒	Kephir	0403.9000	248
酸性油,精炼所得的	Acid oils from refining	3823.1900	6
蒜苗(青蒜),冷冻的	Garlic seedlings, frozen	0710.8020	1
蒜苗(青蒜),鲜或冷藏的	Garlic seedlings, fresh or chilled	0703.2020	1
蒜苔,冷冻的	Garlic stems, frozen	0710.8020	1
蒜苔,鲜或冷藏的	Garlic stems, fresh or chilled	0703.2020	1
蒜头,冷冻的	Garlic bulbs, frozen	0710.8030	1
蒜头,鲜或冷藏的	Garlic bulbs, fresh or chilled	0703.2010	1
sui			
碎玻璃	Cullet	7001.0000	13
碎料板,木质	Particle board, of wood	4410.1100	6
碎料板,麦秸秆制	Particle board, of wheat or rice straw	4410.9011	6
碎料板,木质的,其他	Particle board, of ligneous materials, nes	4410.9019	6
碎料钢铁锭,供再熔的	Scrap ingots, for remelting	7204.5000	46
碎米,其他	Broken rice, nes	1006.4090	35
碎石,通常作混凝土粒料、铺路、铁道路基或其他路基用的	Broken or crushed stone, of a kind commonly used for concrete aggregates, for road metalling or for railway	2517.1000	13
碎石,由矿渣、浮渣及类似的工业残渣制成,不论是否混有子目号 2517.10 所列的材料	Macadam of slag, dross or similar industrial waste, whether or not incorporating the materials cited in subheading No. 2517.10	2517.2000	134
碎织物及其制品, 纺织材料的, 新的或旧的,经分拣的	Rags and their articles, of textile materials, used or new, sorted	6310.1000	146
碎织物及其制品, 纺织材料的, 新的或旧的,其他	Rags and their articles, of textile materials, used or new, nes	6310.9000	146
碎纸机	Paper shrudders	8472.9030	
隧道掘进机,其他	Tunnelling machinery, nes	8430.3900	5
隧道掘进机,自推进的	Tunnelling machinery, self-propelle	8430.3100	5
隧道掘进机零件	Tunnelling machinery parts	8431.4990	3
隧道限界检查车,铁道及电车道用	Inspection vehicles for tunnel clearance, for railway or tramway maintenance or service	8604.0011	37

商品名称	Article Description	税则号列	申报要素
燧石,不论是否热处理	Flint, whether or not bead-treated	2517.1000	13
sun			
笋干丝	Bamboo shoots, dried	0712.9010	4
suo			
梭子,织机用	Shuttles for looms	8448.4930	3
梭子蟹,未冻的	Swimming crab, not frozen	0306.2492	14
梭子蟹,冻的	Swimming crab, frozen	0306.1410	1
羧基丁苯橡胶(XSBR),其他	XSBR, nes	4002.1990	1346
羧基丁苯橡胶,初级形状的	SBR, in primary forms	4002.1919	1346
羧基丁苯橡胶胶乳	XSBR latex	4002.1110	12
羧甲基纤维素及其盐,初级形状的	Carboxymethylcellulose and its salts, in primary forms	3912.3100	16
缩醛,不论是否含有其他含氧基,及其卤化、磺化、硝化或亚硝化衍生物	Acetals, whether or not with other oxygen function, and their haogenated, sulphonated, nitrated or nitrosated derivatives	2911.0000	36
缩缩微胶片阅读机,不论是否可以进行复制	Microform readers, whether or not capable of producing copies	9008.2000	
缩微胶卷阅读机,不论是否可以进行复制	Microfilm readers, whether or not capable of producing copies	9008.2000	
缩微胶片,已曝光已冲洗的,其他	Microfilms, exposed and developed, nes	3705.9029	1238
缩微胶片,已曝光已冲洗的,书籍、报刊的	Microfilms, exposed and developed, for printed books and newspapers	3705.9021	1238
缩微阅读机用零件、附件	Microfilm or microfiche readers parts and accessories	9008.9010	3
缩微照相机,使用缩微胶卷、胶片或其他缩微品的	Cameras of a kind used for recording documents on microfilm, microfiche or other microforms	9006.5210	7
索道用牵引装置,其他	Traction mechanisms for funiculars, nes	8428.6090	
索引标签及类似的办公用品,贱金属制	Indexing tags and similar office articles, of base metal	8305.9000	256
锁,挂锁,贱金属制	Locks, padlocks, of base metal	8301.1000	256
锁,机动车用,贱金属制,其他	Locks of a kind used for motor vehicles, of base metal, nes	8301.2090	256
锁,家具用,贱金属制	Locks of a kind used for furniture, of base metal	8301.3000	256
锁,贱金属制,其他	Locks, of base metal, nes	8301.4000	256
锁,中央控制用,机动车用,贱金属制	Lock for central control, of a kind used for motor vehicles, of base metal	8301.2010	256
锁扣环及扣环框架,贱金属制	Locks clasps and frames with clasps, of base metal	8301.5000	256
锁零件,贱金属制	Locks parts, of base metal	8301.6000	256
锁线机,订书用	Sewing binders for book	8440.1010	
锁线机零件,订书用	Sewing binders parts, for book	8440.9000	3
锁线装订机	Book sewing binders	8440.1010	
锁线装订机零件	Book sewing binders parts	8440.9000	3

S

T

商品名称	Article Description	税则号列	申报要素
ta			
铊,未锻轧	Thallium, unwrought	8112.5100	16
铊粉末	Thallium powders	8112.5100	16
铊制品,其他	Thallium articles, nes	8112.5900	16
塔楼及格构杆,钢铁的	Towers and lattice masts, of iron or steel	7308.2000	6
塔式起重机	Tower cranes	8426.2000	7
鳎鱼,冻的	Sole(Solea spp.), frozen	0303.3300	18
鳎鱼,鲜或冷的	Sole(Solea spp.), fresh or chilled	0302.2300	18
踏板车及类似的带轮玩具	Scooters and similar wheeled toys	9503.0010	
踏板汽车及类似的带轮玩具	Pedal cars and similar wheeled toys	9503.0010	
tai			
胎面补料胎条,轮胎翻新用	Camel-back strips for retreading rubber tyres	4006.1000	13
台布纸,纸浆、纸、纤维素絮纸或纤维素纤维网纸制的	Tablecloths, of paper pulp, paper, cellulose wadding or webs of cellulose fibres	4818.3000	568
台灯,电气的	Table or desk lamps, electric	9405.2000	5
台钳及类似品	Vices and the like	8205.7000	256
台球	Billiards	9504.9090	5
台球用品及附件	Billiards articles and accessories of all kinds	9504.2000	5
台扇,包括风机,本身装有一个输出功率不超过125瓦的电动机	Table fans, with a self-contained electric motor of an output not exceeding 125W	8414.5191	23
苔藓及地衣,制花束或装饰用的	Mosses and lichens, suitable for bouquets or for ornamental purposes	0604.1000	34
太妃糖	Caramels (confectionery)	1704.9000	258
太阳镜	Sunglasses	9004.1000	
太阳镜片,玻璃制	Sunglasses spectacle lenses, of glass	9001.4091	
太阳镜片,其他材料制	Sunglasses spectacle lenses, of other materials	9001.5091	
太阳能电池	Solar cells	8541.4020	5
钛,未锻轧,其他	Titanium, unwrought, nes	8108.2029	16
钛白粉	Titanium white	3206.1110	2368
钛的氧化物	Titanium oxides	2823.0000	4
钛粉末	Titanium powder	8108.2030	16
钛矿砂及其精矿	Titanium ores and concentrates	2614.0000	146
钛铁合金	Ferro-titanium alloys	7202.9100	6
钛铀矿	Brannerite	2612.1000	146
钛制品,其他	Titanium articles, nes	8108.9090	16

商品名称	Article Description	税则号列	申报要素
tan			
摊铺机,沥青混凝土用	Spreading machines, for spreading bituminous concrete	8479.1021	7
摊铺机,其他	Spreading machines, nes	8479.1029	7
摊铺机,稳定土用	Spreading machines for stabilizer	8479.1022	7
坛、瓶及类似品,塑料的	Carboys, bottles, flasks and similar articles, of plastics	3923.3000	23
檀香脑	Santalol	2906.1990	36
坦克的零件和附件	Tanks parts and accessories	8710.0090	3
坦克整车	Tanks, assembled	8710.0010	
钽,未锻轧,包括简单烧结而成的条、杆	Tantalum, unwrought, including bars and rods obtained simply by sintering	8103.2090	16
钽粉,其他	Powders of tantalum, nes	8103.2019	16
钽粉,松装密度小于2.2克/立方厘米的	Powders of tantalum, loose density less than $2.2g/cm^3$	8103.2011	16
钽矿富集物	Enriched materials from tantalum ore	2615.9010	146
钽矿砂及其精矿	Tantalum ores and concentrates	2615.9010	146
钽丝,其他	Wire of tantalum, nes	8103.9019	16
钽丝,直径小于0.5毫米	Wire of tantalum, less than 0.5mm in diameter	8103.9011	16
钽铁矿	Tantalite	2615.9090	146
钽制品,其他	Tantalum articles, nes	8103.9090	16
毯子(电暖毯除外)及旅行毯,合成纤维制的	Blankets(other than electric blankets) and travelling rugs, of synthetic fibres	6301.4000	56
毯子(电暖毯除外)及旅行毯,棉制的	Blankets(other than electric blankets) and travelling rugs, of cotton	6301.3000	56
毯子(电暖毯除外)及旅行毯,羊毛或动物细毛制的	Blankets(other than electric blankets) and travelling rugs, of wool or of fine animal hair	6301.2000	56
毯子及旅行毯,其他	Blankets and travelling rugs, nes	6301.9000	56
炭,其他	Charcoal, nes	4402.9000	
炭,竹的	Charcoal of bamboo	4402.1000	
探伤检测仪,超声波的	Nondestructive examinations apparatus, ultrasonic	9031.8031	
探伤检测仪,磁粉的	Nondestructive examinations apparatus, magnetic	9031.8032	
探伤检测仪,涡流的	Nondestructive examinations apparatus, eddy examinations	9031.8033	
探伤检测仪器(射线探伤仪除外),无损的,其他	Nondestructive examinations apparatus (other than apparatus for radiological examinations), nes	9031.8039	7
探照灯	Search lights	9405.4010	5
碳(碳黑及其他税号未列名的其他形态的碳)	Carbon(carbon blacks and other forms of carbon not elsewhere specified or included)	2803.0000	24
碳布	Carbon fabric	6815.9931	6
碳电极,炉用	Carbon electrodes, of a kind used for furnaces	8545.1100	3
碳电极,其他	Carbon electrodes, nes	8545.1900	3

T

商品名称	Article Description	税则号列	申报要素
碳黑	Channel black	2803.0000	24
碳糊,电极用及炉衬用的类似糊	Carbonaceous pastes for electrodes and similar pastes for furnace linings	3801.3000	134
碳糊及类似糊,炉衬用	Carbonaceous pastes and similar pastes, for furnace linings	3801.3000	134
碳化钙	Calcium carbides	2849.1000	
碳化硅	Silicon carbides	2849.2000	
碳化硼	Boron carbides	2849.9010	
碳化钨	Tungsten carbides	2849.9020	
碳化物,其他	Carbides, nes	2849.9090	
碳精制品,非电气的	Carbon articles, non-electrical	6815.1000	6
碳刷	Carbon brushes	8545.2000	3
碳酸铵,含氨基甲酸铵的	Ammonium carbonate containing ammonium carbamate	2836.9940	
碳酸钡	Barium carbonate	2836.6000	
碳酸镝	Dysprosium carbonate	2846.9043	6
碳酸钙	Calcium carbonate	2836.5000	
碳酸锆	Zirconium carbonate	2836.9950	
碳酸钴	Cobalt carbonate	2836.9930	
碳酸钾	Potassium carbonates	2836.4000	
碳酸镧	Lanthanum carbonate	2846.9041	6
碳酸镁	Magnesium carbonate	2836.9910	
碳酸钠(纯碱)	Disodium carbonate	2836.2000	
碳酸氢钠	Sodium hydrogencarbonate	2836.3000	
碳酸铈	Cerium carbonate	2846.1030	
碳酸铽	Terbium carbonate	2846.9042	6
碳酸稀土,其他	Rare-earth carbonate, nes	2846.9049	6
碳纤维	Carbon fibres	6815.9920	6
碳纤维制品,其他	Carbon fibres articles, nes	6815.9939	6
碳酰二氯	Carbonyl dichloride	2812.1030	
碳制品或半制品,糊状、块状、板状	Carbon preparations or semi-manufactures, in the form of pastes, blocks, plates	3801.9000	134
tang			
汤料及其制品	Soups and broths and preparations therefor	2104.1000	28
汤团,不论是否烹煮或经其他方法制作	Gnocchi, whether or not cooked or otherwise prepared	1902.2000	46
镗床,切削金属的,其他	Boring machines, for removing metal, nes	8459.4090	7
镗床,数控的,切削金属的	Boring machines, numerically controlled, for removing metal	8459.4010	7

商品名称	Article Description	税则号列	申报要素
镗孔或铰孔工具,带有天然或合成金刚石、立方氮化硼制的工作部件,可互换	Boring or broaching tools, with working part of natural or synthetic diamonds or cubic boronnitride, interchangeable	8207.6010	256
镗孔或铰孔用工具,可互换,其他	Boring or broaching tools, interchangeable, nes	8207.6090	256
镗铣机床,切削金属的,其他	Boring-milling machines, for removing metal, nes	8459.3900	7
镗铣机床,数控的,切削金属的	Boring-milling machines, numerically controlled, for removing metal	8459.3100	7
搪瓷玻璃料及其他玻璃,呈粉、粒或粉片状的	Glass frit and other glass, in the form of powder, granules or flakes	3207.4000	13
糖,甘蔗原糖	Sugar, cane sugar, raw	1701.1100	46
糖,加有香料或着色剂	Sugar, containing added flavouring or colouring matter	1701.9100	4
糖,绵白糖	Sugar, superfine	1701.9920	
糖,其他	Sugar, nes	1701.9910	
糖,砂糖	Sugar, granulated	1701.9910	
糖,甜菜原糖	Sugar, beet sugar, raw	1701.1200	46
糖,蔗糖,化学纯	Sucrose, chemically pure	1701.9910	
糖蛋白激素及其衍生物和结构类似物	Glycoprotein hormones, their derivatives and structural analogues	2937.1900	36
糖果生产机器	Confectionery manufacture machinery	8438.2000	
糖果生产机器的零件	Confectionery manufacture machinery parts	8438.9000	3
糖及糖浆,其他	Sygar and sugar syrup, nes	1702.9000	
糖浆	Golden syrup	1702.9000	
糖胶树胶及类似的天然树胶	Chicleand similar natural gums	4001.3000	12
糖精及其盐	Saccharin and its salts	2925.1100	36
糖块夹,镀贵金属的	Sugar tongs, plated with precious metal	8215.9100	256
糖块夹,非镀贵金属的	Sugar tongs, other than plated with precious metal	8215.9900	256
糖醚及其盐,但不包括税号29.37、29.38及29.39的产品	Sugar ethers, and their salts, other than products of heading No. 29.37, 29.38 or 29.39	2940.0000	6
糖蜜,甘蔗糖蜜	Molasses, cane molasses	1703.1000	4
糖蜜,其他	Molasses, nes	1703.9000	4
糖食,不含可可的,其他	Sugar confectionery, nes, not containing cocoa	1704.9000	258
糖缩醛及其盐,但不包括税号29.37、29.38及29.39的产品	Sugar acetals, and their salts, other than products of heading No. 29.37, 29.38 or 29.39	2940.0000	6
糖甜菜子,饲料植物用的	Sugar beet seed	1209.1000	358
糖酯及其盐,但不包括税号29.37、29.38及29.39的产品	Sugar esters, and their salts, other than products of heading No. 29.37, 29.38 or 29.39	2940.0000	6
烫发剂	Hair permanent waving or straightening preparations	3305.2000	23
tao			
桃,罐头,用其他方法制作或保藏的	Peaches, in airtight containers, other wise prepared or preserved	2008.7010	248
桃,其他,用其他方法制作或保藏的	Peaches, otherwise prepared or preserved, nes	2008.7090	248

T

商品名称	Article Description	税则号列	申报要素
桃,鲜的	Peaches, fresh	0809.3000	1
陶瓷槽、缸及类似容器,农业用	Ceramic troughs, tubs and similar receptacles of a kind used in agriculture	6909.9000	5
陶瓷罐、坛及类似品,通常供运输及盛装货物用的	Ceramic pots, jars and similar articles of a kind used for the conveyance or packing of goods	6909.9000	5
陶瓷套管、导管、槽管及管子附件	Ceramic pipes, conduits, guttering and pipe fittings	6906.0000	5
陶瓷贴面砖、铺面砖,包括炉面砖及墙面砖,上釉的,其最大表面以可置入边长小于7厘米的方格为限	Ceramic flags and paving, hearth or wall tiles, glazed, the largest surface area of which is capable of being enclosed in a square, the side of which is less than 7cm	6908.1000	5
陶瓷贴面砖、铺面砖,包括炉面砖及墙面砖,未上釉的,其最大表面以可置入边长小于7厘米的方格为限	Ceramic flags and paving, hearth or wall tiles, unglazed, the largest surface area of which is capable of being enclosed in a square, the side of which is less than 7cm	6907.1000	5
陶瓷贴面砖、铺面砖、镶嵌砖、炉面砖及墙面砖及类似品,上釉的,其他	Ceramic flags, paving, hearth or wall tiles, mosaic cubes and the like, glazed, nes	6908.9000	5
陶瓷贴面砖、铺面砖、镶嵌砖、炉面砖及墙面砖及类似品,未上釉的,其他	Ceramic flags, paving, hearth or wall tiles, mosaic cubes and the like, unglazed, nes	6907.9000	5
陶瓷镶嵌砖(马赛克)及类似品,上釉的,其最大表面以可置入边长小于7厘米的方格为限	Ceramic mosaic cubes and the like, glazed, the largest surface area of which is capable of being enclosed in a square the side of which is less than 7cm	6908.1000	5
陶瓷镶嵌砖(马赛克)及类似品,未上釉的,其最大表面以可置入边长小于7厘米的方格为限	Ceramic mosaic cubes and the like, unglazed, the largest surface area of which is capable of being enclosed in a square the side of which is less than 7cm	6907.1000	5
陶瓷制品,建筑用,其他	Ceramic constructional goods, nes	6905.9000	5
陶瓷砖,建筑用	Ceramic bricks for building	6904.1000	5
陶瓷砖,其他	Ceramic bricks, nes	6904.9000	5
陶器,实验室、化学或其他专门技术用途的,莫氏硬度为9或以上的物品	Pottery wares for laboratory, chemical or other technical uses, having a hardness equivalent to 9 or more on the Mohs scale	6909.1200	5
陶器,实验室、化学或其他专门技术用途的,其他	Pottery wares for laboratory, chemical or other technical uses, nes	6909.1900	5
陶制品,其他	Pottery articles, nes	6914.9000	36
套管,钻探石油或天然气用,外径超过406.4毫米	Casing of a kind used in drilling for oil or gas, the external diameter of which exceeds 406.4mm	7305.2000	6
套管、导管,钻探石油及天然气用,无缝的,不锈钢的	Casing or tubing pipe, of a kind used in drilling for oil or gas, seamless, of stainless steel	7304.2400	6
套管、导管,钻探石油及天然气用,无缝的,其他	Casing or tubing pipe, of a kind used in drilling for oil or gas, seamless, nes	7304.2900	6
套管及导管,钻探石油及天然气用,不锈钢的,焊接的	Casing and tubing of a kind used in drilling for oil or gas, of stainless steel, welded	7306.2100	6

商品名称	Article Description	税则号列	申报要素
套管及导管,钻探石油及天然气用,其他	Casing and tubing of a kind used in drilling for oil or gas, nes	7306. 2900	6
套头衫,针织或钩编的,化学纤维制	Pullovers, knitted or crocheted, of man-made fibres	6110. 3000	2456
套头衫,针织或钩编的,喀什米尔山羊细毛制	Pullovers, knitted or crocheted, of kashmir (cashmere) fine goats hair	6110. 1200	2456
套头衫,针织或钩编的,毛制	Pullovers, knitted or crocheted, of wool	6110. 1100	2456
套头衫,针织或钩编的,棉制	Pullovers, knitted or crocheted, of cotton	6110. 2000	2456
套头衫,针织或钩编的,其他	Pullovers, knitted or crocheted, nes	6110. 9090	2456
套头衫,针织或钩编的,其他动物细毛制	Pullovers, knitted or crocheted, of other fine animal hair	6110. 1990	2456
套头衫,针织或钩编的,其他山羊细毛制	Pullovers, knitted or crocheted, of other fine goats hair	6110. 1910	2456
套头衫,针织或钩编的,丝及绢丝制	Pullovers, knitted or crocheted, of silk or silk waste	6110. 9010	2456
套头衫,针织或钩编的,兔毛制	Pullovers, knitted or crocheted, of rabbit and hare	6110. 1920	2456
te			
特里科经编机	Tricot machines	8447. 2011	7
特种车辆用零件、附件,其他	Motor vehicles parts and accessories, with special purpose, nes	8708. 9960	3
特种照相机,水下、航空测量或体内器官检查用	Cameras specially designed for under-water use, for aerial survey, or for medical or surgical examination of internal organs	9006. 3000	7
铽	Terbium	2805. 3013	56
teng			
藤	Rattans	1401. 2000	3456
藤制家具	Rattan furniture	9403. 8100	6
藤制篮筐	Rattan basketwork	4602. 1200	6
藤制席子	Rattan mats	4601. 2200	6
藤制坐具	Rattan seats	9401. 5100	6
ti			
锑,未锻轧	Antimony unwrought	8110. 1010	16
锑的氧化物	Antimony oxides	2825. 8000	
锑粉末	Antimony powders	8110. 1020	16
锑华	Valentinite	2617. 1090	146
锑精矿	Antimony concentrates	2617. 1010	146
锑矿砂及其精矿,其他	Antimony ores and concentrates, nes	2617. 1090	146
锑制品,其他	Antimony articles, nes	8110. 9000	16
提花机及其所用的卡片缩小、复制、穿孔或汇编机器	Jacquards; card reducing, copying, punching or assembling machines for use there with	8448. 1100	3
提净塔,蒸馏或精馏设备	Stripping towers	8419. 4010	57
提升机,其他	Hoists, nes	8425. 4990	78

T

商品名称	Article Description	税则号列	申报要素
提升机,液压,提升车辆用,其他	Hoists, hydraulic, of a kind used for raising vehicles, nes	8425. 4290	78
提升机的零件	Hoists parts	8431. 1000	3
提箱,以皮革、再生皮革或漆皮作面	Suit-cases, with outer surface of leather, of composition leather or of patent leather	4202. 1190	1458
提箱,以塑料或纺织材料作面	Suit-cases, with outer surface of plastics or of textile materials	4202. 1290	256
蹄及其粉末	Hooves and powder thereof	0507. 9090	14
鳀鱼,盐腌及盐渍的	Anchovies(Engraulis spp.), salted or in brine	0305. 6300	4
鳀鱼,制作或保藏的,整条或切块,但未绞碎	Anchovies, prepared or preserved, whole or in pieces, but not minced	1604. 1600	48
体育用品及设备,其他	Physical exercise, gymnastics or athletics articles, nes	9506. 9900	5
体育用品及设备,一般的,其他	Physical exercise, gymnastics or athletics articles and equipment, for general, nes	9506. 9190	5
体重计,包括婴儿秤;家用秤	Personal weighing machines, including baby scales; household scales	8423. 1000	
剃刀	Razors	8212. 1000	256
剃刀刀片,包括未分开的刀片条	Razor blades, including razor blade blanks in strips	8212. 2000	256
剃刀零件,其他	Razors parts, nes	8212. 9000	256
剃须刀零件,电动的	Shavers parts, with self-contained electric motor	8510. 9000	3
剃须刷	Shaving brushes	9603. 2900	
剃须用制剂	Pre-shave, shaving or after-shave preparations	3307. 1000	23
替利定(INN)及其盐	Tilidine(INN) and its salts	2922. 4400	36
替马西泮(INN)以及盐	Temazepam (INN); salts thereof	2933. 9100	36
tian			
天窗,电动的	Sunroofs, electric	8708. 2941	3
天窗,手动的	Sunroofs, hand-operated	8708. 2942	3
天花板或墙壁上的其他电气照明装置,不包括公共露天场所或街道上的电气照明装置	Ceiling or wall lighting fittings, electric, excluding those of a kind used for lighting public open spaces or thorough-fares	9405. 1000	5
天麻	Rhizoma gastrodiae	1211. 9022	34
天门冬酰胺	Asparagine	2924. 1990	36
天篷,合成纤维制	Awnings, of synthetic fibres	6306. 1200	346
天篷,麻制	Awnings, of bast fibres	6306. 1910	346
天篷,棉制	Awnings, of cotton	6306. 1920	346
天篷,其他	Awnings, nes	6306. 1990	346
天平,感量为0.1毫克或更精密的	Balances of a sensitivity of 0. 1mg or better	9016. 0010	8
天平,感量为50毫克或更精密的,其他	Alances of a sensitivity of 50mg or better, nes	9016. 0090	8
天然粗钾盐,其他	Crude natural potassium salts, nes	3104. 9010	68

T

商品名称	Article Description	税则号列	申报要素
天然粗硼酸,含硼酸干重不超过85%	Natural boric acid, containing not more than 85% of H_3BO_3 calculated on the dry weight	2528.9000	6
天然胶乳,不论是否预硫化	Natural rubber latex, whether or not prevulcanized	4001.1000	12
天然聚合物,初级形状的,其他	Natural polymers, in primary forms, nes	3913.9000	146
天然沥青(地沥青)	Bitumen and asphalt, natural	2714.9010	1346
天然硼砂及其精矿(不论是否煅烧)	Natural sodium borates and concentrates thereof (whether or not calcined)	2528.1000	
天然气,气态的	Natural gas, in gaseous state	2711.2100	1468
天然气,液化的	Natural gas, liquefied	2711.1100	1468
天然砂,其他	Natural sands, nes	2505.9000	
天然石料(包括板岩)制的镶嵌石(马赛克)及类似品,不论是否有衬背,其最大表面以可置入边长小于7厘米的方格为限	Natural stone (including slate) mosaic cubes and the like, whether or not on a backing, the largest surface area of which is capable of being enclosed in a square the side of which is less than 7cm	6802.1090	3468
天然石料的砖、瓦、方块及类似品,不论是否为矩形(包括正方形),其最大表面以可置入边长小于7厘米的方格为限其他	Natural stones tiles, cubes and similar articles, whether or not rectangular (including square), the largest surface area of which is capable of being enclosed in a square the side of which is less than 7cm, nes	6802.1090	3468
天然石料及其制品,已加工的,其他	Natural stone and articles thereof, worked, nes	6802.9990	3468
天然石料经人工染色的石粒、石片及石粉,其他	Natural stones artificially coloured granules, chippings and powder, nes	6802.1090	3468
天然石料石刻	Natural stone carvings	6802.9910	3468
天然树胶	Natural gums	1301.9090	
天然水,未加糖或其他甜物质及未加味的	Natural waters, not containing added sugar or other sweetening matter or flavoured	2201.9010	248
天然橡胶(含胶乳与)合成橡胶(含胶乳)的混合物	Natural rubber (including latex) mixtures with synthetic rubber (including latex)	4002.8000	136
天然橡胶(TSNR),技术分类的	Natural rubber (TSNR), technically specified	4001.2200	12
天然橡胶,其他形状的	Natural rubber in other forms	4001.2900	12
天然橡胶的化学衍生物,初级形状的	Chemical derivatives of natural rubber, in primary forms	3913.9000	146
天文望远镜	Astronomical telescopes	9005.8010	
天文望远镜零件、附件(包括座架)	Astronomical telescopes parts and accessories (including mountings)	9005.9010	3
天文仪器,其他	Astronomical instruments, nes	9005.8010	
天文仪器用零件、附件(包括座架)	Astronomical instruments parts and accessories (including mountings)	9005.9010	3
天文钟,电力驱动的	Astronomical chronometer, electrically operated	9105.9110	5
天线或天线反射器及其零件,雷达设备及无线电导航设备用	Aerials and aerial reflectors of all kinds, and their parts, for radar apparatus and radio navigational aid apparatus	8529.1010	3

T

商品名称	Article Description	税则号列	申报要素
天线或天线反射器及其零件,其他	Aerials and aerial reflectors of all kinds, and their parts, nes	8529. 1090	3
天线或天线反射器及其零件,无线电收音机及其组合机、电视接收机用	Aerials and aerial reflectors of all kinds, and their parts, for radio-broadcast receivers and their combinations, television receivers	8529. 1020	3
天线及其零件,通信设备用	Aerials and parts of communication apparatus	8517. 7070	3
田七	Radix pseudoginseng	1211. 9012	34
甜饼干	Sweet biscuits	1905. 3100	28
甜菜	Sugar beet	1212. 9100	14
甜菜渣、甘蔗渣及制糖过程中的其他残渣	Beet-pulp, bagasses and other waste of sugar manufacture	2303. 2000	56
甜菜子,糖甜菜子除外,饲料植物用的	Beet seed, excluding sugar beet seed, forage plants	1209. 2910	358
甜瓜,其他,鲜的	Melons, nes, fresh	0807. 1990	1
甜瓜子,种用	Seeds of melons	1209. 9920	358
甜椒,干的	Capsicum annuum var. Grossum, dried	0712. 9060	4
甜椒,鲜或冷藏的	Fruits of the genus pimenta, fresh or chilled	0709. 6000	1
甜蜜素	Sodium cyclamate	2929. 9010	36
甜杏仁	Sweet apricot kernels	1212. 9912	134
甜玉米,冷冻的	Sweet corn, frozen	0710. 4000	1
甜玉米,用醋或醋酸以外的其他方法制作或保藏的,未冷冻	Sweet corn (Zea mays var. Saccharata), prepared or preserved otherwise than by vinegar or acetic acid, not frozen	2005. 8000	148
tiao			
条,贱金属制,以焊剂涂面或以焊剂为芯,钎焊或气焊用	Rods, coated with flux material, of base metal, for soldering, brazing or welding by flame	8311. 3000	56
条,硬质合金制,以焊剂涂面或以焊剂为芯,用于焊接或沉积金属、硬质合金	Rods, of metal carbides, coated or cored with flux material, of a kind used for soldering, brazing, welding or deposition of metal or of metal carbides	8311. 9000	56
条、杆,不锈钢的,除冷成形或冷加工外未经进一步加工	Bars and rods, of stainless steel, not further worked than cold-formed or cold-finished	7222. 2000	468
条、杆,不锈钢的,除热轧、热拉拔或热挤压外未经进一步加工,其他	Bars and rods of stainless steel, not further worked than hot-rolled, hot-drawn or extruded, nes	7222. 1900	468
条、杆,不锈钢的,除热轧、热拉拔或热挤压外未经进一步加工,圆形截面的	Bars and rods of stainless steel, not further worked than hot-rolled, hot-drawn or extruded, of circular cross-section	7222. 1100	468
条、杆,不锈钢的,其他	Bars and rods of stainless steel, nes	7222. 3000	468
条、杆,不锈钢热轧的,不规则盘卷	Bars and rods, hot-rolled, of stainless steel, in irregularly wound coils	7221. 0000	468
条、杆,除锻造外未经进一步加工,其他	Bars and rods, not further worked than forged, nes	7228. 4000	468
条、杆,除冷成形或冷加工外未经进一步加工,其他	Bars and rods, not further worked than cold-formed of cold-finished, nes	7228. 5000	468

T

商品名称	Article Description	税则号列	申报要素
条、杆,除热轧、热拉拔或热挤压外未经进一步加工,其他	Bars and rods, not further worked than hot-rolled, hot-drawn or extruded, nes	7228. 3000	468
条、杆,非合金铝制	Bars and rods, of aluminium, not alloyed	7604. 1010	16
条、杆,高速钢的	Bars and rods, of high speed steel	7228. 1000	468
条、杆,高速钢制,热轧的,不规则盘卷的,其他	Bars and rods, of high speed steel hot-rolled, of alloy steel, in irregularly wound coils, nes	7227. 1000	468
条、杆,硅锰钢	Bars and rods, of silico-manganese steel	7228. 2000	468
条、杆,硅锰钢制,热轧的,不规则盘卷的,其他	Bars and rods, of silico-manganese steel hot-rolled, of alloy steel, in irregularly wound coils, nes	7227. 2000	468
条、杆,合金钢的,其他	Bars and rods of alloy steel, nes	7228. 6000	468
条、杆,钼的,但简单烧结而成的除外	Bars and rods, of molybdenum, other than those obtained simply by sintering	8102. 9500	16
条、杆,热轧的,不规则盘卷的,其他	Bars and rods, hot-rolled, of alloy steel, in irregularly wound coils, nes	7227. 9000	468
条、杆,铁或非合金钢的,除锻造、热轧、热拉拔或热挤压外未经进一步加工,包括轧制后扭曲的,带有轧制过程中产生的凹痕、凸缘、槽沟或其他变形以及轧制后扭曲的	Bars and rods, of iron or non-alloy steel, not further worked than forged, hot rolled, hot-drawn or hot-extruded, but including those twisted after rolling, containing indentations, ribs, grooves or other deformations produced during the rolling process or twisted after rolling	7214. 2000	468
条、杆,铁或非合金钢的,除锻造、热轧、热拉拔或热挤压外未经进一步加工,包括轧制后扭曲的,矩形(正方形除外)截面的,其他	Bars and rods of iron or non-alloy steel, not further worked than forged, hot rolled, hot-drawn or hot-extruded, but including those twisted after rolling, of rectangular cross section (other than square), nes	7214. 9100	468
条、杆,铁或非合金钢的,除锻造、热轧、热拉拔或热挤压外未经进一步加工,包括轧制后扭曲的,其他	Bars and rods of iron or non-alloy steel, not further worked than forged, hot rolled, hot-drawn or hot-extruded, but including those twisted after rolling, nes	7214. 9900	468
条、杆,铁或非合金钢的,除锻造、热轧、热拉拔或热挤压外未经进一步加工,包括轧制后扭曲的,易切削钢制,其他	Bars and rods of iron or non-alloy steel, not further worked than forged, hot rolled, hot-drawn or hot-extruded, but including those twisted after rolling, of free-cutting steel, nes	7214. 3000	468
条、杆,铁或非合金钢的,除锻造外未经进一步加工,包括轧制后扭曲的	Bars and rods of iron or non-alloy steel, not further worked than forged, but including those twisted after rolling	7214. 1000	468
条、杆,铁及非合金钢的,除冷成形或冷加工外未经进一步加工,其他	Bars and rods of iron or non-alloy steel, not further worked than cold-formed or cold-finished, nes	7215. 5000	468
条、杆,铁及非合金钢的,其他	Bars and rods of iron or non-alloy steel, nes	7215. 9000	468
条、杆,铁及非合金钢的,热轧的,不规则盘卷的,带有轧制过程中产生的凹痕、凸缘、槽沟及其他变形的	Bars and rods, of iron or non-alloy steel, hot-rolled, in irregulurly wound coils, containing indentations, ribs, grooves or other deformations produced during the rolling process	7213. 1000	468

T

商品名称	Article Description	税则号列	申报要素
条、杆,铁及非合金钢的,热轧的,不规则盘卷的,其他	Bars and rods, of iron or non-alloy steel, hot-rolled, in irregulurly wound coils, nes	7213.9900	468
条、杆,铁及非合金钢的,热轧的,不规则盘卷的,易切削钢制,其他	Bars and rods, of iron or non-alloy steel, hot-rolled, in irregulurly wound coils, of free-cutting steel, nes	7213.2000	468
条、杆,铁及非合金钢的,热轧的,不规则盘卷的,直径小于14毫米圆形截面的,其他	Bars and rods, of iron or non-alloy steel, hot-rolled, in irregulurly wound coils, of circular cross-section measuring less than 14mm in diameter, nes	7213.9100	468
条、杆,铁及非合金钢的,易切削钢制,除冷成形或冷加工外未经进一步加工	Bars and rods of iron or non-alloy steel, of free-cutting steel, not further worked than cold-formed or cold-finished	7215.1000	468
条、杆,钨的,但简单烧结而成的除外	Bars and rods, of tungsten, other than those obtained simply by sintering, profiles, plates, sheets, strip and foil	8101.9910	16
条、杆、型材及异型材,非合金镍制	Bars, rods and profiles, of nickel, not alloyed	7505.1100	46
条、杆、型材及异型材,精炼铜制	Bars, rods and profiles, of refined copper	7407.1000	16
条、杆、型材及异型材,镍合金制	Bars, rods and profiles, of nickel alloys	7505.1200	46
条、杆、型材及异型材,其他铜合金制	Bars, rods and profiles, of copper alloys	7407.2900	16
条、杆、型材及异型材,铜锌合金(黄铜)制	Bars, rods and profiles, of copper-zinc base alloys (brass)	7407.2100	16
条、杆、型材及异型材或丝,铅制	Bars, rods, profiles and wire of lead	7806.0010	16
条、杆、型材及异型材或丝,锡制	Bars, rods, profiles and wire of tin	8003.0000	16
条、杆、型材及异型材或丝,锌的	Bars, rods, profiles and wire of zinc	7904.0000	16
跳棋等棋类用品	Chinese cherkers	9504.9030	
tie			
贴标签的机器,瓶、罐、箱、袋或其他容器的	Labelling machines, for bottles, cans, boxes, bags or other containers, nes	8422.3090	
贴面砖,陶瓷的,上釉的,其最大表面以可置入边长小于7厘米的方格为限	Ceramic flags, glazed, the largest surface area of which is capable of being enclosed in a square the side of which is less than 7cm	6908.1000	5
贴面砖,陶瓷的,未上釉的,其最大表面以可置入边长小于7厘米的方格为限	Ceramic flags, unglazed, the largest surface area of which is capable of being enclosed in a square the side of which is less than 7cm	6907.1000	5
萜品醇	Terpineols	2906.1910	36
萜烯副产品,柑橘属果实精油脱萜所得的	Terpenic byproducts of the deterpenation of essential oils of citrus fruit	3301.9020	34
萜烯副产品,精油脱萜时所得的,其他	Terpenic byproducts of the deterpenation of essential oils, nes	3301.9090	34
萜烯油,用蒸馏或其他方法从针叶木制得	Terpenic oils produced by the distillation or other treatment of coniferous woods	3805.9010	36
铁,按重量计纯度在99.94%及以上的、块、团、团粒及类似形状,其他	Iron, having a minimum purity by weight of 99.94%, in lumps, pellets or similar forms, nes	7203.9000	6

商品名称	Article Description	税则号列	申报要素
铁产品,直接从铁矿还原所得的	Ferrous products obtained by direct reduction of iron ore	7203.1000	6
铁道柴油电力机车,其他	Rail diesel-electric locomotives,nes	8602.1090	37
铁道柴油电力机车,微型机控制的	Rail diesel-electric locomotives, controled by microprocessings	8602.1010	37
铁道电力机车,交流电机驱动的	Rail locomotives,drived by AC motors	8601.1020	37
铁道电力机车,微型机控制的,直流电机驱动的	Rail locomotives, controlled by microprocess-ings, drived by DC motors	8601.1011	37
铁道电力机车,由外部电力驱动,其他	Rail locomotives,powered from an external source of electricity,nes	8601.1090	37
铁道电力机车,由蓄电池驱动	Rail locomotives,powered by electric accumulators	8601.2000	37
铁道电力机车,直流电机驱动的,其他	Rail locomotives,drived by DC motors,nes	8601.1019	37
铁道货车搬运装置	Railway wagon handing equipment	8428.9010	
铁道机车,其他	Rail locomotives,nes	8602.9000	37
铁道机车或货车的转车台	Locmotive or wagon traversers	8428.9010	
铁道及电车道轨道固定装置及附件,其他	Railway or tramway track fixtures and fittings,nes	8608.0090	3
铁道及电车道机车或其他车辆的零件,其他	Railway or tramway locomotives or rolling-stock parts,nes	8607.9900	3
铁道及电车道用的非机动特殊用途车辆,其他	Special purpose railway or tramway coaches,not self-propelled,nes	8605.0090	37
铁道及电车道用的维修或服务车,其他	Railway or tramway maintenance or service vehicles, nes	8604.0099	37
铁道及电车道用的自驱动敞车,其他	Railway or tramway trucks,self-propelled,nes	8603.9000	37
铁道及电车道用的自驱动敞车,由外部电力驱动	Railway or tramway trucks, self-propelled, powered frow an external source of electricity	8603.1000	37
铁道及电车道用的自驱动货车,其他	Railway or tramway vans,self-propelled,nes	8603.9000	37
铁道及电车道用的自驱动货车,由外部电力驱动	Railway or tramway vans,self-propelled,powered frow an external source of electricity	8603.1000	37
铁道及电车道用的自驱动客车,其他	Railway or tramway coaches,self-propelled,nes	8603.9000	37
铁道及电车道用的自驱动客车,由外部电力驱动	Railway or tramway coaches, self-propelled, powered frow an external source of electricity	8603.1000	37
铁道客车	Railway passenger coaches	8605.0010	37
铁道用水泥枕	Railway sleepers of concrete	6810.9910	56
铁的氧化物及氢氧化物	Iron oxides and hydroxides	2821.1000	6
铁合金,其他	Ferro-alloys,nes	7202.9990	6
铁及非合金钢,锭状	Iron and non-alloy steel in ingots	7206.1000	6
铁及非合金钢,其他初级形状	Iron and non-alloy steel in other primary forms	7206.9000	6
铁及非合金钢的半制成品,按重量计含碳量在0.25%及以上	Iron or non-alloy steel, semi-finished, containing by weight 0.25% or more of carbon	7207.2000	468

T

商品名称	Article Description	税则号列	申报要素
铁及非合金钢的半制成品,矩形(包括正方形)截面,宽度小于厚度的两倍	Iron or non-alloy steel, semi-finished, containing by weight less than 0.25% of carbon, of rectangular (including square) cross-section, the width measuring less than twice the thickness	7207.1100	468
铁及非合金钢的半制成品,矩形(正方形除外)截面的,其他	Iron or non-alloy steel, semi-finished, containing by weight less than 0.25% of carbon, of rectangular (other than square) cross-section, nes	7207.1200	468
铁及非合金钢的半制成品,其他	Iron or non-alloy steel, semi-finished, containing by weight less than 0.25% of carbon, nes	7207.1900	468
铁矿砂及其精矿,未烧结,平均粒度不小于0.8毫米,但不大于6.3毫米的	Iron ores and concentrates, non agglomerated, the average grain size not less than 0.8mm, but not more than 6.3mm	2601.1120	13468
铁矿砂及其精矿,未烧结,平均粒度小于0.8毫米的	Iron ores and concentrates, non-agglomerated, the average grain size less than 0.8mm	2601.1110	13468
铁矿砂及其精矿,未烧结,其他	Iron ores and concentrates, non-agglomerated	2601.1190	13468
铁矿砂及其精矿,已烧结	Iron ores and concentrates, agglomerated	2601.1200	1346
铁丝或非合金钢丝,镀或涂贱金属的,其他	Wire of iron or non-alloy steel, plated or coated with base metals, nes	7217.3090	468
铁丝或非合金钢丝,镀或涂铜的	Wire of iron or non-alloy steel, plated or coated with copper	7217.3010	468
铁丝或非合金钢丝,镀或涂锌的	Wire of iron or non-alloy steel, plated or coated with zinc	7217.2000	468
铁丝或非合金钢丝,其他	Wire of iron or non-alloy steel, nes	7217.9000	468
铁丝或非合金钢丝,未经镀或涂层,不论是否抛光	Wire of iron or non-alloy steel, not plated or coated, whether or not polished	7217.1000	468
ting			
听力计	Andiometers	9018.1941	
听力诊断装置,其他	Hearing diagnostic apparatus, nes	9018.1949	3
听诊器	Stethoscopes	9018.9010	
烃的磺化、硝化或亚硝化衍生物,不论是否卤化,其他	Sulphonated, nitrated or nitrosated derivatives of hydrocarbons, whether or not halogenated, nes	2904.9090	36
停车设备,机械式	Parking equipment, mechanical	8428.9020	
tong			
通风帽,陶瓷制	Cowls, ceramic	6905.9000	5
通风罩或循环气罩,罩的平面最大边长不超过120厘米的,其他	Ventilating or recycling hoods, hoods having a maximum horizontal side not exceeding 120cm, nes	8414.6090	23
通心粉,生的,含蛋的	Macaroni, uncooked, containing eggs	1902.1100	46
通心粉,生的,其他	Macaroni, uncooked, nes	1902.1900	46
通心粉生产机器	Macaroni manufacture machinery	8438.1000	
通心粉生产机器的零件	Macaroni manufacture machinery parts	8438.9000	3
通信卡片,纸或纸板制的	Correspondence cards of paper or paperboard	4817.2000	6

商品名称	Article Description	税则号列	申报要素
通信设备用零件,其他	Communication apparatus parts, nes	8517.7090	3
通信网络时钟同步设备	Communication network synchronizing equipments	8517.6231	7
同位素,其他,及其化合物	Isotopes and compounds, nes	2845.9000	
同位素分离机器、装置及其零件	Isotopic separation machinery and apparatus, and parts thereof	8401.2000	2
同位素及其化合物,放射性的,其他	Isotopes and compounds, radioactive, nes	2844.4090	
同样适用于税号 84.69 至 84.72 中两个或两个以上税号所列机器的零件、附件	Parts and accessories equally suitable for use with machines of two or more of the headings No. 84.69 to 84.72	8473.5000	3
同轴电导体,其他	Co-axial electric conductors, nes	8544.2000	35
同轴电缆	Co-axial cable	8544.2000	35
桐油	China wood oil (tung oil)	1515.9030	
桐油及其分离品	Tung oil and its fractions	1515.9030	
铜,精炼的,其他	Copper, refined, nes	7403.1900	146
铜,未精炼的	Copper, unrefined	7402.0000	46
铜箔,精炼铜制,无衬背,厚度不超过 0.15 毫米	Copper foil of refined copper, not backed, of a thickness not exceeding 0.15mm	7410.1100	236
铜箔,精炼铜制,有衬背,铜厚度不超过 0.15 毫米,其他	Copper foil, of refined copper, backed, of a copper thickness not exceeding 0.15mm, nes	7410.2190	236
铜箔,铜合金制,有衬背,铜厚度不超过 0.15 毫米,其他	Copper foil, of copper alloys, backed, of a copper thickness not exceeding 0.15mm, nes	7410.2290	236
铜箔,铜镍合金(白铜),有衬背,铜厚度不超过 0.15 毫米	Copper foil, of copper-nickel base alloys (cupronickel), backed, of a copper thickness not exceeding 0.15mm	7410.2210	236
铜箔,铜镍合金(白铜)或铜镍锌合金(德银),无衬背,厚度不超过 0.15 毫米	Copper foil of copper-nickel base alloys (cupronickel) or copper-nickel-zinc base alloys (nickel silver), not backed, of a thickness not exceeding 0.15mm	7410.1210	236
铜箔,铜镍锌合金(德银),有衬背,铜厚度不超过 0.15 毫米	Copper foil, of copper-nickel-zin cbase alloys (nickel silver), backed, of a copper thickness not exceeding 0.15mm	7410.2210	236
铜箔,无衬背,厚度不超过 0.15 毫米,其他	Copper foil, not backed, of a thickness not exceeding 0.15mm, nes	7410.1290	236
铜的硫酸盐	Copper sulphates	2833.2500	
铜的氯氧化物及氢氧基氯化物	Copper, chloride oxides and chloride hydroxides	2827.4100	
铜的氧化物及氢氧化物	Copper oxides and hydroxides	2825.5000	
铜粉,非片状,精炼铜制	Copper powders of non-lamellar structure, of refined copper	7406.1010	16
铜粉,非片状,其他铜合金制	Copper powders of non-lamellar structure, nes	7406.1090	16
铜粉,非片状,铜镍合金(白铜)制	Copper powders of non-lamellar structure, of copper-nickel base alloys (cupronickel)	7406.1020	16
铜粉,非片状,铜镍锌合金(德银)制	Copper powders of non-lamellar structure, of copper-nickel-zinc base alloys (nickel silver)	7406.1020	16

商品名称	Article Description	税则号列	申报要素
铜粉,非片状,铜锡合金(青铜)制	Copper powders of non-lamellar structure, of copper-tin base alloys (bronze)	7406.1040	16
铜粉,非片状,铜锌合金(黄铜)制	Copper powders of non-lamellar structure, of copper-zinc base alloys (brass)	7406.1030	16
铜粉,片状,精炼铜制	Copper powders of lamellar structure, flakes, of refined copper	7406.2010	16
铜粉,片状,其他铜合金制	Copper powders of lamellar structure, flakes, nes	7406.2090	16
铜粉,片状,铜镍合金(白铜)	Copper powders of lamellar structure, flakes, of copper-nickel base alloys (cupronickel)	7406.2020	16
铜粉,片状,铜镍锌合金(德银)制	Copper powders of lamellar structure, flakes, of copper-nickel-zinc base alloys (nickel silver)	7406.2020	16
铜管乐器	Brass-wind musical instruments	9205.1000	5
铜合金,其他(铜母合金除外)	Copper alloys other than master alloys, nes	7403.2900	146
铜矿砂及其精矿	Copper ores and concentrates	2603.0000	146
铜锍	Copper mattes	7401.0000	46
铜母合金	Copper master alloys	7405.0000	6
铜镍合金	Copper-nickel base alloys	7403.2900	146
铜镍锌合金	Copper-nickel-zinc base alloys	7403.2900	146
铜坯段,精炼铜的	Copper billets, of refined copper	7403.1300	146
铜丝,精炼铜制,其他	Copper wire, of refined copper, nes	7408.1900	16
铜丝,精炼铜制,最大截面尺寸超过6毫米	Copper wire, of refined copper, of which the maximum cross-sectional dimension exceeds 6mm	7408.1100	16
铜丝,其他	Copper wire, nes	7408.2900	16
铜丝,铜合金制,铜镍合金(白铜)	Copper wire, of copper alloys, of copper-nickel base alloys (cupronickel)	7408.2200	16
铜丝,铜合金制,铜镍锌合金(德银)	Copper wire, of copper alloys, of copper-nickel-zinc base alloys (nickel silver)	7408.2200	16
铜丝,铜合金制,铜锌合金(黄铜)	Copper wire, of copper alloys, of copper-zinc base alloys (brass)	7408.2100	16
铜锡合金	Copper-tin base alloys	7403.2200	146
铜线锭,精炼铜的	Copper wire-bars of refined copper	7403.1200	146
铜锌合金	Copper-zinc base alloys	7403.2100	146
铜阳极,电解精炼用的	Copper anodes for electrolytic refining	7402.0000	46
铜阴极,按重量计铜含量超过99.9935%的	Copper anodes containing at least 99.9935% by weight of copper	7403.1111	146
铜阴极,精炼铜的,其他	Copper cathodes of refined copper, nes	7403.1119	146
铜阴极型材,精炼铜的	Copper cathodes sections of refined copper	7403.1190	146
铜制品,工业用,其他	Copper articles, for technical use, nes	7419.9991	4
铜制品,其他	Copper articles, nes	7419.9999	4
铜制品铸造、模压、冲压或锻造,但未经进一步加工的,工业用	Copper articles, cast, moulded, stamped or forged, but not further worked, for technical use	7419.9110	4

T

商品名称	Article Description	税则号列	申报要素
铜制品铸造、模压、冲压或锻造,但未经进一步加工的,其他	Copper articles, cast, moulded, stamped or forged, but not further worked, nes	7419.9190	4
酮,含有其他含氧基的,其他	Ketones with other oxygen function, nes	2914.5090	36
酮,卤化、磺化、硝化或亚硝化衍生物	Ketones, halogenated, sulphonated, nitrated or nitrosated derivatives of	2914.7000	36
酮醇	Ketone-alcohols	2914.4000	36
酮酚,其他	Ketene-phenols, nes	2914.5019	36
酮醛	Ketone-aldehydes	2914.4000	36
筒管、卷轴、纡子及类似品,纸浆、纸或纸板制,纺织纱线用	Bobbins, spools, cops and similar supports of paper pulp, paper or paperboard, of a kind used for winding textile yarn	4822.1000	6
筒管、卷轴、纡子及类似品,纸浆、纸或纸板制,其他	Bobbins, spools, cops and similar supports of paper pulp, paper or paperboard, nes	4822.9000	6
筒管及类似品,木制	Bobbins and the like, of wood	4421.9010	56
tou			
头孢氨苄及其盐	Cefalexin and its salts	2941.9052	
头孢呋辛药品,混合或未混合的,配定剂量或制成零售包装	Cefuroxime medicaments, mixed or unmixed, put up in measured doses or in forms or packings for retail sale	3004.2016	368
头孢呋辛药品,两种或两种以上成分混合而成的,未配定剂量或制成零售包装	Cefuroxime medicaments, consisting of two or more constituents which have been mixed together, not put up in measured doses or in forms or packings for retail sale	3003.2016	368
头孢菌素药品,其他,混合或未混合的,配定剂量或制成零售包装	Cephamycins medicaments, nes, mixed or unmixed, put up in measured doses or in forms or packings for retail sale	3004.2019	368
头孢菌素药品,其他,两种或两种以上成分混合而成的,未配定剂量或制成零售包装	Cephamycins medicaments, nes, consisting of two or more constituents which have been mixed together, not put up in measured doses or in forms or packings for retail sale	3003.2019	368
头孢克罗及其盐	Cefaclor and its salts	2941.9058	
头孢克罗药品,混合或未混合的,配定剂量或制成零售包装	Cefaclor medicaments, mixed or unmixed, put up in measured doses or in forms or packings for retail sale	3004.2015	368
头孢克罗药品,两种或两种以上成分混合而成的,未配定剂量或制成零售包装	Cefaclor medicaments, consisting of two or more constituents which have been mixed together, not put up in measured doses or in forms or packings for retail sale	3003.2015	368
头孢拉啶及其盐	Cefradine and its salts	2941.9054	
头孢哌酮及其盐	Cefoperazone and its salts	2941.9056	

商品名称	Article Description	税则号列	申报要素
头孢哌酮药品，混合或未混合的，配定剂量或制成零售包装	Cefoperazone medicaments, mixed or unmixed, put up in measured doses or in forms or packings for retail sale	3004.2018	368
头孢哌酮药品，两种或两种以上成分混合而成的，未配定剂量或制成零售包装	Cefoperazone medicaments, consisting of two or more constituents which have been mixed together, not put up in measured doses or in forms or packings for retail sale	3003.2018	368
头孢曲松及其盐	Ceftriaxone and its salts	2941.9055	
头孢曲松药品，混合或未混合的，配定剂量或制成零售包装	Ceftriaxone medicaments, mixed or unmixed, put up in measured doses or in forms or packings for retail sale	3004.2017	368
头孢曲松药品，两种或两种以上成分混合而成的，未配定剂量或制成零售包装	Ceftriaxone medicaments, consisting of two or more constituents which have been mixed together, not put up in measured doses or in forms or packings for retail sale	3003.2017	368
头孢噻肟及其盐	Cefotaxime and its salts	2941.9057	
头孢噻肟药品，混合或未混合的，配定剂量或制成零售包装	Cefotaxime medicaments, mixed or unmixed, put up in measured doses or in forms or packings for retail sale	3004.2011	368
头孢噻肟药品，两种或两种以上成分混合而成的，未配定剂量或制成零售包装	Cefotaxime medicaments, consisting of two or more constituents which have been mixed together, not put up in measured doses or in forms or packings for retail sale	3003.2011	368
头孢三嗪及其盐	Ceftriaxone and its salts	2941.9055	
头孢三嗪药品，混合或未混合的，配定剂量或制成零售包装	Ceftriaxone medicaments, mixed or unmixed, put up in measured doses or in forms or packings for retail sale	3004.2017	368
头孢三嗪药品，两种或两种以上成分混合而成的，未配定剂量或制成零售包装	Ceftriaxone medicaments, consisting of two or more constituents which have been mixed together, not put up in measured doses or in forms or packings for retail sale	3003.2017	368
头孢他啶药品，混合或未混合的，未配定剂量或制成零售包装	Ceftazidime medicaments, mixed or unmixed, put up in measured doses or in forms or packings for retail sale	3004.2012	368
头孢他啶药品，两种或两种以上成分混合而成的，未配定剂量或制成零售包装	Ceftazidime medicaments, consisting of two or more constituents which have been mixed together, not put up in measured doses or in forms or packings for retail sale	3003.2012	368
头孢替唑药品，混合或未混合的，配定剂量或制成零售包装	Ceftezole medicaments, mixed or unmixed, put up in measured doses or in forms or packings for retail sale	3004.2014	368

商品名称	Article Description	税则号列	申报要素
头孢替唑药品,两种或两种以上成分混合而成的,未配定剂量或制成零售包装	Ceftezole medicaments, consisting of two or more constituents which have been mixed together, not put up in measured doses or in forms or packings for retail sale	3003.2014	368
头孢西丁药品,混合或未混合的,配定剂量或制成零售包装	Cefoxitin medicaments, mixed or unmixed, put up in measured doses or in forms or packings for retail sale	3004.2013	368
头孢西丁药品,两种或两种以上成分混合而成的,未配定剂量或制成零售包装	Cefoxitin medicaments, consisting of two or more constituents which have been mixed together, not put up in measured doses or in forms or packings for retail sale	3003.2013	368
头孢唑啉及其盐	Cefazolin and its salts	2941.9053	
投梭箱,织机用	Throwing shuttle boxes for looms	8448.4910	3
投影机,彩色的,其他	Projectors, colour, nes	8528.6910	135
投影机,黑白或其他单色的,其他	Projectors, black and white or other monochrome, nes	8528.6990	135
投影机,专用于或主要用于税号84.71的自动数据处理系统的	Projectors of a kind solely or principally used in an automatic data processing system of heading No. 84.71	8528.6100	135
投影掩膜版制作和修复装置	Reticles manufacture or repair apparatus	8486.4010	7
投影掩膜版制作和修复装置零件及附件	Reticles manufacture or repair apparatus parts and accessories	8486.9090	3
投影仪,其他	Projectors for images, nes	9008.3090	
投影仪,正射的	Projectors, orthographical	9008.3010	
投影仪零件、附件	Projectors parts and accessories	9008.9090	3
透镜,未装配的各种材料制	Lenses, of any material, unmounted	9001.9090	5
透镜,已装配的各种材料制,照相机用	Lenses, of any material, mounted, for cameras	9002.9010	3
透镜,已装配的各种材料制,作为仪器或装置的零件、配件	Lenses, of any material, mounted, being parts of or fittings for instruments or apparatus	9002.9090	3
透热疗法设备	Diathermy apparatus	9018.9050	
tu			
凸版印刷机,除卷取进料式以外的,但不包括苯胺印刷机	Letterpress printing machinery, other than reel fed, excluding flexographic printing	8443.1500	57
凸版印刷机,卷取进料式,但不包括苯胺印刷机	Letterpress printing machinery, reel fed, excluding flexographic printing	8443.1400	57
图钉,钢铁制的	Drawing pins, of iron or steel	7317.0000	36
图钉及类似品,铜制或钢铁制带铜头的	Drawing pins and similar articles, of copper or of iron or steel with heads of copper	7415.1000	56
图画碳笔	Drawing charcoals	9609.9000	3
图片、设计图样及照片,印刷品	Pictures, designs and photographs, printed	4911.9100	3
图像增强管	Image intensifiers	8540.2090	35
涂布机器,纺织物的	Coating machines for textile fabrics	8451.8000	
涂布机器零件,纺织物的	Coating machines parts for textile fabrics	8451.9000	

T

商品名称	Article Description	税则号列	申报要素
屠刀	Butchers cleavers	8214.9000	256
土壤电加热器	Electric soil heating apparatus	8516.2910	7
土壤加热器零件	Electric soil heating apparatus parts	8516.9010	3
土色料,按重量计三氧化二铁含量在70%及以上	Earth colours, containing 70% or more by weight of combined iron evaluated as Fe_2O_3	2821.2000	6
吐司烤面包	Toasted bread	1905.4000	28
钍及其化合物	Thorium and its compounds	2844.3000	
钍矿砂及其精矿	Thorium ores and concentrates	2612.2000	146
兔皮,整张的,不论是否带头、尾或爪	Raw furskins of rabbit or hare, whole, with or without head, tail or paws	4301.8010	15
兔肉,兔头除外,家兔的,冻的	Meat of rabbits, frozen, excluding head	0208.1020	1
兔肉,兔头除外,家兔的,鲜或冷的	Meat of rabbits, fresh or chilled, excluding head	0208.1010	1
兔肉,野兔的,鲜或冷或冻的	Meat of hares, fresh, chilled or frozen	0208.1090	145
tuan			
团粒,其他谷物的	Pellets of cereals, nes	1103.2090	4
团粒,小麦的	Pellets of wheat	1103.2010	4
tui			
推进器,船用	Propellers for ships or boats	8487.1000	3
推进器及其零件,航空器用	Propellers and parts thereof, of aircraft	8803.1000	3
推力球轴承	Thrust ball bearings	8482.1040	5
推土机,履带式,其他	Bulldozers, track laying, nes	8429.1190	57
推土机,其他	Bulldozers, nes	8429.1990	57
推土机及侧铲推土机,发动机输出功率超过235.36千瓦(320马力)的	Bulldozers and angledozers, with an engine of an output exceeding 235.36kW(320hp)	8429.1910	57
推土机及侧铲推土机,履带式,发动机输出功率超过235.36千瓦(320马力)的	Bulldozers and angledozers, track laying, with an engine of an output exceeding 235.36kW(320hp)	8429.1110	57
推土机用铲	Bulldozer blades	8431.4200	3
退火处理设备,平板显示器的制造机器及装置	Annealing treatment equipment, flat panel displays manufacture machines and apparatus	8486.3010	7
退火处理设备,制造半导体器件或集成电路的机器及装置	Annealing treatment equipment, semiconductor devices or of electronic integrated circuits manufacture machines and apparatus	8486.2010	7
退绕机器,纺织物的	Unreeling machines for textile fabrics	8451.5000	
退绕机器零件,纺织物的	Unreeling machines parts for textile fabrics	8451.9000	
退热冰	Acetanilide	2924.2990	36
tun			
鲀,活的	Puffer fish, living	0301.9992	15
鲀,鲜或冷的	Puffer fish, fresh or chilled	0302.6950	18

T

商品名称	Article Description	税则号列	申报要素
tuo			
托架及类似品,贱金属制	Brackets and similar fixtures, of base metal	8302.5000	256
托盘护框,辐射松制的	Pallet collars, of radiata pine	4415.2010	56
托盘护框,其他木制的	Pallet collars, of other wood	4415.2090	56
拖把	Mops	9603.9090	3
拖拉机,非轮式	Tractors, other than wheeled	8701.9019	5
拖拉机,轮式	Tractors, wheeled	8701.9011	5
拖拉机用零件、附件	Tractors parts and accessories, nes	8708.9910	3
拖轮	Tugs craft	8904.0000	
脱粒机	Threshing machinery	8433.5200	
脱粒机零件	Threshing machinery parts	8433.9090	
脱毛剂	Depilatories	3307.9000	23
脱毛器,电动的	Hair-removing appliances, with self-contained electric motor	8510.3000	
脱毛器零件,电动的	Hair-removing appliances parts, with self-contained electric motor	8510.9000	3
脱模剂,以润滑剂为基本成分的,含有石油或从沥青矿物提取的油类	Mould release preparations, based on lubricants, containing petroleum oils or oils obtained from bituminous minerals	3403.1900	2368
脱模剂,以润滑剂为基本成分的,其他	Mould release preparations, based on lubricants, nes	3403.9900	2368
脱氢可的松	Dehydrocortisone	2937.2100	36
脱氢可的松	Prednisone(dehydrocortisone)	2937.2100	36
脱氢皮质醇	Dehydrohydrocortisone	2937.2100	36
脱氢皮质醇	Prednisolone(dehydrohydrocortisone)	2937.2100	36
脱水机,离心式	Dewaterers, centrifuges	8421.1910	7
陀螺稳定器,船舶用	Gyroscopic stabilizers for ships	8479.8910	7
陀螺稳定器用零件,船舶用	Gyroscopic stabilizers parts, for ships	8479.9010	3
鸵鸟	Ostrich	0106.3922	3
妥尔油,不论是否精炼	Tall oil, whether or not refined	3803.0000	3
妥尔油脂肪酸,工业用	Tall oil fatty acids, industrial use	3823.1300	6

T

W

商品名称	Article Description	税则号列	申报要素
wa			
挖掘机,履带式,上部结构可旋转 360 度的机械	Excavators, track-mounted, with a 360° revolving superstructure	8429.5212	57
挖掘机,轮胎式,上部结构可旋转 360 度的机械	Excavators, tyre-mounted, with a 360° revolving superstructure	8429.5211	57
挖掘机,上部结构可旋转 360 度的机械,其他	Excavators, with a 360° revolving superstructure, nes	8429.5219	57
挖掘机零件	Excavators parts	8431.4990	3
挖掘机械,对泥土、矿物或矿石的,非自推进的,其他	Excavating machinery, for earth, minerals or ores, not self-propelled, nes	8430.6990	5
挖掘机械,对泥土、矿物或矿石的,自推进的,其他	Excavating machinery, for earth, minerals or ores, self-propelled, nes	8430.5090	5
挖泥船	Dredgers	8905.1000	
蛙苗	Tadpole and young frogs	0106.9011	3
瓦及盖屋板, 木制的	Shingles and shakes, of wood	4418.5000	58
瓦及类似品,用水泥、石膏及其他矿物粘合材料粘合植物纤维、稻草、刨花、木片屑、木粉、锯末或木废料制成	Tiles and similar articles of vegetable fibre, of straw or of shavings, chips, particles, sawdust or other waste, of wood, agglomerated with cement, plaster or other mineral binders	6808.0000	456
瓦楞板, 不含石棉的	Corrugated sheets, not containing asbestos	6811.8100	56
瓦楞板, 含石棉的	Corrugated sheets, containing asbestos	6811.4010	56
瓦楞原纸,半化学浆的	Fluting paper, semi-chemical	4805.1100	
瓦楞原纸,草浆的	Fluting paper, of straw	4805.1200	
瓦楞原纸,其他	Fluting paper, nes	4805.1900	
瓦楞纸及纸板,不论是否穿孔	Corrugated paper and paperboard, whether or not perforated	4808.1000	58
袜,长统或中统的,针织或钩编的,每根单丝细度在 67 分特以下,女式,其他	Hosiery of full-length or knee-length, knitted or crocheted, measuring per single yarn less than 67 decitex, for women or girls, nes	6115.3000	2456
袜,渐紧压的(例如,用以治疗静脉曲张的长统袜)	Hosiery of graduated compression (for example, stockings for varicose veins)	6115.1000	2456
袜,连裤袜及紧身裤袜,针织或钩编的,每根单丝细度在 67 分特及以上的合成纤维制	Panty hose and tights, knitted or crocheted, of synthetic fibres, measuring per single yarn 67 decitex or more	6115.2200	2456
袜,连裤袜及紧身裤袜,针织或钩编的,每根单丝细度在 67 分特以下的合成纤维制	Panty hose and tights, knitted or crocheted, of synthetic fibres, measuring per single yarn less than 67 decitex	6115.2100	2456
袜,连裤袜及紧身裤袜,针织或钩编的,棉制	Panty hose and tights, knitted or crocheted, of cotton	6115.2910	2456

W

商品名称	Article Description	税则号列	申报要素
袜,连裤袜及紧身裤袜,针织或钩编的,其他	Panty hose and tights, knitted or crocheted, nes	6115.2990	2456
袜,丝袜、短袜及其他袜类,针织或钩编的,合成纤维制	Stockings, socks and other hosiery, knitted or crocheted, of synthetic fibres	6115.9600	2456
袜,丝袜、短袜及其他袜类,针织或钩编的,棉制	Stockings, socks and other hosiery, knitted or crocheted, of cotton	6115.9500	2456
袜,丝袜、短袜及其他袜类,针织或钩编的,其他纺织材料制	Stockings, socks and other hosiery, knitted or crocheted, of other textile materials	6115.9900	2456
袜,丝袜、短袜及其他袜类,针织或钩编的,羊毛或动物细毛制	Stockings, socks and other hosiery, knitted or crocheted, of wool or fine animal hair	6115.9400	2456
袜子及袜套,非针织或钩编的	Stocking, socks and socketes, not knitted or crocheted	6217.1010	2456
wai			
外底及鞋跟,橡胶制的	Outer soles and heels, of rubber	6406.2010	6
外底及鞋跟,塑料制的	Outer soles and heels, of plastics	6406.2020	6
外科用仪器及器具,其他	Surgical instruments and appliances, nes	9018.9090	7
外圆磨床,在任一坐标的定位精度至少是0.01毫米,加工金属或金属陶瓷用,其他	Cylindrical grinding machines, in which the positioning in any one axis can be set up to an accuracy of at least 0.01mm, for metal or cermets, nes	8460.2910	7
外圆磨床,在任一坐标的定位精度至少是0.01毫米,数控的,加工金属或金属陶瓷用	Cylindrical grinding machines, in which the positioning in any one axis can be set up to an accuracy of at least 0.01mm, numerically controlled, for metal or cermets	8460.2110	7
wan			
弯曲机,加工金属用,其他	Bending machines, for working metal, nes	8462.2990	7
弯曲机,数控的,加工金属用	Bending machines, numerically controlled, for working metal	8462.2190	7
弯曲机器,加工木材、软木、骨、硬质橡胶、硬质塑料或类似硬质材料的	Bending machines, for working wood, cork, bone, hard rubber, hard plastics or similar hard materials	8465.9400	7
豌豆,冷冻的	Peas (pisum sativum), frozen	0710.2100	1
豌豆,其他,脱荚的,干的	Peas (pisum sativum), nes, dried, shelled	0713.1090	34
豌豆,鲜或冷藏的	Peas (pisum sativum), fresh or chilled	0708.1000	1
豌豆,用醋或醋酸以外的其他方法制作或保藏的,未冷冻	Peas (pisum sativum), prepared or preserved otherwise than by vinegar or acetic acid, not frozen	2005.4000	48
豌豆,种用,脱荚的,干的	Peas (pisum sativum), seed, dried, shelled	0713.1010	34
玩具,电动火车,缩小的成套模型组件	Toys, electric trains, reduced-size model assembly kits	9503.0031	5
玩具,其他	Toys, nes	9503.0089	5
玩具,缩小(按比例缩小)的建筑,成套的	Toys of model assembly kits, of constructional toys	9503.0040	5
玩具,踏板汽车及类似的,带轮的	Toys, pedal cars and similar, wheeled	9503.0010	
玩具,智力玩具	Toys for puzzles	9503.0060	5

W

商品名称	Article Description	税则号列	申报要素
玩具,组装成套或全套的,其他	Toys,put up in sets or outfits,nes	9503.0081	5
玩具动物	Toy animals	9503.0021	5
玩具或模型,带动力装置的,其他	Toys,incorporating a motor,nes	9503.0082	5
玩具乐器	Toy musical instruments and apparatus	9503.0050	5
玩具零件、附件	Toys parts and accessories	9503.0090	5
玩具模型组件,缩小(按比例缩小)的,成套的,其他	Toy of model assembly kits,reduced-size ("scale"),nes	9503.0039	5
玩偶,不论是否着装,动物的	Dolls, whether or not dressed, for representing animals	9503.0021	5
玩偶,不论是否着装,其他	Dolls, whether or not dressed,nes	9503.0029	5
玩偶车	Dolls carriages	9503.0010	
挽具,适合各种动物用,各种材料制成的	Harness for any animal,of any material	4201.0000	1458
挽绳,适合各种动物用	Leads for any animal,of any material	4201.0000	1458
万向节	Universal joints	8483.6000	
万向节零件	Universal joints parts	8483.9000	3
万用表,不带记录装置,量程在五位半及以下的,数字的	Multimeters without a recording device, of measuring range of 5.5 or less,digital	9030.3110	
万用表,不带记录装置,其他	Multimeters without a recording device,nes	9030.3190	7
万用表,带记录装置	Multimeters with a recording device	9030.3200	
万用表的零件、附件	Multimeters parts and accessories	9030.9000	3
wang			
网,纺织材料制,其他	Nets of textile materials,nes	5608.9000	34
网、格栅,铜丝制的	Grill and netting, of copper wire	7419.9940	4
网、篱及格栅,钢铁丝制,镀或涂锌的	Grill,netting and fencing, of iron or steel wire,plated or coated with zinc	7314.4100	36
网、篱及格栅,钢铁丝制,交点焊接的,镀或涂锌的	Grill, netting and fencing, of iron or steel wire, welded at the intersection, plated or coated with zinc	7314.3100	36
网、篱及格栅,钢铁丝制,交点焊接的,其他	Grill, netting and fencing, of iron or steel wire, welded at the intersection,nes	7314.3900	36
网、篱及格栅,钢铁丝制,交点焊接的,丝的最大截面尺寸在3毫米及以上,网眼尺寸在100平方厘米及以上	Grill, netting and fencing, of iron or steel wire, welded at the intersection,of wire with a maximum cross-sectional dimension of 3mm or more and having a mesh size of $100cm^2$ or more	7314.2000	36
网、篱及格栅,钢铁丝制,其他	Grill,netting and fencing, of iron or steel wire,nes	7314.4900	36
网、篱及格栅,钢铁丝制,涂塑的	Grill,netting and fencing, of iron or steel wire,coated whith plastics	7314.4200	36
网及格栅,工业用,其他	Nickel articles, for technical use,nes	7508.1080	6
网及格栅,其他	Grill and netting, of nickel wire,nes	7508.1090	6
网料,化学纤维材料制,其他	Netting of man-made textile materials,nes	5608.1900	34
网料,线、绳或索结制的,其他	Netting,knotted of twine, cordage or rope,nes	5608.9000	34

商品名称	Article Description	税则号列	申报要素
网球,其他	Tennis balls, nes	9506.6900	5
网球拍,其他	Tennis rackets, nes	9506.5900	5
网式印刷机,其他	Screen printing machinery, nes	8443.1929	57
网眼薄纱及其他网眼织物,纺织材料制,其他	Tulles and other net fabrics, of textile materials, nes	5804.1090	468
网眼薄纱及其他网眼织物,化学纤维制	Tulles and other net fabrics, of man-made fibres	5804.1030	468
网眼薄纱及其他网眼织物,棉制	Tulles and other net fabrics, of cotton	5804.1020	468
网眼薄纱及其他网眼织物,丝及绢丝制	Tulles and other net fabrics, of silk or silk waste	5804.1010	468
网眼钢铁板	Expanded metal, of iron or steel	7314.5000	36
网眼铜板	Expanded metal, of copper	7419.9940	4
往复式活塞发动机,车辆用,气缸容量(排气量)超过1000毫升,但不超过3000毫升	Reciprocating piston engines of a kind used for the propulsion of vehicles, of a cylinder capacity exceeding1000cc but not exceeding 3000cc	8407.3410	123
往复式活塞发动机,车辆用,气缸容量(排气量)不超过50毫升	Reciprocating piston engines of a kind used for the propulsion of vehicles, of a cylinder capacity not exceeding 50cc	8407.3100	123
往复式活塞发动机,车辆用,气缸容量(排气量)超过250毫升,但不超过1000毫升	Reciprocating piston engines of a kind used for the propulsion of vehicles, of a cylinder capacity exceeding 250cc but not exceeding 1000cc	8407.3300	123
往复式活塞发动机,车辆用,气缸容量(排气量)超过3000毫升	Reciprocating piston engines of a kind used for the propulsion of vehicles, of a cylinder capacity exceeding 3000cc	8407.3420	123
往复式活塞发动机,车辆用,气缸容量(排气量)超过50毫升,但不超过250毫升	Reciprocating piston engines of a kind used for the propulsion of vehicles, of a cylinder capacity exceeding 50cc but not exceeding 250cc	8407.3200	123
望远镜	Periscopes	9013.1000	
望远镜,作为机器、设备、仪器或器具部件的	Telescopes designed to form parts of machines, appliances, instruments or apparatus	9013.1000	
望远镜盒、照相机套、乐器盒、枪盒、枪套及类似容器,其他	Birocular cases, camera cases, musical instrument cases, gun cases, holsters and similar containers, nes	4202.9900	256
望远镜盒、照相机套、乐器盒、枪盒、枪套及类似容器,以皮革、再生皮革或漆皮作面	Birocular cases, camera cases, musical instrument cases, gun cases, holsters and similar containers, with outer surface of leather, of composition leather or of patent leather	4202.9100	256
望远镜盒、照相机套、乐器盒、枪盒、枪套及类似容器,以塑料片或纺织材料作面	Birocular cases, camera cases, musical instrument cases, gun cases, holsters and similar containers, with outer surface of plastic sheeting or of textile materials	4202.9200	256
望远镜瞄准具,武器用	Telescopic sights for fitting to arms	9013.1000	

商品名称	Article Description	税则号列	申报要素
望远镜瞄准具的零件、附件,武器用	Telescopic sights parts and accessories, for fitting to arms	9013.9010	3
wei			
威士忌酒	Whiskies	2208.3000	2468
微波管,其他	Microwave tubes, nes	8540.7900	35
微波炉	Microwave ovens	8516.5000	7
微晶石蜡	Microcrystalline petroleum wax	2712.9010	6
微型机(计算机)	Microprocessings	8471.4140	26
微型机,以系统形式进口或出口的	Microprocessings, presented in the form of systems	8471.4940	26
微型机的处理部件	Microprocessings processing units	8471.5040	26
薇菜干	Osmund, dried	0712.9020	4
围巾,非针织或钩编的,合成纤维制	Mufflers, not knitted or crocheted, of synthetic fibres	6214.3000	2456
围巾,非针织或钩编的,其他动物细毛制	Mufflers, not knitted or crocheted, of other fine animal hair	6214.2090	2456
围巾,非针织或钩编的,其他纺织材料制	Mufflers, not knitted or crocheted, of other textile materials	6214.9000	2456
围巾,非针织或钩编的,人造纤维制	Mufflers, not knitted or crocheted, of artificial fibres	6214.4000	2456
围巾,非针织或钩编的,山羊绒制	Mufflers, not knitted or crocheted, of goats fine animal hair	6214.2020	2456
围巾,非针织或钩编的,丝或绢丝制	Mufflers, not knitted or crocheted, of silk or silk waste	6214.1000	2456
围巾,非针织或钩编的,羊毛制	Mufflers, not knitted or crocheted, of wool	6214.2010	2456
围巾,针织或钩编的,其他	Mufflers, knitted or crocheted, nes	6117.1090	2456
围巾,针织或钩编的,其他动物细毛制	Mufflers, knitted or crocheted, of other fine animal hair	6117.1019	2456
围巾,针织或钩编的,山羊绒制	Mufflers, knitted or crocheted, of fine goats hair	6117.1011	2456
围巾,针织或钩编的,羊毛制	Mufflers, knitted or crocheted, of wool	6117.1020	2456
帷帘,钩编的,合成纤维制	Drapes, crocheted, of synthetic fibres	6303.1220	346
帷帘,钩编的,棉制	Drapes, crocheted, of cotton	6303.1932	346
帷帘,钩编的,其他纺织材料制	Drapes, crocheted, of other textile materials	6303.1992	346
帷帘,合成纤维制,其他	Drapes, of synthetic fibres, nes	6303.9200	346
帷帘,棉制,其他	Drapes, of cotton, nes	6303.9100	346
帷帘,其他纺织材料制	Drapes, of other textile materials	6303.9900	346
帷帘,针织的,合成纤维制	Drapes, knitted, of synthetic fibres	6303.1210	346
帷帘,针织的,棉制	Drapes, knitted, of cotton	6303.1931	346
帷帘,针织的,其他纺织材料制	Drapes, knitted, of other textile materials	6303.1991	346
维利式信号枪	Very pistols	9303.9000	
维生素,天然浓缩物	Vitamins, natural concentrates	2936.9000	36
维生素 A 及其衍生物	Vitamins A and their derivatives	2936.2100	36
维生素 B_{12} 及其衍生物	Vitamin B_{12} and its derivatives	2936.2600	36
维生素 B_1 及其衍生物	Vitamin B_1 and its derivatives	2936.2200	36
维生素 B_2 及其衍生物	Vitamin B_2 and its derivatives	2936.2300	36

商品名称	Article Description	税则号列	申报要素
维生素 B_3 及其衍生物	Vitamin B_3 and its derivatives	2936. 2400	36
维生素 B_5 及其衍生物	Vitamin B_5 and its derivatives	2936. 2400	36
维生素 B_6 及其衍生物	Vitamin B_6 and its derivatives	2936. 2500	36
维生素 C 及其衍生物	Vitamin C and its derivatives	2936. 2700	36
维生素 E 及其衍生物	Vitamin E and its derivatives	2936. 2800	36
维生素及其衍生物,混合的	Vitamins and their derivatives, mixed	2936. 9000	36
维生素及其衍生物,未混合的,其他	Vitamins and their derivatives, unmixed, nes	2936. 2900	36
维生素类药品,混合或未混合的,配定剂量或制成零售包装,不包括税号 29. 36 的其他产品	Vitamins medicaments, mixed or unmixed, put up in measured doses or in forms of packings for retail sale or other products of heading No. 29. 36	3004. 5000	368
维特罗夫菊苣,鲜或冷藏的	Witloof chicory (cichoriym intybus var. foliosum), fresh or chilled	0705. 2100	1
纬编机,平型的	Weft knitting machines, flat	8447. 2020	7
纬编机的辅助机器	Weft knitting machines auxiliary	8448. 1900	3
苇帘	Screens of reeds	4601. 2921	6
卫生洁具,塑料的,其他	Sanitary ware, of plastics, nes	3922. 9000	236
卫生巾及止血塞、婴儿尿布或尿布垫及类似卫生用品,絮胎制	Sanitary towels and tampons, napkins and napkin liners for babies and similar sanitary articles, of wadding	5601. 1000	6
卫生巾及止血塞及类似的卫生用品,纸浆、纸、纤维素絮纸或纤维素纤维网纸制的	Sanitary towels and tampons and similar sanitary articles, of paper pulp, paper, cellulose wadding or webs of cellulose fibres	4818. 4000	568
卫生器具及其零件,铝制	Sanitary ware and parts thereof, of aluminium	7615. 2000	36
卫生器具及其零件,钢铁制,其他	Sanitary ware and parts thereof, of iron or steel, nes	7324. 9000	24
卫生器具及其零件,铜制	Sanitary ware and parts thereof, of copper	7418. 2000	56
卫生用具,塑料的	Hygienic articles, of plastics	3924. 9000	23
卫生用品,硫化橡胶(硬质橡胶除外)制的	Hygienic articles, of vulcanized rubber other than hard rubber, nes	4014. 9000	23
卫生纸,成卷或成张的	Toilet tissue stock, in rolls or sheets	4803. 0000	58
卫生纸,成卷宽度不超过 36 厘米或切成一定尺寸或形状的	Toilet paper, in rolls of a width not exceeding 36cm, or cut to size or shape	4818. 1000	568
卫星地面站设备,无线电广播、电视用,装有接收装置的	Satellite earth station, for radio-broadcasting or television, incorporating reception apparatus	8525. 6010	7
卫星电视地面接收转播设备用零件	Satellite television ground receiving and relaying apparatus parts	8529. 9010	3
卫星电视接收机,彩色的	Satellite television receivers, colour	8528. 7110	135
卫星及其运载工具、亚轨道运载工具	Satellites and suborbital and spacecraft launch vehicles	8802. 6000	
卫星亚轨道运载工具	Satellites suborbital launch vehicles	8802. 6000	
未烘炒食品,谷物片制成的	Prepared foods obtained from unroasted cereal flakes	1904. 2000	48
未硫化橡胶,其他形状的	Rubber, unvulcanized, in other forms	4006. 9010	13
味精	Gourmet powder	2103. 9010	268

W

商品名称	Article Description	税则号列	申报要素
味美思酒罐装,少于2升	Vermouth, in containers holding 2L or less	2205.1000	248
味美思酒,其他	Vermouth, nes	2205.1000	248
胃,动物的(鱼除外)	Stomachs of animals (other than fish)	0504.0029	14
胃蛋白酶	Pepsin	3507.9090	35
wen			
温度计及高温计,工业用,未与其他仪器组合	Thermometers and pyrometers, for technical use, not combined with other instruments	9025.1910	7
温度计及高温计,未与其他仪器组合,其他	Thermometers and pyrometers, not combined with other instruments, nes	9025.1990	7
温度计及高温计,液体的,可直接读数,未与其他仪器组合	Thermometers and pyrometers, liquid-filled, for direct reading, not combined with other instruments	9025.1100	
温度计及高温计零件、附件	Thermometers or pyrometers parts and accessories	9025.9000	7
榅桲,鲜的	Quinces, fresh	0808.2020	1
文件夹,贱金属制	Paper clips, of base metal	8305.9000	256
文件夹,纸或纸板制的	Folders, of paper or paperboard	4820.3000	
文件篮,贱金属制,办公室家具除外	Paper rests, of base metal, other than office furniture	8304.0000	256
文件盘,贱金属制,办公室家具除外	Paper trays, of base metal, other than office furniture	8304.0000	256
文字处理机	Word-processing machines	8469.0011	
蚊香,零售包装	Mosquito smudges, in forms of packings for retail sale	3808.9111	36
稳定土摊铺机	Stabilizer spreading machines	8479.1022	7
稳压电源,其他	Voltage-stabilized suppliers, nes	8504.4019	78
稳压电源,税号84.71所列机器用	Voltage-stabilized suppliers, of the machines of heading No. 84.71	8504.4013	78
稳压电源用零件	Voltage-stabilized suppliers parts	8504.9020	3
wo			
涡流探伤检测仪	Eddy examinations apparatus, without damaging	9031.8033	
涡轮风扇发动机,推力不超过25千牛顿	Turbo fan engines, of a thrust not exceeding 25kN	8411.1110	27
涡轮风扇发动机,推力超过25千牛顿	Turbo fan engines, of a thrust exceeding 25kN	8411.1210	27
涡轮螺桨发动机,功率不超过1100千瓦	Turbo-propellers, of a power not exceeding 1100kW	8411.2100	27
涡轮螺桨发动机,功率超过1100千瓦,但不超过2238千瓦	Turbo-propellers, of a power exceeding 1100kW but not exceeding 2238kW	8411.2210	27
涡轮螺桨发动机,功率超过2238千瓦,但不超过3730千瓦	Turbo-propellers, of a power exceeding 2238kW but not exceeding 3730kW	8411.2220	27
涡轮螺桨发动机,功率超过3730千瓦	Turbo-propellers, of a power exceeding 3730kW	8411.2230	27
涡轮螺桨发动机用零件	Turbo-propellers parts	8411.9100	27
涡轮喷气发动机,推力不超过25千牛顿,其他	Turbo-jets, of a thrust not exceeding 25kN, nes	8411.1190	27
涡轮喷气发动机,推力超过25千牛顿,其他	Urbo-jets, of a thrust exceeding 25kN, nes	8411.1290	27

W

商品名称	Article Description	税则号列	申报要素
涡轮喷气发动机用零件	Turbo-jets parts	8411.9100	27
涡轮轴发动机用零件	Turboshaft engines parts	8411.9910	27
莴苣,其他,鲜或冷藏的	Lettuce, nes, fresh or chilled	0705.1900	1
蜗牛,种苗	Snails, other than sea snails, for cultivation	0307.6010	8
蜗牛及螺,其他	Snails, other than sea snails, nes	0307.6090	148
wu			
乌龙茶,内包装每件净重不超过3千克	Oolong tea, in immediate packings of a content not exceeding 3kg	0902.3010	248
乌龙茶,其他	Oolong tea, nes	0902.4010	248
屋顶框架,铝制	Roofs, roofing frameworks, of aluminium	7610.9000	56
屋顶瓦,陶瓷制	Roofing tiles, of ceramic	6905.1000	5
钨,未锻轧,包括简单烧结而成的条、杆	Tungsten, unwrought, including bars and rods obtained simply by sintering	8101.9400	16
钨的氧化物及氢氧化物,其他	Tungsten oxides and hydroxides, nes	2825.9019	
钨粉末	Tungsten (wolfram) powders	8101.1000	16
钨矿砂及其精矿	Tungsten ores and concentrates	2611.0000	146
钨锰矿	Hubnerite	2611.0000	146
钨锰铁矿	Wolframite	2611.0000	146
钨丝	Tungsten wire	8101.9600	16
钨酸	Tungstic acid	2825.9011	
钨酸钙	Calcium wolframate	2841.8030	1
钨酸钠	Sodium tungstate	2841.8020	1
钨酸盐,其他	Tungstates (wolframates), nes	2841.8090	1
钨铁合金	Ferro-tungsten alloys	7202.8010	6
钨铁矿	Ferberite	2611.0000	146
钨制品,其他	Tungsten (wolfram) articles, nes	8101.9990	16
无纺产品,玻璃纤维制,其他	Nonwoven products of glass fibres, nes	7019.3900	56
无纺织物,化学纤维长丝制,每平方米重量不超过25克,经浸渍、涂布、包覆或层压	Nonwovens of man-made filaments, weighing not more than $25g/m^2$, impregnated, coated, covered or laminated	5603.1110	46
无纺织物,化学纤维长丝制,每平方米重量不超过25克,其他	Nonwovens of man-made filaments, weighing not more than $25g/m^2$, nes	5603.1190	46
无纺织物,化学纤维长丝制,每平方米重量超过150克,经浸渍、涂布、包覆或层压	Nonwovens of man-made filaments, weighing more than $150g/m^2$, impregnated, coated, covered or laminated	5603.1410	46
无纺织物,化学纤维长丝制,每平方米重量超过150克,其他	Nonwovens of man-made filaments, weighing more than $150g/m^2$, nes	5603.1490	46
无纺织物,化学纤维长丝制,每平方米重量超过25克,但不超过70克,经浸渍、涂布、包覆或层压	Nonwovens of man-made filaments, weighing more than $25g/m^2$ but not more than $70g/m^2$, impregnated, coated, covered or laminated	5603.1210	46

W

商品名称	Article Description	税则号列	申报要素
无纺织物,化学纤维长丝制,每平方米重量超过25克,但不超过70克,其他	Nonwovens of man-made filaments, weighing more than $25g/m^2$ but not more than $70g/m^2$, nes	5603.1290	46
无纺织物,化学纤维长丝制,每平方米重量超过70克,但不超过150克,经浸渍、涂布、包覆或层压	Nonwovens of man-made filaments, weighing more than $70g/m^2$ but not more than $150g/m^2$, impregnated, coated, covered or laminated	5603.1310	46
无纺织物,化学纤维长丝制,每平方米重量超过70克,但不超过150克其他	Nonwovens of man-made filaments, weighing more than $70g/m^2$ but not more than $150g/m^2$, nes	5603.1390	46
无纺织物,每平方米重量不超过25克,经浸渍、涂布、包覆或层压,其他	Nonwovens, weighing not more than $25g/m^2$, impregnated, coated, covered or laminated, nes	5603.9110	46
无纺织物,每平方米重量不超过25克,其他	Nonwovens, weighing not more than $25g/m^2$, nes	5603.9190	46
无纺织物,每平方米重量超过150克,经浸渍、涂布、包覆或层压	Nonwovens, weighing more than $150g/m^2$, impregnated, coated, covered or laminated	5603.9410	46
无纺织物,每平方米重量超过150克,其他	Nonwovens, weighing more than $150g/m^2$, nes	5603.9490	46
无纺织物,每平方米重量超过25克,但不超过70克,经浸渍、涂布、包覆或层压	Nonwovens, weighing more than $25g/m^2$ but not more than $70g/m^2$, impregnated, coated, covered or laminated	5603.9210	46
无纺织物,每平方米重量超过25克,但不超过70克,其他	Nonwovens, weighing more than $25g/m^2$ but not more than $70g/m^2$, nes	5603.9290	46
无纺织物,每平方米重量超过70克,但不超过150克,经浸渍、涂布、包覆或层压	Nonwovens, weighing more than $70g/m^2$ but not more than $150g/m^2$, impregnated, coated, covered or laminated	5603.9310	46
无纺织物,每平方米重量超过70克,但不超过150克,其他	Nonwovens, weighing more than $70g/m^2$ but not more than $150g/m^2$, nes	5603.9390	46
无纺织物整理机器	Nonwovens finishing machinery	8449.0090	7
无根插枝	Unrooted cuttings	0602.1000	3
无轨巷道堆垛机,电动的	Trackless alleyway stackers, powered by an electric motor	8427.1020	7
无花果	Figs	0804.2000	14
无花果蛋白酶	Ficin	3507.9090	35
无环醇的卤化、磺化、硝化或亚硝化衍生物,其他	Halogenated, sulphonated, nitrated ornitrosated derivatives of acyclic alcohols, nes	2905.5900	36
无环单胺及其衍生物以及它们的盐,其他	Acyclic monoamines and their derivatives; salts thereof, nes	2921.1990	36
无环多胺及其衍生物以及它们的盐,其他	Acyclic polyamines and their derivatives; salts thereof, nes	2921.2900	36
无环多元羧酸及其酸酐、酰卤化物、过氧化物和过氧酸以及它们的衍生物,其他	Acyclie polycarboxylic acids, their anhydrides, halides, peroxides, peroxyacids and their derivatives, nes	2917.1900	36
无环醚,其他	Acyclic ethers, nes	2909.1900	36

W

商品名称	Article Description	税则号列	申报要素
无环醛,不含其他含氧基的,其他	Acyclic aldehydes without other oxygen function, nes	2912. 1900	36
无环萜烯醇,其他	Acyclic terpene alcohols, nes	2905. 2290	36
无环烃,饱和的	Acyclic hydrocarbons, saturated	2901. 1000	368
无环烃,不饱和的,其他	Acyclic hydrocarbons, unsaturated, nes	2901. 2990	368
无环烃的饱和氯化衍生物,其他	Saturated chlorinated derivatives of acyclic hydrocarbons, nes	2903. 1990	36
无环烃的不饱和氯化衍生物,其他	Unsaturated chlorinated derivatives of acyclic hydrocarbons, nes	2903. 2990	36
无环烃的氟化、溴化或碘化衍生物,其他	Fluorinated, brominated or iodinated derivatives of acyclic hydrocarbons, nes	2903. 3990	36
无环酮,不含其他含氧基的,其他	Acyclic ketones without other oxygen function, nes	2914. 1900	36
无环酰胺(包括无环氨基甲酸酯)及其衍生物以及它们的盐,其他	Acyclic amides (including acyclic carbamates) and their derivatives; salts thereof, nes	2924. 1990	36
无机化合物,其他	Inorganic compounds, nes	2853. 0090	
无机碱,其他	Inorganic bases, nes	2825. 9090	
无机酸,其他	Inorganic acids, nes	2811. 1990	6
无机酸盐及过氧酸盐,其他	Salts of inorganic acids or peroxoacids, nes	2842. 9090	
无酒精饮料,其他	Non-alcoholic beverages, nes	2202. 9000	268
无螺纹制品,钢铁制的,其他	Non-threaded articles, of iron of steel, nes	7318. 2900	268
无螺纹制品,铜制,其他	Articles, not threaded, of copper, nes	7415. 2900	56
无绳电话机	Line telephone sets with cordless handsets	8517. 1100	
无损探伤检测仪器(射线探伤仪除外),其他	Examinations apparatus without damaging structure (other than apparatus for radiological examinations), nes	9031. 8039	7
无外绱鞋底的鞋类,针织或钩编的,合成纤维制	Footwear without applied soles, knitted or crocheted, of synthetic fibres	6115. 9600	2456
无外绱鞋底的鞋类,针织或钩编的,棉制	Footwear without applied soles, knitted or crocheted, of cotton	6115. 9500	2456
无外绱鞋底的鞋类,针织或钩编的,其他纺织材料制	Footwear without applied soles, knitted or crocheted, of other textile materials	6115. 9900	2456
无外绱鞋底的鞋类,针织或钩编的,羊毛或动物细毛制	Footwear without applied soles, knitted or crocheted, of wool or fine animal hair	6115. 9400	2456
无线电导航设备,机动车辆用	Radio navigational aid apparatus, for motor vehicles	8526. 9110	
无线电导航设备,其他	Radio navigational aid apparatus, nes	8526. 9190	
无线电导航设备用零件	Radio navigational aid apparatus parts	8529. 9050	3
无线电广播接收设备,带时钟的收音机	Radio-broadcasting reception apparatus, not combined with sound recording or reproducing apparatus but combined with a clock	8527. 9200	5
无线电广播接收设备,其他	Radio-broadcasting reception apparatus, nes	8527. 9900	5
无线电广播接收设备,收录(放)音组合机	Radio-broadcasting reception apparatus, combined with sound recording or reproducing apparatus	8527. 9100	5

W

商品名称	Article Description	税则号列	申报要素
无线电话机,手持(包括车载)式	Wireless telephone handsets (including installed in the vehicle)	8517.1210	
无线电话机用(天线除外)零件,手持式	Wireless telephone parts, other than aerials	8517.7030	3
无线电设备零件,其他	Radio apparatus parts, nes	8529.9090	3
无线电收音机,不需外接电源的,其他	Radio-broadcast receivers capable of operating without an external source of power, nes	8527.1900	5
无线电收音机,不需外接电源的,收录(放)音组合机	Radio-broadcast receivers capable of operating without an external source of power, combined with sound recording or reproducing apparatus	8527.1300	5
无线电收音机,需外接电源的,汽车用,其他	Radio-broadcast receivers not capable of operating without an external source of power, of a kind used in motor vehicles, nes	8527.2900	5
无线电收音机,需外接电源的,汽车用,收录(放)音组合机	Radio-broadcast receivers not capable of operating without an external source of power, of a kind used in motor vehicles, combined with sound recording or reproducing apparatus	8527.2100	5
无线电收音机及其组合机用零件	Radio-broadcast receivers and their combinations parts	8529.9060	3
无线电通信车	Radio communication vans	8705.9010	7
无线电遥控设备	Radio remote control apparatus	8526.9200	
无线接入固定台	Fixed wireless access station	8517.6293	7
无线设备,其他	Wireless network equipments, nes	8517.6910	
无线数字通信设备,其他	Wireless digital telecommunication apparatus, nes	8517.6299	7
无线网络接口卡	Wireless network interface cards	8517.6292	7
无烟煤	Anthracite	2701.1100	156
芜菁甘蓝,饲料用	Swedes, forage products	1214.9000	
五氯苯酚(ISO)	Pentachlorophenol (ISO)	2908.1100	36
五氯氟乙烷	Pentachlorofluoroethane	2903.4520	36
五氯化磷	Phosphorus pentachloride	2812.1045	
五氯三氟丙烷	Pentachlorotrifluoropropane	2903.4560	36
五氧化二钒	Divanadium pentaoxide	2825.3010	
五氧化二磷	Diphosphorus pentaoxide	2809.1000	6
武器,其他	Arms, nes	9304.0000	
武器用零件、附件,其他	Arms parts and accessori, nes	9305.9900	3
戊巴比妥(INN)以及盐	Pentobarbital (INN); salts thereof	2933.5300	36
戊酸及其盐和酯	Pentanoic acids, their salts and esters	2915.6000	36
芴	Fluorene	2902.9090	6
物镜,其他	Objective lenses, nes	9002.1990	3
物镜,摄影机或放映机用	Objective lenses, for cinematographic cameras or projectors	9002.1910	3

W

商品名称	Article Description	税则号列	申报要素
物镜,缩微阅读机用	Objective lenses, for microfilm, microfiche or other microform readers	9002.1120	3
物镜,投影仪、照片放大机及缩片机用	Objective lenses, for projectors or photographic enlargers or reducers	9002.1190	3
物镜,照相机用,其他	Objective lenses, for cameras, nes	9002.1139	3
物镜,制版照相机和特种照相机用	Objective lenses, for the cameras of a kind used for preparing printing plates or spelially designed	9002.1110	3
物理气相沉积设备(PVD),平板显示器的制造机器及装置	Physical vapour deposition (PVD) equipment, flat panel displays manufacture machines and apparatus	8486.3022	7
物理气相沉积装置(PVD)零件及附件,制造半导体器件、集成电路、平板显示器的机器及装置	Physical vapour deposition (PVD) equipment parts and accessories, semiconductor devices or of electronic integrated circuits or flat panel displays manufacture machines and apparatus	8486.9090	3
物理气相沉积装置(PVD),制造半导体器件或集成电路的机器及装置	Physical vapour deposition (PVD) equipment, semiconductor devices or of electronic integrated circuits manufacture machines and apparatus	8486.2022	7
物品,宝石或半宝石(天然、合成或再造)制	Articles of precious or semi-precious stones (natural, synthetic or reconstructed)	7116.2000	46
物品,天然或养殖珍珠制	Articles of natural or cultured pearls	7116.1000	46
物品,用纱线、扁条及类似品或线、绳、索、缆制成的,其他	Articles of yarn, strip or the like, twine, cordage, rope or cables, riot, nes	5609.0000	

W

X

商品名称	Article Description	税则号列	申报要素
xi			
西番莲果汁	Passionfruit juice	2009.8013	2468
西服套装,非针织或钩编的,男式,合成纤维制	Suits, not knitted or crocheted, for men or boys, of synthetic fibres	6203.1200	2456
西服套装,非针织或钩编的,男式,其他	Suits, not knitted or crocheted, for men or boys, nes	6203.1990	2456
西服套装,非针织或钩编的,男式,丝及绢丝制	Suits, not knitted or crocheted, for men or boys, of silk or silk waste	6203.1910	2456
西服套装,非针织或钩编的,男式,羊毛或动物细毛制	Suits, not knitted or crocheted, for men or boys, of wool or fine animal hair	6203.1100	2456
西服套装,非针织或钩编的,女式,合成纤维制	Suits, not knitted or crocheted, for women or girls, of synthetic fibres	6204.1300	2456
西服套装,非针织或钩编的,女式,棉制	Suits, not knitted or crocheted, for women or girls, of cotton	6204.1200	2456
西服套装,非针织或钩编的,女式,其他	Suits, not knitted or crocheted, for women or girls, nes	6204.1990	2456
西服套装,非针织或钩编的,女式,丝及绢丝制	Suits, not knitted or crocheted, for women or girls, of silk or silk waste	6204.1910	2456
西服套装,非针织或钩编的,女式,羊毛或动物细毛制	Suits, not knitted or crocheted, for women or girls, of wool or fine animal hair	6204.1100	2456
西服套装,针织或钩编的,男式,合成纤维制	Suits, knitted or crocheted, for men or boys, of synthetic fibres	6103.1020	2456
西服套装,针织或钩编的,男式,其他纺织材料制	Suits, knitted or crocheted, for men or boys, of other textile materials	6103.1090	2456
西服套装,针织或钩编的,男式,羊毛或动物细毛制	Suits, knitted or crocheted, for men or boys, of wool or fine animal hair	6103.1010	2456
西服套装,针织或钩编的,女式,合成纤维制	Suits, knitted or crocheted, for women or girls, of synthetic fibres	6104.1300	2456
西服套装,针织或钩编的,女式,棉制	Suits, knitted or crocheted, for women or girls, of cotton	6104.1920	2456
西服套装,针织或钩编的,女式,其他	Suits, knitted or crocheted, for women or girls, nes	6104.1990	2456
西服套装,针织或钩编的,女式,羊毛或动物细毛制	Suits, knitted or crocheted, for women or girls, of wool or fine animal hair	6104.1910	2456
西谷茎髓	Sago pith	0714.9090	34
西瓜,鲜的	Watermelons, fresh	0807.1100	12
西瓜子,种植用的	Seeds of watermelons	1209.9910	358
西兰花,鲜或冷藏的	Broccolis (brassica oleracea var. Italica), fresh or chilled	0704.9020	1
西梅,干的	Prunes, dried	0813.2000	34

商品名称	Article Description	税则号列	申报要素
西米	Sago	1903.0000	18
西米粉	Sago powder	1106.2000	4
西沙尔麻及其他纺织用龙舌兰类纤维	Sisal and other textile fibres of the genus agave, raw	5305.0091	4
西洋参	American ginseng	1211.2010	34
吸墨纸本	Blotting-pads, of paper or paperboard	4820.9000	
吸音性能的矿物材料的混合物及制品,其他	Sound absorbing mineral materials, mixtures and articles	6806.9000	68
希蒙得木油及其分离品	Jojoba oil and its fractions	1515.9010	
烯丙醇	Allyl alcohol	2905.2900	36
硒,经掺杂用于电子工业的晶体棒	Selenium crystals doped for use in electronics, in the form of cylinders or rods	2804.9010	346
硒,其他	Selenium, nes	2804.9090	346
稀释沥青,以沥青为基本成分的	Cut-backs, based on asphalt or bitumen	2715.0000	1346
稀土金属,其他,未相互混合或相互熔合	Rare-earth metals, nes, not intermixed or interalloyed	2805.3019	56
稀土金属、钪及钇,相互混合或相互熔合,电池级	Rare-earth metals, scandium, yttrium, intermixed or interalloyed, battery grade	2805.3021	56
稀土金属、钪及钇,相互混合或相互熔合,其他	Rare-earth metals, scandium, yttrium, intermixed or interalloyed, nes	2805.3029	56
稀土金属、钇、钪及其混合物的无机或有机化合物,其他	Compounds, inorganic or organic, of rare-earth metals, of yttrium or of scandium or of mixtures of these metals, nes	2846.9090	6
稀土金属矿	Ores of rare earth metals	2530.9020	13456
稀土永磁体	Rare-earth metals permanent magnets	8505.1110	46
稀有气体,其他	Rare gases, nes	2804.2900	
锡,非合金	Tin, not alloyed	8001.1000	16
锡,未锻轧,其他	Tin, unwrought, nes	8001.2090	16
锡箔(不论是否印花或用纸、纸板、塑料或类似材料衬背),厚度(衬背除外)不超过0.2毫米	Tin foil (whether or not printed or backed with paper, paperboard, plastics or similar backing materials), of a thickness (excluding any backing) not exceeding 0.2mm	8007.0030	16
锡合金,其他	Tin alloys, nes	8001.2029	16
锡基巴毕脱合金	Babbitt metal	8001.2010	16
锡矿砂及其精矿	Tin ores and concentrates	2609.0000	146
锡制品,其他	Tin articles, nes	8007.0090	16
嬉戏品	Novelty jokes	9505.9000	5
席,玻璃纤维制	Mats, of glass fibres	7019.3100	56
席子、席料,芦苇制的	Mats, matting of reeds	4601.2929	6
席子、席料及帘子,灯心草属材料制的	Mats, matting and screens of rushes	4601.2911	6
席子、席料及帘子,其他草制的	Mats, matting and screens, of other grass or straw	4601.2919	6
席子、席料及帘子,藤制的	Mats, matting and screens of rattan	4601.2200	6

X

商品名称	Article Description	税则号列	申报要素
席子、席料及帘子,植物材料制的,其他	Mats, matting and screens of vegetable materials, nes	4601.2990	6
席子、席料及帘子,竹制的	Mats, matting and screens of bamboo	4601.2100	6
洗涤槽,塑料的	Sinks, of plastics	3922.1000	236
洗涤槽,瓷制	Sinks, of porcelain or china	6910.1000	268
洗涤槽,陶制	Sinks, of pottery	6910.9000	268
洗涤槽及脸盆,不锈钢制	Sinks and wash basins, of stainless steel	7324.1000	24
洗涤粉,合成的	Detergents in powder form, synthetic	3402.2010	36
洗涤机器,泥土、石料、矿石或其他固体矿物质的	Washing machines, for earth, stone, ores or other mineral substances	8474.1000	
洗涤机器,纱线、织物及纺织制品用	Washing machines, for textile yarns, fabrics or made up textile articles, nes	8451.4000	
洗涤机器零件,纱线、织物及纺织制品用	Washing machines parts, for textile yarns, fabrics or made up textile articles, nes	8451.9000	
洗碟机,家用型	Dish washing machines of the household type	8422.1100	
洗碟机,其他	Dish washing machines, nes	8422.1900	
洗碟机用零件	DIsh washing machines parts	8422.9010	
洗瓶机	Bottles cleaning machinery	8422.2000	
洗刷、擦光用的块垫、手套及类似品,铝制	Scouring or polishing pads, gloves and the like, of aluminium	7615.1100	36
洗刷、擦光用的块垫、手套及类似品,铜制	Scouring or polishing pads, gloves and the like, of copper	7418.1100	56
洗刷擦光用的块垫、手套及类似品	Scouring or polishing pads, gloves and the like	7323.1000	24
洗衣机,干衣量不超过10千克的洗衣机,其他,家用或洗衣房用	Washing machines, each of a dry linen capacity not exceeding 10kg, nes, household or laundry type	8450.1900	7
洗衣机,干衣量超过10千克的,家用或洗衣房用	Washing machines, each of a dry linen capacity exceeding 10kg, household or laundry type	8450.2000	7
洗衣机,全自动的,波轮式,干衣量不超过10千克的洗衣机,家用或洗衣房用	Washing machines, fully-automatic machines, of the continuously rotating impeller, each of a dry linen capacity not exceeding 10kg, household or laundry type	8450.1110	7
洗衣机,全自动的,干衣量不超过10千克的洗衣机,家用或洗衣房用,其他	Washing machines, fully-automatic machines, each of a dry linen capacity not exceeding 10kg, household or laundry type, nes	8450.1190	7
洗衣机,全自动的,滚筒式,干衣量不超过10千克的洗衣机,家用或洗衣房用	Washing machines, fully-automatic machines, of the drum type, each of a dry linen capacity not exceeding 10kg, household or laundry type	8450.1120	7
洗衣机,装有离心甩干机,干衣量不超过10千克的洗衣机,家用或洗衣房用	Washing machines, with built-in centrifugal drier, each of a dry linen capacity not exceeding 10kg, household or laundry type	8450.1200	7
洗衣机用零件,干衣量不超过10千克的,家用或洗衣房用	Washing machines parts, each of a dry linen capacity not exceeding 10kg, household or laundry type	8450.9010	3

X

商品名称	Article Description	税则号列	申报要素
洗衣机用零件,干衣量超过10千克的,家用或洗衣房用	Washing machines parts, each of a dry linen capacity exceeding 10kg, household or laundry type	8450.9090	3
洗印装置及设备,电影用	Apparatus and equipment for photographic laboratories, of a kind used in cinematographic film	9010.5021	7
洗印装置及设备,其他	Apparatus and equipment for photographic laboratories, nes	9010.5029	7
洗印装置及设备,特种照相用	Apparatus and equipment for photographic laboratories, of a kind used in special photographic film or paper	9010.5022	7
铣床,加工木材、软木、骨、硬质橡胶、硬质塑料或类似硬质材料的	Milling machines, for working wood, cork, bone, hard rubber, hard plastics or similar hard materials	8465.9200	7
铣床,龙门式,切削金属的,其他	Milling machines, planomilling machines, for removing metal, nes	8459.6910	7
铣床,龙门式,数控的,切削金属的	Milling machines, planomilling machines, numerically controlled, for removing metal	8459.6110	7
铣床,切削金属的,其他	Milling machines, for removing metal, nes	8459.6990	7
铣床,升降台式,切削金属的,其他	Milling machines, knee-type, for removing metal, nes	8459.5900	7
铣床,数控的,切削金属的,其他	Milling machines, numerically controlled, for removing metal, nes	8459.6190	7
铣床,数控的,升降台式,切削金属的	Milling machines, numerically controlled, for removing metal	8459.5100	7
铣削用工具,可互换,带有金刚石等工作部件的	Milling tools, interchangeable, with working part of diamonds etc.	8207.7010	256
铣削用工具,可互换,其他	Milling tools, interchangeable, nes	8207.7090	256
戏水池	Paddling pools	9506.9190	5
细粉,黑麦的	Flour, of rye	1102.1000	4
细粉,混合麦的	Flour, of maslin	1101.0000	4
细粉,其他谷物的	Flour, of cereal, nes	1102.9090	4
细粉,其他米的	Flour, of rice, nes	1102.9019	4
细粉,籼米的	Flour, of long grain	1102.9011	4
细粉,小麦的	Flour, of wheat	1101.0000	4
细粉,玉米的	Flour, of maize (corn)	1102.2000	4
细粉、粗粉及粉末,用税号07.14的西谷茎髓及植物根茎、块茎制成的	Flour, meal and powder, of sago or of roots or tubers of heading No. 07.14	1106.2000	4
细粉、粗粉及粉末,用第八章的产品制成的	Flour, meal and powder, of the products of chapter 8	1106.3000	4
细粉、粗粉及粉末,用税号07.13的干豆制成的	Flour, meal and powder, of the dried leguminous vegetables of beading No. 07.13	1106.1000	4
细粉、粗粉及团粒,甲壳动物的,适合供人食用的	Flours, meals and pellets of crustaceans, fit for human consumption	0306.2990	14
细粉及粗粉,其他,含油子仁或果实	Flours and meals of oil seeds or oleaginous fruits, nes	1208.9000	4
细菌及病毒	Bacteria and virus	3002.9030	34

X

商品名称	Article Description	税则号列	申报要素
细纱机,环锭式,其他	Spinning frames, for ring, nes	8445.2049	7
细纱机,毛的	Spinning frame, for worsted ring	8445.2042	7
细纱机,棉的	Spinning frame, for cotton ring	8445.2041	7
细筛,手用	Hand riddles	9604.0000	
细丝机织物,其他	Noil silk fabrics, nes	5007.1090	4568
细丝机织物,未漂白或漂白	Noil silk fabrics, unbleached or bleached	5007.1010	4568
细丝纱线	Spun from noil	5005.0010	356
xia			
虾仁,淡水小龙虾的	Shelled, of freshwater crawfish	0306.1911	1
虾仁,冻的	Shelled, of prawns, frozen	0306.1321	18
虾仁,冻的	Shelled, of shrimps, frozen	0306.1311	18
狭幅机织物,按重量计弹性纱线或橡胶线含量在5%及以上的	Narrow woven fabrics, containing by weight 5% or more of elastomeric yarn or rubber thread	5806.2000	468
狭幅机织物,纺织材料制,起绒及绳的,其他	Narrow woven fabrics of textile materials, pile and chenille fabrics, nes	5806.1090	468
狭幅机织物,化学纤维制	Narrow woven fabrics of man-made fibres	5806.3200	468
狭幅机织物,棉或麻制,起绒及绳的	Narrow woven fabrics of cotton or bast fibres, pile and chenille fabrics	5806.1010	468
狭幅机织物,棉制	Narrow woven fabrics of cotton	5806.3100	468
狭幅机织物,其他	Narrow woven fabrics, nes	5806.3990	468
狭幅机织物,丝及绢丝制	Narrow woven fabrics of silk or silk waste	5806.3910	468
狭幅机织物,羊毛或动物细毛制	Narrow woven fabrics of wool or fine animal hair	5806.3920	468
狭幅丝绒织物,用橡胶浸渍的、用于包覆纺缍(织轴)的	Narrow fabrics made of velvet impregnated with rubber, for covering weaving spindles (weaving beams)	5911.1010	
霰石	Aragonite	2530.9099	13456
霞石	Nepheline	2529.3000	13
霰石,加工的	Aragonite, worked	7103.9990	145
霞石正长岩	Nepheline syenite	2529.3000	13
下水道淤泥	Sewage sludge	3825.2000	34
夏威夷果,其他	Macadamia nuts, nes	0802.6090	134
夏威夷果,种用	Macadamia nuts, seed	0802.6010	134
xian			
仙客来,种用,休眠的	Cyclamen, seed, dormant	0601.1091	135
仙人掌果	Cactus figs (prickly pears)	0810.9090	1
先锋霉素及其衍生物以及它们的盐,其他	Cephamycin and its derivatives; salts thereof, nes	2941.9059	3
纤维缝编织物	Stitch-bonded fibre fabrics	5602.1000	46
纤维浆,从回收(废碎)纸或纸板提取的	Pulps of fibres derived from recovered (waste and scrap) paper or paperboard	4706.2000	4

商品名称	Article Description	税则号列	申报要素
纤维素及其化学衍生物,初级形状的,其他	Cellulose and its chemical derivatives, in primary forms, nes	3912.9000	16
纤维素醚,初级形状的,其他	Cellulose ethers, in primary forms, nes	3912.3900	16
纤维素水泥管子及附件,含石棉的	Cellulose fibre-cement tubes, pipes and fittings, containing asbestos	6811.4030	56
纤维素水泥或类似材料制管子及附件,不含石棉的	Cellulose fibre-cement tubes, pipes and fittings, not containing asbestos	6811.8300	56
纤维素水泥或类似材料制片、板、砖、瓦及类似制品,不含石棉的	Cellulose fibre-cement sbeets, panels, tiles and similar ahicles, not containing asbestos	6302.5990	346
纤维素水泥或类似材料制片、板、砖、瓦及类似制品,含石棉的	Cellulose fibre-cement sheets, panels, tiles and similar articles, containing asbestos	6302.5990	346
纤维素水泥或类似材料制品,不含石棉的	Cellulose fibre-cement articles or the like, not containing asbestos	6811.8900	56
纤维素水泥或类似材料制品,其他	Cellulose fibre-cement articles or the like	6811.4090	56
纤维素纤维网	Webs of cellulose fibres	4811.9000	458
纤维素絮料	Cellulose wadding	4811.9000	458
纤维素絮纸,成卷或成张的	Cellulose wadding, in rolls or sheets	4803.0000	58
纤维屑、纤维粉末及球结,长度不超过5毫米	Textile flock and dust and mill neps, not exceeding 5mm in length	5601.3000	6
籼米,半精米或精米	Long grain, semi-milled or wholly milled	1006.3010	35
籼米,糙米	Long grain, husked	1006.2010	35
籼米,其他	Long grain, nes	1006.1091	35
籼米,碎米	Long grain, broken	1006.4010	35
籼米,种用	Long grain, seed, in husk (paddy or rough)	1006.1011	35
酰脲及其衍生物以及它们的盐	Ureides and their derivatives; salts thereof	2924.2100	36
酰亚胺及其衍生物以及它们的盐,其他	Imides and their derivatives; salts thereof, nes	2925.1900	36
鲜蜂王浆	Pure royal jelley	0410.0041	12
鲜蜂王浆粉	Pure royal jelley, in powder	0410.0042	12
鲜乳酪(未熟化或未固化的)	Fresh(unripened or uncured) cheese	0406.1000	24
弦,乐器用的	Strings for musical instruments	9209.3000	
弦乐器,键盘的,其他	String musical instruments, keyboard, nes	9201.9000	5
弦乐器,其他	String musical instruments, nes	9202.9000	5
弦乐器,用弓演奏的	String musical instruments, played with a bow	9202.1000	5
咸蛋	Eggs, salted	0407.0091	14
咸藠头,用醋或醋酸以外的其他方法制作或保藏的,未冷冻	Scallion, salted, prepared or preserved otherwise than by vinegar or acetic acid, not frozen	2005.9960	148
咸蕨菜,用醋或醋酸以外的其他方法制作或保藏的,未冷冻	Chueh Tsai (fiddlehead), salted, prepared or preserved otherwise than by vinegar or acetic acid, not frozen	2005.9950	148
显示管,雷达的,阴极射线管	Display tubes for radar, cathode-ray tubes	8540.6010	35

X

X

商品名称	Article Description	税则号列	申报要素
显示管,数据/图形的,彩色的,屏幕荧光点间距小于0.4毫米	Display tubes for data/graphic, colour, with a phosphor dot screen pitch smaller than 0.4mm	8540.4000	35
显示管,数据/图形的,黑白的或其他单色的	Display tubes for data/graphic, black and white or other monochrome	8540.5000	35
显示管用零件,雷达的	Display tubes parts for radar	8540.9120	3
显微镜,光学的,其他	Microscopes, optical, nes	9011.8000	
显微镜,光学显微镜除外	Microscopes other than optical microscopes	9012.1000	
显微镜,立体的,光学的	Microscopes, stereoscopic, optical	9011.1000	
显微镜,显微电影摄影用,光学的	Microscopes, for cinephotomicrography, optical	9011.2000	
显微镜,显微投影用,光学的	Microscopes, for microprojection, optical	9011.2000	
显微镜,显微照相用,光学的	Microscopes, for photomicrography, optical	9011.2000	
显微镜的零件、附件,光学显微镜除外	Microscopes parts and accessories, other than optical microscopes	9012.9000	3
显微镜零件、附件,光学的	Microscopes parts and accessories, optical	9011.9000	3
显像管玻壳及其零件	Glass envelopes for kinescope and glass parts thereof	7011.2010	4
显影装置,平板显示器的制造机器及装置	Developing apparatus, flat panel displays manufacture machines and apparatus	8486.3049	7
显影装置及设备,自动的,电影用	Developing apparatus and equipment, automatically, of a kind used in cinematographic film	9010.1010	7
显影装置及设备,自动的,照相胶卷或成卷感光纸用,彩色胶卷用	Developing apparatus and equipment, automatically, for photographic film or paper in rolls, for the colour photographic film in rolls	9010.1091	7
显影装置及设备,自动的,照相胶卷或成卷感光纸用,其他	Developing apparatus and equipment, automatically, for photographic film or paper in rolls, nes	9010.1099	7
显影装置及设备,自动的,照相胶卷或成卷感光纸用,特种照相用	Developing apparatus and equipment, automatically, for photographic film or paper in rolls, of a kind used in special photographic film or paper	9010.1020	7
现金出纳机,其他	Cash registers, nes	8470.5090	
线、绳、索、缆,合成纤维制,其他	Twine, cordage, rope sand cables, of synthetic fibres, nes	5607.5000	368
线、绳、索、缆,蕉麻或其他硬质纤维纺制	Twine, cordage, rope sand cables, of abaca or other hard fibres	5607.9010	368
线、绳、索、缆,聚乙烯或聚丙烯制,其他	Twine, cordage, rope sand cables, of polyethylene or polypropylene, nes	5607.4900	368
线、绳、索、缆,其他	Twine, cordage, rope sand cables, nes	5607.9090	368
线、绳、索、缆,西沙尔麻或其他纺织用龙舌兰类纤维制,其他	Twine, cordage, rope sand cables, of sisal or other texile fibres of the genus Agave, nes	5607.2900	368
线材轧机	Wire mills	8455.2130	7
线路导管及其接头,内衬绝缘材料的,贱金属制	Electrical conduit tubing and joints therefor, of base metal lined with insulating material	8547.9010	3
线轴及类似品,缝纫用,木制	Sewing thread reels and the like, of wood	4421.9010	56

商品名称	Article Description	税则号列	申报要素
腺体,其他,供配制药用的,鲜、冷、冻或用其他方法暂时保藏的	Glands, of animal, used in the preparation of pharmaceutical products, fresh, chilled, frozen or otherwise provisionally preserved	0510.0090	14
腺体及其分泌物的提取物	Glands extracts and secretions	3001.2000	34
腺体及其他器官,已干燥的,器官疗法用,不论是否制成粉末	Glands and other organs for organotherapeutic uses, dried, whether or not powdered	3001.9090	34
xiang			
相框,贱金属制	Photograph, of base metal	8306.3000	256
相框及类似品,辐射松制的	Frames for photographs or similar objects, of radiata pine	4414.0010	56
相框及类似品,其他木制的	Frames for photographs or similar objects, of other wood	4414.0090	56
香波	Shampoos	3305.1000	23
香薄荷	Savory, french savory	0910.9900	6
香薄荷,干的	Savory, dried	0712.9090	4
香薄荷,冷冻的	Savory, frozen	0710.8090	1
香薄荷,鲜或冷藏的	Savory, fresh or chilled	0709.9090	1
香菜,鲜或冷藏的	Coriander, fresh or chilled	0709.9090	1
香菜子	Seeds of caraway	0909.4000	
香菜子	Caraway Seeds	0909.4000	
香草醛	Vanillin	2912.4100	36
香肠及类似产品,其他	Sausages and similar products, nes	1601.0020	48
香肠及类似产品,用天然肠衣做外包装的	Sausages and similar products, with a natural casing	1601.0010	348
香肠用肠衣	Casings for sausage	3917.1000	6
香肠制成的食品及类似产品	Sausages food preparations and similar products	1601.0030	48
香豆素	Coumarin	2932.2100	36
香膏,其他	Resinoids, nes	3301.3090	34
香菇,干的	Shiitake, dried	0712.3910	4
香菇,鲜或冷藏的	Shiitake, fresh or chilled	0709.5920	1
香瓜	Casaba melons	0807.1990	1
香蕉,鲜或干的香蕉	Bananas, fresh or dried	0803.0000	1245
香梨,鲜的	Xiang pears, fresh	0808.2013	1
香料混合物,其他	Odoriferous substances mixtures, nes	3302.9000	36
香料混合物,食品或饮料工业用,其他	Odoriferous substances mixtures, of a kind used in the food or drink industry, nes	3302.1090	36
香料为基本成分的制品,生产饮料用,按容量计酒精浓度不超过0.5%的	Odoriferous substances preparations, of a kind used for the manufacture of beverages, alcoholic strength by volume not exceeding 0.5% vol.	3302.1010	36
香茅醇(3,7-二甲基-6辛烯-1-醇)	Citronellol(3,7-dimethyl-6-octen-1-ol)	2905.2220	36
香茅油	Essential oils of citronella	3301.2920	34

X

X

商品名称	Article Description	税则号列	申报要素
香气制品,通过燃烧散发的,其他	Odoriferous preparations which operate by burning, nes	3307. 4100	23
香气制品,宗教仪式用	Odoriferous preparations used during religious rites	3307. 4100	23
香芹酚	Carvacrol	2907. 1990	36
香树脂	Oleoresins	1301. 9090	
香水	Perfumes	3303. 0000	2
香水喷雾器及其座架、喷头	Scent sprays and similar, and mounts and heads thereof	9616. 1000	
香烟打火机,其他	Cigarette lighters, nes	9613. 8000	5
香烟打火机零件	Cigarette lighters parts	9613. 9000	3
香叶醇、橙花醇(3,7-二甲基-2,6-辛二烯-1-醇)	Geraniol, nerol(cis-3,7-dimethyl-2,6-octadien-1-ol)	2905. 2210	36
香叶油	Essential oils of geranium	3301. 2991	34
香浴盐及其他沐浴用制剂	Perfumed bath salts and other bath preparations	3307. 3000	23
香子兰豆	Vanilla	0905. 0000	
箱、盒、匣,非瓦楞纸或纸板制的,可折叠	Cartons, boxes and cases, of noncorrugated paper or paperboard, folding	4819. 2000	68
箱、盒、匣,瓦楞纸或纸板制的	Cartons, boxes and cases, of corrugated paper or paperboard	4819. 1000	68
箱形托盘及其他装载用木板,辐射松制的	Box pallets and other load boards, of radiata pine	4415. 2010	56
箱形托盘及其他装载用木板,其他木制的	Box pallets and other load boards, of other wood	4415. 2090	56
镶板及类似品,用水泥、石膏及其他矿物粘合材料粘合植物纤维、稻草、刨花、木片屑、木粉、锯末或木废料制成	Panels and similar articles of vegetable fibre, of straw or of shavings, chips, particles, sawdust or other waste, of wood, agglomerated with cement, plaster or other mineral binders	6808. 0000	456
镶嵌木	Wood marquetry and inlaid wood	4420. 9010	56
镶嵌石及类似品,天然石料(包括板岩)制的,不论是否有衬背,其最大表面以可置入边长小于7厘米的方格为限	Mosaic cubes and the like, of natural stone (including slate), whether or not on a backing, the largest surface area of which is capable of being enclosed in a square the side of which is less than 7cm	6802. 1090	3468
响板	Castanets	9206. 0000	5
响葫芦	Maracas	9206. 0000	5
橡胶促进剂,配制的	Rubber accelerators, prepared	3812. 1000	36
橡胶防老剂	Rubber antioxidants	3812. 3010	36
橡胶或塑料产品用加工机器,其他	Rubber or plastics products working machinery, nes	8477. 8000	7
橡胶或塑料加工机器,其他	Rubber or plastics working machinery, nes	8477. 8000	7
橡胶或塑料加工机器的零件	Rubber or plastics working machinery parts	8477. 9000	7
橡胶轮胎衬带	Tyre flaps, of rubber	4012. 9090	234
橡胶内胎,航空器用	Inner tubes, of rubber, of a kind used on aircraft	4013. 9010	23

商品名称	Article Description	税则号列	申报要素
橡胶内胎,机动小客车(包括旅行小客车及赛车)、客运、机动车辆或货运机动车辆用	Inner tubes, of rubber, of a kind used on motor cars (including staton wagons and racing cars), buses or lorries	4013.1000	23
橡胶内胎,其他	Inner tubes, of rubber, nes	4013.9090	23
橡胶内胎,自行车用	Inner tubes, of rubber, of a kind used on bicycles	4013.2000	23
橡胶溶剂油	Rubber solvent	2710.1130	6
橡胶胎面	Tyre treads, of rubber	4012.9090	234
橡胶线及绳,硫化的	Rubber thread and cord, vulcanized	4007.0000	18
橡胶线及绳,用纺织材料包覆的	Rubber thread and cord, textile covered	5604.1000	46
橡胶制品,硫化橡胶(硬质橡胶除外)的,其他	Articles of vulcanized rubber other than hard rubber, nes	4016.9990	236
橡胶制品,未硫化	Rubber articles, unvulcanized	4006.9020	13
橡皮擦	Erasers	4016.9200	
橡皮膏	Adhesive plasters	3005.1010	1346
橡皮扫帚	Squeegees	9603.9090	3
xiao			
削铅笔机	Pencil-sharpening machines	8472.9090	
消毒剂	Disinfectants	3808.9400	36
消毒器具,利用温度变化处理,医用或实验室用	Sterilizers, with a process involving a change of temperature, for medical, surgical or laboratory use	8419.2000	57
消防船	Fire-floats	8905.9090	37
消声器(消音器)、排气管及其零件,机动车辆用	Silencers (mufflers), exhaust pipes and parts, of motor vehicles	8708.9200	3
硝铵炸药	Explosives, based on ammonals nitrate	3602.0010	6
硝化淀粉	Nitrostarch	3505.1000	36
硝基苯	Nitrobenzene	2904.2010	36
硝基胍	Nitroguanidine	2929.9090	36
硝基甲苯	Nitrotoluene and nitrochlorobenzene	2904.2020	36
硝基氯仿	Trichloronitromethane (chloropicrin, nitrochloroform)	2904.9030	36
硝甲西泮(INN)以及盐	Nimetazepam (INN); salts thereof	2933.9100	36
硝酸	Nitric acid	2808.0000	6
硝酸铵,不论是否水溶液	Ammonium nitrate, whether or not in aqueous solution	3102.3000	68
硝酸铵与碳酸钙或其他无肥效无机物的混合物	Mixtures of ammonium nitrate with calcium carbonate or other inorganic nonfertilizing substances	3102.4000	68
硝酸钙和硝酸铵的复盐及混合物	Double salts and mixtures of calcium nitrate and ammonium nitrate	3102.6000	68
硝酸钴	Cobalt, nitrate	2834.2910	
硝酸钾,肥料用	Potassium nitrate, for use as fertilizer	2834.2110	
硝酸钾,其他	Potassium nitrate, nes	2834.2190	3
硝酸钠	Sodium nitrate	3102.5000	68

商品名称	Article Description	税则号列	申报要素
硝酸纤维素,初级形状的	Cellulose nitrates, in primary forms	3912.2000	16
硝酸盐,其他	Nitrates, nes, inorganic	2834.2990	
硝酸银	Silver nitrate	2843.2100	
硝西泮(INN)以及盐	Nitrazepam (INN); salts thereof	2933.9100	36
销,铝制	Cotters, of aluminium	7616.1000	36
销及开尾销,钢铁制的	Cotters and cotter-pins, of iron or steel	7318.2400	268
销售点终端出纳机	Terminal registers for market	8470.5010	
小便池及类似的固定卫生设备,陶制	Urinals and similar sanitary fixtures, of pottery	6910.9000	268
小便池及类似的固定卫生设备,瓷制	Urinals and similar sanitary fixtures, of porcelain or china	6910.1000	268
小雕塑品及其他装饰品,塑料的	Statuettes and other ornamental articles, of plastics	3926.4000	236
小号	Trumpets	9205.1000	5
小黄瓜	Gherkins, prepared or preserved by vinegar or acetic acid	2001.1000	48
小黄瓜,鲜或冷藏的	Gherkins, fresh or chilled	0707.0000	1
小黄瓜,暂时保藏,但不适合直接使用的	Gherkins, provisionally preserved, but unsuitable in that state for immediate consumption	0711.4000	34
小茴香子	Seeds of fennel	0909.5000	
小脚轮,贱金属制,用于家具、门窗、楼梯、百叶窗、车厢、鞍具、衣箱、盒子及类似品的	Castors, of base metal, suitable for furniture, doors, staircases, windows, blinds, coachwork, saddlery, trunks, chests, caskets, or the like	8302.2000	256
小轿车,气缸容量(排气量)不超过1000毫升,装有点燃往复式活塞内燃发动机的	Saloon cars, of a cylinder capacity not exceeding 1000cc, with spark-ignition internal combustion reciprocating piston engine	8703.2130	58
小轿车,气缸容量(排气量)不超过1000毫升,装有压燃式活塞内燃发动机的	Saloon cars, of a cylinder capacity not exceeding 1000cc, with compression-ignition internal combustion piston engine	8703.3111	58
小轿车,气缸容量(排气量)超过1000毫升,但不超过1500毫升,装有点燃往复式活塞内燃发动机的	Saloon cars, of a cylinder capacity exceeding 1000cc but not exceeding 1500cc, with spark-ignition internal combustion reciprocating piston	8703.2230	58
小轿车,气缸容量(排气量)超过1000毫升,但不超过1500毫升,装有压燃式活塞内燃发动机的	Saloon cars, of a cylinder capacity exceeding 1000cc but not exceeding 1500cc, with compression-ignition internal combustion piston engine	8703.3121	58
小轿车,气缸容量(排气量)超过1500毫升,但不超过2000毫升,装有点燃往复式活塞内燃发动机的	Saloon cars, of a cylinder capacity exceeding 1500cc but not exceeding 2000cc, with spark-ignition internal combustion reciprocating piston	8703.2341	58
小轿车,气缸容量(排气量)超过1500毫升,但不超过2000毫升,装有压燃式活塞内燃发动机的	Saloon cars, of a cylinder capacity exceeding 1500cc but not exceeding 2000cc, with compression-ignition internal combustion piston engine	8703.3211	58
小轿车,气缸容量(排气量)超过2000毫升,但不超过2500毫升,装有点燃往复式活塞内燃发动机的	Saloon cars, of a cylinder capacity exceeding 2000cc but not exceeding 2500cc, with spark-ignition internal combustion reciprocating piston	8703.2351	58

商品名称	Article Description	税则号列	申报要素
小轿车，气缸容量（排气量）超过2000毫升，但不超过2500毫升，装有压燃式活塞内燃发动机的	Saloon cars, of a cylinder capacity exceeding 2000cc but not exceeding 2500cc, with compression-ignition internal combustion piston engine	8703. 3221	58
小轿车，气缸容量（排气量）超过2500毫升，但不超过3000毫升，装有点燃往复式活塞内燃发动机的	Saloon cars, of a cylinder capacity exceeding 2500cc but not exceeding 3000cc, with spark-ignition internal combustion reciprocating piston	8703. 2361	58
小轿车，气缸容量（排气量）超过2500毫升，但不超过3000毫升，装有压燃式活塞内燃发动机的	Saloon cars, of a cylinder capacity exceeding 2500cc, but not exceeding 3000cc, with compression-ignition internal combustion piston engine	8703. 3311	58
小轿车，气缸容量（排气量）超过3000毫升，但不超过4000毫升，装有点燃往复式活塞内燃发动机的	Saloon cars, of a cylinder capacity exceeding 3000cc, but not exceeding 4000cc, with spark-ignition internal combustion reciprocating piston	8703. 2411	58
小轿车，气缸容量（排气量）超过3000毫升，但不超过4000毫升，装有压燃式活塞内燃发动机的	Saloon cars, of a cylinder capacity exceeding 3000cc, but not exceeding 4000cc, with compression-ignition internal combustion piston engine	8703. 3321	58
小轿车，气缸容量（排气量）超过4000毫升，装有点燃往复式活塞内燃发动机的	Saloon cars, of a cylinder capacity exceeding 4000cc, with spark-ignition internal combustion reciprocating piston	8703. 2421	58
小轿车，气缸容量（排气量）超过4000毫升，装有压燃式活塞内燃发动机的	Saloon cars, of a cylinder capacity exceeding 4000cc, with compression-ignition internal combustion piston engine	8703. 3361	58
小轿车用零件、附件，其他	Saloon cars parts and accessories, nes	8708. 9949	3
小客车，9座及以下的，气缸容量（排气量）不超过1000毫升，装有点燃往复式活塞内燃发动机的	Station wagons (with 9 seats or less), of a cylinder capacity not exceeding 1000cc, with spark-ignition internal combustion reciprocating piston engine	8703. 2150	58
小客车，9座及以下的，气缸容量（排气量）超过1000毫升，但不超过1500毫升，装有点燃往复式活塞内燃发动机的	Station wagons (with 9 seats or less), of a cylinder capacity exceeding 1000cc but not exceeding 1500cc, with spark-ignition internal combustion reciprocating piston	8703. 2250	58
小客车，9座及以下的，气缸容量（排气量）超过1000毫升，但不超过1500毫升，装有压燃式活塞内燃发动机的	Station wagons (with 9 seats or less), of a cylinder capacity exceeding 1000cc but not exceeding 1500cc, with compression-ignition internal combustion piston engine	8703. 3123	58
小客车，9座及以下的，气缸容量（排气量）超过1500毫升，但不超过2000毫升，装有点燃往复式活塞内燃发动机的	Station wagons (with 9 seats or less), of a cylinder capacity exceeding 1500cc but not exceeding 2000cc, with spark-ignition internal combustion reciprocating piston	8703. 2343	58
小客车，9座及以下的，气缸容量（排气量）超过1500毫升，但不超过2000毫升，装有压燃式活塞内燃发动机的	Station wagons (with 9 seats or less), of a cylinder capacity exceeding 1500cc but not exceeding 2000cc, with compression-ignition internal combustion piston engine	8703. 3213	58

X

商品名称	Article Description	税则号列	申报要素
小客车,9座及以下的,气缸容量(排气量)超过2000毫升,但不超过2500毫升,装有点燃往复式活塞内燃发动机的	Station wagons (with 9 seats or less), of a cylinder capacity exceeding 2000cc but not exceeding 2500cc, with spark-ignition internal combustion reciprocating piston	8703. 2353	58
小客车,9座及以下的,气缸容量(排气量)超过2000毫升,但不超过2500毫升,装有压燃式活塞内燃发动机的	Station wagons (with 9 seats or less), of a cylinder capacity exceeding 2000cc but not exceeding 2500cc, with compression-ignition internal combustion piston engine	8703. 3223	58
小客车,9座及以下的,气缸容量(排气量)超过2500毫升,但不超过3000毫升,装有点燃往复式活塞内燃发动机的	Station wagons (with 9 seats or less), of a cylinder capacity exceeding 2500cc but not exceeding 3000cc, with spark-ignition internal combustion reciprocating piston	8703. 2363	58
小客车,9座及以下的,气缸容量(排气量)超过2500毫升,但不超过3000毫升,装有压燃式活塞内燃发动机的	Station wagons (with 9 seats or less), of a cylinder capacity exceeding 2500cc, but not exceeding 3000cc, with compression-ignition internal combustion piston engine	8703. 3313	58
小客车,9座及以下的,气缸容量(排气量)超过3000毫升,但不超过4000毫升,装有点燃往复式活塞内燃发动机的	Station wagons (with 9 seats or less), of a cylinder capacity exceeding 3000cc, but not exceeding 4000cc, with spark-ignition internal combustion reciprocating piston	8703. 2413	58
小客车,9座及以下的,气缸容量(排气量)超过3000毫升,但不超过4000毫升,装有压燃式活塞内燃发动机的	Station wagons (with 9 seats or less), of a cylinder capacity exceeding 3000cc, but not exceeding 4000cc, with compression-ignition internal combustion piston engine	8703. 3323	58
小客车,9座及以下的,气缸容量(排气量)超过4000毫升,装有点燃往复式活塞内燃发动机的	Station wagons (with 9 seats or less), of a cylinder capacity exceeding 4000cc, with spark-ignition internal combustion reciprocating piston	8703. 2423	58
小客车,9座及以下的,气缸容量(排气量)超过4000毫升,装有压燃式活塞内燃发动机的	Station wagons (with 9 seats or less), of a cylinder capacity exceeding 4000cc, with compression-ignition internal combustion piston engine	8703. 3363	58
小萝卜,鲜或冷藏的	Radishes, fresh or chilled	0706. 9000	1
小麦,其他	Wheat, nes	1001. 9090	356
小麦,其他,种用	Wheat, nes, seed	1001. 9010	356
小麦的	Starch of wheat	1108. 1100	
小手袋,以皮革、再生皮革或漆皮作面	Vanity-cases, with outer surface of leather, of composition leather or of patent leather	4202. 1190	1458
小手袋,以塑料或纺织材料作面	Vanity-cases, with outer surface of plastics or of textile materials	4202. 1290	256
小苏打	Sodium bicarbonate	2836. 3000	
小提琴	Violins	9202. 1000	5
小提琴的零件、附件	Violins parts and accessories	9209. 9200	3
小虾,其他,冻的	Shrimps, nes, frozen	0306. 1319	18
小虾,其他,未冻的	Shrimps, nes, not frozen	0306. 2399	14

商品名称	Article Description	税则号列	申报要素
小虾及对虾,制作或保藏的	Shrimps and prawns, prepared or preserved	1605.2000	48
小虾种苗	Shrimps, for cultivation	0306.2310	3
小型机(计算机)	Mini-computers	8471.4120	26
小型机,以系统形式进口或出口的	Mini-computers, presented in the form of systems	8471.4920	26
小型机的处理部件	Mini-computers processing units	8471.5020	26
xie			
楔子,伐木用	Timber wedges	8201.9000	256
斜锆石	Baddeleyite	2615.1000	1346
携带器具,弥补生理缺陷或残疾的	Carried appliances, to compensate for a defect or disability	9021.9000	3
缬氨酸	Valine	2922.4910	36
鞋面及其零件,但硬衬除外	Footwear uppers and parts, other than stiffeners	6406.1000	6
鞋靴,纺织材料制鞋面的	Footwear with uppers of textile materials	6405.2000	26
鞋靴,皮革或再生皮革制外底的,纺织材料制鞋面的	Footwear with outer soles of leather or composition leather and uppers of textile materials	6404.2000	26
鞋靴,皮革制外底的,皮革制鞋面的,其他	Footwear, with outer soles of leather and upers of leather, nes	6403.5900	26
鞋靴,其他材料制外底的	Footwear with outer soles of other materials, nes	6405.9090	26
鞋靴,其他材料制外底的,皮革或再生皮革制鞋面的	Footwear with outer soles of other materials and uppers of leather or composition leather	6405.1090	26
鞋靴,橡胶、塑料、皮革或再生皮革制外底,皮革制鞋面的,其他	Footwear, with outer soles of rubber, plastics, leather or composition leather and upers of leather, nes	6403.9900	26
鞋靴,橡胶、塑料、皮革及再生皮革制外底的	Footwear with outer soles of rubber, plastics, leather or composition leather	6405.9010	26
鞋靴,橡胶、塑料、皮革及再生皮革制外底的,皮革或再生皮革制鞋面的	Footwear with outer soles of rubber, plastics, leather or composition leather and uppers of leather or composition leather	6405.1010	26
鞋靴,橡胶或塑料制外底的鞋靴,纺织材料制鞋面的,其他	Footwear with outer soles of rubber or plastics and uppers of textile materials, nes	6404.1900	26
鞋靴,橡胶或塑料制外底及塑料制鞋面的	Footwear with outer soles and uppers of rubber or plastics and uppers of plastics	6402.9920	26
鞋靴,橡胶或塑料制外底及橡胶制鞋面的	Footwear with outer soles and uppers of rubber or plastics and uppers of rubber	6402.9910	26
鞋靴,用栓塞方法将鞋面条带装配在鞋底上的,橡胶或塑料制外底及鞋面的其他鞋靴	Footwear with upper straps or thongs assembled to the sole by means of plugs, with outer soles and uppers of rubber or plastics	6402.2000	26
鞋靴,由交叉于脚背并绕大脚趾的皮革条带构成鞋面的,皮革制外底	Footwear with outer soles of leather, and uppers which consist of leather straps across the instep and around the big toe	6403.2000	26
鞋靴,装有金属防护鞋头的,橡胶、塑料、皮革或再生皮革制外底,皮革制鞋面的,其他	Footwear, incorporating a protective metal toe-cap, with outer soles of rubber, plastics, leather or composition leather and upers of leather, nes	6403.4000	26

X

X

商品名称	Article Description	税则号列	申报要素
鞋靴修理机器	Footwear repairing machinery	8453. 2000	
鞋靴修理机器零件	Footwear repairing machinery parts	8453. 9000	3
鞋靴制作机器	Footwear making machinery	8453. 2000	
鞋靴制作机器零件	Footwear making machinery parts	8453. 9000	3
鞋眼,贱金属制	Footwear eyes, of base metal	8308. 1000	256
泻盐矿(天然硫酸镁)	Epsomite (natural magnesium sulphates)	2530. 2000	13456
卸船机,其他	Ship unloading cranes, nes	8426. 1929	7
卸船机,抓斗式	Ship unloading cranes, grab	8426. 1921	7
蟹,其他,冻的	Crabs, nes, frozen	0306. 1490	1
蟹,其他,未冻的	Crabs, nes, not frozen	0306. 2499	14
蟹,制作或保藏的	Crab, prepared or preserved	1605. 1000	48
蟹种苗	Crabs, for cultivation	0306. 2410	3
xin			
心电图记录仪	Electro-cardiographs	9018. 1100	
心理功能测验装置	Psychological aptitudetesting apparatus	9019. 1090	7
心脏起搏器,不包括零件、附件	Pacemakers for stimulating heart muscles, excluding parts and accessories	9021. 5000	
辛醇及其异构体,其他	Octanol(octyl alcohol) and isomers thereof, nes	2905. 1690	36
辛基酚	Octylphenol	2907. 1390	36
锌,按重量计含锌量低于99. 99%	Zinc, containing by weight less than 99. 99% of zinc	7901. 1200	16
锌,按重量计含锌量在99. 99%及以上,但少于99. 995%	Zinc, containing by weight 99. 99% or more of zinc, but less than 99. 995%	7901. 1190	16
锌,按重量计含锌量在99. 995%及以上	Zinc, containing by weight 99. 995% or more of zinc	7901. 1110	16
锌白	Zinc white (zinc oxide)	2817. 0010	34
锌钡白	Lithopone	3206. 4210	2368
锌废碎料	Zinc waste and scrap	7902. 0000	16
锌合金	Zinc alloys	7901. 2000	16
锌矿砂及其精矿	Zinc ores and concentrates	2608. 0000	146
锌末	Zinc dust	7903. 1000	16
锌制品,其他	Zinc articles, nes	7907. 0090	16
新闻纸,所含用机械或化学-机械方法制得的纤维超过全部纤维重量的10%,成卷的	Newsprint, of which more than 10% by weight of the total fibre content consists of fibres obtained by a mechanical or chemi-mechanical process, in rolls	4802. 6110	3468
新闻纸,成卷或成张的,卷宽度超过36厘米,或长超过36厘米且宽超过15厘米	Newsprint, in rolls or sheets, of width exceeding 36cm or in roll or one side exceeding 36cm and other side exceeding 15cm in rectangular sheets	4801. 0000	68
新闻纸,所含用机械或化学-机械方法制得的纤维超过全部纤维重量的10%	Newsprint, of which more than 10% by weight of the total fibre content consists of fibres obtained by a mechanical or chemi-mechanical process	4802. 6910	3468

商品名称	Article Description	税则号列	申报要素
薪柴(圆木段、块、枝、成捆或类似形状)	Fuel wood, in logs, in billets, in twigs, in faggots or in similar forms	4401.1000	15
信封,纸或纸板制的	Envelopes of paper or paperboard	4817.1000	6
信封制造机器,纸制的	Envelopes making machines, of paper	8441.2000	
信封制造机器零件,纸制的	Envelopes making machines parts, of paper	8441.9090	
信号玻璃器,未经光学加工的	Signalling glassware, not optically worked	7014.0090	345
信号弹	Signalling flares	3604.9000	
信号弹的发射装置	Signal flares project devices	9303.9000	
信号发生器,其他	Signal generators, nes	8543.2090	37
信号发生器,输出信号频率在1500兆赫兹以下的通用信号发生器	Signal generators, universal signal generators, with a frequency range of less than 1500MHz	8543.2010	37
信号发生器用零件,其他	Signal generators parts, nes	8543.9029	3
信号发生器用零件,输出信号频率在1500兆赫兹以下的通用信号发生器用	Signal generators parts, with a frequency range of less than 1500MHz	8543.9021	3
信号器,口吹音响的	Signalling instruments, mouth-blown sound	9208.9000	5
信号枪,维利式	Very pistols	9303.9000	
信号设备,电气的,道路的	Signalling electrical equipment for roads	8530.8000	
信号设备,电气的,电车道的	Signalling electrical equipment for tramways	8530.1000	
信号设备,电气的,港口的	Signalling electrical equipment for port installations	8530.8000	
信号设备,电气的,机场的	Signalling electrical equipment for airfields	8530.8000	
信号设备,电气的,内河航道的	Signalling electrical equipment for inland waterways	8530.8000	
信号设备,电气的,铁道的	Signalling electrical equipment for railways	8530.1000	
信号设备,电气的,停车场的	Signalling electrical equipment for parking facilities	8530.8000	
信号设备的零件	Signalling electrical equipment parts	8530.9000	3
信号设备及其零件,机械的,道路用	Signalling equipment and parts, for roads	8608.0090	3
信号设备及其零件,机械的,电车道用	Signalling equipment and parts, for tramways	8608.0090	3
信号设备及其零件,机械的,港口用	Signalling equipment and parts, for port installations	8608.0090	3
信号设备及其零件,机械的,机场用	Signalling equipment and parts, for airfields	8608.0090	3
信号设备及其零件,机械的,内河航道用	Signalling equipment and parts, for inland water-ways	8608.0090	3
信号设备及其零件,机械的,铁道用	Signalling equipment and parts, for railways	8608.0090	3
信号设备及其零件,机械的,停车场用	Signalling equipment and parts, for parking facilities	8608.0090	3
信夹,贱金属制	Letter clips, of base metal	8305.9000	256
信笺本,纸或纸板制的	Letter pads, of paper or paperboard	4820.1000	
信件盘及类似品,办公室、商店及类似场所使用的,纸制的	Letter trays and similar articles, of a kind used in offices, shops or the like, of paper, paperboard,	4819.6000	68
信角,贱金属制	Letter corners, of base metal	8305.9000	256
xing			
行波管	Travelling wave tubes	8540.7900	35

X

商品名称	Article Description	税则号列	申报要素
行李车,铁道及电车道用,非机动	Luggage vans, railway or tramway coaches, not self-propelled	8605.0090	37
行李箱盖(或背门),机动车辆的	Rear compartment covers(or rear door), of the motor vehicles	8708.2955	3
行星齿轮减速器	Planet decelerators	8483.4020	7
型材及异型材,板、片、带、箔,钨的	Profiles, plates, sheets, strip and foil, of tungsten	8101.9910	16
型材及异型材,铝合金制,其他	Profiles, of aluminium alloys, nes	7604.2990	16
型材及异型材、板、片、带、箔,钼的	Profiles, plates, sheets, strip and foil, of molybdenum	8102.9500	16
型材及异型材,非合金铝制	Profiles of aluminium, not alloyed	7604.1090	16
型钢轧机	Rolled-steel section mills	8455.2120	7
型模,玻璃用	Moulds for glass	8480.5000	7
型模,矿物材料用	Moulds for mineral materials	8480.6000	7
型模底板	Mould bases	8480.2000	7
型箱,金属铸造用	Moulding boxes for metal foundry	8480.1000	7
杏,干的	Apricots, dried	0813.1000	34
杏,鲜的	Apricots, fresh	0809.1000	1
杏,用其他方法制作或保藏的	Apricots, otherwise prepared, or preserved	2008.5000	248
xiong			
胸罩,化学纤维制	Brassières of man-made fibres	6212.1010	2456
胸罩,其他纺织材料制	Brassières of other textile materials	6212.1090	2456
熊,改良种用	Bears, pure-bred breeding	0106.1910	34
xiu			
修脚用具	Pedicure sets and instruments	8214.2000	256
修饰免疫制品	Modified immunological products	3002.1000	34
修枝剪及类似的单手操作剪刀	Secateurs and similar one- handed pruners and shears	8201.5000	256
修指甲锉	Nail files	8214.2000	256
修指甲用具	Manicure sets and instruments	8214.2000	256
绣花机	Embroidery machines	8447.9020	7
绣花机的辅助机器	Embroidery machines auxiliary	8448.1900	3
袖扣、仿首饰,贱金属制,不论是否镀费金属	Cuff-links, imitation jewellery, of base metal, whether or not plated with precious metal	7117.1100	46
袖珍盒式收放机,无线电收音机,不需外接电源的	Pocket-size radio cassette-players, radio-broadcast receivers capable of operating without an external source of power	8527.1200	5
袖珍气体打火机,可充气的	Pocket lighters, gas fuelled, refillable	9613.2000	
袖珍气体打火机,一次性的	Pocket lighters, gas fuelled, non refillable	9613.1000	
溴	Bromine	2801.3020	
溴仿	Bromoform	2903.3990	36
溴化钾	Potassium bromides	2827.5100	
溴化钠	Sodium bromides	2827.5100	

商品名称	Article Description	税则号列	申报要素
溴化物及溴氧化物,其他,无机的	Bromides and bromide oxides, nes, inorganic	2827.5900	
溴氯二氟甲烷	Bromochlorodifluoromethane	2903.4600	36
溴三氟甲烷	Bromotrifluoromethane	2903.4600	36
溴酸盐,无机的	Bromates, inorganic	2829.9000	
溴替唑仑(INN)及盐	Brotizolam (INN); salts thereof	2934.9100	36
溴西泮(INN)以及盐	Bromazepam (INN); salts thereof	2933.3300	36
xu			
絮胎及制品,化学纤维制	Wadding and articles, of man-made fibres	5601.2290	6
絮胎及制品,棉制	Wadding and articles of cotton	5601.2100	6
絮胎及制品,其他	Wadding and articles, nes	5601.2900	6
蓄电池,废的	Electric accumulators, spent	8548.1000	3
蓄电池,锂离子的	Accumulators of lithium ion	8507.8020	68
蓄电池,镍镉的	Accumulators of nickel-cadmium	8507.3000	68
蓄电池,镍氢的	Accumulators of nickel-hydrogen	8507.8010	68
蓄电池,镍铁的	Accumulators of nickel-iron	8507.4000	68
蓄电池,其他	Accumulators, nes	8507.8090	68
蓄电池,铅酸的,其他	Accumulators of lead-acid, nes	8507.2000	68
蓄电池,铅酸的,用于起动活塞式发动机	Accumulators of lead-acid, of a kind used for starting piston engines	8507.1000	68
蓄电池零件,其他	Accumulators parts, nes	8507.9090	3
蓄电池用零件,铅酸的	Accumulators parts, lead-acid	8507.9010	3
xuan			
宣纸	Xuan paper	4802.1010	3458
玄武岩	Basalt	2516.9000	148
悬挂滑翔机	Hang gliders	8801.0010	
悬挂系统及其零件(包括减震器),10座以下客车用	Uspension systems and parts thereof (including shock-absorbers), of motor vehicles with seats less than 10	8708.8010	3
悬挂系统及其零件(包括减震器),其他	Suspension systems and parts thereof (including shock-absorbers), nes	8708.8090	3
旋风式除尘器	Cyclone dust collectors for industry uses	8421.3923	7
旋塞,用于管道、锅炉、罐、桶或类似品的	Cocks, for pipes, boiler shells, tanks, vats or the like	8481.8090	
旋塞用零件	Cocks parts	8481.9090	3
旋梭,家用型缝纫机用	Rotating shuttles, of the household type	8452.9011	3
旋梭,其他缝纫机用	Rotating shuttles, nes	8452.9091	3
旋翼降落伞及其零件、附件	Rotochutes, parts and accessories	8804.0000	3
旋转木马	Roundabouts	9508.9000	5
旋转式变流机	Electric rotary converters	8502.4000	8

X

商品名称	Article Description	税则号列	申报要素
xue			
雪	Snow	2201.9090	248
雪地行走专用车	Snow travelling vehicles	8703.1090	58
雪地行走专用车	Vehicles specially designed for travelling on snow	8703.1090	58
雪梨,鲜的	Hsueh pears, fresh	0808.2012	1
雪利酒	Sherry wine	2204.2900	24568
雪莲花,种用,休眠的	Galanthus (snow-drop)	0601.1091	135
雪茄烟,烟草代用品制成的	Cigars, cheroots, cigarillos and cigarettes, of tobacco substitutes	2402.9000	245
雪茄烟,烟草制的	Cigars, cheroots and cigarillos, containing tobacco	2402.1000	245
鳕鱼(大西洋鳕鱼、太平洋鳕鱼、格陵兰鳕鱼),冻的	Cod (gadus morhua, gadus ogac, gadus macrocephalus), frozen	0303.5200	18
鳕鱼,但鱼肝及鱼卵除外,鲜或冷的	God (gadus morhua, gadus ogac, gadus macrocephalus), excluding livers and roes, fresh or chilled	0302.5000	18
鳕鱼,盐腌及盐渍的	God (gadus morhua, gadus ogac, gadus macrocephalus), salted or in brine	0305.6200	4
血份,其他	Blood fractions, nes	3002.1000	34
血竭	Dragon's blood	1301.9020	
血清球蛋白	Serum globulins	3002.1000	34
血栓烷及其衍生物和结构类似物	Thromboxanes, their derivatives and structural analogues	2937.5000	36
血型试剂	Blood-grouping reagents	3006.2000	36
血压测量仪器及器具	Sphygmomanometers and appliances	9018.9020	
xun			
熏鱼,包括鱼片,大马哈鱼	Smoked fish, including fillet, pacific salmon	0305.4120	4
熏鱼,包括鱼片,大西洋鲑鱼	Smoked fish, including fillet, atlantic salmon	0305.4110	4
熏鱼,包括鱼片,多瑙哲罗鱼	Smoked fish, including fillet, danube salmon	0305.4120	4
熏鱼,包括鱼片,鲱鱼(大西洋鲱鱼、太平洋鲱鱼)	Smoked fish, including fillet, herrings (clupea harengus, clupea pallasii)	0305.4200	4
熏鱼,包括鱼片,其他	Smoked fish, including fillet, nes	0305.4900	4
薰肠,有天然肠衣	Frankfurters (meat sausages), with a natural casing	1601.0010	348
巡航船,非机动船舶	Cruise ships, not motorized vessels	8901.1090	5
巡航船,机动船舶	Cruise ships, motor vessels	8901.1010	5
鲟鱼苗	Fry, of sturgeon	0301.9912	15
鲟鱼子酱	Caviar	1604.3000	248
鲟鱼子酱代用品	Caviar substitutes	1604.3000	248

Y

Y

商品名称	Article Description	税则号列	申报要素
ya			
压电晶体,已装配的	Piezo-electrie crystals, mounted	8541.6000	5
压力/差压变送器	Pressure/differential pressure transmitters	9026.2010	7
压力表	Manometers	9026.2090	7
压力表零件、附件	Manometers parts and accessories	9026.9000	3
压力测量、检验仪器及装置,其他	Pressure measuring or checking instruments and apparatus, nes	9026.2090	7
压力机,机械的,加工金属或硬质合金用	Presses of mechanical, for working metal or metal carbides	8462.9910	7
压力机,加工金属或硬质合金用,其他	Presses for working metal or metal carbides, nes	8462.9990	7
压力机,液压的,加工金属或硬质合金用,其他	Presses of hydraulic, for working metal or metal carbides, nes	8462.9190	7
压力机,自动模式数控步冲的,加工金属用	Punch press, cnc automatic tool change, numerically controlled, for working metal	8462.4111	7
压滤机,液体用	Press filters, for liquids	8421.2910	7
压路机,机动的,机重 18 吨及以上的,振动式	Road rollers, self-propelled, of a deadweight of 18t or more, vibration type	8429.4011	57
压路机,机动的,其他	Road rollers, self-propelled, nes	8429.4019	57
压路机零件	Road rollers parts	8431.4990	3
压模,金属、硬质合金用型模	Moulds of compression types, for metal or metal carbides	8480.4100	7
压模,塑料或橡胶用	Moulds for rubber or plastics, compression types	8480.7100	7
压舌片及类似一次性制品,木制	Spatula and the like, of wood	4421.9021	56
压舌片及类似一次性制品,其他	Spatula and the like, nes	4421.9029	56
压舌片及类似一次性制品,竹制	Spatula and the like, of bamboo	4421.9022	56
压实机,放射性废物用	Presses for radioactive waste material	8479.8950	7
压实机械,对泥土、矿物或矿石的,自推进的,其他	Compacting machinery, for earth, minerals or ores, self-propelled, nes	8430.5090	5
压实机械,非自推进的	Compacting machinery, not self-propelled	8430.6100	5
压缩机,空气调节器用,电动机额定功率超过 0.4 千瓦,但不超过 5 千瓦	Compressors for air conditioning machines, of a motor power exceeding 0.4kW but not exceeding 5kW	8414.3013	27
压缩机,空气调节器用,电动机额定功率超过 5 千瓦	Compressors for air conditioning machines, of a motor power exceeding 5kW	8414.3014	27
压缩机,冷藏箱或冷冻箱用,电动机额定功率超过 0.4 千瓦,但不超过 5 千瓦	Compressors for refrigerators or freezers, of a motor power exceeding 0.4kW but not exceeding 5kW	8414.3012	27
压缩机,冷藏箱或冷冻箱用,电动机额定功率不超过 0.4 千瓦	Compressors for refrigerators or freezers, of a motor power not exceeding 0.4kW	8414.3011	27

Y

商品名称	Article Description	税则号列	申报要素
压缩机,冷冻或冷藏设备用,电动机额定功率超过5千瓦	Compressors for refrigerators or freezers, of a motor power exceeding 5kW	8414.3015	27
压缩机,用于制冷设备的,电动机驱动的,其他	Compressors of a kind used in refrigerating equipment, driven by a motor, nes	8414.3019	27
压缩机,用于制冷设备的,非电动机驱动的	Compressors of a kind used in refrigerating equipment, driven by a non-motor	8414.3090	27
压缩机进、排气阀片,冷藏箱、冷冻箱用或空气调节器的	In take valve leaf or discharge valve leaf, for refrigerators or freezers or air conditioning machines	8414.9011	23
压印箔	Stamping foils	3212.1000	136
压榨机,制酒、制果汁或制类似饮料用	Presses machinery used in the manufacture of wine, cider, fruit juices or similar beverages	8435.1000	
压榨机,制酒、制果汁或制类似饮料用	Presses machinery, used in the manufacture of wine, cider, fruit juices or similar beverages	8435.1000	
压榨机零件,制酒、制果或制类似饮料用	Presses machinery parts, used in the manufacture of wine, cider, fruit juices or similar beverages	8435.9000	3
压制软木及其制品,其他	Articles of agglomerated cork, nes	4504.9000	
压铸机,冷室的	Casting machines, cold chamber, die- casting	8454.3010	
压铸机用零件	Casting machines parts, cold chamber, die- casting	8454.9090	3
鸦片碱及其衍生物以及它们的盐,其他	Opium alkaloids and their derivatives; salts thereof	2939.1900	34
鸭,改良种用,重量不超过185克	Ducks, pure-bred breeding, weighing not more than 185g	0105.1910	48
鸭,改良种用,重量超过185克	Ducks, pure-bred breeding, weighing more than 185g	0105.9910	48
鸭,改良种用除外,重量超过185克	Ducks, ex. pure-bred breeding, weighing more than 185g	0105.9991	48
鸭,整只,冻的	Ducks, not cut in pieces, frozen	0207.3310	1
鸭,整只,鲜或冷的	Ducks, not cut in pieces, fresh or chilled	0207.3210	1
鸭蛋	Eggs, of ducks, in shell, fresh	0407.0022	1
鸭块,冻的	Cuts of ducks, frozen	0207.3610	1
鸭块,鲜或冷的	Cuts of ducks, fresh or chilled	0207.3510	1
鸭梨,鲜的	Ya pears, fresh	0808.2012	1
鸭绒被	Eiderdowns	9404.9010	6
牙齿固定件	Dental fittings	9021.2900	3
牙膏	Toothpastes	3306.1010	23
牙科填料,其他	Dental fillings	3006.4000	36
牙科用蜡	Dental wax	3407.0010	13
牙科用其他仪器及器具,其他	Dental sciences instruments and appliances, nes	9018.4990	7
牙科用仪器及器具,其他	Dental instruments and appliances, nes	9018.9090	7
牙科用椅,装有牙科设备的	Dentists chairs incorporating dental equipment	9018.4910	
牙科用椅及其零件	Dentists chairs and parts thereof	9402.1090	3

商品名称	Article Description	税则号列	申报要素
牙科用造型膏	Dental impression compounds	3407.0010	13
牙科用制品,以熟石膏为基本成分的	Dentistry preparations, with a basis of plaster	3407.0020	13
牙科粘固剂	Dental cements	3006.4000	36
牙刷,包括齿板刷	Tooth brushes, including ventalplate brushes	9603.2100	5
牙线,单独零售包装的	Dental floss, in individual retail package	3306.2000	23
牙钻机,不论是否与其他牙科设备组装在同一底座上	Dental drill engines, whether or not combined on a single base with other dental equipment	9018.4100	
芽子碱,它的盐、酯及其他衍生物	Ecgonine, salts, esters and other derivatives thereof	2939.9190	34
亚胺及其衍生物以及它们的盐,其他	Imines and their derivatives; salts thereof, nes	2925.2900	36
亚磷酸二甲酯	Dimethyl phosphite	2920.9013	36
亚磷酸二乙酯	Diethyl phosphite	2920.9014	36
亚磷酸三甲酯	Trimethyl phosphite	2920.9011	36
亚磷酸三乙酯	Trimethyl phosphite	2920.9012	36
亚磷酸盐,无机的	Phosphonates(phosphites), inorganic	2835.1000	
亚磷酸酯,其他	Phosphites, nes	2920.9019	36
亚硫酸盐,其他,无机的	Sulphites, nes, inorganic	2832.2000	
亚硫酸盐木浆,但溶解级的除外,半漂白或漂白,非针叶木的	Chemical wood pulp, sulphite, other than dissolving grades, semi-bleached or bleached, non-coniferous	4704.2900	46
亚硫酸盐木浆,但溶解级的除外,半漂白或漂白,针叶木的	Chemical wood pulp, sulphite, other than dissolving grades, semi-bleached or bleached, coniferous	4704.2100	46
亚硫酸盐木浆,但溶解级的除外,未漂白,非针叶木的	Chemical wood pulp, sulphite, other than dissolving grades, unbleached, non-coniferous	4704.1900	46
亚硫酸盐木浆,但溶解级的除外,未漂白,针叶木的	Chemical wood pulp, sulphite, other than dissolving grades, unbleached, coniferous	4704.1100	46
亚硫酸盐松节油及其他粗制对异丙基苯甲烷;	Sulphite turpentine and other crude paracymene	3805.9090	36
亚氯酸盐,无机的	Chlorites, inorganic	2828.9000	
亚麻,破开的或打成但未纺制的亚麻	Flax, broken or scutched, but not spun	5301.2100	4
亚麻,生的或经沤制的	Flax, raw or retted	5301.1000	4
亚麻,栉梳或经其他加工但未纺制的	Flax, hackled or otherwise processed, but not spun	5301.2900	4
亚麻短纤	Flax tow	5301.3000	4
亚麻废麻	Flax waste	5301.3000	4
亚麻机织物,按重量计亚麻含量在85%及以上,漂白	Flax woven fabrics, containing 85% or more by weight of flax, bleached	5309.1120	2468
亚麻机织物,按重量计亚麻含量在85%及以上,其他	Flax woven fabrics, containing 85% or more by weight of flax, nes	5309.1900	2468
亚麻机织物,按重量计亚麻含量在85%及以上,未漂白	Flax woven fabrics, containing 85% or more by weight of flax, unbleached	5309.1110	2468
亚麻机织物,按重量计亚麻含量在85%以下,漂白	Flax woven fabrics, containing less than 85% by weight of flax, bleached	5309.2120	2468
亚麻机织物,按重量计亚麻含量在85%以下,其他	Flax woven fabrics, containing less than 85% by weight of flax, nes	5309.2900	2468

Y

商品名称	Article Description	税则号列	申报要素
亚麻机织物,按重量计亚麻含量在85%以下,未漂白	Flax woven fabrics, containing less than 85% by weight of flax, unbleached	5309.2110	2468
亚麻纱线,单纱	Flax yarn, single	5306.1000	4
亚麻纱线,多股纱线或缆线	Flax yarn, multiple(folded) or cabled	5306.2000	4
亚麻酸及其盐和酯	Linotenic acids, their salts and esters	2916.1500	36
亚麻油地毡	Linoleum	5904.1000	
亚麻籽,不论是否破碎	Linseed, whether or not broken	1204.0000	
亚麻子油及其分离品,初榨的	Linseed oil and its fractions, crude oil	1515.1100	4
亚麻子油及其分离品,其他	Linseed oil and its fractions, nes	1515.1900	4
亚锰酸盐	Manganites	2841.6900	1
亚硝酸盐,无机的	Nitrites, inorganic	2834.1000	
亚油酸及其盐和酯	Linoleic acids, their salts and esters	2916.1500	36
砑光机,加工金属或玻璃用的除外	Calendering machines, other than for metals or glass, and cylinders	8420.1000	
砑光机滚筒	Calendering machines cylinders	8420.9100	3
砑光机零件,其他	Calendering machines parts, nes	8420.9900	3
氩	Argon	2804.2100	
yan			
烟草,供吸用的,不论是否含有任何比例的烟草代用品	Smoking tobacco, whether or not containing tobacco substitutes in any proportion	2403.1000	3
烟草,其他,部分或全部去梗的	Tobacco, partly or wholly stemmed/stripped, nes	2401.2090	4
烟草,其他,未去梗的	Tobacco, not stemmed/stripped, nes	2401.1090	4
烟草废料	Tobacco refuse	2401.3000	
烟草加工及制作机器	Tobacco preparing or making machinery	8478.1000	7
烟草加工及制作机器的零件	Tobacco preparing or making machinery parts	8478.9000	7
烟草精汁	Tobacco extracts and essences	2403.9900	
烟囱衬壁,陶瓷制	Chimney liners, ceramic	6905.9000	5
烟囱罩,陶瓷制	Chimney-pots, ceramic	6905.9000	5
烟斗及烟斗头	Pipes and pipe bowls for smoking	9614.0010	
烟斗及烟斗头	Smoking pipes and pipe bowls	9614.0010	
烟斗零件	Smoking pipes parts	9614.0090	5
烟盒、烟袋,以皮革、再生皮革或漆皮作面	Cigarette-cases, tobacco-pouches, with outer surface of leather, of composition leather or of patent leather	4202.3100	256
烟盒、烟袋,以塑料片或纺织材料作面	Cigarette-cases, tobacco-pouches, with outer surface of plastic sheeting or of textile materials	4202.3200	256
烟花	Fireworks	3604.1000	
烟火制品其他	Pyrotechnic articles other	3604.9000	
烟碱及其盐	Nicotine and its salts	2939.9910	34
烟胶片	Smoked sheets	4001.2100	12
烟卷纸,成小本或管状	Cigarette paper, in the form of booklets or tubes	4813.1000	8

商品名称	Article Description	税则号列	申报要素
烟卷纸,宽度不超过5厘米成卷的	Cigarette paper, in rolls of a width not exceeding 5cm	4813.2000	8
烟卷纸,其他	Cigarette paper, nes	4813.9000	8
烟煤,其他	Bituminous coal, nes	2701.1290	156
烟气脱硫装置	Flue gas desulfurization apparatus	8421.3940	7
烟气脱硝装置	Flue gas denitration apparatus	8421.3950	7
烟雾分析仪	Smoke analysis apparatus	9027.1000	8
烟嘴	Cigarette holders	9614.0090	5
胭脂虫	Cochineal	0511.9990	34
胭脂虫提取物	Cochineal extract	3203.0020	34
芫荽子	Seeds of coriander	0909.2000	
研磨机,其他	Grinding machines, nes	8479.8200	7
研磨机,食品用,家用电动器具	Grinders for food, electro-mechanical domestic appliances	8509.4090	
研磨机床,玻璃用	Grinding machines for glass or glassware	8464.2010	7
研磨机床,加工金属或金属陶瓷用	Lapping machines, for metal or cermets	8460.4020	7
研磨机床,加工石料、陶瓷、混凝土、石棉水泥或类似矿物材料的,其他	Grinding machines for working stone, ceramics, concrete, asbestos-cement or like mineral materials, nes	8464.2090	7
研磨机器,加工木材、软木、骨、硬质橡胶、硬质塑料或类似硬质材料的	Grinding machines, for working wood, cork, bone, hard rubber, hard plastics or similar hard materials	8465.9300	7
研磨球及类似品,经锻造或冲压,但未经进一步加工,研磨机用的	Grinding balls and similar articles, forged or stamped, but not further worked, for mills	7326.1100	346
研磨球及类似品,铸造制品,研磨机用的	Grinding balls and similar cast articles for mills	7325.9100	346
研磨设备,单晶硅柱或硅晶片的制造机器及装置	Grinding machines, boules or wafers manufacture machines and apparatus	8486.1020	7
盐,其他,氯化钠的	Salt, nes, of sodium chloride	2501.0019	1368
盐酸	Hydrochloric acid	2806.1000	6
盐渍绵羊肠衣	Sheep casings, salted	0504.0012	14
盐渍山羊肠衣	Goat casings, salted	0504.0013	14
盐渍猪肠衣(猪大肠头除外)	Hog casings, salted (excluding hog fatends)	0504.0011	14
盐渍猪大肠头	Hog fatends, salted	0504.0014	14
颜料(包括金属粉末或金属粉片),分散于非水介质中呈液状或浆状的,制造油漆(含瓷漆)用的	Pigments (including metallic powders and flakes) dispersed in non-aqueous media, in liquid or paste form, of a kind used in the manufacture of paints (including enamels)	3212.9000	136
颜料,成套的	Colours in sets	3213.1000	3
颜料,加工皮革用的,水性的	Pigments of a kind used for finishing leather, prepared, water based	3210.0000	36

Y

商品名称	Article Description	税则号列	申报要素
颜料、调色料、文娱颜料及类似品，片状、管装、罐装、瓶装、扁盒装以及类似形状或包装的，艺术家、学生和广告美工用的	Painters'colours, modifying tints, amusement colours and the like, in tablets, tubes, jars, bottles, pans or in similar forms or packings, for artists, students or signboard use	3213.9000	3
颜料和制品，硫化锌为基本成分的	Pigments and preparations based on zinc sulphide	3206.4290	2368
颜料及类似制品，调制的，陶瓷、搪瓷及玻璃工业用	Pigments and similar preparations, prepared, of a kind used in the ceramic, enamelling or glass industry	3207.1000	13
颜料及以其为基本成分的制品	Pigments and preparations based thereon	3204.1700	345
颜料及制品，以二氧化钛为基本成分的，其他	Pigments and preparations, based on titanium dioxide, nes	3206.1900	2368
颜料及制品，以干物质计二氧化钛含量在80%及以上的，其他	Pigments and preparations containing 80% or more by weight of titanium dioxide calculated on the dry matter, nes	3206.1190	2368
颜料及制品，以铬化合物为基本成分的	Pigments and preparations based on chromium compounds	3206.2000	2368
衍射设备	Diffraction apparatus	9012.1000	
衍射设备的零件、附件	Diffraction apparatus parts and accessories	9012.9000	3
掩膜版制作和修复装置	Masks manufacture or repair apparatus	8486.4010	7
掩膜版制作和修复装置零件及附件	Masks manufacture or repair apparatus parts and accessories	8486.9090	3
眼，贱金属制，用于衣着、鞋靴、天篷、提包、旅行用品或其他制成品	Eyes, of base metal, of a kind used for clothing, footwear, awnings, handbags, travel goods or other made up articles	8308.1000	256
眼镜，矫正视力用	Spectacles, corrective	9004.9090	5
眼镜盒，以皮革、再生皮革或漆皮作面	Spectacle cases, with outer surface of leather, of composition leather or of patent leather	4202.3100	256
眼镜盒，以塑料片或纺织材料作面	Spectacle cases, with outer surface of plastic sheeting or of textile materials	4202.3200	256
眼镜盒、化妆包、钱夹、钱包、烟盒、烟袋、粉盒，其他	Spectacle cases, toilet bags, wallets, purses, cigarette-cases, tobacco-pouches, powder-boxes, nes	4202.3900	256
眼镜架，其他材料制	Spectacles frames and mountings of other materials	9003.1900	3
眼镜架，塑料制	Spectacles frames and mountings of plastics	9003.1100	3
眼镜架零件	Spectacles frames and mountings parts	9003.9000	3
眼镜片，玻璃制，其他	Spectacle lenses of glass, nes	9001.4099	5
眼镜片，其他材料制，其他	Spectacle lenses of other materials	9001.5099	
眼科用其他仪器及器具	Ophthalmic instruments and appliances	9018.5000	7
燕麦，滚压或制片的	Oats, rolled or flaked	1104.1200	4
燕麦，其他	Oats, nes	1004.0090	3
燕麦，其他加工的	Oats, other worked	1104.2200	4
燕麦，种用	Oats, seed	1004.0010	3

商品名称	Article Description	税则号列	申报要素
燕窝	Birds' nests, edible	0410.0010	3
燕窝	Salanganes' nests	0410.0010	3
yang			
扬声器,单喇叭音箱	Loudspeakers, single loudspeakers, mounted in their enclosures	8518.2100	5
扬声器,多喇叭音箱	Loudspeakers, multiple loudspeakers, mounted in the same enclosure	8518.2200	5
扬声器,其他	Loudspeakers, nes	8518.2900	5
扬声器零件	Loudspeakers parts	8518.9000	3
羊毛,粗梳的	Wool, carded	5105.1000	5
羊毛,精梳的,片毛	Wool, combed in fragments	5105.2100	5
羊毛,精梳的,其他	Wool, combed, nes	5105.2900	5
羊毛,碳化的	Wool, not carded or combed, carbonized	5101.3000	48
羊毛,未梳的,含脂的,剪羊毛	Wool, not carded or combed, greasy, shorn wool	5101.1100	48
羊毛,未梳的,含脂的,其他	Wool, not carded or combed, greasy, nes	5101.1900	48
羊毛,未梳的,脱脂的,未碳化,剪羊毛	Wool, not carded or combed, degreased, not carbonized, shorn wool	5101.2100	48
羊毛,未梳的,脱脂的,未碳化,其他	Wool, not carded or combed, degreased, not carbonized, nes	5101.2900	48
羊毛、其他动物毛或其他纺织材料,作假发及类似品用的	Wool or other animal hair or other textile materials, prepared for use in making wigs or the like	6703.0000	4
羊毛的回收纤维	Garnetted stock of wool	5104.0010	5
羊毛的机织物,粗梳的,按重量计羊毛或动物细毛含量在85%及以上	Woven fabrics of carded wool, containing 85% or more by weight of wool or of fine animal hair	5111.1990	4568
羊毛的机织物,粗梳的,按重量计羊毛或动物细毛含量在85%及以上,每平方米重量不超过300克	Woven fabrics of carded wool, containing 85% or more by weight of wool or of fine animal hair, of a weight not exceeding 300g/m^2	5111.1190	4568
羊毛的机织物,粗梳的,其他	Woven fabrics of carded wool, nes	5111.9000	4568
羊毛的机织物,粗梳的,主要或仅与化学纤维长丝混纺	Woven fabrics of carded wool, mixed mainly or solely with man-made filaments	5111.2000	4568
羊毛的机织物,粗梳的,主要或仅与化学纤维短纤混纺	Woven fabrics of carded wool, mixed mainly or solely with man-made staple fibres	5111.3000	4568
羊毛的机织物,精梳的,按重量计羊毛或动物细毛含量在85%及以上,每平方米重量不超过200克	Woven fabrics of combed wool, containing 85% or more by weight of wool or of fine animal hair, of a weight not exceeding 200g/m^2	5112.1100	4568
羊毛的机织物,精梳的,按重量计羊毛或动物细毛含量在85%及以上,其他	Woven fabrics of combed wool, containing 85% or more by weight of wool or of fine animal hair, nes	5112.1900	4568
羊毛的机织物,精梳的,其他	Woven fabrics of combed wool, nes	5112.9000	4568
羊毛的机织物,精梳的,主要或仅与化学纤维长丝混纺	Woven fabrics of combed wool, mixed mainly or solely with man-made filaments	5112.2000	4568

Y

Y

商品名称	Article Description	税则号列	申报要素
羊毛的机织物,精梳的,主要或仅与化学纤维短纤混纺	Woven fabrics of combed wool, mixed mainly or solely with man-made staple fibres	5112.3000	4568
羊毛废料	Waste of wool	5103.2010	5
羊毛落毛	Noils of wool	5103.1010	5
羊毛纱线,粗梳的,非供零售用,按重量计羊毛含量在85%及以上	Yarn of carded wool, not put up for retail sale, containing 85% or more by weight of wool	5106.1000	346
羊毛纱线,粗梳的,非供零售用,按重量计羊毛含量在85%以下	Yarn of carded wool, not put up for retail sale, containing less than 85% by weight of wool	5106.2000	346
羊毛纱线,供零售用	Yarn of wool, put up for retail sale	5109.9090	346
羊毛纱线,精梳的,非供零售用,按重量计羊毛含量在85%及以上	Yarn of combed wool, not put up for retail sale, containing 85% or more by weight of wool	5107.1000	346
羊毛纱线,精梳的,非供零售用,按重量计羊毛含量在85%以下	Yarn of combed wool, not put up for retail sale, containing less than 85% by weight of wool	5107.2000	346
羊毛条	Wool tops	5105.2900	5
羊毛脂	Wool grease	1505.0000	
羊毛脂,纯净的	Lanolin	1505.0000	
羊茅子,饲料植物用的	Fescue seed, forage plants	1209.2300	358
羊乳干酪	Roquefort cheese	0406.4000	2468
羊脂肪,其他	Fats of sheep or goats, nes	1502.0090	4
羊脂肪,未炼制的	Fats of sheep or goats, raw	1502.0010	4
阳极,镍制,电镀用	Anodes of nickel for electroplating	7508.9010	6
阳模	Moulding patterns	8480.3000	7
杨桃,鲜的	Carambola, fresh	0810.9060	1
洋葱,干的	Onions, dried	0712.2000	4
洋葱,鲜或冷藏的	Onions, fresh or chilled	0703.1010	1
洋姜	Jerusalem artichokes	0714.9090	34
养蜂业用机器	Bee-keeping machinery	8436.8000	
养蜂业用机器零件,其他	Bee-keeping machinery parts, nes	8436.9900	3
氧	Oxygen	2804.4000	
氧化、扩散、退火及其他热处理设备,制造半导体器件或集成电路的机器及装置	Oxidation, diffusion, annealing and other heat treatment equipment, semiconductor devices or of electronic integrated circuits manufacture machines and apparatus	8486.2010	7
氧化钡	Baryta water	2816.4000	
氧化丙烯	Propylene oxide	2910.2000	36
氧化处理设备,平板显示器的制造机器及装置	Diffusion treatment equipment, flat panel displays manufacture machines and apparatus	8486.3010	7
氧化处理设备,制造半导体器件或集成电路的机器及装置	Oxidation treatment equipment, semiconductor devices or of electronic integrated circuits manufacture machines and apparatus	8486.2010	7
氧化镝	Dysprosium oxide	2846.9015	
氧化铬绿	Chromium sesquioxide [chromium (Ⅲ) oxide]	2819.9000	

商品名称	Article Description	税则号列	申报要素
氧化镧	Lanthanum oxide	2846.9012	
氧化铝,但人造刚玉除外	Aluminium oxide, other than artificial corundum	2818.2000	136
氧化镁,化学纯	Magnesium oxide, chemically pure	2519.9091	146
氧化镁,其他	Magnesium oxide, nes	2519.9099	146
氧化镍烧结物及镍冶炼的中间产品,其他	Nickel oxide sinters and intermediate products of nickel metallurgy, nes	7501.2090	4
氧化钕	Neodymium oxide	2846.9013	
氧化偶氮化合物	Azoxy-compounds	2927.0000	36
氧化皮,冶炼钢铁所产生的	Scalings from the manufacture of iron or steel	2619.0000	134
氧化铈	Cerium oxide	2846.1010	
氧化铽	Terbium oxide	2846.9016	
氧化稀土,其他	Rare-earth oxides, nes	2846.9019	
氧化锌	Flowers of zinc (zinc oxide)	2817.0010	34
氧化锌	Zinc oxide	2817.0010	34
氧化亚麻油	Linoxyn	1518.0000	46
氧化乙烯	Ethylene oxide	2910.1000	36
氧化钇	Yttrium oxide	2846.9011	
氧化铕	Eurapium oxide	2846.9014	
氧氯化磷	Phosphorus oxychloride	2812.1020	
氧气治疗器	Oxygen therapy apparatus	9019.2000	
氧氰化钠	Sodium cyanide oxide	2837.1120	6
样品簿,纸或纸板制的	Albums for samples, of paper or paperboard	4820.5000	
yao			
腰带,皮革或再生皮革制的	Belts, of leather or of composition leather	4203.3010	456
腰果,去壳	Cashew nuts, shelled	0801.3200	134
腰果,未去壳	Cashew nuts, in shell	0801.3100	134
摇纱机	Textile reeling machines	8445.4090	7
摇纱机的辅助机器	Textile reeling machines auxiliary	8448.1900	3
药棉,供医疗、外科、牙科或兽医用	Absorbent cotton, medical, surgical, dental or veterinary purposes	3005.9010	1346
药品,其他,混合或未混合的,配定剂量或制成零售包装	Medicaments, nes, mixed or unmixed, put up in measured doses or in forms or packings for retail sale	3004.9090	368
药品,其他,两种或两种以上成分混合而成的,未配定剂量或制成零售包装	Medicaments, nes, consisting of two or more constituents which have been mixed together, not put up in measured doses or in forms or packings for retail sale	3003.9090	368
ye			
椰壳	Coconut (coir)	5305.0092	4
椰壳纤维纱线	Coir yarn	5308.1000	568

Y

商品名称	Article Description	税则号列	申报要素
椰枣	Dates	0804.1000	14
椰子,干的	Coconuts, desiccated	0801.1100	134
椰子,其他	Coconuts, nes	0801.1990	134
椰子,种用	Coconuts, seedlings	0801.1910	134
椰子油及其分离品,初榨的	Coconut (copra) oil and its fractions, crude oil	1513.1100	4
椰子油及其分离品,其他	Coconut (copra) oil and its fractions, nes	1513.1900	4
椰子汁	Coconut juice	2106.9040	268
耶稣兹茶	Jesuits' tea	0903.0000	
野山参(西洋参除外)	Wild ginseng (other than american ginseng)	1211.2020	34
野鸭	Teals	0106.3923	34
野营用品,化学纤维制,其他	Camping goods, of man-made fibres, nes	6306.9920	346
野营用品,麻制,其他	Camping goods, of bast fibres, nes	6306.9910	346
野营用品,棉制,其他	Camping goods, of cotton, nes	6306.9100	346
野营用品,其他	Camping goods, nes	6306.9990	346
叶黄素,胡萝卜醇	Xanthophyll	3203.0019	34
叶绿素	Chlorophyll	3203.0019	34
页状蛭石	Exfoliated vermiculite	6806.2000	68
页状蛭石、膨胀粘土、泡沫矿渣及类似的膨胀矿物材料(包括其相互混合物)	Exfoliated vermiculite, expanded clays, foamed slag and similar expanded mineral materials (including intermixtures thereof)	6806.2000	68
液化空气或其他气体的机器,其他	Liquefying air or other gases machinery, nes	8419.6090	57
液化气体燃料,直接灌注香烟打火机及类似打火器用的,包装容器的容积不超过300立方厘米	Liquefied-gas fuels in containers of a kind used for filling or refilling cigarette or similar lighters and of a capacity not exceeding 300cm³	3606.1000	38
液化石油气船,容积在20000立方米及以下	Liquified petroleum gas ships, volume with 20000m³ or less	8901.2031	8
液化石油气船,容积在20000立方米以上	Liquified petroleum gas ships, volume more than 20000m³	8901.2032	8
液化天然气船,容积在20000立方米及以下	Liquified natural gas ships, volume with 20000m³ or less	8901.2041	8
液化天然气船,容积在20000立方米以上	Liquified natural gas ships, volume more than 20000m³	8901.2042	8
液货船,其他	Tanker ships, nes	8901.2090	8
液晶显示板	Liquid crystal display panel	9013.8030	
液量计,生产或供应计量仪表,其他	Liquid meters, supply or production meters, nes	9028.2090	7
液量计零件、附件,工业用	Liquid meters parts and accessories, for industrial use	9028.9010	3
液量计零件、附件,其他	Liquid meters parts and accessories, nes	9028.9090	3
液体流量测量、检验仪器及装置	Flow measuring or checking instruments and apparatus, of liquids	9026.1000	7
液体燃料,直接灌注香烟打火机及类似打火器用的,包装容器的容积不超过300立方厘米	Liquid fuels in containers of a kind used for filling or refilling cigarette or similar lighters and of a capacity not exceeding 300cm³	3606.1000	38

商品名称	Article Description	税则号列	申报要素
液体石蜡	Liquid paraffin	2710. 1994	8
液体提升机	Liquid elevators	8413. 8200	27
液体提升机用零件	Liquid elevators parts	8413. 9200	27
液体猪油,未经乳化、混合或其他方法制作	Lard oil, not emulsified or mixed or otherwise prepared	1503. 0000	4
液位的测量、检验仪器及装置	Level measuring or checking instruments and apparatus, of liquids	9026. 1000	7
液位计,测量或检验变化量的	Level, measuring or checking variables of liquids or gases	9026. 1000	7
液位计零件、附件	Level meter parts and accessories	9026. 9000	3
液相色谱仪	Liquid chromatographs instruments	9027. 2012	
液压传动用液体,不含石油或从沥青矿物提取的油类,或者按重量计石油或从沥青矿物提取的油类含量低于70%	Liquids for hydraulic transmission, prepared, not containing or containing less than 70% by weight of petroleum oils or oils obtained from bituminous minerals	3819. 0000	36
液压动力装置,其他	Hydraulic power engines, nes	8412. 2990	27
液压马达	Hydraulic motors	8412. 2910	27
液压千斤顶	Jacks, hydraulic	8425. 4210	78
液压压力机,加工金属或硬质合金用,其他	Hydraulic presses, for working metal or metal carbides, nes	8462. 9190	7
液压自动调节或控制仪器及装置,其他	Hydraulic automatic regulating or controlling instruments and apparatus, nes	9032. 8100	7
液汁及浸膏,除虫菊的或含鱼藤酮植物根茎的	Vegetable saps and extracts, of pyrethrum or of the roots of plants containing rotenone	1302. 1930	14
液汁及浸膏,甘草的	Vegetable saps and extracts, of liquorice	1302. 1200	14
液汁及浸膏,啤酒花的	Vegetable saps and extracts, of hops	1302. 1300	146
液汁及浸膏,其他	Vegetable saps and extracts, nes	1302. 1990	
液汁及浸膏,生漆的	Vegetable saps and extracts, crude lacquer	1302. 1910	14
液汁及浸膏,鸦片的	Vegetable saps and extracts, opium	1302. 1100	14
液汁及浸膏,印楝素	Vegetable saps and extracts, azadirachtin	1302. 1920	14
yi			
一般的体育用品及设备,其他	Articles and equipment for general physical exercise, gymnastics or athletics, nes	9506. 9190	5
一次成像卷片,未曝光的,无齿孔的,宽度不超过105毫米,涂卤化银乳液的	Instant print film, unexposed, without perforations, of a width not exceeding 105mm, with silver halide emulsion	3702. 3210	12368
一次成像卷片,未曝光的,无齿孔的,宽度不超过105毫米,彩色摄影用	Instant print film, unexposed, without perforations, of a width not exceeding 105mm, for colour photography	3702. 3110	12368
一次成像平片,未曝光的	Instant print film, unexposed	3701. 2000	12368
一次成像照相机	Instant print cameras	9006. 4000	7
一硫化二烃氨基硫羰	Thiuram monosulphide	2930. 3000	36

Y

商品名称	Article Description	税则号列	申报要素
一氯代乙酸及其盐和酯	Mono-chloroacetic acids, their salts and esters	2915.4000	36
一氯化硫(氯化硫)	Sulfur monochloride	2812.1041	
一氯甲烷	Chloromethane(methyl chloride)	2903.1100	36
一氧化铅	Lead monoxide	2824.1000	
一元酚,其他	Monophenols, nes	2907.1990	36
伊红	Eosins (as synthetic organic colouring matter)	3204.1200	345
衣服,毛皮的	Apparel of furskin	4303.1010	456
衣服,皮革或再生皮革制的	Apparel, of leather or of composition leather	4203.1000	456
衣服及衣着附件,塑料的,其他	Apparel articles and clothing accessories, of plastics, nes	3926.2090	236
衣服及衣着附件,纸浆、纸、纤维素絮纸或纤维素纤维网纸制的	Articles of apparel and clothing accessories, of paper pulp, paper, cellulose wadding or webs of cellulose fibres	4818.5000	568
衣架,木制	Clothes hangers of wood	4421.1000	56
衣箱,以皮革、再生皮革或漆皮作面	Trunks, with outer surface of leather, of composition leather or of patent leather	4202.1110	1458
衣箱,以塑料或纺织材料作面	Trunks and suit-cases, with outer surface of plastics or of textile materials	4202.1210	256
衣箱、提箱、小手袋、公文箱、公文包、书包及类似容器,其他	Trunks, suit-cases, vanity-cases, executive-cases, briefcases, school satchels and similar containers, nes	4202.1900	256
衣着附件,非针织或钩编的,制成的,其他	Clothing accessories, not knitted or crocheted, made up, nes	6217.1090	2456
衣着附件,毛皮的	Clothing accessories, of furskin	4303.1020	456
衣着附件,皮革或再生皮革制的,其他	Clothing accessories, of leather or of composition leather, nes	4203.4000	456
衣着附件,针织或钩编的,制成的,其他	Clothing accessories, knitted or crocheted, made up, nes	6117.8090	2456
衣着附件的零件,非针织或钩编的	Clothing accessories parts, not knitted or crocheted	6217.9000	2456
衣着附件的零件,针织或钩编的	Clothing accessories parts, knitted or crocheted	6117.9000	2456
衣着用品及附件,硫化橡胶(硬质橡胶除外)制的,其他	Articles of apparel and clothing accessories, of vulcanized rubber other than hard rubber, nes	4015.9090	23
衣着用品及附件,硫化橡胶(硬质橡胶除外)制的,医疗用	Articles of apparel and clothing accessories, of vulcanized rubber other than hard rubber, for medical purpose	4015.9010	23
医疗车	Mobile clinics	8705.9040	7
医疗废物	Clinical waste	3825.3000	34
医疗用品,硫化橡胶(硬质橡胶除外)制的,其他	Pharmaceutical articles, of vulcanized rubber other than hard rubber, nes	4014.9000	23
医疗用仪器及器具,其他	Medical instruments and appliances, nes	9018.9090	7
依发韦仑及盐	Efavirenz and their salts	2934.9940	36
铱,板、片	Iridium, plates and sheets	7110.4910	46

商品名称	Article Description	税则号列	申报要素
铱,其他	Iridium, nes	7110.4990	46
铱,未锻造或粉末状	Iridium, unwrought or in powder form	7110.4100	46
仪表板钟及车辆、航空器、航天器或船舶用的类似钟	Instrument panel clocks and clocks of a similar type for vehicles, aircraft, spacecraft or vessels	9104.0000	5
贻贝,其他,冻、干、盐腌或盐渍的	Mussels (Mytilus spp., Perna spp.), frozen, dried, salted or in brine	0307.3900	14
贻贝,其他,活或鲜或冷的	Mussels (Mytilus spp., Perna spp.), live, fresh or chilled	0307.3190	1
贻贝,种苗	Mussels (Mytilus spp., Perna spp.), for cultivation	0307.3110	3
胰岛素及其盐,其他	Insulin and its salts, nes	2937.1290	36
胰岛素及其盐,重组的	Insulin and its salts, recombinant	2937.1210	36
胰岛素药品,混合或未混合的,配定剂量或制成零售包装,其他	Insulin medicaments, mixed or unmixed, put up in measured doses or in forms or packings for retail sale, nes	3004.3190	368
胰岛素药品,两种或两种以上成分混合而成的,未配定剂量或制成零售包装	Insulin medicaments, consisting of two or more constituents which have been mixed together, not put up in measured doses or in forms or packings for retail sale	3003.3100	368
胰岛素药品,重组的,混合或未混合的,配定剂量或制成零售包装	Insulin medicaments, recombinant, mixed or unmixed, put up in measured doses or in forms or packings for retail sale	3004.3110	368
移动式吊运架及跨运车,带胶轮的	Mobile lifting frames on tyres and straddle carriers	8426.1200	7
移动通信基站	Mobile communication base stations	8517.6110	
移动通信交换机	Mobile communication switching system	8517.6212	
移植机,农业、园艺及林业用	Transplanters, for agricultural, horticultural or forestry use	8432.3000	
遗传物质和基因修饰生物体	Genetics material and gene modified organism	3002.9040	34
乙胺丁醇	Ethylamino butanol (ethambutol)	2922.1910	36
乙苯	Ethylbenzene	2902.6000	6
乙丙非共轭二烯橡胶(EPDM),初级形状的	Ethylene-propylene-non-conjugated diene rubber (EPDM), in primary forms	4002.7010	136
乙丙非共轭二烯橡胶(EPDM),其他	Ethylene-propylene-non-conjugated diene rubber (EPDM), nes	4002.7090	136
乙丙橡胶	Ethylene-propylene copolymers, predominated by propylene monomer unit	3902.3010	1256
乙丙橡胶,初级形状的	Ethylene-propylene copolymers, in primary forms, predominated by ethylene monomer unit	3901.9010	1256
乙醇,改性的,及其他酒精	Ethyl alcohol and other spirits, denatured of any strength	2207.2000	246
乙醇,未改性的,按容量计酒精浓度在80%及以上	Ethyl alcohol, undenatured, of an alcoholic strength by volume of 80% vol or higher	2207.1000	246
乙醇,未改性的,按容量计酒精浓度在80%及以下,其他	Ethyl alcohol, undenatured, of an alcoholic strength by volume of less than 80% vol	2208.9090	2468

Y

商品名称	Article Description	税则号列	申报要素
乙二胺	Ethylenediamine	2921. 2110	36
乙二胺盐	Ethylenediamine salts	2921. 2190	36
乙二醇或二甘醇的单丁醚	Monobutyl ethers of ethylene glycol or of diethylene glycol	2909. 4300	36
乙二醇或二甘醇的其他单烷基醚	Other monoalkylethers of ethylene glycol or of diethylene glycol	2909. 4400	36
乙非他明以及它们的盐	Etilamfetamine (INN), salts thereof	2921. 4600	36
乙基二乙醇胺	Ethyldiethanolamine	2922. 1930	36
乙基吗啡及盐	Ethylmorphine and salts	2939. 1100	34
乙基香草醛	Ethylvanillin	2912. 4200	36
乙基香豆素	Ethylcoumarins	2932. 2100	36
乙氯维诺(INN)	Ethchlorvynol(INN)	2905. 5100	36
乙醚	Diethyl ether	2909. 1100	36
乙内酰脲及其衍生物	Hydantoin and its derivatives	2933. 2100	36
乙醛	Acetaldehyde	2912. 1200	36
乙醛	Ethanal(acetaldehyde)	2912. 1200	36
乙醛肟	Acetaldoxime	2928. 0000	36
乙炔	Acetylene	2901. 2920	368
乙炔发生器,不论有无净化器	Acetylene gas generators, with or without their purifiers	8405. 1000	3
乙炔发生器的零件	Acetylene gas generators parts	8405. 9000	3
乙酸(正)丁酯	N-butyl acetate	2915. 3300	36
乙酸,其他	Acetic acid, nes	2915. 2190	36
乙酸酐	Acetic anhydride	2915. 2400	36
乙酸钠	Sodium acetate	2915. 2910	36
乙酸纤维素,未塑化,初级形状的	Cellulose acetates, non-plasticized, in primary forms	3912. 1100	16
乙酸纤维素,已塑化,初级形状的	Cellulose acetates, plasticized, in primary forms	3912. 1200	16
乙酸盐,其他	Acetic acid salts, nes	2915. 2990	36
乙酸乙烯酯	Vinyl acetate	2915. 3200	36
乙酸乙烯酯共聚物,初级形状的;其他	Vinyl acetate copolymers, in primary forms, nes	3905. 2900	1256
乙酸乙烯酯共聚物,水分散体,初级形状的	Vinyl acetate copolymers, in aqueous dispersion, in primary forms	3905. 2100	1256
乙酸乙烯酯或其他乙烯酯聚合物,初级形状的,其他	Vinyl acetate or of other vinyl esters polymers, in primary forms, nes	3905. 9900	1256
乙酸乙烯酯或其他乙烯酯聚合物的共聚物,初级形状的	Vinyl acetate or of other vinyl esters copolymers, in primary forms	3905. 9100	1256
乙酸乙酯	Ethyl acetate	2915. 3100	36
乙酸酯,其他	Esters of acetic acid, nes	2915. 3900	36
乙烯	Ethylene	2901. 2100	368
乙烯,液化的	Ethylene, liquefied	2711. 1400	1468
乙烯比妥(INN)以及盐	Vinylbital(INN); salts thereof	2933. 5300	36

商品名称	Article Description	税则号列	申报要素
乙烯-丙烯共聚物	Ethylene-propylene copolymers, predominated by propylene monomer unit	3902.3010	1256
乙烯-丙烯共聚物,初级形状的,乙烯单体单元为主	Ethylene-propylene copolymers, in primary forms, predominated by ethylene monomer unit	3901.9010	1256
乙烯基聚合物,其他	Vinyl polymers in primary forms, nes	3905.9900	1256
乙烯基聚合物的共聚物,初级形状的	Vinyl copolymers, in primary forms	3905.9100	1256
乙烯聚合物,初级形状的,其他	Ethylene polymers, in primary forms, nes	3901.9090	1256
乙烯-乙酸乙烯酯共聚物,初级形状的	Ethylene-vinyl acetate copolymers, in primary forms	3901.3000	1256
乙酰甲胺磷	Acephate	2929.9040	36
乙酰螺旋霉素及其衍生物以及它们的盐	Acetyl-spiramycin and its derivatives; salts thereof	2941.9070	
乙酰替苯胺	Acetanilide	2924.2990	36
乙酯杀螨醇(ISO)	Chlorobenzilate (ISO)	2918.1800	36
乙字钢,除热轧、热拉拔或热挤压外未经进一步加工	Z sections, not further worked than hot-rolled, hot-drawn or extruded	7216.5010	468
已绘制画布,作舞台、摄影布景或类似用途的	Painted canvas being theatrical scenery, studio backcloths or the like	5907.0020	4
已加工的板岩	Slate, worked	6803.0010	4
已鞣毛皮,羔羊的(阿斯特拉罕、喀拉科尔、波斯羔羊及类似羔羊、印度、中国或蒙古羔羊),未缝制的整张毛皮,不论是否带头、尾或爪	Tanned or dressed furskins of lamb, (astrakhan, broadtail, caracul, persian and similar lamb, indian, chinese, mongolian or tibetan lamb), whole skins, with or without head, tail or paws, not assembled	4302.1930	15
已鞣毛皮,灰鼠、白鼬、貂、狐、水獭、旱獭及猞猁的整张毛皮及其块、片,已缝制的	Tanned or dressed furskins of grey squirrel, ermine, other marten, fox, otter, marmot and lynx, whole skins and pieces or cuttings thereof, assembled	4302.3010	15
已鞣毛皮,灰鼠皮、白鼬皮、其他貂皮、狐皮、水獭皮、旱獭皮及猞猁皮,未缝制的整张毛皮,不论是否带头、尾或爪	Tanned or dressed furskins of grey squirrel, ermine, other marten, fox, otter, marmot and lynx, whole skins, with or without head, tail or paws, not assembled	4302.1910	15
已鞣毛皮,水貂的,未缝制的整张毛皮,不论是否带头、尾或爪	Tanned or dressed furskins whole skins, with or without head, tail or paws, not assembled	4302.1100	15
已鞣毛皮,兔皮,未缝制的整张毛皮,不论是否带头、尾或爪	Tanned or dressed furskins of rabbit or hare, whole skins, with or without head, tail or paws, not assembled	4302.1920	15
已鞣毛皮,未缝制的头、尾、爪及其他块、片	Tanned or dressed furskins, heads, tails, paws and other pieces or cuttings, not assembled	4302.2000	15
已鞣毛皮,未缝制的整张毛皮,不论是否带头、尾或爪,其他	Tanned or dressed furskins, whole skins, with or without head, tail or paws, not assembled, nes	4302.1990	15
已鞣毛皮,整张的,已缝制的,其他	Tanned or dressed furskins, whole skins and pieces or cuttings thereof, assembled, nes	4302.3090	15
以太网络交换机	Ethernet exchangers	8517.6232	7
钇	Yttrium	2805.3019	56

Y

商品名称	Article Description	税则号列	申报要素
钇,与稀土相互混合或相互熔合,电池级	Yttrium, intermixed or interalloyed with rare-earth metals, battery grade	2805. 3021	56
钇,与稀土相互混合或相互熔合,其他	Yttrium, intermixed or interalloyed with rare-earth metals, nes	2805. 3029	56
异冰片	Isoborneol	2906. 1990	36
异丙胺	Isopropyl amine	2921. 1920	36
异丙醇	Propan-2-ol(isopropyl alcohol)	2905. 1220	36
异丙基苯	Cumene	2902. 7000	6
异丁醇	Isobutanol	2905. 1410	36
异丁烯-异戊二烯(丁基)橡胶(IIR),初级形状的	Isobutene-isoprene (butyl) rubber (IIR), in primary forms	4002. 3110	136
异丁烯-异戊二烯(丁基)橡胶(IIR),其他	Isobutene-isoprene (butyl) rubber (IIR), nes	4002. 3190	136
异花青	Isocyanines, a synthetic organic colouring matter	3204. 9090	345
异黄樟脑	Isosafrole	2932. 9100	36
异极矿	Hemimorphite	2608. 0000	146
异喹啉环系化合物,结构上含有,未经进一步稠合的,不论是否氢化,其他	Isoquinoline ring-system compounds, not further fused in the structure, whether or not hydrogenated, nes	2933. 4990	36
异氰	Isocyanides	2929. 9090	36
异氰化物	Isocyanides	2929. 9090	36
异氰脲酸氯化衍生物,其他	Chloroisocyanurate, nes	2933. 6929	36
异氰酸酯,其他	Isocyanates, nes	2929. 1090	36
异戊巴比妥(INN)以及盐	Amobarbital(INN); salts thereof	2933. 5300	36
异戊二烯	Isoprene	2901. 2400	368
异戊二烯橡胶(IR),初级形状的	Isoprene rubber(IR), in primary forms	4002. 6010	136
异戊二烯橡胶(IR),其他	Isoprene rubber(IR), nes	4002. 6090	136
异戊烯	Isopentene	2901. 2910	368
易拉罐及罐体	Tear tab ends and bodies thereof	7612. 9010	368
易燃材料制品	Combustible materials articles	3606. 9090	13
意大利面条,生的,含蛋的	Spaghetti, uncooked, containing eggs	1902. 1100	46
意大利面条,生的,其他	Spaghetti, uncooked, nes	1902. 1900	46
溢流阀	Relief valves	8481. 4000	6
翼子板(或叶子板),机动车辆的	Running-boards, of the motor vehicles	8708. 2957	3
yin			
阴极射线电视显像管,包括视频监视器用阴极射线管,彩色的	Cathode-ray television picture tubes, including video monitor cathode-ray tubes, colour	8540. 1100	35
阴极射线电视显像管,包括视频监视器用阴极射线管,黑白的或其他单色的	Cathode-ray television picture tubes, including video monitor cathode-ray tubes, black and white or other monochrome	8540. 1200	35
阴极射线管,其他	Cathode-ray tubes, nes	8540. 6090	35

Y

商品名称	Article Description	税则号列	申报要素
阴极射线管用零件	Cathode-ray tubes parts	8540.9190	3
音叉	Tuning forks	9209.9910	3
音频扩大器	Audio-frequency electric amplifiers	8518.4000	5
音频扩大器零件	Audio-frequency electric amplifiers parts	8518.9000	3
音响或视觉信号装置,电气的,其他	Sound or visual signalling apparatus, electric, nes	8531.8090	3
音响信号器,口吹的	Sound signalling instruments, mouth-blown	9208.9000	5
音响信号装置,机动车辆用,其他	Sound signalling equipment for motor vehicles, nes	8512.3019	7
音响信号装置,自行车用	Sound signalling equipment for bicycles	8512.3090	7
音响信号装置零件,自行车或机动车辆用	Sound signalling equipment parts for cycles or motor vehicles	8512.9000	3
铟,未锻轧	Indium, unwrought	8112.9230	16
铟粉末	Indium powders	8112.9230	16
铟制品,其他	Indium articles, nes	8112.9930	16
银(包括镀金、镀铂的银),半制成,纯度达 99.99% 及以上	Silver (including silver plated with gold or platinum), semi-manufactured, of a purity of 99.99% or more	7106.9210	145
银(包括镀金、镀铂的银),半制成,其他	Silver (including silver plated with gold or platinum), semi-manufactured, nes	7106.9290	145
银(包括镀金、镀铂的银),未锻造,纯度达 99.99% 及以上	Silver (including silver plated with gold or platinum), unwrought, of a purity of 99.99% or more	7106.9110	145
银(包括镀金、镀铂的银),未锻造,其他	Silver (including silver plated with gold or platinum), unwrought, nes	7106.9190	145
银,以贱金属为底的,未加工成半成品的	Silver clothing base metals, not further worked than semi-manufactured	7107.0000	46
银耳,干的	Jelly fungi (tremella spp.), dried	0712.3300	4
银粉,非片状,平均粒径小于 3 微米	Silver powder, not flake, average diameter less than 3μm	7106.1011	145
银粉,非片状,其他	Silver powder, not flake, nes	7106.1019	145
银粉,片状,平均粒径小于 10 微米	Silver powder, flake, average diameter less than 10μm	7106.1021	145
银粉,片状,其他	Silver powder, flake, nes	7106.1029	145
银化合物,其他	Silver compounds, nes	2843.2900	
银或银化合物的灰	Silver or silver compounds ash	7112.3010	46
银胶菊胶、糖胶树胶及类似的天然树胶	Guayule gums	4001.3000	12
银矿砂及其精矿	Silver ores and concentrates	2616.1000	146
银幕及其他投影屏幕	Projection screens	9010.6000	7
引爆器	Igniters	3603.0000	
引火合金,其他	Pyrophoric alloys, nes	3606.9019	13
引火合金,其他,已切成形可直接使用	Pyrophoric alloys, nes, cut to shape, for immediate use	3606.9011	13
引纬装置,织机用	Weft insertion for looms	8448.4920	3

Y

商品名称	Article Description	税则号列	申报要素
引线键合装置,主要用于或专用于装配与封装半导体器件或集成电路	Wire bonders, solely or principally of a kind used for assembling or encapsulating semiconductor devices	8486. 4022	7
引线键合装置用零件及附件,主要用于或专用于装配与封装半导体器件或集成电路	Wire bonders parts and accessories, solely or principally of a kind used for assembling or encapsulating semiconductor devices	8486. 9020	3
引针,钢铁制的,手工用	Bod-kins, for use in the hand, of iron or steel	7319. 9000	
饮料充气机	Machinery for aerating beverages	8422. 3090	
饮料充气机零件	Aerating beverages machinery parts	8422. 9090	
饮料灌装设备	Machinery for bottling or canning beverages	8422. 3010	
饮料生产或加工机器	Drink preparation or manufacture machinery	8438. 8000	
饮料生产或加工机器的零件	Drink preparation or manufacture machinery parts	8438. 9000	3
饮水机,电热的	Water dispensers, electro-thermic	8516. 7910	7
饮用蒸馏水	Distilled water for human consumption	2853. 0010	3
隐形眼镜片	Contact lenses	9001. 3000	
印戳,手用,其他	Stamps for printing or embossing, designed for operating in the hand, nes	9611. 0000	
印花税票	Revenue stamps	9704. 0090	5
印花税票,未经使用的	Revenue stamps, unused	4907. 0090	5
印楝油及其分离品	Neemoil and its fractions	1515. 9020	
印刷版(片)的制造机器、器具及设备,其他	Plates preparing or making machinery, nes	8442. 3090	
印刷版制造机零件	Plates making machinery parts	8442. 4000	3
印刷版制造设备,计算机直接制	Plates preparing machines for CTP	8442. 3021	
印刷部件,其他	Printing components, nes	8442. 5000	
印刷部件的制造机器、器具及设备,其他	Printing components preparing or making machinery, nes	8442. 3090	
印刷部件制造机器零件	Printing components making machinery parts	8442. 4000	3
印刷电路,4 层以上的	Printed circuits, of more than 4 layers	8534. 0010	5
印刷电路,其他	Printed circuits, nes	8534. 0090	5
印刷电路板制造用光致抗蚀干膜,未曝光的,无齿孔的,宽度超过 105 毫米,但不超过 610 毫米	Narrow anticorrosive photographic plate for printed circuit processing, unexposed, without perforations, of a width exceeding 105mm but not exceeding 610mm	3702. 4422	12368
印刷电路板制造用光致抗蚀干膜,未曝光的,无齿孔的,宽度超过 610 毫米,长度超过 200 米	Wide anticorrosive photographic plate for printed circuit processing, unexposed, without perforations, of a width exceeding 610mm and of a length exceeding 200 m	3702. 4221	12368
印刷滚筒	Cylinders for printing machinery	8442. 5000	
印刷机,凹版的	Printing machinery of gravure	8443. 1700	57
印刷机,苯胺的	Printing machinery of flexographic	8443. 1600	57
印刷机,激光数字式	Printing machines, laser, digital	8443. 3222	57

商品名称	Article Description	税则号列	申报要素
印刷机,静电照相(激光印刷机),数字式	Printing machines (laser printing machines), electrostatic photographic, digital	8443.3222	57
印刷机,喷墨数字式	Printing machines, ink-jet, digital	8443.3221	57
印刷机,平网的	Printing machinery of platen screen	8443.1922	57
印刷机,凸版的,除卷取进料式以外的,但不包括苯胺印刷机	Printing machinery of letterpress, other than reel fed, excluding flexographic printing	8443.1500	57
印刷机,凸版的,卷取进料式,但不包括苯胺印刷机	Printing machinery of letterpress, reel fed, excluding flexographic printing	8443.1400	57
印刷机,网式的,其他	Printing machinery of screen, nes	8443.1929	57
印刷机,圆网的	Printing machinery of cylinder screen	8443.1921	57
印刷机器,用印刷用版(片)、滚筒及其他印刷部件进行的,其他	Printing machinery, used for printing by means of plates, cylinders and other printing components, nes	8443.1980	57
印刷机器零件及附件,其他	Printing machinery parts and accessories, nes	8443.9190	3
印刷品,其他	Printed matter, nes	4911.9900	346
印刷设备,数字式,其他	Digital printing machines, nes	8443.3939	57
印刷设备,数字式,可与自动数据处理设备或网络连接的,其他	Printing machines, digital, capelle of connecting to an APP machine or to a network, nes	8443.3229	57
印刷设备,数字式,可与自动数据处理设备或网络连接的	Digital printing machines, capable of connecting to an APP machine or to a network, nes	8443.3229	57
印刷设备的零件,数字式,其他	Printing machines parts, digital, nes	8443.9929	3
印刷用版	Plates for printing machinery	8442.5000	
印刷用辅助机器,其他	Printing ancillary machines, nes	8443.9110	3
印刷用辅助机器,数字式	Printing ancillary machines, digital	8443.9910	3
印刷用石板	Printing lithographic stones	8442.5000	
印刷油墨,黑色	Printing ink, black	3215.1100	3
印刷油墨,其他	Printing ink, nes	3215.1900	3
印台,不论是否已加印油或带盒子	Ink-pads, whether or not inked, with or without boxes	9612.2000	
印有邮票或印花税票的纸品	Stamp-impressed paper	4907.0090	5
印制电路用覆铜板,精炼铜制,铜厚度不超过0.15毫米	Copper-clad board used to print circuit, of refined copper, of a copper thickness not exceeding 0.15mm	7410.2110	236
印制画的原本	Prints, original	9702.0000	
茚树脂,初级形状的	Indene resins, in primary forms	3911.1000	16
ying			
婴儿服装及衣着附件,针织或钩编的,合成纤维制	Babies garments and clothing accessories, knitted or crocheted, of synthetic fibres	6111.3000	2456
婴儿服装及衣着附件,针织或钩编的,棉制	Babies garments and clothing accessories, knitted or crocheted, of cotton	6111.2000	2456
婴儿服装及衣着附件,针织或钩编的,其他	Babies garments and clothing accessories, knitted or crocheted, nes	6111.9090	2456

Y

商品名称	Article Description	税则号列	申报要素
婴儿服装及衣着附件,针织或钩编的,羊毛或动物细毛制	Babies garments and clothing accessories, knitted or crocheted, of wool or fine animal hair	6111.9010	2456
婴儿尿布、尿布衬里及类似的卫生用品,纸浆、纸、纤维素絮纸或纤维素纤维网纸制的	Napkins and napkin liners for babies and similar sanitary articles, of paper pulp, paper, cellulose wadding or webs of cellulose fibres	4818.4000	568
婴孩车及其零件	Baby carriages and parts thereof	8715.0000	3
婴幼儿食品,零售包装的	Preparations for infant use, put up for retail sale	1901.1000	2368
罂粟秆	Poppy straw	1211.4000	34
罂粟秆浓缩物及盐	Poppy straw concentrates and salts	2939.1100	34
罂粟籽	Poppy seeds	1207.9100	3
樱桃,罐头	Cherries, in airtight containers	2008.6010	248
樱桃,鲜的	Cherries, fresh	0809.2000	1
樱桃,用其他方法制作或保藏的	Cherries, otherwise prepared, or preserved	2008.6090	248
樱桃,暂时保藏,但不适于直接食用的	Cherries, provisionally preserved, but unsuitable in that state for immediate consumption	0812.1000	34
鹦鹉,改良种用除外	Psittaciformes, ex. pure-bred breeding	0106.3290	
鹦鹉,改良种用	Psittaciformes, pure-bred breeding	0106.3210	3
鹦鹉,普通,改良种用	Parrots, pure-bred breeding	0106.3210	3
鹰嘴豆,其他,脱荚的,干的	Chickpeas(garbanzos), nes, dried, shelled	0713.2090	34
鹰嘴豆,种用,脱荚的,干的	Chickpeas(garbanzos), seed, dried, shelled	0713.2010	34
荧蒽	Fluoranthene	2902.9090	6
荧光素,荧光黄	Fluorescein (synthetic organic colouring matter)	3204.1990	345
荧光增白剂,有机合成的	Flourescent brightening agents, synthetic organic products	3204.2000	345
萤石,按重量计氟化钙含量在97%及以下	Fluorspar, containing by weight 97% or less of calcium fluoride	2529.2100	138
萤石,按重量计氟化钙含量在97%以上	Fluorspar, containing by weight more than 97% of calcium fluoride	2529.2200	138
硬币(金币除外),非法定货币的	Coin(other than gold coin), not being legal tender	7118.1000	46
硬币,其他	Coin, nes	7118.9000	46
硬币分类、计数及包装机	Coin-sorting, counting or wrapping machines	8472.9090	
硬衬布及类似硬挺纺织物,化学纤维制	Buckram and similar stiffened textile fabrics of a kind used for hat foundations of man-made fibres	5901.9092	
硬衬布及类似硬挺纺织物,棉或麻制	Buckram and similar stiffened textile fabrics of a kind used for hat foundations of cotton or bast fibres	5901.9091	
硬衬布及类似硬挺纺织物,其他	Buckram and similar stiffened textile fabrics of a kind used for hat foundations, nes	5901.9099	
硬度计,金属材料试验用	Hardness testing machines and applinances, or testing metals	9024.1020	
硬管,丙烯聚合物制	Tubes, pipes and hoses, rigid, of polymers of propylene	3917.2200	36

商品名称	Article Description	税则号列	申报要素
硬管,氯乙烯聚合物制	Tubes, pipes and hoses, rigid, of polymers of vinyl chloride	3917.2300	36
硬管,其他塑料制	Tubes, pipes and hoses, rigid, of other plastics	3917.2900	36
硬管,乙烯聚合物制	Tubes, pipes and hoses, rigid, of polymers of ethylene	3917.2100	36
硬花甘蓝,鲜或冷藏的	Headed broccoli, fresh or chilled	0704.1000	1
硬化蛋白,初级形状的	Hardened proteins, in primary forms	3913.9000	146
硬粒小麦	Durum wheat	1001.1000	356
硬锰矿	Psilomelane	2602.0000	1346
硬盘驱动器	Rigid disk drivers	8471.7010	
硬石膏	Anhydrite	2520.1000	34
硬糖	Boiled sweets	1704.9000	258
硬脂酸	Stearic acid	2915.7010	36
硬脂酸,工业用	Stearic acid, industrial use	3823.1100	6
硬脂酸盐和酯	Stearic acid salts and esters	2915.7090	36
硬质橡胶,各种形状的包括废碎料	Hard rubber in all forms, including waste and scrap	4017.0010	14
硬质橡胶制品	Hard rubber articles	4017.0020	14
yong			
庸鲽鱼,其他,冻的	Halibut (reinhardtius hippoglossoides, hippoglossus hippoglossus, hippoglossus stenolepis), nes, frozen	0303.3190	18
庸鲽鱼,鲜或冷的	Halibut (Reinhardtius hippoglossoides, Hippoglossus hippoglossus, Hippoglossus stenolepis), fresh or chilled	0302.2100	18
永磁体,金属的,其他	Permanent magnets of metal, nes	8505.1190	47
永磁体,稀土的	Permanent magnets of rare-earth metals	8505.1110	46
永磁铁的物品,未磁化	Permanent magnets articles, intended to become after magnetization	8505.1900	48
永磁直流发电机,点燃式或压燃式内燃发动机用的,其他	Magneto-dynamos, for electrical ignition or starting equipment, nes	8511.2090	7
永磁直流发电机,机车、航空器及船舶用,点燃式或压燃式内燃发动机用的	Magneto-dynamos, for locomotives, aircraft or ships, for electrical ignition or starting equipment	8511.2010	7
you			
邮戳盖销印	Stamp-post-marks	9704.0090	5
邮票	Postage	9704.0010	
邮票,未经使用的	Postage, unused	4907.0010	1
邮政信笺	Postal stationery	9704.0090	5
邮政用分拣设备	Post offices sorting machines used in	8479.8940	7
邮资盖戳机	Postage franking machines	8470.9000	
油,从乳中提取的	Oils, derived from milk	0405.9000	268
油、脂及其分离品,海生哺乳动物的	Fats and oils and their fractions, of marine mammals	1504.3000	4

Y

商品名称	Article Description	税则号列	申报要素
油、脂及其分离品,其他动物的,不论是否精制,但未经化学改性	Fats and oils and their fractions, of other animal, whether or not refined, but not chemically modified	1506.0000	4
油、脂及其分离品除鱼肝油以外的鱼的	Fats and oils and their fractions, of fish, other than liver oils	1504.2000	346
油菜籽,其他	Colza, nes	1205.9090	3
油菜籽,其他	Rape, nes	1205.9090	3
油菜籽,其他,低芥子酸的	Rape, nes, low erucic acid	1205.1090	36
油菜籽,种用	Colza, seed	1205.9010	3
油菜籽,种用	Rape, seed	1205.9010	3
油菜籽,种用,低芥子酸的	Colza, seed, low erucic acid	1205.1010	36
油菜籽,种用,低芥子酸的	Rape, seed, low erucic acid	1205.1010	36
油醇(纯度大于90%)	Oleyl alcohol (of a purity of 90% or more)	2905.2900	36
油橄榄,用醋或醋酸以外的其他方法制作或保藏的,未冷冻	Olives, prepared or preserved otherwise than by vinegar or acetic acid, not frozen	2005.7000	148
油橄榄,暂时保藏,但不适合直接使用的	Olives, provisionally preserved, but unsuitable in that state for immediate consumption	0711.2000	34
油橄榄油及其分离品,初榨的	Olive oil and its fractions, virgin	1509.1000	4
油橄榄油及其分离品,其他	Olive oil and its fractions, nes	1509.9000	4
油罐挂车及半挂车	Oil tanker trailers and semi-trailers	8716.3110	
油罐货车及类似车	Tank wagons and the like	8606.1000	37
油画、粉画及其他手绘画复制品	Paintings, drawings and pastels, reproductions	9701.1020	
油画、粉画及其他手绘画原件	Paintings, drawings and pastels, the orginals	9701.1010	
油画棒	Crayons	9609.1020	
油画布,制成的	Painting canvas, prepared	5901.9010	
油类及其他产品,芳族成分重量超过非芳族成分的	Oils and other products in which the weight of the aromatic constituents exceeds that of the non-aromatic constituents	2707.9990	6
油类及其他产品,蒸馏高温煤焦油所得的	Oils and other products of the distillation of high temperature coal tar	2707.9990	6
油漆滚筒及块垫	Paint pads and rollers	9603.4020	
油漆及清漆(包括瓷漆、大漆及水浆涂料),其他	Paints and varnishes (including enamels, lacquers and distempers), nes	3210.0000	36
油漆及清漆(包括瓷漆及大漆),其他,分散于或溶于非水介质的	Paints and varnishes (including enamels and lacquers), nes, dispersed or dissolved in a nonaqueous medium	3208.9090	136
油漆及清漆(包括瓷漆及大漆),其他,分散于或溶于水介质的	Paints and varnishes (including enamels and lacquers), nes, dispersed or dissolved in an aqueous medium	3209.9090	36
油漆及清漆(包括瓷漆及大漆),以丙烯酸聚合物或乙烯聚合物为基本成分,分散于或溶于水介质的	Paints and varnishes (including enamels and lacquers), based on acrylic or vinyl polymers, dispersed or dissolved in an aqueous medium	3209.1000	36

商品名称	Article Description	税则号列	申报要素
油漆及清漆(包括瓷漆及大漆),以丙烯酸聚合物为基本成分,分散于或溶于非水介质的	Paints and varnishes (including enamels and lacquers), based on acrylic polymers, dispersed or dissolved in a nonaqueous medium	3208.2010	136
油漆及清漆(包括瓷漆及大漆),以氟树脂为基本成分,分散于或溶于水介质的	Paints and varnishes (including enamels and lacquers), based on fluororesin, dispersed or dissolved in an aqueous medium	3209.9020	36
油漆及清漆(包括瓷漆及大漆),以环氧树脂为基本成分,分散于或溶于水介质的	Paints and varnishes (including enamels and lacquers), based on epoxy resin, dispersed or dissolved in an aqueous medium	3209.9010	36
油漆及清漆(包括瓷漆及大漆),以聚胺酯类化合物为基本成分,分散于或溶于非水介质的	Paints and varnishes (including enamels and lacquers), based on polyurethane polymers, dispersed or dissolved in a nonaqueous medium	3208.9010	136
油漆及清漆(包括瓷漆及大漆),以聚酯为基本成分,分散于或溶于非水介质的	Paints and varnishes (including enamels and lacquers), based on polyesters, dispersed or dissolved in a nonaqueous medium	3208.1000	136
油漆及清漆(包括瓷漆及大漆),以乙烯聚合物为基本成分,分散于或溶于非水介质的	Paints and varnishes (including enamels and lacquers), based on vinyl polymers, dispersed or dissolved in a nonaqueous medium	3208.2020	136
油漆溶剂油	Paint solvent	2710.1130	6
油漆刷,其他	Paint brushes, nes	9603.4019	3
油漆刷,猪鬃制	Paint brushes of pigs, hogs or boars bristle	9603.4011	
油鞣回收脂	Degras	1522.0000	4
油鞣皮革(包括结合鞣制的油鞣皮革)	Chamois (including combination chamois) leather	4114.1000	1458
油苫布,合成纤维制	Tarpaulins, of synthetic fibres	6306.1200	346
油苫布,麻制	Tarpaulins, of bast fibres	6306.1910	346
油苫布,棉制	Tarpaulins, of cotton	6306.1920	346
油苫布,其他	Tarpaulins, nes	6306.1990	346
油树脂,天然的	Balsams, of natural	1301.9090	
油树脂,提取的	Oleoresins extracted	3301.9010	34
油酸,工业用	Oleic acid, industrial use	3823.1200	6
油酸及其盐和酯	Oleic acids, their salts and esters	2916.1500	36
油桃,鲜的	Nectarines, fresh	0809.3000	1
油桐子	Tung nuts (oleococca seeds)	1207.9999	3
油页岩及焦油砂	Oil shale	2714.1000	1346
油印机	Stencil duplicating machines	8472.1000	
油印蜡纸,成卷或成张的,卷宽度超过36厘米,或长超过36厘米且宽超过15厘米	Duplicator stencils, in rolls or sheets, of width exceeding 36cm in roll or one side exceeding 36cm and other side exceeding 15cm in rectangular sheets	4809.9000	458
油印蜡纸,其他	Duplicator stencils, nes	4816.9090	58

Y

Y

商品名称	Article Description	税则号列	申报要素
油硬脂,未经乳化、混合或其他方法制作	Oleostearin, not emulsified or mixed or otherwise prepared	1503.0000	4
油渣,不适于供人食用的	Greaves	2301.1020	136
油渣饼	Oil cake, resulting from the extraction of soyabean oil	2304.0010	46
油渣饼,提炼花生油所得的	Oil cake, resulting from the extraction of groundnut oil	2305.0000	46
油渣饼及其他固体残渣,低芥子酸油菜子的	Oil cake and other solid residues, resulting from the extraction of low erucic acid rape or colza seeds	2306.4100	46
油渣饼及其他固体残渣,葵花子的	Oil cake and other solid residues, resulting from the extraction of sunflower seeds	2306.3000	46
油渣饼及其他固体残渣,棉子的	Oil cake and other solid residues, resulting from the extraction of cotton seeds	2306.1000	46
油渣饼及其他固体残渣,其他	Oil cake and other solid residues, resulting from the extraction of vegetable fats or oils, nes	2306.9000	46
油渣饼及其他固体残渣,亚麻子的	Oil cake and other solid residues, resulting from the extraction of linseed	2306.2000	46
油渣饼及其他固体残渣,椰子或干椰肉的	Oil cake and other solid residues, resulting from the extraction of coconut or copra	2306.5000	46
油渣饼及其他固体残渣,油菜子的,其他	Oil cake and other solid residues, resulting from the extraction of rape or colza seeds, nes	2306.4900	46
油渣饼及其他固体残渣,油棕果或油棕仁的	Oil cake and other solid residues, resulting from the extraction of palm nuts or kernels	2306.6000	46
油脂处理制剂,处理纺织材料、皮革、毛皮或其他材料的,含有石油或从沥青矿物提取的油类	Grease treatment preparations for textile materials, leather, furskins or other materials, containing petroleum oils or oils obtained from bituminous minerals	3403.1100	2368
油脂处理制剂,处理纺织材料、皮革、毛皮或其他材料的,其他	Grease treatment preparations for textile materials, leather, furskins or other materials, nes	3403.9100	2368
油棕果	Palm nuts	1207.9992	3
油棕仁	Kernels	1207.9992	3
柚	Pomelos	0805.4000	14
铀及其化合物,天然的	Uranium and its compounds, natural	2844.1000	
铀矿砂及其精矿	Uranium ores and concentrates	2612.1000	146
铀云母	Autunite	2612.1000	146
游览船,非机动船舶	Excursion boats, nes	8901.1090	5
游览船,机动船舶	Excursion boats, motor vessels	8901.1010	5
游乐场的娱乐设备,其他	Fairground amusements, nes	9508.9000	5
游丝,钟、表的	Hairsprings, of clock or watch	9114.1000	6
游戏机,其他	Video games, nes	9504.9010	5
游戏机,用硬币、钞票、银行卡、代币或其他支付方式使其工作的	Video games, operated by coins, bank notes, bank cards, tokens or by other means of payment	9504.3010	5
游戏机,与电视接收机配套使用的	Video games of a kind used with a television receiver	9504.1000	5

Y

商品名称	Article Description	税则号列	申报要素
游戏用品,用硬币、钞票、银行卡、代币或其他支付方式使其工作的,其他	Games, operated by coins, bank notes, bank cards, tokens or by other means of payment, nes	9504.3090	5
游戏用品,桌上的	Games, playing on the table	9504.9040	
游戏专用桌	Games tables, special designed	9504.9090	5
游艺场风琴	Fairground organs	9208.9000	5
游泳池	Swimming pools	9506.9900	5
游泳服,非针织或钩编的,男式	Swimwear, not knitted or crocheted, for men or boys	6211.1100	2456
游泳服,非针织或钩编的,女式	Swimwear, not knitted or crocheted, for women or girls	6211.1200	2456
游泳服,针织或钩编的,男式,合成纤维制	Swimwear, knitted or crocheted, for men or boys, of synthetic fibres	6112.3100	2456
游泳服,针织或钩编的,男式,其他纺织材料制	Swimwear, knitted or crocheted, for men or boys, of other textile materials	6112.3900	2456
游泳服,针织或钩编的,女式,合成纤维制	Swimwear, knitted or crocheted, for women or girls, of synthetic fibres	6112.4100	2456
游泳服,针织或钩编的,女式,其他纺织材料制	Swimwear, knitted or crocheted, for women or girls, of other textile materials	6112.4900	2456
鱿鱼,其他,冻、干、盐腌或盐渍的	Squid (Ommastrephes spp., Loligo spp., Nototodarus spp., Sepioteuthis spp.), frozen, dried, salted or in brine	0307.4900	148
鱿鱼,其他,活、鲜或冷的	Squid (Ommastrephes spp., Loligo spp., Nototodarus spp., Sepioteuthis spp.), live, fresh or chilled	0307.4190	18
鱿鱼,制作的	Squid, preserved	1605.9090	48
鱿鱼,种苗	Squid (Ommastrephes spp., Loligo spp., Nototodarus spp., Sepioteuthis spp.), for cultivation	0307.4110	3
鱿鱼粉,不适合食用	Squid flour, unfit for human consumption	2301.2090	136
鱿鱼粉,食用	Squid meal, fit for human consumption	0307.9990	14
鱿鱼制作的饵料	Squid for bait	0511.9190	34
有轨巷道堆垛机,电动的	Track alleyway stackers, powered by an electric motor	8427.1010	7
有机表面活性产品及制品,洁肤用的,液状或膏状并制成零售包装的,不论是否含有肥皂	Organic surface-active products and preparations for washing the skin, in the form of liquid or cream and put up for retail sale, whether or not containing soap	3401.3000	
有机表面活性产品及制品,条状、块状或模制形状的,盥洗用	Organic surface-active products and preparations, in the form of bars, cakes, moulded pieces or shapes, for toilet use	3401.1100	123
有机表面活性产品及制品浸渍、涂面或包覆的纸、絮胎、毡呢及无纺织物,盥洗用	Organic surface-active products and preparations impregnated (coated or covered) paper (wadding, felt and non-wovens), for toilet use	3401.1100	123
有机表面活性剂,不论是否零售包装,非离子型	Organic surface-active agents, whether or not put up for retail sale, non-ionic	3402.1300	56
有机表面活性剂,不论是否零售包装,其他	Organic surface-active agents, whether or not put up for retail sale, other	3402.1900	56

Y

商品名称	Article Description	税则号列	申报要素
有机表面活性剂,不论是否零售包装,阳离子型	Organic surface-active agents, whether or not put up for retail sale, cationic	3402.1200	56
有机表面活性剂,不论是否零售包装,阴离子型	Organic surface-active agents, whether or not put up for retail sale, anionic	3402.1100	56
有机表面活性剂制品,零售包装的,其他	Organic surface-active agents, preparations put up for retail sale, nes	3402.2090	36
有机表面活性剂制品,其他	Organic surface-active agents preparations, nes	3402.9000	36
有机复合溶剂,其他	Organic composite solvents, nes	3814.0000	36
有机复合稀释剂,其他	Organic composite thinners, nes	3814.0000	36
有机化合物,其他	Organic compounds, nes	2942.0000	
有机硫化合物,其他	Organo-sulphur compounds, nes	2930.9090	36
有机-无机化合物,其他	Organo-inorganic compounds, nes	2931.0000	36
有线设备,其他	Wired network equipments, nes	8517.6990	
有线数字通信设备,其他	Telecommunication apparatus for digital line system, nes	8517.6239	7
有线网络接口卡,有线数字通信设备	Wired network interface cards, telecommunication apparatus for digital line system	8517.6237	7
黝锰矿	Polianite	2602.0000	1346
黝铜矿	Tetrahedrite	2603.0000	146
右苯丙胺(INN)以及它们的盐	Dexamfetamine (INN), salts thereof	2921.4600	36
右丙氧吩(INN)及其盐	Dextropropoxyphene (INN) and its salts	2922.1400	36
右吗拉胺(INN)及盐	Dextromoramide (INN); salts thereof	2934.9100	36
釉底料及类似制品,陶瓷、搪瓷及玻璃工业用	Engobes and similar preparations, of a kind used in the ceramic, enamelling or glass industry	3207.2000	13
釉料及类似制品,陶瓷、搪瓷及玻璃工业用	Glazes and similar preparations, of a kind used in the ceramic, enamelling or glass industry	3207.2000	13
釉转印贴花纸(移画印花法用图案纸)	Transfers (decalcomanias), vitrifiable	4908.1000	4
yu			
纡子及类似品,木制	Cops and the like, of wood	4421.9010	56
鱼,活的,其他	Fish, living, nes	0301.9999	15
鱼,其他,冻的	Fish, nes, frozen	0303.7990	18
鱼,其他,鲜或冷的	Fishes, nes, fresh or chilled	0302.6990	18
鱼,其他,盐腌及盐渍的	Fish, nes, salted or in brine	0305.6990	4
鱼,其他,制作或保藏的	Fish, nes, prepared or preserved	1604.2099	48
鱼,其他,制作或保藏的,整条或切块,但未绞碎	Fish, nes, prepared or preserved, whole or in pieces, but not minced	1604.1990	48
鱼鳔胶	Isinglass	3503.0090	13
鱼翅,干的	Shark's fin, dried	0305.5920	4
鱼翅,制作或保藏的,其他	Shark's fin, nes, prepared or preserved	1604.2091	48
鱼刀,镀贵金属的	Fish knives, plated with precious metal	8215.9100	256

商品名称	Article Description	税则号列	申报要素
鱼刀,非镀贵金属的	Fish knives,other than plated with precious metal	8215.9900	256
鱼的产品,其他	Products of fish,nes	0511.9119	34
鱼粉,适合供人食用的	Flours, meals and pellets of fish, fit for human consumption	0305.1000	3
鱼粉,饲料用	Flours and meals of fish, of a kind used in animal feeding	2301.2010	1356
鱼肝,干、熏、盐腌或盐渍的	Livers of fish,dried,smoked, salted or in brine	0305.2000	4
鱼肝及鱼卵	Livers and roes	0303.8000	1
鱼肝及鱼卵,鲜或冷的	Livers and roes,fresh or chilled	0302.7000	1
鱼肝油及其分离品	Fish-liver oils and their fractions	1504.1000	346
鱼酱,罐头	Anchovy paste,in airtight container	1604.2019	48
鱼雷发射管及类似发射装置自推进的	Torpedo tubes and similar projectors	9301.2000	
鱼雷及其零件	Torpedoes and parts	9306.9000	3
鱼卵,干、熏、盐腌或盐渍的	Roes of fish,dried,smoked, salted or in brine	0305.2000	4
鱼苗,其他	Fry,nes	0301.9919	15
鱼苗,鳟鱼	Fry,of oncorhynchus aguabonita	0301.9110	15
鱼苗,鳟鱼	Fry,of oncorhynchus apache	0301.9110	15
鱼苗,鳟鱼	Fry,of oncorhynchus chrysogaster	0301.9110	15
鱼苗,鳟鱼	Fry,of oncorhynchus clarki	0301.9110	15
鱼苗,鳟鱼	Fry,of oncorhynchus gilae	0301.9110	15
鱼苗,鳟鱼	Fry,of oncorhynchus my kiss	0301.9110	15
鱼苗,鳟鱼	Fry,of salmo trutta	0301.9110	15
鱼片,斑点叉尾鮰鱼的,冻的	Fillets,channel catfish(Ictalurus Punctatus),frozen	0304.2921	18
鱼片,叉尾鮰鱼的,其他,冻的	Fillets of ictalurus,nes,frozen	0304.2929	18
鱼片,剑鱼的,冻的	Fillets,swordfish (Xiphias gladius),frozen	0304.2100	18
鱼片,剑鱼的,鲜或冷的,不论是否绞碎	Fish fillets, swordfish (Xiphias gladius), fresh or chilled	0304.1100	18
鱼片,罗非鱼的,冻的	Fillets of tilapia,frozen	0304.2910	18
鱼片,南极犬牙鱼的,冻的	Fillets,toothfish (Dissostichus spp.),frozen	0304.2200	18
鱼片,南极犬牙鱼的,鲜或冷的,不论是否绞碎	Fish fillets, toothfish (Dissostichus spp.), fresh or chilled	0304.1200	18
鱼片,其他,冻的	Fillets,nes,frozen	0304.2990	18
鱼片,其他,鲜或冷的,不论是否绞碎	Fish fillets,nes,fresh or chilled	0304.1900	18
鱼片,盐腌或盐渍的	Fish fillets,dried, salted or in brine	0305.3000	4
鱼肉,剑鱼,冻的	Fish meat,swordfish,whether or not minced,frozen	0304.9100	18
鱼肉,剑鱼的,鲜或冷的,不论是否绞碎	Fish meat (whether or not minced), swordfish (Xiphias gladius),fresh or chilled	0304.1100	18
鱼肉,南极犬牙鱼,冻的	Fish meat, toothfish,whether or not minced,frozen	0304.9200	18
鱼肉,南极犬牙鱼的,鲜或冷的,不论是否绞碎	Fish meat (whether or not minced), toothfish (Dissostichus spp.),fresh or chilled	0304.1200	18
鱼肉,其他,冻的	Fish meat,nes,whether or not minced,frozen	0304.9900	18

Y

Y

商品名称	Article Description	税则号列	申报要素
鱼肉,其他,鲜或冷的,不论是否绞碎	Fish meat (whether or not minced), nes, fresh or chilled	0304.1900	18
鱼藤根	Derris roots	1211.9091	34
鱼尾板及钢轨垫板	Fish-plates and sole plates	7302.4000	6
渔网,化学纤维材料制	Fishing nets of man-made textile materials	5608.1100	34
宇宙射线的测量或检验仪器及装置	Cosmic radiations measuring or detecting instruments and apparatus	9030.1000	
羽管键琴	Clavichords	9201.9000	5
羽毛,不完整,粉末及废料	Feathers, powder and waste or parts of feathers	0505.9010	34
羽毛,填充用	Feathers of a kind used for stuffing	0505.1000	34
羽毛、部分羽毛及其制品	Feathers, parts of feathers and articles thereof	6701.0000	
羽毛及其鸟皮或鸟体其他部分	Feathers with their skins and other parts of birds	6701.0000	
羽毛球拍	Badminton rackets	9506.5900	5
羽绒	Down, of birds	0505.1000	34
羽绒服,非针织或钩编的,男式	Downwear, not knitted or crocheted, for men or boys, padded with feathers or down	6201.1310	2456
羽绒服,非针织或钩编的,男式,充绒,化学纤维制,其他	Downwear, not knitted or crocheted, for men or boys, padded with feathers or down, of man-made fibres, nes	6201.9310	2456
羽绒服,非针织或钩编的,男式,充绒,棉制,大衣式	Downwear, not knitted or crocheted, for men or boys, padded with feathers or down, of cotton, overcoats	6201.1210	2456
羽绒服,非针织或钩编的,男式,充绒,棉制,其他	Downwear, not knitted or crocheted, for men or boys, padded with feathers or down, of cotton, nes	6201.9210	2456
羽绒服,非针织或钩编的,女式,充绒	Downwear, not knitted or crocheted, for women or girls, padded with feathers or down	6202.1310	2456
羽绒服,非针织或钩编的,女式,充绒,化学纤维制,其他	Downwear, not knitted or crocheted, for women or girls, padded with feathers or down, of man-made fibres, nes	6202.9310	2456
羽绒服,非针织或钩编的,女式,充绒,棉制,大衣式	Downwear, not knitted or crocheted, for women or girls, padded with feathers or down, of cotton, overcoats	6202.1210	2456
羽绒服,非针织或钩编的,女式,充绒,棉制,其他	Downwear, not knitted or crocheted, for women or girls, padded with feathers or down, of cotton, nes	6202.9210	2456
羽绒及其鸟皮或鸟体其他部分	Down with their skins and other parts of birds	6701.0000	
羽绒及其制品	Down and articles thereof	6701.0000	
羽扇豆,饲料用	Lupines, forage products	1214.9000	
羽衣甘蓝,鲜或冷藏的	Kale, fresh or chilled	0704.9090	1
雨伞及阳伞,其他	Umbrellas and sun umbrellas, nes	6601.9900	
雨伞及阳伞,折叠	Umbrellas and sun umbrellas, having a telescopic shaft	6601.9100	
雨衣,非针织或钩编的,男式	Raincoats, not knitted or crocheted, for men or boys, of man-made fibres	6201.1390	2456

商品名称	Article Description	税则号列	申报要素
雨衣,非针织或钩编的,男式,棉制	Raincoats, not knitted or crocheted, for men or boys, of cotton	6201. 1290	2456
雨衣,非针织或钩编的,男式,其他纺织材料制	Raincoats, not knitted or crocheted, for men or boys, of other textile materials	6201. 1900	2456
雨衣,非针织或钩编的,男式,羊毛或动物细毛制	Raincoats, not knitted or crocheted, for men or boys, of wool or fine animal hair	6201. 1100	2456
雨衣,非针织或钩编的,女式,化学纤维制	Raincoats, not knitted or crocheted, for women or girls, of man-made fibres	6202. 1390	2456
雨衣,非针织或钩编的,女式,棉制	Raincoats, not knitted or crocheted, for women or girls, of cotton	6202. 1290	2456
雨衣,非针织或钩编的,女式,其他纺织材料制	Raincoats, not knitted or crocheted, for women or girls, of other textile materials	6202. 1900	2456
雨衣,非针织或钩编的,女式,羊毛或动物细毛制	Raincoats, not knitted or crocheted, for women or girls, of wool or fine animal hair	6202. 1100	2456
玉米,其他	Maize(corn), nes	1005. 9000	3
玉米,其他加工的	Maize corn, other worked	1104. 2300	4
玉米,种用	Maize(corn), seed	1005. 1000	3
玉米蛋白	Zein	3504. 0090	1346
玉米片,经膨化或烘炒制成的	Corn flakes, obtained by the swelling or roasting	1904. 1000	48
玉米油及其分离品,初榨的	Maize (corn) oil and its fractions, crude oil	1515. 2100	4
玉米油及其分离品,其他	Maize (corn) oil and its fractions, nes	1515. 2900	4
芋头	Dasheens	0714. 9030	34
芋头	Taroes(Colocasia esculenta)	0714. 9030	34
芋头	Taros	0714. 9030	34
育雏器,家禽用	Brooders for poultry	8436. 2100	
浴缸, 陶制	Baths, of pottery	6910. 9000	268
浴缸,瓷制	Baths, of porcelain or china	6910. 1000	268
浴缸,钢铁制,其他	Baths, of iron or steel, nes	7324. 2900	24
浴缸,铸铁制,不论是否搪瓷	Baths, of cast iron, whether or not enamelled	7324. 2100	24
浴巾,毛巾织物或类似的毛圈织物的,棉制	Bath towels of terry towelling or similar terry fabrics, of cotton	6302. 6010	346
浴衣、晨衣及类似品,非针织或钩编的,男式,化学纤维制	Bathrobes, dressing gowns and similar articles, not knitted or crocheted, for men or boys, of man-made fibres	6207. 9920	2456
浴衣、晨衣及类似品,非针织或钩编的,男式,棉制	Bathrobes, dressing gowns and similar articles, not knitted or crocheted, for men or boys, of cotton	6207. 9100	2456
浴衣、晨衣及类似品,非针织或钩编的,男式,其他	Bathrobes, dressing gowns and similar articles, not knitted or crocheted, for men or boys, nes	6207. 9990	2456
浴衣、晨衣及类似品,非针织或钩编的,女式,化学纤维制	Bathrobes, dressing gowns and similar articles, not knitted or crocheted, for women or girls, of man-made fibres	6208. 9200	2456
浴衣、晨衣及类似品,非针织或钩编的,女式,棉制	Bathrobes, dressing gowns and similar articles, not knitted or crocheted, for women or girls, of cotton	6208. 9100	2456

Y

商品名称	Article Description	税则号列	申报要素
浴衣、晨衣及类似品，非针织或钩编的，女式，其他	Bathrobes, dressing gowns and similar articles, not knitted or crocheted, for women or girls, nes	6208.9990	2456
浴衣、晨衣及类似品，非针织或钩编的，女式，丝及绢丝制	Bathrobes, dressing gowns and similar articles, not knitted or crocheted, for women or girls, of silk or silk waste	6208.9910	2456
浴衣、晨衣及类似品，针织或钩编的，女式，化学纤维制	Bathrobes, dressing gowns and similar articles, knitted or crocheted, for women or girls, of man-made fibres	6108.9200	2456
浴衣、晨衣及类似品，针织或钩编的，女式，棉制	Bathrobes, dressing gowns and similar articles, knitted or crocheted, for women or girls, of cotton	6108.9100	2456
浴衣、晨衣及类似品，针织或钩编的，女式，其他纺织材料制	Bathrobes, dressing gowns and similar articles, knitted or crocheted, for women or girls, of other textile materials	6108.9900	2456
浴衣、晨衣及类似品，针织或钩编的男式，化学纤维制	Bathrobes, dressing gowns and similar articles, knitted or crocheted, for men or boys, of man-made fibres	6107.9910	2456
浴衣、晨衣及类似品，针织或钩编的男式，棉制	Bathrobes, dressing gowns and similar articles, knitted or crocheted, for men or boys, of cotton	6107.9100	2456
浴衣、晨衣及类似品，针织或钩编的男式，其他	Bathrobes, dressing gowns and similar articles, knitted or crocheted, for men or boys, nes	6107.9990	2456
浴衣、晨衣及类似品非针织或钩编的，男式，丝及绢丝制	Bathrobes, dressing gowns and similar articles, not knitted or crocheted, for men or boys, of silk or silk waste	6207.9910	2456
预处理机器，纺织纤维的，其他	Preparing machines for textile fibres, nes	8445.1900	7
预应力混凝土管、杆、板、桩等	Prestressed concrete tubes, pipes, rods, plates, piles and similar articles	6810.9110	56
预制结构件，建筑或土木工程用的，其他	Prefabricated structural components for building or civil engineering, nes	6810.9190	56
愈创木酚	Guaiacol	2909.5000	36
yuan			
鸢尾，种用，休眠的	Iris, seed, dormant	0601.1091	135
鸢尾凝脂	Balsam of irises	3301.3010	34
鸢尾酮	Irone	2914.2300	36
园艺用机器，包括装有机械或热力装置的催芽设备，其他	Horticultural machinery, including germination plant fitted with mechanical or thermal equipment, nes	8436.8000	
园艺用机器零件，其他	Horticultural machinery parts, nes	8436.9900	3
原电池，废的	Primary cells, spent	8548.1000	3
原电池及原电池组，二氧化锰的，其他	Primary cells and primary batteries, manganese dioxide, nes	8506.1090	68
原电池及原电池组，碱性锌锰的，扣式	Button shape primary cells and primary batteries, alkaline zinc-manganese dioxide	8506.1011	68
原电池及原电池组，碱性锌锰的，其他	Primary cells and primary batteries, alkaline zinc-manganese dioxide, nes	8506.1019	68

商品名称	Article Description	税则号列	申报要素
原电池及原电池组,碱性锌锰的,圆柱型	Cylindrical shape primary cells and primary batteries, alkaline zinc-manganese dioxide	8506.1012	68
原电池及原电池组,锂的	Primary cells and primary batteries, lithium	8506.5000	68
原电池及原电池组,其他	Primary cells and primary batteries, nes	8506.8000	68
原电池及原电池组,锌空气的	Primary cells and primary batteries, air-zinc	8506.6000	68
原电池及原电池组,氧化汞的	Primary cells and primary batteries, mercuric oxide	8506.3000	68
原电池及原电池组,氧化银的	Primary cells and primary batteries, silver oxide	8506.4000	68
原电池及原电池组零件,二氧化锰的	Primary cells and primary batteries parts, manganese dioxide	8506.9010	3
原电池及原电池组零件,其他	Primary cells and primary batteries parts, nes	8506.9090	3
原电池组,废的	Primary batteries, spent	8548.1000	3
原木,奥克曼(奥克榄)	Wood in the rough, okoume(Aukoumed Klaineana)	4403.4920	458
原木,白松(云杉和冷杉)	Wood in the rough, white pine (spruce and fir)	4403.2020	458
原木,北美硬阔叶木(包括樱桃木、黑胡桃木、枫木)	Wood in the rough, north american hard wood (including cherry, walnut, and maple)	4403.9960	458
原木,大干巴豆(门格里斯或康派斯)	Wood in the rough, Koompassia spp. (Mengaris or Kempas)	4403.4960	458
原木,辐射松	Wood in the rough, radiata pine	4403.2030	458
原木,红木	Wood in the rough, of rosewood	4403.9930	458
原木,红松和樟子松	Wood in the rough, korean pine and Mongolian scotch pine	4403.2010	458
原木,栎木(橡木)	Wood in the rough, of oak(Quercus spp.)	4403.9100	458
原木,柳桉木(深红、浅红、巴栲红)	Wood in the rough, Meranti(Dark Red Meranti, Light Red Metanti and Meranti Bakau)	4403.4100	458
原木,龙脑香木(克隆)	Wood in the rough, Dipterocarpus spp. Keruing	4403.4930	458
原木,落叶松	Wood in the rough, larch	4403.2040	458
原木,楠木	Wood in the rough, of nan mu(Phoebe)	4403.9910	458
原木,泡桐木	Wood in the rough, of Kiri(Paulownia)	4403.9940	458
原木,其他	Wood in the rough, nes	4403.9990	458
原木,热带非针叶木,其他	Wood in the rough, tropical non-coniferous, nes	4403.4990	458
原木,山毛榉木	Wood in the rough, of beech(Fagus spp.)	4403.9200	458
原木,山樟(香木)	Wood in the rough, Kapur(Dryobalanops spp.)	4403.4940	458
原木,水曲柳	Wood in the rough, ash	4403.9950	458
原木,温带非针叶木,其他	Wood in the rough, temperate non-coniferous, nes	4403.9980	458
原木,异翅香木	Wood in the rough, Anisopter spp.	4403.4970	458
原木,印加木(波罗格)	Wood in the rough, Intsia spp. (Mengaris)	4403.4950	458
原木,用油漆、着色剂、杂酚油或其他防腐剂处理	Wood in the rough, treated with paint, stains, creosote or other preservatives	4403.1000	458
原木,柚木	Wood in the rough, teak	4403.4910	458
原木,樟木	Wood in the rough, of camphor wood	4403.9920	458
原木,针叶木,其他	Wood in the rough, coniferous, nes	4403.2090	458
原油,从沥青矿物提取的	Crude oils obtained from bituminous minerals	2709.0000	56

Y

Y

商品名称	Article Description	税则号列	申报要素
原油船,载重量不超过 15 万吨	Crude oil tanker ships, loading not exceeding 150000t	8901.2021	8
原油船,载重量超过 15 万吨,但不超过 30 万吨	Crude oil tanker ships, loading exceeding 150000t, but not exceeding 300000t	8901.2022	8
原油船,载重量超过 30 万吨	Crude oil tanker ships, loading exceeding 300000t	8901.2023	8
圆锯片,包括部件,其他	Circular saw blades, including parts, nes	8202.3900	256
圆锯片,带有钢制工作部件	Circular saw blades, with working part of steel	8202.3100	256
圆帽片及制帽用的毡呢筒(包括裁开的毡呢筒),毡呢制的	Plateaux and manchons (including slit manchons), of felt	6501.0000	26
圆盘锯,加工石料、陶瓷、混凝土、石棉水泥或类似矿物材料的	Disk sawing machines, for working stone, ceramics, concrete, asbestos-cement or like mineral materials	8464.1010	7
圆盘耙,农业、园艺及林业用	Disc harrows, for agricultural, horticultural or forestry use	8432.2100	
圆签、圆棒及类似一次性制品,木制	Circle sticks, circle bars and the like, of wood	4421.9021	56
圆签、圆棒及类似一次性制品,其他	Circle sticks, circle bars and the like, nes	4421.9029	56
圆签、圆棒及类似一次性制品,竹制	Circle sticks, circle bars and the like, of bamboo	4421.9022	56
圆网印刷机	Cylinder screen press	8443.1921	57
圆型针织机,圆筒直径不超过 165 毫米	Circular knitting machines, with cylinder diameter not exceeding 165mm	8447.1100	
圆型针织机,圆筒直径超过 165 毫米	Circular knitting machines, with cylinder diameter exceeding165mm	8447.1200	
圆珠笔	Ball point pens	9608.1000	
圆珠笔芯,由圆珠笔头和墨芯构成	Ball point pens refills	9608.6000	
圆柱形滚子轴承,其他	Cylindrical roller bearings, nes	8482.5000	5
圆柱型原电池及原电池组,碱性锌锰的	Cylindrical shape primary cells and primary batteries, alkaline zinc-manganese dioxide	8506.1012	68
yue			
月桂叶	Bay leaves	0910.9900	6
钥匙,单独报验的,贱金属制	Keys presented separately, of base metal	8301.7000	256
越桔,鲜的	Bilberries, fresh	0810.4000	1
越野车(4 轮驱动),气缸容量(排气量)超过 2500 毫升,但不超过 3000 毫升,装有点燃往复式活塞内燃发动机的	Cross-country cars (4WD), of a cylinder capacity exceeding 2500cc but not exceeding 3000cc, with spark-ignition internal combustion reciprocating piston	8703.2362	58
越野车(4 轮驱动),气缸容量(排气量)超过 4000 毫升,装有点燃往复式活塞内燃发动机的	Cross-country cars (4WD), of a cylinder capacity exceeding 4000cc, with spark-ignition internal combustion reciprocating piston	8703.2422	58
越野车(4 轮驱动),气缸容量(排气量)不超过 1000 毫升,装有点燃往复式活塞内燃发动机的	Cross-country cars (4WD), of a cylinder capacity not exceeding 1000cc, with spark-ignition internal combustion reciprocating piston engine	8703.2140	58

商品名称	Article Description	税则号列	申报要素
越野车(4 轮驱动),气缸容量(排气量)超过 1000 毫升,但不超过 1500 毫升,装有点燃往复式活塞内燃发动机的	Cross-country cars (4WD), of a cylinder capacity exceeding 1000cc but not exceeding 1500cc, with spark-ignition internal combustion reciprocating piston	8703.2240	58
越野车(4 轮驱动),气缸容量(排气量)超过 1000 毫升,但不超过 1500 毫升,装有压燃式活塞内燃发动机的	Cross-country cars (4WD), of a cylinder capacity exceeding 1000cc but not exceeding 1500cc, with compression-ignition internal combustion piston engine	8703.3122	58
越野车(4 轮驱动),气缸容量(排气量)超过 1500 毫升,但不超过 2000 毫升,装有点燃往复式活塞内燃发动机的	Cross-country cars (4WD), of a cylinder capacity exceeding 1500cc but not exceeding 2000cc, with spark-ignition internal combustion reciprocating piston	8703.2342	58
越野车(4 轮驱动),气缸容量(排气量)超过 1500 毫升,但不超过 2000 毫升,装有压燃式活塞内燃发动机的	Cross-country cars (4WD), of a cylinder capacity exceeding 1500cc but not exceeding 2000cc, with compression-ignition internal combustion piston engine	8703.3212	58
越野车(4 轮驱动),气缸容量(排气量)超过 2000 毫升,但不超过 2500 毫升,装有点燃往复式活塞内燃发动机的	Cross-country cars (4WD), of a cylinder capacity exceeding 2000cc but not exceeding 2500cc, with spark-ignition internal combustion reciprocating piston	8703.2352	58
越野车(4 轮驱动),气缸容量(排气量)超过 2000 毫升,但不超过 2500 毫升,装有压燃式活塞内燃发动机的	Cross-country cars (4WD), of a cylinder capacity exceeding 2000cc but not exceeding 2500cc, with compression-ignition internal combustion piston engine	8703.3222	58
越野车(4 轮驱动),气缸容量(排气量)超过 2500 毫升,但不超过 3000 毫升,装有压燃式活塞内燃发动机的	Cross-country cars (4WD), of a cylinder capacity exceeding 2500cc, but not exceeding 3000cc, with compression-ignition internal combustion piston engine	8703.3312	58
越野车(4 轮驱动),气缸容量(排气量)超过 3000 毫升,但不超过 4000 毫升,装有点燃往复式活塞内燃发动机的	Cross-country cars (4WD), of a cylinder capacity exceeding 3000cc, but not exceeding 4000cc, with spark-ignition internal combustion reciprocating piston	8703.2412	58
越野车(4 轮驱动),气缸容量(排气量)超过 3000 毫升,但不超过 4000 毫升,装有压燃式活塞内燃发动机的	Cross-country cars (4WD), of a cylinder capacity exceeding 3000cc, but not exceeding 4000cc, with compression-ignition internal combustion piston engine	8703.3322	58
越野车(4 轮驱动),气缸容量(排气量)超过 4000 毫升,装有压燃式活塞内燃发动机的	Cross-country cars (4WD), of a cylinder capacity exceeding 4000cc, with compression-ignition internal combustion piston engine	8703.3362	58
越野车(4 轮驱动)用零件、附件,其他	Cross-country cars (4wd) parts and accessories, nes	8708.9959	3
越野滑雪鞋靴,橡胶、塑料、皮革或再生皮革制外底,皮革制鞋面的	Cross-country ski footwear, with outer soles of rubber, plastics, leather or composition leather and upers of leather	6403.1200	26

Y

商品名称	Article Description	税则号列	申报要素
越野滑雪鞋靴及滑雪板靴,橡胶或塑料制外底及鞋面的	Cross-country ski footwear, with outer soles and uppers of rubber or plastics	6402.1200	26
乐锯	Musical saws	9208.9000	5
乐谱原稿或印本,不论是否装订或印有插图	Music, printed or in manuscript, whether or not bound or illustrated	4904.0000	5
乐器,通过电产生或扩大声音的,其他	Musical instruments, the sound of which is produced or must be amplified electrically, nes	9207.9000	5
yun			
云母,已加工的,其他	Mica, worked, nes	6814.9000	6
云母,原状的	Mica, crude	2525.1000	13
云母废料	Mica waste	2525.3000	13
云母粉	Mica powder	2525.2000	13
云母片,劈开的	Mica rifted into sheets or splittings	2525.1000	13
云母制的板、片、带,粘聚或再制云母的,不论是否附于其他材料上	Mica plates, sheets and strips of agglomerated or reconstituted mica, whether or not on a support	6814.1000	6
云母制品,已加工的,其他	Mica articles, worked, nes	6814.9000	6
芸豆,其他,脱荚的,干的	Kidney beans, including white pea beans (phaseolus vulgaris), nes, dried, shelled	0713.3390	34
芸豆,种用,脱荚的,干的	Kidney beans, including white pea beans (phaseolus vulgaris), seed, dried, shelled	0713.3310	34
芸香苷及其衍生物	Rutoside (rutin) and its derivatives	2938.1000	34
孕激素	Progestogens	2937.2300	36
运动服,非针织或钩编的,男式,化学纤维制	Track suits, not knitted or crocheted, for men or boys, of man-made fibres	6211.3320	2456
运动服,非针织或钩编的,男式,棉制	Track suits, not knitted or crocheted, for men or boys, of cotton	6211.3220	2456
运动服,非针织或钩编的,女式,化学纤维制,其他	Track suits, not knitted or crocheted, for women or girls, of man-made fibres, nes	6211.4310	2456
运动服,非针织或钩编的,女式,棉制,其他	Track suits, not knitted or crocheted, for women or girls, of cotton, nes	6211.4210	2456
运动服,针织或钩编的,合成纤维制	Track suits, knitted or crocheted, of synthetic fibres	6112.1200	2456
运动服,针织或钩编的,棉制	Track suits, knitted or crocheted, of cotton	6112.1100	2456
运动服,针织或钩编的,其他纺织材料制	Track suits, knitted or crocheted, of other textile materials	6112.1900	2456
运动鞋靴,橡胶、塑料、皮革或再生皮革制外底,皮革制鞋面的,其他	Sports footwear, with outer soles of rubber, plastics, leather or composition leather and upers of leather, nes	6403.1900	26
运动鞋靴,橡胶或塑料制外底及鞋面的,其他	Sports footwear, with outer soles and uppers of rubber or plastics, nes	6402.1900	26
运动鞋靴;网球鞋、篮球鞋、体操鞋、训练鞋及类似鞋,橡胶或塑料制外底的鞋靴,纺织材料制鞋面的	Sports footwear, tennis shoes, basketball shoes, gym shoes, training shoes and the like	6404.1100	26

商品名称	Article Description	税则号列	申报要素
运动用步枪,其他	Sporting rifles, nes	9303.3000	
运动用猎枪,包括组合式滑膛来复枪	Sporting shotguns, including combination shotgun rifles	9303.2000	
运送机械,对泥土、矿物或矿石的,非自推进的,其他	Moving machinery, for earth, minerals or ores, not self-propelled, nes	8430.6990	5
运送机械,对泥土、矿物或矿石的,自推进的,其他	Moving machinery, for earth, minerals or ores, self-propelled, nes	8430.5090	5
熨烫机	Ironing machines	8451.3000	
熨烫机零件	Ironing machines parts	8451.9000	

Z

Z

商品名称	Article Description	税则号列	申报要素
za			
杂醇油	Fusel oil	3824. 9010	36
杂酚油	Creosote oils	2707. 9100	6
杂环化合物，其他	Heteroeyclic compounds, nes	2934. 9990	36
杂碎，鹅的，鲜或冷的	Offal of geese, fresh or chilled	0207. 3520	1
杂碎，鹅的，冻的	Offal of geese, frozen	0207. 3620	1
杂碎，海牛的，鲜或冷或冻的，食用	Offal of manatees, fresh, chilled or frozen, edible	0208. 4000	15
杂碎，海豚的，鲜或冷或冻的，食用	Offal of dolphins, fresh, chilled or frozen, edible	0208. 4000	15
杂碎，火鸡的，冻的	Offal of turkeys, frozen	0207. 2700	1
杂碎，火鸡的，鲜或冷的	Offal of turkeys, fresh or chilled	0207. 2600	1
杂碎，鸡的，其他，冻的	Offal of fowls of the species gallus domesticus, nes, frozen	0207. 1429	1
杂碎，鸡的，其他，鲜或冷的	Offal of fowls of the species gallus domesticus, nes, fresh or chilled	0207. 1329	1
杂碎，家兔的，食用	Offal of rabbits, edible	0208. 1090	145
杂碎，鲸的，鲜或冷或冻的，食用	Offal of whales, fresh, chilled or frozen, edible	0208. 4000	15
杂碎，灵长目的，鲜或冷或冻的，食用	Offal of primates and, fresh, chilled or frozen, edible	0208. 3000	15
杂碎，驴的，冻的，食用	Offal of asses, frozen, edible	0206. 9000	15
杂碎，驴的，鲜或冷的，食用	Offal of asses, fresh or chilled, edible	0206. 8000	15
杂碎，骡的，冻的，食用	Offal of mules or hinnies, frozen, edible	0206. 9000	15
杂碎，骡的，鲜或冷的，食用	Offal of mules or hinnies, fresh or chilled, edible	0206. 8000	15
杂碎，马的，冻的，食用	Offal of horses, frozen, edible	0206. 9000	15
杂碎，马的，鲜或冷的，食用	Offal of horses, fresh or chilled, edible	0206. 8000	15
杂碎，绵羊的，冻的，食用	Offal of goats, frozen, edible	0206. 9000	15
杂碎，绵羊的，鲜或冷的，食用	Offal of goats, fresh or chilled, edible	0206. 8000	15
杂碎，牛的，冻的，食用，其他	Offal of bovine animals, frozen, edible, nes	0206. 2900	15
杂碎，牛的，鲜或冷的，食用	Offal of bovine animals, fresh or chilled, edible	0206. 1000	15
杂碎，爬行动物（包括蛇及龟鳖）的，食用	Offal, of reptiles (including snakes and turtles), fresh, chilled or frozen, edible	0208. 5000	15
杂碎，其他，鲜或冷或冻的，食用	Offal nes, fresh, chilled or frozen, edible	0208. 9090	145
杂碎，儒艮（海牛目哺乳动物）的，鲜或冷或冻的，食用	Offal of dugongs (mammals of the order sirenia), fresh, chilled or frozen, edible	0208. 4000	15
杂碎，乳鸽的，鲜或冷或冻的，食用	Offal of squabs, fresh, chilled or frozen, edible	0208. 9010	15
杂碎，山羊的，冻的	Offal of sheep, frozen, edible	0206. 9000	15
杂碎，山羊的，鲜或冷的	Offal of sheep, fresh or chilled, edible	0206. 8000	15
杂碎，鼠海豚（鲸目哺乳动物）的，鲜或冷或冻的，食用	Offal of porpoises (mammals of the order cetacea), fresh, chilled or frozen, edible	0208. 4000	15

商品名称	Article Description	税则号列	申报要素
杂碎,鸭的,冻的	Offal of ducks,frozen	0207.3610	1
杂碎,鸭的,鲜或冷的	Offal of ducks,fresh or chilled	0207.3510	1
杂碎,野兔的,食用	Offal of hares,edible	0208.1090	145
杂碎,珍珠鸡的,冻的	Offal of guinea fowls,frozen	0207.3630	1
杂碎,珍珠鸡的,鲜或冷的	Offal of guinea fowls,fresh or chilled	0207.3530	1
杂碎,猪的,冻的,其他	Offal of swine,frozen,edible,nes	0206.4900	15
杂碎,猪的,鲜或冷的,食用	Offal of swine,fresh or chilled,edible	0206.3000	15
杂碎粉,灵长目的,食用	Flours and meals of offal of primates,edible	0210.9100	14
杂碎粉,爬行动物(包括蛇及龟鳖)的,食用	Flours and meals of offal of reptiles(including snakes and turtles),edible	0210.9300	14
杂碎粉,食用,其他	Flours and meals of offal,edible,nes	0210.9900	14
甾族激素及其衍生物和结构类似物,其他	Steroidal hormones, their derivatives and structural analogues,nes	2937.2900	36
zai			
载体催化剂,其他	Supported catalysts,nes	3815.1900	36
载体催化剂,以贵金属及其化合物为活性物的	Supported catalysts, with precious metal or precious metal compounds as the active substance	3815.1200	36
载体催化剂,以镍及其化合物为活性物的	Supported catalysts,with nickel or nickel compounds as the active substance	3815.1100	36
再熔胶	Run gums	3806.9000	4
再生皮革,以皮革或皮革纤维为基本成分的,成块、成张或成条,不论是否成卷	Composition leather with a basis of leather or leather fibre, in slabs, sheets or strip, whether or not in rolls	4115.1000	1458
再生橡胶,初级形状或板、片、带	Reclaimed rubber in primary forms or in plates, sheets or strip	4003.0000	14
再造烟草	Reconstituted tobacco	2403.9100	
zao			
凿井机械的零件,其他	Parts of sinking machinery,nes	8431.4390	3
凿榫机器,加工木材、软木、骨、硬质橡胶、硬质塑料或类似硬质材料的	Mortising machines, for working wood, cork, bone, hard rubber, hard plastics or similar hard materials	8465.9500	7
凿岩或钻探工具,带有金属陶瓷制的工作部件,可互换	Rock drilling or earth boring tools,with working part of cermets,interchangeable	8207.1300	256
凿岩或钻探工具,带有天然或合成金刚石、立方氮化硼制的工作部件,可互换	Rock drilling or earth boring tools,with working part of natural or synthetic diamonds or cubic boron nitride,interchangeable	8207.1910	256
凿岩或钻探工具,可互换,其他	Rock drilling or earth boring tools, interchangeable, nes	8207.1990	256
凿岩机,其他	Rock cutters,nes	8430.3900	5
凿岩机,自推进的	Rock cutters,self-propelled	8430.3100	5
凿岩机零件	Rock cutters parts	8431.4990	3
凿子,木工用	Chisels, for working wood	8205.3000	256

Z

商品名称	Article Description	税则号列	申报要素
凿子及类似切削工具,木工用	Gouges and similar cutting tools for working wood	8205.3000	256
枣,水晶枣,用糖保存的	Jujubes, crystallised jujubes, preserved by sugar	2006.0090	48
枣,医药级	Jujubes, used in pharmacy	1211.9039	34
枣,暂时保藏的	Jujubes, provisionally preserved	0812.9000	34
枣,鲜的	Jujubes, fresh	0810.9090	1
藻酸及其盐和酯,初级形状的	Alginic acid, its salts and esters, in primary forms	3913.1000	146
皂石,破碎或研粉	Soapstone, crushed or powdered	2526.2010	4
皂石,未破碎及未研粉	Soapstone, not crushed, not powdered	2526.1010	4
造口术用具	Ostomy use appliances	3006.9100	3
噪声计,通讯专用的	Psophometers, specially designed for telecommunications	9030.4090	7
zeng			
增湿器,空气的	Humidifiers for air	8479.8920	7
增湿器用零件,空气的	Humidifiers parts, for air	8479.9020	3
增炭剂	Carburetant	3824.9030	36
增压器,发动机用	Superchargers for engines	8414.8030	23
增益测量仪,通讯专用的	Gain measuring instruments, specially designed for telecommunications	9030.4090	7
甑,含有按重量计超过50%的三氧化二铝或三氧化二铝和二氧化硅的混合物或化合物	Retorts, containing by weight more than 50% of alumina(Al_2O_3) or of a mixture of compound of alumina and of silica(SiO_2)	6903.2000	6
甑,含有按重量计超过50%的石墨、其他碳或其混合物	Retorts, containing by weight more than 50% of graphite or other carbon or of a mixture of these pro-ducts	6903.1000	6
甑炭	Retort carbon	2704.0090	34
zang			
藏红花,种用,休眠的	Crocus bulbs, seed, dormant	0601.1091	135
藏花醛	Safranal	2912.2990	36
zha			
渣粉及团粒,甲壳动物、软体动物或其他水生无脊椎动物的	Flours, meals and pellets, of crustaceans, molluscs or other aquatic invertebrates	2301.2090	136
渣粉及团粒,肉的或杂碎的,其他,不适于供人食用的	Flours, meals and pellets, of meat or meat offal, nes	2301.1090	136
轧管机,定减径的	Tube mills, fixed and reduced	8455.1030	7
轧管机,冷轧的	Tube mills for cold-rolled	8455.1020	7
轧管机,其他	Tube mills, nes	8455.1090	7
轧管机,热轧的	Tube mills, for hot-rolled	8455.1010	7
轧管机零件	Tube mills parts	8455.9000	3

Z

商品名称	Article Description	税则号列	申报要素
轧辊磨床,在任一坐标的定位精度至少是0.01毫米,加工金属或金属陶瓷用,其他	Grinding machines of roll, in which the positioning in any one axis can be set up to an accuracy of at least 0.01mm, for metal or cermets, nes	8460.2930	7
轧机,冷热联合的	Mills, combination hot and cold-rolled	8455.2190	7
轧机,冷轧的,板材的	Mills, cold-rolled, for sheet	8455.2210	7
轧机,热轧的,板材的	Mills, hot-rolled, for sheet	8455.2110	7
轧机,热轧的,其他	Mills, hot-rolled, nes	8455.2190	7
轧机,线材的	Mills, for wire	8455.2130	7
轧机,型钢的	Mills, for rolled-steel section	8455.2120	7
轧机零件	Mills parts	8455.9000	3
轧机用轧辊	Rolling mills rolls	8455.3000	3
轧碎机,其他	Crushing machines, nes	8479.8200	7
轧碎机,制酒、制果汁或制类似饮料用	Crushing machinery, used in the manufacture of wine, cider, fruit juices or similar beverages	8435.1000	
轧碎机,制酒、制果汁或制类似饮料用	Machinery for crushing, used in the manufacture of wine, cider, fruit juices or similar beverages	8435.1000	
轧碎机零件,制酒、制果或制类似饮料用	Machinery for crushing parts, used in the manufacture of wine, cider, fruit juices or similar beverages	8435.9000	3
扎头带,棉或麻制	Bolducs of cotton or bast fibres	5806.4010	468
扎头带,其他纺织材料制	Bolducs of other textile materials	5806.4090	468
闸衬,不含石棉的	Brake linings, not containing asbestos	6813.8100	6
闸衬,含石棉的	Brake linings, containing asbestos	6813.2010	6
闸垫,不含石棉的	Brake pads, not containing asbestos	6813.8100	6
闸垫,含石棉的	Brake pads, containing asbestos	6813.2010	6
闸门,钢铁的	Lock-gates, of iron or steel	7308.9000	6
闸用液压油,不含石油或从沥青矿物提取的油类,或者按重量计石油或从沥青矿物提取的油类含量低于70%	Huydraulic brake fluids, not containing or containing less than 70% by weight of petroleum oils or oils obtaines from bituminous minerals	3819.0000	36
炸弹及其零件	Bombs and parts	9306.9000	3
炸薯条,冻的	French fries, frozen	2004.1000	48
炸薯条,未冻的	French fries, not frozen	2005.2000	48
榨菜,用醋或醋酸以外的其他方法制作或保藏的,未冷冻	Hot pickled mustard tubers, prepared or preserved otherwise than by vinegar or acetic acid, not frozen	2005.9940	148
榨汁机,蔬菜用,家用电动器具	Juice extractors for vegetable, electro-mechanical domestic appliances	8509.4010	
榨汁机,水果用,家用电动器具	Juice extractors for fruit, electro-mechanical domestic appliances	8509.4010	
榨汁机,制酒、制果或制类似饮料用	Presses machinery, used in the manufacture of wine, cider, fruit juices or similar beverages	8435.1000	
榨汁机零件,制酒、制果或制类似饮料用	Presses machinery parts, used in the manufacture of wine, cider, fruit juices or similar beverages	8435.9000	3

Z

商品名称	Article Description	税则号列	申报要素
zhan			
毡尖笔	Felt tipped pens	9608. 2000	
毡呢,其他	Felt, nes	5602. 9000	46
毡呢,其他纺织材料制,未浸渍、涂布、包覆或层压	Felt of other textile materials, not impregnated, coated, covered or laminated	5602. 2900	46
毡呢,羊毛或动物细毛制,未浸渍、涂布、包覆或层压	Felt of wool or fine animal hair, not impregnated, coated, covered or laminated	5602. 2100	46
毡呢帽模	Felt hats making blocks	8449. 0090	7
毡呢帽生产机器	Felt hats making machinery	8449. 0090	7
毡呢整理机器	Felt finishing machinery	8449. 0090	7
毡纸及纸板	Felt paper and paperboard	4805. 5000	458
粘贴簿,纸或纸板制的	Albums for collections, of paper or paperboard	4820. 5000	
粘贴邮票机	Sealing or affixing mail machines	8472. 3090	
展览专示范而无其他用途的仪器、装置及模型	Exhibitions instruments, designed for demonstrational purposes, unsuitable for other uses	9023. 0000	
展示及存储(柜、箱、展示台、陈列箱及类似品),装有冷藏或冷冻装置的,其他	Furniture (chests, cabinets, display counters, show-cases and the like) for storage and display, incorporating refrigerating or freezing equipment, nes	8418. 5000	57
zhang			
章鱼,冻、干、盐腌或盐渍的	Octopus (Octopus spp.), frozen, dried, salted or in brine	0307. 5900	148
章鱼,活、鲜及冷的	Octopus(Octopus spp.), live, fresh or chilled	0307. 5100	18
章鱼,制作或保藏的	Octopus, prepared or preserved	1605. 9090	48
章鱼粉,不适合食用	Octopus flour, unfit for human consumption	2301. 2090	136
章鱼粉,食用	Octopus flour, fit for human consumption	0307. 9990	14
樟脑	Camphor	2914. 2100	36
樟脑油	Essential oils of camphor	3301. 2910	34
帐幔,钩编的,合成纤维制	Interior blinds, crocheted, of synthetic fibres	6303. 1220	346
帐幔,钩编的,棉制	Interior blinds, crocheted, of cotton	6303. 1932	346
帐幔,钩编的,其他纺织材料制	Interior blinds, crocheted, of other textile materials	6303. 1992	346
帐幔,合成纤维制,其他	Interior blinds, of synthetic fibres, nes	6303. 9200	346
帐幔,棉制,其他	Interior blinds, of cotton, nes	6303. 9100	346
帐幔,其他纺织材料制	Interior blinds, of other textile materials	6303. 9900	346
帐幔,针织的,合成纤维制	Interior blinds, knitted, of synthetic fibres	6303. 1210	346
帐幔,针织的,棉制	Interior blinds, knitted, of cotton	6303. 1931	346
帐幔,针织的,其他纺织材料制	Interior blinds, knitted, of other textile materials	6303. 1991	346
帐篷,合成纤维制	Tents, of synthetic fibres	6306. 2200	346
帐篷,棉制	Tents, of cotton	6306. 2910	346
帐篷,其他	Tents, nes	6306. 2990	346

商品名称	Article Description	税则号列	申报要素
账本,纸或纸板制的	Account books, of paper or paperboard	4820.1000	
zhao			
沼气发动机,活塞内燃发动机,点燃往复式或旋转式	Firedamp engines, internal combustion piston engines, spark-ignition reciprocating or rotary	8407.9010	25
照明装置,电的,其他	Lighting fittings, electric, nes	9405.4090	5
照明装置,非电气的,其他	Lighting fittings, non-electrical lamps, nes	9405.5000	5
照明装置,机动车辆用	Lighting equipment of a kind used for motor vehicles	8512.2010	57
照明装置,天花板或墙壁上的,电气的,不包括公共露天场所或街道上的电气照明装置	Lighting fittings, for ceiling or wall, electric, excluding those of a kind used for lighting public open spaces or thorough-fares	9405.1000	5
照明装置,自行车用	Lighting equipment of a kind used on bicycles	8512.1000	7
照明装置零件,玻璃制	Lighting fittings parts, of glass	9405.9100	36
照明装置零件,其他	Lighting fittings parts, nes	9405.9900	36
照明装置零件,塑料制	Lighting fittings parts, of plastics	9405.9200	36
照明装置零件,自行车或机动车辆用	Lighting equipment parts for cycles or motor vehicles	8512.9000	3
照片(电影片除外)放大机	Photographic(other than cinematographic)enlargers	9008.4000	
照片(电影片除外)缩片机	Photographic(other than cinematographic)reducers	9008.4000	
照片放大机及缩片机用零件、附件	Photographic enlargers and reducers parts and accessories	9008.9020	3
照相机,比较法庭或犯罪学用的	Cameras for comparison of forensic or criminological purposes	9006.3000	7
照相机,其他	Cameras, nes	9006.5990	7
照相机,使用胶片宽度为35毫米	Cameras, for roll film of a width of 35mm	9006.5300	7
照相机,使用胶片宽度小于35毫米	Cameras, for roll film of a width less than 35mm	9006.5290	7
照相机,特种的,水下、航空测量或体内器官检查用	Cameras specially designed for under-water use, for aerial survey or for medical or surgical examination of internal organs	9006.3000	7
照相机,通过镜头取景[单镜头反光式(SLR)],使用胶片宽度不超过35毫米	Cameras, with a through-the-lens viewfinder [single lens reflex (SLR)], for roll film of a width not exceeding 35mm	9006.5100	7
照相机,一次成像的	Cameras, instant print	9006.4000	7
照相机,制版的,其他	Cameras of a kind used for preparing printing plates or cylinders, nes	9006.1090	7
照相机用零件、附件,其他	Cameras parts and accessories, nes	9006.9199	3
照相机用零件、附件,一次成像照相机用	Cameras parts and accessories, for instant print cameras	9006.9120	3
照相机用零件、附件,制版照相机和特种照相机用	Cameras parts and accessories, for the photographic cameras	9006.9110	3
照相闪光灯,放电式(电子式)	Photographic flashlight discharge lamp(electronic)	9006.6100	7
照相用装置及设备的零件、附件,其他	Photographic apparatus and equipment parts and accessories, nes	9010.9090	3

Z

商品名称	Article Description	税则号列	申报要素
照相用装置及设备的零件、附件,特种的	Photographic apparatus and equipment parts and accessories, with special purposes	9010. 9020	3
照相原纸	Photo paper bese	4802. 2010	3458
zhe			
遮光剂及类似制品,调制的,陶瓷、搪瓷及玻璃工业用	Opacifiers and similar preparations, prepared, of a kind used in the ceramic, enamelling or glass industry	3207. 1000	13
遮阳篷,合成纤维制	Sunblinds, of synthetic fibres	6306. 1200	346
遮阳篷,麻制	Sunblinds, of bast fibres	6306. 1910	346
遮阳篷,棉制	Sunblinds, of cotton	6306. 1920	346
遮阳篷,其他	Sunblinds, nes	6306. 1990	346
折叠机,加工金属用,其他	Folding machines, for working metal, nes	8462. 2990	7
折叠机,数控的,加工金属用	Folding machines, numerically controlled, for working metal	8462. 2190	7
折叠机或装封机,信件用	Folding mail or inserting mail in envelopes or bands machines	8472. 3090	
折叠机器,纺织物的	Folding machines for textile fabrics	8451. 5000	
折叠机器零件,纺织物的	Folding machines parts for textile fabrics	8451. 9000	
折叠伞	Umbrellas and sun umbrellas, having a telescopic shaft	6601. 9100	
锗,未锻轧	Germanium, unwrought	8112. 9210	16
锗的氧化物	Germanium oxides	2825. 6000	
锗粉末	Germanium powders	8112. 9210	16
锗制品	Germanium articles, nes	8112. 9910	16
赭石	Germanite	2617. 9090	146
zhen			
针,缝合用	Needles for sutures	9018. 3220	
针刺机,毡呢或无纺织物制造用	Stitch machinery, for the manufacture of felt or non-wovens	8449. 0010	7
针刺机制毡呢	Needleloom felt	5602. 1000	46
针式打印机,专用于自动数据处理设备的	Stylus printers, of a kind solely used for automatic data processing machine	8443. 3211	57
针头,金属管状,医疗、外科、牙科或兽医用	Needles, tubular metal, used in medical, surgical, dental or veterinary sciences	9018. 3210	
针织或钩编织物,合成纤维制,染色	Knitted or crocheted fabrics of synthetic fibres, dyed	6006. 3200	46
针织或钩编织物,合成纤维制,色织	Knitted or crocheted fabrics of synthetic fibres, of yarns of different colours	6006. 3300	46
针织或钩编织物,合成纤维制,未漂白或漂白	Knitted or crocheted fabrics of synthetic fibres, unbleached or bleached	6006. 3100	46
针织或钩编织物,合成纤维制,印花	Knitted or crocheted fabrics of synthetic fibres, printed	6006. 3400	46

商品名称	Article Description	税则号列	申报要素
针织或钩编织物,宽度不超过30厘米,合成纤维制	Knitted or crocheted fabrics of a width not exceeding 30cm, of synthetic fibres	6003.3000	46
针织或钩编织物,宽度不超过30厘米,棉制	Knitted or crocheted fabrics of a width not exceeding 30cm, of cotton	6003.2000	46
针织或钩编织物,宽度不超过30厘米,其他	Knitted or crocheted fabrics of a width not exceeding 30cm, nes	6003.9000	46
针织或钩编织物,宽度不超过30厘米,人造纤维制	Knitted or crocheted fabrics of a width not exceeding 30cm, of artificial fibres	6003.4000	46
针织或钩编织物,宽度不超过30厘米,羊毛或动物细毛制	Knitted or crocheted fabrics of a width not exceeding 30cm, of wool or fine animal hair	6003.1000	46
针织或钩编织物,棉制,染色	Knitted or crocheted fabrics of cotton, dyed	6006.2200	46
针织或钩编织物,棉制,色织	Knitted or crocheted fabrics of cotton, of yarns of different colours	6006.2300	46
针织或钩编织物,棉制,未漂白或漂白	Knitted or crocheted fabrics of cotton, unbleached or bleached	6006.2100	46
针织或钩编织物,棉制,印花	Knitted or crocheted fabrics of cotton, printed	6006.2400	46
针织或钩编织物,其他	Knitted or crocheted fabrics, nes	6006.9000	46
针织或钩编织物,人造纤维制,染色	Knitted or crocheted fabrics of artificial fibres, dyed	6006.4200	46
针织或钩编织物,人造纤维制,色织	Knitted or crocheted fabrics of artificial fibres, of yarns of different colours	6006.4300	46
针织或钩编织物,人造纤维制,未漂白或漂白	Knitted or crocheted fabrics of artificial fibres, unbleached or bleached	6006.4100	46
针织或钩编织物,人造纤维制,印花	Knitted or crocheted fabrics of artificial fibres, printed	6006.4400	46
针织或钩编织物,羊毛或动物细毛制	Knitted or crocheted fabrics of wool or fine animal hair	6006.1000	46
针织机,圆型的,圆筒直径不超过165毫米	Knitting machines, circular, with cylinder diameter not exceeding 165mm	8447.1100	
针织机,圆型的,圆筒直径超过165毫米	Knitting machines, circular, with cylinder diameter exceeding 165mm	8447.1200	
针织机的辅助机器	Circular knitting machines auxiliary	8448.1900	3
针织机及其辅助机器的零件、附件,其他	Knitting machines or of their auxiliary machinery's parts and accessories, nes	8448.5900	3
针织物或钩编织物,宽度不超过30厘米,按重量计弹性纱线含量在5%及以上,但不含橡胶线,合成纤维制	Knitted or crocheted fabrics of a width not exceeding 30cm, containing by weight 5% or more of elastomeric yarn but not containing rubber thread, of synthetic fibres	6002.4030	46
针织物或钩编织物,宽度不超过30厘米,按重量计弹性纱线含量在5%及以上,但不含橡胶线,棉制	Knitted or crocheted fabrics of a width not exceeding 30cm, containing by weight 5% or more of elastomeric yarn but not containing rubber thread, of cotton	6002.4010	46

Z

商品名称	Article Description	税则号列	申报要素
针织物或钩编织物，宽度不超过30厘米，按重量计弹性纱线含量在5%及以上，但不含橡胶线，其他	Knitted or crocheted fabrics of a width not exceeding 30cm, containing by weight 5% or more of elastomeric yarn but not containing rubber thread, nes	6002.4090	46
针织物或钩编织物，宽度不超过30厘米，按重量计弹性纱线含量在5%及以上，但不含橡胶线，人造纤维制	Knitted or crocheted fabrics of a width not exceeding 30cm, containing by weight 5% or more of elastomeric yarn but not containing rubber thread, of artificial fibres	6002.4040	46
针织物或钩编织物，宽度不超过30厘米，按重量计弹性纱线含量在5%及以上，但不含橡胶线，丝及绢丝制	Knitted or crocheted fabrics of a width not exceeding 30cm, containing by weight 5% or more of elastomeric yarn but not containing rubber thread, of silk or silk waste	6002.4020	46
针织物或钩编织物，宽度不超过30厘米，按重量计弹性纱线或橡胶线含量在5%及以上的，合成纤维制，其他	Knitted or crocheted fabrics of a width not exceeding 30cm, containing by weight 5% or more of elastomeric yarn or rubber thread, of synthetic fibres, nes	6002.9030	46
针织物或钩编织物，宽度不超过30厘米，按重量计弹性纱线或橡胶线含量在5%及以上的，棉制，其他	Knitted or crocheted fabrics of a width not exceeding 30cm, containing by weight 5% or more of elastomeric yarn or rubber thread, of cotton, nes	6002.9010	46
针织物或钩编织物，宽度不超过30厘米，按重量计弹性纱线或橡胶线含量在5%及以上的，其他	Knitted or crocheted fabrics of a width not exceeding 30cm, containing by weight 5% or more of elastomeric yarn or rubber thread, nes	6002.9090	46
针织物或钩编织物，宽度不超过30厘米，按重量计弹性纱线或橡胶线含量在5%及以上的，人造纤维制，其他	Knitted or crocheted fabrics of a width not exceeding 30cm, containing by weight 5% or more of elastomeric yarn or rubber thread, of artificial fibres, nes	6002.9040	46
针织物或钩编织物，宽度不超过30厘米，按重量计弹性纱线或橡胶线含量在5%及以上的，丝及绢丝制，其他	Knitted or crocheted fabrics of a width not exceeding 30cm, containing by weight 5% or more of elastomeric yarn or rubber thread, of silk or silk waste, nes	6002.9020	46
针织物或钩编织物，宽度超过30厘米，按重量计弹性纱线含量在5%及以上，但不含橡胶线，合成纤维制	Knitted or crocheted fabrics of a width exceeding 30cm, containing by weight 5% or more of elastomeric yarn but not containing rubber thread, of synthetic fibres	6004.1030	46
针织物或钩编织物，宽度超过30厘米，按重量计弹性纱线含量在5%及以上，但不含橡胶线，棉制	Knitted or crocheted fabrics of a width exceeding 30cm, containing by weight 5% or more of elastomeric yarn but not containing rubber thread, of cotton	6004.1010	46
针织物或钩编织物，宽度超过30厘米，按重量计弹性纱线含量在5%及以上，但不含橡胶线，其他	Knitted or crocheted fabrics of a width exceeding 30cm, containing by weight 5% or more of elastomeric yarn but not containing rubber thread, nes	6004.1090	46

商品名称	Article Description	税则号列	申报要素
针织物或钩编织物,宽度超过30厘米,按重量计弹性纱线含量在5%及以上,但不含橡胶线,人造纤维制	Knitted or crocheted fabrics of a width exceeding 30cm, containing by weight 5% or more of elastomeric yarn but not containing rubber thread, of artificial fibres	6004.1040	46
针织物或钩编织物,宽度超过30厘米,按重量计弹性纱线含量在5%及以上,但不含橡胶线,丝及绢丝制	Knitted or crocheted fabrics of a width exceeding 30cm, containing by weight 5% or more of elastomeric yarn but not containing rubber thread, of silk or silk waste	6004.1020	46
针织物或钩编织物,宽度超过30厘米,按重量计弹性纱线或橡胶线含量在5%及以上的,合成纤维制,其他	Knitted or crocheted fabrics of a width exceeding 30cm, containing by weight 5% or more elastomeric yarn or rubber thread, of synthetic fibres, nes	6004.9030	46
针织物或钩编织物,宽度超过30厘米,按重量计弹性纱线或橡胶线含量在5%及以上的,棉制,其他	Knitted or crocheted fabrics of a width exceeding 30cm, containing by weight 5% or more elastomeric yarn or rubber thread, of cotton, nes	6004.9010	46
针织物或钩编织物,宽度超过30厘米,按重量计弹性纱线或橡胶线含量在5%及以上的,其他	Knitted or crocheted fabrics of a width exceeding 30cm, containing by weight 5% or more elastomeric yarn or rubber thread, nes	6004.9090	46
针织物或钩编织物,宽度超过30厘米,按重量计弹性纱线或橡胶线含量在5%及以上的,人造纤维制,其他	Knitted or crocheted fabrics of a width exceeding 30cm, containing by weight 5% or more elastomeric yarn or rubber thread, of artificial fibres, nes	6004.9040	46
针织物或钩编织物,宽度超过30厘米,按重量计弹性纱线或橡胶线含量在5%及以上的,丝及绢丝制,其他	Knitted or crocheted fabrics of a width exceeding 30cm, containing by weight 5% or more elastomeric yarn or rubber thread, of silk or silk waste, nes	6004.9020	46
珍粉及淀粉制成的珍粉代用品,片、粒、珠、粉或类似形状的	Tapioca and substitutes therefor prepared from starch, in the form of flakes, grains, pearls, siftings or in similar forms	1903.0000	18
珍珠,天然的,其他	Pearls, natural, nes	7101.1099	145
珍珠,天然的,未分级,其他	Pearls, natural, ungraded, nes	7101.1019	145
珍珠,养殖的,未加工,其他	Pearls, cultured pearls, unworked, nes	7101.2190	145
珍珠,养殖的,未加工,未分级	Pearls, cultured pearls, unworked, ungraded	7101.2110	145
珍珠,养殖的,已加工,其他	Pearls, cultured pearls, worked, nes	7101.2290	145
珍珠,养殖的,已加工,未分级	Pearls, cultured pearls, worked, ungraded	7101.2210	145
珍珠鸡,改良种用,重量不超过185克	Guinea fowls, pure-bred breeding, weighing not more than 185g	0105.1910	48
珍珠鸡,改良种用,重量超过185克	Guinea fowls, pure-bred breeding, weighing more than 185g	0105.9910	48
珍珠鸡,改良种用除外,重量超过185克	Guinea fowls, ex. pure-bred breeding, weighing more than 185g	0105.9993	48
珍珠鸡,整只,冻的	Guinea fowls, not cut in pieces, frozen	0207.3330	1
珍珠鸡,整只,鲜或冷的	Guinea fowls, not cut in pieces, fresh or chilled	0207.3230	1

Z

商品名称	Article Description	税则号列	申报要素
珍珠鸡块,冻的	Cuts of guinea fowls, frozen	0207.3630	1
珍珠鸡块,鲜或冷的	Cuts of guinea fowls, fresh or chilled	0207.3530	1
珍珠母,已加工的	Mother-of-pearl, worked	9601.9000	5
珍珠陶土	Nacrite	2507.0090	1346
珍珠岩,未膨胀的	Perlite, unexpanded	2530.1020	13456
真空泵	Vacuum pumps	8414.1000	27
真空泵零件	Vacuum pumps parts	8414.9090	23
真空模塑机器,加工橡胶或塑料及其产品用,其他	Vacuum moulding machines, for working rubber or plastics or for the manufacture of products from these materials, nes	8477.4090	7
真空容器及其零件,玻璃瓶胆除外	Vacuum vessels and parts thereof, other than glass inners	9617.0090	5
真空吸尘器,电动的,功率不超过1500瓦,且带有容积不超过20升的集尘袋或其他集尘容器	Vacuum cleaners, with self-contained electric motor, of a power not exceeding 1500W and having a dust bag or other receptacle capacity not exceeding 20L	8508.1100	78
真空吸尘器,电动的,其他	Vacuum cleaners, with self-contained electric motor, nes	8508.1900	78
真空吸尘器,其他	Vacuum cleaners, nes	8508.6000	78
真空吸尘器零件,电动吸尘器的,功率不超过1500瓦,且带有容积不超过20升的集尘袋或其他集尘容器,子目8508.1100所列吸尘器用	Vacuum cleaners parts, of vacuum cleaners which having self-contained electric motor, of a power not exceeding 1500W and having a dust bag or other receptacle capacity not exceeding 20L, of the cleaners of subheading 8508.1100	8508.7010	3
真空吸尘器零件,其他	Vacuum cleaners parts, nes	8508.7090	3
砧	Anvils	8205.8000	256
榛子,去壳	Hazelnuts or filberts (Corylus spp.), shelled	0802.2200	134
榛子,未去壳	Hazelnuts or filberts (Corylus spp.), in shell	0802.2100	134
诊断或实验用配制试剂,其他	Diagnostic or laboratory reagents, prepared, nes	3822.0090	36
诊断或实验用试剂,附于衬背上的	Diagnostic or laboratory reagents on a backing	3822.0010	36
诊断试剂,用于病人的	Diagnostic reagents designed to be administered to the patient	3006.3000	36
诊断装置(包括功能检查或生理参数检查用装置),电气的,其他	Diagnostic apparatus (including apparatus for functional exploratory examination or for checking physiological parameters), electro-diagnostic, nes	9018.1990	
枕木,铁道及电车道,其他	Sleepers (crossties) of wood, for railway or tramway, nes	4406.9000	4
枕木,铁道及电车道,未浸渍	Sleepers (crossties) of wood, for railway or tramway, not impregnated	4406.1000	4
枕头,化纤棉填充的	Pillows, stuffed with man-made fibres	9404.9040	6
枕头,其他	Pillows, nes	9404.9090	6
枕头,兽毛填充的	Pillows, stuffed with animal hair	9404.9020	6
枕头,丝棉填充的	Pillows, stuffed with silk wadding	9404.9030	6
枕头,羽毛或羽绒填充的	Pillows, stuffed with feathers or down	9404.9010	6

商品名称	Article Description	税则号列	申报要素
振动装置,钢坯连铸机用	Vibrating devices, for ingot continuous casting machines	8454.9022	3
镇流器,放电灯或放电管用,电子的	Ballasts, for discharge lamps or tubes, electronic	8504.1010	
镇流器,放电灯或放电管用,其他	Ballasts, for discharge lamps or tubes, nes	8504.1090	
zheng			
蒸发式空气冷却器	Evaporative air coolers	8479.6000	7
蒸馏或精馏设备,其他	Distilling or rectifying plant, nes	8419.4090	57
蒸馏渗滤式咖啡机,电热的	Steam espresso makers, electro-thermic	8516.7120	7
蒸汽锅炉,包括混合式锅炉,其他	Steam or other vapour generating boilers, including hybrid boilers, nes	8402.1900	27
蒸汽锅炉,蒸发量不超过45吨/时的水管锅炉	Steam or other vapour generating watertube boilers, with a steam production not exceeding 45t per hour	8402.1200	27
蒸汽锅炉,蒸发量超过45吨/时的水管锅炉,其他	Steam or other vapour generating watertube boilers, with a steam production exceeding 45t per hour, nes	8402.1190	27
蒸汽锅炉,蒸发量在900吨/时及以上的发电用水管锅炉	Steam or other vapour generating watertube boilers, with a steam production 900t or more per hour, for generating electricity	8402.1110	27
蒸汽锅炉的辅助设备	Steam or other vapour generating watertube boilers auxiliary plant	8404.1010	3
蒸汽锅炉的辅助设备的零件	Steam or other vapour generating watertube boilers auxiliary plant parts	8404.9090	3
蒸汽锅炉零件	Steam or other vapour generating boilers parts	8402.9000	27
整经机	Warping machines	8445.9010	7
整经机的辅助机器	Warping machines auxiliary	8448.1900	3
整理机器,纺织物的	Finishing machines for textile fabrics	8451.8000	
整理机器零件,纺织物的	Finishing machines parts for textile fabrics	8451.9000	
整理剂,纺织工业及类似工业用,其他	Finishing agents, of a kind used in the textile or like industries, nes	3809.9100	236
整理剂,以淀粉物质为基本成分	Finishing agents, with a basis of amylaceous substances	3809.1000	236
整理剂,造纸工业及类似工业用,其他	Finishing agents, of a kind used in the paper or like industries, nes	3809.9200	236
整理剂,制革工业及类似工业用,其他	Finishing agents, of a kind used in the leather or like industries, nes	3809.9300	236
整头假发,合成纤维纺织材料制	Wigs, complete, of synthetic textile materials	6704.1100	4
整只火鸡,冻的	Turkeys, not cut in pieces, frozen	0207.2500	1
整只火鸡,鲜或冷的	Turkeys, not cut in pieces, fresh or chilled	0207.2400	1
正丁巴比妥(INN)以及盐	Butobarbital; salts thereof	2933.5300	36
正丁醇	Butan-1-ol(n-butyl alcohol)	2905.1300	36
正磷酸氢钙(磷酸二钙),其他	Calcium hydrogenorthophosphate (dicalcium phosphate), nes	2835.2590	3

Z

商品名称	Article Description	税则号列	申报要素
正磷酸氢钙(磷酸二钙),食品级的	Calcium hydrogenorthophosphate (dicalcium phosphate), food grade	2835.2520	
正磷酸氢钙(磷酸二钙),饲料级的	Calcium hydrogenorthophosphate (dicalcium phosphate), feed grade	2835.2510	
正射投影仪	Orthographical projectors	9008.3010	
正辛醇	N-octanol	2905.1610	36
zhi			
支票	Cheque forms	4907.0090	5
芝麻,其他	Sesamum seeds, nes	1207.4090	3
芝麻,用其他方法制作或保藏的	Sesame, otherwise prepared, or preserved	2008.1992	248
芝麻,种用	Sesamum seeds for cultivation	1207.4010	3
芝麻油及其分离品	Sesame oil and its fractions	1515.5000	4
枝形吊灯,不包括公共露天场所或街道上的电气照明装置	Chandeliers, excluding those of a kind used for lighting public open spaces or thorough-fares	9405.1000	5
织机,地毯用,动力的,所织织物宽度超过30厘米的梭织机	Weaving machines (looms), for making carpets or rugs, powered, for weaving fabrics of a width exceeding 30cm, shuttle type	8446.2110	7
织机,动力的,所织织物宽度超过30厘米的梭织机,其他	Weaving machines (looms), powered, for weaving fabrics of a width exceeding 30cm, shuttle type, nes	8446.2190	7
织机,剑杆式,所织织物宽度超过30厘米的无梭织机	Looms, rapier, for weaving fabrics of a width exceeding 30cm, shuttleless type	8446.3020	7
织机,喷气式,所织织物宽度超过30厘米的无梭织机	Looms, air jet, for weaving fabrics of a width exceeding 30cm, shuttleless type	8446.3050	7
织机,喷水式,所织织物宽度超过30厘米的无梭织机	Looms, water jet, for weaving fabrics of a width exceeding 30cm, shuttleless type	8446.3040	7
织机,片梭式,所织织物宽度超过30厘米的无梭织机	Looms, carrier, for weaving fabrics of a width exceeding 30cm, shuttleless type	8446.3030	7
织机,所织织物宽度不超过30厘米的织机	Weaving machines (looms), for weaving fabrics of a width not exceeding 30cm	8446.1000	7
织机,所织织物宽度超过30厘米的梭织机,其他	Weaving machines (looms), for weaving fabrics of a width exceeding 30cm, shuttle type, nes	8446.2900	7
织机,所织织物宽度超过30厘米的无梭织机,其他	Weaving machines (looms), for weaving fabrics of a width exceeding 30cm, shuttleless type, nes	8446.3090	7
织机的辅助机器	Weaving machines (looms) auxiliary	8448.1900	3
织机及其辅助机器的零件、附件,其他	Weaving machines or of their auxiliary machinery's parts and accessories, nes	8448.4990	3
织物,棉或麻制,用粘合剂粘合制成的有经纱而无纬纱的	Fabrics consisting of warp without weft assembled by means of an adhesive, of cotton or bast fibres	5806.4010	468
织物,用粘合剂粘合制成的有经纱而无纬纱的,其他	Fabrics consisting of warp without weft assembled by means of an adhesive of textile materials, nes	5806.4090	468
织针,针织机的	Needles for knitting machines	8448.5190	3
脂,从乳中提取的	Fats, derived from milk	0405.9000	268

商品名称	Article Description	税则号列	申报要素
脂肪醇,工业用	Atty alcohols, industrial use	3823.7000	6
脂肪酶,其他	Lipase	3507.9090	35
脂肪物质,从羊毛脂制得的,其他	Fatty substances derived therefrom, nes	1505.0000	
脂松节油	Gum turpentine oils	3805.1000	36
直缝焊管机,全自动或半自动的	Aligning tube welding machines, fully or partly automatic	8515.2110	
直接灌注香烟打火机及类似打火器用的燃料,其包装容器的容积超过300立方厘米	Liquefied gas fuels, nes, in containers of a kind used for filling or refilling cigarette or similar lighters and of a capacity exceeding 300cm^3	2711.1910	1468
直锯片,机械锯用	Straight saw blades, for sawing machines	8202.9110	256
直锯片,加工金属用,其他	Saw blades, straight, for working metal, nes	8202.9190	256
直流稳压电源,功率小于1千瓦,精度低于万分之一,其他	DC voltage-stabilized suppliers, of a power of less than 1kW and an accuracy of not better than 0.0001, nes	8504.4014	78
直升机,空载重量不超过2000千克	Helicopters, of an unladen weight not exceeding 2000kg	8802.1100	
直升机,空载重量超过2000千克,但不超过7000千克	Helicopters, of an unladen weight exceeding 2000kg but not exceeding 7000kg	8802.1210	
直升机,空载重量超过7000千克	Helicopters, of an unladen weight exceeding 7000kg	8802.1220	
直升机的零件,其他	Helicopters parts, nes	8803.3000	3
直线作用(气压缸)的	Pneumatic power engines, linear acting (cylinders)	8412.3100	27
直线作用(液压缸)的	Hydraulic power engines, linear acting (cylinders)	8412.2100	27
植入人体内的其他器具,弥补生理缺陷或残疾的	Implanted appliances, to compensate for a defect or disability	9021.9000	3
植物部分,其他,制花束或装饰用的	Parts of plants, nes, suitable for bouquets or for ornamental purposes	0604.9900	34
植物部分,其他,用糖保藏的,沥干、糖渍或裹糖的	Parts of plants, nes, preserved by sugar (drained, glace or crystallized)	2006.0090	48
植物部分,食用的,其他,用醋或醋酸制作或保藏的	Parts of plants, edible, nes, prepared or preserved by vinegar or acetic acid	2001.9090	48
植物部分,食用的,其他,用其他方法制作或保藏的	Parts of plants, edible, nes, otherwise prepared, or preserved	2008.9990	248
植物部分,鲜的,制花束或装饰用的	Parts of plants, fresh, suitable for bouquets or for ornamental purposes	0604.9100	34
植物材料,灯心草属的	Vegetable materials, rushes	1401.9039	3
植物材料,主要作编结用的	Vegetable materials, primarily for plaiting	1401.9090	3
植物产品,其他	Vegetable products, nes	1404.9090	
植物纺织纤维纱线,其他	Vegetable textile fibres yarn, nes	5308.9099	568
植物固定油脂加工的机器	Fixed vegetable fats or oils preparation machinery	8479.2000	7
植物固定油脂提取的机器	Fixed vegetable fats or oils extraction machinery	8479.2000	7
植物及其某部分,主要用作香料的	Plants and parts of plants of a kind used primarily in perfumery	1211.9050	34

Z

商品名称	Article Description	税则号列	申报要素
植物及其某部分,其他	Plants and parts of plants, nes	1211.9099	34
植物及其某部分,主要用作药料的	Plants and parts of plants of a kind used primarily in pharmacy	1211.9039	34
植物蜡	Vegetable waxes	1521.1000	6
植物沥青	Vegetable pitch	3807.0000	3
植物生长调节剂,零售包装	Plant-growth regulators, put up for retail sale	3808.9391	36
植物生长调节剂,其他	Plant-growth regulators, nes	3808.9399	36
植物纤维机织物,纺织用,其他	Vegetable textile fibres yarn, nes	5311.0090	2468
植物纤维及其短纤、落麻及废料,纺织用,其他	Vegetable textile fibres, tow, noils and waste of these fibres, nes	5305.0099	4
植物羊皮纸	Vegetable parchment	4806.1000	58
植物叶,鲜的,制花束或装饰用的	Foliage, fresh, suitable for bouquets or for ornamental purposes	0604.9100	34
植物油脂及其分离品,全部或部分氢化,相互酯化,再酯化或反油酸化,不论是否精制,但未经进一步加工	Vegetable fats and oil and fractions thereof, partly or wholly hydrogenated, interesterified, reesterified or elaidinized, whether or not refined, but not further prepared	1516.2000	
植物油脂及其分离品,其他	Vegetable fats and oils and fractions thereof, nes	1518.0000	46
植物原料,主要供染料、鞣料用的	Raw vegetable materials of a kind used primarily in dyeing or tanning	1404.9010	3
植物甾醇类	Phytosterols	2906.1310	36
植物枝,鲜的,制花束或装饰用的	Branches, fresh, suitable for bouquets or for ornamental purposes	0604.9100	34
植物质海绵,天然的	Sponges of vegetable origin, natural	1404.9090	
止汗剂,人体用	Antiperspirants, for personal use	33097.2000	23
止回阀	Check (nonreturn) valves	8481.3000	
止血材料,外科或牙科用,无菌,吸收性	Haemostatics, for surgical or dental use, sterile, absorbable	3006.1000	3
纸板抄造机器	Paper board making machinery	8439.2000	
纸板抄造机器的零件	Paper board making machinery parts	8439.9900	3
纸板整理机器	Paper board finishing machinery	8439.3000	
纸板整理机器的零件	Paper board finishing machinery parts	8439.9900	3
纸抄造机器	Paper making machinery	8439.2000	
纸抄造机器的零件	Paper making machinery parts	8439.9900	3
纸袋,底宽40厘米及以上的	Sacks and hags, having a base of a width of 40cm or more, of paper, paperboard	4819.3000	68
纸袋,其他	Sacks and bags, of paper, paperboard, nes	4819.4000	68
纸袋制造机器	Paper bags making machines	8441.2000	
纸袋制造机器零件	Paper bags making machines parts	8441.9090	
纸袋子,内装各种纸制文具	Pouches of paper or paperboard, containing an assortment of paper stationery	4817.3000	6

商品名称	Article Description	税则号列	申报要素
纸和纸板,主要由漂白化学木浆制成未经本体染色的	Paper or paperboard made mainly of bleached chemical pulp, not coloured in the mass	4707.2000	125
纸盒子,内装各种纸制文具	Boxes of paper or paperboard, containing an assortment of paper stationery	4817.3000	6
纸或纸板,主要由机械浆制成的(例如,报纸、杂志及类似印刷品)	Paper or paperboard made mainly of mechanical pulp (for example, newspapers, journals and similar printed matter)	4707.3000	125
纸及纸板,成卷的,书写、印刷或类似用途的,不含用机械或化学-机械方法制得的纤维或所含前述纤维不超过全部纤维重量的10%,单面或双面涂布高岭土或其他无机物质的	Paper and paperboard, In rolls, of a kind used for writing, printing or other graphic purposes, not containing fibres obtained by a mechanical or chemi-mechanical process or of which not more than 10% by weight of the total fibre content consists of such fibres, coated on one or both sides with kaolin or other inorganic substances	4810.1300	14568
纸及纸板,穿孔的	Paper and paperboard, perforated	4808.9000	58
纸及纸板,但书写、印刷或类似用途的除外,单面或双面涂布高岭土或其他无机物质的,其他	Paper and paperboard, other than that of a kind used for writing, printing or other graphic purposes, coated on one or both sides with kaolin or other inorganic substances, nes	4810.9900	14568
纸及纸板,但书写、印刷或类似用途的除外,多层的,单面或双面涂布高岭土或其他无机物质的	Paper and paperboard, other than that of a kind used for writing, printing or other graphic purposes, multiply, coated on one or both sides with kaolin or other inorganic substances	4810.9200	14568
纸及纸板,胶粘的,其他	Paper and paperboard, gummed or adhesive, nes	4811.4900	458
纸及纸板,书写、印刷或类似用途的,不含用机械或化学-机械方法制得的纤维或所含前述纤维不超过全部纤维重量的10%,成张的,一边不超过435毫米,另一边不超过297毫米(以未折叠计),单面或双面涂布高岭土或其他无机物质的	Paper and paperboard, In sheets with one side not exceeding 435mm and the other side not exceeding 297mm in the unfolded state, of a kind used for writing, printing or other graphic purposes, not containing fibres obtained by a mechanical or chemi-mechanical process or of which not more than 10% by weight of the total fibre content consists of such fibres, coated on one or both sides with kaolin or other inorganic substances	4810.1400	14568
纸及纸板,书写、印刷或类似用途的,不含用机械或化学-机械方法制得的纤维或所含前述纤维不超过全部纤维重量的10%,单面或双面涂布高岭土或其他无机物质的,其他	Paper and paperboard of a kind used for writing, printing or other graphic purposes, not containing fibres obtained by a mechanical or chemi-mechanical process or of which not more than 10% by weight of the total fibre content consists of such fibres, coated on one or both sides with kaolin or other inorganic substances, nes	4810.1900	14568

Z

商品名称	Article Description	税则号列	申报要素
纸及纸板,书写、印刷或类似用途的,所含用机械或化学-机械方法制得的纤维超过全部纤维重量的10%,单面或双面涂布高岭土或其他无机物质的,其他	Paper and paperboard of a kind used for writing, printing or other graphic purposes, of which more than 10% by weight of the total fibre content consists of fibres obtained by a mechanical or chemi-mechanical process, coated on one or both sides with kaolin or other inorganic substances, nes	4810. 2900	14568
纸及纸板,未经涂布的,不含用机械或化学-机械方法制得的纤维或所含前述纤维不超过全部纤维重量的10%,每平方米重量超过150克	Paper and paperboard, uncoated, not containing fibres obtained by a mechanical or chemi-mechanical process or of which not more than 10% by weight of the total fibre content consists of such fibres, weighing more than 150g/m^2	4802. 5800	3468
纸及纸板,未经涂布的,不含用机械或化学-机械方法制得的纤维或所含前述纤维不超过全部纤维重量的10%,每平方米重量小于40克	Paper and paperboard, uncoated, not containing fibres obtained by a mechanical or chemi-mechanical process or of which not more than 10% by weight of the total fibre content consists of such fibres, weighing less than 40g/m^2	4802. 5400	3468
纸及纸板,未经涂布的,不含用机械或化学-机械方法制得的纤维或所含前述纤维不超过全部纤维重量的10%,每平方米重量在40克及以上,但不超过150克,一边不越过435毫米,另一边不超过297毫米(以未折叠计)成张的	Paper and paperboard, Uncoated, not containing fibres obtained by a mechanical or chemi-mechanical process or of which not more than 10% by weight of the total fibre content consists of such fibres, Weighing 40g/m^2 or more but not more than 150g/m^2, in sheets with one side not exceeding 435mm and the other side not exceeding 297mm in the unfolded state	4802. 5600	3468
纸及纸板,未经涂布的,不含用机械或化学-机械方法制得的纤维或所含前述纤维不超过全部纤维重量的10%,每平方米重量在40克及以上,但不超过150克,成卷	Paper and paperboard, Uncoated, not containing fibres obtained by a mechanical or chemi-mechanical process or of which not more than 10% by weight of the total fibre content consists of such fibres, Weighing 40g/m^2 or more but not more than 150g/m^2, in rolls	4802. 5500	3468
纸及纸板,未经涂布的,不含用机械或化学-机械方法制得的纤维或所含前述纤维不超过全部纤维重量的10%,每平方米重量在40克及以上,但不超过150克,其他	Paper and paperboard, uncoated, not containing fibres obtained by a mechanical or chemi-mechanical process or of which not more than 10% by weight of the total fibre content consists of such fibres, weighing 40g/m^2 or more but not more than 150g/m^2	4802. 5700	3468
纸及纸板,未经涂布的,每平方米重量超过150克,但小于225克	Paper and paperboard, uncoated, weighing more than 150g/m^2 but less than 225g/m^2	4805. 9200	458
纸及纸板,未经涂布的,每平方米重量在150克及以下,其他	Paper and paperboard, uncoated, weighing 150g/m^2 or less, nes	4805. 9190	458
纸及纸板,未经涂布的,每平方米重量在225克及以上	Paper and paperboard, uncoated, weighing 225g/m^2 or more	4805. 9300	458
纸及纸板,未经涂布的,手工制,其他	Paper and paperboard, uncoated, hand-made, nes	4802. 1090	3458

商品名称	Article Description	税则号列	申报要素
纸及纸板,未经涂布的,所含用机械或化学-机械方法制得的纤维超过全部纤维重量的10%,成卷的,其他	Paper and paperboard, uncoated, of which more than 10% by weight of the total fibre content consists of fibres obtained by a mechanical or chemi-mechanical process, in rolls, nes	4802.6190	3468
纸及纸板,未经涂布的,所含用机械或化学-机械方法制得的纤维超过全部纤维重量的10%,成张的,一边不超过435毫米,另一边不超过297毫米(以未折叠计)	Paper and paperboard, Uncoated, of which more than 10% by weight of the total fibre content consists of fibres obtained by a mechanical or chemi-mechanical process, In sheets with one side not exceeding 435mm and the other side not exceeding 297mm in the unfolded state	4802.6200	3468
纸及纸板,未经涂布的,所含用机械或化学-机械方法制得的纤维超过全部纤维重量的10%,其他	Paper and paperboard, uncoated, of which more than 10% by weight of the total fibre content consists of fibres obtained by a mechanical or chemi-mechanical process, nes	4802.6990	3468
纸及纸板,压纹的	Paper and paperboard, embossed	4808.9000	58
纸及纸板,用蜡、石蜡、硬脂精、油或甘油涂布、浸渍、覆盖的,其他	Paper and paperboard, coated, impregnated or covered with wax, paraffin wax, stearin, oil or glycerol, nes	4811.6090	458
纸及纸板,用塑料(不包括粘合剂)涂布、浸渍或覆盖的,漂白的,每平方米重量超过150克,其他	Paper and paperboard, coated, impregnated or covered with plastics (excluding adhesives), bleached, weighing more than 150g/m^2, nes	4811.5190	458
纸及纸板,用塑料(不包括粘合剂)涂布、浸渍或覆盖的,其他	Paper and paperboard, coated, impregnated or covered with plastics (excluding adhesives), nes	4811.5990	458
纸及纸板,自粘的	Paper and paperboard, self-adhesive	4811.4100	458
纸及纸板的原纸和原纸板,光敏、热敏、电敏,其他	Paper and paperboard of a kind used as a base for photo-sensitive, heat-sensitive or electro-sensitive paper or paperboard, nes	4802.2090	3458
纸夹子,内装各种纸制文具	Wallets of paper or paperboard, containing an assortment of paper stationery	4817.3000	6
纸浆、纸或纸板制品模制成型机器	Paper pulp, paper or paperboard articles moulding machines	8441.4000	
纸浆制品,压制或模制	Articles of paper pulp, moulded or pressed	4823.7000	68
纸浆制造机器,纤维素材料用	Pulp making machinery of fibrous cellulosic material	8439.1000	
纸浆制造机器的零件,纤维素材料用	Pulp making machinery parts, of fibrous cellulosic material	8439.9100	3
纸纱线	Paper yarn	5308.9091	568
纸纱线机织物	Paper yarn woven fabrics	5311.0020	2468
纸扇	Paper fans	4823.9030	68
纸塑铝复合罐的生产设备	Composite can manufacture machines for paper, plastic and aluminium	8441.3010	
纸塑铝软包装生产设备	Paper plastic and aluminium flexible packaging manufacture machines	8441.8010	
纸整理机器	Paper finishing machinery	8439.3000	
纸整理机器的零件	Paper finishing machinery parts	8439.9900	3

商品名称	Article Description	税则号列	申报要素
纸制品模制成型机器	Paper articles moulding machines	8441.4000	
纸质物品,纸浆、纸、纸板、纤维素絮纸及纤维素纤维网纸制的,其他	Articles of paper pulp, paper, paperboard, cellulose wadding or webs of cellulose fibres, nes	4823.9090	68
芷香酮	Ionones	2914.2300	36
指甲刷	Nail brushes	9603.2900	
指示板,电气的,其他	Indicator panels, electric, nes	8531.8090	3
指示板,装有液晶装置(LCD)或发光二极管(LED)的音响或视觉信号装置	Indicator panels incorporating liquid crystal devices (LCD) or light emitting diodes (LED), sound or visual signalling apparatus, electric	8531.2000	3
酯胶	Ester gums	3806.3000	4
制版机器、器具及设备,其他	Typesetting machinery, apparatus and equipment, nes	8442.3029	
制版照相机,其他	Cameras of a kind used for preparing printing plates or cylinders, nes	9006.1090	7
制动器(包括倒轮制动毂及毂闸)及其零件,自行车及脚踏车的	Brakes, including coaster braking hubs and hub brakes, and parts thereof, of bicycles and other cycles	8714.9400	3
制动器、助力制动器及其零件,30座及以上客运机动车辆用	Brakes, servo-brakes and parts of motor vehicles with 30 seats or more	8708.3092	3
制动器、助力制动器及其零件,其他车辆用	Brakes, servo-brakes and parts of motor vehicles, nes	8708.3099	3
制动器、助力制动器及其零件,特种车辆用	Brakes, servo-brakes and parts of motor vehicles with special purpose	8708.3096	3
制动器、助力制动器及其零件,拖拉机的	Brakes, servo-brakes and parts of tractors	8708.3091	3
制动器、助力制动器及其零件,小轿车用	Brakes, servo-brakes and parts of saloon cars	8708.3094	3
制动器、助力制动器及其零件,越野车(4轮驱动)用	Brakes, servo-brakes and parts of cross-country cars (4WD)	8708.3095	3
制动器、助力制动器及其零件,自卸车用	Brakes, servo-brakes and parts of dumpers	8708.3093	3
制动装置及其零件,铁道及电车道机车或其他车辆的,其他	Brakes and parts, of railway or tramway locomotives or rolling-stock, nes	8607.2900	3
制冷机组	Refrigerating units	8418.6920	57
制冷机组及热泵用零件	Refrigerating units and heat pumps parts	8418.9910	3
制冷设备,其他	Refrigerating or freezing equipment, nes	8418.6990	57
制冷设备零件,其他	Refrigerating or freezing equipment parts, nes	8418.9999	3
制冷温度在-40℃及以下的冷冻设备用零件	Freezing equipment parts, of a refrigerating temperature of -40℃ or lower	8418.9991	3
制冷温度在-40℃以上,但容积超过500升的冷藏或冷冻设备用零件	Refrigerating or freezing equipment parts, of a refrigerating temperature higher than -40℃ and a capacity exceeding 500L	8418.9992	3
制糖机器	Sugar manufacture machinery	8438.3000	
制糖机器的零件	Sugar manufacture machinery parts	8438.9000	3

商品名称	Article Description	税则号列	申报要素
制氧机,利用温度变化处理,其他	Oxygen producers, with a process involving a change of temperature, nes	8419.6019	57
制氧机,利用温度变化处理,制氧量在15000立方米/小时及以上	Oxygen producers, with a process involving a change of temperature, oxygen preparation volume no less than 15000m^3/h	8419.6011	57
制造半导体器件或集成电路的机器及装置,其他	Semiconductor devices or of electronic integrated circuits manufacture machines and apparatus, nes	8486.2090	7
制造淀粉过程中的残渣及类似的残渣	Residues of starch manufacture and similar residues	2303.1000	56
制造碳酸饮料的浓缩物	Beverage bases	2106.9010	268
制造箱、盒、管、桶或类似容器的机器,纸浆、纸或纸板制的,模制成型机器除外,其他	Machines for making cartons, boxes, cases, tubes, drums or similar containers, of paper pulp, paper or paperboard, other than by moulding, nes	8441.3090	
制造纸浆制品、纸制品或纸板制品的机器,其他	Machinery for making up paper pulp, paper or paperboard, nes	8441.8090	
质谱仪,集成电路生产用氦质谱检漏台	Mass spectrograph, integrated circuit belium spectra leak detectors	9027.8011	
质谱仪,其他	Mass spectrograph, nes	9027.8019	7
质谱仪零件、附件	Mass spectrograph parts and accessories	9027.9000	3
智力玩具	Toys for intelligence	9503.0060	5
智能卡,其他	Smart cards, nes	8523.5290	37
智能卡,未录制	Smart cards, unrecorded	8523.5210	37
蛭石,未膨胀的	Vermiculite, unexpanded	2530.1020	13456
zhong			
中耕机,农业、园艺及林业用,其他	Cultivators, for agricultural, horticultural or forestry use, nes	8432.2900	
中国象棋等棋类用品	Chinese chess and other board games	9504.9030	
中华绒螯蟹,未冻的	Freshwater crabs, not frozen	0306.2491	14
中空或真空隔温、隔音玻璃	Sealed or vacuum insulating glass	7008.0010	234
中密度纤维板,厚度不超过5毫米,密度不超过每立方厘米0.5克,其他	Medium density fibreboard (MDF), of a thickness not exceeding 5mm, of a density not exceeding 0.5g/cm^3, nes	4411.1299	48
中密度纤维板,厚度不超过5毫米,密度不超过每立方厘米0.5克,未经机械加工或盖面的	Medium density fibreboard (MDF), of a thickness not exceeding 5mm, of a density not exceeding 0.5g/cm^3, not mechanically worked or surface covered	4411.1291	48
中密度纤维板,厚度不超过5毫米,密度超过每立方厘米0.5克,但未超过每立方厘米0.8克,辐射松制的	Medium density fibreboard (MDF), of a thickness not exceeding 5mm, of a density exceeding 0.5g/cm^3 but not exceeding 0.8g/cm^3, of radiata pine	4411.1221	48
中密度纤维板,厚度不超过5毫米,密度超过每立方厘米0.5克,但未超过每立方厘米0.8克,其他	Medium density fibreboard (MDF), of a thickness not exceeding 5mm, of a density exceeding 0.5g/cm^3 but not exceeding 0.8g/cm^3, nes	4411.1229	48

Z

商品名称	Article Description	税则号列	申报要素
中密度纤维板,厚度不超过5毫米,密度超过每立方厘米0.8克,其他	Medium density fibreboard (MDF), of a thickness not exceeding 5mm, of a density exceeding 0.8g/cm³, nes	4411.1219	48
中密度纤维板,厚度不超过5毫米,密度超过每立方厘米0.8克,未经机械加工或盖面的	Medium density fibreboard (MDF), of a thickness not exceeding 5mm, of a density exceeding 0.8g/cm³, not mechanically worked or surface covered	4411.1211	48
中密度纤维板,厚度超过5毫米但未超过9毫米,密度不超过每立方厘米0.5克,其他	Medium density fibreboard (MDF), of a thickness exceeding 5mm but not exceeding 9mm, of a density not exceeding 0.5g/cm³, nes	4411.1399	48
中密度纤维板,厚度超过5毫米但未超过9毫米,密度不超过每立方厘米0.5克,未经机械加工或盖面的	Medium density fibreboard (MDF), of a thickness exceeding 5mm but not exceeding 9mm, of a density not exceeding 0.5g/cm³, not mechanically worked or surface covered	4411.1391	48
中密度纤维板,厚度超过5毫米但未超过9毫米,密度超过每立方厘米0.5克,但未超过每立方厘米0.8克,辐射松制的	Medium density fibreboard (MDF), of a thickness exceeding 5mm but not exceeding 9mm, of a density exceeding 0.5g/cm³ but not exceeding 0.8g/cm³, of radiata pine	4411.1321	48
中密度纤维板,厚度超过5毫米但未超过9毫米,密度超过每立方厘米0.5克,但未超过每立方厘米0.8克,其他	Medium density fibreboard (MDF), of a thickness exceeding 5mm but not exceeding 9mm, of a density exceeding 0.5g/cm³ but not exceeding 0.8g/cm³, nes	4411.1329	48
中密度纤维板,厚度超过5毫米但未超过9毫米,密度超过每立方厘米0.8克,其他	Medium density fibreboard (MDF), of a thickness exceeding 5mm but not exceeding 9mm, of a density exceeding 0.8g/cm³, nes	4411.1319	48
中密度纤维板,厚度超过5毫米但未超过9毫米,密度超过每立方厘米0.8克,未经机械加工或盖面的	Medium density fibreboard (MDF), of a thickness exceeding 5mm but not exceeding 9mm, of a density exceeding 0.8g/cm³, not mechanically worked or surface covered	4411.1311	48
中密度纤维板,厚度超过9毫米,密度超过每立方厘米0.5克,但未超过每立方厘米0.8克,辐射松制的	Medium density fibreboard (MDF), of a thickness exceeding 9mm, of a density exceeding 0.5g/cm³ but not exceeding 0.8g/cm³, of radiata pine	4411.1421	48
中密度纤维板,厚度超过9毫米,密度超过每立方厘米0.5克,但未超过每立方厘米0.8克,其他	Medium density fibreboard (MDF), of a thickness exceeding 9mm, of a density exceeding 0.5g/cm³ but not exceeding 0.8g/cm³, nes	4411.1429	48
中密度纤维板,厚度超过9毫米,密度超过每立方厘米0.8克,其他	Medium density fibreboard (MDF), of a thickness exceeding 9mm, of a density exceeding 0.8g/cm³, nes	4411.1419	48
中密度纤维板,厚度超过9毫米,密度超过每立方厘米0.8克,未经机械加工或盖面的	Medium density fibreboard (MDF), of a thickness exceeding 9mm, of a density exceeding 0.8g/cm³, not mechanically worked or surface covered	4411.1411	48
中密度纤维板,厚度超过9毫米,其他	Medium density fibreboard (MDF), of a thickness exceeding 9mm, nes	4411.1499	48

商品名称	Article Description	税则号列	申报要素
中密度纤维板,厚度超过9毫米,未经机械加工或盖面的	Medium density fibreboard (MDF), of a thickness exceeding 9mm, not mechanically worked or surface covered	4411.1491	48
中频放大器	Intermediate frequency amplifiers	8543.7092	37
中频放大器用零件	Intermediate frequency amplifiers parts	8543.9040	3
中式成药,其他	Medicaments of chinese type, nes	3004.9059	368
中型机(计算机)	Mid-sized computer machine	8471.4110	26
中型机(计算机),以系统形式进口或出口的	Mid-sized computer machine, presented in the form of systems	8471.4910	26
中型机的处理部件	Mid-sized computer machine processing units	8471.5010	26
中央控制门锁,机动车用,贱金属制	Central control door lock of a kind used for motor vehicles, of base metal	8301.2010	256
中药酒	Medicated liquors or wines, chinese type	3004.9051	368
终端,巨型机、大型机、中型机及小型机用	Terminating machines for the huge computers, mainframes and minicomputers	8471.6040	
钟,带仪表板的	Clocks, with instrument panel	9104.0000	5
钟,带仪表板的,车辆、航空器、航天器或船舶用的类似钟	Clocks, with instrument panel, and clocks of similar type for vehicles, aircraft, spacecraft or vessels	9104.0000	5
钟,电力驱动的,其他	Clocks, electrically operated, nes	9105.9190	5
钟,挂钟,电力驱动的	Clocks, wall clocks, electrically operated	9105.2100	5
钟,挂钟,其他	Clocks, wall clocks, nes	9105.2900	5
钟,闹钟,电力驱动的	Clocks, alarm clocks, electrically operated	9105.1100	5
钟,闹钟,其他	Clocks, alarm clocks, nes	9105.1900	5
钟,其他	Clocks, nes	9105.9900	5
钟,天文钟,电力驱动的	Clocks, astronomical chronometer, electrically operated	9105.9110	5
钟,以表芯装成的,电力驱动的	Clocks with watch movements, electrically operated	9103.1000	5
钟,以表芯装成的,其他	Clocks with watch movements, nes	9103.9000	5
钟、表零件,其他	Clock or watch parts, nes	9114.9000	6
钟表玻璃	Clock and watch glasses	7015.9010	1345
钟及类似品,贱金属制,非电动的	Gongs and the like, of base metal, non-electric	8306.1000	256
钟壳	Clock cases	9112.2000	3
钟壳零件	Clock cases parts	9112.9000	3
钟面或表面,钟、表的	Dials, of clock or watch	9114.3000	6
钟芯,不完整的	Clock movements, incomplete	9110.9090	1
钟芯,完整的,未组装或部分组装的	Clock movements, complete, unassembled or partly assembled	9110.9010	1
钟芯,完整的,未组装或部分组装的	Clock movements, complete, unassembled or partly assembled	9110.9010	1
钟芯,已组装完整的,电力驱动的,其他	Clock movements, complete and assembled, electrically operated, nes	9109.1900	5

Z

商品名称	Article Description	税则号列	申报要素
钟芯,已组装完整的,其他	Clock movements, complete and assembled, nes	9109.9000	5
种苗,其他,软体动物和水生无脊椎动物(甲壳动物除外)的,	Aquatic invertebrates and molluscs, other than crustaceans, nes, for cultivation	0307.9110	8
种苗,其他,适合供人食用的甲壳动物的	Crustaceans, nes, fit for human consumption, for cultivation	0306.2910	3
种用蛋	Eggs, for hatching	0407.0010	34
种用苗木,其他	Seedlings, nes	0602.9091	3
种植机,农业、园艺及林业用	Planters, for agricultural, horticultural or forestry use	8432.3000	5
种植土	Garden earth	2530.9099	13456
种子、果实及孢子,其他,饲料植物用的	Seeds, fruit and spores, nes, of forage plants	1209.2990	358
种子、果实及孢子,其他,种植用的	Seeds, fruit and spores, nes, of a kind used for sowing	1209.9990	358
仲丁巴比妥(INN)以及盐	Secbutabarbital (INN); salts thereof	2933.5300	36
仲丁醇	Secbutanol	2905.1420	36
仲钨酸铵	Ammonium paratungstate	2841.8010	1
重氮化合物	Diazo-compounds	2927.0000	36
重铬酸钠	Sodium dichromate	2841.3000	1
重铬酸盐,其他	Dichromates, nes	2841.5000	1
重过磷酸钙	Triple superphosphates	3103.1010	68
重晶石	Barytes	2511.1000	45
重烧镁	Magnesia, sintered	2519.9020	146
重水(氧化氘)	Heavy water (deuterium oxide)	2845.1000	5
重油,其他	Heavy oils, nes	2710.1999	8
重质液体石蜡	Heavy liquid paraffin	2710.1994	8
zhou			
轴,铁道及电车道机车或其他车辆的	Axles, of railway or tramway locomotives or rolling-stock	8607.1910	3
轴承,宝石的,钟、表的	Bearings of jewel, of clock or watch	9114.2000	6
轴承,调心球的	Bearings of self-aligning ball	8482.1010	5
轴承,鼓形滚子的	Bearings of spherical roller	8482.3000	5
轴承,滚针的	Bearings of needle roller	8482.4000	5
轴承,滚珠的,其他	Bearings of ball, nes	8482.1090	5
轴承,滑动的	Bearings of plain shaft	8483.3000	5
轴承,角接触的	Bearings of angular contact	8482.1030	5
轴承,球柱混合的	Bearings of combined ball/roller	8482.8000	5
轴承,深沟球的	Bearings of deep groove ball	8482.1020	5
轴承,推力球的	Bearings of thrust ball	8482.1040	5
轴承,圆柱形滚子的,其他	Bearings of cylindrical roller, nes	8482.5000	5
轴承,锥形滚子的,包括锥形滚子组件	Bearings of tapered roller, including cone and tapered roller assemblies	8482.2000	5

商品名称	Article Description	税则号列	申报要素
轴承零件,滚针的	Bearings parts of needles	8482. 9100	3
轴承零件,滚珠的	Bearings parts of balls	8482. 9100	3
轴承零件,滚柱的	Bearings parts of rollers	8482. 9100	3
轴承零件,滑动的	Bearings of plain shaft parts	8483. 9000	3
轴承零件,其他	Bearings parts, nes	8482. 9900	3
轴承座,未装有滚珠或滚子轴承的	Bearing housings, not incorporating ball or roller bearings	8483. 3000	
轴承座,装有滚珠或滚子轴承的	Bearing housings, incorporating ball or roller bearings	8483. 2000	
轴向柱塞泵,排液回转式	Axial plunger pump, for positive displacement, rotary	8413. 6060	27
肘管, 塑料的	Elbows, of plastics	3917. 4000	
帚及刷,用枝条或其他植物材料捆扎而成的不论是否有把	Brooms and brushes, consisting of twigs or other vegetable materials bound together, with or without handles	9603. 1000	
皱胃膜	Rennet bags	0504. 0090	14
zhu			
朱砂	Cinnabar	2617. 9010	146
珠子,贱金属制	Beads, of base metal	8308. 9000	256
猪,改良种用	Swine, live, pure-bred breeding	0103. 1000	34
猪,重量在10千克及以上,但在50千克以下	Swine, live, weighing 10kg or more, but less than 50kg	0103. 9120	48
猪,重量在10千克以下	Swine, live, weighing less than 10kg	0103. 9110	48
猪,重量在50千克及以上	Swine, live, weighing 50kg or more	0103. 9200	48
猪肝,冻的	Livers of swine, frozen	0206. 4100	15
猪毛	Hair	0502. 1020	
猪肉,冻的,其他	Meat of swine, frozen, nes	0203. 2900	14
猪肉,冻的,整头及半头,其他	Meat of swine, frozen, carcasses and halfcarcasses, nes	0203. 2190	14
猪肉,其他,干、熏、盐腌或盐渍的	Meat of swine, nes, salted, in brine, dried or smoked	0210. 1900	14
猪肉,鲜或冷的,其他	Meat of swine, fresh or chilled, nes	0203. 1900	14
猪肉,鲜或冷的,整头及半头,其他	Meat of swine, fresh or chilled, carcasses and halfcarcasses, nes	0203. 1190	14
猪肉块,冻的,带骨	Cuts, with bone in, of swine, frozen	0203. 2200	14
猪肉块,鲜或冷的,带骨	Cuts, with bone in, of swine, fresh or chilled	0203. 1200	14
猪腿,带骨的,干、熏、盐腌或盐渍的	Hams and shoulders of swine, with bone in, salted, in brine, dried or smoked	0210. 1110	14
猪油,已炼制,但税号02. 09及15. 03的货品除外	Lard, other than that of heading No. 02. 09 or 15. 03	1501. 0000	
猪油硬脂,未经乳化、混合或其他方法制作	Lard stearin, not emulsified or mixed or otherwise prepared	1503. 0000	4
猪脂肪(包括的猪油),但税号02. 09及15. 03的货品除外	Pig fat (including lard), other than that of heading No. 02. 09 or 15. 03	1501. 0000	

Z

商品名称	Article Description	税则号列	申报要素
猪脂肪,未炼制或用其他方法提取的不带瘦肉的,鲜、冷、冻、干、熏、盐腌或盐渍的	Pig fat, free of lean meat, not rendered or otherwise extracted, fresh, chilled, frozen, salted, in brine, dried or smoked	0209. 0000	14
猪鬃	Bristles	0502. 1010	
竹	Bamboos	1401. 1000	3
竹浆,从回收(废碎)纸或纸板提取的	Pulp, of bamboo, derived from recovered (waste and scrap) paper or paperboard	4706. 3000	4
竹刻	Bamboo carvings	4420. 1012	56
竹笋,其他,用醋或醋酸以外的其他方法制作或保藏的,未冷冻	Bamboo shoots, nes, prepared or preserved otherwise than by vinegar or acetic acid, not frozen	2005. 9190	148
竹笋,鲜或冷藏的	Bamboo shoots, fresh or chilled	0709. 9010	1
竹笋,盐水的,暂时保藏,但不适合直接使用的	Bamboo shoots, in brine, provisionally preserved, but unsuitable in that state for immediate consumption	0711. 9031	34
竹笋罐头,用醋或醋酸以外的其他方法制作或保藏的,未冷冻	Bamboo shoots, in airtight containers, prepared or preserved otherwise than by vinegar or acetic acid, not frozen	2005. 9110	1248
竹芋	Arrowroot	0714. 9090	34
竹制人造纤维单纱,捻度每米超过120转,非供零售用	Bamboo artificial single yarn, not put up for retail sale, with a twist exceeding 120 turns per metre	5403. 3210	3468
竹制人造纤维单纱,未加捻或捻度每米不超过120转,非供零售用	Bamboo artificial single yarn, untwisted or with a twist not exceeding 120 turns per metre, not put up for retail sale	5403. 3110	3468
竹制人造纤维短纤,未梳或未经其他纺前加工	Bamboo artificial staple fibres, not carded, combed or otherwise processed for spinning	5504. 1010	68
烛芯或类似品,用纺织材料机织、编结或针织而成的	Wicks, of woven textile, plaited or knitted, for candles or the like	5908. 0000	
助听器,不包括零件、附件	Hearing aids, excluding parts and accessories	9021. 4000	
苎麻,短纤及废料	Remie, tow and waste	5305. 0013	4
苎麻,经加工但未纺制的	Remie, processed but not spun	5305. 0012	4
苎麻,其他	Remie, nes	5305. 0019	4
苎麻,生的	Remie, raw	5305. 0011	4
苎麻机织物,按重量计苎麻含量在85%及以上的,其他	Ramie woven fabrics, containing 85% or more by weight of ramie, nes	5311. 0013	2468
苎麻机织物,按重量计苎麻含量在85%及以上的,未漂白	Ramie woven fabrics, containing 85% or more by weight of ramie, unbleached	5311. 0012	2468
苎麻机织物,按重量计苎麻含量在85%以下的,其他	Ramie woven fabrics, containing less than 85% by weight of ramie, nes	5311. 0015	2468
苎麻机织物,按重量计苎麻含量在85%以下的,未漂白	Ramie woven fabrics, containing less than 85% by weight of ramie, unbleached	5311. 0014	2468
苎麻纱线,按重量计苎麻含量在85%及以上的色纱线	Ramie yarn, containing 85% or more by weight of ramie, coloured yarn	5308. 9012	568

商品名称	Article Description	税则号列	申报要素
苎麻纱线,按重量计苎麻含量在85%及以上的未漂白或漂白纱线	Ramie yarn, containing 85% or more by weight of ramie, unbleached or bleached yarn	5308.9011	568
苎麻纱线,按重量计苎麻含量在85%以下的色纱线	Ramie yarn, containing less than 85% by weight of coloured yarn	5308.9014	568
苎麻纱线,按重量计苎麻含量在85%以下的未漂白或漂白纱线	Ramie yarn, containing less than 85% by weight of ramie, unbleached or bleached yarn	5308.9013	568
注模,金属、硬质合金用型模	Moulds of injection types, for metal or metal carbides	8480.4100	7
注模,塑料或橡胶用	Moulds for rubber or plastics, injection types	8480.7100	7
注射机,加工橡胶或塑料及其产品用,其他	Injection-moulding machines, for working rubber or plastics or for the manufacture of products from these materials, nes	8477.1090	7
注射器,不论是否装有针头	Syringes, with or without needles	9018.3100	
注塑机,用来加工塑料	Injection-moulding machines, for working plastics	8477.1010	7
柱和梁,木制的	Posts and beams, of wood	4418.6000	58
柱塞泵,排液泵回转式,径向的	Plunger pumps, positive displacement pumps, rotary, radial	8413.6050	27
柱塞泵,排液泵回转式,轴向的	Plunger pumps, positive displacement pumps, rotary, axial	8413.6060	27
柱塞泵,排液往复式	Plunger pumps, for positive displacement, reciprocating	8413.5031	23
筑路机,发动机输出功率超过235.36千瓦(320马力)的	Graders, with an engine of an output exceeding 235.36kW(320hp)	8429.2010	57
筑路机,其他	Graders, nes	8429.2090	57
筑路机零件	Graders parts	8431.4990	3
铸造机,连铸,板坯的	Casting machines for ingot slab, continuous	8454.3022	
铸造机,连铸,方坯的	Casting machines for ingot block, continuous	8454.3021	
铸造机,连铸,钢坯,其他	Casting machines for ingot, continuous, nes	8454.3029	
铸造机,其他	Casting machines, nes	8454.3090	
铸造机,压铸,冷室的	Casting machines, cold chamber, die- casting	8454.3010	
铸造用砂模的成形机器	Foundry moulds of sand forming machines	8474.8090	7
铸造制品,钢铁制,工业用,其他	Cast articles of iron or steel, for technical use, nes	7325.9910	346
铸造制品,钢铁制,其他	Cast articles of iron or steel, nes	7325.9990	346
铸造制品,无可锻性铸铁制,工业用	Cast articles of non-malleable cast iron, for technical use	7325.1010	346
铸造制品,无可锻性铸铁制,其他	Cast articles of non-malleable cast iron, nes	7325.1090	346
铸字机	Type casters	8442.3010	
zhua			
抓斗,推土机或起重机零件	Grabs, parts of bulldozer or cranes	8431.4100	3
爪及其粉末	Claws and powder thereof	0507.9090	14

Z

商品名称	Article Description	税则号列	申报要素
zhuan			
砖及类似品,用水泥、石膏及其他矿物粘合材料粘合植物纤维、稻草、刨花、木片屑、木粉、锯末或木废料制成	Blocks and similar articles of vegetable fibre, of straw or of shavings, chips, particles, sawdust or other waste, of wood, agglomerated with cement, plaster or other mineral binders	6808.0000	456
转笔刀	Pencile sharpener	8472.9090	
转杯纺纱机	Rotor spinning machine	8445.2031	7
转动坐具,可调高度的	Swivel seats with variable height adjustment	9401.3000	6
转化糖	Invert sugar	1702.9000	
转炉,金属冶炼及铸造用	Converters, of a kind used in metallurgy or in metal foundries	8454.1000	
转炉用零件	Converters parts	8454.9090	3
转录数据的机器	Transcribing machines for data	8471.9000	
转盘(唱机唱盘)	Turntables (record-decks)	8519.3000	
转盘或唱机用零件、附件	Turntables(record-decks) or record-players parts and accessories	8522.9010	3
转数计	Revolution counters	9029.1010	
转数计零件、附件	Revolution counters parts and accessories	9029.9000	3
转速表	Tachometers	9029.2090	7
转速表零件、附件	Tachometers parts and accessories	9029.9000	3
转向架及轴,铁道及电车道机车或其他车辆的,其他	Other bogies and bissel-bogies, of railway or tramway locomotives or rolling-stock, nes	8607.1200	3
转向盘、转向柱、转向器及其零件,30座及以上客运机动车辆用	Steering wheels, steering columns, steering boxes and parts of motor vehicles with 30 seats or more	8708.9420	3
转向盘、转向柱、转向器及其零件,其他	Steering wheels, steering columns, steering boxes and parts, nes	8708.9490	3
转向盘、转向柱、转向器及其零件,特种车辆用	Steering wheels, steering columns, steering boxes and parts of motor vehicles with special purpose	8708.9460	3
转向盘、转向柱、转向器及其零件,拖拉机的	Steering wheels, steering columns, steering boxes and parts of tractors	8708.9410	3
转向盘、转向柱、转向器及其零件,小轿车用	Steering wheels, steering columns, steering boxes and parts of saloon cars	8708.9440	3
转向盘、转向柱、转向器及其零件,越野车(4轮驱动)用	Steering wheels, steering columns, steering boxes and parts of cross-country cars(4WD)	8708.9450	3
转向盘、转向柱、转向器及其零件,自卸车用	Steering wheels, steering columns, steering boxes and parts of dumpers	8708.9430	3
转印贴花纸,其他	Transfers, nes	4908.9000	4
转印纸,成卷或成张的,卷宽度超过36厘米,或长超过36厘米且宽超过15厘米	Transfer papers, in rolls or sheets, of width exceeding 36cm or in roll or one side exceeding 36cm and other side exceeding 15cm in rectangular sheets	4809.9000	458

商品名称	Article Description	税则号列	申报要素
zhuang			
装船机	Ship loading cranes	8426.1910	7
装订机,书本用,其他	Binding machinery for book, nes	8440.1090	
装订机零件,书本用,其他	Binding machinery parts, for book, nes	8440.9000	3
装订用机器,其他	Stapling machines, nes	8472.9029	
装甲战斗车辆的零件和附件	Armoured fighting vehicles parts and accessories	8710.0090	3
装甲战斗车辆整车,机动的	Armoured fighting vehicles, assembled	8710.0010	
装配半导体器件或集成电路的设备,其他	Assembling machines for semiconductor devices, nes	8486.4029	7
装配机器,加工木材、软木、骨、硬质橡胶、硬质塑料或类似硬质材料的	Assembling machines, for working wood, cork, bone, hard rubber, hard plastics or similar hard materials	8465.9400	7
装配机器,印刷电路装配用,其他	Assemblying machines, for assemblying elements on printed circuit boards, nes	8479.8969	7
装饰带机	Trimmings making machines	8447.9090	7
装饰毯,"奥步生"及类似式样的手织装饰毯	Tapestries, Aubusson type hand-woven and the like	5805.0090	468
装饰用织物制品,非针织或非钩编的,刺绣的,合成纤维制	Furnishing articles, not knitted or crocheted, embroidered, of synthetic fibres	6304.9310	346
装饰用织物制品,非针织或非钩编的,刺绣的,麻制	Furnishing articles, not knitted or crocheted, embroidered, of bast fibres	6304.9921	346
装饰用织物制品,非针织或非钩编的,刺绣的,棉制	Furnishing articles, not knitted or crocheted, embroidered, of cotton	6304.9210	346
装饰用织物制品,非针织或非钩编的,合成纤维制,其他	Furnishing articles, not knitted or crocheted, of synthetic fibres, nes	6304.9390	346
装饰用织物制品,非针织或非钩编的,麻制,其他	Furnishing articles, not knitted or crocheted, of bast fibres, nes	6304.9929	346
装饰用织物制品,非针织或非钩编的,棉制,其他	Furnishing articles, not knitted or crocheted, of cotton, nes	6304.9290	346
装饰用织物制品,非针织或非钩编的,其他	Furnishing articles, not knitted or crocheted, nes	6304.9990	346
装饰用织物制品,非针织或非钩编的,丝及绢丝制	Furnishing articles, not knitted or crocheted, of silk or silk waste	6304.9910	346
装饰用织物制品,钩编的,其他	Furnishing articles, crocheted, nes	6304.9139	346
装饰用织物制品,钩编的,手工制	Furnishing articles, crocheted, hand-worked	6304.9131	346
装饰用织物制品,针织的,其他	Furnishing articles, knitted, nes	6304.9129	346
装饰用织物制品,针织的,手工制	Furnishing articles, knitted, hand-worked	6304.9121	346
装填机器,瓶、罐、箱、袋或其他容器的	Filling machines, for bottles, cans, boxes, bags or other containers	8422.3090	
装卸桥,其他	Loading and unloading bridges, nes	8426.1949	7
装卸装置,集成电路工厂用的,其他	Lifting or loading machines solely or principally of a kind used in the electronic integrated circuits factories, nes	8486.4039	7

商品名称	Article Description	税则号列	申报要素
装卸装置零件及附件,集成电路工厂用的	Lifting or loading machines parts and accessories, solely or principally of a kind used in the electronic integrated circuits factories	8486.9010	3
装药空囊	Empty cachets of a kind suitable for pharmaceutical use	1905.9000	28
装在蹄片上的制动摩擦片	Mounted brake linings	8708.3010	3
zhui			
追击炮,其他	Mortars, nes	9301.1900	7
追击炮,自推进的	Mortars, self-propelled	9301.1100	7
锥冰晶石	Chiolite, natural	2530.9099	13456
锥形袋,纸制的	Cones, of paper, paperboard, nes	4819.4000	68
锥形滚子轴承,包括锥形滚子组件	Tapered roller bearings, including cone and tapered roller assemblies	8482.2000	5
zhuo			
着色剂及类似制品,调制的,陶瓷、搪瓷及玻璃工业用	Colours and similar preparations, prepared, of a kind used in the ceramic, enamelling or glass industry	3207.1000	13
着色料及其他制品,其他	Colouring matter and other preparations, nes	3206.4900	2368
着色料及以其为基本成分的制品,动物质的	Colouring matter of animal origin and preparations based thereon	3203.0020	34
着色料及以其为基本成分的制品,植物质的,其他	Colouring matter of vegetable origin and preparations based thereon, nes	3203.0019	34
着色料为基本成分的制品,有机合成的,其他	Colouring matter preparations, based on synthetic organic products, nes	3204.9090	345
着色料组成的混合物	Colouring matter, mixed	3204.1990	345
琢磨油石	Oilstones	6804.3010	36
zi			
籽黄	Rhubarb	1211.9024	34
子弹,猎枪的	Cartridges for shotgun	9306.2100	
子弹带,皮革或再生皮革制的	Bandoliers, of leather or of composition leather	4203.3020	456
子弹及其零件,铆接机或类似工具用	Cartridges for riveting or similar tools, and parts thereof	9306.3080	3
子弹及其零件,弩枪式人道捕杀器用	Cartridges for captive-bolt humane killers, and parts thereof	9306.3080	3
子弹及其零件,其他	Cartridges and parts thereof, other	9306.3090	3
子弹零件,猎枪的	Cartridges parts for shotgun	9306.2900	3
紫菜,调味的	Laver, seasoned	2008.9931	248
紫菜,干的	Laver, dried	1212.2041	14
紫菜,其他	Laver, nes	1212.2049	14
紫菜,鲜的	Laver, fresh	1212.2042	14
紫苜蓿,其他,饲料用	Lucerne (alfalfa), nes, forage products	1214.9000	

商品名称	Article Description	税则号列	申报要素
紫苜蓿粗粉及团粒,饲料用	Lucerne(alfalfa) meal and pellets, forage products	1214.1000	1
紫苜蓿子,种植用的	Lucerne(alfalfa) seed, for sowing	1209.2100	358
紫萁,干的	Osmund, dried	0712.9020	4
紫苏子	Perilla seeds	1207.9999	3
紫外线灯	Ultra-violet lamps	8539.4900	35
紫外线分光仪、分光光度计及摄谱仪	UV spectrometers, spectrophotometers and spectrographs	9027.3000	
紫外线装置,医疗、外科、牙科或兽医用	Ultra-violet ray apparatus, used in medical, surgical, dental or veterinary sciences	9018.2000	
字典	Dictionaries	4901.9100	15
字母标志,贱金属制,税号94.05的货品除外	Letters symbols, of base metal, excluding those of heading No. 94.05	8310.0000	256
自动搬运机器,集成电路工厂用的	Automated material handling machines solely or principally of a kind used in the electronic integrated circuits factories	8486.4031	7
自动闭门器,贱金属制	Automatic door closets, of base metal	8302.6000	256
自动插件机,印刷电路装配用	Automatic plug-in machines, for assemblying elements on printed circuit boards	8479.8961	7
自动调焦组件,照相机用	Automatic focal setting units for cameras	9006.9191	3
自动调节或控制仪器及装置,其他	Automatic regulating or controlling instruments and apparatus, nes	9032.8900	7
自动调节或控制仪器及装置的零件、附件	Automatic regulating or controlling instruments and apparatus parts and accessories	9032.9000	3
自动断路器,用于电压不超过1000伏的线路	Automatic circuit breakers, for a voltage not exceeding 1000V	8536.2000	8
自动断路器,用于电压超过1000伏的线路,其他	Automatic circuit breakers, for a voltage exceeding 1000V, nes	8535.2900	8
自动断路器,用于电压低于72.5千伏的线路	Automatic circuit breakers, for a voltage of less than 72.5 kV	8535.2100	8
自动付钞机	Automatic banknote dispensers	8472.9090	
自动钢琴	Automatic pianos	9201.9000	5
自动柜员机	Automated teller	8472.9010	
自动柜员机用出钞器的零件、附件	Banknote dispenser of automated teller's parts and accessories	8473.4010	3
自动化立体仓储设备	Automatic warehouse equipments	8479.8992	7
自动换挡变速箱及其零件,小轿车用	Automatic gearshift for saloon cars and parts thereof	8708.4091	3
自动驾驶仪	Automatic pilots	9014.2010	
自动驾驶仪用零件、附件	Automatic pilots parts and accessories	9014.9010	3
自动络筒机	Automatic bobbin winders	8445.4010	7
自动络筒机的辅助机器	Automatic bobbin winders auxiliary machinery	8448.1900	3
自动模式数控步冲压力机,数控的,加工金属用	Cnc automatic tool change punch press, numerically controlled, for working metal	8462.4111	7

Z

商品名称	Article Description	税则号列	申报要素
自动模型,橱窗装饰用的	Automata used for shop window dressing	9618.0000	
自动售货机,其他	Automatic goods-vending machines, nes	8476.8900	5
自动售货机,装有加热或制冷装置的,其他	Automatic goods-vending machines, incorporating heating or refrigerating devices, nes	8476.8100	5
自动售货机的零件	Automatic goods-vending machines parts	8476.9000	3
自动数据处理设备,同一机壳内至少有一个中央处理部件及一个输入和输出部件,不论是否组合式,其他	Automatic data processing machines, comprising in the same housing at least a central processing unit and an input and output unit, whether or not combined, nes	8471.4190	26
自动数据处理设备,以系统形式进口或出口的,其他	Automatic data processing machines, presented in the form of systems, nes	8471.4999	26
自动数据处理设备,重量不超过10千克的,便携式,至少由一个中央处理部件、一个键盘及一个显示器组成	Automatic data processing machines, weighing not more than 10kg, portable, consisting of at least a central processing unit, a keyboard and a display	8471.3000	
自动数据处理设备部件的零件、附件,其他	Automatic data processing machines units's parts and accessories, nes	8473.3090	3
自动数据处理设备储存部件的零件、附件	Automatic data processing machines storage units's parts and accessories	8473.3010	3
自动数据处理设备处理部件,其他	Automatic data processing machines processing units, nes	8471.5090	26
自动数据处理设备存储部件,其他	Automatic data processing machines storage units, nes	8471.7090	
自动数据处理设备的其他部件	Units of automatic data processing machines, nes	8471.8000	
自动数据处理设备输入或输出部件,其他	Automatic data processing machines input or output units, nes	8471.6090	
自动数据处理设备输入输出部件的零件、附件	Automatic data processing machines input or output units's parts and accessories	8473.3010	3
自动梯的零件	Escalators parts	8431.3100	3
自动梯及自动人行道	Escalators and moving walkways	8428.4000	57
自动贴片机,印刷电路装配用	Automatic coreslice adhering machines, for assemblying elements on printed circuit boards	8479.8962	7
自动销售机,饮料的,其他	Automatic beverage-vending machines, nes	8476.2900	5
自动销售机,饮料的,装有加热或制冷装置的	Automatic beverage-vending machines, incorporating heating or refrigerating devices	8476.2100	5
自动抓棉机	Bale plucker, for cotton type fibres	8445.1112	7
自攻螺钉,钢铁制的	Self-tapping screws, of iron of steel	7318.1400	268
自来水笔	Fountain pens	9608.3910	
自启板牙切头	Self-opening dieheads	8466.1000	3
自停装置,织机的辅助机器	Automatic stop motions, weaving auxiliary machines	8448.1900	3
自推进机动车,装有升降或搬运装置的,其他	Self-propelled trucks, fitted with lifting or handing equipment, nes	8427.2090	7
自推进机动车,装有升降或搬运装置的电动的,其他	Self-propelled trucks, fitted with lifting or handing equipment, powered by an electric motor, nes	8427.1090	7

Z

商品名称	Article Description	税则号列	申报要素
自卸车,电动轮货运,非公路用	Dumpers for the transport of goods, electromobile, for off-highway use	8704.1030	58
自卸车,非公路用,其他	Dumpers designed for off-highway use, nes	8704.1090	58
自卸车用零件、附件,其他	Dumpers parts and accessories, nes	8708.9939	3
自卸货车,子目 8606.1000 的货品除外	Self-discharging wans and wagons, other than those of subheading 8606.1000	8606.3000	37
自行车,16 英寸及以下	Bicycles, not larger than 16″	8712.0081	8
自行车,竞赛型	Bicycle for racing	8712.0020	8
自行车,其他	Bicycles, nes	8712.0089	8
自行车,山地型	Bicycle, mountain type	8712.0030	8
自行车,越野型,16、18 及 20 英寸	Bicycles, cross-country type, 16″, 18″or 20″	8712.0041	8
自行车,越野型,其他	Bicycles, cross-country type, nes	8712.0049	8
自行车及其他脚踏车的零件,其他	Bicycles and other cycles' parts, nes	8714.9900	3
自行车用视觉信号装置	Bicycles visual signalling equipment	8512.1000	7
自行车用照明装置	Bicycles lighting equipment	8512.1000	7
自印复写纸,成卷或成张的,卷宽度超过 36 厘米,或长超过 36 厘米且宽超过 15 厘米	Self-copy paper, in rolls or sheets, of a width exceeding 36cm or in roll or one side exceeding 36cm and other side exceeding 15cm in rectangular sheets	4809.2000	458
自印复写纸,其他	Self-copy paper, nes	4816.2000	58
自由端纺纱机,其他	Open-end spinner, nes	8445.2039	7
自由活塞式发生器,燃气轮机用的	Free piston generators for gas turbines	8414.8010	23
zong			
综丝及综框,织机用	Healds and heald-frames for looms	8448.4200	3
棕刚玉,人造的	Brown fused alumina, artificial	2818.1010	136
棕榈蜡	Palm wax	1521.1000	6
棕榈仁油及其分离品,初榨的	Palm kernel oil and fractions thereof, crude oil	1513.2100	4
棕榈仁油及其分离品,其他	Palm kernel oil and fractions thereof, nes	1513.2900	4
棕榈酸及其盐和酯	Palmitic acid, their salts and esters	2915.7090	36
棕榈芯,用其他方法制作或保藏的	Palm hearts, otherwise prepared, or preserved	2008.9100	248
棕榈液油(熔点 19℃~24℃)	Palm olein	1511.9010	4
棕榈硬脂(熔点 44℃~56℃)	Palm stearin	1511.9020	48
棕榈油及其分离品,初榨的	Palm oil and its fractions, crude oil	1511.1000	4
棕榈油及其分离品,其他	Palm oil and its fractions, nes	1511.9090	48
纵行起圈纱线	Loopwale yarn	5606.0000	
zou			
走带机构(机芯),不论是否装有磁头,盒式磁带录音机或放声机用	Transport mechanisms, whether or not incorporating a magnetic head, of cassette magnetic tape recorders or reproducers	8522.9021	3

Z

商品名称	Article Description	税则号列	申报要素
zu			
足球	Footballs	9506.6210	
组合机,具有打印、复印或传真中两种及以上功能的,可与自动数据处理设备或网络连接,静电感光式	Combined machines, which perform two or more of the functions of printing, copying or facsimile transmission, capable of connecting to an automatic data processing machine or to a network, electrostatic photosensitive-type	8443.3110	57
组合机,具有打印、复印或传真中两种及以上功能的,可与自动数据处理设备或网络连接,其他	Combined machines, which perform two or more of the functions of printing, copying or facsimile transmission, capable of connecting to an automatic data processing machine or to a network, nes	8443.3190	57
组合机床,单工位的,加工金属的	Single station construction machines, for working metal	8457.2000	7
组合机床,多工位的,加工金属的	Multi station transfer machines, for working metal	8457.3000	7
组合机零件及附件,具有打印、复印或传真中两种及以上功能的,可与自动数据处理设备或网络连接,其他	Combined machines parts and accessories, which perform two or more of the functions of printing, copying or facsimile transmission, capable of connecting to an automatic data processing machine or to a network, nes	8443.9990	3
组织化处理机,化学纺织纤维的	Texturing machinery for man-made textile materials	8444.0090	
zuan			
钻,手提式,本身装有电动动力装置的	Drills, hand tools, with self-contained electric motor	8467.2100	57
钻床,切削金属的,其他	Drilling machines, for removing metal, nes	8459.2900	7
钻床,数控的,切削金属的	Drilling machines, numerically controlled, for removing metal	8459.2100	7
钻床,直线移动式动力头,切削金属的	Drilling machines, way-type unit head machines, for removing metal	8459.1000	7
钻钢,空心的,合金钢或非合金钢制的	Bars and rods, hollow, for drill, of alloy or non-alloy steel	7228.8000	468
钻管,钻探石油及天然气用,无缝的,不锈钢制,其他	Drill pipe, of a kind used in drilling for oil or gas, seamless, of stainless steel, nes	7304.2290	6
钻管,钻探石油及天然气用,无缝的,不锈钢制,外径不超过168.3毫米	Drill pipe, of a kind used in drilling for oil or gas, of stainless steel, seamless, having an outside diameter not exceeding 168.3mm	7304.2210	6
钻管,钻探石油及天然气用,无缝的,其他	Drill pipe, of a kind used in drilling for oil or gas, seamless, nes	7304.2390	6
钻管,钻探石油及天然气用,无缝的,外径不超过168.3毫米	Drill pipe, of a kind used in drilling for oil or gas, seamless, having an outside diameter not exceeding 168.3mm	7304.2310	6
钻孔工具	Drilling tools, hand tools	8205.1000	256

商品名称	Article Description	税则号列	申报要素
钻孔工具,但凿岩及钻探用的除外,带有天然或合成金刚石、立方氮化硼制的工作部件,可互换	Drilling tools, other than for rock drilling, with working part of natural or synthetic diamonds or cubic boron nitride, interchangeable	8207.5010	256
钻孔工具,但凿岩及钻探用的除外,可互换,其他	Drilling tools, other than for rock drilling, interchangeable, nes	8207.5090	256
钻孔机器,加工木材、软木、骨、硬质橡胶、硬质塑料或类似硬质材料的	Drilling machines, for working wood, cork, bone, hard rubber, hard plastics or similar hard materials	8465.9500	7
钻石,非工业用,其他	Diamonds, non-industrial, nes	7102.3900	145
钻石,非工业用,未加工或经简单锯开、劈开或粗磨	Diamonds, non-industrial, unworked or simply sawn, cleaved or bruted	7102.3100	145
钻石,工业用,合成或再造的	Diamonds, for technical use, synthetic or reconstructed	7104.9011	145
钻石,工业用,其他	Diamonds, industrial, nes	7102.2900	145
钻石,工业用,未加工或经简单锯开、劈开或粗磨	Diamonds, industrial, unworked or simply sawn, cleaved or bruted	7102.2100	145
钻石,合成或再造的,其他	Diamonds, synthetic or reconstructed, nes	7104.9091	145
钻石,合成或再造的,未加工或经简单锯开或粗制成形	Diamonds, synthetic or reconstructed, unworked or simply sawn or roughly shaped	7104.2010	145
钻石,未分级	Diamonds, unsorted	7102.1000	145
钻石的粉末,人工合成的	Diamonds dust and powder, synthetic	7105.1020	145
钻石的粉末,天然的	Diamonds dust and powder, natural	7105.1010	145
钻探车,流动的	Drilling derricks, mobile	8705.2000	7
钻探或凿井机械,其他	Boring or sinking machinery, nes	8430.4900	5
钻探或凿井机械,自推进的,其他	Boring or sinking machinery, self-propelled, nes	8430.4190	5
钻探或凿井机械,自推进的,钻探深度在6000米及以上的	Boring or sinking machinery, self-propelled, of drilling depth of 6000m or more	8430.4121	5
钻探或凿井机械,自推进的,钻探深度在6000米以下的履带式自推进钻机	Boring or sinking machinery, self-propelled, crawler boring machinery of drilling depth not exceeding 6000m	8430.4122	5
钻探或凿井机械,自推进的,钻探深度在6000米以下的其他钻探机	Boring or sinking machinery, self-propelled, other boring machinery of drilling depth not exceeding 6000m	8430.4129	5
钻探机零件,其他	Of other drilling machinery	8431.4320	3
钻探机零件,石油或天然气钻探用	Of oil and natural gas drilling machinery	8431.4310	3
钻探平台,浮动式	Drilling platforms, floating	8905.2000	
钻探平台,潜水式	Drilling platforms, submersible	8905.2000	
zun			
鳟鱼,冻的	Trout (Salmo trutta, Oncorhynchus mykiss, oncorhynchus clarki, Oncorhynchus aguabonita, Oncorhynchus gilae, Oncorhynchus apache and Oncorhynchus chrysogaster), frozen	0303.2100	18
鳟鱼,其他,活的	Trout, nes, living	0301.9190	15

Z

商品名称	Article Description	税则号列	申报要素
鳟鱼,鲜或冷的,	Trout (Salmo trutta, Oncorhynchus my kiss, Oncorhynchus clarki, Oncorhynchus aguabonita, Oncorhynchus gilae, Oncorhynchus apache and Oncohynchus chrysogaster), fresh or chilled	0302. 1100	18
鳟鱼苗	Fry, of trout	0301. 9110	15
zuo			
左苯丙胺(INN)以及它们的盐	Levamfetamine(INN); salts thereof	2921. 4600	36
左非诺(INN)及其盐	Levorpharol(INN) and its salts	2933. 4100	36
左甲苯丙胺,它的盐、酯及其他衍生物	Levometamfe-tamine, salts, esters and other derivatives thereof	2939. 9190	34
左轮手枪	Revolvers	9302. 0000	
左轮手枪和其他手枪,发射空包弹的	Pistols and revolvers for firing blank ammunition	9303. 9000	
左轮手枪用零件、附件	Revolvers parts and accessories	9305. 1000	3
作焊条芯子或焊条涂料用的制品	Preparations of a kind used as cores or coatings for welding electrodes or rods	3810. 9000	36
坐标测量仪	Coordinate measuring machine	9031. 8020	
坐具,飞机用	Seats of a kind used for aircraft	9401. 1000	
坐具,机动车辆用,皮革或再生皮革面的	Seats of a kind used for motor vehicles, with outer surface of leather or composition leather	9401. 2010	6
坐具,机动车辆用,其他	Seats of a kind used for motor vehicles, nes	9401. 2090	6
坐具,金属框架的,其他	Seats, with metal frames, nes	9401. 7900	6
坐具,金属框架的,装软垫的,皮革或再生皮革面的	Seats, with metal frames upholstered, with outer surface of leather or composition leather	9401. 7110	6
坐具,金属框架的,装软垫的,其他	Seats, with metal frames upholstered, nes	9401. 7190	6
坐具,可调高度的,转动的	Seats with variable height adjustment, swivel	9401. 3000	6
坐具,柳条及类似材料制	Seats of osier or similar materials	9401. 5900	6
坐具,木框架的,其他	Seats, with wooden frames, nes	9401. 6900	6
坐具,木框架的,装软垫的,皮革或再生皮革面的	Seats, with wooden frames upholstered, with outer surface of leather or composition leather	9401. 6110	6
坐具,木框架的,装软垫的,其他	Seats, with wooden frames upholstered, nes	9401. 6190	6
坐具,其他	Seats, nes	9401. 8090	6
坐具,石制的	Seats of stone	9401. 8010	6
坐具,竹制或藤制的	Seats of bamboo or rattan	9401. 5100	6
坐具零件,机动车辆用,其他	Seats parts, of the motor vehicles, nes	9401. 9019	3
坐具零件,其他	Seats parts, nes	9401. 9090	3
坐具套,皮革或再生皮革的	Cover of seat, of leather or of composition leather	4205. 0010	456
坐浴盆,塑料的	Bidets, of plastics	3922. 9000	236
坐浴盆,陶制	Bidets, of pottery	6910. 9000	268
坐浴盆,瓷制	Bidets, of porcelain or china	6910. 1000	268
柞蚕丝	Tussah silk	5002. 0020	45

商品名称	Article Description	税则号列	申报要素
柞蚕丝机织物,按重量计丝或绢丝含量在85%及以上,其他	Tussah silk fabrics, containing 85% or more by weight of silk or of silk waste, nes	5007. 2029	4568
柞蚕丝机织物,未漂白或漂白,按重量计丝或绢丝含量在85%及以上	Tussah silk fabrics, unbleached or bleached, containing 85% or more by weight of silk or of silk waste	5007. 2021	4568
座垫,化纤棉填充的	Pouffes, stuffed with man-made fibres	9404. 9040	6
座垫,其他	Pouffes, nes	9404. 9090	6
座垫,兽毛填充的	Pouffes, stuffed with animal hair	9404. 9020	6
座垫,丝棉填充的	Pouffes, stuffed with silk wadding	9404. 9030	6
座垫,羽毛或羽绒填充的	Pouffes, stuffed with feathers or down	9404. 9010	6
座式升降机,其他	Chair-lifts, nes	8428. 6090	
座式旋臂起重机	Pedestal jib cranes	8426. 3000	7
座椅安全带	Safety seat belts	8708. 2100	3
座椅调角器,机动车辆用	Seat angle regulating devices, of the motor vehicles	9401. 9011	3

其　他

商品名称	Article Description	税则号列	申报要素
1-(1,3-苯并二噁茂-5 基)丙烷-2 酮	1-(1,3-benzodioxol-5-yl) propan-2-one	2932. 9200	36
1,1,1-三氯-2,2-双(4-氯苯基)乙烷	1,1,1-trichloro-2,2-bis(p-chlorophenyl)ethane	2903. 6200	36
1,1,1-三氯-2,2-双(4-氯苯基)乙烷	Clofenotane (INN)	2903. 6200	36
1,1,1-三氯乙烷(甲基氯仿)	1,1,1-trichloroethane(methylchloro form)	2903. 1910	36
1,1,3,3,3-五氟-2 三氟甲基-1-丙烯	1,1,3,3,3-pentafluro-2-trifluromethyl-1-propene	2903. 3910	36
1,2,3,4,5,6-六氯环已烷	1,2,3,4,5,6-hexachlorocyclohexane	2903. 5100	36
1,2-丙二醇	Propylene glycol(propane-1,2-diol)	2905. 3200	36
1,2-二氯乙烷	1,2-dichloroethane(ethylene dichloride)	2903. 1500	36
1,2-二溴乙烷(ISO)	Ethylene dibromide (ISO)(1,2-dibromoethane)	2903. 3100	36
1,2-乙二醇	Ethylene glycol(ethanediol)	2905. 3100	36
1,3 丁二烯	Buta-1,3-diene	2901. 2400	368
1,8-桉树脑	Eucalgptol	2909. 2081	36
1-丁烯	1-butene	2901. 2310	368
1-氯-2,3-环氧丙烷	1-chloro-2,3-epoxypropane	2910. 3000	36
1-萘胺(α-萘胺)及其衍生物以及它们的盐	1-naphthylamine (α-naphthy lamine) and their derivatives;salts thereof	2921. 4500	36
1-氰基胍	1-cyanoguanidine	2926. 2000	36
2,2-二苯基-2-羟基乙酸	2,2-diphenyl-2-hydroxyacetic acid	2918. 1910	36
2,2'-双甲氧羰基-4,4',-双甲氧基-5,6,5',6'-双亚甲二氧基联苯	Bifendate	2932. 9920	36
2,2'-氧联二乙醇	2,2'-oxydiethanol	2909. 4100	36
2,4,5-三氯苯氧基乙酸及其盐或酯	2, 4, 5-trichlorophenoxyacetic acid, its salts and esters	2918. 9100	36
2,4,5-涕(ISO)及其盐或酯	2,4,5-T(ISO), its salts and esters	2918. 9100	36
2,4-和 2,6-甲苯二异氰酸酯混合物	Toluene diisocyanate	2929. 1010	36
2,5-二甲基已二醇	2,5-dimethyl hexandiol	2905. 3910	36
2,6-二乙基苯胺	2,6-diethylaniline	2921. 4940	36
2,6-甲基乙基苯胺	2,6-methyl ethyl aniline	2921. 4930	36
2-苯基乙醇	2-phenylethyl alcohol	2906. 2910	36
2-丁烯	2-butene	2901. 2320	368
2-甲基丙烯	2-methylpropylene	2901. 2330	368
2-糠醛	2-furaldehyde(furfuraldehyde)	2932. 1200	36
2-萘胺(β-萘胺)及其衍生物以及它们的盐	2-naphthylamine (β-naphthylamine) and their derivatives;salts thereof	2921. 4500	36
2-萘酚	2-naphthols	2907. 1510	36
2-羟基-4-甲氧基二苯甲酮	2-hydroxy-4-methoxydibenzophenone	2914. 5020	36

商品名称	Article Description	税则号列	申报要素
2-乙基-2-(羟甲基)丙烷-1,3-二醇(三羟甲基丙烷)	2-ethyl-2-(hydroxymethyl) propane-1, 3-diol (trimethylolpropane)	2905.4100	36
2-乙酰氨基苯甲酸及其盐	2-acetamidobenzoic acid and its salts	2924.2300	36
3,3-二甲基丁-2-醇(频哪基醇)	3,3-dimethyl-2-butanol(pinacolyl alcohol)	2905.1910	36
3,4-二氯三氟甲苯	3,4-dichlorotrifluoride toluene	2903.6920	36
3,4-亚甲二氧基苯甲醛	Piperonal	2932.9300	36
30座及以上客运机动车辆用零件、附件,其他	Motor vehicles parts and accessories, with 30 seats or more, nes	8708.9929	3
3-甲氧基-4-羟基苯甲醛	4-hydroxy-3-methoxybenzaldehyde	2912.4100	36
3-氯-1-丙烯	3-chloro-1-propene	2903.2910	36
3-乙氧基-4-羟基苯甲醛	3-ethoxy-4-hydroxyben-zaldehyde	2912.4200	36
4-(4'-烷基苯基)-1-(4'-烷基苯基)-2-氟苯	4-(4'-alkylphenyl)-1-(4'-alkylphenyl)-2-fluorobenzene	2903.6930	36
4-(4'-烷基环己基)环己基乙烯	4-(4'-alkylcyclohexyl) cyclohexyl ethylene	2902.9040	6
4,4'-异亚丙基联苯酚及其盐	4,4-isopropylidenediphenol and its salts	2907.2300	36
4-丙烯基-1,2-亚甲二氧基苯	Isosafrole	2932.9100	36
4-甲基-2-戊酮	4-methl1-2-pentanone	2914.1300	36
4-氰基-2-二甲氨基-4,4-二苯基丁烷	4-cyano-2-dimethylamino-4,4-diphenylbutane	2926.3000	36
4-烯丙基-1,2-亚甲二氧基苯	Safrole	2932.9400	36
5～7号燃料油	Fuel oils No. 5～No. 7	2710.1922	6
6-氨基青霉烷酸(6APA)	6-aminopenicillanic acid	2941.1093	
6-己内酰胺	6-hexanolactam (epsilon-caprolactam)	2933.7100	36
7-氨基头孢烷酸	7-aminocephalosporianic acid	2941.9051	
7-氨基脱乙酰氧基头孢烷酸	7-aminodeacetoxycefanoic acid	2941.9051	
7-羟基苯并呋喃	Furan phenol	2932.9910	36
B型超声波诊断仪	B-ultrasonic diagnostic equipment	9018.1210	
CTP版,未曝光的	CTP plate, unexposed	3701.3023	12368
DL-泛酸及其衍生物	DL-pantothenic acid and its derivatives	2936.2400	36
DVD播放机	Digital video disc player	8521.9012	5
DV菊酸甲酯	DVchrysanthemimono carboxylate	2916.2010	36
D-泛酸及其衍生物	D-pantothenic acid and its derivatives	2936.2400	36
D-去甲假麻黄碱(INN)及其盐	D-norpseudoephedrine and its salts	2939.4300	34
H型钢,除热轧、热拉拔或热挤压外未经进一步加工,截面高度低于80毫米	H sections, not further worked than hot-rolled, hot-drawn or extruded, of a height of less than 80mm	7216.1010	468
H型钢,除热轧、热拉拔或热挤压外未经进一步加工,截面高度在200毫米以上,且不超过800毫米	H sections, not further worked than hot-rolled, hot-drawn or extruded of a height of 200mm or more, and not exceeding 800mm	7216.3319	468
H型钢,除热轧、热拉拔或热挤压外未经进一步加工,截面高度在80毫米及以上,且不超过200毫米	H sections, not further worked than hot-rolled, hot-drawn or extruded of a height of 80mm or more, and not exceeding 200mm	7216.3390	468

商品名称	Article Description	税则号列	申报要素
H 型钢,除热轧、热拉拔或热挤压外未经进一步加工,截面高度在 800 毫米以上	H sections, not further worked than hot-rolled, hot-drawn or extruded of a height exceeding 800mm	7216.3311	468
IP 电话信号转换设备	IP telephone signal converters	8517.6233	7
MDI,粗制	MDI, crude	3909.3010	1256
MDI,聚合的	MDI, polymeric	3909.3010	1256
N,N-二(2-氯乙基)甲胺	N,N-bis(2-chloroethyl) methylamine	2921.1940	36
N,N-二(2-氯乙基)乙胺	N,N-bis(2-chloroethyl) ethylamine	2921.1930	36
N-乙酰邻氨基苯甲酸及其盐	N-acety-lanthranilic acid and its salts	2924.2300	36
PS 版,未曝光的	Precoated sensitized plate, unexposed	3701.3022	12368
TDI	Toluene diisocyanate	2929.1010	36
TODI	O-xylene diisocyanate	2929.1020	36
T 恤衫,针织或钩编的,及绢丝制	T-shirts, knitted or crocheted, of silk or silk waste	6109.9010	2456
T 恤衫,针织或钩编的,棉制	T-shirts, knitted or crocheted, of cotton	6109.1000	2456
T 恤衫,针织或钩编的,其他	T-shirts, knitted or crocheted, nes	6109.9090	2456
U235 浓缩铀及其化合物	Uranium enriched in U235 and its compounds	2844.2000	
U235 贫化铀及其化合物	Uranium depleted in U235 and its compounds	2844.3000	
U 形钉,钢铁制的	Staples, of iron or steel	7317.0000	36
U 形钉,铝制	Staples of aluminium	7616.1000	36
U 形钉及类似品,铜制或钢铁制带铜头的	Staples and similar articles, of copper or of iron or steel with heads of copper	7415.1000	56
VCD 播放机	Video compact disc player	8521.9011	5
X 光检查造影剂	Opacifying preparations for X-ray examinations	3006.3000	36
X 射线安全检查设备,低剂量	X-ray security inspecting equipment, low dosage	9022.1910	
X 射线的应用设备,其他	X-rays apparatus, nes	9022.1990	3
X 射线的应用设备,牙科用,其他	X-rays apparatus, for dental uses, nes	9022.1300	3
X 射线的应用设备,医疗、外科或兽医用,其他	X-rays apparatus, for medical, surgical or veterinary uses, nes	9022.1400	3
X 射线断层检查仪	X-rays computed tomography apparatus	9022.1200	
X 射线管	X-ray tubes	9022.3000	
X 射线影像增强器	X-ray intensifiers	9022.9010	
X 射线的测量或检验仪器及装置	X-ray measuring or detecting instruments and apparatus	9030.1000	
α 射线的测量或检验仪器及装置	Alpha measuring or detecting instruments and apparatus	9030.1000	
α 射线的应用设备,其他	Alpha radiations apparatus, nes	9022.2900	3
α 射线的应用设备,医疗、外科、牙科或兽医用	Alpha radiations apparatus, for medical, surgical, dental or veterinary uses	9022.2100	
β-萘酚	β-naphthol	2907.1510	36
β 射线的测量或检验仪器及装置	Beta measuring or detecting instruments and apparatus	9030.1000	
β 射线的应用设备,其他	Beta radiations apparatus, nes	9022.2900	3

商品名称	Article Description	税则号列	申报要素
β 射线的应用设备,医疗、外科、牙科或兽医用	Beta radiations apparatus, for medical, surgical, dental or veterinary uses	9022. 2100	
γ 射线的测量或检验仪器及装置	Gamma measuring or detecting instruments and apparatus	9030. 1000	
γ 射线的应用设备,其他	Gamma radiations apparatus, nes	9022. 2900	3
γ 射线的应用设备,医疗、外科、牙科或兽医用	Gamma radiations apparatus, for medical, surgical, dental or veterinary uses	9022. 2100	

Engilish—Chinese

英汉对照

A

A

Article Description	商品名称	Tariff Code	D. R. ①
A carotene	胡萝卜素,天然 α 型	3203.0019	34
Abaca	蕉麻	5305.0020	4
Abalone, frozen, dried, salted or in brine	鲍鱼,冻、干、盐腌或盐渍的	0307.9910	14
Abalone, live, fresh or chilled	鲍鱼,活、鲜或冷的	0307.9191	1
Abrasive powder or grain, natural or artificial, on a base of woven textile fabric only	砂布	6805.1000	246
Abrasive powder or grain, natural or artificial, on a base of other materials	磨料或颗粒,天然或人造的,以其他材料为底的	6805.3000	246
Abrasive powder or grain, natural or artificial, on a base of woven textile fabric only	磨料或颗粒,天然或人造的,以纺织材料为底的	6805.1000	246
Abrasives, natural, nes	磨料,天然,其他	2513.2000	
Absinth	苦艾酒	2208.9090	2468
Absorbent cotton, medical, surgical, dental or veterinary purposes	药棉,供医疗、外科、牙科或兽医用	3005.9010	1346
Ac voltage-stabilized suppliers, of a power of less than 10kW and an accuracy of not better than 0.001, nes	交流稳压电源,功率小于 10 千瓦,精度低于千分之一,其他	8504.4015	78
Accordions and similar instruments	手风琴及类似乐器	9205.9020	5
Account balances, having a maximum weighing capacity not exceeding 30kg	计价秤,最大称量不超过 30 千克	8423.8110	
Account books, of paper or paperboard	账本,纸或纸板制的	4820.1000	
Accounting machines	会计计算机,装有计算装置的	8470.3000	
Accumulators of lead-acid, nes	蓄电池,铅酸的,其他	8507.2000	68
Accumulators of lead-acid, of a kind used for starting piston engines	蓄电池,铅酸的,用于起动活塞式发动机	8507.1000	68
Accumulators of lithium ion	蓄电池,锂离子的	8507.8020	68
Accumulators of nickel-cadmium	蓄电池,镍镉的	8507.3000	68
Accumulators of nickel-hydrogen	蓄电池,镍氢的	8507.8010	68
Accumulators of nickel-iron	蓄电池,镍铁的	8507.4000	68
Accumulators parts, lead-acid	蓄电池用零件,铅酸的	8507.9010	3
Accumulators parts, nes	蓄电池零件,其他	8507.9090	3
Accumulators, nes	蓄电池,其他	8507.8090	68
Acenaphthene	苊	2902.9090	6
Acephate	乙酰甲胺磷	2929.9040	36
Acetaldehyde	乙醛	2912.1200	36
Acetaldoxime	乙醛肟	2928.0000	36

① D. R. = Declaration Requirement(s). There are primary declaration requirements in this colume. In case of policy changes, readers are requested to refer the latest version published by General Administration of Customs.

A

Article Description	商品名称	Tariff Code	D. R.
Acetals, whether or not with other oxygen function, and their haogenated, sulphonated, nitrated or nitrosated derivatives	缩醛,不论是否含有其他含氧基,及其卤化、磺化、硝化或亚硝化衍生物	2911.0000	36
Acetanilide	萨罗芬	2924.2990	36
Acetanilide	退热冰	2924.2990	36
Acetanilide	乙酰替苯胺	2924.2990	36
Acetic acid salts, nes	乙酸盐,其他	2915.2990	36
Acetic acid, glacial, food grade	冰乙酸,食品级	2915.2111	36
Acetic acid, glacial, nes	冰乙酸,其他	2915.2119	36
Acetic acid, nes	乙酸,其他	2915.2190	36
Acetic anhydride	乙酸酐	2915.2400	36
Acetone	丙酮	2914.1100	36
Acetophenone	苯乙酮	2914.3910	36
Acetoxime	丙酮肟	2928.0000	36
Acetylene	乙炔	2901.2920	368
Acetylene gas generators parts	乙炔发生器的零件	8405.9000	3
Acetylene gas generators, with or without their purifiers	乙炔发生器,不论有无净化器	8405.1000	3
Acetylsalicylic acid	阿斯匹林	2918.2210	36
Acetylsalicylic acid	邻乙酰水杨酸	2918.2210	36
Acetyl-spiramycin and its derivatives; salts thereof	乙酰螺旋霉素及其衍生物以及它们的盐	2941.9070	
Achine-tools for working wood, cork, bone, hard rubber, hard plastics or similar hard materials, nes	加工机床,加工木材、软木、骨、硬质橡胶、硬质塑料或类似硬质材料的,其他	8465.9900	7
Acid oils from refining	酸性油,精炼所得的	3823.1900	6
Acrylic acid and its salts	丙烯酸及其盐	2916.1100	36
Acrylic or modacrylic filament tow	聚丙烯腈或变性聚丙烯腈长丝丝束	5501.3000	68
Acrylic or modacrylic staple fibres woven fabrics, mixed mainly or solely with man-made filaments, nes	聚丙烯腈或变性聚丙烯腈短机织物,主要或仅与化学纤维长丝混纺	5515.2100	2468
Acrylic or modacrylic staple fibres woven fabrics, mixed mainly or solely with wool or fine animal hair, nes	聚丙烯腈或变性聚丙烯腈短机织物,主要或仅与羊毛或动物细毛混纺	5515.2200	2468
Acrylic or modacrylic staple fibres woven fabrics, nes	聚丙烯腈或变性聚丙烯腈短机织物,其他	5515.2900	2468
Acrylic or modacrylic staple fibres yarn, mixed mainly or solely with cotton	聚丙烯腈或变性聚丙烯腈短纤纱线,主要或仅与棉混纺	5509.6200	68
Acrylic or modacrylic staple fibres yarn, mixed mainly or solely with wool or fine animal hair	聚丙烯腈或变性聚丙烯腈短纤纱线,主要或仅与羊毛或动物细毛混纺	5509.6100	68
Acrylic or modacrylic staple fibres yarn, nes	聚丙烯腈或变性聚丙烯腈短纤纱线,其他	5509.6900	68

Article Description	商品名称	Tariff Code	D. R.
Acrylic or modacrylic staple fibres, carded, combed or otherwise processed for spinning	聚丙烯腈或变性聚丙烯腈短纤，已梳或经其他纺前加工	5506.3000	68
Acrylic or modacrylie staple fibres, not carded, combed or otherwise processed for spinning	聚丙烯腈或变性聚丙烯腈短纤，未梳或未经其他纺前加工	5503.3000	68
Acrylic polymers, in primary forms, nes	丙烯酸聚合物，初级形状的，其他	3906.9090	1256
Acrylonitrile	丙烯腈	2926.1000	36
Acrylonitrile-butadiene-styrene (ABS) copolymers, in primary forms, nes	丙烯腈-丁二烯-苯乙烯(ABS)共聚物，初级形状的，其他	3903.3090	1256
Acrylonitrile-butadiene-styrene (ABS) copolymers, modified, in primary forms	丙烯腈-丁二烯-苯乙烯(ABS)共聚物，改性的，初级形状的	3903.3010	1256
Acrylonitrile-butadient rubber (NBR) latex	丁腈橡胶(NBR)胶乳	4002.5100	136
Acrylonitrile-butadient rubber (NBR), in primary forms	丁腈橡胶(NBR)，初级形状的	4002.5910	136
Acrylonitrile-butadient rubber (NBR), nes	丁腈橡胶(NBR)，其他	4002.5990	136
Activated carbon, nes	活性碳，其他	3802.1090	34
Activated carbon, wood based	活性碳，木质的	3802.1010	34
Activated natural mineral products	活性天然矿产品	3802.9000	34
Active yeasts	酵母，活性	2102.1000	28
Acyclic aldehydes without other oxygen function, nes	无环醛，不含其他含氧基的，其他	2912.1900	36
Acyclic ethers, nes	无环醚，其他	2909.1900	36
Acyclic hydrocarbons, saturated	无环烃，饱和的	2901.1000	368
Acyclic hydrocarbons, unsaturated, nes	无环烃，不饱和的，其他	2901.2990	368
Acyclic ketones without other oxygen function, nes	无环酮，不含其他含氧基的，其他	2914.1900	36
Acyclic monoamines and their derivatives; salts thereof, nes	无环单胺及其衍生物以及它们的盐，其他	2921.1990	36
Acyclic polyamines and their derivatives; salts thereof, nes	无环多胺及其衍生物以及它们的盐，其他	2921.2900	36
Acyclic terpene alcohols, nes	无环萜烯醇，其他	2905.2290	36
Acyclie polycarboxylic acids, their anhydrides, halides, peroxides, peroxyacids and their derivatives, nes	无环多元羧酸及其酸酐、酰卤化物、过氧化物和过氧酸以及它们的衍生物，其他	2917.1900	36
Additives for lubricating oils, containing petroleum oils or oils obtained from bituminous minerals	润滑油添加剂，含有石油或从沥青矿物提取的油类	3811.2100	236
Additives for lubricating oils, for mineral oils and alike, nes	润滑油添加剂，用于矿物油及类似液体，其他	3811.2900	236
Address plate embossing machines	地址铭牌压印机	8472.9040	
Addressing machines	地址印写机	8472.9040	
Address-plates, of base metal, excluding those of heading No. 94.05	地名牌，贱金属制，税号 94.05 的货品除外	8310.0000	256
Adenophora axilliflora	沙参	1211.9034	34
Adermin	吡哆醇	2936.2500	36

A

Article Description	商品名称	Tariff Code	D. R.
Adhesion barriers, for surgical or dental use, sterile, whether or not absorbable	抗粘连阻隔材料,外科或牙科用,无菌,不论是否可吸收	3006.1000	3
Adhesive dressings	胶粘敷料	3005.1090	1346
Adhesive plasters	橡皮膏	3005.1010	1346
Adhesive tape of a width not exceeding 20cm, rubberized, nes	胶带,宽度不超过20厘米的,用橡胶处理的,其他	5906.1090	48
Adhesives based on epoxy resin	粘合剂,以环氧树脂为基本成分的	3506.9120	36
Adhesives based on polyamide	粘合剂,以聚酰胺为基本成分的	3506.9110	36
Adhesives, prepared, nes	粘合剂,调制的,其他	3506.9900	36
Adhesives, adhesives based on polymers or on rubber, nes	粘合剂,以橡胶或聚合物为基本成分的,其他	3506.9190	36
Adipic acid, its salts and esters	已二酸及其盐和酯	2917.1200	36
Aerated waters, containing added sugar or other sweetening matter or flavoured	汽水,加味、加糖或其他甜物质的	2202.1000	248
Aerated waters, not containing added sugar or other sweetening matter or flavoured	汽水,未加糖或其他甜物质及未加味的	2201.1020	28
Aerating beverages machinery parts	饮料充气机零件	8422.9090	
Aerials and aerial reflectors of all kinds, and their parts, for radar apparatus and radio navigational aid apparatus	天线或天线反射器及其零件,雷达设备及无线电导航设备用	8529.1010	3
Aerials and aerial reflectors of all kinds, and their parts, for radio-broadcast receivers and their combinations, television receivers	天线或天线反射器及其零件,无线电收音机及其组合机、电视接收机用	8529.1020	3
Aerials and aerial reflectors of all kinds, and their parts, nes	天线或天线反射器及其零件,其他	8529.1090	3
Aerials and parts of communication apparatus	天线及其零件,通信设备用	8517.7070	3
Aeroplanes and other aircraft, of an unladen weight exceeding 15000kg but not exceeding 45000kg	飞机及其他航空器,空载重量超过15000千克,但不超过45000千克	8802.4010	
Aeroplanes and other aircraft, of an unladen weight exceeding 2000kg but not exceeding 15000kg	飞机及其他航空器,空载重量超过2000千克,但不超过15000千克	8802.3000	
Aeroplanes and other aircraft, of an unladen weight exceeding 45000kg	飞机及其他航空器,空载重量超过45000千克	8802.4020	
Aeroplanes and other aircraft, of an unladen weight not exceeding 2000kg	飞机及其他航空器,空载重量不超过2000千克	8802.2000	
Aeroplanes parts, nes	飞机的零件,其他	8803.3000	3
Aerosol therapy apparatus	喷雾治疗器	9019.2000	
Aeyclic amides (including acyclic carbamates) and their derivatives; salts thereof, nes	无环酰胺(包括无环氨基甲酸酯)及其衍生物以及它们的盐,其他	2924.1990	36
Agaragar	琼脂	1302.3100	5
Agarbatti	神香	3307.4100	23
Agricultural machinery parts, nes	农业用机器零件,其他	8436.9900	3
Agricultural machinery, including germination plant fitted with mechanical or thermal equipment, nes	农业用机器,包括装有机械或热力装置的催芽设备,其他	8436.8000	

Article Description	商品名称	Tariff Code	D. R.
Ahydroxydiphenylacetic acid	二苯羟乙酸	2918. 1910	36
Air brakes and parts, of railway or tramway locomotives or rolling-stock	空气制动器及其零件,铁道及电车道机车或其他车辆的	8607. 2100	3
Air combat simulators and parts thereof	空战模拟器及其零件	8805. 2100	3
Air compressors mounted on a wheeled chassis for towing	空气压缩机,装在拖车底盘上的	8414. 4000	23
Air conditioning machines parts, of a kind used for persons, in motor vehicles	空气调节器零件,机动车辆上供人使用的	8415. 9090	23
Air conditioning machines parts, other than a kind used for persons, in motor vehicles	空气调节器零件,非机动车辆上供人使用的	8415. 9010	23
Air conditioning machines, incorporating a refrigerating unit and a valve for reversal of the cooling/heat cycle (reversible heat pumps), of a refrigerating effect exceeding 4000Cal per hour	空气调节器,装有制冷装置及一个冷热循环换向阀的(可逆式热泵),制冷量超过4000大卡/时	8415. 8120	25
Air conditioning machines, incorporating a refrigerating unit and a valve for reversal of the cooling/heat cycle (reversible heat pumps), of a refrigerating effect not exceeding 4000Cal per hour	空气调节器,装有制冷装置及一个冷热循环换向阀的(可逆式热泵),制冷量不超过4000大卡/时	8415. 8110	25
Air conditioning machines, incorporating a refrigerating unit, of a refrigerating effect exceeding 4000Cal per hour	空气调节器,装有制冷装置的,制冷量超过4000大卡/时	8415. 8220	25
Air conditioning machines, incorporating a refrigerating unit, of a refrigerating effect not exceeding 4000Cal per hour	空气调节器,装有制冷装置的,制冷量不超过4000大卡/时	8415. 8210	25
Air conditioning machines, not incorporating a refrigerating unit	空气调节器,未装有制冷装置的	8415. 8300	25
Air conditioning machines, of a kind used for persons, in motor vehicles	空气调节器,机动车辆上供人使用的	8415. 2000	25
Air conditioning machines, window or wall types, self-contained	空气调节器,窗式或壁式,独立式	8415. 1010	25
Air conditioning machines, window or wall types, split systerm, of a refrigerating effect exceeding 4000Cal per hour	空气调节器,窗式或壁式,分体式,制冷量超过4000大卡/时	8415. 1022	25
Air conditioning machines, window or wall types, split systerm, of a refrigerating effect not exceeding 4000Cal per hour	空气调节器,窗式或壁式,分体式,制冷量不超过4000大卡/时	8415. 1021	25
Air coolers, evaporative	空气冷却器,蒸发式的	8479. 6000	7
Air dehumidifiers	空气减湿器	8479. 8920	7
Air gun pellets	气枪弹丸	9306. 2900	3
Air heaters and parts thereof, of iron or steel, not electrically heated, incorporating a motor-dirven fan or blower	空气加热器及其零件,钢铁制,非电热的,装有电动风扇或鼓风机	7322. 9000	7
Air humidifiers	空气增湿器	8479. 8920	7

A

Article Description	商品名称	Tariff Code	D. R.
Air jet looms, for weaving fabrics of a with exceeding 30cm, shuttleless type	喷气织机,所织织物宽度超过30厘米的无梭织机	8446.3050	7
Air or gas guns	气枪	9304.0000	
Air or gas pistols	气手枪	9304.0000	
Air pumps parts	空气泵零件	8414.9090	23
Air pumps, hand-operated or foot-operated	空气泵,手动或脚踏式	8414.2000	27
Air twisting devices	空气捻接器	8448.3930	3
Air, compressed	空气,压缩的	2853.0090	
Air, liquid	空气,液态的	2853.0090	
Aircraft engines, spark-ignition reciprocating or rotary, of an output exceeding 298kW	航空器发动机,点燃往复式或旋转式,输出功率超过298千瓦	8407.1020	3
Aircraft engines, spark-ignition reciprocating or rotary, of an output not exceeding 298kW	航空器发动机,点燃往复式或旋转式,输出功率不超过298千瓦	8407.1010	3
Aircraft launching gear and parts thereof	航空器的发射装置及其零件	8805.1000	3
Aircraft parts, nes	航空器的零件,其他	8803.9000	3
Aircraft, non-powered	航空器,无动力的	8801.0090	
Airtight containers of bovine animals	罐头,牛的	1602.5010	248
Airtight containers of swine	罐头,猪的	1602.4910	248
Airtight containers, of any animal, nes	罐头,其他	1602.9010	248
Airtight containers, of fowls of the species gallus domesticus	罐头,鸡的	1602.3210	48
Airtight containers, of poultry of heading 01.05, nes	罐头,其他家禽的	1602.3910	248
Airtight containers, of tomatoes, whole or in pieces	罐头,番茄的,整个或切片	2002.1010	248
Alabaster	蜡石	2515.2000	148
Alabaster and articles thereof, worked, nes	蜡石及其制品,已加工的,其他	6802.9190	3468
Alabaster carvings	蜡石石刻	6802.9110	3468
Alabaster monumental or building stone and articles thereof, simply cut or sawn, with a flat or even surface	蜡石碑石或建筑用石及其制品,简单切削或锯开并具有一个平面的	6802.2190	3468
Alances of a sensitivity of 50mg or better, nes	天平,感量为50毫克或更精密的,其他	9016.0090	8
Alarm clocks movements, complete and assembled, elcetrically operated	闹钟芯,已组装完整的,电力驱动的	9109.1100	5
Alarm clocks, electrically operated	闹钟,电力驱动的	9105.1100	5
Alarm clocks, nes	闹钟,其他	9105.1900	5
Albacore or longfinned tunas (thunnus alalunga), fresh or chilled	长鳍金枪鱼,鲜或冷的,	0302.3100	18
Albacore tunas (thunnus alalunga), frozen	长鳍金枪鱼,冻的	0303.4100	18
Albumin derivatives, nes	白蛋白衍生物,其他	3502.9000	13
Albumin from egg, dried	白蛋白,卵清蛋白,干的	3502.1100	13
Albumin from egg, nes	白蛋白,卵清蛋白,其他	3502.1900	13

Article Description	商品名称	Tariff Code	D. R.
Albumin from milk, including concentrates of two or more whey proteins	白蛋白,乳白蛋白,包括两种或两种以上的乳清蛋白浓缩物	3502. 2000	13
Albuminates	白蛋白盐	3502. 9000	13
Albums for collections, of paper or paperboard	粘贴簿,纸或纸板制的	4820. 5000	
Albums for samples, of paper or paperboard	样品簿,纸或纸板制的	4820. 5000	
Alcohol peroxides and their halogenated, sulphonated, nitrated or nitrosated derivatives	过氧化醇及其卤化、磺化、硝化或亚硝化衍生物	2909. 6000	36
Alcoholic preparations of a kind used for the manufacture of beverages, compound	酒精制品,制造饮料用,复合的	2106. 9020	268
Aldehydes with other oxygen function, nes	醛,含氧基的,其他	2912. 4900	36
Aldehyde-alcohols	醛醇	2912. 3000	36
Aldrin (ISO)	艾氏剂(ISO)	2903. 5200	36
Alfentanil(INN); salts thereof	阿芬太尼(INN)以及盐	2933. 3300	36
Algin	褐藻胶	1302. 3912	3
Alginic acid, its salts and esters, in primary forms	藻酸及其盐和酯,初级形状的	3913. 1000	146
Aligning tube welding machines, fully or partly automatic	直缝焊管机,全自动或半自动的	8515. 2110	
Alizarin	茜素	3204. 1200	345
Alkali metals, nes	碱金属,其他	2805. 1900	
Alkaline-earth metals, nes	碱土金属,其他	2805. 1900	
Alkaloids or derivatives medicaments, nes, consisting of two or more constituents which have been mixed together, not put up in measured doses or in forms or packings for retail sale	生物碱及其衍生物药品,其他,两种或两种以上成分混合而成的,未配定剂量或制成零售包装	3003. 4090	368
Alkaloids or derivatives medicaments, nes, mixed or unmixed, put up in measured doses or in forms or packings for retail sale	生物碱及其衍生物药品,其他,混合或未混合的,配定剂量或制成零售包装	3004. 4090	368
Alkaloids, natural or reproduced by synthesis, and their salts, ethers, esters and other derivatives, nes	生物碱及其盐、醚、酯和其他衍生物,天然或合成再制的	2939. 9990	34
Alkyd resins, in primary forms	醇酸树脂,初级形状的	3907. 5000	1256
Alkylbenzenes, mixed, from alkylation process	混合烷基苯,烷基化制得	3817. 0000	36
Alkylnaphthalenes, mixed, from alkylation process	混合烷基萘,烷基化制得	3817. 0000	36
All terrain vehicles	全地形车	8703. 1011	58
Allene	丙二烯	2901. 2990	368
Alliaceous vegetables, nes, fresh or chilled	葱属蔬菜,其他,鲜或冷藏的	0703. 9090	1
Allobarbital (INN); salts thereof	阿洛巴比妥(INN)以及盐	2933. 5300	36
Alloy steel in ingots and other primary forms, nes	合金钢,锭状及其他初级形状,其他	7224. 1000	468
Alloy steel powders, nes	合金钢粉末,其他	7205. 2100	6
Alloy steel semi-finished products, nes	合金钢制的半制成品,其他	7224. 9090	468
Alloy steel semi-finished products, raw casting forging stocks, individual piece weight of 10t or more, nes	合金钢制的半制成品,单件重量在10吨及以上的粗铸锻件坯	7224. 9010	468

A

Article Description	商品名称	Tariff Code	D. R.
Alloys dispersion (including cermets), ceramic products and mixtures containing uranium enriched in U235, plutonium or compounds of these products	合金、分散体(包括金属陶瓷)、陶瓷产品及混合物,含U235浓缩铀、钚或它们的化合物的	2844. 2000	
Alloys, dispersions (including cermets), ceramic products and mixtures containing uranium depleted in U235, thorium or compounds of these products	合金、分散体(包括金属陶瓷)、陶瓷产品及混合物,含U235贫化铀、钍或它们的化合物的	2844. 3000	
Allyl alcohol	烯丙醇	2905. 2900	36
Almonds, in shell	巴旦杏,未去壳	0802. 1100	134
Almonds, shelled	巴旦杏,去壳	0802. 1200	134
Aloes wood	沉香	1211. 9033	34
Aloys, dispersions (including cermets), ceramic products and mixtures containing natural uranium or natural uranium compouds	合金、分散体(包括金属陶瓷)、陶瓷产品及混合物,含天然铀或天然铀化合物的	2844. 1000	
Alpha measuring or detecting instruments and apparatus	α射线的测量或检验仪器及装置	9030. 1000	
Alpha radiations apparatus, for medical, surgical, dental or veterinary uses	α射线的应用设备,医疗、外科、牙科或兽医用	9022. 2100	
Alpha radiations apparatus, nes	α射线的应用设备,其他	9022. 2900	3
Alprazolam (INN); salts thereof	阿普唑仑(INN)以及盐	2933. 9100	36
Aluminium alloys	铝合金	7601. 2000	6
Aluminium articles for technical use	铝制品,工业用	7616. 9910	36
Aluminium articles, nes	铝制品,其他	7616. 9990	36
Aluminium calcium phosphates, natural, ground	磷酸铝钙,天然的,碾磨	2510. 2090	46
Aluminium calcium phosphates, natural, unground	磷酸铝钙,天然的,未碾磨	2510. 1090	46
Aluminium chlorides	氯化铝	2827. 3200	
Aluminium fluorides, anhydrous	氟化铝,无水的	2826. 1210	
Aluminium fluorides, nes	氟化铝,其他	2826. 1290	
Aluminium foil, backed, of a thickness not exceeding 0. 2mm	铝箔,有衬背,铝厚度不超过0. 2毫米	7607. 2000	68
Aluminium foil, not backed, of a thickness not exceeding 0. 2mm, nes	铝箔,无衬背,厚度不超过0. 2毫米,其他	7607. 1900	68
Aluminium foil, not backed, rolled but not further worked, of a thickness exceeding 0. 007mm but not exceeding 0. 01mm	铝箔,无衬背,轧制后未经进一步加工的,厚度大于0. 007毫米,但不超过0. 01毫米	7607. 1120	68
Aluminium foil, not backed, rolled but not further worked, of a thickness not exceeding 0. 007mm	铝箔,无衬背,轧制后未经进一步加工的,厚度不超过0. 007毫米	7607. 1110	68
Aluminium foil, not backed, rolled but not further worked, of a thickness not exceeding 0. 2mm, nes	铝箔,无衬背,轧制后未经进一步加工的,厚度不超过0. 2毫米,其他	7607. 1190	68
Aluminium hydroxide	氢氧化铝	2818. 3000	26
Aluminium ores and concentrates	铝矿砂及其精矿	2606. 0000	146
Aluminium oxide, other than artificial corundum	氧化铝,但人造刚玉除外	2818. 2000	136

Article Description	商品名称	Tariff Code	D. R.
Aluminium plates, rods profiles, tubes and the like, prepared for use in structures, worked	铝板、杆、型材、异型材、管子及类似品,结构体用的,已加工	7610.9000	56
Aluminium structures, nes	铝制结构体,其他	7610.9000	56
Aluminium sulphates	硫酸铝	2833.2200	
Aluminium, not alloyed, containing by weight 99.95% or more of aluminium	铝,非合金的,按重量计含铝量在99.95%及以上	7601.1010	6
Aluminium, not alloyed, nes	铝,非合金的,其他	7601.1090	6
Aluminosilicates whether or not chemically defined	硅铝酸盐,不论是否已有化学定义的	2842.1000	
Aluminous cement	矾土水泥	2523.3000	3
Alums, nes	矾,其他	2833.3090	
Alumstone	明矾石	2530.9099	13456
Amalgams of precious metals	汞齐,贵金属的	2843.9000	
Amalgams, other than amalgams of precious metals	汞齐,非贵金属的	2853.0090	
Ambergris	龙涎香	0510.0020	14
Ambroid (agglomerated amber)	琥珀	2530.9099	13456
American ginseng	西洋参	1211.2010	34
Amfepramone (INN) and salts thereof	安非拉酮以及它们的盐	2922.3100	36
Amfetamine (INN), salts thereof	安非他明(INN)以及它们的盐	2921.4600	36
Amidines, nes	脒,其他	2925.2900	36
Amino acids, nes	氨基酸,其他	2922.4910	36
Aminohydroxynaphthalenesulphonic acid and their salts	氨基羟基萘磺酸及其盐	2922.2100	36
Aminophylline (theophylline-ethylenediamine) and their derivatives; salts thereof, nes	氨茶碱及其衍生物以及它们的盐,其他	2939.5900	34
Aminorex(INN); salts thereof	阿米雷司(INN)及盐	2934.9100	36
Amino-acid derivatives(as hormones)	氨基酸衍生物(用作激素)	2937.4000	36
Amino-acidphenols	氨基酸酚	2922.5000	36
Amino-acids, other than those containing more than one kind of oxygen function, and their esters; salts thereof, nes	氨基酸及其酯,但含有一种以上含氧基的除外,以及它们的盐,其他	2922.4999	36
Amino-alcohols, other than those containing more than one kind of oxygen function, their ethers and esters; salts thereof, nes	氨基醇(但含有一种以上含氧基的除外)及其醚和酯,以及它们的盐,其他	2922.1990	36
Amino-alcohol-phenols	氨基醇酚	2922.5000	36
Amino-aldehydes, other than those containing more than one kind of oxygen function; salts thereof, nes	氨基醛,但含有一种以上含氧基的除外,以及它们的盐,其他	2922.3900	36
Amino-ketones, other than those containing more than one kind of oxygen function; salts thereof, nes	氨基酮,但含有一种以上含氧基的除外,以及它们的盐,其他	2922.3900	36
Amino-naphthols, other than those containing more than one kind of oxygen function, their ethers and esters; salts thereof, nes	氨基萘酚(但含有一种以上含氧基的除外)及其醚和酯,以及它们的盐,其他	2922.2990	36

A

Article Description	商品名称	Tariff Code	D. R.
Amino-phenols, other than those containing more than one kind of oxygen function, their ethers and esters; salts thereof, nes	氨基酚(但含有一种以上含氧基的除外)及其醚和酯,以及它们的盐,其他	2922.2990	36
Amino-quinones, other than those containing more than one kind of oxygen function; salts thereof, nes	氨基醌,但含有一种以上含氧基的除外,以及它们的盐,其他	2922.3900	36
Amino-resins, in primary forms, nes	氨基树脂,初级形状的,其他	3909.3090	1256
Ammeters, of measuring range of 5.5 or less, digital, without a recording device	电流表,量程在五位半及以下的,数字的,不带记录装置	9030.3310	
Ammeters, with a recording device	电流表,带记录装置	9030.3900	7
Ammonia, anhydrous	氨,无水的	2814.1000	6
Ammonia, in aqueous solution	氨水	2814.2000	6
Ammonia, in aqueous solution	氨,水溶液的	2814.2000	6
Ammonium carbonate containing ammonium carbamate	碳酸铵,含氨基甲酸铵的	2836.9940	
Ammonium carbonates, nes	铵的碳酸盐,其他	2836.9940	
Ammonium chloride, for use as fertilizer	氯化铵,肥料用	2827.1010	13
Ammonium chloride, nes	氯化铵,其他	2827.1090	13
Ammonium dihydrogenorthophosphate (monoammonium phosphate)	磷酸二氢铵	3105.4000	68
Ammonium dihydrogenorthophosphate (monoammonium phosphate) mixtures with diammonium hydrogenorthophosphate (diammonium phosphate)	磷酸二氢铵与磷酸氢二铵的混合物	3105.4000	68
Ammonium fluorides	氟化铵	,2826.1910	
Ammonium metatungstate	偏钨酸铵	2841.8040	1
Ammonium molybdates	钼酸铵	2841.7010	1
Ammonium nitrate, whether or not in aqueous solution	硝酸铵,不论是否水溶液	3102.3000	68
Ammonium paratungstate	仲钨酸铵	2841.8010	1
Ammonium sulphate	硫酸铵	3102.2100	68
Ammonium sulphate and ammonium nitrate, double salts or mixtures of	硫酸铵和硝酸铵的复盐及混合物	3102.2900	68
Amobarbital (INN); salts thereof	异戊巴比妥(INN)以及盐	2933.5300	36
Amoxycillin	羟氨苄青霉素	2941.1091	
Amoxycillin medicaments, mixed or unmixed, put up in measured doses or in forms or packings for retail sale	羟氨苄青霉素药品,混合或未混合的,配定剂量或制成零售包装	3004.1012	368
Amoxycillin medicaments, consisting of two or more constituents which have been mixed together, not put up in measured doses or in forms or packings for retail sale	羟氨苄青霉素药品,两种或两种以上成分混合而成的,未配定剂量或制成零售包装	3003.1012	368
Amoxycillin trihydrate	羟氨苄青霉素三水酸	2941.1092	

Article Description	商品名称	Tariff Code	D. R.
Ampicillin	氨苄青霉素	2941. 1011	
Ampicillin and its salts, nes	氨苄青霉素及其盐,其他	2941. 1019	
Ampicillin medicaments, consisting of two or more constituents which have been mixed together, not put up in measured doses or in forms or packings for retail sale	氨苄青霉素药品,两种或两种以上成分混合而成的,未配定剂量或制成零售包装	3003. 1011	368
Ampicillin medicaments, mixed or unmixed, put up in measured doses or in forms or packings for retail sale	氨苄青霉素药品,混合或未混合的,配定剂量或制成零售包装	3004. 1011	368
Ampicillin trihydrate	氨苄青霉素三水酸	2941. 1012	
Amplifier valves and tubes	放大管	8540. 8100	35
Amplifiers, electronic integrated circuits	放大器,集成电路	8542. 3300	37
Ampoules	安瓿	7010. 1000	8
Anaesthetic apparatus and instruments	麻醉设备	9018. 9070	
Analgin	安乃近	2933. 1920	36
Analysis apparatus parts and accessories	分析仪零件、附件	9027. 9000	3
Anatase	锐钛矿	2614. 0000	146
Anchors and parts thereof, of iron or steel	锚及其零件,钢铁的	7316. 0000	36
Anchovies(Engraulis spp.), salted or in brine	鳀鱼,盐腌及盐渍的	0305. 6300	4
Anchovies, prepared or preserved, whole or in pieces, but not minced	鳀鱼,制作或保藏的,整条或切块,但未绞碎	1604. 1600	48
Anchovy paste, in airtight container	鱼酱,罐头	1604. 2019	48
Andalusite	红柱石	2508. 5000	134
Andiometers	听力计	9018. 1941	
Anethole	茴香脑	2909. 3000	36
Angledozer blades	侧铲推土机用铲	8431. 4200	3
Angledozers, nes	侧铲推土机,其他	8429. 1990	57
Angledozers, track laying, nes	侧铲推土机,履带式,其他	8429. 1190	57
Angles, shapes and sections of iron or nonalloy steel, cold-formed or cold-finished from flatrolled products	角材、型材及异型材,铁或非合金钢的,平板轧材经冷成形或冷加工制的	7216. 9100	468
Angles, shapes and sections of iron or nonalloy steel, nes	角材、型材及异型材,铁或非合金钢的,其他	7216. 9900	468
Angles, shapes and sections of stainless steel	角材、型材及异型材,不锈钢的	7222. 4000	468
Angles, shapes and sections, nes	角材、型材及异型材,合金钢,其他	7228. 7090	468
Angles, shapes and sections, not further worked than hot-rolled, hot-drawn or extruded, nes	角材、型材及异型材,除热轧、热拉拔或热挤压外未经进一步加工,其他	7216. 5090	468
Angles, shapes and sections, of flat-rolled iron or non-alloy steel, not further worked than cold-formed or cold-finished	角材、型材及异型材,铁或非合金钢的平板轧材制的,除冷成形或冷加工外未经进一步加工	7216. 6100	468

A

Article Description	商品名称	Tariff Code	D. R.
Angles, shapes and sections, of iron or non-alloy steel, not further worked than cold-formed or cold-finished, nes	角材、型材及异型材,铁或非合金钢的,除冷成形或冷加工外未经进一步加工,其他	7216.6900	468
Angles, shapes and sections, of iron or steel, welded	角材、型材及异型材,钢铁的,焊接的	7301.2000	6
Angles, shapes and sections, shapes of crawler tread	角材、型材及异型材,履带板型钢	7228.7010	468
Anglesite	硫酸铅矿	2607.0000	146
Angular contact bearings	角接触轴承	8482.1030	5
Anhydrite	硬石膏	2520.1000	34
Anileridine (INN); salts thereof	阿尼利定(INN)以及盐	2933.3300	36
Aniline	苯胺	2921.4110	36
Aniline derivatives and their salts	苯胺衍生物及其盐	2921.4200	36
Aniline salts	苯胺盐	2921.4190	36
Animal black	动物炭黑	3802.9000	34
Animal black, spent	动物炭黑,废的	3802.9000	34
Animal blood prepared for therapeutic, prophylactic or diagnostic uses	动物血制品,治病、防病或诊断用的	3002.9090	34
Animal embryo	动物胚胎	0511.9920	4
Animal fats and oil and fractions thereof	动物油脂及其分离品	1516.1000	46
Animal fats and oils and fractions thereof, nes	动物油脂及其分离品,其他	1518.0000	46
Animal fats or oils extraction machinery	动物油脂提取的机器	8479.2000	7
Animal fats or oils preparation machinery	动物油脂加工的机器	8479.2000	7
Animal or vegetable fertilizers, nes	动物或植物肥料,其他	3101.0090	1346
Animal or vegetable fertilizers, not chemically treated	动物或植物肥料,未经化学处理	3101.0019	1346
Animal products, nes	动物产品,其他	0511.9990	34
Animal semen, other than bovine semen	动物精液(牛的精液除外)	0511.9910	4
Animals of Chapter 1, dead, unfit for human consumption	动物,死的,第一章的,不适合供人食用的	0511.9990	34
Animals of Chapter 3, dead, unfit for human consumption	动物,死的,第三章的,不适合供人食用的	0511.9190	34
Animated displays used for shop window dressing	活动陈列品,橱窗装饰用的	9618.0000	
Anisaldehyde	茴香醛	2912.4900	36
Anisette	茴香酒	2208.7000	2468
Anisidines, dianisidines, phenetidines, and their salts	茴香胺、二茴香胺、氨基苯乙醚及其盐	2922.2910	36
Annealing treatment equipment, flat panel displays manufacture machines and apparatus	退火处理设备,平板显示器的制造机器及装置	8486.3010	7
Annealing treatment equipment, semiconductor devices or of electronic integrated circuits manufacture machines and apparatus	退火处理设备,制造半导体器件或集成电路的机器及装置	8486.2010	7
Anodes of nickel for electroplating	阳极,镍制,电镀用	7508.9010	6
Anoraks (including ski-jackets) and similar articles, knitted or crocheted, for men or boys, of cotton	带风帽的防寒短上衣(包括滑雪短上衣)及类似品,针织或钩编的,男式,棉制	6101.2000	2456

Article Description	商品名称	Tariff Code	D. R.
Anoraks (including ski-jackets) and similar articles, knitted or crocheted, for men or boys, of man-made fibres	带风帽的防寒短上衣(包括滑雪短上衣)及类似品,针织或钩编的,男式,化学纤维制	6101. 3000	2456
Anoraks (including ski-jackets) and similar articles, knitted or crocheted, for men or boys, of other textile materials	带风帽的防寒短上衣(包括滑雪短上衣)及类似品,针织或钩编的,男式,其他	6101. 9090	2456
Anoraks (including ski-jackets) and similar articles, knitted or crocheted, for men or boys, of wool or fine animal hair	带风帽的防寒短上衣(包括滑雪短上衣)及类似品,针织或钩编的,男式,羊毛或动物细毛制	6101. 9010	2456
Anoraks (including ski-jackets) and similar articles, knitted or crocheted, for women or girls, of cotton	带风帽的防寒短上衣(包括滑雪短上衣)及类似品,针织或钩编的,女式,棉制	6102. 2000	2456
Anoraks (including ski-jackets) and similar articles, knitted or crocheted, for women or girls, of man-made fibres	带风帽的防寒短上衣(包括滑雪短上衣)及类似品,针织或钩编的,女式,化学纤维制	6102. 3000	2456
Anoraks (including ski-jackets) and similar articles, knitted or crocheted, for women or girls, of other textile materials	带风帽的防寒短上衣(包括滑雪短上衣)及类似品,针织或钩编的,女式,其他	6102. 9000	2456
Anoraks (including ski-jackets) and similar articles, knitted or crocheted, for women or girls, of wool or fine animal hair	带风帽的防寒短上衣(包括滑雪短上衣)及类似品,针织或钩编的,女式,羊毛或动物细毛制	6102. 1000	2456
Anoraks (including skijackets), not knitted or crocheted, for men or boys, of cotton	带风帽的防寒短上衣(包括滑雪短上衣),非针织或钩编的,男式,棉制	6201. 9290	2456
Anoraks (including skijackets), not knitted or crocheted, for men or boys, of man-made fibres	带风帽的防寒短上衣(包括滑雪短上衣),非针织或钩编的,男式,化学纤维制	6201. 9390	2456
Anoraks (including skijackets), not knitted or crocheted, for men or boys, of other textile materials	带风帽的防寒短上衣(包括滑雪短上衣),非针织或钩编的,男式,其他纺织材料制	6201. 9900	2456
Anoraks (including skijackets), not knitted or crocheted, for men or boys, of wool or fine animal hair	带风帽的防寒短上衣(包括滑雪短上衣),男式,羊毛或动物细毛制非针织或钩编的	6201. 9100	2456
Anoraks (including skijackets), not knitted or crocheted, for women or girls, of cotton	带风帽的防寒短上衣(包括滑雪短上衣),非针织或钩编的,女式,棉制	6202. 9290	2456
Anoraks (including skijackets), not knitted or crocheted, for women or girls, of man-made fibres	带风帽的防寒短上衣(包括滑雪短上衣),非针织或钩编的,女式,化学纤维制	6202. 9390	2456
Anoraks (including skijackets), not knitted or crocheted, for women or girls, of other textile materials	带风帽的防寒短上衣(包括滑雪短上衣),非针织或钩编的,女式,其他纺织材料制	6202. 9900	2456
Anoraks (including skijackets), not knitted or crocheted, for women or girls, of wool or fine animal hair	带风帽的防寒短上衣(包括滑雪短上衣),女式,羊毛或动物细毛制非针织或钩编的	6202. 9100	2456

A

Article Description	商品名称	Tariff Code	D. R.
Antelope horns and powder or waste thereof	羚羊角及其粉末和废料	0507.9010	14
Antelopes, pure-bred breeding	羚羊,改良种用	0106.1910	34
Anthracite	无烟煤	2701.1100	156
Anthranilic acid	邻氨基苯甲酸(氨茴酸)	2922.4310	36
Anthranilic acid salts	邻氨基苯甲酸(氨茴酸)盐	2922.4390	36
Anthraquinone	蒽醌	2914.6100	36
Antibiotics medicaments, nes, consisting of two or more constituents which have been mixed together, not put up in measured doses or in forms or packings for retail sale	抗菌素药品,其他,两种或两种以上成分混合而成的,未配定剂量或制成零售包装	3003.2090	368
Antibiotics medicaments, nes, mixed or unmixed, put up in measured doses or in forms or packings for retail sale	抗菌素药品,其他,混合或未混合的,配定剂量或制成零售包装	3004.2090	368
Antibiotics, nes	抗菌素,其他	2941.9090	
Antimonite	辉锑矿	2617.1090	146
Antimony articles, nes	锑制品,其他	8110.9000	16
Antimony concentrates	锑精矿	2617.1010	146
Antimony ores and concentrates, nes	锑矿砂及其精矿,其他	2617.1090	146
Antimony oxides	锑的氧化物	2825.8000	
Antimony powders	锑粉末	8110.1020	16
Antimony sulphide	硫化锑	2830.9020	
Antimony unwrought	锑,未锻轧	8110.1010	16
Antiperspirants, for personal use	止汗剂,人体用	33097.2000	23
Antipyrin and its derivatives	安替比林及其衍生物	2933.1100	36
Antiques of an age exceeding one hundred years	古物,超过100年的	9706.0000	5
Antisera	抗血清	3002.1000	34
Anti-corrosive preparations, for mineral oils and alike	防腐蚀制剂,用于矿物油及类似液体	3811.9000	236
Anti-freezing preparations	防冻剂	3820.0000	36
Anti-knock preparations, for mineral oils and alike, based on lead compounds	抗震剂,用于矿物油及类似液体,以铅化合物为基本成分	3811.1100	236
Anti-knock preparations, for mineral oils and alike, nes	抗震剂,用于矿物油及类似液体,其他	3811.1900	236
Anti-oxidizing preparations and other compound stabilizers for rubber or plastics, nes	抗氧制剂及其他复合稳定剂,橡胶或塑料用,其他	3812.3090	36
Anti-rust or anticorrosion preparations, based on lubricants, containing petroleum oils or oils obtained from bituminous minerals	防锈或防腐蚀制剂,以润滑剂为基本成分的,含有石油或从沥青矿物提取的油类	3403.1900	2368
Anti-rust or anticorrosion preparations, based on lubricants, nes	防锈或防腐蚀制剂,以润滑剂为基本成分的,其他	3403.9900	2368
Anti-slid brake system(ABS), nes	防抱死制动系统(ABS),其他	8708.3029	3
Anti-slid brake system(ABS), of dumpers	防抱死制动系统(ABS),自卸车的	8708.3021	3
Anti-slid brake system(ABS), of tractors	防抱死制动系统(ABS),拖拉机的	8708.3021	3

Article Description	商品名称	Tariff Code	D. R.
Anti-sprouting products, nes	抗萌剂,其他	3808.9399	36
Anti-sprouting products, put up for retail sale	抗萌剂,零售包装	3808.9391	36
Antlers, worked	鹿角,已加工的	9601.9000	5
Anvils	砧	8205.8000	256
Apatite, ground	磷灰石,已碾磨	2510.2010	46
Apatite, unground	磷灰石,未碾磨	2510.1010	46
Apparatus and equipment for photographic laboratories, nes	洗印装置及设备,其他	9010.5029	7
Apparatus and equipment for photographic laboratories, of a kind used in cinematographic film	洗印装置及设备,电影用	9010.5021	7
Apparatus and equipment for photographic laboratories, of a kind used in special photographic film or paper	洗印装置及设备,特种照相用	9010.5022	7
Apparatus for the projection or drawing of circuit patterns on sensitized semiconductor materials, flat panel displays manufacture machines and apparatus, nes	将电路图投影或绘制到感光半导体材料上的装置,平板显示器的制造机器及装置,其他	8486.3039	7
Apparatus for the projection or drawing of circuit patterns on sensitized semiconductor materials, semiconductor devices or of electronic integrated circuits manufacture machines and apparatus, nes	将电路图投影或绘制到感光半导体材料上的装置,制造半导体器件或集成电路的机器及装置,其他	8486.2039	7
Apparel articles and clothing accessories, of plastics, nes	衣服及衣着附件,塑料的,其他	3926.2090	236
Apparel of furskin	衣服,毛皮的	4303.1010	456
Apparel, of leather or of composition leather	衣服,皮革或再生皮革制的	4203.1000	456
Apple juice, nes	苹果汁,其他	2009.7900	2468
Apple juice, of a brix value not exceeding 20	苹果汁,白利糖度值不超过20的	2009.7100	2468
Apples, dried	苹果,干的	0813.3000	34
Apples, fresh	苹果,鲜的	0808.1000	125
Apricots, dried	杏,干的	0813.1000	34
Apricots, fresh	杏,鲜的	0809.1000	1
Apricots, otherwise prepared, or preserved	杏,用其他方法制作或保藏的	2008.5000	248
Aquatic invertebrates and molluscs (other than crustaceans), frozen, dried, salted or in brine	软体动物和水生无脊椎动物(甲壳动物除外),冻、干、盐腌或盐渍的	0307.9990	14
Aquatic invertebrates and molluscs (other than crustaceans), nes	软体动物和水生无脊椎动物(甲壳动物除外),其他	0307.9199	1
Aquatic invertebrates and molluscs, other than crustaceans, nes, for cultivation	种苗,其他,软体动物和水生无脊椎动物(甲壳动物除外)的,	0307.9110	8
Aquatic invertebrates, nes, prepared or preserved	水生无脊椎动物,其他,制作或保藏的	1605.9090	48
Arabian robes, not knitted or crocheted, for men or boys, of cotton	阿拉伯袍,非针织或钩编的,男式,棉制	6211.3210	2456

A

Article Description	商品名称	Tariff Code	D. R.
Arabian robes, not knitted or crocheted, for men or boys, of man-made fibres	阿拉伯袍,非针织或钩编的,男式,化学纤维制	6211.3310	2456
Arabian trousers, not knitted or crocheted, for men or boys, of cotton	阿拉伯裤,非针织或钩编的,男式,棉制	6203.4210	2456
Arabian trousers, not knitted or crocheted, for men or boys, of other textile material	阿拉伯裤,非针织或钩编的,男式,其他纺织材料制	6203.4910	2456
Arabian trousers, not knitted or crocheted, for men or boys, of synthetic fibres	阿拉伯裤,非针织或钩编的,男式,合成纤维制	6203.4310	2456
Aragonite	霰石	2530.9099	13456
Aragonite, worked	霰石,加工的	7103.9990	145
Aramides elastic filament, measuring per single yarn more than 50 tex, not put up for retail sale	聚酰胺(芳香族)弹力丝,每根单纱细度超过50特,芳香族聚酰胺纺制,非供零售用	5402.3213	3468
Aramides elastic filament, measuring per single yarn not more than 50 rex, not put up for retail sale	聚酰胺(芳香族)弹力丝,每根单纱细度不超过50特,非供零售用	5402.3113	3468
Aramides multiple or cabled yarn, not put up for retail sale	聚酰胺(芳香族)多股纱线或缆线,非供零售用	5402.6130	3468
Aramides single yarn, untwisted or with a twist not exceeding 50 turns per metre, not put up for retail sale	聚酰胺(芳香族)单纱,未加捻或捻度每米不超过50转,非供零售用	5402.4530	3468
Aramides single yarn, with a twist exceeding 50 turns per metre, not put up for retail sale	聚酰胺(芳香族)单纱,捻度每米超过50转,非供零售用	5402.5130	3468
Aramids high tenacity yarn, not put up for retail sale, nes	聚酰胺(芳香族)高强力纱,非供零售用,其他	5402.1190	3468
Aramids high tenacity yarn, of poly isophthaloyl metaphenylene daimine, not put up for retail sale	聚酰胺(芳香族)高强力纱,聚间苯二甲酰间苯二胺,非供零售用	5402.1110	3468
Aramids high tenacity yarn, of poly-p-phenylene terephthamide, not put up for retail sale	聚酰胺(芳香族)高强力纱,聚对苯二甲酰对苯二胺,非供零售用	5402.1120	3468
Aramids staple fibres, of poly isophthaloyl metaphenylene daimine, not carded, combed or otherwise processed for spinning	聚酰胺(芳族)短纤,聚间苯二甲酰间苯二胺,未梳或未经其他纺前加工	5503.1110	68
Aramids staple fibres, of poly-p-phenylene terephthamide, not carded, combed or otherwise processed for spinning	聚酰胺(芳族)短纤,聚对苯二甲酰对苯二胺,未梳或未经其他纺前加工	5503.1190	68
Architectural ornaments, ceramic	建筑装饰物,陶瓷制	6905.9000	5
Arc-lamps	弧光灯	8539.4100	35
Argentite	辉银矿	2616.1000	146
Argol	粗酒石	2307.0000	
Argon	氩	2804.2100	
Armoured fighting vehicles parts and accessories	装甲战斗车辆的零件和附件	8710.0090	3
Armoured fighting vehicles, assembled	装甲战斗车辆整车,机动的	8710.0010	
Arms parts and accessori, nes	武器用零件、附件,其他	9305.9900	3
Arms, nes	武器,其他	9304.0000	

Article Description	商品名称	Tariff Code	D. R.
Aromatic bitters	别特酒	2103. 9020	268
Aromatic ethers and their halogenated, sulphonated, nitrated or nitrosated derivatives	芳香醚及其卤化、磺化、硝化或亚硝化衍生物	2909. 3000	36
Aromatic hydrocarbon mixtures of which 65% or more by volume(including losses) distils at 250℃ by the ASTM D86 method, nes	芳烃混合物,其他,温度在250℃时蒸馏量以体积计(包括损耗)在65%及以上(以美国标准试验法D86为准)	2707. 5000	6
Aromatic ketones without other oxygen function, nes	芳香酮,不含其他含氧基的,其他	2914. 3990	36
Aromatic monoamines and their derivatives; salts thereof, nes	芳香单胺及其衍生物以及它们的盐,其他	2921. 4990	36
Aromatic monocarboxylic acids, their anhydrides, halides, peroxides, peroxyacids and their derivatives, nes	芳香一元羧酸及其酸酐、酰卤化物、过氧化物和过氧酸以及它们的衍生物,其他	2916. 3990	36
Aromatic polyamines and their derivatives; salts thereof, nes	芳香多胺及其衍生物以及它们的盐,其他	2921. 5900	36
Aromatic polycarboxylic acids, their anhydrides, halides, peroxides, peroxyacids and their derivatives, nes	芳香多元羧酸及其酸酐、酰卤化物、过氧化物和过氧酸以及它们的衍生物,其他	2917. 3990	36
Arrowroot	竹芋	0714. 9090	34
Arsenic	砷	2804. 8000	
Arsenic trichloride	三氯化砷	2812. 1044	
Artemisinins and their derivatives medicaments, consisting of two or more constituents which have been mixed together, not put up in measured doses or in forms or packings for retail sale	青蒿素及其衍生物药品,两种或两种以上成分混合而成的,未配定剂量或制成零售包装	3003. 9020	368
Artemisinins and their derivatives medicaments, mixed or unmixed, put up in measured doses or in forms or packings for retail sale	青蒿素及其衍生物药品,混合或未混合的,配定剂量或制成零售包装	3004. 9060	368
Arters and similar articles, of man-made fibres	束袜带和类似品,化学纤维制	6212. 9010	2456
Arters and similar articles, of other textile materials	束袜带和类似品,其他纺织材料制	6212. 9090	2456
Articles and equipment for general physical exercise, gymnastics or athletics, nes	一般的体育用品及设备,其他	9506. 9190	5
Articles intended to become permanent magnets after magnetization	磁化后准备制永磁铁的物品	8505. 1900	48
Articles of a kind used in machines or instruments of vulcanized rubber other than hard rubber, nes	机器及仪器用零件,硫化橡胶(硬质橡胶除外)的,其他	4016. 9910	236
Articles of a kind used in machines or instruments, of cellular rubber	机器及仪器用零件,海绵橡胶制	4016. 1010	236
Articles of a kind used in machines or instruments, of cellular rubber, nes	机器及仪器用零件,海绵橡胶制	4016. 1090	236
Articles of agglomerated cork, nes	压制软木及其制品,其他	4504. 9000	

A

Article Description	商品名称	Tariff Code	D. R.
Articles of apparel and clothing accessories, of paper pulp, paper, cellulose wadding or webs of cellulose fibres	衣服及衣着附件,纸浆、纸、纤维素絮纸或纤维素纤维网纸制的	4818.5000	568
Articles of apparel and clothing accessories, of vulcanized rubber other than hard rubber, for medical purpose	衣着用品及附件,硫化橡胶(硬质橡胶除外)制的,医疗用	4015.9010	23
Articles of apparel and clothing accessories, of vulcanized rubber other than hard rubber, nes	衣着用品及附件,硫化橡胶(硬质橡胶除外)制的,其他	4015.9090	23
Articles of artificial fur	人造毛皮制品	4304.0020	6
Articles of gut (other than silkwormgut), of goldbeater's skin, of bladders or of tendons	肠线(蚕胶丝除外)、肠膜、膀胱或筋腱制品	4206.0000	23
Articles of household, sanitary or hospital, of paper pulp, paper, cellulose wadding or webs of cellulose fibres, nes	家庭、卫生或医院用品,纸浆、纸、纤维素絮纸或纤维素纤维网纸制的,其他	4818.9000	568
Articles of natural or cultured pearls	物品,天然或养殖珍珠制	7116.1000	46
Articles of paper pulp, paper, paperboard, cellulose wadding or webs of cellulose fibres, nes	纸质物品,纸浆、纸、纸板、纤维素絮纸及纤维素纤维网纸制的,其他	4823.9090	68
Articles of paper pulp, moulded or pressed	纸浆制品,压制或模制	4823.7000	68
Articles of precious or semi-precious stones (natural, synthetic or reconstructed)	物品,宝石或半宝石(天然、合成或再造)制	7116.2000	46
Articles of vulcanized rubber other than hard rubber, nes	橡胶制品,硫化橡胶(硬质橡胶除外)的,其他	4016.9990	236
Articles of wood, nes	木制品,其他	4421.9090	56
Articles of yarn, strip or the like, twine, cordage, rope or cables, riot, nes	物品,用纱线、扁条及类似品或线、绳、索、缆制成的,其他	5609.0000	23
Articles, not threaded, of copper, nes	无螺纹制品,铜制,其他	7415.2900	56
Articles, threaded, of copper, nes	螺纹制品,铜制,其他	7415.3900	56
Articulated link chain parts, of iron or steel	铰接链零件,钢铁的	7315.1900	36
Articulated link chain, of iron or steel, nes	铰接链,钢铁的,其他	7315.1200	36
Artificial fibres waste	人造纤维的废料	5505.2000	68
Artificial filament tow, nes	人造纤维长丝丝束,其他	5502.0090	68
Artificial filament yarn woven fabrics, containing 85% or more by weight of artificial filament or strip or the like, dyed, nes	人造纤维长丝纱线机织物,按重量计人造纤维长丝、扁条或类似品含量在85%及以上,染色,其他	5408.2290	2468
Artificial filament yarn woven fabrics, containing 85% or more by weight of artificial filament or strip or the like, of yarns of different colours, nes	人造纤维长丝纱线机织物,按重量计人造纤维长丝、扁条或类似品含量在85%及以上,色织,其他	5408.2390	2468
Artificial filament yarn woven fabrics, containing 85% or more by weight of artificial filament or strip or the like, of yarns of different colours, printed, nes	人造纤维长丝纱线机织物,按重量计人造纤维长丝、扁条或类似品含量在85%及以上,色织,印花,其他	5408.2490	2468

Article Description	商品名称	Tariff Code	D. R.
Artificial filament yarn woven fabrics, containing 85% or more by weight of artificial filament or strip or the like, unbleached or bleached	人造纤维长丝纱线机织物,按重量计人造纤维长丝、扁条或类似品含量在85%及以上,未漂白或漂白	5408.2190	2468
Artificial filament yarn woven fabrics, dyed	人造纤维长丝纱线机织物,染色	5408.3200	2468
Artificial filament yarn woven fabrics, of yarns of different colours	人造纤维长丝纱线机织物,色织	5408.3300	2468
Artificial filament yarn woven fabrics, printed	人造纤维长丝纱线机织物,印花	5408.3400	2468
Artificial filament yarn woven fabrics, unbleached or bleached	人造纤维长丝纱线机织物,未漂白或漂白	5408.3100	2468
Artificial filament yarn, put up for retail sale	人造纤维长丝纱线,供零售用	5406.0020	
Artificial flowers, foliage and fruit and parts thereof, nes	人造花、叶、果实及其零件,其他	6702.9090	
Artificial flowers, foliage and fruit and parts thereof, of feathers or down	人造花、叶、果实及其零件,羽毛制	6702.9010	
Artificial flowers, foliage and fruit and parts thereof, of man-made fibres	人造花、叶、果实及其零件,化学纤维制	6702.9030	
Artificial flowers, foliage and fruit and parts thereof, of silk or silk waste	人造花、叶、果实及其零件,丝及绢丝制	6702.9020	
Artificial flowers, foliage or fruit articles, nes	人造花、叶或果实制成的物品,其他	6702.9090	
Artificial flowers, foliage or fruit articles, of feathers or down	人造花、叶或果实制成的物品,羽毛制	6702.9010	
Artificial flowers, foliage or fruit articles, of man-made fibres	人造花、叶或果实制成的物品,化学纤维制	6702.9030	
Artificial flowers, foliage or fruit articles, of plastics	人造花、叶或果实制成的物品,塑料制	6702.1000	
Artificial flowers, foliage or fruit articles, of silk or silk waste	人造花、叶或果实制成的物品,丝及绢丝制	6702.9020	
Artificial flowers, foliage and fruit and parts thereof, of plastics	人造花、叶、果实及其零件,塑料制	6702.1000	
Artificial fur	人造毛皮	4304.0010	6
Artificial guts, of hardened protein or of cellulosic materials	人造肠衣,硬化蛋白或纤维素材料制的	3917.1000	6
Artificial joints	人造关节	9021.3100	
Artificial kidney(dialysis) apparatus	肾脏透析设备(人工肾)	9018.9040	
Artificial monofilament of 67 decitex or more and of which no cross-sectional dimension exceeds 1mm	人造纤维单丝,截面尺寸不超过1毫米,细度在67分特及以上	5405.0000	568
Artificial multiple or cabled yarn, nes	人造纤维多股纱线或缆线,其他	5403.4900	3468
Artificial parts of the body, nes	人造的人体部分,其他	9021.3900	3
Artificial respiration apparatus	人工呼吸器	9019.2000	
Artificial single yarn, not put up for retail sale, nes	人造纤维单纱,非供零售用,其他	5403.3900	3468
Artificial staple fibres multiple or cabled yarn, containing 85% or more by weight of artificial staple fibres, not put up for retail sale	人造纤维短纤多股纱线或缆线,按重量计人造纤维短纤含量在85%及以上,非供零售用	5510.1200	68

A

Article Description	商品名称	Tariff Code	D. R.
Artificial staple fibres sewing thread, whether or not put up for retail sale	人造纤维短纤缝纫线,不论是否供零售用	5508. 2000	68
Artificial staple fibres single yarn, containing 85% or more by weight of artificial staple fibres, not put up for retail sale	人造纤维短纤单纱,按重量计人造纤维短纤含量在85%及以上,非供零售用	5510. 1100	68
Artificial staple fibres woven fabrics, containing 85% or more by weight of artificial staple fibres, dyed	人造纤维短机织物,按重量计人造纤维短纤含量在85%及以上,染色	5516. 1200	2468
Artificial staple fibres woven fabrics, containing 85% or more by weight of artificial staple fibres, of yarns of different colours	人造纤维短机织物,按重量计人造纤维短纤含量在85%及以上,色织	5516. 1300	2468
Artificial staple fibres woven fabrics, containing 85% or more by weight of artificial staple fibres, printed	人造纤维短机织物,按重量计人造纤维短纤含量在85%及以上,印花	5516. 1400	2468
Artificial staple fibres woven fabrics, containing 85% or more by weight of artificial staple fibres, unbleached or bleached	人造纤维短机织物,按重量计人造纤维短纤含量在85%及以上,未漂白或漂白	5516. 1100	2468
Artificial staple fibres woven fabrics, containing less than 85% by weight of artificial staple fibres, mixed mainly or solely with cotton, dyed	人造纤维短机织物,按重量计人造纤维短纤含量在85%以下,主要或仅与棉混纺,染色	5516. 4200	2468
Artificial staple fibres woven fabrics, containing less than 85% by weight of artificial staple fibres, mixed mainly or solely with cotton, of yarns of different colours	人造纤维短机织物,按重量计人造纤维短纤含量在85%以下,主要或仅与棉混纺,色织	5516. 4300	2468
Artificial staple fibres woven fabrics, containing less than 85% by weight of artificial staple fibres, mixed mainly or solely with cotton, printed	人造纤维短机织物,按重量计人造纤维短纤含量在85%以下,主要或仅与棉混纺,印花	5516. 4400	2468
Artificial staple fibres woven fabrics, containing less than 85% by weight of artificial staple fibres, mixed mainly or solely with cotton, unbleached or bleached	人造纤维短机织物,按重量计人造纤维短纤含量在85%以下,主要或仅与棉混纺,未漂白或漂白	5516. 4100	2468
Artificial staple fibres woven fabrics, containing less than 85% by weight of artificial staple fibres, mixed mainly or solely with man-made filaments, dyed	人造纤维短机织物,按重量计人造纤维短纤含量在85%以下,主要或仅与化学纤维长丝混纺,染色	5516. 2200	2468
Artificial staple fibres woven fabrics, containing less than 85% by weight of artificial staple fibres, mixed mainly or solely with man-made filaments, of yarns of different colours	人造纤维短机织物,按重量计人造纤维短纤含量在85%以下,主要或仅与化学纤维长丝混纺,色织	5516. 2300	2468
Artificial staple fibres woven fabrics, containing less than 85% by weight of artificial staple fibres, mixed mainly or solely with man-made filaments, printed	人造纤维短机织物,按重量计人造纤维短纤含量在85%以下,主要或仅与化学纤维长丝混纺,印花	5516. 2400	2468

A

Article Description	商品名称	Tariff Code	D. R.
Artificial staple fibres woven fabrics, containing less than 85% by weight of artificial staple fibres, mixed mainly or solely with man-made filaments, unbleached or bleached	人造纤维短机织物,按重量计人造纤维短纤含量在85%以下,主要或仅与化学纤维长丝混纺,未漂白或漂白	5516. 2100	2468
Artificial staple fibres woven fabrics, containing less than 85% by weight of artificial staple fibres, mixed mainly or solely with wool or fine animal hair, dyed	人造纤维短机织物,按重量计人造纤维短纤含量在85%以下,主要或仅与羊毛或动物细毛混纺,染色	5516. 3200	2468
Artificial staple fibres woven fabrics, containing less than 85% by weight of artificial staple fibres, mixed mainly or solely with wool or fine animal hair, of yarns of different colours	人造纤维短机织物,按重量计人造纤维短纤含量在85%以下,主要或仅与羊毛或动物细毛混纺,色织	5516. 3300	2468
Artificial staple fibres woven fabrics, containing less than 85% by weight of artificial staple fibres, mixed mainly or solely with wool or fine animal hair, printed	人造纤维短机织物,按重量计人造纤维短纤含量在85%以下,主要或仅与羊毛或动物细毛混纺,印花	5516. 3400	2468
Artificial staple fibres woven fabrics, containing less than 85% by weight of artificial staple fibres, mixed mainly or solely with wool or fine animal hair, unbleached or bleached	人造纤维短机织物,按重量计人造纤维短纤含量在85%以下,主要或仅与羊毛或动物细毛混纺,未漂白或漂白	5516. 3100	2468
Artificial staple fibres woven fabrics, dyed, nes	人造纤维短机织物,染色,其他	5516. 9200	2468
Artificial staple fibres woven fabrics, of yarns of different colours, nes	人造纤维短机织物,色织,其他	5516. 9300	2468
Artificial staple fibres woven fabrics, printed, nes	人造纤维短机织物,印花,其他	5516. 9400	2468
Artificial staple fibres woven fabrics, unbleached or bleached, nes	人造纤维短机织物,未漂白或漂白,其他	5516. 9100	2468
Artificial staple fibres yarn, mixed mainly or solely with cotton, not put up for retail sale, nes	人造纤维短纤纱线,主要或仅与棉混纺,非供零售用,其他	5510. 3000	68
Artificial staple fibres yarn, mixed mainly or solely with wool or fine animal hair, not put up for retail sale, nes	人造纤维短纤纱线,主要或仅与羊毛或动物细毛混纺,非供零售用,其他	5510. 2000	68
Artificial staple fibres yarn, not put up for retail sale, nes	人造纤维短纤纱线,非供零售用,其他	5510. 9000	68
Artificial staple fibres yarn, put up for retail sale	人造纤维短纤纱线,供零售用	5511. 3000	68
Artificial staple fibres, carded, combed or otherwise processed for spinning	人造纤维短纤,已梳或经其他纺前加工	5507. 0000	68
Artificial staple fibres, not carded, combed or otherwise processed for spinning, nes	人造纤维短纤,未梳或未经其他纺前加工,其他	5504. 9000	68
Artificial stone articles, nes	人造石制品,其他	6810. 9990	56
Artificial stone blocks and bricks, for building	人造石砖及块,建筑用	6810. 1100	56
Artificial stone flagstones and similar articles	人造扁平石及类似品	6810. 1910	56
Artificial stone tiles	人造石瓦	6810. 1910	56

A

Article Description	商品名称	Tariff Code	D. R.
Artificial straw, of artificial textile materials of an apparent width not exceeding 5mm	人造草,表观宽度不超过5毫米的人造纤维纺织材料制	5405. 0000	568
Artificial straw, of synthetic textile materials of an apparent width not exceeding 5mm	人造草,表观宽度不超过5毫米,合成纤维纺织材料制	5404. 9000	568
Artificial teeth	假牙	9021. 2100	
Artillery weapons parts and accessories	火炮武器用零件、附件	9305. 9100	3
Artillery weapons, nes	火炮武器,其他	9301. 1900	7
Artillery weapons, self-propelled, nes	火炮武器,自推进的,其他	9301. 1100	7
Artists brushes	画笔	9603. 3010	
Asafoetida	阿魏	1301. 9030	
Asbestos articles of mixtures with a basis of crocidolite or with a basis of crocidolite and magnesium carbonate, nes	石棉为基本成分或以石棉和碳酸镁混合物为基本成分的制品,其他	6812. 9900	56
Asbestos brake linings	石棉闸衬	6813. 2010	6
Asbestos brake pads	石棉闸垫	6813. 2010	6
Asbestos clothing, clothing accessories, footwear and headgear, with a basis of asbestos or with a basis of asbestos and magnesium carbonate	石棉服装、衣着附件、帽类及鞋靴,以石棉为基本成分或以石棉和碳酸镁混合物为基本成分的	6812. 9100	56
Asbestos corrugated sheets	石棉瓦楞板	6811. 4010	56
Asbestos fibre jointing, in sheets or rolls, compressed	石棉纤维接合材料,成片或成卷的,压缩的	6812. 9300	56
Asbestos friction material and articles thereof, not mpunted, for brakes, for clutches or the like, nes	石棉摩擦材料及其制品,未装配,适于作制动器、离合器及类似品,其他	6813. 2090	6
Asbestos of long staple, ex. crocidolite	石棉,长纤维的,青石棉除外	2524. 9010	148
Asbestos paper, millboard and felt, with a basis of asbestos or with a basis of asbestos and magnesium carbonate	石棉纸、麻丝板及毡子,以石棉为基本成分或以石棉和碳酸镁混合物为基本成分的	6812. 9200	56
Asbestos tubes, pipes and fittings	石棉水泥管子及附件	6811. 4030	56
Asbestos, mineral substances or cellulose friction material and articles thereof, not mpunted, for brakes, for clutches or the like, containing asbestos, nes	石棉、矿物质或纤维素为基本成分的未装配摩擦材料及其制品,适于作制动器、离合器及类似品,含石棉的,其他	6813. 2090	6
Asbestos, nes	石棉,其他	2524. 9090	148
Asbestos-cement articles or the like, nes	石棉水泥或类似材料制品,其他	6811. 4090	56
Asbestos-cement sheets, panels, tiles and similar articles	石棉水泥片、板、砖、瓦及类似制品	6302. 5990	346
Ash and residues from the incineration of municipal waste	灰、渣,焚化城市垃圾所产生的	2621. 1000	134
Asparagine	天门冬酰胺	2924. 1990	36
Asparagus crowns, seed, dormant	芦笋,种用,休眠的	0601. 1091	135
Asparagus, fresh or chilled	芦笋,鲜或冷藏的	0709. 2000	1
Asparagus, in airtight containers	芦笋罐头	2005. 6010	148

A

Article Description	商品名称	Tariff Code	D. R.
Asparagus, prepared or preserved otherwise than by vinegar or acetic acid, not frozen, nes	芦笋,用醋或醋酸以外的其他方法制作或保藏的,未冷冻	2005.6090	148
Asphalt or of similar material articles, in rolls	沥青或类似原料的制品,成卷	6807.1000	
Asphalt or of similar material articles, nes	沥青或类似原料的制品,其他	6807.9000	
Asphaltites and asphaltic rocks	沥青岩	2714.9090	1346
Assembling machines for electric or electronic lamps, tubes or valves or flashbulbs, in glass envelopes	封装机器,电灯泡、灯管、电子管、闪光灯泡及类似品的	8475.1000	
Assembling machines for semiconductor devices, nes	装配半导体器件或集成电路的设备,其他	8486.4029	7
Assembling machines parts, for electric lamps	封装机器的零件,灯泡的	8475.9000	3
Assembling machines, for working wood, cork, bone, hard rubber, hard plastics or similar hard materials	装配机器,加工木材、软木、骨、硬质橡胶、硬质塑料或类似硬质材料的	8465.9400	7
Assemblying machines, for assemblying elements on printed circuit boards, nes	装配机器,印刷电路装配用,其他	8479.8969	7
Asses, ex. pure-bred breeding	驴,改良种用除外	0101.9090	34
Asses, pure-bred breeding	驴,改良种用	0101.1020	34
Astronomical chronometer, electrically operated	天文钟,电力驱动的	9105.9110	5
Astronomical instruments parts and accessories (including mountings)	天文仪器用零件、附件(包括座架)	9005.9010	3
Astronomical instruments, nes	天文仪器,其他	9005.8010	
Astronomical telescopes	天文望远镜	9005.8010	
Astronomical telescopes parts and accessories (including mountings)	天文望远镜零件、附件(包括座架)	9005.9010	3
Atlantic salmon (salmo salar), frozen	大西洋鲑鱼,冻的	0303.2210	18
Atlantic salmon, fresh or chilled	大西洋鲑鱼,鲜或冷的,	0302.1210	18
Atlantic salmon, prepared or preserved, nes	大西洋鲑鱼,制作或保藏的,其他	1604.1190	48
Atlantic salmon, prepared or preserved, whole or in pieces, but not minced	大西洋鲑鱼,制作或保藏的,整条或切块,但未绞碎	1604.1110	48
Atty alcohols, industrial use	脂肪醇,工业用	3823.7000	6
Aubepine	茴香醛	2912.4900	36
Aubergines (eggplants), fresh or chilled	茄子,鲜或冷藏的	0709.3000	1
Aubusson type hand-woven tapestries	奥步生及类似式样的手织装饰毯	5805.0090	468
Audio-frequency electric amplifiers	音频扩大器	8518.4000	5
Audio-frequency electric amplifiers parts	音频扩大器零件	8518.9000	3
Automata used for shop window dressing	自动模型,橱窗装饰用的	9618.0000	
Automated material handling machines solely or principally of a kind used、in the electronic integrated circuits factories	自动搬运机器,集成电路工厂用的	8486.4031	7
Automated teller	自动柜员机	8472.9010	
Automatic banknote dispensers	自动付钞机	8472.9090	
Automatic beverage-vending machines, incorporating heating or refrigerating devices	自动销售机,饮料的,装有加热或制冷装置的	8476.2100	5

A

Article Description	商品名称	Tariff Code	D. R.
Automatic beverage-vending machines, nes	自动销售机,饮料的,其他	8476.2900	5
Automatic bobbin winders	自动络筒机	8445.4010	7
Automatic bobbin winders auxiliary machinery	自动络筒机的辅助机器	8448.1900	3
Automatic circuit breakers, for a voltage exceeding 1000V, nes	自动断路器,用于电压超过1000伏的线路,其他	8535.2900	8
Automatic circuit breakers, for a voltage not exceeding 1000V	自动断路器,用于电压不超过1000伏的线路	8536.2000	8
Automatic circuit breakers, for a voltage of less than 72.5 kV	自动断路器,用于电压低于72.5千伏的线路	8535.2100	8
Automatic coreslice adhering machines, for assemblying elements on printed circuit boards	自动贴片机,印刷电路装配用	8479.8962	7
Automatic data processing machines input or output units, nes	自动数据处理设备输入或输出部件,其他	8471.6090	
Automatic data processing machines input or output units's parts and accessories	自动数据处理设备输入输出部件的零件、附件	8473.3010	3
Automatic data processing machines processing units, nes	自动数据处理设备处理部件,其他	8471.5090	26
Automatic data processing machines storage units, nes	自动数据处理设备存储部件,其他	8471.7090	
Automatic data processing machines storage units's parts and accessories	自动数据处理设备储存部件的零件、附件	8473.3010	3
Automatic data processing machines units's parts and accessories, nes	自动数据处理设备部件的零件、附件,其他	8473.3090	3
Automatic data processing machines, weighing not more than 10kg, portable, consisting of at least a central processing unit, a keyboard and a display	自动数据处理设备,重量不超过10千克的,便携式,至少由一个中央处理部件、一个键盘及一个显示器组成	8471.3000	
Automatic data processing machines, comprising in the same housing at least a central processing unit and an input and output unit, whether or not combined, nes	自动数据处理设备,同一机壳内至少有一个中央处理部件及一个输入和输出部件,不论是否组合式,其他	8471.4190	26
Automatic data processing machines, presented in the form of systems, nes	自动数据处理设备,以系统形式进口或出口的,其他	8471.4999	26
Automatic door closets, of base metal	自动闭门器,贱金属制	8302.6000	256
Automatic focal setting units for cameras	自动调焦组件,照相机用	9006.9191	3
Automatic gearshift for saloon cars and parts thereof	自动换挡变速箱及其零件,小轿车用	8708.4091	3
Automatic goods-vending machines parts	自动售货机的零件	8476.9000	3
Automatic goods-vending machines, incorporating heating or refrigerating devices, nes	自动售货机,装有加热或制冷装置的,其他	8476.8100	5
Automatic goods-vending machines, nes	自动售货机,其他	8476.8900	5
Automatic pianos	自动钢琴	9201.9000	5
Automatic pilots	自动驾驶仪	9014.2010	
Automatic pilots parts and accessories	自动驾驶仪用零件、附件	9014.9010	3
Automatic plug-in machines, for assemblying elements on printed circuit boards	自动插件机,印刷电路装配用	8479.8961	7

Article Description	商品名称	Tariff Code	D. R.
Automatic regulating or controlling instruments and apparatus parts and accessories	自动调节或控制仪器及装置的零件、附件	9032. 9000	3
Automatic regulating or controlling instruments and apparatus, nes	自动调节或控制仪器及装置,其他	9032. 8900	7
Automatic stop motions, weaving auxiliary machines	自停装置,织机的辅助机器	8448. 1900	3
Automatic warehouse equipments	自动化立体仓储设备	8479. 8992	7
Autunite	铀云母	2612. 1000	146
Aviation gasoline	航空汽油	2710. 1110	6
Aviation kerosene	航空煤油	2710. 1911	6
Avocados	鳄梨	0804. 4000	14
Awnings, nes	天篷,其他	6306. 1990	346
Awnings, of bast fibres	天篷,麻制	6306. 1910	346
Awnings, of cotton	天篷,棉制	6306. 1920	346
Awnings, of synthetic fibres	天篷,合成纤维制	6306. 1200	346
Axes and similar hewing tools	斧子及类似砍伐工具	8201. 4000	256
Axial plunger pump, for positive displacement, rotary	轴向柱塞泵,排液回转式	8413. 6060	27
Axles, of railway or tramway locomotives or rolling-stock	轴,铁道及电车道机车或其他车辆的	8607. 1910	3
Azelaic acid, its salts and esters	壬二酸及其盐和酯	2917. 1390	36
Azides, whether or not chemically defined	叠氮化物,不论是否已有化学定义	2850. 0000	
Azoxy-compounds	氧化偶氮化合物	2927. 0000	36
Azo-compounds	偶氮化合物	2927. 0000	36

B

B

Article Description	商品名称	Tariff Code	D. R.
B carotene, sythetic orgaric colouring	胡萝卜素,合成有机着色料	3204.1700	345
Babassu oil and fractions thereof, crude oil	巴巴苏棕榈果油及其分离品,初榨的	1513.2100	4
Babassu oil and fractions thereof, nes	巴巴苏棕榈果油及其分离品,其他	1513.2900	4
Babbitt metal	锡基巴毕脱合金	8001.2010	16
Babies garments and clothing accessories, knitted or crocheted, nes	婴儿服装及衣着附件,针织或钩编的,其他	6111.9090	2456
Babies garments and clothing accessories, knitted or crocheted, of cotton	婴儿服装及衣着附件,针织或钩编的,棉制	6111.2000	2456
Babies garments and clothing accessories, knitted or crocheted, of synthetic fibres	婴儿服装及衣着附件,针织或钩编的,合成纤维制	6111.3000	2456
Babies garments and clothing accessories, knitted or crocheted, of wool or fine animal hair	婴儿服装及衣着附件,针织或钩编的,羊毛或动物细毛制	6111.9010	2456
Baby carriages and parts thereof	婴孩车及其零件	8715.0000	3
Bacteria and virus	细菌及病毒	3002.9030	34
Baddeleyite	斜锆石	2615.1000	1346
Badger hair	獾毛	0502.9019	3
Badminton rackets	羽毛球拍	9506.5900	5
Bag pipes	风笛	9205.9090	5
Baghoused dust collectors, for industry uses	袋式除尘器	8421.3922	7
Bai yao	白药	3004.9053	368
Bakers wares	烘焙糕饼	1905.9000	28
Bakers' yeast	发面酵母	2102.1000	28
Bakery machinery	糕点加工机器	8438.1000	
Bakery machinery parts	糕点加工机器的零件	8438.9000	3
Bakery ovens, including biscuit ovens	烘箱,面包房用及包括做饼干用的	8417.2000	7
Bakery ovens, including biscuit ovens	烤炉,面包房用及包括做饼干用的	8417.2000	7
Baking powders, prepared	发酵粉	2102.3000	28
Balances of a sensitivity of 0.1mg or better	天平,感量为0.1毫克或更精密的	9016.0010	8
Balata gums	巴拉塔胶	4001.3000	12
Bale plucker, for cotton type fibres	自动抓棉机	8445.1112	7
Ball bearings, nes	滚珠轴承,其他	8482.1090	5
Ball point pens	圆珠笔	9608.1000	
Ball point pens refills	圆珠笔芯,由圆珠笔头和墨芯构成	9608.6000	
Ballast tampers, for railway or tramway maintenance or service	道碴捣固车,铁道及电车道用	8604.0099	37
Ballast, whether or not bead-treated	沙石,不论是否热处理	2517.1000	13
Ballasts, for discharge lamps or tubes, electronic	镇流器,放电灯或放电管用,电子的	8504.1010	
Ballasts, for discharge lamps or tubes, nes	镇流器,放电灯或放电管用,其他	8504.1090	

Article Description	商品名称	Tariff Code	D. R.
Balloons	气球	8801. 0090	
Balls bearings parts	滚珠轴承零件	8482. 9100	3
Balls, inflatable, sports articles, nes	可充气的球,体育用品,其他	9506. 6290	5
Balls, sports articles, nes	球,体育用品,其他	9506. 6900	5
Balsam of irises	鸢尾凝脂	3301. 3010	34
Balsams, of natural	油树脂,天然的	1301. 9090	
Bamboo artificial single yarn, untwisted or with a twist not exceeding 120 turns per metre, not put up for retail sale	竹制人造纤维单纱,未加捻或捻度每米不超过 120 转,非供零售用	5403. 3110	3468
Bamboo artificial single yarn, not put up for retail sale, with a twist exceeding 120 turns per metre	竹制人造纤维单纱,捻度每米超过 120 转,非供零售用	5403. 3210	3468
Bamboo artificial staple fibres, not carded, combed or otherwise processed for spinning	竹制人造纤维短纤,未梳或未经其他纺前加工	5504. 1010	68
Bamboo carvings	竹刻	4420. 1012	56
Bamboo shoots, fresh or chilled	竹笋,鲜或冷藏的	0709. 9010	1
Bamboo shoots, dried	笋干丝	0712. 9010	4
Bamboo shoots, in airtight containers, prepared or preserved otherwise than by vinegar or acetic acid, not frozen	竹笋罐头,用醋或醋酸以外的其他方法制作或保藏的,未冷冻	2005. 9110	1248
Bamboo shoots, in brine, provisionally preserved, but unsuitable in that state for immediate consumption	竹笋,盐水的,暂时保藏,但不适合直接使用的	0711. 9031	34
Bamboo shoots, nes, prepared or preserved otherwise than by vinegar or acetic acid, not frozen	竹笋,其他,用醋或醋酸以外的其他方法制作或保藏的,未冷冻	2005. 9190	148
Bamboos	竹	1401. 1000	3
Bananas, fresh or dried	香蕉,鲜或干的香蕉	0803. 0000	1245
Band saw blades	带锯片	8202. 2000	256
Bandages for medical, surgical, dental or veterinary purposes	绷带,供医疗、外科、牙科或兽医用	3005. 9010	1346
Bandoliers, of leather or of composition leather	子弹带,皮革或再生皮革制的	4203. 3020	456
Banknote dispenser of automated teller's parts and accessories	自动柜员机用出钞器的零件、附件	8473. 4010	3
Banknotes	钞票	4907. 0020	1
Bantaroi seeds	大海子	1211. 9032	34
Barbecue and parts thereof, of iron or steel, for household, for solid fuel	烧烤炉及其零件,钢铁制,家用,使用固体燃料的	7321. 8900	7
Barbecues, of iron or steel, non-electric domestic appliances, for gas fuel or for both gas and other fuels	烤肉架,钢铁制,非电热的家用,使用气体燃料或可使用气体燃料及其他燃料的	7321. 1100	7
Barbecues, of iron or steel, non-electric domestic appliances, for liquid fuel	烤肉架,钢铁制,非电热的家用,使用液体燃料的	7321. 1290	7
Barbecues, of iron or steel, non-electric domestic appliances, nes, including appliances for solid fuel	烤肉架,钢铁制,非电热的家用,其他,包括使用固体燃料的	7321. 1900	7

B

Article Description	商品名称	Tariff Code	D. R.
Barbed wire of iron or steel	带刺钢铁丝	7313.0000	36
Barbered needles for knitting machines, smaler than gauge No. 28	弹簧针,针织机用28号以下的	8448.5120	3
Barbers chairs and parts thereof	理发用椅及其零件	9402.1010	3
Barbital (INN); salts thereof	巴比妥(INN)以及盐	2933.5300	36
Barbituric acid and its salts	巴比土酸及其盐	2933.5200	36
Barbituric acid derivatives; salts thereof, nes	巴比土酸衍生物以及它们的盐,其他	2933.5400	36
Barium carbonate	碳酸钡	2836.6000	
Barium chloride	氯化钡	2827.3920	
Barium sulphates	硫酸钡	2833.2700	
Barium, oxides, hydroxides and peroxides	钡的氧化物、氢氧化物及过氧化物	2816.4000	
Barley, nes	大麦,其他	1003.0090	3
Barley, other worked	大麦,其他加工的	1104.2910	4
Barley, rolled or flaked	大麦,滚压或制片的	1104.1910	4
Barley, seed	大麦,种用	1003.0010	3
Barometers	气压计	9025.8000	3
Barometers parts and accessories	气压计零件、附件	9025.9000	7
Barrels, of other wood	琵琶桶,其他木制的	4416.0090	56
Barrels, of radiata pine	琵琶桶,辐射松制的	4416.0010	56
Bars and rods of alloy steel, nes	条、杆,合金钢的,其他	7228.6000	468
Bars and rods of aluminium alloys	铝合金条、杆,铝合金制	7604.2910	16
Bars and rods of iron or non-alloy steel, not further worked than cold-formed or cold-finished, nes	条、杆,铁及非合金钢的,除冷成形或冷加工外未经进一步加工,其他	7215.5000	468
Bars and rods of iron or non-alloy steel, not further worked than forged, but including those twisted after rolling	条、杆,铁或非合金钢的,除锻造外未经进一步加工,包括轧制后扭曲的	7214.1000	468
Bars and rods of iron or non-alloy steel, not further worked than forged, hot rolled, hot-drawn or hot-extruded, but including those twisted after rolling, containing indentations, ribs, grooves or other deformations produced during the rolling process or twisted after rolling	条、杆,铁或非合金钢的,除锻造、热轧、热拉拔或热挤压外未经进一步加工,包括轧制后扭曲的,带有轧制过程中产生的凹痕、凸缘、槽沟或其他变形以及轧制后扭曲的	7214.2000	468
Bars and rods of iron or non-alloy steel, not further worked than forged, hot rolled, hot-drawn or hot-extruded, but including those twisted after rolling, nes	条、杆,铁或非合金钢的,除锻造、热轧、热拉拔或热挤压外未经进一步加工,包括轧制后扭曲的,其他	7214.9900	468
Bars and rods of iron or non-alloy steel, not further worked than forged, hot rolled, hot-drawn or hot-extruded, but including those twisted after rolling, of free-cutting steel, nes	条、杆,铁或非合金钢的,除锻造、热轧、热拉拔或热挤压外未经进一步加工,包括轧制后扭曲的,易切削钢制,其他	7214.3000	468

Article Description	商品名称	Tariff Code	D. R.
Bars and rods of iron or non-alloy steel, not further worked than forged, hot rolled, hot-drawn or hot-extruded, but including those twisted after rolling, of rectangular cross section (other than square), nes	条、杆,铁或非合金钢的,除锻造、热轧、热拉拔或热挤压外未经进一步加工,包括轧制后扭曲的,矩形(正方形除外)截面的,其他	7214.9100	468
Bars and rods of iron or non-alloy steel, of free-cutting steel, not further worked than cold-formed or cold-finished	条、杆,铁及非合金钢的,易切削钢制,除冷成形或冷加工外未经进一步加工	7215.1000	468
Bars and rods of stainless steel, nes	条、杆,不锈钢的,其他	7222.3000	468
Bars and rods of stainless steel, not further worked than hot-rolled, hot-drawn or extruded, nes	条、杆,不锈钢的,除热轧、热拉拔或热挤压外未经进一步加工,其他	7222.1900	468
Bars and rods of stainless steel, not further worked than hot-rolled, hot-drawn or extruded, of circular cross-section	条、杆,不锈钢的,除热轧、热拉拔或热挤压外未经进一步加工,圆形截面的	7222.1100	468
Bars and rods, hot-rolled, of alloy steel, in irregularly wound coils, nes	条、杆,热轧的,不规则盘卷的,其他	7227.9000	468
Bars and rods, of iron or non-alloy steel, hot-rolled, in irregulurly wound coils, containing indentations, ribs, grooves or other deformations produced during the rolling process	条、杆,铁及非合金钢的,热轧的,不规则盘卷的,带有轧制过程中产生的凹痕、凸缘、槽沟及其他变形的	7213.1000	468
Bars and rods, of iron or non-alloy steel, hot-rolled, in irregulurly wound coils, nes	条、杆,铁及非合金钢的,热轧的,不规则盘卷的,其他	7213.9900	468
Bars and rods, of iron or non-alloy steel, hot-rolled, in irregulurly wound coils, of free-cutting steel, nes	条、杆,铁及非合金钢的,热轧的,不规则盘卷的,易切削钢制,其他	7213.2000	468
Bars and rods, of iron or non-alloy steel, hot-rolled, in irregulurly wound coils, of circular cross-section measuring less than 14mm in diameter, nes	条、杆,铁及非合金钢的,热轧的,不规则盘卷的,直径小于 14 毫米圆形截面的,其他	7213.9100	468
Bars and rods, of iron or non-alloy steel, nes	条、杆,铁及非合金钢的,其他	7215.9000	468
Bars and rods, of molybdenum, other than those obtained simply by sintering	条、杆,钼的,但简单烧结而成的除外	8102.9500	16
Bars and rods, of tungsten, other than those obtained simply by sintering, profiles, plates, sheets, strip and foil	条、杆,钨的,但简单烧结而成的除外	8101.9910	16
Bars and rods, hollow, for drill, of alloy or non-alloy steel	钻钢,空心的,合金钢或非合金钢制的	7228.8000	468
Bars and rods, hot-rolled, of stainless steel, in irregularly wound coils	条、杆,不锈钢热轧的,不规则盘卷	7221.0000	468
Bars and rods, not further worked than cold-formed of cold-finished, nes	条、杆,除冷成形或冷加工外未经进一步加工,其他	7228.5000	468
Bars and rods, not further worked than forged, nes	条、杆,除锻造外未经进一步加工,其他	7228.4000	468
Bars and rods, not further worked than hot-rolled, hot-drawn or extruded, nes	条、杆,除热轧、热拉拔或热挤压外未经进一步加工,其他	7228.3000	468

B

B

Article Description	商品名称	Tariff Code	D. R.
Bars and rods, of aluminium, not alloyed	条、杆,非合金铝制	7604.1010	16
Bars and rods, of high speed steel	条、杆,高速钢的	7228.1000	468
Bars and rods, of high speed steel hot-rolled, of alloy steel, in irregularly wound coils, nes	条、杆,高速钢制,热轧的,不规则盘卷的,其他	7227.1000	468
Bars and rods, of silico-manganese steel	条、杆,硅锰钢	7228.2000	468
Bars and rods, of silico-manganese steel hot-rolled, of alloy steel, in irregularly wound coils, nes	条、杆,硅锰钢制,热轧的,不规则盘卷的,其他	7227.2000	468
Bars and rods, of stainless steel, not further worked than cold-formed or cold-finished	条、杆,不锈钢的,除冷成形或冷加工外未经进一步加工	7222.2000	468
Bars, rods and profiles, of copper alloys	条、杆、型材及异型材,其他铜合金制	7407.2900	16
Bars, rods and profiles, of copper-zinc base alloys (brass)	条、杆、型材及异型材,铜锌合金(黄铜)制	7407.2100	16
Bars, rods and profiles, of nickel alloys	条、杆、型材及异型材,镍合金制	7505.1200	46
Bars, rods and profiles, of nickel, not alloyed	条、杆、型材及异型材,非合金镍制	7505.1100	46
Bars, rods and profiles, of refined copper	条、杆、型材及异型材,精炼铜制	7407.1000	16
Bars, rods, profiles and wire of lead	条、杆、型材及异型材或丝,铅制	7806.0010	16
Bars, rods, profiles and wire of tin	条、杆、型材及异型材或丝,锡制	8003.0000	16
Bars, rods, profiles and wire of zinc	条、杆、型材及异型材或丝,锌的	7904.0000	16
Baryta water	氧化钡	2816.4000	
Barytes	重晶石	2511.1000	45
Basalt	玄武岩	2516.9000	148
Base stations for mobile communication	基站,移动通信用	8517.6110	
Base stations, for wired or wireless network, nes	基站,有线或无线网络的,其他	8517.6190	
Basic lipase	碱性脂肪酶	3507.9020	35
Basic oils for lubricating oils	润滑油基础油	2710.1993	238
Basic proteinase	碱性蛋白酶	3507.9010	35
Basin and parts thereof, of iron or steel, for household, enamelled	面盆及其零件,钢铁制,家用,已搪瓷	7323.9410	24
Basketballs	篮球	9506.6210	
Basketwork, made directly to shape from plaiting materials or made up from goods, of bamboo	篮筐,用编结材料直接编成,竹制的	4602.1100	6
Basketwork, made directly to shape from plaiting materials or made up from goods, of grass or straw	篮筐,用编结材料直接编成,草制的	4602.1910	6
Basketwork, made directly to shape from plaiting materials or made up from goods, of maize-shuck	篮筐,用编结材料直接编成,玉米皮制的	4602.1920	6
Basketwork, made directly to shape from plaiting materials or made up from goods, of other vegetable materials	篮筐,用编结材料直接编成,其他植物材料制	4602.1990	6
Basketwork, made directly to shape from plaiting materials or made up from goods, of rattan	篮筐,用编结材料直接编成,藤制的	4602.1200	6
Bath towels of terry towelling or similar terry fabrics, of cotton	浴巾,毛巾织物或类似的毛圈织物的,棉制	6302.6010	346

Article Description	商品名称	Tariff Code	D. R.
Bathrobes, dressing gowns and similar articles, not knitted or crocheted, for women or girls, nes	浴衣、晨衣及类似品,非针织或钩编的,女式,其他	6208.9990	2456
Bathrobes, dressing gowns and similar articles, not knitted or crocheted, for women or girls, of cotton	浴衣、晨衣及类似品,非针织或钩编的,女式,棉制	6208.9100	2456
Bathrobes, dressing gowns and similar articles, not knitted or crocheted, for women or girls, of man-made fibres	浴衣、晨衣及类似品,非针织或钩编的,女式,化学纤维制	6208.9200	2456
Bathrobes, dressing gowns and similar articles, not knitted or crocheted, for women or girls, of silk or silk waste	浴衣、晨衣及类似品,非针织或钩编的,女式,丝及绢丝制	6208.9910	2456
Bathrobes, dressing gowns and similar articles, knitted or crocheted, for men or boys, nes	浴衣、晨衣及类似品,针织或钩编的男式,其他	6107.9990	2456
Bathrobes, dressing gowns and similar articles, knitted or crocheted, for men or boys, of cotton	浴衣、晨衣及类似品,针织或钩编的男式,棉制	6107.9100	2456
Bathrobes, dressing gowns and similar articles, knitted or crocheted, for men or boys, of man-made fibres	浴衣、晨衣及类似品,针织或钩编的男式,化学纤维制	6107.9910	2456
Bathrobes, dressing gowns and similar articles, knitted or crocheted, for women or girls, of cotton	浴衣、晨衣及类似品,针织或钩编的,女式,棉制	6108.9100	2456
Bathrobes, dressing gowns and similar articles, knitted or crocheted, for women or girls, of man-made fibres	浴衣、晨衣及类似品,针织或钩编的,女式,化学纤维制	6108.9200	2456
Bathrobes, dressing gowns and similar articles, knitted or crocheted, for women or girls, of other textile materials	浴衣、晨衣及类似品,针织或钩编的,女式,其他纺织材料制	6108.9900	2456
Bathrobes, dressing gowns and similar articles, not knitted or crocheted, for men or boys, nes	浴衣、晨衣及类似品,非针织或钩编的,男式,其他	6207.9990	2456
Bathrobes, dressing gowns and similar articles, not knitted or crocheted, for men or boys, of cotton	浴衣、晨衣及类似品,非针织或钩编的,男式,棉制	6207.9100	2456
Bathrobes, dressing gowns and similar articles, not knitted or crocheted, for men or boys, of man-made fibres	浴衣、晨衣及类似品,非针织或钩编的,男式,化学纤维制	6207.9920	2456
Bathrobes, dressing gowns and similar articles, not knitted or crocheted, for men or boys, of silk or silk waste	浴衣、晨衣及类似品非针织或钩编的,男式,丝及绢丝制	6207.9910	2456
Baths, of porcelain or china	浴缸,瓷制	6910.1000	268
Baths, of pottery	浴缸, 陶制	6910.9000	268
Baths, of cast iron, whether or not enamelled	浴缸,铸铁制,不论是否搪瓷	7324.2100	24
Baths, of iron or steel, nes	浴缸,钢铁制,其他	7324.2900	24
Battery carbons	电池碳棒	8545.9000	3
Battery separator, of polymers of ethylene, non-cellular and not reinforced, laminated, supported or similarly combined with other materials	电池隔膜,乙烯聚合物制,非泡沫,未用其他材料强化、层压、支撑或用类似方法合制	3920.1010	16

B

Article Description	商品名称	Tariff Code	D. R.
Battery separator, of polymers of propylene, non-cellular and not reinforced, laminated, supported or similarly combined with other materials	电池隔膜,丙烯聚合物制,非泡沫,未用其他材料强化、层压、支撑或用类似方法合制	3920. 2010	16
Bay leaves	月桂叶	0910. 9900	6
Bayonets and parts	刺刀及其零件	9307. 0000	
Beacons, floating structures	航标,浮动结构体	8907. 9000	5
Beads, of base metal	珠子,贱金属制	8308. 9000	256
Beaks and powder thereof	喙及其粉末	0507. 9090	14
Bean vermicelli, cooked	粉丝	1902. 3020	46
Bean, in airtight containers, nes	豇豆及菜豆罐头,其他	2005. 5910	148
Bean, in airtight containers, shelled, nes	豇豆及菜豆罐头,脱荚的,其他	2005. 5119	148
Bean, prepared or preserved otherwise than by vinegar or acetic acid, not frozen, nes	豇豆及菜豆,用醋或醋酸以外的其他方法制作或保藏的,未冷冻,其他	2005. 5990	148
Bean, shelled, prepared or preserved otherwise than by vinegar or acetic acid, not frozen, nes	豇豆及菜豆,脱荚的,用醋或醋酸以外的其他方法制作或保藏的,未冷冻,其他	2005. 5199	148
Beans (Vigna spp., Phaseolus spp.), nes, dried, shelled	豇豆及菜豆,其他,脱荚的,干的	0713. 3900	34
Beans of the species vigna mungo (L.) hepper or vigna radiata (L.) Wilczek, nes, dried, shelled	绿豆,其他,脱荚的,干的	0713. 3190	34
Beans of the species vigna mungo (L.) hepper or vigna radiata (L.) Wilczek, seed, dried, shelled	绿豆,种用,脱荚的,干的	0713. 3110	34
Beans (phaseolus spp.), fresh or chilled	菜豆,鲜或冷藏的	0708. 2000	1
Beans (Vigna spp.), fresh or chilled	豇豆,鲜或冷藏的	0708. 2000	1
Bearing housings, incorporating ball or roller bearings	轴承座,装有滚珠或滚子轴承的	8483. 2000	
Bearing housings, not incorporating ball or roller bearings	轴承座,未装有滚珠或滚子轴承的	8483. 3000	
Bearings of angular contact	轴承,角接触的	8482. 1030	5
Bearings of ball, nes	轴承,滚珠的,其他	8482. 1090	5
Bearings of combined ball/roller	轴承,球柱混合的	8482. 8000	5
Bearings of cylindrical roller, nes	轴承,圆柱形滚子的,其他	8482. 5000	5
Bearings of deep groove ball	轴承,深沟球的	8482. 1020	5
Bearings of jewel, of clock or watch	轴承,宝石的,钟、表的	9114. 2000	6
Bearings of needle roller	轴承,滚针的	8482. 4000	5
Bearings of plain shaft	轴承,滑动的	8483. 3000	
Bearings of plain shaft parts	轴承零件,滑动的	8483. 9000	3
Bearings of self-aligning ball	轴承,调心球的	8482. 1010	5
Bearings of spherical roller	轴承,鼓形滚子的	8482. 3000	5
Bearings of tapered roller, including cone and tapered roller assemblies	轴承,锥形滚子的,包括锥形滚子组件	8482. 2000	5
Bearings of thrust ball	轴承,推力球的	8482. 1040	5
Bearings parts of balls	轴承零件,滚珠的	8482. 9100	3

Article Description	商品名称	Tariff Code	D. R.
Bearings parts of needles	轴承零件,滚针的	8482. 9100	3
Bearings parts of rollers	轴承零件,滚柱的	8482. 9100	3
Bearings parts, nes	轴承零件,其他	8482. 9900	3
Bearnaise (sauce)	蛋黄酱	2103. 9090	268
Bears, pure-bred breeding	熊,改良种用	0106. 1910	34
Beauvais type hand-woven tapestries	"波威"及类似式样的手织装饰毯	5805. 0090	468
Bed linen, embroidered, nes	床上用织物制品,刺绣的,其他	6302. 3991	346
Bed linen, embroidered, of bast fibres, nes	床上用织物制品,刺绣的,麻制,其他	6302. 3921	346
Bed linen, embroidered, of cotton	床上用织物制品,刺绣的,棉制	6302. 3110	346
Bed linen, embroidered, of cotton, nes	床上用织物制品,棉制,其他	6302. 3199	346
Bed linen, embroidered, of man-made fibres	床上用织物制品,刺绣的,化学纤维制	6302. 3210	346
Bed linen, knitted or crocheted, of cotton	床上用织物制品,针织或钩编的,棉制	6302. 1010	346
Bed linen, knitted or crocheted, of other textile materials	床上用织物制品,针织或钩编的,其他纺织材料制	6302. 1090	346
Bed linen, nes	床上用织物制品,其他	6302. 3999	346
Bed linen, of bast fibres, nes	床上用织物制品,麻制,其他	6302. 3929	346
Bed linen, of man-made fibres, nes	床上用织物制品,化学纤维制,其他	6302. 3290	346
Bed linen, of silk or silk waste, nes	床上用织物制品,丝及绢丝制,其他	6302. 3910	346
Bed linen, printed, of bast fibres	床上用织物制品,印花的,麻制	6302. 2920	346
Bed linen, printed, of cotton, nes	床上用织物制品,印花的,棉制,其他	6302. 2190	346
Bed linen, printed, of man-made fibres, nes	床上用织物制品,印花的,化学纤维制,其他	6302. 2290	346
Bed linen, printed, of other textile materials	床上用织物制品,印花的,其他纺织材料制	6302. 2990	346
Bed linen, printed, of silk or silk waste	床上用织物制品,印花的,丝及绢丝制	6302. 2910	346
Bed sheets, of cotton, nes	床单,棉制,其他	6302. 3191	346
Bed sheets, printed, of cotton	床单,印花的,棉制	6302. 2110	346
Bed sheets, printed, of man-made fibres	床单,印花的,化学纤维制	6302. 2210	346
Bed valances, crocheted, of cotton	床帷,钩编的,棉制	6303. 1932	346
Bed valances, crocheted, of other textile materials	床帷,钩编的,其他纺织材料制	6303. 1992	346
Bed valances, crocheted, of synthetic fibres	床帷,钩编的,合成纤维制	6303. 1220	346
Bed valances, knitted, of cotton	床帷,针织的,棉制	6303. 1931	346
Bed valances, knitted, of other textile materials	床帷,针织的,其他纺织材料制	6303. 1991	346
Bed valances, knitted, of synthetic fibres	床帷,针织的,合成纤维制	6303. 1210	346
Bed valances, of cotton, nes	床帷,棉制,其他	6303. 9100	346
Bed valances, of other textile materials	床帷,其他纺织材料制	6303. 9900	346
Bed valances, of synthetic fibres, nes	床帷,合成纤维制,其他	6303. 9200	346
Bedside lamps, electric	床头灯,电气的	9405. 2000	5
Bedspreads, crocheted, hand-worked	床罩,钩编的,手工制	6304. 1131	346
Bedspreads, crocheted, nes	床罩,钩编的,其他	6304. 1139	346
Bedspreads, embroidered, of cotton or bast fibres	床罩,刺绣的,棉或麻制	6304. 1921	346

Article Description	商品名称	Tariff Code	D. R.
Bedspreads, embroidered, of man-made fibres	床罩,刺绣的,化学纤维制	6304. 1931	346
Bedspreads, embroidered, of other textile materials	床罩,刺绣的,其他纺织材料制	6304. 1991	346
Bedspreads, knitted, hand-worked	床罩,针织的,手工制	6304. 1121	346
Bedspreads, knitted, nes	床罩,针织的,其他	6304. 1129	346
Bedspreads, of cotton or bast fibres, nes	床罩,棉或麻制,其他	6304. 1929	346
Bedspreads, of man-made fibres, nes	床罩,化学纤维制,其他	6304. 1939	346
Bedspreads, of other textile materials, nes	床罩,其他纺织材料制,其他	6304. 1999	346
Bedspreads, of silk or silk waste	床罩,丝及绢丝制	6304. 1910	346
Bee pollen	蜂花粉	0410. 0043	12
Bee products, nes	蜂产品,其他	0410. 0049	12
Beer made from malt	啤酒,麦芽酿造的	2203. 0000	268
Bees, live, nes	蜜蜂,其他	0106. 9090	4
Bees, pure-bred breeding	蜜蜂,改良种用	0106. 9019	4
Beeswax	蜂蜡	1521. 9010	
Beet seed, excluding sugar beet seed, forage plants	甜菜子,糖甜菜子除外,饲料植物用的	1209. 2910	358
Beet-pulp, bagasses and other waste of sugar manufacture	甜菜渣、甘蔗渣及制糖过程中的其他残渣	2303. 2000	56
Bee-keeping machinery	养蜂业用机器	8436. 8000	
Bee-keeping machinery parts, nes	养蜂业用机器零件,其他	8436. 9900	3
Bellies (streaky) and cuts thereof, of pig salted, in brine, dried or smoked	腹肉(五花肉),猪的,干、熏、盐腌或盐渍的	0210. 1200	14
Bells and the like, of base metal, non-electric	铃及类似品,贱金属制,非电动的	8306. 1000	256
Bells parts, electric	电铃零件,电气的	8531. 9090	3
Bells, electric	电铃,电气的	8531. 8090	3
Belt sander, hand tools, with self-contained electric motor	砂光机,手提式,本身装有电动动力装置的	8467. 2910	57
Belts, of leather or of composition leather	腰带,皮革或再生皮革制的	4203. 3010	456
Bending machines, for working metal, nes	弯曲机,加工金属用,其他	8462. 2990	7
Bending machines, for working wood, cork, bone, hard rubber, hard plastics or similar hard materials	弯曲机器,加工木材、软木、骨、硬质橡胶、硬质塑料或类似硬质材料的	8465. 9400	7
Bending machines, numerically controlled, for working metal	弯曲机,数控的,加工金属用	8462. 2190	7
Benflumetol	本芴醇	2922. 1950	36
Bentonite	膨润土	2508. 1000	1345
Benzaldehyde	苯甲醛	2912. 2100	36
Benzene	苯	2902. 2000	6
Benzfetamine (INN), salts thereof	苄非他明(INN)以及它们的盐	2921. 4600	36
Benzilic acid	二苯乙醇酸	2918. 1910	36
Benzilic acid-3-quinuclidinate	二苯乙醇酸-3-奎宁环脂	2933. 3910	36
Benzoic acid, its salts and esters	苯甲酸及其盐和酯	2916. 3100	36
Benzole	粗苯	2707. 1000	6

Article Description	商品名称	Tariff Code	D. R.
Benzothiazole ring-system compounds, not further fused in the structure, whether or not hydrogenated	苯并噻唑环系化合物,结构上含有,未经进一步稠合的,不论是否氢化	2934. 2000	36
Benzoyl peroxied and benzoyl chloride	过氧化苯甲酰及苯甲酰氯	2916. 3200	36
Benzyl alcohol	苄醇	2906. 2100	36
Bertrandite	羟硅铍石	2617. 9090	146
Beryllium articles, nes	铍制品,其他	8112. 1900	16
Beryllium powders	铍粉末	8112. 1200	16
Beryllium, unwrought	铍,未锻轧	8112. 1200	16
Beta measuring or detecting instruments and apparatus	β射线的测量或检验仪器及装置	9030. 1000	
Beta radiations apparatus, for medical, surgical, dental or veterinary uses	β射线的应用设备,医疗、外科、牙科或兽医用	9022. 2100	
Beta radiations apparatus, nes	β射线的应用设备,其他	9022. 2900	3
Betel nuts, fresh or dried	槟榔,鲜的或干的	0802. 9010	134
Betel nuts, frozen	槟榔,冷冻的	0811. 9090	1
Betel nuts, in airtight containers	槟榔罐头	2008. 1920	248
Beverage bases	制造碳酸饮料的浓缩物	2106. 9010	268
Bezitramide (INN); salts thereof	苯氰米特(INN)以及盐	2933. 3300	36
Bezoar	黄药	0510. 0010	14
Bib and brace overalls, knitted or crocheted, of men or boys, of cotton	护胸背带工装裤,针织或钩编的,男式,棉制	6103. 4200	2456
Bib and brace overalls, knitted or crocheted, of men or boys, of other textile materials	护胸背带工装裤,针织或钩编的,男式,其他纺织材料制	6103. 4900	2456
Bib and brace overalls, knitted or crocheted, of men or boys, of synthetic fibres	护胸背带工装裤,针织或钩编的,男式,合成纤维制	6103. 4300	2456
Bib and brace overalls, knitted or crocheted, of men or boys, of wool or fine animal hair	护胸背带工装裤,针织或钩编的,男式,羊毛或动物细毛制	6103. 4100	2456
Bib and brace overalls, knitted or crocheted, of women or girls, of cotton	护胸背带工装裤,针织或钩编的,女式,棉制	6104. 6200	2456
Bib and brace overalls, knitted or crocheted, of women or girls, of other textile materials	护胸背带工装裤,针织或钩编的,女式,其他纺织材料制	6104. 6900	2456
Bib and brace overalls, knitted or crocheted, of women or girls, of synthetic fibres	护胸背带工装裤,针织或钩编的,女式,合成纤维制	6104. 6300	2456
Bib and brace overalls, knitted or crocheted, of women or girls, of wool or fine animal hair	护胸背带工装裤,针织或钩编的,女式,羊毛或动物细毛制	6104. 6100	2456
Bib and brace overalls, not knitted or crocheted, for men or boys, of cotton	护胸背带工装裤,非针织或钩编的,男式,棉制	6203. 4290	2456
Bib and brace overalls, not knitted or crocheted, for men or boys, of other textile material	护胸背带工装裤,非针织或钩编的,男式,其他纺织材料制	6203. 4990	2456
Bib and brace overalls, not knitted or crocheted, for men or boys, of synthetic fibres	护胸背带工装裤,非针织或钩编的,男式,合成纤维制	6203. 4390	2456
Bib and brace overalls, not knitted or crocheted, for men or boys, of wool or fine animal hair	护胸背带工装裤,非针织或钩编的,男式,羊毛或动物细毛制	6203. 4100	2456

B

Article Description	商品名称	Tariff Code	D. R.
Bib and brace overalls, not knitted or crocheted, for women or girls, of cotton	护胸背带工装裤,非针织或钩编的,女式,棉制	6204. 6200	2456
Bib and brace overalls, not knitted or crocheted, for women or girls, of other textile materials	护胸背带工装裤,非针织或钩编的,女式,其他纺织材料制	6204. 6900	2456
Bib and brace overalls, not knitted or crocheted, for women or girls, of synthetic fibres	护胸背带工装裤,非针织或钩编的,女式,合成纤维制	6204. 6300	2456
Bib and brace overalls, not knitted or crocheted, for women or girls, of wool or fine animal hair	护胸背带工装裤,非针织或钩编的,女式,羊毛或动物细毛制	6204. 6100	2456
Bicycle for racing	自行车,竞赛型	8712. 0020	8
Bicycle, mountain type	自行车,山地型	8712. 0030	8
Bicycles and other cycles' parts, nes	自行车及其他脚踏车的零件,其他	8714. 9900	3
Bicycles lighting equipment	自行车用照明装置	8512. 1000	7
Bicycles visual signalling equipment	自行车用视觉信号装置	8512. 1000	7
Bicycles, cross-country type, 16″, 18″or 20″	自行车,越野型,16、18 及 20 英寸	8712. 0041	8
Bicycles, cross-country type, nes	自行车,越野型,其他	8712. 0049	8
Bicycles, nes	自行车,其他	8712. 0089	8
Bicycles, not larger than 16″	自行车,16 英寸及以下	8712. 0081	8
Bidets, of porcelain or china	坐浴盆,瓷制	6910. 1000	268
Bidets, of pottery	坐浴盆, 陶制	6910. 9000	268
Bidets, of plastics	坐浴盆, 塑料的	3922. 9000	236
Bifendate	联苯双酯	2932. 9920	36
Bifendate	2,2'-双甲氧羰基 -4,4',-双甲氧基-5,6,5',6'-双亚甲二氧基联苯	2932. 9920	36
Bifurcated rivets, of base metal	开口铆钉,贱金属制,	8308. 2000	256
Bigeye tunas(thunnus obesus), fresh or chilled	大眼金枪鱼,鲜或冷的,	0302. 3400	18
Bigeye tunas(thunnus obesus), frozen	大眼金枪鱼,冻的	0303. 4400	18
Bilberries, fresh	越桔,鲜的	0810. 4000	1
Bile, whether of not dried	胆汁,不论是否干制;	0510. 0090	14
Bill hooks and similar hewing tools	钩刀及类似砍伐工具	8201. 4000	256
Billiards	台球	9504. 9090	5
Billiards articles and accessories of all kinds	台球用品及附件	9504. 2000	5
Binapacryl (ISO)	乐杀螨(ISO)	2916. 3600	36
Binder or baler twine, of polyethylene or polypropylene	包扎用绳,聚乙烯或聚丙烯制	5607. 4100	368
Binder or baler twine, of sisal or other textile fibres of the genus agave	包扎用绳,西沙尔麻或其他纺织用龙舌兰类纤维制	5607. 2100	368
Binders for foundry cores, prepared	粘合剂,铸芯用	3824. 1000	36
Binders for foundry moulds, prepared	粘合剂,铸模用	3824. 1000	36
Binders (other than book covers), of paper or paperboard	活动封面(书籍封面除外),纸或纸板制的	4820. 3000	
Binding machinery for book, nes	装订机,书本用,其他	8440. 1090	
Binding machinery parts, for book, nes	装订机零件,书本用,其他	8440. 9000	3

B

Article Description	商品名称	Tariff Code	D. R.
Binoculars	双筒望远镜	9005. 1000	
Binoculars parts and accessories (including mountings), nes	双筒望远镜零件、附件(包括座架),其他	9005. 9090	3
Biological stains	生物染色剂	3204. 9010	345
Biphenyl	联苯	2902. 9090	6
Biphenyl dicarbxybte medicaments, mixed or unmixed, put up in measured doses or in forms or packings for retail sale	联苯双酯类药品,混合或未混合的,配定剂量或制成零售包装	3004. 9020	368
Birds of prey, nes	猛禽,其他	0106. 3190	
Birds of prey, pure-bred breeding	猛禽,改良种用	0106. 3110	3
Birds' nests, edible	燕窝	0410. 0010	3
Birocular cases, camera cases, musical instrument cases, gun cases, holsters and similar containers, nes	望远镜盒、照相机套、乐器盒、枪盒、枪套及类似容器,其他	4202. 9900	256
Birocular cases, camera cases, musical instrument cases, gun cases, holsters and similar containers, with outer surface of leather, of composition leather or of patent leather	望远镜盒、照相机套、乐器盒、枪盒、枪套及类似容器,以皮革、再生皮革或漆皮作面	4202. 9100	256
Birocular cases, camera cases, musical instrument cases, gun cases, holsters and similar containers, with outer surface of plastic sheeting or of textile materials	望远镜盒、照相机套、乐器盒、枪盒、枪套及类似容器,以塑料片或纺织材料作面	4202. 9200	256
Birs, for human consumption, nes	鸟,食用,其他	0106. 3929	34
Birs, nes	鸟,其他	0106. 3990	34
Birs, pure-bred breeding, nes	鸟,改良种用,其他	0106. 3910	34
Biscuits	饼干	1905. 9000	28
Bismite	铋华	2617. 9090	146
Bismuth articles, nes	铋制品,其他	8106. 0090	16
Bismuth glance	辉铋矿	2617. 9090	146
Bismuth powders	铋粉末	8106. 0010	16
Bismuth, unwrought	铋,未锻轧	8106. 0010	16
Bismutite	泡铋矿	2617. 9090	146
Bismutite	泡铋矿	2617. 9090	146
Bisphenol A and its salts	双酚 A 及其盐	2907. 2300	36
Bitter apricot kernels	苦杏仁	1212. 9911	134
Bitumen and asphalt, emulsified	乳化沥青	2714. 9020	1346
Bitumen and asphalt, natural	天然沥青(地沥青)	2714. 9010	1346
Bituminised or asphalted paper and paperboard	沥青纸及纸板	4811. 1000	458
Bituminous coal, nes	烟煤,其他	2701. 1290	156
Bituminous concrete spreading machines	沥青混凝土摊铺机	8479. 1021	7
Bituminous mastics, based on asphalt or bitumen	沥青胶粘剂,以沥青为基本成分的	2715. 0000	1346
Bituminous mixtures based on asphalt or bitumen	沥青混合物,以沥青为基本成分的	2715. 0000	1346

B

Article Description	商品名称	Tariff Code	D. R.
Bituminous shale	沥青页岩	2714.1000	1346
Black boards, whether or not framed	黑板,不论是否镶框	9610.0000	
Black moss	发菜	1212.2020	14
Black tea (fermented), nes	红茶(已发酵),其他	0902.4090	248
Black tea (fermented), nes, in immediate packings of a content not exceeding 3kg	红茶(已发酵),内包装每件净重不超过3千克,其他	0902.3090	248
Black watermelon seeds	瓜子,黑的	1212.9991	134
Blackberries, frozen	黑莓,冷冻的	0811.2000	1
Blackberries, fresh	黑莓,鲜的	0810.2000	1
Bladders of animals (other than fish)	膀胱,动物的(鱼除外)	0504.0090	14
Blades for angledozer	铲,侧铲推土机用	8431.4200	3
Blades for bulldozer	铲,推土机用	8431.4200	3
Blades for scissors, tailors' shears and similar shears	剪刀片,剪刀、裁缝剪刀用	8213.0000	256
Blades for ships or boats	桨叶,船用	8487.1000	3
Blades, other than knives of heading No. 82.08, and blades therefor	刀片,税号82.08的刀除外	8211.9400	256
Blank ammunition firing pistols and revolvers	空包弹发射的左轮手枪和其他手枪	9303.9000	
Blankets and travelling rugs, nes	毯子及旅行毯,其他	6301.9000	56
Blankets (other than electric blankets) and travelling rugs, of cotton	毯子(电暖毯除外)及旅行毯,棉制的	6301.3000	56
Blankets (other than electric blankets) and travelling rugs, of synthetic fibres	毯子(电暖毯除外)及旅行毯,合成纤维制的	6301.4000	56
Blankets (other than electric blankets) and travelling rugs, of wool or of fine animal hair	毯子(电暖毯除外)及旅行毯,羊毛或动物细毛制的	6301.2000	56
Blanks for photochromic spectacles, of glass	镜片坯件,变色眼镜用,未经光学加工的,玻璃制	7015.1010	13457
Blanks for plane photochromic spectacles, of glass	镜片坯件,平光变色眼镜用,未经光学加工的,玻璃制	7015.9020	13457
Blanks of optical elements, for optical instruments	光学元件毛坯,光学仪器用,玻璃制,未经光学加工的	7014.0010	345
Bleaching machines parts, for textile yarns, fabrics or made up textile articles	漂白机器零件,纱线、织物及纺织制品用	8451.9000	
Bleaching machines, for textile yarns, fabrics or made up textile articles	漂白机器,纱线、织物及纺织制品用	8451.4000	
Blende	闪锌矿	2608.0000	146
Blinds (including venetian blinds) and similar articles and parts thereof, of plastics	百叶窗(包括威尼斯式百叶窗)或类似制品及其零件,塑料的	3925.3000	23
Blockboard, laminboard and battenboard, containing at least one layer of particle board	木块芯胶合板,侧板条芯胶合板及板条芯胶合板,至少含有一层木碎料板	4412.9492	48
Blockboard, laminboard and battenboard, nes	木块芯胶合板,侧板条芯胶合板及板条芯胶合板,其他	4412.9499	48

Article Description	商品名称	Tariff Code	D. R.
Blockboard, laminboard and battenboard, with at least one outer ply of non-coniferous wood	木块芯胶合板,侧板条芯胶合板及板条芯胶合板,至少有一表层是非针叶木	4412.9410	48
Blockboard, laminboard and battenboard, with at least one outer ply of tropical wood specified in Subheading Note to this Chapter	木块芯胶合板,侧板条芯胶合板及板条芯胶合板,至少有一层是本章子目注释所列的热带木	4412.9491	48
Blocks and similar articles of vegetable fibre, of straw or of shavings, chips, particles, sawdust or other waste, of wood, agglomerated with cement, plaster or other mineral binders	砖及类似品,用水泥、石膏及其他矿物粘合材料粘合植物纤维、稻草、刨花、木片屑、木粉、锯末或木废料制成	6808.0000	456
Blocks, plates, sheets and strip, tiles of any shape, of agglomerated cork	块、板、片及条,任何形状的砖、瓦,压制软木制	4504.1000	16
Blood fractions, nes	血份,其他	3002.1000	34
Blood transfusion apparatus	输血设备	9018.9060	
Blood-grouping reagents	血型试剂	3006.2000	36
Blotting-pads, of paper or paperboard	吸墨纸本	4820.9000	
Blow lamps	喷灯	8205.6000	256
Blow moulding machines, for working plastics	吹塑机	8477.3000	7
Blow pipes, hand-held	喷焊器,手提式	8468.1000	57
Blowing-carding machinery, for cotton type fibres	清梳联合机	8445.1111	7
Bluefin tunas(thunnus thynnus), fresh or chilled	蓝鳍金枪鱼,鲜或冷的,	0302.3500	18
Bluefin tunas(thunnus thynnus), frozen	金枪鱼(蓝鳍金枪鱼),冻的	0303.4500	18
Bluefin tunas, nes, living	蓝鳍金枪鱼,其他,活的	0301.9490	15
Bluetooth headphones	蓝牙耳机	8518.3010	5
Blueveined cheese	蓝纹乳酪	0406.4000	2468
Blueveined cheese and other cheese containing veins produced by penicillium roqueforti	蓝纹乳酪和娄地青霉生产的带有纹理的其他乳酪	0406.4000	2468
Boards and similar articles of vegetable fibre, of straw or of shavings, chips, particles, sawdust or other waste, of wood, agglomerated with cement, plaster or other mineral binders	板及类似品,用水泥、石膏及其他矿物粘合材料粘合植物纤维、稻草、刨花、木片屑、木粉、锯末或木废料制成	6808.0000	456
Boards, with writing or drawing surfaces	黑板,具有书写或绘画面的	9610.0000	
Boat or dock fenders, whether or not inflatable	船舶或码头的碰垫,不论是否可充气	4016.9400	236
Bobbins and the like, of wood	筒管及类似品,木制	4421.9010	56
Bobbins, spools, cops and similar supports of paper pulp, paper or paperboard, nes	筒管、卷轴、纡子及类似品,纸浆、纸或纸板制,其他	4822.9000	6
Bobbins, spools, cops and similar supports of paper pulp, paper or paperboard, of a kind used for winding textile yarn	筒管、卷轴、纡子及类似品,纸浆、纸或纸板制,纺织纱线用	4822.1000	6
Bodies covered parts, of the motor vehicles, nes	车身覆盖件,机动车辆的,其他	8708.2959	3
Bodies parts and accessories, of the motor vehicles, nes	车身(包括驾驶室)的其他零件、附件,其他	8708.2990	3

B

B

Article Description	商品名称	Tariff Code	D. R.
Bodies (including cabs), for motor vehicles with special purpose	车身(包括驾驶室),特种车辆用	8707.9090	7
Bodies (including cabs), for the motor vehicles, with 10 seats or more	车身(包括驾驶室),10座以上客车用	8707.9010	7
Bodies (including cabs), for the motor vehicles, with seats less than 10	车身(包括驾驶室),10座以下客车用	8707.1000	7
Bod-kins, for use in the hand, of iron or steel	引针,钢铁制的,手工用	7319.9000	
Boiled sweets	硬糖	1704.9000	258
Boiler tubes and pipes, seamless, of alloy steel, of circular cross-section, cold-drawn or cold-rolled, nes	锅炉管,无缝的,合金钢的,圆形截面管,冷拔或冷轧的,其他	7304.5110	6
Boiler tubes and pipes, seamless, of alloy steel, of circular cross-section, nes	锅炉管,无缝的,合金钢的,圆形截面管,其他	7304.5910	6
Boiler tubes and pipes, seamless, of iron or non-alloysteel, of circular cross-section, cold-drawn or cold-rolled	锅炉管,无缝的,铁或非合金钢的,圆形截面,冷拔或冷轧的	7304.3110	6
Boiler tubes and pipes, seamless, of iron or non-alloysteel, of circular cross-section, nes	锅炉管,无缝的,铁或非合金钢的,圆形截面,其他	7304.3910	6
Boiler tubes and pipes, seamless, of stainless steel, of circular cross-section, cold-drawn or cold-rolled	锅炉管,无缝的,不锈钢的,圆形截面,冷拔或冷轧的	7304.4110	6
Boiler tubes and pipes, seamless, of stainless steel, of circular cross-section, nes	锅炉管,无缝的,不锈钢的,圆形截面,其他	7304.4910	6
Bolducs of cotton or bast fibres	扎头带,棉或麻制	5806.4010	468
Bolducs of other textile materials	扎头带,其他纺织材料制	5806.4090	468
Boletus, dried	牛肝菌,干的	0712.3950	4
Bolognas, with a natural casing	腊肠,有天然肠衣	1601.0010	348
Bolt croppers, hand tools	螺栓切头器	8203.4000	256
Bolt or nut release preparations, based on lubricants, containing petroleum oils or oils obtained from bituminous minerals	螺栓或螺母松开剂,以润滑剂为基本成分的,含有石油或从沥青矿物提取的油类	3403.1900	2368
Bolt or nut release preparations, based on lubricants, nes	螺栓或螺母松开剂,以润滑剂为基本成分的,其他	3403.9900	2368
Bolting cloth, whether or not made up	筛布,不论是否制成的	5911.2000	
Bolts, of aluminium	螺栓,铝制	7616.1000	36
Bolts, of copper	螺栓,铜制	7415.3390	56
Bolts, whether or not with their nuts or washers, of iron of steel, nes	螺栓,不论是否带有螺母或垫圈,钢铁制的,其他	7318.1500	268
Bombs and parts	炸弹及其零件	9306.9000	3
Bone reconstruction cements	骨骼粘固剂	3006.4000	36
Bone, worked	兽骨,已加工的	9601.9000	5
Bones treated with acid	骨,经酸处理的	0506.1000	4
Bones, nes	骨,其他	0506.9090	146

B

Article Description	商品名称	Tariff Code	D. R.
Bones, powder, nes	骨粉,其他	0506.9019	14
Bones, powder, of bovine and sheep	骨粉,含牛羊成分的	0506.9011	146
Bones, waste, nes	骨废料,其他	0506.9019	14
Bones, waste, of bovine and sheep	骨废料,含牛羊成分的	0506.9011	146
Bonnets, of the motor vehicles	发动机罩盖,机动车辆的	8708.2953	3
Book binding machinery parts, nes	书本装订机器零件,其他	8440.9000	3
Book binding machinery, nes	书本装订机器,其他	8440.1090	
Book covers, of paper or paperboard	书籍封面,纸或纸板制的	4820.9000	
Book sewing binders	订书机,锁线式	8440.1010	
Book sewing binders	锁线装订机	8440.1010	
Book sewing binders parts	订书机零件,锁线式	8440.9000	3
Book sewing binders parts	锁线装订机零件	8440.9000	3
Boot or shoe lasts and trees, of other wood	木制鞋靴楦及楦头,其他木制的	4417.0090	56
Boot or shoe lasts and trees, of radiata pine	木制鞋靴楦及楦头,辐射松制的	4417.0010	56
Borates, nes	硼酸盐,其他	2840.2000	
Boric acids	硼酸	2810.0020	6
Borides, whether or not chemically defined	硼化物,不论是否已有化学定义	2850.0000	
Boring machines, for removing metal, nes	镗床,切削金属的,其他	8459.4090	7
Boring machines, numerically controlled, for removing metal	镗床,数控的,切削金属的	8459.4010	7
Boring or broaching tools, interchangeable, nes	镗孔或铰孔用工具,可互换,其他	8207.6090	256
Boring or broaching tools, with working part of natural or synthetic diamonds or cubic boronnitride, interchangeable	镗孔或铰孔工具,带有天然或合成金刚石、立方氮化硼制的工作部件,可互换	8207.6010	256
Boring or sinking machinery, nes	钻探或凿井机械,其他	8430.4900	5
Boring or sinking machinery, self-propelled, crawler boring machinery of drilling depth not exceeding 6000m	钻探或凿井机械,自推进的,钻探深度在6000米以下的履带式自推进钻机	8430.4122	5
Boring or sinking machinery, self-propelled, nes	钻探或凿井机械,自推进的,其他	8430.4190	5
Boring or sinking machinery, self-propelled, of drilling depth of 6000m or more	钻探或凿井机械,自推进的,钻探深度在6000米及以上的	8430.4121	5
Boring or sinking machinery, self-propelled, other boring machinery of drilling depth not exceeding 6000m	钻探或凿井机械,自推进的,钻探深度在6000米以下的其他钻探机	8430.4129	5
Boring-milling machines, for removing metal, nes	镗铣机床,切削金属的,其他	8459.3900	7
Boring-milling machines, numerically controlled, for removing metal	镗铣机床,数控的,切削金属的	8459.3100	7
Borneol	冰片	2906.1990	36
Bornite(erubescite)	斑铜矿	2603.0000	146
Boron	硼	2804.5000	
Boron carbides	碳化硼	2849.9010	
Boron, oxides thereof	硼的氧化物	2810.0010	6

B

Article Description	商品名称	Tariff Code	D. R.
Bottles cleaning machinery	洗瓶机	8422. 2000	
Bottles drying machinery	干瓶机	8422. 2000	
Bottles or other containers cleaning or drying machinery	瓶子或其他容器的洗涤或干燥机器	8422. 2000	
Bottling machinery parts, for beverages or liquid food	食品灌装设备用零件,饮料及液体用	8422. 9020	
Bottling or canning machinery for beverages or liquid food	灌装设备,饮料及液体用	8422. 3010	
Boules or wafers manufacture machines and apparatus, chemical mechanical polishers (CMP)	单晶硅柱或硅晶片的制造机器及装置,化学机械抛光设备(CMP)	8486. 1040	7
Boules or wafers manufacture machines and apparatus, for the treatment of monocrystalline sillicon by a process involving a change of temperature	单晶硅柱或硅晶片的制造机器及装置,利用温度变化处理单晶硅的机器及装置	8486. 1010	7
Boules or wafers manufacture machines and apparatus, grinding machines	单晶硅柱或硅晶片的制造机器及装置,研磨设备	8486. 1020	7
Boules or wafers manufacture machines and apparatus, nes	单晶硅柱或硅晶片的制造机器及装置,其他	8486. 1090	7
Boules or wafers manufacture machines and apparatus, sawing machines	单晶硅柱或硅晶片的制造机器及装置,切割设备	8486. 1030	7
Bovine animals, live, ex. pure-bred breeding	牛,改良种用除外	0102. 9000	34
Bovine animals, live, pure-bred breeding	牛,改良种用	0102. 1000	34
Bow string musical instruments	弓弦乐器	9202. 1000	5
Bowling alley equipments and appliances, automatic, nes	保龄球自动球道设备及器具,其他	9504. 9029	5
Bowling balls	保龄球	9504. 9022	
Bowling pin distributing machines, automatic	保龄球自动分瓶机	9504. 9021	
Bowling pins	保龄球瓶	9504. 9023	
Box files and similar articles, of a kind used in offices, shops or the like, of paper, paperboard,	卷宗盒类似品,办公室、商店及类似场所使用的,纸制的	4819. 6000	68
Box pallets and other load boards, of radiata pine	箱形托盘及其他装载用木板,辐射松制的	4415. 2010	56
Box pallets and other load boards, of other wood	箱形托盘及其他装载用木板,其他木制的	4415. 2090	56
Boxes of paper or paperboard, containing an assortment of paper stationery	纸盒子,内装各种纸制文具	4817. 3000	6
Boxes packings, of wood	包装盒,木制的	4415. 1000	56
Boxes, cases, crates and similar articles, of plastics	盒、箱(包括板条箱)及类似品,塑料的	3923. 1000	23
Braces, of man-made fibres	吊裤带,化学纤维制	6212. 9010	2456
Braces, of other textile materials	吊裤带,其他纺织材料制	6212. 9090	2456
Brackets and similar fixtures, of base metal	托架及类似品,贱金属制	8302. 5000	256
Braid making machines	编织带机	8447. 9090	7
Braids in the piece	成匹的编带	5808. 1000	468

Article Description	商品名称	Tariff Code	D. R.
Brake linings, containing asbestos	闸衬,含石棉的	6813. 2010	6
Brake linings, not containing asbestos	闸衬,不含石棉的	6813. 8100	6
Brake pads, containing asbestos	闸垫,含石棉的	6813. 2010	6
Brake pads, not containing asbestos	闸垫,不含石棉的	6813. 8100	6
Brakes and parts, of railway or tramway locomotives or rolling-stock, nes	制动装置及其零件,铁道及电车道机车或其他车辆的,其他	8607. 2900	3
Brakes, including coaster braking hubs and hub brakes, and parts thereof, of bicycles and other cycles	制动器(包括倒轮制动毂及毂闸)及其零件,自行车及脚踏车的	8714. 9400	3
Brakes, servo-brakes and parts of cross-country cars (4WD)	制动器、助力制动器及其零件,越野车(4 轮驱动)用	8708. 3095	3
Brakes, servo-brakes and parts of dumpers	制动器、助力制动器及其零件,自卸车用	8708. 3093	3
Brakes, servo-brakes and parts of motor vehicles with 30 seats or more	制动器、助力制动器及其零件,30 座及以上客运机动车辆用	8708. 3092	3
Brakes, servo-brakes and parts of motor vehicles with special purpose	制动器、助力制动器及其零件,特种车辆用	8708. 3096	3
Brakes, servo-brakes and parts of motor vehicles, nes	制动器、助力制动器及其零件,其他车辆用	8708. 3099	3
Brakes, servo-brakes and parts of saloon cars	制动器、助力制动器及其零件,小轿车用	8708. 3094	3
Brakes, servo-brakes and parts of tractors	制动器、助力制动器及其零件,拖拉机的	8708. 3091	3
Bran, sharps and other residues, of leguminous plants	糠、麸及其他残渣,豆类植物的	2302. 5000	56
Bran, sharps and other residues, of maize (corn)	糠、麸及其他残渣,玉米的	2302. 1000	56
Bran, sharps and other residues, of other cereals	糠、麸及其他残渣,其他谷物的	2302. 4000	56
Bran, sharps and other residues, of wheat	糠、麸及其他残渣,小麦的	2302. 3000	56
Branches, fresh, suitable for bouquets or for ornamental purposes	植物枝,鲜的,制花束或装饰用的	0604. 9100	34
Brandy	白兰地酒	2208. 2000	2468
Brannerite	钛铀矿	2612. 1000	146
Brass	黄铜	7403. 2100	146
Brassicas, edible, fresh or chilled, nes	芥菜类蔬菜,食用,鲜或冷藏的,其他	0704. 9090	1
Brassières of man-made fibres	胸罩,化学纤维制	6212. 1010	2456
Brassières of other textile materials	胸罩,其他纺织材料制	6212. 1090	2456
Brass-wind musical instruments	铜管乐器	9205. 1000	5
Braunite	褐锰矿	2602. 0000	1346
Braziers, of iron or steel, non-electric domestic appliances, for liquid fuel	烤炉,钢铁制,非电热的家用,使用液体燃料的	7321. 1290	7
Braziers, of iron or steel, non-electric domestic appliances, for gas fuel or for both gas and other fuels	烤炉,钢铁制,非电热的家用,使用气体燃料或可使用气体燃料及其他燃料的	7321. 1100	7

B

Article Description	商品名称	Tariff Code	D. R.
Braziers, of iron or steel, non-electric domestic appliances, nes, including appliances for solid fuel	烤炉,钢铁制,非电热的家用,其他,包括使用固体燃料的	7321. 1900	7
Brazil nuts, in shell	巴西果,未去壳	0801. 2100	134
Brazil nuts, shelled	巴西果,去壳	0801. 2200	134
Brazing or soldering machines and apparatus	钎焊机器及装置零件	8515. 9000	3
Brazing or soldering machines and apparatus, nes	钎焊机器及装置,其他	8515. 1900	
Bread makers, household automated	面包机,家用自动的	8516. 7210	7
Breakdown lorries	抢修车	8705. 9090	7
Breathing appliances, excluding protective masks having neither mechanical parts nor replaceable filters	呼吸器具,不包括既无机械零件又无可互换过滤器的防护面具	9020. 0000	
Breeches, knitted or crocheted, for men or boys, of wool or fine animal hair	马裤,针织或钩编的,男式,羊毛或动物细毛制	6103. 4100	2456
Breeches, knitted or crocheted, for women or girls, of cotton	马裤,针织或钩编的,女式,棉制	6104. 6200	2456
Breeches, knitted or crocheted, for women or girls, of other textile materials	马裤,针织或钩编的,女式,其他纺织材料制	6104. 6900	2456
Breeches, knitted or crocheted, for women or girls, of synthetic fibres	马裤,针织或钩编的,女式,合成纤维制	6104. 6300	2456
Breeches, knitted or crocheted, for women or girls, of wool or fine animal hair	马裤,针织或钩编的,女式,羊毛或动物细毛制	6104. 6100	2456
Breeches, knitted or crocheted, for men or boys, of cotton	马裤,针织或钩编的,男式,棉制	6103. 4200	2456
Breeches, knitted or crocheted, for men or boys, of other textile materials	马裤,针织或钩编的,男式,其他纺织材料制	6103. 4900	2456
Breeches, knitted or crocheted, for men or boys, of synthetic fibres	马裤,针织或钩编的,男式,合成纤维制	6103. 4300	2456
Breeches, not knitted or crocheted, for men or boys, of cotton	马裤,非针织或钩编的,男式,棉制	6203. 4290	2456
Breeches, not knitted or crocheted, for men or boys, of other textile material	马裤,非针织或钩编的,男式,其他纺织材料制	6203. 4990	2456
Breeches, not knitted or crocheted, for men or boys, of synthetic fibres	马裤,非针织或钩编的,男式,合成纤维制	6203. 4390	2456
Breeches, not knitted or crocheted, for men or boys, of wool or fine animal hair	马裤,非针织或钩编的,男式,羊毛或动物细毛制	6203. 4100	2456
Breeches, not knitted or crocheted, for women or girls, of cotton	马裤,非针织或钩编的,女式,棉制	6204. 6200	2456
Breeches, not knitted or crocheted, for women or girls, of other textile materials	马裤,非针织或钩编的,女式,其他纺织材料制	6204. 6900	2456
Breeches, not knitted or crocheted, for women or girls, of synthetic fibres	马裤,非针织或钩编的,女式,合成纤维制	6204. 6300	2456
Breeches, not knitted or crocheted, for women or girls, of wool or fine animal hair	马裤,非针织或钩编的,女式,羊毛或动物细毛制	6204. 6100	2456

Article Description	商品名称	Tariff Code	D. R.
Brewers'pitch and similar preparations based on rosin, resin acids or on vegetable pitch	啤酒桶沥青及类似制品,以松香、树脂酸或植物沥青为基本成分的	3807. 0000	3
Brewery machinery	酿酒机器	8438. 4000	
Brewery machinery parts	酿酒机器的零件	8438. 9000	3
Brewery yeast	啤酒酵母	2102. 1000	28
Brewing or distilling dregs and waste	酿造及蒸馏过程中的糟粕及残渣	2303. 3000	56
Bridge cranes, all-purpose	桥式起重机,通用型	8426. 1120	7
Bridges and bridge-sections, of iron or steel	桥梁及桥梁体段,钢铁的	7308. 1000	6
Bridges and bridge-sections, of aluminium	桥梁及桥梁体段,铝制	7610. 9000	56
Bridges, of clock or watch	横担(过桥),钟、表的	9114. 4000	6
Brie cheese, unworked	布里乳酪,未加工	0406. 9000	2468
Briefcases, with outer surface of leather, of composition leather or of patent leather	公文包,以皮革、再生皮革或漆皮作面	4202. 1190	1458
Briefcases, with outer surface of plastics or of textile materials	公文包,以塑料或纺织材料作面	4202. 1290	256
Briefs and panties, knitted or crocheted, for women or girls, nes	三角裤及短衬裤,针织或钩编的,女式,其他	6108. 2990	2456
Briefs and panties, knitted or crocheted, for women or girls, of cotton	三角裤及短衬裤,针织或钩编的,女式,棉制	6108. 2100	2456
Briefs and panties, knitted or crocheted, for women or girls, of man-made fibres	三角裤及短衬裤,针织或钩编的,女式,化学纤维制	6108. 2200	2456
Briefs and panties, knitted or crocheted, for women or girls, of silk or silk waste	三角裤及短衬裤,针织或钩编的,女式,丝及绢丝制	6108. 2910	2456
Briefs, panties, not knitted or crocheted, for women or girls, nes	三角裤、短衬裤,非针织或钩编的,女式,其他	6208. 9990	2456
Briefs, panties, not knitted or crocheted, for women or girls, of cotton	三角裤、短衬裤,非针织或钩编的,女式,棉制	6208. 9100	2456
Briefs, panties, not knitted or crocheted, for women or girls, of man-made fibres	三角裤、短衬裤,非针织或钩编的,女式,化学纤维制	6208. 9200	2456
Briefs, panties, not knitted or crocheted, for women or girls, of silk or silk waste	三角裤、短衬裤,非针织或钩编的,女式,丝及绢丝制	6208. 9910	2456
Brine	海水	2501. 0030	1368
Briquettes manufactured from coal	煤砖	2701. 2000	156
Brisling or sprats (Sprattus), fresh or chilled	黍鲱鱼,鲜或冷的	0302. 6100	18
Brisling or sprats (Sprattus), frozen	黍鲱鱼,冻的	0303. 7100	18
Bristles	猪鬃	0502. 1010	
Bristles and hair, nes, for brush making	兽毛,其他,制刷用	0502. 9019	3
Broaching machines, for removing metal or cermets	拉床,切削金属或金属陶瓷用	8461. 3000	7
Broad beans (Vicia fabavar Major) and horse beans (Viciafaba var. Equina, Vicia fabavar. minor, nes, dried, shelled)	蚕豆,其他,脱荚的,干的	0713. 5090	34

B

B

Article Description	商品名称	Tariff Code	D. R.
Broad beans (Vicia fabavar Major) and horse beans (Viciafaba var. Equina, vicia fabavar. minor, seed, dried, shelled)	蚕豆,种用,脱荚的,干的	0713.5010	34
Broad beans, in airtight containers, prepared or preserved otherwise than by vinegar or acetic acid, not frozen	蚕豆罐头,用醋或醋酸以外的其他方法制作或保藏的,未冷冻	2005.9920	1248
Broccolis (brassica oleracea var. Italica), fresh or chilled	西兰花,鲜或冷藏的	0704.9020	1
Broken or crushed stone, of a kind commonly used for concrete aggregates, for road metalling or for railway	碎石,通常作混凝土粒料、铺路、铁道路基或其他路基用的	2517.1000	13
Broken rice, nes	碎米,其他	1006.4090	35
Bromates, inorganic	溴酸盐,无机的	2829.9000	
Bromazepam (INN); salts thereof	溴西泮(INN)以及盐	2933.3300	36
Bromides and bromide oxides, nes, inorganic	溴化物及溴氧化物,其他,无机的	2827.5900	
Bromine	溴	2801.3020	
Bromochlorodifluoromethane	溴氯二氟甲烷	2903.4600	36
Bromoform	溴仿	2903.3990	36
Bromotrifluoromethane	溴三氟甲烷	2903.4600	36
Bronze	青铜	7403.2200	146
Brooders for poultry	育雏器,家禽用	8436.2100	
Brookite	板钛矿	2614.0000	146
Broom or brush bodies and handles, of other wood	扫帚及刷子的身及柄,其他木制的	4417.0090	56
Broom or brush bodies and handles, of radiata pine	扫帚及刷子的身及柄,辐射松制的	4417.0010	56
Brooms and brushes, consisting of twigs or other vegetable materials bound together, with or without handles	帚及刷,用枝条或其他植物材料捆扎而成的不论是否有把	9603.1000	
Brotizolam (INN); salts thereof	溴替唑仑(INN)及盐	2934.9100	36
Brown fused alumina, artificial	棕刚玉,人造的	2818.1010	136
Brown haematite, agglomerated	赤铁矿,已烧结	2601.1200	1346
Brufen (Ibuprofen)	布洛芬	2916.3920	36
Brushes for the application of cosmetics, nes	化妆用笔,其他	9603.3090	3
Brushes of metal wire, constituting parts of machines or appliances	金属丝刷,作为机器、器具零件的	9603.5011	3
Brushes of metal wire, nes	金属丝刷,其他	9603.5019	3
Brushes, constituting parts of machines or appliances	刷,作为机器、器具零件的	9603.5091	3
Brushes, nes	刷,其他	9603.5099	3
Brussels sprouts, fresh or chilled	抱子甘蓝,鲜或冷藏的	0704.2000	1
Buckets, parts of bulldozer or cranes	戽斗,推土机或起重机零件	8431.4100	3
Buckles, of base metal, of a kind used for clothing, footwear, awnings, handbags, travel goods or other made up articles	扣,贱金属制,用于衣着、鞋靴、天篷、提包、旅行用品或其他制成品	8308.9000	256

Article Description	商品名称	Tariff Code	D. R.
Buckle-clasps, of base metal, of a kind used for clothing, footwear, awnings, handbags, travel goods or other made up articles	扣,带栓的,贱金属制,用于衣着、鞋靴、天篷、提包、旅行用品或其他制成品	8308.9000	256
Buckram and similar stiffened textile fabrics of a kind used for hat foundations of cotton or bast fibres	硬衬布及类似硬挺纺织物,棉或麻制	5901.9091	
Buckram and similar stiffened textile fabrics of a kind used for hat foundations of man-made fibres	硬衬布及类似硬挺纺织物,化学纤维制	5901.9092	
Buckram and similar stiffened textile fabrics of a kind used for hat foundations, nes	硬衬布及类似硬挺纺织物,其他	5901.9099	
Buckwheat	荞麦	1008.1000	3
Buffers and parts, of railway or tramway locomotives or rolling-stock	缓冲器及其零件,铁道及电车道机车或其他车辆的	8607.3000	3
Builders joinery and carpentry of wood, nes	木工制品,建筑用,其他	4418.9000	
Builders ware of plastics, nes	塑料制品,建筑用,其他	3925.9000	23
Bulbs fritillariae thunbergii	贝母	1211.9017	34
Bulbs, in growth or in flower	鳞茎,生长或开花的	0601.2000	
Bulbs, nes, dormant	鳞茎,其他,休眠的	0601.1099	135
Bulbs, seed, dormant	鳞茎,种用,休眠的	0601.1091	135
Bulgur wheet	干小麦,碾碎的	1904.3000	48
Bulk ships, motor powered, loading exceeding 150000t, not exceeding 300000t	散货船,机动的,载重量超过 15 万吨,但不超过 30 万吨	8901.9042	8
Bulk ships, motor powered, loading exceeding 300000t	散货船,机动的,载重量超过 30 万吨	8901.9043	8
Bulk ships, motor powered, loading not exceeding 150000t	散货船,机动的,载重量不超过 15 万吨	8901.9041	8
Bulldozer blades	推土机用铲	8431.4200	3
Bulldozers and angledozers, track laying, with an engine of an output exceeding 235.36kW(320hp)	推土机及侧铲推土机,履带式,发动机输出功率超过 235.36 千瓦(320 马力)的	8429.1110	57
Bulldozers and angledozers, with an engine of an output exceeding 235.36kW(320hp)	推土机及侧铲推土机,发动机输出功率超过 235.36 千瓦(320 马力)的	8429.1910	57
Bulldozers, nes	推土机,其他	8429.1990	57
Bulldozers, track laying, nes	推土机,履带式,其他	8429.1190	57
Bumpers and parts thereof	保险杠及其零件	8708.1000	3
Bung covers, of base metal	塞子帽,贱金属制	8309.9000	256
Buoys	浮筒	8907.9000	5
Buprenorphine (INN) and salts	丁丙诺啡(INN)及盐	2939.1100	34
Burglar alarm for motor vehicles	防盗报警器,机动车辆用	8512.3012	7
Burglar alarms and similar apparatus	防盗报警器及类似装置	8531.1000	3
Burglar alarms parts	防盗报警器及类似装置用零件	8531.9010	3
Burn furnaces for radioactive waste	焚烧炉,放射性废物	8417.8020	7

B

Article Description	商品名称	Tariff Code	D. R.
Burnisher, hand tools, with self-contained electric motor	磨光机,手提式,本身装有电动动力装置的	8467. 2910	57
Buses for transport passengers at airport, with compression-ignition internal combustion piston engine	机坪客车,装有压燃式活塞内燃发动机的	8702. 1020	58
Butadiene rubber(BR), in primary forms	丁二烯橡胶(BR),初级形状的	4002. 2010	136
Butadiene rubber(BR), nesr	丁二烯橡胶(BR),其他	4002. 2090	136
Butadiene, liquefied	丁二烯,液化的	2711. 1400	1468
Butalbital (INN); salts thereof	布他比妥(INN)以及盐	2933. 5300	36
Butanes, liquefied, in containers of a kind used for filling or refilling cigarette or similar lighters and of a capacity exceeding 300cm^3	丁烷,液化的,直接灌注香烟打火机及类似打火器用,其包装容器的容积超过300立方厘米	2711. 1310	1468
Butanes, liquefied, nes	丁烷,液化的,其他	2711. 1390	1468
Butanoic, their salts and esters	丁酸及其盐和酯	2915. 6000	36
Butanone	丁酮	2914. 1200	36
Butan-1-ol(n-butyl alcohol)	正丁醇	2905. 1300	36
Buta-1,3-diene	1,3 丁二烯	2901. 2400	368
Butchers cleavers	刀,屠刀	8214. 9000	256
Butchers cleavers	屠刀	8214. 9000	256
Butobarbital; salts thereof	正丁巴比妥(INN)以及盐	2933. 5300	36
Butt welding fittings, of iron or steel, nes	对焊件,钢铁的,其他	7307. 9300	6
Butt welding fittings, of stainless steel	对焊件,不锈钢制	7307. 2300	6
Butter	黄油	0405. 1000	268
Butter knives, other than plated with precious metal	黄油刀,非镀贵金属的	8215. 9900	256
Butter knives, plated with precious metal	黄油刀,镀贵金属的	8215. 9100	256
Butterfish(pampus), frozen	鲳鱼,冻的	0303. 7930	18
Butterfish(pampus), salted or in brine	鲳鱼,盐腌及盐渍的	0305. 6930	4
Butterfish(pamus), fresh or chilled	鲳鱼,鲜或冷的	0302. 6930	18
Butterfly nets	捕蝶网	9507. 9000	5
Buttermilk	酪乳	0403. 9000	248
Button blanks	钮扣坯	9606. 3000	5
Button moulds and other parts of buttons	钮扣芯及钮扣的其他零件	9606. 3000	5
Button shape primary cells and primary batteries, alkaline zinc-manganese dioxide	扣式原电池及原电池组,碱性锌锰的	8506. 1011	68
Button shape primary cells and primary batteries, alkaline zinc-manganese dioxide	原电池及原电池组,碱性锌锰的,扣式	8506. 1011	68
Buttons, of base metal, not covered with textile material	钮扣,金属制,未用纺织材料包裹	9606. 2200	5
Buttons, of plastics, not covered with textile material	钮扣,塑料制,未用纺织材料包裹	9606. 2100	5
Buttons, nes	钮扣,其他	9606. 2900	5
Butyl acrylate	丙烯酸丁酯	2916. 1230	36
Butylene, liquefied	丁烯,液化的	2711. 1400	1468

Article Description	商品名称	Tariff Code	D. R.
Buzzers parts, electric	蜂鸣器零件,电气的	8531. 9090	3
Buzzers, electric	蜂鸣器,电气的	8531. 8010	3
Buzzers, for motor vehicles	蜂鸣器,机动车辆用	8512. 3011	7
B-ultrasonic diagnostic equipment	B 型超声波诊断仪	9018. 1210	

C

Article Description	商品名称	Tariff Code	D. R.
Cabbage lettuce, fresh or chilled	结球莴苣,鲜或冷藏的	0705.1100	1
Cabbages (brassica oleracea var. Capitata), fresh or chilled	卷心菜,鲜或冷藏的	0704.9010	1
Cable making machines	缆的制造机器	8479.4000	7
Cable-drums, of wood	电缆卷筒,木制的	4415.1000	56
Cachous	口香糖	1704.1000	268
Cactus figs (prickly pears)	仙人掌果	0810.9090	1
Cadmium articles, nes	镉制品,其他	8107.9000	16
Cadmium powders	镉粉末	8107.2000	16
Cadmium telluride	碲化镉	2842.9020	
Cadmium, unwrought	镉,未锻轧	8107.2000	16
Caffeine and its salts	咖啡因及其盐	2939.3000	34
Cake servers, other than plated with precious metal	糕点夹,非镀贵金属的	8215.9900	256
Cake servers, plated with precious metal	糕点夹,镀贵金属的	8215.9100	256
Cakes	糕饼	1905.9000	28
Calamine (hemimorphite)	菱锌矿	2608.0000	146
Calaverite	碲金矿	2616.9000	146
Calcareous monumental or building stone, nes	石灰质碑用或建筑用石,其他	2515.2000	148
Calcareous stone and articles thereof, worked, nes	石灰石及其制品,已加工的,其他	6802.9290	3468
Calcareous stone carvings, nes	石灰石石刻,其他	6802.9210	3468
Calcareous stone monumental or building stone and articles thereof, simply cut or sawn, with a flat or even surface, nes	石灰石碑石或建筑用石及其制品,简单切削或锯开并具有一个平面的,其他	6802.2910	3468
Calcite	冰洲石	2530.9099	13456
Calcium	钙	2805.1200	6
Calcium carbides	碳化钙	2849.1000	
Calcium carbonate	碳酸钙	2836.5000	
Calcium chloride	氯化钙	2827.2000	
Calcium cyanamide	氰氨化钙	3102.9010	68
Calcium hydrogenorthophosphate (dicalcium phosphate), feed grade	正磷酸氢钙(磷酸二钙),饲料级的	2835.2510	
Calcium hydrogenorthophosphate (dicalcium phosphate), food grade	正磷酸氢钙(磷酸二钙),食品级的	2835.2520	
Calcium hydrogenorthophosphate (dicalcium phosphate), nes	正磷酸氢钙(磷酸二钙),其他	2835.2590	3
Calcium hypochlorite, commercial	次氯酸钙,商品级	2828.1000	
Calcium hypochlorites, nes	钙的次氯酸盐,其他	2828.1000	
Calcium wolframate	钨酸钙	2841.8030	1

Article Description	商品名称	Tariff Code	D. R.
Calculating machines parts and accessories, nes	计算器具的零件、附件,其他	8473. 2900	3
Calculating machines, electronic, incorporating a printing device	计算器,电子式,装有打印装置的	8470. 2100	
Calculating machines, electronic, nes	计算器,电子式,其他	8470. 2900	
Calculating machines, nes	计算机器,其他	8470. 3000	
Calculators, electronic, capable of operation without an external source of electric power	计算器,电子式,不需外接电源的	8470. 1000	
Calendars of any kind, printed, including calendar blocks	日历,包括日历芯,印刷的	4910. 0000	
Calendering machines cylinders	研光机滚筒	8420. 9100	3
Calendering machines parts, nes	研光机零件,其他	8420. 9900	3
Calendering machines, other than for metals or glass, and cylinders	研光机,加工金属或玻璃用的除外	8420. 1000	
Calia melons, fresh	加勒比甜瓜,鲜的	0807. 1920	1
Call horns	号角	9208. 9000	5
Callipers	卡尺	9017. 3000	
Camazepam(INN); salts thereof	卡马西泮(INN)以及盐	2933. 9100	36
Camel-back strips for retreading rubber tyres	胎面补料胎条,轮胎翻新用	4006. 1000	13
Cameras for comparison of forensic or criminological purposes	照相机,比较法庭或犯罪学用的	9006. 3000	7
Cameras lens for single lens reflex	单反相机镜头	9002. 1131	3
Cameras of a kind used for preparing printing plates or cylinders, nes	照相机,制版的,其他	9006. 1090	7
Cameras of a kind used for preparing printing plates or cylinders, nes	制版照相机,其他	9006. 1090	7
Cameras of a kind used for recording documents on microfilm, microfiche or other microforms	缩微照相机,使用缩微胶卷、胶片或其他缩微品的	9006. 5210	7
Cameras parts and accessories	摄影机用零件、附件	9007. 9100	3
Cameras parts and accessories, for instant print cameras	照相机用零件、附件,一次成像照相机用	9006. 9120	3
Cameras parts and accessories, for the photographic cameras	照相机用零件、附件,制版照相机和特种照相机用	9006. 9110	3
Cameras parts and accessories, nes	照相机用零件、附件,其他	9006. 9199	3
Cameras specially designed for under-water use, for aerial survey or for medical or surgical examination of internal organs	照相机,特种的,水下、航空测量或体内器官检查用	9006. 3000	7
Cameras specially designed for under-water use, for aerial survey, or for medical or surgical examination of internal organs	特种照相机,水下、航空测量或体内器官检查用	9006. 3000	7
Cameras, for roll film of a width of 35mm	照相机,使用胶片宽度为35毫米	9006. 5300	7
Cameras, for film of less than 16mm width or for double-8mm film	摄影机,胶片宽度小于16毫米或双8毫米	9007. 1100	8
Cameras, for roll film of a width less than 35mm	照相机,使用胶片宽度小于35毫米	9006. 5290	7

C

Article Description	商品名称	Tariff Code	D. R.
Cameras, high speed	摄影机,高速的	9007.1910	8
Cameras, instant print	照相机,一次成像的	9006.4000	7
Cameras, nes	摄影机,其他	9007.1990	8
Cameras, nes	照相机,其他	9006.5990	7
Cameras, with a through-the-lens viewfinder [single lens reflex (SLR)], for roll film of a width not exceeding 35mm	照相机,通过镜头取景[单镜头反光式(SLR)],使用胶片宽度不超过35毫米	9006.5100	7
Camphene	莰烯	2902.1990	6
Camphor	樟脑	2914.2100	36
Camping goods, nes	野营用品,其他	6306.9990	346
Camping goods, of bast fibres, nes	野营用品,麻制,其他	6306.9910	346
Camping goods, of cotton, nes	野营用品,棉制,其他	6306.9100	346
Camping goods, of man-made fibres, nes	野营用品,化学纤维制,其他	6306.9920	346
Canary seed	加那利草子	1008.3000	3
Cancelling postage stamps machines	盖销邮票机	8472.3090	
Candies, not containing cocoa	冰糖	1702.9000	
Candles and the like	蜡烛	3406.0000	
Canna bulbs, seed, dormant	美人蕉,种用,休眠的	0601.1091	135
Cannelloni, whether or not cooked or otherwise prepared	奶油面卷,不论是否烹煮或经其他方法制作	1902.2000	46
Cannulae and the like, used in medical, surgical, dental or veterinary sciences	插管及类似品,医疗、外科、牙科或兽医用	9018.3900	3
Canoes, inflatable	轻舟,充气的	8903.1000	58
Canoes, nes	轻舟,其他	8903.9900	58
Cans, of iron or steel, for any material, of a capacity of less than 50L, closed by soldering or crimping, whether or not lined or heat-insulated, but not fitted with mechanical or thermal equipment	罐,钢铁的,盛装物料用,容积在50升以下,焊边或卷边接合的,不论是否衬里或隔热,但无机械或热力装置	7310.2100	36
Cantaloupe melons, fresh	罗马甜瓜,鲜的	0807.1920	1
Cantharides	斑蝥	0510.0040	14
Canthaxanthin	角黄素	3204.1700	345
Capacitances measuring instruments and apparatus, nes	电容测试仪,其他	9030.8910	
Capacitances measuring instruments and apparatus, with a recording device	电容测试仪,带记录装置	9030.8410	
Capacitors parts, fixed, designed for use in 50/60Hz circuits and having a reactive power handling capacity of not less than 0.5kVar (power capacitors)	电容器零件,固定式,用于50/60赫兹电路,其额定无功功率不低于0.5千瓦(电力电容器)	8532.9010	3
Capacitors parts, nes	电容器零件,其他	8532.9090	3
Capacitors, ceramic dielectric, multilayer, laminate	电容器,多层瓷介,片式	8532.2410	56
Capacitors, ceramic dielectric, multilayer, nes	电容器,多层瓷介,其他	8532.2490	56

Article Description	商品名称	Tariff Code	D. R.
Capacitors, ceramic dielectric, single layer	电容器,单层瓷介的	8532. 2300	56
Capacitors, dielectric of paper or plastics,	电容器,纸介质或塑料介质,其他	8532. 2590	56
Capacitors, dielectric of paper or plastics, laminate	电容器,纸介质或塑料介质,片式	8532. 2510	56
Capacitors, fixed, designed for use in 50/60Hz circuits and having a reactive power handling capacity of not less than 0. 5kVar (power capacitors)	电容器,固定式,用于50/60赫兹电路,其额定无功功率不低于0.5千瓦(电力电容器)	8532. 1000	56
Capacitors, fixed, nes	电容器,固定式,其他	8532. 2900	56
Capacitors, of aluminium electrolytic, laminate	电容器,铝电解式,片式	8532. 2210	56
Capacitors, of aluminium electrolytic, nes	电容器,铝电解式,其他	8532. 2290	56
Capacitors, of tantalum, fixed, nes	电容器,钽的,其他	8532. 2190	56
Capacitors, of tantalum, laminate	电容器,钽的,片式	8532. 2110	56
Capacitors, variable or adjustable (pre-set)	电容器,可变或可调(微调)	8532. 3000	56
Capes and similar articles, knitted or crocheted, for men or boys, for man-made fibres	斗篷及类似品,针织或钩编的,男式,化学纤维制	6101. 3000	2456
Capes and similar articles, knitted or crocheted, for men or boys, nes	斗篷及类似品,针织或钩编的,男式,其他	6101. 9090	2456
Capes and similar articles, knitted or crocheted, for men or boys, of cotton	斗篷及类似品,针织或钩编的,男式,棉制	6101. 2000	2456
Capes and similar articles, knitted or crocheted, for men or boys, of wool or fine animal hair	斗篷及类似品,针织或钩编的,男式,羊毛或动物细毛制	6101. 9010	2456
Capes and similar articles, knitted or crocheted, for women or girls, nes	斗篷及类似品,针织或钩编的,女式,其他	6102. 9000	2456
Capes and similar articles, knitted or crocheted, for women or girls, of cotton	斗篷及类似品,针织或钩编的,女式,棉制	6102. 2000	2456
Capes and similar articles, knitted or crocheted, for women or girls, of man-made fibres	斗篷及类似品,针织或钩编的,女式,化学纤维制	6102. 3000	2456
Capes and similar articles, knitted or crocheted, for women or girls, of wool or fine animal hair	斗篷及类似品,针织或钩编的,女式,羊毛或动物细毛制	6102. 1000	2456
Capes, not knitted or crocheted, for men or boys, of cotton	斗篷,非针织或钩编的,男式,棉制	6201. 1290	2456
Capes, not knitted or crocheted, for men or boys, of man-made fibres	斗篷,非针织或钩编的,男式,化学纤维制	6201. 1390	2456
Capes, not knitted or crocheted, for men or boys, of other textile materials	斗篷,非针织或钩编的,男式,其他纺织材料制	6201. 1900	2456
Capes, not knitted or crocheted, for men or boys, of wool or fine animal hair	斗篷,非针织或钩编的,男式,羊毛或动物细毛制	6201. 1100	2456
Capes, not knitted or crocheted, for women or girls, of cotton	斗篷,非针织或钩编的,女式,棉制	6202. 1290	2456
Capes, not knitted or crocheted, for women or girls, of man-made fibres	斗篷,非针织或钩编的,女式,化学纤维制	6202. 1390	2456
Capes, not knitted or crocheted, for women or girls, of other textile materials	斗篷,非针织或钩编的,女式,其他纺织材料制	6202. 1900	2456

C

C

Article Description	商品名称	Tariff Code	D. R.
Capes, not knitted or crocheted, for women or girls, of wool or fine animal hair	斗篷,非针织或钩编的,女式,羊毛或动物细毛制	6202.1100	2456
Caps, of base metal	盖子,贱金属制	8309.9000	256
Capsicum annuum var. Grossum, dried	甜椒,干的	0712.9060	4
Capstans, nes	绞盘,其他	8425.3990	78
Capstans, pit-head winding gear, powered by electric motor	绞盘,电动的,矿井口用	8425.3110	78
Capstans, powered by electric motor, specially designed for use underground	绞盘,电动的,专为井下使用设计的	8425.3110	78
Capstans, powered by electric motor, nes	绞盘,电动的,其他	8425.3190	78
Capsules for bottles, of base metal	瓶帽,贱金属制	8309.9000	256
Capsules, pharmaceutical	胶囊,装药用	9602.0010	
Captafol (ISO)	敌菌丹(ISO)	2930.5000	36
Captive-bolt humane killers	弩枪式人道捕杀器	9303.9000	
Carambola, fresh	杨桃,鲜的	0810.9060	1
Caramel	焦糖	1702.9000	
Caramelised sugars	焦糖	1702.9000	
Caramels (confectionery)	太妃糖	1704.9000	258
Caraway Seeds	香菜子	0909.4000	
Carbides, nes	碳化物,其他	2849.9090	
Carbon articles, non-electrical	碳精制品,非电气的	6815.1000	6
Carbon brushes	碳刷	8545.2000	3
Carbon dioxide	二氧化碳	2811.2100	36
Carbon disulphide	二硫化碳	2813.1000	
Carbon electrodes, nes	碳电极,其他	8545.1900	3
Carbon electrodes, of a kind used for furnaces	碳电极,炉用	8545.1100	3
Carbon fabric	碳布	6815.9931	6
Carbon fibres	碳纤维	6815.9920	6
Carbon fibres articles, nes	碳纤维制品,其他	6815.9939	6
Carbon paper, in rolls or sheets, of width exceeding 36cm or in roll or one side exceeding 36cm and other side exceeding 15cm in rectangular sheets	复写纸,成卷或成张的,卷宽度超过36厘米,或长超过36厘米且宽超过15厘米	4809.9000	458
Carbon paper, nes	复写纸,其他	4816.9090	58
Carbon preparations or semi-manufactures, in the form of pastes, blocks, plates	碳制品或半制品,糊状、块状、板状	3801.9000	134
Carbon tetrachloride	四氯化碳	2903.1400	36
Carbon (carbon blacks and other forms of carbon not elsewhere specified or included)	碳(碳黑及其他税号未列名的其他形态的碳)	2803.0000	24
Carbonaceous pastes and similar pastes, for furnace linings	碳糊及类似糊,炉衬用	3801.3000	134
Carbonaceous pastes for electrodes and similar pastes for furnace linings	碳糊,电极用及炉衬用的类似糊	3801.3000	134

Article Description	商品名称	Tariff Code	D. R.
Carbonyl dichloride	碳酰二氯	2812.1030	
Carboxylic acids with additional oxygen function and their anhydrides, halides, peroxides and peroxyacids; their halogenated, sulphonated, nitrated or nitrosated derivatives, nes	含附加含氧基的羧酸及其酸酐、酰卤化物、过氧化物和过氧酸以及它们的卤化、磺化、硝化或亚硝化衍生物,其他	2918.9900	36
Carboxylic acids with alcohol function but without other oxygen function, their anhydrides, halides, peroxides, peroxyacids and their derivatives, nes	含醇基但不含其他含氧基的羧酸及其酸酐、酰卤化物、过氧化物和过氧酸以及它们的衍生物,其他	2918.1990	36
Carboxylic acids with aldehyde or ketone function but without other oxygen function, their anhydrides, halides, peroxides, peroxyacids and their derivatives	含醛基或酮基但不含其他含氧基的羧酸及其酸酐、酰卤化物、过氧化物和过氧酸以及它们的衍生物	2918.3000	36
Carboxylic acids with phenol function but without other oxygen function, their anhydrides, halides, peroxides, peroxyacids and their derivatives, nes	含酚基但不含其他含氧基的羧酸及其酸酐、酰卤化物、过氧化物和过氧酸以及它们的衍生物,其他	2918.2900	36
Carboxymethylcellulose and its salts, in primary forms	羧甲基纤维素及其盐,初级形状的	3912.3100	16
Carboys, bottles, flasks and similar articles, of plastics	坛、瓶及类似品,塑料的	3923.3000	23
Carburetant	增炭剂	3824.9030	36
Carcinotrons	返波管	8540.7900	35
Card clothing	钢丝针布	8448.3100	3
Card or carding machine, for cotton type fibres	梳棉机	8445.1113	7
Cardamoms	豆蔻	0908.3000	
Cardigans, knitted or crocheted, nes	开襟衫,针织或钩编的,其他	6110.9090	2456
Cardigans, knitted or crocheted, of cotton	开襟衫,针织或钩编的,棉制	6110.2000	2456
Cardigans, knitted or crocheted, of fine animal hair	开襟衫,针织或钩编的,其他动物细毛制	6110.1990	2456
Cardigans, knitted or crocheted, of kashmir (cashmere) goats	开襟衫,针织或钩编的,喀什米尔山羊细毛制	6110.1200	2456
Cardigans, knitted or crocheted, of man-made fibres	开襟衫,针织或钩编的,化学纤维制	6110.3000	2456
Cardigans, knitted or crocheted, of other goats	开襟衫,针织或钩编的,其他山羊细毛制	6110.1910	2456
Cardigans, knitted or crocheted, of rabbit and hare	开襟衫,针织或钩编的,兔毛制	6110.1920	2456
Cardigans, knitted or crocheted, of silk or silk waste	开襟衫,针织或钩编的,丝及绢丝制	6110.9010	2456
Cardigans, knitted or crocheted, of wool	开襟衫,针织或钩编的,毛制	6110.1100	2456
Carding machines, for cotton type fibres, nes	梳理机,棉纤维型,其他	8445.1119	7
Carding machines, for wool type fibres	梳理机,毛纤维型	8445.1120	7
Carding machines, nes	梳理机,其他	8445.1190	7
Cards, discs and rolls for mechanical instruments	卡片、盘及带卷,机械乐器用的	9209.9990	3
Card-index cabinets, of base metal, other than office furniture	卡片索引柜,贱金属制,办公室家具除外	8304.0000	256
Cargo aerial cableways	货运架空索道	8428.6010	
Carnallite	光卤石	3104.9010	68

C

Article Description	商品名称	Tariff Code	D. R.
Carnation, nes	康乃馨,其他	0602. 9095	
Carnation, seedlings	康乃馨,种用	0602. 9091	3
Carnations, fresh, suitable for bouquets or for ornamental purposes	康乃馨,鲜的,制花束或装饰用的	0603. 1200	34
Carnival entertainment articles	狂欢节用品	9505. 9000	5
Carp, nes, living	鲤鱼,其他	0301. 9390	15
Carpets and other textile floor coverings knotted of man-made textile materials	地毯及铺地制品,纺织材料结织栽绒的,化学纤维制	5701. 9010	468
Carpets and other textile floor coverings knotted, nes	地毯及铺地制品,纺织材料结织栽绒的,其他	5701. 9090	468
Carpets and other textile floor coverings knotted, of silk	地毯及铺地制品,纺织材料结织栽绒的,丝制	5701. 9020	468
Carpets and other textile floor coverings knotted, of wool or fine animal hair	地毯及铺地制品,纺织材料结织栽绒的,羊毛或动物细毛制	5701. 1000	468
Carpets and other textile floor coverings, of felt, nes	地毯及铺地制品,毡呢纺织材料的,其他	5704. 9000	468
Carpets and other textile floor coverings, of felt, tiles, having a maximum surface area of 0. 3m^2	地毯及铺地制品,毡呢纺织材料的,最大铺装表面面积不超过0.3平方米	5704. 1000	468
Carpets and other textile floor coverings, of nylon or other polyamides, tufted	地毯及铺地制品,尼龙或聚酰胺制,簇绒纺织材料的	5703. 2000	468
Carpets and other textile floor coverings, of other man-made textile materials, tufted	地毯及铺地制品,其他化学纤维制,簇绒纺织材料的	5703. 3000	468
Carpets and other textile floor coverings, of other textile materials, tufted, nes	地毯及铺地制品,纺织材料制,簇绒纺织材料的,其他	5703. 9000	468
Carpets and other textile floor coverings, of wool or fine animal hair, tufted	地毯及铺地制品,羊毛或动物细毛制,簇绒纺织材料的	5703. 1000	468
Carpets and textile floor coverings, nes	地毯及铺地制品,其他	5705. 0090	468
Carpets and textile floor coverings, of man-made textile materials, nes	地毯及铺地制品,化学纤维制,其他	5705. 0020	468
Carpets and textile floor coverings, of wool or fine animal hair, nes	地毯及铺地制品,羊毛或动物细毛制,其他	5705. 0010	468
Carpets or rugs making machines	地毯织机	8447. 9011	7
Carpets or rugs making machines auxiliary	地毯织机的辅助机器	8448. 1900	3
Carrageenan	卡拉胶	1302. 3911	35
Carriages for disabled persons, nes	残疾人用车,其他	8713. 9000	7
Carriages for disabled persons, not mechanically propelled	残疾人用车,非机械驱动	8713. 1000	7
Carried appliances, to compensate for a defect or disability	携带器具,弥补生理缺陷或残疾的	9021. 9000	3
Carrier looms, for weaving fabrics of a with exceeding 30cm, shuttleless type	片梭织机,所织织物宽度超过30厘米的无梭织机	8446. 3030	7
Carrots, fresh or chilled	胡萝卜,鲜或冷藏的	0706. 1000	1

Article Description	商品名称	Tariff Code	D. R.
Cartons, boxes and cases, of corrugated paper or paperboard	箱、盒、匣,瓦楞纸或纸板制的	4819. 1000	68
Cartons, boxes and cases, of noncorrugated paper or paperboard, folding	箱、盒、匣,非瓦楞纸或纸板制的,可折叠	4819. 2000	68
Cartridges and parts thereof, other	子弹及其零件,其他	9306. 3090	3
Cartridges for captive-bolt humane killers, and parts thereof	弩枪式人道捕杀器用子弹及其零件	9306. 3080	3
Cartridges for captive-bolt humane killers, and parts thereof	子弹及其零件,弩枪式人道捕杀器用	9306. 3080	3
Cartridges for riveting or similar tools, and parts thereof	铆接机或类似工具用子弹及其零件	9306. 3080	3
Cartridges for riveting or similar tools, and parts thereof	子弹及其零件,铆接机或类似工具用	9306. 3080	3
Cartridges for shotgun	子弹,猎枪的	9306. 2100	
Cartridges parts for shotgun	子弹零件,猎枪的	9306. 2900	3
Cartridges, for nuclear reactors, non-irradiated	释热元件,核反应堆的,未辐照	8401. 3010	2
Carvacrol	香芹酚	2907. 1990	36
Carved or moulded articles of modelling pastes	雕刻模塑或制品,塑型膏制成的	9602. 0090	5
Carved or moulded articles of natural gums	雕刻模塑或制品,天然树胶的	9602. 0090	5
Carved or moulded articles of natural resins	雕刻模塑或制品,天然树脂的	9602. 0090	5
Carved or moulded articles of stearin	雕刻模塑或制品,硬脂的	9602. 0090	5
Carved or moulded articles of wax	雕刻模塑或制品,蜡的	9602. 0090	5
Carved or moulded articles, nes	雕刻或模塑制品,其他	9602. 0090	5
Carving machines, for cold-working glass or glassware	刻花机,玻璃冷加工用	8464. 9012	7
Carving material and articles of animal, worked	雕刻材料及其制品,动物质的,已加工的	9601. 9000	5
Carving material and articles of mineral, worked	雕刻材料及其制品,矿物质的,已加工的	9602. 0090	5
Carving material and articles of vegetable, worked	雕刻材料及其制品,植物质的,已加工的	9602. 0090	5
Car-coats and similar articles, knitted or crocheted, for men or boys, for man-made fibres	短大衣及类似品,针织或钩编的,男式,化学纤维制	6101. 3000	2456
Car-coats and similar articles, knitted or crocheted, for men or boys, nes	短大衣及类似品,针织或钩编的,男式,其他	6101. 9090	2456
Car-coats and similar articles, knitted or crocheted, for men or boys, of cotton	短大衣及类似品,针织或钩编的,男式,棉制	6101. 2000	2456
Car-coats and similar articles, knitted or crocheted, for men or boys, of wool or fine animal hair	短大衣及类似品,针织或钩编的,男式,羊毛或动物细毛制	6101. 9010	2456
Car-coats and similar articles, knitted or crocheted, for women or girls, nes	短大衣及类似品,针织或钩编的,女式,其他	6102. 9000	2456
Car-coats and similar articles, knitted or crocheted, for women or girls, of cotton	短大衣及类似品,针织或钩编的,女式,棉制	6102. 2000	2456

C

Article Description	商品名称	Tariff Code	D. R.
Car-coats and similar articles, knitted or crocheted, for women or girls, of man-made fibres	短大衣及类似品,针织或钩编的,女式,化学纤维制	6102. 3000	2456
Car-coats and similar articles, knitted or crocheted, for women or girls, of wool or fine animal hair	短大衣及类似品,针织或钩编的,女式,羊毛或动物细毛制	6102. 1000	2456
Car-coats, not knitted or crocheted, for men or boys, of cotton	短大衣,非针织或钩编的,男式,棉制	6201. 1290	2456
Car-coats, not knitted or crocheted, for men or boys, of man-made fibres	短大衣,非针织或钩编的,男式,化学纤维制	6201. 1390	2456
Car-coats, not knitted or crocheted, for men or boys, of other textile materials	短大衣,非针织或钩编的,男式,其他纺织材料制	6201. 1900	2456
Car-coats, not knitted or crocheted, for men or boys, of wool or fine animal hair	短大衣,非针织或钩编的,男式,羊毛或动物细毛制	6201. 1100	2456
Car-coats, not knitted or crocheted, for women or girls, of cotton	短大衣,非针织或钩编的,女式,棉制	6202. 1290	2456
Car-coats, not knitted or crocheted, for women or girls, of man-made fibres	短大衣,非针织或钩编的,女式,化学纤维制	6202. 1390	2456
Car-coats, not knitted or crocheted, for women or girls, of other textile materials	短大衣,非针织或钩编的,女式,其他纺织材料制	6202. 1900	2456
Car-coats, not knitted or crocheted, for women or girls, of wool or fine animal hair	短大衣,非针织或钩编的,女式,羊毛或动物细毛制	6202. 1100	2456
Casaba melons	香瓜	0807. 1990	1
Casein	酪蛋白	3501. 1000	
Casein derivatives, nes	酪蛋白衍生物,其他	3501. 9000	
Casein glues	酪蛋白胶	3501. 9000	
Caseinates	酪蛋白酸盐	3501. 9000	
Cases packings, of wood	包装箱,木制的	4415. 1000	56
Cash registers, nes	现金出纳机,其他	8470. 5090	
Cashew nuts, in shell	腰果,未去壳	0801. 3100	134
Cashew nuts, shelled	腰果,去壳	0801. 3200	134
Casing and tubing of a kind used in drilling for oil or gas, nes	套管及导管,钻探石油及天然气用,其他	7306. 2900	6
Casing and tubing of a kind used in drilling for oil or gas, of stainless steel, welded	套管及导管,钻探石油及天然气用,不锈钢的,焊接的	7306. 2100	6
Casing of a kind used in drilling for oil or gas, the external diameter of which exceeds 406. 4mm	套管,钻探石油或天然气用,外径超过406. 4 毫米	7305. 2000	6
Casing or tubing pipe, of a kind used in drilling for oil or gas, seamless, nes	套管、导管,钻探石油及天然气用,无缝的,其他	7304. 2900	6
Casing or tubing pipe, of a kind used in drilling for oil or gas, seamless, of stainless steel	套管、导管,钻探石油及天然气用,无缝的,不锈钢的	7304. 2400	6
Casings for sausage	香肠用肠衣	3917. 1000	6
Casings, nes	肠衣,其他	0504. 0019	14
Caskets and cases for jewellery or cutlery, and similar articles, of wood	盒子和匣子及类似品,装珠宝或刀具用的,木制	4420. 9090	56

Article Description	商品名称	Tariff Code	D. R.
Casks, of other wood	大桶,其他木制的	4416.0090	56
Casks, of radiata pine	大桶,辐射松制的	4416.0010	56
Casserole and parts thereof, of iron or steel, for household, enamelled	烧锅及其零件,钢铁制,家用,已搪瓷	7323.9420	24
Cassette magnetic tape recorders or reproducers parts and accessories, nes	盒式磁带录音机或放声机用零件、附件,其他	8522.9029	3
Cassette-type recorders, incorporating sound reproducing apparatus	录音机,装有声音重放装置的,盒带型	8519.8112	5
Cast articles of iron or steel, for technical use, nes	铸造制品,钢铁制,工业用,其他	7325.9910	346
Cast articles of iron or steel, nes	铸造制品,钢铁制,其他	7325.9990	346
Cast articles of non-malleable cast iron, for technical use	铸造制品,无可锻性铸铁制,工业用	7325.1010	346
Cast articles of non-malleable cast iron, nes	铸造制品,无可锻性铸铁制,其他	7325.1090	346
Castanets	响板	9206.0000	5
Casting machines for ingot block, continuous	连铸机,方坯的	8454.3021	
Casting machines for ingot block, continuous	铸造机,连铸,方坯的	8454.3021	
Casting machines for ingot slab, continuous	连铸机,板坯的	8454.3022	
Casting machines for ingot slab, continuous	铸造机,连铸,板坯的	8454.3022	
Casting machines for ingot, continuous, nes	连铸机,钢坯,其他	8454.3029	
Casting machines for ingot, continuous, nes	铸造机,连铸,钢坯,其他	8454.3029	
Casting machines parts, cold chamber, die- casting	压铸机用零件	8454.9090	3
Casting machines parts, for ingot continuous casting machines, nes	连铸机用零件,钢坯的,其他	8454.9029	3
Casting machines parts, nes	连铸机用零件,其他	8454.9090	3
Casting machines, cold chamber, die- casting	压铸机,冷室的	8454.3010	
Casting machines, cold chamber, die- casting	铸造机,压铸,冷室的	8454.3010	
Casting machines, nes	铸造机,其他	8454.3090	
Castor oil and its fractions	蓖麻油及其分离品	1515.3000	4
Castor oil seeds	蓖麻籽	1207.9993	3
Castoreum	海狸香	0510.0020	14
Castors, of base metal, suitable for furniture, doors, staircases, windows, blinds, coachwork, saddlery, trunks, chests, caskets, or the like	小脚轮,贱金属制,用于家具、门窗、楼梯、百叶窗、车厢、鞍具、衣箱、盒子及类似品的	8302.2000	256
Catalysts in the form of wire cloth or grill, of platinum	金属丝布或格栅形状的铂催化剂	7115.1000	46
Catching shuttle boxes for looms	接梭箱,织机用	8448.4910	3
Catechol, pyrocatechol	邻苯二酚	2907.2910	36
Catecholamine hormones, their derivatives and structural analogues, nes	儿茶酚胺激素及其衍生物和结构类似物,其他	2937.3900	36
Catgut, for surgical sterile	肠线,外科用无菌	3006.1000	3
Catheters and the like, used in medical, surgical, dental or veterinary sciences	导管及类似品,医疗、外科、牙科或兽医用	9018.3900	3

Article Description	商品名称	Tariff Code	D. R.
Cathode-ray television picture tubes, including video monitor cathode-ray tubes, black and white or other monochrome	阴极射线电视显像管,包括视频监视器用阴极射线管,黑白的或其他单色的	8540. 1200	35
Cathode-ray television picture tubes, including video monitor cathode-ray tubes, colour	阴极射线电视显像管,包括视频监视器用阴极射线管,彩色的	8540. 1100	35
Cathode-ray tubes parts	阴极射线管用零件	8540. 9190	3
Cathode-ray tubes, nes	阴极射线管,其他	8540. 6090	35
Cauliflowers, fresh or chilled	菜花,鲜或冷藏的	0704. 1000	1
Caulking compounds and other mastics	嵌缝胶及其他类似胶粘剂	3214. 1090	3
Caustic potash	苛性钾	2815. 2000	136
Caustic soda, in aqueous solution	烧碱,水溶液	2815. 1200	136
Caustic soda, solid	烧碱,固体	2815. 1100	136
Caviar	鲟鱼子酱	1604. 3000	248
Caviar substitutes	鲟鱼子酱代用品	1604. 3000	248
CD drivers	光盘驱动器	8471. 7030	
Cefaclor and its salts	头孢克罗及其盐	2941. 9058	
Cefaclor medicaments, consisting of two or more constituents which have been mixed together, not put up in measured doses or in forms or packings for retail sale	头孢克罗药品,两种或两种以上成分混合而成的,未配定剂量或制成零售包装	3003. 2015	368
Cefaclor medicaments, mixed or unmixed, put up in measured doses or in forms or packings for retail sale	头孢克罗药品,混合或未混合的,配定剂量或制成零售包装	3004. 2015	368
Cefalexin and its salts	头孢氨苄及其盐	2941. 9052	
Cefazolin and its salts	头孢唑啉及其盐	2941. 9053	
Cefoperazone and its salts	头孢哌酮及其盐	2941. 9056	
Cefoperazone medicaments, consisting of two or more constituents which have been mixed together, not put up in measured doses or in forms or packings for retail sale	头孢哌酮药品,两种或两种以上成分混合而成的,未配定剂量或制成零售包装	3003. 2018	368
Cefoperazone medicaments, mixed or unmixed, put up in measured doses or in forms or packings for retail sale	头孢哌酮药品,混合或未混合的,配定剂量或制成零售包装	3004. 2018	368
Cefotaxime and its salts	头孢噻肟及其盐	2941. 9057	
Cefotaxime medicaments, consisting of two or more constituents which have been mixed together, not put up in measured doses or in forms or packings for retail sale	头孢噻肟药品,两种或两种以上成分混合而成的,未配定剂量或制成零售包装	3003. 2011	368
Cefotaxime medicaments, mixed or unmixed, put up in measured doses or in forms or packings for retail sale	头孢噻肟药品,混合或未混合的,配定剂量或制成零售包装	3004. 2011	368

Article Description	商品名称	Tariff Code	D. R.
Cefoxitin medicaments, consisting of two or more constituents which have been mixed together, not put up in measured doses or in forms or packings for retail sale	头孢西丁药品,两种或两种以上成分混合而成的,未配定剂量或制成零售包装	3003. 2013	368
Cefoxitin medicaments, mixed or unmixed, put up in measured doses or in forms or packings for retail sale	头孢西丁药品, 混合或未混合的,配定剂量或制成零售包装	3004. 2013	368
Cefradine and its salts	头孢拉啶及其盐	2941. 9054	
Ceftazidime medicaments, consisting of two or more constituents which have been mixed together, not put up in measured doses or in forms or packings for retail sale	头孢他啶药品,两种或两种以上成分混合而成的,未配定剂量或制成零售包装	3003. 2012	368
Ceftazidime medicaments, mixed or unmixed, put up in measured doses or in forms or packings for retail sale	头孢他啶药品, 混合或未混合的,未配定剂量或制成零售包装	3004. 2012	368
Ceftezole medicaments, consisting of two or more constituents which have been mixed together, not put up in measured doses or in forms or packings for retail sale	头孢替唑药品,两种或两种以上成分混合而成的,未配定剂量或制成零售包装	3003. 2014	368
Ceftezole medicaments, mixed or unmixed, put up in measured doses or in forms or packings for retail sale	头孢替唑药品, 混合或未混合的,配定剂量或制成零售包装	3004. 2014	368
Ceftriaxone and its salts	头孢曲松及其盐	2941. 9055	
Ceftriaxone and its salts	头孢三嗪及其盐	2941. 9055	
Ceftriaxone medicaments, consisting of two or more constituents which have been mixed together, not put up in measured doses or in forms or packings for retail sale	头孢曲松药品,两种或两种以上成分混合而成的,未配定剂量或制成零售包装	3003. 2017	368
Ceftriaxone medicaments, consisting of two or more constituents which have been mixed together, not put up in measured doses or in forms or packings for retail sale	头孢三嗪药品,两种或两种以上成分混合而成的,未配定剂量或制成零售包装	3003. 2017	368
Ceftriaxone medicaments, mixed or unmixed, put up in measured doses or in forms or packings for retail sale	头孢曲松药品, 混合或未混合的,配定剂量或制成零售包装	3004. 2017	368
Ceftriaxone medicaments, mixed or unmixed, put up in measured doses or in forms or packings for retail sale	头孢三嗪药品, 混合或未混合的,配定剂量或制成零售包装	3004. 2017	368
Cefuroxime medicaments, consisting of two or more constituents which have been mixed together, not put up in measured doses or in forms or packings for retail sale	头孢呋辛药品,两种或两种以上成分混合而成的,未配定剂量或制成零售包装	3003. 2016	368

C

C

Article Description	商品名称	Tariff Code	D. R.
Cefuroxime medicaments, mixed or unmixed, put up in measured doses or in forms or packings for retail sale	头孢呋辛药品，混合或未混合的，配定剂量或制成零售包装	3004. 2016	368
Ceiling or roof fans, nes	吊扇，其他	8414. 5910	23
Ceiling or roof fans, with a self-contained electric motor of an output not exceeding 125W	吊扇，包括风机，本身装有一个输出功率不超过125瓦的电动机	8414. 5110	23
Ceiling or wall lighting fittings, electric, excluding those of a kind used for lighting public open spaces or thorough-fares	天花板或墙壁上的其他电气照明装置，不包括公共露天场所或街道上的电气照明装置	9405. 1000	5
Celeriac, fresh or chilled	块根芹，鲜或冷藏的	0706. 9000	1
Celery other than celeriac, fresh or chilled	芹菜，但块根芹除外，鲜或冷藏的	0709. 4000	1
Celery salt	芹盐	2103. 9090	268
Cellpacking blanks (zinc biscuits), of zinc	电池壳体坯料，锌制	7907. 0030	16
Cellular wood panels	蜂窝结构木镶板	4418. 9000	
Cellulose acetate multiple or cabled yarn	醋酸纤维多股纱线或缆线	5403. 4200	3468
Cellulose acetate woven fabrics, containing 85% or more by weight of artificial filament or strip or the like, dyed	醋纤纤维制机织物，按重量计人造纤维长丝、扁条或类似品含量在85%及以上，染色	5408. 2220	2468
Cellulose acetate woven fabrics, containing 85% or more by weight of artificial filament or strip or the like, of yarns of different colours	醋纤纤维制机织物，按重量计人造纤维长丝、扁条或类似品含量在85%及以上，色织	5408. 2320	2468
Cellulose acetate woven fabrics, containing 85% or more by weight of artificial filament or strip or the like, printed	醋纤纤维制机织物，按重量计人造纤维长丝、扁条或类似品含量在85%及以上，印花	5408. 2420	2468
Cellulose acetate woven fabrics, containing 85% or more by weight of artificial filament or strip or the like, unbleached or bleached	醋纤纤维制机织物，按重量计人造纤维长丝、扁条或类似品含量在85%及以上，未漂白或漂白	5408. 2120	2468
Cellulose acetates, non-plasticized, in primary forms	乙酸纤维素，未塑化，初级形状的	3912. 1100	16
Cellulose acetates, plasticized, in primary forms	乙酸纤维素，已塑化，初级形状的	3912. 1200	16
Cellulose and its chemical derivatives, in primary forms, nes	纤维素及其化学衍生物，初级形状的，其他	3912. 9000	16
Cellulose diacetate filament tow	二醋酸纤维丝束	5502. 0010	68
Cellulose diacetate single yarn, not put up for retail sale	二醋酸纤维单纱，非供零售用	5403. 3310	3468
Cellulose ethers, in primary forms, nes	纤维素醚，初级形状的，其他	3912. 3900	16
Cellulose fibre-cement articles or the like	纤维素水泥或类似材料制品，其他	6811. 4090	56
Cellulose fibre-cement articles or the like, not containing asbestos	纤维素水泥或类似材料制品，不含石棉的	6811. 8900	56
Cellulose fibre-cement sheets, panels, tiles and similar ahicles, not containing asbestos	纤维素水泥或类似材料制片、板、砖、瓦及类似制品，不含石棉的	6302. 5990	346
Cellulose fibre-cement sheets, panels, tiles and similar articles, containing asbestos	纤维素水泥或类似材料制片、板、砖、瓦及类似制品，含石棉的	6302. 5990	346

Article Description	商品名称	Tariff Code	D. R.
Cellulose fibre-cement tubes, pipes and fittings, containing asbestos	纤维素水泥管子及附件,含石棉的	6811.4030	56
Cellulose fibre-cement tubes, pipes and fittings, not containing asbestos	纤维素水泥或类似材料制管子及附件,不含石棉的	6811.8300	56
Cellulose nitrates, in primary forms	硝酸纤维素,初级形状的	3912.2000	16
Cellulose wadding	纤维素絮料	4811.9000	458
Cellulose wadding, in rolls or sheets	纤维素絮纸,成卷或成张的	4803.0000	58
Cement articles, nes	水泥制品,其他	6810.9990	56
Cement blocks and bricks, for building	水泥砖及块,建筑用	6810.1100	56
Cement clinkers	水泥熟料	2523.1000	3
Cement copper	沉积铜	7401.0000	46
Cement flagstones and similar articles	水泥扁平石及类似品	6810.1990	56
Cement packing machinery parts	水泥包装机零件	8422.9090	
Cement packing machinery, automatic filling and sacking machines	水泥包装机,全自动灌包机	8422.3021	
Cement packing machinery, nes	水泥包装机,其他	8422.3029	
Cement rotary kilns	水泥回转窑	8417.8030	7
Cement tiles and similar articles	水泥瓦及类似品	6810.1990	56
Cements, for refractory	水泥,耐火的	3816.0000	36
Cements, mortars or concretes additives, nes	水泥、灰泥及混凝土用添加剂,其他	3824.4090	36
Central control door lock of a kind used for motor vehicles, of base metal	中央控制门锁,机动车用,贱金属制	8301.2010	256
Central heating boilers auxiliary plant	集中供暖用的热水锅炉辅助设备	8404.1020	3
Central heating boilers auxiliary plant parts	集中供暖用的热水锅炉辅助设备的零件	8404.9010	3
Central heating boilers parts	集中供暖用的热水锅炉零件	8403.9000	27
Central heating boilers, household type	集中供暖用的热水锅炉,家用型	8403.1010	27
Central heating boilers, nes	集中供暖用的热水锅炉,其他	8403.1090	27
Centrifugal dryers, nes	离心机,其他	8421.1990	7
Centrifugal pumps, electric submersible oil pumps and electric submersible pumps	离心泵,电动潜油泵及潜水电泵	8413.7091	27
Centrifugal pumps, nes	离心泵,其他	8413.7099	27
Centrifugal pumps, rotational speed no less than 10000r/min	离心泵,转速在10000转/分及以上	8413.7010	27
Centrifugal ventilation fans, nes	离心通风机,其他	8414.5930	23
Cephamycin and its derivatives; salts thereof, nes	先锋霉素及其衍生物以及它们的盐,其他	2941.9059	
Cephamycins medicaments, nes, mixed or unmixed, put up in measured doses or in forms or packings for retail sale	头孢菌素药品,其他,混合或未混合的,配定剂量或制成零售包装	3004.2019	368

C

Article Description	商品名称	Tariff Code	D. R.
Cephamycins medicaments, nes, consisting of two or more constituents which have been mixed together, not put up in measured doses or in forms or packings for retail sale	头孢菌素药品,其他,两种或两种以上成分混合而成的,未配定剂量或制成零售包装	3003. 2019	368
Ceramic bricks for building	瓷砖,建筑用	6904. 1000	5
Ceramic bricks for building	陶瓷砖,建筑用	6904. 1000	5
Ceramic bricks, nes	陶瓷砖,其他	6904. 9000	5
Ceramic constructional goods, nes	陶瓷制品,建筑用,其他	6905. 9000	5
Ceramic flags and paving, hearth or wall tiles, glazed, the largest surface area of which is capable of being enclosed in a square, the side of which is less than 7cm	陶瓷贴面砖、铺面砖,包括炉面砖及墙面砖,上釉的,其最大表面以可置入边长小于7厘米的方格为限	6908. 1000	5
Ceramic flags and paving, hearth or wall tiles, unglazed, the largest surface area of which is capable of being enclosed in a square, the side of which is less than 7cm	陶瓷贴面砖、铺面砖,包括炉面砖及墙面砖,未上釉的,其最大表面以可置入边长小于7厘米的方格为限	6907. 1000	5
Ceramic flags, glazed, the largest surface area of which is capable of being enclosed in a square the side of which is less than 7cm	贴面砖,陶瓷的,上釉的,其最大表面以可置入边长小于7厘米的方格为限	6908. 1000	5
Ceramic flags, paving, hearth or wall tiles, mosaic cubes and the like, glazed, nes	陶瓷贴面砖、铺面砖、镶嵌砖、炉面砖及墙面砖及类似品,上釉的,其他	6908. 9000	5
Ceramic flags, paving, hearth or wall tiles, mosaic cubes and the like, unglazed, nes	陶瓷贴面砖、铺面砖、镶嵌砖、炉面砖及墙面砖及类似品,未上釉的,其他	6907. 9000	5
Ceramic flags, unglazed, the largest surface area of which is capable of being enclosed in a square the side of which is less than 7cm	贴面砖,陶瓷的,未上釉的,其最大表面以可置入边长小于7厘米的方格为限	6907. 1000	5
Ceramic mosaic cubes and the like, glazed, the largest surface area of which is capable of being enclosed in a square the side of which is less than 7cm	陶瓷镶嵌砖(马赛克)及类似品,上釉的,其最大表面以可置入边长小于7厘米的方格为限	6908. 1000	5
Ceramic mosaic cubes and the like, unglazed, the largest surface area of which is capable of being enclosed in a square the side of which is less than 7cm	陶瓷镶嵌砖(马赛克)及类似品,未上釉的,其最大表面以可置入边长小于7厘米的方格为限	6907. 1000	5
Ceramic paving, glazed, the largest surface area of which is capable of being enclosed in a square the side of which is less than 7cm	铺面砖,陶瓷的,上釉的,其最大表面以可置入边长小于7厘米的方格为限	6908. 1000	5
Ceramic paving, unglazed, the largest surface area of which is capable of being enclosed in a square the side of which is less than 7cm	铺面砖,陶瓷的,未上釉的,其最大表面以可置入边长小于7厘米的方格为限	6907. 1000	5
Ceramic pipes, conduits, guttering and pipe fittings	陶瓷套管、导管、槽管及管子附件	6906. 0000	5
Ceramic pots, jars and similar articles of a kind used for the conveyance or packing of goods	陶瓷罐、坛及类似品,通常供运输及盛装货物用的	6909. 9000	5

Article Description	商品名称	Tariff Code	D. R.
Ceramic troughs, tubs and similar receptacles of a kind used in agriculture	陶瓷槽、缸及类似容器，农业用	6909.9000	5
Cerargyrites	角银矿	2616.1000	146
Cereal grains, other worked	谷物,其他,其他加工的	1104.2990	4
Cereal grains, rolled or flaked	谷物,其他,滚压或制片的	1104.1990	4
Cereal husks, unprepared	谷壳,未经处理的	1213.0090	4
Cereal straw (other than wheat straw)	谷类植物的茎秆(麦秸除外)	1401.9010	3
Cereal straw, nes	稻草的茎杆,其他的	1213.0090	4
Cereal straw, unprepared	稻草的茎杆,未经处理的	1213.0010	4
Cereals (other than maize (corn)) in grain form or in the form of flakes or other worked grains (except flour, groats and meal), precooked or otherwise prepared, not elsewhere specified or included	谷粒(玉米除外)或谷物片,预煮或经其他方法制作的,细粉及粗粉除外	1904.9000	48
Cereals, nes	谷物,其他	1008.9090	3
Cereals, nes, seed	谷物,其他,种用	1008.9010	3
Ceric compounds, nes	铈的化合物,其他	2846.1090	
Cerium carbonate	碳酸铈	2846.1030	
Cerium hydroxide	氢氧化铈	2846.1020	
Cerium oxide	氧化铈	2846.1010	
Cermets articles, in granules or powder	金属陶瓷制品,颗粒或粉末	8113.0010	16
Cermets articles, nes	金属陶瓷制品,其他	8113.0090	16
Cermets for tools, unmounted, nes	金属陶瓷制品,未装配的工具用,其他	8209.0090	256
Cermets plates for tools, unmounted	金属陶瓷板,未装配的工具用	8209.0010	256
Cermets sticks for tools, unmounted	金属陶瓷杆,未装配的工具用	8209.0020	256
Cermets tips for tools, unmounted	金属陶瓷刀头,未装配的工具用	8209.0030	256
Cermets, in granules or powder	金属陶瓷,颗粒或粉末	8113.0010	16
Cermets, nes	金属陶瓷,其他	8113.0090	16
Certified reference materials	检定参照物	3822.0090	36
Cerussite	白铅矿	2607.0000	146
Cervantite	白安矿	2617.1090	146
Chain and parts thereof, of copper	链条及其零件,铜制	7419.1000	4
Chain parts, of iron or steel	链零件,钢铁的	7315.9000	36
Chain saw blades	链锯片	8202.4000	256
Chain saws parts, for hand tools, nes	链锯零件,手提式,其他	8467.9190	3
Chain saws parts, with self-contained electric motor, for hand tools	链锯零件,电动的,手提式	8467.9110	3
Chain saws, hand tools, nes	链锯,手提式,其他	8467.8100	57
Chain saws, hand tools, with self-contained electric motor	链锯,手提式,本身装有电动动力装置的	8467.2210	57
Chain, of iron or steel, nes	链,钢铁的,其他	7315.8900	36

C

Article Description	商品名称	Tariff Code	D. R.
Chairs, chair wedges, specialized for jointing or fixing rails	轨座、轨座楔	7302. 9090	6
Chair-lifts, nes	座式升降机,其他	8428. 6090	
Chalcocite	辉铜矿	2603. 0000	146
Chalcopyrite	黄铜矿	2603. 0000	146
Chalk	白垩	2509. 0000	
Chalks	粉笔	9609. 9000	3
Chamois (including combination chamois) leather	油鞣皮革(包括结合鞣制的油鞣皮革)	4114. 1000	1458
Chamotte	火泥	2508. 7000	134
Chandeliers, excluding those of a kind used for lighting public open spaces or thorough-fares	枝形吊灯,不包括公共露天场所或街道上的电气照明装置	9405. 1000	5
Channel black	碳黑	2803. 0000	24
Channel catfish (ictalurus punctatus), prepared or preserved, whole or in pieces, but not minced	斑点叉尾鱼,制作或保藏的,整条或切块,但未绞碎	1604. 1931	48
Charcoal of bamboo	炭,竹的	4402. 1000	
Charcoal, nes	炭,其他	4402. 9000	
Charging vehicles (frequency 400Hz) for airplane	电源车(频率为 400 赫兹),航空用	8705. 9051	7
Charging vehicles, nes	电源车,其他	8705. 9059	7
Chassis fitted with engines, for the motor vehicles, nes	底盘,装有发动机的机动车辆用,其他	8706. 0090	7
Chassis for crane lorries, fitted with engines	底盘,汽车起重机的,装有发动机的	8706. 0040	7
Chassis for motor vehicles of goods transportation, for vehicles g. v. w less than 14 tons, fitted with engines	底盘,货车的,车辆总重量在 14 吨以下的,装有发动机的	8706. 0022	7
Chassis for motor vehicles of goods transportation, for vehicles g. v. w of 14 tons or more, fitted with engines	底盘,货车的,车辆总重量在 14 吨及以上的,装有发动机的	8706. 0021	7
Chassis for off-road dumpers, fitted with engines	底盘,非公路用自卸车用,装有发动机的	8706. 0010	7
Chassis for passenger motor vehicles with 30 seats or more, fitted with engines	底盘,大型客车的,装有发动机的	8706. 0030	7
Check(nonreturn) valves	止回阀	8481. 3000	
Check-rails and rack rails	护轨、齿轨	7302. 9090	6
Cheddar cheese, not processed	车达乳酪,未加工	0406. 9000	2468
Cheddar cheese, powdered	车达乳酪,粉化	0406. 2000	24
Cheese, grated or powdered, of all kinds	乳酪,各种磨碎或粉化的	0406. 2000	24
Cheese, nes	乳酪,其他	0406. 9000	2468
Cheese, nes, containing veins produced by penicillium roqueforti	乳酪,其他,娄地青霉生产的带有纹理的乳酪	0406. 4000	2468
Cheese, processed, not grated or powdered	乳酪,经加工的乳酪,但磨碎或粉化的除外	0406. 3000	24

Article Description	商品名称	Tariff Code	D. R.
Chemical derivatives of natural rubber, in primary forms	天然橡胶的化学衍生物,初级形状的	3913. 9000	146
Chemical mechanical polishers (CMP) parts and accessories, semiconductor devices or of electronic integrated circuits manufacture machines and apparatus	化学机械抛光设备(CMP)零件及附件,制造半导体器件或集成电路的机器及装置	8486. 9090	3
Chemical mechanical polishers (CMP), boules or wafers manufacture machines and apparatus	化学机械抛光设备(CMP),单晶硅柱或硅晶片的制造机器及装置	8486. 1040	7
Chemical preparations for photographic uses, for use in developing photographic film and photographs	摄影用化学制剂,冲洗照相胶卷及相片用	3707. 9010	36
Chemical preparations for photographic uses, nes	摄影用化学制剂,其他	3707. 9090	36
Chemical products and preparations of the chemical or allied industries, nes	化学工业及其相关工业的化学产品及配制品,其他	3824. 9099	36
Chemical pulp, derived from recovered (waste and scrap) paper or paperboard	化学浆,从回收(废碎)纸或纸板提取的	4706. 9200	46
Chemical vapour deposition (CVD) equipment parts and accessories, semiconductor devices or of electronic integrated circuits or flat panel displays manufacture machines and apparatus	化学气相沉积装置(CVD)零件及附件,制造半导体器件、集成电路、平板显示器的机器及装置	8486. 9090	3
Chemical vapour deposition (CVD) equipment, flat panel displays manufacture machines and apparatus	化学气相沉积设备(CVD),平板显示器的制造机器及装置	8486. 3021	7
Chemical vapour deposition (CVD) equipment, semiconductor devices or of electronic integrated circuits manufacture machines and apparatus	化学气相沉积装置(CVD),制造半导体器件或集成电路的机器及装置	8486. 2021	7
Chemical wood pulp, dissolving grades	化学木浆,溶解级	4702. 0000	
Chemical wood pulp, soda, other than dissolving grades, semi-bleached or bleached, coniferous	碱木浆,但溶解级的除外,半漂白或漂白,针叶木的	4703. 2100	46
Chemical wood pulp, soda, other than dissolving grades, semi-bleached or bleached, non-coniferous	碱木浆,但溶解级的除外,半漂白或漂白,非针叶木的	4703. 2900	46
Chemical wood pulp, soda, other than dissolving grades, unbleached, coniferous	碱木浆,但溶解级的除外,未漂白,针叶木的	4703. 1100	46
Chemical wood pulp, soda, other than dissolving grades, unbleached, non-coniferous	碱木浆,但溶解级的除外,未漂白,非针叶木的	4703. 1900	46
Chemical wood pulp, sulphite, other than dissolving grades, semi-bleached or bleached, coniferous	亚硫酸盐木浆,但溶解级的除外,半漂白或漂白,针叶木的	4704. 2100	46
Chemical wood pulp, sulphite, other than dissolving grades, semi-bleached or bleached, non-coniferous	亚硫酸盐木浆,但溶解级的除外,半漂白或漂白,非针叶木的	4704. 2900	46
Chemical wood pulp, sulphite, other than dissolving grades, unbleached, coniferous	亚硫酸盐木浆,但溶解级的除外,未漂白,针叶木的	4704. 1100	46
Chemical wood pulp, sulphite, other than dissolving grades, unbleached, non-coniferous	亚硫酸盐木浆,但溶解级的除外,未漂白,非针叶木的	4704. 1900	46

C

Article Description	商品名称	Tariff Code	D. R.
Chemical wood pulp, sul-phate, other than dissolving grades, semi-bleached or bleached, coniferous	硫酸盐木浆,但溶解级的除外,半漂白或漂白,针叶木的	4703. 2100	46
Chemical wood pulp, sul-phate, other than dissolving grades, semi-bleached or bleached, non-coniferous	硫酸盐木浆,但溶解级的除外,半漂白或漂白,非针叶木的	4703. 2900	46
Chemical wood pulp, sul-phate, other than dissolving grades, unbleached, coniferous	硫酸盐木浆,但溶解级的除外,未漂白,针叶木的	4703. 1100	46
Chemical wood pulp, sul-phate, other than dissolving grades, unbleached, non-coniferous	硫酸盐木浆,但溶解级的除外,未漂白,非针叶木的	4703. 1900	46
Chenille yarn	绳绒线	5606. 0000	
Cheque forms	支票	4907. 0090	5
Cherries, fresh	樱桃,鲜的	0809. 2000	1
Cherries, in airtight containers	樱桃,罐头	2008. 6010	248
Cherries, otherwise prepared, or preserved	樱桃,用其他方法制作或保藏的	2008. 6090	248
Cherries, provisionally preserved, but unsuitable in that state for immediate consumption	樱桃,暂时保藏,但不适于直接食用的	0812. 1000	34
Chestnut seed, otherwise prepared, or preserved	栗仁,用其他方法制作或保藏的	2008. 1991	248
Chestnuts	板栗	0802. 4010	134
Chestnuts(Castanea spp.), nes	栗子,其他	0802. 4090	134
Chestnuts, in shell, frozen	栗子,未去壳,冷冻的	0811. 9010	14
Chewing gum, whether or not sugarcoated, not containing cocoa	口香糖,不论是否裹糖	1704. 1000	268
Chewing tobacco	嚼烟	2403. 9900	
Chiaokan	蕉柑	0805. 2010	14
Chicken breast filets, prepared or preserved, nes	鸡胸肉,制作或保藏的,其他	1602. 3291	48
Chicken leg meat, prepared or preserved, nes	鸡腿肉,制作或保藏的,其他	1602. 3292	48
Chickpeas(garbanzos), nes, dried, shelled	鹰嘴豆,其他,脱荚的,干的	0713. 2090	34
Chickpeas(garbanzos), seed, dried, shelled	鹰嘴豆,种用,脱荚的,干的	0713. 2010	34
Chicleand similar natural gums	糖胶树胶及类似的天然树胶	4001. 3000	12
Chicory plants and roots	菊苣植物及其根	0601. 2000	
Chicory roots of the variety cichorium intybus sativum, unroasted	菊苣根,未焙制的	1212. 9999	134
Chicory, nes, fresh or chilled	菊苣,其他,鲜或冷藏的	0705. 2900	1
Chicory, roasted	菊苣,烘焙的	2101. 3000	268
Children's picture, drawing or colouring books	儿童图画书、绘画或涂色书	4903. 0000	35
Chimney liners, ceramic	烟囱衬壁,陶瓷制	6905. 9000	5
Chimney-pots, ceramic	烟囱罩,陶瓷制	6905. 9000	5
China wood oil (tung oil)	桐油	1515. 9030	
Chinese artichokes, fresh or chilled	甘露,鲜或冷藏的	0706. 9000	1
Chinese artichokes, frozen	甘露,冷冻的	0710. 8090	1
Chinese artichokes, frozen, prepared or preserved, not by vinegar or acetic acid	甘露,冷冻的,用醋或醋酸以外的其他方法制作或保藏的	2004. 9000	48

Article Description	商品名称	Tariff Code	D. R.
Chinese artichokes, prepared or preserved otherwise than by vinegar or acetic acid, nes	甘露,用醋或醋酸以外的其他方法制作或保藏的,其他	2005.9999	148
Chinese cherkers	跳棋等棋类用品	9504.9030	
Chinese chess and other board games	中国象棋等棋类用品	9504.9030	
Chinese wax	白蜡	1521.9090	
Chiolite, natural	锥冰晶石	2530.9099	13456
Chipwood and the like, coniferous	木片条及类似品,针叶木的	4404.1000	15
Chipwood and the like, non-coniferous	木片条及类似品,非针叶木的	4404.2000	15
Chisels, for working wood	凿子,木工用	8205.3000	256
Chloramphenicol and its derivatives; salts thereof	氯霉素及其衍生物以及它们的盐	2941.4000	
Chlorates, nes	氯酸盐,其他	2829.1990	
Chlordane (ISO)	氯丹(ISO)	2903.5200	36
Chlordiazepoxide (INN); salts thereof	氯氮卓(INN)以及盐	2933.9100	36
Chlordimeform (ISO)	杀虫脒(ISO)	2925.2100	36
Chloride oxides and chloride hydroxides, inorganic, nes	氯氧化物及氢氧基氯化物,其他,无机的	2827.4990	
Chlorides and chloride oxides, nes	氯化物及氯氧化物,其他	2812.1090	
Chlorides of non-metals, nes	非金属氯化物,其他	2812.1049	
Chlorides, nes, inorganic	氯化物,其他,无机的	2827.3990	
Chlorine	氯	2801.1000	
Chlorites, inorganic	亚氯酸盐,无机的	2828.9000	
Chlorites, unexpanded	绿泥石,未膨胀的	2530.1010	13456
Chloro propene	氯丙烯	2903.2910	36
Chlorobenzene	氯苯	2903.6190	36
Chlorobenzilate (ISO)	乙酯杀螨醇(ISO)	2918.1800	36
Chlorocyanogen, cyanogen chloride	氯化氰	2853.0020	3
Chloroethane(ethyl chloride)	氯乙烷	2903.1100	36
Chloroform(trichloromethane)	氯仿(三氯甲烷)	2903.1300	36
Chloroheptafluoropropane	氯七氟丙烷	2903.4592	36
Chloroisocyanurate, nes	异氰脲酸氯化衍生物,其他	2933.6929	36
Chloromethane(methyl chloride)	一氯甲烷	2903.1100	36
Chloropenta-fluoroethane	氯五氟乙烷	2903.4400	36
Chlorophyll	叶绿素	3203.0019	34
Chloropicrin	氯化苦	2904.9030	36
Chloroprene (ehlorobutadiene) rubber (CR), in primary forms	氯丁二烯(氯丁)橡胶(CR),初级形状的	4002.4910	136
Chloroprene (ehlorobutadiene) rubber(CR) latex	氯丁二烯(氯丁)橡胶(CR)胶乳	4002.4100	136
Chloroprene (ehlorobutadiene) rubber(CR), nes	氯丁二烯(氯丁)橡胶(CR),其他	4002.4990	136
Chlorosulphuric acid	氯磺酸	2806.2000	6
Chlorotrifluoromethane	氯三氟甲烷	2903.4510	36
Chocolate, filled, in blocks, slabs or bars	巧克力,夹心,块状或条状的	1806.3100	12468

C

C

Article Description	商品名称	Tariff Code	D. R.
Chocolate, Not filled, in blocks, slabs or bars	巧克力,不夹心,块状或条状的	1806. 3200	12468
Chocolate and other food preparations containing cocoa, filled, in blocks, slabs or bars	可可食品,其他,夹心,块状或条状的	1806. 3100	12468
Chocolate and other food preparations containing cocoa, nes	可可食品,其他	1806. 9000	268
Chocolate and other food preparations containing cocoa, nes, in blocks, slabs or bars weighing more than 2kg or in liquid, paste, powder, granular or other bulk form in containers or immediate packings, of a content exceeding 2kg	巧克力及其他含可可的食品,其他,重量超过2千克的块状或条状含可可食品,或液状、膏状、粉状、粒状或其他散装形状的含可可食品,容器包装或内包装每件净重超过2千克的	1806. 2000	1268
Chocolate and other food preparations containing cocoa, not filled, in blocks, slabs or bars	可可食品,其他,不夹心,块状或条状的	1806. 3200	12468
Chocolate manufacture machinery	巧克力生产机器	8438. 2000	
Chocolate manufacture machinery parts	巧克力生产机器的零件	8438. 9000	3
Chocolate spreads, of a weight less than 2kg	巧克力酱,重量小于2kg	1806. 9000	268
Chocolate, nes	巧克力,其他	1806. 9000	268
Chocolate, white	巧克力,白色的	1704. 9000	258
Cholesterol	胆固醇	2906. 1310	36
Choline and its salts	胆碱及其盐	2923. 1000	36
Choppers	切肉刀	8214. 9000	256
Chopsticks, for one-time use, of bamboo	筷子,一次性的,竹制	4419. 0032	6
Chopsticks, for one-time use, of other wooden materials	筷子,一次性的,其他木质材料制	4419. 0039	6
Chopsticks, for one-time use, of wood	筷子,一次性的,木制	4419. 0031	6
Christmas festivities articles	圣诞节用品	9505. 1000	5
Christmas trees lighting sets	圣诞树用成套灯具	9405. 3000	5
Chromates	铬酸盐	2841. 5000	1
Chromatographs instruments parts and accessories	色谱仪零件、附件	9027. 9000	3
Chromatographs instruments, nes	色谱仪,其他	9027. 2019	7
Chromite	铬铁矿	2610. 0000	1346
Chromium articles, nes	铬制品,其他	8112. 2900	16
Chromium hydroxides, nes	铬的氢氧化物,其他	2819. 9000	
Chromium ores and concentrates	铬矿砂及其精矿	2610. 0000	1346
Chromium oxides, nes	铬的氧化物,其他	2819. 9000	
Chromium powders	铬粉末	8112. 2100	16
Chromium sesquioxide [chromium (Ⅲ) oxide]	氧化铬绿	2819. 9000	
Chromium sulphates	铬的硫酸盐	2833. 2920	
Chromium trioxide	三氧化铬	2819. 1000	6
Chromium, unwrought	铬,未锻轧	8112. 2100	16
Chromoscope ultrasonic diagnostic equipment	彩色超声波诊断仪	9018. 1291	
Chrysanthemums, fresh, suitable for bouquets or for ornamental purposes	菊花,鲜的,制花束或装饰用的	0603. 1400	34

Article Description	商品名称	Tariff Code	D. R.
Chrysathemum, nes	菊花,其他	0602.9093	.
Chrysathemum, seedlings	菊花,种用	0602.9091	3
Chueh Tsai (fiddlehead), salted, prepared or preserved otherwise than by vinegar or acetic acid, not frozen	咸蕨菜,用醋或醋酸以外的其他方法制作或保藏的,未冷冻	2005.9950	148
Cider	苹果酒	2206.0090	2468
Cigarette filter tips	卷烟滤嘴	5601.2210	6
Cigarette holders	烟嘴	9614.0090	5
Cigarette lighters parts	香烟打火机零件	9613.9000	3
Cigarette lighters, nes	香烟打火机,其他	9613.8000	5
Cigarette paper, in rolls of a width not exceeding 5cm	烟卷纸,宽度不超过5厘米成卷的	4813.2000	8
Cigarette paper, in the form of booklets or tubes	烟卷纸,成小本或管状	4813.1000	8
Cigarette paper, nes	烟卷纸,其他	4813.9000	8
Cigarettes containing tobacco	卷烟,烟草制的	2402.2000	245
Cigarettes, of tobacco substitutes	卷烟,烟草代用品制成的	2402.9000	245
Cigarette-cases, tobacco-pouches, with outer surface of leather, of composition leather or of patent leather	烟盒、烟袋,以皮革、再生皮革或漆皮作面	4202.3100	256
Cigarette-cases, tobacco-pouches, with outer surface of plastic sheeting or of textile materials	烟盒、烟袋,以塑料片或纺织材料作面	4202.3200	256
Cigars, cheroots and cigarillos, containing tobacco	雪茄烟,烟草制的	2402.1000	245
Cigars, cheroots, cigarillos and cigarettes, of tobacco substitutes	雪茄烟,烟草代用品制成的	2402.9000	245
Cinchona alkaloids and their derivatives; salts thereof	金鸡纳生物碱及其衍生物以及它们的盐	2939.2000	34
Cinematographic apparatus and equipment parts and accessories	电影用装置及设备的零件、附件	9010.9010	3
Cinematographic film, unexposed, for colour photography, of a width exceeding 16mm but not exceeding 35mm and of a length exceeding 30m	电影胶片,未曝光的,彩色摄影用的,宽度超过16毫米,但不超过35毫米,长度超过30米	3702.5520	12368
Cinematographic film, unexposed, for colour photography, of a width exceeding 35mm	电影胶片,未曝光的,彩色摄影用的,宽度超过35毫米	3702.5620	12368
Cinematographic film, exposed and developed, for educational use only, nes	电影胶片,已曝光已冲洗的,教学专用,其他	3706.9010	1238
Cinematographic film, exposed and developed, nes	电影胶片,已曝光已冲洗的,其他	3706.9090	1238
Cinematographic film, exposed and developed, of a width of 35mm or more, for educational use only	电影胶片,已曝光已冲洗的,宽度在35毫米及以上,教学专用	3706.1010	1238
Cinematographic film, exposed and developed, of a width of 35mm or more, nes	电影胶片,已曝光已冲洗的,宽度在35毫米及以上,其他	3706.1090	1238
Cinematographic film, exposed but not developed	电影胶片,已曝光未冲洗的	3704.0010	1238
Cinematographic film, unexposed, of a width exceeding 16mm but not exceeding 35mm and of a length exceeding 30m, nes	电影胶片,未曝光的,宽度超过16毫米,但不超过35毫米,长度超过30米,其他	3702.9420	12368

C

C

Article Description	商品名称	Tariff Code	D. R.
Cinematographic film, unexposed, of a width exceeding 35mm, nes	电影胶片,未曝光的,宽度超过35毫米,其他	3702.9520	12368
Cinnabar	辰砂	2617.9010	146
Cinnabar	朱砂	2617.9010	146
Cinnamon, cinnamomum zeylanicum blume, neither crushed nor ground	肉桂,锡兰,未磨	0906.1100	4
Cinnamon, crushed or ground	肉桂,已磨	0906.2000	4
Cinnamon, nes, neither crushed nor ground	肉桂,其他,未磨	0906.1900	4
Cinnamontree flowers, crushed or ground	肉桂花,已磨	0906.2000	4
Cinnamontree flowers, neither crushed nor ground	肉桂花,未磨	0906.1900	4
Ciprofloxacin	环丙氟哌酸	2933.4910	36
Circle sticks, circle bars and the like, nes	圆签、圆棒及类似一次性制品,其他	4421.9029	56
Circle sticks, circle bars and the like, of bamboo	圆签、圆棒及类似一次性制品,竹制	4421.9022	56
Circle sticks, circle bars and the like, of wood	圆签、圆棒及类似一次性制品,木制	4421.9021	56
Circular knitting machines auxiliary	针织机的辅助机器	8448.1900	3
Circular knitting machines, with cylinder diameter exceeding165mm	圆型针织机,圆筒直径超过165毫米	8447.1200	
Circular knitting machines, with cylinder diameter not exceeding 165mm	圆型针织机,圆筒直径不超过165毫米	8447.1100	
Circular saw blades, including parts, nes	圆锯片,包括部件,其他	8202.3900	256
Circular saw blades, with working part of steel	圆锯片,带有钢制工作部件	8202.3100	256
Citral	柠檬醛	2912.1900	36
Citric acid	柠檬酸	2918.1400	36
Citronellol(3,7-dimethyl-6-octen-1-ol)	香茅醇(3,7-二甲基-6 辛烯-1-醇)	2905.2220	36
Citrus fruit, in airtight containers	柑橘属水果,罐头	2008.3010	248
Citrus fruit, nes, otherwise prepared, or preserved	柑橘属水果,其他,用其他方法制作或保藏的	2008.3090	248
Civet	灵猫香	0510.0020	14
Clam, frozen, dried, salted or in brine	蛤,冻、干、盐腌或盐渍的	0307.9930	14
Clam, live, fresh or chilled	蛤,活、鲜或冷的	0307.9193	1
Clam, prepared or preserved	蛤,制作或保藏的	1605.9020	48
Clamps and the like	夹钳及类似品	8205.7000	256
Clamworm, live, fresh or chilled	沙蚕,活、鲜或冷的	0307.9192	1
Clarinets	单簧管	9205.9090	5
Clasps and frames with clasps, incorporating locks, of base metal	扣环及扣环框架,带锁的,贱金属制	8301.5000	256
Clasps, of base metal, of a kind used for clothing, footwear, awnings, handbags, travel goods or other made up articles	栓,贱金属制,用于衣着、鞋靴、天篷、提包、旅行用品或其他制成品	8308.9000	256
Clavichords	羽管键琴	9201.9000	5
Clavulanic acid and its salts	克拉维酸及其盐	2934.9950	36
Claw of fowls of the species gallus domesticus, frozen	鸡爪,冻的	0207.1422	1

Article Description	商品名称	Tariff Code	D. R.
Claws and powder thereof	爪及其粉末	0507. 9090	14
Clayey sands	粘土砂	2505. 9000	
Clays, nes	粘土,其他	2508. 4000	145
Cleaning apparatus, flat panel displays manufacture machines and apparatus, nes	清洗装置,平板显示器的制造机器及装置,其他	8486. 3049	7
Cleaning machines for eggs, fruit or other agricultural produce	清洁机器,对蛋类、水果或其他农产品的	8433. 6000	
Cleaning machines for seed, grain or dried leguminous vegetables	清洁机器,种子、谷物或干豆用	8437. 1090	3
Cleaning machines parts, for seed, grain or dried leguminous vegetables	清洁机器零件,种子、谷物或干豆用	8437. 9000	3
Cleaning machines parts, for egg, fruit or other agricultural produce	清洁机器零件,对蛋类、水果或其他农产品的	8433. 9090	
Clementines, wilkings and similar citrus hybrids, nes	柑橘,杂交,其他	0805. 2090	14
Clinical waste	医疗废物	3825. 3000	34
Cloaks and similar articles not knitted or crocheted, for men or boys, for man-made fibres	短斗篷及类似品,非针织或钩编的,男式,化学纤维制	6201. 1390	2456
Cloaks and similar articles not knitted or crocheted, for men or boys, of other textile materials	短斗篷及类似品,非针织或钩编的,男式,其他纺织材料制	6201. 1900	2456
Cloaks and similar articles not knitted or crocheted, for men or boys, of wool or fine animal hair	短斗篷及类似品,非针织或钩编的,男式,羊毛或动物细毛制	6201. 1100	2456
Cloaks and similar articles not knitted or crocheted, for women or girls, of man-made fibres	短斗篷及类似品,非针织或钩编的,女式,化学纤维制	6202. 1390	2456
Cloaks and similar articles not knitted or crocheted, for women or girls, of other textile materials	短斗篷及类似品,非针织或钩编的,女式,其他纺织材料制	6202. 1900	2456
Cloaks and similar articles not knitted or crocheted, for women or girls, of wool or fine animal hair	短斗篷及类似品,非针织或钩编的,女式,羊毛或动物细毛制	6202. 1100	2456
Cloaks and similar articles, knitted or crocheted, for men or boys, for man-made fibres	短斗篷及类似品,针织或钩编的,男式,化学纤维制	6101. 3000	2456
Cloaks and similar articles, knitted or crocheted, for men or boys, of cotton	短斗篷及类似品,针织或钩编的,男式,棉制	6101. 2000	2456
Cloaks and similar articles, knitted or crocheted, for men or boys, of other textile materials	短斗篷及类似品,针织或钩编的,男式,其他	6101. 9090	2456
Cloaks and similar articles, knitted or crocheted, for men or boys, of wool or fine animal hair	短斗篷及类似品,针织或钩编的,男式,羊毛或动物细毛制	6101. 9010	2456
Cloaks and similar articles, knitted or crocheted, for women or girls, of cotton	短斗篷及类似品,针织或钩编的,女式,棉制	6102. 2000	2456
Cloaks and similar articles, knitted or crocheted, for women or girls, of man-made fibres	短斗篷及类似品,针织或钩编的,女式,化学纤维制	6102. 3000	2456
Cloaks and similar articles, knitted or crocheted, for women or girls, of other textile materials	短斗篷及类似品,针织或钩编的,女式,其他	6102. 9000	2456
Cloaks and similar articles, knitted or crocheted, for women or girls, of wool or fine animal hair	短斗篷及类似品,针织或钩编的,女式,羊毛或动物细毛制	6102. 1000	2456

C

C

Article Description	商品名称	Tariff Code	D. R.
Cloaks and similar articles, not knitted or crocheted, for men or boys, of cotton	短斗篷及类似品,非针织或钩编的,男式,棉制	6201.1290	2456
Cloaks and similar articles, not knitted or crocheted, for women or girls, of cotton	短斗篷及类似品,非针织或钩编的,女式,棉制	6202.1290	2456
Clobazam (INN)	氯巴占(INN)	2933.7200	36
Clock and watch glasses	钟表玻璃	7015.9010	1345
Clock cases	钟壳	9112.2000	3
Clock cases parts	钟壳零件	9112.9000	3
Clock movements, complete and assembled, electrically operated, nes	钟芯,已组装完整的,电力驱动的,其他	9109.1900	5
Clock movements, complete and assembled, nes	钟芯,已组装完整的,其他	9109.9000	5
Clock movements, complete, unassembled or partly assembled	钟芯,完整的,未组装或部分组装的	9110.9010	1
Clock movements, complete, unassembled or partly assembled	钟芯,完整的,未组装或部分组装的	9110.9010	1
Clock movements, incomplete	钟芯,不完整的	9110.9090	1
Clock or watch parts, nes	钟、表零件,其他	9114.9000	6
Clocks with watch movements, electrically operated	钟,以表芯装成的,电力驱动的	9103.1000	5
Clocks with watch movements, nes	钟,以表芯装成的,其他	9103.9000	5
Clocks, alarm clocks, electrically operated	钟,闹钟,电力驱动的	9105.1100	5
Clocks, alarm clocks, nes	钟,闹钟,其他	9105.1900	5
Clocks, astronomical chronometer, electrically operated	钟,天文钟,电力驱动的	9105.9110	5
Clocks, electrically operated, nes	钟,电力驱动的,其他	9105.9190	5
Clocks, nes	钟,其他	9105.9900	5
Clocks, wall clocks, electrically operated	钟,挂钟,电力驱动的	9105.2100	5
Clocks, wall clocks, nes	钟,挂钟,其他	9105.2900	5
Clocks, with instrument panel	钟,带仪表板的	9104.0000	5
Clocks, with instrument panel, and clocks of similar type for vehicles, aircraft, spacecraft or vessels	钟,带仪表板的,车辆、航空器、航天器或船舶用的类似钟	9104.0000	5
Clofenotane (INN)	1,1,1-三氯-2,2-双(4-氯苯基)乙烷	2903.6200	36
Cloisonne statuettes and other ornaments of base metal	景泰蓝雕塑像及其他装饰品,贱金属制	8306.2910	256
Clonazepam (INN); salts thereof	氯硝西泮(INN)以及盐	2933.9100	36
Clorazepate; salts thereof	氯拉卓酸以及盐	2933.9100	36
Closing machines, for bottles, cans, boxes, bags or other containers, nes	密封机器,瓶、罐、箱、袋或其他容器的	8422.3090	
Cloth, grill, netting and fencing, of aluminium wire	布、网、篱及格栅,铝丝制的	7616.9100	36
Cloth, of copper wire	布,铜丝制	7419.9930	4
Cloth, of nickel wire	布,镍丝制	7508.1010	6
Clothes hangers of wood	衣架,木制	4421.1000	56

C

Article Description	商品名称	Tariff Code	D. R.
Clothes-dryers of a dry linen capacity not exceeding 10kg, centrifuges	干衣机,离心式,干衣量不超过 10 千克	8421. 1210	7
Clothes-dryers parts, of a dry linen capacity not exceeding 10kg	干衣机用零件,干衣量不超过 10 千克的	8421. 9110	3
Clothes-dryers, centrifuges, nes	干衣机,离心式,其他	8421. 1290	
Clothing accessories parts, knitted or crocheted	衣着附件的零件,针织或钩编的	6117. 9000	2456
Clothing accessories parts, not knitted or crocheted	衣着附件的零件,非针织或钩编的	6217. 9000	2456
Clothing accessories, of furskin	衣着附件,毛皮的	4303. 1020	456
Clothing accessories, knitted or crocheted, made up, nes	衣着附件,针织或钩编的,制成的,其他	6117. 8090	2456
Clothing accessories, not knitted or crocheted, made up, nes	衣着附件,非针织或钩编的,制成的,其他	6217. 1090	2456
Clothing accessories, of leather or of composition leather, nes	衣着附件,皮革或再生皮革制的,其他	4203. 4000	456
Clothing eyes, of base metal	扣眼,贱金属制,用于衣着	8308. 1000	256
Clotiazepam (INN); salts thereof	氯噻西泮(INN)及盐	2934. 9100	36
Clover(Trifblium spp.) seed, forage plants	三叶草子,饲料植物用的	1209. 2200	358
Clover, forage products	三叶草,饲料用	1214. 9000	
Cloves(whole fruit, cloves and stems)	丁香(母丁香、公丁香及丁香梗)	0907. 0000	
Cloxacillin	邻氯青霉素	2941. 1096	
Cloxazolam(INN); salts thereof	氯恶唑仑(INN)及盐	2934. 9100	36
Clutches	离合器	8483. 6000	
Clutches and parts of cross-country cars(4WD)	离合器及其零件,越野车(4 轮驱动)用	8708. 9350	3
Clutches and parts of dumpers	离合器及其零件,自卸车用	8708. 9330	3
Clutches and parts of motor vehicles with 30 seats or more	离合器及其零件,30 座及以上客运机动车辆用	8708. 9320	3
Clutches and parts of motor vehicles with special purpose	离合器及其零件,特种车辆用	8708. 9360	3
Clutches and parts of saloon cars	离合器及其零件,小轿车用	8708. 9340	3
Clutches and parts of tractors	离合器及其零件,拖拉机的	8708. 9310	3
Clutches and parts, nes	离合器及其零件,其他	8708. 9390	3
Clutches parts	离合器零件	8483. 9000	3
Cnc automatic tool change punch press, numerically controlled, for working metal	自动模式数控步冲压力机,数控的,加工金属用	8462. 4111	7
CO_2 compressors	二氧化碳压缩机	8414. 8020	23
Coach screws, of iron of steel	方头螺钉,钢铁制的	7318. 1100	268
Coal cutters parts	截煤机零件	8431. 4990	3
Coal cutters, nes	截煤机,其他	8430. 3900	5
Coal cutters, self-propelled	截煤机,自推进的	8430. 3100	5
Coal gas	煤气	2705. 0000	4
Coal gas meters	煤气表	9028. 1010	

C

Article Description	商品名称	Tariff Code	D. R.
Coal gas meters parts and accessories, for industrial use	煤气表零件、附件,工业用	9028. 9010	3
Coal gas meters parts and accessories, nes	煤气表零件、附件,其他	9028. 9090	3
Coal, nes, whether or not pulverized, but not agglomerated	煤,其他,不论是否粉化,但未制成型	2701. 1900	156
Coalfish (pollachius virens), fresh or chilled	绿青鳕鱼,鲜或冷的	0302. 6300	18
Coalfish (pollachius virens), frozen	绿青鳕鱼,冻的	0303. 7300	18
Coarse animal hair, carded or combed	动物粗毛,已梳的	5105. 4000	5
Coarse animal hair, not carded orcombed	动物粗毛,未梳的	5102. 2000	48
Coaster braking hubs and parts, of bicycles and other cycles	倒轮制动毂及其零件,自行车及脚踏车的	8714. 9400	3
Coating machines for textile fabrics	涂布机器,纺织物的	8451. 8000	
Coating machines parts for textile fabrics	涂布机器零件,纺织物的	8451. 9000	
Cobalamins	钴胺素	2936. 2600	36
Cobalt and its salts	钴及钴盐,放射性的	2844. 4020	
Cobalt articles, nes	钴制品,其他	8105. 9000	16
Cobalt carbonate	碳酸钴	2836. 9930	
Cobalt chloride	氯化钴	2827. 3930	
Cobalt mattes	钴锍	8105. 2090	16
Cobalt ores and concentrates	钴矿砂及其精矿	2605. 0000	146
Cobalt oxalate	草酸钴	2917. 1120	36
Cobalt oxides and hydroxides, nes	钴的氧化物及氢氧化物,其他	2822. 0090	
Cobalt powders	钴粉末	8105. 2090	16
Cobalt sulphide	硫化钴	2830. 9030	
Cobalt tetroxide	四氧化三钴	2822. 0010	
Cobalt, nitrate	硝酸钴	2834. 2910	
Cobalt, unwrought	钴,未锻轧	8105. 2090	16
Cobaltite	辉钴矿	2605. 0000	146
Coca leaf	古柯叶	1211. 3000	34
Cocaine and its salts	可卡因及其盐	2939. 9110	34
Cochineal	胭脂虫	0511. 9990	34
Cochineal extract	胭脂虫提取物	3203. 0020	34
Cockatoos, pure-bred breeding	美冠鹦鹉,改良种用	0106. 3210	3
Cocks parts	旋塞用零件	8481. 9090	3
Cocks, for pipes, boiler shells, tanks, vats or the like	旋塞,用于管道、锅炉、罐、桶或类似品的	8481. 8090	
Cocoa beans, whole or broken, raw or roasted	可可豆,整颗或破碎的,生的或焙炒的	1801. 0000	4
Cocoa butter, fat	可可脂	1804. 0000	
Cocoa manufacture machinery	可可粉生产机器	8438. 2000	
Cocoa manufacture machinery parts	可可粉生产机器的零件	8438. 9000	3
Cocoa oil	可可油	1804. 0000	

Article Description	商品名称	Tariff Code	D. R.
Cocoa paste, not defatted	可可膏,未脱脂	1803. 1000	6
Cocoa paste, wholly or partly defatted	可可膏,全脱脂或部分脱脂	1803. 2000	6
Cocoa powder, containing added sugar or other sweetening matter	可可粉,加糖或其他甜物质的	1806. 1000	248
Cocoa powder, not containing added sugar or other sweetening matter	可可粉,未加糖或其他甜物质的	1805. 0000	468
Cocoa shells, husks, skins and other cocoa waste	可可荚、壳、皮及废料	1802. 0000	4
Coconut (coir)	椰壳	5305. 0092	4
Coconut (copra) oil and its fractions, crude oil	椰子油及其分离品,初榨的	1513. 1100	4
Coconut (copra) oil and its fractions, nes	椰子油及其分离品,其他	1513. 1900	4
Coconut juice	椰子汁	2106. 9040	268
Coconuts, desiccated	椰子,干的	0801. 1100	134
Coconuts, nes	椰子,其他	0801. 1990	134
Coconuts, seedlings	椰子,种用	0801. 1910	134
Cod (gadus morhua, gadus ogac, gadus macrocephalus), frozen	鳕鱼(大西洋鳕鱼、太平洋鳕鱼、格陵兰鳕鱼),冻的	0303. 5200	18
Codeine and salts	可待因及盐	2939. 1100	34
Coffee extracts, essences and concentrates	咖啡浓缩精汁	2101. 1100	268
Coffee husks	咖啡豆荚	0901. 9010	5
Coffee makers, electro-thermic, drip	咖啡机,电热的,滴液式	8516. 7110	7
Coffee makers, electro-thermic, nes	咖啡壶,电热的,其他	8516. 7190	7
Coffee makers, electro-thermic, pump espresso	咖啡机,电热的,泵压式	8516. 7130	7
Coffee makers, electro-thermic, steam espresso	咖啡机,电热的,蒸馏渗滤式	8516. 7120	7
Coffee preparations with a basis of extracts, essences or concentrates or with a basis of coffee	咖啡浓缩精汁为基本成分的制品	2101. 1200	268
Coffee skins	咖啡豆皮	0901. 9010	5
Coffee substitutes containing coffee	含咖啡的咖啡代用品	0901. 9020	6
Coffee substitutes, and extracts, essences and concentrates thereof	咖啡代用品及其浓缩精汁	2101. 3000	268
Coffee, not roasted, decaffeinated	咖啡,未焙炒的,已浸除咖啡碱	0901. 1200	14
Coffee, not roasted, not decaffeinated	咖啡,未焙炒的,未浸除咖啡碱	0901. 1100	14
Coffee, roasted, decaffeinated	咖啡,已焙炒的,已浸除咖啡碱	0901. 2200	14
Coffee, roasted, not decaffeinated	咖啡,已焙炒的,未浸除咖啡碱	0901. 2100	14
Coffer-dams	潜水箱	8907. 9000	5
Coffinite	水硅铀矿	2612. 1000	146
Coin of gold	金币	7108. 2000	46
Coin (other than gold coin), not being legal tender	硬币(金币除外),非法定货币的	7118. 1000	46
Coin, nes	硬币,其他	7118. 9000	46
Coin-sorting, counting or wrapping machines	硬币分类、计数及包装机	8472. 9090	
Coir yarn	椰壳纤维纱线	5308. 1000	568
Coke and semi-coke, of lignite or of peat, whether or not agglomerated	焦炭及半焦炭,煤、褐煤或泥煤制成的	2704. 0010	34

C

C

Article Description	商品名称	Tariff Code	D. R.
Coke ovens	炼焦炉	8417.8010	7
Coke ovens parts	炼焦炉用零件	8417.9020	3
Coking coal	炼焦煤	2701.1210	156
Cold cathode parts, nes	冷阴极管零件,其他	8540.9990	3
Cold chamber die-casting machines	冷室压铸机	8454.3010	
Cold-drawing tube benches, for working metal or cermets, without removing material, nes	冷拔管机,金属或金属陶瓷用,非切削,其他	8463.1019	7
Cold-drawing tube benches, with 300t or less, for working metal or cermets, without removing material	冷拔管机,300 吨及以下,金属或金属陶瓷用,非切削	8463.1011	7
Collages and similar decorative plaques	拼贴画及类似装饰板	9701.9000	5
Collapsible tubular containers, of aluminium, of a capacity not exceeding 300L, whether or not lined or heat-insulated, but not fitted with mechanical or thermal equipment	软管容器,铝制,容积不超过 300 升,不论是否衬里或隔热,但无机械或热力装置	7612.1000	368
Collections and collectors pieces of zoological, botanical, mineralogical, anatomical, historical, archaeolohical, palaeontological, ethnographic or numismatic interest	收集品及珍藏品,具有动物学、植物学、矿物学、解剖学、历史学、考古学、古生物学、人种学或钱币学意义的	9705.0000	5
Collodions, in primary forms	胶棉,初级形状的	3912.2000	16
Colloidal sulphur	胶态硫磺	2802.0000	
Color filters	彩色滤光片	9001.9010	
Colour lakes	色淀	3205.0000	
Colour lakes preparations	色淀制品	3205.0000	
Colouring matter and other preparations, nes	着色料及其他制品,其他	3206.4900	2368
Colouring matter of animal origin and preparations based thereon	着色料及以其为基本成分的制品,动物质的	3203.0020	34
Colouring matter of vegetable origin and preparations based thereon, nes	着色料及以其为基本成分的制品,植物质的,其他	3203.0019	34
Colouring matter preparations, based on synthetic organic products, nes	着色料为基本成分的制品,有机合成的,其他	3204.9090	345
Colouring matter, mixed	着色料组成的混合物	3204.1990	345
Colours and similar preparations, prepared, of a kind used in the ceramic, enamelling or glass industry	着色剂及类似制品,调制的,陶瓷、搪瓷及玻璃工业用	3207.1000	13
Colours in sets	颜料,成套的	3213.1000	3
Columbite	铌铁矿	2615.9090	146
Colza oil and fractions thereof, nes	菜子油及其分离品,其他	1514.9900	4
Colza oil and its fractions, low erucic acid, crude oil	菜子油及其分离品,低芥子酸的,初榨的	1514.1100	46
Colza oil and its fractions, low erucic acid, nes	菜子油及其分离品,低芥子酸的,其他	1514.1900	46
Colza, nes	油菜籽,其他	1205.9090	3
Colza, seed	油菜籽,种用	1205.9010	3

Article Description	商品名称	Tariff Code	D. R.
Colza, seed, low erucic acid	油菜籽,种用,低芥子酸的	1205. 1010	36
Combine harvester-threshers	联合收割机	8433. 5100	
Combine harvester-threshers parts	联合收割机用零件	8433. 9010	
Combined ball/roller bearings	球柱混合轴承	8482. 8000	5
Combined machines parts and accessories, which perform two or more of the functions of printing, copying or facsimile transmission, capable of connecting to an automatic data processing machine or to a network, nes	组合机零件及附件,具有打印、复印或传真中两种及以上功能的,可与自动数据处理设备或网络连接,其他	8443. 9990	3
Combined machines, which perform two or more of the functions of printing, copying or facsimile transmission, capable of connecting to an automatic data processing machine or to a network, electrostatic photosensitive-type	组合机,具有打印、复印或传真中两种及以上功能的,可与自动数据处理设备或网络连接,静电感光式	8443. 3110	57
Combined machines, which perform two or more of the functions of printing, copying or facsimile transmission, capable of connecting to an automatic data processing machine or to a network, nes	组合机,具有打印、复印或传真中两种及以上功能的,可与自动数据处理设备或网络连接,其他	8443. 3190	57
Combined punching and shearing machines, for working metal	冲剪两用机,加工金属用	8462. 4900	7
Combined punching and shearing machines, numerically controlled, for working metal	冲剪两用机,数控的,加工金属用	8462. 4190	7
Combing machines, for cotton	精梳机,棉的	8445. 1210	7
Combing machines, for worsted	精梳机,毛的	8445. 1220	7
Combing machines, nes	精梳机,其他	8445. 1290	7
Combs, nes	梳子,其他	9615. 1900	6
Combs, of hard rubber or plastics	梳子,硬质橡胶或塑料制	9615. 1100	6
Combustible materials articles	易燃材料制品	3606. 9090	13
Communication apparatus parts, nes	通信设备用零件,其他	8517. 7090	3
Communication network synchronizing equipments	通信网络时钟同步设备	8517. 6231	7
Compact disc players, not incorporating a sound recording device, using optical media	激光唱机,未装有声音录制装置,使用光学媒体的	8519. 8121	5
Compact set of ring spinning frames	环定细纱机紧密纺装置	8448. 3940	3
Compacting machinery, for earth, minerals or ores, self-propelled, nes	压实机械,对泥土、矿物或矿石的,自推进的,其他	8430. 5090	5
Compacting machinery, not self-propelled	压实机械,非自推进的	8430. 6100	5
Comparison cameras for forensic or criminological purposes	比较照相机,法庭或犯罪学用的	9006. 3000	7
Compasses parts and accessories	罗盘零件、附件,其他	9014. 9090	3
Compasses, for direction finding	罗盘,定向用	9014. 1000	
Complex cyanides	氰络合物	2837. 2000	6
Complex fluorine salts, nes	氟络盐,其他	2826. 9090	

C

C

Article Description	商品名称	Tariff Code	D. R.
Complex needles for knitting machines, smaler than gauge No. 28	复合针,针织机用28号以下的	8448.5120	3
Composing sticks, hand-operated	排字盘,手工操作的	9611.0000	
Composite can manufacture machines for paper, plastic and aluminium	复合罐生产设备,纸塑铝的	8441.3010	
Composite can manufacture machines for paper, plastic and aluminium	纸塑铝复合罐的生产设备	8441.3010	
Composite can manufacture machines parts, for paper, plastic and aluminium	复合罐生产设备零件,纸塑铝的	8441.9090	
Composite paper and paperboard, in rolls or sheets, not surface-coated or impregnated, whether or not internally reinforced	复合纸及纸板,成卷或成张的,未经表面涂布或未浸渍,不论内层是否有加强材料	4807.0000	48
Composition leather with a basis of leather or leather fibre, in slabs, sheets or strip, whether or not in rolls	再生皮革,以皮革或皮革纤维为基本成分的,成块、成张或成条,不论是否成卷	4115.1000	1458
Compound plasticizers for rubber or plastics	复合增塑剂,橡胶或塑料用	3812.2000	36
Compounded rubber solutions, unvulcanized	复合橡胶溶液,未硫化的	4005.2000	16
Compounded rubber, unvulcanized, compounded with carbon black or silica	复合橡胶,未硫化的,与碳黑或硅石混合	4005.1000	16
Compounded rubber, unvulcanized, in plates, sheets and strip	复合橡胶,未硫化的,板、片、带	4005.9100	16
Compounded rubber, unvulcanized, in primary forms	复合橡胶,未硫化的,初级形状的	4005.9900	16
Compounds with other nitrogen function, nes	含氮基化合物,其他	2929.9090	36
Compounds, inorganic or organic, of rare-earth metals, of yttrium or of scandium or of mixtures of these metals, nes	稀土金属、钇、钪及其混合物的无机或有机化合物,其他	2846.9090	6
Compressors for air conditioning machines, of a motor power exceeding 0.4kW but not exceeding 5kW	压缩机,空气调节器用,电动机额定功率超过0.4千瓦,但不超过5千瓦	8414.3013	27
Compressors for air conditioning machines, of a motor power exceeding 5kW	压缩机,空气调节器用,电动机额定功率超过5千瓦	8414.3014	27
Compressors for refrigerators or freezers, of a motor power exceeding 0.4kW but not exceeding 5kW	压缩机,冷藏箱或冷冻箱用,电动机额定功率超过0.4千瓦,但不超过5千瓦	8414.3012	27
Compressors for refrigerators or freezers, of a motor power exceeding 5kW	压缩机,冷冻或冷藏设备用,电动机额定功率超过5千瓦	8414.3015	27
Compressors for refrigerators or freezers, of a motor power not exceeding 0.4kW	压缩机,冷藏箱或冷冻箱用,电动机额定功率不超过0.4千瓦	8414.3011	27
Compressors of a kind used in refrigerating equipment, driven by a motor, nes	压缩机,用于制冷设备的,电动机驱动的,其他	8414.3019	27
Compressors of a kind used in refrigerating equipment, driven by a non-motor	压缩机,用于制冷设备的,非电动机驱动的	8414.3090	27

Article Description	商品名称	Tariff Code	D. R.
Concentrates of essential oils in fats, in fixedoils, in waxes or the like, obtained by enfleurage or maceration	含浓缩精油的脂肪、固定油、蜡及类似品,用花香吸取法或浸渍法制成的	3301.9090	34
Concrete articles, nes	混凝土制品,其他	6810.9990	56
Concrete blocks and bricks, for building	混凝土砖及块,建筑用	6810.1100	56
Concrete flagstones and similar articles	混凝土扁平石及类似品	6810.1990	56
Concrete mixer lorries	混凝土搅拌车	8705.4000	7
Concrete mixers	混凝土混合机器	8474.3100	56
Concrete pumps	混凝土泵	8413.4000	23
Concrete tiles and similar articles	混凝土瓦及类似品	6810.1990	56
Concrete tubes, pipes, rods, plates, piles and similar articles, prestressed	混凝土管、杆、板、桩等,预应力的	6810.9110	56
Concrete tubes, pipes, rods, plates, piles and similar articles, reinforced by steel	混凝土管、杆、板、桩等,钢筋加强的	6810.9110	56
Concretes and similar compositions for refractory	混凝土及类似耐火混合制品	3816.0000	36
Concretes, non-refractory	混凝土,非耐火的	3824.5000	36
Condensers for steam or other vapour power units	冷凝器,水蒸气或其他蒸汽动力装置的	8404.2000	3
Condensers for steam or other vapour power units parts	冷凝器零件,水蒸气或其他蒸汽动力装置的	8404.9090	3
Condiments, mixed	混合调味品	2103.9090	268
Conductivity glass, for technical use	导电玻璃,工业用	7020.0011	6
Conductivity water	导电水	2853.0090	3
Cones, of paper, paperboard, nes	锥形袋,纸制的	4819.4000	68
Confectionery manufacture machinery	糖果生产机器	8438.2000	3
Confectionery manufacture machinery parts	糖果生产机器的零件	8438.9000	3
Conjuring tricks	魔术道具	9505.9000	5
Constant weight scales, for rationed packing	恒定秤,定量包装用	8423.3010	3
Constant weight scales, for rationed sorting	恒定秤,定量分选用	8423.3020	3
Contact lenses	隐形眼镜片	9001.3000	3
Container loading and unloading bridges	集装箱装卸桥	8426.1942	7
Container vessels, motor powered, capable loading standard containers more than 6000	集装箱船,机动的,可载标准集装箱在6000箱以上	8901.9022	8
Container vessels, motor powered, capable loading standard containers with 6000 or less	集装箱船,机动的,可载标准集装箱在6000箱及以下	8901.9021	8
Containers for compressed or liquefied gas, of iron or steel, for retail packing	容器,钢铁的,装压缩气体或液化气体用的,零售包装用	7311.0010	36
Containers for compressed or liquefied gas, of iron or steel, nes	容器,钢铁的,装压缩气体或液化气体用的,其他	7311.0090	36
Containers of aluminium, for compressed or liquefied gas, for retail packing	容器,铝制,装压缩气体或液化气体用的,零售包装用	7613.0010	368

Article Description	商品名称	Tariff Code	D. R.
Containers of aluminium, for compressed or liquefied gas, nes	容器,铝制,装压缩气体或液化气体用的,其他	7613. 0090	368
Containers, nes	集装箱,其他	8609. 0090	58
Containers, of 20 feet, insulated	集装箱,20 英尺的,保温式	8609. 0011	58
Containers, of 20 feet, nes	集装箱,20 英尺的,其他	8609. 0019	58
Containers, of 20 feet, tank type	集装箱,20 英尺的,罐式	8609. 0012	58
Containers, of 40 feet, insulated	集装箱,40 英尺的,保温式	8609. 0021	58
Containers, of 40 feet, nes	集装箱,40 英尺的,其他	8609. 0029	58
Containers, of 40 feet, tank type	集装箱,40 英尺的,罐式	8609. 0022	58
Containers, of 45, 48, 53 feet	集装箱,45、48、53 英尺的	8609. 0030	58
Continuous hot bending furnaces, for hot working glass or glasswares	连续式玻璃热弯炉	8475. 2911	
Contraceptive preparations based on hormones	避孕药,以激素为基本成分的	3006. 6010	36
Controlled valves, thermostatically	控制阀,恒温的	8481. 8040	
Controllers, electronic integrated circuits, whether or not combined with memories, converters, logic circuits, amplifiers, clock and timing circuits, or other circuits	控制器,集成电路,不论是否带有存储器、转换器、逻辑电路、放大器、时钟及时序电路或其他电路	8542. 3100	37
Converters parts	转炉用零件	8454. 9090	3
Converters, of a kind used in metallurgy or in metal foundries	转炉,金属冶炼及铸造用	8454. 1000	
Converters, electric rotary	变流机,旋转式	8502. 4000	8
Conveyor belts or belting, of vulcanized rubber, nes	输送带及带料,硫化橡胶制的,其他	4010. 1900	1368
Conveyor belts or belting, of vulcanized rubber, reinforced only with metal	输送带及带料,硫化橡胶制的,仅用金属加强的	4010. 1100	1368
Conveyor belts or belting, of vulcanized rubber, reinforced only with textile materials	输送带及带料,硫化橡胶制的,仅用纺织材料加强的	4010. 1200	1368
Conveyors parts	输送机零件	8431. 3900	3
Cooking apparatus, of copper, of a kind used for domestic purposes, non-electric, and parts thereof, of copper	烹饪器具及其零件,铜制,非电热的,家用	7418. 1910	56
Cooking appliances and plate warmers, of iron or steel, non-electric domestic appliances, for gas fuel or for both gas and other fuels	烹饪器具及加热板,钢铁制,非电热的家用,使用气体燃料或可使用气体燃料及其他燃料的	7321. 1100	7
Cooking appliances and plate warmers, of iron or steel, non-electric domestic appliances, for liquid fuel, nes	烹饪器具及加热板,钢铁制,非电热的家用,使用液体燃料的,其他	7321. 1290	7
Cooking appliances and plate warmers, of iron or steel, non-electric domestic appliances, nes, including appliances for solid fuel	烹饪器具及加热板,钢铁制,非电热的家用,其他,包括使用固体燃料的	7321. 1900	7
Cooling medium pumps for internal combustion piston engines	冷却剂泵,活塞式内燃发动机用	8413. 3090	23
Coordinate measuring machine	坐标测量仪	9031. 8020	

Article Description	商品名称	Tariff Code	D. R.
Copper alloys other than master alloys, nes	铜合金,其他(铜母合金除外)	7403.2900	146
Copper anodes containing at least 99.9935% by weight of copper	铜阴极,按重量计铜含量超过99.9935%的	7403.1111	146
Copper anodes for electrolytic refining	铜阳极,电解精炼用的	7402.0000	46
Copper articles, cast, moulded, stamped or forged, but not further worked, for technical use	铜制品铸造、模压、冲压或锻造,但未经进一步加工的,工业用	7419.9110	4
Copper articles, cast, moulded, stamped or forged, but not further worked, nes	铜制品铸造、模压、冲压或锻造,但未经进一步加工的,其他	7419.9190	4
Copper articles, for technical use, nes	铜制品,工业用,其他	7419.9991	4
Copper articles, nes	铜制品,其他	7419.9999	4
Copper billets, of refined copper	铜坯段,精炼铜的	7403.1300	146
Copper cathodes of refined copper, nes	铜阴极,精炼铜的,其他	7403.1119	146
Copper cathodes sections of refined copper	铜阴极型材,精炼铜的	7403.1190	146
Copper foil of copper-nickel base alloys (cupronickel) or copper-nickel-zinc base alloys (nickel silver), not backed, of a thickness not exceeding 0.15mm	铜箔,铜镍合金(白铜)或铜镍锌合金(德银),无衬背,厚度不超过0.15毫米	7410.1210	236
Copper foil of refined copper, not backed, of a thickness not exceeding 0.15mm	铜箔,精炼铜制,无衬背,厚度不超过0.15毫米	7410.1100	236
Copper foil, not backed, of a thickness not exceeding 0.15mm, nes	铜箔,无衬背,厚度不超过0.15毫米,其他	7410.1290	236
Copper foil, of copper alloys, backed, of a copper thickness not exceeding 0.15mm, nes	铜箔,铜合金制,有衬背,铜厚度不超过0.15毫米,其他	7410.2290	236
Copper foil, of copper-nickel base alloys (cupronickel), backed, of a copper thickness not exceeding 0.15mm	铜箔,铜镍合金(白铜),有衬背,铜厚度不超过0.15毫米	7410.2210	236
Copper foil, of copper-nickel-zin cbase alloys (nickel silver), backed, of a copper thickness not exceeding 0.15mm	铜箔,铜镍锌合金(德银),有衬背,铜厚度不超过0.15毫米	7410.2210	236
Copper foil, of refined copper, backed, of a copper thickness not exceeding 0.15mm, nes	铜箔,精炼铜制,有衬背,铜厚度不超过0.15毫米,其他	7410.2190	236
Copper master alloys	铜母合金	7405.0000	6
Copper mattes	铜锍	7401.0000	46
Copper ores and concentrates	铜矿砂及其精矿	2603.0000	146
Copper oxides and hydroxides	铜的氧化物及氢氧化物	2825.5000	
Copper powders of lamellar structure, flakes, nes	铜粉,片状,其他铜合金制	7406.2090	16
Copper powders of lamellar structure, flakes, of copper-nickel base alloys (cupronickel)	铜粉,片状,铜镍合金(白铜)	7406.2020	16
Copper powders of lamellar structure, flakes, of copper-nickel-zinc base alloys (nickel silver)	铜粉,片状,铜镍锌合金(德银)制	7406.2020	16
Copper powders of lamellar structure, flakes, of refined copper	铜粉,片状,精炼铜制	7406.2010	16
Copper powders of non-lamellar structure, nes	铜粉,非片状,其他铜合金制	7406.1090	16

C

Article Description	商品名称	Tariff Code	D. R.
Copper powders of non-lamellar structure, of copper-nickel base alloys (cupronickel)	铜粉，非片状，铜镍合金（白铜）制	7406.1020	16
Copper powders of non-lamellar structure, of copper-nickel-zinc base alloys (nickel silver)	铜粉，非片状，铜镍锌合金（德银）制	7406.1020	16
Copper powders of non-lamellar structure, of copper-tin base alloys (bronze)	铜粉，非片状，铜锡合金（青铜）制	7406.1040	16
Copper powders of non-lamellar structure, of copper-zinc base alloys (brass)	铜粉，非片状，铜锌合金（黄铜）制	7406.1030	16
Copper powders of non-lamellar structure, of refined copper	铜粉，非片状，精炼铜制	7406.1010	16
Copper sulphates	铜的硫酸盐	2833.2500	
Copper wire, nes	铜丝，其他	7408.2900	16
Copper wire, of copper alloys, of copper-nickel base alloys (cupronickel)	铜丝，铜合金制，铜镍合金（白铜）	7408.2200	16
Copper wire, of copper alloys, of copper-nickel-zinc base alloys (nickel silver)	铜丝，铜合金制，铜镍锌合金（德银）	7408.2200	16
Copper wire, of copper alloys, of copper-zinc base alloys (brass)	铜丝，铜合金制，铜锌合金（黄铜）	7408.2100	16
Copper wire, of refined copper, nes	铜丝，精炼铜制，其他	7408.1900	16
Copper wire, of refined copper, of which the maximum cross-sectional dimension exceeds 6mm	铜丝，精炼铜制，最大截面尺寸超过 6 毫米	7408.1100	16
Copper wire-bars of refined copper	铜线锭，精炼铜的	7403.1200	146
Copper, chloride oxides and chloride hydroxides	铜的氯氧化物及氢氧基氯化物	2827.4100	
Copper, refined, nes	铜，精炼的，其他	7403.1900	146
Copper, unrefined	铜，未精炼的	7402.0000	46
Copper-clad board used to print circuit, of refined copper, of a copper thickness not exceeding 0.15mm	印制电路用覆铜板，精炼铜制，铜厚度不超过 0.15 毫米	7410.2110	236
Copper-nickel base alloys	铜镍合金	7403.2900	146
Copper-nickel-zinc base alloys	铜镍锌合金	7403.2900	146
Copper-tin base alloys	铜锡合金	7403.2200	146
Copper-zinc base alloys	铜锌合金	7403.2100	146
Copra	干椰子肉	1203.0000	3
Cops and the like, of wood	纡子及类似品，木制	4421.9010	56
Copying apparatus, electrostatic photocopying, operating by reproducing the original image directly onto the copy (direct process)	复印设备，静电感光的，将原件直接复印的（直接法）	8443.3911	57
Copying apparatus, electrostatic photocopying, operating by reproducing the original image via an intermediate onto the copy (indirect process)	复印设备，静电感光的，将原件通过中间体转印的（间接法）	8443.3912	57
Copying apparatus, photocopying, incorporating an optical system	复印设备，感光的，带有光学系统的	8443.3921	57
Copying apparatus, photocopying, of the contact type	复印设备，感光的，接触式的	8443.3922	57

Article Description	商品名称	Tariff Code	D. R.
Copying apparatus, thermocopying	复印设备,热敏的	8443. 3923	57
Copying apparatus, thermo-sublime	复印设备,热升华的	8443. 3924	57
Copying machines parts and accessories, nes	复印设备零件及附件,其他	8443. 9990	3
Copying machines, nes	复印设备,其他	8443. 3990	57
Copying or transfer papers, nes	拷贝或转印纸,其他	4816. 9090	58
Copying papers, in rolls or sheets, of width exceeding 36cm or in roll or one side exceeding 36cm and other side exceeding 15cm in rectangular sheets	拷贝纸,成卷或成张的,卷宽度超过36厘米,或长超过36厘米且宽超过15厘米	4809. 9000	458
Coral and similar materials	珊瑚及类似品	0508. 0090	14
Coral, worked	珊瑚,已加工的	9601. 9000	5
Cordials	柯迪尔酒	2208. 7000	2468
Cordyceps sinensis	冬虫夏草	1211. 9016	34
Cored wire of base metal, for electric arcwelding	焊丝,贱金属制,以焊剂为芯,电弧焊用	8311. 2000	56
Coriander, fresh or chilled	香菜,鲜或冷藏的	0709. 9090	1
Cork articles of natural, nes	软木制品,天然的,其他	4503. 9000	568
Cork blanks, sharp-edged for corks or stoppers	软木方块坯料,作塞子用的	4502. 0000	146
Cork treating machinery	软木处理机	8479. 3000	7
Cork waste	软木废料	4501. 9010	46
Cork, crushed, granulated or ground	软木,碎的、粒状的或粉状的	4501. 9020	46
Cork, natrual, raw or simply prepared	软木,天然的,未加工或简单加工的	4501. 1000	46
Cork, natural, debarked or roughly squared, or in rectangular (including square) blocks, plates, sheets or strip	软木,天然的,除去表皮或粗切成方形,或成长方块、正方块、板、片或条状	4502. 0000	146
Corms, in growth or in flower	球茎,生长或开花的	0601. 2000	135
Corms, nes, dormant	球茎,其他,休眠的	0601. 1099	135
Corms, seed, dormant	球茎,种用,休眠的	0601. 1091	135
Corn flakes, obtained by the swelling or roasting	玉米片,经膨化或烘炒制成的	1904. 1000	48
Correspondence cards of paper or paperboard	通信卡片,纸或纸板制的	4817. 2000	6
Corrugated nails, of iron or steel	波纹钉,钢铁制的	7317. 0000	36
Corrugated paper and paperboard, whether or not perforated	瓦楞纸及纸板,不论是否穿孔	4808. 1000	58
Corrugated sheets, containing asbestos	瓦楞板,含石棉的	6811. 4010	56
Corrugated sheets, not containing asbestos	瓦楞板,不含石棉的	6811. 8100	56
Corselettes of man-made fibres	束腰胸衣,化学纤维制	6212. 3010	2456
Corselettes of other textile materials	束腰胸衣,其他纺织材料制	6212. 3090	2456
Cortex eucommiae	杜仲	1211. 9028	34
Corticosteroid hormones, their derivatives and structural analogues medicaments, nes, mixed or unmixed, put up in measured doses or in forms or packings for retail sale	皮质甾类激素及其衍生物或结构类似物药品,其他,混合或未混合的,配定剂量或制成零售包装	3004. 3200	368
Cortisone	可的松	2937. 2100	36

C

C

Article Description	商品名称	Tariff Code	D. R.
Corundum, artificial, nes, whether or not chemically defined	刚玉,人造的,其他	2818. 1090	136
Corundum, natural	刚玉砂,天然	2513. 2000	
Cosmic radiations measuring or detecting instruments and apparatus	宇宙射线的测量或检验仪器及装置	9030. 1000	
Cotters and cotter-pins, of iron or steel	销及开尾销,钢铁制的	7318. 2400	268
Cotters, of aluminium	销,铝制	7616. 1000	36
Cotter-pins, of aluminium	开尾销,铝制	7616. 1000	36
Cotton comber	棉精梳机	8445. 1210	7
Cotton garnetted stock	废棉回收纤维	5202. 9100	46
Cotton linters	棉短绒	1404. 2000	6
Cotton linters pulp	棉短绒纸浆	4706. 1000	5
Cotton picker	棉花采摘机	8433. 5920	
Cotton ring spinning frame	棉细纱机	8445. 2041	7
Cotton roving frames	棉纺粗纱机	8445. 1321	7
Cotton seeds, for cultivation	棉籽,种用	1207. 2010	3
Cotton seeds, nes	棉籽,其他	1207. 2090	3
Cotton sewing thread, not put up for retail sale, containing 85% or more by weight of cotton	棉制缝纫线,非供零售用,按重量计含棉量在85%及以上	5204. 1100	3468
Cotton sewing thread, not put up for retail sale, nes	棉制缝纫线,非供零售用,其他	5204. 1900	3468
Cotton sewing thread, put up for retail sale	棉制缝纫线,供零售用	5204. 2000	3468
Cotton thread waste	废棉线	5202. 1000	46
Cotton waste, nes	废棉,其他	5202. 9900	46
Cotton wax [see also wax(es)]	棉蜡	1521. 1000	6
Cotton yarn waste	废棉纱线	5202. 1000	46
Cotton yarn, containing 85% or more by weight of cotton, not put up for retail sale, multiple (folded) or cabled yarn, of combed fibres, measuring per single yarn 714. 29 decitex or more (not exceeding 14 metric number per single yarn)	棉纱线,按重量计含棉量在85%及以上,非供零售用,精梳纤维纺制的多股纱线或缆线,每根单纱细度在714. 29分特及以上(每根单纱不超过14公支)	5205. 4100	3468
Cotton yarn, containing 85% or more by weight of cotton, not put up for retail sale, multiple (folded) or cabled yarn, of combed fibres, measuring per single yarn less than 125 decitex but not less than 106. 38 decitex (exceeding 80 metric number but not exceeding 94 metric number per single yarn)	棉纱线,按重量计含棉量在85%及以上,非供零售用,精梳纤维纺制的多股纱线或缆线,每根单纱细度在125分特以下,但不细于106. 38分特(每根单纱超过80公支,但不超过94公支)	5205. 4600	3468
Cotton yarn, containing 85% or more by weight of cotton, not put up for retail sale, multiple (folded) or cabled yarn, of combed fibres, measuring per single yarn less than 192. 31 decitex but not less than 125 decitex (exceeding 52 metric number but not exceeding 80 metric number per single yarn)	棉纱线,按重量计含棉量在85%及以上,非供零售用,精梳纤维纺制的多股纱线或缆线,每根单纱细度在192. 31分特以下,但不细于125分特(每根单纱超过52公支,但不超过80公支)	5205. 4400	3468

Article Description	商品名称	Tariff Code	D. R.
Cotton yarn, containing 85% or more by weight of cotton, not put up for retail sale, multiple (folded) or cabled yarn, of combed fibres, measuring per single yarn less than 714.29 decitex but not less than 232.56 decitex (exceeding 14 metric number but not exceeding 43 metric number per single yarn)	棉纱线,按重量计含棉量在85%及以上,非供零售用,精梳纤维纺制的多股纱线或缆线,每根单纱细度在714.29分特以下,但不细于232.56分特(每根单纱超过14公支,但不超过43公支)	5205.4200	3468
Cotton yarn, containing 85% or more by weight of cotton, not put up for retail sale, multiple (folded) or cabled yarn, of combed fibres, measuring per single yarn less than 83.33 decitex (exceeding 120 metric number per single yarn)	棉纱线,按重量计含棉量在85%及以上,非供零售用,精梳纤维纺制的多股纱线或缆线,每根单纱细度在83.33分特以下(每根单纱超过120公支)	5205.4800	3468
Cotton yarn, containing 85% or more by weight of cotton, not put up for retail sale, multiple (folded) or cabled yarn, of combed fibres, measuring per singleyarn less than 106.38 decitex but not less than 83.33 decitex (exceeding 94 metric number but not exceeding 120 metric number per single yarn)	棉纱线,按重量计含棉量在85%及以上,非供零售用,精梳纤维纺制的多股纱线或缆线,每根单纱细度在106.38分特以下,但不细于83.33分特(每根单纱超过94公支,但不超过120公支)	5205.4700	3468
Cotton yarn, containing 85% or more by weight of cotton, not put up for retail sale, multiple (folded) or cabled yarn, of combed fibres, measuring per singleyarn less than 232.56 decitex but not less than 192.31 decitex (exceeding 43 metric number but not exceeding 52 metric number per single yarn)	棉纱线,按重量计含棉量在85%及以上,非供零售用,精梳纤维纺制的多股纱线或缆线,每根单纱细度在232.56分特以下,但不细于192.31分特(每根单纱超过43公支,但不超过52公支)	5205.4300	3468
Cotton yarn, containing 85% or more by weight of cotton, not put up for retail sale, multiple (folded) or cabled yarn, of uncombed fibres, measuring per single yarn 714.29 decitex or more (not exceeding 14 metric number per single yarn)	棉纱线,按重量计含棉量在85%及以上,非供零售用,未精梳纤维纺制的多股纱线或缆线,每根单纱细度在714.29分特及以上(每根单纱不超过14公支)	5205.3100	3468
Cotton yarn, containing 85% or more by weight of cotton, not put up for retail sale, multiple (folded) or cabled yarn, of uncombed fibres, measuring per single yarn less than 125 decitex (exceeding 80metric number per single yarn)	棉纱线,按重量计含棉量在85%及以上,非供零售用,未精梳纤维纺制的多股纱线或缆线,每根单纱细度在125分特以下(每根单纱超过80公支)	5205.3500	3468
Cotton yarn, containing 85% or more by weight of cotton, not put up for retail sale, multiple (folded) or cabled yarn, of uncombed fibres, measuring per single yarn less than 192.31 decitex but not less than 125 decitex (exceeding 52 metric number but not exceeding 80 metric number per single yarn)	棉纱线,按重量计含棉量在85%及以上,非供零售用,未精梳纤维纺制的多股纱线或缆线,每根单纱细度在192.31分特以下,但不细于125分特(每根单纱超过52公支,但不超过80公支)	5205.3400	3468

C

C

Article Description	商品名称	Tariff Code	D. R.
Cotton yarn, containing 85% or more by weight of cotton, not put up for retail sale, multiple (folded) or cabled yarn, of uncombed fibres, measuring per single yarn less than 232.56 decitex but not less than 192.31 decitex (exceeding 43 metric number but not exceeding 52 metric number per single yarn)	棉纱线,按重量计含棉量在85%及以上,非供零售用,未精梳纤维纺制的多股纱线或缆线,每根单纱细度在232.56分特以下,但不细于192.31分特(每根单纱超过43公支,但不超过52公支)	5205.3300	3468
Cotton yarn, containing 85% or more by weight of cotton, not put up for retail sale, multiple (folded) or cabled yarn, of uncombed fibres, measuring per single yarn less than 714.29 decitex but not less than 232.56 decitex (exceeding 14 metric number but not exceeding 43 metric number per single yarn)	棉纱线,按重量计含棉量在85%及以上,非供零售用,未精梳纤维纺制的多股纱线或缆线,每根单纱细度在714.29分特以下,但不细于232.56分特(每根单纱超过14公支,但不超过43公支)	5205.3200	3468
Cotton yarn, containing 85% or more by weight of cotton, not put up for retail sale, single yarn, of combed fibres, measuring 714.29 decitex or more (not exceeding 14 metric number)	棉纱线,按重量计含棉量在85%及以上,非供零售用,精梳纤维纺制的单纱,细度在714.29分特及以上(不超过14公支)	5205.2100	3468
Cotton yarn, containing 85% or more by weight of cotton, not put up for retail sale, single yarn, of combed fibres, measuring less than 106.38 decitex but not less than 83.33 decitex (exceeding 94 metric number but not exceeding 120 metric number)	棉纱线,按重量计含棉量在85%及以上,非供零售用,精梳纤维纺制的单纱,细度在106.38分特以下,但不细于83.33分特(超过94公支,但不超过120公支)	5205.2700	3468
Cotton yarn, containing 85% or more by weight of cotton, not put up for retail sale, single yarn, of combed fibres, measuring less than 125 decitex but not less than 106.38 decitex (exceeding 80 metric number but not exceeding 94 metric number)	棉纱线,按重量计含棉量在85%及以上,非供零售用,精梳纤维纺制的单纱,细度在125分特以下,但不细于106.38分特(超过80公支,但不超过94公支)	5205.2600	3468
Cotton yarn, containing 85% or more by weight of cotton, not put up for retail sale, single yarn, of combed fibres, measuring less than 192.31 decitex but not less than 125 decitex (exceeding 52 metric number but not exceeding 80 metric number)	棉纱线,按重量计含棉量在85%及以上,非供零售用,精梳纤维纺制的单纱,细度在192.31分特以下,但不细于125分特(超过52公支,但不超过80公支)	5205.2400	3468
Cotton yarn, containing 85% or more by weight of cotton, not put up for retail sale, single yarn, of combed fibres, measuring less than 232.56 decitex but not less than 192.31 decitex (exceeding 43 metric number but not exceeding 52 metric number)	棉纱线,按重量计含棉量在85%及以上,非供零售用,精梳纤维纺制的单纱,细度在232.56分特以下,但不细于192.31分特(超过43公支,但不超过52公支)	5205.2300	3468
Cotton yarn, containing 85% or more by weight of cotton, not put up for retail sale, single yarn, of combed fibres, measuring less than 714.29 decitex but not less than 232.56 decitex (exceeding 14 metric number but not exceeding 43 metric number)	棉纱线,按重量计含棉量在85%及以上,非供零售用,精梳纤维纺制的单纱,细度在714.29分特以下,但不细于232.56分特(超过14公支,但不超过43公支)	5205.2200	3468

Article Description	商品名称	Tariff Code	D. R.
Cotton yarn, containing 85% or more by weight of cotton, not put up for retail sale, single yarn, of combed fibres, measuring less than 83.33 decitex (exceeding 120 metric number)	棉纱线,按重量计含棉量在85%及以上,非供零售用,精梳纤维纺制的单纱,细度在83.33分特以下(超过120公支)	5205.2800	3468
Cotton yarn, containing 85% or more by weight of cotton, not put up for retail sale, single yarn, of uncombed fibres, measuring 714.29 decitex or more (not exceeding 14 metric number)	棉纱线,按重量计含棉量在85%及以上,非供零售用,未精梳纤维纺制的单纱,细度在714.29分特及以上(不超过14公支)	5205.1100	3468
Cotton yarn, containing 85% or more by weight of cotton, not put up for retail sale, single yarn, of uncombed fibres, measuring less than 125 decitex (exceeding 80 metric number)	棉纱线,按重量计含棉量在85%及以上,非供零售用,未精梳纤维纺制的单纱,细度在125分特以下(超过80公支)	5205.1500	3468
Cotton yarn, containing 85% or more by weight of cotton, not put up for retail sale, single yarn, of uncombed fibres, measuring less than 192.31 decitex but not less than 125 decitex (exceeding 52 metric number but not exceeding 80 metric number)	棉纱线,按重量计含棉量在85%及以上,非供零售用,未精梳纤维纺制的单纱,细度在192.31分特以下,但不细于125分特(超过52公支,但不超过80公支)	5205.1400	3468
Cotton yarn, containing 85% or more by weight of cotton, not put up for retail sale, single yarn, of uncombed fibres, measuring less than 232.56 decitex but not less than 192.31 decitex (exceeding 43 metric number but not exceeding 52 metric number)	棉纱线,按重量计含棉量在85%及以上,非供零售用,未精梳纤维纺制的单纱,细度在232.56分特以下,但不细于192.31分特(超过43公支,但不超过52公支)	5205.1300	3468
Cotton yarn, containing 85% or more by weight of cotton, not put up for retail sale, single yarn, of uncombed fibres, measuring less than 714.29 decitex but not less than 232.56 decitex (exceeding 14 metric number but not exceeding 43 metric number)	棉纱线,按重量计含棉量在85%及以上,非供零售用,未精梳纤维纺制的单纱,细度在714.29分特以下,但不细于232.56分特(超过14公支,但不超过43公支)	5205.1200	3468
Cotton yarn, containing less than 85% by weight of cotton, not put up for retail sale, multiple (folded) or cabled yarn, of combed fibres, measuring per single yarn 714.29 decitex or more (not exceeding 14 metric number per single yarn)	棉纱线,按重量计含棉量在85%以下,非供零售用,精梳纤维纺制的多股纱线或缆线,每根单纱细度在714.29分特及以上(每根单纱不超过14公支)	5206.4100	3468
Cotton yarn, containing less than 85% by weight of cotton, not put up for retail sale, multiple (folded) or cabled yarn, of combed fibres, measuring per single yarn less than 125 decitex (exceeding 80 metric number per single yarn)	棉纱线,按重量计含棉量在85%以下,非供零售用,精梳纤维纺制的多股纱线或缆线,每根单纱细度在125分特以下(每根单纱超过80公支)	5206.4500	3468

Article Description	商品名称	Tariff Code	D. R.
Cotton yarn, containing less than 85% by weight of cotton, not put up for retail sale, multiple (folded) or cabled yarn, of combed fibres, measuring per single yarn less than 192. 31 decitex but not less than 125 decitex (exceeding 52 metric number but not exceeding 80 metric number per single yarn)	棉纱线,按重量计含棉量在85%以下,非供零售用,精梳纤维纺制的多股纱线或缆线,每根单纱细度在192. 31分特以下,但不细于125分特(每根单纱超过52公支,但不超过80公支)	5206. 4400	3468
Cotton yarn, containing less than 85% by weight of cotton, not put up for retail sale, multiple (folded) or cabled yarn, of combed fibres, measuring per single yarn less than 232. 56 decitex but not less then 192. 31 decitex (exceeding 43 metric number but not exceeding 52 metric number per single yarn)	棉纱线,按重量计含棉量在85%以下,非供零售用,精梳纤维纺制的多股纱线或缆线,每根单纱细度在232. 56分特以下,但不细于192. 31分特(每根单纱超过43公支,但不超过52公支)	5206. 4300	3468
Cotton yarn, containing less than 85% by weight of cotton, not put up for retail sale, multiple (folded) or cabled yarn, of combed fibres, measuring per single yarn less than 714. 29 deeitex but not less than 232. 56 decitex (exceeding 14 metric number but not exceeding 43 metric number per single yarn)	棉纱线,按重量计含棉量在85%以下,非供零售用,精梳纤维纺制的多股纱线或缆线,每根单纱细度在714. 29分特以下,但不细于232. 56分特(每根单纱超过14公支,但不超过43公支)	5206. 4200	3468
Cotton yarn, containing less than 85% by weight of cotton, not put up for retail sale, multiple (folded) or cabled yarn, of uncombed fibres, measuring per single yarn 714. 29 decitex or more (not exceeding 14 metric number per single yarn)	棉纱线,按重量计含棉量在85%以下,非供零售用,未精梳纤维纺制的多股纱线或缆线,每根单纱细度在714. 29分特及以上,(每根单纱不超过14公支)	5206. 3100	3468
Cotton yarn, containing less than 85% by weight of cotton, not put up for retail sale, multiple (folded) or cabled yarn, of uncombed fibres, measuring per single yarn less than 125 decitex (exceeding 80 metric number per single yarn)	棉纱线,按重量计含棉量在85%以下,非供零售用,未精梳纤维纺制的多股纱线或缆线,每根单纱细度在125分特以下(每根单纱超过80公支)	5206. 3500	3468
Cotton yarn, containing less than 85% by weight of cotton, not put up for retail sale, multiple (folded) or cabled yarn, of uncombed fibres, measuring per single yarn less than 192. 31 decitex but not less than 125 decitex (exceeding 52 metric number but not exceeding 80 metric number per single yarn)	棉纱线,按重量计含棉量在85%以下,非供零售用,未精梳纤维纺制的多股纱线或缆线,每根单纱细度在192. 31分特以下,但不细于125分特(每根单纱超过52公支,但不超过80公支)	5206. 3400	3468
Cotton yarn, containing less than 85% by weight of cotton, not put up for retail sale, multiple (folded) or cabled yarn, of uncombed fibres, measuring per single yarn less than 714. 29 decitex but not less than 232. 56 decitex (exceeding 14 metric number but not exceeding 43 metric number per single yarn)	棉纱线,按重量计含棉量在85%以下,非供零售用,未精梳纤维纺制的多股纱线或缆线,每根单纱细度在232. 56分特以下,但不细于192. 31分特(每根单纱超过43公支,但不超过52公支)	5206. 3300	3468

Article Description	商品名称	Tariff Code	D. R.
Cotton yarn, containing less than 85% by weight of cotton, not put up for retail sale, multiple (folded) or cabled yarn, of uncombed fibres, measuring per single yarn less than 714. 29 decitex but not less than 232. 56 decitex (exceeding 14 metric number but not exceeding 43 metric number per single yarn)	棉纱线,按重量计含棉量在85%以下,非供零售用,未精梳纤维纺制的多股纱线或缆线,每根单纱细度在714. 29分特以下,但不细于232. 56分特(每根单纱超过14公支,但不超过43公支)	5206. 3200	3468
Cotton yarn, containing less than 85% by weight of cotton, not put up for retail sale, single yarn, of combed fibres, measuring 714. 29 decitex or more (not exceeding 14 metric number)	棉纱线,按重量计含棉量在85%以下,非供零售用,精梳纤维纺制的单纱,细度在714. 29分特及以上(不超过14公支)	5206. 2100	3468
Cotton yarn, containing less than 85% by weight of cotton, not put up for retail sale, single yarn, of combed fibres, measuring less than 125 decitex (exceeding 80 metric number)	棉纱线,按重量计含棉量在85%以下,非供零售用,精梳纤维纺制的单纱,细度在125分特以下(超过80公支)	5206. 2500	3468
Cotton yarn, containing less than 85% by weight of cotton, not put up for retail sale, single yarn, of combed fibres, measuring less than 192. 31 decitex but not less than 125 decitex (exceeding 52 metric number but not exceeding 80 metric number)	棉纱线,按重量计含棉量在85%以下,非供零售用,精梳纤维纺制的单纱,细度在192. 31分特以下,但不细于125分特(超过52公支,但不超过80公支)	5206. 2400	3468
Cotton yarn, containing less than 85% by weight of cotton, not put up for retail sale, single yarn, of combed fibres, measuring less than 232. 56 decitex but not less than 192. 31 decitex (exceeding 43 metric number but not exceeding 52 metric number)	棉纱线,按重量计含棉量在85%以下,非供零售用,精梳纤维纺制的单纱,细度在232. 56分特以下,但不细于192. 31分特(超过43公支,但不超过52公支)	5206. 2300	3468
Cotton yarn, containing less than 85% by weight of cotton, not put up for retail sale, single yarn, of combed fibres, measuring less than 714. 29 decitex but not less than 232. 56 decitex (exceeding 14 metric number but not exceeding 43 metric number)	棉纱线,按重量计含棉量在85%以下,非供零售用,精梳纤维纺制的单纱,细度在714. 29分特以下,但不细于232. 56分特(超过14公支,但不超过43公支)	5206. 2200	3468
Cotton yarn, containing less than 85% by weight of cotton, not put up for retail sale, single yarn, of uncombed fibres, measuring 714. 29 decitex or more (not exceeding 14 metric number)	棉纱线,按重量计含棉量在85%以下,非供零售用,未精梳纤维纺制的单纱,细度在714. 29分特及以上(不超过14公支)	5206. 1100	3468
Cotton yarn, containing less than 85% by weight of cotton, not put up for retail sale, single yarn, of uncombed fibres, measuring less than 125 decitex (exceeding 80 metric number)	棉纱线,按重量计含棉量在85%以下,非供零售用,未精梳纤维纺制的单纱,细度在125分特以下(超过80公支)	5206. 1500	3468

C

Article Description	商品名称	Tariff Code	D. R.
Cotton yarn, containing less than 85% by weight of cotton, not put up for retail sale, single yarn, of uncombed fibres, measuring less than 192.31 decitex but not less than 125 decitex (exceeding 52 metric number but not exceeding 80 metric number)	棉纱线,按重量计含棉量在85%以下,非供零售用,未精梳纤维纺制的单纱,细度在192.31分特以下,但不细于125分特(超过52公支,但不超过80公支)	5206.1400	3468
Cotton yarn, containing less than 85% by weight of cotton, not put up for retail sale, single yarn, of uncombed fibres, measuring less than 232.56 decitex but not less than 192.31 decitex (exceeding 43 metric number but not exceeding 52 metric number)	棉纱线,按重量计含棉量在85%以下,非供零售用,未精梳纤维纺制的单纱,细度在232.56分特以下,但不细于192.31分特(超过43公支,但不超过52公支)	5206.1300	3468
Cotton yarn, containing less than 85% by weight of cotton, not put up for retail sale, single yarn, of uncombed fibres, measuring less than 714.29 decitex but not less than 232.56 decitex (exceeding 14 metric number but not exceeding 43 metric number)	棉纱线,按重量计含棉量在85%以下,非供零售用,未精梳纤维纺制的单纱,细度在714.29分特以下,但不细于232.56分特(超过14公支,但不超过43公支)	5206.1200	3468
Cotton yarn, put up for retail sale, containing 85% or more by weight of cotton	棉纱线,供零售用,按重量计含棉量在85%及以上	5207.1000	36
Cotton yarn, put up for retail sale, nes	棉纱线,供零售用,其他	5207.9000	36
Cotton, carded or combed	棉花,已梳的	5203.0000	48
Cotton, not carded or combed	棉花,未梳的	5201.0000	48
Cottonseed oil and fractions thereof, crued, whether or not gossypol has been removed	棉子油及其分离品,初榨的,不论是否去除棉子酚	1512.2100	4
Cottonseed oil and its fractions, nes	棉子油及其分离品,其他	1512.2900	4
Coumarin	香豆素	2932.2100	36
Coumarone, in primary forms	苯并呋喃树脂,初级形状的	3911.1000	16
Coumarone-indene resins and polyterpenes, in primary forms	苯并呋喃一茚树脂,初级形状的	3911.1000	16
Coupling agent between the body and medical instruments	偶合剂,躯体和医疗器械之间用的	3006.7000	36
Coupling devices and parts, of railway or tramway locomotives or rolling-stock	联结器及其零件,铁道及电车道机车或其他车辆的	8607.3000	3
Couscous	古斯古斯面食	1902.4000	46
Covellite	靛铜矿	2603.0000	146
Cover of seat, of leather or of composition leather	坐具套,皮革或再生皮革的	4205.0010	456
Cowls, ceramic	通风帽,陶瓷制	6905.9000	5
Co-axial cable	同轴电缆	8544.2000	35
Co-axial electric conductors, nes	同轴电导体,其他	8544.2000	35
Crab, prepared or preserved	蟹,制作或保藏的	1605.1000	48
Crabs, for cultivation	蟹种苗	0306.2410	3
Crabs, nes, frozen	蟹,其他,冻的	0306.1490	1

Article Description	商品名称	Tariff Code	D. R.
Crabs, nes, not frozen	蟹,其他,未冻的	0306. 2499	14
Cranberries, fresh	蔓越桔,鲜的	0810. 4000	1
Crane lorries of all-road, of a maxium lifting capacity exceeding 100 tons	起重车,全路面,最大起重重量超过100吨	8705. 1023	7
Crane lorries of all-road, of a maxium lifting capacity exceeding 50 tons but not exceeding 100 tons	起重车,全路面,最大起重重量超过50吨,但不超过100吨	8705. 1022	7
Crane lorries of all-road, of maxium lifting capacity not more than 50 tons	起重车,全路面,最大起重重量不超过50吨	8705. 1021	7
Crane lorries, of a maxium lifting capacity exceeding 100 tons, nes	起重车,最大起重重量超过100吨,其他	8705. 1093	7
Crane lorries, of a maxium lifting capacity exceeding 50 tons but not exceeding 100 tons, nes	起重车,最大起重重量超过50吨,但不超过100吨,其他	8705. 1092	7
Crane lorries, of maxium lifting capacity not more than 50 tons, nes	起重车,最大起重重量不超过50吨,其他	8705. 1091	7
Cranes on fixed support, overhead travelling, nes	起重机,固定支架的高架移动式,其他	8426. 1190	7
Cranes parts	起重机零件	8431. 4990	3
Cranes, bridge cranes, all-purpose	起重机,通用型,桥式	8426. 1120	7
Cranes, crawler cranes	起重机,履带式	8426. 4910	7
Cranes, designed for mounting on road vehicles	起重机,供装于公路车辆的	8426. 9100	7
Cranes, for railway or tramway maintenance or service	起重机车,铁道及电车道用	8604. 0099	37
Cranes, gantry cranes	起重机,龙门式	8426. 1930	7
Cranes, nes	起重机,其他	8426. 9900	7
Cranes, pedestal jib cranes	起重机,座式旋臂的	8426. 3000	7
Cranes, portal cranes	起重机,门座式	8426. 3000	7
Cranes, self-propelled, nes	起重机,自推进的,其他	8426. 4990	7
Cranes, self-propelled, on tyres, nes	起重机,自推进的,带胶轮的,其他	8426. 4190	7
Cranes, self-propelled, wheel mounted	起重机,自推进的,轮胎式	8426. 4110	7
Cranes, tower cranes	起重机,塔式	8426. 2000	7
Cranes, transporter cranes	起重机,桁架桥式	8426. 1990	7
Crank shafts of diesel engine, for ships	柴油机曲轴,船舶用	8483. 1010	
Cranks	曲柄	8483. 1090	
Cranks parts	曲柄零件	8483. 9000	3
Crank-gear and parts thereof, of bicycles and other cycles	曲柄链轮及其零件,自行车及脚踏车的	8714. 9620	3
Crates packings, of wood	包装板条箱,木制的	4415. 1000	56
Crawler cranes	履带式起重机	8426. 4910	7
Crayons	油画棒	9609. 1020	
Cream separators, centrifuges	奶油分离器,离心式	8421. 1100	7
Cream, curdled	奶油,凝固的	0403. 9000	248
Cream, fermented or acidified, nes	奶油,发酵或酸化的,其他	0403. 9000	248

C

Article Description	商品名称	Tariff Code	D. R.
Cream, in powder, granules or other solid forms, of a fat content, by weight, exceeding 1.5%, containing added sugar or other sweetening matter	奶油,粉状、粒状或其他固体形状,按重量计脂肪含量超过1.5%,加糖或其他甜物质	0402.2900	12468
Cream, in powder, granules or other solid forms, of a fat content, by weight, exceeding 1.5%, not containing added sugar or other sweetening matter	奶油,粉状、粒状或其他固体形状,按重量计脂肪含量超过1.5%,未加糖或其他甜物质	0402.2100	12468
Cream, in powder, granules or other solid forms, of a fat content, by weight, not exceeding 1.5%	奶油,粉状、粒状或其他固体形状,按重量计脂肪含量不超过1.5%	0402.1000	12468
Cream, not in solid forms, containing added sugar or other sweetening matter	奶油,非固体形状,加糖或其他甜物质	0402.9900	12468
Cream, not in solid forms, not containing added sugar or other sweetening matter	奶油,非固体形状,未加糖或其他甜物质	0402.9100	12468
Cream, of a fat content, by weight, exceeding 1% but not exceeding 6%, not concentrated nor containing added sugar or other sweetening matter	奶油,按重量计脂肪含量超过1%,但不超过6%,未浓缩及未加糖或其他甜物质的	0401.2000	12468
Cream, of a fat content, by weight, exceeding 6%, not concentrated nor containing added sugar or other sweetening matter	奶油,按重量计脂肪含量超过6%,未浓缩及未加糖或其他甜物质的	0401.3000	12468
Cream, of a fat content, by weight, not exceeding 1%, not concentrated nor containing added sugar or other sweetening matter	奶油,按重量计脂肪含量不超过1%,未浓缩及未加糖或其他甜物质的	0401.1000	12468
Creosote oils	杂酚油	2707.9100	6
Cresol salts	甲酚的盐	2907.1290	36
Cresol, nes	甲酚,其他	2907.1219	36
Crimping machinery auxiliary, for man-made filaments	变形机的辅助机器,化学纤维的	8448.1900	3
Crimping machinery for man-made filaments	变形机,化学纤维的	8444.0040	
Crispbread	面包片,脆的	1905.1000	28
Crochet hooks, for use in the hand, of iron or steel	钩针,钢铁制的,手工用	7319.9000	
Crocidolite	青石棉	2524.1000	148
Crocidolite articles of mixtures with a basis of crocidolite or with a basis of crocidolite and magnesium carbonate	青石棉制品,以青石棉为基本成分或以青石棉和碳酸镁混合物为基本成分的	6812.8000	56
Crocidolite fibres, fabricated	青石棉纤维,已加工的	6812.8000	56
Crocidolite mixtures with a basis of crocidoliteor with a basis of crocidolite and magnesium carbonate	青石棉为基本成分或以石棉和碳酸镁为基本成分的混合物	6812.8000	56
Crocodiles for cultivation, pure-bred breeding	鳄鱼苗	0106.2011	3
Crocus bulbs, seed, dormant	藏红花,种用,休眠的	0601.1091	135
Cross-country cars (4WD), of a cylinder capacity exceeding 1000cc but not exceeding 1500cc, with compression-ignition internal combustion piston engine	越野车(4轮驱动),气缸容量(排气量)超过1000毫升,但不超过1500毫升,装有压燃式活塞内燃发动机的	8703.3122	58

Article Description	商品名称	Tariff Code	D. R.
Cross-country cars (4WD), of a cylinder capacity exceeding 1500cc but not exceeding 2000cc, with spark-ignition internal combustion reciprocating piston	越野车(4 轮驱动),气缸容量(排气量)超过 1500 毫升,但不超过 2000 毫升,装有点燃往复式活塞内燃发动机的	8703. 2342	58
Cross-country cars (4WD), of a cylinder capacity exceeding 2000cc but not exceeding 2500cc, with spark-ignition internal combustion reciprocating piston	越野车(4 轮驱动),气缸容量(排气量)超过 2000 毫升,但不超过 2500 毫升,装有点燃往复式活塞内燃发动机的	8703. 2352	58
Cross-country cars (4WD), of a cylinder capacity exceeding 2500cc but not exceeding 3000cc, with spark-ignition internal combustion reciprocating piston	越野车(4 轮驱动),气缸容量(排气量)超过 2500 毫升,但不超过 3000 毫升,装有点燃往复式活塞内燃发动机的	8703. 2362	58
Cross-country cars(4wd) parts and accessories, nes	越野车(4 轮驱动)用零件、附件,其他	8708. 9959	3
Cross-country cars (4WD), of a cylinder capacity exceeding 1000cc but not exceeding 1500cc, with spark-ignition internal combustion reciprocating piston	越野车(4 轮驱动),气缸容量(排气量)超过 1000 毫升,但不超过 1500 毫升,装有点燃往复式活塞内燃发动机的	8703. 2240	58
Cross-country cars (4WD), of a cylinder capacity exceeding 1500cc but not exceeding 2000cc, with compression-ignition internal combustion piston engine	越野车(4 轮驱动),气缸容量(排气量)超过 1500 毫升,但不超过 2000 毫升,装有压燃式活塞内燃发动机的	8703. 3212	58
Cross-country cars (4WD), of a cylinder capacity exceeding 2000cc but not exceeding 2500cc, with compression-ignition internal combustion piston engine	越野车(4 轮驱动),气缸容量(排气量)超过 2000 毫升,但不超过 2500 毫升,装有压燃式活塞内燃发动机的	8703. 3222	58
Cross-country cars (4WD), of a cylinder capacity exceeding 2500cc, but not exceeding 3000cc, with compression-ignition internal combustion piston engine	越野车(4 轮驱动),气缸容量(排气量)超过 2500 毫升,但不超过 3000 毫升,装有压燃式活塞内燃发动机的	8703. 3312	58
Cross-country cars (4WD), of a cylinder capacity exceeding 3000cc, but not exceeding 4000cc, with compression-ignition internal combustion piston engine	越野车(4 轮驱动),气缸容量(排气量)超过 3000 毫升,但不超过 4000 毫升,装有压燃式活塞内燃发动机的	8703. 3322	58
Cross-country cars (4WD), of a cylinder capacity exceeding 3000cc, but not exceeding 4000cc, with spark-ignition internal combustion reciprocating piston	越野车(4 轮驱动),气缸容量(排气量)超过 3000 毫升,但不超过 4000 毫升,装有点燃往复式活塞内燃发动机的	8703. 2412	58
Cross-country cars (4WD), of a cylinder capacity exceeding 4000cc, with compression-ignition internal combustion piston engine	越野车(4 轮驱动),气缸容量(排气量)超过 4000 毫升,装有压燃式活塞内燃发动机的	8703. 3362	58
Cross-country cars (4WD), of a cylinder capacity exceeding 4000cc, with spark-ignition internal combustion reciprocating piston	越野车(4 轮驱动),气缸容量(排气量)超过 4000 毫升,装有点燃往复式活塞内燃发动机的	8703. 2422	58

Article Description	商品名称	Tariff Code	D. R.
Cross-country cars(4WD), of a cylinder capacity not exceeding 1000cc, with spark-ignition internal combustion reciprocating piston engine	越野车(4 轮驱动),气缸容量(排气量)不超过 1000 毫升,装有点燃往复式活塞内燃发动机的	8703. 2140	58
Cross-country ski footwear, with outer soles and uppers of rubber or plastics	越野滑雪鞋靴及滑雪板靴,橡胶或塑料制外底及鞋面的	6402. 1200	26
Cross-country ski footwear, with outer soles of rubber, plastics, leather or composition leather and upers of leather	越野滑雪鞋靴,橡胶、塑料、皮革或再生皮革制外底,皮革制鞋面的	6403. 1200	26
Cross-talk meters, specially designed for telecommunications	串音测试器,通讯专用的	9030. 4090	7
Crotchet hooks for knitting machines, smaler than gauge No. 28	钩针,针织机用 28 号以下的	8448. 5120	3
Crown corks, of base metal	冠形瓶塞,贱金属制	8309. 1000	256
Crowns, in growth or in flower	根茎,生长或开花的	0601. 2000	11
Crowns, nes, dormant	根茎,其他,休眠的	0601. 1099	135
Crowns, seed, dormant	根茎,种用,休眠的	0601. 1091	135
Crucibles, containing by weight more than 50% of alumina(Ai_2O_3) or of a mixture of compound of alumina and of silica(SiO_2)	坩埚,含有按重量计超过 50% 的三氧化二铝或三氧化二铝和二氧化硅的混合物或化合物	6903. 2000	6
Crucibles, containing by weight more than 50% of graphite or other carbon or of a mixture of these products	坩埚,含有按重量计超过 50% 的石墨、其他碳或其混合物	6903. 1000	6
Crude antimony	生锑	2617. 1010	146
Crude dipentene	粗制二聚戊烯	3805. 9090	36
Crude natural potassium salts, nes	天然粗钾盐,其他	3104. 9010	68
Crude oil tanker ships, loading exceeding 150000t, but not exceeding 300000t	原油船,载重量超过 15 万吨,但不超过 30 万吨	8901. 2022	8
Crude oil tanker ships, loading exceeding 300000t	原油船,载重量超过 30 万吨	8901. 2023	8
Crude oil tanker ships, loading not exceeding 150000t	原油船,载重量不超过 15 万吨	8901. 2021	8
Crude oils obtained from bituminous minerals	原油,从沥青矿物提取的	2709. 0000	56
Cruise ships, motor vessels	巡航船,机动船舶	8901. 1010	5
Cruise ships, not motorized vessels	巡航船,非机动船舶	8901. 1090	5
Crushing machinery, used in the manufacture of wine, cider, fruit juices or similar beverages	轧碎机,制酒、制果汁或制类似饮料用	8435. 1000	
Crushing machines, for earth, stone, ores or other mineral substances, nes	破碎机器,泥土、石料、矿石或其他固体矿物质的,其他	8474. 2090	7
Crushing machines, em-peters type, for earth, stone, ores or other mineral substances	破碎机器,球磨式,泥土、石料、矿石或其他固体矿物质的	8474. 2020	7
Crushing machines, nes	轧碎机,其他	8479. 8200	7
Crushing machines, toothing roller type, for earth, stone, ores or other mineral substances	破碎机器,齿辊式,泥土、石料、矿石或其他固体矿物质的	8474. 2010	7
Crustaceans, nes, fit for human consumption, for cultivation	种苗,其他,适合供人食用的甲壳动物的	0306. 2910	3

Article Description	商品名称	Tariff Code	D. R.
Crustaceans, nes, frozen	甲壳动物,其他,冻的	0306. 1990	1
Crustaceans, nes, not frozen	甲壳动物,其他,未冻的	0306. 2990	14
Crustaceans, nes, prepared or preserved	甲壳动物,其他,制作或保藏的	1605. 4090	48
Crystallizers, for ingot continuous casting machines	结晶器,钢坯连铸机用	8454. 9021	3
CTP plate, unexposed	CTP 版,未曝光的	3701. 3023	12368
CTP plates preparing machines	计算机直接制版设备	8442. 3021	
Cucumbers, fresh or chilled	黄瓜,鲜或冷藏的	0707. 0000	1
Cucumbers, prepared or preserved by vinegar or acetic acid	黄瓜,用醋或醋酸保存或制作的	2001. 1000	48
Cucumbers, provisionally preserved, but unsuitable in that state for immediate consumption	黄瓜,暂时保藏,但不适合直接使用的	0711. 4000	34
Cuff-links, imitation jewellery, of base metal, whether or not plated with precious metal	袖扣、仿首饰,贱金属制,不论是否镀贵金属	7117. 1100	46
Cullet	玻璃,碎的	7001. 0000	13
Cullet	碎玻璃	7001. 0000	13
Cultivators, for agricultural, horticultural or forestry use, nes	中耕机,农业、园艺及林业用,其他	8432. 2900	
Culture media, prepared for the development or maintenance of micro-organisms (including viruses and the like) or of plant, human or animal cells	培养基,制成的供微生物(包括病毒及类似品)或植物、人体、动物细胞生长或维持用的	3821. 0000	36
Culture yeast	培养酵母	2102. 1000	28
Cultures of micro-organisms (excluding yeasts) and similar products	培养微生物(不包括酵母)及类似产品	3002. 9090	34
Cumene	异丙基苯	2902. 7000	6
Cuprite	赤铜矿	2603. 0000	146
Cupronickel	白铜	7403. 2900	146
Curbstones, of natural stone (except slate)	路缘石,天然石料(不包括板岩)制的	6801. 0000	46
Curd	凝乳	0406. 1000	24
Curling grips	卷发器	9615. 9000	
Curling tong heaters, electro-thermic	热发钳,电热的	8516. 3300	7
Currants, black, white or red, fresh	醋栗,黑、白或红的,鲜的	0810. 9020	1
Currants, black, white or red, fresh	加仑子,黑、白或红的,鲜的	0810. 9020	1
Currants, black, white or red, frozen	醋栗,黑、白或红的,冷冻的	0811. 2000	1
Currants, black, white or red, frozen	加仑子,黑、白或红的,冷冻的	0811. 2000	1
Curry	咖喱	0910. 9900	6
Curtains, crocheted, of cotton	窗帘,钩编的,棉制	6303. 1932	346
Curtains, crocheted, of other textile materials	窗帘,钩编的,其他纺织材料制	6303. 1992	346
Curtains, crocheted, of synthetic fibres	窗帘,钩编的,合成纤维制	6303. 1220	346
Curtains, knitted, of cotton	窗帘,针织的,棉制	6303. 1931	346
Curtains, knitted, of other textile materials	窗帘,针织的,其他纺织材料制	6303. 1991	346
Curtains, knitted, of synthetic fibres	窗帘,针织的,合成纤维制	6303. 1210	346
Curtains, of cotton, nes	窗帘,棉制,其他	6303. 9100	346

C

C

Article Description	商品名称	Tariff Code	D. R.
Curtains, of other textile materials	窗帘,其他纺织材料制	6303.9900	346
Curtains, of synthetic fibres, nes	窗帘,合成纤维制,其他	6303.9200	346
Cushions, nes	靠垫,其他	9404.9090	6
Cushions, stuffed with animal hair	靠垫,兽毛填充的	9404.9020	6
Cushions, stuffed with feathers or down	靠垫,羽毛或羽绒填充的	9404.9010	6
Cushions, stuffed with man-made fibres	靠垫,化纤棉填充的	9404.9040	6
Cushions, stuffed with silk wadding	靠垫,丝棉填充的	9404.9030	6
Cut flowers and flower buds, fresh, suitable for bouquets or for ornamental purposes, nes	插花及花蕾,鲜的,制花束或装饰用的,其他	0603.1990	34
Cut flowers and flower buds, nes, suitable for bouquets or for ornamental purposes	插花及花蕾,其他,制花束或装饰用的	0603.9000	34
Cut of fowls of the species gallus domesticus, nes, fresh or chilled	鸡块,其他,鲜或冷的	0207.1319	1
Cut of fowls of the species gallus domesticus, nes, frozen	鸡块,其他,冻的	0207.1419	1
Cut of fowls of the species gallus domesticus, with bone, fresh or chilled	鸡块,带骨的,鲜或冷的	0207.1311	1
Cut of fowls of the species gallus domesticus, with bone, frozen	鸡块,带骨的,冻的	0207.1411	1
Cutlasses and parts	短弯刀及其零件	9307.0000	
Cutlery articles, nes	利口器,其他	8214.9000	256
Cutouts, for electrical ignition or starting equipment	断流器,点燃式或压燃式内燃发动机用的	8511.8000	7
Cuts of ducks, fresh or chilled	鸭块,鲜或冷的	0207.3510	1
Cuts of ducks, frozen	鸭块,冻的	0207.3610	1
Cuts of geese, fresh or chilled	鹅块,鲜或冷的	0207.3520	1
Cuts of geese, frozen	鹅块,冻的	0207.3620	1
Cuts of guinea fowls, fresh or chilled	珍珠鸡块,鲜或冷的	0207.3530	1
Cuts of guinea fowls, frozen	珍珠鸡块,冻的	0207.3630	1
Cuts of swine, with bone in, salted, in brine, dried or smoked	肉块,猪的,带骨的,干、熏、盐腌或盐渍的	0210.1190	14
Cuts of turkeys, fresh or chilled	火鸡块,鲜或冷的	0207.2600	1
Cuts of turkeys, frozen	火鸡块,冻的	0207.2700	1
Cuts, with bone in, of swine, fresh or chilled	猪肉块,鲜或冷的,带骨	0203.1200	14
Cuts, with bone in, of swine, frozen	猪肉块,冻的,带骨	0203.2200	14
Cutting machinery auxiliary, for man-made filaments	切断机的辅助机器,化学纤维的	8448.1900	3
Cutting machinery, for man-made filaments	切断机,化学纤维的	8444.0050	
Cutting machines for making up paper pulp, paper or paperboard	切纸机	8441.1000	
Cutting machines for textile fabrics	剪切机器,纺织物的	8451.5000	
Cutting machines of plasma arc	等离子切割机	8456.9010	7
Cutting machines parts	切纸机用零件	8441.9010	

Article Description	商品名称	Tariff Code	D. R.
Cutting machines parts for textile fabrics	剪切机器零件,纺织物的	8451.9000	
Cutting pliers and similar tools	剪钳及类似工具	8203.2000	256
Cutting-off machines, for cold-working glass or glassware	切割机,玻璃冷加工用	8464.9011	7
Cutting-off machines, for removing metal or cermets	切断机,切削金属或金属陶瓷用	8461.5000	7
Cutting-oil preparations, based on lubricants, containing petroleum oils or oils obtained from bituminous minerals	切削油制剂,以润滑剂为基本成分的,含有石油或从沥青矿物提取的油类	3403.1900	2368
Cutting-oil preparations, based on lubricants, nes	切削油制剂,以润滑剂为基本成分的,其他	3403.9900	2368
Cuttle fish bone powder	墨鱼骨粉	0508.0010	14
Cuttle fish meal, fit for human consumption	墨鱼粉,食用	0307.9990	14
Cuttle fish (Sepia of ficinalis, Rossia macrosoma, Sepiola spp.), for cultivation	墨鱼,种苗	0307.4110	3
Cuttle fish (Sepia of ficinalis, Rossia macrosoma, Sepiola spp.), frozen, dried, salted or in brine	墨鱼,其他,冻、干、盐腌或盐渍的	0307.4900	148
Cuttle fish (Sepia of ficinalis, Rossia macrosoma, Sepiola spp.), live, fresh or chilled	墨鱼,其他,活、鲜或冷的	0307.4190	18
Cuttle fish, prepared	墨鱼,制作的	1605.9090	48
Cuttlebone	墨鱼骨	0508.0090	14
Cut-backs, based on asphalt or bitumen	稀释沥青,以沥青为基本成分的	2715.0000	1346
Cyanates	氰酸盐	2842.9010	
Cyanides and cyanide oxides, nes, inorganic	氰化物及氧氰化物,其他,无机的	2837.1990	6
Cyanuric chloride	三聚氰氯	2933.6910	36
Cyclamen, seed, dormant	仙客来,种用,休眠的	0601.1091	135
Cyclanes, cyclenes and cycloterpenes, nes	环烷烃、环烯及环萜烯,其他	2902.1990	6
Cyclanic ketones, without other oxygen function, nes	环烷酮,不含其他含氧基的,其他	2914.2900	36
Cyclanic, cyclenic or cycloterpenic alcohols, nes	环烷醇、环烯醇及环萜烯醇,其他	2906.1990	36
Cyclanic, cyclenic or cycloterpenic ethers and their halogenated, sulphonated, nitrated or nitrosated derivatives, nes	环烷醚、环烯醚或环萜烯醚及其卤化、磺化、硝化或亚硝化衍生物,其他	2909.2090	36
Cyclanic, cyclenic or cycloterpenic monocarboxylic acids, their anhydrides, halides, peroxides, peroxyacids and their derivatives, nes	环烷一元羧酸、环烯一元羧酸或环萜烯一元羧酸及其酸酐、酰卤化物、过氧化物和过氧酸以及它们的衍生物,其他	2916.2090	36
Cyclanic, cyclenic or cycloterpenic monoor polyamines, and their derivatives; salts thereof	环烷单胺或多胺、环烯单胺或多胺、环萜烯单胺或多胺及其衍生物以及它们的盐	2921.3000	36
Cyclanic, eyclenic or cycloterpenic polycarboxylic acids, their anhydrides, halides, peroxides, peroxyacids and their derivatives, nes	环烷多元羧酸、环烯多元羧酸、环萜烯多元羧酸及其酸酐、酰卤化物、过氧化物和过氧酸以及它们的衍生物,其他	2917.2090	36

C

C

Article Description	商品名称	Tariff Code	D. R.
Cyclenic ketones without other oxygen function, nes	环烯酮,不含其他含氧基的,其他	2914. 2900	36
Cycles, not motorized	脚踏车,非机动	8712. 0090	8
Cyclic alcohols, aromatic	芳香醇	2906. 2990	36
Cyclic aldehydes without other oxygen function, nes	环醛,不含其他含氧基的,其他	2912. 2990	36
Cyclic amides (including cyclic carbamates) and their derivatives; salts thereof, nes	环酰胺(包括环氨基甲酸酯)及其衍生物以及它们的盐,其他	2924. 2990	36
Cyclic hydrocarbons, nes	环烃,其他	2902. 9090	6
Cyclic polymers of aldehydes	环聚醛	2912. 5000	36
Cyclobarbital (INN); salts thereof	环已巴比妥(INN)以及盐	2933. 5300	36
Cyclohexane	环已烷	2902. 1100	6
Cyclohexanol	环已醇	2906. 1200	36
Cyclohexanone	环已酮	2914. 2200	36
Cyclone dust collectors for industry uses	旋风式除尘器	8421. 3923	7
Cycloterpenic ethers, nes	环萜烯醚,其他	2909. 2089	36
Cycloterpenic ketones without other oxygen function, nes	环萜烯酮,不含其他含氧基的,其他	2914. 2900	36
Cylinder screen press	圆网印刷机	8443. 1921	57
Cylinders for calendering machines	滚筒,研光机用	8420. 9100	3
Cylinders for printing machinery	印刷滚筒	8442. 5000	
Cylinders for rolling machines	滚筒,滚压机用	8420. 9100	3
Cylinders making machinery parts	滚筒制造机器零件	8442. 4000	3
Cylinders preparing or making machinery, nes	滚筒的制造机器、器具及设备,其他	8442. 3090	
Cylindrical grinding machines, in which the positioning in any one axis can be set up to an accuracy of at least 0. 01mm, for metal or cermets, nes	外圆磨床,在任一坐标的定位精度至少是0. 01 毫米,加工金属或金属陶瓷用,其他	8460. 2910	7
Cylindrical grinding machines, in which the positioning in any one axis can be set up to an accuracy of at least 0. 01mm, numerically controlled, for metal or cermets	外圆磨床,在任一坐标的定位精度至少是0. 01 毫米,数控的,加工金属或金属陶瓷用	8460. 2110	7
Cylindrical roller bearings, nes	圆柱形滚子轴承,其他	8482. 5000	5
Cylindrical shape primary cells and primary batteries, alkaline zinc-manganese dioxide	原电池及原电池组,碱性锌锰的,圆柱型	8506. 1012	68
Cylindrical shape primary cells and primary batteries, alkaline zinc-manganese dioxide	圆柱型原电池及原电池组,碱性锌锰的	8506. 1012	68
Cymbals	铙钹	9206. 0000	5
Cystine	胱氨酸	2930. 9010	36
Cystine	双巯丙氨酸	2930. 9010	36
Cytosine	胞嘧啶	2933. 5910	36

D

Article Description	商品名称	Tariff Code	D. R.
Dahlia, seed, dormant	大丽花,种用,休眠的	0601.1091	135
Dairy machinery	乳品加工机器	8434.2000	
Dairy machinery parts	乳品加工机器零件	8434.9000	3
Dairy spreads	乳酱	0405.2000	268
Danube salmon (hucho hucho), fresh or chilled	多瑙哲罗鱼,鲜或冷的	0302.1220	18
Danube salmon, frozen	多瑙哲罗鱼,冻的	0303.2220	18
Dasheens	芋头	0714.9030	34
Data recording, reproducing and displaying machines with calculating functions, pocket-size	数据记录、重现及显示机器,具有计算功能的,袖珍式	8470.1000	
Data/graphic display tubes, black and white or other monochrome	数据/图形显示管,黑白的或其他单色的	8540.5000	35
Data/graphic display tubes, colour, with a phosphor dot screen pitch smaller than 0.4mm	数据/图形显示管,彩色的,屏幕荧光点间距小于0.4毫米	8540.4000	35
Date stamps, designed for operating in the hand	日期戳,手用	9611.0000	
Dates	椰枣	0804.1000	14
Day lily flowers, dried	黄花菜,干的	0712.9030	4
Day lily flowers, dried	金针菜,干的	0712.9030	4
DC voltage-stabilized suppliers, of a power of less than 1kW and an accuracy of not better than 0.0001, nes	直流稳压电源,功率小于1千瓦,精度低于万分之一,其他	8504.4014	78
DDT (ISO, INN)	滴滴涕(ISO, INN)	2903.6200	36
Decahydronaphthalene	萘烷	2902.1990	6
Deck-arrestor or similar gear and parts thereof	甲板停机装置或类似装置及其零件	8805.1000	3
Decoy birds and similar hunting or shooting requisites	捕鸟用品及类似的狩猎用品	9507.9000	5
Decoy calls	媒诱音响器	9208.9000	5
Deep groove ball bearings	深沟球轴承	8482.1020	5
Defrosters for motor vehicles	除霜器,机动车辆用	8512.4000	7
Degras	油鞣回收脂	1522.0000	4
Dehumidifiers for air	减湿器,空气的	8479.8920	7
Dehumidifiers parts, for air	减湿器用零件,空气的	8479.9020	3
Dehydrocortisone	脱氢可的松	2937.2100	36
Dehydrohydrocortisone	脱氢皮质醇	2937.2100	36
Delorazepam (INN); salts thereof	地洛西泮(INN)以及盐	2933.9100	36
Demisters, for motor vehicles	去雾器,机动车辆用	8512.4000	7
Denim (woven fabrics of cotton, containing 85% or more by weight of cotton, weighing more than 200g/m², of yarns of different colours)	劳动布(棉机织物,按重量计含棉量在85%及以上,每平方米重量超过200克,色织)	5209.4200	468

D

Article Description	商品名称	Tariff Code	D. R.
Denim(woven fabrics of cotton, containing less than 85% by weight of cotton, mixed mainly or solely with man-made fibres, weighing more than $200g/m^2$, of yarns of different colours)	劳动布(棉机织物,按重量计含棉量在85%以下,主要或仅与化学纤维混纺,每平方米重量超过200克,色织,粗斜纹布)	5211.4200	468
Densified wood, in blocks, plates, strips or profile shapes	强化木,成块、板、条或异型的	4413.0000	14
Dental cements	牙科粘固剂	3006.4000	36
Dental drill engines, whether or not combined on a single base with other dental equipment	牙钻机,不论是否与其他牙科设备组装在同一底座上	9018.4100	
Dental fillings	牙科填料, 其他	3006.4000	36
Dental fittings	牙齿固定件	9021.2900	3
Dental floss, in individual retail package	牙线,单独零售包装的	3306.2000	23
Dental impression compounds	牙科用造型膏	3407.0010	13
Dental instruments and appliances, nes	牙科用仪器及器具,其他	9018.9090	7
Dental sciences instruments and appliances, nes	牙科用其他仪器及器具,其他	9018.4990	7
Dental wax	牙科用蜡	3407.0010	13
Dental yarns, for surgical sterile, absorbable	缝线,无菌,可吸收的	3006.1000	3
Dentifrices, nes	洁齿品,其他	3306.1090	23
Dentistry preparations, with a basis of plaster	牙科用制品,以熟石膏为基本成分的	3407.0020	13
Dentists chairs and parts thereof	牙科用椅及其零件	9402.1090	3
Dentists chairs incorporating dental equipment	牙科用椅,装有牙科设备的	9018.4910	
Denture fixative pastes and powders	假牙模膏及粉	3306.9000	23
Deodorants, for personal use	除臭剂,人体用	3307.2000	23
Depilatories	脱毛剂	3307.9000	23
Derivatives containing only nitro or nitroso groups, their salts and ethyl esters	仅含硝基或亚硝基的衍生物	2904.2090	36
Derivatives containing only sulpho groups, their salts and ethyl esters	仅含磺基的衍生物及其盐和乙酯	2904.1000	36
Derivatives perhalogenated only with fluorine and chloirine, nes	仅含氟和氯的全卤化衍生物,其他	2903.4599	36
Derrick loading and unloading bridges, nes	动臂式装卸桥,其他	8426.1943	7
Derris roots	鱼藤根	1211.9091	34
Descloizite	钒铅锌矿	2615.9090	146
Detergents in powder form, synthetic	洗涤粉,合成的	3402.2010	36
Detonating fuses	导爆索	3603.0000	
Developing apparatus and equipment, automatically, for photographic film or paper in rolls, for the colour photographic film in rolls	显影装置及设备,自动的,照相胶卷或成卷感光纸用,彩色胶卷用	9010.1091	7
Developing apparatus and equipment, automatically, for photographic film or paper in rolls, nes	显影装置及设备,自动的,照相胶卷或成卷感光纸用,其他	9010.1099	7

Article Description	商品名称	Tariff Code	D. R.
Developing apparatus and equipment, automatically, for photographic film or paper in rolls, of a kind used in special photographic film or paper	显影装置及设备,自动的,照相胶卷或成卷感光纸用,特种照相用	9010.1020	7
Developing apparatus and equipment, automatically, of a kind used in cinematographic film	显影装置及设备,自动的,电影用	9010.1010	7
Developing apparatus, flat panel displays manufacture machines and apparatus	显影装置,平板显示器的制造机器及装置	8486.3049	7
Dewaterers, centrifuges	脱水机,离心式	8421.1910	7
Dexamethasone	地塞米松	2937.2210	36
Dexamfetamine (INN), salts thereof	右苯丙胺(1NN)以及它们的盐	2921.4600	36
Dextrins	糊精	3505.1000	36
Dextromoramide (INN); salts thereof	右吗拉胺(INN)及盐	2934.9100	36
Dextropropoxyphene (INN) and its salts	右丙氧吩(INN)及其盐	2922.1400	36
De-icing fluids, prepared	解冻剂	3820.0000	36
Diacs, other than photosensitive devices	两端交流开关元件,但光敏器件除外	8541.3000	5
Diagnostic apparatus (including apparatus for functional exploratory examination or for checking physiological parameters), electro-diagnostic, nes	诊断装置(包括功能检查或生理参数检查用装置),电气的,其他	9018.1990	
Diagnostic or laboratory reagents on a backing	诊断或实验用试剂,附于衬背上的	3822.0010	36
Diagnostic or laboratory reagents, prepared, nes	诊断或实验用配制试剂,其他	3822.0090	36
Diagnostic reagents designed to be administered to the patient	诊断试剂,用于病人的	3006.3000	36
Dialkyl (me, et, n-pr or i-pr) N, N-dialkyl (me, et, n-pr or i-pr)-phosphoramidates	二烷(甲、乙、正丙或异丙)氨基膦酸二烷(甲、乙、正丙或异丙)酯	2929.9030	36
Dialogite (rhodocrosite)	菱锰矿	2602.0000	1346
Dials, of clock or watch	钟面或表面,钟、表的	9114.3000	6
Dialysis	人工肾	9018.9040	
Diammonium hydrogenorthophosphate (diammonium phosphate)	磷酸氢二铵	3105.3000	68
Diamonds dust and powder, natural	钻石的粉末,天然的	7105.1010	145
Diamonds dust and powder, synthetic	钻石的粉末,人工合成的	7105.1020	145
Diamonds, for technical use, synthetic or reconstructed	钻石,工业用,合成或再造的	7104.9011	145
Diamonds, industrial, nes	钻石,工业用,其他	7102.2900	145
Diamonds, industrial, unworked or simply sawn, cleaved or bruted	钻石,工业用,未加工或经简单锯开、劈开或粗磨	7102.2100	145
Diamonds, non-industrial, nes	钻石,非工业用,其他	7102.3900	145
Diamonds, non-industrial, unworked or simply sawn, cleaved or bruted	钻石,非工业用,未加工或经简单锯开、劈开或粗磨	7102.3100	145
Diamonds, synthetic or reconstructed, nes	钻石,合成或再造的,其他	7104.9091	145
Diamonds, synthetic or reconstructed, unworked or simply sawn or roughly shaped	钻石,合成或再造的,未加工或经简单锯开或粗制成形	7104.2010	145

D

D

Article Description	商品名称	Tariff Code	D. R.
Diamonds, unsorted	钻石,未分级	7102. 1000	145
Diaries and similar articles, of paper or paperboard	日记本及类似品,纸或纸板制的	4820. 1000	
Diathermy apparatus	透热疗法设备	9018. 9050	
Diazepam (INN); salts thereof	地西泮(INN)以及盐	2933. 9100	36
Diazo-compounds	重氮化合物	2927. 0000	36
Dibromochrysanthermic acid	二溴菊酸	2916. 2010	36
Dibromotetraf luoroethane	二溴四氟乙烷	2903. 4600	36
Dibutyl orthophthalates	邻苯二甲酸二丁酯	2917. 3410	36
Dichlorodifluoromethane	二氯二氟甲烷	2903. 4200	36
Dichlorohexafluoropropane	二氯六氟丙烷	2903. 4591	36
Dichloroisooyanurate acid	二氯异氰脲酸	2933. 6921	36
Dichloromethane (methylene chloride)	二氯甲烷	2903. 1200	36
Dichlorotetrafluoroethanes	二氯四氟乙烷	2903. 4400	36
Dichromates, nes	重铬酸盐,其他	2841. 5000	1
Dictionaries	字典	4901. 9100	15
Dicyandiamide	双氰胺	2926. 2000	36
Didanosine and their salts	地达诺新及它们的盐	2938. 9010	34
Didecyl orthophthalates	邻苯二甲酸二癸酯	2917. 3300	36
Dieldrin (ISO, INN)	狄氏剂(ISO, INN)	2910. 4000	36
Dies for drawing or extruding metal, interchangeable, nes	金属拉拔或挤压用模,其他	8207. 2090	256
Dies for drawing or extruding metal, with working part of natural or synthetic diamonds or cubic boron nitride, interchangeable	金属拉拔或挤压用模,带有天然或合成金刚石、立方氮化硼制的工作部件,可互换	8207. 2010	256
Diesel oils and other fuel oils, nes	柴油及其他燃料油,其他	2710. 1929	6
Diethanolamine and its salts	二乙醇胺及其盐	2922. 1200	36
Diethyl ether	乙醚	2909. 1100	36
Diethyl phosphite	亚磷酸二乙酯	2920. 9014	36
Diethylene glycol, digol	二甘醇	2909. 4100	36
Die-stamping machines, for working metal, nes	冲压机床,加工金属用,其他	8462. 1090	7
Die-stamping machines, numerically controlled, for working metal	冲压机床,数控的,加工金属用	8462. 1010	7
Difenoxin (INN); salts thereof	地芬诺新 (INN)以及盐	2933. 3300	36
Diffraction apparatus	衍射设备	9012. 1000	
Diffraction apparatus parts and accessories	衍射设备的零件、附件	9012. 9000	3
Diffusion treatment equipment, flat panel displays manufacture machines and apparatus	氧化处理设备,平板显示器的制造机器及装置	8486. 3010	7
Diffusion treatment equipment, semiconductor devices or of electronic integrated circuits manufacture machines and apparatus	扩散处理设备,制造半导体器件或集成电路的机器及装置	8486. 2010	7
Digital cameras parts, camera modules without special purposes	数字照相机用零件,非特种用途的取像模块	8529. 9042	3

Article Description	商品名称	Tariff Code	D. R.
Digital cameras parts, nes	数字照相机用零件,其他	8529. 9049	3
Digital cameras parts, of special purposes	数字照相机用零件,特种用途的	8529. 9041	3
Digital cameras, not for special purposes	数字照相机,非特种用途的其他类型	8525. 8029	7
Digital cameras, for special purposes	数字照相机,特种用途的	8525. 8021	7
Digital cameras, single lens reflex, not for special purposes	数字照相机,非特种用途的单镜头反光型	8525. 8022	7
Digital printing machines, capable of connecting to an APP machine or to a network, nes	印刷设备,数字式,可与自动数据处理设备或网络连接的	8443. 3229	57
Digital printing machines, nes	印刷设备,数字式,其他	8443. 3939	57
Digital video disc player	数字化视频光盘(DVD)播放机	8521. 9012	5
Digital video disc player	DVD 播放机	8521. 9012	5
Digitizer	数字化仪	8471. 6060	
Dihydrocodeine (INN) and salts	双氢可待因(INN) 及盐	2939. 1100	34
Dill powder	莳萝粉	0910. 9900	6
Dill, fresh or chilled	莳萝,鲜或冷藏的	0709. 9090	1
Dill, frozen	莳萝,冷冻的	0710. 8090	1
Dimethyl phosphite	亚磷酸二甲酯	2920. 9013	36
Dimethyl terephthalate	对苯二甲酸二甲酯	2917. 3700	36
Dimethylamine and their salts	二甲胺及其盐	2921. 1100	36
Dimethylanilines	二甲基苯胺	2921. 4920	36
Dimethylcyctohexanols	二甲基环已醇	2906. 1200	36
Dinas earths	第纳斯土	2508. 7000	134
Dinitrochlorobenzene	二硝基氯化苯	2904. 9020	36
Dinitrotoluene and dinitrochlorobenzene	二硝基甲苯	2904. 2030	36
Dinonyl orthophthalates	邻苯二甲酸二壬酯	2917. 3300	36
Dinoseb (ISO) acetate	地乐酚(ISO)乙酸酯	2915. 3600	36
Dinoseb (ISO) and its salts	地乐酚(ISO)及其盐	2908. 9100	36
Dioctyl orthophthalates	邻苯二甲酸二辛酯	2917. 3200	36
Diodes, other than photosensitive or light emitting diodes	二极管,但光敏二极管或发光二极管除外	8541. 1000	
Diols, nes	二元醇,其他	2905. 3990	36
Dioptase	绿铜矿	2603. 0000	146
Diphenols	联苯酚	2907. 1990	36
Diphenoxylate(INN); salts thereof	地芬诺酯 (INN)以及盐	2933. 3300	36
Diphenylamine and its derivatives; salts thereof	二苯胺及其衍生物以及它们的盐	2921. 4400	36
Diphenylmethane diisocyanate	纯 MDI	2929. 1030	36
Diphenylmethane diisocyanate	二苯基甲烷二异氰酸酯	2929. 1030	36
Diphenylolpropane and its salts	二苯基酚丙烷及其盐	2907. 2300	36
Diphosphorus pentaoxide	五氧化二磷	2809. 1000	6
Dipipanone (INN); salts thereof	地匹哌酮(INN)以及盐	2933. 3300	36
Direction finding compasses	定向罗盘	9014. 1000	

D

Article Description	商品名称	Tariff Code	D. R.
Directional control valves, electromagnetic	换向阀,电磁式	8481. 8021	
Directional control valves, nes	换向阀,其他	8481. 8029	
Dirigibles	飞艇	8801. 0090	
Disabled persons carriages parts and accessoris	残疾人车辆用零件、附件	8714. 2000	3
Disabled persons carriages, nes	残疾人车,其他	8713. 9000	7
Disabled persons carriages, not mechanically propelled	残疾人车,非机械驱动	8713. 1000	7
Disc harrows, for agricultural, horticultural or forestry use	圆盘耙,农业、园艺及林业用	8432. 2100	
Discharge lamps, other than ultra-violet lamps, for locomotives and rolling-stock, aircraft or ships	放电灯,但紫外线灯除外,火车、航空器及船舶用	8539. 3920	35
Discharge lamps, other than ultra-violet lamps, for scientific or medical uses only	放电灯,但紫外线灯管除外,科研、医疗专用	8539. 3910	35
Discharge lamps, other than ultra-violet lamps, nes	放电灯,但紫外线灯除外,其他	8539. 3990	35
Dish washing machines of the household type	洗碟机,家用型	8422. 1100	
DIsh washing machines parts	洗碟机用零件	8422. 9010	
Dish washing machines, nes	洗碟机,其他	8422. 1900	
Dish-cloths and similar cleaning cloths	擦碗布及类似擦拭用布	6307. 1000	346
Disinfectants	消毒剂	3808. 9400	36
Disk sawing machines, for working stone, ceramics, concrete, asbestos-cement or like mineral materials	圆盘锯,加工石料、陶瓷、混凝土、石棉水泥或类似矿物材料的	8464. 1010	7
Disodium carbonate	纯碱	2836. 2000	
Disodium carbonate	碳酸钠(纯碱)	2836. 2000	
Disodium phosphates	磷酸二钠	2835. 2200	
Disodium sulphate	硫酸钠	2833. 1100	
Disodium tetraborate, anhydrous	四硼酸钠,无水的	2840. 1100	
Disodium tetraborate, nes	四硼酸钠,其他	2840. 1900	
Display tubes for data/graphic, black and white or other monochrome	显示管,数据/图形的,黑白的或其他单色的	8540. 5000	35
Display tubes for data/graphic, colour, with a phosphor dot screen pitch smaller than 0. 4mm	显示管,数据/图形的,彩色的,屏幕荧光点间距小于0. 4毫米	8540. 4000	35
Display tubes for radar, cathode-ray tubes	显示管,雷达的,阴极射线管	8540. 6010	35
Display tubes parts for radar	显示管用零件,雷达的	8540. 9120	3
Distilled water for human consumption	饮用蒸馏水	2853. 0010	3
Distilling or rectifying plant, nes	蒸馏或精馏设备,其他	8419. 4090	57
Distortion factor meters, specially designed for telecommunications	失真度表,通讯专用的	9030. 4090	7
Distributors, for electrical ignition or starting equipment, nes	分电器,点燃式或压燃式内燃发动机用的,其他	8511. 3090	7
Distributors, for locomotives, aircraft or ships, for electrical ignition or starting equipment	分电器,机车、航空器及船舶用,点燃式或压燃式内燃发动机用的	8511. 3010	7
Dithiocarbamates	二硫代氨基甲酸盐	2930. 2000	36

Article Description	商品名称	Tariff Code	D. R.
Dithiocarbonates	二硫代碳酸酯(或盐)	2930. 9020	36
Dithionites, nes, inorganic	连二亚硫酸盐,其他,无机的	2831. 9000	
Divanadium pentaoxide	五氧化二钒	2825. 3010	
Dividing heads for machine-tools	分度头,机床的附件	8466. 3000	3
Di-chloroacetic acids, their salts and esters	二氯乙酸或三氯乙酸及其盐和酯	2915. 4000	36
Di-n-propylamine	二正丙胺	2921. 1910	36
DL-pantothenic acid and its derivatives	DL-泛酸及其衍生物	2936. 2400	36
Dobbies and card reducing, copying, punching or assembling machines for use there with	多臂机及其所用的卡片缩小、复制、穿孔或汇编机器	8448. 1100	3
Dodecan-1-ol(lauryl alcohol), hexade can-1-ol(cetyl alcohol) and octadecan-1-ol(stearyl alcohol)	十二醇、十六醇及十八醇	2905. 1700	36
Dodecylbenzene	十二烷基苯	2902. 9030	6
Dog coats and the like	狗外套及类似品	4201. 0000	1458
Dog or cat food, put up for retail sale, in airtight containers	零售包装的狗食或猫食,罐头	2309. 1010	23468
Dog or cat food, put up for retail sale, nes	零售包装的狗食或猫食,其他	2309. 1090	23468
Dogfish, fresh or chilled	角鲨,鲜或冷的	0302. 6500	18
Dogfish, frozen	角鲨,冻的	0303. 7500	18
Dolls carriages	玩偶车	9503. 0010	
Dolls, whether or not dressed, for representing animals	玩偶,不论是否着装,动物的	9503. 0021	5
Dolls, whether or not dressed, nes	玩偶,不论是否着装,其他	9503. 0029	5
Dolomite ramming mix	白云石,夯混	2518. 3000	14
Dolomite, calcined or sintered dolomite	白云石,已煅烧或烧结的	2518. 2000	14
Dolomite, not calcinecd or sintered	白云石,未煅烧或烧结的	2518. 1000	14
Dolphins	海豚	0106. 1200	
Domestic appliances parts, of iron or steel, non-electric	家用器具零件,非电热的家用	7321. 9000	7
Domestic appliances, of iron or steel, non-electric, for gas fuel or for both gas and other fuels	家用器具,非电热的家用,使用气体燃料或可使用气体燃料及其他燃料的	7321. 8100	7
Domestic appliances, of iron or steel, non-electric, for liquid fuel	家用器具,非电热的家用,使用液体燃料的	7321. 8200	7
Domestic appliances, of iron or steel, non-electric, nes, including appliances for solid fuel	家用器具,非电热的家用,其他,包括使用固体燃料的	7321. 8900	7
Door eyes, optical	门眼,光学的	9013. 8020	
Doors and their frames and thresholds, wooden	门及其框架和门槛,木制的	4418. 2000	58
Doors and their frames, of plastics	门及其框架,塑料的	3925. 2000	23
Doors thresholds, of plastics	门槛,塑料的	3925. 2000	23
Doors, of the motor vehicles	车门,机动车辆的	8708. 2952	3
Doors, windows and their frames and thresholds for doors, of aluminium	门窗及其框架、门槛,铝制	7610. 1000	56

D

Article Description	商品名称	Tariff Code	D. R.
Doors, windows and their frames and thresholds for doors, of iron or steel	门窗及其框架、门槛,钢铁的	7308. 3000	6
Double column planing machines, for removing metal or cermets	龙门刨床,切削金属或金属陶瓷用	8461. 9011	7
Double salts and mixtures of calcium nitrate and ammonium nitrate	硝酸钙和硝酸铵的复盐及混合物	3102. 6000	68
Down and articles thereof	羽绒及其制品	6701. 0000	
Down with their skins and other parts of birds	羽绒及其鸟皮或鸟体其他部分	6701. 0000	
Down, of birds	羽绒	0505. 1000	34
Downwear, not knitted or crocheted, for men or boys, padded with feathers or down	羽绒服,非针织或钩编的,男式	6201. 1310	2456
Downwear, not knitted or crocheted, for men or boys, padded with feathers or down, of cotton, nes	羽绒服,非针织或钩编的,男式,充绒,棉制,其他	6201. 9210	2456
Downwear, not knitted or crocheted, for men or boys, padded with feathers or down, of cotton, overcoats	羽绒服,非针织或钩编的,男式,充绒,棉制,大衣式	6201. 1210	2456
Downwear, not knitted or crocheted, for men or boys, padded with feathers or down, of man-made fibres, nes	羽绒服,非针织或钩编的,男式,充绒,化学纤维制,其他	6201. 9310	2456
Downwear, not knitted or crocheted, for women or girls, padded with feathers or down	羽绒服,非针织或钩编的,女式,充绒	6202. 1310	2456
Downwear, not knitted or crocheted, for women or girls, padded with feathers or down, of cotton, nes	羽绒服,非针织或钩编的,女式,充绒,棉制,其他	6202. 9210	2456
Downwear, not knitted or crocheted, for women or girls, padded with feathers or down, of cotton, overcoats	羽绒服,非针织或钩编的,女式,充绒,棉制,大衣式	6202. 1210	2456
Downwear, not knitted or crocheted, for women or girls, padded with feathers or down, of man-made fibres, nes	羽绒服,非针织或钩编的,女式,充绒,化学纤维制,其他	6202. 9310	2456
Drafting tables and machines, whether or not automatic	绘图台及绘图机,不论是否自动	9017. 1000	
Dragon fruit, fresh	火龙果,鲜的	0810. 9080	1
Dragon's blood	血竭	1301. 9020	
Drapes, crocheted, of cotton	帷帘,钩编的,棉制	6303. 1932	346
Drapes, crocheted, of other textile materials	帷帘,钩编的,其他纺织材料制	6303. 1992	346
Drapes, crocheted, of synthetic fibres	帷帘,钩编的,合成纤维制	6303. 1220	346
Drapes, knitted, of cotton	帷帘,针织的,棉制	6303. 1931	346
Drapes, knitted, of other textile materials	帷帘,针织的,其他纺织材料制	6303. 1991	346
Drapes, knitted, of synthetic fibres	帷帘,针织的,合成纤维制	6303. 1210	346
Drapes, of cotton, nes	帷帘,棉制,其他	6303. 9100	346
Drapes, of other textile materials	帷帘,其他纺织材料制	6303. 9900	346
Drapes, of synthetic fibres, nes	帷帘,合成纤维制,其他	6303. 9200	346
Drawing benches, for working metal or cermets, without removing material, nes	拉拔机,金属或金属陶瓷用,非切削,其他	8463. 1090	7

Article Description	商品名称	Tariff Code	D. R.
Drawing charcoals	图画碳笔	9609. 9000	3
Drawing instruments parts and accessories	绘图器具的零件、附件	9017. 9000	3
Drawing instruments, nes	绘图器具,其他	9017. 2000	
Drawing machinery auxiliary, for man-made textile materials	拉伸机的辅助机器,化学纺织纤维的	8448. 1900	3
Drawing machinery for man-made textile materials	拉伸机,化学纺织纤维的	8444. 0090	
Drawing machines for wire, for working metal or cermets, without removing material	拔丝机,金属或金属陶瓷用,非切削	8463. 1020	7
Drawing machines, for textile fibres	拉伸机,纺织纤维的	8445. 1310	7
Drawing pins and similar articles, of copper or of iron or steel with heads of copper	图钉及类似品,铜制或钢铁制带铜头的	7415. 1000	56
Drawing pins, of iron or steel	图钉,钢铁制的	7317. 0000	36
Drawing tube benches, cold drawing, for working metal or cermets, without removing material, nes	拔管机,冷拔的,金属或金属陶瓷用,非切削,其他	8463. 1019	7
Drawing tube benches, cold drawing, with 300t or less, for working metal or cermets, without removing material	拔管机,冷拔的,300 吨及以下,金属或金属陶瓷用,非切削	8463. 1011	7
Dredgers	挖泥船	8905. 1000	
Dress patterns	服装裁剪样	6307. 9000	346
Dresses, knitted or crocheted, of women or girls, of artificial fibres	连衣裙,针织或钩编的,女式,人造纤维制	6104. 4400	2456
Dresses, knitted or crocheted, of women or girls, of cotton	连衣裙,针织或钩编的,女式,棉制	6104. 4200	2456
Dresses, knitted or crocheted, of women or girls, of other textile materials	连衣裙,针织或钩编的,女式,其他纺织材料制	6104. 4900	2456
Dresses, knitted or crocheted, of women or girls, of synthetic fibres	连衣裙,针织或钩编的,女式,合成纤维制	6104. 4300	2456
Dresses, knitted or crocheted, of women or girls, of wool or fine animal hair	连衣裙,针织或钩编的,女式,羊毛或动物细毛制	6104. 4100	2456
Dresses, not knitted or crocheted, for women or girls, nes	连衣裙,非针织或钩编的,女式,其他	6204. 4990	2456
Dresses, not knitted or crocheted, for women or girls, of artificial fibres	连衣裙,非针织或钩编的,女式,人造纤维制	6204. 4400	2456
Dresses, not knitted or crocheted, for women or girls, of cotton	连衣裙,非针织或钩编的,女式,棉制	6204. 4200	2456
Dresses, not knitted or crocheted, for women or girls, of silk or silk waste	连衣裙,非针织或钩编的,女式,丝及绢丝制	6204. 4910	2456
Dresses, not knitted or crocheted, for women or girls, of synthetic fibres	连衣裙,非针织或钩编的,女式,合成纤维制	6204. 4300	2456
Dresses, not knitted or crocheted, for women or girls, of wool or fine animal hair	连衣裙,非针织或钩编的,女式,羊毛或动物细毛制	6204. 4100	2456
Dressing machines for textile fabrics	上浆机器,纺织物的	8451. 8000	
Dressing machines parts for textile fabrics	上浆机器零件,纺织物的	8451. 9000	

D

Article Description	商品名称	Tariff Code	D. R.
Dressings, medical, surgical, dental or veterinary purposes	敷料,供医疗、外科、牙科或兽医用	3005. 9090	1346
Dried fish, cod (gadus morhua, gadus ogac, gadus macrocephalus)	干鱼,鳕鱼的	0305. 5100	4
Dried fish, nes	干鱼,其他	0305. 5990	4
Driers, prepared, for paints and varnishes	催干剂,配制的,油漆及清漆用	3211. 0000	36
Drill pipe, of a kind used in drilling for oil or gas, of stainless steel, seamless, having an outside diameter not exceeding 168. 3mm	钻管,钻探石油及天然气用,无缝的,不锈钢制,外径不超过 168. 3 毫米	7304. 2210	6
Drill pipe, of a kind used in drilling for oil or gas, seamless, having an outside diameter not exceeding 168. 3mm	钻管,钻探石油及天然气用,无缝的,外径不超过 168. 3 毫米	7304. 2310	6
Drill pipe, of a kind used in drilling for oil or gas, seamless, nes	钻管,钻探石油及天然气用,无缝的,其他	7304. 2390	6
Drill pipe, of a kind used in drilling for oil or gas, seamless, of stainless steel, nes	钻管,钻探石油及天然气用,无缝的,不锈钢制,其他	7304. 2290	6
Drilling derricks, mobile	钻探车,流动的	8705. 2000	7
Drilling machinery, of oil and natual gos	钻探机零件,石油或天然气钻探用	8431. 4310	3
Drilling machinery, nes	钻探机零件,其他	8431. 4320	3
Drilling machines, for removing metal, nes	钻床,切削金属的,其他	8459. 2900	7
Drilling machines, for working wood, cork, bone, hard rubber, hard plastics or similar hard materials	钻孔机器,加工木材、软木、骨、硬质橡胶、硬质塑料或类似硬质材料的	8465. 9500	7
Drilling machines, numerically controlled, for removing metal	钻床,数控的,切削金属的	8459. 2100	7
Drilling machines, way-type unit head machines, for removing metal	钻床,直线移动式动力头,切削金属的	8459. 1000	7
Drilling platforms, floating	钻探平台,浮动式	8905. 2000	
Drilling platforms, submersible	钻探平台,潜水式	8905. 2000	
Drilling tools, other than for rock drilling, interchangeable, nes	钻孔工具,但凿岩及钻探用的除外,可互换,其他	8207. 5090	256
Drilling tools, other than for rock drilling, with working part of natural or synthetic diamonds or cubic boron nitride, interchangeable	钻孔工具,但凿岩及钻探用的除外,带有天然或合成金刚石、立方氮化硼制的工作部件,可互换	8207. 5010	256
Drilling tools, hand tools	钻孔工具	8205. 1000	256
Drills, hand tools, with self-contained electric motor	钻,手提式,本身装有电动动力装置的	8467. 2100	57
Drink preparation or manufacture machinery	饮料生产或加工机器	8438. 8000	
Drink preparation or manufacture machinery parts	饮料生产或加工机器的零件	8438. 9000	3
Drinking glasses, other than of glass ceramics, nes	玻璃杯子,但玻璃陶瓷制的除外,其他	7013. 3700	356
Drinking glasses, other than of glass ceramics, of lead crystal	玻璃杯子,但玻璃陶瓷制的除外,铅晶质玻璃制	7013. 3300	356
Drip coffee makers, electro-thermic	滴液式咖啡机,电热的	8516. 7110	7
Drive-axles with differential and parts of cross-country cars(4WD)	驱动桥及其零件,装有差速器的,越野车(4 轮驱动)用	8708. 5075	3

Article Description	商品名称	Tariff Code	D. R.
Drive-axles with differential and parts of dumpers	驱动桥及其零件,装有差速器的,自卸车用	8708.5073	3
Drive-axles with differential and parts of motor vehicles with 30 seats or more	驱动桥及其零件,装有差速器的,30座及以上客运机动车辆用	8708.5072	3
Drive-axles with differential and parts of motor vehicles with special purpose	驱动桥及其零件,装有差速器的,特种车辆用	8708.5076	3
Drive-axles with differential and parts of motor vehicles, nes	驱动桥及其零件,装有差速器的,其他	8708.5079	3
Drive-axles with differential and parts of saloon cars	驱动桥及其零件,装有差速器的,小轿车用	8708.5074	3
Drive-axles with differential and parts of tractors	驱动桥及其零件,装有差速器的,拖拉机的	8708.5071	3
Driving bogies and bissel-bogies, of railway or tramway locomotives or rolling-stock	驾驶转向架及轴,铁道及电车道机车或其他车辆的	8607.1100	3
Dross (other than granulated slag), from the manufacture of iron or steel	浮渣(粒状熔渣除外),冶炼钢铁所产生的	2619.0000	134
Drums	鼓	9206.0000	5
Drums and similar packing containers, of wood	包装圆桶及类似的包装容器,木制的	4415.1000	56
Dry plasma etching equipment parts and accessories, semiconductor devices or of electronic integrated circuits manufacture machines and apparatus	等离子体干法刻蚀机零件及附件,制造半导体器件或集成电路的机器及装置	8486.9090	3
Dry plasma etching equipment, semiconductor devices or of electronic integrated circuits manufacture machines and apparatus	等离子体干法刻蚀机,制造半导体器件或集成电路的机器及装置	8486.2041	7
Dryers, with a process involving a change of temperature, for agricultural products	干燥器,利用温度变化处理,农产品干燥用	8419.3100	57
Dryers, with a process involving a change of temperature, for breeze pottery blanks use	干燥器,利用温度变化处理,微空气流动陶瓷坯件用	8419.3910	57
Dryers, with a process involving a change of temperature, for wood, paper pulp, paper or paperboard	干燥器,利用温度变化处理,木材、纸浆、纸或纸板干燥用	8419.3200	57
Dryers, with a process involving a change of temperature, nes	干燥器,利用温度变化处理,其他	8419.3990	57
Drying machines parts	干燥机零件	8451.9000	
Drying machines, each of a dry linen capacity exceeding 10kg	干燥机,干衣量超过10千克	8451.2900	
Drying machines, each of a dry linen capacity not exceeding 10kg	干燥机,干衣量不超过10千克	8451.2100	
Dry-cleaning machines	干洗机	8451.1000	
Dry-cleaning machines parts	干洗机零件	8451.9000	
Dual purpose starter generators, for electrical ignition or starting equipment, nes	两用启动发电机,点燃式或压燃式内燃发动机用的,其他	8511.4099	7

Article Description	商品名称	Tariff Code	D. R.
Dual purpose starter generators, for locomotives, aircraft or ships, for electrical ignition or starting equipment	两用启动发电机,机车、航空器及船舶用,点燃式或压燃式内燃发动机用的	8511.4010	7
Ducks Ducks, ex. pure-bred breeding, weighing more than 185g	鸭,改良种用除外,重量超过185克	0105.9991	48
Ducks, not cut in pieces, fresh or chilled	鸭,整只,鲜或冷的	0207.3210	1
Ducks, not cut in pieces, frozen	鸭,整只,冻的	0207.3310	1
Ducks, pure-bred breeding, weighing more than 185g	鸭,改良种用,重量超过185克	0105.9910	48
Ducks, pure-bred breeding, weighing not more than 185g	鸭,改良种用,重量不超过185克	0105.1910	48
Dugongs (mammals of the order sirenia)	儒艮(海牛目哺乳动物)	0106.1200	
Dumpers designed for off-highway use, nes	自卸车,非公路用,其他	8704.1090	58
Dumpers for the transport of goods, electromobile, for off-highway use	自卸车,电动轮货运,非公路用	8704.1030	58
Dumpers parts and accessories, nes	自卸车用零件、附件,其他	8708.9939	3
Duplicating machines of hectograph	复印机,胶版的	8472.1000	
Duplicating stylos	蜡纸铁笔	9608.9920	
Duplicator stencils, in rolls or sheets, of width exceeding 36cm in roll or one side exceeding 36cm and other side exceeding 15cm in rectangular sheets	油印蜡纸,成卷或成张的,卷宽度超过36厘米,或长超过36厘米且宽超过15厘米	4809.9000	458
Duplicator stencils, nes	油印蜡纸,其他	4816.9090	58
Durian, fresh	榴莲,鲜的	0810.6000	12
Durum wheat	硬粒小麦	1001.1000	356
Dust collectors for industry uses, baghoused	除尘器,工业用,袋式	8421.3922	7
Dust collectors for industry uses, cyclone	除尘器,工业用,旋风式	8421.3923	7
Dust collectors for industry uses, electrostatic	除尘器,工业用,静电式	8421.3921	7
Dust collectors for industry uses, nes	除尘器,工业用,其他	8421.3929	7
Dust collectors for industry uses, nes	工业用除尘器,其他	8421.3929	7
Dusters and similar cleaning cloths	抹布及类似擦拭用布	6307.1000	346
DVchrysanthemimono carboxylate	DV菊酸甲酯	2916.2010	36
Dye carriers to accelerate the dyeing or fixing of dyestuffs, of a kind used in the leather or like industries, nes	染料加速着色或固色助剂,制革工业及类似工业用,其他	3809.9300	236
Dye carriers to accelerate the dyeing or fixing of dyestuffs, of a kind used in the paper or like industries, nes	染料加速着色或固色助剂,造纸工业及类似工业用,其他	3809.9200	236
Dye carriers to accelerate the dyeing or fixing of dyestuffs, of a kind used in the textile or like industries, nes	染料加速着色或固色助剂,纺织工业及类似工业用,其他	3809.9100	236
Dye carriers to accelerate the dyeing or fixing of dyestuffs, with a basis of amylaceous substances	染料加速着色或固色助剂,以淀粉物质为基本成分	3809.1000	236

D

Article Description	商品名称	Tariff Code	D. R.
Dye indicators	染料指示剂	3204. 9010	345
Dyeing extracts, but excluding animal black	染料浸膏,但动物炭黑除外	3203. 0020	34
Dyeing extracts, of vegetable origin	染料浸膏,植物质的	3203. 0019	34
Dyeing machines parts, for textile yarns, fabrics or made up textile articles	染色机器零件,纱线、织物及纺织制品用	8451. 9000	
Dyeing machines, for textile yarns, fabrics or made up textile articles	染色机器,纱线、织物及纺织制品用	8451. 4000	
Dyes (including those usable in that state as pigments) and preparations based thereon, vat dyes or reductive dyes, nes	染料(包括颜料用的)及以其为基本成分的制品,其他,瓮染料或还原染料	3204. 1590	345
Dyes and colouring matter put up in forms or packings for retail sale	染料或着色料,零售形状及零售包装的	3212. 9000	136
Dyes and preparations based thereon, basic type	染料及以其为基本成分的制品,碱性型	3204. 1300	345
Dyes and preparations based thereon, direct type	染料及以其为基本成分的制品,直接型	3204. 1400	345
Dyes and preparations based thereon, disperse type	染料及以其为基本成分的制品,分散型	3204. 1100	345
Dyes and preparations based thereon, mordant type	染料及以其为基本成分的制品,媒染型	3204. 1200	345
Dyes and preparations based thereon, reactive	染料及以其为基本成分的制品, 活性的	3204. 1600	345
Dyes and preparations based thereon, sulphur type, nes	硫化染料及以其为基本成分的制品,其他	3204. 1919	345
Dyes, whether or not premetallized, and preparations based thereon acid type	染料(不论是否预金属络合)及以其为基本成分的制品,酸性型	3204. 1200	345
Dysprosium	镝	2805. 3012	56
Dysprosium carbonate	碳酸镝	2846. 9043	6
Dysprosium chloride	氯化镝	2846. 9022	
Dysprosium oxide	氧化镝	2846. 9015	
D-glucitol(sorbitol), separate chemically defined	山梨醇,单独有化学定义的	2905. 4400	36
D-norpseudoephedrine and its salts	D-去甲假麻黄碱(INN)及其盐	2939. 4300	34
D-pantothenic acid and its derivatives	D-泛酸及其衍生物	2936. 2400	36

E

Article Description	商品名称	Tariff Code	D. R.
Earth colours, containing 70% or more by weight of combined iron evaluated as Fe_2O_3	土色料,按重量计三氧化二铁含量在70%及以上	2821. 2000	6
Ecaussine	艾克辛	2515. 2000	148
Ecgonine, salts, esters and other derivatives thereof	芽子碱,它的盐、酯及其他衍生物	2939. 9190	34
Echinoderms	棘皮动物壳	0508. 0090	14
Economizers, auxiliary plant for use with central heating boilers	节热器,集中供暖用的热水锅炉的辅助设备	8404. 1020	3
Economizers, auxiliary plant for use with steam or other vapour generating watertube boilers	节热器,蒸汽锅炉的辅助设备	8404. 1010	3
Economizers, auxiliary plant for use with super-heated water boilers	节热器,过热水锅炉的辅助设备	8404. 1010	3
Eddy examinations apparatus, without damaging	涡流探伤检测仪	9031. 8033	
Education instruments, designed for demonstrational purposes, unsuitable for other uses	教学示范而无其他用途的仪器、装置及模型	9023. 0000	
Eel fry	鳗鱼苗	0301. 9210	15
Eels (Anguilla spp.), fresh or chilled	鳗鱼,鲜或冷的	0302. 6600	18
Eels (Anguilla spp.), frozen	鳗鱼,冻的	0303. 7600	18
Eels (Anguilla spp.), nes, living	鳗鱼,其他,活的	0301. 9290	15
Eels, prepared or preserved, whole or in pieces, but not minced	鳗鱼,制作或保藏的,整条或切块,但未绞碎	1604. 1910	48
Efavirenz and their salts	依发韦仑及盐	2934. 9940	36
Egg yolks, dried	蛋黄,干的	0408. 1100	14
Egg yolks, nes	蛋黄,其他	0408. 1900	14
Eggs, for hatching	种用蛋	0407. 0010	34
Eggs, limepreserved	皮蛋	0407. 0092	14
Eggs, of birds, nes, in shell, fresh	蛋,禽的,其他,带壳的,鲜的	0407. 0029	1
Eggs, of birds, nes, in shell, fresh, preserved or cooked	蛋,禽的,其他,带壳的、腌制或煮过的	0407. 0099	14
Eggs, of birds, not in shell, dried	蛋,禽的,去壳的,干的	0408. 9100	14
Eggs, of birds, not in shell, nes	蛋,禽的,去壳的,其他	0408. 9900	14
Eggs, of ducks, in shell, fresh	鸭蛋	0407. 0022	1
Eggs, of geese, in shell, fresh	鹅蛋,鲜的、带壳	0407. 0023	1
Eggs, of hens, in shell, fresh	鸡蛋,带壳的,鲜的	0407. 0021	1
Eggs, salted	咸蛋	0407. 0091	14
Eiderdowns	鸭绒被	9404. 9010	6
Elastomeric monofilament, synthetic, of 67 decitex or more and of which no cross-sectional dimension exceeding 1mm	弹性单丝,合成纤维,截面尺寸不超过1毫米,细度在67分特及以上	5404. 1100	568

Article Description	商品名称	Tariff Code	D. R.
Elastomeric single yarn, untwisted or with a twist not exceeding 50 turns per metre, not put up for retail sale, nes	弹性单纱,未加捻或捻度每米不超过50转,非供零售用,其他	5402.4490	3468
Elbows, of plastics	肘管,塑料的	3917.4000	
Electric accumulators, spent	蓄电池,废的	8548.1000	3
Electric blankets	电暖毯	6301.1000	56
Electric cable, insulated, fitted with connectors, for a voltage not exceeding 80V	电缆,绝缘的,有接头,额定电压不超过80伏	8544.4211	35
Electric cable, insulated, fitted with connectors, for a voltage exceeding 80V but not exceeding 1000V	电缆,绝缘的,额定电压超过80伏,但不超过1000伏,有接头	8544.4221	35
Electric cable, insulated, for a voltage exceeding 1000V	电缆,绝缘的,额定电压超过1000伏,其他	8544.6019	35
Electric cable, insulated, for a voltage exceeding 110kV but not exceeding 220kV	电缆,绝缘的,额定电压超过110千伏,但不超过220千伏	8544.6014	35
Electric cable, insulated, for a voltage exceeding 35kV but not exceeding 110kV	电缆,绝缘的,额定电压超过35千伏,但不超过110千伏	8544.6013	35
Electric cable, insulated, for a voltage exceeding 80V but not exceeding 1000V, nes	电缆,绝缘的,额定电压超过80伏,但不超过1000伏,其他	8544.4921	35
Electric cable, insulated, for a voltage not exceeding 35kV	电缆,绝缘的,额定电压不超过35千伏	8544.6012	35
Electric cable, insulated, for a voltage not exceeding 80V, nes	电缆,绝缘的,额定电压不超过80伏,其他	8544.4911	35
Electric conductors, insulated, fitted with connectors, for a voltage not exceeding 80V, nes	电导体,绝缘的,有接头,额定电压不超过80伏,其他	8544.4219	35
Electric conductors, insulated, fitted with connectors, for a voltage exceeding 80V but not exceeding 1000V, nes	电导体,绝缘的,额定电压超过80伏,但不超过1000伏,有接头,其他	8544.4229	35
Electric conductors, insulated, for a voltage exceeding 1000V, nes	电导体,绝缘的,额定电压超过1000伏,其他	8544.6090	35
Electric conductors, insulated, for a voltage exceeding 80V but not exceeding 1000V, nes	电导体,绝缘的,额定电压超过80伏,但不超过1000伏,其他	8544.4929	35
Electric conductors, insulated, for a voltage not exceeding 80V, nes	电导体,绝缘的,额定电压不超过80伏,其他	8544.4919	35
Electric control boards, panels, consoles, desks, cabinets and other bases, for a voltage exceeding 1000V, equipped with two or more switching or protecting or connecting apparatus, nes	电气控制盘、板、台、柜及其他基座,用于电压超过1000伏的线路,装有两个或多个开关、保护或连接用的电器装置,其他	8537.2090	78
Electric control boards, panels, consoles, desks, cabinets and other bases, for a voltage not exceeding 1000V, equipped with two or more switching or protecting or connecting apparatus, nes	电气控制盘、板、台、柜及其他基座,用于电压不超过1000伏的线路,装有两个或多个开关、保护或连接用的电器装置,其他	8537.1090	78

E

Article Description	商品名称	Tariff Code	D. R.
Electric control boards, panels, consoles, desks, cabinets and other bases' parts, for a voltage exceeding 1000V, not equipped with their apparatus	电气控制盘、板、台、柜及其他基座的零件,用于电压超过 1000 伏的线路,但未装有关装置	8538. 1090	3
Electric convection space heating apparatus, fan type	对流式空间电加热器,风扇式	8516. 2931	7
Electric convection space heating apparatus, nes	对流式空间电加热器,其他	8516. 2939	7
Electric convection space heating apparatus, oil-filled types	对流式空间电加热器,充液式	8516. 2932	7
Electric cooking plates	电热板	8516. 6090	7
Electric detonators	电雷管	3603. 0000	
Electric fence energizers	电篱网激发器	8543. 7093	37
Electric frying pans	电炒锅	8516. 6040	7
Electric fuel injection devices	电控燃油喷射装置	8409. 9191	2
Electric heating resistors	加热电阻器	8516. 8000	3
Electric heating resistors parts	加热电阻器用零件	8516. 9010	3
Electric immersion heaters	浸入式液体加热器,电热的	8516. 1090	7
Electric instantaneous waterheaters	即热式电热水器	8516. 1020	7
Electric machines and apparatus for hot spraying of metals or cermets	热喷金属或金属陶瓷的电气机器及装置	8515. 8000	
Electric multitesting machines, for testing metals	电子万能试验机,金属材料试验用	9024. 1010	
Electric radiant space heating apparatus	辐射式空间电加热器	8516. 2920	7
Electric rice cookers	电饭锅	8516. 6030	7
Electric roaster oven	电烤箱	8516. 6050	7
Electric rotary converters	旋转式变流机	8502. 4000	8
Electric smoothing irons	电熨斗	8516. 4000	7
Electric soil heating apparatus	土壤电加热器	8516. 2910	7
Electric soil heating apparatus parts	土壤加热器零件	8516. 9010	3
Electric sound amplifier sets	电气扩音机组	8518. 5000	5
Electric sound amplifier sets parts	电气扩音机组零件	8518. 9000	3
Electric space heating apparatus, nes	电加热器,空间的,其他	8516. 2990	7
Electric space heating apparatus, nes	电气空间电加热器,其他	8516. 2990	7
Electric storage heating radiators	储存式电散热器	8516. 2100	7
Electric storage waterheaters	储存式电热水器	8516. 1010	7
Electric trains, reduced-size ("scale") model assembly kits	电动火车,缩小(按比例缩小)的成套模型组件	9503. 0031	5
Electrical apparatus for making connections to or in electrical circuits, for a voltage exceeding 1000V	电路的连接用电气装置,用于电压超过 1000 伏的线路	8535. 9000	8
Electrical apparatus for protecting electrical circuits, for a voltage exceeding 1000V	电路的保护装置,用于电压超过 1000 伏的线路	8535. 9000	8
Electrical apparatus for protecting electrical circuits, for a voltage not exceeding 1000V	电路的保护装置,用于电压不超过 1000 伏的线路	8536. 9000	8

Article Description	商品名称	Tariff Code	D. R.
Electrical apparatus for switching electrical circuits, for a voltage exceeding 1000V	电路的开关装置,用于电压超过1000伏的线路	8535.9000	8
Electrical apparatus for switching electrical circuits, for a voltage not exceeding 1000V	电路的开关装置,用于电压不超过1000伏的线路	8536.9000	8
Electrical apparatus parts for making connections to or in electrical circuits	电路的连接用电气装置的零件	8538.9000	3
Electrical apparatus parts for protecting electrical circuits	电路的保护装置的零件	8538.9000	3
Electrical apparatus parts for switching electrical circuits	电路的开关装置的零件	8538.9000	3
Electrical conduit tubing and joints therefor, of base metal lined with insulating material	线路导管及其接头,内衬绝缘材料的,贱金属制	8547.9010	3
Electrical energy	电力	2716.0000	
Electrical ignition or starting equipment parts, for electrical ignition or starting equipment, nes	电点火及电起动装置零件,点燃式或压燃式内燃发动机用的,其他	8511.9090	3
Electrical ignition or starting equipment parts, for locomotives, aircraft or ships, for electrical ignition or starting equipment	电点火及电起动装置零件,供机车、航空器及船舶用,点燃式或压燃式内燃发动机用的	8511.9010	3
Electrical insulators of ceramics, nes	绝缘子,陶瓷制,其他	8546.2090	3
Electrical insulators of ceramics, power transmission and converting ceramic bushings	绝缘子,陶瓷制,输变电线路绝缘瓷套管	8546.2010	3
Electrical insulators of glass	绝缘子,玻璃制	8546.1000	3
Electrical insulators, nes	绝缘子,其他	8546.9000	3
Electrical machines and apparatus parts, nes	电气设备及装置的零件,其他	8543.9090	3
Electrical machines and apparatus, having individual functions, nes	电气设备及装置,具有独立功能的,其他	8543.7099	37
Electrical parts of machinery or apparatus, nes	电气零件,其他	8548.9000	3
Electrical quantities measuring or checking instruments and apparatus parts and accessories, nes	电量测量或检验的仪器和装置的零件、附件,其他	9030.9000	3
Electrical quantities measuring or checking instruments and apparatus, nes	电量测量或检验的仪器和装置,其他	9030.8990	7
Electrical quantities measuring or checking instruments and apparatus, with a recording device, nes	电量测量或检验的仪器和装置,带记录装置,其他	9030.8490	7
Electricity distribution boards, panels, consoles, desks, cabinets and other bases, for a voltage exceeding 1000V, equipped with two or more switching or protecting or connecting apparatus, nes	电力分配盘、板、台、柜及其他基座,用于电压超过1000伏的线路,装有两个或多个开关、保护或连接用的电器装置,其他	8537.2090	78
Electricity distribution boards, panels, consoles, desks, cabinets and other bases, for a voltage not exceeding 1000V, equipped with two or more switching or protecting or connecting apparatus, nes	电力分配盘、板、台、柜及其他基座,用于电压不超过1000伏的线路,装有两个或多个开关、保护或连接用的电器装置,其他	8537.1090	78

Article Description	商品名称	Tariff Code	D. R.
Electricity distribution boards, panels, consoles, desks, cabinets and other bases' parts, for a voltage exceeding 1000V, not equipped with their apparatus	电力分配盘、板、台、柜及其他基座的零件,用于电压超过1000伏的线路,但未装有关装置	8538.1090	3
Electricity meters parts and accessories, for industrial use	电量计零件、附件,工业用	9028.9010	3
Electricity meters parts and accessories, nes	电量计零件、附件,其他	9028.9090	3
Electricity meters, supply or production meters, nes	电量计,生产或供应计量仪表,其他	9028.3090	7
Electrodes of base metal, coated with flux material, for electric arc-welding	电极,贱金属制,以焊剂涂面,电弧焊用	8311.1000	56
Electrodes of metal carbides, coated or cored with flux material, of a kind used for soldering, brazing, welding or deposition of metal or of metal carbides	电极,硬质合金制,以焊剂涂面或以焊剂为芯,用于焊接或沉积金属、硬质合金	8311.9000	56
Electrolysis machines and apparatus	电解设备及装置	8543.3000	37
Electromagnetic ovens	电磁炉	8516.6010	7
Electronic ballats, for discharge lamps or tubes	电子镇流器,放电灯或放电管用	8504.1010	
Electronic belt weighing machines	电子皮带秤	8423.2010	
Electronic calculating machines parts and accessories	电子计算器的零件、附件	8473.2100	3
Electronic calculators capable of operation without an external source of electric power	电子计算器,不需外接电源的	8470.1000	
Electronic colour scanners	电子分色机	9006.1010	7
Electronic expansion valves	电子膨胀阀	8481.8031	
Electronic integrated circuits parts	集成电路零件	8542.9000	37
Electronic integrated circuits, nes	集成电路,其他	8542.3900	37
Electronic yarn clearers	电子清纱器	8448.3920	3
Electrophoresis instruments	电泳仪	9027.2020	
Electrophoresis instruments parts and accessories	电泳仪零件、附件	9027.9000	3
Electrophoresis machines and apparatus	电泳设备及装置	8543.3000	37
Electroplating machines and apparatus	电镀设备及装置	8543.3000	37
Electrostatic dust collectors for industry uses	静电除尘器	8421.3921	7
Electrostatic photocopying apparatus, operating by reproducing the original image directly onto the copy (direct process)	静电感光复印设备,将原件直接复印的(直接法)	8443.3911	57
Electrostatic photocopying apparatus, operating by reproducing the original image via an intermediate onto the copy (indirect process)	静电感光复印设备,将原件通过中间体转印的(间接法)	8443.3912	57
Electrostatic photographic printing machines (laser printing machines), digital	静电照相印刷机(激光印刷机),数字式	8443.3932	57
Electrostatic photographic printing machines (laser printing machines), digital, capable of connecting to an ADP machine or to a network	静电照相印刷机(激光印刷机),数字式,可与自动数据处理设备或网络连接的	8443.3222	57
Electro-cardiographs	心电图记录仪	9018.1100	

Article Description	商品名称	Tariff Code	D. R.
Electro-magnetic brakes	电磁制动器	8505. 2000	
Electro-magnetic clutches	电磁离合器	8505. 2000	
Electro-magnetic couplings	电磁联轴节	8505. 2000	
Electro-magnetic lifting heads	电磁起重吸盘	8505. 9010	3
Electro-magnetic or permanent magnet chucks	电磁铁或永磁铁卡盘	8505. 9090	3
Electro-magnetic or permanent magnet clamps and similar holding devices	电磁铁或永磁铁夹具及类似的工件夹具	8505. 9090	3
Electro-magnets	电磁铁	8505. 9090	3
Electro-mechanical domestic appliances parts	家用电动器具零件	8509. 9000	3
Electro-mechanical domestic appliances, nes	家用电动器具,其他	8509. 8090	
Electro-thermic appliances parts, of a kind used for domestic purposes	电热器具用零件,家用	8516. 9090	3
Electro-thermic appliances parts, of a kind used for domestic purposes	家用电热器具用零件	8516. 9090	3
Electro-thermic appliances, nes	电热器具,其他	8516. 7990	7
Electro-thermichair-dressing apparatus parts	电热的理发器具用零件	8516. 9090	3
Elements, radioactive, nes	化学元素,放射性的,其他	2844. 4090	
Elevators and conveyors, continuous-action for goods or materials, belt type	升降机及输送机,用于连续运送货物或材料的,带式	8428. 3300	57
Elevators and conveyors, continuous-action for goods or materials, bucket type	升降机及输送机,用于连续运送货物或材料的,斗式	8428. 3200	57
Elevators and conveyors, continuous-action for goods or materials, chain type	升降机及输送机,用于连续运送货物或材料的,链式	8428. 3910	57
Elevators and conveyors, continuous-action for goods or materials, nes	升降机及输送机,用于连续运送货物或材料的,其他	8428. 3990	57
Elevators and conveyors, continuous-action for goods or materials, roller type	升降机及输送机,用于连续运送货物或材料的,辊式	8428. 3920	57
Elevators and conveyors, continuous-action for goods or materials, specially designed for underground use	升降机及输送机,用于连续运送货物或材料的,地下专用的	8428. 3100	57
Elevators and conveyors, pneumatic type	升降机及输送机,气压式	8428. 2000	7
Embroidery in the piece, in strips or in motifs, nes	刺绣品,成匹、成条或成小块图案的,其他	5810. 9900	46
Embroidery in the piece, in strips or in motifs, of cotton	刺绣品,成匹、成条或成小块图案的,棉制	5810. 9100	46
Embroidery in the piece, in strips or in motifs, of man-made fibres	刺绣品,成匹、成条或成小块图案的,化学纤维制	5810. 9200	46
Embroidery in the piece, in strips or in motifs, without visible ground	刺绣品,成匹、成条或成小块图案的,不见底布的	5810. 1000	46
Embroidery machines	绣花机	8447. 9020	7
Embroidery machines auxiliary	绣花机的辅助机器	8448. 1900	3
Embroidery stilettos and similar articles, for use in the hand	刺绣穿孔锥及类似制品,手工用	7319. 9000	

E

Article Description	商品名称	Tariff Code	D. R.
Emeralds dust and powder	绿宝石的粉末	7105. 9000	145
Emeralds, unworked	绿宝石,未加工	7103..1000	145
Emeralds, worked	绿宝石,加工的	7103. 9100	145
Emery	刚玉岩	2513. 2000	
Empty cachets of a kind suitable for pharmaceutical use	装药空囊	1905. 9000	28
Emulsifying machines, nes	乳化机,其他	8479. 8200	7
Enamels and similar preparations, vitrifiable, of a kind used in the ceramic, enamelling or glass industry	珐琅及类似制品,陶瓷、搪瓷及玻璃工业用	3207. 2000	13
Encapsulant reflective film, in rolls, self-adhesive plates, of a width not exceeding 20cm	胶囊型反光膜,成卷,自粘的,宽度不超过20厘米	3919. 1091	16
Encapsulant reflective film, self-adhesive plates, nes	胶囊型反光膜,自粘的,其他	3919. 9010	16
Encapsulating machines for semiconductor devices, nes	封装半导体器件或集成电路的设备,其他	8486. 4029	7
Encapsulation material for semiconductor devices	半导体器件封装材料	3214. 1010	3
Encyclopaedias, and serial instalments thereof	百科全书及其连续出版的分册	4901. 9100	15
Endless bands for machinery, of stainless steel wire	环形带,机器用,不锈钢丝制	7314. 1200	36
Endless hands, of copper wire	环形带,铜丝制	7419. 9930	4
Endless synchronous belts, of an outside circumference exceeding 60cm but notexceeding 150cm	环形同步带,外周长超过60厘米,但不超过150厘米	4010. 3500	1368
Endless synchronous belts, of an outside circumference exceeding 150cm but not exceeding 198cm	环形同步带,外周长超过150厘米,但不超过198厘米	4010. 3600	1368
Endless transmission belts of trapezoidal cross - section (V-belts), other than V-ribbed, of an outside circumference exceeding 60cm but not exceeding 180cm	环形传动带(三角带),梯形截面的,V形肋状的除外外周长超过60厘米,但不超过180厘米	4010. 3200	1368
Endless transmission belts of trapezoidal cross - section (V-belts), V-ribbed, of an outside circumference exceeding 180cm but not exceeding 240cm	环形传动带(三角带),梯形截面的,V形肋状的,外周长超过180厘米,但不超过240厘米	4010. 3300	1368
Endless transmission belts of trapezoidal cross-section (V-belts), V-ribbed, of an outside circumference exceeding 180cm but not exceeding 240cm	环形传动带(三角带),梯形截面的,外周长超过180厘米,但不超过240厘米,V形肋状的除外	4010. 3400	1368
Endless transmission belts of trapezoidal cross-section (V-belts), V-ribbed, whether or not grooved, of a circumference exceeding 60cm but not exceeding 180cm	环形传动带(三角带),梯形截面的,V形肋状的,外周长超过60厘米,但不超过180厘米	4010. 3100	1368
Endoscopes	内窥镜	9018. 9030	
Engineering drills, not self-propelled, boring casing diameter more than 3m	工程钻机,非自推进的,钻筒直径3米及以上	8430. 6911	5

E

Article Description	商品名称	Tariff Code	D. R.
Engineering drills, not self-propelled, nes	工程钻机,非自推进的,其他	8430. 6919	5
Engines and motors parts, nes	发动机及动力装置的零件,其他	8412. 9090	
Engines and motors, nes	发动机及动力装置,其他	8412. 8000	27
Engines for aircraft, spark-ignition reciprocating or rotary, of an output exceeding 298kW	发动机,航空器用,点燃往复式或旋转式,输出功率超过298 千瓦	8407. 1020	3
Engines for aircraft, spark-ignition reciprocating or rotary, of an output not exceeding 298kW	发动机,航空器用,点燃往复式或旋转式,输出功率不超过298 千瓦	8407. 1010	3
Engines for locomotive, compression-ignition	发动机,机车用,压燃式	8408. 9010	2
Engines for marine outboard, spark-ignition reciprocating or rotary	发动机,船舶舷外用,活塞内燃发动机,点燃往复式或旋转式,	8407. 2100	3
Engines for marine, compression-ignition	发动机,船舶用,压燃式	8408. 1000	
Engines for marine, spark-ignition reciprocating or rotary, nes	发动机,船舶用,活塞内燃发动机,点燃往复式或旋转式,其他	8407. 2900	3
Engines for vehicles, compression-ignition, nes	发动机,车辆用,压燃式,其他	8408. 2090	123
Engines for vehicles, compression-ignition, of an output of 132. 39kW (180hp) or more	车辆发动机,压燃式,输出功率在132. 39 千瓦(180 马力)及以 上	8408. 2010	123
Engines for vehicles, compression-ignition, of an output of 132. 39kW (180hp) or more	发动机,车辆用,压燃式,输出功率在132. 39 千瓦(180 马力)及以 上	8408. 2010	123
Engines for vehicles, reciprocating, of a cylinder capacity exceeding 250cc but not exceeding 1000cc	发动机,车辆用,往复式,气缸容量(排气量)超过250 毫升,但不超过1000 毫升	8407. 3300	123
Engines for vehicles, reciprocating, of a cylinder capacity exceeding 3000cc	发动机,车辆用,往复式,气缸容量(排气量)超过3000 毫升	8407. 3420	123
Engines for vehicles, reciprocating, of a cylinder capacity exceeding 50cc but not exceeding 250cc	发动机,车辆用,往复式,气缸容量(排气量)超过 50 毫升,但不超过 250 毫升	8407. 3200	123
Engines for vehicles, reciprocating, of a cylinder capacity exceeding1000cc but not exceeding 3000cc	发动机,车辆用,往复式,气缸容量(排气量) 超过 1000 毫升,但不超过 3000 毫升	8407. 3410	123
Engines for vehicles, reciprocating, of a cylinder capacity not exceeding 50cc	发动机,车辆用,往复式,气缸容量(排气量)不超过50 毫升	8407. 3100	123
Engines of firedamp, internal combustion piston engines, spark-ignition reciprocating or rotary	发动机,用沼气的,活塞内燃发动机,点燃往复式或旋转式	8407. 9010	25
Engines of jet other than turbo-jets, for aircraft or spacecraft	发动机,喷气的,但涡轮喷气发动机除外,航空器及航天器用	8412. 1010	27
Engines of jet other than turbo-jets, nes	发动机,喷气的,但涡轮喷气发动机除外,其他	8412. 1090	27
Engines of turbo fan, of a thrust exceeding 25kN	发动机,涡轮风扇的,推力超过 25 千牛顿	8411. 1210	27
Engines of turbo fan, of a thrust not exceeding 25kN	发动机,涡轮风扇的,推力不超过 25 千牛顿	8411. 1110	27
Engines of turbo-jets, of a thrust exceeding 25kN, nes	发动机,涡轮喷气的,推力超过 25 千牛顿,其他	8411. 1290	27

Article Description	商品名称	Tariff Code	D. R.
Engines of turbo-jets, of a thrust not exceeding 25kN, nes	发动机,涡轮喷气的,推力不超过25千牛顿,其他	8411. 1190	27
Engines of turbo-propellers, of a power exceeding 1100kW but not exceeding 2238kW	发动机,涡轮螺桨的,功率超过1100千瓦,但不超过2238千瓦	8411. 2210	27
Engines of turbo-propellers, of a power exceeding 2238kW but not exceeding 3730kW	发动机,涡轮螺桨的,功率超过2238千瓦,但不超过3730千瓦	8411. 2220	27
Engines of turbo-propellers, of a power exceeding 3730kW	发动机,涡轮螺桨的,功率超过3730千瓦	8411. 2230	27
Engines of turbo-propellers, of a power not exceeding 1100kW	发动机,涡轮螺桨的,功率不超过1100千瓦	8411. 2100	27
Engines parts of jet other than turbo-jets, for aircraft or spacecraft	发动机零件,喷气的,但涡轮喷气发动机除外,航空器及航天器用的	8412. 9010	23
Engines parts of turboshaft engines	发动机零件,涡轮轴发动机的	8411. 9910	27
Engines parts of turbo-jets	发动机零件,涡轮喷气发动机的	8411. 9100	27
Engines parts of turbo-propellers	发动机零件,涡轮螺桨发动机的	8411. 9100	27
Engines parts, for aircraft engines	发动机零件,航空器发动机用	8409. 1000	2
Engines parts, for engines with an output of 132. 39kW(180hp) or more	发动机零件,输出功率在132. 39千瓦(180马力)及以上的发动机用	8409. 9991	2
Engines parts, for locomotive engines	发动机零件,机车发动机用	8409. 9920	2
Engines parts, for marine propulsion engines, nes	发动机零件,船舶发动机用,其他	8409. 9910	2
Engines parts, for marine propulsion engines, suitable for use solely or principally with spark-ignition internal combustion piston engines	发动机零件,船舶发动机用,专用于或主要用于点燃式活塞内燃发动机的	8409. 9110	2
Engines parts, nes	发动机零件,其他	8409. 9999	2
Engines parts, suitable for use solely or principally with spark-ignition internal combustion piston engines, nes	发动机零件,专用于或主要用于点燃式活塞内燃发动机的,其他	8409. 9199	2
Engines vehicles, compression-ignition, nes	车辆发动机,压燃式,其他	8408. 2090	123
Engines, compression-ignition, of an output exceeding 14kw but not exceeding 132. 39kW (180hp), nes	发动机,压燃式,输出功率超过14千瓦,但小于132. 39千瓦(180马力),其他	8408. 9092	2
Engines, compression-ignition, of an output not exceeding 14kW, nes	发动机,压燃式,输出功率不超过14千瓦,其他	8408. 9091	2
Engines, compression-ignition, of an output of 132. 39kW(180hp) or more, nes	发动机,压燃式,输出功率在132. 39千瓦(180马力)及 以上,其他	8408. 9093	2
Engines, spark-ignition reciprocating or rotary, nes	发动机,点燃往复式或旋转式,其他	8407. 9090	25
Engobes and similar preparations, of a kind used in the ceramic, enamelling or glass industry	釉底料及类似制品,陶瓷、搪瓷及玻璃工业用	3207. 2000	13
Engravings, original	雕版画的原本	9702. 0000	
Enriched materials from niobium ore	铌矿富集物	2615. 9010	146
Enriched materials from tantalum ore	钽矿富集物	2615. 9010	146
Ensembles, knitted or crocheted, of men or boys, of cotton	便服套装,针织或钩编的,男式,棉制	6103. 2200	2456

Article Description	商品名称	Tariff Code	D. R.
Ensembles, knitted or crocheted, of men or boys, of other textile materials	便服套装,针织或钩编的,男式,其他纺织材料制	6103.2990	2456
Ensembles, knitted or crocheted, of men or boys, of synthetic fibres	便服套装,针织或钩编的,男式,合成纤维制	6103.2300	2456
Ensembles, knitted or crocheted, of men or boys, of wool or fine animal hair	便服套装,针织或钩编的,男式,羊毛或动物细毛制	6103.2910	2456
Ensembles, knitted or crocheted, of women or girls, nes	便服套装,针织或钩编的,女式,其他	6104.2990	2456
Ensembles, knitted or crocheted, of women or girls, of cotton	便服套装,针织或钩编的,女式,棉制	6104.2200	2456
Ensembles, knitted or crocheted, of women or girls, of synthetic fibres	便服套装,针织或钩编的,女式,合成纤维制	6104.2300	2456
Ensembles, knitted or crocheted, of women or girls, of wool or fine animal hair	便服套装,针织或钩编的,女式,羊毛或动物细毛制	6104.2910	2456
Ensembles, not knitted or crocheted, for men or boys, nes	便服套装,非针织或钩编的,男式,其他	6203.2990	2456
Ensembles, not knitted or crocheted, for men or boys, of cotton	便服套装,非针织或钩编的,男式,棉制	6203.2200	2456
Ensembles, not knitted or crocheted, for men or boys, of silk or silk waste	便服套装,非针织或钩编的,男式,丝及绢丝制	6203.2910	2456
Ensembles, not knitted or crocheted, for men or boys, of synthetic fibres	便服套装,非针织或钩编的,男式,合成纤维制	6203.2300	2456
Ensembles, not knitted or crocheted, for men or boys, of wool or fine animal hair	便服套装,非针织或钩编的,男式,羊毛或动物细毛制	6203.2920	2456
Ensembles, not knitted or crocheted, for women or girls, nes	便服套装,非针织或钩编的,女式,其他	6204.2990	2456
Ensembles, not knitted or crocheted, for women or girls, of cotton	便服套装,非针织或钩编的,女式,棉制	6204.2200	2456
Ensembles, not knitted or crocheted, for women or girls, of silk or silk waste	便服套装,非针织或钩编的,女式,丝及绢丝制	6204.2910	2456
Ensembles, not knitted or crocheted, for women or girls, of synthetic fibres	便服套装,非针织或钩编的,女式,合成纤维制	6204.2300	2456
Ensembles, not knitted or crocheted, for women or girls, of wool or fine animal hair	便服套装,非针织或钩编的,女式,羊毛或动物细毛制	6204.2100	2456
Envelopes making machines parts, of paper	信封制造机器零件,纸制的	8441.9090	
Envelopes making machines, of paper	信封制造机器,纸制的	8441.2000	
Envelopes of paper or paperboard	信封,纸或纸板制的	4817.1000	6
Enzymatic preparations for pre-tanning	酶制剂,预鞣用	3202.9000	68
Enzymes and prepared enzymes, nes	酶及酶制品,其他	3507.9090	35
Eosins (as synthetic organic colouring matter)	曙红	3204.1200	345
Eosins (as synthetic organic colouring matter)	伊红	3204.1200	345
Ephedrine and its salts	麻黄碱及其盐	2939.4100	34
Ephedrines and their salts, nes	麻黄碱类及其盐,其他	2939.4900	34

Article Description	商品名称	Tariff Code	D. R.
Epichlorohydrin	表氯醇	2910. 3000	36
Epinephrine	肾上腺素	2937. 3100	36
Epoxide resins, in primary forms	环氧树脂,初级形状的	3907. 3000	1256
Epoxides, with a three-membered ring	环氧化物,三节环	2910. 9000	36
Epoxyalcohols, with a three-membered ring	环氧醇,三节环	2910. 9000	36
Epoxyethers, with a three-membered ring	环氧醚,三节环	2910. 9000	36
Epoxyphenols, with a three-membered ring	环氧酚,三节环	2910. 9000	36
Epsomite (natural magnesium sulphates)	泻盐矿(天然硫酸镁)	2530. 2000	13456
Equipment for scaffolding, shuttering, propping or pit-propping, of iron or steel	脚手架、模板或坑道支撑用的支柱及类似设备,钢铁的	7308. 4000	6
Erasers	橡皮擦	4016. 9200	
Erasing knives and blades thereof	改错刀及其刀片	8214. 1000	256
Ergometrine(INN) and its salts	麦角新碱及其盐	2939. 6100	34
Ergotamine(INN) and its salts	麦角胺及其盐	2939. 6200	34
Erythromycin and its derivatives, salts thereof	红霉素及其衍生物以及它们的盐	2941. 5000	
Escalators and moving walkways	自动梯及自动人行道	8428. 4000	57
Escalators parts	自动梯的零件	8431. 3100	3
Essential balm	清凉油	3004. 9054	368
Essential oils aqueous distillates and aqueous solutions	精油水馏液及水溶液	3301. 9090	34
Essential oils of aniseed	茴香油	3301. 2930	34
Essential oils of camphor	樟脑油	3301. 2910	34
Essential oils of cassia	桂油	3301. 2940	34
Essential oils of citronella	香茅油	3301. 2920	34
Essential oils of citrus fruit, nes	柑橘属果实的精油,其他	3301. 1990	34
Essential oils of eucalyptus	桉叶油	3301. 2960	34
Essential oils of geranium	老鹳草油	3301. 2991	34
Essential oils of geranium	香叶油	3301. 2991	34
Essential oils of lemon	柠檬油	3301. 1300	34
Essential oils of lime	白柠檬油	3301. 1910	34
Essential oils of lime	酸橙油	3301. 1910	34
Essential oils of litsea cubeba	山苍子油	3301. 2950	34
Essential oils of mentha piperita	胡椒薄荷油	3301. 2400	34
Essential oils of orange	橙油	3301. 1200	34
Essential oils of other mints	其他薄荷油	3301. 2500	34
Essential oils of peppermint	胡椒薄荷油	3301. 2400	34
Essential oils other than those of citrus fruit, nes	精油,柑橘属果实的,其他	3301. 2999	34
Estazolam (INN); salts thereof	艾司唑仑(INN)以及盐	2933. 9100	36
Ester gums	酯胶	3806. 3000	4
Esters of acetic acid, nes	乙酸酯,其他	2915. 3900	36
Esters of acrylic acid, nes	丙烯酸酯,其他	2916. 1290	36

E

Article Description	商品名称	Tariff Code	D. R.
Esters of formic acid	甲酸酯	2915. 1300	36
Esters of inorganic acids of nonmetals (excluding esters of hydrogen halides) and their salts; their halogenated, sulphonated, nitrated or nitrosated derivatives, nes	非金属无机酸酯(不包括卤化氢的酯)及其盐以及它们的卤化、磺化、硝化或亚硝化衍生物,其他	2920. 9090	36
Esters of orthophthalic acid, nes	邻苯二甲酸酯,其他	2917. 3490	36
Esters of phenylacetic acid	苯乙酸酯	2916. 3500	36
Esters of salicylic acid and their salts, nes	水杨酸的其他酯及其盐	2918. 2300	36
Etching and stripping equipment parts and accessories, semiconductor devices or of electronic integrated circuits manufacture machines and apparatus	刻蚀及剥离设备零件及附件,制造半导体器件或集成电路的机器及装置	8486. 9090	3
Etching and stripping equipment, semiconductor devices or of electronic integrated circuits manufacture machines and apparatus, nes	刻蚀及剥离设备,制造半导体器件或集成电路的机器及装置,其他	8486. 2049	7
Ethanal(acetaldehyde)	乙醛	2912. 1200	36
Ethchlorvynol(INN)	乙氯维诺(INN)	2905. 5100	36
Ether peroxides and their halogenated, sulphonated, nitrated or nitrosated derivatives	过氧化醚及其卤化、磺化、硝化或亚硝化衍生物	2909. 6000	36
Ethernet exchangers	以太网络交换机	8517. 6232	7
Ether-alcohols and their halogenated, sulphonated, nitrated or nitrosated derivatives, nes	醚醇及其卤化、磺化、硝化或亚硝化衍生物,其他	2909. 4990	36
Ether-alcohol-phenols and their halogenated, sulphonated, nitrated or nitrosated derivatives	醚醇酚及其卤化、磺化、硝化或亚硝化衍生物	2909. 5000	36
Ether-phenols and their halogenated, sulphonated, nitrated or nitrosated derivatives	醚酚及其卤化、磺化、硝化或亚硝化衍生物	2909. 5000	36
Ethinamate(INN)	炔已蚁胺(INN)	2924. 2400	36
Ethyl acetate	乙酸乙酯	2915. 3100	36
Ethyl acrylate	丙烯酸乙酯	2916. 1220	36
Ethyl alcohol and other spirits, denatured of any strength	乙醇,改性的,及其他酒精	2207. 2000	246
Ethyl alcohol, undenatured, of an alcoholic strength by volume of 80% vol or higher	乙醇,未改性的,按容量计酒精浓度在80%及以上	2207. 1000	246
Ethyl alcohol, undenatured, of an alcoholic strength by volume of less than 80% vol	乙醇,未改性的,按容量计酒精浓度在80%及以下,其他	2208. 9090	2468
Ethyl loflazepate(INN); salts thereof	氯氟卓乙酯(INN)以及盐	2933. 9100	36
Ethylamino butanol(ethambutol)	乙胺丁醇	2922. 1910	36
Ethylbenzene	乙苯	2902. 6000	6
Ethylcoumarins	乙基香豆素	2932. 2100	36
Ethyldiethanolamine	乙基二乙醇胺	2922. 1930	36
Ethylene	乙烯	2901. 2100	368
Ethylene dibromide (ISO)(1,2-dibromoethane)	1,2-二溴乙烷(ISO)	2903. 3100	36

E

Article Description	商品名称	Tariff Code	D. R.
Ethylene glycol(ethanediol)	1,2-乙二醇	2905.3100	36
Ethylene oxide	氧化乙烯	2910.1000	36
Ethylene polymers, in primary forms, nes	乙烯聚合物,初级形状的,其他	3901.9090	1256
Ethylene, liquefied	乙烯,液化的	2711.1400	1468
Ethylenediamine	乙二胺	2921.2110	36
Ethylenediamine salts	乙二胺盐	2921.2190	36
Ethylene-propylene copolymers, in primary forms, predominated by ethylene monomer unit	乙丙橡胶,初级形状的	3901.9010	1256
Ethylene-propylene copolymers, in primary forms, predominated by ethylene monomer unit	乙烯-丙烯共聚物,初级形状的,乙烯单体单元为主	3901.9010	1256
Ethylene-propylene copolymers, predominated by propylene monomer unit	乙丙橡胶	3902.3010	1256
Ethylene-propylene copolymers, predominated by propylene monomer unit	乙烯-丙烯共聚物	3902.3010	1256
Ethylene-propylene-non-conjugated diene rubber (EPDM), in primary forms	乙丙非共轭二烯橡胶(EPDM),初级形状的	4002.7010	136
Ethylene-propylene-non-conjugated diene rubber (EPDM), nes	乙丙非共轭二烯橡胶(EPDM),其他	4002.7090	136
Ethylene-vinyl acetate copolymers, in primary forms	乙烯-乙酸乙烯酯共聚物,初级形状的	3901.3000	1256
Ethylmorphine and salts	乙基吗啡及盐	2939.1100	34
Ethylvanillin	乙基香草醛	2912.4200	36
Etilamfetamine (INN), salts thereof	乙非他明以及它们的盐	2921.4600	36
Etorphine(INN) and salts	埃托啡(INN)及盐	2939.1100	34
Eucalgptol	1,8-桉树脑	2909.2081	36
Eucheuma, dried	麒麟菜,干的	1212.2061	14
Eucheuma, nes	麒麟菜,其他	1212.2069	14
Eurapium oxide	氧化铕	2846.9014	
Evaporative air coolers	蒸发式空气冷却器	8479.6000	7
Examination tables, for medical, surgical, dental or veterinary usages	检查台,医疗、外科、牙科或兽医用	9402.9000	3
Examinations apparatus without damaging structure (other than apparatus for radiological examinations), nes	无损探伤检测仪器(射线探伤仪除外),其他	9031.8039	7
Excavating machinery, for earth, minerals or ores, not self-propelled, nes	挖掘机械,对泥土、矿物或矿石的,非自推进的,其他	8430.6990	5
Excavating machinery, for earth, minerals or ores, self-propelled, nes	挖掘机械,对泥土、矿物或矿石的,自推进的,其他	8430.5090	5
Excavators parts	挖掘机零件	8431.4990	3
Excavators, track-mounted, with a 360° revolving superstructure	挖掘机,履带式,上部结构可旋转360度的机械	8429.5212	57
Excavators, tyre-mounted, with a 360° revolving superstructure	挖掘机,轮胎式,上部结构可旋转360度的机械	8429.5211	57

Article Description	商品名称	Tariff Code	D. R.
Excavators, with a 360° revolving superstructure, nes	挖掘机,上部结构可旋转 360 度的机械,其他	8429.5219	57
Excursion boats, motor vessels	游览船,机动船舶	8901.1010	5
Excursion boats, nes	游览船,非机动船舶	8901.1090	5
Executive-cases, with outer surface of leather, of composition leather or of patent leather	公文箱,以皮革、再生皮革或漆皮作面	4202.1190	1458
Executive-cases, with outer surface of plastics or of textile materials	公文箱,以塑料或纺织材料作面	4202.1290	256
Exercise and recovery equipments	健身及康复器械	9506.9110	
Exercise books, of paper or paperboard	练习本,纸或纸板制的	4820.2000	
Exfoliated vermiculite	页状蛭石	6806.2000	68
Exfoliated vermiculite, expanded clays, foamed slag and similar expanded mineral materials (including intermixtures thereof)	页状蛭石、膨胀粘土、泡沫矿渣及类似的膨胀矿物材料(包括其相互混合物)	6806.2000	68
Exhibitions instruments, designed for demonstrational purposes, unsuitable for other uses	展览专示范而无其他用途的仪器、装置及模型	9023.0000	
Expanded clays	膨胀粘土	6806.2000	68
Expanded metal, of copper	网眼铜板	7419.9940	4
Expanded metal, of iron or steel	网眼钢铁板	7314.5000	36
Explosives, based on ammonals nitrate	硝铵炸药	3602.0010	6
Explosives, prepared, nes, other than propellent powders	配制炸药,其他,但发射药除外	3602.0090	6
Exposing apparatus and equipment, automatically, for developed film to rolls of photographic paper, for the colour photographic film in rolls	曝光装置及设备,自动将已冲洗胶卷曝光到成卷感光纸上的,彩色胶卷用	9010.1091	7
Exposing apparatus and equipment, automatically, for developed film to rolls of photographic paper, nes	曝光装置及设备,自动将已冲洗胶卷曝光到成卷感光纸上的,其他	9010.1099	7
Exposing apparatus and equipment, automatically, for developed film to rolls of photographic paper, of a kind used in cinematographic film	曝光装置及设备,自动将已冲洗胶卷曝光到成卷感光纸上的,电影用	9010.1010	7
Exposing apparatus and equipment, automatically, for developed film to rolls of photographic paper, of a kind used in special photographic film or paper	曝光装置及设备,自动将已冲洗胶卷曝光到成卷感光纸上的,特种照相用	9010.1020	7
Exposure meters	曝光表	9027.8091	
Extracts and juices of meat, fish or crustaceans, molluscs or other aquatic invertebrates	精汁,肉、鱼、甲壳动物、软体动物或其他水生无脊椎动物的	1603.0000	48
Extruders, for working rubber or plastics or for the manufacture of products from these materials, nes	挤出机,加工橡胶或塑料及其产品用,其他	8477.2090	7
Extruding machinery auxiliary, for man-made textile materials	挤压机的辅助机器,化学纺织纤维的	8448.1900	3
Extruding machinery for man-made textile materials	挤压机,化学纺织纤维的	8444.0090	
Extruding nipples or spinnerets	喷丝头或喷丝板	8448.2020	3
Eyelash brushes	睫毛刷	9603.2900	

E

Article Description	商品名称	Tariff Code	D. R.
Eyelets, of base metal, of a kind used for clothing, footwear, awnings, handbags, travel goods or other made up articles	环,贱金属制,用于衣着、鞋靴、天篷、提包、旅行用品或其他制成品	8308. 1000	256
Eyes, of base metal, of a kind used for clothing, footwear, awnings, handbags, travel goods or other made up articles	眼,贱金属制,用于衣着、鞋靴、天篷、提包、旅行用品或其他制成品	8308. 1000	256

E

F

Article Description	商品名称	Tariff Code	D. R.
Fabrics consisting of warp without weft assembled by means of an adhesive of textile materials, nes	织物,用粘合剂粘合制成的有经纱而无纬纱的,其他	5806.4090	468
Fabrics consisting of warp without weft assembled by means of an adhesive, of cotton or bast fibres	织物,棉或麻制,用粘合剂粘合制成的有经纱而无纬纱的	5806.4010	468
Fabrics specified in Note 9 to section XI	机织物,第十一类注释九所列的	5407.3000	2468
Facial tissue stock, in rolls or sheets	面巾纸,成卷或成张的	4803.0000	58
Facial tissues, of paper pulp, paper, cellulose wadding or webs of cellulose fibres	面巾纸,纸浆、纸、纤维素絮纸或纤维素纤维网纸制的	4818.2000	568
Factice derived from oils	从油类提取的油膏	4002.9990	136
Factory ships, motor vessels, for processing or preserving fishery products	加工船,机动船舶,加工保藏鱼类产品的	8902.0010	5
Factory ships, not-motorized vessels, for processing or preserving fishery products	加工船,非机动船舶,加工保藏鱼类产品的	8902.0090	5
Fairground amusements, nes	游乐场的娱乐设备,其他	9508.9000	5
Fairground organs	游艺场风琴	9208.9000	5
False beards and the like, of animal hair or textile materials, nes	假胡须类似品,动物毛或纺织材料制的,其他	6704.9000	4
False beards and the like, of human hair	假胡须及类似品,人发制	6704.2000	4
False beards and the like, of synthetic textile materials, nes	假胡须及类似品,合成纤维纺织材料制,其他	6704.1900	4
False eyebrows and the like, of animal hair or textile materials, nes	假眉毛及类似品,动物毛或纺织材料制的,其他	6704.9000	4
False eyebrows and the like, of human hair	假眉毛及类似品,人发制	6704.2000	4
False eyebrows and the like, of synthetic textile materials, nes	假眉毛及类似品,合成纤维纺织材料制,其他	6704.1900	4
False eyelashes and the like, of animal hair or textile materials, nes	假睫毛及类似品,动物毛或纺织材料制的,其他	6704.9000	4
False eyelashes and the like, of human hair	假睫毛及类似品,人发制	6704.2000	4
Fans, nes	风机、风扇,其他	8414.5990	23
Fans, with a self-contained electric motor of an output not exceeding 125W, nes	风机、风扇,包括风机,本身装有一个输出功率不超过125瓦的电动机,其他	8414.5199	23
Fasteners for pressing or snapping	揿扣	9606.1000	5
Fats and oils and their fractions, of fish, other than liver oils	油、脂及其分离品除鱼肝油以外的鱼的	1504.2000	346
Fats and oils and their fractions, of marine mammals	油、脂及其分离品,海生哺乳动物的	1504.3000	4
Fats and oils and their fractions, of other animal, whether or not refined, but not chemically modified	油、脂及其分离品,其他动物的,不论是否精制,但未经化学改性	1506.0000	4
Fats of bovine animals, nes	牛脂肪,其他	1502.0090	4

F

Article Description	商品名称	Tariff Code	D. R.
Fats of bovine animals, raw	牛脂肪,未炼制的	1502. 0010	4
Fats of sheep or goats, nes	羊脂肪,其他	1502. 0090	4
Fats of sheep or goats, raw	羊脂肪,未炼制的	1502. 0010	4
Fats, derived from milk	脂,从乳中提取的	0405. 9000	268
Fatty livers (foie gras), fresh or chilled	肥肝,鲜或冷的	0207. 3400	1
Fatty substances derived therefrom, nes	脂肪物质,从羊毛脂制得的,其他	1505. 0000	
Feather dusters	毛掸	9603. 9010	
Feathers of a kind used for stuffing	羽毛,填充用	0505. 1000	34
Feathers with their skins and other parts of birds	羽毛及其鸟皮或鸟体其他部分	6701. 0000	
Feathers, parts of feathers and articles thereof	羽毛、部分羽毛及其制品	6701. 0000	
Feathers, powder and waste or parts of feathers	羽毛,不完整,粉末及废料	0505. 9010	34
Feeding stuffs preparations for use in making the complete feeds or supplementary feeds	饲料添加剂,制成的	2309. 9010	2468
Feeding stuffs preparing machinery for animal	饲料配制机,动物用	8436. 1000	
Feeds stuffs of plants, nes	饲料,植物的,其他	1214. 9000	
Felspar	长石	2529. 1000	13
Felt finishing machinery	毡呢整理机器	8449. 0090	7
Felt hats making blocks	毡呢帽模	8449. 0090	7
Felt hats making machinery	毡呢帽生产机器	8449. 0090	7
Felt of other textile materials, not impregnated, coated, covered or laminated	毡呢,其他纺织材料制,未浸渍、涂布、包覆或层压	5602. 2900	46
Felt of wool or fine animal hair, not impregnated, coated, covered or laminated	毡呢,羊毛或动物细毛制,未浸渍、涂布、包覆或层压	5602. 2100	46
Felt paper and paperboard	毡纸及纸板	4805. 5000	458
Felt tipped pens	毡尖笔	9608. 2000	
Felt, nes	毡呢,其他	5602. 9000	46
Fencamfamin (INN); salts thereof	芬坎法明(INN)以及它们的盐	2921. 4600	36
Fenchone	葑酮	2914. 2900	36
Fenetylline (INN) and its salts	芬乙茶碱(INN)及其盐	2939. 5100	34
Fenproporex (INN) and its salts	芬普雷司(INN)及其盐	2926. 3000	36
Fentanyl (INN); salts thereof	芬太尼(INN)以及盐	2933. 3300	36
Ferberite	钨铁矿	2611. 0000	146
Fermented beverages, nes	发酵饮料,其他	2206. 0090	2468
Ferrous products obtained by direct reduction of iron ore	铁产品,直接从铁矿还原所得的	7203. 1000	6
Ferrous sulphate	硫酸亚铁	2833. 2910	
Ferro-alloys, nes	铁合金,其他	7202. 9990	6
Ferro-cerium alloys, cut to shape, for immediate use	铈铁合金,已切成形,可直接使用	3606. 9011	13
Ferro-cerium alloys, nes	铈铁合金,其他	3606. 9019	13
Ferro-chromium alloys, containing by weight more than 4% of carbon	铬铁合金,按重量计含碳量在 4% 以上	7202. 4100	6

F

Article Description	商品名称	Tariff Code	D. R.
Ferro-chromium alloys, nes	铬铁合金,其他	7202.4900	6
Ferro-manganese alloys, containing by weight more than 2% of carbon	锰铁合金,按重量计含碳量在2%以上	7202.1100	6
Ferro-manganese alloys, nes	锰铁合金,其他	7202.1900	6
Ferro-molybdenum alloys	钼铁合金	7202.7000	6
Ferro-nickel alloys	镍铁合金	7202.6000	6
Ferro-niobium alloys	铌铁合金	7202.9300	6
Ferro-silicon alloys, containing by weight more than 55% of silicon	硅铁合金,按重量计含硅量在55%以上	7202.2100	6
Ferro-silicon alloys, nes	硅铁合金,其他	7202.2900	6
Ferro-silico-chromium alloys	硅铬铁合金	7202.5000	6
Ferro-silico-manganese alloys	硅锰铁合金	7202.3000	6
Ferro-silico-titanium alloys	硅钛铁合金	7202.9100	6
Ferro-silico-tungsten alloys	硅钨铁合金	7202.8020	6
Ferro-titanium alloys	钛铁合金	7202.9100	6
Ferro-tungsten alloys	钨铁合金	7202.8010	6
Ferro-vanadium alloys, containing by weight more than 75% of vanadium	钒铁合金,按重量计含钒量在75%及以上	7202.9210	6
Ferro-vanadium alloys, nes	钒铁合金,其他	7202.9290	6
Ferryboats, motor vessels	渡船,机动船舶	8901.1010	5
Ferryboats, nes	渡船,非机动船舶	8901.1090	5
Fertilized fish eggs	受精鱼卵	0511.9111	4
Fertilizers containing nitrates and phosphates	复合肥,含有硝酸盐及磷酸盐	3105.5100	68
Fertilizers containing the three fertilizing elements nitrogen, phosphorus and potassium, mineral or chemical	复合肥,含氮、磷、钾三种肥效元素的矿物肥料或化学肥料	3105.2000	68
Fertilizers containing the two fertilizing elements phosphorus and potassium, mineral or chemical fertilizers	复合肥,含磷、钾两种肥效元素的矿物肥料或化学肥料	3105.6000	68
Fertilizers in packages of a gross weight not exceeding 10kg	肥料,毛重不超过10千克的,	3105.1000	68
Fertilizers in tablets or similar forms	肥料,制成片及类似形状的	3105.1000	68
Fertilizers, nes	肥料,其他	3105.9000	68
Fertilizers, nes, containing the two fertilizing elements nitrogen and phosphorus, mineral or chemical	复合肥,其他,含氮、磷两种肥效元素的矿物肥料或化学肥料	3105.5900	68
Fescue seed, forage plants	羊茅子,饲料植物用的	1209.2300	358
Festive entertainment articles	节日用品	9505.9000	5
Fiber glass winder (excluding opticaefiber winder)	玻璃纤维拉丝机(光纤拉丝机除外)	8475.2912	
Fibre building board manufacture presses	木纤维板挤压机	8479.3000	7
Fibreboard of wood or other ligneous materials, nes	木纤维板或其他木质材料纤维板,其他	4411.9429	48

F

Article Description	商品名称	Tariff Code	D. R.
Fibreboard of wood or other ligneous materials, of a density exceeding 0. 35g/cm³ but not exceeding 0. 5g/cm³	木纤维板或其他木质材料纤维板,密度超过每立方厘米0. 35克,但未超过每立方厘米0. 5克	4411. 9410	48
Fibreboard of wood or other ligneous materials, of a density exceeding 0. 5g/cm³ but not exceeding 0. 8g/cm³, nes	木纤维板或其他木质材料纤维板,密度超过每立方厘米0. 5克,但未超过每立方厘米0. 8克,其他	4411. 9390	48
Fibreboard of wood or other ligneous materials, of a density exceeding 0. 5g/cm³ but not exceeding 0. 8g/cm³, of radiata pine	木纤维板或其他木质材料纤维板,密度超过每立方厘米0. 5克,但未超过每立方厘米0. 8克,辐射松制的	4411. 9310	48
Fibreboard of wood or other ligneous materials, of a density exceeding 0. 8g/cm³, not mechanically worked or surface covered	木纤维板或其他木质材料纤维板,密度超过每立方厘米0. 8克,未经机械加工或盖面的	4411. 9210	48
Fibreboard of wood or other ligneous materials, of a density exceeding 0. 8g/cm³, not mechanically worked or surface covered, nes	木纤维板或其他木质材料纤维板,密度超过每立方厘米0. 8克,其他	4411. 9290	48
Fibreboard of wood or other ligneous materials, of a density not exceeding 0. 35g/cm³, not mechanically worked or surface covered	木纤维板或其他木质材料纤维板,密度未超过每立方厘米0. 35克,未经机械加工或盖面的	4411. 9421	48
Ficin	无花果蛋白酶	3507. 9090	35
Figs	无花果	0804. 2000	14
Filament lamps, excluding ultraviolet or infra-red lamps, for locomotives and roiling-stock, aircraft or ships	灯,不包括紫外线灯或红外线灯,火车、航空器及船舶用	8539. 2920	35
Filament lamps, excluding ultraviolet or infra-red lamps, for motor vehicles	灯,不包括紫外线灯或红外线灯,机动车辆用	8539. 2930	35
Filament lamps, excluding ultraviolet or infra-red lamps, for scientific or medical uses only	灯,不包括紫外线灯或红外线灯,科研、医疗专用	8539. 2910	35
Filament lamps, excluding ultraviolet or infra-red lamps, nes	灯,不包括紫外线灯或红外线灯,其他	8539. 2999	35
Filament lamps, excluding ultraviolet or infra-red lamps, of a voltage 12V or less	灯,不包括紫外线灯或红外线灯,12伏及以下的	8539. 2991	35
Filament lamps, of a power not exceeding 200W and for a voltage exceeding 100V, excluding ultraviolet or infra-red lamps, for scientific or medical uses only	灯,功率不超过200瓦,但额定电压超过100伏,不包括紫外线灯或红外线灯,科研、医疗专用	8539. 2210	35
Filament lamps, of a power not exceeding 200W and for a voltage exceeding 100V, excluding ultraviolet or infra-red lamps, nes	灯,功率不超过200瓦,但额定电压超过100伏,不包括紫外线灯或红外线灯,其他	8539. 2290	35
Filament winding machines	绕线机	8479. 8110	7
File covers, of paper or paperboard	卷宗皮,纸或纸板制的	4820. 3000	
Files and similar tools	钢锉及类似工具	8203. 1000	256
Filing cabinets, of base metal, other than office furniture	档案柜,贱金属制,办公室家具除外	8304. 0000	256

Article Description	商品名称	Tariff Code	D. R.
Fillets of ictalurus, nes, frozen	鱼片,叉尾鮰鱼的,其他,冻的	0304.2929	18
Fillets of tilapia, frozen	鱼片,罗非鱼的,冻的	0304.2910	18
Fillets, channel catfish (Ictalurus Punctatus), frozen	鱼片,斑点叉尾鮰鱼的,冻的	0304.2921	18
Fillets, nes, frozen	鱼片,其他,冻的	0304.2990	18
Fillets, swordfish (Xiphias gladius), frozen	鱼片,剑鱼的,冻的	0304.2100	18
Fillets, toothfish (Dissostichus spp.), frozen	鱼片,南极犬牙鱼的,冻的	0304.2200	18
Filling machines, for bottles, cans, boxes, bags or other containers	装填机器,瓶、罐、箱、袋或其他容器的	8422.3090	
Film deposition equipment parts and accessories, semiconductor devices or of electronic integrated circuits or flat panel displays manufacture machines and apparatus	薄膜沉积设备零件及附件,制造半导体器件、集成电路、平板显示器的机器及装置	8486.9090	3
Film deposition equipment, flat panel displays manufacture machines and apparatus, nes	薄膜沉积设备,制造平板显示器用的机器及装置,其他	8486.3029	7
Film deposition equipment, semiconductor devices or of electronic integrated circuits manufacture machines and apparatus, nes	薄膜沉积设备,制造半导体器件或集成电路的机器及装置,其他	8486.2029	7
Filter blocks, slabs and plates, of paper pulp	滤块、滤板及滤片,纸浆制的	4812.0000	16
Filter paper and paperboard	滤纸及纸板	4805.4000	458
Filter paper and paperboard, of width not exceeding 36cm or in roll or no side exceeding 36cm in unfoled state	滤纸及纸板,成卷或成张的,卷宽度不超过36厘米,或任何一边不超过36厘米	4823.2000	68
Filtering apparatus for exhaust air, for internal combustion engines	过滤装置,内燃发动机排气用	8421.3930	7
Filtering apparatus for gases, nes	过滤装置,气体用,其他	8421.3990	7
Filtering machinery and apparatus, for filtering or purifying beverages other than water	过滤机器及装置,过滤或净化饮料(水除外)用	8421.2200	7
Filtering machinery and apparatus, for filtering or purifying water, nes	过滤机器及装置,过滤或净化水用,其他	8421.2190	7
Filtering machinery and apparatus, for liquids, nes	过滤机器及装置,液体用,其他	8421.2990	7
Filtering machinery and apparatus, of the household type, for filtering or purifying water	过滤机器及装置,家用型,过滤或净化水用	8421.2110	7
Filtering machinery and apparatus, of the household type, for gases	过滤机器及装置,家用型,气体用	8421.3910	7
Filtering machines parts, nes	过滤装置用零件,其他	8421.9990	3
Filtering machines parts, of household-type	过滤装置用零件,家用型	8421.9910	3
Filters, for cameras	滤色镜,照相机用	9002.2010	3
Filters, nes	滤色镜,其他	9002.2090	3
Fine animal hair, carded or combed, nes	动物细毛,已梳的,其他	5105.3990	5
Fine animal hair, carded or combed, of dehaired goats	动物细毛,已梳的,无毛山羊绒	5105.3921	5
Fine animal hair, carded or combed, of goats, nes	动物细毛,已梳的,山羊绒,其他	5105.3929	5
Fine animal hair, carded or combed, of kashmir goats	动物细毛,已梳的,喀什米尔山羊的	5105.3100	5

Article Description	商品名称	Tariff Code	D. R.
Fine animal hair, carded or combed, of rabbit and hare	动物细毛,已梳的,兔毛	5105. 3910	5
Fine animal hair, not carded or combed, nes	动物细毛,未梳的,其他	5102. 1990	48
Fine animal hair, not carded or combed, of goats, nes	动物细毛,未梳的,山羊绒,其他	5102. 1920	48
Fine animal hair, not carded or combed, of camel	动物细毛,未梳的,骆驼毛、骆驼绒	5102. 1930	48
Fine animal hair, not carded or combed, of kashmir goats	动物细毛,未梳的,喀什米尔山羊的	5102. 1100	48
Fine animal hair, not carded or combed, of rabbit and hare	动物细毛,未梳的,兔毛	5102. 1910	48
Fining equipments outside converters	炉外精炼设备	8454. 2010	
Fining equipments outside converters parts	炉外精炼设备用零件	8454. 9010	3
Finished oil tanker ships, loading exceeding 100000t, but not exceeding 300000t	成品油船,载重量超过 10 万吨,但不超过 30 万吨	8901. 2012	8
Finished oil tanker ships, loading exceeding 300000t	成品油船,载重量超过 30 万吨	8901. 2013	8
Finished oil tanker ships, loading not exceeding 100000t	成品油船,载重量不超过 10 万吨	8901. 2011	8
Finishing agents, of a kind used in the leather or like industries, nes	整理剂,制革工业及类似工业用,其他	3809. 9300	236
Finishing agents, of a kind used in the paper or like industries, nes	整理剂,造纸工业及类似工业用,其他	3809. 9200	236
Finishing agents, of a kind used in the textile or like industries, nes	整理剂,纺织工业及类似工业用,其他	3809. 9100	236
Finishing agents, with a basis of amylaceous substances	整理剂,以淀粉物质为基本成分	3809. 1000	236
Finishing machines for textile fabrics	整理机器,纺织物的	8451. 8000	
Finishing machines of gear, for removing metal or cermets, nes	精加工机床,齿轮的,切削金属或金属陶瓷用,其他	8461. 4090	7
Finishing machines of gear, numerically controlled, for removing metal or cermets	精加工机床,齿轮的,数控的,切削金属或金属陶瓷用	8461. 4010	7
Finishing machines parts for textile fabrics	整理机器零件,纺织物的	8451. 9000	
Finishing machine-tools, for metal or cermets, nes	精加工的机床,加工金属或金属陶瓷用,其他	8460. 9090	7
Fire alarms and similar apparatus	防火报警器及类似装置	8531. 1000	3
Fire alarms parts and parts of similar apparatus	防火报警器及类似装置用零件	8531. 9010	3
Fire fighting vehicles, mounted with scaling ladder	救火车,装有云梯的	8705. 3010	7
Fire fighting vehicles, nes	救火车,其他	8705. 3090	7
Firedamp engines, internal combustion piston engines, spark-ignition reciprocating or rotary	沼气发动机,活塞内燃发动机,点燃往复式或旋转式	8407. 9010	25
Fireworks	爆竹	3604. 1000	
Fireworks	烟花	3604. 1000	
Fire-clay	耐火粘土	2508. 3000	145
Fire-extinguishers charges	灭火器的装配药	3813. 0010	36

Article Description	商品名称	Tariff Code	D. R.
Fire-extinguishers parts	灭火器零件	8424. 9010	
Fire-extinguishers, whether or not charged	灭火器,不论是否装药	8424. 1000	
Fire-extinguishing grenades, charged	灭火弹,已装药的	3813. 0020	36
Fire-floats	消防船	8905. 9090	37
First-aid boxes and kits	急救药箱、药包	3006. 5000	36
First-day covers	首日封	9704. 0090	5
Fish fillets, dried, salted or in brine	鱼片,盐腌或盐渍的	0305. 3000	4
Fish fillets, nes, fresh or chilled	鱼片,其他,鲜或冷的,不论是否绞碎	0304. 1900	18
Fish fillets, swordfish (Xiphias gladius), fresh or chilled	鱼片,剑鱼的,鲜或冷的,不论是否绞碎	0304. 1100	18
Fish fillets, toothfish (Dissostichus spp.), fresh or chilled	鱼片,南极犬牙鱼的,鲜或冷的,不论是否绞碎	0304. 1200	18
Fish knives, other than plated with precious metal	鱼刀,非镀贵金属的	8215. 9900	256
Fish knives, plated with precious metal	鱼刀,镀贵金属的	8215. 9100	256
Fish landing nets	捞鱼网	9507. 9000	5
Fish meat (whether or not minced), nes, fresh or chilled	鱼肉,其他,鲜或冷的,不论是否绞碎	0304. 1900	18
Fish meat (whether or not minced), swordfish (Xiphias gladius), fresh or chilled	鱼肉,剑鱼的,鲜或冷的,不论是否绞碎	0304. 1100	18
Fish meat (whether or not minced), toothfish (Dissostichus spp.), fresh or chilled	鱼肉,南极犬牙鱼的,鲜或冷的,不论是否绞碎	0304. 1200	18
Fish meat, toothfish, whether or not minced, frozen	鱼肉,南极犬牙鱼,冻的	0304. 9200	18
Fish meat, nes, whether or not minced, frozen	鱼肉,其他,冻的	0304. 9900	18
Fish meat, swordfish, whether or not minced, frozen	鱼肉,剑鱼,冻的	0304. 9100	18
Fish, living, nes	鱼,活的,其他	0301. 9999	15
Fish, nes, frozen	鱼,其他,冻的	0303. 7990	18
Fish, nes, in airtight containers	罐头,其他鱼的	1604. 2019	48
Fish, nes, prepared or preserved	鱼,其他,制作或保藏的	1604. 2099	48
Fish, nes, prepared or preserved, whole or in pieces, but not minced	鱼,其他,制作或保藏的,整条或切块,但未绞碎	1604. 1990	48
Fish, nes, salted or in brine	鱼,其他,盐腌及盐渍的	0305. 6990	4
Fishes, nes, fresh or chilled	鱼,其他,鲜或冷的	0302. 6990	18
Fishing nets of man-made textile materials	渔网,化学纤维材料制	5608. 1100	34
Fishing reels	钓线轮	9507. 3000	
Fishing rods	钩鱼竿	9507. 1000	
Fishing vessels, motor vessels	捕鱼船,机动船舶	8902. 0010	5
Fishing vessels, not-motorized vessels	捕鱼船,非机动船舶	8902. 0090	5
Fish-hooks, whether or not snelled	钓鱼钩,不论有无系钩丝	9507. 2000	
Fish-liver oils and their fractions	鱼肝油及其分离品	1504. 1000	346
Fish-plates and sole plates	鱼尾板及钢轨垫板	7302. 4000	6
Fittings for coachwork or the like, of plastics	车厢或类似品的附件,塑料的	3926. 3000	236
Fittings for furniture, or the like, of plastics	家具或类似品的附件,塑料的	3926. 3000	236

F

Article Description	商品名称	Tariff Code	D. R.
Fittings for loose-leaf binders	活页夹的附件	8305. 1000	256
Fittings for loose-leaf files	卷宗夹的附件	8305. 1000	256
Fittings of plastics	管子附件,塑料的	3917. 4000	
Fixed and reduced tube mills	定减径轧管机	8455. 1030	7
Fixed vegetable fats and oils and fractions thereof, nes	固定植物油脂及其分离品,其他	1515. 9090	
Fixed vegetable fats or oils extraction machinery	植物固定油脂提取的机器	8479. 2000	7
Fixed vegetable fats or oils preparation machinery	植物固定油脂加工的机器	8479. 2000	7
Fixed wireless access station	无线接入固定台	8517. 6293	7
Flagstones, of natural stone (except slate)	扁平石,天然石料(不包括板岩)制的	6801. 0000	46
Flame-throwers	火焰喷射器	9301. 2000	
Flammulina Velutipes, dried	金针菇,干的	0712. 3920	4
Flammulina Velutipes, fresh or chilled	金针菇,鲜或冷藏的	0709. 5930	1
Flanders type hand-woven tapestries	弗朗德及类似式样的手织装饰毯	5805. 0090	468
Flanges, of iron or steel, nes	法兰,钢铁的,其他	7307. 9100	6
Flanges, of plastics	法兰,塑料的	3917. 4000	
Flanges, of stainless steel	法兰,不锈钢制	7307. 2100	6
Flash bulbs, photographic	闪光灯泡,照相用	9006. 6910	7
Flash memory cards, recorded	闪速存储器,已录制	8523. 5120	37
Flash memory cards, unrecorded	闪速存储器,未录制	8523. 5110	37
Flashlight apparatus and flashbulbs parts and accessories, photographic, nes	闪光灯装置及闪光灯泡的零件、附件,照相用,其他	9006. 9900	3
Flashlight, discharge lamp (electronic), photographic	闪光灯,放电式(电子式),照相用	9006. 6100	7
Flashlight, photographic, nes	闪光灯,照相用,其他	9006. 6990	7
Flat fish, nes, fresh or chilled	比目鱼,其他,鲜或冷的,	0302. 2900	18
Flat panel displays manufacture machines and apparatus, nes	平板显示器的制造机器及装置,其他	8486. 3090	7
Flat panel displays manufacture machines and apparatus, oxidation, diffusion, annealing and other heat treatment equipment	平板显示器的制造机器及装置,扩散、氧化、退火及其他热处理设备	8486. 3010	7
Flat seam machines	平缝机	8452. 2110	
Flat weft knitting machines	平型纬编机	8447. 2020	7
Flatfish, nes, frozen	比目鱼,其他,冻的	0303. 3900	18
Flat-rolled products of grain-oriented silicon-electrical steel, of a width of 600mm or more	平板轧材,取向性硅电钢,宽度在 600 毫米及以上	7225. 1100	468
Flat-rolled products of grain-oriented silicon-electrical steel, of a width of less than 600mm	平板轧材,取向性硅电钢,宽度小于 600 毫米	7226. 1100	468
Flat-rolled products of high speed steel, of a width of 600mm or less	平板轧材,高速钢制,宽度小于 600 毫米	7226. 2000	468
Flat-rolled products of high speed steel, of a width of 600mm or more	平板轧材,高速钢制,宽度在 600 毫米及以上	7225. 9910	468

Article Description	商品名称	Tariff Code	D. R.
Flat-rolled products of iron or non-alloy steel of a width of 600mm or more, hot-rolled, not clad, plated or coated, in coils, with patterns in relief, not further worked than hot rolled	平板轧材,铁或非合金钢的,宽度在600毫米及以上的,经热轧,但未经包覆、镀层或涂层,已轧压花纹,卷状,除热轧外未经进一步加工的	7208.1000	468
Flat-rolled products of iron or non-alloy steel of a width of 600mm or more, hot-rolled, not clad, plated or coated, in coils, not further worked than hot-rolled, nes	平板轧材,铁或非合金钢的,宽度在600毫米及以上的,经热轧,但未经包覆、镀层或涂层,卷材,除热轧外未经进一步加工,其他	7208.3990	468
Flat-rolled products of iron or non-alloy steel of a width of 600mm or more, hot-rolled, not clad, plated or coated, in coils, not further worked than hot-rolled, of a thickness exceeding 10mm	平板轧材,铁或非合金钢的,宽度在600毫米及以上的,经热轧,但未经包覆、镀层或涂层,卷材,除热轧外未经进一步加工,厚度超过10毫米	7208.3600	468
Flat-rolled products of iron or non-alloy steel of a width of 600mm or more, hot-rolled, not clad, plated or coated, in coils, not further worked than hot-rolled, of a thickness of 3mm or more but less than 4.75mm, nes	平板轧材,铁或非合金钢的,宽度在600毫米及以上的,经热轧,但未经包覆、镀层或涂层,卷材,除热轧外未经进一步加工,厚度在3毫米及以上,但小于4.75毫米,其他	7208.3890	468
Flat-rolled products of iron or non-alloy steel of a width of 600mm or more, hot-rolled, not clad, plated or coated, in coils, not further worked than hot-rolled, of a thickness of 3mm or more but less than 4.75mm, of a yield strength exceeding $355N/mm^2$	平板轧材,铁或非合金钢的,宽度在600毫米及以上的,经热轧,但未经包覆、镀层或涂层,卷材,除热轧外未经进一步加工,厚度在3毫米及以上,但小于4.75毫米,屈服强度大于355牛顿/平方毫米	7208.3810	468
Flat-rolled products of iron or non-alloy steel of a width of 600mm or more, hot-rolled, not clad, plated or coated, in coils, not further worked than hot-rolled, of a thickness of 4.75mm or more but not exceeding 10mm	平板轧材,铁或非合金钢的,宽度在600毫米及以上的,经热轧,但未经包覆、镀层或涂层,卷材,除热轧外未经进一步加工,厚度在4.75毫米及以上,但不超过10毫米	7208.3700	468
Flat-rolled products of iron or non-alloy steel of a width of 600mm or more, hot-rolled, not clad, plated or coated, in coils, not further worked than hot-rolled, of a thickness of less than 1.5mm	平板轧材,铁或非合金钢的,宽度在600毫米及以上的,经热轧,但未经包覆、镀层或涂层,卷材,除热轧外未经进一步加工,厚度小于1.5毫米	7208.3910	468
Flat-rolled products of iron or non-alloy steel of a width of 600mm or more, hot-rolled, not clad, plated or coated, in coils, not further worked than hot-rolled, pickled, of a thickness of 4.75mm or more	平板轧材,铁或非合金钢的,宽度在600毫米及以上的,经热轧,但未经包覆、镀层或涂层,经酸洗的卷材,除热轧外未经进一步加工,厚度在4.75毫米及以上	7208.2500	468
Flat-rolled products of iron or non-alloy steel of a width of 600mm or more, hot-rolled, not clad, plated or coated, nes	平板轧材,铁或非合金钢的,宽度在600毫米及以上的,经热轧,但未经包覆、镀层或涂层,其他	7208.9000	468

F

Article Description	商品名称	Tariff Code	D. R.
Flat-rolled products of iron or non-alloy steel of a width of 600mm or more, hot-rolled, not clad, plated or coated, not in coils, not further worked than hotrolled, with patterns in relief	平板轧材,铁或非合金钢的,宽度在600毫米及以上的,经热轧,但未经包覆、镀层或涂层,已轧压花纹的非卷材,除热轧外未经进一步加工	7208. 4000	468
Flat-rolled products of iron or non-alloy steel of a width of 600mm or more, hot-rolled, not clad, plated or coated, not in coils, not further worked than hot-rolled, of a thickness exceeding 10mm, nes	平板轧材,铁或非合金钢的,宽度在600毫米及以上的,经热轧,但未经包覆、镀层或涂层,非卷材,除热轧外未经进一步加工,厚度超过10毫米,其他	7208. 5190	468
Flat-rolled products of iron or non-alloy steel of a width of 600mm or more, hot-rolled, not clad, plated or coated, not in coils, not further worked than hot-rolled, of a thickness exceeding 20mm but not exceeding 50mm	平板轧材,铁或非合金钢的,宽度在600毫米及以上的,经热轧,但未经包覆、镀层或涂层,非卷材,除热轧外未经进一步加工,厚度在20毫米以上,但不超过50毫米	7208. 5120	468
Flat-rolled products of iron or non-alloy steel of a width of 600mm or more, hot-rolled, not clad, plated or coated, not in coils, not further worked than hot-rolled, of a thickness exceeding 50mm	平板轧材,铁或非合金钢的,宽度在600毫米及以上的,经热轧,但未经包覆、镀层或涂层,非卷材,除热轧外未经进一步加工,厚度超过50毫米	7208. 5110	468
Flat-rolled products of iron or non-alloy steel of a width of 600mm or more, hot-rolled, not clad, plated or coated, not in coils, not further worked than hot-rolled, of a thickness of 3mm or more but less than 4. 75mm, nes	平板轧材,铁或非合金钢的,宽度在600毫米及以上的,经热轧,但未经包覆、镀层或涂层,非卷材,除热轧外未经进一步加工,厚度在3毫米及以上,但小于4.75毫米,其他	7208. 5390	468
Flat-rolled products of iron or non-alloy steel of a width of 600mm or more, hot-rolled, not clad, plated or coated, not in coils, not further worked than hot-rolled, of a thickness of 3mm or more but less than 4. 75mm, of a yield strength exceeding 355N/mm^2	平板轧材,铁或非合金钢的,宽度在600毫米及以上的,经热轧,但未经包覆、镀层或涂层,非卷材,除热轧外未经进一步加工,厚度在3毫米及以上,但小于4.75毫米,屈服强度大于355牛顿/平方毫米	7208. 5310	468
Flat-rolled products of iron or non-alloy steel of a width of 600mm or more, hot-rolled, not clad, plated or coated, not in coils, not further worked than hot-rolled, of a thickness of 4. 75mm or more but not exceeding 10mm	平板轧材,铁或非合金钢的,宽度在600毫米及以上的,经热轧,但未经包覆、镀层或涂层,非卷材,除热轧外未经进一步加工,厚度在4.75毫米及以上,但不超过10毫米	7208. 5200	468
Flat-rolled products of iron or non-alloy steel of a width of 600mm or more, hot-rolled, not clad, plated or coated, not in coils, not further worked than hot-rolled, of a thickness of less than 3mm, nes	平板轧材,铁或非合金钢的,宽度在600毫米及以上的,经热轧,但未经包覆、镀层或涂层,非卷材,除热轧外未经进一步加工,厚度小于3毫米,其他	7208. 5490	468

F

Article Description	商品名称	Tariff Code	D. R.
Flat-rolled products of iron or non-alloy steel of a width of 600mm or more, hot-rolled, not clad, plated or coated, not in coils, not further worked than hot-rolled, of a thickness of less than 3mm, of a thickness of less than 1.5mm	平板轧材,铁或非合金钢的,宽度在600毫米及以上的,经热轧,但未经包覆、镀层或涂层,非卷材,除热轧外未经进一步加工,厚度小于3毫米,厚度小于1.5毫米	7208.5410	468
Flat-rolled products of iron or non-alloy steel of a width of 600mm or more, hot-rolled, not clad, plated or coated, pickled in coils, not further worked than hot-rolled, of a thickness of less than 3mm, nes	平板轧材,铁或非合金钢的,宽度在600毫米及以上的,经热轧,但未经包覆、镀层或涂层,经酸洗的卷材,除热轧外未经进一步加工,厚度小于3毫米,其他	7208.2790	468
Flat-rolled products of iron or non-alloy steel of a width of 600mm or more, hot-rolled, not clad, plated or coated, pickled, in coils, not further worked than hot-rolled, of a thickness of 3mm or more but less than 4.75mm, nes	平板轧材,铁或非合金钢的,宽度在600毫米及以上的,经热轧,但未经包覆、镀层或涂层,经酸洗的卷材,除热轧外未经进一步加工,厚度在3毫米及以上,但小于4.75毫米,其他	7208.2690	468
Flat-rolled products of iron or non-alloy steel of a width of 600mm or more, hot-rolled, not clad, plated or coated, pickled, in coils, not further worked than hot-rolled, of a thickness of 3mm or more but less than 4.75mm, of a yield strength exceeding 355N/mm^2	平板轧材,铁或非合金钢的,宽度在600毫米及以上的,经热轧,但未经包覆、镀层或涂层,经酸洗的卷材,除热轧外未经进一步加工,厚度在3毫米及以上,但小于4.75毫米,屈服强度大于355牛顿/平方毫米	7208.2610	468
Flat-rolled products of iron or non-alloy steel of a width of 600mm or more, hot-rolled, not clad, plated or coated, pickled, in coils, not further worked than hot-rolled, of a thickness of less than 3mm, of a thickness of less than 1.5mm	平板轧材,铁或非合金钢的,宽度在600毫米及以上的,经热轧,但未经包覆、镀层或涂层,经酸洗的卷材,除热轧外未经进一步加工,厚度小于3毫米,厚度小于1.5毫米	7208.2710	468
Flat-rolled products of iron or non-alloy steel, of a width of 600mm of more, electrolytically plated or coated with zinc	平板轧材,铁或非合金钢的宽度在600毫米及以上的,电镀锌的	7210.3000	468
Flat-rolled products of iron or non-alloy steel, of a width of 600mm of more, nes	平板轧材,铁或非合金钢的宽度在600毫米及以上的,经包覆、镀层或涂层,其他	7210.9000	468
Flat-rolled products of iron or non-alloy steel, of a width of 600mm of more, painted, varnished or coated with plastics	平板轧材,铁或非合金钢的宽度在600毫米及以上的,涂漆或涂塑的	7210.7000	468
Flat-rolled products of iron or non-alloy steel, of a width of 600mm of more, plated or coated with aluminium, nes	平板轧材,铁或非合金钢的宽度在600毫米及以上的,镀或涂铝的,其他	7210.6900	468
Flat-rolled products of iron or non-alloy steel, of a width of 600mm of more, plated or coated with aluminium, plated or coated with aluminium-zinc alloys	平板轧材,铁或非合金钢的宽度在600毫米及以上的,镀或涂铝的,镀或涂铝锌合金的	7210.6100	468

F

Article Description	商品名称	Tariff Code	D. R.
Flat-rolled products of iron or non-alloy steel, of a width of 600mm of more, plated or coated with chromium oxides or with chromium and chromium oxides	平板轧材,铁或非合金钢的宽度在600毫米及以上的,镀或涂氧化铬或铬及氧化铬的	7210.5000	468
Flat-rolled products of iron or non-alloy steel, of a width of 600mm of more, plated or coated with lead, including terneplate	平板轧材,铁或非合金钢的宽度在600毫米及以上的,镀或涂铅的,包括镀铅锡钢板	7210.2000	468
Flat-rolled products of iron or non-alloy steel, of a width of 600mm of more, plated or coated with tin, of a thickness of 0.5mm or more	平板轧材,铁或非合金钢的宽度在600毫米及以上的,镀或涂锡的,厚度在0.5毫米及以上	7210.1100	468
Flat-rolled products of iron or non-alloy steel, of a width of 600mm of more, plated or coated with tin, of a thickness of less than 0.5mm	平板轧材,铁或非合金钢的宽度在600毫米及以上的,镀或涂锡的,厚度小于0.5毫米	7210.1200	468
Flat-rolled products of iron or non-alloy steel, of a width of 600mm of more, plated or coated with zinc, corrugated	平板轧材,铁或非合金钢的宽度在600毫米及以上的,用其他方法镀或涂锌的,瓦楞形	7210.4100	468
Flat-rolled products of iron or non-alloy steel, of a width of 600mm of more, plated or coated with zinc, nes	平板轧材,铁或非合金钢的宽度在600毫米及以上的,用其他方法镀或涂锌的,其他	7210.4900	468
Flat-rolled products of iron or non-alloy steel, of a width of 600mm or more, cold rolled, not clad, plated or coated, in coils, not further worked than cold-rolled, of a thickness exceeding 1mm but less than 3mm, nes	平板轧材,铁或非合金钢的,宽度在600毫米及以上的,经冷轧,但未经包覆、镀层或涂层,卷材,除冷轧外未经进一步加工,厚度超过1毫米,但小于3毫米,其他	7209.1690	468
Flat-rolled products of iron or non-alloy steel, of a width of 600mm or more, cold rolled, not clad, plated or coated, in coils, not further worked than cold-rolled, of a thickness exceeding 1mm but less than 3mm, of a yield strength exceeding $275N/mm^2$	平板轧材,铁或非合金钢的,宽度在600毫米及以上的,经冷轧,但未经包覆、镀层或涂层,卷材,除冷轧外未经进一步加工,厚度超过1毫米,但小于3毫米,屈服强度大于275牛顿/平方毫米	7209.1610	468
Flat-rolled products of iron or non-alloy steel, of a width of 600mm or more, cold rolled, not clad, plated or coated, in coils, not further worked than cold-rolled, of a thickness less than 0.3mm	平板轧材,铁或非合金钢的宽度在600毫米及以上的,经冷轧,但未经包覆、镀层或涂层,卷材,除冷轧外未经进一步加工,厚度小于0.3毫米	7209.1810	468
Flat-rolled products of iron or non-alloy steel, of a width of 600mm or more, cold rolled, not clad, plated or coated, in coils, not further worked than cold-rolled, of a thickness of 0.5mm or more but not exceeding 1mm, nes	平板轧材,铁或非合金钢的宽度在600毫米及以上的,经冷轧,但未经包覆、镀层或涂层,卷材,除冷轧外未经进一步加工,厚度在0.5毫米及以上,但不超过1毫米,其他	7209.1790	468
Flat-rolled products of iron or non-alloy steel, of a width of 600mm or more, cold rolled, not clad, plated or coated, in coils, not further worked than cold-rolled, of a thickness of 0.5mm or more but not exceeding 1mm, of a yield strength exceeding $275N/mm^2$	平板轧材,铁或非合金钢的宽度在600毫米及以上的,经冷轧,但未经包覆、镀层或涂层,卷材,除冷轧外未经进一步加工,厚度在0.5毫米及以上,但不超过1毫米,屈服强度大于275牛顿/平方毫米	7209.1710	468

F

Article Description	商品名称	Tariff Code	D. R.
Flat-rolled products of iron or non-alloy steel, of a width of 600mm or more, cold rolled, not clad, plated or coated, in coils, not further worked than cold-rolled, of a thickness of 3mm or more, nes	平板轧材,铁或非合金钢的,宽度在600毫米及以上的,经冷轧,但未经包覆、镀层或涂层,卷材,除冷轧外未经进一步加工,厚度在3毫米及以上,其他	7209.1590	468
Flat-rolled products of iron or non-alloy steel, of a width of 600mm or more, cold rolled, not clad, plated or coated, in coils, not further worked than cold-rolled, of a thickness of 3mm or more, of a yield strength exceeding 355N/mm^2	平板轧材,铁或非合金钢的,宽度在600毫米及以上的,经冷轧,但未经包覆、镀层或涂层,卷材,除冷轧外未经进一步加工,厚度在3毫米及以上,屈服强度大于355牛顿/平方毫米	7209.1510	468
Flat-rolled products of iron or non-alloy steel, of a width of 600mm or more, cold rolled, not clad, plated or coated, in coils, not further worked than cold-rolled, of a thickness of less than 0.5mm but of 0.3mm or exceeding 0.3mm, nes	平板轧材,铁或非合金钢的宽度在600毫米及以上的,经冷轧,但未经包覆、镀层或涂层,卷材,除冷轧外未经进一步加工,厚度小于0.5毫米但等于或大于0.3毫米,其他	7209.1890	468
Flat-rolled products of iron or non-alloy steel, of a width of 600mm or more, cold rolled, not clad, plated or coated, nes	平板轧材,铁或非合金钢的宽度在600毫米及以上的,经冷轧,但未经包覆、镀层或涂层,其他	7209.9000	468
Flat-rolled products of iron or non-alloy steel, of a width of 600mm or more, cold rolled, not clad, plated or coated, not in coils, not further worked than cold-rolled, of a thickness exceeding 1mm but less than 3mm	平板轧材,铁或非合金钢的宽度在600毫米及以上的,经冷轧,但未经包覆、镀层或涂层,非卷材,除冷轧外未经进一步加工,厚度超过1毫米,但小于3毫米	7209.2600	468
Flat-rolled products of iron or non-alloy steel, of a width of 600mm or more, cold rolled, not clad, plated or coated, not in coils, not further worked than cold-rolled, of a thickness of 0.5mm or more but not exceeding 1mm	平板轧材,铁或非合金钢的宽度在600毫米及以上的,经冷轧,但未经包覆、镀层或涂层,非卷材,除冷轧外未经进一步加工,厚度在0.5毫米及以上,但不超过1毫米	7209.2700	468
Flat-rolled products of iron or non-alloy steel, of a width of 600mm or more, cold rolled, not clad, plated or coated, not in coils, not further worked than cold-rolled, of a thickness of 3mm or more	平板轧材,铁或非合金钢的宽度在600毫米及以上的,经冷轧,但未经包覆、镀层或涂层,非卷材,除冷轧外未经进一步加工,厚度在3毫米及以上	7209.2500	468
Flat-rolled products of iron or non-alloy steel, of a width of 600mm or more, cold rolled, not clad, plated or coated, not in coils, not further worked than cold-rolled, of a thickness of less than 0.5mm	平板轧材,铁或非合金钢的宽度在600毫米及以上的,经冷轧,但未经包覆、镀层或涂层,非卷材,除冷轧外未经进一步加工,厚度小于0.5毫米	7209.2800	468
Flat-rolled products of iron or non-alloy steel, of a width of less than 600mm, clad	平板轧材,铁或非合金钢的宽度小于600毫米的,经包覆的	7212.6000	468

F

Article Description	商品名称	Tariff Code	D. R.
Flat-rolled products of iron or non-alloy steel, of a width of less than 600mm, electrolytically plated or coated with zinc	平板轧材,铁或非合金钢的宽度小于600毫米的,电镀锌的	7212. 2000	468
Flat-rolled products of iron or non-alloy steel, of a width of less than 600mm, not clad, plated or coated, nes	平板轧材,铁或非合金钢的宽度小于600毫米的,但未经包覆、镀层或涂层,其他	7211. 9000	468
Flat-rolled products of iron or non-alloy steel, of a width of less than 600mm, not clad, plated or coated, not further worked than cold-rolled, containing by weight less than 0. 25% of carbon	平板轧材,铁或非合金钢的宽度小于600毫米的,但未经包覆、镀层或涂层,除冷轧外未经进一步加工,按重量计含碳量低于0. 25%	7211. 2300	468
Flat-rolled products of iron or non-alloy steel, of a width of less than 600mm, not clad, plated or coated, not further worked than cold-rolled, nes	平板轧材,铁或非合金钢的宽度小于600毫米的,但未经包覆、镀层或涂层,除冷轧外未经进一步加工,其他	7211. 2900	468
Flat-rolled products of iron or non-alloy steel, of a width of less than 600mm, not clad, plated or coated, not further worked than hot-rolled, nes	平板轧材,铁或非合金钢的宽度小于600毫米的,但未经包覆、镀层或涂层,除热轧外未经进一步加工,其他	7211. 1900	468
Flat-rolled products of iron or non-alloy steel, of a width of less than 600mm, not clad, plated or coated, not further worked than hot-rolled, of a thickness of 4. 75mm or more, nes	平板轧材,铁或非合金钢的宽度小于600毫米的,但未经包覆、镀层或涂层,除热轧外未经进一步加工,厚度在4. 75毫米及以上,其他	7211. 1400	468
Flat-rolled products of iron or non-alloy steel, of a width of less than 600mm, not clad, plated or coated, not further worked than hot-rolled, rolled on four faces or in a closed box pass, of a width exceeding 150mm and a thickness of not less than 4mm, not in coils and without patterns in relief	平板轧材,铁或非合金钢的宽度小于600毫米的,但未经包覆、镀层或涂层,除热轧外未经进一步加工,经四面轧制或在闭合匣内轧制的非卷材,宽度超过150毫米,厚度不小于4毫米,未轧压花纹	7211. 1300	468
Flat-rolled products of iron or non-alloy steel, of a width of less than 600mm, otherwise plated or coated	平板轧材,铁或非合金钢的宽度小于600毫米的,镀或涂其他材料的	7212. 5000	468
Flat-rolled products of iron or non-alloy steel, of a width of less than 600mm, otherwise plated or coated with zinc	平板轧材,铁或非合金钢的宽度小于600毫米的,用其他方法镀或涂锌的	7212. 3000	468
Flat-rolled products of iron or non-alloy steel, of a width of less than 600mm, painted, varnished or coated with plastics	平板轧材,铁或非合金钢的宽度小于600毫米的,涂漆或涂塑的	7212. 4000	468
Flat-rolled products of iron or non-alloy steel, of a width of less than 600mm, plated or coated with tin	平板轧材,铁或非合金钢的宽度小于600毫米的,镀或涂锡的	7212. 1000	468
Flat-rolled products of other alloy steel, of a width of 600mm or more, electrolytically plated or coated with zinc, nes	平板轧材,合金钢的,宽度在600毫米及以上,电镀或涂锌的,其他	7225. 9100	468
Flat-rolled products of other alloy steel, of a width of 600mm or more, nes	平板轧材,合金钢的,宽度在600毫米及以上,其他	7225. 9990	468

F

Article Description	商品名称	Tariff Code	D. R.
Flat-rolled products of other alloy steel, of a width of 600mm or more, not further worked than cold-rolled, nes	平板轧材,合金钢的,宽度在600毫米及以上,除冷轧外未经进一步加工,其他	7225. 5000	468
Flat-rolled products of other alloy steel, of a width of 600mm or more, not further worked than hot-rolled, in coils, nes	平板轧材,合金钢的,宽度在600毫米及以上,卷材,除热轧外未经进一步加工,其他	7225. 3000	468
Flat-rolled products of other alloy steel, of a width of 600mm or more, not further worked than hot-rolled, not in coils, nes	平板轧材,合金钢的,宽度在600毫米及以上,非卷材,除热轧外未经进一步加工,其他	7225. 4000	468
Flat-rolled products of other alloy steel, of a width of 600mm or more, otherwise plated or coated with zinc, nes	平板轧材,合金钢的,宽度在600毫米及以上,用其他方法镀或涂锌的,其他	7225. 9200	468
Flat-rolled products of other alloy steel, of a width of less than 600mm, electrolytically plated or coated with zinc, nes	平板轧材,合金钢,宽度小于600毫米,电镀锌的,其他	7226. 9910	468
Flat-rolled products of other alloy steel, of a width of less than 600mm, nes	平板轧材,合金钢,宽度小于600毫米,其他	7226. 9990	468
Flat-rolled products of other alloy steel, of a width of less than 600mm, not further worked than cold-rolled, nes	平板轧材,合金钢,宽度小于600毫米,除冷轧外未经进一步加工,其他	7226. 9200	468
Flat-rolled products of other alloy steel, of a width of less than 600mm, not further worked than hot-rolled, nes	平板轧材,合金钢,宽度小于600毫米,除热轧外未经进一步加工,其他	7226. 9100	468
Flat-rolled products of other alloy steel, of a width of less than 600mm, otherwise plated or coated with zinc, nes	平板轧材,合金钢,宽度小于600毫米,用其他方法镀或涂锌的,其他	7226. 9920	468
Flat-rolled products of silicon-electrical steel, of a width of 600mm or more, nes	平板轧材,硅电钢制,宽度在600毫米及以上,其他	7225. 1900	468
Flat-rolled products of silicon-electrical steel, of a width of less than 600mm	平板轧材,硅电钢制,宽度小于600毫米,其他	7226. 1900	468
Flat-rolled products of stainless steel, of a width of 600mm or more, nes	平板轧材,不锈钢的,宽度在600毫米及以上,其他	7219. 9000	468
Flat-rolled products of stainless steel, of a width of 600mm or more, not further worked than hot-rolled, in coils, of a thickness exceeding 10mm	平板轧材,不锈钢的,宽度在600毫米及以上,除热轧外未经进一步加工的卷材,厚度超过10毫米	7219. 1100	468
Flat-rolled products of stainless steel, of a width of 600mm or more, not further worked than hot-rolled, in coils, of a thickness of 3mm or less, acid pickled, containing more than 5.5% by weight of manganese of ferro-chromium-manganese steel	平板轧材,不锈钢的,宽度在600毫米及以上,除热轧外未经进一步加工的卷材,厚度在3毫米及以下,经酸洗的,按重量计含锰量在5.5%及以上的铬锰系不锈钢	7219. 1422	468
Flat-rolled products of stainless steel, of a width of 600mm or more, not further worked than hot-rolled, in coils, of a thickness of 3mm or less, acid pickled, nes	平板轧材,不锈钢的,宽度在600毫米及以上,除热轧外未经进一步加工的卷材,厚度在3毫米及以下,经酸洗的,其他	7219. 1429	468

Article Description	商品名称	Tariff Code	D. R.
Flat-rolled products of stainless steel, of a width of 600mm or more, not further worked than hot-rolled, in coils, of a thickness of 3mm or less, not acid pickled, containing more than 5.5% by weight of manganese of ferro-chromium-manganese steel	平板轧材,不锈钢的,宽度在 600 毫米及以上,除热轧外未经进一步加工的卷材,厚度在 3 毫米及以下,未经酸洗的,按重量计含锰量在 5.5% 及以上的铬锰系不锈钢	7219.1412	468
Flat-rolled products of stainless steel, of a width of 600mm or more, not further worked than hot-rolled, in coils, of a thickness of 3mm or less, not acid pickled, nes	平板轧材,不锈钢的,宽度在 600 毫米及以上,除热轧外未经进一步加工的卷材,厚度在 3 毫米及以下,未经酸洗的,其他	7219.1419	468
Flat-rolled products of stainless steel, of a width of 600mm or more, Not further worked than hot-rolled, in coils, Of a thickness of 3mm or more but less than 4.75mm, Acid pickled, Containing more than 5.5% by weight of manganese of Ferro-chromium-manganese steel	平板轧材,不锈钢的,宽度在 600 毫米及以上,除热轧外未经进一步加工的卷材,厚度在 3 毫米及以上,但小于 4.75 毫米,经酸洗的,按重量计含锰量在 5.5% 及以上的铬锰系不锈钢	7219.1322	468
Flat-rolled products of stainless steel, of a width of 600mm or more, not further worked than hot-rolled, in coils, of a thickness of 3mm or more but less than 4.75mm, acid pickled, nes	平板轧材,不锈钢的,宽度在 600 毫米及以上,除热轧外未经进一步加工的卷材,厚度在 3 毫米及以上,但小于 4.75 毫米,经酸洗的,其他	7219.1329	468
Flat-rolled products of stainless steel, of a width of 600mm or more, Not further worked than hot-rolled, in coils, Of a thickness of 3mm or more but less than 4.75mm, Not acid picked, Containing more than 5.5% by weight of manganese of Ferro-chromium-manganese steel	平板轧材,不锈钢的,宽度在 600 毫米及以上,除热轧外未经进一步加工的卷材,厚度在 3 毫米及以上,但小于 4.75 毫米,未经酸洗的,按重量计含锰量在 5.5% 及以上的铬锰系不锈钢	7219.1312	468
Flat-rolled products of stainless steel, of a width of 600mm or more, not further worked than hot-rolled, in coils, of a thickness of 3mm or more but less than 4.75mm, not acid picked, nes	平板轧材,不锈钢的,宽度在 600 毫米及以上,除热轧外未经进一步加工的卷材,厚度在 3 毫米及以上,但小于 4.75 毫米,未经酸洗的,其他	7219.1319	468
Flat-rolled products of stainless steel, of a width of 600mm or more, not further worked than hot-rolled, in coils, of a thickness of 4.75mm or more but not exceeding 10mm	平板轧材,不锈钢的,宽度在 600 毫米及以上,除热轧外未经进一步加工的卷材,厚度在 4.75 毫米及以上,但不超过 10 毫米	7219.1200	468
Flat-rolled products of stainless steel, of a width of 600mm or more, not further worked than hot-rolled, not in coils, of a thickness exceeding 10mm	平板轧材,不锈钢的,宽度在 600 毫米及以上,除热轧外未经进一步加工的非卷材,厚度超过 10 毫米	7219.2100	468
Flat-rolled products of stainless steel, of a width of 600mm or more, not further worked than hot-rolled, not in coils, of a thickness exceeding 1mm but less than 3mm	平板轧材,不锈钢的,宽度在 600 毫米及以上,除热轧外未经进一步加工的非卷材,厚度超过 1 毫米但小于 3 毫米	7219.2410	468

F

Article Description	商品名称	Tariff Code	D. R.
Flat-rolled products of stainless steel, of a width of 600mm or more, not further worked than hot-rolled, not in coils, of a thickness of 0.5mm or more but not exceeding 1mm	平板轧材,不锈钢的,宽度在600毫米及以上,除热轧外未经进一步加工的非卷材,厚度在0.5毫米及以上,但不超过1毫米	7219.2420	468
Flat-rolled products of stainless steel, of a width of 600mm or more, not further worked than hot-rolled, not in coils, of a thickness of 3mm or more but less than 4.75mm	平板轧材,不锈钢的,宽度在600毫米及以上,除热轧外未经进一步加工的非卷材,厚度在3毫米及以上,但小于4.75毫米	7219.2300	468
Flat-rolled products of stainless steel, of a width of 600mm or more, not further worked than hot-rolled, not in coils, of a thickness of 4.75mm or more but not exceeding 10mm	平板轧材,不锈钢的,宽度在600毫米及以上,除热轧外未经进一步加工的非卷材,厚度在4.75毫米及以上,但不超过10毫米	7219.2200	468
Flat-rolled products of stainless steel, of a width of 600mm or more, not further worked than hot-rolled, not in coils, of a thickness of less than 0.5mm	平板轧材,不锈钢的,宽度在600毫米及以上,除热轧外未经进一步加工的非卷材,厚度小于0.5毫米	7219.2430	468
Flat-rolled products of stainless steel, of a width of 600mm or more, not further worked than than cold-rolled, of a thickness exceeding 1mm but less than 3mm	平板轧材,不锈钢的,宽度在600毫米及以上,除冷轧外未经进一步加工,厚度超过1毫米,但小于3毫米	7219.3300	468
Flat-rolled products of stainless steel, of a width of 600mm or more, not further worked than than cold-rolled, of a thickness of 0.5mm or more but not exceeding 1mm	平板轧材,不锈钢的,宽度在600毫米及以上,除冷轧外未经进一步加工,厚度在0.5毫米及以上,但不超过1毫米	7219.3400	468
Flat-rolled products of stainless steel, of a width of 600mm or more, not further worked than than cold-rolled, of a thickness of 3mm or more but less than 4.75mm	平板轧材,不锈钢的,宽度在600毫米及以上,除冷轧外未经进一步加工,厚度在3毫米及以上,但小于4.75毫米	7219.3200	468
Flat-rolled products of stainless steel, of a width of 600mm or more, not further worked than than cold-rolled, of a thickness of 4.75mm or more	平板轧材,不锈钢的,宽度在600毫米及以上,除冷轧外未经进一步加工,厚度在4.75毫米及以上	7219.3100	468
Flat-rolled products of stainless steel, of a width of 600mm or more, not further worked than than cold-rolled, of a thickness of less than 0.5mm	平板轧材,不锈钢的,宽度在600毫米及以上,除冷轧外未经进一步加工,厚度小于0.5毫米	7219.3500	468
Flat-rolled products stainless steel, of a width of less than 600mm, nes	平板轧材,不锈钢的,宽度小于600毫米,其他	7220.9000	468
Flat-rolled products stainless steel, of a width of less than 600mm, not further worked than cold-rolled, nes	平板轧材,不锈钢的,宽度小于600毫米,除冷轧外未经进一步加工,厚度在3毫米及以上	7220.2040	468
Flat-rolled products stainless steel, of a width of less than 600mm, not further worked than cold-rolled, of a thickness of 0.35mm or less	平板轧材,不锈钢的,宽度小于600毫米,除冷轧外未经进一步加工,厚度在0.35毫米及以下	7220.2020	468

F

Article Description	商品名称	Tariff Code	D. R.
Flat-rolled products stainless steel, of a width of less than 600mm, not further worked than cold-rolled, of a thickness of more than 0.35mm but less than 3mm	平板轧材,不锈钢的,宽度小于600毫米,除冷轧外未经进一步加工,厚度在0.35毫米以上但小于3毫米	7220.2030	468
Flat-rolled products stainless steel, of a width of less than 600mm, not further worked than hot-rolled, of a thickness of 4.75mm or more	平板轧材,不锈钢的,宽度小于600毫米,除热轧外未经进一步加工,厚度在4.75毫米及以上	7220.1100	468
Flat-rolled products stainless steel, of a width of less than 600mm, not further worked than hot-rolled, of a thickness of less than 4.75mm	平板轧材,不锈钢的,宽度小于600毫米,除热轧外未经进一步加工,厚度小于4.75毫米	7220.1200	468
Flat-surface grinding machines, in which the positioning in any one axis can be set up to an accuracy of at least 0.01mm, for metal or cermets, nes	平面磨床,在任一坐标的定位精度至少是0.01毫米,加工金属或金属陶瓷用,其他	8460.1900	7
Flat-surface grinding machines, in which the positioning in any one axis can be set up to an accuracy of at least 0.01mm, numerically controlled, for metal or cermets	平面磨床,在任一坐标的定位精度至少是0.01毫米,数控的,加工金属或金属陶瓷用	8460.1100	7
Flax tow	亚麻短纤	5301.3000	4
Flax waste	亚麻废麻	5301.3000	4
Flax woven fabrics, containing 85% or more by weight of flax, bleached	亚麻机织物,按重量计亚麻含量在85%及以上,漂白	5309.1120	2468
Flax woven fabrics, containing 85% or more by weight of flax, nes	亚麻机织物,按重量计亚麻含量在85%及以上,其他	5309.1900	2468
Flax woven fabrics, containing 85% or more by weight of flax, unbleached	亚麻机织物,按重量计亚麻含量在85%及以上,未漂白	5309.1110	2468
Flax woven fabrics, containing less than 85% by weight of flax, bleached	亚麻机织物,按重量计亚麻含量在85%以下,漂白	5309.2120	2468
Flax woven fabrics, containing less than 85% by weight of flax, nes	亚麻机织物,按重量计亚麻含量在85%以下,其他	5309.2900	2468
Flax woven fabrics, containing less than 85% by weight of flax, unbleached	亚麻机织物,按重量计亚麻含量在85%以下,未漂白	5309.2110	2468
Flax yarn, multiple (folded) or cabled	亚麻纱线,多股纱线或缆线	5306.2000	4
Flax yarn, single	亚麻纱线,单纱	5306.1000	4
Flax, hackled or otherwise processed, but not spun	亚麻,栉梳或经其他加工但未纺制的	5301.2900	4
Flax, raw or retted	亚麻,生的或经沤制的	5301.1000	4
Flax, broken or scutched, but not spun	亚麻,破开的或打成但未纺制的亚麻	5301.2100	4
Flexible intermediate bulk containers, of man-made textile materials	散装货物储运软袋,化学纤维材料制	6305.3200	346
Flexible packaging manufacture machines parts, for paper plastic and aluminium	软包装生产设备零件,纸塑铝的	8441.9090	
Flexible packaging manufacture machines, for paper plastic and aluminium	软包装生产设备,纸塑铝的	8441.8010	

F

Article Description	商品名称	Tariff Code	D. R.
Flexible tubing of iron or steel, with or without fittings	软管,钢铁制,不论是否有附件	8307.1000	256
Flexible tubing of other base metal, with or without fittings, nes	软管,贱金属制,不论是否有附件,其他	8307.9000	256
Flexographic printing machinery	苯胺印刷机	8443.1600	57
Flint, whether or not bead-treated	燧石,不论是否热处理	2517.1000	13
Float glass, coloured throughout the mass (body tinted), opacified, flashed or merely surface ground	浮法玻璃板片,整块着色、不透明、镶色或仅表面研磨的非夹丝玻璃,其他	7005.2100	134
Float glass, non-wired glass, having an absorbent, reflecting or non-reflecting layer	浮法玻璃板片,具有吸收、反射或非反射层的非夹丝玻璃	7005.1000	134
Float glass, non-wired, nes	浮法玻璃板片,非夹丝玻璃,其他	7005.2900	134
Float glass, wired	浮法玻璃板片,夹丝玻璃	7005.3000	134
Floating cranes	起重船	8905.9090	37
Floating docks	浮船坞	8905.9010	
Floating drilling or production platforms	浮动式钻探或生产平台	8905.2000	
Floating structures for breaking up	浮动结构体,供拆卸的	8908.0000	5
Floating structures, nes	浮动结构体,其他	8907.9000	5
Floor board strips, coniferous	地板条(块),针叶木	4409.1010	158
Floor board strips, non-coniferous	地板条(块),非针叶木	4409.2910	158
Floor board strips, of bamboo	地板条(块),竹的	4409.2110	158
Floor coverings and mats of vulcanized rubber other than hard rubber	铺地制品及门垫,硫化橡胶(硬质橡胶除外)的	4016.9100	
Floor coverings consisting of a coating or covering applied on a textile backing	铺地制品,以织物为底布经涂布或覆面的	5904.9000	
Floor coverings of coconut fibres (coir)	铺地制品,椰壳纤维制的	5702.2000	468
Floor coverings of man-made textile materials, not of pile construction, made up	铺地制品,化学纤维制,非起绒结构的铺地制品,制成的	5702.9200	468
Floor coverings of man-made textile materials, not of pile construction, not made up	铺地制品,化学纤维制,非起绒结构的,未制成的	5702.5020	468
Floor coverings of man-made textile materials, of pile construction, made up	铺地制品,化学纤维制,起绒结构的,制成的	5702.4200	468
Floor coverings of man-made textile materials, of pile construction, not made up	铺地制品,化学纤维制,起绒结构的,未制成的	5702.3200	468
Floor coverings of other textile materials, not of pile construction, made up, nes	铺地制品,其他纺织材料制,非起绒结构的铺地制品,制成的,其他	5702.9900	468
Floor coverings of other textile materials, not of pile construction, not made up, nes	铺地制品,其他纺织材料制,非起绒结构的,未制成的,其他	5702.5090	468
Floor coverings of plastics, whether or not self-adhesive, nes	铺地制品,塑料的,不论是否胶粘,其他	3918.9090	36
Floor coverings of plastics, whether or not self-adhesive, of polymers of vinyl chloride	铺地制品,塑料的,不论是否胶粘,氯乙烯聚合物制	3918.1090	36

F

Article Description	商品名称	Tariff Code	D. R.
Floor coverings of textile materials, of pile construction, made up, nes	铺地制品,纺织材料制,起绒结构的,制成的,其他	5702. 4900	468
Floor coverings of textile materials, of pile construction, not made up, nes	铺地制品,纺织材料制,起绒结构的,未制成的,其他	5702. 3900	468
Floor coverings of wool or fine animal hair, not of pile construction, made up	铺地制品,羊毛或动物细毛制,非起绒结构的铺地制品,制成的	5702. 9100	468
Floor coverings of wool or fine animal hair, not of pile construction, not made up	铺地制品,羊毛或动物细毛制,非起绒结构的,未制成的	5702. 5010	468
Floor coverings of wool or fine animal hair, of pile construction, made up	铺地制品,羊毛或动物细毛制,起绒结构的,制成的	5702. 4100	468
Floor coverings of wool or fine animal hair, of pile construction, not made up	铺地制品,羊毛或动物细毛制,起绒结构的,未制成的	5702. 3100	468
Floor coverings on a base of paper or of paperboard, whether or not cut to size	铺地制品,以纸或纸板为底制成的	4823. 9010	68
Floor fans, with a self-contained electric motor of an output not exceeding 125W	落地扇,包括风机,本身装有一个输出功率不超过 125 瓦的电动机	8414. 5192	23
Floor polishers, electro-mechanical domestic appliances	地板打蜡机,家用电动器具	8509. 8010	
Floor sweepers, hand-operated, mechanical	地板清扫器,手工操作的,机械的	9603. 9090	3
Flooring blocks for building	地砖,建筑用	6904. 1000	5
Flooring blocks for building	铺地砖,建筑用	6904. 1000	5
Flooring panels, assembled, for mosaic floors, of wood	地板,已装拼的,马赛克地板用,木制的	4418. 7100	58
Flooring panels, assembled, multilayer, nes	地板,已装拼的,多层的,其他	4418. 7290	58
Flooring panels, assembled, multilayer, of bamboo	地板,已装拼的,多层的,竹制	4418. 7210	58
Flooring panels, assembled, nes	地板,已装拼的,其他	4418. 7990	58
Flooring panels, assembled, of bamboo	地板,已装拼的,竹制	4418. 7910	58
Floorstanding lamps, electric	落地灯,电气的	9405. 2000	5
Floor-cloths and similar cleaning cloths	擦地布及类似擦拭用布	6307. 1000	346
Floppy disk drivers	软盘驱动器	8471. 7020	
Flos chrysanthemi	菊花	1211. 9015	34
Flos sophorae	槐米	1211. 9027	34
Flour, meal and powder, of sago or of roots or tubers of heading No. 07. 14	细粉、粗粉及粉末,用税号 07. 14 的西谷茎髓及植物根茎、块茎制成的	1106. 2000	4
Flour, meal and powder, of the dried leguminous vegetables of beading No. 07. 13	细粉、粗粉及粉末,用税号 07. 13 的干豆制成的	1106. 1000	4
Flour, meal and powder, of the products of chapter 8	细粉、粗粉及粉末,用第八章的产品制成的	1106. 3000	4
Flour, of maslin	细粉,混合麦的	1101. 0000	4
Flour, of cereal, nes	细粉,其他谷物的	1102. 9090	4
Flour, of long grain	细粉,籼米的	1102. 9011	4
Flour, of maize (corn)	细粉,玉米的	1102. 2000	4

F

Article Description	商品名称	Tariff Code	D. R.
Flour, of rice, nes	细粉,其他米的	1102. 9019	4
Flour, of rye	细粉,黑麦的	1102. 1000	4
Flour, of wheat	细粉,小麦的	1101. 0000	4
Flourescent brightening agents, synthetic organic products	荧光增白剂,有机合成的	3204. 2000	345
Flours and meals of fish, of a kind used in animal feeding	鱼粉,饲料用	2301. 2010	1356
Flours and meals of meat of dolphins, edible	海豚肉粉,食用	0210. 9200	14
Flours and meals of meat of dugongs (mammals of the order sirenia), edible	儒艮(海牛目哺乳动物)的肉粉,食用	0210. 9200	14
Flours and meals of meat of manatees, edible	海牛肉粉,食用	0210. 9200	14
Flours and meals of meat of porpoises (mammals of the order cetacea), edible	鼠海豚(鲸目哺乳动物)肉粉,食用	0210. 9200	14
Flours and meals of meat of whales, edible	鲸肉粉,食用	0210. 9200	14
Flours and meals of meat, edible, nes	肉粉,食用,其他	0210. 9900	14
Flours and meals of meat, of primates, edible	肉粉,灵长目的,食用	0210. 9100	14
Flours and meals of meat, of reptiles (including snakes and turtles), edible	肉粉,爬行动物(包括蛇及龟鳖)的,食用	0210. 9300	14
Flours and meals of offal of primates, edible	杂碎粉,灵长目的,食用	0210. 9100	14
Flours and meals of offal of reptiles (including snakes and turtles), edible	杂碎粉,爬行动物(包括蛇及龟鳖)的,食用	0210. 9300	14
Flours and meals of offal, edible, nes	杂碎粉,食用,其他	0210. 9900	14
Flours and meals of oil seeds or oleaginous fruits, nes	细粉及粗粉,其他,含油子仁或果实	1208. 9000	4
Flours and meals, of meat bones, nes, unfit for human consumption	肉骨粉,其他,不适于供人食用的	2301. 1019	136
Flours and meals, of meat bones, of bovine and sheep unfit for human consumption	肉骨粉,含牛羊成分的,不适于供人食用的	2301. 1011	136
Flours and meals, of soya beans	大豆粉	1208. 1000	4
Flours, meals and pellets of aquatic invertebrates, fit for human consumption	水生无脊椎动物(甲壳动物除外)的细粉、粗粉及团粒,适合供人食用的	0307. 9990	14
Flours, meals and pellets of crustaceans, fit for human consumption	细粉、粗粉及团粒,甲壳动物的,适合供人食用的	0306. 2990	14
Flours, meals and pellets of fish, fit for human consumption	鱼粉,适合供人食用的	0305. 1000	3
Flours, meals and pellets, of crustaceans, molluscs or other aquatic invertebrates	渣粉及团粒,甲壳动物、软体动物或其他水生无脊椎动物的	2301. 2090	136
Flours, meals and pellets, of meat or meat offal, nes	渣粉及团粒,肉的或杂碎的,其他,不适于供人食用的	2301. 1090	136
Flow control valves, nes	流量阀,其他	8481. 8039	
Flow measuring or checking instruments and apparatus, of liquids	液体流量测量、检验仪器及装置	9026. 1000	7
Flow meter parts and accessories	流量计零件、附件	9026. 9000	3

F

Article Description	商品名称	Tariff Code	D. R.
Flow, measuring or checking variables of liquids or gases	流量计,测量或检验液体变化量的	9026. 1000	7
Flowers of zinc (zinc oxide)	氧化锌	2817. 0010	34
Fludiazepam (INN); salts thereof	氟地西泮(INN)以及盐	2933. 9100	36
Flue gas denitration apparatus	烟气脱硝装置	8421. 3950	7
Flue gas desulfurization apparatus	烟气脱硫装置	8421. 3940	7
Flunitrazepam (INN); salts thereof	氟硝西泮(INN)以及盐	2933. 9100	36
Fluoranthene	荧蒽	2902. 9090	6
Fluorene	芴	2902. 9090	6
Fluorescein (synthetic organic colouring matter)	荧光素,荧光黄	3204. 1990	345
Fluorescent, hot cathode, compact type	热阴极荧光灯,紧凑型	8539. 3191	35
Fluorescent, hot cathode, for locomotives and rolling-stock, aircraft or ships	热阴极荧光灯,火车、航空器及船舶用	8539. 3120	35
Fluorescent, hot cathode, for scientific or medical uses only	热阴极荧光灯,科研、医疗专用	8539. 3110	35
Fluorescent, hot cathode, nes	热阴极荧光灯,其他	8539. 3199	35
Fluorides, nes, inorganic	氟化物,其他,无机的	2826. 1990	
Fluorinated, brominated or iodinated derivatives of acyclic hydrocarbons, nes	无环烃的氟化、溴化或碘化衍生物,其他	2903. 3990	36
Fluorine	氟	2801. 3010	
Fluoroacetamide (ISO)	氟乙酰胺(ISO)	2924. 1200	36
Fluoroaluminates	氟铝酸盐	2826. 9090	
Fluorosilicates	氟硅酸盐	2826. 9010	
Fluoro-polymers, in primary forms, nes	氟聚合物,初级形状的,其他	3904. 6900	1256
Fluorspar, containing by weight 97% or less of calcium fluoride	萤石,按重量计氟化钙含量在97%及以下	2529. 2100	138
Fluorspar, containing by weight more than 97% of calcium fluoride	萤石,按重量计氟化钙含量在97%以上	2529. 2200	138
Flurazepam (INN); salts thereof	氟西泮(INN),以及盐	2933. 9100	36
Flushing cisterns, of porcelain or china	水箱,瓷制	6910. 1000	268
Flushing cisterns, of pottery	水箱, 陶制	6910. 9000	268
Fluting paper, nes	瓦楞原纸,其他	4805. 1900	
Fluting paper, of straw	瓦楞原纸,草浆的	4805. 1200	
Fluting paper, semi-chemical	瓦楞原纸,半化学浆的	4805. 1100	
Flywheels	飞轮	8483. 5000	
Flywheels parts	飞轮零件	8483. 9000	3
Fly-papers, put up for retail sale	捕蝇纸,零售包装	3808. 9910	36
Foamed slag	泡沫矿渣	6806. 2000	68
Fodder roots, forage products	草料根,饲料用	1214. 9000	
Fog signals	浓雾信号弹	3604. 9000	
Folders, of paper or paperboard	文件夹,纸或纸板制的	4820. 3000	
Folding machines for textile fabrics	折叠机器,纺织物的	8451. 5000	

F

Article Description	商品名称	Tariff Code	D. R.
Folding machines parts for textile fabrics	折叠机器零件,纺织物的	8451.9000	
Folding machines, for working metal, nes	折叠机,加工金属用,其他	8462.2990	7
Folding machines, numerically controlled, for working metal	折叠机,数控的,加工金属用	8462.2190	7
Folding mail or inserting mail in envelopes or bands machines	折叠机或装封机,信件用	8472.3090	
Foliage, fresh, suitable for bouquets or for ornamental purposes	植物叶,鲜的,制花束或装饰用的	0604.9100	34
Fondants and fondant pastes	软糖	1704.9000	258
Food grinders, electro-mechanical domestic appliances	食品研磨机,家用电动器具	8509.4090	
Food mixers, electro-mechanical domestic appliances	食品搅拌器,家用电动器具	8509.4090	
Food preparation or manufacture machinery	食品生产或加工机器	8438.8000	
Food preparation or manufacture machinery parts	食品生产或加工机器的零件	8438.9000	3
Food preparations, nes	食品,其他	2106.9090	268
Footballs	足球	9506.6210	
Footwear eyes, of base metal	鞋眼,贱金属制	8308.1000	256
Footwear making machinery	鞋靴制作机器	8453.2000	
Footwear making machinery parts	鞋靴制作机器零件	8453.9000	3
Footwear repairing machinery	鞋靴修理机器	8453.2000	
Footwear repairing machinery parts	鞋靴修理机器零件	8453.9000	3
Footwear uppers and parts, other than stiffeners	鞋面及其零件,但硬衬除外	6406.1000	6
Footwear with outer soles and uppers of rubber or plastics and uppers of plastics	鞋靴,橡胶或塑料制外底及塑料制鞋面的	6402.9920	26
Footwear with outer soles and uppers of rubber or plastics and uppers of rubber	鞋靴,橡胶或塑料制外底及橡胶制鞋面的	6402.9910	26
Footwear with outer soles and uppers of rubber or plastics, covering the ankle	短统靴(过踝),橡胶或塑料制外底及鞋面的其他鞋靴	6402.9100	26
Footwear with outer soles of leather or composition leather and uppers of textile materials	鞋靴,皮革或再生皮革制外底的,纺织材料制鞋面的	6404.2000	26
Footwear with outer soles of leather, and uppers which consist of leather straps across the instep and around the big toe	鞋靴,由交叉于脚背并绕大脚趾的皮革条带构成鞋面的,皮革制外底	6403.2000	26
Footwear with outer soles of other materials and uppers of leather or composition leather	鞋靴,其他材料制外底的,皮革或再生皮革制鞋面的	6405.1090	26
Footwear with outer soles of other materials, nes	鞋靴,其他材料制外底的	6405.9090	26
Footwear with outer soles of rubber or plastics and uppers of textile materials, nes	鞋靴,橡胶或塑料制外底的鞋靴,纺织材料制鞋面的,其他	6404.1900	26
Footwear with outer soles of rubber, plastics, leather or composition leather	鞋靴,橡胶、塑料、皮革及再生皮革制外底的	6405.9010	26
Footwear with outer soles of rubber, plastics, leather or composition leather and uppers of leather or composition leather	鞋靴,橡胶、塑料、皮革及再生皮革制外底的,皮革或再生皮革制鞋面的	6405.1010	26

F

Article Description	商品名称	Tariff Code	D. R.
Footwear with upper straps or thongs assembled to the sole by means of plugs, with outer soles and uppers of rubber or plastics	鞋靴,用栓塞方法将鞋面条带装配在鞋底上的,橡胶或塑料制外底及鞋面的其他鞋靴	6402. 2000	26
Footwear with uppers of textile materials	鞋靴,纺织材料制鞋面的	6405. 2000	26
Footwear without applied soles, knitted or crocheted, of cotton	无外绱鞋底的鞋类,针织或钩编的,棉制	6115. 9500	2456
Footwear without applied soles, knitted or crocheted, of other textile materials	无外绱鞋底的鞋类,针织或钩编的,其他纺织材料制	6115. 9900	2456
Footwear without applied soles, knitted or crocheted, of synthetic fibres	无外绱鞋底的鞋类,针织或钩编的,合成纤维制	6115. 9600	2456
Footwear without applied soles, knitted or crocheted, of wool or fine animal hair	无外绱鞋底的鞋类,针织或钩编的,羊毛或动物细毛制	6115. 9400	2456
Footwear, incorporating a protective metal toe-cap, with outer soles of rubber, plastics, leather or composition leather and upers of leather, nes	鞋靴,装有金属防护鞋头的,橡胶、塑料、皮革或再生皮革制外底,皮革制鞋面的,其他	6403. 4000	26
Footwear, with outer soles of leather and upers of leather, nes	鞋靴,皮革制外底的,皮革制鞋面的,其他	6403. 5900	26
Footwear, covering the ankle but not covering the calf, length of inner soles less than 24cm, with outer soles of leather and upers of leather	短统靴(过踝),但低于小腿的,内底长度小于24厘米的,皮革制外底的,皮革制鞋面的	6403. 5111	26
Footwear, covering the ankle but not covering the calf, length of inner soles less than 24cm, with outer soles of rubber, plastics, leather or composition leather and upers of leather	短统靴(过踝),但低于小腿的,内底长度小于24厘米的,橡胶、塑料、皮革或再生皮革制外底,皮革制鞋面的	6403. 9111	26
Footwear, covering the ankle but not covering the calf, with outer soles of leather and upers of leather, nes	短统靴(过踝),但低于小腿的,皮革制外底的,皮革制鞋面的,其他	6403. 5119	26
Footwear, covering the ankle but not covering the calf, with outer soles of rubber, plastics, leather or composition leather and upers of leather, nes	短统靴(过踝),但低于小腿的,橡胶、塑料、皮革或再生皮革制外底,皮革制鞋面的,其他	6403. 9119	26
Footwear, covering the ankle, length of inner soles less than 24cm, with outer soles of leather and upers of leather, nes	短统靴(过踝),内底长度小于24厘米的,皮革制外底的,皮革制鞋面的,其他	6403. 5191	26
Footwear, covering the ankle, length of inner soles less than 24cm, with outer soles of rubber, plastics, leather or composition leather and upers of leather, nes	短统靴(过踝),内底长度小于24厘米的,橡胶、塑料、皮革或再生皮革制外底,皮革制鞋面的,其他	6403. 9191	26
Footwear, covering the ankle, with outer soles of leather and upers of leather, nes	短统靴(过踝),皮革制外底的,皮革制鞋面的,其他	6403. 5199	26
Footwear, covering the ankle, with outer soles of rubber, plastics, leather or composition leather and upers of leather, nes	短统靴(过踝),橡胶、塑料、皮革或再生皮革制外底,皮革制鞋面的,其他	6403. 9199	26

Article Description	商品名称	Tariff Code	D. R.
Footwear, with outer soles of rubber, plastics, leather or composition leather and upers of leather, nes	鞋靴,橡胶、塑料、皮革或再生皮革制外底,皮革制鞋面的,其他	6403.9900	26
For making carpets or rugs, powered, for weaving fabrics of width exceeding 30cm, shuttle type	地毯织机,动力的,所织织物宽度超过30厘米的梭织机	8446.2110	7
For wet etching apparatus, flat panel displays manufacture machines and apparatus	湿法蚀刻装置,平板显示器的制造机器及装置	8486.3049	7
Forestry machinery parts, nes	林业用机器零件,其他	8436.9900	3
Forestry machinery, including germination plant fitted with mechanical or thermal equipment, nes	林业用机器,包括装有机械或热力装置的催芽设备,其他	8436.8000	
Forging machines, for working metal, nes	锻造机床,加工金属用,其他	8462.1090	7
Forging machines, numerically controlled, for working metal	锻造机床,数控的,加工金属用	8462.1010	7
Forks, hand tools of a kind used in agriculture, horticulture or foresty	叉子,农业、园艺、林业用手工工具	8201.2000	256
Forks, other than plated with precious metal, kitchen or tableware	餐叉,非镀贵金属的,厨房或餐桌用具	8215.9900	256
Forks, plated with precious metal, kitchen or tableware	餐叉,镀贵金属的,厨房或餐桌用具	8215.9100	256
Fork-lift trucks, for lifting or handing containers, self-propelled	集装箱叉车,自推进的	8427.2010	7
Formaldehyde	甲醛	2912.1100	36
Formic acid	甲酸	2915.1100	36
Forming machines parts	成形机器的零件	8474.9000	3
Foundry moulds of sand forming machines	铸造用砂模的成形机器	8474.8090	7
Fountain pens	自来水笔	9608.3910	
Fowls of the species gallus domesticus, ex. pure-bred breeding, weighing more than 185g	鸡,改良种用除外,重量超过185克	0105.9490	48
Fowls of the species gallus domesticus, ex. pure-bred breeding, weighing not more than 185g	鸡,改良种用除外,重量不超过185克	0105.1190	48
Fowls of the species gallus domesticus, not cut in pieces, fresh or chilled	鸡,整只,鲜或冷的	0207.1100	1
Fowls of the species gallus domesticus, not cut in pieces, frozen	鸡,整只,冻的	0207.1200	1
Fowls of the species gallus domesticus, pure-bred breeding, weighing more than 185g	鸡,改良种用,重量超过185克	0105.9410	48
Fowls of the species gallus domesticus, pure-bred breeding, weighing not more than 185g	鸡,改良种用,重量不超过185克	0105.1110	48
Foxes, for human consumption	松鸡,食用	0106.1920	48
Foxes, pure-bred breeding	松鸡,改良种用	0106.1910	34
Fracture appliances	骨折用器具	9021.1000	
Frame loading and unloading bridges	门式装卸桥	8426.1941	7
Frames and forks, and parts thereof, of bicycles and other cycles	车架、轮叉及其零件,自行车及脚踏车的	8714.9100	3

F

Article Description	商品名称	Tariff Code	D. R.
Frames for mirrors or similar objects, of other wood	镜框及类似品,其他木制的	4414.0090	56
Frames for mirrors or similar objects, of radiata pine	镜框及类似品,辐射松制的	4414.0010	56
Frames for paintings or similar objects, of other wood	画框及类似品,其他木制的	4414.0090	56
Frames for paintings or similar objects, of radiata pine	画框及类似品,辐射松制的	4414.0010	56
Frames for photographs or similar objects, of other wood	相框及类似品,其他木制的	4414.0090	56
Frames for photographs or similar objects, of radiata pine	相框及类似品,辐射松制的	4414.0010	56
Frames with clasps, of base metal, of a kind used for clothing, footwear, awnings, handbags, travel goods or other made up articles	框,带栓的,贱金属制,用于衣着、鞋靴、天篷、提包、旅行用品或其他制成品	8308.9000	256
Frames, of cross-country cars (4WD)	车架,越野车(4 轮驱动)用	8708.9951	3
Frames, of dumpers	车架,自卸车用	8708.9931	3
Frames, of motor vehicles with 30 seats or more	车架,30 座及以上客运机动车辆用	8708.9921	3
Frames, of motor vehicles, nes	车架,机动车辆用,其他	8708.9991	3
Frames, of saloon cars	车架,小轿车用	8708.9941	3
Frankfurters (meat sausages), with a natural casing	熏肠,有天然肠衣	1601.0010	348
Free piston generators for gas turbines	自由活塞式发生器,燃气轮机用的	8414.8010	23
Free wheel, of bicycles and other cycles	飞轮,自行车及脚踏车的	8714.9320	3
Freezers of the chest type, not exceeding 800l capacity, of a refrigerating temperature higher than -40℃, nes	柜式冷冻箱,容积不超过 800 升,制冷温度在 -40℃以上,其他	8418.3029	57
Freezers of the chest type, not exceeding 800L capacity, of a refrigerating temperature of -40℃ or lower	柜式冷冻箱,容积不超过 800 升,制冷温度在 -40℃及以下	8418.3010	57
Freezers of the chest type, of a capacity exceeding 500l, of a refrigerating temperature higher than -40℃	柜式冷冻箱,容积超过 500 升,制冷温度在 -40℃以上	8418.3021	57
Freezers of the upright type, not exceeding 900L capacity, of a refrigerating temperature higher than -40℃, nes	立式冷冻箱,容积不超过 900 升,制冷温度在 -40℃以上,其他	8418.4029	57
Freezers of the upright type, of a capacity exceeding 500L, of a refrigerating temperature higher than -40℃	立式冷冻箱,容积超过 500 升,制冷温度在 -40℃以上	8418.4021	57
Freezers of the upright type, of a refrigerating temperature of -40°c or lower	立式冷冻箱,容积不超过 900 升,制冷温度在 -40℃及以下	8418.4010	57
Freezing equipment parts, of a refrigerating temperature of -40℃ or lower	制冷温度在 -40℃及以下的冷冻设备用零件	8418.9991	3
French fries, frozen	炸薯条,冻的	2004.1000	48
French fries, not frozen	炸薯条,未冻的	2005.2000	48
Frequency meters, nes	频率计,其他	9030.4090	7
Frequency meters, of test frequency less than 12.4 GHz, digital	频率计,测试频率在 12.4 吉赫兹以下的,数字式	9030.4010	

F

Article Description	商品名称	Tariff Code	D. R.
Fresh(unripened or uncured) cheese	鲜乳酪(未熟化或未固化的)	0406. 1000	24
Freshwater crabs, not frozen	中华绒螯蟹,未冻的	0306. 2491	14
Freshwater crawfish, nes	淡水小龙虾,其他	0306. 1919	1
Freshwater crawfish, nes, prepared or preserved	淡水小龙虾,其他,制作或保藏的	1605. 4019	48
Freshwater crawfish, shelled, prepared or preserved	淡水小龙虾,虾仁,制作或保藏的	1605. 4011	48
Fritillaria, used in pharmacy	贝母,药用	1211. 9017	34
Frontal appearance of bodies, of the motor vehicles	前围,机动车辆的	8708. 2954	3
Front-end shovel loaders	前铲装载机	8429. 5100	57
Fructose and fructose syrup, nes, containing in the dry state more than 50% by weight of fructose	果糖及果糖浆,其他,按重量计干燥状态的果糖含量在50%以上	1702. 6000	356
Fructose, chemically pure	果糖,化学纯	1702. 5000	6
Fructus lycii	枸杞	1211. 9031	34
Fruit jellies, sweets, not containing cocoa	果冻,不含可可,糖食	1704. 9000	258
Fruit jellies, being cooked preparations, nes	果冻,烹煮的,其他	2007. 9990	248
Fruit jellies, citrus fruit, being cooked preparations	果冻,烹煮的,柑橘属水果的	2007. 9100	248
Fruit jellies, citrus fruit, being cooked preparations, in airtight containers	果冻,烹煮的,柑橘属水果的,罐头	2007. 9910	248
Fruit juice extractors, electro-mechanical domestic appliances	水果榨汁机,家用电动器具	8509. 4010	
Fruit juice, of any other single fruit	水果汁,其他单一水果的	2009. 8019	2468
Fruit juices, mixtures	水果汁,混合汁	2009. 9010	2468
Fruit pastes sweets not containing cocoa	果泥,不含可可,糖食	1704. 9000	258
Fruit stones and kernels and other vegetable products, of a kind used primarily for human consumption	果核、果仁及植物产品,主要供人食用的	1212. 9999	134
Fruit, citrus, nes	水果,柑橘属,其他	0805. 9000	14
Fruits of the genus capsicum or of the genus pimenta, dried	辣椒干	0904. 2010	4
Fruits of the genus capsicum or of the genus pimenta, in powder	辣椒粉	0904. 2020	4
Fruits of the genus capsicum, fresh or chilled	辣椒,鲜或冷藏的	0709. 6000	1
Fruits of the genus pimenta, fresh or chilled	甜椒,鲜或冷藏的	0709. 6000	1
Fruits preparation machinery	水果加工机器	8438. 6000	
Fruits preparation machinery parts	水果加工机器的零件	8438. 9000	3
Fruits, nes, frozen	水果,其他,冷冻的	0811. 9090	1
Fruits, nes, fresh	水果,其他,鲜的	0810. 9090	1
Fruits, nes, provisionally preserved, but unsuitable in that state for immediate consumption	水果,其他,暂时保藏,但不适于直接食用的	0812. 9000	34
Fry, bluefin tunas	蓝鳍金枪鱼苗	0301. 9410	15
Fry, eels(Anguilla spp.)	鳗鱼苗	0301. 9210	15
Fry, nes	鱼苗,其他	0301. 9919	15
Fry, of carp	鲤鱼苗	0301. 9310	15

F

Article Description	商品名称	Tariff Code	D. R.
Fry, of oncorhynchus aguabonita	鱼苗,鳟鱼	0301.9110	15
Fry, of oncorhynchus apache	鱼苗,鳟鱼	0301.9110	15
Fry, of oncorhynchus chrysogaster	鱼苗,鳟鱼	0301.9110	15
Fry, of oncorhynchus clarki	鱼苗,鳟鱼	0301.9110	15
Fry, of oncorhynchus gilae	鱼苗,鳟鱼	0301.9110	15
Fry, of oncorhynchus my kiss	鱼苗,鳟鱼	0301.9110	15
Fry, of perches	鲈鱼苗	0301.9911	15
Fry, of salmo trutta	鱼苗,鳟鱼	0301.9110	15
Fry, of sturgeon	鲟鱼苗	0301.9912	15
Fry, of trout	鳟鱼苗	0301.9110	15
Fry, southern bluefin tunas	南方蓝鳍金枪鱼苗	0301.9510	15
Fry, thunnus maccoyii	南方蓝鳍金枪鱼苗	0301.9510	15
Fry, thunnus thynnus	蓝鳍金枪鱼苗	0301.9410	15
Fuchsine as synthetic organic colouring matter	品红,洋红	3204.1300	345
Fucose	海藻糖	2940.0000	6
Fuel elements parts, for nuclear reactors, non-irradiated	燃料元件的零件,核反应堆的,未辐照	8401.3090	2
Fuel elements, for nuclear reactors, non-irradiated	燃料元件,核反应堆的,未辐照	8401.3010	2
Fuel oils, nes	燃料油,其他	2917.1929	6
Fuel oils, No. 5 ~7	燃料油 5 ~7 号	2917.1922	6
Fuel pumps for internal combustion piston engines, for engines of an output of 132.39kW (180hp) or more	燃油泵,活塞式内燃发动机用的,输出功率在 132.39 千瓦(180 马力)及以上的发动机用	8413.3021	23
Fuel pumps for internal combustion piston engines, nes	燃油泵,活塞式内燃发动机用的,其他	8413.3029	23
Fuel wood, in logs, in billets, in twigs, in faggots or in similar forms	薪柴(圆木段、块、枝、成捆或类似形状)	4401.1000	15
Full-length or knee-length hosiery, knitted or crocheted, measuring per single yarn less than 67 decitex, for women or girls, nes	长统袜或中统袜,针织或钩编的,每根单丝细度在 67 分特以下,女式,其他	6115.3000	2456
Fulminates	雷酸盐	2842.9010	
Fungicides, nes	杀菌剂,其他	3808.9290	36
Fungicides, put up for retail sale	杀菌剂,零售包装	3808.9210	36
Furan phenol	呋喃酚	2932.9910	36
Furan phenol	7-羟基苯并呋喃	2932.9910	36
Furan ring compounds, unfused in the structure, whether or not hydrogenated, nes	呋喃环化合物,结构上含有,非稠合的,不论是否氢化,其他	2932.1900	36
Furazan	呋咱	2934.9990	36
Furazolidone	呋喃唑酮	2934.9920	36
Furfuryl alcohol and tetrahydrofurfuryl alcohol	糠醇及四氢糠醇	2932.1300	36
Furnace burners for liquid fuel	炉用燃烧器,使用液体燃料的	8416.1000	5
Furnace burners parts	炉用燃烧器零件	8416.9000	

Article Description	商品名称	Tariff Code	D. R.
Furnace burners, for gas, nes	炉用燃烧器,使用气体的,其他	8416. 2019	5
Furnace burners, including combination burners, nes	炉用燃烧器,包括复式燃烧器,其他	8416. 2090	5
Furnace burners, of using natural gas	炉用燃烧器,使用天然气的	8416. 2011	5
Furnaces and ovens for industrial or laboratory, non-electric, nes	烘箱及炉,非电热的工业或实验室用,其他	8417. 8090	7
Furnaces and ovens for the roasting, melting or other heat-treatment of ores, pyrites or of metals	烘箱及炉,焙烧熔化或其他热处理矿砂、黄铁矿或金属用	8417. 1000	7
Furnaces and ovens parts, for industrial or laboratory, non-electric, nes	烘箱及炉零件,非电热的工业或实验室用,其他	8417. 9090	3
Furnaces functioning by induction or dielectric loss, for industrial or laboratory use, electric	炉,通过感应或介质损耗工作的,工业或实验室用	8514. 2000	7
Furnaces, for industrial or laboratory use, electric, nes	炉,工业或实验室用,电的,其他	8514. 3000	7
Furnaces, resistance heated, for industrial or laboratory use, electric, nes	炉,电阻加热的,工业或实验室用,其他	8514. 1090	7
Furnishing articles, crocheted, hand-worked	装饰用织物制品,钩编的,手工制	6304. 9131	346
Furnishing articles, crocheted, nes	装饰用织物制品,钩编的,其他	6304. 9139	346
Furnishing articles, knitted, hand-worked	装饰用织物制品,针织的,手工制	6304. 9121	346
Furnishing articles, knitted, nes	装饰用织物制品,针织的,其他	6304. 9129	346
Furnishing articles, not knitted or crocheted, embroidered, of bast fibres	装饰用织物制品,非针织或非钩编的,刺绣的,麻制	6304. 9921	346
Furnishing articles, not knitted or crocheted, nes	装饰用织物制品,非针织或非钩编的,其他	6304. 9990	346
Furnishing articles, not knitted or crocheted, of bast fibres, nes	装饰用织物制品,非针织或非钩编的,麻制,其他	6304. 9929	346
Furnishing articles, not knitted or crocheted, of silk or silk waste	装饰用织物制品,非针织或非钩编的,丝及绢丝制	6304. 9910	346
Furnishing articles, not knitted or crocheted, embroidered, of cotton	装饰用织物制品,非针织或非钩编的,刺绣的,棉制	6304. 9210	346
Furnishing articles, not knitted or crocheted, embroidered, of synthetic fibres	装饰用织物制品,非针织或非钩编的,刺绣的,合成纤维制	6304. 9310	346
Furnishing articles, not knitted or crocheted, of cotton, nes	装饰用织物制品,非针织或非钩编的,棉制,其他	6304. 9290	346
Furnishing articles, not knitted or crocheted, of synthetic fibres, nes	装饰用织物制品,非针织或非钩编的,合成纤维制,其他	6304. 9390	346
Furniture (chests, cabinets, display counters, show-cases and the like) for storage and display, incorporating refrigerating or freezing equipment, nes	展示及存储(柜、箱、展示台、陈列箱及类似品),装有冷藏或冷冻装置的,其他	8418. 5000	57
Furniture of a kind used in offices, of metal	家具,办公室用,金属的	9403. 1000	6
Furniture of a kind used in offices, wooden	家具,办公室用,木的	9403. 3000	6
Furniture of a kind used in the bedroom, of lacquered wood	家具,卧室用,漆木的	9403. 5091	6

F

Article Description	商品名称	Tariff Code	D. R.
Furniture of a kind used in the bedroom, of rose wood	家具,卧室用,红木制	9403. 5010	6
Furniture of a kind used in the bedroom, of wood, nes	家具,卧室用,木制,其他	9403. 5099	6
Furniture of a kind used in the kitchen, wooden	家具,厨房用,木的	9403. 4000	6
Furniture of bamboo or rattan	家具,竹制或藤制的	9403. 8100	6
Furniture of lacquered wood, nes	家具,漆木的,其他	9403. 6091	6
Furniture of osier or similar materials	家具,柳条及类似材料制的	9403. 8910	6
Furniture of plastics	家具,塑料的	9403. 7000	6
Furniture of rose wood, nes	家具,红木制,其他	9403. 6010	6
Furniture of stone	家具,石制的	9403. 8920	6
Furniture of wood, nes	家具,木的,其他	9403. 6099	6
Furniture parts	家具零件	9403. 9000	3
Furniture parts, designed to receive refrigerating or freezing equipment	冷藏或冷冻设备专用设备零件	8418. 9100	3
Furniture, nes	家具,其他	9403. 8990	6
Furniture, of metal, nes	家具,金属的,其他	9403. 2000	6
Furskin articles, nes	毛皮制物品,其他	4303. 9000	456
Fusel oil	杂醇油	3824. 9010	36
Fuses, for a voltage exceeding 1000V	熔断器,用于电压超过 1000 伏的线路	8535. 1000	8
Fuses, for a voltage not exceeding 1000V	熔断器,用于电压不超过 1000 伏的线路	8536. 1000	8
Fusing presses machines parts, for textile yarns, fabrics or made up textile articles	熔压机零件,纱线、织物及纺织制品用	8451. 9000	
Fusing presses machines, for textile yarns, fabrics or made up textile articles	熔压机,纱线、织物及纺织制品用	8451. 3000	

F

G

Article Description	商品名称	Tariff Code	D. R.
Gadolinite	硅铍钇矿	2530. 9020	13456
Gain measuring instruments, specially designed for telecommunications	增益测量仪,通讯专用的	9030. 4090	7
Gaiters, leggings and similar articles, and parts thereof, of other materials	护腿、裹腿和类似品及其零件,其他材料制	6406. 9900	6
Gaiters, leggings and similar articles, and parts thereof, of wood	护腿、裹腿和类似品及其零件,木制	6406. 9100	6
Galactose	半乳糖	2940. 0000	6
Galanthus (snow-drop)	雪莲花,种用,休眠的	0601. 1091	135
Galena	方铅矿	2607. 0000	146
Gallium articles	镓制品	8112. 9990	16
Gallium powders	镓粉末	8112. 9290	16
Gallium, unwrought	镓,未锻轧	8112. 9290	16
Games tables, special designed	游戏专用桌	9504. 9090	5
Games, operated by coins, bank notes, bank cards, tokens or by other means of payment, nes	游戏用品,用硬币、钞票、银行卡、代币或其他支付方式使其工作的,其他	9504. 3090	5
Games, playing on the table	游戏用品,桌上的	9504. 9040	
Gamma measuring or detecting instruments and apparatus	γ射线的测量或检验仪器及装置	9030. 1000	
Gamma radiations apparatus, for medical, surgical, dental or veterinary uses	γ射线的应用设备,医疗、外科、牙科或兽医用	9022. 2100	
Gamma radiations apparatus, nes	γ射线的应用设备,其他	9022. 2900	3
Gantry cranes	龙门式起重机	8426. 1930	7
Garden earth	种植土	2530. 9099	13456
Garlic bulbs, frozen	蒜头,冷冻的	0710. 8030	1
Garlic bulbs, fresh or chilled	蒜头,鲜或冷藏的	0703. 2010	1
Garlic seedlings, frozen	蒜苗(青蒜),冷冻的	0710. 8020	1
Garlic seedlings, fresh or chilled	蒜苗(青蒜),鲜或冷藏的	0703. 2020	1
Garlic stems, frozen	蒜苔,冷冻的	0710. 8020	1
Garlic stems, fresh or chilled	蒜苔,鲜或冷藏的	0703. 2020	1
Garlic, dried	大蒜,干的	0712. 9050	4
Garlic, in brine, provisionally preserved, but unsuitable in that state for immediate consumption	大蒜,盐水的,暂时保藏,但不适合直接使用的	0711. 9034	34
Garlic, nes	大蒜,其他	0703. 2090	1
Garlic, prepared or preserved by vinegar or acetic acid	大蒜,用醋或醋酸制作或保藏的	2001. 9010	48
Garments accessories parts	服装附件的零件,针织或钩编的	6117. 9000	2456

G

Article Description	商品名称	Tariff Code	D. R.
Garments and clothing accessories, not knitted or crocheted, for babies, of cotton, nes	服装及衣着附件,非针织或钩编的,婴儿的,棉制,其他	6209. 2090	2456
Garments and clothing accessories, not knitted or crocheted, for babies, of other textile materials	服装及衣着附件,非针织或钩编的,婴儿的,其他纺织材料制	6209. 9090	2456
Garments and clothing accessories, not knitted or crocheted, for babies, of synthetic fibres	服装及衣着附件,非针织或钩编的,婴儿的,合成纤维制	6209. 3000	2456
Garments and clothing accessories, not knitted or crocheted, for babies, of wool or fine animal hair	服装及衣着附件,非针织或钩编的,婴儿的,羊毛或动物细毛制	6209. 9010	2456
Garments parts, not knitted or crocheted	服装的零件,非针织或钩编的	6217. 9000	2456
Garments, for men or boys, fabrics treated, nes	服装,男式,织物经处理的,其他	6210. 4000	2456
Garments, for women or girls, fabrics treated, nes	服装,女式,织物经处理的,其他	6210. 5000	2456
Garments, knitted or crocheted, nes	服装,针织或钩编的,其他	6114. 9090	2456
Garments, knitted or crocheted, of cotton	服装,针织或钩编的,棉制	6114. 2000	2456
Garments, knitted or crocheted, of man-made fibres	服装,针织或钩编的,化学纤维制	6114. 3000	2456
Garments, knitted or crocheted, of wool or fine animal hair	服装,针织或钩编的,羊毛或动物细毛制	6114. 9010	2456
Garments, made up of felt or Non-wovens treated, of cotton or bast fibres	服装,用毡呢或无纺织物制成的,织物经处理的,棉或麻制	6210. 1020	2456
Garments, made up of felt or Non-wovens treated, of man-made fibres	服装,用毡呢或无纺织物制成的,织物经处理的,化学纤维制	6210. 1030	2456
Garments, made up of felt or Non-wovens treated, of other textile materials	服装,用毡呢或无纺织物制成的,织物经处理的,其他纺织材料制	6210. 1090	2456
Garments, made up of felt or Non-wovens treated, of wool or fine animal hair	服装,用毡呢或无纺织物制成的,织物经处理的,羊毛或动物细毛制	6210. 1010	2456
Garments, made up of knitted or crocheted fabrics treated	服装,针织物或钩编织物制成的,织物经处理的	6113. 0000	2456
Garments, not knitted or crocheted, for men or boys, of cotton, nes	服装,非针织或钩编的,男式,棉制,其他	6211. 3290	2456
Garments, not knitted or crocheted, for men or boys, of man-made fibres, nes	服装,非针织或钩编的,男式,化学纤维制,其他	6211. 3390	2456
Garments, not knitted or crocheted, for men or boys, of other textile materials	服装,非针织或钩编的,男式,其他纺织材料制	6211. 3990	2456
Garments, not knitted or crocheted, for men or boys, of silk or silk waste, nes	服装,非针织或钩编的,男式,丝及绢丝制,其他	6211. 3910	2456
Garments, not knitted or crocheted, for men or boys, of wool or fine animal hair, nes	服装,非针织或钩编的,男式,羊毛或动物细毛制,其他	6211. 3920	2456
Garments, not knitted or crocheted, for women or girls, of cotton, nes	服装,非针织或钩编的,女式,棉制,其他	6211. 4290	2456
Garments, not knitted or crocheted, for women or girls, of man-made fibres, nes	服装,非针织或钩编的,女式,化学纤维制,其他	6211. 4390	2456
Garments, not knitted or crocheted, for women or girls, of other textile materials	服装,非针织或钩编的,女式,其他纺织材料制	6211. 4990	2456

Article Description	商品名称	Tariff Code	D. R.
Garments, not knitted or crocheted, for women or girls, of silk or silk waste, nes	服装,非针织或钩编的,女式,丝及绢丝制,其他	6211.4910	2456
Garments, not knitted or crocheted, for women or girls, of wool or fine animal hair, nes	服装,非针织或钩编的,女式,羊毛或动物细毛制,其他	6211.4100	2456
Garments, of the type described in subheadings 6201.11 to 6201.19, fabrics treated	服装,子目号6201.11至6201.19所列类型的,织物经处理的	6210.2000	2456
Garments, of the type described in subheadings 6202.11 to 6202.19, fabrics treated	服装,子目号6202.11至6202.19所列类型的,织物经处理的	6210.3000	2456
Garnet, natural	石榴石,天然	2513.2000	
Garnetted stock of coarse animal hair	动物粗毛的回收纤维	5104.0090	5
Garnetted stock of fine animal hair	动物细毛的回收纤维	5104.0090	5
Garnetted stock of wool	羊毛的回收纤维	5104.0010	5
Garnierite	硅镁镍矿	2604.0000	146
Gas analysis apparatus	气体分析仪	9027.1000	
Gas chromatographs instruments	气相色谱仪	9027.2011	
Gas compressors parts	气体压缩机零件	8414.9090	23
Gas compressors, nes	气体压缩机,其他	8414.8090	23
Gas insulated switch gear parts, for a voltage of 500kV or more	全封闭组合式高压开关装置零件,用于电压在500千伏及以上的线路	8538.1010	3
Gas insulated switch gear, for a voltage of 500kV or more	全封闭组合式高压开关装置,用于电压在500千伏及以上的线路	8537.2010	78
Gas masks, excluding protective masks having neither mechanical parts nor replaceable filters	防毒面具,不包括既无机械零件又无可互换过滤器的防护面具	9020.0000	
Gas meter parts and accessories, for industrial use	气量计零件、附件,工业用	9028.9010	3
Gas meter parts and accessories, nes	气量计零件、附件,其他	9028.9090	3
Gas meters, supply or production meters, nes	气量计,生产或供应计量仪表,其他	9028.1090	7
Gas producer or generators parts	煤气发生器的零件	8405.9000	3
Gas producer or generators, with or without their purifiers	煤气发生器,不论有无净化器	8405.1000	3
Gas recoverers, auxiliary plant for use with central heating boilers	气体回收器,集中供暖用的热水锅炉的辅助设备	8404.1020	3
Gas recoverers, auxiliary plant for use with steam or other vapour generating watertube boilers	气体回收器,蒸汽锅炉的辅助设备	8404.1010	3
Gas recoverers, auxiliary plant for use with super-heated water boilers	气体回收器,过热水锅炉的辅助设备	8404.1010	3
Gas turbines parts, nes	燃气轮机零件,其他	8411.9990	27
Gas turbines, of a power exceeding 5000kW, nes	燃气轮机,功率超过5000千瓦,其他	8411.8200	27
Gas turbines, of a power not exceeding 5000kW, nes	燃气轮机,功率不超过5000千瓦,其他	8411.8100	27
Gaskets of metal sheeting combined with other material or of two or more layers of metal	密封垫,用金属片与其他材料制成或用双层或多层金属片制成	8484.1000	56
Gaskets sets	密封垫成套物品	8484.9000	56

G

Article Description	商品名称	Tariff Code	D. R.
Gaskets, washers and other seals of a kind used in machines or instruments, of vulcanized rubber other than hard rubber	垫片、垫圈及其他密封垫,机器及仪器用,硫化橡胶(硬质橡胶除外)的	4016.9310	236
Gaskets, washers and other seals, of vulcanized rubber other than hard rubber, nes	垫片、垫圈及其他密封垫,硫化橡胶(硬质橡胶除外)的,其他	4016.9390	236
Gas-rings, of iron or steel, non-electric domestic appliances, for gas fuel or for both gas and other fuels	煤气灶,钢铁制,非电热的家用,使用气体燃料或可使用气体燃料及其他燃料的	7321.1100	7
Gas-rings, of iron or steel, non-electric domestic appliances, for liquid fuel	煤气灶,钢铁制,非电热的家用,使用液体燃料的	7321.1290	7
Gas-rings, of iron or steel, non-electric domestic appliances, nes, including appliances for solid fuel	煤气灶,钢铁制,非电热的家用,其他,包括使用固体燃料的	7321.1900	7
Gauges	量规	9017.3000	
Gauze, other than narrow fabrics, nes	纱罗,狭幅织物除外,其他	5803.0090	468
Gauze, other than narrow fabrics, of cotton	纱罗,狭幅织物除外,棉制	5803.0010	468
Gauze, other than narrow fabrics, of man-made fibres	纱罗,狭幅织物除外,化学纤维制	5803.0030	468
Gauze, other than narrow fabrics, of silk or silk waste	纱罗,狭幅织物除外,丝及绢丝制	5803.0020	468
Gauze, medical, surgical, dental or veterinary purposes	纱布,供医疗、外科、牙科或兽医用	3005.9010	1346
Gear boxes and other speed changers	齿轮箱及其他变速装置	8483.4090	7
Gear boxes and parts of cross-country cars(4WD)	变速箱及其零件,越野车(4 轮驱动)用	8708.4050	3
Gear boxes and parts of dumpers	变速箱及其零件,自卸车用	8708.4030	3
Gear boxes and parts of motor vehicles with 30 seats or more	变速箱及其零件,30 座及以上客运机动车辆用	8708.4020	3
Gear boxes and parts of motor vehicles with special purpose	变速箱及其零件,特种车辆用	8708.4060	3
Gear boxes and parts of saloon cars	变速箱及其零件,小轿车用	8708.4040	3
Gear boxes and parts of tractors	变速箱及其零件,拖拉机的	8708.4010	3
Gear boxes and parts, nes	变速箱及其零件,其他	8708.4099	3
Gear cutting machines, numerically controlled, for removing metal or cermets	切齿机,数控的,切削金属或金属陶瓷用	8461.4010	7
Gear cutting machines, for removing metal or cermets, nes	切齿机,切削金属或金属陶瓷用,其他	8461.4090	7
Gear finishing machines, for removing metal or cermets, nes	齿轮精加工机床,切削金属或金属陶瓷用,其他	8461.4090	7
Gear finishing machines, numerically controlled, for removing metal or cermets	齿轮精加工机床,数控的,切削金属或金属陶瓷用	8461.4010	7
Gear grinding machines, for removing metal or cermets, nes	齿轮磨床,切削金属或金属陶瓷用,其他	8461.4090	7
Gear grinding machines, numerically controlled, for removing metal or cermets	齿轮磨床,数控的,切削金属或金属陶瓷用	8461.4010	7
Gear pumps, for positive displacement, rotary, electric	齿轮泵,排液回转式,电动式	8413.6021	27

Article Description	商品名称	Tariff Code	D. R.
Gear pumps, for positive displacement, rotary, hydraulic	齿轮泵,排液回转式,液压式	8413. 6022	27
Gear pumps, for positive displacement, rotary, nes	齿轮泵,排液回转式,其他	8413. 6029	27
Gears and gearing parts	齿轮及齿轮传动装置零件	8483. 9000	3
Gears and gearing, nes	齿轮及齿轮传动装置,其他	8483. 4090	7
Geese, ex. pure-bred breeding, weighing more than 185g	鹅,改良种用除外,重量超过185克	0105. 9992	48
Geese, not cut in pieces, fresh or chilled	鹅,整只,鲜或冷的	0207. 3220	1
Geese, not cut in pieces, frozen	鹅,整只,冻的	0207. 3320	1
Geese, pure-bred breeding, weighing more than 185g	鹅,改良种用,重量超过185克	0105. 9910	48
Geese, pure-bred breeding, weighing not more than 185g	鹅,改良种用,重量不超过185克	0105. 1910	48
Gel preparations designed to be used in human or veterinary medicine	凝胶制品,专用于人类或作兽药用的	3006. 7000	36
Gelatin and gelatin derivatives	明胶及其衍生物	3503. 0010	13
Gelatin articles, unhardened	明胶制品,未硬化	9602. 0090	5
Gelatin, unhardened, worked	明胶,未硬化的,已加工的	9602. 0090	5
Generating sets parts, nes	发电机组的零件,其他	8503. 0090	3
Generating sets parts, wind-powered	发电机组的零件,风力驱动的	8503. 0030	3
Generating sets with compression-ignition internal combustion piston engines (diesel or semi-diesel engines), of an output exceeding 75kVA but not exceeding 375kVA	发电机组,装有压燃式活塞内燃发动机(柴油或半柴油发动机)的,输出功率超过75千伏安,但不超过375千伏安	8502. 1200	8
Generating sets with compression-ignition internal combustion piston engines (diesel or semi-diesel engines), of an output not exceeding 75kVA	发电机组,装有压燃式活塞内燃发动机(柴油或半柴油发动机)的,输出功率不超过75千伏安	8502. 1100	8
Generating sets with compression-ignition internal combustion piston engines (diesel or semi-diesel engines) of an output exceeding 2MVA	发电机组,装有压燃式活塞内燃发动机(柴油或半柴油发动机)的,输出功率超过2兆伏安	8502. 1320	8
Generating sets with compression-ignition internal combustion piston engines (diesel or semi-diesel engines) of an output exceeding 375kVA but not exceeding 2MVA	发电机组,装有压燃式活塞内燃发动机(柴油或半柴油发动机)的,输出功率超过375千伏安,但不超过2兆伏安	8502. 1310	8
Generating sets with spark-ignition internal combustion piston engines	发电机组,装有点燃式活塞内燃发动机的	8502. 2000	8
Generating sets, nes	发电机组,其他	8502. 3900	8
Generating sets, wind-powered	发电机组,风力驱动的	8502. 3100	8
Generators of an output exceeding 350MVA but not exceeding 665MVA, AC	发电机,输出功率超过350兆伏安,但不超过665兆伏安,交流	8501. 6420	8
Generators of an output exceeding 375kVA but not exceeding 750kVA, AC	发电机,输出功率超过375千伏安,但不超过750千伏安,交流	8501. 6300	8
Generators of an output exceeding 375kW, DC	发电机,输出功率超过375千瓦,直流	8501. 3400	8

G

Article Description	商品名称	Tariff Code	D. R.
Generators of an output exceeding 665MVA, AC	发电机,输出功率超过665兆伏安,交流	8501.6430	8
Generators of an output exceeding 750kVA but not exceeding 350MVA, AC	发电机,输出功率超过750千伏安,但不超过350兆伏安,交流	8501.6410	8
Generators of an output exceeding 750W but not exceeding 75kW, DC	发电机,输出功率超过750瓦,但不超过75千瓦,直流	8501.3200	8
Generators of an output exceeding 75kVA but not exceeding 375kVA, AC	发电机,输出功率超过75千伏安,但不超过375千伏安,交流	8501.6200	8
Generators of an output exceeding 75kW but not exceeding 375kW, DC	发电机,输出功率超过75千瓦,但不超过375千瓦,直流	8501.3300	8
Generators of an output not exceeding 750W, DC	发电机,输出功率不超过750瓦,直流	8501.3100	8
Generators of an output not exceeding 75kVA, AC	发电机,输出功率不超过75千伏安,交流	8501.6100	8
Generators parts, for electrical ignition or starting equipment, nes	发电机零件,点燃式或压燃式内燃发动机用的,其他	8511.9090	3
Generators parts, for locomotives, aircraft or ships, for electrical ignition or starting equipment	发电机零件,供机车、航空器及船舶用,点燃式或压燃式内燃发动机用的	8511.9010	3
Generators parts, nes	发电机的零件,其他	8503.0090	3
Generators parts, of an output exceeding 350MVA but not exceeding 665MVA, AC	发电机的零件,输出功率超过350兆伏安,但不超过665兆伏安,交流	8503.0020	3
Generators, for electrical ignition or starting equipment, nes	发电机,点燃式或压燃式内燃发动机用的,其他	8511.5090	7
Generators, for locomotives, aircraft or ships, for electrical ignition or starting equipment, nes	发电机,机车、航空器及船舶用,点燃式或压燃式内燃发动机用的,其他	8511.5010	7
Genetics material and gene modified organism	遗传物质和基因修饰生物体	3002.9040	34
Geneva	杜松子酒	2208.5000	2468
Gentamycin and its derivatives; salts thereof	庆大霉素及其衍生物以及它们的盐	2941.9010	6
Geological casing and drill pipes, seamless, of alloy steel, of circular cross-section, cold-drawn or cold-rolled, nes	地质钻管、套管,无缝的,合金钢的,圆形截面管,冷拔或冷轧的,其他	7304.5120	6
Geological casing and drill pipes, seamless, of alloy steel, of circular cross-section, nes	地质钻管、套管,无缝的,合金钢的,圆形截面管,其他	7304.5920	6
Geological casing and drill pipes, seamless, of iron or non-alloysteel, of circular cross-section, cold-drawn or cold-rolled	地质钻管、套管,无缝的,铁或非合金钢的,圆形截面,冷拔或冷轧的	7304.3120	6
Geological casing and drill pipes, seamless, of iron or non-alloysteel, of circular cross-section, nes	地质钻管、套管,无缝的,铁或非合金钢的,圆形截面,其他	7304.3920	6
Geraniol, nerol (cis-3,7-dimethyl-2,6-octadien-1-ol)	香叶醇、橙花醇(3,7-二甲基-2,6-辛二烯-1-醇)	2905.2210	36
Germ of cereals, whole, rolled, flaked or ground	谷物胚芽,整粒、滚压、制片或磨碎的	1104.3000	4
Germanite	赭石	2617.9090	146
Germanium articles, nes	锗制品	8112.9910	16

G

Article Description	商品名称	Tariff Code	D. R.
Germanium oxides	锗的氧化物	2825. 6000	
Germanium powders	锗粉末	8112. 9210	16
Germanium, unwrought	锗,未锻轧	8112. 9210	16
Ghee	酥油	0405. 9000	268
Gherkins, fresh or chilled	小黄瓜,鲜或冷藏的	0707. 0000	1
Gherkins, prepared or preserved by vinegar or acetic acid	小黄瓜	2001. 1000	48
Gherkins, provisionally preserved, but unsuitable in that state for immediate consumption	小黄瓜,暂时保藏,但不适合直接使用的	0711. 4000	34
Gimped horsehair yarn, whether or not put up for retail sale	马毛粗松螺旋花线,不论是否供零售用	5110. 0000	56
Gimped yarn making machines	螺旋花线机	8447. 9090	7
Gimped yarn, and strip and the like, gimped	粗松螺旋花线,扁条及类似品制的螺旋花线	5606. 0000	
Gin	杜松子酒	2208. 5000	2468
Ginger	姜	0910. 1000	
Gingerbread and the like	姜饼及类似品	1905. 2000	28
Gingko nuts	白果	0802. 9020	134
Ginseng roots, fresh	人参,鲜的	1211. 2091	34
Ginseng roots, nes	人参,其他	1211. 2099	34
Girdles and panty-girdles, of man-made fibres	束腰带及腹带,化学纤维制	6212. 2010	2456
Girdles and panty-girdles, of other textile materials	束腰带及腹带,其他纺织材料制	6212. 2090	2456
Gizzard, of chicken, cold, frozen	鸡胗,冷、冻的	0504. 0021	14
Glands and other organs for organotherapeutic uses, dried, whether or not powdered	腺体及其他器官,已干燥的,器官疗法用,不论是否制成粉末	3001. 9090	34
Glands extracts and secretions	腺体及其分泌物的提取物	3001. 2000	34
Glands, of animal, used in the preparation of pharmaceutical products, fresh, chilled, frozen or otherwise provisionally preserved	腺体,其他,供配制药用的,鲜、冷、冻或用其他方法暂时保藏的	0510. 0090	14
Glass articles, for technical use, nes	玻璃制品,工业用,其他	7020. 0019	6
Glass articles, nes	玻璃制品,其他	7020. 0099	6
Glass beads	玻璃珠	7018. 1000	3458
Glass chopped strands, of a length of not more than 50mm	玻璃短切纤维,长度不超过 50 毫米的	7019. 1100	568
Glass containers, exceeding 0. 15L but not exceeding 0. 33L	玻璃容器,超过 0. 15 升,但不超过 0. 33 升	7010. 9030	8
Glass containers, exceeding 0. 33L but not exceeding 1L	玻璃容器,超过 0. 33 升,但不超过 1 升	7010. 9020	8
Glass containers, exceeding 1L	玻璃容器,超过 1 升	7010. 9010	8
Glass containers, not exceeding 0. 15L	玻璃容器,不超过 0. 15 升	7010. 9090	8
Glass cubes and other glass smallwares, for mosaics or similar decorative purposes, pressed or moulded	玻璃马赛克及其他小件玻璃品,供镶嵌或类似装饰用的,压制或模制的	7016. 1000	345

G

Article Description	商品名称	Tariff Code	D. R.
Glass envelopes and glass parts thereof, for cathode-ray tubes, open, without fittings, nes	玻璃外壳及其玻璃零件,制阴极射线管用,未封口,未装有配件,其他	7011. 2090	4
Glass envelopes and glass parts thereof, for electric lighting, open, without fittings	玻璃外壳及其玻璃零件,制电灯用,未封口,未装有配件	7011. 1000	4
Glass envelopes and glass parts thereof, for electronic tubes and valves (other than cathode-ray tubes), open, without fittings	玻璃外壳及其玻璃零件,电子管用(阴极射线管用的除外),未封口,未装有配件	7011. 9010	4
Glass envelopes and glass parts thereof, open, without fittings, nes	玻璃外壳及其玻璃零件,未封口,未装有配件,其他	7011. 9090	4
Glass envelopes for kinescope and glass parts thereof	显像管玻壳及其零件	7011. 2010	4
Glass eyes other than prosthetic articles	玻璃假眼,但医用假眼除外	7018. 9000	3458
Glass fibres articles, nes	玻璃纤维制品,其他	7019. 9000	6
Glass frit and other glass, in the form of powder, granules or flakes	搪瓷玻璃料及其他玻璃,呈粉、粒或粉片状的	3207. 4000	13
Glass in balls, unworked	玻璃球,未加工的	7002. 1000	3
Glass in blocks, panels, plates, shells or similar forms, pressed or moulded, multicellular or foam	玻璃块、板、片及类似品,压制或模制的,多孔或泡沫	7016. 9090	345
Glass in rods, unworked, nes	玻璃棒,未加工的,其他	7002. 2090	238
Glass in the mass	玻璃块料	7001. 0000	13
Glass inners for vacuum flasks or for other vacuum vessels	保温瓶或其他保温容器用的玻璃胆	7020. 0091	6
Glass microspheres, not exceeding 1mm in diameter	玻璃球,微型的,直径不超过 1 毫米	7018. 2000	3458
Glass mirrors, framed	玻璃镜,已镶框	7009. 9200	4
Glass mirrors, unframed	玻璃镜,未镶框	7009. 9100	4
Glass optical elements, not optically worked	光学元件,玻璃制,未经光学加工的	7014. 0090	345
Glass or glassware grinding machines	玻璃研磨机床	8464. 2010	7
Glass or glassware hot working or manufacturing machines parts, nes	玻璃或玻璃制品的制造或热加工机器的零件,其他	8475. 9000	3
Glass or glassware hot working or manufacturing machines, nes	玻璃或玻璃制品的制造或热加工机器,其他	8475. 2990	
Glass or glassware polishing machines	玻璃抛光机床	8464. 2010	7
Glass or glasswares hot working equipments, nes	玻璃的热加工设备,其他	8475. 2919	
Glass pavingblocks, slabs, bricks, squares, tiles and other articles of a kind used for building or construction purposes, pressed or moulded, nes	玻璃块、砖、片、瓦及其他制品,建筑用,压制或模制的,其他	7016. 9090	345
Glass profiles, cast and rolled	玻璃型材及异型材,铸制或轧制的	7003. 3000	134
Glass rovings	玻璃粗纱	7019. 1200	568
Glass sheets, drawn and blown, coloured throughout the mass (body tinted), opacified, flashed or having an absorbent, reflecting or non-reflecting layer	玻璃板片,拉制或吹制的,整块着色、不透明、镶色或具有吸收、反射或非反射层的	7004. 2000	134
Glass sheets, drawn and blown, nes	玻璃板片,拉制或吹制的,其他	7004. 9000	134

G

Article Description	商品名称	Tariff Code	D. R.
Glass sheets, non-wired, cast and rolled, coloured throughout the mass (body tinted), opacified, flashed or having an absorbent, or non-reflecting reflecting layer	玻璃板片,非夹丝的,铸制或轧制的,整块着色、不透明、镶色或具有吸收、反射或非反射层的	7003.1200	134
Glass sheets, non-wired, cast and rolled, nes	玻璃板片,非夹丝的,铸制或轧制的,其他	7003.1900	134
Glass sheets, wired, cast and rolled	玻璃板片,夹丝的,铸制或轧制的	7003.2000	134
Glass slivers, yarn	玻璃梳条、纱线	7019.1900	568
Glass stoppers, lids and other closures	玻璃塞、盖及类似的封口器	7010.2000	8
Glass tubes for optical fibres use, of quartz, waveguide grade	玻璃管,石英的,光导纤维用,波导级	7002.3110	238
Glass tubes, nes	玻璃管,其他	7002.3900	238
Glass tubes, of fused quartz or other fused silica, nes	玻璃管,熔融石英或其他熔融硅石制,其他	7002.3190	238
Glass tubes, of other glass having a linear coefficient of expansion not exceeding 5×10^{-6} per Kelvin within a temperature range of 0℃ to 300℃	玻璃管,温度在0℃ 至 300℃ 时线膨胀系数不超过 5×10^{-6}/开尔文的其他玻璃制	7002.3200	238
Glass umbrella for insulator, for technical use	绝缘子用玻璃伞盘,工业用	7020.0012	6
Glass waste and scrap	玻璃,废的	7001.0000	13
Glass, bent, edge-worked, engraved, drilled, enamelled or otherwise worked, but not framed or fitted with other materials	玻璃,经弯曲、磨边、镂刻、钻孔、涂珐琅或其他加工的,但未用其他材料镶框或装配	7006.0000	134
Glass, by float process, coloured throughout the mass (body tinted), opacified, flashed or merely surface ground, nes	玻璃板片,浮法工艺制造,整块着色、不透明、镶色或仅表面研磨的非夹丝玻璃,其他	7005.2100	134
Glass, by float process, non-wired glass, having an absorbent, reflecting or non-reflecting layer	玻璃板片,浮法工艺制造,具有吸收、反射或非反射层的非夹丝玻璃	7005.1000	134
Glass, by float process, non-wired, nes	玻璃板片,浮法工艺制造,非夹丝玻璃,其他	7005.2900	134
Glass, by float process, wired	玻璃板片,浮法工艺制造,夹丝玻璃	7005.3000	134
Glass, surface ground or polished, coloured throughout the mass (body tinted), opacified, flashed or merely surface ground, non-wired, nes	玻璃板片,表面研磨或抛光,整块着色、不透明、镶色或仅表面研磨的非夹丝玻璃,其他	7005.2100	134
Glass, surface ground or polished, non-wired glass, having an absorbent, reflecting or non-reflecting layer	玻璃板片,表面研磨或抛光,具有吸收、反射或非反射层的非夹丝玻璃	7005.1000	134
Glass, surface ground or polished, non-wired, nes	玻璃板片,表面研磨或抛光,非夹丝玻璃,其他	7005.2900	134
Glass, surface ground or polished, wired	玻璃板片,表面研磨或抛光,夹丝玻璃	7005.3000	134
Glasses for corrective spectacles, not optically worked, of glass, nes	玻璃,视力矫正眼镜用,未经光学加工的,玻璃制,其他	7015.1090	1345
Glassine and other glazed transparent or translucent papers	高光泽透明或半透明纸	4806.4000	58

G

Article Description	商品名称	Tariff Code	D. R.
Glassware of a kind used for decoration or similar purposes, of glass-ceramics	玻璃器,装饰或类似用途,玻璃陶瓷制	7013. 1000	356
Glassware of a kind used for table (other than drinking glasses) or kitchen purposes, other than of glass-ceramics, nes	玻璃器皿(不包括杯子),餐桌或厨房用,但玻璃陶瓷制的除外,其他	7013. 4900	356
Glassware of a kind used for table (other than drinking glasses) or kitchen purposes, other than of glass-ceramics, of glass having a linear coefficient of expansion not exceeding 5×10^{-6} per Kelvin within a temperature range of 0℃ to 300℃	玻璃器皿(不包括杯子),餐桌或厨房用,但玻璃陶瓷制的除外,温度在0℃至300℃时线膨胀系数不超过5×10^{-6}/开尔文的其他玻璃制	7013. 4200	356
Glassware of a kind used for table (other than drinking glasses) or kitchen purposes, other than of glass-ceramics, of lead crystal	玻璃器皿(不包括杯子),餐桌或厨房用,但玻璃陶瓷制的除外,铅晶质玻璃制	7013. 4100	356
Glassware of lead crystal, nes	玻璃器,铅晶质玻璃制,其他	7013. 9100	356
Glassware, for laboratory, hygienic or pharmaceutical, whether or not graduated or calibrated, nes	玻璃器,实验室、卫生及配药用,不论有无刻度或标量,其他	7017. 9000	356
Glassware, for laboratory, hygienic or pharmaceutical, whether or not graduated or calibrated, of fused quartz or other fused silica	玻璃器,实验室、卫生及配药用,不论有无刻度或标量,熔融石英或其他熔融硅石制	7017. 1000	356
Glassware, for laboratory, hygienic or pharmaceutical, whether or not graduated or calibrated, of other glass having a linear coefficient of expansion not exceeding 5×10^{-6} per Kelvin within a temperature range of 0℃ to 300℃	玻璃器,实验室、卫生及配药用,不论有无刻度或标量,温度在0℃至300℃时线膨胀系数不超过5×10^{-6}/开尔文的其他玻璃制	7017. 2000	356
Glassware, nes	玻璃器,其他	7013. 9900	356
Glazes and similar preparations, of a kind used in the ceramic, enamelling or glass industry	釉料及类似制品,陶瓷、搪瓷及玻璃工业用	3207. 2000	13
Glaziers' diamonds for household	玻璃刀,家用	8205. 5100	256
Glaziers' putty	安装玻璃用油灰	3214. 1090	3
Gliders	滑翔机	8801. 0010	
Globes, printed	地球仪,印制的	4905. 1000	
Gloves for surgical	手套,外科用	4015. 1100	23
Gloves of other plastics	手套,其他塑料的	3926. 2019	236
Gloves of poly (vinyl chloride)	手套,聚氯乙烯制	3926. 2011	236
Gloves, mittens and mitts, impregnated, coated or covered with plastics or rubber	分指手套、连指手套及露指手套,针织或钩编的,用塑料或橡胶浸渍、涂布或包覆的	6116. 1000	2456
Gloves, mittens and mitts, knitted or crocheted, of cotton	分指手套、连指手套及露指手套,针织或钩编的,棉制	6116. 9200	2456
Gloves, mittens and mitts, knitted or crocheted, of other textile materials	分指手套、连指手套及露指手套,针织或钩编的,其他纺织材料制	6116. 9900	2456

G

Article Description	商品名称	Tariff Code	D. R.
Gloves, mittens and mitts, knitted or crocheted, of synthetic fibres	分指手套、连指手套及露指手套,针织或钩编的,合成纤维制	6116.9300	2456
Gloves, mittens and mitts; knitted or crocheted, of wool of fine animal hair	分指手套、连指手套及露指手套,针织或钩编的,羊毛或动物细毛制	6116.9100	2456
Gloves, mittens and mitts, not knitted or crocheted	分指手套、连指手套及露指手套,非针织或钩编的,	6216.0000	2456
Gloves, mittens and mitts, of leather or composition leather, nes	手套,包括连指或露指的,皮革或再生皮革制的,其他	4203.2990	456
Gloves, mittens and mitts, specially designed for use in sports, of leather or composition leather	手套,包括连指或露指的,专供运动用,皮革或再生皮革制的	4203.2100	456
Gloves, mittens and mitts, working gloves, of leather or of composition leather	劳保手套,皮革或再生皮革制的	4203.2910	456
Gloves, of vulcanized rubber other than hard rubber, nes	手套,硫化橡胶(硬质橡胶除外)制的,其他	4015.1900	23
Glow plugs, for electrical ignition or starting equipment	电热塞,点燃式或压燃式内燃发动机用的	8511.8000	7
Gluconic acid, its salts and esters	葡糖酸及其盐和酯	2918.1600	36
Glucose syrup, containing in the dry state at least 20% but less than 50% by weight of fructose	葡萄糖浆,按重量计干燥状态的果糖含量在20%及以上,但在50%以下	1702.4000	6
Glucose syrup, not containing fructose or containing in the dry state less than 20% by weight of fructose	葡萄糖浆,不含果糖或按重量计干燥状态的果糖含量在20% 以下	1702.3000	36
Glucose, containing in the dry state at least 20% but less than 50% by weight of fructose	葡萄糖,按重量计干燥状态的果糖含量在20%及以上,但在50%以下	1702.4000	6
Glucose, not containing fructose or containing in the dry state less than 20% by weight of fructose	葡萄糖,不含果糖或按重量计干燥状态的果糖含量在20% 以下	1702.3000	36
Glueing binders parts, for book	胶订机零件	8440.9000	3
Glueing binders, for book	胶订机	8440.1020	
Glues of animal origin, nes, excluding casein glues of heading No. 35.01	动物胶,其他,但不包括税号35.01的酪蛋白胶	3503.0090	13
Glues or adhesives, put up for retail sale, not exceeding a net weight, of 1 kg	胶或粘合剂,零售包装每件净重不超过1千克	3506.1000	36
Glues, based on starches, or on dextrins or other modified starches	胶,以淀粉、糊精或其他改性淀粉为基本成分的	3505.2000	36
Glues, prepared, nes	胶,调制的,其他	3506.9900	36
Glutamic acid	谷氨酸	2922.4210	36
Glutamic acid salts, nes	谷氨酸盐,其他	2922.4290	36
Glutethimide(INN)	格鲁米特(INN)	2925.1200	36
Glycerol lyes	甘油碱液	1520.0000	6
Glycerol waters	甘油水	1520.0000	6
Glycerol, crude	粗甘油	1520.0000	6
Glycerol, separate chemically defined	丙三醇(甘油),单独有化学定义的	2905.4500	36

Article Description	商品名称	Tariff Code	D. R.
Glycoprotein hormones, their derivatives and structural analogues	糖蛋白激素及其衍生物和结构类似物	2937. 1900	36
Glycosides, natural or reproduced bysynthesis, and their salts, ethers, esters and other derivatives, nes	苷(配糖物)及其盐、醚、酯和其他衍生物,天然或合成再制的,其他	2938. 9090	34
Gnocchi, whether or not cooked or otherwise prepared	汤团,不论是否烹煮或经其他方法制作	1902. 2000	46
Goat casings, salted	盐渍山羊肠衣	0504. 0013	14
Goat hair	山羊毛	0502. 9011	3
Goats, live, ex. pure-bred breeding	山羊,活的,改良种用除外	0104. 2090	3
Goats, live, pure-bred breeding	山羊,活的,改良种用	0104. 2010	3
Gobelins type hand-woven tapestries	哥白林及类似式样的手织装饰毯	5805. 0090	468
God (gadus morhua, gadus ogac, gadus macrocephalus), excluding livers and roes, fresh or chilled	鳕鱼,但鱼肝及鱼卵除外,鲜或冷的	0302. 5000	18
God (gadus morhua, gadus ogac, gadus macrocephalus), salted or in brine	鳕鱼,盐腌及盐渍的	0305. 6200	4
Goggles	挡风镜	9004. 9090	5
Gold clothing base metals or silver, not further worked than semi-manufactured	金包覆材料,以贱金属或银为底的,未加工成半成品的	7109. 0000	46
Gold compounds	金化合物	2843. 3000	
Gold ores and concentrates	金矿砂及其精矿	2616. 9000	146
Gold powder, non-monetary	金粉,非货币用	7108. 1100	46
Gold(including gold plated with platinum), monetary	金(包括镀铂的金),货币用	7108. 2000	46
Gold (including gold plated with platinum), non-monetary, semi-manufactured forms, non-monetary, nes	金(包括镀铂的金),半制成形状,非货币用,其他	7108. 1300	46
Gold (including gold plated with platinum), unwrought forms, non-monetary, nes	金(包括镀铂的金),未锻造形状,非货币用,其他	7108. 1200	46
Golden syrup	糖浆	1702. 9000	
Goldsmiths or silversmiths' wares and parts thereof, of base metal clad with precious metal	金银器及其零件,以贱金属为底的包贵金属制	7114. 2000	46
Goldsmiths or silversmiths' wares and parts thereof, of precious metal, whether or not plated or clad with precious metal, nes	金银器及其零件,贵金属制,不论是否包、镀贵金属,其他	7114. 1900	46
Goldsmiths or silversmiths' wares and parts thereof, of silver, whether or not pla-ted or clad with other precious metal	金银器及其零件,银制,不论是否包、镀其他贵金属	7114. 1100	46
Golf balls	高尔夫球	9506. 3200	
Golf cars and similar vehicles, nes	高尔夫球车及类似车辆,其他	8703. 1019	58
Golf clubs, complete	高尔夫球棍,全套	9506. 3100	
Golf equipment, nes	高尔夫球用具,其他	9506. 3900	5
Gongs and the like, of base metal, non-electric	钟及类似品,贱金属制,非电动的	8306. 1000	256

Article Description	商品名称	Tariff Code	D. R.
Gongs and the like, of base metal, non-electric	锣及类似品,贱金属制,非电动的	8306.1000	256
Goods vans and wagons, covered and closed, for railway or tramway, not self-propelled	货车,带篷及封闭的,铁道及电车道用的,非机动	8606.9100	37
Goods vans and wagons, for railway or tramway, not self-propelled, nes	货车,铁道及电车道用的非机动,其他	8606.9900	37
Goods vans and wagons, open, with non-removable sides of a height exceeding 60cm, for railway or tramway, not self-propelled	货车,敞篷的,厢壁固定且高度超过60厘米,铁道及电车道用的,非机动	8606.9200	37
Gooseberries, fresh	鹅莓,鲜的	0810.9020	1
Gooseberries, frozen	鹅莓,冷冻的	0811.2000	1
Gouges and similar cutting tools for working wood	凿子及类似切削工具,木工用	8205.3000	256
Gourmet powder	味精	2103.9010	268
Grabs, parts of bulldozer or cranes	抓斗,推土机或起重机零件	8431.4100	3
Gracilaria, dried	江蓠,干的	1212.2071	14
Gracilaria, nes	江蓠,其他	1212.2079	14
Graders parts	筑路机零件	8431.4990	3
Graders, nes	筑路机,其他	8429.2090	57
Graders, with an engine of an output exceeding 235.36kW(320hp)	筑路机,发动机输出功率超过235.36千瓦(320马力)的	8429.2010	57
Grading machines for eggs, fruit or other agricultural produce	分级机器,对蛋类、水果或其他农产品的	8433.6000	
Grading machines for seed, grain or dried leguminous vegetables	分级机器,种子、谷物或干豆用	8437.1090	3
Grading machines parts, for seed, grain or dried leguminous vegetables	分级机器零件,种子、谷物或干豆用	8437.9000	3
Grading machines parts, for gees, furits or other agricultural products	分级机器零件,对蛋类、水果或其他农产品的	8433.9090	3
Graduated compression hosiery (for example, stockings for varicose veins)	渐紧压袜类(例如,用以治疗静脉曲张的长统袜)	6115.1000	2456
Grafting putty	接缝用油灰	3214.1090	3
Grain sorghum, nes	高粱,其他	1007.0090	35
Grain sorghum, seed	高粱,种用	1007.0010	35
Gramophone records, nes	唱片,其他	8523.8019	37
Gramophone records, recorded	唱片,已录制	8523.8011	37
Grand pianos	大钢琴	9201.2000	5
Grand pianos	平台式钢琴	9201.2000	5
Granite and articles thereof, worked, nes	花岗岩及其制品,已加工的,其他	6802.9390	3468
Granite carvings	花岗岩石刻	6802.9310	3468
Granite monumental or building stone and articles thereof, simply cut or sawn, with a flat or even surface	花岗岩碑石或建筑用石及其制品,简单切削或锯开并具有一个平面的	6802.2300	3468
Granite, crude or roughly trimmed	花岗岩,原状或粗加修整	2516.1100	148

G

Article Description	商品名称	Tariff Code	D. R.
Granite, merely cut, by sawing or otherwise, into blocks or slabs of a rectangular (including square) shape	花岗岩,仅用锯或其他方法切割成矩形,包括正方形	2516.1200	148
Granulated slag, nes, from the manufacture of iron or steel	熔渣,粒状,其他,冶炼钢铁所产生的	2618.0090	146
Granules, chippings and powder, stones of heading No. 25.15 or 25.16, nes, whether or not heat-treated	石料的碎粒、碎屑及粉末,不论是否热处理,税号25.15及25.16所列,其他	2517.4900	1
Granules, of pig iron, spiegeleisen, iron or steel	颗粒,生铁、镜铁及钢铁的	7205.1000	6
Grape juice (including grape must), of a brix value not exceeding 20	葡萄汁,包括酿酒葡萄汁,白利糖度值不超过20的	2009.6100	2468
Grape juice, nes	葡萄汁,包括酿酒葡萄汁,其他	2009.6900	2468
Grape must, with fermentation prevented or arrested by the addition of alcohol	酿酒葡萄汁	2204.3000	268
Grapefruit	葡萄柚	0805.4000	14
Grapefruit (including pomelo) juice, nes	葡萄柚(包括柚)汁,其他	2009.2900	2468
Grapefruit (including pomelo) juice, of a brix value not exceeding 20	葡萄柚(包括柚)汁,白利糖度值不超过20的	2009.2100	2468
Grapes, dried	葡萄,干的	0806.2000	24
Grapes, fresh	葡萄,鲜的	0806.1000	1245
Graphite articles, non-electrical	石墨制品,非电气的	6815.1000	6
Graphite or other carbon articles of a kind used for electrical purposes, nes	石墨或碳精制品,电气设备用,其他	8545.9000	3
Graphite preparations or semi-manufactures, in the form of pastes, blocks, plates	石墨制品或半制品,糊状、块状、板状	3801.9000	134
Graphite, artificial	石墨,人造的	3801.1000	134
Graphite, colloidal or semi-colloidal	石墨,胶态或半胶态	3801.2000	134
Graphite, natural, in flakes	石墨,天然的,粉片	2504.1010	13468
Graphite, natural, in powder	石墨,天然的,粉末	2504.1099	13468
Graphite, natural, nes	石墨,天然的,其他	2504.9000	13468
Graphite, natural, spheroidized	石墨,天然的,球化的	2504.1091	13468
Grapnels and parts thereof, of iron or steel	多爪锚及其零件,钢铁的	7316.0000	36
Gravel, of a kind commonly used for concrete aggregates, for road metalling or for railway	砾石,通常作混凝土粒料、铺路、铁道路基或其他路基用的	2517.1000	13
Gravure printing machinery	凹版印刷机	8443.1700	57
Grease treatment preparations for textile materials, leather, furskins or other materials, containing petroleum oils or oils obtained from bituminous minerals	油脂处理制剂,处理纺织材料、皮革、毛皮或其他材料的,含有石油或从沥青矿物提取的油类	3403.1100	2368
Grease treatment preparations for textile materials, leather, furskins or other materials, nes	油脂处理制剂,处理纺织材料、皮革、毛皮或其他材料的,其他	3403.9100	2368
Greaseproof papers	防油纸	4806.2000	58

Article Description	商品名称	Tariff Code	D. R.
Greaves	油渣,不适于供人食用的	2301. 1020	136
Green tea (not fermented), flavoured, in immediate packings of a content not exceeding 3kg	花茶,内包装每件净重不超过3千克	0902. 1010	248
Green tea (not fermented), flavoured, nes	花茶,其他	0902. 2010	248
Green tea (not fermented), nes	绿茶(未发酵),其他	0902. 2090	248
Green tea (not fermented), nes, in immediate packings of a content not exceeding 3kg	绿茶(未发酵),内包装每件净重不超过3千克	0902. 1090	248
Greenland halibut, frozen	格陵兰庸鲽鱼,冻的	0303. 3110	18
Grenade launchers	手榴弹发射器	9301. 2000	
Grenades and parts	手榴弹及其零件	9306. 9000	3
Grill and netting, of copper wire	网、格栅,铜丝制的	7419. 9940	4
Grill and netting, of nickel wire, nes	网及格栅,其他	7508. 1090	6
Grill, netting and fencing, of iron or steel wire, welded at the intersection, nes	网、篱及格栅,钢铁丝制,交点焊接的,其他	7314. 3900	36
Grill, netting and fencing, of iron or steel wire, welded at the intersection, of wire with a maximum cross-sectional dimension of 3mm or more and having a mesh size of $100cm^2$ or more	网、篱及格栅,钢铁丝制,交点焊接的,丝的最大截面尺寸在3毫米及以上,网眼尺寸在100平方厘米及以上	7314. 2000	36
Grill, netting and fencing, of iron or steel wire, welded at the intersection, plated or coated with zinc	网、篱及格栅,钢铁丝制,交点焊接的,镀或涂锌的	7314. 3100	36
Grill, netting and fencing, of iron or steel wire, coated whith plastics	网、篱及格栅,钢铁丝制,涂塑的	7314. 4200	36
Grill, netting and fencing, of iron or steel wire, nes	网、篱及格栅,钢铁丝制,其他	7314. 4900	36
Grill, netting and fencing, of iron or steel wire, plated or coated with zinc	网、篱及格栅,钢铁丝制,镀或涂锌的	7314. 4100	36
Grindding wheels, hand or pedal operated, with frameworks	砂轮,带支架的手摇或脚踏	8205. 8000	256
Grinders for food, electro-mechanical domestic appliances	研磨机,食品用,家用电动器具	8509. 4090	
Grinding balls and similar articles, forged or stamped, but not further worked, for mills	研磨球及类似品,经锻造或冲压,但未经进一步加工,研磨机用的	7326. 1100	346
Grinding balls and similar cast articles for mills	研磨球及类似品,铸造制品,研磨机用的	7325. 9100	346
Grinding machines for glass or glassware	研磨机床,玻璃用	8464. 2010	7
Grinding machines for working stone, ceramics, concrete, asbestos-cement or like mineral materials, nes	研磨机床,加工石料、陶瓷、混凝土、石棉水泥或类似矿物材料的,其他	8464. 2090	7
Grinding machines of gear, for removing metal or cermets, nes	磨床,齿轮的,切削金属或金属陶瓷用,其他	8461. 4090	7
Grinding machines of gear, numerically controlled, for removing metal or cermets	磨床,齿轮的,数控的,切削金属或金属陶瓷用	8461. 4010	7

G

Article Description	商品名称	Tariff Code	D. R.
Grinding machines of roll, in which the positioning in any one axis can be set up to an accuracy of at least 0. 01mm, for metal or cermets, nes	轧辊磨床,在任一坐标的定位精度至少是0.01 毫米,加工金属或金属陶瓷用,其他	8460. 2930	7
Grinding machines of roll, in which the positioning in any one axis can be set up to an accuracy of at least 0. 01mm, for metal or cermets, nes	磨床,轧辊的,在任一坐标的定位精度至少是0.01 毫米,加工金属或金属陶瓷用,其他	8460. 2930	7
Grinding machines, boules or wafers manufacture machines and apparatus	研磨设备,单晶硅柱或硅晶片的制造机器及装置	8486. 1020	7
Grinding machines, cylindrical, in which the positioning in any one axis can be set up to an accuracy of at least 0. 01mm, for metal or cermets, nes	磨床,外圆的,在任一坐标的定位精度至少是0.01 毫米,加工金属或金属陶瓷用,其他	8460. 2910	7
Grinding machines, cylindrical, in which the positioning in any one axis can be set up to an accuracy of at least 0. 01mm, numerically controlled, for metal or cermets	磨床,外圆的,在任一坐标的定位精度至少是0.01 毫米,数控的,加工金属或金属陶瓷用	8460. 2110	7
Grinding machines, em-peters type, for earth, stone, ores or other mineral substances	磨粉机器,球磨式,泥土、石料、矿石或其他固体矿物质的	8474. 2010	7
Grinding machines, flat-surface, in which the positioning in any one axis can be set up to an accuracy of at least 0. 01mm, for metal or cermets, nes	磨床,平面的,在任一坐标的定位精度至少是0.01 毫米,加工金属或金属陶瓷用,其他	8460. 1900	7
Grinding machines, flat-surface, in which the positioning in any one axis can be set up to an accuracy of at least 0. 01mm, numerically controlled, for metal or cermets	磨床,平面的,在任一坐标的定位精度至少是0.01 毫米,数控的,加工金属或金属陶瓷用	8460. 1100	7
Grinding machines, for earth, stone, ores or other mineral substances, nes	磨粉机器,泥土、石料、矿石或其他固体矿物质的,其他	8474. 2090	7
Grinding machines, for working wood, cork, bone, hard rubber, hard plastics or similar hard materials	研磨机器,加工木材、软木、骨、硬质橡胶、硬质塑料或类似硬质材料的	8465. 9300	7
Grinding machines, in which the positioning in any one axis can be set up to an accuracy of at least 0. 01mm, for metal or cermets, nes	磨床,在任一坐标的定位精度至少是0.01 毫米,加工金属或金属陶瓷用,其他	8460. 2990	7
Grinding machines, in which the positioning in any one axis can be set up to an accuracy of at least 0. 01mm, numerically controlled, for metal or cermets, nes	磨床,在任一坐标的定位精度至少是0.01 毫米,数控的,加工金属或金属陶瓷用,其他	8460. 2190	7
Grinding machines, internal, in which the positioning in any one axis can be set up to an accuracy of at least 0. 01mm, for metal or cermets, nes	磨床,内圆的,在任一坐标的定位精度至少是0.01 毫米,加工金属或金属陶瓷用,其他	8460. 2920	7
Grinding machines, internal, in which the positioning in any one axis can be set up to an accuracy of at least 0. 01mm, numerically controlled, for metal or cermets	磨床,内圆的,在任一坐标的定位精度至少是0.01 毫米,数控的,加工金属或金属陶瓷用	8460. 2120	7

Article Description	商品名称	Tariff Code	D. R.
Grinding machines, nes	研磨机,其他	8479.8200	7
Grinding machines, toothing roller type, for earth, stone, ores or other mineral substances	磨粉机器,齿辊式,泥土、石料、矿石或其他固体矿物质的	8474.2010	7
Grinding wheel machines, for metal or cermets	砂轮机,加工金属或金属陶瓷用	8460.9010	7
Grinding wheels and the like, of agglomerated synthetic or natural diamond	砂轮及类似品,粘聚合成或天然金刚石制	6804.2100	236
Grinding wheels, of natural stone	砂轮,天然石料制	6804.2310	236
Grinding wheels, of other agglomerated abrasives or of ceramics	砂轮,其他粘聚磨料制或陶瓷制	6804.2210	236
Grips, parts of bulldozer or cranes	夹斗,推土机或起重机零件	8431.4100	3
Groats and meal of cereal, nes	粗粒及粗粉,其他谷物的	1103.1990	4
Groats and meal of long grain	粗粒及粗粉,籼米的	1103.1921	4
Groats and meal of maize(corn)	粗粒及粗粉,玉米的	1103.1300	4
Groats and meal of oats	粗粒及粗粉,燕麦的	1103.1910	4
Groats and meal of rice, nes	粗粒及粗粉,其他米的	1103.1929	4
Groats and meal of wheat	粗粒及粗粉,小麦的	1103.1100	4
Ground flying trainers and parts, nes	地面飞行训练器及其零件,其他	8805.2900	3
Groundnut butter	花生酱	2008.1130	248
Groundnut kernels, in airtight containers	花生米,罐头	2008.1110	248
Groundnut oil and its fractions, crude oil	花生油及其分离品,初榨的	1508.1000	
Groundnut oil and its fractions, nes	花生油及其分离品,其他	1508.9000	
Groundnuts, nes, in shell, not roasted or otherwise cooked	花生,其他,未去壳,未焙炒或未烹煮的	1202.1090	34
Groundnuts, nes, otherwise prepared, or preserved	花生,其他,用其他方法制作或保藏的	2008.1190	248
Groundnuts, roasted	花生,烘焙的	2008.1120	248
Groundnuts, seed	花生,种用	1202.1010	34
Groundnuts, shelled, not roasted or otherwise cooked, whether or not broken	花生,去壳的,未焙炒或未烹煮的,不论是否破碎	1202.2000	34
Guaiacol	愈创木酚	2909.5000	36
Guano, not chemically treated	鸟粪, 未经化学处理	3101.0011	1346
Guavas	番石榴	0804.5010	14
Guayule gums	银胶菊胶、糖胶树胶及类似的天然树胶	4001.3000	12
Guinea fowls, ex. pure-bred breeding, weighing more than 185g	珍珠鸡,改良种用除外,重量超过185克	0105.9993	48
Guinea fowls, not cut in pieces, fresh or chilled	珍珠鸡,整只,鲜或冷的	0207.3230	1
Guinea fowls, not cut in pieces, frozen	珍珠鸡,整只,冻的	0207.3330	1
Guinea fowls, pure-bred breeding, weighing more than 185g	珍珠鸡,改良种用,重量超过185克	0105.9910	48
Guinea fowls, pure-bred breeding, weighing not more than 185g	珍珠鸡,改良种用,重量不超过185克	0105.1910	48
Guitars	吉他	9202.9000	5

G

Article Description	商品名称	Tariff Code	D. R.
Guitars parts and accessories	吉他的零件、附件	9209. 9200	3
Gum arabic	阿拉伯胶	1301. 2000	3
Gum inhibitors, for mineral oils and alike	防胶剂,用于矿物油及类似液体	3811. 9000	236
Gum tragacanth	胶黄耆树胶	1301. 9010	
Gum tragacanth	卡喇杆胶	1301. 9010	
Gum turpentine oils	脂松节油	3805. 1000	36
Gumresins	树胶脂	1301. 9090	
Guts of animals (other than fish)	肠,动物的(鱼除外)	0504. 0090	14
Gutta-percha gums	古塔波胶	4001. 3000	12
Guva juice	番石榴果汁	2009. 8014	2468
Gypsum	生石膏	2520. 1000	34
Gyroscopic stabilizers for ships	陀螺稳定器,船舶用	8479. 8910	7
Gyroscopic stabilizers parts, for ships	陀螺稳定器用零件,船舶用	8479. 9010	3

G

H

Article Description	商品名称	Tariff Code	D. R.
H sections, not further worked than hot-rolled, hot-drawn or extruded of a height exceeding 800mm	H 型钢,除热轧、热拉拔或热挤压外未经进一步加工,截面高度在 800 毫米以上	7216. 3311	468
H sections, not further worked than hot-rolled, hot-drawn or extruded of a height of 200mm or more, and not exceeding 800mm	H 型钢,除热轧、热拉拔或热挤压外未经进一步加工,截面高度在 200 毫米以上,且不超过 800 毫米	7216. 3319	468
H sections, not further worked than hot-rolled, hot-drawn or extruded of a height of 80mm or more, and not exceeding 200mm	H 型钢,除热轧、热拉拔或热挤压外未经进一步加工,截面高度在 80 毫米及以上,且不超过 200 毫米	7216. 3390	468
H sections, not further worked than hot-rolled, hot-drawn or extruded, of a height of less than 80mm	H 型钢,除热轧、热拉拔或热挤压外未经进一步加工,截面高度低于 80 毫米	7216. 1010	468
Haddock (melanogrammus aeglefinus), fresh or chilled	黑线鳕鱼,鲜或冷的	0302. 6200	18
Haddock(melanogrammus aeglefinus), frozen	黑线鳕鱼,冻的	0303. 7200	18
Haematein	苏木红,正铁血红素	3203. 0019	34
Haemostatics, for surgical or dental use, sterile, absorbable	止血材料,外科或牙科用,无菌,吸收性	3006. 1000	3
Hafnium articles	铪制品	8112. 9990	16
Hafnium powders	铪粉末	8112. 9290	16
Hafnium, unwrought	铪,未锻轧	8112. 9290	16
Hair	猪毛	0502. 1020	
Hair brushes	发刷	9603. 2900	
Hair clippers	理发推剪	8214. 9000	256
Hair clippers parts, with self-contained electric motor	毛发推剪零件,电动的	8510. 9000	3
Hair clippers, with self-contained electric motor	毛发推剪,电动的	8510. 2000	
Hair curlers, electro-thermic	卷发器、电热的	8516. 3300	7
Hair dryers, hair-dressing apparatus, electro-thermic	吹风机,理发器具,电热的	8516. 3100	7
Hair lacquers	定型剂	3305. 3000	23
Hair permanent waving or straightening preparations	烫发剂	3305. 2000	23
Hair use preparations, nes	护发品,其他	3305. 9000	23
Haircurlers or curling pins	卷发夹	9615. 9000	
Hairsprings, of clock or watch	游丝,钟、表的	9114. 1000	6
Hair-dressing apparatus implements, electro-thermic	理发器具用零件,电热的	8516. 9090	3
Hair-dressing apparatus, electro-thermic, nes	理发器具,电热的,其他	8516. 3200	7
Hair-nets	发网	6505. 1000	26
Hair-pins	发卡	9615. 9000	

Article Description	商品名称	Tariff Code	D. R.
Hair-removing appliances parts, with self-contained electric motor	脱毛器零件,电动的	8510. 9000	3
Hair-removing appliances, with self-contained electric motor	脱毛器,电动的	8510. 3000	
Hair-slide, nes	发夹,其他	9615. 1900	6
Hair-slide, of hard rubber or plastics	发夹,硬质橡胶或塑料制	9615. 1100	6
Hake(merluccius spp. Urophycis spp.), frozen	狗鳕鱼(无须鳕鱼、长鳍鳕鱼),冻的	0303. 7800	18
Halazepam (INN); salts thereof	哈拉西泮(INN)以及盐	2933. 9100	36
Halibut (Reinhardtius hippoglossoides, Hippoglossus hippoglossus, Hippoglossus stenolepis), fresh or chilled	庸鲽鱼,鲜或冷的	0302. 2100	18
Halibut (reinhardtius hippoglossoides, hippoglossus hippoglossus, hippoglossus stenolepis), nes, frozen	庸鲽鱼,其他,冻的	0303. 3190	18
Halides and halide oxides of non-metals, nes	非金属卤化物及卤氧化物,其他	2812. 9000	
Halogenated derivatives of acyclic hydrocarbons containing two or more different halogens, nes	含有两种或两种以上不同卤素的无环烃卤化衍生物,其他	2903. 4990	36
Halogenated derivatives of aromatic hydrocarbons, nes	芳烃卤化衍生物,其他	2903. 6990	36
Halogenated derivatives of corticosteroidal hormones, nes	皮质(甾)类激素的卤化衍生物,其他	2937. 2290	36
Halogenated derivatives of cyclanic, cyclenic or cycloter penic hydrocarbons, nes	环烷烃、环烯烃或萜烯烃的卤化衍生物,其他	2903. 5900	36
Halogenated olefins polymers, in primary forms, nes	卤化烯烃聚合物,初级形状的,其他	3904. 9000	1256
Halogenated, sulphonated, nitrated or nitrosated derivatives of Aldehydes	醛的卤化、磺化、硝化或亚硝化衍生物	2913. 0000	36
Halogenated, sulphonated, nitrated ornitrosated derivatives of acyclic alcohols, nes	无环醇的卤化、磺化、硝化或亚硝化衍生物,其他	2905. 5900	36
Haloxazolam (INN); salts thereof	卤恶唑仑(INN)及盐	2934. 9100	36
Halo-isobutene-iso prene rubber(CIIR or BIIR), in pimary forms	卤代丁基橡胶(CIIR 或 BIIR),初级形状的	4002. 3910	136
Halo-isobutene-iso prene rubber(CIIR or BIIR), nes	卤代丁基橡胶(CIIR 或 BIIR),其他	4002. 3990	136
Hami melons, fresh	哈蜜瓜,鲜的	0807. 1910	1
Hammers and sledge hammers	锤子	8205. 2000	256
Hammers, for forging or die-stamping machines, for working metal	锻锤,锻造或冲压机床用,加工金属用	8462. 1090	7
Hams and cuts thereof, of swine	后腿及其肉块,猪的,制作或保藏的	1602. 4100	48
Hams and cuts thereof, with bone in, of swine, fresh or chilled	后腿及其肉块,猪的,鲜或冷的,带骨	0203. 1200	14
Hams and shoulders of swine, with bone in, salted, in brine, dried or smoked	猪腿,带骨的,干、熏、盐腌或盐渍的	0210. 1110	14
Hams, shoulders and cuts thereof, with bone in, of swine, frozen	后腿及其肉块,猪的,冻的,带骨	0203. 2200	14
Hand magnifying glasses	放大镜	9013. 8010	

H

Article Description	商品名称	Tariff Code	D. R.
Hand printing sets incorporating such composing sticks	手印器,带有排字盘的	9611. 0000	
Hand pumps, other than those of subheading No. 8413. 11 or 8413. 19	手泵,但子目号 8413. 11 或 8413. 19 的货品除外	8413. 2000	23
Hand riddles	细筛,手用	9604. 0000	
Hand saws	手工锯	8202. 1000	256
Hand sieves	粗筛,手用	9604. 0000	
Hand tools for household, nes	手工工具,家用,其他	8205. 5100	256
Hand tools of a kind used in agriculture, horticulture or forestry, nes	手工工具,用于农业、园艺或林业的,其他	8201. 9000	256
Hand tools parts, for self-contained electric motor tools, nes	手提式工具用零件,电动工具的,其他	8467. 9910	3
Hand tools parts, nes	手提式工具用零件,其他	8467. 9990	3
Hand tools, chain saws	手提式工具,链锯	8467. 8100	57
Hand tools, chain saws, with self-contained electric motor	手提式工具,链锯,本身装有电动动力装置的	8467. 2210	57
Hand tools, drills of all kinds, with self-contained electric motor	手提式工具,各种钻,本身装有电动动力装置的	8467. 2100	57
Hand tools, grinding tools (including burnisher, belt sander, wheel-sander)	手提式工具,砂磨工具(包括磨光机,砂光机,砂轮机等),本身装有电动动力装置的	8467. 2910	57
Hand tools, nes	手工工具,其他	8205. 5900	256
Hand tools, nes	手提式工具,其他	8467. 8900	57
Hand tools, planings, with self-contained electric motor	手提式工具,电刨,本身装有电动动力装置的	8467. 2920	57
Hand tools, pneumatic, nes	手提式工具,气动的,其他	8467. 1900	57
Hand tools, pneumatic, rotary type (including combined rotarypercussion)	手提式工具,气动的,旋转式(包括旋转冲击式的)	8467. 1100	57
Hand tools, saws, with self-contained electric motor, nes	手提式工具,锯,本身装有电动动力装置的,其他	8467. 2290	57
Hand tools, with self-contained electric motor, nes	手提式工具,本身装有电动动力装置的,其他	8467. 2990	57
Handbags, nes	手提包,其他	4202. 2900	256
Handbags, with outer surface of leather, composition leather or patent leather	手提包,以皮革、再生皮革或漆皮作面	4202. 2100	256
Handbags, with outer surface of plastic sheeting or textile materials	手提包,以塑料片或纺织材料作面	4202. 2200	256
Handkerchiefs, of paper pulp, paper, cellulose wadding or webs of cellulose fibres	手帕纸,纸浆、纸、纤维素絮纸或纤维素纤维网纸制的	4818. 2000	568
Handkerchiefs, not knitted or crocheted, embroidered, nes	手帕,非针织或钩编的,刺绣的,其他	6213. 9020	2456
Handkerchiefs, not knitted or crocheted, embroidered, of cotton	手帕,非针织或钩编的,刺绣的,棉制	6213. 2010	2456

Article Description	商品名称	Tariff Code	D. R.
Handkerchiefs, not knitted or crocheted, nes	手帕,非针织或钩编的,其他	6213.9090	2456
Handkerchiefs, not knitted or crocheted, of cotton, nes	手帕,非针织或钩编的,棉制,其他	6213.2090	2456
Handling machines, automated, solely or principally of a kind used in the electronic integrated circuits factories	搬运机器,自动的,集成电路工厂用的	8486.4031	7
Hand-drying apparatus, electro-thermic	干手器,电热的	8516.3300	7
Hand-operated mechanical appliances, weighing 10kg or less, used in the preparation, conditioning or serving of food or drink	手动机械器具,重量不超过10千克,用于加工或调制食品或饮料的	8210.0000	256
Hand-written text	手稿	4906.0000	
Hand-written text copies, photographic reprodced on sensitized paper and carbon	手稿复制件,用感兴纸照相复印或用复写纸眷写的	4906.0000	
Hang gliders	悬挂滑翔机	8801.0010	
Hanging scales	吊秤	8423.8930	
Hard rubber articles	硬质橡胶制品	4017.0020	14
Hard rubber in all forms, including waste and scrap	硬质橡胶,各种形状的包括废碎料	4017.0010	14
Hardened proteins, in primary forms	硬化蛋白,初级形状的	3913.9000	146
Hardness testing machines and applinances, or testing metals	硬度计,金属材料试验用	9024.1020	
Harmoniums and similar keyboard instruments with free metal reeds	簧风琴及类似的游离金属簧片键盘乐器	9205.9010	5
Harness for any animal, of any material	挽具,适合各种动物用,各种材料制成的	4201.0000	1458
Harps	竖琴	9202.9000	5
Harps parts and accessories	竖琴的零件、附件	9209.9200	3
Harpsichords	拨弦古钢琴	9201.9000	5
Harrows, machinary for agricultural, horticultural or forestry use, nes	耙,农业、园艺及林业用耕作机械,其他	8432.2900	
Harvesting machinery parts	收割机零件	8433.9090	
Harvesting machinery, combine type	收割机,联合脱粒式	8433.5990	
Harvesting machinery, for root or tuber	收割机,收获根茎或块茎用	8433.5990	
Harvesting machinery, for sugarcane	收割机,收获甘蔗用	8433.5990	
Harvesting machinery, nes	收割机,其他	8433.5990	
Harvesting machines for root or tuber	收获机,收获根茎或块茎用	8433.5300	
Harvesting machines for sugarcane	甘蔗收获机	8433.5910	
Hats and other headgear of felt, made from the hat bodies, hoods or plateaux of felt, whether or not lined or trimmed	帽类,用毡呢帽身、帽兜或圆帽片制成的,不论有无衬里或装饰物	6302.5990	346
Hats and other headgear, knitted	帽类,针织的	6505.9090	26
Hats and other headgear, knitted or crocheted	帽类,钩编的	6505.9010	26

H

Article Description	商品名称	Tariff Code	D. R.
Hats and other headgear, plaited or made by assembling strips of any material, whether or not lined or trimmed	帽类,不论有无衬里或装饰物,编结帽或用任何材料的条带拼制而成的	6504.0000	24
Hat-forms, hat bodies and hoods of felt, neither blocked to shape nor with made brims	帽坯、帽身及帽兜,未楦制成形,也未加帽边,毡呢制的	6501.0000	26
Hat-pegs and similar fixtures, of base metal	帽钩及类似品,贱金属制	8302.5000	256
Hat-racks and similar fixtures, of base metal	帽架及类似品,贱金属制	8302.5000	256
Hat-shapes, plaited or made by assembling strips of any material, neither blocked to shape, nor with made brims, nor lined, nor trimmed	帽坯,未楦制成形,也未加帽边、衬里或装饰物,用任何材料的条带拼制而成或编结的	6502.0000	246
Hausmannite	黑锰矿	2602.0000	1346
Hay knives	秣刀	8201.9000	256
Hay, forage products	干草,饲料用	1214.9000	
Haymaking machinery, nes	干草加工机器,其他	8433.3000	
Hazelnuts or filberts (Corylus spp.), in shell	榛子,未去壳	0802.2100	134
Hazelnuts or filberts (Corylus spp.), shelled	榛子,去壳	0802.2200	134
HCH (ISO)	六六六(ISO)	2903.5100	36
Head lettuce, fresh or chilled	包心生菜,鲜或冷藏的	0705.1100	1
Headed broccoli, fresh or chilled	硬花甘蓝,鲜或冷藏的	0704.1000	1
Headgear, nes	帽类,其他	6506.9990	26
Headgear, of furskin, nes	帽类,毛皮制,其他	6506.9920	26
Headgear, of leather, nes	帽类,皮革制,其他	6506.9910	26
Headgear, of rubber or of plastics, nes	帽类,橡胶或塑料制,其他	6506.9100	26
Headphones and earphones, nes	耳机、耳塞机,其他	8518.3090	5
Headphones parts	耳机零件	8518.9000	3
Head-bands, linings, covers, hat foundations, hat frames, peaks and chinstraps, for headgear	帽圈、帽衬、帽套、帽帮、帽骨架、帽舌及帽颏带	6507.0000	
Healds and heald-frames for looms	综丝及综框,织机用	8448.4200	3
Hearing aids, excluding parts and accessories	助听器,不包括零件、附件	9021.4000	
Hearing diagnostic apparatus, nes	听力诊断装置,其他	9018.1949	3
Heat exchange units	热交换装置	8419.5000	57
Heat meters	热量计	9026.8000	7
Heat meters parts and accessories	热量计零件、附件	9026.9000	3
Heat pumps other than air conditioning machines, compression-type	热泵,空气调节器除外,压缩式	8418.6120	57
Heat pumps other than air conditioning machines, nes	热泵,空气调节器除外,其他	8418.6190	57
Heat transfer paper	热敏转印纸	4816.9010	58
Heat treatment equipment parts, for industrial or laboratory use, electric, nes	热处理设备零件,工业或实验室用,电的,其他	8514.9090	3
Heat treatment equipment, by dielectric loss, for industrial or laboratory use, electric	热处理设备,通过介质损耗进行的,工业或实验室用,电的	8514.4000	7

H

Article Description	商品名称	Tariff Code	D. R.
Heat treatment equipment, by induction, for industrial or laboratory use, electric	热处理设备,通过感应进行的,工业或实验室用,电的	8514.4000	7
Heat treatment equipment, flat panel displays manufacture machines and apparatus	热处理设备,平板显示器的制造机器及装置	8486.3010	7
Heat treatment equipment, semiconductor devices or of electronic integrated circuits manufacture machines and apparatus	热处理设备,制造半导体器件或集成电路的机器及装置	8486.2010	7
Heat treatment furnaces, atmosphere controllable, for industrial or laboratory use, electric	热处理炉,可控气氛的,工业或实验室用,电的	8514.1010	7
Heating apparatus for soil, electric	电加热器,土壤的	8516.2910	7
Heating apparatus of a kind used for domestic purposes, non-electric, and parts thereof, of copper	供暖器具及其零件,铜制,非电热的,家用	7419.9950	4
Heat-insulating mineral materials, mixtures and articles, nes	隔热的矿物材料的混合物及制品,其他	6806.9000	68
Heat-shrink wrapping machinery	热缩包装机器	8422.4000	
Heavy liquid paraffin	重质液体石蜡	2710.1994	8
Heavy oils, nes	重油,其他	2710.1999	8
Heavy water (deuterium oxide)	重水(氧化氘)	2845.1000	
Hectograph duplicating machines	胶版复印机	8472.1000	
Hedge shears	树篱剪	8201.6000	256
Helical springs, of iron or steel, for railway locomotives and rollingstock	螺旋弹簧,钢铁制,铁道车辆用	7320.2010	36
Helical springs, of iron or steel, nes	螺旋弹簧,钢铁制,其他	7320.2090	36
Helicopters parts, nes	直升机的零件,其他	8803.3000	3
Helicopters, of an unladen weight exceeding 2000kg but not exceeding 7000kg	直升机,空载重量超过2000千克,但不超过7000千克	8802.1210	
Helicopters, of an unladen weight exceeding 7000kg	直升机,空载重量超过7000千克	8802.1220	
Helicopters, of an unladen weight not exceeding 2000kg	直升机,空载重量不超过2000千克	8802.1100	
Hemiacetals, whether or not with other oxygen function, and their haogenated, sulphonated, nitrated or nitrosated derivatives	半缩醛,不论是否含有其他含氧基,及其卤化、磺化、硝化或亚硝化衍生物	2911.0000	36
Hemimorphite	异极矿	2608.0000	146
Heparin and its salts	肝素及其盐	3001.9010	34
Heptachlor (ISO)	七氯(ISO)	2903.5200	36
Heptachlorofluoropropane	七氯氟丙烷	2903.4540	36
Herbicides, nes	除草剂,其他	3808.9319	36
Herbicides, put up for retail sale	除草剂,零售包装	3808.9311	36
Hermoforming machines, for working rubber or plastics or for the manufacture of products from these materials, nes	热成型机器,加工橡胶或塑料及其产品用,其他	8477.4090	7
Heroin and salts	海洛因及盐	2939.1100	34

H

Article Description	商品名称	Tariff Code	D. R.
Herrings (clupea harengus, clupea pallasii), excluding livers and roes, fresh or chilled	鲱鱼(大西洋鲱鱼、太平洋鲱鱼),但鱼肝及鱼卵除外,鲜或冷的	0302. 4000	18
Herrings(clupea harengus, clupea pallasii), salted or in brine	鲱鱼(大西洋鲱鱼、太平洋鲱鱼),盐腌及盐渍的	0305. 6100	4
Herrings, prepared or preserved, whole or in pieces, but not minced	鲱鱼,制作或保藏的,整条或切块,但未绞碎	1604. 1200	48
Heterocyclic compounds with nitrogen hetero-atom (s) only, nes	仅含有氮杂原子的杂环化合物,其他	2933. 9900	36
Heterocyclic compounds with oxygen hetero-atom (s) only, nes	仅含有氧杂原子的杂环化合物,其他	2932. 9990	36
Heteroeyclic compounds, nes	杂环化合物,其他	2934. 9990	36
Heterogenite	水钴矿	2605. 0000	146
Hexachlorobenzene (ISO)	六氯苯(ISO)	2903. 6200	36
Hexachlorodifluoropropane	六氯二氟丙烷	2903. 4550	36
Hexahydropyridine	六氢吡啶	2933. 3210	36
Hexamethelene diisocyanate	六亚甲基二异氰酸酯	2929. 1040	36
Hexamethylenediamine and its salts, nes	六亚甲基二胺及其盐,其他	2921. 2290	36
Hide powder, whether or not chromed	皮粉,不论是否加入铬矾	3504. 0090	1346
Hides and skins of bovine animals, tanned, without hair on, full grains, unsplit; grain splits, nes	皮,牛的,鞣制的,不带毛,全粒面未剖层革;粒面剖层革,其他	4104. 1119	1458
Hides and skins of bovine animals, tanned, without hair on, nes	皮,牛的,鞣制的,不带毛,其他	4104. 1919	1458
Hides and skins of bovine animals, tanned, without hair on, wet-blue, full grains, unsplit; grain splits	皮,牛的,鞣制的,不带毛,蓝湿的,全粒面未剖层革;粒面剖层革	4104. 1111	1458
Hides and skins of bovine animals, tanned, without hair on, wet-blue, nes	皮,牛的,鞣制的,不带毛,蓝湿的,其他	4104. 1911	1458
Hides and skins of bovine or equine animals, for machinery belting	皮,牛或马的,机器带用	4104. 4910	1458
Hides and skins of bovine or equine animals, in the dry state, full grain, unsplit; grain splits	皮,牛或马的,干革,全粒面未剖层革粒面剖层革的	4104. 4100	1458
Hides and skins of bovine or equine animals, nes	皮,牛或马的,其他	4104. 4990	1458
Hides and skins of equine animals, tanned, without hair on, in the wet state, full grains, unsplit; grain splits	皮,马的,鞣制的,不带毛,湿革,全粒面未剖层革;粒面剖层革	4104. 1120	1458
Hides and skins of equine animals, tanned, without hair on, in the wet state, nes	皮,马的,鞣制的,不带毛,湿革,其他	4104. 1920	1458
Hides and skins of goats or kids, tanned or crust, without wool or hair on, in the dry state	皮及其坯革,山羊或小山羊的,鞣制的,不带毛,干革	4106. 2200	1458
Hides and skins of goats or kids, tanned or crust, without wool or hair on, in the wet state	皮及其坯革,山羊或小山羊的,鞣制的,不带毛,湿革	4106. 2100	1458
Hides and skins of reptiles, tanned or crust, without wool or hair on	皮及其坯革,爬行动物的,鞣制的,不带毛	4106. 4000	1458

H

Article Description	商品名称	Tariff Code	D. R.
Hides and skins of swine, tanned or crust, without wool or hair on, in the dry state (crust)	皮及其坯革,猪的,鞣制的,不带毛,干革(坯革)	4106. 3200	1458
Hides and skins of swine, tanned or crust, without wool or hair on, nes	皮及其坯革,猪的,鞣制的,不带毛,其他	4106. 3190	1458
Hides and skins of swine, tanned or crust, without wool or hair on, wet-blue	皮及其坯革,猪的,鞣制的,不带毛,蓝湿的	4106. 3110	1458
Hides and skins, tanned or crust, without wool or hair on, in the dry state (crust), nes	皮及其坯革,鞣制的,不带毛,干革(坯革),其他	4106. 9200	1458
Hides and skins, tanned or crust, without wool or hair on, in the wet state, nes	皮及其坯革,鞣制的,不带毛,湿革,其他	4106. 9100	1458
High efficiency water reducing agent	高效减水剂	3824. 4010	36
High frequency amplifiers	高频放大器	8543. 7092	37
High frequency amplifiers parts	高频放大器用零件	8543. 9040	3
High speed cameras	高速摄影机	9007. 1910	8
Hinges, of base metal, suitable for furniture, doors, staircases, windows, blinds, coachwork, saddlery, trunks, chests, caskets, or the like	铰链(折叶),贱金属制,用于家具、门窗、楼梯、百叶窗、车厢、鞍具、衣箱、盒子及类似品的	8302. 1000	256
Hinnies	骒	0101. 9090	34
Hippocampi, dried	海马,干的	0305. 5910	4
Hoes	掘头	8201. 3000	256
Hoes, for agricultural, horticultural or forestry use, nes	耕耘机,农业、园艺及林业用,其他	8432. 2900	
Hog casings, salted (excluding hog fatends)	盐渍猪肠衣(猪大肠头除外)	0504. 0011	14
Hog fatends, salted	盐渍猪大肠头	0504. 0014	14
Hoists parts	提升机的零件	8431. 1000	3
Hoists, hydraulic, of a kind used for raising vehicles, nes	提升机,液压,提升车辆用,其他	8425. 4290	78
Hoists, nes	提升机,其他	8425. 4990	78
Hollow drill bars and rods, of alloy or non-alloy steel	空心钻钢,合金钢或非合金钢制的	7228. 8000	468
Hollow glass spheres and their segments, for the manufacture of clock, watch or spectacles glasses	空心玻璃球面及片段,制造钟表玻璃及眼镜用玻璃的凹面用	7015. 9090	1345
Hollow profiles of aluminium alloys	空心异型材,铝合金制	7604. 2100	16
Homogenized composite food preparations	均化混合食品	2104. 2000	28
Homogenized preparations, being cooked preparations	均化食品,烹煮的	2007. 1000	248
Homogenized preparations, prepared or preserved	均化食品,制作或保藏的	1602. 1000	48
Homogenized tobacco	均化烟草	2403. 9100	
Homogenized vegetables, prepared or preserved otherwise than by vinegar or acetic acid, not frozen	均化蔬菜,用醋或醋酸以外的其他方法制作或保藏的,未冷冻	2005. 1000	48
Homogenizing machines, nes	均化机,其他	8479. 8200	7
Honey, artificial, whether or not mixed with natural honey	人造蜂蜜,不论是否含有天然蜂蜜	1702. 9000	
Honey, natural	蜂蜜,天然的	0409. 0000	24
Honing machines, for metal or cermets	珩磨机床,加工金属或金属陶瓷用	8460. 4010	7

H

Article Description	商品名称	Tariff Code	D. R.
Hooks, of base metal, of a kind used for clothing, footwear, awnings, handbags, travel goods or other made up articles	钩,贱金属制,用于衣着、鞋靴、天篷、提包、旅行用品或其他制成品	8308. 1000	256
Hooks, of railway or tramway locomotives or rolling-stock	钩,铁道及电车道机车或其他车辆的	8607. 3000	3
Hoopwood, coniferous	箍木,针叶木的	4404. 1000	15
Hoopwood, non-coniferous	箍木,非针叶木的	4404. 2000	15
Hooves and powder thereof	蹄及其粉末	0507. 9090	14
Hop cones, ground, powdered or in the form of pellets	啤酒花,经研磨或制成团粒	1210. 2000	14
Hop cones, neither ground nor powdered nor in the form of pellets	啤酒花,未经研磨也未制成团粒	1210. 1000	14
Hopper scales	库秤	8423. 3090	
Horese, ex. pure-bred breeding	马,改良种用除外	0101. 9010	34
Hormones medicaments, nes, consisting of two or more constituents which have been mixed together, not put up in measured doses or in forms or packings for retail sale	激素药品,其他,两种或两种以上成分混合而成的,未配定剂量或制成零售包装	3003. 3900	368
Hormones medicaments, nes, mixed or unmixed, put up in measured doses or in forms or packings for retail sale	激素药品,其他,混合或未混合的,配定剂量或制成零售包装	3004. 3900	368
Horn, worked	角,已加工的	9601. 9000	5
Horncores, nes	角柱,其他	0506. 9090	146
Horns and powder thereof	角及其粉末	0507. 9090	14
Horsehair and horsehair waste, whether or not put up as a layer with or without supporting material	马毛及废马毛,不论是否制成有或无衬垫的毛片	0511. 9940	
Horseradish, fresh or chilled	山葵,鲜或冷藏的	0706. 9000	1
Horseradish, fresh or chilled	辣根,鲜或冷藏的	0706. 9000	1
Horseradish, frozen	辣根,冷冻的	0710. 8090	1
Horseradish, prepared or preserved otherwise than by vinegar or acetic acid	辣根,用醋或醋酸以外的其他方法制作或保藏的	2005. 9999	148
Horses, pure-bred breeding	马,改良种用	0101. 1010	34
Horticultural machinery parts, nes	园艺用机器零件,其他	8436. 9900	3
Horticultural machinery, including germination plant fitted with mechanical or thermal equipment, nes	园艺用机器,包括装有机械或热力装置的催芽设备,其他	8436. 8000	
Hosepiping and similar tubing, of textile, with or without lining, armour or accessories of other materials	水龙软管及类似的管子,纺织材料制的,不论有无其他材料作衬里、护套或附件	5909. 0000	
Hosiery of full-length or knee-length, knitted or crocheted, measuring per single yarn less than 67 decitex, for women or girls, nes	袜,长统或中统的,针织或钩编的,每根单丝细度在 67 分特以下,女式,其他	6115. 3000	2456
Hosiery of graduated compression (for example, stockings for varicose veins)	袜,渐紧压的(例如,用以治疗静脉曲张的长统袜)	6115. 1000	2456

H

Article Description	商品名称	Tariff Code	D. R.
Hospital beds with mechanical fittings	病床,带机械装置的	9402.9000	3
Hot air distributors (including distributors which can also distribute fresh or con-ditioned air) and parts thereof, of iron or steel, not electrically heated, incorporating a motor-dirven fan or blower	暖气分布器(包括可分布新鲜空气或调节空气的)及其零件,钢铁制,非电热的,装有电动风扇或鼓风机	7322.9000	7
Hot pickled mustard tubers, prepared or preserved otherwise than by vinegar or acetic acid, not frozen	榨菜,用醋或醋酸以外的其他方法制作或保藏的,未冷冻	2005.9940	148
Household articles and toilet articles, of porcelain, nes	家用或盥洗用器,瓷制,其他	6911.9000	268
Household articles and toilet articles, of pottery, nes	家用或盥洗用器,陶制,其他	6912.0090	268
Household articles, of plastics	家庭用具,塑料的	3924.9000	23
Household automated bread makers	家用自动面包机	8516.7210	7
Howitzers, nes	榴弹炮,其他	9301.1900	7
Howitzers, self-propelled	榴弹炮,自推进的	9301.1100	7
Hsueh pears, fresh	雪梨,鲜的	0808.2012	1
Hub brakes and parts, of bicycles and other cycles	毂闸及其零件,自行车及脚踏车的	8714.9400	3
Hubnerite	钨锰矿	2611.0000	146
Hubs, of bicycles and other cycles, other than coaster braking hubs and hub brakes	轮毂(倒轮制动毂及毂闸除外),自行车及脚踏车的	8714.9310	3
Hubs, telecommunication apparatus for digital line system	集线器,有线数字通信设备	8517.6235	7
Human blood	人血	3002.9090	34
Human hair, dressed, thinned, bleached or otherwise worked	人发,经梳理、稀疏、脱色或其他方法加工的	6703.0000	4
Human hair, unworked, whether or not washed or scoured	人发,未经加工的,不论是否洗涤	0501.0000	4
Human hair, wasted	人发,废的	0501.0000	4
Human or animal substances, prepared for therapeutic or prophylactic uses, not elsewhere specified or included	人体或动物制品,供治疗或预防疾病用的,其他税号未列名的	3001.9090	34
Humidifiers for air	增湿器,空气的	8479.8920	7
Humidifiers parts, for air	增湿器用零件,空气的	8479.9020	3
Humming birds, pure-bred breeding	蜂鸟,改良种用	0106.3910	34
Hunting rifles, nes	狩猎用步枪,其他	9303.3000	7
Hunting shotguns, including combination shotgun rifles	狩猎用猎枪,包括组合式滑膛来复枪	9303.2000	7
Husked (brown) rice, nes	糙米,其他	1006.2090	35
Huydraulic brake fluids, not containing or containing less than 70% by weight of petroleum oils or oils obtaines from bituminous minerals	闸用液压油,不含石油或从沥青矿物提取的油类,或者按重量计石油或从沥青矿物提取的油类含量低于70%	3819.0000	36
Hydantoin and its derivatives	乙内酰脲及其衍生物	2933.2100	36

Article Description	商品名称	Tariff Code	D. R.
Hydrated tantalum/niobium materials	水合钽铌原料	2615. 9010	146
Hydraulic automatic regulating or controlling instruments and apparatus, nes	液压自动调节或控制仪器及装置,其他	9032. 8100	7
Hydraulic cements, nes	水凝水泥,其他	2523. 9000	3
Hydraulic lime	水硬石灰	2522. 3000	
Hydraulic motors	液压马达	8412. 2910	27
Hydraulic power engines, linear acting(cylinders)	直线作用(液压缸)的	8412. 2100	27
Hydraulic power engines, nes	液压动力装置,其他	8412. 2990	27
Hydraulic presses, for working metal or metal carbides, nes	液压压力机,加工金属或硬质合金用,其他	8462. 9190	7
Hydraulic turbines and water wheels of a power exceeding 200000kW, pumping	水轮机及水轮,功率超过 200000 千瓦,水泵的	8410. 1330	27
Hydraulic turbines and water wheels of a power exceeding 30000kW, impulse	水轮机及水轮,功率超过 30000 千瓦,冲击式的	8410. 1310	27
Hydraulic turbines and water wheels of a power exceeding 35000kW, radial	水轮机及水轮,功率超过 35000 千瓦,贯流式的	8410. 1320	27
Hydraulic turbines and water wheels parts, nes	水轮机及水轮零件,其他	8410. 9090	27
Hydraulic turbines and water wheels regulators	水轮机及水轮调节器	8410. 9010	27
Hydraulic turbines and water wheels, of a power not exceeding 1000kW	水轮机及水轮,功率不超过 1000 千瓦	8410. 1100	2
Hydraulic turbines and water wheels, of a power exceeding 10000kW	水轮机及水轮,功率超过 10000 千瓦,其他	8410. 1390	
Hydraulic turbines and water wheels, of a power exceeding 1000kW but not exceeding 10000kW	水轮机及水轮,功率超过 1000 千瓦,但不超过 10000 千瓦	8410. 1200	2
Hydrazine and their inorganic salts	肼(联氨)及其无机盐	2825. 1090	
Hydrazine hydrate	水合肼	2825. 1010	
Hydrides, whether or not chemically defined	氢化物,不论是否已有化学定义	2850. 0000	
Hydrochloric acid	盐酸	2806. 1000	6
Hydrocodone(INN) and salts	氢可酮(INN) 及盐	2939. 1100	34
Hydrocortisone	氢化可的松	2937. 2100	36
Hydrocyanic acid	氢氰酸	2811. 1910	6
Hydrofluoric acid	氢氟酸	2811. 1100	6
Hydrofluorid	氟化氢	2811. 1100	6
Hydroformer vessels, with a process involving a change of temperature	加氢反应器,利用温度变化处理	8419. 8910	57
Hydrogen	氢	2804. 1000	
Hydrogen chloride	氯化氢	2806. 1000	6
Hydrogen peroxide, whether or not solidified with urea	过氧化氢,不论是否用尿素固化	2847. 0000	6
Hydrographic or similar charts of all kinds, printed	水道图及类似图表,印制的	4905. 9900	1
Hydrometers	流速仪	9025. 8000	3
Hydrometers parts and accessories	流速仪零件、附件	9025. 9000	7
Hydromorphone(INN) and salts	氢吗啡酮 (INN) 及盐	2939. 1100	34

Article Description	商品名称	Tariff Code	D. R.
Hydroquinone	对苯二酚	2907. 2210	36
Hydroxylamine and their inorganic salts	胲(羟胺)及其无机盐	2825. 1090	
Hydroxylamine sulfate	硫酸羟胺	2825. 1020	
Hygienic articles, of plastics	卫生用具,塑料的	3924. 9000	23
Hygienic articles, of vulcanized rubber other than hard rubber, nes	卫生用品,硫化橡胶(硬质橡胶除外)制的	4014. 9000	23
Hygrometers	湿度计	9025. 8000	3
Hygrometers parts and accessories	湿度计零件、附件	9025. 9000	7
Hypobromites, inorganic	次溴酸盐,无机的	2828. 9000	
Hypochlorites, nes, inorganic	次氯酸盐,其他,无机的	2828. 9000	

H

I

Article Description	商品名称	Tariff Code	D. R.
I sections, not further worked than hot-rolled, hot-drawn or extruded of a height	工字钢,除热轧、热拉拔或热挤压外未经进一步加工,截面高度在200毫米以上	7216.3210	468
I sections, not further worked than hot-rolled, hot-drawn or extruded of a height of 80mm or more, and not exceeding 200mm	工字钢,除热轧、热拉拔或热挤压外未经进一步加工,截面高度在80毫米及以上,且不超过200毫米	7216.3290	468
I sections, not further worked than hot-rolled, hot-drawn or extruded, of a height of less than 80mm	工字钢,除热轧、热拉拔或热挤压外未经进一步加工,截面高度低于80毫米	7216.1020	468
Ice	冰	2201.9090	248
Ice cream and other edible ice, whether or not containing cocoa	冰淇淋及其他冰制食品,不论是否含可可	2105.0000	28
Ice skates and articles	溜冰鞋及用品	9506.7010	
Iceland spar (calcite)	冰洲石	2530.9099	13456
Ictalurus, nes, prepared or preserved, whole or in pieces, but not minced	叉尾鮰鱼,其他,制作或保藏的,整条或切块,但未绞碎	1604.1939	48
Igniters	引爆器	3603.0000	
Ignition coils, for electrical ignition or starting equipment, nes	点火线圈,点燃式或压燃式内燃发动机用的,其他	8511.3090	7
Ignition coils, for locomotives, aircraft or ships, for electrical ignition or starting equipment	点火线圈,机车、航空器及船舶用,点燃式或压燃式内燃发动机用的	8511.3010	7
Ignition magnetos, for electrical ignition or starting equipment, nes	点火磁电机,点燃式或压燃式内燃发动机用的,其他	8511.2090	7
Ignition magnetos, for locomotives, aircraft or ships, for electrical ignition or starting equipment	点火磁电机,机车、航空器及船舶用,点燃式或压燃式内燃发动机用的	8511.2010	7
Ignition wiring sets, for motor vehicles	点火布线组,机动车辆用	8544.3020	35
Ignition wiring sets, nes	点火布线组,其他	8544.3090	35
Illuminated nameplates and the like, having a permanently fixed light source	发光铭牌及类似品,装有固定光源的	9405.6000	5
Illuminated signs and the like, having a permanently fixed light source	发光标志及类似品,装有固定光源的	9405.6000	5
Image converters	变像管	8540.2090	35
Image intensifiers	图像增强管	8540.2090	35
Imidazole ring compounds, unfused in the structure, whether or not hydrogenated, nes	咪唑环化合物,结构上含有,非稠合的,不论是否氢化,其他	2933.2900	36
Imides and their derivatives; salts thereof, nes	酰亚胺及其衍生物以及它们的盐,其他	2925.1900	36
Imines and their derivatives; salts thereof, nes	亚胺及其衍生物以及它们的盐,其他	2925.2900	36
Imitation jewellery, nes	仿首饰,其他	7117.9000	46

I

Article Description	商品名称	Tariff Code	D. R.
Imitation jewellery, of base metal, whether or not plated with precious metal, nes	仿首饰,贱金属制,不论是否镀贵金属,其他	7117. 1900	46
Imitation leather, impregnated, coated, covered or laminated with plastics, nes	人造革,用塑料浸渍、涂布、包覆或层压的,其他	5903. 9020	
Imitation leather, impregnated, coated, covered or laminated with poly(vinyl chloride)	人造革,用聚氯乙烯浸渍、涂布、包覆或层压的	5903. 1020	
Imitation leather, impregnated, coated, covered or laminated with polyurethane	人造革,用聚氨基甲酸酯浸渍、涂布、包覆或层压的	5903. 2020	
Imitation pearls, of glass	仿珍珠	7018. 1000	3458
Imitation precious or semi-precious stones and similar glass smallwares	仿宝石或仿半宝石及类似小件玻璃品	7018. 1000	3458
Implanted appliances, to compensate for a defect or disability	植入人体内的其他器具,弥补生理缺陷或残疾的	9021. 9000	3
Impregnating machines for textile fabrics	浸渍机器,纺织物的	8451. 8000	
Impregnating machines parts for textile fabrics	浸渍机器零件,纺织物的	8451. 9000	
In take valve leaf or discharge valve leaf, for refrigerators or freezers or air conditioning machines	压缩机进、排气阀片,冷藏箱、冷冻箱用或空气调节器的	8414. 9011	23
Inactive yeasts	酵母,非活性	2102. 2000	28
Incandescent gas mantles and tubular knitted gas mantle fabric therefor, whether or not impregnated	煤气灯纱筒及纱罩,不论是否浸渍	5908. 0000	
Incubators for poultry	孵卵器,家禽用	8436. 2100	
Indene resins, in primary forms	茚树脂,初级形状的	3911. 1000	16
Indexing tags and similar office articles, of base metal	索引标签及类似的办公用品,贱金属制	8305. 9000	256
Indian ink drawing pens	墨汁画笔	9608. 3100	
Indicator panels incorporating liquid crystal devices (LCD) or light emitting diodes (LED), sound or visual signalling apparatus, electric	指示板,装有液晶装置(LCD)或发光二极管(LED)的音响或视觉信号装置	8531. 2000	3
Indicator panels, electric, nes	指示板,电气的,其他	8531. 8090	3
Indigo and preparations based thereon, natural	靛蓝及以其为基本成分的制品,天然的	3203. 0011	34
Indigo, reductive	靛蓝,还原型	3204. 1510	345
Indigo, synthetic	靛蓝,合成的	3204. 1510	345
Indium articles, nes	铟制品,其他	8112. 9930	16
Indium powders	铟粉末	8112. 9230	16
Indium, unwrought	铟,未锻轧	8112. 9230	16
Inductances measuring instruments and apparatus, nes	电感测试仪,其他	9030. 8910	
Inductances measuring instruments and apparatus, with a recording device	电感测试仪,带记录装置	9030. 8410	
Inductors parts	电感器零件	8504. 9090	3
Inductors, nes	电感器,其他	8504. 5000	

Article Description	商品名称	Tariff Code	D. R.
Industrial robots for multiple uses	工业机器人,多功能的	8479.5010	7
Industrial robots, nes	工业机器人,其他	8479.5090	7
Inflatable articles of vulcanized rubber other than hard rubber, nes	可充气制品,硫化橡胶(硬质橡胶除外)的,其他	4016.9500	236
Inflatable rafts	充气筏	8907.1000	5
Infra-red lamps	红外线灯	8539.4900	35
Infra-red ray apparatus, used in medical, surgical, dental or veterinary sciences	红外线装置,医疗、外科、牙科或兽医用	9018.2000	
Infra-res or helium-neon laser film, unexposed, without perforations, of a width exceeding 610mm and of a length exceeding 200 m	红外或氦氖激光胶片,未曝光的,无齿孔的,宽度超过610毫米,长度超过200米	3702.4291	12368
Ingot block continuous casting machines	方坯连铸机	8454.3021	
Ingot continuous casting machines, nes	钢坯连铸机,其他	8454.3029	
Ingot moulds	锭模	8454.2090	
Ingot slab continuous casting machines	板坯连铸机	8454.3022	
Ingrain paper	壁纸,用木粒或草粒等饰面的	4814.1000	4
Injection-moulding machines, for working plastics	注塑机,用来加工塑料	8477.1010	7
Injection-moulding machines, for working rubber or plastics or for the manufacture of products from these materials, nes	注射机,加工橡胶或塑料及其产品用,其他	8477.1090	7
Inks for writing or drawing	墨水,书写或绘图用	3215.9010	3
Inks, nes, whether or not concentrated or solid	墨类,其他,不论是否固体或浓缩	3215.9090	3
Ink-jet printers, of a kind solely used for automatic data processing machine	喷墨打印机,专用于自动数据处理设备的	8443.3213	57
Ink-jet printing machines, digital	喷墨印刷机,数字式	8443.3931	57
Ink-jet printing machines, digital, capable of connecting to an APP machine or to a network	喷墨印刷机,数字式,可与自动数据处理设备或网络连接	8443.3221	57
Ink-pads, whether or not inked, with or without boxes	印台,不论是否已加印油或带盒子	9612.2000	
Ink-removers and the like	除墨剂及类似品	3824.9020	36
Inner tubes, of rubber, nes	橡胶内胎,其他	4013.9090	23
Inner tubes, of rubber, of a kind used on aircraft	橡胶内胎,航空器用	4013.9010	23
Inner tubes, of rubber, of a kind used on bicycles	橡胶内胎,自行车用	4013.2000	23
Inner tubes, of rubber, of a kind used on motor cars (including staton wagons and racing cars), buses or lorries	橡胶内胎,机动小客车(包括旅行小客车及赛车)、客运、机动车辆或货运机动车辆用	4013.1000	23
Inorganic acids, nes	无机酸,其他	2811.1990	6
Inorganic bases, metal oxides, hydroxides and peroxides, nes	金属氧化物、氢氧化物及过氧化物,其他	2825.9090	
Inorganic bases, nes	无机碱,其他	2825.9090	
Inorganic compounds, nes	无机化合物,其他	2853.0090	
Inorganic oxygen compounds of nonmetals, nes	非金属无机氧化物,其他	2811.2900	
Inositol	肌醇	2906.1320	36

I

Article Description	商品名称	Tariff Code	D. R.
Insect waxes, nes	虫蜡,其他	1521.9090	
Insecticides, nes	杀虫剂,其他	3808.9190	36
Insecticides, put up for retail sale, nes	杀虫剂,零售包装,其他	3808.9119	36
Inspection vehicles for tunnel clearance, for railway or tramway maintenance or service	隧道限界检查车,铁道及电车道用	8604.0011	37
Installing vehicles for suspension of contact wire (running on rails), for railway or tramway maintenance or service	电气化接触网架线机(轨行式),铁道及电车道用	8604.0091	37
Instant noodle	即食或快熟面条	1902.3030	2468
Instant print cameras	一次成像照相机	9006.4000	7
Instant print film, unexposed	一次成像平片,未曝光的	3701.2000	12368
Instant print film, unexposed, without perforations, of a width not exceeding 105mm, for colour photography	一次成像卷片,未曝光的,无齿孔的,宽度不超过105毫米,彩色摄影用	3702.3110	12368
Instant print film, unexposed, without perforations, of a width not exceeding 105mm, with silver halide emulsion	一次成像卷片,未曝光的,无齿孔的,宽度不超过105毫米,涂卤化银乳液的	3702.3210	12368
Instrument panel clocks and clocks of a similar type for vehicles, aircraft, spacecraft or vessels	仪表板钟及车辆、航空器、航天器或船舶用的类似钟	9104.0000	5
Insulated switch gear of gas, for a voltage of 500kV or more	高压开关装置,全封闭组合式,用于电压在500千伏及以上的线路	8537.2010	78
Insulated switch gear parts of gas, for a voltage of 500kV or more	高压开关装置零件,全封闭组合式,用于电压在500千伏及以上的线路	8538.1010	3
Insulating cloth or tape, impregnated, coated, covered or laminated with poly(vinyl chloride)	绝缘布或带,用聚氯乙烯浸渍、涂布包覆或层压的	5903.1010	
Insulating cloth or tape, impregnated, coated or covered, nes	绝缘布或带,浸渍、涂布或包覆的,其他	5907.0010	4
Insulating cloth or tape, impregnated, coated, covered or laminated with plastics, nes	绝缘布或带,用塑料浸渍、涂布、包覆或层压的,其他	5903.9010	
Insulating cloth or tape, impregnated, coated, covered or laminated with polyurethane	绝缘布或带,用聚氨基甲酸酯浸渍、涂布、包覆或层压的	5903.2010	
Insulating cloth or tape, rubberized	绝缘布或带,用橡胶处理的	5906.9910	48
Insulating fittings for electrical machines, appliances or equipment, being fittings wholly of insulating material	绝缘零件,电气机器、器具或设备用,全部用绝缘材料制成	8547.9090	3
Insulating fittings of ceramics	绝缘零件,陶瓷制	8547.1000	3
Insulating fittings of plastics	绝缘零件,塑料制	8547.2000	3
Insulating paper and paperboard, coated, impregnated or covered with plastics (excluding adhesives)	绝缘纸及纸板,用塑料(不包括粘合剂)涂布、浸渍或覆盖的	4811.5910	458
Insulating paper and paperboard, coated, impregnated or covered with wax, paraffin wax, stearin, oil or glyecrol	绝缘纸及纸板,用蜡、石蜡、硬脂精、油或甘油涂布、浸渍、覆盖的	4811.6010	458

I

Article Description	商品名称	Tariff Code	D. R.
Insulating tape, of a width not exceeding 20cm, rubberized	绝缘带,宽度不超过 20 厘米的,用橡胶处理的	5906. 1010	48
Insulin and its salts, nes	胰岛素及其盐,其他	2937. 1290	36
Insulin and its salts, recombinant	胰岛素及其盐,重组的	2937. 1210	36
Insulin medicaments, consisting of two or more constituents which have been mixed together, not put up in measured doses or in forms or packings for retail sale	胰岛素药品,两种或两种以上成分混合而成的,未配定剂量或制成零售包装	3003. 3100	368
Insulin medicaments, mixed or unmixed, put up in measured doses or in forms or packings for retail sale, nes	胰岛素药品,混合或未混合的,配定剂量或制成零售包装,其他	3004. 3190	368
Insulin medicaments, recombinant, mixed or unmixed, put up in measured doses or in forms or packings for retail sale	胰岛素药品,重组的,混合或未混合的,配定剂量或制成零售包装	3004. 3110	368
Intake air filters for internal combustion engines	过滤器,内燃发动机进气用	8421. 3100	7
Interchangeable tools, nes	可互换工具,其他	8207. 9090	256
Interchangeable tools, with working part of natural or synthetic diamonds or cubic boron nitride	可互换工具,带有天然或合成金刚石、立方氮化硼制的工作部件	8207. 9010	256
Interior blinds, crocheted, of cotton	帐幔,钩编的,棉制	6303. 1932	346
Interior blinds, crocheted, of other textile materials	帐幔,钩编的,其他纺织材料制	6303. 1992	346
Interior blinds, crocheted, of synthetic fibres	帐幔,钩编的,合成纤维制	6303. 1220	346
Interior blinds, knitted, of cotton	帐幔,针织的,棉制	6303. 1931	346
Interior blinds, knitted, of other textile materials	帐幔,针织的,其他纺织材料制	6303. 1991	346
Interior blinds, knitted, of synthetic fibres	帐幔,针织的,合成纤维制	6303. 1210	346
Interior blinds, of cotton, nes	帐幔,棉制,其他	6303. 9100	346
Interior blinds, of other textile materials	帐幔,其他纺织材料制	6303. 9900	346
Interior blinds, of synthetic fibres, nes	帐幔,合成纤维制,其他	6303. 9200	346
Interleaved carbon sets, of paper or paperboard	复写本,页间夹有纸的,纸或纸板制的	4820. 4000	
Interlock machines	绷缝机	8452. 2130	
Intermediate frequency amplifiers	中频放大器	8543. 7092	37
Intermediate frequency amplifiers parts	中频放大器用零件	8543. 9040	3
Intermediate products of cobalt matallurgy, nes	钴冶炼时所得的中间产品,其他	8105. 2090	16
Intermediate products of cobalt metallurgy by wet process	钴湿法冶炼中间品	8105. 2010	16
Intermediate products of nickel metallurgy by wet process	镍湿法冶炼中间品	7501. 2010	4
Internal combustion piston engines, spark-ignition reciprocating or rotary, for aircraft, of an output exceeding 298kW	活塞内燃发动机,点燃往复式或旋转式,航空器用,输出功率超过 298 千瓦	8407. 1020	3
Internal combustion piston engines, spark-ignition reciprocating or rotary, for aircraft, of an output not exceeding 298kW	活塞内燃发动机,点燃往复式或旋转式,航空器用,输出功率不超过 298 千瓦	8407. 1010	3

I

Article Description	商品名称	Tariff Code	D. R.
Internal combustion piston engines, spark-ignition reciprocating or rotary, for marine, nes	活塞内燃发动机,点燃往复式或旋转式,船舶发动机,其他	8407.2900	3
Internal combustion piston engines, spark-ignition reciprocating or rotary, for marine, outboard motors	活塞内燃发动机,点燃往复式或旋转式,船舶舷外发动机	8407.2100	3
Internal combustion piston engines, spark-ignition reciprocating or rotary, nes	活塞内燃发动机,点燃往复式或旋转式,其他	8407.9090	25
Internal grinding machines, in which the positioning in any one axis can be set up to an accuracy of at least 0.01mm, for metal or cermets, nes	内圆磨床,在任一坐标的定位精度至少是0.01毫米,加工金属或金属陶瓷用,其他	8460.2920	7
Internal grinding machines, in which the positioning in any one axis can be set up to an accuracy of at least 0.01mm, numerically controlled, for metal or cermets	内圆磨床,在任一坐标的定位精度至少是0.01毫米,数控的,加工金属或金属陶瓷用	8460.2120	7
International chess and other board games	国际象棋等棋类用品	9504.9030	
Intrauterine contraceptive device	宫内节育器	9018.9080	
Inulin	菊粉	1108.2000	
Invert sugar	转化糖	1702.9000	
Inverter	逆变器	8504.4030	
Iodates, inorganic	碘酸盐,无机的	2829.9000	
Iodides and iodide oxides	碘化物及碘氧化物	2827.6000	
Iodine	碘	2801.2000	
Ion implanters parts and accessories, semiconductor devices or of electronic integrated circuits manufacture machines and apparatus	离子注入机零件及附件,制造半导体器件或集成电路的机器及装置	8486.9090	3
Ion implanters, semiconductor devices or of electronic integrated circuits manufacture machines and apparatus	离子注入机,制造半导体器件或集成电路的机器及装置	8486.2050	7
Ionizing radiations measuring or detecting instruments and apparatus	离子射线的测量或检验仪器及装置	9030.1000	
Ionones	芷香酮	2914.2300	36
Ion-exchangers based on polymers, in primary forms	离子交换剂,以聚合物为基本成分的,初级形状的	3914.0000	136
IP telephone signal converters	IP电话信号转换设备	8517.6233	7
IR spectrometers, spectrophotometers and spectrographs	红外线分光仪、分光光度计及摄谱仪	9027.3000	
Iridium, nes	铱,其他	7110.4990	46
Iridium, plates and sheets	铱,板、片	7110.4910	46
Iridium, unwrought or in powder form	铱,未锻造或粉末状	7110.4100	46
Iris, seed, dormant	鸢尾,种用,休眠的	0601.1091	135
Iron and non-alloy steel in ingots	铁及非合金钢,锭状	7206.1000	6
Iron and non-alloy steel in other primary forms	铁及非合金钢,其他初级形状	7206.9000	6
Iron citrate	枸橼酸铁	2918.1500	36

I

Article Description	商品名称	Tariff Code	D. R.
Iron citrate	柠檬酸铁	2918. 1500	36
Iron or non-alloy steel, semi-finished, containing by weight 0. 25% or more of carbon	铁及非合金钢的半制成品,按重量计含碳量在 0. 25% 及以上	7207. 2000	468
Iron or non-alloy steel, semi-finished, containing by weight less than 0. 25% of carbon, nes	铁及非合金钢的半制成品,其他	7207. 1900	468
Iron or non-alloy steel, semi-finished, containing by weight less than 0. 25% of carbon, of rectangular (including square) cross-section, the width measuring less than twice the thickness	铁及非合金钢的半制成品,矩形(包括正方形)截面,宽度小于厚度的两倍	7207. 1100	468
Iron or non-alloy steel, semi-finished, containing by weight less than 0. 25% of carbon, of rectangular (other than square) cross-section, nes	铁及非合金钢的半制成品,矩形(正方形除外)截面的,其他	7207. 1200	468
Iron or steel articles, for technical use, nes	钢铁制品,工业用,其他	7326. 9010	346
Iron or steel articles, forged or stamped, but not further worked, for technical use	钢铁制品,经锻造或冲压,但未经进一步加工,工业用	7326. 1910	346
Iron or steel articles, forged or stamped, but not further worked, nes	钢铁制品,经锻造或冲压,但未经进一步加工,其他	7326. 1990	346
Iron or steel articles, nes	钢铁制品,其他	7326. 9090	346
Iron or steel wire articles, for technical use	钢铁丝制品,工业用	7326. 2010	346
Iron or steel wire articles, nes	钢铁丝制品,其他	7326. 2090	346
Iron or steel wool	钢铁丝绒	7323. 1000	24
Iron ores and concentrates, agglomerated	铁矿砂及其精矿,已烧结	2601. 1200	1346
Iron ores and concentrates, non agglomerated, the average grain size not less than 0. 8mm, but not more than 6. 3mm	铁矿砂及其精矿,未烧结,平均粒度不小于 0. 8 毫米,但不大于 6. 3 毫米的	2601. 1120	13468
Iron ores and concentrates, non-agglomerated	铁矿砂及其精矿,未烧结,其他	2601. 1190	13468
Iron ores and concentrates, non-agglomerated, the average grain size less than 0. 8mm	铁矿砂及其精矿,未烧结,平均粒度小于 0. 8 毫米的	2601. 1110	13468
Iron oxides and hydroxides	铁的氧化物及氢氧化物	2821. 1000	6
Iron pyrites, unroasted	黄铁矿,未焙烧的	2502. 0000	4
Iron vats and similar containers for any material, of a capacity exceeding 300L, whether or not lined or heat-insulated, but not fitted with mechanical or thermal equipment	钢铁桶及类似容器,容积超过 300 升,不论是否衬里或隔热,但无机械或热力装置,盛装物料用的	7309. 0000	36
Iron, having a minimum purity by weight of 99. 94%, in lumps, pellets or similar forms, nes	铁,按重量计纯度在 99. 94% 及以上的、块、团、团粒及类似形状,其他	7203. 9000	6
Irone	鸢尾酮	2914. 2300	36
Ironing machines	熨烫机	8451. 3000	
Ironing machines parts	熨烫机零件	8451. 9000	
Isinglass	鱼鳔胶	3503. 0090	13
Isoborneol	异冰片	2906. 1990	36
Isobutanol	异丁醇	2905. 1410	36

I

Article Description	商品名称	Tariff Code	D. R.
Isobutene-isoprene (butyl) rubber (IIR), in primary forms	异丁烯-异戊二烯(丁基)橡胶(IIR),初级形状的	4002. 3110	136
Isobutene-isoprene (butyl) rubber (IIR), nes	异丁烯-异戊二烯(丁基)橡胶(IIR),其他	4002. 3190	136
Isobutylene octafluoride	八氟异丁烯	2903. 3910	36
Isobutylmethyl ketone	甲基异丁基(甲)酮	2914. 1300	36
Isocyanates, nes	异氰酸酯,其他	2929. 1090	36
Isocyanides	胩	2929. 9090	36
Isocyanides	异氰	2929. 9090	36
Isocyanides	异氰化物	2929. 9090	36
Isocyanines, a synthetic organic colouring matter	异花青	3204. 9090	345
Isolating switches, for a voltage exceeding 1000V	隔离开关,用于电压超过 1000 伏的线路	8535. 3000	8
Isoniazidum	六氢吡啶盐	2933. 3220	36
Isooctyl acrylate	丙烯酸异辛酯	2916. 1240	36
Isopentene	异戊烯	2901. 2910	368
Isoprene	异戊二烯	2901. 2400	368
Isoprene rubber (IR), in primary forms	异戊二烯橡胶(IR),初级形状的	4002. 6010	136
Isoprene rubber (IR), nes	异戊二烯橡胶(IR),其他	4002. 6090	136
Isopropyl amine	异丙胺	2921. 1920	36
Isoquinoline ring-system compounds, not further fused in the structure, whether or not hydrogenated, nes	异喹啉环系化合物,结构上含有,未经进一步稠合的,不论是否氢化,其他	2933. 4990	36
Isosafrole	异黄樟脑	2932. 9100	36
Isosafrole	4-丙烯基-1,2-亚甲二氧基苯	2932. 9100	36
Isotopes and compounds, nes	同位素,其他,及其化合物	2845. 9000	
Isotopes and compounds, radioactive, nes	同位素及其化合物,放射性的,其他	2844. 4090	
Isotopic separation machinery and apparatus, and parts thereof	同位素分离机器、装置及其零件	8401. 2000	2
Ivory	兽牙	0507. 1000	14
Ivory and articles of ivory, worked	兽牙及其制品,已加工的	9601. 1000	
Ivory powder	兽牙粉末	0507. 1000	14
Ivory waste	兽牙废料	0507. 1000	14

I

J

Article Description	商品名称	Tariff Code	D. R.
Jackets and blazers, not knitted or crocheted, for men or boys, nes	上衣,非针织或钩编的,男式,其他	6203. 3990	2456
Jackets and blazers, not knitted or crocheted, for men or boys, of cotton	上衣,非针织或钩编的,男式,棉制	6203. 3200	2456
Jackets and blazers, not knitted or crocheted, for men or boys, of silk or silk waste	上衣,非针织或钩编的,男式,丝及绢丝制	6203. 3910	2456
Jackets and blazers, not knitted or crocheted, for men or boys, of synthetic fibres	上衣,非针织或钩编的,男式,合成纤维制	6203. 3300	2456
Jackets and blazers, not knitted or crocheted, for men or boys, of wool or fine animal hair	上衣,非针织或钩编的,男式,羊毛或动物细毛制	6203. 3100	2456
Jackets and blazers, knitted or crocheted, for men or boys, of cotton	上衣,针织或钩编的,男式,棉制	6103. 3200	2456
Jackets and blazers, knitted or crocheted, for men or boys, of other textile materials	上衣,针织或钩编的,男式,其他纺织材料制	6103. 3900	2456
Jackets and blazers, knitted or crocheted, for men or boys, of synthetic fibres	上衣,针织或钩编的,男式,合成纤维制	6103. 3300	2456
Jackets and blazers, knitted or crocheted, for men or boys, of wool or fine animal hair	上衣,针织或钩编的,男式,羊毛或动物细毛制	6103. 3100	2456
Jackets and blazers, knitted or crocheted, for women or girls, of cotton	上衣,针织或钩编的,女式,棉制	6104. 3200	2456
Jackets and blazers, knitted or crocheted, for women or girls, of other textile materials	上衣,针织或钩编的,女式,其他纺织材料制	6104. 3900	2456
Jackets and blazers, knitted or crocheted, for women or girls, of synthetic fibres	上衣,针织或钩编的,女式,合成纤维制	6104. 3300	2456
Jackets and blazers, knitted or crocheted, for women or girls, of wool or fine animal hair	上衣,针织或钩编的,女式,羊毛或动物细毛制	6104. 3100	2456
Jackets and blazers, not knitted or crocheted, for women or girls, nes	上衣,非针织或钩编的,女式,其他	6204. 3990	2456
Jackets and blazers, not knitted or crocheted, for women or girls, of cotton	上衣,非针织或钩编的,女式,棉制	6204. 3200	2456
Jackets and blazers, not knitted or crocheted, for women or girls, of silk or silk waste	上衣,非针织或钩编的,女式,丝及绢丝制	6204. 3910	2456
Jackets and blazers, not knitted or crocheted, for women or girls, of synthetic fibres	上衣,非针织或钩编的,女式,合成纤维制	6204. 3300	2456
Jackets and blazers, not knitted or crocheted, for women or girls, of wool or fine animal hair	上衣,非针织或钩编的,女式,羊毛或动物细毛制	6204. 3100	2456
Jacking systems of a type used in garages, built-in	千斤顶系统,车库中固定使用的	8425. 4100	78
Jacks, hydraulic	千斤顶,液压的	8425. 4210	78
Jacks, hydraulic	液压千斤顶	8425. 4210	78
Jacks, nes	千斤顶,其他	8425. 4910	78

Article Description	商品名称	Tariff Code	D. R.
Jacquards; card reducing, copying, punching or assembling machines for use there with	提花机及其所用的卡片缩小、复制、穿孔或汇编机器	8448. 1100	3
Jadeite dust and powder	翡翠的粉末	7105. 9000	145
Jadeite, unworked	翡翠,未加工	7103. 1000	145
Jadeite, worked	翡翠,加工的	7103. 9910	145
Jams, being cooked preparations, nes	果酱,烹煮的,其他	2007. 9990	248
Jams, citrus fruit, being cooked preparations	果酱,烹煮的,柑橘属水果的	2007. 9100	248
Jams, citrus fruit, being cooked preparations, in airtight containers	果酱,烹煮的,柑橘属水果的,罐头	2007. 9910	248
Jasmone	茉莉酮	2914. 2900	36
Jelly fish, prepared or preserved	海蜇,制作或保藏的	1605. 9010	48
Jelly fungi (tremella spp.), dried	银耳,干的	0712. 3300	4
Jerseys, knitted or crocheted, nes	球衣,针织或钩编的,其他	6110. 9090	2456
Jerseys, knitted or crocheted, of cotton	球衣,针织或钩编的,棉制	6110. 2000	2456
Jerseys, knitted or crocheted, of kashmir (cashmere) fine goats hair	球衣,针织或钩编的,喀什米尔山羊细毛制	6110. 1200	2456
Jerseys, knitted or crocheted, of man-made fibres	球衣,针织或钩编的,化学纤维制	6110. 3000	2456
Jerseys, knitted or crocheted, of other fine animal hair	球衣,针织或钩编的,其他动物细毛制	6110. 1990	2456
Jerseys, knitted or crocheted, of other fine goats hair	球衣,针织或钩编的,其他山羊细毛制	6110. 1910	2456
Jerseys, knitted or crocheted, of rabbit and hare	球衣,针织或钩编的,兔毛制	6110. 1920	2456
Jerseys, knitted or crocheted, of silk or silk waste	球衣,针织或钩编的,丝及绢丝制	6110. 9010	2456
Jerseys, knitted or crocheted, of wool	球衣,针织或钩编的,毛制	6110. 1100	2456
Jerusalem artichokes	菊芋	0714. 9090	34
Jerusalem artichokes	洋姜	0714. 9090	34
Jesuits' tea	耶稣兹茶	0903. 0000	
Jet spinner	喷气纺纱机	8445. 2032	7
Jewel bearings, of clock or watch	宝石轴承,钟、表的	9114. 2000	6
Jewellery articles and parts thereof, of base metal clad with precious metal, diamond mounted or set, nes	首饰及其零件,以贱金属为底的包贵金属制,镶嵌钻石的	7113. 2010	46
Jewellery articles and parts thereof, of base metal clad with precious metal, nes	首饰及其零件,以贱金属为底的包贵金属制,其他	7113. 2090	46
Jewellery articles and parts thereof, of gold, whether or not plated or clad with precious metal, diamond mounted	首饰及其零件,黄金制,不论是否包、镀贵金属,镶嵌钻石的	7113. 1911	46
Jewellery articles and parts thereof, of gold, whether or not plated or clad with precious metal, nes	首饰及其零件,黄金制,不论是否包、镀贵金属,其他	7113. 1919	46
Jewellery articles and parts thereof, of platinium, whether or not plated or clad with precious metal, diamond mounted or set	首饰及其零件,铂制,不论是否包、镀贵金属,镶嵌钻石的	7113. 1921	46

J

Article Description	商品名称	Tariff Code	D. R.
Jewellery articles and parts thereof, of platinium, whether or not plated or clad with precious metal, nes	首饰及其零件,铂制,不论是否包、镀贵金属,其他	7113. 1929	46
Jewellery articles and parts thereof, of precious metal, whether or not plated or clad with precious metal, diamond mounted or set, nes	首饰及其零件,贵金属制,不论是否包、镀贵金属,镶嵌钻石的	7113. 1991	46
Jewellery articles and parts thereof, of precious metal, whether or not plated or clad with precious metal, nes	首饰及其零件,贵金属制,不论是否包、镀贵金属,其他	7113. 1999	46
Jewellery articles and parts thereof, of silver, whether or not plated or clad with other precious metal, diamond mounted or set	首饰及其零件,银制,不论是否包、镀其他贵金属,镶嵌钻石的	7113. 1110	46
Jewellery articles and parts thereof, of silver, whether or not plated or clad with other precious metal, nes	首饰及其零件,银制,不论是否包、镀其他贵金属,其他	7113. 1190	46
Jewellery boxes, nes	首饰盒,其他	4202. 9900	256
Jewellery boxes, with outer surface of leather, composition leather or patent leather	首饰盒,以皮革、再生皮革或漆皮作面	4202. 9100	256
Jewellery boxes, with outer surface of plastic sheeting or textile materials	首饰盒,以塑料片或纺织材料作面	4202. 9200	256
Joints assortments, dissimilar in composition	接合衬垫,各种不同材料制	8484. 9000	56
Joints of metal sheeting combined with other material or of two or more layers of metal	接合衬垫,用金属片与其他材料制成或用双层或多层金属片制成	8484. 1000	56
Joints, of plastics	接头,塑料的	3917. 4000	
Jojoba oil and its fractions	霍霍巴油及其分离品	1515. 9010	
Jojoba oil and its fractions	希蒙得木油及其分离品	1515. 9010	
Joss paper and the like	神纸及类似用品	4823. 9020	68
Juice extractors for fruit, electro-mechanical domestic appliances	榨汁机,水果用,家用电动器具	8509. 4010	
Juice extractors for vegetable, electro-mechanical domestic appliances	榨汁机,蔬菜用,家用电动器具	8509. 4010	
Juice of any other single citrus fruit, nes	柑橘属水果汁,其他	2009. 3990	2468
Juice of any other single citrus fruit, nes, of a brix value not exceeding 20	柑橘属水果汁,其他,白利糖度值不超过 20 的	2009. 3190	2468
Juice, mixtures, nes	混合汁	2009. 9090	2468
Jujubes, crystallised jujubes, preserved by sugar	枣,水晶枣,用糖保存的	2006. 0090	48
Jujubes, fresh	枣,鲜的	0810. 9090	1
Jujubes, provisionally preserved	枣,暂时保藏的	0812. 9000	34
Jujubes, used in pharmacy	枣,医药级	1211. 9039	34
Junction boxes, for a voltage exceeding 1000V	接线盒,用于电压超过 1000 伏的线路	8535. 9000	8
Junction boxes, for a voltage not exceeding 1000V	接线盒,用于电压不超过 1000 伏的线路	8536. 9000	8
Juniper berries	杜松果	0909. 5000	
Jute and other textile bast fibres tow	黄麻及纺织用韧皮纤维短纤	5303. 9000	4

Article Description	商品名称	Tariff Code	D. R.
Jute and other textile bast fibres waste	黄麻及纺织用韧皮纤维废麻	5303.9000	4
Jute or textilebast fibres woven fabrics, nes	黄麻或纺织用韧皮纤维机织物,其他	5310.9000	2468
Jute or textilebast fibres woven fabrics, unbleached	黄麻或纺织用韧皮纤维机织物,未漂白	5310.1000	2468
Jute yarn or textile bast fibres yarn, multiple(folded) or cabled	黄麻纱线或纺织用韧皮纤维纱线,多股纱线或缆线	5307.2000	58
Jute yarn or textile bast fibres yarn, single	黄麻纱线或纺织用韧皮纤维纱线,单纱	5307.1000	58
Jute, raw or retted	黄麻,生的或经沤制的	5303.1000	4

K

Article Description	商品名称	Tariff Code	D. R.
Kakis, fresh	柿子,鲜的	0810. 9090	1
Kale, forage products	饲料羽衣甘蓝	1214. 9000	
Kale, fresh or chilled	羽衣甘蓝,鲜或冷藏的	0704. 9090	1
Kanamycin and its derivatives; salts thereof	卡那霉素及其衍生物以及它们的盐	2941. 9020	
Kaolin clays	高岭土	2507. 0010	1346
Kaolinic clays	高岭类似土	2507. 0090	1346
Kapok seeds	木棉子	1207. 9999	3
Karamanieand and similar handwoven rugs	卡拉马尼及类似的手织地毯	5702. 1000	468
Karite nuts	牛油树果	1207. 9991	3
Kelem and similar handwoven rugs	开来姆及类似的手织地毯	5702. 1000	468
Kentucky blue grass (poa pratensis L.) Seed, forage plants	草地早熟禾子,饲料植物用的	1209. 2400	358
Kephir	酸乳酒	0403. 9000	248
Keratins	角蛋白	3504. 0090	1346
Kermesite	红锑矿	2617. 1090	146
Kernels	油棕仁	1207. 9992	3
Kerosene cooking stoves, of iron or steel, domestic appliances	煤油炉,钢铁制,家用	7321. 1210	7
Kerosene distillages, nes	煤油馏分,其他	2710. 1919	6
Ketazolam(INN); salts thereof	凯他唑仑(INN)及盐	2934. 9100	36
Ketchup, of tomato and other tomato sauces	番茄沙司及其他番茄调味汁	2103. 2000	268
Ketene-phenols, nes	酮酚,其他	2914. 5019	36
Ketobemidone (INN); salts thereof	凯托米酮(INN)及盐	2933. 3300	36
Ketone peroxides and their halogenated, sulphonated, nitrated or nitrosated derivatives	过氧化酮及其卤化、磺化、硝化或亚硝化衍生物	2909. 6000	36
Ketones with other oxygen function, nes	酮,含有其他含氧基的,其他	2914. 5090	36
Ketones, halogenated, sulphonated, nitrated or nitrosated derivatives of	酮,卤化、磺化、硝化或亚硝化衍生物	2914. 7000	36
Ketone-alcohols	酮醇	2914. 4000	36
Ketone-aldehydes	酮醛	2914. 4000	36
Keyboard musical instruments parts and accessories	键盘乐器零件、附件	9209. 9400	3
Keyboard musical instruments, other than accordions, the sound of which is produced or must be amplified electrically	键盘乐器,手风琴除外,通过电产生或扩大声音的	9207. 1000	5
Keyboard pipe organs	键盘管风琴	9205. 9010	5
Keyboard string musical instruments, nes	键盘弦乐器,其他	9201. 9000	5
Keyboards	键盘	8471. 6071	
Keys presented separately, of base metal	钥匙,单独报验的,贱金属制	8301. 7000	256

K

Article Description	商品名称	Tariff Code	D. R.
Kidney beans, including white pea beans (phaseolus vulgaris), nes, dried, shelled	芸豆,其他,脱荚的,干的	0713. 3390	34
Kidney beans, including white pea beans (phaseolus vulgaris), seed, dried, shelled	芸豆,种用,脱荚的,干的	0713. 3310	34
Kieselguhr	硅藻土	2512. 0010	1234568
Kieserite	硫镁矾矿	2530. 2000	13456
Kimono belts, not knitted or crocheted	和服腰带,非针织或钩编的	6217. 1020	2456
Kitchen cleavers	砍骨刀	8214. 9000	256
Kitchen linen, nes	厨房用制品,其他	6302. 5990	346
Kitchen linen, of cotton, nes	厨房用制品,棉制,其他	6302. 9100	346
Kitchen linen, of flax, nes	厨房用制品,亚麻制,其他	6302. 9910	346
Kitchen linen, of man-made fibres, nes	厨房用制品,化学纤维制,其他	6302. 9300	346
Kitchen linen, of terry towelling or similar terry fabrics, of cotton	厨房用制品,毛巾织物或类似的毛圈织物的,棉制	6302. 6090	346
Kitchen waste disposers, electro-mechanical domestic appliances	厨房废物处理器,家用电动器具	8509. 8020	346
Kitchenware plated with precious metal	厨房用具,镀贵金属的	8215. 9100	256
Kitchenware sets of assorted articles containing at least one article plated with precious metal	厨房用具,成套货品,至少其中一件物品是镀贵金属的	8215. 1000	256
Kitchenware sets of assorted articles, nes	厨房用具,成套货品,其他	8215. 2000	256
Kitchenware, nes	厨房用具,其他	8215. 9900	256
Kitchenware, of plastics	厨房用具,塑料的	3924. 1000	23
Kitchenware, of porcelain	厨房器具,瓷制	6911. 1020	268
Kitchenware, of pottery	厨房器具,陶制	6912. 0090	268
Kiwifruit, fresh	猕猴桃,鲜的	0810. 5000	15
Klystrons	速调管	8540. 7200	35
Kneading machines, for earth, stone, ores or other mineral substances, nes	搅拌机器,泥土、石料、矿石或其他固体矿物质的,其他	8474. 3900	346
Kneading machines, nes	搅拌机,其他	8479. 8200	7
Knee pads for any animal, of any material	护膝垫,适合各种动物用	4201. 0000	1458
Knitted or crocheted fabrics of a width exceeding 30cm, containing by weight 5% or more elastomeric yarn or rubber thread, of artificial fibres, nes	针织物或钩编织物,宽度超过30厘米,按重量计弹性纱线或橡胶线含量在5%及以上的,人造纤维制,其他	6004. 9040	46
Knitted or crocheted fabrics of a width exceeding 30cm, containing by weight 5% or more elastomeric yarn or rubber thread, of cotton, nes	针织物或钩编织物,宽度超过30厘米,按重量计弹性纱线或橡胶线含量在5%及以上的,棉制,其他	6004. 9010	46
Knitted or crocheted fabrics of a width exceeding 30cm, containing by weight 5% or more elastomeric yarn or rubber thread, of silk or silk waste, nes	针织物或钩编织物,宽度超过30厘米,按重量计弹性纱线或橡胶线含量在5%及以上的,丝及绢丝制,其他	6004. 9020	46

Article Description	商品名称	Tariff Code	D. R.
Knitted or crocheted fabrics of a width exceeding 30cm, containing by weight 5% or more elastomeric yarn or rubber thread, of synthetic fibres, nes	针织物或钩编织物，宽度超过30厘米，按重量计弹性纱线或橡胶线含量在5%及以上的，合成纤维制，其他	6004.9030	46
Knitted or crocheted fabrics of a width exceeding 30cm, containing by weight 5% or more elastomeric yarn or rubber thread, nes	针织物或钩编织物，宽度超过30厘米，按重量计弹性纱线或橡胶线含量在5%及以上的，其他	6004.9090	46
Knitted or crocheted fabrics of a width exceeding 30cm, containing by weight 5% or more of elastomeric yarn but not containing rubber thread, nes	针织物或钩编织物，宽度超过30厘米，按重量计弹性纱线含量在5%及以上，但不含橡胶线，其他	6004.1090	46
Knitted or crocheted fabrics of a width exceeding 30cm, containing by weight 5% or more of elastomeric yarn but not containing rubber thread, of artificial fibres	针织物或钩编织物，宽度超过30厘米，按重量计弹性纱线含量在5%及以上，但不含橡胶线，人造纤维制	6004.1040	46
Knitted or crocheted fabrics of a width exceeding 30cm, containing by weight 5% or more of elastomeric yarn but not containing rubber thread, of cotton	针织物或钩编织物，宽度超过30厘米，按重量计弹性纱线含量在5%及以上，但不含橡胶线，棉制	6004.1010	46
Knitted or crocheted fabrics of a width exceeding 30cm, containing by weight 5% or more of elastomeric yarn but not containing rubber thread, of silk or silk waste	针织物或钩编织物，宽度超过30厘米，按重量计弹性纱线含量在5%及以上，但不含橡胶线，丝及绢丝制	6004.1020	46
Knitted or crocheted fabrics of a width exceeding 30cm, containing by weight 5% or more of elastomeric yarn but not containing rubber thread, of synthetic fibres	针织物或钩编织物，宽度超过30厘米，按重量计弹性纱线含量在5%及以上，但不含橡胶线，合成纤维制	6004.1030	46
Knitted or crocheted fabrics of a width not exceeding 30cm, containing by weight 5% or more of elastomeric yarn but not containing rubber thread, nes	针织物或钩编织物，宽度不超过30厘米，按重量计弹性纱线含量在5%及以上，但不含橡胶线，其他	6002.4090	46
Knitted or crocheted fabrics of a width not exceeding 30cm, containing by weight 5% or more of elastomeric yarn but not containing rubber thread, of artificial fibres	针织物或钩编织物，宽度不超过30厘米，按重量计弹性纱线含量在5%及以上，但不含橡胶线，人造纤维制	6002.4040	46
Knitted or crocheted fabrics of a width not exceeding 30cm, containing by weight 5% or more of elastomeric yarn but not containing rubber thread, of cotton	针织物或钩编织物，宽度不超过30厘米，按重量计弹性纱线含量在5%及以上，但不含橡胶线，棉制	6002.4010	46
Knitted or crocheted fabrics of a width not exceeding 30cm, containing by weight 5% or more of elastomeric yarn but not containing rubber thread, of silk or silk waste	针织物或钩编织物，宽度不超过30厘米，按重量计弹性纱线含量在5%及以上，但不含橡胶线，丝及绢丝制	6002.4020	46

Article Description	商品名称	Tariff Code	D. R.
Knitted or crocheted fabrics of a width not exceeding 30cm, containing by weight 5% or more of elastomeric yarn but not containing rubber thread, of synthetic fibres	针织物或钩编织物,宽度不超过30厘米,按重量计弹性纱线含量在5%及以上,但不含橡胶线,合成纤维制	6002. 4030	46
Knitted or crocheted fabrics of a width not exceeding 30cm, containing by weight 5% or more of elastomeric yarn or rubber thread, nes	针织物或钩编织物,宽度不超过30厘米,按重量计弹性纱线或橡胶线含量在5%及以上的,其他	6002. 9090	46
Knitted or crocheted fabrics of a width not exceeding 30cm, containing by weight 5% or more of elastomeric yarn or rubber thread, of artificial fibres, nes	针织物或钩编织物,宽度不超过30厘米,按重量计弹性纱线或橡胶线含量在5%及以上的,人造纤维制,其他	6002. 9040	46
Knitted or crocheted fabrics of a width not exceeding 30cm, containing by weight 5% or more of elastomeric yarn or rubber thread, of cotton, nes	针织物或钩编织物,宽度不超过30厘米,按重量计弹性纱线或橡胶线含量在5%及以上的,棉制,其他	6002. 9010	46
Knitted or crocheted fabrics of a width not exceeding 30cm, containing by weight 5% or more of elastomeric yarn or rubber thread, of silk or silk waste, nes	针织物或钩编织物,宽度不超过30厘米,按重量计弹性纱线或橡胶线含量在5%及以上的,丝及绢丝制,其他	6002. 9020	46
Knitted or crocheted fabrics of a width not exceeding 30cm, containing by weight 5% or more of elastomeric yarn or rubber thread, of synthetic fibres, nes	针织物或钩编织物,宽度不超过30厘米,按重量计弹性纱线或橡胶线含量在5%及以上的,合成纤维制,其他	6002. 9030	46
Knitted or crocheted fabrics of a width not exceeding 30cm, nes	针织或钩编织物,宽度不超过30厘米,其他	6003. 9000	46
Knitted or crocheted fabrics of a width not exceeding 30cm, of artificial fibres	针织或钩编织物,宽度不超过30厘米,人造纤维制	6003. 4000	46
Knitted or crocheted fabrics of a width not exceeding 30cm, of cotton	针织或钩编织物,宽度不超过30厘米,棉制	6003. 2000	46
Knitted or crocheted fabrics of a width not exceeding 30cm, of synthetic fibres	针织或钩编织物,宽度不超过30厘米,合成纤维制	6003. 3000	46
Knitted or crocheted fabrics of a width not exceeding 30cm, of wool or fine animal hair	针织或钩编织物,宽度不超过30厘米,羊毛或动物细毛制	6003. 1000	46
Knitted or crocheted fabrics of artificial fibres, dyed	针织或钩编织物,人造纤维制,染色	6006. 4200	46
Knitted or crocheted fabrics of artificial fibres, of yarns of different colours	针织或钩编织物,人造纤维制,色织	6006. 4300	46
Knitted or crocheted fabrics of artificial fibres, printed	针织或钩编织物,人造纤维制,印花	6006. 4400	46
Knitted or crocheted fabrics of artificial fibres, unbleached or bleached	针织或钩编织物,人造纤维制,未漂白或漂白	6006. 4100	46
Knitted or crocheted fabrics of cotton, dyed	针织或钩编织物,棉制,染色	6006. 2200	46
Knitted or crocheted fabrics of cotton, of yarns of different colours	针织或钩编织物,棉制,色织	6006. 2300	46
Knitted or crocheted fabrics of cotton, printed	针织或钩编织物,棉制,印花	6006. 2400	46

K

Article Description	商品名称	Tariff Code	D. R.
Knitted or crocheted fabrics of cotton, unbleached or bleached	针织或钩编织物,棉制,未漂白或漂白	6006. 2100	46
Knitted or crocheted fabrics of synthetic fibres, dyed	针织或钩编织物,合成纤维制,染色	6006. 3200	46
Knitted or crocheted fabrics of synthetic fibres, of yarns of different colours	针织或钩编织物,合成纤维制,色织	6006. 3300	46
Knitted or crocheted fabrics of synthetic fibres, printed	针织或钩编织物,合成纤维制,印花	6006. 3400	46
Knitted or crocheted fabrics of synthetic fibres, unbleached or bleached	针织或钩编织物,合成纤维制,未漂白或漂白	6006. 3100	46
Knitted or crocheted fabrics of wool or fine animal hair	针织或钩编织物,羊毛或动物细毛制	6006. 1000	46
Knitted or crocheted fabrics, nes	针织或钩编织物,其他	6006. 9000	46
Knitting machines or of their auxiliary machinery's parts and accessories, nes	针织机及其辅助机器的零件、附件,其他	8448. 5900	3
Knitting machines, circular, with cylinder diameter exceeding 165mm	针织机,圆型的,圆筒直径超过165毫米	8447. 1200	
Knitting machines, circular, with cylinder diameter not exceeding 165mm	针织机,圆型的,圆筒直径不超过165毫米	8447. 1100	
Knitting needles, for use in the hand, of iron or steel	编织针,钢铁制的,手工用	7319. 9000	
Knives and cutting blades, for agricultural, horticultural or forestry machines	刀及刀片,农业、园艺或林业机器用	8208. 4000	256
Knives and cutting blades, for kitchen appliances or for machines used by the food industry	刀及刀片,厨房器具或食品工业机器用	8208. 3000	256
Knives and cutting blades, for machines or for mechanical appliances, for metal working, nes	刀及刀片,机器或机械器具的,金属加工用,其他	8208. 1090	256
Knives and cutting blades, for machines or for mechanical appliances, for metal working, of metal carbides, nes	刀及刀片,机器或机械器具的,金属加工用,硬质合金制的,其他	8208. 1019	256
Knives and cutting blades, for machines or for mechanical appliances, for metal working, of metal carbides, plated or coated	刀及刀片,机器或机械器具的,金属加工用,硬质合金制的,经镀或涂层的	8208. 1011	256
Knives and cutting blades, for machines or for mechanical appliances, nes	刀及刀片,机器或机械器具的,其他	8208. 9000	256
Knives and cutting blades, for wood working machines	刀及刀片,木器加工机械用	8208. 2000	256
Knives handles of base metal	刀柄,贱金属制的	8211. 9500	256
Knives having fixed blades, nes	刀,刃面固定的,其他	8211. 9200	256
Knives having other than fixed blades	刀,刃面不固定的	8211. 9300	256
Knives with cutting blades, serrated or not (including pruning knives), sets of assorted articles, other than knives of heading No. 82. 08, and blades therefor	刀及刀片,不论是否有锯齿(包括整枝刀),成套货品,税号82. 08的刀除外	8211. 1000	256
Knives with cutting blades, sets of assorted articles, serrated or not	刀及刀片成套货品,不论是否有锯齿	8211. 1000	256

K

Article Description	商品名称	Tariff Code	D. R.
Knots and tufts for broom or brush making, prepared	成束或成簇的材料,供制帚、刷用的	9603.9090	3
Kohlrabi, fresh or chilled	球茎甘蓝,鲜或冷藏的	0704.9090	1
Krafliner, nes	牛皮挂面纸,其他	4804.1900	24568
Krafliner, unbleached	牛皮挂面纸,未漂白	4804.1100	24568
Kraft paper and paperboard, bleached uniformly throughout the mass, other than that of a kind used for writing, printing or other graphic purposes, of which more than 95% by weight of the total fibre content consists of wood fibres obtained by a chemical process, and weighing 150 g/m^2 or less, coated on one or both sides with kaolin or other inorganic substances	牛皮纸及纸板,本体均匀漂白,但书写、印刷或类似用途的除外,所含用化学方法制得的木纤维超过全部纤维重量的95%,每平方米重量不超过150克,单面或双面涂布高岭土或其他无机物质的	4810.3100	14568
Kraft paper and paperboard, bleached uniformly throughout the mass, other than that of a kind used for writing, printing or other graphic purposes, of which more than 95% by weight of the total fibre content consists of wood fibres obtained by a chemical process, and weighing more than 150 g/m^2, coated on one or both sides with kaolin or other inorganic substances	牛皮纸及纸板,本体均匀漂白,但书写、印刷或类似用途的除外,所含用化学方法制得的木纤维超过全部纤维重量的95%,每平方米重量超过150克,单面或双面涂布高岭土或其他无机物质的	4810.3200	14568
Kraft paper and paperboard, bleached uniformly throughout the mass, uncoated, weighing $225g/m^2$ or more, of which more than 95% by weight of the total fibre content consists of wood fibres obtained by a chemical process	牛皮纸及纸板,未经涂布的,本体均匀漂白,每平方米重量在225克及以上,所含用化学方法制得的木纤维超过全部纤维重量的95%	4804.5200	24568
Kraft paper and paperboard, bleached uniformly throughout the mass, uncoated, weighing more than $150g/m^2$ but less than $225g/m^2$, of which more than 95% by weight of the total fibre content consists of wood fibres obtained by a chemical process	牛皮纸及纸板,本体均匀漂白,未经涂布的,每平方米重量超过150克,但小于225克,所含用化学方法制得的木纤维超过全部纤维重量的95%	4804.4200	24568
Kraft paper and paperboard, unbleached, uncoated, weighing $225g/m^2$ or more	牛皮纸及纸板,未经涂布的,未漂白,每平方米重量在225克及以上	4804.5100	24568
Kraft paper and paperboard, uncoated, weighing $150g/m^2$ or less	牛皮纸及纸板,未经涂布的,每平方米重量不超过150克,其他	4804.3900	24568
Kraft paper and paperboard, uncoated, unbleached, weighing $150g/m^2$ or less	牛皮纸及纸板,未经涂布的,未漂白,每平方米重量不超过150克	4804.3100	24568
Kraft paper and paperboard, uncoated, weighing $225g/m^2$ or more, nes	牛皮纸及纸板,未经涂布的,每平方米重量在225克及以上,其他	4804.5900	24568
Kraft paper and paperboard, uncoated, weighing more than $150g/m^2$ but less than $225g/m^2$, nes	牛皮纸及纸板,未经涂布的,每平方米重量超过150克,但小于225克,其他	4804.4900	24568

Article Description	商品名称	Tariff Code	D. R.
Kraft paper and paperboard, other than that of a kind used for writing, printing or other graphic purposes, coated on one or both sides with kaolin or other inorganic substances, nes	牛皮纸及纸板,但书写、印刷或类似用途的除外,单面或双面涂布高岭土或其他无机物质的,其他	4810.3900	14568
Kraft paper and paperboard, unbleached, uncoated, weighing more than $150g/m^2$ but less than $225g/m^2$	牛皮纸及纸板,未经涂布的,未漂白,每平方米重量超过150克,但小于225克	4804.4100	24568
Kraft paper or paperboard or of corrugated paper or paperboard, unbleached	牛皮纸或纸板及瓦楞纸或纸板,未漂白的	4707.1000	125
Kraft paper, creped or crinkled, whether or not embossed or perforated, nes	牛皮纸,起皱的,不论是否压花或穿孔,其他	4808.3000	58
Kumquats marmalade	金橘果酱	2007.9100	248
Kumquats, fresh or dried	金橘,鲜或干的	0805.9000	14
Kumquats, frozen	金橘	0811.9090	1
Kumquats, prepared or preserved	金橘,制作的	2008.3010	248
Kyanite	蓝晶石	2508.5000	134

L

Article Description	商品名称	Tariff Code	D. R.
L sections, not further worked than hot-rolled, hot-drawn or extruded, of a height of 80mm or more	角钢,除热轧、热拉拔或热挤压外未经进一步加工,截面高度在 80 毫米及以上	7216.4010	468
L sections, not further worked than hot-rolled, hot-drawn or extruded, of a height of less than 80mm	角钢,除热轧、热拉拔或热挤压外未经进一步加工,截面高度低于 80 毫米	7216.2100	468
Labelling machines, for bottles, cans, boxes, bags or other containers, nes	贴标签的机器,瓶、罐、箱、袋或其他容器的	8422.3090	
Labels of all kinds, of paper or paperboard, nes	标签,纸或纸板制的,其他	4821.9000	4
Labels of all kinds, of paper or paperboard, printed	标签,纸或纸板制的,印制	4821.1000	4
Labels, badges and similar articles of textile materials, in the piece, in strips or cut to shape or size, not embroidered, nes	标签、徽章及类似品,纺织材料制,成匹、成条或裁成一定形状或尺寸,非绣制,其他	5807.9000	468
Labels, badges and similar articles of textile materials, in the piece, in strips or cut to shape or size, not embroidered, woven	标签、徽章及类似品,纺织材料制,成匹、成条或裁成一定形状或尺寸,非绣制,机织	5807.1000	468
Lac	虫胶	1301.9090	
Lace, hand-made	花边,手工制	5804.3000	468
Lace, mechanically made, nes	花边,机制,其他	5804.2990	468
Lace, mechanically made, of cotton	花边,机制,棉制	5804.2920	468
Lace, mechanically made, of man-made fibres	花边,机制,化学纤维制	5804.2100	468
Lace, mechanically made, of silk or silk waste	花边,机制,丝及绢丝制	5804.2910	468
Lactams, nes	内酰胺,其他	2933.7900	36
Lactic acid, its salts and esters	乳酸及其盐和酯	2918.1100	36
Lactoflavine (vitamin B_2)	核黄素	2936.2300	36
Lactoglobulins	乳球蛋白	3504.0090	1346
Lactones, nes	内酯,其他	2932.2900	36
Lactophosphates, their halogenated, sulphonated, nitrated or nitrosated derivatives	乳磷酸盐,以及它们的卤化、磺化、硝化或亚硝化衍生物	2919.9000	36
Lactose syrup, containing by weight 99% or more lactose, expressed as anhydrous lactose, calculated on the dry matter	乳糖浆,按重量计干燥无水乳糖含量在 99% 及以上	1702.1100	68
Lactose, containing by weight 99% or more lactose, expressed as anhydrous lactose, calculated on the dry matter	乳糖,按重量计干燥无水乳糖含量在 99% 及以上	1702.1100	68
Ladles	浇包	8454.2090	
Ladles, other than plated with precious metal, kitchen or tableware	长柄勺,非镀贵金属的,厨房或餐桌用具	8215.9900	256
Ladles, plated with precious metal, kitchen or tableware	长柄勺,镀贵金属的,厨房或餐桌用具	8215.9100	256

Article Description	商品名称	Tariff Code	D. R.
Laminaria and sterile laminaria tents, sterile	昆布及无菌昆布塞条,无菌	3006. 1000	3
Laminated safety glass, for aircraft, spacecraft or vessels	层压安全玻璃,航空器、航天器及船舶用	7007. 2110	234
Laminated safety glass, nes	层压安全玻璃,其他	7007. 2900	234
Laminated safety glass, of size and shape suitable for vehicles	层压安全玻璃,车辆用	7007. 2190	234
Lamivudine and their salts	拉米夫定及它们的盐	2938. 9010	34
Lamp carbons	灯碳棒	8545. 9000	3
Lamps parts	灯的零件	8539. 9000	3
Lamps parts, nes	灯具零件,其他	9405. 9900	36
Lamps parts, of glass	灯具零件,玻璃制	9405. 9100	36
Lamps parts, of plastics	灯具零件,塑料制	9405. 9200	36
Lamp-holders, for a voltage not exceeding 1000V	灯座,用于电压不超过1000伏的线路	8536. 6100	8
Lamp-kerosene	灯用煤油	2710. 1912	6
Lances and parts	长矛及其零件	9307. 0000	
Landing stages	浮码头	8907. 9000	5
Lanolin	羊毛脂,纯净的	1505. 0000	
Lantern slides, for educational use only, exposed and developed	教学专用幻灯片,已曝光已冲洗的	3705. 9010	1238
Lanthanum carbonate	碳酸镧	2846. 9041	6
Lanthanum oxide	氧化镧	2846. 9012	6
Lapping machines, for metal or cermets	研磨机床,加工金属或金属陶瓷用	8460. 4020	7
Lard oil, not emulsified or mixed or otherwise prepared	液体猪油,未经乳化、混合或其他方法制作	1503. 0000	4
Lard stearin, not emulsified or mixed or otherwise prepared	猪油硬脂,未经乳化、混合或其他方法制作	1503. 0000	4
Lard, other than that of heading No. 02. 09 or 15. 03	猪油,已炼制,但税号 02. 09 及 15. 03 的货品除外	1501. 0000	
Lasagne, uncooked, containing eggs	烤宽面条,生的,含蛋的	1902. 1100	46
Lasagne, uncooked, nes	烤宽面条,生的,其他	1902. 1900	46
Laser photo typesetting equipments	激光照相排版设备	9006. 5910	7
Laser phototypesetting film, unexposed	激光照排片,未曝光的	3701. 3021	12368
Laser phototypesetting film, unexposed, without perforations, of a width exceeding 105mm but not exceeding 610mm	激光照排片,未曝光的,无齿孔的,宽度超过 105 毫米,但不超过 610 毫米	3702. 4421	12368
Laser phototypesetting film, unexposed, without perforations, of a width exceeding 610mm and of a length not exceeding 200 m	激光照排片,未曝光的,无齿孔的,宽度超过 610 毫米,长度不超过 200 米	3702. 4321	12368
Laser printers, of a kind solely used for automatic data processing machine	激光打印机,专用于自动数据处理设备的	8443. 3212	57
Laser printing machines, digital	激光印刷机,数字式	8443. 3222	57

Article Description	商品名称	Tariff Code	D. R.
Laser transmitting and receiving unit of optical communication equipments	光通信设备的激光收发模块	8517.7060	3
Laser video compact disk player, nes	激光视盘机,其他	8521.9019	5
Lasers parts and accessories, other than laser diodes	激光器的零件、附件,激光二极管除外	9013.9010	3
Lasers, other than laser diodes	激光器,激光二极管除外	9013.2000	
Lathes, for removing metal, nes	车床,切削金属的,其他	8458.9900	7
Lathes, horizontal, for removing metal, nes	车床,卧式,切削金属的,其他	8458.1900	7
Lathes, horizontal, numerically controlled, for removing metal	车床,卧式,数控的,切削金属的	8458.1100	7
Lathes, numerically controlled, for removing metal, nes	车床,数控的,切削金属的,其他	8458.9100	7
Latifolia citrus	阔叶柑橘	0805.2020	14
Lavatory pans, of plastics	便盆,塑料的	3922.9000	236
Lavatory seats and covers, of plastics	马桶座圈及盖,塑料的	3922.2000	236
Laver, dried	紫菜,干的	1212.2041	14
Laver, fresh	紫菜,鲜的	1212.2042	14
Laver, nes	紫菜,其他	1212.2049	14
Laver, seasoned	紫菜,调味的	2008.9931	248
Lawn or sports-ground rollers	草坪及运动场地滚压机	8432.8010	
Lawn-tennis balls	草地网球	9506.6100	
Lawn-tennis rackets, whether or not strung	草地网球拍,不论是否装弦	9506.5100	
Lead articles of lead, nes	铅制品,其他	7806.0090	16
Lead azide	叠氮化铅	2850.0000	
Lead monoxide	一氧化铅	2824.1000	
Lead ores and concentrates	铅矿砂及其精矿	2607.0000	146
Lead oxides, nes	铅的氧化物,其他	2824.9090	
Lead unwrought, containing by weight antimony as the principal other element	铅,未锻轧,按重量计所含其他元素是以锑为主的	7801.9100	46
Lead unwrought, nes	铅,未锻轧,其他	7801.9900	46
Lead, refined	铅,精炼的	7801.1000	46
Leaded anti-knock compound sludges	含铅抗震化合物的淤渣	2620.2100	134
Leaded gasoline sludges	含铅汽油的淤渣	2620.2100	134
Leaded lights and the like, pressed or moulded	花饰铅条窗玻璃及类似品,压制或模制的	7016.9010	345
Leads for any animal, of any material	挽绳,适合各种动物用	4201.0000	1458
Lead-acid accumulators parts	铅酸蓄电池用零件	8507.9010	3
Lead-acid accumulators, nes	铅酸蓄电池,其他	8507.2000	68
Lead-acid accumulators, of a kind used for starting piston engines	铅酸蓄电池,用于起动活塞式发动机	8507.1000	68
Leaf moulds	腐叶土	2530.9099	13456
Leaflets and similar printed matter, in single sheets, whether or not folded	散页印刷品及类似印刷品,单张的,不论是否折叠	4901.1000	15

L

Article Description	商品名称	Tariff Code	D. R.
Leaf-springs and leaves thereof, of iron or steel, for motor vehicles	片簧及簧片,钢铁制,汽车用	7320. 1020	36
Leaf-springs and leaves thereof, of iron or steel, for railway locomotives and rollingstock	片簧及簧片,钢铁制,铁道车辆用	7320. 1010	36
Leaf-springs and leaves thereof, of iron or steel, nes	片簧及簧片,钢铁制,其他	7320. 1090	36
Leather articles of a kind used in machinery or mechanical appliances or for other technical uses	皮革或再生皮革的制品,机器、机械器具或其他专门技术用途的	4205. 0020	456
Leather articles or composition leather articles, nes	皮革或再生皮革的制品,其他	4205. 0090	456
Leather dust, powder and flour	皮革粉末	4115. 2000	1458
Leather of bovine animals, further prepared after tanning or crusting, without hair on, whole, full grains, unsplit	皮,牛的,经鞣制或半硝处理后进一步加工的,不带毛的,整张的,全粒面未剖层革	4107. 1110	1458
Leather of bovine animals, further prepared after tanning or crusting, without hair on, whole, grain splits	皮,牛的,经鞣制或半硝处理后进一步加工的,不带毛的,整张的,粒面剖层革	4107. 1210	1458
Leather of bovine or quine animals, further prepared after tanning or crusting, without hair on, for machinery belting, nes, including sides	皮,牛或马的,经鞣制或半硝处理后进一步加工的,不带毛的,机器带用,其他,包括半张的	4107. 9910	1458
Leather of bovine or quine animals, further prepared after tanning or crusting, without hair on, full grains, unsplit, nes, including sides	皮,牛或马的,经鞣制或半硝处理后进一步加工的,不带毛的,全粒面未剖层革,其他,包括半张的	4107. 9100	1458
Leather of bovine or quine animals, further prepared after tanning or crusting, without hair on, grain splits, nes, including sides	皮,牛或马的,经鞣制或半硝处理后进一步加工的,不带毛的,粒面剖层革,其他,包括半张的	4107. 9200	1458
Leather of bovine or quine animals, further prepared after tanning or crusting, without hair on, nes, including sides	皮,牛或马的,经鞣制或半硝处理后进一步加工的,不带毛的,其他,包括半张的	4107. 9990	1458
Leather of bovine or quine animals, further prepared after tanning or crusting, without hair on, whole, for machinery belting	皮,牛或马的,整张的,经鞣制或半硝处理后进一步加工的,不带毛的,机器带用	4107. 1910	1458
Leather of bovine or quine animals, further prepared after tanning or crusting, without hair on, whole, nes	皮,牛或马的,整张的,经鞣制或半硝处理后进一步加工的,不带毛的,其他	4107. 1990	1458
Leather of equine animals, further prepared after tanning or crusting, without hair on, whole, full grains, unsplit	皮,马的,整张的,经鞣制或半硝处理后进一步加工的,不带毛的,整张的,全粒面未剖层革	4107. 1120	1458
Leather of equine animals, further prepared after tanning or crusting, without hair on, whole, grain splits	皮,马的,整张的,经鞣制或半硝处理后进一步加工的,不带毛的,整张的,粒面剖层革	4107. 1220	1458
Leather of goats or kids, further prepared after tanning or crusting, without wool on	皮革,山羊或小山羊皮的,经鞣制或半硝处理后进一步加工的,不带毛的	4113. 1000	1458
Leather of reptiles, further prepared after tanning or crusting, without wool on	皮革,爬行动物皮的,经鞣制或半硝处理后进一步加工的,不带毛的	4113. 3000	1458

Article Description	商品名称	Tariff Code	D. R.
Leather of sheep or lamb, further prepared after tanning or crusting, without wool on	皮革,绵羊或羔羊的,经鞣制或半硝处理后进一步加工的,不带毛的	4112. 0000	1458
Leather of swine, further prepared after tanning or crusting, without wool on	皮革,猪的,经鞣制或半硝处理后进一步加工的,不带毛的	4113. 2000	1458
Leather or of composition leather's parings and other waste o, not suitable for the manufacture of leather articles	皮革或再生皮革的边角废料,不适宜作皮革制品用	4115. 2000	1458
Leather, further prepared after tanning or crusting, without wool on, nes	皮革,经鞣制或半硝处理后进一步加工的,不带毛的,其他	4113. 9000	1458
Leaven, alsatian	面肥	2102. 3000	28
Lecithins	卵磷脂	2923. 2000	36
Leeks, fresh or chilled	韭葱,鲜或冷藏的	0703. 9010	1
Lefetamine (INN); salts thereof	利非他明以及它们的盐	2921. 4600	36
Leguminous vegetables, nes, fresh or chilled	豆类蔬菜,其他,鲜或冷藏的	0708. 9000	1
Leguminous vegetables, nes, frozen	豆类蔬菜,其他,冷冻的	0710. 2900	1
Leguminous vegetables, nes, seed, shelled, dried	豆类,其他,种用,脱荚的,干的	0713. 9010	34
Leguminous vegetables, nes, shelled, dried	豆类,其他,脱荚的,干的	0713. 9090	34
Lemon juice, nes	柠檬汁,其他	2009. 3910	2468
Lemon juice, of a brix value not exceeding 20	柠檬汁,白利糖度值不超过 20 的	2009. 3110	2468
Lemonade	柠檬汽水	2202. 1000	248
Lemons (Citrus limon, Citrus limonum)	柠檬	0805. 5000	124
Lenses, of any material, mounted, for cameras	透镜,已装配的各种材料制,照相机用	9002. 9010	3
Lenses, of any material, mounted, being parts of or fittings for instruments or apparatus	透镜,已装配的各种材料制,作为仪器或装置的零件、配件	9002. 9090	3
Lenses, of any material, unmounted	透镜,未装配的各种材料制	9001. 9090	5
Lentils, nes, dried, shelled	扁豆,其他,脱荚的,干的	0713. 4090	34
Lentils, seed, dried, shelled	扁豆,种用,脱荚的,干的	0713. 4010	34
Lepidolite	锂云母	2530. 9099	13456
Letter cards of paper or paperboard	封缄信片,纸或纸板制的	4817. 2000	6
Letter clips, of base metal	信夹,贱金属制	8305. 9000	256
Letter corners, of base metal	信角,贱金属制	8305. 9000	256
Letter openers and blades thereof	开信刀及其刀片	8214. 1000	256
Letter pads, of paper or paperboard	信笺本,纸或纸板制的	4820. 1000	256
Letter trays and similar articles, of a kind used in offices, shops or the like, of paper, paperboard,	信件盘及类似品,办公室、商店及类似场所使用的,纸制的	4819. 6000	68
Letterpress printing machinery, other than reel fed, excluding flexographic printing	凸版印刷机,除卷取进料式以外的,但不包括苯胺印刷机	8443. 1500	57
Letterpress printing machinery, reel fed, excluding flexographic printing	凸版印刷机,卷取进料式,但不包括苯胺印刷机	8443. 1400	57
Letters symbols, of base metal, excluding those of heading No. 94. 05	字母标志,贱金属制,税号 94. 05 的货品除外	8310. 0000	256
Lettuce, nes, fresh or chilled	莴苣,其他,鲜或冷藏的	0705. 1900	1

L

Article Description	商品名称	Tariff Code	D. R.
Let-off motions for looms	送经装置,织机用	8448. 4920	3
Leucite	白榴石	2529. 3000	13
Leukotrienes, their derivatives and structural analogues	白细胞三烯及其衍生物和结构类似物	2937. 5000	36
Levamfetamine(INN); salts thereof	左苯丙胺(INN)以及它们的盐	2921. 4600	36
Level measuring or checking instruments and apparatus, of liquids	液位的测量、检验仪器及装置	9026. 1000	7
Level meter parts and accessories	液位计零件、附件	9026. 9000	3
Level, measuring or checking variables of liquids or gases	液位计,测量或检验变化量的	9026. 1000	7
Levellers parts	平地机零件	8431. 4990	3
Levellers, nes	平地机,其他	8429. 2090	57
Levellers, with an engine of an output exceeding 235. 36kW(320hp)	平地机,发动机输出功率超过235. 36千瓦(320马力)的	8429. 2010	57
Levels	水平仪	9015. 3000	
Levometamfe-tamine, salts, esters and other derivatives thereof	左甲苯丙胺,它的盐、酯及其他衍生物	2939. 9190	34
Levorphanol(INN) and its salts	左非诺(INN)及其盐	2933. 4100	36
Lids, of base metal	盖子,贱金属制	8309. 9000	256
Lifeboats, motor vessels	救生船,机动船舶	8906. 9010	5
Lifeboats, not-motorized vessels	救生船,非机动船舶	8906. 9020	5
Life-belts	安全带	6307. 2000	346
Life-jackets	救生衣	6307. 2000	346
Lifting or loading machines parts and accessories, solely or principally of a kind used in the electronic integrated circuits factories	装卸装置零件及附件,集成电路工厂用的	8486. 9010	3
Lifting or loading machines solely or principally of a kind used in the electronic integrated circuits factories, nes	装卸装置,集成电路工厂用的,其他	8486. 4039	7
Lifting, handling, loading or unloading machinery, nes	升降、搬运、装卸机械,其他	8428. 9090	
Lifts and skip hoists, nes	升降机及倒卸式起重机,其他	8428. 1090	
Lifts parts	升降机的零件	8431. 3100	3
Lifts, designed for the transport of persons	电梯,载客用	8428. 1010	
Light diesel oil	轻柴油	2710. 1921	6
Light emitting diodes (LED), photosensitive semiconductor devices	发光二极管,光敏半导体器件	8541. 4010	5
Light oils and preparations, nes	轻油及其制品,其他	2710. 1199	6
Lighters, nes	打火机,其他	9613. 8000	5
Lighters, pocket, gas fuelled, non refillable	打火机,一次性袖珍型气体的	9613. 1000	
Lighters, pocket, gas fuelled, refillable	打火机,袖珍型,可充气的	9613. 2000	
Lighting equipment of a kind used for motor vehicles	照明装置,机动车辆用	8512. 2010	57

L

Article Description	商品名称	Tariff Code	D. R.
Lighting equipment of a kind used on bicycles	照明装置,自行车用	8512. 1000	7
Lighting equipment parts for cycles or motor vehicles	照明装置零件,自行车或机动车辆用	8512. 9000	3
Lighting fittings parts, nes	照明装置零件,其他	9405. 9900	36
Lighting fittings parts, of glass	照明装置零件,玻璃制	9405. 9100	36
Lighting fittings parts, of plastics	照明装置零件,塑料制	9405. 9200	36
Lighting fittings, for ceiling or wall, electric, excluding those of a kind used for lighting public open spaces or thorough-fares	照明装置,天花板或墙壁上的,电气的,不包括公共露天场所或街道上的电气照明装置	9405. 1000	5
Lighting fittings, electric, nes	照明装置,电的,其他	9405. 4090	5
Lighting fittings, non-electrical lamps, nes	照明装置,非电气的,其他	9405. 5000	5
Lighting sets of a kind used for christmas trees	灯具,成套的,圣诞树用	9405. 3000	5
Lightning arresters, for a voltage exceeding 1000V	避雷器,用于电压超过 1000 伏的线路	8535. 4000	8
Light-vessels	灯船	8905. 9090	37
Light-weight coated paper, of a kind used for writing, printing or other graphic purposes, of which more than 10% by weight of the total fibre content consists of fibres obtained by a mechanical or chemi-mechanical process, coated on one or both sides with kaolin or other inorganic substances	轻质涂布纸,书写、印刷或类似用途的纸及纸板,所含用机械或化学-机械方法制得的纤维超过全部纤维重量的 10%,单面或双面涂布高岭土或其他无机物质的	4810. 2200	14568
Lignin sulphonates, but excluding tall oil	木素磺酸盐,但不包括妥尔油	3804. 0000	
Lignite wax	褐煤蜡	2712. 9090	6
Lignite, agglomerated	褐煤,制成型的	2702. 2000	1
Lignite, whether or not pulverized, but not agglomerated	褐煤,不论是否粉化,但未制成型	2702. 1000	1
Lilial	铃兰醛	2912. 2910	36
Lily corms, dormant, nes	百合球茎,其他,休眠的	0601. 1029	135
Lily corms, dormant, seed	百合球茎,种用,休眠的	0601. 1021	135
Lily, fresh, suitable for bouquets or for ornamental purposes	百合花,鲜的,制花束或装饰用的	0603. 1910	34
Lily, nes	百合,其他	0602. 9094	
Lily, seedlings	百合,种用	0602. 9091	3
Lima beans or butter beans, fresh or chilled	利马豆,鲜或冷藏的	0708. 9000	1
Lime bark	椴树皮	1401. 9090	3
Limes (citrus aurantifolia)	酸橙	0805. 5000	124
Limestone and other calcareous stone, of a kind used for the manufacture of lime or cement	石灰石及其他钙质石,通常用于制造石灰或水泥的	2521. 0000	3
Limestone decomposition furnace	石灰石分解炉	8417. 8040	7
Limestone flux	石灰石助熔剂	2521. 0000	3
Limonite, agglomerated	褐铁矿,已烧结	2601. 1200	1346
Linalool	芳樟醇	2905. 2230	36
Lincomycin and its derivatives; salts thereof	林可霉素及其衍生物以及它们的盐	2941. 9040	
Lindane (ISO, INN)	林丹(ISO, INN)	2903. 5100	36

L

Article Description	商品名称	Tariff Code	D. R.
Line pipe of a kind used for oil or gas pipelines, longitudinally submerged arc welded, the external diameter of which exceeds 406. 4mm	管道管,石油或天然气用,纵向埋弧焊接的,外径超过406. 4 毫米	7305. 1100	6
Line pipe of a kind used for oil or gas pipelines, longitudinally welded, the external diameter of which exceeds 406. 4mm	管道管,石油或天然气用,其他纵向焊接的,外径超过406. 4 毫米	7305. 1200	6
Line pipe of a kind used for oil or gas pipelines, nes	管道管,石油及天然气用,其他	7306. 1900	6
Line pipe of a kind used for oil or gas pipelines, of stainless steel, welded, nes	管道管,石油及天然气用,焊接的,不锈钢的,其他	7306. 1100	6
Line pipe of a kind used for oil or gas pipelines, seamless, having an outside diament not exceeding 114. 3mm	管道管,石油或天然气用,无缝的,外径不超过114. 3 毫米	7304. 1930	6
Line pipe of a kind used for oil or gas pipelines, seamless, having an outside diameter exceeding 114. 3mm but less than 215. 9mm	管道管,石油或天然气用,无缝的,外径超过 114. 3 毫米,但小于 215. 9 毫米	7304. 1920	6
Line pipe of a kind used for oil or gas pipelines, seamless, having an outside diameter of 215. 9mm or more but not exceeding 406. 4mm	管道管,石油或天然气用,无缝的,外径大于等于 215. 9 毫米,但不超过406. 4 毫米	7304. 1910	6
Line pipe of a kind used for oil or gas pipelines, seamless, nes	管道管,石油或天然气用,无缝的,其他	7304. 1990	6
Line pipe of a kind used for oil or gas pipelines, seamless, of stainless steel, having an outside diament not exceeding 114. 3mm	管道管,石油或天然气用,无缝的,不锈钢制,外径不超过114. 3 毫米	7304. 1130	6
Line pipe of a kind used for oil or gas pipelines, seamless, of stainless steel, having an outside diameter exceeding 114. 3mm but less than 215. 9mm	管道管,石油或天然气用,无缝的,不锈钢制,外径超过114. 3 毫米,但小于215. 9 毫米	7304. 1120	6
Line pipe of a kind used for oil or gas pipelines, seamless, of stainless steel, having an outside diameter of 215. 9mm or more but not exceeding 406. 4mm	管道管,石油或天然气用,无缝的,不锈钢制,外径大于等于 215. 9 毫米,但不超过406. 4 毫米	7304. 1110	6
Line pipe of a kind used for oil or gas pipelines, seamless, of stainless steel, nes	管道管,石油或天然气用,无缝的,不锈钢制,其他	7304. 1190	6
Line pipe of a kind used for oil or gas pipelines, the external diameter of which exceeds 406. 4mm, nes	管道管,石油或天然气用,外径超过406. 4 毫米,其他	7305. 1900	6
Line telephone sets with cordless handsets	无绳电话机	8517. 1100	
Line throwing guns	抛缆枪	9303. 9000	
Linnaeite	硫钴矿	2605. 0000	146
Linoleic acids, their salts and esters	亚油酸及其盐和酯	2916. 1500	36
Linoleum	列诺伦	5904. 1000	
Linoleum	亚麻油地毡	5904. 1000	
Linotenic acids, their salts and esters	亚麻酸及其盐和酯	2916. 1500	36
Linoxyn	氧化亚麻油	1518. 0000	46

Article Description	商品名称	Tariff Code	D. R.
Linseed oil and its fractions, crude oil	亚麻子油及其分离品,初榨的	1515. 1100	4
Linseed oil and its fractions, nes	亚麻子油及其分离品,其他	1515. 1900	4
Linseed, whether or not broken	亚麻籽,不论是否破碎	1204. 0000	
Lipase	脂肪酶,其他	3507. 9090	35
Liquefied gas fuels, nes, in containers of a kind used for filling or refilling cigarette or similar lighters and of a capacity exceeding $300cm^3$	直接灌注香烟打火机及类似打火器用的燃料,其包装容器的容积超过300立方厘米	2711. 1910	1468
Liquefied-gas fuels in containers of a kind used for filling or refilling cigarette or similar lighters and of a capacity not exceeding $300cm^3$	液化气体燃料,直接灌注香烟打火机及类似打火器用的,包装容器的容积不超过300立方厘米	3606. 1000	38
Liquefying air or other gases machinery, nes	液化空气或其他气体的机器,其他	8419. 6090	57
Liqueurs	利口酒	2208. 7000	2468
Liquid chromatographs instruments	液相色谱仪	9027. 2012	
Liquid crystal display panel	液晶显示板	9013. 8030	
Liquid elevators	液体提升机	8413. 8200	27
Liquid elevators parts	液体提升机用零件	8413. 9200	27
Liquid fuels in containers of a kind used for filling or refilling cigarette or similar lighters and of a capacity not exceeding $300cm^3$	液体燃料,直接灌注香烟打火机及类似打火器用的,包装容器的容积不超过300立方厘米	3606. 1000	38
Liquid lustres and similar preparations, of a kind used in the ceramic, enamelling or glass industry	光瓷釉及类似制品,陶瓷、搪瓷及玻璃工业用	3207. 3000	13
Liquid meters parts and accessories, for industrial use	液量计零件、附件,工业用	9028. 9010	3
Liquid meters parts and accessories, nes	液量计零件、附件,其他	9028. 9090	3
Liquid meters, supply or production meters, nes	液量计,生产或供应计量仪表,其他	9028. 2090	7
Liquid paraffin	液体石蜡	2710. 1994	8
Liquids for hydraulic transmission, prepared, not containing or containing less than 70% by weight of petroleum oils or oils obtained from bituminous minerals	液压传动用液体,不含石油或从沥青矿物提取的油类,或者按重量计石油或从沥青矿物提取的油类含量低于70%	3819. 0000	36
Liquified natural gas ships, volume more than $20000m^3$	液化天然气船,容积在20000立方米以上	8901. 2042	8
Liquified natural gas ships, volume with $20000m^3$ or less	液化天然气船,容积在20000立方米及以下	8901. 2041	8
Liquified petroleum gas ships, volume more than $20000m^3$	液化石油气船,容积在20000立方米以上	8901. 2032	8
Liquified petroleum gas ships, volume with $20000m^3$ or less	液化石油气船,容积在20000立方米及以下	8901. 2031	8
Liquorice roots	甘草	1211. 9036	34
Litharge	铅黄	2824. 1000	
Lithium carbonates	锂的碳酸盐	2836. 9100	
Lithium chloride	氯化锂	2827. 3910	
Lithium hydroxide	氢氧化锂	2825. 2010	

Article Description	商品名称	Tariff Code	D. R.
Lithium ion accumulators	锂离子蓄电池	8507.8020	68
Lithium mica	锂云母	2530.9099	13456
Lithium oxide and hydroxide, nes	锂的氧化物和氢氧化物,其他	2825.2090	
Lithographic stones, prepared for printing purposes	石板,制成供印刷用	8442.5000	
Lithographs, original	石印画的原本	9702.0000	
Lithopone	锌钡白	3206.4210	2368
Live plants(including their roots), nes	活植物(包括其根),其他	0602.9099	
Liver of any animal, prepared or preserved	动物肝,制作或保藏的	1602.2000	48
Livers and roes	鱼肝及鱼卵	0303.8000	1
Livers and roes, fresh or chilled	鱼肝及鱼卵,鲜或冷的	0302.7000	1
Livers of bovine animals, frozen, edible	牛肝,冻的,可食用的	0206.2200	15
Livers of fish, dried, smoked, salted or in brine	鱼肝,干、熏、盐腌或盐渍的	0305.2000	4
Livers of swine, frozen	猪肝,冻的	0206.4100	15
Living animals, for human consumption, nes	动物,活的,食用,其他	0106.9020	34
Living animals, nes	动物,活的,其他	0106.9090	4
Living animals, pure-bred breeding, nes	动物,活的,改良种用,其他	0106.9019	4
Loading and unloading bridges, nes	装卸桥,其他	8426.1949	7
Lobster, prepared or preserved	龙虾,制作或保藏的	1605.3000	48
Lobsters(homarus spp.), for cultivation	大螯虾种苗	0306.2210	3
Lobsters(homarus spp.), frozen	大螯虾,冻的	0306.1200	1
Lobsters(homarus spp.), nes, not frozen	大螯虾,其他,未冻的	0306.2290	14
Lock for central control, of a kind used for motor vehicles, of base metal	锁,中央控制用,机动车用,贱金属制	8301.2010	256
Lock washers, of iron or steel, nes	防松垫圈,钢铁制的,其他	7318.2100	268
Locks clasps and frames with clasps, of base metal	锁扣环及扣环框架,贱金属制	8301.5000	256
Locks of a kind used for furniture, of base metal	锁,家具用,贱金属制	8301.3000	256
Locks of a kind used for motor vehicles, of base metal, nes	锁,机动车用,贱金属制,其他	8301.2090	256
Locks parts, of base metal	锁零件,贱金属制	8301.6000	256
Locks, of base metal, nes	锁,贱金属制,其他	8301.4000	256
Locks, padlocks, of base metal	锁,挂锁,贱金属制	8301.1000	256
Lock-gates, of iron or steel	闸门,钢铁的	7308.9000	6
Locmotive or wagon traversers	铁道机车或货车的转车台	8428.9010	
Locomotive engines, compression-ignition	机车发动机,压燃式	8408.9010	2
Locomotives parts	机车用零件	8607.9100	3
Locomot-ive tenders	机车煤水车	8602.9000	37
Locust beans, including locust bean seeds	刺槐豆,包括刺槐豆子	1212.9920	134
Loganberries, fresh	罗甘莓,鲜的	0810.2000	1
Loganberries, frozen	罗甘莓,冷冻的	0811.2000	1
Lollipops, iced	棒糖,冰的	2105.0000	28
Long grain, broken	籼米,碎米	1006.4010	35

Article Description	商品名称	Tariff Code	D. R.
Long grain, husked	籼米,糙米	1006. 2010	35
Long grain, nes	籼米,其他	1006. 1091	35
Long grain, seed, in husk (paddy or rough)	籼米,种用	1006. 1011	35
Long grain, semi-milled or wholly milled	籼米,半精米或精米	1006. 3010	35
Long pepper	荜拨,调味料	0904. 1100	4
Long pepper, used in pharmacy	荜拨,医药级	1211. 9039	34
Long pilefabrics, knitted or crocheted	长毛绒织物	6001. 1000	46
Longan can	龙眼罐头	2008. 9920	248
Longan pulps, dried	龙眼肉,干的	0813. 4010	345
Longan, fresh	龙眼,鲜的	0810. 9030	1
Longans, dried	龙眼干	0813. 4010	345
Longfinned tunas (thunnus alalunga)	长鳍金枪鱼,鲜或冷的,	0302. 3100	18
Longfinned tunas (thunnus alalunga), frozen	长鳍金枪鱼,冻的	0303. 4100	18
Loofah articles	丝瓜络制品	4602. 9000	6
Looms, air jet, for weaving fabrics of a width exceeding 30cm, shuttleless type	织机,喷气式,所织织物宽度超过30厘米的无梭织机	8446. 3050	7
Looms, carrier, for weaving fabrics of a width exceeding 30cm, shuttleless type	织机,片梭式,所织织物宽度超过30厘米的无梭织机	8446. 3030	7
Looms, rapier, for weaving fabrics of a width exceeding 30cm, shuttleless type	织机,剑杆式,所织织物宽度超过30厘米的无梭织机	8446. 3020	7
Looms, water jet, for weaving fabrics of a width exceeding 30cm, shuttleless type	织机,喷水式,所织织物宽度超过30厘米的无梭织机	8446. 3040	7
Looped pile fabrics of cotton, knitted or crocheted	毛圈绒织物,棉制,针织或钩编的	6001. 2100	46
Looped pile fabrics of man-made fibres, knitted or crocheted	毛圈绒织物,化学纤维制,针织或钩编的	6001. 2200	46
Looped pile fabrics of textile materials, knitted or crocheted, nes	毛圈绒织物,纺织材料制,针织或钩编的,其他	6001. 2900	46
Loopwale yarn	纵行起圈纱线	5606. 0000	
Loosely twisted double wire, of a kind used for fencing, of iron or steel	松绞双股丝,钢铁的,围篱用的	7313. 0000	36
Loprazolam (INN); salts thereof	氯普唑仑(INN)以及盐	2933. 5500	36
Lorazepam (INN); salts thereof	劳拉西泮(INN)以及盐	2933. 9100	36
Lormetazepam (INN); salts thereof	氯甲西泮(INN)以及盐	2933. 9100	36
Lotus (Nelumbo nucifera) rootstock, for cultivation	藕,种用	0714. 9021	34
Lotus (Nelumbo nucifera) rootstock, nes	藕,其他	0714. 9029	34
Lotus seeds (Semen Nelurnbinis)	莲子	1212. 9994	134
Loudspeaker for motor vehicles	喇叭,机动车辆用	8512. 3011	7
Loudspeakers parts	扬声器零件	8518. 9000	3
Loudspeakers, multiple loudspeakers, mounted in the same enclosure	扬声器,多喇叭音箱	8518. 2200	5
Loudspeakers, single loudspeakers, mounted in their enclosures	扬声器,单喇叭音箱	8518. 2100	5

Article Description	商品名称	Tariff Code	D. R.
Loudspeakers, nes	扬声器,其他	8518. 2900	5
Low dosage X-ray security inspecting equipment	低剂量 X 射线安全检查设备	9022. 1910	
Lubricant for parts of the body for surgical operations or physical examinations	润滑剂,外科手术或体检时躯体部位用	3006. 7000	36
Lubricating grease	润滑油	2710. 1991	2368
Lubricating oils	润滑脂	2710. 1992	2368
Lubricating preparations (including cutting-oil preparations, bolt or nutrelease preparations, anti-rust or anticorrosion preparations and mould release preparations, based on lubricants), containing petroleum oils or oils obtained from bituminous minerals	润滑剂(包括以润滑剂为基本成分的切削油制剂、螺栓或螺母松开剂、防锈或防腐蚀制剂及脱模剂),含有石油或从沥青矿物提取的油类	3403. 1900	2368
Lubricating preparations (including cutting-oil preparations, bolt or nutrelease preparations, anti-rust or anticorrosion preparations and mould release preparations, based on lubricants), nes	润滑剂(包括以润滑剂为基本成分的切削油制剂、螺栓或螺母松开剂、防锈或防腐蚀制剂及脱模剂),其他	3403. 9900	2368
Lubricating pumps for internal combustion piston engines	润滑油泵,活塞式内燃发动机用	8413. 3030	23
Lucerne (alfalfa), nes, forage products	紫苜蓿,其他,饲料用	1214. 9000	
Lucerne(alfalfa) seed, for sowing	紫苜蓿子,种植用的	1209. 2100	358
Lucerne(alfalfa) meal and pellets, forage products	紫苜蓿粗粉及团粒,饲料用	1214. 1000	1
Luggage vans, railway or tramway coaches, not self-propelled	行李车,铁道及电车道用,非机动	8605. 0090	37
Luminophores, inorganic products	发光体,无机产品	3206. 5000	2368
Lupines, forage products	羽扇豆,饲料用	1214. 9000	
Lupulin	蛇麻腺	1210. 2000	14
Lychee can	荔枝罐头	2008. 9910	248
Lychee, fresh	荔枝,鲜的	0810. 9010	1
Lydite	璧玄岩	2530. 9099	13456
Lydite	璧玄岩制品	6815. 9990	6
Lysergic acid and its salts	麦角酸及其盐	2939. 6300	34
Lysine	赖氨酸	2922. 4110	36
Lysine esters; salts thereof	赖氨酸酯以及它们的盐	2922. 4190	36

M

Article Description	商品名称	Tariff Code	D. R.
Macadam of slag, dross or similar industrial waste, whether or not incorporating the materials cited in subheading No. 2517. 10	碎石,由矿渣、浮渣及类似的工业残渣制成,不论是否混有子目号 2517. 10 所列的材料	2517. 2000	134
Macadamia nuts, nes	马卡达姆坚果,其他	0802. 6090	134
Macadamia nuts, nes	夏威夷果,其他	0802. 6090	134
Macadamia nuts, seed	马卡达姆坚果,种用	0802. 6010	134
Macadamia nuts, seed	夏威夷果,种用	0802. 6010	134
Macaroni manufacture machinery	通心粉生产机器	8438. 1000	
Macaroni manufacture machinery parts	通心粉生产机器的零件	8438. 9000	3
Macaroni, uncooked, containing eggs	通心粉,生的,含蛋的	1902. 1100	46
Macaroni, uncooked, nes	通心粉,生的,其他	1902. 1900	46
Macaws, pure-bred breeding	金刚鹦鹉,改良种用	0106. 3210	3
Mace	肉豆蔻衣	0908. 2000	
Machinery for aerating beverages	饮料充气机	8422. 3090	
Machinery for agricultural, horticultural or forestry use, nes	机械,农业、园艺及林业用,其他	8432. 8090	
Machinery for bottling or canning beverages	饮料灌装设备	8422. 3010	
Machinery for crushing parts, used in the manufacture of wine, cider, fruit juices or similar beverages	轧碎机零件,制酒、制果或制类似饮料用	8435. 9000	3
Machinery for crushing, used in the manufacture of wine, cider, fruit juices or similar beverages	轧碎机,制酒、制果汁或制类似饮料用	8435. 1000	
Machinery for making up paper pulp, paper or paperboard, nes	制造纸浆制品、纸制品或纸板制品的机器,其他	8441. 8090	
Machinery parts, for agricultural, horticultural or forestry use	机械零件,农业、园艺及林业用	8432. 9000	
Machinery parts, not containing electrical connectors, insulators, coils, contacts or other electrical features, nes	机器零件,不具有电气接插件、绝缘体、线圈、触点或其他电气器材特征的,其他	8487. 9000	3
Machinery parts, with a process involving a change of temperature, nes	机器设备零件,利用温度变化处理,其他	8419. 9090	3
Machinery with a 360° revolving superstructure, nes	机械,上部结构可旋转 360 度的,其他	8429. 5290	57
Machinery, plant and equipment, for making hot drinks of for cooking or heating food	机器设备,加工热饮料或烹调、加热食品用	8419. 8100	57
Machinery, with a process involving a change of temperature, nes	机器设备,利用温度变化处理,其他	8419. 8990	57
Machines and mechanical appliances having individual functions, nes	具有独立功能的机器及机械器具,其他	8479. 9090	3
Machines and mechanical appliances, nes	机器及机械器具,其他	8479. 8999	7
Machines for balancing mechanical parts	机械零件平衡试验机	9031. 1000	

M

Article Description	商品名称	Tariff Code	D. R.
Machines for cold-working glass or glassware, nes	加工机床,玻璃冷加工用,其他	8464.9019	7
Machines for making bags, sacks or envelopes, of paper pulp, paper or paperboard	包、袋或信封的制造机器,纸浆、纸或纸板制的	8441.2000	
Machines for making cartons, boxes, cases, tubes, drums or similar containers, of paper pulp, paper or paperboard, other than by moulding, nes	制造箱、盒、管、桶或类似容器的机器,纸浆、纸或纸板制的,模制成型机器除外,其他	8441.3090	
Machines for preparing textile yarns, nes	处理纺织纱线的机器,其他	8445.9090	7
Machines, appliances, instruments or apparatus parts and accessories, nes	机器、器具、仪器或装置用的零件、附件,其他	9033.0000	3
Machine-tools for working metal or cermets, without removing material, nes	加工机床,金属或金属陶瓷用,非切削的,其他	8463.9000	7
Machine-tools for working stone, ceramics, concrete, asbestos-cement or like mineral materials, nes	加工机床,加工石料、陶瓷、混凝土、石棉水泥或类似矿物材料的,其他	8464.9090	7
Machine-tools for working wood, cork, bone, hard rubber, hard plastics or similar hard materials, which can carry out different types of machining operations without tool change between such operations	加工机床,加工木材、软木、骨、硬质橡胶、硬质塑料或类似硬质材料的,不需更换工具即可进行不同机械加工的机器	8465.1000	7
Machine-tools parts and accessories, for removing metal or other materials	加工机床的零件及附件,切削加工金属或其他材料的	8466.9300	3
Machine-tools parts and accessories, for working stone, ceramics, concrete, asbestos-cement or like mineral materials	加工机床的零件及附件,加工石料、陶瓷、混凝土、石棉水泥或类似矿物材料的	8466.9100	3
Machine-tools parts and accessories, for working wood, cork, bone, hard rubber, hard plastics or similar hard materials	加工机床的零件及附件,加工木材、软木、骨、硬质橡胶、硬质塑料或类似硬质材料的	8466.9200	3
Machine-tools parts and accessories, without removing metal or other materials	加工机床的零件及附件,非切削加工金属或其他材料的	8466.9400	3
Machine-tools special attachments	机床专用附件	8466.3000	3
Machine-tools, nes	加工机床,其他	8456.9090	7
Machine-tools, operated by electro-discharge processes, nes	加工机床,用放电处理的,其他	8456.3090	7
Machine-tools, operated by electro-discharge processes, numerically controlled	加工机床,用放电处理的,数控的	8456.3010	7
Machine-tools, operated by laser or other light or photon beam processes	加工机床,用激光、其他光或光子束处理的	8456.1000	7
Machine-tools, operated by ultrasonic processes	加工机床,用超声波处理的	8456.2000	7
Machining centres, for working metal, nes	加工中心,加工金属的,其他	8457.1090	7
Machining centres, horizontal, for working metal	加工中心,卧式,加工金属的	8457.1020	7
Machining centres, plano, for working metal	加工中心,龙门式,加工金属的	8457.1030	7
Machining centres, vertical, for working metal	加工中心,立式,加工金属的	8457.1010	7
Mackerel (Scomber scombrus, Scomber australasicus, Scomber japonicus), fresh or chilled	鲭鱼,鲜或冷的	0302.6400	18

M

Article Description	商品名称	Tariff Code	D. R.
Mackerel (Scomber scombrus, Scomber australasicus, Scomber japonicus), frozen	鲭鱼,冻的	0303. 7400	18
Mackerel, prepared or preserved, whole or in pieces, but not minced	鲭鱼,制作或保藏的,整条或切块,但未绞碎	1604. 1500	48
Magnesia, fused	镁氧矿,熔凝的	2519. 9010	146
Magnesia, light-burned	轻烧镁	2519. 9030	146
Magnesia, sintered	重烧镁	2519. 9020	146
Magnesite	菱镁矿	2519. 1000	146
Magnesium articles	镁制品	8104. 9020	16
Magnesium carbonate	碳酸镁	2836. 9910	
Magnesium chlorides	氯化镁	2827. 3100	
Magnesium hydroxide	氢氧化镁	2816. 1000	
Magnesium oxide, chemically pure	氧化镁,化学纯	2519. 9091	146
Magnesium oxide, nes	氧化镁,其他	2519. 9099	146
Magnesium peroxide	过氧化镁	2816. 1000	
Magnesium, sulphates	硫酸镁	2833. 2100	
Magnesium, unwrought, containing at least 99. 8% by weight of magnesium	镁,未锻轧,按重量计含镁量至少为 99. 8%	8104. 1100	16
Magnesium, unwrought, nes	镁,未锻轧,其他	8104. 1900	16
Magnesium, wrought	镁,已锻轧	8104. 9010	16
Magnetic discs, nes	磁盘,其他	8523. 2919	37
Magnetic discs, unrecorded	磁盘,未录制	8523. 2911	37
Magnetic examinations apparatus	磁粉探伤检测仪	9031. 8032	
Magnetic flywheels, for electrical ignition or starting equipment, nes	磁飞轮,点燃式或压燃式内燃发动机用的,其他	8511. 2090	7
Magnetic flywheels, for locomotives, aircraft or ships, for electrical ignition or starting equipment	磁飞轮,机车、航空器及船舶用,点燃式或压燃式内燃发动机用的	8511. 2010	7
Magnetic heads, of cassette magnetic tape recorders or reproducers	磁头,盒式磁带录音机或放声机用	8522. 9022	3
Magnetic resonance imaging apparatus, used in medical, surgical, dental or veterinary sciences	核磁共振成像装置,医疗、外科、牙科或兽医用	9018. 1300	
Magnetic stripe cards, recorded	磁条卡,已录制	8523. 2120	37
Magnetic stripe cards, unrecorded	磁条卡,未录制	8523. 2110	37
Magnetic tapes, for reproducing sound or image phenomena	磁带,重放声音或图像信息的	8523. 2928	37
Magnetic tapes, nes	磁带,其他	8523. 2990	37
Magnetic tapes, of a width exceeding 4mm, but not exceeding 6. 5mm, unrecorded	磁带,未录制的宽度超过 4 毫米,但不超过 6. 5 毫米的	8523. 2922	37
Magnetic tapes, of a width exceeding 6. 5mm, unrecorded	磁带,未录制的宽度超过 6. 5 毫米的	8523. 2923	37
Magnetic tapes, of a width not exceeding 4mm, unrecorded	磁带,未录制的宽度不超过 4 毫米的	8523. 2921	37

Article Description	商品名称	Tariff Code	D. R.
Magnetic tapes, recorded, nes	磁带,已录制的,其他	8523. 2929	37
Magneto-dynamos, for electrical ignition or starting equipment, nes	永磁直流发电机,点燃式或压燃式内燃发动机用的,其他	8511. 2090	7
Magneto-dynamos, for locomotives, aircraft or ships, for electrical ignition or starting equipment	永磁直流发电机,机车、航空器及船舶用,点燃式或压燃式内燃发动机用的	8511. 2010	7
Magnetrons	磁控管	8540. 7100	35
Mahjong and similiar table games	麻将及类似桌上游戏用品	9504. 9040	
Mainframe	大型机(计算机)	8471. 4110	26
Mainframe, presented in the form of systems	大型机(计算机),以系统形式进口或出口的	8471. 4910	26
Mainframes processing units	大型机处理部件	8471. 5010	26
Maize (corn) oil and its fractions, crude oil	玉米油及其分离品,初榨的	1515. 2100	4
Maize (corn) oil and its fractions, nes	玉米油及其分离品,其他	1515. 2900	4
Maize corn, other worked	玉米,其他加工的	1104. 2300	4
Maize(corn), nes	玉米,其他	1005. 9000	3
Maize(corn), seed	玉米,种用	1005. 1000	3
Make-and-break switches, for a voltage exceeding 1000V	断续开关,用于电压超过 1000 伏的线路	8535. 3000	8
Make-up preparations for eye	化妆品,眼用	3304. 2000	23
Make-up preparations for lip	化妆品,唇用	3304. 1000	23
Make-up preparations, nes, in powders, whether or not compressed	化妆品,其他,粉状,不论是否压紧	3304. 9100	23
Maleic anhydride	马来酐	2917. 1400	36
Malonylurea and its salts	丙二酰脲及其盐	2933. 5200	36
Malonylurea derivatives; salts thereof, nes	丙二酰脲衍生物以及它们的盐,其他	2933. 5400	36
Malt extract	麦精	1901. 9000	68
Malt, not roasted	麦芽,未焙制	1107. 1000	4
Malt, roasted	麦芽,已焙制	1107. 2000	4
Malted milk, other than for infant use	麦乳精,非幼儿食品	1901. 9000	68
Maltose and maltose syrup	麦芽糖及糖浆	1702. 9000	
Mammals, for human consumption, nes	哺乳动物,食用	0106. 1920	48
Mammals, nes	哺乳动物,其他	0106. 1990	48
Mammals, pure-bred breeding, nes	哺乳动物,改良种用	0106. 1910	34
Manatees	海牛	0106. 1200	
Mandarins (including tangerines and satsumas), nes	柑橘,其他	0805. 2090	14
Manganates	锰酸盐	2841. 6900	1
Manganese articles, nes	锰制品,其他	8111. 0090	16
Manganese dioxide	二氧化锰	2820. 1000	6
Manganese granulated slag, from the manufacture of iron or steel	锰渣,粒状	2618. 0010	146

M

Article Description	商品名称	Tariff Code	D. R.
Manganese ores and concentrates, including ferruginous manganese ores and concentrates with a manganese content of 20% or more, calculated on the dry weight	锰矿砂及其精矿,包括以干重计含锰量在20%及以上的锰铁矿及其精矿	2602.0000	1346
Manganese oxide, nes	锰的氧化物,其他	2820.9000	6
Manganese, unwrought	锰,未锻轧	8111.0010	16
Manganites	亚锰酸盐	2841.6900	1
Mango juice	芒果汁	2009.8012	2468
Mangoes	芒果	0804.5020	14
Mangosteens	山竹果	0804.5030	14
Manicture or pedicure preparations	化妆品,指(趾)甲用	3304.3000	23
Manicure sets and instruments	修指甲用具	8214.2000	256
Manifold business forms, of paper or paperboard	多联商业表格纸,纸或纸板制的	4820.4000	
Manigolds, forage products	饲料甜菜,饲料用	1214.9000	
Manioc (cassava), chilled or frozen	木薯,冷或冻的	0714.1030	34
Manioc (cassava), dried	木薯,干的	0714.1020	34
Manioc (cassava), fresh	木薯,鲜的	0714.1010	34
Mannitol	甘露糖醇	2905.4300	36
Manometers	压力表	9026.2090	7
Manometers parts and accessories	压力表零件、附件	9026.9000	3
Manostats	恒压器	9032.2000	
Mantillas, knitted or crocheted, nes	披纱,针织或钩编的,其他	6117.1090	2456
Mantillas, knitted or crocheted, of fine animal hair, nes	披纱,针织或钩编的,其他动物细毛制	6117.1019	2456
Mantillas, knitted or crocheted, of goats fine animal hair	披纱,针织或钩编的,山羊绒制	6117.1011	2456
Mantillas, knitted or crocheted, of wool	披纱,针织或钩编的,羊毛制	6117.1020	2456
Mantillas, not knitted or crocheted, of artificial fibres	披纱,非针织或钩编的,人造纤维制	6214.4000	2456
Mantillas, not knitted or crocheted, of goats fine animal hair	披纱,非针织或钩编的,山羊绒制	6214.2020	2456
Mantillas, not knitted or crocheted, of other fine animal hair	披纱,非针织或钩编的,其他动物细毛制	6214.2090	2456
Mantillas, not knitted or crocheted, of other textile materials	披纱,非针织或钩编的,其他纺织材料制	6214.9000	2456
Mantillas, not knitted or crocheted, of silk or silk waste	披纱,非针织或钩编的,丝或绢丝制	6214.1000	2456
Mantillas, not knitted or crocheted, of synthetic fibres	披纱,非针织或钩编的,合成纤维制	6214.3000	2456
Mantillas, not knitted or crocheted, of wool	披纱,非针织或钩编的,羊毛制	6214.2010	2456
Manure spreaders and fertilizer distributors, used in agriaulture, horticulture and forestry	施肥机,农业、园艺及林业用	8432.4000	
Man-made or synthetic leather, of polyurethanes	人造革及合成革,泡沫塑料的,氨酯聚合物制	3921.1310	16

M

Article Description	商品名称	Tariff Code	D. R.
Man-made or synthetic leather, nes	人造革及合成革,其他	3921. 1910	16
Man-made or synthetic leather, of polymers, of vinyl chloride	人造革及合成革,泡沫塑料的,氯乙烯聚合物制	3921. 1210	16
Maple sugar	槭糖	1702. 2000	
Maple syrup	槭糖浆	1702. 2000	
Maps for wall, printed	地图挂图,印制的	4905. 9900	1
Maps, printed, in book form	地图册,印制的,成册的	4905. 9100	1
Map-cases, bottle-cases, cutlery cases and similar containers, nes	地图盒、瓶盒、刀叉餐具盒及类似容器,其他	4202. 9900	256
Map-cases, bottle-cases, cutlery cases and similar containers, with outer surface of leather, of composition leather or of patent leather	地图盒、瓶盒、刀叉餐具盒及类似容器,以皮革、再生皮革或漆皮作面	4202. 9100	256
Map-cases, bottle-cases, cutlery cases and similar containers, with outer surface of plastic sheeting or of textile materials	地图盒、瓶盒、刀叉餐具盒及类似容器,以塑料片或纺织材料作面	4202. 9200	256
Maracas	沙球	9206. 0000	5
Maracas	响葫芦	9206. 0000	5
Marble and articles thereof, worked, nes	大理石及其制品,已加工的,其他	6802. 9190	3468
Marble artificially coloured granules, chippings and powder	大理石经人工染色的石粒、石片及石粉	6802. 1010	3468
Marble carvings	大理石石刻	6802. 9110	3468
Marble granules, chippings and powder, whether or not heat treated	大理石碎粒、碎屑及粉末,不论是否热处理	2517. 4100	1
Marble monumental or building stone and articles thereof, simply cut or sawn, with a flat or even surface	大理石碑石或建筑用石及其制品,简单切削或锯开并具有一个平面的	6802. 2110	3468
Marble tiles, cubes and similar articles, whether or not rectangular (including square), the largest surface area of which is capable of being enclosed in a square the side of which is less than 7cm	大理石砖、瓦、方块及类似品,不论是否为矩形(包括正方形),其最大表面以可置入边长小于7厘米的方格为限	6802. 1010	3468
Marble, crude or roughly trimmed	大理石,原状或粗加修整	2515. 1100	148
Marble, merely cut, by sawing or otherwise, into blocks or slabs of a rectangular (including square) shape	大理石,用锯或其他方法切割成矩形,包括正方形	2515. 1200	148
Margarine, excluding liquid margarine	人造黄油,但不包括液态的	1517. 1000	24
Marine cabinet washer, spraying mechanical appliances	船用洗舱机,喷雾喷射机械器具	8424. 8991	7
Marine outboard motors, spark-ignition reciprocating or rotary	船舶舷外发动机,点燃往复式或旋转式	8407. 2100	3
Marine propulsion engines, compression-ignition	船舶发动机,压燃式	8408. 1000	
Marine propulsion engines, spark-ignition reciprocating or rotary, nes	船舶发动机,点燃往复式或旋转式,其他	8407. 2900	3
Markers	记号笔	9608. 2000	

Article Description	商品名称	Tariff Code	D. R.
Markers	唛头笔	9608.2000	
Marking-out instruments	划线器具	9017.2000	
Marking-out instruments parts and accessories	划线器具的零件、附件	9017.9000	3
Marmalades, being cooked preparations	柑橘酱,烹煮的	2007.9100	248
Masks manufacture or repair apparatus	掩膜版制作和修复装置	8486.4010	7
Masks manufacture or repair apparatus parts and accessories	掩膜版制作和修复装置零件及附件	8486.9090	3
Maslin	混合麦	1001.9090	356
Mass spectrograph parts and accessories	质谱仪零件、附件	9027.9000	3
Mass spectrograph, integrated circuit belium spectra leak detectors	质谱仪,集成电路生产用氦质谱检漏台	9027.8011	
Mass spectrograph, nes	质谱仪,其他	9027.8019	7
Massage apparatus	按摩器具	9019.1010	
Massicot	黄丹	2824.1000	
Mat rush	蔺草	1401.9031	3
Matches, other than pyrotechnic articles	火柴,但烟火制品除外	3605.0000	
Mate	马黛茶	0903.0000	
Mathematical calculating instruments	数学计算器具	9017.2000	
Mathematical calculating instruments parts and accessories	数学计算器具的零件、附件	9017.9000	3
Mats, matting and screens of bamboo	席子、席料及帘子,竹制的	4601.2100	6
Mats, matting and screens of rattan	席子、席料及帘子,藤制的	4601.2200	6
Mats, matting and screens of rushes	席子、席料及帘子,灯心草属材料制的	4601.2911	6
Mats, matting and screens of vegetable materials, nes	席子、席料及帘子,植物材料制的,其他	4601.2990	6
Mats, matting and screens, of other grass or straw	席子、席料及帘子,其他草制的	4601.2919	6
Mats, matting of reeds	席子、席料,芦苇制的	4601.2929	6
Mats, of glass fibres	席,玻璃纤维制	7019.3100	56
Mattocks	镐	8201.3000	256
Mattress supports	床垫支架	9404.1000	
Mattresses, of cellular rubber or plastics, whether or not covered	床垫,海绵橡胶或泡沫塑料制,不论是否包面	9404.2100	6
Mattresses, of other materials	床垫,其他材料制	9404.2900	6
Mayonnaise	蛋黄酱	2103.9090	268
Mazindol(INN) ; salts thereof	马吲哚(INN)以及盐	2933.9100	36
MDI, crude	MDI,粗制	3909.3010	1256
MDI, polymeric	MDI,聚合的	3909.3010	1256
Mead	蜂蜜酒	2206.0090	2468
Measuring or checking instruments, appliances and machines parts and accessories, nes	测量或检验仪器、器具及机器零件、附件,其他	9031.9000	3
Measuring or checking instruments, appliances and machines, nes	测量或检验仪器、器具及机器,其他	9031.8090	7

M

Article Description	商品名称	Tariff Code	D. R.
Measuring rods and tapes	量尺、量带	9017.8000	7
Meat of asses, fresh, chilled or frozen	驴肉,鲜或冷或冻的	0205.0000	14
Meat of bovine animals, fresh of chilled, boneless	牛肉,鲜或冷的,去骨	0201.3000	14
Meat of bovine animals, fresh of chilled, carcasses and halfcarcasses	牛肉,鲜或冷的,整头及半头	0201.1000	14
Meat of bovine animals, fresh of chilled, other cuts with bone in	牛肉,鲜或冷的,带骨	0201.2000	14
Meat of bovine animals, frozen, boneless	牛肉,冻的,去骨	0202.3000	14
Meat of bovine animals, frozen, carcasses and halfcarcasses	牛肉,冻的,整头及半头	0202.1000	14
Meat of bovine animals, frozen, other cuts with bone in	牛肉,冻的,带骨	0202.2000	14
Meat of bovine animals, salted, in brine, dried or smoked	牛肉,干、熏、盐腌或盐渍的	0210.2000	14
Meat of dolphins, fresh, chilled or frozen	海豚肉,鲜或冷或冻的	0208.4000	15
Meat of dugongs (mammals of the order sirenia)	儒艮(海牛目哺乳动物)的肉	0208.4000	15
Meat of goats	山羊肉	0204.5000	14
Meat of hares, fresh, chilled or frozen	兔肉,野兔的,鲜或冷或冻的	0208.1090	145
Meat of horses, fresh, chilled or frozen	马肉,鲜或冷或冻的	0205.0000	14
Meat of lamb, fresh or chilled, carcasses and half carcasses	羔羊肉,鲜或冷的,整头及半头	0204.1000	14
Meat of lamb, frozen, carcasses and half carcasses	羔羊肉,冻的,整头及半头	0204.3000	14
Meat of manatees, fresh, chilled or frozen	海牛肉,鲜或冷或冻的	0208.4000	15
Meat of mules or hinnies, fresh, chilled or frozen	骡肉,鲜或冷或冻的	0205.0000	14
Meat of porpoises (mammals of the order cetacea), fresh, chilled or frozen	鼠海豚(鲸目哺乳动物)的肉,鲜或冷或冻的	0208.4000	15
Meat of rabbits, fresh or chilled, excluding head	兔肉,兔头除外,家兔的,鲜或冷的	0208.1010	1
Meat of rabbits, frozen, excluding head	兔肉,兔头除外,家兔的,冻的	0208.1020	1
Meat of reptiles (including snakes and turtles), fresh, chilled or frozen	爬行动物(包括蛇及龟鳖)的肉	0208.5000	15
Meat of sheep, fresh or chilled, carcasses and halfcarcasses	绵羊肉,鲜或冷的,整头及半头	0204.2100	14
Meat of sheep, fresh or chilled, nes, boneless	绵羊肉,鲜或冷的,其他,去骨	0204.2300	14
Meat of sheep, fresh or chilled, nes, other cuts with bone in	绵羊肉,鲜或冷的,其他,带骨	0204.2200	14
Meat of sheep, frozen, carcasses and halfcarcasses	绵羊肉,冻的,整头及半头	0204.4100	14
Meat of sheep, frozen, nes, boneless	绵羊肉,冻的,其他,去骨	0204.4300	14
Meat of sheep, frozen, nes, other cuts with bone in	绵羊肉,冻的,其他,带骨	0204.4200	14
Meat of squabs, fresh, chilled or frozen	乳鸽肉,鲜或冷或冻的,	0208.9010	15
Meat of swine, fresh or chilled, carcasses and halfcarcasses, nes	猪肉,鲜或冷的,整头及半头,其他	0203.1190	14
Meat of swine, fresh or chilled, nes	猪肉,鲜或冷的,其他	0203.1900	14

Article Description	商品名称	Tariff Code	D. R.
Meat of swine, frozen, carcasses and halfcarcasses, nes	猪肉,冻的,整头及半头,其他	0203. 2190	14
Meat of swine, frozen, nes	猪肉,冻的,其他	0203. 2900	14
Meat of swine, nes, salted, in brine, dried or smoked	猪肉,其他,干、熏、盐腌或盐渍的	0210. 1900	14
Meat of whales, fresh, chilled or frozen	鲸肉,鲜或冷或冻的	0208. 4000	15
Meat preparation machinery	肉类加工机器	8438. 5000	
Meat preparation machinery parts	肉类加工机器的零件	8438. 9000	3
Meat, nes, fresh, chilled or frozen	肉,其他,鲜或冷或冻的	0208. 9090	145
Meat, of primatesand, fresh, chilled or frozen	肉,灵长目的,鲜或冷或冻的	0208. 3000	15
Meat, offal and blood of any animals, prepared or preserved, nes	肉、杂碎及血,其他,制作或保藏的	1602. 9090	48
Meat, offal and blood of bovine animals, prepared or preserved	肉、杂碎及血,牛的,制作或保藏的	1602. 5090	48
Meat, offal and blood of duck, prepared or preserved	肉、杂碎及血,鸭的,制作或保藏的	1602. 3991	248
Meat, offal and blood of fowls of the species gallus domesticus, prepared or preserved	肉、杂碎及血,鸡的,制作或保藏的	1602. 3299	48
Meat, offal and blood of swine, prepared or preserved	肉、杂碎及血,猪的,制作或保藏的	1602. 4990	48
Mechanical presses, for working metal or metal carbides	机械压力机,加工金属或硬质合金用	8462. 9910	7
Mechanical properties testing machines and appliances	机械性能试验机器及器具,非金属材料试验用	9024. 8000	7
Mechanical properties testing machines and appliances parts and accessories	机械性能试验机器及器具的零件、附件	9024. 9000	7
Mechanical properties testing machines and appliances, for testing metals, nes	机械性能试验机器及器具,金属材料试验用,其他	9024. 1090	7
Mechanical pulp, derived from recovered (waste and scrap) paper or paperboard	机械浆,从回收(废碎)纸或纸板提取的	4706. 9100	46
Mechanical seals	机械密封件	8484. 2000	56
Mechanical shovels	机械铲	8429. 5900	57
Mechanical singing birds	机械鸣禽	9208. 9000	5
Mechanical stokers	机械加煤机	8416. 3000	
Mechanical stokers ash dischargers and similar appliances	机械加煤机出灰器	8416. 3000	
Mechanical stokers grates	机械加煤机炉篦	8416. 3000	
Mechanical stokers parts	机械加煤机零件	8416. 9000	
Mechanical street organs	手摇风琴	9208. 9000	5
Mechanical wood pulp	机械木浆	4701. 0000	
Mechanisms for musical boxes	百音盒的机械装置	9209. 9920	3
Mechano-therapy appliances	机械疗法器具	9019. 1090	7
Mecloqualone (INN); salts thereof	甲氯喹酮(INN)以及盐	2933. 5500	36
Medazepam (INN); salts thereof	美达西泮(INN)以及盐	2933. 9100	36
Media, for the machines of heading 84. 71, nes	媒体,税号 84. 71 所列机器用,其他	8523. 8029	37
Media, nes	媒体,其他	8523. 8099	37

Article Description	商品名称	Tariff Code	D. R.
Media, unrecorded	媒体,未录制	8523. 8091	37
Media, unrecorded, for the machines of heading 84. 71	媒体,未录制,税号 84. 71 所列机器用	8523. 8021	37
Medical instruments and appliances, nes	医疗用仪器及器具,其他	9018. 9090	7
Medicaments of chinese type, nes	中式成药,其他	3004. 9059	368
Medicaments, nes, consisting of two or more constituents which have been mixed together, not put up in measured doses or in forms or packings for retail sale	药品,其他,两种或两种以上成分混合而成的,未配定剂量或制成零售包装	3003. 9090	368
Medicaments, nes, mixed or unmixed, put up in measured doses or in forms or packings for retail sale	药品,其他,混合或未混合的,配定剂量或制成零售包装	3004. 9090	368
Medicated liquors or wines, chinese type	中药酒	3004. 9051	368
Medium density fibreboard (MDF), of a thickness exceeding 5mm but not exceeding 9mm, of a density not exceeding 0. 5g/cm^3, nes	中密度纤维板,厚度超过 5 毫米但未超过 9 毫米,密度不超过每立方厘米 0. 5 克,其他	4411. 1399	48
Medium density fibreboard (MDF), of a thickness exceeding 5mm but not exceeding 9mm, of a density not exceeding 0. 5g/cm^3, not mechanically worked or surface covered	中密度纤维板,厚度超过 5 毫米但未超过 9 毫米,密度不超过每立方厘米 0. 5 克,未经机械加工或盖面的	4411. 1391	48
Medium density fibreboard (MDF), of a thickness exceeding 5mm but not exceeding 9mm, of a density exceeding 0. 5g/cm^3 but not exceeding 0. 8g/cm^3, nes	中密度纤维板,厚度超过 5 毫米但未超过 9 毫米,密度超过每立方厘米 0. 5 克,但未超过每立方厘米 0. 8 克,其他	4411. 1329	48
Medium density fibreboard (MDF), of a thickness exceeding 5mm but not exceeding 9mm, of a density exceeding 0. 5g/cm^3 but not exceeding 0. 8g/cm^3, of radiata pine	中密度纤维板,厚度超过 5 毫米但未超过 9 毫米,密度超过每立方厘米 0. 5 克,但未超过每立方厘米 0. 8 克,辐射松制的	4411. 1321	48
Medium density fibreboard (MDF), of a thickness exceeding 5mm but not exceeding 9mm, of a density exceeding 0. 8g/cm^3, nes	中密度纤维板,厚度超过 5 毫米但未超过 9 毫米,密度超过每立方厘米 0. 8 克,其他	4411. 1319	48
Medium density fibreboard (MDF), of a thickness exceeding 5mm but not exceeding 9mm, of a density exceeding 0. 8g/cm^3, not mechanically worked or surface covered	中密度纤维板,厚度超过 5 毫米但未超过 9 毫米,密度超过每立方厘米 0. 8 克,未经机械加工或盖面的	4411. 1311	48
Medium density fibreboard (MDF), of a thickness exceeding 9mm, nes	中密度纤维板,厚度超过 9 毫米,其他	4411. 1499	48
Medium density fibreboard (MDF), of a thickness exceeding 9mm, not mechanically worked or surface covered	中密度纤维板,厚度超过 9 毫米,未经机械加工或盖面的	4411. 1491	48
Medium density fibreboard (MDF), of a thickness exceeding 9mm, of a density exceeding 0. 5g/cm^3 but not exceeding 0. 8g/cm^3, nes	中密度纤维板,厚度超过 9 毫米,密度超过每立方厘米 0. 5 克,但未超过每立方厘米 0. 8 克,其他	4411. 1429	48

Article Description	商品名称	Tariff Code	D. R.
Medium density fibreboard (MDF), of a thickness exceeding 9mm, of a density exceeding 0.5g/cm^3 but not exceeding 0.8g/cm^3, of radiata pine	中密度纤维板,厚度超过9毫米,密度超过每立方厘米0.5克,但未超过每立方厘米0.8克,辐射松制的	4411.1421	48
Medium density fibreboard (MDF), of a thickness exceeding 9mm, of a density exceeding 0.8g/cm^3, nes	中密度纤维板,厚度超过9毫米,密度超过每立方厘米0.8克,其他	4411.1419	48
Medium density fibreboard (MDF), of a thickness exceeding 9mm, of a density exceeding 0.8g/cm^3, not mechanically worked or surface covered	中密度纤维板,厚度超过9毫米,密度超过每立方厘米0.8克,未经机械加工或盖面的	4411.1411	48
Medium density fibreboard (MDF), of a thickness not exceeding 5mm, of a density exceeding 0.5g/cm^3 but not exceeding 0.8g/cm^3, nes	中密度纤维板,厚度不超过5毫米,密度超过每立方厘米0.5克,但未超过每立方厘米0.8克,其他	4411.1229	48
Medium density fibreboard (MDF), of a thickness not exceeding 5mm, of a density exceeding 0.5g/cm^3 but not exceeding 0.8g/cm^3, of radiata pine	中密度纤维板,厚度不超过5毫米,密度超过每立方厘米0.5克,但未超过每立方厘米0.8克,辐射松制的	4411.1221	48
Medium density fibreboard (MDF), of a thickness not exceeding 5mm, of a density exceeding 0.8g/cm^3, nes	中密度纤维板,厚度不超过5毫米,密度超过每立方厘米0.8克,其他	4411.1219	48
Medium density fibreboard (MDF), of a thickness not exceeding 5mm, of a density exceeding 0.8g/cm^3, not mechanically worked or surface covered	中密度纤维板,厚度不超过5毫米,密度超过每立方厘米0.8克,未经机械加工或盖面的	4411.1211	48
Medium density fibreboard (MDF), of a thickness not exceeding 5mm, of a density not exceeding 0.5g/cm^3, nes	中密度纤维板,厚度不超过5毫米,密度不超过每立方厘米0.5克,其他	4411.1299	48
Medium density fibreboard (MDF), of a thickness not exceeding 5mm, of a density not exceeding 0.5g/cm^3, not mechanically worked or surface covered	中密度纤维板,厚度不超过5毫米,密度不超过每立方厘米0.5克,未经机械加工或盖面的	4411.1291	48
Mefenorex (INN); salts thereof	美芬雷司(INN)以及它们的盐	2921.4600	36
Melamine	蜜胺	2933.6100	36
Melamine	三聚氰胺	2933.6100	36
Melamine resins, in primary forms	蜜胺树脂,初级形状的	3909.2000	1256
Melons, nes, fresh	甜瓜,其他,鲜的	0807.1990	1
Memorandum pads, of paper or paperboard	记事本,纸或纸板制的	4820.1000	
Memories, electronic integrated circuits	存储器,集成电路	8542.3200	37
Menthol	薄荷醇	2906.1100	36
Meprobamate (INN)	甲丙氨酯(INN)	2924.1100	36
Mercaptans	硫醇	2930.9090	36
Mercuric cyanide	氰化汞	2852.0000	
Mercuric thiocyanate	硫氰酸汞	2852.0000	
Mercury	汞	2805.4000	
Mercury albuminate	白阮化汞	2852.0000	

Article Description	商品名称	Tariff Code	D. R.
Mercury compounds, inorganic or organic, excluding amalgams	汞的无机或有机化合物,汞齐除外	2852.0000	
Mercury fulminate	雷酸汞	2852.0000	
Mercury lactate	乳酸汞	2852.0000	
Mercury tannate	单宁酸汞	2852.0000	
Mercury vapour lamps	汞蒸汽灯	8539.3240	35
Mesocarb (INN); salts thereof	美索卡(INN)及盐	2934.9100	36
Metal carbides mixed with metallic binders, non-agglomerated	金属碳化物,与金属粘合剂混合的,未烧结	3824.3000	36
Metal carbides, mixed, non-agglomerated	金属碳化物,混合的,未烧结	3824.3000	36
Metal cutting shears and similar tools, hand tools	白铁剪及类似工具	8203.3000	256
Metal detectors	金属探测器	8543.7091	37
Metal detectors parts	金属探测器用零件	8543.9030	3
Metal gaskets	金属密封垫	8484.1000	56
Metal halide lamps	金属卤化物灯	8539.3290	35
Metal section squeezing machine	金属型材挤压机	8462.9110	7
Metal thread woven fabrics, combined with cotton, of a kind used in apparel, as furnishing fabrics or for similar purposes	金属线机织物,与棉混制,用于衣着、装饰及类似用途	5809.0010	468
Metal thread woven fabrics, combined with man-made fibres, of a kind used in apparel, as furnishing fabrics or for similar purposes	金属线机织物,与化学纤维混制,用于衣着、装饰及类似用途	5809.0020	468
Metal thread woven fabrics, of a kind used in apparel, as furnishing fabrics or for similar purposes, nes	金属线机织物,用于衣着、装饰及类似用途,其他	5809.0090	468
Metal treating machines and mechanical appliances, nes	金属处理的机械,其他	8479.8190	7
Metallised leather	镀金属皮革	4114.2000	1458
Metallized yarn, whether or not gimped, being textile yarn, or strip or the like, combined with metal in the form of thread, strip or powder or covered with metal	含金属纱线,不论是否螺旋花线,由纺织纱线或扁条及类似品与金属线、扁条或粉末混合制得或用金属包覆制得	5605.0000	6
Metamfetamine (INN); salts, esters and other derivatives thereof	去氧麻黄碱(INN),它的盐、酯及其他衍生物	2939.9190	34
Metamfetamine racemate; salts, esters and other derivatives thereof	去氧麻黄碱外消旋体,它们的盐、酯及其他衍生物	2939.9190	34
Metaphosphoric acid	偏磷酸	2809.2019	6
Methacrylie acid and its salts	甲基丙烯酸及其盐	2916.1300	36
Methacrylie acid esters	甲基丙烯酸酯	2916.1400	36
Methadone (INN) and salts thereof	美沙酮以及它们的盐	2922.3100	36
Methadone (INN) intermediate	美沙酮中间体	2926.3000	36
Methamidophos (ISO)	甲胺磷(ISO)	2930.5000	36

Article Description	商品名称	Tariff Code	D. R.
Methanal	甲醛	2912. 1100	36
Methane, ethane and propane halogenated derivatives only with fluorine and chlorine, nes	仅含氟和氯的甲烷、乙烷及丙烷的卤化衍生物,其他	2903. 4910	36
Methane, ethane and propane halogenated derivatives with fluorine and bromine, nes	仅含氟和溴的甲烷、乙烷及丙烷的卤化衍生物,其他	2903. 4920	36
Methanol(methyl alcohol)	甲醇	2905. 1100	36
Methaqualone (INN); salts thereof	甲喹酮 (INN)以及盐	2933. 5500	36
Methionine	蛋氨酸	2930. 4000	36
Methionine	甲硫氨酸	2930. 4000	36
Methyl acrylate	丙烯酸甲酯	2916. 1210	36
Methyl ethyl ketone	甲基乙基(甲) 酮	2914. 1200	36
Methylamine and their salts	甲胺及其盐	2921. 1100	36
Methylcoumarins	甲基香豆素	2932. 2100	36
Methylcyclohexanols	甲基环已醇	2906. 1200	36
Methylcyclohexanone	甲基环已酮	2914. 2200	36
Methyldiethanolamine	甲基二乙醇胺	2922. 1940	36
Methylionones	甲基芷香酮	2914. 2300	36
Methyloxirane	甲基环氧乙烷	2910. 2000	36
Methylphenidate (INN); salts thereof	哌醋甲酯(INN)以及盐	2933. 3300	36
Methylphenobarbital(INN); salts thereof	甲苯巴比妥(INN)以及盐	2933. 5300	36
Methyprylon(INN)	甲乙哌酮(INN)	2933. 7200	36
Metronomes	节拍器	9209. 9910	3
Mica articles, worked, nes	云母制品,已加工的,其他	6814. 9000	6
Mica plates, sheets and strips of agglomerated or reconstituted mica, whether or not on a support	云母制的板、片、带,粘聚或再制云母的,不论是否附于其他材料上	6814. 1000	6
Mica powder	云母粉	2525. 2000	13
Mica rifted into sheets or splittings	云母片,劈开的	2525. 1000	13
Mica waste	云母废料	2525. 3000	13
Mica, crude	云母,原状的	2525. 1000	13
Mica, worked, nes	云母,已加工的,其他	6814. 9000	6
Microcrystalline petroleum wax	微晶石蜡	2712. 9010	6
Microfilm or microfiche readers parts and accessories	缩微阅读机用零件、附件	9008. 9010	3
Microfilm readers, whether or not capable of producing copies	缩微胶卷阅读机,不论是否可以进行复制	9008. 2000	
Microfilms, exposed and developed, for printed books and newspapers	缩微胶片,已曝光已冲洗的,书籍、报刊的	3705. 9021	1238
Microfilms, exposed and developed, nes	缩微胶片,已曝光已冲洗的,其他	3705. 9029	1238
Microform readers, whether or not capable of producing copies	缩缩微胶片阅读机,不论是否可以进行复制	9008. 2000	
Micrometers	千分尺	9017. 3000	
Microphones and stands thereof	麦克风及其座架	8518. 1000	
Microphones parts	麦克风零件	8518. 9000	3

M

Article Description	商品名称	Tariff Code	D. R.
Microprocessings	微型机(计算机)	8471. 4140	26
Microprocessings processing units	微型机的处理部件	8471. 5040	26
Microprocessings, presented in the form of systems	微型机,以系统形式进口或出口的	8471. 4940	26
Microscopes other than optical microscopes	显微镜,光学显微镜除外	9012. 1000	
Microscopes parts and accessories, optical	显微镜零件、附件,光学的	9011. 9000	3
Microscopes parts and accessories, other than optical microscopes	显微镜的零件、附件,光学显微镜除外	9012. 9000	3
Microscopes, for cinephotomicrography, optical	显微镜,显微电影摄影用,光学的	9011. 2000	
Microscopes, for microprojection, optical	显微镜,显微投影用,光学的	9011. 2000	
Microscopes, for photomicrography, optical	显微镜,显微照相用,光学的	9011. 2000	
Microscopes, optical, nes	显微镜,光学的,其他	9011. 8000	
Microscopes, stereoscopic, optical	显微镜,立体的,光学的	9011. 1000	
Microtomes	检镜切片机	9027. 9000	3
Microwave ovens	微波炉	8516. 5000	7
Microwave tubes, nes	微波管,其他	8540. 7900	35
Midazolam(INN); salts thereof	咪达唑仑(INN)以及盐	2933. 9100	36
Midecamycin and its derivatives; salts thereof	麦迪霉素及其衍生物以及它们的盐	2941. 9060	
Midjoint wing of fowls of the species gallus domesticus, fresh or chilled	鸡翼(不包括翼尖),鲜或冷的	0207. 1321	1
Midjoint wing of fowls of the species gallus domesticus, frozen	鸡翼(不包括翼尖),冻的	0207. 1421	1
Mid-sized computer machine	中型机(计算机)	8471. 4110	26
Mid-sized computer machine processing units	中型机的处理部件	8471. 5010	26
Mid-sized computer machine, presented in the form of systems	中型机(计算机),以系统形式进口或出口的	8471. 4910	26
Mileometers	里程计	9029. 1020	
Mileometers parts and accessories	里程计零件、附件	9029. 9000	3
Military weapons, other than revolvers, pistols, nes	军用武器,手枪除外,其他	9301. 9000	7
Milk, curdled	乳,凝固的	0403. 9000	248
Milk, fermented or acidified, nes	乳,发酵或酸化的,其他	0403. 9000	248
Milk, in powder, granules or other solid forms, of a fat content, by weight, exceeding 1. 5%, containing added sugar or other sweetening matter	乳,粉状、粒状或其他固体形状,按重量计脂肪含量超过1. 5%,加糖或其他甜物质	0402. 2900	12468
Milk, in powder, granules or other solid forms, of a fat content, by weight, exceeding 1. 5%, not containing added sugar or other sweetening matter	乳,粉状、粒状或其他固体形状,按重量计脂肪含量超过1. 5%,未加糖或其他甜物质	0402. 2100	12468
Milk, in powder, granules or other solid forms, of a fat content, by weight, not exceeding 1. 5%	乳,粉状、粒状或其他固体形状,按重量计脂肪含量不超过1. 5%	0402. 1000	12468
Milk, not in solid forms, containing added sugar or other sweetening matter	乳,非固体形状,加糖或其他甜物质	0402. 9900	12468
Milk, not in solid forms, not containing added sugar or other sweetening matter	乳,非固体形状,未加糖或其他甜物质	0402. 9100	12468

M

Article Description	商品名称	Tariff Code	D. R.
Milk, of a fat content, by weight, exceeding 1% but not exceeding 6%, not concentrated nor containing added sugar or other sweetening matter	乳,按重量计脂肪含量超过1%,但不超过6%,未浓缩及未加糖或其他甜物质的	0401.2000	12468
Milk, of a fat content, by weight, exceeding 6%, not concentrated nor containing added sugar or other sweetening matter	乳,按重量计脂肪含量超过6%,未浓缩及未加糖或其他甜物质的	0401.3000	12468
Milk, of a fat content, by weight, not exceeding 1%, not concentrated nor containing added sugar or other sweetening matter	乳,按重量计脂肪含量不超过1%,未浓缩及未加糖或其他甜物质的	0401.1000	12468
Milking machines	挤奶机	8434.1000	
Milking machines parts	挤奶机零件	8434.9000	3
Millet	谷子	1008.2000	3
Milling machinery parts, used in the industry	磨粉业加工机器零件	8437.9000	3
Milling machinery used in the industry	磨粉业加工机器	8437.8000	3
Milling machines, knee-type, for removing metal, nes	铣床,升降台式,切削金属的,其他	8459.5900	7
Milling machines, numerically controlled, for removing metal	铣床,数控的,升降台式,切削金属的	8459.5100	7
Milling machines, planomilling machines, numerically controlled, for removing metal	铣床,龙门式,数控的,切削金属的	8459.6110	7
Milling machines, planomilling machines, for removing metal, nes	铣床,龙门式,切削金属的,其他	8459.6910	7
Milling machines, for removing metal, nes	铣床,切削金属的,其他	8459.6990	7
Milling machines, for working wood, cork, bone, hard rubber, hard plastics or similar hard materials	铣床,加工木材、软木、骨、硬质橡胶、硬质塑料或类似硬质材料的	8465.9200	7
Milling machines, numerically controlled, for removing metal, nes	铣床,数控的,切削金属的,其他	8459.6190	7
Milling tools, interchangeable, nes	铣削用工具,可互换,其他	8207.7090	256
Milling tools, interchangeable, with working part of diamonds etc.	铣削用工具,可互换,带有金刚石等工作部件的	8207.7010	256
Mills parts	轧机零件	8455.9000	3
Mills, hot-rolled, for sheet	轧机,热轧的,板材的	8455.2110	7
Mills, cold-rolled, for sheet	轧机,冷轧的,板材的	8455.2210	7
Mills, combination hot and cold-rolled	轧机,冷热联合的	8455.2190	7
Mills, for rolled-steel section	轧机,型钢的	8455.2120	7
Mills, for wire	轧机,线材的	8455.2130	7
Mills, hot-rolled, nes	轧机,热轧的,其他	8455.2190	7
Millstones and grindstones and the like, of natural stone, nes	石磨、石碾及类似品,天然石料制,其他	6804.2390	236
Millstones and grindstones and the like, of other agglomerated abrasives or ceramics	石磨、石碾及类似品,其他粘聚磨料制或陶瓷制	6804.2290	236
Millstones and grindstones and the like, of agglomerated synthetic or natural diamond, nes	石磨、石碾及类似品,粘聚合成或天然金刚石制,其他	6804.2100	236

Article Description	商品名称	Tariff Code	D. R.
Millstones and grindstones, for milling, grinding or pulping, without frameworks	石磨、石碾,碾磨或磨浆用,未装支架的	6804. 1000	36
Mincing knives	切菜刀	8214. 9000	256
Mine detectors	矿藏探测器	8543. 7091	37
Mine detectors parts	矿藏探测器用零件	8543. 9030	3
Mine wagon pushers	矿车推动机	8428. 9010	3
Mineral medicinal substances	矿物性药材	2530. 9010	13456
Mineral or chemical fertilizers, nitrogenous, nes	矿物氮肥及化学氮肥,其他	3102. 9090	68
Mineral or chemical fertilizers, phosphatic, nes	矿物磷肥及化学磷肥,其他	3103. 9000	68
Mineral or chemical fertilizers, potassic, nes	矿物钾肥及化学钾肥,其他	3104. 9090	68
Mineral substances or cellulose friction material and articles thereof, not mpunted, for brakes, for clutches or the like, not containing asbestos	矿物质或纤维素为基本成分的未装配摩擦材料及其制品,适于作制动器、离合器及类似品,不含石棉的,其他	6813. 8900	6
Mineral substances with bitumen mixing machines	矿物与沥青的混合机器	8474. 3200	3
Mineral substances, nes	矿产品,其他	2530. 9099	13456
Mineral waters, containing added sugar or other sweetening matter or flavoured	矿泉水,加味、加糖或其他甜物质的	2202. 1000	248
Mineral waters, not containing added sugar or other sweetening matter or flavoured	矿泉水,未加糖或其他甜物质及未加味的	2201. 1010	28
Mineral waxes, nes	矿物蜡,其他	2712. 9090	6
Mines and parts	地雷及其零件	9306. 9000	3
Mining drills, self-propelled, gear wheel diameter more than 380mm	采矿钻机,自推进的,牙轮直径 380 毫米及以上	8430. 5031	5
Mining drills, self-propelled, nes	采矿钻机,自推进的,其他	8430. 5039	5
Mining power shovels parts	矿用电铲用零件	8431. 4910	3
Mining power shovels, self-propelled	矿用电铲,自推进的	8430. 5020	5
Mini-computers	小型机(计算机)	8471. 4120	26
Mini-computers processing units	小型机的处理部件	8471. 5020	26
Mini-computers, presented in the form of systems	小型机,以系统形式进口或出口的	8471. 4920	26
Mink, for human consumption	貂,食用	0106. 1920	48
Mink, live, nes	貂,其他	0106. 1990	48
Mink, pure-bred breeding	貂,改良种用	0106. 1910	34
Mirrors and other optical elements, of any material, unmounted	反射镜,未装配的各种材料制	9001. 9090	5
Mirrors of base metal	镜子,贱金属制	8306. 3000	256
Mirrors, of any material, mounted, being parts of or fittings for instruments or apparatus	反射镜,已装配的各种材料制,作为仪器或装置的零件、配件	9002. 9090	3
Mirrors, of any material, mounted, for cameras	反射镜,已装配的各种材料制,照相机用	9002. 9010	3
Missiles and parts	导弹及其零件	9306. 9000	3
Mixed xylene isomers	混合二甲苯异构体	2902. 4400	6

Article Description	商品名称	Tariff Code	D. R.
Mixers for food, electro-mechanical domestic appliances	搅拌器,食品用,家用电动器具	8509. 4090	
Mixes and doughs for the preparation of bakers' wares of heading No. 19. 05	面团及调制品,供烘焙税号 19. 05 所列面包糕饼用的	1901. 2000	368
Mixing machines, for earth, stone, ores or other mineral substances, nes	混合机器,泥土、石料、矿石或其他固体矿物质的,其他	8474. 3900	
Mixing machines, nes	混合机,其他	8479. 8200	7
Mixture of rare-earth carbonate	混合碳酸稀土	2846. 9048	6
Mixture of rare-earth chlorides	混合氯化稀土	2846. 9028	6
Mixtures and preparations containing oxirane (ethylene oxide)	混合物及制品,含环氧乙烷(氧化乙烯)的	3824. 8100	36
Mixtures and preparations containing polychlorinated biphenyls (PCBs), polychlorinated terphenyls (PCTs) or polybrominated biphenyls (PBBs)	混合物及制品,含多氯联苯(PCBs)、多氯三联苯(PCTs)或多溴联苯(PBBs)的	3824. 8200	36
Mixtures and preparations containing tris (2, 3-dibromopropyl) phosphate	混合物及制品,含三(2,3-二溴丙基)磷酸酯的	3824. 8300	36
Mixtures containing 1, 1, 1-trichloroethane (methyl chloroform)	混合物,含 1,1,1-三氯乙烷(甲基氯仿)的	3824. 7600	36
Mixtures containing bromochlorodifluoromethane, bromotrifluoromethane or dibromotetrafluoroethanes	混合物,含溴氯二氟甲烷、溴三氟甲烷或二溴四氟乙烷的	3824. 7200	36
Mixtures containing bromomethane (methyl bromide) or bromochloro methane	混合物,含溴化甲烷(甲基溴)或溴氯甲烷的	3824. 7700	36
Mixtures containing carbon tetrachloride	混合物,含四氯化碳的	3824. 7500	36
Mixtures containing halogenated derivatives of methane, ethane or propane, nes	混合物,含有甲烷、乙烷或丙烷的卤化衍生物的混合物,其他	3824. 7900	36
Mixtures containing hydrobromofluorocarbons (HBFCs)	混合物,含氢溴氟烃(HBFCs)的	3824. 7300	36
Mixtures containing hydrochlorofluorocarbons (HCFCs), whether or not containing perfluorocarbons (PFCs) or hydrofluorocarbons (HFCs), but not containing chlorofluorocarbons (CFCs)	混合物,含氢氯氟烃(HCFCs)的,不论是否含全氟烃(PFCs)或氢氟烃(HFCs),但不含全氯氟烃(CFCs)	3824. 7400	36
Mixtures containing more than 50% by weight of talc	混合物,按重量计含滑石 50%以上的	3824. 9091	36
Mixtures containing more than 70% by weight of magnesium oxide	混合物,按重量计含氧化镁 70%以上的	3824. 9092	36
Mixtures containing perfluorocarbons (PFCs) or hydrofluorocarbons (HFCs), but not containing chlorofluorocarbons (CFCs) or hydrochlorofluorocarbons (HCFCs)	混合物,含全氟烃(PFCs)或氢氟烃(HFCs)的,但不含全氯氟烃(CFCs)或氢氯氟烃(HCFCs)的	3824. 7800	36
Mixtures of ammonium nitrate with calcium carbonate or other inorganic nonfertilizing substances	硝酸铵与碳酸钙或其他无肥效无机物的混合物	3102. 4000	68
Mixtures of nuts	什锦干果	0813. 5000	345
Mixtures of nuts	什锦果仁	2008. 1999	248

Article Description	商品名称	Tariff Code	D. R.
Mixtures of nuts, dried	什锦坚果,干的	0813.5000	345
Mixtures of parts of plants, edible	什锦植物部分,食用的	2008.9200	248
Mixtures of urea and ammonium nitrate in aqueous or ammoniacal solution	尿素及硝酸铵混合物的水溶液或氨水溶液	3102.8000	68
Mixtures of vegetables, frozen	什锦蔬菜,冷冻的	0710.9000	16
Mixtures of vegetables, dried	什锦蔬菜,干的	0712.9090	4
Mixtures of vegetables, prepared or preserved otherwise than by vinegar or acetic acid	什锦蔬菜,用醋或醋酸以外的其他方法制作或保藏的	2004.9000	48
Mixtures of vegetables, provisionally preserved, but unsuitable in that state for immediate consumption	什锦蔬菜,暂时保藏,但不适合直接使用的	0711.9090	34
Mixtures or preparations of fats or oils of this chapter, nes, edible, other than edible fats or oils or their fracitions of heading No. 15.16	混合油脂或制品,其他,食用,但税号15.16的食用油脂及其分离品除外	1517.9090	24
Mixtures spices	调味香料,混合的	0910.9100	6
Mixturescontaining chlorofluorocarbons (CFCs), whether or not containing hydrochlorofluorocarbons (HCFCs), perfluorocarbons (PFCs) or hydrofluorocarbons (HFCs)	混合物,含全氯氟烃(CFCs)的,不论是否含氢氯氟烃(HCFCs)、全氟烃(PFCs)或氢氟烃(HFCs)	3824.7100	36
Mobile clinics	医疗车	8705.9040	7
Mobile communication base stations	移动通信基站	8517.6110	
Mobile communication switching system	移动通信交换机	8517.6212	
Mobile electric generator sets, nes	电源车,其他	8705.9059	7
Mobile environmental monitoring units	环境监测车	8705.9030	7
Mobile lifting frames on tyres and straddle carriers	移动式吊运架及跨运车,带胶轮的	8426.1200	7
Mobile radiological units	放射线检查车	8705.9020	7
Mobile vehicles for aircraft air-conditioning	飞机调温车	8705.9060	7
Mobile vehicles for aircraft deicing	飞机除冰车	8705.9060	7
Mobile vehicles for aircraft refuelling	飞机加油车	8705.9060	7
Mobile workshops	流动工场车	8705.9090	7
Model assembly kits, of construction toys sets	建筑玩具套件,缩小(按比例缩小)的,成套的	9503.0040	5
Model assembly kits, of constructional toys	建筑玩具,缩小(按比例缩小)的,成套的	9503.0040	5
Model assembly kits, reduced-size ("scale"), nes	模型组件,缩小(按比例缩小)的,成套的,其他	9503.0039	5
Modelling pastes, including those put up for children's amusement	塑型用膏,包括供儿童娱乐用的在内	3407.0090	13
Modem, telecommunication apparatus for digital line system	调制解调器,有线数字通信设备	8517.6234	7
Modified immunological products	修饰免疫制品	3002.1000	34
Molasses, cane molasses	糖蜜,甘蔗糖蜜	1703.1000	4
Molasses, nes	糖蜜,其他	1703.9000	4

Article Description	商品名称	Tariff Code	D. R.
Molluscs, nes, prepared or preserved	软体动物,其他,制作或保藏的	1605.9090	48
Molybdates, nes	钼酸盐,其他	2841.7090	1
Molybdenite, non-metallurgical uses	辉钼矿,非冶金用途	2530.9099	13456
Molybdenite, roasted	辉钼矿,已焙烧	2613.1000	146
Molybdenum articles, nes	钼制品,其他	8102.9900	16
Molybdenum ores and concentrates, nes	钼矿砂及其精矿,其他	2613.9000	146
Molybdenum ores and concentrates, roasted	钼矿砂及其精矿,已焙烧	2613.1000	146
Molybdenum oxides and hydroxides	钼的氧化物及氢氧化物	2825.7000	
Molybdenum powders	钼粉末	8102.1000	16
Molybdenum wire	钼丝	8102.9600	16
Molybdenum, unwrought, including bars and rods obtained simply by sintering	钼,未锻轧,包括简单烧结而成的条、杆	8102.9400	16
Monazites	独居石	2612.2000	146
Money-changing machines	钱币兑换机	8476.8900	5
Monitor parts, nes	监视器零件,其他	8529.9090	3
Monitors of cathode-ray tube, black and white or other monochrome	监视器,阴极射线管的,黑白或其他单色的	8528.4990	135
Monitors of cathode-ray tube, colour	监视器,阴极射线管的,彩色的	8528.4910	135
Monitors of cathode-ray tube, of a kind solely or principally used in an automatic data processing system of heading 84.71	监视器,阴极射线管的,专用于或主要用于税号 84.71 的自动数据处理系统的	8528.4100	135
Monitors of lcd, of a kind solely or principally used in an automatic data processing system of heading 84.71, nes	监视器,液晶的,专用于或主要用于税号 84.71 的自动数据处理系统的	8528.5110	135
Monitors, black and white or other monochrome, nes	监视器,黑白或单色的,其他	8528.5990	135
Monitors, colour, nes	监视器,彩色的,其他	8528.5910	135
Monitors, of a kind solely or principally used in an automatic data processing system of heading 84.71, nes	监视器,专用于或主要用于税号 84.71 的自动数据处理系统的,其他	8528.5190	135
Monobutyl ethers of ethylene glycol or of diethylene glycol	乙二醇或二甘醇的单丁醚	2909.4300	36
Monocrotophos (ISO)	久效磷(ISO)	2924.1200	36
Monocrystalline sillicon, diameter exceeding 15.24cm, doped	单晶硅切片,直径在 15.24 厘米及以上的,掺杂的	3818.0019	13468
Monocrystalline sillicon, diameter not exceeding 15.24cm, doped	单晶硅切片,直径在 15.24 厘米及以下的,掺杂的	3818.0011	13468
Monocrystalline sillicon, diameter not exceeding 7.5cm, doped	单晶硅切片,直径在 7.5 厘米及以下的,掺杂的	3818.0090	13468
Monocrystals doped for use in electronics, containing by weight not less than 99.99% of silicon, in the form of cylinders or rods, 30cm or more in diameter	单晶硅棒,按重量计含硅量不少于 99.99%,经掺杂用于电子工业的,直径在 30 厘米及以上的	2804.6117	3468

M

Article Description	商品名称	Tariff Code	D. R.
Monocrystals doped for use in electronics, containing by weight not less than 99.99% of silicon, in the form of cylinders or rods, 7.5cm or more in diameter, less than 30cm	单晶硅棒,按重量计含硅量不少于99.99%,经掺杂用于电子工业的,直径在7.5厘米及以上但小于30厘米的	2804.6119	3468
Monocrystals doped for use in electronics, containing by weight not less than 99.99% of silicon, in the form of cylinders or rods, nes	单晶硅棒,按重量计含硅量不少于99.99%,经掺杂用于电子工业的,其他	2804.6120	3468
Monoculars	单筒望远镜	9005.8090	5
Monoculars parts and accessories (including mountings), nes	单筒望远镜零件、附件(包括座架),其他	9005.9090	3
Monoethanolamine and its salts, nes	单乙醇胺及其盐,其他	2922.1190	36
Monofilament rods, sticks and profile shapes, of other plastics	单丝、条、杆、型材及异型材,其他塑料制	3916.9090	168
Monofilament rods, sticks and profile shapes, of polyamides	单丝、条、杆、型材及异型材,聚酰胺制	3916.9010	168
Monofilament rods, sticks and profile shapes, of polymers of ethylene	单丝、条、杆、型材及异型材,乙烯聚合物制	3916.1000	168
Monofilament rods, sticks and profile shapes, of polymers of vinyl chloride	单丝、条、杆、型材及异型材,氯乙烯聚合物制	3916.2000	168
Monophenols, nes	一元酚,其他	2907.1990	36
Mono-chloroacetic acids, their salts and esters	一氯代乙酸及其盐和酯	2915.4000	36
Mono-sodium phosphates	磷酸一钠	2835.2200	
Monumental or building stone and articles thereof, simply cut or sawn, with a flat or even surface, nes	碑石或建筑用石及其制品,简单切削或锯开并具有一个平面的,其他	6802.2990	3468
Monumental or building stone, ecaussine and other calcareous, nes	碑用或建筑用石,石灰质,其他	2515.2000	148
Monumental or building stone, nes	碑用或建筑用石,其他	2516.9000	148
Mops	拖把	9603.9090	3
Morphine and salts	吗啡及盐	2939.1100	34
Mortar mixers	砂浆混合机器	8474.3100	
Mortars for refractory	灰泥,耐火的	3816.0000	36
Mortars, nes	追击炮,其他	9301.1900	7
Mortars, non-refractory	灰泥,非耐火的	3824.5000	36
Mortars, self-propelled	追击炮,自推进的	9301.1100	7
Mortising machines, for working wood, cork, bone, hard rubber, hard plastics or similar hard materials	凿榫机器,加工木材、软木、骨、硬质橡胶、硬质塑料或类似硬质材料的	8465.9500	7
Mosaic cubes and the like, ceramic, glazed, the largest surface area of which is capable of being enclosed in a square the side of which is less than 7cm	马赛克及类似品,陶瓷的,上釉的,其最大表面以可置入边长小于7厘米的方格为限	6908.1000	5
Mosaic cubes and the like, ceramic, unglazed, the largest surface area of which is capable of being enclosed in a square the side of which is less than 7cm	马赛克及类似品,陶瓷的,未上釉的,其最大表面以可置入边长小于7厘米的方格为限	6907.1000	5

Article Description	商品名称	Tariff Code	D. R.
Mosaic cubes and the like, of natural stone (including slate), whether or not on a backing, the largest surface area of which is capable of being enclosed in a square the side of which is less than 7cm	镶嵌石及类似品,天然石料(包括板岩)制的,不论是否有衬背,其最大表面以可置入边长小于7厘米的方格为限	6802.1090	3468
Mosaic cubes and the like, of natural stone (including slate), whether or not on a backing, the largest surface area of which is capable of being enclosed in a square the side of which is less than 7cm	马赛克及类似品,天然石料(包括板岩)制的,不论是否有衬背,其最大表面以可置入边长小于7厘米的方格为限	6802.1090	3468
Mosaic cubes of glass and other glass smallwares, for decorative or similar purposes, pressed or moulded	马赛克及其他小件玻璃品,供镶嵌或类似装饰用,压制或模制的	7016.1000	345
Mosquito smudges, in forms of packings for retail sale	蚊香,零售包装	3808.9111	36
Mosses and lichens, suitable for bouquets or for ornamental purposes	苔藓及地衣,制花束或装饰用的	0604.1000	34
Mother-of-pearl, worked	珍珠母,已加工的	9601.9000	5
Motor cars, of a cylinder capacity exceeding 1000cc but not exceeding 1500cc, with spark-ignition internal combustion reciprocating piston, for the transport of persons, nes	机动车辆,客运,气缸容量(排气量)超过1000毫升,但不超过1500毫升,装有点燃往复式活塞内燃发动机的,其他	8703.2290	58
Motor cars, of a cylinder capacity exceeding 1500cc but not exceeding 2000cc, with compression-ignition internal combustion piston engine, for the transport of persons, nes	机动车辆,客运,气缸容量(排气量)超过1500毫升,但不超过2000毫升,装有压燃式活塞内燃发动机的,其他	8703.3219	58
Motor cars, of a cylinder capacity exceeding 1500cc but not exceeding 2000cc, with spark-ignition internal combustion reciprocating piston, for the transport of persons, nes	机动车辆,客运,气缸容量(排气量)超过1500毫升,但不超过2000毫升,装有点燃往复式活塞内燃发动机的,其他	8703.2349	58
Motor cars, of a cylinder capacity exceeding 1500cc but not exceeding 2500cc, with compression-ignition internal combustion piston engine, for the transport of persons, nes	机动车辆,客运,气缸容量(排气量)超过1000毫升,但不超过1500毫升,装有压燃式活塞内燃发动机的,其他	8703.3129	58
Motor cars, of a cylinder capacity exceeding 2000cc but not exceeding 2500cc, with compression-ignition internal combustion piston engine, for the transport of persons, nes	机动车辆,客运,气缸容量(排气量)超过2000毫升,但不超过2500毫升,装有压燃式活塞内燃发动机的,其他	8703.3229	58
Motor cars, of a cylinder capacity exceeding 2000cc but not exceeding 2500cc, with spark-ignition internal combustion reciprocating piston, for the transport of persons, nes	机动车辆,客运,气缸容量(排气量)超过2000毫升,但不超过2500毫升,装有点燃往复式活塞内燃发动机的,其他	8703.2359	58

Article Description	商品名称	Tariff Code	D. R.
Motor cars, of a cylinder capacity exceeding 2500cc but not exceeding 3000cc, with spark-ignition internal combustion reciprocating piston, for the transport of persons, nes	机动车辆,客运,气缸容量(排气量)超过2500毫升,但不超过3000毫升,装有点燃往复式活塞内燃发动机的,其他	8703.2369	58
Motor cars, of a cylinder capacity exceeding 2500cc, but not exceeding 3000cc, with compression-ignition internal combustion piston engine, for the transport of persons, nes	机动车辆,客运,气缸容量(排气量)超过2500毫升,但不超过3000毫升,装有压燃式活塞内燃发动机的,其他	8703.3319	58
Motor cars, of a cylinder capacity exceeding 3000cc, but not exceeding 4000cc, with compression-ignition internal combustion piston engine, for the transport of persons, nes	机动车辆,客运,气缸容量(排气量)超过3000毫升,但不超过4000毫升,装有压燃式活塞内燃发动机的,其他	8703.3329	58
Motor cars, of a cylinder capacity exceeding 3000cc, but not exceeding 4000cc, with spark-ignition internal combustion reciprocating piston, for the transport of persons, nes	机动车辆,客运,气缸容量(排气量)超过3000毫升,但不超过4000毫升,装有点燃往复式活塞内燃发动机的,其他	8703.2419	58
Motor cars, of a cylinder capacity exceeding 3000cc, but not exceeding 4000cc, with spark-ignition internal combustion reciprocating piston, for the transport of persons, nes	机动车辆,客运,气缸容量(排气量)超过4000毫升,装有点燃往复式活塞内燃发动机的,其他	8703.2429	58
Motor cars, of a cylinder capacity exceeding 4000cc, with compression-ignition internal combustion piston engine, for the transport of persons, nes	机动车辆,客运,气缸容量(排气量)超过4000毫升,装有压燃式活塞内燃发动机的,其他	8703.3369	58
Motor cars, of a cylinder capacity not exceeding 1000cc, with compression-ignition internal combustion piston engine, for the transport of persons, nes	机动车辆,客运,气缸容量(排气量)不超过1000毫升,装有压燃式活塞内燃发动机的,其他	8703.3119	58
Motor cars, of a cylinder capacity not exceeding 1000cc, with spark-ignition internal combustion reciprocating piston engine, for the transport of persons, nes	机动车辆,客运,气缸容量(排气量)不超过1000毫升,装有点燃往复式活塞内燃发动机的,其他	8703.2190	58
Motor cars, principally designed for the transport of persons, nes	机动车辆,主要用于载人的,其他	8703.9000	58
Motor gasoline	车用汽油	2710.1110	6
Motor vehicles for the transport of goods, with compression-ignition internal combustion piston engine, g. v. w. Exceeding 20 tons	机动车辆,货运,车辆总重量超过20吨,装有压燃式活塞内燃发动机	8704.2300	58
Motor vehicles for the transport of goods, with compression-ignition internal combustion piston engine, g. v. w. exceeding 5 tons but not exceeding 14 tons	机动车辆,货运,车辆总重量超过5吨,但小于14吨,装有压燃式活塞内燃发动机	8704.2230	58

Article Description	商品名称	Tariff Code	D. R.
Motor vehicles for the transport of goods, with compression-ignition internal combustion piston engine, g. v. w. not exceeding 5 tons	机动车辆,货运,车辆总重量不超过5吨,装有压燃式活塞内燃发动机	8704. 2100	58
Motor vehicles for the transport of goods, with compression-ignition internal combustion piston engine, g. v. w. of 14 tons or more but not exceeding 20 tons	机动车辆,货运,车辆总重量在14吨及以上,但不超过20吨,装有压燃式活塞内燃发动机	8704. 2240	58
Motor vehicles for the transport of goods, with spark-ignition internal combustion piston engine, g. v. w. exceeding 8 tons	机动车辆,货运,车辆总重量超过8吨,装有点燃式活塞内燃发动机的其他货车	8704. 3240	58
Motor vehicles for the transport of goods, with spark-ignition internal combustion piston engine, g. v. w. not exceeding 5 tons	机动车辆,货运,车辆总重量不超过5吨,装有点燃式活塞内燃发动机的其他货车	8704. 3100	58
Motor vehicles for the transport of goods, with spark-ignition internal combustion piston engine, g. v. w. exceeding 5 tons, but not exceeding 8 tons.	机动车辆,货运,车辆总重量超过5吨,但不超过8吨,装有点燃式活塞内燃发动机的其他货车	8704. 3230	58
Motor vehicles for the transport of goods, with spark-ignition internal combustion piston engine, nes	机动车辆,货运,装有点燃式活塞内燃发动机的其他货车,其他	8704. 9000	58
Motor vehicles for the transport of persons, with 10 seats or more, but not exceeding 19 seats, nes	机动车辆,客运,10座及以上,但不超过19座,其他	8702. 9030	58
Motor vehicles for the transport of persons, with 10 seats or more, but not exceeding 19 seats, with compression-ignition internal combustion piston engine	机动车辆,客运,10座及以上,但不超过19座,装有压燃式活塞内燃发动机的	8702. 1093	58
Motor vehicles for the transport of persons, with 20 seats or more, but not exceeding 29 seats, nes	机动车辆,客运,20座及以上,但不超过29座,其他	8702. 9020	58
Motor vehicles for the transport of persons, with 20 seats or more, but not exceeding 29 seats, with compression-ignition internal combustion piston engine	机动车辆,客运,20座及以上,但不超过29座,装有压燃式活塞内燃发动机的	8702. 1092	58
Motor vehicles for the transport of persons, with 30 seats or more, nes	机动车辆,客运,30座及以上,其他	8702. 9010	58
Motor vehicles for the transport of persons, with 30 seats or more, with compression-ignition internal combustion piston engine	机动车辆,客运,30座及以上(大型客车),装有压燃式活塞内燃发动机的	8702. 1091	58
Motor vehicles lighting equipment	机动车辆用照明装置	8512. 2010	57
Motor vehicles parts and accessories, with 30 seats or more, nes	30座及以上客运机动车辆用零件、附件,其他	8708. 9929	3
Motor vehicles parts and accessories, nes	机动车辆用零件、附件,其他	8708. 9999	3
Motor vehicles parts and accessories, with special purpose, nes	特种车辆用零件、附件,其他	8708. 9960	3
Motor vehicles visual signalling equipment	机动车辆用视觉信号装置	8512. 2090	7
Motor vehicles, special purpose, nes	机动车辆,特殊用途的,其他	8705. 9090	7

Article Description	商品名称	Tariff Code	D. R.
Motorboats, other than outboard motorboats for pleasure or sports	汽艇,但装有舷外发动机的除外,娱乐或运动用	8903.9200	58
Motorcycles (including mopeds) and cycles fitted with an auxiliary motor, electric or with electrical assistant	摩托车(包括机器脚踏两用车)及装有辅助发动机的脚踏车,电动及电动助力的	8711.9010	58
Motorcycles (including mopeds) and cycles fitted with an auxiliary motor, nes	摩托车(包括机器脚踏两用车)及装有辅助发动机的脚踏车,其他	8711.9090	58
Motorcycles (including mopeds) and cycles fitted with an auxiliary motor, with reciprocating internal combustion piston engine of a cylinder capacity exceeding 100cc but not exceeding 125cc	摩托车(包括机器脚踏两用车)及装有辅助发动机的脚踏车,装有往复式活塞内燃发动机,气缸容量超过100毫升,但不超过125毫升	8711.2020	58
Motorcycles (including mopeds) and cycles fitted with an auxiliary motor, with reciprocating internal combustion piston engine of a cylinder capacity exceeding 125cc but not exceeding 150cc	摩托车(包括机器脚踏两用车)及装有辅助发动机的脚踏车,装有往复式活塞内燃发动机,气缸容量超过125毫升,但不超过150毫升	8711.2030	58
Motorcycles (including mopeds) and cycles fitted with an auxiliary motor, with reciprocating internal combustion piston engine of a cylinder capacity exceeding 150cc but not exceeding 200cc	摩托车(包括机器脚踏两用车)及装有辅助发动机的脚踏车,装有往复式活塞内燃发动机,气缸容量超过150毫升,但不超过200毫升	8711.2040	58
Motorcycles (including mopeds) and cycles fitted with an auxiliary motor, with reciprocating internal combustion piston engine of a cylinder capacity exceeding 200cc but not exceeding 250cc	摩托车(包括机器脚踏两用车)及装有辅助发动机的脚踏车,装有往复式活塞内燃发动机,气缸容量超过200毫升,但不超过250毫升	8711.2050	58
Motorcycles (including mopeds) and cycles fitted with an auxiliary motor, with reciprocating internal combustion piston engine of a cylinder capacity exceeding 250cc but not exceeding 400cc	摩托车(包括机器脚踏两用车)及装有辅助发动机的脚踏车,装有往复式活塞内燃发动机,气缸容量超过250毫升,但不超过400毫升	8711.3010	58
Motorcycles (including mopeds) and cycles fitted with an auxiliary motor, with reciprocating internal combustion piston engine of a cylinder capacity exceeding 400cc but not exceeding 500cc	摩托车(包括机器脚踏两用车)及装有辅助发动机的脚踏车,装有往复式活塞内燃发动机,气缸容量超过400毫升,但不超过500毫升	8711.3020	58
Motorcycles (including mopeds) and cycles fitted with an auxiliary motor, with reciprocating internal combustion piston engine of a cylinder capacity exceeding 500cc but not exceeding 800cc	摩托车(包括机器脚踏两用车)及装有辅助发动机的脚踏车,装有往复式活塞内燃发动机,气缸容量(排气量)超过500毫升,但不超过800毫升	8711.4000	58
Motorcycles (including mopeds) and cycles fitted with an auxiliary motor, with reciprocating internal combustion piston engine of a cylinder capacity exceeding 50cc but not exceeding 100cc	摩托车(包括机器脚踏两用车)及装有辅助发动机的脚踏车,装有往复式活塞内燃发动机,气缸容量超过50毫升,但不超过100毫升	8711.2010	58
Motorcycles (including mopeds) and cycles fitted with an auxiliary motor, with reciprocating internal combustion piston engine of a cylinder capacity exceeding 800cc	摩托车(包括机器脚踏两用车)及装有辅助发动机的脚踏车,装有往复式活塞内燃发动机,气缸容量(排气量)超过800毫升	8711.5000	58

Article Description	商品名称	Tariff Code	D. R.
Motorcycles (including mopeds) and cycles fitted with an auxiliary motor, with reciprocating internal combustion piston engine of a cylinder capacity not exceeding 50cc	摩托车(包括机器脚踏两用车)及装有辅助发动机的脚踏车,装有往复式活塞内燃发动机,气缸容量(排气量)不超过50毫升	8711.1000	58
Motorcycles(including mopeds) parts and accessoris, nes	摩托车(包括机器脚踏两用车)用零件、附件,其他	8714.1900	3
Motors of an output exceeding 375kW, DC	电动机,输出功率超过375千瓦,直流	8501.3400	8
Motors of an output exceeding 37.5W, universal AC/DC	电动机,输出功率超过37.5瓦,交直流两用	8501.2000	8
Motors of an output exceeding 750W but not exceeding 75kW, AC, multi-phase	电动机,输出功率超过750瓦,但不超过75千瓦,多相交流	8501.5200	8
Motors of an output exceeding 750W but not exceeding 75kW, DC	电动机,输出功率超过750瓦,但不超过75千瓦,直流	8501.3200	8
Motors of an output exceeding 75kW but not exceeding 375kW, DC	电动机,输出功率超过75千瓦,但不超过375千瓦,直流	8501.3300	8
Motors of an output exceeding 75kW, AC, multi-phase	电动机,输出功率超过75千瓦,多相交流	8501.5300	8
Motors of an output not exceeding 37.5W, for use in toys	电动机,输出功率不超过37.5瓦的,玩具用	8501.1010	8
Motors of an output not exceeding 37.5W, micromotors with a housing size of 20mm or more but not exceeding 39mm	电动机,输出功率不超过37.5瓦的,微电机,机座尺寸在20毫米及以上,但不超过39毫米	8501.1091	8
Motors of an output not exceeding 37.5W, nes	电动机,输出功率不超过37.5瓦的,其他	8501.1099	8
Motors of an output not exceeding 750W, AC, multi-phase	电动机,输出功率不超过750瓦,多相交流	8501.5100	8
Motors of an output not exceeding 750W, DC	电动机,输出功率不超过750瓦,直流	8501.3100	8
Motors parts, nes	电动机的零件,其他	8503.0090	3
Motors parts, of an output not exceeding 37.5W, for use in toys	电动机的零件,输出功率不超过37.5瓦的,玩具用	8503.0010	3
Motors parts, of an output not exceeding 37.5W, micromotors with a housing size of 20mm or more but not exceeding 39mm	电动机的零件,输出功率不超过37.5瓦的,微电机,机座尺寸在20毫米及以上,但不超过39毫米	8503.0010	3
Motors, AC, single-phase, nes	电动机,单相交流,其他	8501.4000	8
Mould bases	型模底板	8480.2000	7
Mould release preparations, based on lubricants, containing petroleum oils or oils obtained from bituminous minerals	脱模剂,以润滑剂为基本成分的,含有石油或从沥青矿物提取的油类	3403.1900	2368
Mould release preparations, based on lubricants, nes	脱模剂,以润滑剂为基本成分的,其他	3403.9900	2368
Moulding boxes for metal foundry	金属铸造用型箱	8480.1000	7
Moulding boxes for metal foundry	型箱,金属铸造用	8480.1000	7

Article Description	商品名称	Tariff Code	D. R.
Moulding forming machines, for agglomerating, shaping or moulding solid mineral fuels, ceramic paste, unhardened cements, plastering materials or other mineral products in powder or paste form	模压成型机,固体矿物燃料、陶瓷坯泥、未硬化水泥、石膏材料或其他粉状、浆状矿产品的粘聚或成形用	8474.8020	7
Moulding machines, for working wood, cork, bone, hard rubber, hard plastics or similar hard materials	切削成形机器,加工木材、软木、骨、硬质橡胶、硬质塑料或类似硬质材料的	8465.9200	7
Moulding or forming machinery, for moulding or retreading pneumatic tyres or for moulding otherwise forming inner tubes	模塑或成型的机器,用于充气轮胎模塑或翻新的机器及内胎的	8477.5100	7
Moulding or forming machinery, nes	模塑或成型机器,其他	8477.5900	7
Moulding patterns	阳模	8480.3000	7
Moulds for glass	玻璃用型模	8480.5000	7
Moulds for glass	型模,玻璃用	8480.5000	7
Moulds for metal or metal carbides, nes	金属、硬质合金用型模,其他	8480.4900	7
Moulds for mineral materials	矿物材料用型模	8480.6000	7
Moulds for mineral materials	型模,矿物材料用	8480.6000	7
Moulds for rubber or plastics, compression types	压模,塑料或橡胶用	8480.7100	7
Moulds for rubber or plastics, injection types	注模,塑料或橡胶用	8480.7100	7
Moulds for rubber or plastics, nes	塑料或橡胶用,其他	8480.7900	7
Moulds of compression types, for metal or metal carbides	压模,金属、硬质合金用型模	8480.4100	7
Moulds of injection types, for metal or metal carbides	注模,金属、硬质合金用型模	8480.4100	7
Mountain bicycle	山地自行车	8712.0030	8
Mounted brake linings	装在蹄片上的制动摩擦片	8708.3010	3
Mountings, fittings and similar articles suitable for motor vehicles	附件及架座,贱金属制,机动车辆用	8302.3000	256
Mountings, fittings and similar articles, of base metal, nes	附件及架座,贱金属制,其他	8302.4900	256
Mountings, fittings and similar articles, of base metal, suitable for furniture	附件及架座,贱金属制,家具用	8302.4200	256
Mountings, fittings and similar articles, suitable for buildings, of base metal	附件及架座,建筑用,贱金属制	8302.4100	256
Mouses	鼠标器	8471.6072	
Mouth organs	口琴	9205.9030	5
Mouth-blown sound signalling instruments	口吹音响信号器	9208.9000	5
Movement sets, of clock	机芯套装件,钟的	9110.9090	1
Movement sets, of watches	机芯套装件,表的	9110.1100	1
Movements for laser video compact disk player, of video recording or reproducing apparatus	激光视盘机的机芯	8522.9031	3
Moving machinery, for earth, minerals or ores, not self-propelled, nes	运送机械,对泥土、矿物或矿石的,非自推进的,其他	8430.6990	5

Article Description	商品名称	Tariff Code	D. R.
Moving machinery, for earth, minerals or ores, self-propelled, nes	运送机械,对泥土、矿物或矿石的,自推进的,其他	8430. 5090	5
Mowers for lawns, parks or sports grounds, nes	割草机,草坪、公园或运动场地用,其他	8433. 1900	7
Mowers for lawns, parks or sports grounds, powered, with the cutting device rotating in a horizontal plane	割草机,草坪、公园或运动场地用,机动的,切割装置在同一水平面上旋转的	8433. 1100	7
Mowers parts	割草机零件	8433. 9090	
Mowers, including cutter bars for tractor mounting, nes	割草机,包括牵引装置用的刀具杆,其他	8433. 2000	
Mucilages and thickeners, nes	胶液及增稠剂,其他	1302. 3990	34
Mucilages and thickeners, preparations of seaweeds and other algae	胶液及增稠剂,海草及其他藻类制品	1302. 3919	3
Mucilages and thickeners, whether or not modified, derived from locust beans, locust bean seeds or guar seeds	胶液及增稠剂,从刺槐豆、刺槐豆子或瓜尔豆制得的,不论是否改性	1302. 3200	4
Mufflers, knitted or crocheted, nes	围巾,针织或钩编的,其他	6117. 1090	2456
Mufflers, knitted or crocheted, of fine goats hair	围巾,针织或钩编的,山羊绒制	6117. 1011	2456
Mufflers, knitted or crocheted, of other fine animal hair	围巾,针织或钩编的,其他动物细毛制	6117. 1019	2456
Mufflers, knitted or crocheted, of wool	围巾,针织或钩编的,羊毛制	6117. 1020	2456
Mufflers, not knitted or crocheted, of artificial fibres	围巾,非针织或钩编的,人造纤维制	6214. 4000	2456
Mufflers, not knitted or crocheted, of goats fine animal hair	围巾,非针织或钩编的,山羊绒制	6214. 2020	2456
Mufflers, not knitted or crocheted, of other fine animal hair	围巾,非针织或钩编的,其他动物细毛制	6214. 2090	2456
Mufflers, not knitted or crocheted, of other textile materials	围巾,非针织或钩编的,其他纺织材料制	6214. 9000	2456
Mufflers, not knitted or crocheted, of silk or silk waste	围巾,非针织或钩编的,丝或绢丝制	6214. 1000	2456
Mufflers, not knitted or crocheted, of synthetic fibres	围巾,非针织或钩编的,合成纤维制	6214. 3000	2456
Mufflers, not knitted or crocheted, of wool	围巾,非针织或钩编的,羊毛制	6214. 2010	2456
Muffles, containing by weight more than 50% of alumina(Al_2O_3) or of a mixture of compound of alumina and of silica(SiO_2)	马弗罩,含有按重量计超过50%的三氧化二铝或三氧化二铝和二氧化硅的混合物或化合物	6903. 2000	6
Muffles, containing by weight more than 50% of graphite or other carbon or of a mixture of these products	马弗罩,含有按重量计超过50%的石墨、其他碳或其混合物	6903. 1000	6
Mulberries, fresh	桑椹,鲜的	0810. 2000	1
Mulberries, frozen	桑椹,冷冻的	0811. 2000	1
Mulberry silk-worm silk fabrics, containing 85% or more by weight of silk or silk waste, nes	桑蚕丝机织物,按重量计丝或绢丝含量在85%及以上,其他	5007. 2019	4568

Article Description	商品名称	Tariff Code	D. R.
Mulberry silk-worm silk fabrics, unbleached (unscoured or scoured) or bleached, containing 85% or more by weight of silk or silk waste	桑蚕丝机织物,未漂白或漂白,按重量计丝或绢丝含量在85%及以上	5007.2011	4568
Mulberry silk-worm silk, doupion	桑蚕丝,双宫丝	5002.0013	45
Mulberry silk-worm silk, home reeled	桑蚕丝,土丝	5002.0012	45
Mulberry silk-worm silk, nes	桑蚕丝,其他	5002.0019	45
Mulberry silk-worm silk, plant reeled (filature silk)	桑蚕丝,厂丝	5002.0011	45
Mules	骡	0101.9090	34
Mullite	富铝红柱石	2508.6000	134
Multi station transfer machines, for working metal	组合机床,多工位的,加工金属的	8457.3000	7
Multimeters parts and accessories	万用表的零件、附件	9030.9000	3
Multimeters with a recording device	万用表,带记录装置	9030.3200	
Multimeters without a recording device, of measuring range of 5.5 or less, digital	万用表,不带记录装置,量程在五位半及以下的,数字的	9030.3110	
Multimeters without a recording device, nes	万用表,不带记录装置,其他	9030.3190	7
Multiple or cabled yarn, not put up for retail sale, nes	多股纱线或缆线,非供零售用,其他	5402.6990	3468
Multiplewalled insulating units of glass, nes	多层隔温、隔音玻璃组件,其他	7008.0090	234
Multi-station transfer machines, for working metal	多工位组合机床,加工金属的	8457.3000	7
Municipal waste	城市垃圾	3825.1000	34
Mushroom sauce	磨菇酱油	2103.9090	268
Mushroom spawn	蘑菇菌丝	0602.9010	
Mushrooms and truffles, dried, nes	蘑菇及块菌,其他,干的	0712.3990	4
Mushrooms and truffles, in airtight containers, nes	罐头,蘑菇及块菌,其他	2003.9010	248
Mushrooms and truffles, nes, in brine, provisionally preserved, but unsuitable in that state for immediate consumption	蘑菇及块菌,其他,盐水的,暂时保藏,但不适合直接使用的	0711.5919	34
Mushrooms and truffles, nes, prepared or preserved otherwise than by vinegar or acetic acid	蘑菇及块菌,其他,用醋或醋酸以外的其他方法制作或保藏的	2003.9090	248
Mushrooms and truffles, nes, provisionally preserved, but unsuitable in that state for immediate consumption	蘑菇及块菌,其他,暂时保藏,但不适合直接使用的	0711.5990	34
Mushrooms of the genus agaricus, dried	伞菌属蘑菇,干的	0712.3100	4
Mushrooms of the genus agaricus, fresh or chilled	伞菌属蘑菇,鲜或冷藏的	0709.5100	1
Mushrooms of the genus agaricus, nes, in brine, provisionally preserved, but unsuitable in that state for immediate consumption	伞菌属蘑菇,其他,盐水的,暂时保藏,但不适合直接使用的	0711.5119	34
Mushrooms of the genus agaricus, nes, provisionally preserved, but unsuitable in that state for immediate consumption	伞菌属蘑菇,其他,暂时保藏,但不适合直接使用的	0711.5190	34
Mushrooms, nes	蘑菇,其他	0709.5990	1
Mushrooms, of agaricus, in airtight containers	罐头,蘑菇,伞菌属	2003.1090	248
Mushrooms, of agaricus, in airtight containers, nes	罐头,蘑菇,伞菌属,其他	2003.1019	248

M

Article Description	商品名称	Tariff Code	D. R.
Music, printed or in manuscript, whether or not bound or illustrated	乐谱原稿或印本,不论是否装订或印有插图	4904.0000	5
Musical boxes	八音盒	9208.1000	5
Musical boxes	百音盒	9208.1000	5
Musical instruments, the sound of which is produced or must be amplified electrically, nes	乐器,通过电产生或扩大声音的,其他	9207.9000	5
Musical saws	乐锯	9208.9000	5
Musk	麝香	0510.0030	14
Mussels (Mytilus spp., Perna spp.), for cultivation	贻贝,种苗	0307.3110	3
Mussels (Mytilus spp., Perna spp.), frozen, dried, salted or in brine	贻贝,其他,冻、干、盐腌或盐渍的	0307.3900	14
Mussels (Mytilus spp., Perna spp.), live, fresh or chilled	贻贝,其他,活或鲜或冷的	0307.3190	1
Mustard flour and meal and prepared mustard	芥子粉及其调制品	2103.3000	268
Mustard oil and frac tions thereof, nes	芥子油及其分离品,其他	1514.9900	4
Mustard oil, crude, nes	芥子油,其他,初榨的	1514.9190	4
Mustard pickles	酸菜	2001.9090	48
Mustard seeds for cultivation	芥菜籽,种用	1207.5010	3
Mustard seeds, nes	芥菜籽,其他	1207.5090	3
Mutual inductor, having a power handling capacity exceeding 1kVA but not exceeding 16kVA	互感器,额定容量超过1千伏安,但不超过16千伏安	8504.3210	78
Mutual inductor, having a power handling capacity not exceeding 1kVA	互感器,额定容量不超过1千伏安	8504.3110	78
Muzzles for any animal, of any material	口套,适合各种动物用	4201.0000	1458
Muzzle-loading firearms	前装枪	9303.1000	
Myrrh	没药	1301.9020	
M-cresol	间甲酚	2907.1211	36
M-dihydroxybenzene (resorcinol) and its salts	间苯二酚及其盐	2907.2100	36
M-methylbenzoic acid	邻甲基苯甲酸	2916.3910	36
M-nitrochlorobenzene	间硝基氯化苯	2904.9012	36
M-phenoxy benzalcohol	间苯氧基苄醇	2909.4910	36
M-phthalic acid	间苯二甲酸	2917.3910	36
M-phthalonitrile	间苯二甲腈	2926.9020	36
M-xylene	间二甲苯	2902.4200	6

M

N

Article Description	商品名称	Tariff Code	D. R.
N,N-bis(2-chloroethyl) ethylamine	N,N-二(2-氯乙基)乙胺	2921.1930	36
N,N-bis(2-chloroethyl) methylamine	N,N-二(2-氯乙基)甲胺	2921.1940	36
N,N-dialkyl (me, et, n-pr or i-pr) aminoethyl-2-chlorides and corresponding protonated salts	二烷(甲、乙、正丙或异丙)氨基乙基-2-氯及其质子化盐	2921.1960	36
N,N-dialkyl(me, et, n-pr or i-pr) phosphoramidic dihalides	二烷(甲、乙、正丙或异丙)氨基膦酰二卤	2929.9020	36
N,N-dialkyl-(me,et,n-pr or i-pr) aminoethane-2-ols and corresponding protonated salts,nes	二烷(甲、乙、正丙或异丙)氨基乙-2-醇及其质子化盐,其他	2922.1929	36
N, N-diethylaminoethanol and corresponding protonated salts	二乙氨基乙醇及其质子化盐	2922.1922	36
N,N-dimetheylformamide	二甲基甲酰胺	2924.1910	36
N, N-dimethylaminoethanol and corresponding protonated salts	二甲氨基乙醇及其质子化盐	2922.1921	36
Nacrite	珍珠陶土	2507.0090	1346
Nail brushes	指甲刷	9603.2900	
Nail files	修指甲锉	8214.2000	256
Nails and powder thereof	甲及其粉末	0507.9090	14
Nails and similar articles,of copper or of iron or steel with heads of copper	钉及类似品,铜制或钢铁制带铜头的	7415.1000	56
Nails and similar articles, of iron or steel, whether or not with heads of other material, but excluding such articles with heads of copper	钢铁制的钉及类似品,不论钉头是否用其他材料制成,但不包括铜头钉	7317.0000	36
Nails,of aluminium	钉,铝制	7616.1000	36
Name-plates, of base metal, excluding those of heading No. 94.05	铭牌,贱金属制,税号 94.05 的货品除外	8310.0000	256
Naphtha	石脑油	2710.1120	6
Naphthalene, crude	萘,粗萘	2707.4000	6
Naphthalene, refined	萘,精萘	2902.9020	6
Naphthalene,crude	粗萘	2707.4000	6
Naphthalene,refined	精萘	2902.9020	6
Naphthols salts	萘酚盐	2907.1590	36
Naphthols,nes	萘酚,其他	2907.1590	36
Napkins and napkin liners for babies and similar sanitary articles, of paper pulp, paper, cellulose wadding or webs of cellulose fibres	婴儿尿布、尿布衬里及类似的卫生用品,纸浆、纸、纤维素絮纸或纤维素纤维网纸制的	4818.4000	568
Napkins(diapers),for babies,of cotton	尿布,非针织或钩编的,婴儿的,棉制,	6209.2010	2456

Article Description	商品名称	Tariff Code	D. R.
Narrow anticorrosive photographic plate for printed circuit processing, unexposed, without perforations, of a width exceeding 105mm but not exceeding 610mm	印刷电路板制造用光致抗蚀干膜,未曝光的,无齿孔的,宽度超过105毫米,但不超过610毫米	3702.4422	12368
Narrow fabrics made of velvet impregnated with rubber, for covering weaving spindles (weaving beams)	狭幅丝绒织物,用橡胶浸渍的、用于包覆纺锤(织轴)的	5911.1010	
Narrow woven fabrics of cotton	狭幅机织物,棉制	5806.3100	468
Narrow woven fabrics of cotton or bast fibres, pile and chenille fabrics	狭幅机织物,棉或麻制,起绒及绳的	5806.1010	468
Narrow woven fabrics of man-made fibres	狭幅机织物,化学纤维制	5806.3200	468
Narrow woven fabrics of silk or silk waste	狭幅机织物,丝及绢丝制	5806.3910	468
Narrow woven fabrics of textile materials, pile and chenille fabrics, nes	狭幅机织物,纺织材料制,起绒及绳的,其他	5806.1090	468
Narrow woven fabrics of wool or fine animal hair	狭幅机织物,羊毛或动物细毛制	5806.3920	468
Narrow woven fabrics, containing by weight 5% or more of elastomeric yarn or rubber thread	狭幅机织物,按重量计弹性纱线或橡胶线含量在5%及以上的	5806.2000	468
Narrow woven fabrics, nes	狭幅机织物,其他	5806.3990	468
Natural boric acid, containing not more than 85% of H_3BO_3 calculated on the dry weight	天然粗硼酸,含硼酸干重不超过85%	2528.9000	6
Natural gas, in gaseous state	天然气,气态的	2711.2100	1468
Natural gas, liquefied	天然气,液化的	2711.1100	1468
Natural gums	天然树胶	1301.9090	
Natural or artificial abrasive powder or grain, on a base of paper or paperboard only	砂纸	6805.2000	246
Natural or artificial abrasive powder or grain, on a base of paper or paperboard only	磨料或颗粒,天然或人造的,以纸为底的	6805.2000	246
Natural polymers, in primary forms, nes	天然聚合物,初级形状的,其他	3913.9000	146
Natural polymers, modified, in primary forms	改性天然聚合物,初级形状的	3913.9000	146
Natural rubber in other forms	天然橡胶,其他形状的	4001.2900	12
Natural rubber latex, whether or not prevulcanized	天然胶乳,不论是否预硫化	4001.1000	12
Natural rubber (including latex) mixtures with synthetic rubber (including latex)	天然橡胶(含胶乳与)合成橡胶(含胶乳)的混合物	4002.8000	136
Natural rubber (TSNR), technically specified	天然橡胶(TSNR),技术分类的	4001.2200	12
Natural sands, nes	天然砂,其他	2505.9000	
Natural sodium borates and concentrates thereof (whether or not calcined)	天然硼砂及其精矿(不论是否煅烧)	2528.1000	
Natural steatite, crushed or powdered	冻石,已破碎或已研粉	2526.2010	4
Natural steatite, not crushed, not powdered	冻石,未破碎及未研粉	2526.1010	4

N

Article Description	商品名称	Tariff Code	D. R.
Natural stone (including slate) mosaic cubes and the like, whether or not on a backing, the largest surface area of which is capable of being enclosed in a square the side of which is less than 7cm	天然石料(包括板岩)制的镶嵌石(马赛克)及类似品,不论是否有衬背,其最大表面以可置入边长小于7厘米的方格为限	6802. 1090	3468
Natural stone and articles thereof, worked, nes	天然石料及其制品,已加工的,其他	6802. 9990	3468
Natural stone carvings	天然石料石刻	6802. 9910	3468
Natural stones artificially coloured granules, chippings and powder, nes	天然石料经人工染色的石粒、石片及石粉,其他	6802. 1090	3468
Natural stones tiles, cubes and similar articles, whether or not rectangular (including square), the largest surface area of which is capable of being enclosed in a square the side of which is less than 7cm, nes	天然石料的砖、瓦、方块及类似品,不论是否为矩形(包括正方形),其最大表面以可置入边长小于7厘米的方格为限其他	6802. 1090	3468
Natural waters, not containing added sugar or other sweetening matter or flavoured	天然水,未加糖或其他甜物质及未加味的	2201. 9010	248
Navigation instruments and appliances parts and accessories, nes	导航仪器及装置的零件、附件,其他	9014. 9090	3
Navigation instruments and appliances (other than compasses), for aeronautical or space, nes	导航仪器及装置(罗盘除外),航空或航天用,其他	9014. 2090	7
Navigation instruments and appliances (other than compasses), nes	导航仪器及装置(罗盘除外),其他	9014. 8000	7
Nd-Fe-B alloy, nes	钕铁硼合金,其他	7202. 9919	
Nd-Fe-B magnetic powder	钕铁硼磁粉	7202. 9912	6
Nd-Fe-B rapidly solidified permenent megnetic powder	钕铁硼速凝永磁片	7202. 9911	6
Nectarines, fresh	油桃,鲜的	0809. 3000	1
Needle roller bearings	滚针轴承	8482. 4000	5
Needleloom felt	针刺机制毡呢	5602. 1000	46
Needles bearings parts	滚针轴承零件	8482. 9100	3
Needles for knitting machines	织针,针织机的	8448. 5190	3
Needles for sutures	缝合用针	9018. 3220	
Needles for sutures	针,缝合用	9018. 3220	
Needles, tubular metal, used in medical, surgical, dental or veterinary sciences	针头,金属管状,医疗、外科、牙科或兽医用	9018. 3210	
Needle-worked tapestries	手工针绣嵌花装饰毯	5805. 0010	468
Neemoil and its fractions	印楝油及其分离品	1515. 9020	
Negatoscopes	负片显示器	9010. 5010	7
Neodymium	钕	2805. 3011	56
Neodymium oxide	氧化钕	2846. 9013	
Nepheline	霞石	2529. 3000	13
Nepheline syenite	霞石正长岩	2529. 3000	13
Nests, salanganes	金丝燕窝	0410. 0010	3

Article Description	商品名称	Tariff Code	D. R.
Net making machines	编织网机	8447. 9090	7
Nets of textile materials, nes	网,纺织材料制,其他	5608. 9000	34
Netting of man-made textile materials, nes	网料,化学纤维材料制,其他	5608. 1900	34
Netting, knotted of twine, cordage or rope, nes	网料,线、绳或索结制的,其他	5608. 9000	34
Nevirapine and their salts	奈韦拉平及盐	2934. 9940	36
Newspapers, journals and periodicals, appearing at least four times a week	报纸、杂志及期刊,每周至少出版四次	4902. 1000	
Newspapers, journals and periodicals, nes	报纸、杂志及期刊,其他	4902. 9000	
Newsprint, in rolls or sheets, of width exceeding 36cm or in roll or one side exceeding 36cm and other side exceeding 15cm in rectangular sheets	新闻纸,成卷或成张的,卷宽度超过36厘米,或长超过36厘米且宽超过15厘米	4801. 0000	68
Newsprint, of which more than 10% by weight of the total fibre content consists of fibres obtained by a mechanical or chemi-mechanical process	新闻纸,所含用机械或化学-机械方法制得的纤维超过全部纤维重量的10%	4802. 6910	3468
Newsprint, of which more than 10% by weight of the total fibre content consists of fibres obtained by a mechanical or chemi-mechanical process, in rolls	新闻纸,所含用机械或化学-机械方法制得的纤维超过全部纤维重量的10%,成卷的	4802. 6110	3468
Niccolite	红砷镍矿	2604. 0000	146
Nickel anodes for electroplating	镍阳极,电镀用	7508. 9010	6
Nickel articles, for technical use	镍制品,工业用,其他	7508. 9080	6
Nickel articles, for technical use, nes	网及格栅,工业用,其他	7508. 1080	6
Nickel articles, nes	镍制品,其他	7508. 9090	6
Nickel chlorides	氯化镍	2827. 3500	
Nickel mattes	镍锍	7501. 1000	4
Nickel ores and concentrates	镍矿砂及其精矿	2604. 0000	146
Nickel oxide sinters and intermediate products of nickel metallurgy, nes	氧化镍烧结物及镍冶炼的中间产品,其他	7501. 2090	4
Nickel oxides and hydroxides	镍的氧化物及氢氧化物	2825. 4000	
Nickel powders and flakes, not alloyed	镍粉及片状粉末,非合金的	7504. 0010	46
Nickel powders and flakes, of alloys	镍粉及片状粉末,合金的	7504. 0020	
Nickel silver	德银	7403. 2900	146
Nickel sulphates	镍的硫酸盐	2833. 2400	
Nickel, alloys, unwrought	镍合金,未锻轧的	7502. 2000	46
Nickel, not alloyed, containing 99. 99% or more by total weight of nickel and cobalt, but containing cobalt not exceeding 0. 005%	镍,非合金的,按重量计镍、钴总量在99. 99%及以上的,但钴含量不超过0. 005%	7502. 1010	46
Nickel, not alloyed, nes	镍,非合金的,其他	7502. 1090	46
Nickel-cadmium accumulators	镍镉蓄电池	8507. 3000	68
Nickel-hydrogen accumulators	镍氢蓄电池	8507. 8010	68
Nickel-iron accumulators	镍铁蓄电池	8507. 4000	68
Nicomorphine (INN) and salts	尼可吗啡(INN)及盐	2939. 1100	34
Nicotine and its salts	烟碱及其盐	2939. 9910	34

Article Description	商品名称	Tariff Code	D. R.
Nightdresses and pyjamas, knitted or crocheted, for women or girls, nes	睡衣及睡衣裤,针织或钩编的,女式,其他	6108.3990	2456
Nightdresses and pyjamas, knitted or crocheted, for women or girls, of cotton	睡衣及睡衣裤,针织或钩编的,女式,棉制	6108.3100	2456
Nightdresses and pyjamas, knitted or crocheted, for women or girls, of man-made fibres	睡衣及睡衣裤,针织或钩编的,女式,化学纤维制	6108.3200	2456
Nightdresses and pyjamas, knitted or crocheted, for women or girls, of silk or silk waste	睡衣及睡衣裤,针织或钩编的,女式,丝及绢丝制	6108.3910	2456
Nightdresses and pyjamas, not knitted or crocheted, for women or girls, nes	睡衣及睡衣裤,非针织或钩编的,女式,其他	6208.2990	2456
Nightdresses and pyjamas, not knitted or crocheted, for women or girls, of cotton	睡衣及睡衣裤,非针织或钩编的,女式,棉制	6208.2100	2456
Nightdresses and pyjamas, not knitted or crocheted, for women or girls, of man-made fibres	睡衣及睡衣裤,非针织或钩编的,女式,化学纤维制	6208.2200	2456
Nightdresses and pyjamas, not knitted or crocheted, for women or girls, of silk or silk waste	睡衣及睡衣裤,非针织或钩编的,女式,丝及绢丝制	6208.2910	2456
Nightshirts and pyjamas, knitted or crocheted, for men or boys, nes	长睡衣及睡衣裤,针织或钩编的男式,其他	6107.2990	2456
Nightshirts and pyjamas, knitted or crocheted, for men or boys, of cotton	长睡衣及睡衣裤,针织或钩编的男式,棉制	6107.2100	2456
Nightshirts and pyjamas, knitted or crocheted, for men or boys, of man-made fibres	长睡衣及睡衣裤,针织或钩编的男式,化学纤维制	6107.2200	2456
Nightshirts and pyjamas, knitted or crocheted, for men or boys, of silk or silk waste	长睡衣及睡衣裤,针织或钩编的男式,丝及绢丝制	6107.2910	2456
Nightshirts and pyjamas, not knitted or crocheted, for men or boys, nes	长睡衣及睡衣裤,非针织或钩编的,男式,其他	6207.2990	2456
Nightshirts and pyjamas, not knitted or crocheted, for men or boys, of cotton	长睡衣及睡衣裤,非针织或钩编的,男式,棉制	6207.2100	2456
Nightshirts and pyjamas, not knitted or crocheted, for men or boys, of man-made fibres	长睡衣及睡衣裤,非针织或钩编的,男式,化学纤维制	6207.2200	2456
Nightshirts and pyjamas, not knitted or crocheted, for men or boys, of silk or silk waste	长睡衣及睡衣裤,非针织或钩编的,男式,丝及绢丝制	6207.2910	2456
Nigrosines, as synthetic organic colouring matter	苯胺黑	3204.1300	345
Nimetazepam (INN) ; salts thereof	硝甲西泮(INN)以及盐	2933.9100	36
Niobite	铌铁矿	2615.9090	146
Niobium articles, nes	铌制品	8112.9940	16
Niobium ores and concentrates	铌矿砂及其精矿	2615.9010	146
Niobium powders	铌粉末	8112.9240	16
Niobium, unwrought	铌,未锻轧	8112.9240	16
Nitrates, nes, inorganic	硝酸盐,其他	2834.2990	
Nitrazepam (INN); salts thereof	硝西泮(INN)以及盐	2933.9100	36
Nitric acid	硝酸	2808.0000	6
Nitrides, whether or not chemically defined	氮化物,不论是否已有化学定义	2850.0000	

Article Description	商品名称	Tariff Code	D. R.
Nitrile-function compounds, nes	腈基化合物,其他	2926.9090	36
Nitrites, inorganic	亚硝酸盐,无机的	2834.1000	
Nitrobenzene	硝基苯	2904.2010	36
Nitrogen	氮	2804.3000	
Nitroguanidine	硝基胍	2929.9090	36
Nitrostarch	硝化淀粉	3505.1000	36
Nitrotoluene and nitrochlorobenzene	硝基甲苯	2904.2020	36
Noil silk fabrics, nes	细丝机织物,其他	5007.1090	4568
Noil silk fabrics, unbleached or bleached	细丝机织物,未漂白或漂白	5007.1010	4568
Noils of fine animal hair	动物细毛落毛	5103.1090	5
Noils of wool	羊毛落毛	5103.1010	5
Nondestructive examinations apparatus (other than apparatus for radiological examinations), nes	探伤检测仪器(射线探伤仪除外),无损的,其他	9031.8039	7
Nondestructive examinations apparatus, eddy examinations	探伤检测仪,涡流的	9031.8033	
Nondestructive examinations apparatus, magnetic	探伤检测仪,磁粉的	9031.8032	
Nondestructive examinations apparatus, ultrasonic	探伤检测仪,超声波的	9031.8031	
Nonene, light oils	壬烯,轻油	2710.1191	6
Nonthreaded articles, of iron of steel, nes	无螺纹制品,钢铁制的,其他	7318.2900	268
Nonwoven products of glass fibres, nes	无纺产品,玻璃纤维制,其他	7019.3900	56
Nonwovens finishing machinery	无纺织物整理机器	8449.0090	7
Nonwovens of man-made filaments, weighing more than $25g/m^2$ but not more than $70g/m^2$, impregnated, coated, covered or laminated	无纺织物,化学纤维长丝制,每平方米重量超过25克,但不超过70克,经浸渍、涂布、包覆或层压	5603.1210	46
Nonwovens of man-made filaments, weighing more than $25g/m^2$ but not more than $70g/m^2$, nes	无纺织物,化学纤维长丝制,每平方米重量超过25克,但不超过70克,其他	5603.1290	46
Nonwovens of man-made filaments, weighing not more than $25g/m^2$, impregnated, coated, covered or laminated	无纺织物,化学纤维长丝制,每平方米重量不超过25克,经浸渍、涂布、包覆或层压	5603.1110	46
Nonwovens of man-made filaments, weighing not more than $25g/m^2$, nes	无纺织物,化学纤维长丝制,每平方米重量不超过25克,其他	5603.1190	46
Nonwovens of man-made filaments, weighing more than $150g/m^2$, impregnated, coated, covered or laminated	无纺织物,化学纤维长丝制,每平方米重量超过150克,经浸渍、涂布、包覆或层压	5603.1410	46
Nonwovens of man-made filaments, weighing more than $150g/m^2$, nes	无纺织物,化学纤维长丝制,每平方米重量超过150克,其他	5603.1490	46
Nonwovens of man-made filaments, weighing more than $70g/m^2$ but not more than $150g/m^2$, impregnated, coated, covered or laminated	无纺织物,化学纤维长丝制,每平方米重量超过70克,但不超过150克,经浸渍、涂布、包覆或层压	5603.1310	46

Article Description	商品名称	Tariff Code	D. R.
Nonwovens of man-made filaments, weighing more than 70g/m² but not more than 150g/m², nes	无纺织物,化学纤维长丝制,每平方米重量超过 70 克,但不超过 150 克其他	5603. 1390	46
Nonwovens, weighing more than 150g/m², impregnated, coated, covered or laminated	无纺织物,每平方米重量超过 150 克,经浸渍、涂布、包覆或层压	5603. 9410	46
Nonwovens, weighing more than 150g/m², nes	无纺织物,每平方米重量超过 150 克,其他	5603. 9490	46
Nonwovens, weighing more than 25g/m² but not more than 70g/m², impregnated, coated, covered or laminated	无纺织物,每平方米重量超过 25 克,但不超过 70 克,经浸渍、涂布、包覆或层压	5603. 9210	46
Nonwovens, weighing more than 25g/m² but not more than 70g/m², nes	无纺织物,每平方米重量超过 25 克,但不超过 70 克,其他	5603. 9290	46
Nonwovens, weighing more than 70g/m² but not more than 150g/m², impregnated, coated, covered or laminated	无纺织物,每平方米重量超过 70 克,但不超过 150 克,经浸渍、涂布、包覆或层压	5603. 9310	46
Nonwovens, weighing more than 70g/m² but not more than 150g/m², nes	无纺织物,每平方米重量超过 70 克,但不超过 150 克,其他	5603. 9390	46
Nonwovens, weighing not more than 25g/m², impregnated, coated, covered or laminated, nes	无纺织物,每平方米重量不超过 25 克,经浸渍、涂布、包覆或层压,其他	5603. 9110	46
Nonwovens, weighing not more than 25g/m², nes	无纺织物,每平方米重量不超过 25 克,其他	5603. 9190	46
Nonylphenol	壬基酚	2907. 1310	36
Non-alcoholic beverages, nes	无酒精饮料,其他	2202. 9000	268
Non-driving axles and parts of cross-country cars (4WD)	非驱动的桥及其零件,越野车(4 轮驱动)用	8708. 5085	3
Non-driving axles and parts of dumpers	非驱动的桥及其零件,自卸车用	8708. 5083	3
Non-driving axles and parts of motor vehicles with 30 seats or more	非驱动的桥及其零件,30 座及以上客运机动车辆用	8708. 5082	3
Non-driving axles and parts of motor vehicles with special purpose	非驱动的桥及其零件,特种车辆用	8708. 5086	3
Non-driving axles and parts of saloon cars	非驱动的桥及其零件,小轿车用	8708. 5084	3
Non-driving axles and parts of tractors	非驱动的桥及其零件,拖拉机的	8708. 5081	3
Non-driving axles and parts, nes	非驱动的桥及其零件,其他	8708. 5089	3
Non-refractory surfacing preparations for facades, indoor walls, floors, ceilings or the like	非耐火涂面制剂,涂门面、内墙、地板、天花板等用	3214. 9000	36
Noodles, uncooked, containing eggs	面条,生的,含蛋的	1902. 1100	46
Noodles, uncooked, nes	面条,生的,其他	1902. 1900	46
Nordazepam(INN); salts thereof	去甲西泮(INN)以及盐	2933. 9100	36
Normethadone (INN) and salts thereof	去甲美沙酮以及它们的盐	2922. 3100	36
Northem pandalus(pandalus), frozen	北方长额虾,冻的	0306. 1312	18
Notching machines, for working metal, nes	开槽机床,加工金属用,其他	8462. 4900	7
Notching machines, numerically controlled, for working metal	开槽机床,数控的,加工金属用,其他	8462. 4190	7

Article Description	商品名称	Tariff Code	D. R.
Note books, of paper or paperboard	笔记本,纸或纸板制的	4820. 1000	
Novelty jokes	嬉戏品	9505. 9000	5
Nuclear reactors fuel elements, non-irradiated	核反应堆燃料元件,未辐照	8401. 3010	2
Nuclear reactor internals	核反应堆的堆内构件	8401. 4020	2
Nuclear reactors	核反应堆	8401. 1000	2
Nuclear reactors associated assembly, non-irradiated	核反应堆的相关组件,未辐照	8401. 4010	2
Nuclear reactors cartridges, non-irradiated	核反应堆释热元件,的未辐照	8401. 3010	2
Nuclear reactors fuel elements parts, non-irradiated	核反应堆燃料元件的零件,未辐照	8401. 3090	2
Nuclear reactors parts, nes	核反应堆零件,其他	8401. 4090	2
Nucleic acids and their salts	核酸及其盐	2934. 9930	36
Numbering stamps, designed for operating in the hand	编号戳,手用	9611. 0000	
Numbers, of base metal, excluding those of heading No. 94. 05	号码,贱金属制,税号 94. 05 的货品除外	8310. 0000	256
Numerical control panels, for a voltage not exceeding 1000V, equipped with two or more switching or protecting or connecting apparatus, nes	数控装置,用于电压不超过 1000 伏的线路,装有两个或多个开关、保护或连接用的电器装置,其他	8537. 1019	78
Nutmeg	肉豆蔻	0908. 1000	
Nuts preparation machinery	坚果加工机器	8438. 6000	
Nuts preparation machinery parts	坚果加工机器的零件	8438. 9000	3
Nuts, nes	干果,其他	0813. 4090	34
Nuts, nes, fresh or dried	坚果,其他,鲜或干的	0802. 9090	134
Nuts, nes, frozen	坚果,其他,冷冻的	0811. 9090	1
Nuts, nes, in airtight containers	果仁,其他,罐头	2008. 1920	248
Nuts, nes, otherwise prepared, or preserved	果仁,其他,用其他方法制作或保藏的	2008. 1999	248
Nuts, nes, provisionally preserved, but unsuitable in that state for immediate consumption	坚果,其他,暂时保藏,但不适于直接食用的	0812. 9000	34
Nuts, of aluminium	螺母,铝制	7616. 1000	36
Nuts, of copper	螺母,铜制	7415. 3390	56
Nuts, of iron of steel	螺母,钢铁制的	7318. 1600	268
Nylon or other polyamides filament tow	尼龙或聚酰胺长丝丝束	5501. 1000	68
Nylon or other polyamides high tenacity yarn woven fabrics	尼龙或聚酰胺高强力纱纺制的机织物	5407. 1010	2468
Nylon or other polyamides staple fibres, carded, combed or otherwise processed for spinning	尼龙或聚酰胺短纤,已梳或经其他纺前加工	5506. 1000	68
Nylon or other polyamides woven fabrics, containing 85% or more by weight of filaments, dyed	尼龙或聚酰胺机织物,按重量计长丝含量在 85% 及以上,染色	5407. 4200	2468
Nylon or other polyamides woven fabrics, containing 85% or more by weight of filaments, of yarns of different colours	尼龙或聚酰胺机织物,按重量计长丝含量在 85% 及以上,色织	5407. 4300	2468
Nylon or other polyamides woven fabrics, containing 85% or more by weight of filaments, printed	尼龙或聚酰胺机织物,按重量计长丝含量在 85% 及以上,印花	5407. 4400	2468

Article Description	商品名称	Tariff Code	D. R.
Nylon or other polyamides woven fabrics, containing 85% or more by weight of filaments, unbleached or bleached	尼龙或聚酰胺机织物,按重量计长丝含量在85%及以上,未漂白或漂白	5407. 4100	2468
Nylon or polyamides elastic filament, measuring per single yarn more than 50 tex, not put up for retail sale	尼龙或聚酰胺弹力丝,每根单纱细度超过50特,非供零售用,其他	5402. 3219	3468
Nylon or polyamides elastic filament, measuring per single yarn not more than 50 tex, not put up for retail sale, nes	尼龙或聚酰胺弹力丝,每根单纱细度不超过50特,非供零售用,其他	5402. 3119	3468
Nylon or polyamides high tenacity yarn, not put up for retail sale, nes	尼龙或聚酰胺高强力纱,非供零售用,其他	5402. 1990	3468
Nylon or polyamides multiple or cabled yarn, not put up for retail sale, nes	尼龙或聚酰胺多股纱线或缆线,非供零售用,其他	5402. 6190	3468
Nylon or polyamides single yarn, with a twist exceeding 50 turns per metre, not put up for retail sale, nes	尼龙或聚酰胺单纱,捻度每米超过50转,非供零售用,其他	5402. 5190	3468
Nylon or polyamides single yarn, untwisted or with a twist not exceeding 50 turns per metre, not put up for retail sale, nes	尼龙或聚酰胺单纱,未加捻或捻度每米不超过50转,非供零售用,其他	5402. 4590	3468
Nylon or polyamides staple fibres, not carded, combed or otherwise processed for spinning, nes	尼龙或聚酰胺短纤,未梳或未经其他纺前加工,其他	5503. 1900	68
Nylon or polyamides textured yarn of measuring per single yarn more than 50 tex, not put up for retail sale, nes	尼龙或聚酰胺变形纱线,每根单纱细度超过50特,非供零售用,其他	5402. 3290	3468
Nylon or polyamides textured yarn, measuring per single yarn not more than 50 tex, not put up for retail sale, nes	尼龙或聚酰胺变形纱线,每根单纱细度不超过50特,非供零售用,其他	5402. 3190	3468
Nylon-6 elastic filament, measuring per single yarn more than 50 tex, not put up for retail sale	尼龙-6弹力丝,每根单纱细度超过50特,非供零售用	5402. 3211	3468
Nylon-6 elastic filament, measuring per single yarn not more than 50 tex, not put up for retail sale	尼龙-6弹力丝,每根单纱细度不超过50特,非供零售用	5402. 3111	3468
Nylon-6 multiple or cabled yarn, not put up for retail sale	尼龙-6多股纱线或缆线,非供零售用	5402. 6110	3468
Nylon-6 single yarn, with a twist exceeding 50 turns per metre, not put up for retail sale	尼龙-6单纱,捻度每米超过50转,非供零售用	5402. 5110	3468
Nylon-6,6 elastic filament, measuring per single yarn more than 50 tex, not put up for retail sale	尼龙-6,6弹力丝,每根单纱细度超过50特,非供零售用	5402. 3212	3468
Nylon-6,6 elastic filament, measuring per single yarn not more than 50 tex, not put up for retail sale	尼龙-6,6弹力丝,每根单纱细度不超过50特,非供零售用	5402. 3112	3468
Nylon-6,6 high tenacity yarn, not put up for retail sale	尼龙-6,6高强力纱,非供零售用	5402. 1920	3468
Nylon-6,6 multiple or cabled yarn, not put up for retail sale	尼龙-6,6多股纱线或缆线,非供零售用	5402. 6120	3468

N

Article Description	商品名称	Tariff Code	D. R.
Nylon-6,6 single yarn, untwisted or with a twist not exceeding 50 turns per metre, not put up for retail sale	尼龙 -6,6 单纱,未加捻或捻度每米不超过 50 转,非供零售用	5402. 4520	3468
Nylon-6,6 single yarn, with a twist exceeding 50 turns per metre, not put up for retail sale	尼龙 -6,6 单纱,捻度每米超过 50 转,非供零售用	5402. 5120	3468
Nylon-66 salt	己二酸己二胺盐	2921. 2210	36
Nylon-66 salt	尼龙 -66 盐	2921. 2210	36
Nylon-6high tenacity yarn, not put up for retail sale	尼龙 -6 高强力纱,非供零售用	5402. 1910	3468
Nylon-6single yarn, untwisted or with a twist not exceeding 50 turns per metre, not put up for retail sale	尼龙 -6 单纱,未加捻或捻度每米不超过 50 转,非供零售用	5402. 4510	3468
N-acety-lanthranilic acid and its salts	N-乙酰邻氨基苯甲酸及其盐	2924. 2300	36
N-butyl acetate	乙酸(正)丁酯	2915. 3300	36
N-octanol	正辛醇	2905. 1610	36

O

Article Description	商品名称	Tariff Code	D. R.
Oats, nes	燕麦,其他	1004. 0090	3
Oats, other worked	燕麦,其他加工的	1104. 2200	4
Oats, rolled or flaked	燕麦,滚压或制片的	1104. 1200	4
Oats, seed	燕麦,种用	1004. 0010	3
Objective lenses, for cameras, nes	物镜,照相机用,其他	9002. 1139	3
Objective lenses, for cinematographic cameras or projectors	物镜,摄影机或放映机用	9002. 1910	3
Objective lenses, for microfilm, microfiche or other microform readers	物镜,缩微阅读机用	9002. 1120	3
Objective lenses, for projectors or photographic enlargers or reducers	物镜,投影仪、照片放大机及缩片机用	9002. 1190	3
Objective lenses, for the cameras of a kind used for preparing printing plates or spelially designed	物镜,制版照相机和特种照相机用	9002. 1110	3
Objective lenses, nes	物镜,其他	9002. 1990	3
Octanol(octyl alcohol) and isomers thereof, nes	辛醇及其异构体,其他	2905. 1690	36
Octopus flour, fit for human consumption	章鱼粉,食用	0307. 9990	14
Octopus flour, unfit for human consumption	章鱼粉,不适合食用	2301. 2090	136
Octopus(Octopus spp.), frozen, dried, salted or in brine	章鱼,冻、干、盐腌或盐渍的	0307. 5900	148
Octopus(Octopus spp.), live, fresh or chilled	章鱼,活、鲜及冷的	0307. 5100	18
Octopus, prepared or preserved	章鱼,制作或保藏的	1605. 9090	48
Octylphenol	辛基酚	2907. 1390	36
Odoriferous preparations used during religious rites	香气制品,宗教仪式用	3307. 4100	23
Odoriferous preparations which operate by burning, nes	香气制品,通过燃烧散发的,其他	3307. 4100	23
Odoriferous substances mixtures, nes	香料混合物,其他	3302. 9000	36
Odoriferous substances mixtures, of a kind used in the food or drink industry, nes	香料混合物,食品或饮料工业用,其他	3302. 1090	36
Odoriferous substances preparations, of a kind used for the manufacture of beverages, alcoholic strength by volume not exceeding 0. 5% vol.	香料为基本成分的制品,生产饮料用,按容量计酒精浓度不超过 0. 5% 的	3302. 1010	36
Oestrogens	雌(甾)激素	2937. 2300	36
Offal nes, fresh, chilled or frozen, edible	杂碎,其他,鲜或冷或冻的,食用	0208. 9090	145
Offal of asses, fresh or chilled, edible	杂碎,驴的,鲜或冷的,食用	0206. 8000	15
Offal of asses, frozen, edible	杂碎,驴的,冻的,食用	0206. 9000	15
Offal of bovine animals, fresh or chilled, edible	杂碎,牛的,鲜或冷的,食用	0206. 1000	15
Offal of bovine animals, frozen, edible, nes	杂碎,牛的,冻的,食用,其他	0206. 2900	15
Offal of dolphins, fresh, chilled or frozen, edible	杂碎,海豚的,鲜或冷或冻的,食用	0208. 4000	15

Article Description	商品名称	Tariff Code	D. R.
Offal of ducks, fresh or chilled	杂碎,鸭的,鲜或冷的	0207. 3510	1
Offal of ducks, frozen	杂碎,鸭的,冻的	0207. 3610	1
Offal of dugongs (mammals of the order sirenia), fresh, chilled or frozen, edible	杂碎,儒艮(海牛目哺乳动物)的,鲜或冷或冻的,食用	0208. 4000	15
Offal of fowls of the species gallus domesticus, nes, fresh or chilled	杂碎,鸡的,其他,鲜或冷的	0207. 1329	1
Offal of fowls of the species gallus domesticus, nes, frozen	杂碎,鸡的,其他,冻的	0207. 1429	1
Offal of geese, fresh or chilled	杂碎,鹅的,鲜或冷的	0207. 3520	1
Offal of geese, frozen	杂碎,鹅的,冻的	0207. 3620	1
Offal of goats, fresh or chilled, edible	杂碎,绵羊的,鲜或冷的,食用	0206. 8000	15
Offal of goats, frozen, edible	杂碎,绵羊的,冻的,食用	0206. 9000	15
Offal of guinea fowls, fresh or chilled	杂碎,珍珠鸡的,鲜或冷的	0207. 3530	1
Offal of guinea fowls, frozen	杂碎,珍珠鸡的,冻的	0207. 3630	1
Offal of hares, edible	杂碎,野兔的,食用	0208. 1090	145
Offal of horses, fresh or chilled, edible	杂碎,马的,鲜或冷的,食用	0206. 8000	15
Offal of horses, frozen, edible	杂碎,马的,冻的,食用	0206. 9000	15
Offal of manatees, fresh, chilled or frozen, edible	杂碎,海牛的,鲜或冷或冻的,食用	0208. 4000	15
Offal of mules or hinnies, fresh or chilled, edible	杂碎,骡的,鲜或冷的,食用	0206. 8000	15
Offal of mules or hinnies, frozen, edible	杂碎,骡的,冻的,食用	0206. 9000	15
Offal of porpoises (mammals of the order cetacea), fresh, chilled or frozen, edible	杂碎,鼠海豚(鲸目哺乳动物)的,鲜或冷或冻的,食用	0208. 4000	15
Offal of primates and, fresh, chilled or frozen, edible	杂碎,灵长目的,鲜或冷或冻的,食用	0208. 3000	15
Offal of rabbits, edible	杂碎,家兔的,食用	0208. 1090	145
Offal of sheep, fresh or chilled, edible	杂碎,山羊的,鲜或冷的	0206. 8000	15
Offal of sheep, frozen, edible	杂碎,山羊的,冻的	0206. 9000	15
Offal of squabs, fresh, chilled or frozen, edible	杂碎,乳鸽的,鲜或冷或冻的,食用	0208. 9010	15
Offal of swine, fresh or chilled, edible	杂碎,猪的,鲜或冷的,食用	0206. 3000	15
Offal of swine, frozen, edible, nes	杂碎,猪的,冻的,其他	0206. 4900	15
Offal of turkeys, fresh or chilled	杂碎,火鸡的,鲜或冷的	0207. 2600	1
Offal of turkeys, frozen	杂碎,火鸡的,冻的	0207. 2700	1
Offal of whales, fresh, chilled or frozen, edible	杂碎,鲸的,鲜或冷或冻的,食用	0208. 4000	15
Offal, of reptiles (including snakes and turtles), fresh, chilled or frozen, edible	杂碎,爬行动物(包括蛇及龟鳖)的,食用	0208. 5000	15
Office articles, of base metal, nes	办公用品,其他,贱金属制	8305. 9000	256
Office machines, nes	办公室用机器,其他	8472. 9090	
Office machines' parts and accessories, nes	办公室用机器的零件、附件,其他	8473. 4090	3
Office or desk equipment, of base metal, other than office furniture	办公用具,贱金属制,办公室家具除外	8304. 0000	256
Office-stamp stands and similar office or desk equipment, of base metal, other than office furniture	公章架及类似的办公用具,贱金属制,办公室家具除外	8304. 0000	256

Article Description	商品名称	Tariff Code	D. R.
Offset plates, in rolls or sheets, of width exceeding 36cm or in roll or one side exceeding 36cm and other side exceeding 15cm in rectangular sheets	胶印版纸,成卷或成张的,卷宽度超过36厘米,或长超过36厘米且宽超过15厘米	4809.9000	458
Offset plates, nes	胶印版纸,其他	4816.9090	58
Offset printing machinery, nes	胶印机,其他	8443.1390	57
Offset printing machinery, reel-fed	胶印机,卷取进料式	8443.1100	57
Offset printing machinery, sheet fed, four colors	胶印机,平张纸进料式,四色机	8443.1313	57
Offset printing machinery, sheet fed, nes	胶印机,平张纸进料式,其他	8443.1319	57
Offset printing machinery, sheet fed, single color	胶印机,平张纸进料式,单色机	8443.1311	57
Offset printing machinery, sheet fed, two colors	胶印机,平张纸进料式,双色机	8443.1312	57
Offset printing machinery, sheet-fed, office type (using sheets with one side not exceeding 22cm and the other side not exceeding 36cm in the unfolded state)	胶印机,片取进料式,办公室用(以未折叠计,片尺寸一边长不超过22cm,另一边长不超过36cm)	8443.1200	57
Oil and natural gas drilling machinery, self-propelled, nes	石油及天然气钻探机,自推进的,其他	8430.4119	5
Oil and natural gas drilling machinery, self-propelled, of drilling depth of 6000m or more	石油及天然气钻探机,自推进的,钻探深度在6000米及以上的	8430.4111	5
Oil cake and other solid residues, resulting from the extraction of coconut or copra	油渣饼及其他固体残渣,椰子或干椰肉的	2306.5000	46
Oil cake and other solid residues, resulting from the extraction of cotton seeds	油渣饼及其他固体残渣,棉子的	2306.1000	46
Oil cake and other solid residues, resulting from the extraction of linseed	油渣饼及其他固体残渣,亚麻子的	2306.2000	46
Oil cake and other solid residues, resulting from the extraction of low erucic acid rape or colza seeds	油渣饼及其他固体残渣,低芥子酸油菜子的	2306.4100	46
Oil cake and other solid residues, resulting from the extraction of palm nuts or kernels	油渣饼及其他固体残渣,油棕果或油棕仁的	2306.6000	46
Oil cake and other solid residues, resulting from the extraction of rape or colza seeds, nes	油渣饼及其他固体残渣,油菜子的,其他	2306.4900	46
Oil cake and other solid residues, resulting from the extraction of sunflower seeds	油渣饼及其他固体残渣,葵花子的	2306.3000	46
Oil cake and other solid residues, resulting from the extraction of vegetable fats or oils, nes	油渣饼及其他固体残渣,其他	2306.9000	46
Oil cake, resulting from the extraction of groundnut oil	油渣饼,提炼花生油所得的	2305.0000	46
Oil cake, resulting from the extraction of soyabean oil	油渣饼	2304.0010	46
Oil coolers, of motor vehicles	机油冷却器,机动车辆用	8708.9120	3
Oil or petrol-filters for internal combustion engines	滤油器,内燃发动机的	8421.2300	7
Oil production machinery, self-propelled, nes	采油机械,自推进的,其他	8430.5010	5
Oil seeds and oleaginous fruits, nes	含油子仁及果实,其他	1207.9999	3
Oil seeds and oleaginous fruits, nes, seed	含油子仁及果实,其他,种用	1207.9910	3
Oil shale	油页岩及焦油砂	2714.1000	1346

Article Description	商品名称	Tariff Code	D. R.
Oil tanker trailers and semi-trailers	油罐挂车及半挂车	8716. 3110	
Oils and other products in which the weight of the aromatic constituents exceeds that of the non-aromatic constituents	油类及其他产品，芳族成分重量超过非芳族成分的	2707. 9990	6
Oils and other products of the distillation of high temperature coal tar	油类及其他产品，蒸馏高温煤焦油所得的	2707. 9990	6
Oils and their fractions, nes, obtained solely from olives, whether or not refined, but not chemically modified, including blends of these oils or fractions with oils or fractions of heading No. 15. 09	橄榄油及其分离品，其他，不论是否精制，但未经化学改性，包括掺有税号 15. 09 的油或分离品的混合物	1510. 0000	24
Oils, derived from milk	油，从乳中提取的	0405. 9000	268
Oilstones	琢磨油石	6804. 3010	36
Oleic acid, industrial use	油酸，工业用	3823. 1200	6
Oleic acids, their salts and esters	油酸及其盐和酯	2916. 1500	36
Oleooil, not emulsified or mixed or otherwise prepared	食用脂油，未经乳化、混合或其他方法制作	1503. 0000	4
Oleoresins	香树脂	1301. 9090	
Oleoresins extracted	油树脂，提取的	3301. 9010	34
Oleostearin, not emulsified or mixed or otherwise prepared	油硬脂，未经乳化、混合或其他方法制作	1503. 0000	4
Oleum	发烟硫酸	2807. 0000	346
Oleyl alcohol (of a purity of 90% or more)	油醇(纯度大于 90%)	2905. 2900	36
Olibanum	乳香	1301. 9020	
Olive oil and its fractions, nes	油橄榄油及其分离品，其他	1509. 9000	4
Olive oil and its fractions, virgin	油橄榄油及其分离品，初榨的	1509. 1000	4
Olives, prepared or preserved otherwise than by vinegar or acetic acid, not frozen	油橄榄，用醋或醋酸以外的其他方法制作或保藏的，未冷冻	2005. 7000	148
Olives, provisionally preserved, but unsuitable in that state for immediate consumption	油橄榄，暂时保藏，但不适合直接使用的	0711. 2000	34
Onions, dried	洋葱，干的	0712. 2000	4
Onions, fresh or chilled	洋葱，鲜或冷藏的	0703. 1010	1
Oolong tea, in immediate packings of a content not exceeding 3kg	乌龙茶，内包装每件净重不超过 3 千克	0902. 3010	248
Oolong tea, nes	乌龙茶，其他	0902. 4010	248
Opacifiers and similar preparations, prepared, of a kind used in the ceramic, enamelling or glass industry	遮光剂及类似制品，调制的，陶瓷、搪瓷及玻璃工业用	3207. 1000	13
Opacifying preparations for X-ray examinations	X 光检查造影剂	3006. 3000	36
Opening or closing mail machines	开封或闭封机，信件用	8472. 3090	
Open-end rotors	气流杯	8448. 3910	3
Open-end spinner, nes	自由端纺纱机，其他	8445. 2039	7

Article Description	商品名称	Tariff Code	D. R.
Operating tables, for medical, surgical, dental or veterinary usages	手术台,医疗、外科、牙科或兽医用	9402. 9000	3
Ophthalmic instruments and appliances	眼科用其他仪器及器具	9018. 5000	7
Opium alkaloids and their derivatives; salts thereof	鸦片碱及其衍生物以及它们的盐,其他	2939. 1900	34
Optical communication equipments, nes	光通讯设备,其他	8517. 6229	7
Optical devices (or appliances and instruments) parts and accessories, nes	光学装置、仪器及器具的零件、附件,其他	9013. 9090	3
Optical devices, appliances and instruments, nes	光学装置、仪器及器具,其他	9013. 8090	
Optical disks, for reproducing sound only, recorded	光盘,仅用于重放声音信息的,已录制	8523. 4010	37
Optical elements, nes	光学元件,其他	9001. 9090	5
Optical elements, of any material, mounted, being parts of or fittings for instruments or apparatus	光学元件,已装配的各种材料制,作为仪器或装置的零件、配件	9002. 9090	3
Optical elements, of any material, mounted, for cameras	光学元件,已装配的各种材料制,照相机用	9002. 9010	3
Optical fibre bundles	光导纤维束	9001. 1000	6
Optical fibre bundles connectors, for a voltage not exceeding 1000V	光导纤维束用连接器,用于电压不超过1000伏的线路	8536. 7000	8
Optical fibre cables connectors, for a voltage not exceeding 1000V	光缆用连接器,用于电压不超过1000伏的线路	8536. 7000	8
Optical fibre cables, made up of individually sheathed fibres	光缆,单根被覆的	8544. 7000	35
Optical fibre cables, nes	光缆,其他	9001. 1000	6
Optical fibres	光导纤维	9001. 1000	6
Optical fibres and preforms making machines	光导纤维及其预制棒的制造机器	8475. 2100	
Optical fibres connectors, for a voltage not exceeding 1000V	光导纤维用连接器,用于电压不超过1000伏的线路	8536. 7000	8
Optical line terminal equipments	光端机	8517. 6221	7
Optical line terminal equipments parts	光端机用零件	8517. 7020	3
Optical measuring or checking instruments and appliances, for inspecting semiconductor wafers or devices or for inspecting photomasks or reticles used in manufacturing semiconductor devices	光学测量或检验仪器及器具,制造半导体器件时检验半导体晶片、器件或检测光掩模或光栅用	9031. 4100	
Optical measuring or checking instruments and appliances, nes	光学测量或检验仪器及器具,其他	9031. 4990	7
Optical media, for reproducing phenomena other than sound or image, for the machines of heading 84. 71	光学媒体,用于重放声音、图像以外信息的,税号84. 71所列机器用	8523. 4020	37
Optical media, nes	光学媒体,其他	8523. 4099	37
Optical media, unrecorded	光学媒体,未录制	8523. 4091	37
Optical telecommunication and optical fibre performance testing instruments	光纤通信及光纤性能测试仪	9031. 8010	
Optical transmission equipments for wave-division multiplexing	波分复用光传输设备	8517. 6222	7

Article Description	商品名称	Tariff Code	D. R.
Optical transmission equipments for wave-division multiplexing	光传输设备,波分复用的	8517. 6222	7
Orange juice, frozen	橙汁,冷冻的	2009. 1100	2468
Orange juice, nes	橙汁,其他	2009. 1900	2468
Orange juice, not frozen, of a brix value not exceeding 20	橙汁,非冷冻的,白利糖度值不超过20	2009. 1200	2468
Orange lead	铅橙	2824. 9010	
Orangeade	橙汁饮料	2202. 1000	248
Oranges	橙	0805. 1000	1245
Orchid, nes	兰花,其他	0602. 9092	
Orchid, seedlings	兰花,种用	0602. 9091	3
Orchids, fresh, suitable for bouquets or for ornamental purposes	兰花,鲜的,制花束或装饰用的	0603. 1300	34
Order books, of paper or paperboard	定货本,纸或纸板制的	4820. 1000	
Ores and concentrates, nes	矿砂及其精矿,其他	2617. 9090	146
Ores of rare earth metals	稀土金属矿	2530. 9020	13456
Organic composite solvents, nes	有机复合溶剂,其他	3814. 0000	36
Organic composite thinners, nes	有机复合稀释剂,其他	3814. 0000	36
Organic compounds, nes	有机化合物,其他	2942. 0000	
Organic derivatives of hydrazine	肼(联氨)的有机衍生物	2928. 0000	36
Organic derivatives of hydroxylamine	胲(羟胺)的有机衍生物	2928. 0000	36
Organic surface-active agents preparations, nes	有机表面活性剂制品,其他	3402. 9000	36
Organic surface-active agents, preparations put up for retail sale, nes	有机表面活性剂制品,零售包装的,其他	3402. 2090	36
Organic surface-active agents, whether or not put up for retail sale, anionic	有机表面活性剂,不论是否零售包装,阴离子型	3402. 1100	56
Organic surface-active agents, whether or not put up for retail sale, cationic	有机表面活性剂,不论是否零售包装,阳离子型	3402. 1200	56
Organic surface-active agents, whether or not put up for retail sale, non-ionic	有机表面活性剂,不论是否零售包装,非离子型	3402. 1300	56
Organic surface-active agents, whether or not put up for retail sale, other	有机表面活性剂,不论是否零售包装,其他	3402. 1900	56
Organic surface-active products and preparations for washing the skin, in the form of liquid or cream and put up for retail sale, whether or not containing soap	有机表面活性产品及制品,洁肤用的,液状或膏状并制成零售包装的,不论是否含有肥皂	3401. 3000	
Organic surface-active products and preparations impregnated (coated or covered) paper (wadding, felt and non-wovens), for toilet use	有机表面活性产品及制品浸渍、涂面或包覆的纸、絮胎、毡呢及无纺织物,盥洗用	3401. 1100	123
Organic surface-active products and preparations, in the form of bars, cakes, moulded pieces or shapes, for toilet use	有机表面活性产品及制品,条状、块状或模制形状的,盥洗用	3401. 1100	123

O

Article Description	商品名称	Tariff Code	D. R.
Organo-inorganic compounds, nes	有机-无机化合物,其他	2931. 0000	36
Organo-sulphur compounds, nes	有机硫化合物,其他	2930. 9090	36
Organs extracts and secretions	器官及其分泌物的提取物	3001. 2000	34
Oriented strand board (osb) of wood	定向刨花板	4410. 1200	6
Oriented strand board (osb), of ligneous materials	定向刨花板	4410. 9090	6
Ornamental fish	观赏鱼	0301. 1000	15
Ornamental trimmings in the piece, without embroidery	成匹装饰带,非绣制的其他	5808. 9000	468
Orthographical projectors	正射投影仪	9008. 3010	
Orthopaedic appliances	矫形器具	9021. 1000	
Oscilloscopes and oscillographs parts and accessories	示波器的零件、附件	9030. 9000	3
Oscilloscopes and oscillographs, for general use, of test frequency less than 300 MHz	示波器,通用的,测试频率在 300 兆赫兹以下的	9030. 2010	
Oscilloscopes and oscillographs, nes	示波器,其他	9030. 2090	7
Osier	柳条	1401. 9090	3
Osmium, nes	锇,其他	7110. 4990	46
Osmium, plates and sheets	锇,板、片	7110. 4910	46
Osmium, unwrought or in powder form	锇,未锻造或粉末状	7110. 4100	46
Osmund, dried	薇菜干	0712. 9020	4
Osmund, dried	紫萁,干的	0712. 9020	4
Ossein treated with acid	骨胶原,经酸处理的	0506. 1000	4
Ostomy use appliances	造口术用具	3006. 9100	3
Ostrich	鸵鸟	0106. 3922	3
Other	离心机零件,其他	8421. 9190	3
Other bogies and bissel-bogies, of railway or tramway locomotives or rolling-stock, nes	转向架及轴,铁道及电车道机车或其他车辆的,其他	8607. 1200	3
Other monoalkylethers of ethylene glycol or of diethylene glycol	乙二醇或二甘醇的其他单烷基醚	2909. 4400	36
Other pins, of iron or steel, nes	别针,钢铁制的,其他	7319. 3000	
Outer soles and heels, of plastics	外底及鞋跟,塑料制的	6406. 2020	6
Outer soles and heels, of rubber	外底及鞋跟,橡胶制的	6406. 2010	6
Ovens functioning by induction or dielectric loss, for industrial or laboratory use, electric	烘箱,通过感应或介质损耗工作的,工业或实验室用	8514. 2000	7
Ovens, for industrial or laboratory use, electric, nes	烘箱,工业或实验室用,电的,其他	8514. 3000	7
Ovens, resistance heated, for industrial or laboratory use, electric, nes	烘箱,电阻加热的,工业或实验室用,其他	8514. 1090	7
Overcoats and similar articles, knitted or crocheted, for men or boys, for man-made fibres	大衣及类似品,针织或钩编的,男式,化学纤维制	6101. 3000	2456
Overcoats and similar articles, knitted or crocheted, for men or boys, of cotton	大衣及类似品,针织或钩编的,男式,棉制	6101. 2000	2456
Overcoats and similar articles, knitted or crocheted, for men or boys, of other textile materials	大衣及类似品,针织或钩编的,男式,其他	6101. 9090	2456

Article Description	商品名称	Tariff Code	D. R.
Overcoats and similar articles, knitted or crocheted, for men or boys, of wool or fine animal hair	大衣及类似品,针织或钩编的,男式,羊毛或动物细毛制	6101. 9010	2456
Overcoats and similar articles, knitted or crocheted, for women or girls, for man-made fibres	大衣及类似品,针织或钩编的,女式,化学纤维制	6102. 3000	2456
Overcoats and similar articles, knitted or crocheted, for women or girls, of cotton	大衣及类似品,针织或钩编的,女式,棉制	6102. 2000	2456
Overcoats and similar articles, knitted or crocheted, for women or girls, of other textile materials	大衣及类似品,针织或钩编的,女式,其他	6102. 9000	2456
Overcoats and similar articles, knitted or crocheted, for women or girls, of wool or fine animal hair	大衣及类似品,针织或钩编的,女式,羊毛或动物细毛制	6102. 1000	2456
Overcoats, not knitted or crocheted, for men or boys, of cotton, nes	大衣,非针织或钩编的,男式,棉制,其他	6201. 1290	2456
Overcoats, not knitted or crocheted, for men or boys, of other textile materials	大衣,非针织或钩编的,男式,其他纺织材料制	6201. 1900	2456
Overcoats, not knitted or crocheted, for men or boys, of wool or fine animal hair	大衣,非针织或钩编的,男式,羊毛或动物细毛制	6201. 1100	2456
Overcoats, not knitted or crocheted, for men or boys, padded with feathers or down, of man-made fibres	大衣,非针织或钩编的,男式,充绒,化学纤维制	6201. 1390	2456
Overcoats, not knitted or crocheted, for women or girls, of cotton, nes	大衣,非针织或钩编的,女式,棉制,其他	6202. 1290	2456
Overcoats, not knitted or crocheted, for women or girls, of other textile materials	大衣,非针织或钩编的,女式,其他纺织材料制	6202. 1900	2456
Overcoats, not knitted or crocheted, for women or girls, of wool or fine animal hair	大衣,非针织或钩编的,男式,羊毛或动物细毛制	6202. 1100	2456
Overcoats, not knitted or crocheted, for women or girls, padded with feathers or down, of man-made fibres	大衣,非针织或钩编的,女式,充绒,化学纤维制	6202. 1390	2456
Overlock machines	包缝机	8452. 2120	
Ovoids manufactured from coal	煤球	2701. 2000	156
Oxalie acid	草酸	2917. 1110	36
Oxalie acid salts and esters, nes	草酸盐和酯,其他	2917. 1190	36
Oxazepam(INN); salts thereof	奥沙西泮(INN)以及盐	2933. 9100	36B
Oxazolam(INN); salts thereof	恶唑仑(INN)及盐	2934. 9100	36
Oxidation inhibitors, for mineral oils and alike	抗氧剂,用于矿物油及类似液体	3811. 9000	236
Oxidation treatment equipment, flat panel displays manufacture machines and apparatus	扩散处理设备,平板显示器的制造机器及装置	8486. 3010	7
Oxidation treatment equipment, semiconductor devices or of electronic integrated circuits manufacture machines and apparatus	氧化处理设备,制造半导体器件或集成电路的机器及装置	8486. 2010	7
Oxidation, diffusion, annealing and other heat treatment equipment, semiconductor devices or of electronic integrated circuits manufacture machines and apparatus	氧化、扩散、退火及其他热处理设备,制造半导体器件或集成电路的机器及装置	8486. 2010	7

Article Description	商品名称	Tariff Code	D. R.
Oxirane	环氧乙烷	2910. 1000	36
Oxometanic salts, nes	金属酸盐,其他	2841. 9000	1
Oxycodone(INN) and salts	羟考酮(INN)及盐	2939. 1100	34
Oxygen	氧	2804. 4000	
Oxygen producers, with a process involving a change of temperature, nes	制氧机,利用温度变化处理,其他	8419. 6019	57
Oxygen producers, with a process involving a change of temperature, oxygen preparation volume no less than 15000m^3/h	制氧机,利用温度变化处理,制氧量在15000立方米/小时及以上	8419. 6011	57
Oxygen therapy apparatus	氧气治疗器	9019. 2000	
Oxymorphone(INN) and salts	羟吗啡酮(INN)及盐	2939. 1100	34
Oyster extract	牡蛎提取物	1603. 0000	48
Oyster flour, fit for human consumption	牡蛎粉,食用	0307. 9990	14
Oyster shells, crushed	牡蛎壳,碎的	0508. 0010	14
Oysters, for cultivation	蚝,种苗	0307. 1010	3
Oysters, for cultivation	牡蛎,种苗	0307. 1010	3
Oysters, nes	蚝,其他	0307. 1090	14
Oysters, nes	牡蛎,其他	0307. 1090	14
Oysters, prepared or preserved	牡蛎,制作或保藏的	1605. 9090	48
Ozokerite	地蜡	2712. 9090	6
Ozone therapy apparatus	臭氧治疗器	9019. 2000	
O-, m-, p-diaminotoluener and their derivatives; salts thereof, nes	邻-、间-、对-二氨基甲苯及其衍生物以及它们的盐,其他	2921. 5190	36
O-, m-, p-phenylenediamine and their derivatives; salts thereof, nes	邻-、间-、对-苯二胺及其衍生物以及它们的盐,其他	2921. 5190	36
O-acetylsalicylic acid salts and esters, nes	邻乙酰水杨酸盐和酯,其他	2918. 2290	36
O-cresol	邻甲酚	2907. 1212	36
O-dichlorobenzene	邻二氯苯	2903. 6110	36
O-dihydroxybenzene(catechol, pyrocatechol)	邻苯二酚	2907. 2910	36
O-isopropyl phenol	邻异丙基酚	2907. 1910	36
O-nitrochlorobenzene	邻硝基氯化苯	2904. 9011	36
O-phenylenediamine	邻苯二胺	2921. 5110	36
O-sec-butyl phenol	邻仲丁基酚	2907. 1910	36
O-xylene	邻二甲苯	2902. 4100	6
o-Xylene diisocyanate	二甲苯二异氰酸酯	2929. 1020	36
O-xylene diisocyanate	TODI	2929. 1020	36

P

Article Description	商品名称	Tariff Code	D. R.
Pacemakers for stimulating heart muscles, excluding parts and accessories	心脏起搏器,不包括零件、附件	9021. 5000	
Pacific salmon (oncorhynchus nerka, oncorhynchus gorbuscha, oncorhynchus keta, oncorhynchus tschawytscha, oncorhynchus kisutch, oncorhynchus masou and oncorhynchus rhodurus), fresh or chilled	大马哈鱼,鲜或冷的,	0302. 1220	18
Pacific salmon, nes, frozen	大马哈鱼,其他,冻的	0303. 1900	18
Packing containers, of paper, nes	包装容器,纸制的,其他	4819. 5000	68
Packing machines parts	包装机零件	8422. 9090	
Packing machines, for bottles, cans, boxes, bags or other containers	包装机,瓶、罐、箱、袋或其他容器的	8422. 3030	
Packing or wrapping machinery, nes	包装或打包机器,其他	8422. 4000	
Paddling pools	戏水池	9506. 9190	5
Paddy straw mushroom, dried	草菇,干的	0712. 3930	4
Paddy straw mushroom, fresh or chilled	草菇,鲜或冷藏的	0709. 5940	1
Padlocks, of base metal	挂锁,贱金属制	8301. 1000	256
Paint brushes of pigs, hogs or boars bristle	油漆刷,猪鬃制	9603. 4011	
Paint brushes, nes	油漆刷,其他	9603. 4019	3
Paint pads and rollers	油漆滚筒及块垫	9603. 4020	
Paint solvent	油漆溶剂油	2710. 1130	6
Painted canvas being theatrical scenery, studio backcloths or the like	已绘制画布,作舞台、摄影布景或类似用途的	5907. 0020	4
Painters' colours, modifying tints, amusement colours and the like, in tablets, tubes, jars, bottles, pans or in similar forms or packings, for artists, students or signboard use	颜料、调色料、文娱颜料及类似品,片状、管装、罐装、瓶装、扁盒装以及类似形状或包装的,艺术家、学生和广告美工用的	3213. 9000	3
Painters' fillings	漆工用填料	3214. 1090	3
Painting canvas, prepared	油画布,制成的	5901. 9010	
Paintings, drawings and pastels, reproductions	油画、粉画及其他手绘画复制品	9701. 1020	
Paintings, drawings and pastels, the orginals	油画、粉画及其他手绘画原件	9701. 1010	
Paints and varnishes (including enamels and lacquers), based on acrylic polymers, dispersed or dissolved in a nonaqueous medium	油漆及清漆(包括瓷漆及大漆),以丙烯酸聚合物为基本成分,分散于或溶于非水介质的	3208. 2010	136
Paints and varnishes (including enamels and lacquers), based on polyesters, dispersed or dissolved in a nonaqueous medium	油漆及清漆(包括瓷漆及大漆),以聚酯为基本成分,分散于或溶于非水介质的	3208. 1000	136

Article Description	商品名称	Tariff Code	D. R.
Paints and varnishes (including enamels and lacquers), based on polyurethane polymers, dispersed or dissolved in a nonaqueous medium	油漆及清漆(包括瓷漆及大漆),以聚胺酯类化合物为基本成分,分散于或溶于非水介质的	3208. 9010	136
Paints and varnishes (including enamels and lacquers), based on vinyl polymers, dispersed or dissolved in a nonaqueous medium	油漆及清漆(包括瓷漆及大漆),以乙烯聚合物为基本成分,分散于或溶于非水介质的	3208. 2020	136
Paints and varnishes (including enamels and lacquers), nes, dispersed or dissolved in a nonaqueous medium	油漆及清漆(包括瓷漆及大漆),其他,分散于或溶于非水介质的	3208. 9090	136
Paints and varnishes (including enamels, lacquers and distempers), nes	油漆及清漆(包括瓷漆、大漆及水浆涂料),其他	3210. 0000	36
Paints and varnishes (including enamels and lacquers), based on acrylic or vinyl polymers, dispersed or dissolved in an aqueous medium	油漆及清漆(包括瓷漆及大漆),以丙烯酸聚合物或乙烯聚合物为基本成分,分散于或溶于水介质的	3209. 1000	36
Paints and varnishes (including enamels and lacquers), based on epoxy resin, dispersed or dissolved in an aqueous medium	油漆及清漆(包括瓷漆及大漆),以环氧树脂为基本成分,分散于或溶于水介质的	3209. 9010	36
Paints and varnishes (including enamels and lacquers), based on fluororesin, dispersed or dissolved in an aqueous medium	油漆及清漆(包括瓷漆及大漆),以氟树脂为基本成分,分散于或溶于水介质的	3209. 9020	36
Paints and varnishes (including enamels and lacquers), nes, dispersed or dissolved in an aqueous medium	油漆及清漆(包括瓷漆及大漆),其他,分散于或溶于水介质的	3209. 9090	36
Palladium, nes	钯,其他	7110. 2990	46
Palladium, plates and sheets	钯,板、片	7110. 2910	46
Palladium, unwrought or in powder form	钯,未锻造或粉末状	7110. 2100	46
Pallet collars, of radiata pine	托盘护框,辐射松制的	4415. 2010	56
Pallet collars, of other wood	托盘护框,其他木制的	4415. 2090	56
Pallets, of other wood	木托板木,其他木制的	4415. 2090	56
Pallets, of radiata pine	木托板木,辐射松制的	4415. 2010	56
Palm hearts, otherwise prepared, or preserved	棕榈芯,用其他方法制作或保藏的	2008. 9100	248
Palm kernel oil and fractions thereof, crude oil	棕榈仁油及其分离品,初榨的	1513. 2100	4
Palm kernel oil and fractions thereof, nes	棕榈仁油及其分离品,其他	1513. 2900	4
Palm nuts	油棕果	1207. 9992	3
Palm oil and its fractions, crude oil	棕榈油及其分离品,初榨的	1511. 1000	4
Palm oil and its fractions, nes	棕榈油及其分离品,其他	1511. 9090	48
Palm olein	棕榈液油(熔点 19℃ ~24℃)	1511. 9010	4
Palm stearin	棕榈硬脂(熔点 44℃ ~56℃)	1511. 9020	48
Palm wax	棕榈蜡	1521. 1000	6
Palmitic acid, their salts and esters	棕榈酸及其盐和酯	2915. 7090	36

Article Description	商品名称	Tariff Code	D. R.
Panels and similar articles of vegetable fibre, of straw or of shavings, chips, particles, sawdust or other waste, of wood, agglomerated with cement, plaster or other mineral binders	镶板及类似品,用水泥、石膏及其他矿物粘合材料粘合植物纤维、稻草、刨花、木片屑、木粉、锯末或木废料制成	6808.0000	456
Pantographs	比例缩放仪	9017.8000	7
Panty hose and tights, knitted or crocheted, nes	袜,连裤袜及紧身裤袜,针织或钩编的,其他	6115.2990	2456
Panty hose and tights, knitted or crocheted, of cotton	袜,连裤袜及紧身裤袜,针织或钩编的,棉制	6115.2910	2456
Panty hose and tights, knitted or crocheted, of synthetic fibres, measuring per single yarn 67 decitex or more	袜,连裤袜及紧身裤袜,针织或钩编的,每根单丝细度在67分特及以上的合成纤维制	6115.2200	2456
Panty hose and tights, knitted or crocheted, of synthetic fibres, measuring per single yarn less than 67 decitex	袜,连裤袜及紧身裤袜,针织或钩编的,每根单丝细度在67分特以下的合成纤维制	6115.2100	2456
Panty hose and tights, knitted or crocheted, nes	连裤袜及紧身裤袜,针织或钩编的,其他	6115.2990	2456
Panty hose and tights, knitted or crocheted, of cotton	连裤袜及紧身裤袜,针织或钩编的,棉制	6115.2910	2456
Panty hose and tights, knitted or crocheted, of synthetic fibres, measuring per single yarn 67 decitex or more	连裤袜及紧身裤袜,针织或钩编的,每根单丝细度在67分特及以上的合成纤维制	6115.2200	2456
Panty hose and tights, knitted or crocheted, of synthetic fibres, measuring per single yarn less than 67 decitex	连裤袜及紧身裤袜,针织或钩编的,每根单丝细度在67分特以下的合成纤维制	6115.2100	2456
Papain	木瓜蛋白酶	3507.9090	35
Papaws (Papayas), fresh	木瓜,鲜的	0807.2000	12
Paper and paperboard of a kind used as a base for photo-sensitive, heat-sensitive or electro-sensitive paper or paperboard, nes	纸及纸板的原纸和原纸板,光敏、热敏、电敏,其他	4802.2090	3458
Paper and paperboard of a kind used for writing, printing or other graphic purposes, not containing fibres obtained by a mechanical or chemi-mechanical process or of which not more than 10% by weight of the total fibre content consists of such fibres, coated on one or both sides with kaolin or other inorganic substances, nes	纸及纸板,书写、印刷或类似用途的,不含用机械或化学-机械方法制得的纤维或所含前述纤维不超过全部纤维重量的10%,单面或双面涂布高岭土或其他无机物质的,其他	4810.1900	14568
Paper and paperboard of a kind used for writing, printing or other graphic purposes, of which more than 10% by weight of the total fibre content consists of fibres obtained by a mechanical or chemi-mechanical process, coated on one or both sides with kaolin or other inorganic substances, nes	纸及纸板,书写、印刷或类似用途的,所含用机械或化学-机械方法制得的纤维超过全部纤维重量的10%,单面或双面涂布高岭土或其他无机物质的,其他	4810.2900	14568

P

Article Description	商品名称	Tariff Code	D. R.
Paper and paperboard of a kind used for writing, printing or other graphic purposes, of which more than 10% by weight of the total fibre content, consists of fibres obtained by a mechanical or chemi-mechanical process, coated on one or both sides with kaolin or other inorganic substances, nes	书写、印刷或类似用途的纸及纸板，所含用机械或化学-机械方法制得的纤维超过全部纤维重量的10%，单面或双面涂布高岭土或其他无机物质的，其他	4810. 2900	14568
Paper and paperboard, uncoated, not containing fibres obtained by a mechanical or chemi-mechanical process or of which not more than 10% by weight of the total fibre content consists of such fibres, weighing $40g/m^2$ or more but not more than $150g/m^2$	纸及纸板，未经涂布的，不含用机械或化学-机械方法制得的纤维或所含前述纤维不超过全部纤维重量的10%，每平方米重量在40克及以上，但不超过150克，其他	4802. 5700	3468
Paper and paperboard, Uncoated, not containing fibres obtained by a mechanical or chemi-mechanical process or of which not more than 10% by weight of the total fibre content consists of such fibres, Weighing $40g/m^2$ or more but not more than $150g/m^2$, in sheets with one side not exceeding 435mm and the other side not exceeding 297mm in the unfolded state	纸及纸板，未经涂布的，不含用机械或化学-机械方法制得的纤维或所含前述纤维不超过全部纤维重量的10%，每平方米重量在40克及以上，但不超过150克，一边不越过435毫米，另一边不超过297毫米（以未折叠计）成张的	4802. 5600	3468
Paper and paperboard, uncoated, not containing fibres obtained by a mechanical or chemi-mechanical process or of which not more than 10% by weight of the total fibre content consists of such fibres, weighing less than $40g/m^2$	纸及纸板，未经涂布的，不含用机械或化学-机械方法制得的纤维或所含前述纤维不超过全部纤维重量的10%，每平方米重量小于40克	4802. 5400	3468
Paper and paperboard, uncoated, of which more than 10% by weight of the total fibre content consists of fibres obtained by a mechanical or chemi-mechanical process, in rolls, nes	纸及纸板，未经涂布的，所含用机械或化学-机械方法制得的纤维超过全部纤维重量的10%，成卷的，其他	4802. 6190	3468
Paper and paperboard, Uncoated, not containing fibres obtained by a mechanical or chemi-mechanical process or of which not more than 10% by weight of the total fibre content consists of such fibres, Weighing $40g/m^2$ or more but not more than $150g/m^2$, in rolls	纸及纸板，未经涂布的，不含用机械或化学-机械方法制得的纤维或所含前述纤维不超过全部纤维重量的10%，每平方米重量在40克及以上，但不超过150克，成卷	4802. 5500	3468
Paper and paperboard, uncoated, not containing fibres obtained by a mechanical or chemi-mechanical process or of which not more than 10% by weight of the total fibre content consists of such fibres, weighing more than $150g/m^2$	纸及纸板，未经涂布的，不含用机械或化学-机械方法制得的纤维或所含前述纤维不超过全部纤维重量的10%，每平方米重量超过150克	4802. 5800	3468
Paper and paperboard, Uncoated, of which more than 10% by weight of the total fibre content consists of fibres obtained by a mechanical or chemi-mechanical process, In sheets with one side not exceeding 435mm and the other side not exceeding 297mm in the unfolded state	纸及纸板，未经涂布的，所含用机械或化学-机械方法制得的纤维超过全部纤维重量的10%，成张的，一边不超过435毫米，另一边不超过297毫米（以未折叠计）	4802. 6200	3468

Article Description	商品名称	Tariff Code	D. R.
Paper and paperboard, uncoated, of which more than 10% by weight of the total fibre content consists of fibres obtained by a mechanical or chemi-mechanical process, nes	纸及纸板,未经涂布的,所含用机械或化学-机械方法制得的纤维超过全部纤维重量的10%,其他	4802.6990	3468
Paper and paperboard, coated, impregnated or covered with plastics (excluding adhesives), bleached, weighing more than 150g/m^2, nes	纸及纸板,用塑料(不包括粘合剂)涂布、浸渍或覆盖的,漂白的,每平方米重量超过150克,其他	4811.5190	458
Paper and paperboard, coated, impregnated or covered with plastics (excluding adhesives), nes	纸及纸板,用塑料(不包括粘合剂)涂布、浸渍或覆盖的,其他	4811.5990	458
Paper and paperboard, coated, impregnated or covered with wax, paraffin wax, stearin, oil or glycerol, nes	纸及纸板,用蜡、石蜡、硬脂精、油或甘油涂布、浸渍、覆盖的,其他	4811.6090	458
Paper and paperboard, embossed	纸及纸板,压纹的	4808.9000	58
Paper and paperboard, gummed or adhesive, nes	纸及纸板,胶粘的,其他	4811.4900	458
Paper and paperboard, In rolls, of a kind used for writing, printing or other graphic purposes, not containing fibres obtained by a mechanical or chemi-mechanical process or of which not more than 10% by weight of the total fibre content consists of such fibres, coated on one or both sides with kaolin or other inorganic substances	纸及纸板,成卷的,书写、印刷或类似用途的,不含用机械或化学-机械方法制得的纤维或所含前述纤维不超过全部纤维重量的10%,单面或双面涂布高岭土或其他无机物质的	4810.1300	14568
Paper and paperboard, In sheets with one side not exceeding 435mm and the other side not exceeding 297mm in the unfolded state, of a kind used for writing, printing or other graphic purposes, not containing fibres obtained by a mechanical or chemi-mechanical process or of which not more than 10% by weight of the total fibre content consists of such fibres, coated on one or both sides with kaolin or other inorganic substances	纸及纸板,书写、印刷或类似用途的,不含用机械或化学-机械方法制得的纤维或所含前述纤维不超过全部纤维重量的10%,成张的,一边不超过435毫米,另一边不超过297毫米(以未折叠计),单面或双面涂布高岭土或其他无机物质的	4810.1400	14568
Paper and paperboard, other than that of a kind used for writing, printing or other graphic purposes, coated on one or both sides with kaolin or other inorganic substances, nes	纸及纸板,但书写、印刷或类似用途的除外,单面或双面涂布高岭土或其他无机物质的,其他	4810.9900	14568
Paper and paperboard, other than that of a kind used for writing, printing or other graphic purposes, multiply, coated on one or both sides with kaolin or other inorganic substances	纸及纸板,但书写、印刷或类似用途的除外,多层的,单面或双面涂布高岭土或其他无机物质的	4810.9200	14568
Paper and paperboard, perforated	纸及纸板,穿孔的	4808.9000	58
Paper and paperboard, self-adhesive	纸及纸板,自粘的	4811.4100	458
Paper and paperboard, uncoated, hand-made, nes	纸及纸板,未经涂布的,手工制,其他	4802.1090	3458
Paper and paperboard, uncoated, weighing 150g/m^2 or less, nes	纸及纸板,未经涂布的,每平方米重量在150克及以下,其他	4805.9190	458
Paper and paperboard, uncoated, weighing 225g/m^2 or more	纸及纸板,未经涂布的,每平方米重量在225克及以上	4805.9300	458

Article Description	商品名称	Tariff Code	D. R.
Paper and paperboard, uncoated, weighing more than 150g/m^2 but less than 225g/m^2	纸及纸板,未经涂布的,每平方米重量超过150克,但小于225克	4805.9200	458
Paper articles moulding machines	纸制品模制成型机器	8441.4000	
Paper bags making machines	纸袋制造机器	8441.2000	
Paper bags making machines parts	纸袋制造机器零件	8441.9090	
Paper board finishing machinery	纸板整理机器	8439.3000	
Paper board finishing machinery parts	纸板整理机器的零件	8439.9900	3
Paper board making machinery	纸板抄造机器	8439.2000	
Paper board making machinery parts	纸板抄造机器的零件	8439.9900	3
Paper clips, of base metal	文件夹,贱金属制	8305.9000	256
Paper coated on both sides with plastics for colour photography, bleached, weighing more than 150g/m^2	彩色相纸用双面涂塑纸,漂白的,每平方米重量超过150克	4811.5110	458
Paper cutting machines	切纸机	8441.1000	
Paper fans	纸扇	4823.9030	68
Paper finishing machinery	纸整理机器	8439.3000	
Paper finishing machinery parts	纸整理机器的零件	8439.9900	3
Paper for electrolytic capacitor, weighing 150g/m^2 or less	电解电容器原纸,每平方米重量在150克及以下	4805.9110	458
Paper knives and blades therefor	裁纸刀及其刀片	8214.1000	256
Paper making machinery	纸抄造机器	8439.2000	
Paper making machinery parts	纸抄造机器的零件	8439.9900	3
Paper or paperboard made mainly of bleached chemical pulp, not coloured in the mass	纸和纸板,主要由漂白化学木浆制成未经本体染色的	4707.2000	125
Paper or paperboard made mainly of mechanical pulp (for example, newspapers, journals and similar printed matter)	纸或纸板,主要由机械浆制成的(例如,报纸、杂志及类似印刷品)	4707.3000	125
Paper plastic and aluminium flexible packaging manufacture machines	纸塑铝软包装生产设备	8441.8010	
Paper pulp, paper or paperboard articles moulding machines	纸浆、纸或纸板制品模制成型机器	8441.4000	
Paper rests, of base metal, other than office furniture	文件篮,贱金属制,办公室家具除外	8304.0000	256
Paper shrudders	碎纸机	8472.9030	
Paper trays, of base metal, other than office furniture	文件盘,贱金属制,办公室家具除外	8304.0000	256
Paper yarn	纸纱线	5308.9091	568
Paper yarn woven fabrics	纸纱线机织物	5311.0020	2468
Paracetanol	扑热息痛	2924.2920	36
Parachutes (including dirigible parachutes), parts and accessories	降落伞(包括可操纵降落伞)及其零件、附件	8804.0000	3
Paraffin wax, containing by weight less than 0.75% of oil	石蜡,按重量计含油量小于0.75%	2712.2000	146
Paraffin wax, nes	石蜡,其他	2712.9090	6

P

Article Description	商品名称	Tariff Code	D. R.
Paraformaldehyde	多聚甲醛	2912. 6000	136
Paragliders parts and accessories	滑翔伞及其零件、附件	8804. 0000	3
Paraguay tea	巴拉圭茶	0903. 0000	
Parakeets, pure-bred breeding	长尾鹦鹉,改良种用	0106. 3210	3
Parathion (ISO)	对硫磷(ISO)	2920. 1100	36
Parathion-methyl (ISO) (methyl-parathion)	甲基对硫磷(ISO)	2920. 1100	36
Paring machines, for working wood, cork, bone, hard rubber, hard plastics or similar hard materials	刮削机器,加工木材、软木、骨、硬质橡胶、硬质塑料或类似硬质材料的	8465. 9600	7
Parking equipment, mechanical	停车设备,机械式	8428. 9020	
Parrots, pure-bred breeding	鹦鹉,普通,改良种用	0106. 3210	3
Particle accelerators	粒子加速器	8543. 1000	37
Particle accelerators parts	粒子加速器用零件	8543. 9010	3
Particle board manufacture presses	木碎料板挤压机	8479. 3000	7
Particle board, of ligneous materials, nes	碎料板,木质的,其他	4410. 9019	6
Particle board, of wheat or rice straw	碎料板,麦秸秆制	4410. 9011	6
Particle board, of wood	碎料板,木质	4410. 1100	6
Partly fermented tea, in immediate packings of a content not exceeding 3kg, nes	半发酵茶,内包装每件净重不超过3千克,其他	0902. 3090	248
Partly fermented tea, nes	半发酵茶,其他	0902. 4090	248
Parts and accessories equally suitable for use with machines of two or more of the headings No. 84. 69 to 84. 72	零件、附件,同样适用于税号84. 69至84. 72中两个或两个以上税号所列机器的	8473. 5000	3
Parts and accessories equally suitable for use with machines of two or more of the headings No. 84. 69 to 84. 72	同样适用于税号84. 69至84. 72中两个或两个以上税号所列机器的零件、附件	8473. 5000	3
Parts and accessories of the type writer	打字机的零件、附件	8473. 1000	3
Parts and accessories, for machines of heading No. 84. 62 or 84. 63	零件及附件,税号84. 62或84. 63所列机器用	8466. 9400	3
Parts and accessories, for machines of heading No. 84. 64	零件及附件,税号84. 64所列机器用	8466. 9100	3
Parts and accessories, for machines of heading No. 84. 65	零件及附件,税号84. 65所列机器用	8466. 9200	3
Parts and accessories, for machines of headings No. 84. 56 to 84. 61	零件及附件,税号84. 56至84. 61所列机器用	8466. 9300	3
Parts of birds, nes	鸟体,其他	0505. 9090	34
Parts of magnetic heads, of cassette magnetic tape recorders or reproducers	磁头零件,盒式磁带录音机或放声机用	8522. 9023	3
Parts of plants, edible, nes, otherwise prepared, or preserved	植物部分,食用的,其他,用其他方法制作或保藏的	2008. 9990	248
Parts of plants, edible, nes, prepared or preserved by vinegar or acetic acid	植物部分,食用的,其他,用醋或醋酸制作或保藏的	2001. 9090	48

Article Description	商品名称	Tariff Code	D. R.
Parts of plants, fresh, suitable for bouquets or for ornamental purposes	植物部分,鲜的,制花束或装饰用的	0604. 9100	34
Parts of plants, nes, preserved by sugar (drained, glace or crystallized)	植物部分,其他,用糖保藏的,沥干、糖渍或裹糖的	2006. 0090	48
Parts of plants, nes, suitable for bouquets or for ornamental purposes	植物部分,其他,制花束或装饰用的	0604. 9900	34
Parts of sinking machinery, nes	凿井机械的零件,其他	8431. 4390	3
Parts, for fans or ventilating or recycling hoods	零件,风机、风扇或循环气罩的	8414. 9020	23
Parts, for refrigerators or freezers or air conditioning machines	零件,冷藏箱、冷冻箱用或空气调节器的,其他	8414. 9019	23
Passanger aerial cableways, monocable endless	客运架空索道,单线循环式	8428. 6021	
Passanger aerial cableways, nes	客运架空索道,其他	8428. 6029	
Passenger boarding bridge used at airport	机场用旅客登机桥	8479. 8991	7
Passenger boarding bridge used at airport	旅客登机桥,机场用	8479. 8991	7
Passionfruit juice	西番莲果汁	2009. 8013	2468
Pasta, nes	面食,其他	1902. 3090	246
Pasta, stuffed, nes, whether or not cooked or otherwise prepared	包馅面食,其他,不论是否烹煮或经其他方法制作	1902. 2000	46
Pasta, uncooked, nes, not stuffed or other wise prepared	面食,其他,生的,未包馅或未经其他方法制作	1902. 1900	46
Paste applying machines for the base fabric or other support used in the manufacture of floor coverings	浆料涂布机器,涂布铺地制品的布基或其他底布用	8451. 8000	
Paste applying machines parts	浆料涂布机器零件	8451. 9000	
Pastels	蜡笔(粉)	9609. 9000	3
Pastes, being cooked preparations, nes	果膏,烹煮的,其他	2007. 9990	248
Pastes, citrus fruit, being cooked preparations	果膏,烹煮的,柑橘属水果的	2007. 9100	248
Pastes, citrus fruit, being cooked preparations, in airtight containers	果膏,烹煮的,柑橘属水果的,罐头	2007. 9910	248
Pastry	糕点	1905. 9000	28
Patent leather and patent laminated leather	漆皮及层压漆皮	4114. 2000	1458
Patient monitors	病员监护仪	9018. 1930	
Pawpaws, edible, otherwise prepared, or preserved	木瓜,食用的,用其他方法制作或保藏的	2008. 9990	248
Pawpaws, fresh	木瓜,鲜的	0810. 9090	1
Pawpaws, frozen	木瓜,冷冻的	0811. 9090	1
Pawpaws, provisionally preserved, unsuitable for immediate consumption	木瓜,暂时保藏,但不适于直接食用的	0812. 9000	34
PBT(Polybutylene terephthalate), in primary forms	聚对苯二甲酸丁二酯,初级形状的	3907. 9910	1256
Pdyethylene glycol tevephthalate waste, parings and scrap	聚对苯二甲酸乙二酯的废碎料及下脚料	3915. 9010	146
Peaches, fresh	桃,鲜的	0809. 3000	1
Peaches, otherwise prepared or preserved, nes	桃,其他,用其他方法制作或保藏的	2008. 7090	248

Article Description	商品名称	Tariff Code	D. R.
Peaches, in airtight containers, other wise prepared or preserved	桃,罐头,用其他方法制作或保藏的	2008. 7010	248
Peanut butter	花生酱	2008. 1130	248
Pearls, cultured pearls, unworked, nes	珍珠,养殖的,未加工,其他	7101. 2190	145
Pearls, cultured pearls, unworked, ungraded	珍珠,养殖的,未加工,未分级	7101. 2110	145
Pearls, cultured pearls, worked, nes	珍珠,养殖的,已加工,其他	7101. 2290	145
Pearls, cultured pearls, worked, ungraded	珍珠,养殖的,已加工,未分级	7101. 2210	145
Pearls, natural, nes	珍珠,天然的,其他	7101. 1099	145
Pearls, natural, ungraded, nes	珍珠,天然的,未分级,其他	7101. 1019	145
Pears, in airtight containers	梨,罐头	2008. 4010	248
Pears, nes, fresh	梨,其他,鲜的	0808. 2019	1
Pears, nes, otherwise prepared, or preserved	梨,其他,用其他方法制作或保藏的	2008. 4090	248
Peas (pisum sativum), frozen	豌豆,冷冻的	0710. 2100	1
Peas (pisum sativum), nes, dried, shelled	豌豆,其他,脱荚的,干的	0713. 1090	34
Peas (pisum sativum), seed, dried, shelled	豌豆,种用,脱荚的,干的	0713. 1010	34
Peas (pisum sativum), prepared or preserved otherwise than by vinegar or acetic acid, not frozen	豌豆,用醋或醋酸以外的其他方法制作或保藏的,未冷冻	2005. 4000	48
Peas (pisum sativum), fresh or chilled	豌豆,鲜或冷藏的	0708. 1000	1
Peat articles	泥煤制品	6815. 2000	6
Peat wax	泥煤蜡	2712. 9090	6
Peat (including peat litter), whether or not agglomerated	泥煤(包括肥料用泥煤),不论是否制成型	2703. 0000	14
Pebbles, of a kind commonly used for concrete aggregates, for road metalling or for railway	卵石,通常作混凝土粒料、铺路、铁道路基或其他路基用的	2517. 1000	13
Pecan nuts, fresh or dried	山核桃,鲜或干的	0802. 9090	134
Pectates	果胶酸酯	1302. 2000	3
Pectic substances	果胶	1302. 2000	3
Pectinates and pectates	果胶酸盐	1302. 2000	3
Pedal cars and similar wheeled toys	踏板汽车及类似的带轮玩具	9503. 0010	
Pedals and parts thereof, of bicycles and other cycles	脚蹬及其零件,自行车及脚踏车的	8714. 9610	3
Pedestal jib cranes	座式旋臂起重机	8426. 3000	7
Pedestrian controlled tractors	手扶拖拉机	8701. 1000	
Pedicure sets and instruments	修脚用具	8214. 2000	256
Pedometers and the like	步数计及类似仪表	9029. 1090	7
Pedometers parts and accessories	步数计零件、附件	9029. 9000	3
Peel of citrus fruit or melons (including watermelons), fresh, frozen, dried or provisionally preserved in brine, in sulphur water or in other preservative solutions	果皮,柑橘属水果或甜瓜(包括西瓜)的,鲜、冻、干或用盐水、亚硫酸水或其他防腐液暂时保藏的	0814. 0000	14
Pellets for air gun	弹丸,气枪的	9306. 2900	3
Pellets of cereals, nes	团粒,其他谷物的	1103. 2090	4
Pellets of wheat	团粒,小麦的	1103. 2010	4

P

Article Description	商品名称	Tariff Code	D. R.
Pemoline (INN); salts thereof	匹莫林(INN)盐	2934. 9100	36
Pen nibs and nib points	笔头及笔尖粒,钢笔的	9608. 9100	
Pen nibs and nib points	钢笔头及笔尖粒	9608. 9100	
Pen of a kind used on machines or instruments	笔,机器、仪器用	9608. 9910	
Pen or pencil parts	笔的零件	9608. 9990	3
Pen trays, of base metal, other than office furniture	笔盘,贱金属制,办公室家具除外	8304. 0000	256
Pen, in sets of two or more pens	笔,成套的,由上述两个或多个组成的	9608. 5000	
Pencil leads, black or other colour	铅笔芯,黑的或其他颜色的	9609. 2000	
Pencil sharpeners and blades there of	铅笔刀及其刀片	8214. 1000	256
Pencile sharpener	转笔刀	8472. 9090	
Pencils	铅笔	9609. 1010	
Pencils, propelling or sliding	铅笔,活动铅笔	9608. 4000	
Pencil-holders	铅笔套	9608. 9920	
Pencil-sharpening machines	削铅笔机	8472. 9090	
Penicillanic acid structure, or streptomycins or their derivatives medicaments, mixed or unmixed, put up in measured doses or in forms of packings for retail sale	青霉烷酸结构的青霉素衍生物或链霉素及其衍生物的药品,混合或未混合的,配定剂量或制成零售包装	3004. 1090	368
Penicillanic acid structure, or streptomycins or their derivatives medicaments, consisting of two or more constituents which have been mixed together, not put up in measured doses or in forms of packings for retail sale	青霉烷酸结构的青霉素衍生物或链霉素及其衍生物的药品,两种或两种以上成分混合而成的,未配定剂量或制成零售包装	3003. 1090	368
Penicillin V	青霉素 V	2941. 1094	
Penicillin V medicaments, consisting of two or more constituents which have been mixed together, not put up in measured doses or in forms of packings for retail sale	青霉素 V 药品,两种或两种以上成分混合而成的,未配定剂量或制成零售包装	3003. 1013	368
Penicillin V medicaments, mixed or unmixed, put up in measured doses or in forms of packings for retail sale	青霉素 V 药品,混合或未混合的,配定剂量或制成零售包装	3004. 1013	368
Penicillins and their derivatives medicaments, nes, consisting of two or more constituents which have been mixed together, not put up in measured doses or in forms of packings for retail sale	青霉素及其衍生物药品,其他,两种或两种以上成分混合而成的,未配定剂量或制成零售包装	3003. 1019	368
Penicillins and their derivatives medicaments, nes, mixed or unmixed, put up in measured doses or in forms of packings for retail sale	青霉素及其衍生物药品,其他,混合或未混合的,配定剂量或制成零售包装	3004. 1019	368
Penicillins and their derivatives with a penicillanic acid structure; salts thereof, nes	青霉素和具有青霉烷酸结构的青霉素衍生物及其盐,其他	2941. 1099	
Pens refills of ball point pens	笔芯,圆珠笔的	9608. 6000	
Pens, ball point pens	笔,圆珠笔	9608. 1000	

P

Article Description	商品名称	Tariff Code	D. R.
Pens, duplicating stylos	笔,蜡纸铁笔	9608.9920	
Pens, felt tipped pens	笔,毡尖笔	9608.2000	
Pens, fountain pens	笔,自来水笔	9608.3910	
Pens, indian ink drawing pens	笔,墨汁画笔	9608.3100	
Pens, markers	笔,记号笔	9608.2000	
Pens, markers	笔,唛头笔	9608.2000	
Pens, nes	笔,钢笔,其他	9608.3990	3
Pens, porous-tipped pens	笔,渗水式笔	9608.2000	
Pens, propelling or sliding pencils	笔,活动铅笔	9608.4000	
Pentachlorofluoroethane	五氯氟乙烷	2903.4520	36
Pentachlorophenol (ISO)	五氯苯酚(ISO)	2908.1100	36
Pentachlorotrifluoropropane	五氯三氟丙烷	2903.4560	36
Pentaerythritol	季戊四醇	2905.4200	36
Pentanoic acids, their salts and esters	戊酸及其盐和酯	2915.6000	36
Pentazocine (INN); salts thereof	喷他左辛(INN)以及盐	2933.3300	36
Pentlandite	镍黄铁矿	2604.0000	146
Pentobarbital (INN); salts thereof	戊巴比妥(INN)以及盐	2933.5300	36
Pen-holders, pencil-holders and similar holders	笔套	9608.9920	
Pen-holders, pencil-holders and similar holders	钢笔套、铅笔套及类似的笔套	9608.9920	
Pepper, crushed or ground	胡椒,已磨	0904.1200	4
Pepper, neither crushed nor ground	胡椒,未磨	0904.1100	4
Pepsin	胃蛋白酶	3507.9090	35
Peptones	蛋白胨	3504.0010	1346
Peptones derivatives	蛋白胨衍生物	3504.0090	1346
Perbromates, inorganic	过溴酸盐,无机的	2829.9000	
Perchlorates, inorganic	高氯酸盐,无机的	2829.9000	
Perchloroethylene	全氯乙烯	2903.2300	36
Percussion musical instruments, nes	打击乐器,其他	9206.0000	5
Percussion or detonating caps	火帽或雷管	3603.0000	
Perfluorolisobutylene	全氟异丁烯	2903.3910	36
Perforating punches and similar tools	打孔冲子及类似工具	8203.4000	256
Perforator, for stapling	打孔机,装订用	8472.9021	
Perfumed bath salts and other bath preparations	香浴盐及其他沐浴用制剂	3307.3000	23
Perfumery, cosmetic or toilet preparations, nes	芳香料制品及化妆盥洗品,其他	3307.9000	23
Perfumes	香水	3303.0000	2
Perfuming or deodorizing preparations for rooms, nes	室内散香或除臭制品,其他	3307.4900	23
Perhalogenated derivatives, nes	全卤化衍生物,其他	2903.4700	36
Perilla seeds	紫苏子	1207.9999	3
Periodates, inorganic	高碘酸盐,无机的	2829.9000	
Periscopes	潜望镜式望远镜	9013.1000	
Periscopes	望远镜	9013.1000	

P

Article Description	商品名称	Tariff Code	D. R.
Perlite, unexpanded	珍珠岩,未膨胀的	2530.1020	13456
Permanent magnets articles, intended to become after magnetization	永磁铁的物品,未磁化	8505.1900	48
Permanent magnets of metal, nes	永磁体,金属的,其他	8505.1190	47
Permanent magnets of rare-earth metals	永磁体,稀土的	8505.1110	46
Permanganates, nes	高锰酸盐,其他	2841.6900	1
Peroxoborates (perborates)	过硼酸盐	2840.3000	
Peroxocarbonates (percarbonates)	过碳酸盐	2836.9990	
Peroxochromates	过铬酸盐	2841.5000	1
Peroxometallicacids salts, nes	过金属酸盐,其他	2841.9000	1
Peroxosulphates, inorganic	过硫酸盐,无机的	2833.4000	
Perry	梨酒	2206.0090	2468
Persimmons, dried	柿饼,干的	0813.4020	34
Persimmons, fresh	柿子,鲜的	0810.9090	1
Persimmons, edible, otherwise prepared or preserved	柿子,食用的,用其他方法制作或保藏的	2008.9990	248
Personal deodorants and antiperspirants	人体除臭剂及止汗剂	3307.2000	23
Personal weighing machines, including baby scales; household scales	体重计,包括婴儿秤;家用秤	8423.1000	
Persulphates, inorganic	过硫酸盐,无机的	2833.4000	
Pethidine (INN) intermediate A; salts thereof	哌替啶中间体 A(INN)以及盐	2933.3300	36
Pethidine (INN); salts thereof	哌替啶(INN)以及盐	2933.3300	36
Petroleum bitumen	石油沥青	2713.2000	12348
Petroleum coke, calcined, containing by weight less than 0.8% of sulphur	石油焦,已煅烧,硫的重量百分比小于0.8%的	2713.1210	134
Petroleum coke, calcined, nes	石油焦,已煅烧,其他	2713.1290	134
Petroleum coke, not calcined, containing by weight less than 3% of sulphur	石油焦,未煅烧,硫的重量百分比小于3%的	2713.1110	134
Petroleum coke, not calcined, nes	石油焦,未煅烧,其他	2713.1190	134
Petroleum fracturing unit trucks	石油压裂车	8705.9080	7
Petroleum gases and gaseous hydrocarbons, nes, in gaseous state	石油气及烃类气,其他,气态的	2711.2900	1468
Petroleum gases and gaseous hydrocarbons, nes, liquid	石油气及烃类气,其他,液态的	2711.1990	1468
Petroleum jelly	凡士林	2712.1000	
Petroleum mixing sand trucks	石油混沙车	8705.9080	7
Petroleum oils, crude	石油原油	2709.0000	56
Petroleum resins, in primary forms	石油树脂,初级形状的	3911.1000	16
Petroleum well logging trucks	石油测井车	8705.9080	7
Pharmaceutical articles, of vulcanized rubber other than hard rubber, nes	医疗用品,硫化橡胶(硬质橡胶除外)制的,其他	4014.9000	23
Phenacetin	对乙酰氨基苯乙醚	2924.2910	36

P

Article Description	商品名称	Tariff Code	D. R.
Phenacetin	非那西丁	2924. 2910	36
Phenazone and its derivatives	二甲基苯基吡唑酮及其衍生物	2933. 1100	36
Phencyclidine (INN) (pcp); salts thereof	苯环利定(INN)以及盐	2933. 3300	36
Phendimet razine (INN); salts thereof	苯巴曲嗪(INN)及盐	2934. 9100	36
Phenmetrazine (INN) ; salts thereof	芬美曲嗪(INN) 及盐	2934. 9100	36
Phenobarbital (INN); salts thereof	苯巴比妥(INN)以及盐	2933. 5300	36
Phenol	苯酚	2907. 1110	36
Phenol salts	苯酚盐	2907. 1190	36
Phenolic resins	酚醛树脂	3909. 4000	1256
Phenols or phenol alcohols, derivatives containing only halogen substituents and their salts, nes	酚及酚醇,仅含卤素取代基的衍生物及其盐,其他	2908. 1990	36
Phenols or phenolalcohols, halogenated, sulphonated, nitrated ornitrosated derivatives of, nes	酚及酚醇的卤化、磺化、硝化或亚硝化衍生物,其他	2908. 9990	36
Phenols, of the distillation of high temperature coal tar	酚,蒸馏高温煤焦油所得的	2707. 9910	6
Phenol-alcohols	酚醇	2907. 2990	36
Phenoperidine (INN); salts thereof	苯哌利定(INN)以及盐	2933. 3300	36
Phenothiazine ring-system compounds, not further fused in the structure, whether or not hydrogenated	吩噻嗪环系化合物,结构上含有,未经进一步稠合的,不论是否氢化	2934. 3000	36
Phentermine(INN); salts thereof	苯丁胺(INN)以及它们的盐	2921. 4600	36
Phenyl propan-2-one	苯基丙-2-酮	2914. 3100	36
Phenylacetic acid and its salts	苯乙酸及其盐	2916. 3400	36
Pholcodine (INN) and salts	福尔可定(INN) 及盐	2939. 1100	34
Phorones	佛尔酮	2914. 1900	36
Phosgene	光气	2812. 1030	
Phosphamidon (ISO)	磷胺(ISO)	2924. 1200	36
Phosphates of calcium, nes	磷酸钙,其他	2835. 2600	
Phosphates, nes, inorganic	磷酸盐,其他,无机的	2835. 2990	
Phosphatic chalk, ground	磷酸盐白垩,碾磨	2510. 2090	46
Phosphatic chalk, unground	磷酸盐白垩,未碾磨	2510. 1090	46
Phosphides, whether or not chemically defined, excluding ferrophophorus	磷化物,不论是否已有化学定义,但不包括磷铁	2848. 0000	6
Phosphinates (hypophosphites), inorganic	次磷酸盐,无机的	2835. 1000	
Phosphites, nes	亚磷酸酯,其他	2920. 9019	36
Phosphoam-inolipids, nes	磷氨基类脂,其他	2923. 2000	36
Phosphonates(phosphites), inorganic	亚磷酸盐,无机的	2835. 1000	
Phosphoric acid, food grade	磷酸,食品级	2809. 2011	6
Phosphoric acid, nes	磷酸,其他	2809. 2019	6
Phosphoric esters and their salts, their halogenated, sulphonated, nitrated or nitrosated derivatives	磷酸酯及其盐,以及它们的卤化、磺化、硝化或亚硝化衍生物	2919. 9000	36
Phosphorus oxychloride	氧氯化磷	2812. 1020	
Phosphorus oxytrichloride	三氯氧磷	2812. 1020	

P

Article Description	商品名称	Tariff Code	D. R.
Phosphorus pentachloride	五氯化磷	2812. 1045	
Phosphorus trichloride	三氯化磷	2812. 1043	
Phosphorus trisuiphides, commercial type	三硫化二磷,商品级	2813. 9000	
Phosphorus, nes	磷,其他	2804. 7090	6
Phosphorus, white	白磷	2804. 7010	6
Phosphorus, yellow	黄磷	2804. 7010	6
Phosphoryl monochloride	磷酰氯	2812. 1020	
Photo paper bese	照相原纸	4802. 2010	3458
Photocathode parts, nes	光阴极管零件,其他	8540. 9990	3
Photocathode tubes, nes	光阴极管,其他	8540. 2090	35
Photochromic spectacle lenses, of glass	变色镜片,玻璃制	9001. 4010	
Photochromic spectacle lenses, of other materials	变色镜片,其他材料制	9001. 5010	
Photochromic spectacles	变色镜	9004. 9010	
Photocopying apparatus, incorporating an optical system	感光复印设备,带有光学系统的	8443. 3921	57
Photocopying apparatus, of the contact type	感光复印设备,接触式的	8443. 3922	57
Photograph, of base metal	相框,贱金属制	8306. 3000	256
Photographic apparatus and equipment parts and accessories, nes	照相用装置及设备的零件、附件,其他	9010. 9090	3
Photographic apparatus and equipment parts and accessories, with special purposes	照相用装置及设备的零件、附件,特种的	9010. 9020	3
Photographic enlargers and reducers parts and accessories	照片放大机及缩片机用零件、附件	9008. 9020	3
Photographic film in rolls, sensitized, unexposed, for X-ray	感光卷片,未曝光的,X 光用	3702. 1000	12368
Photographic film in rolls, sensitized, unexposed, without perforations,, of a width not exceeding 105mm, for preparing printing plates or cylinders, nes	感光卷片,未曝光的,无齿孔的,宽度不超过 105 毫米,照相制版用,其他	3702. 3920	12368
Photographic film in rolls, sensitized, unexposed, without perforations, for preparing printing plates or cylinders, of a width exceeding 610mm and of a length exceeding 200m, nes	感光卷片,未曝光的,无齿孔的,照相制版用,宽度超过 610 毫米,长度超过 200 米,其他	3702. 4229	12368
Photographic film in rolls, sensitized, unexposed, without perforations, of a width exceeding 610mm and of a length exceeding 200 m, for colour photography	感光卷片,未曝光的,无齿孔的,彩色摄影用,宽度超过 610 毫米,长度超过 200 米	3702. 4100	12368
Photographic film in rolls, sensitized, unexposed, without perforations, of a width not exceeding 105mm, for colour photography, nes	感光卷片,未曝光的,无齿孔的,宽度不超过 105 毫米,彩色摄影用,其他	3702. 3190	12368

P

Article Description	商品名称	Tariff Code	D. R.
Photographic film in rolls, sensitized, unexposed, without perforations, of a width not exceeding 105mm, for preparing printing plates or cylinders, with silver halide emulsion	感光卷片,未曝光的,无齿孔的,宽度不超过105毫米,照相制版用,涂卤化银乳液的	3702. 3220	12368
Photographic film in rolls, sensitized, unexposed, without perforations, of a width not exceeding 105mm, nes	感光卷片,未曝光的,无齿孔的,宽度不超过105毫米,其他	3702. 3990	12368
Photographic film in rolls, sensitized, unexposed, without perforations, of a width not exceeding 105mm, with silver halide emulsion, nes	感光卷片,未曝光的,无齿孔的,宽度不超过105毫米,涂卤化银乳液的,其他	3702. 3290	12368
Photographic film in rolls, unexposed, for colour photography, other than for slides, of a width 34mm and of a length not exceeding 2m	感光卷片,未曝光的,彩色摄影用的,非幻灯片用,宽度为35毫米,长度不超过2米	3702. 5410	12368
Photographic film in rolls, unexposed, for colour photography, of a width exceeding 16mm but not exceeding 35mm and of a length exceeding 30m, nes	感光卷片,未曝光的,彩色摄影用的,宽度超过16毫米,但不超过35毫米,长度超过30米,其他	3702. 5590	12368
Photographic film in rolls, unexposed, for colour photography, of a width exceeding 16mm but not exceeding 35mm and of a length not exceeding 30m, for slides	感光卷片,未曝光的,彩色摄影用的,幻灯片用,宽度超过16毫米,但不超过35毫米,长度不超过30米	3702. 5300	12368
Photographic film in rolls, unexposed, for colour photography, of a width exceeding 16mm but not exceeding 35mm and of a length not exceeding 30m, other than for slides, nes	感光卷片,未曝光的,彩色摄影用的,非幻灯片用,宽度超过16毫米,但不超过35毫米,长度不超过30米,其他	3702. 5490	12368
Photographic film in rolls, unexposed, for colour photography, of a width exceeding 35mm, nes	感光卷片,未曝光的,彩色摄影用的,宽度超过35毫米,其他	3702. 5690	12368
Photographic film in rolls, unexposed, for colour photography, of a width not exceeding 16mm and of a length exceeding 14m	感光卷片,未曝光的,彩色摄影用的,宽度不超过16毫米,长度超过14米	3702. 5200	12368
Photographic film in rolls, unexposed, for colour photography, of a width not exceeding 16mm and of a length not exceeding 14m	感光卷片,未曝光的,彩色摄影用的,宽度不超过16毫米,长度不超过14米	3702. 5100	12368
Photographic film in rolls, unexposed, of a width 35mm and of a length not exceeding 2m	感光卷片,未曝光的,宽度为35毫米,长度不超过2米	3702. 9310	12368
Photographic film in rolls, unexposed, of a width exceeding 16mm but not exceeding 35mm and of a length exceeding 30m, nes	感光卷片,未曝光的,宽度超过16毫米,但不超过35毫米,长度超过30米,其他	3702. 9490	12368
Photographic film in rolls, unexposed, of a width exceeding 16mm but not exceeding 35mm and of a length not exceeding 30m, nes	感光卷片,未曝光的,宽度超过16毫米,但不超过35毫米,长度不超过30米,其他	3702. 9390	12368
Photographic film in rolls, unexposed, of a width exceeding 35mm, nes	感光卷片,未曝光的,宽度超过35毫米,其他	3702. 9590	12368

Article Description	商品名称	Tariff Code	D. R.
Photographic film in rolls, unexposed, of a width not exceeding 16mm, nes	感光卷片，未曝光的，宽度不超过16毫米，其他	3702.9100	12368
Photographic film in rolls, unexposed, without perforations, for preparing printing plates or cylinders, of a width exceeding 105mm but not exceeding 610mm, nes	感光卷片，未曝光的，无齿孔的，照相制版用，宽度超过105毫米，但不超过610毫米，其他	3702.4429	12368
Photographic film in rolls, unexposed, without perforations, for preparing printing plates or cylinders, of a width exceeding 610mm and of a length not exceeding 200m, nes	感光卷片，未曝光的，无齿孔的，照相制版用，宽度超过610毫米，长度不超过200米，其他	3702.4329	12368
Photographic film in rolls, unexposed, without perforations, of a width exceeding 105mm but not exceeding 610mm, nes	感光卷片，未曝光的，无齿孔的，宽度超过105毫米，但不超过610毫米，其他	3702.4490	12368
Photographic film in rolls, unexposed, without perforations, of a width exceeding 610mm and of a length exceeding 200 m, other than for colour photography, nes	感光卷片，未曝光的，无齿孔的，非彩色摄影用，宽度超过610毫米，长度超过200米，其他	3702.4299	12368
Photographic film in rolls, unexposed, without perforations, of a width exceeding 610mm and of a length not exceeding 200m, nes	感光卷片，未曝光的，无齿孔的，宽度超过610毫米，长度不超过200米，其他	3702.4390	12368
Photographic flashlight discharge lamp (electronic)	照相闪光灯，放电式（电子式）	9006.6100	7
Photographic paper and paperboard, unexposed, for colour photography	感光纸及纸板，未曝光的，彩色摄影用	3703.2010	1238
Photographic paper and paperboard, unexposed, in rolls of a width exceeding 610mm	感光纸及纸板，未曝光的，成卷，宽度超过610毫米	3703.1010	1238
Photographic paper and paperboard, unexposed, nes	感光纸及纸板，未曝光的，其他	3703.9010	1238
Photographic plates and film in the flat, sensitized, unexposed, for colour photography (polychrome)	感光硬片及平面软片，未曝光的，彩色摄影用	3701.9100	12368
Photographic plates and film in the flat, sensitized, unexposed, for preparing printing plates or cylinders, nes	感光硬片及平面软片，未曝光的，照相制版用，其他	3701.9920	12368
Photographic plates and film in the flat, sensitized, unexposed, for X-ray	感光硬片及平面软片，未曝光的，X光用	3701.1000	12368
Photographic plates and film in the flat, sensitized, unexposed, nes	感光硬片及平面软片，未曝光的，其他	3701.9990	12368
Photographic plates and film in the flat, sensitized, unexposed, with any side exceeding 255mm, for preparing printing plates or cylinders, nes	感光硬片及平面软片，未曝光的，任何一边超过255毫米，照相制版用，其他	3701.3029	12368
Photographic plates and film in the flat, sensitized, unexposed, with any side exceeding 255mm, nes	感光硬片及平面软片，未曝光的，任何一边超过255毫米，其他	3701.3090	12368
Photographic plates and film, for offset reproduction, exposed and developed	摄影硬片及软片，供复制胶版用，已曝光已冲洗的	3705.1000	1238

Article Description	商品名称	Tariff Code	D. R.
Photographic plates and film, exposed and developed, other than cinematographic film, nes	摄影硬片及软片,已曝光已冲洗的,电影胶片除外,其他	3705. 9090	1238
Photographic plates, film, paper, paperboard and textiles, exposed but not developed, nes	摄影硬片、软片、纸、纸板及纺织物,已曝光未冲洗的,其他	3704. 0090	1238
Photographic textiles, unexposed, for colour photography	感光纺织物,未曝光的,彩色摄影用	3703. 2090	1238
Photographic textiles, unexposed, in rolls of a width exceeding 610mm	感光纺织物,未曝光的,成卷,宽度超过 610 毫米	3703. 1090	1238
Photographic textiles, unexposed, nes	感光纺织物,未曝光的,其他	3703. 9090	1238
Photographic(other than cinematographic) enlargers	照片(电影片除外)放大机	9008. 4000	
Photographic(other than cinematographic) reducers	照片(电影片除外)缩片机	9008. 4000	
Photosensitive semiconductor devices, nes	光敏半导体器件,其他	8541. 4090	5
Phthalic anhydride	邻苯二甲酸酐	2917. 3500	36
Physical exercise, gymnastics or athletics articles and equipment, for general, nes	体育用品及设备,一般的,其他	9506. 9190	5
Physical exercise, gymnastics or athletics articles, nes	体育用品及设备,其他	9506. 9900	5
Physical or chemical analysis instruments and apparatus parts and accessories	理化分析仪器及装置零件、附件	9027. 9000	3
Physical or chemical analysis instruments and apparatus, nes	理化分析仪器及装置,其他	9027. 8099	7
Physical or chemical analysis instruments and apparatus, using optical radiations (UV, visible, IR), nes	理化分析仪器及装置,使用光学射线(紫外线、可见光、红外线)的,其他	9027. 5000	7
Physical vapour deposition (PVD) equipment parts and accessories, semiconductor devices or of electronic integrated circuits or flat panel displays manufacture machines and apparatus	物理气相沉积装置(PVD)零件及附件,制造半导体器件、集成电路、平板显示器的机器及装置	8486. 9090	3
Physical vapour deposition (PVD) equipment, semiconductor devices or of electronic integrated circuits manufacture machines and apparatus	物理气相沉积装置(PVD),制造半导体器件或集成电路的机器及装置	8486. 2022	7
Physical vapour deposition (PVD) equipment, flat panel displays manufacture machines and apparatus	物理气相沉积设备(PVD),平板显示器的制造机器及装置	8486. 3022	7
Phytosterols	植物甾醇类	2906. 1310	36
Pianos parts and accessories	钢琴的零件、附件	9209. 9100	3
Pianos, automatic	钢琴,自动的	9201. 9000	5
Pianos, grand	钢琴,大钢琴	9201. 2000	5
Pianos, grand	钢琴,平台式	9201. 2000	5
Pianos, upright	钢琴,竖式的	9201. 1000	5
Pickling preparations for metal surfaces	金属表面酸洗剂	3810. 1000	36
Picks	锄	8201. 3000	256
Pick-up cartridges	拾音头	8522. 1000	3

P

Article Description	商品名称	Tariff Code	D. R.
Picture or similar frames, of base metal	画框及类似框架,贱金属制	8306. 3000	256
Pictures, designs and photographs, printed	图片、设计图样及照片,印刷品	4911. 9100	3
Pien tzu huang	片仔癀	3004. 9052	368
Piezo-electrie crystals, mounted	压电晶体,已装配的	8541. 6000	5
Pig fat (including lard), other than that of heading No. 02. 09 or 15. 03	猪脂肪(包括的猪油),但税号 02. 09 及 15. 03 的货品除外	1501. 0000	
Pig fat, free of lean meat, not rendered or otherwise extracted, fresh, chilled, frozen, salted, in brine, dried or smoked	猪脂肪,未炼制或用其他方法提取的不带瘦肉的,鲜、冷、冻、干、熏、盐腌或盐渍的	0209. 0000	14
Pig iron powders, spiegeleisen powders, iron or steel powders, nes	生铁、镜铁及钢铁的粉末,其他	7205. 2900	6
Pig iron, alloy	生铁,合金的	7201. 5000	6
Pig iron, non-alloy, containing by weight 0. 5% or less of phosphorus	生铁,非合金,按重量计含磷量在 0. 5% 及以下	7201. 1000	6
Pig iron, non-alloy, containing by weight more than 0. 5% of phosphorus	生铁,非合金,按重量计含磷量在 0. 5% 以上	7201. 2000	6
Pigments (including metallic powders and flakes) dispersed in non-aqueous media, in liquid or paste form, of a kind used in the manufacture of paints (including enamels)	颜料(包括金属粉末或金属粉片),分散于非水介质中呈液状或浆状的,制造油漆(含瓷漆)用的	3212. 9000	136
Pigments and preparations based on chromium compounds	颜料及制品,以铬化合物为基本成分的	3206. 2000	2368
Pigments and preparations based on zinc sulphide	颜料和制品,硫化锌为基本成分的	3206. 4290	2368
Pigments and preparations based thereon	颜料及以其为基本成分的制品	3204. 1700	345
Pigments and preparations containing 80% or more by weight of titanium dioxide calculated on the dry matter, nes	颜料及制品,以干物质计二氧化钛含量在 80% 及以上的,其他	3206. 1190	2368
Pigments and preparations, based on titanium dioxide, nes	颜料及制品,以二氧化钛为基本成分的,其他	3206. 1900	2368
Pigments and similar preparations, prepared, of a kind used in the ceramic, enamelling or glass industry	颜料及类似制品,调制的,陶瓷、搪瓷及玻璃工业用	3207. 1000	13
Pigments of a kind used for finishing leather, prepared, water based	颜料,加工皮革用的,水性的	3210. 0000	36
Pile and chenille woven fabrics, other than terry or narrow fabrics, nes	起绒及绳绒织物,毛圈及狭幅织物除外,其他	5801. 9090	468
Pile and chenille woven fabrics, other than terry or narrow fabrics, of cotton, chenille fabrics	起绒及绳绒织物,毛圈及狭幅织物除外,棉制,绳绒织物	5801. 2600	468
Pile and chenille woven fabrics, other than terry or narrow fabrics, of cotton, cut corduroy	起绒及绳绒织物,毛圈及狭幅织物除外,棉制,割绒的灯芯绒	5801. 2200	468
Pile and chenille woven fabrics, other than terry or narrow fabrics, of cotton, uncut weft pile fabrics	起绒及绳绒织物,毛圈及狭幅织物除外,棉制,不割绒的纬起绒织物	5801. 2100	468

Article Description	商品名称	Tariff Code	D. R.
Pile and chenille woven fabrics, other than terry or narrow fabrics, of cotton, warp pile fabrics, cut	起绒及绳绒织物,毛圈及狭幅织物除外,棉制,割绒的经起绒织物	5801. 2500	468
Pile and chenille woven fabrics, other than terry or narrow fabrics, of cotton, warp pile fabrics, èpinglè (uncut)	起绒及绳绒织物,毛圈及狭幅织物除外,棉制,不割绒的经起绒织物(棱纹绸)	5801. 2400	468
Pile and chenille woven fabrics, other than terry or narrow fabrics, of cotton, weft pile fabrics, nes	起绒及绳绒织物,毛圈及狭幅织物除外,棉制,纬起绒织物,其他	5801. 2300	468
Pile and chenille woven fabrics, other than terry or narrow fabrics, of man-made fibres, chenille fabrics	起绒及绳绒织物,毛圈及狭幅织物除外,化学纤维制,绳绒织物	5801. 3600	468
Pile and chenille woven fabrics, other than terry or narrow fabrics, of man-made fibres, cut corduroy	起绒及绳绒织物,毛圈及狭幅织物除外,化学纤维制,割绒的灯芯绒	5801. 3200	468
Pile and chenille woven fabrics, other than terry or narrow fabrics, of man-made fibres, uncut weft pile fabrics	起绒及绳绒织物,毛圈及狭幅织物除外,化学纤维制,不割绒的纬起绒织物	5801. 3100	468
Pile and chenille woven fabrics, other than terry or narrow fabrics, of man-made fibres, warp pile fabrics, cut	起绒及绳绒织物,毛圈及狭幅织物除外,化学纤维制,割绒的经起绒织物	5801. 3500	468
Pile and chenille woven fabrics, other than terry or narrow fabrics, of man-made fibres, warp pile fabrics, èpinglè (uncut)	起绒及绳绒织物,毛圈及狭幅织物除外,化学纤维制,不割绒的经起绒织物(棱纹绸)	5801. 3400	468
Pile and chenille woven fabrics, other than terry or narrow fabrics, of man-made fibres, weft pile fabrics, nes	起绒及绳绒织物,毛圈及狭幅织物除外,化学纤维制,纬起绒织物,其他	5801. 3300	468
Pile and chenille woven fabrics, other than terry or narrow fabrics, of silk or silk waste	起绒及绳绒织物,毛圈及狭幅织物除外,丝及绢丝制	5801. 9010	468
Pile and chenille woven fabrics, other than terry or narrow fabrics, of wool or fine animal hair	起绒及绳绒织物,毛圈及狭幅织物除外,羊毛或动物细毛制	5801. 1000	468
Pile fabrics, of cotton, knitted or crocheted	起绒织物,针织或钩编的,棉制	6001. 9100	46
Pile fabrics, of man-made fibres, knitted or crocheted	起绒织物,针织或钩编的,化学纤维制	6001. 9200	46
Pile fabrics, of textile materials, knitted or crocheted, nes	起绒织物,针织或钩编的,其他纺织材料制	6001. 9900	46
Piles, pickets and stakes of wood, pointed but not sawn lengthwise, coniferous	木桩,已削尖但未经纵锯的木桩,针叶木的	4404. 1000	15
Piles, pickets and stakes of wood, pointed but not sawn lengthwise, non-coniferous	木桩,已削尖但未经纵锯的木桩,非针叶木的	4404. 2000	15
Pile-drivers	打桩机	8430. 1000	5
Pile-drivers parts	打桩机零件	8431. 4990	3
Pile-extractors	拔桩机	8430. 1000	5
Pile-extractors parts	拔桩机零件	8431. 4990	3
Pillows, nes	枕头,其他	9404. 9090	6
Pillows, stuffed with animal hair	枕头,兽毛填充的	9404. 9020	6
Pillows, stuffed with feathers or down	枕头,羽毛或羽绒填充的	9404. 9010	6
Pillows, stuffed with man-made fibres	枕头,化纤棉填充的	9404. 9040	6

Article Description	商品名称	Tariff Code	D. R.
Pillows, stuffed with silk wadding	枕头,丝棉填充的	9404. 9030	6
Pilose antlers and powder thereof	鹿茸及其粉末	0507. 9020	14
Pinazepam(INN); salts thereof	匹那西泮(INN)以及盐	2933. 9100	36
Pincers and similar tools	钳子及类似工具	8203. 2000	256
Pine oil	松油	3805. 9010	36
Pineapple juice, nes	菠萝汁,其他	2009. 4900	2468
Pineapple juice, of a brix value not exceeding 20	菠萝汁,白利糖度值不超过 20 的	2009. 4100	2468
Pineapples	菠萝	0804. 3000	145
Pineapples, in airtight containers	菠萝,罐头	2008. 2010	248
Pineapples, nes, otherwise prepared, or preserved	菠萝,其他,用其他方法制作或保藏的	2008. 2090	248
Pinene	蒎烯	2902. 1910	6
Pinenuts, shelled	松子仁	0802. 9030	134
Pineresin	松脂	1301. 9040	
Pinking machines for textile fabrics	剪齿边机器,纺织物的	8451. 5000	
Pinking machines parts, for textile fabrics	剪齿边机器零件,纺织物的	8451. 9000	
Pinnatifida, dried	裙带菜,干的	1212. 2031	14
Pinnatifida, fresh	裙带菜,鲜的	1212. 2032	14
Pinnatifida, nes	裙带菜,其他	1212. 2039	14
Pinnatifida, salted	裙带菜,盐腌的	2008. 9933	248
Pintables	弹球机	9504. 9090	5
Pipefish, dried	海龙,干的	0305. 5910	4
Piperazine ring compounds, in the structure, whether or not hydrogenated, nes	哌嗪环化合物,结构上含有,其他	2933. 5990	36
Piperidine	哌啶	2933. 3210	36
Piperonal	胡椒醛	2932. 9300	36
Piperonal	3,4-亚甲二氧基苯甲醛	2932. 9300	36
Pipes and pipe bowls for smoking	烟斗及烟斗头	9614. 0010	
Pipe-cutters, hand tools	切管器	8203. 4000	256
Pipradrol (INN); salts thereof	哌苯甲醇(INN)以及盐	2933. 3300	36
Piritramide (INN); salts thereof	哌氰米特(INN)以及盐	2933. 3300	36
Pistachios	阿月浑子果(开心果)	0802. 5000	134
Pistols and revolvers for firing blank ammunition	左轮手枪和其他手枪,发射空包弹的	9303. 9000	
Pistols parts and accessories, nes	手枪用零件、附件,其他	9305. 1000	3
Pistols, nes	手枪,其他	9302. 0000	
Pitch	沥青	2708. 1000	14
Pitch coke	沥青焦	2708. 2000	14
Pitch pipes	定音管	9209. 9910	3
Pit-head winding gear	卷扬装置,矿井口用	8425. 3910	78
Pit-head winding gear, powered by electric motor	卷扬装置,电动的,矿井口用	8425. 3110	78
Plaice (pleuronectes platessa), fresh or chilled	鲽鱼,鲜或冷的,	0302. 2200	18
Plaice (pleuronectes platessa), frozen	鲽鱼,冻的	0303. 3200	18

P

Article Description	商品名称	Tariff Code	D. R.
Plain shaft bearings	滑动轴承	8483. 3000	
Plaited bands, slings and the like, of iron or steel, not electrically insulated	编带、吊索及类似品,非绝缘钢铁的	7312. 9000	36
Plaiting materials, plaits and similar products of plaiting materials, bound together in parallel strands or woven, in sheet form, nes	平行连结或编结的成片材料、缏条或类似的编结材料产品,其他	4601. 9990	6
Plaiting materials, plaits and similar products of plaiting materials, bound together in parallel strands or woven, in sheet form, of bamboo	平行连结或编结的成片材料、缏条或类似的编结材料产品,竹制的	4601. 9290	6
Plaiting materials, plaits and similar products of plaiting materials, bound together in parallel strands or woven, in sheet form, of other vegetable materials	平行连结或编结的成片材料、缏条或类似的编结材料产品,其他植物材料制的	4601. 9499	6
Plaiting materials, plaits and similar products of plaiting materials, bound together in parallel strands or woven, in sheet form, of rattan	平行连结或编结的成片材料、缏条或类似的编结材料产品,藤制的	4601. 9390	6
Plaiting materials, plaits and similar products of plaiting materials, bound together in parallel strands or woven, in sheet form, of straw, nes	平行连结或编结的成片材料、缏条或类似的编结材料产品,稻草制的,其他	4601. 9419	6
Plaits and similar products of plaiting materials, whether or not assembled into strips, nes	鞭条及类似产品,不论是否缝合成宽条,其他	4601. 9910	6
Plaits and similar products of plaiting meterials, whether or not assembled into strips, of bamboo	缏条及类似产品,不论是否缝合成宽条,竹制的	4601. 9210	6
Plaits and similar products of plaiting meterials, whether or not assembled into strips, of other vegetable materials	缏条及类似产品,不论是否缝合成宽条,其他植物材料制的	4601. 9491	6
Plaits and similar products of plaiting meterials, whether or not assembled into strips, of rattan	缏条及类似产品,不论是否缝合成宽条,藤制的	4601. 9310	6
Plaits of straw	缏条(绳),稻草制的	4601. 9411	6
Planes, for working wood	刨子,木工用	8205. 3000	256
Planet decelerators	行星齿轮减速器	8483. 4020	7
Planing machines, double column, for removing metal or cermets	刨床,龙门式,切削金属或金属陶瓷用	8461. 9011	7
Planing machines, for removing metal or cermets, nes	刨床,切削金属或金属陶瓷用,其他	8461. 9019	7
Planing machines, for working wood, cork, bone, hard rubber, hard plastics or similar hard materials	刨床,加工木材、软木、骨、硬质橡胶、硬质塑料或类似硬质材料的	8465. 9200	7
Planings, hand tools, with self-contained electric motor	电刨,手提式	8467. 2920	57
Planomilling machines, numerically controlled, for removing metal	龙门铣床,数控的,切削金属的	8459. 6110	7
Planomilling machines, for removing metal, nes	龙门铣床,切削金属的,其他	8459. 6910	7
Plans and drawings copies, photographic reqrodued on sensitized paper and carbon	设计图纸复制件,用感兴纸照相复印或用复写纸眷写的	4906. 0000	

P

Article Description	商品名称	Tariff Code	D. R.
Plans and drawings for architectural, engineering, industrial, commercial topographical or similar purposes, being originals drawn by hand	设计图纸原稿,手绘的,建筑、工程、工业、商业、地形或类似用途的	4906.0000	
Plantains, fresh or dried	芭蕉,鲜或干的	0803.0000	1245
Planters, for agricultural, horticultural or forestry use	种植机,农业、园艺及林业用	8432.3000	
Plants and parts of plants of a kind used primarily in perfumery	植物及其某部分,主要用作香料的	1211.9050	34
Plants and parts of plants of a kind used primarily in pharmacy	植物及其某部分,主要用作药料的	1211.9039	34
Plants and parts of plants, nes	植物及其某部分,其他	1211.9099	34
Plant-growth regulators, nes	植物生长调节剂,其他	3808.9399	36
Plant-growth regulators, put up for retail sale	植物生长调节剂,零售包装	3808.9391	36
Plasma arc welding of metals machines and apparatus parts	等离子弧焊接机器及装置零件	8515.9000	3
Plasma arc welding of metals machines and apparatus, fully or partly automatic, nes	等离子弧焊接机器及装置,全自动或半自动的,其他	8515.3190	
Plasma display modules and part thereof, television receivers parts	等离子显像组件及其零件电视接收机用零件	8529.9082	3
Plaster articles or articles of compositions based on plaster, nes	石膏制品及以石膏为基本成分的混合材料制品,其他	6809.9000	46
Plaster articles or articles of compositions based on plaster, not ornamented, faced or reinforced with paper or paper board only	石膏制品及以石膏为基本成分的混合材料制品,未经装饰的,仅用纸、纸板贴面或加强的,其他	6809.1900	46
Plaster boards, not ornamented, faced or reinforced with paper or paper board only	石膏板,未经装饰的,仅用纸、纸板贴面或加强的	6809.1100	46
Plaster panels, not ornamented, faced or reinforced with paper or paper board only	石膏镶板,未经装饰的,仅用纸、纸板贴面或加强的	6809.1100	46
Plaster tiles and similar articles, not ornamented, faced or reinforced with paper or paper board only	石膏瓦及类似品,未经装饰的,仅用纸、纸板贴面或加强的	6809.1100	46
Plasters, for dental use	熟石膏,牙科用	2520.2010	34
Plasters, nes	熟石膏,其他	2520.2090	34
Plastic articles for the conveyance or packing of goods, nes	塑料制品,供运输或包装货物用的,其他	3923.9000	23
Plastic articles, nes	塑料制品,其他	3926.9090	236
Plastic articles, for office or school supplies	办公室或学校用品,塑料的	3926.1000	236
Plastic articles, of a kind for used in machines or instruments, of plastics	机器及仪器用零件,塑料的	3926.9010	236
Plastic bags, of polymers of ethylene	塑料袋,乙烯聚合物制	3923.2100	23
Plastic bottles	塑料瓶	3923.3000	23
Plastic lids	塑料盖	3923.5000	23
Plastic pelletizers	塑料造粒机	8477.2010	7
Plastics brideg-die-forming machines	塑料中空成型机	8477.4010	7
Plastics calender-forming machines	塑料压延成型机	8477.4020	7

Article Description	商品名称	Tariff Code	D. R.
Plastics encapsulating machines parts and accessories, solely or principally of a kind used for assembling or encapsulating semiconductor devices	塑封机零件及附件,主要用于或专用于装配与封装半导体器件或集成电路	8486.9090	3
Plastics encapsulating machines, solely or principally of a kind used for assembling or encapsulating semiconductor devices	塑封机,主要用于或专用于装配与封装半导体器件或集成电路	8486.4021	7
Plastics waste, parings and scrap, nes	塑料的废碎料及下脚料,其他	3915.9090	146
Plateaux and manchons (including slit manchons), of felt	圆帽片及制帽用的毡呢筒(包括裁开的毡呢筒),毡呢制的	6501.0000	26
Platen screen press	平网印刷机	8443.1922	57
Plates for printing machinery	印刷用版	8442.5000	
Plates making machinery parts	印刷版制造机零件	8442.4000	3
Plates preparing machines for CTP	印刷版制造设备,计算机直接制	8442.3021	
Plates preparing or making machinery, nes	印刷版(片)的制造机器、器具及设备,其他	8442.3090	
Plates, foil exceeding 0.2mm, of lead	板,超过0.2毫米的箔,铅制	7804.1900	16
Plates, of clock or watch	夹板,钟、表的	9114.4000	6
Plates, of metal carbides, coated or cored with flux material, of a kind used for soldering, brazing, welding or deposition of metal or of metal carbides	板,硬质合金制,以焊剂涂面或以焊剂为芯,用于焊接或沉积金属、硬质合金	8311.9000	56
Plates, rods, angles, shapes, sections, tubes and the like, prepared for use in structures, of iron or steel, worked	板、杆、角材、型材、异型材、管子及类似品,结构体用,钢铁的,已加工	7308.9000	6
Plates, sheets and strip of cellular rubber	板、片、带,海绵橡胶制	4008.1100	18
Plates, sheets and strip of non-cellular rubber	板、片、带,非海绵橡胶制	4008.2100	18
Plates, sheets and strip, of a thickness exceeding 0.2mm, of tin	板、片及带,厚度超过0.2毫米,锡制	8007.0020	16
Plates, sheets and strip, of aluminium alloys, rectangular (including square), of a thickness exceeding 0.2mm, nes	板、片及带,铝合金制,矩形(包括正方形),铝厚度超过0.2毫米,其他	7606.1290	246
Plates, sheets and strip, of aluminium alloys, rectangular (including square), of a thickness less than 0.28mm, of a thickness exceeding 0.2mm	板、片及带,铝合金制,矩形(包括正方形),厚度小于0.28毫米,铝厚度超过0.2毫米	7606.1220	246
Plates, sheets and strip, of aluminium alloys, rectangular (including square), of a thickness more than 0.35mm but not exceeding 4mm	板、片及带,铝合金制,矩形(包括正方形),厚度在0.35毫米以上,但不超过4毫米	7606.1250	246
Plates, sheets and strip, of aluminium alloys, rectangular (including square), of a thickness of 0.28mm or more but not exceeding 0.35mm	板、片及带,铝合金制,矩形(包括正方形),厚度在0.28毫米及以上,但不超过0.35毫米	7606.1230	246
Plates, sheets and strip, of aluminium alloys, of a thickness exceeding 0.2mm, nes	板、片及带,铝合金制,铝厚度超过0.2毫米,其他	7606.9200	246
Plates, sheets and strip, of aluminium, not alloyed, of a thickness exceeding 0.2mm, nes	板、片及带,非合金铝制,铝厚度超过0.2毫米,其他	7606.9100	246

P

Article Description	商品名称	Tariff Code	D. R.
Plates, sheets and strip, of aluminium, not alloyed, rectangular (including square), of a thickness exceeding 0. 2mm, nes	板、片及带,非合金铝制,矩形(包括正方形),铝厚度超过 0. 2 毫米,其他	7606. 1190	246
Plates, sheets and strip, of aluminium, not alloyed, rectangular(including square), of a thickness of 0. 30mm or more but not exceeding 0. 36mm	板、片及带,非合金铝制,矩形(包括正方形),厚度在 0. 30 毫米及以上,但不超过 0. 36 毫米	7606. 1120	246
Plates, sheets and strip, of copper-nickel base alloys (cupronickel), of a thickness exceeding 0. 15mm	板、片及带,铜镍合金(白铜),厚度超过 0. 15 毫米,	7409. 4000	16
Plates, sheets and strip, of copper-nickel-zinc base alloys (nickel silver), of a thickness exceeding 0. 15mm	板、片及带,镍锌合金(德银)制,厚度超过 0. 15 毫米,	7409. 4000	16
Plates, sheets and strip, of copper-tin base alloys (bronze), in coils, of a thickness exceeding 0. 15mm	板、片及带,铜锡合金(青铜)制,盘卷的厚度超过 0. 15 毫米,	7409. 3100	16
Plates, sheets and strip, of copper-tin base alloys (bronze), of a thickness exceeding 0. 15mm, nes	板、片及带,铜锡合金(青铜)制,厚度超过 0. 15 毫米,其他	7409. 3900	16
Plates, sheets and strip, of copper-zinc base alloys (brass), in coils, of a thickness exceeding 0. 15mm	板、片及带,铜锌合金(黄铜)制,盘卷的,厚度超过 0. 15 毫米,	7409. 2100	16
Plates, sheets and strip, of copper-zinc base alloys (brass), of a thickness exceeding 0. 15mm, nes	板、片及带,铜锌合金(黄铜)制,厚度超过 0. 15 毫米,其他	7409. 2900	16
Plates, sheets and strip, of other copper alloys, of a thickness exceeding 0. 15mm	板、片及带,其他铜合金制厚度超过 0. 15 毫米,	7409. 9000	16
Plates, sheets and strip, of refined copper, in coils, of a thickness exceeding 0. 15mm, containing oxygen not exceeding 10PPM	板、片及带,精炼铜制,盘卷的,厚度超过 0. 15 毫米,含氧量不超过 10PPM 的	7409. 1110	16
Plates, sheets and strip, of refined copper, in coils, of a thickness exceeding 0. 15mm, nes	板、片及带,精炼铜制,盘卷的,厚度超过 0. 15 毫米,其他	7409. 1190	16
Plates, sheets and strip, of refined copper, of a thickness exceeding 0. 15mm, nes	板、片及带,精炼铜制,厚度超过 0. 15 毫米,其他	7409. 1900	16
Plates, sheets of polyethylene with glass fibres	塑料板、片,聚乙烯制,嵌有玻璃纤维的	3921. 9020	16
Plates, sheets, coils of poly-isobutylene with man-made felt	塑料板、片、卷材,聚异丁烯为基本成分的,附有人造毛毡的	3921. 9030	16
Plates, sheets, film, foil and strip, of plastics, cellular, nes	塑料板、片、膜、箔、扁条,泡沫塑料的,其他	3921. 1990	16
Plates, sheets, film, foil and strip, of plastics, cellular, of polymers of styrene	塑料板、片、膜、箔、扁条,泡沫塑料的,苯乙烯聚合物制	3921. 1100	16
Plates, sheets, film, foil and strip, of plastics, cellular, of polymers of vingl chloride, nes	塑料板、片、膜、箔、扁条,泡沫塑料的,氯乙烯聚合物制,其他	3921. 1290	16
Plates, sheets, film, foil and strip, of plastics, cellular, of polyurethanes, nes	塑料板、片、膜、箔、扁条,泡沫塑料的,氨酯聚合物制,其他	3921. 1390	16
Plates, sheets, film, foil and strip, of plastics, cellular, of regenerated cellulose	塑料板、片、膜、箔、扁条,泡沫塑料的,再生纤维素制	3921. 1400	16

Article Description	商品名称	Tariff Code	D. R.
Plates, sheets, film, foil and strip, of plastics, nes	塑料板、片、膜、箔、扁条,其他	3921.9090	16
Plates, sheets, film, foil and strip, of plastics, non-cellular and not reinforced, laminated, supported or similarly combined with other materials, of acrylic polymers, nes	塑料板、片、膜、箔及扁条,非泡沫,未用其他材料强化、层压、支撑或用类似方法合制,丙烯酸聚合物制,其他	3920.5900	16
Plates, sheets, film, foil and strip, of plastics, non-cellular and not reinforced, laminated, supported or similarly combined with other materials, of amino-resins	塑料板、片、膜、箔及扁条,非泡沫,未用其他材料强化、层压、支撑或用类似方法合制,氨基树脂制	3920.9300	16
Plates, sheets, film, foil and strip, of plastics, non-cellular and not reinforced, laminated, supported or similarly combined with other materials, of cellulose acetate	塑料板、片、膜、箔及扁条,非泡沫,未用其他材料强化、层压、支撑或用类似方法合制,乙酸纤维素制	3920.7300	16
Plates, sheets, film, foil and strip, of plastics, non-cellular and not reinforced, laminated, supported or similarly combined with other materials, of other cellulose derivatives	塑料板、片、膜、箔及扁条,非泡沫,未用其他材料强化、层压、支撑或用类似方法合制,其他纤维素衍生物制	3920.7900	16
Plates, sheets, film, foil and strip, of plastics, non-cellular and not reinforced, laminated, supported or similarly combined with other materials, of other plastics	塑料板、片、膜、箔及扁条,非泡沫,未用其他材料强化、层压、支撑或用类似方法合制,其他塑料制	3920.9990	16
Plates, sheets, film, foil and strip, of plastics, non-cellular and not reinforced, laminated, supported or similarly combined with other materials, of other polyesters	塑料板、片、膜、箔及扁条,非泡沫,未用其他材料强化、层压、支撑或用类似方法合制,其他聚酯制	3920.6900	16
Plates, sheets, film, foil and strip, of plastics, non-cellular and not reinforced, laminated, supported or similarly combined with other materials, of phenolic resins	塑料板、片、膜、箔及扁条,非泡沫,未用其他材料强化、层压、支撑或用类似方法合制,酚醛树脂制	3920.9400	16
Plates, sheets, film, foil and strip, of plastics, non-cellular and not reinforced, laminated, supported or similarly combined with other materials, of poly (ethylene terephthalate)	塑料板、片、膜、箔及扁条,非泡沫,未用其他材料强化、层压、支撑或用类似方法合制,聚对苯二甲酸乙二酯制	3920.6200	16
Plates, sheets, film, foil and strip, of plastics, non-cellular and not reinforced, laminated, supported or similarly combined with other materials, of poly (methyl methacrylate)	塑料板、片、膜、箔及扁条,非泡沫,未用其他材料强化、层压、支撑或用类似方法合制,聚甲基丙烯酸甲酯制	3920.5100	16
Plates, sheets, film, foil and strip, of plastics, non-cellular and not reinforced, laminated, supported or similarly combined with other materials, of poly (vinyl butyral)	塑料板、片、膜、箔及扁条,非泡沫,未用其他材料强化、层压、支撑或用类似方法合制,聚乙烯醇缩丁醛制	3920.9100	16

P

Article Description	商品名称	Tariff Code	D. R.
Plates, sheets, film, foil and strip, of plastics, non-cellular and not reinforced, laminated, supported or similarly combined with other materials, of polyamides	塑料板、片、膜、箔及扁条,非泡沫,未用其他材料强化、层压、支撑或用类似方法合制,聚酰胺制	3920.9200	16
Plates, sheets, film, foil and strip, of plastics, non-cellular and not reinforced, laminated, supported or similarly combined with other materials, of polycarbonates	塑料板、片、膜、箔及扁条,非泡沫,未用其他材料强化、层压、支撑或用类似方法合制,聚碳酸酯制	3920.6100	16
Plates, sheets, film, foil and strip, of plastics, non-cellular and not reinforced, laminated, supported or similarly combined with other materials, of polymers of ethylene, nes	塑料板、片、膜、箔及扁条,非泡沫,未用其他材料强化、层压、支撑或用类似方法合制,乙烯聚合物制,其他	3920.1090	16
Plates, sheets, film, foil and strip, of plastics, non-cellular and not reinforced, laminated, supported or similarly combined with other materials, of polymers of propylene, nes	塑料板、片、膜、箔及扁条,非泡沫,未用其他材料强化、层压、支撑或用类似方法合制,丙烯聚合物制,其他	3920.2090	16
Plates, sheets, film, foil and strip, of plastics, non-cellular and not reinforced, laminated, supported or similarly combined with other materials, of polymers of styrene	塑料板、片、膜、箔及扁条,非泡沫,未用其他材料强化、层压、支撑或用类似方法合制,苯乙烯聚合物制	3920.3000	16
Plates, sheets, film, foil and strip, of plastics, non-cellular and not reinforced, laminated, supported or similarly combined with other materials, of polymers of vinyl chloride, containing by weight not less than 6% of plasticisers	塑料板、片、膜、箔及扁条,非泡沫,未用其他材料强化、层压、支撑或用类似方法合制,氯乙烯聚合物制,按重量计增塑剂含量不小于6%	3920.4300	16
Plates, sheets, film, foil and strip, of plastics, non-cellular and not reinforced, laminated, supported or similarly combined with other materials, of polymers of vinyl chloride, nes	塑料板、片、膜、箔及扁条,非泡沫,未用其他材料强化、层压、支撑或用类似方法合制,氯乙烯聚合物制,其他	3920.4900	16
Plates, sheets, film, foil and strip, of plastics, non-cellular and not reinforced, laminated, supported or similarly combined with other materials, of potytetrafluoroethylene	塑料板、片、膜、箔及扁条,非泡沫,未用其他材料强化、层压、支撑或用类似方法合制,聚四氟乙烯制	3920.9910	16
Plates, sheets, film, foil and strip, of plastics, non-cellular and not reinforced, laminated, supported or similarly combined with other materials, of regenerated cellulose	塑料板、片、膜、箔及扁条,非泡沫,未用其他材料强化、层压、支撑或用类似方法合制,再生纤维素制	3920.7100	16
Plates, sheets, film, foil and strip, of plastics, non-cellular and not reinforced, laminated, supported or similarly combined with other materials, of unsaturated polyesters	塑料板、片、膜、箔及扁条,非泡沫,未用其他材料强化、层压、支撑或用类似方法合制,不饱和聚酯制	3920.6300	16
Plates, sheets, strap, foil, of titanium, of a thickness more than 0.8mm	板、片、带、箔,钛的,厚度超过0.8毫米	8108.9032	16

Article Description	商品名称	Tariff Code	D. R.
Plates, sheets, strap, foil, of titanium, of a thickness not more than 0.8mm	板、片、带、箔,钛的,厚度不超过0.8毫米	8108.9031	16
Plates, sheets, strip and foil, of nickel alloys	板、片、带、箔,镍合金制	7506.2000	46
Plates, sheets, strip and foil, of nickel, not alloyed	板、片、带、箔,非合金镍制	7506.1000	46
Plates, sheets, strip and foil, of zinc	板、片、带、箔,锌的	7905.0000	16
Platinum clothing base metals, silver or gold, not further worked than semi-manufactured	铂包覆材料,以贱金属、银或金为底的,未加工成半成品的	7111.0000	46
Platinum ores and concentrates	铂矿砂及其精矿	2616.9000	146
Platinum, nes	铂,其他	7110.1990	46
Platinum, plates and sheets	铂,板、片	7110.1910	46
Platinum, unwrought or in powder form	铂,未锻造或粉末状	7110.1100	46
Playing cards	扑克牌	9504.4000	
Pliers and similar tools	钳子及类似工具	8203.2000	256
Ploughs, for agricultural, horticultural or forestry use	犁,农业、园艺及林业用	8432.1000	
Plugs and other connectors, for a voltage exceeding 1000V	插头及其他连接器,用于电压超过1000伏的线路	8535.9000	8
Plugs and sockets, for a voltage not exceeding 1000V	插头及插座,用于电压不超过1000伏的线路	8536.6900	8
Plums, fresh	梅,鲜的	0809.4000	1
Plunger pumps, for positive displacement, reciprocating	柱塞泵,排液往复式	8413.5031	23
Plunger pumps, positive displacement pumps, rotary, axial	柱塞泵,排液泵回转式,轴向的	8413.6060	27
Plunger pumps, positive displacement pumps, rotary, radial	柱塞泵,排液泵回转式,径向的	8413.6050	27
Plutonium and its compounds	钚及其化合物	2844.2000	
Plywood consisting solely of sheets of wood, of bamboo, each ply not exceeding 6mm thickness, nes	胶合板,仅由薄板制的,竹制的,每层厚度不超过6毫米,其他	4412.1019	48
Plywood consisting solely of sheets of wood, of bamboo, each ply not exceeding 6mm thickness, with at least one outer ply of tropical wood specified in subheading note to this chapter	胶合板,仅由薄板制的,竹制的,每层厚度不超过6毫米,至少有一表层是本章子目注释所列的热带木	4412.1011	48
Plywood, consisting solely of sheets of wood (other than bamboo), each ply not exceeding 6mm thickness, nes	胶合板,仅由薄木板制的(竹制除外),每层厚度不超过6毫米,其他	4412.3900	48
Plywood, consisting solely of sheets of wood (other than bamboo), each ply not exceeding 6mm thickness, with at least one outer ply of non-coniferous wood, nes	胶合板,仅由薄木板制的(竹制除外),每层厚度不超过6毫米,至少有一表层是非针叶木,其他	4412.3290	48

P

Article Description	商品名称	Tariff Code	D. R.
Plywood, consisting solely of sheets of wood (other than bamboo), each ply not exceeding 6mm thickness, with at least one outer ply of temperate non-coniferous wood	胶合板,仅由薄木板制的(竹制除外),每层厚度不超过6毫米,至少有一表层是温带非针叶木	4412.3210	48
Plywood, consisting solely of sheets of wood (other than bamboo), each ply not exceeding 6mm thickness, with at least one outer ply of tropical wood specified in subheading note to this chapter	胶合板,仅由薄木板制的(竹制除外),每层厚度不超过6毫米,至少有一表层是本章子目注释所列的热带木	4412.3100	48
Plywood, veneered panels and similar laminated wood, containing at least one layer of particle board, nes	胶合板、单板饰面板及类似的多层板,至少含有一层木碎料板,其他	4412.9992	48
Plywood, veneered panels and similar laminated wood, nes	胶合板、单板饰面板及类似的多层板,其他	4412.9999	48
Plywood, veneered panels and similar laminated wood, of bamboo, containing at least one layer of particle board, nes	胶合板、单板饰面板及类似的多层板,竹制的,至少含有一层木碎料板,其他	4412.1092	48
Plywood, veneered panels and similar laminated wood, of bamboo, nes	胶合板、单板饰面板及类似的多层板,竹制的,其他	4412.1099	48
Plywood, veneered panels and similar laminated wood, of bamboo, with at least one outer ply of non-coniferous wood, nes	胶合板、单板饰面板及类似的多层板,竹制的,至少有一表层是非针叶木,其他	4412.1020	48
Plywood, veneered panels and similar laminated wood, of bamboo, with at least one outer ply of tropical wood, nes	胶合板、单板饰面板及类似的多层板,竹制的,至少有一层是热带木,其他	4412.1091	48
Plywood, veneered panels and similar laminated wood, with at least one outer ply of non-coniferous wood, nes	胶合板、单板饰面板及类似的多层板,至少有一表层是非针叶木,其他	4412.9910	48
Plywood, veneered panels and similar laminated wood, with at least one outer ply of tropical wood, nes	胶合板、单板饰面板及类似的多层板,至少有一层是热带木,其他	4412.9991	48
Pneumatic automatic regulating or controlling instruments and apparatus, nes	气压的自动调节或控制仪器及装置,其他	9032.8100	7
Pneumatic elevators and conveyors	气压升降机及输送机	8428.2000	7
Pneumatic mattresses, nes	充气褥垫,其他	6306.4090	346
Pneumatic mattresses, of cotton	充气褥垫,棉制	6302.5990	346
Pneumatic mattresses, of man-made fibres	充气褥垫,化学纤维制	6306.4020	346
Pneumatic power engines and motors, nes	气压动力装置,其他	8412.3900	27
Pneumatic power engines, linear acting (cylinders)	直线作用(气压缸)的	8412.3100	27
Pneumatic tools parts, for hand tools	气动工具用零件,手提式	8467.9200	3
Pneumatic tools, working in the hand, rotary type (including combined rotarypercussion)	气动工具,手提式,旋转式(包括旋转冲击式的)	8467.1100	57
Pneumatic tools, working in the hand, nes	气动工具,手提式,其他	8467.1900	57

Article Description	商品名称	Tariff Code	D. R.
Pneumatic tyres, new, of rubber of a kind used on aircraft	充气橡胶轮胎,新的,航空器用	4011. 3000	1238
Pneumatic tyres, new, of rubber of a kind used on bicycles	充气橡胶轮胎,新的,自行车用	4011. 5000	1238
Pneumatic tyres, new, of rubber of a kind used on buses or lorries	充气橡胶轮胎,新的,客运机动车辆或货运机动车辆用	4011. 2000	1238
Pneumatic tyres, new, of rubber of a kind used on motor cars (including station wagons and racing cars)	充气橡胶轮胎,新的,机动小客车(包括旅行小客车及赛车)用	4011. 1000	1238
Pneumatic tyres, new, of rubber of a kind used on motorcycles	充气橡胶轮胎,新的,摩托车用	4011. 4000	1238
Pneumatic tyres, new, of rubber, having a "herring-bone" or similar tread, nes	充气橡胶轮胎,新的,人字形胎面或类似胎面的,其他	4011. 6900	1238
Pneumatic tyres, new, of rubber, having a "herring-bone" or similar tread, of a kind used on agricultural or forestry vehicles and machines	充气橡胶轮胎,新的,人字形胎面或类似胎面的,农业或林业车辆及机器用	4011. 6100	1238
Pneumatic tyres, new, of rubber, having a "herring-bone" or similar tread, of a kind used on construction or industrial handling vehicles and machines and having a rim size exceeding 61cm	充气橡胶轮胎,新的,人字形胎面或类似胎面的,建筑业或工业搬运车辆及机器用,辋圈尺寸超过61 厘米	4011. 6300	1238
Pneumatic tyres, new, of rubber, having a "herring-bone" or similar tread, of a kind used on construction or industrial handling vehicles and machines and having a rim size not exceeding 61cm	充气橡胶轮胎,新的,人字形胎面或类似胎面的,建筑业或工业搬运车辆及机器用,辋圈尺寸不超过61 厘米	4011. 6200	1238
Pneumatic tyres, new, of rubber, nes	充气橡胶轮胎,新的,其他	4011. 9900	
Pneumatic tyres, new, of rubber, of a kind used on agricultural or forestry vehicles and machines	充气橡胶轮胎,新的,农业或林业车辆及机器用	4011. 9200	1238
Pneumatic tyres, new, of rubber, of a kind used on construction or industrial handling vehicles and machines and having a rim size exceeding 61cm, nes	充气橡胶轮胎,新的,建筑业或工业搬运车辆及机器用,辋圈尺寸超过61 厘米	4011. 9400	1238
Pneumatic tyres, new, of rubber, of a kind used on construction or industrial handling vehicles and machines and having a rim size not exceeding 61cm, nes	充气橡胶轮胎,新的,建筑业或工业搬运车辆及机器用,辋圈尺寸不超过61 厘米	4011. 9300	1238
Pneumatic tyres, retreaded, nes	充气橡胶轮胎,翻新的,其他	4012. 1900	234
Pneumatic tyres, retreaded, of a kind used on aircratr	充气橡胶轮胎,翻新的,航空器用	4012. 1300	234
Pneumatic tyres, retreaded, of a kind used on buses or corries	充气橡胶轮胎,翻新的,机动大客车或货运机动车辆用	4012. 1200	234
Pneumatic tyres, retreaded, of a kind used on motor cars (including station wagons and racing cars)	充气橡胶轮胎,翻新的,机动小客车(包括旅行小客车及赛车)用	4012. 1100	234
Pneumatic tyres, used, nes	充气橡胶轮胎,旧的,其他	4012. 2090	234

P

Article Description	商品名称	Tariff Code	D. R.
Pneumatic tyres, used, of a kind used on motor cars, buses or lorries	充气橡胶轮胎,旧的,汽车用	4012. 2010	234
Pocket lighters, gas fuelled, non refillable	袖珍气体打火机,一次性的	9613. 1000	
Pocket lighters, gas fuelled, refillable	袖珍气体打火机,可充气的	9613. 2000	
Pocket-size radio cassette-players, radio-broadcast receivers capable of operating without an external source of power	袖珍盒式收放机,无线电收音机,不需外接电源的	8527. 1200	5
Pocket-watches, electrically operated, nes	怀表,电力驱动的,其他	9102. 9100	56
Pocket-watches, electrically operated, with case of precious metal or of metal clad with precious metal	怀表,电力驱动的,表壳用贵金属或包贵金属制成的	9101. 9100	56
Pocket-watches, nes	怀表,其他	9102. 9900	56
Pocket-watches, with case of precious metal or of metal clad with precious metal, nes	怀表,表壳用贵金属或包贵金属制成的,其他	9101. 9900	56
Polarizing material sheets and plates	偏振材料制的片及板	9001. 2000	6
Polianite	黝锰矿	2602. 0000	1346
Polishes and creams, nes	光洁剂及类似制品,其他	3405. 9000	36
Polishes and similar preparations for coachwork, other than metal polishes	上光剂及类似制品,车身用的,但金属用的光洁剂除外	3405. 3000	36
Polishes, creams and similar preparations for footwear or leather	上光剂及类似制品,鞋靴或皮革用的	3405. 1000	36
Polishes, creams and similar preparations for the maintenance of wooden furniture, floors or other woodwork	上光剂及类似制品,保养木制家具、地板或其他木制品用的	3405. 2000	36
Polishing machines for glass or glassware	抛光机床,玻璃用	8464. 2010	7
Polishing machines for working stone, ceramics, concrete, asbestos-cement or alike mineral materials, nes	抛光机床,加工石料、陶瓷、混凝土、石棉水泥或类似矿物材料的,其他	8464. 2090	7
Polishing machines, for metal or cermets	抛光机床,加工金属或金属陶瓷用	8460. 9020	7
Polishing machines, for working wood, cork, bone, hard rubber, hard plastics or similar hard materials	抛光机器,加工木材、软木、骨、硬质橡胶、硬质塑料或类似硬质材料的	8465. 9300	7
Polishing stones, hand used	抛光石,手用	6804. 3090	36
Poly (vinyl alcohol), whether or not containing unhydrolyzed acetate groups, in primary forms	聚乙烯醇,不论是否含有未水解的乙酸酯基,初级形状的	3905. 3000	1256
Poly (vinyl chloride), not mixed with any other substances, in primary forms, nes	聚氯乙烯,未掺其他物质,初级形状的,其他	3904. 1090	1256
Poly (vinyl chloride), not mixed with any other substances, paste resins	聚氯乙烯,未掺其他物质,糊树脂	3904. 1010	1256
Poly(ethylene terephthalate) slices or chips, high viscosity	聚对苯二甲酸乙二酯切片,高粘度	3907. 6011	1256
Poly(ethylene terephthalate) slices or chips, nes	聚对苯二甲酸乙二酯切片,其他	3907. 6019	1256
Poly(ethylene terephthalate), in primary forms, nes	聚对苯二甲酸乙二酯,初级形状的,其他	3907. 6090	1256
Poly(lactic acid), in primary forms	聚乳酸,初级形状的	3907. 7000	1256

Article Description	商品名称	Tariff Code	D. R.
Poly(methyl methacrylate)	聚甲基丙烯酸甲酯	3906. 1000	1256
Poly(methylene phenyl isocyanate)	聚(亚甲基苯基异氰酸酯)	3909. 3010	1256
Poly (vinyl acetate), in aqueous dispersion, in primary forms	聚乙酸乙烯酯,水分散体,初级形状的	3905. 1200	1256
Poly(vinyl acetate),in primary forms,nes	聚乙酸乙烯酯,初级形状的,其他	3905. 1900	1256
Poly(vinyl chloride) (including polymers of vinyl chloride) waste,parings and scrap	聚氯乙烯(含氯乙烯聚合物)的废碎料及下脚料	3915. 3000	146
Poly (vinyl chloride), non-plasticized, in primary forms	聚氯乙烯,未塑化,初级形状的	3904. 2100	1256
Poly(vinyl chloride),plasticized,in primary forms	聚氯乙烯,已塑化,初级形状的	3904. 2200	1256
Polyacetals,in primary forms,nes	初级形状的,其他	3907. 1090	1256
Polyacrylamide	聚丙烯酰胺	3906. 9010	1256
Polyallyl esters,in primary forms	聚烯丙基酯,初级形状的	3907. 9990	1256
Polyamide slices or chips,nes	聚酰胺切片,其他	3908. 1019	1256
Polyamide -6,6 slices or chips	聚酰胺 -6,6 切片	3908. 1011	1256
Polyamides in primary forms,nes	聚酰胺,初级形状的,其他	3908. 9000	1256
Polyamide-6,-11,-12,-6 , 6,-6 , 9,-6,10 or -6, 12,in primary forms,nes	聚酰胺 -6、-11、-12、-6,6、-6,9、-6,10 或-6,12,初级形状的,其他	3908. 1090	1256
Polybasite	硫锑铜银矿	2616. 1000	146
Polycarbonates,in primary forms	聚碳酸酯,初级形状的	3907. 4000	1256
Polycarbonates,in primary forms	聚碳酸酯,初级形状的	3907. 9990	1256
Polyester staple fibres 3-thread or 4-thread twill, including cross twill,containing less than 85% by weight of such fibres,mixed mainly or solely with cotton,of a weight exceeding 170g/m², bleached	聚酯短纤三线或四线斜纹机织物,包括双面斜纹机织物,按重量计合成纤维短纤含量在85%以下,主要或仅与棉混纺,每平方米重量超过170克,漂白	5514. 1220	2468
Polyester staple fibres 3-thread or 4-thread twill, including cross twill,containing less than 85% by weight of such fibres,mixed mainly or solely with cotton,of a weight exceeding 170g/m², dyed	聚酯短纤三线或四线斜纹机织物,包括双面斜纹机织物,按重量计合成纤维短纤含量在85%以下,主要或仅与棉混纺,每平方米重量超过170克,染色	5514. 2200	2468
Polyester staple fibres 3-thread or 4-thread twill, including cross twill,containing less than 85% by weight of such fibres,mixed mainly or solely with cotton,of a weight exceeding 170g/m², of yarns of different colours	聚酯短纤三线或四线斜纹机织物,包括双面斜纹机织物,按重量计合成纤维短纤含量在85%以下,主要或仅与棉混纺,每平方米重量超过170克,色织	5514. 3020	2468
Polyester staple fibres 3-thread or 4-thread twill, including cross twill,containing less than 85% by weight of such fibres,mixed mainly or solely with cotton,of a weight exceeding 170g/m², printed	聚酯短纤三线或四线斜纹机织物,包括双面斜纹机织物,按重量计合成纤维短纤含量在85%以下,主要或仅与棉混纺,每平方米重量超过170克,印花	5514. 4200	2468

Article Description	商品名称	Tariff Code	D. R.
Polyester staple fibres 3-thread or 4-thread twill, including cross twill, containing less than 85% by weight of such fibres, mixed mainly or solely with cotton, of a weight exceeding 170g/m^2, unbleached	聚酯短纤三线或四线斜纹机织物,包括双面斜纹机织物,按重量计合成纤维短纤含量在85%以下,主要或仅与棉混纺,每平方米重量超过170克,未漂白	5514.1210	2468
Polyester staple fibres 3-thread or 4-thread twill, including cross twill, containing less than 85% by weight of such fibres, mixed mainly or solely with cotton, of a weight not exceeding 170g/m^2, bleached	聚酯短纤三线或四线斜纹机织物,包括双面斜纹机织物,按重量计合成纤维短纤含量在85%以下,主要或仅与棉混纺,每平方米重量不超过170克,漂白	5513.1220	2468
Polyester staple fibres 3-thread or 4-thread twill, including cross twill, containing less than 85% by weight of such fibres, mixed mainly or solely with cotton, of a weight not exceeding 170g/m^2, dyed	聚酯短纤三线或四线斜纹机织物,包括双面斜纹机织物,按重量计合成纤维短纤含量在85%以下,主要或仅与棉混纺,每平方米重量不超过170克,染色	5513.2310	2468
Polyester staple fibres 3-thread or 4-thread twill, including cross twill, containing less than 85% by weight of such fibres, mixed mainly or solely with cotton, of a weight not exceeding 170g/m^2, of yarns of different colours	聚酯短纤三线或四线斜纹机织物,包括双面斜纹机织物,按重量计合成纤维短纤含量在85%以下,主要或仅与棉混纺,每平方米重量不超过170克,色织	5513.3910	2468
Polyester staple fibres 3-thread or 4-thread twill, including cross twill, containing less than 85% by weight of such fibres, mixed mainly or solely with cotton, of a weight not exceeding 170g/m^2, printed	聚酯短纤三线或四线斜纹机织物,包括双面斜纹机织物,按重量计合成纤维短纤含量在85%以下,主要或仅与棉混纺,每平方米重量不超过170克,印花	5513.4910	2468
Polyester staple fibres 3-thread or 4-thread twill, including cross twill, containing less than 85% by weight of such fibres, mixed mainly or solely with cotton, of a weight not exceeding 170g/m^2, unbleached	聚酯短纤三线或四线斜纹机织物,包括双面斜纹机织物,按重量计合成纤维短纤含量在85%以下,主要或仅与棉混纺,每平方米重量不超过170克,未漂白	5513.1210	2468
Polyester staple fibres plain weave, containing less than 85% by weight of such fibres, mixed mainly or solely with cotton, of a weight exceeding 170g/m^2, unbleached	聚酯短纤平纹机织物,按重量计合成纤维短纤含量在85%以下,主要或仅与棉混纺,每平方米重量超过170克,未漂白	5514.1110	2468
Polyester staple fibres plain weave, containing less than 85% by weight of such fibres, mixed mainly or solely with cotton, of a weight exceeding 170g/m^2, bleached	聚酯短纤平纹机织物,按重量计合成纤维短纤含量在85%以下,主要或仅与棉混纺,每平方米重量超过170克,漂白	5514.1120	2468
Polyester staple fibres plain weave, containing less than 85% by weight of such fibres, mixed mainly or solely with cotton, of a weight exceeding 170g/m^2, dyed	聚酯短纤平纹机织物,按重量计合成纤维短纤含量在85%以下,主要或仅与棉混纺,每平方米重量超过170克,染色	5514.2100	2468

P

Article Description	商品名称	Tariff Code	D. R.
Polyester staple fibres plain weave, containing less than 85% by weight of such fibres, mixed mainly or solely with cotton, of a weight exceeding 170g/m^2, of yarns of different colours	聚酯短纤平纹机织物,按重量计合成纤维短纤含量在85%以下,主要或仅与棉混纺,每平方米重量超过170克,色织	5514.3010	2468
Polyester staple fibres plain weave, containing less than 85% by weight of such fibres, mixed mainly or solely with cotton, of a weight exceeding 170g/m^2, printed	聚酯短纤平纹机织物,按重量计合成纤维短纤含量在85%以下,主要或仅与棉混纺,每平方米重量超过170克,印花	5514.4100	2468
Polyester staple fibres plain weave, containing less than 85% by weight of such fibres, mixed mainly or solely with cotton, of a weight not exceeding 170g/m^2, bleached	聚酯短纤平纹机织物,按重量计合成纤维短纤含量在85%以下,主要或仅与棉混纺,每平方米重量不超过170克,漂白	5513.1120	2468
Polyester staple fibres plain weave, containing less than 85% by weight of such fibres, mixed mainly or solely with cotton, of a weight not exceeding 170g/m^2, dyed	聚酯短纤平纹机织物,按重量计合成纤维短纤含量在85%以下,主要或仅与棉混纺,每平方米重量不超过170克,染色	5513.2100	2468
Polyester staple fibres plain weave, containing less than 85% by weight of such fibres, mixed mainly or solely with cotton, of a weight not exceeding 170g/m^2, of yarns of different colours	聚酯短纤平纹机织物,按重量计合成纤维短纤含量在85%以下,主要或仅与棉混纺,每平方米重量不超过170克,色织	5513.3100	2468
Polyester staple fibres plain weave, containing less than 85% by weight of such fibres, mixed mainly or solely with cotton, of a weight not exceeding 170g/m^2, printed	聚酯短纤纺制的平纹机织物,按重量计合成纤维短纤含量在85%以下,主要或仅与棉混纺,每平方米重量不超过170克,印花	5513.4100	2468
Polyester staple fibres plain weave, ontaining less than 85% by weight of such fibres, mixed mainly or solely with cotton, of a weight not exceeding 170g/m^2, unbleached	聚酯短纤平纹机织物,按重量计合成纤维短纤含量在85%以下,主要或仅与棉混纺,每平方米重量不超过170克,未漂白	5513.1110	2468
Polyester staple fibres woven fabrics, containing less than 85% by weight of such fibres, mixed mainly or solely with cotton, of a weight not exceeding 170g/m^2, of yarns of different colours, nes	聚酯短纤机织物,按重量计合成纤维短纤含量在85%以下,主要或仅与棉混纺,每平方米重量不超过170克,色织,其他	5513.3920	2468
Polyester staple fibres woven fabrics, containing less than 85% by weight of such fibres, mixed mainly or solely with cotton, of a weight exceeding 170g/m^2, bleached, nes	聚酯短纤机织物,按重量计合成纤维短纤含量在85%以下,主要或仅与棉混纺,每平方米重量超过170克,漂白,其他	5514.1912	2468
Polyester staple fibres woven fabrics, containing less than 85% by weight of such fibres, mixed mainly or solely with cotton, of a weight exceeding 170g/m^2, dyed, nes	聚酯短纤机织物,按重量计合成纤维短纤含量在85%以下,主要或仅与棉混纺,每平方米重量超过170克,染色,其他	5514.2300	2468
Polyester staple fibres woven fabrics, containing less than 85% by weight of such fibres, mixed mainly or solely with cotton, of a weight exceeding 170g/m^2, of yarns of different colours, nes	聚酯短纤机织物,按重量计合成纤维短纤含量在85%以下,主要或仅与棉混纺,每平方米重量超过170克,色织,其他	5514.3030	2468

P

Article Description	商品名称	Tariff Code	D. R.
Polyester staple fibres woven fabrics, containing less than 85% by weight of such fibres, mixed mainly or solely with cotton, of a weight exceeding 170g/m², printed, nes	聚酯短纤机织物,按重量计合成纤维短纤含量在85%以下,主要或仅与棉混纺,每平方米重量超过170克,印花,其他	5514.4300	2468
Polyester staple fibres woven fabrics, containing less than 85% by weight of such fibres, mixed mainly or solely with cotton, of a weight exceeding 170g/m², unbleached, nes	聚酯短纤机织物,按重量计合成纤维短纤含量在85%以下,主要或仅与棉混纺,每平方米重量超过170克,未漂白,其他	5514.1911	2468
Polyester staple fibres woven fabrics, containing less than 85% by weight of such fibres, mixed mainly or solely with cotton, of a weight not exceeding 170g/m², bleached	聚酯短纤机织物,按重量计合成纤维短纤含量在85%以下,主要或仅与棉混纺,每平方米重量不超过170克,漂白	5513.1320	2468
Polyester staple fibres woven fabrics, containing less than 85% by weight of such fibres, mixed mainly or solely with cotton, of a weight not exceeding 170g/m², dyed, nes	聚酯短纤机织物,按重量计合成纤维短纤含量在85%以下,主要或仅与棉混纺,每平方米重量不超过170克,染色,其他	5513.2390	2468
Polyester staple fibres woven fabrics, containing less than 85% by weight of such fibres, mixed mainly or solely with cotton, of a weight not exceeding 170g/m², printed, nes	聚酯短纤机织物,按重量计合成纤维短纤含量在85%以下,主要或仅与棉混纺,每平方米重量不超过170克,印花,其他	5513.4920	2468
Polyester staple fibres woven fabrics, containing less than 85% by weight of such fibres, mixed mainly or solely with cotton, of a weight not exceeding 170g/m², unbleached	聚酯短纤机织物,按重量计合成纤维短纤含量在85%以下,主要或仅与棉混纺,每平方米重量不超过170克,未漂白	5513.1310	2468
Polyester staple fibres woven fabrics, mixed mainly or solely with man-made filaments	聚酯短纤机织物,主要或仅与化学纤维长丝混纺	5515.1200	2468
Polyester staple fibres woven fabrics, mixed mainly or solely with viscose rayon staple fibres	聚酯短纤机织物,主要或仅与粘胶纤维短纤混纺	5515.1100	2468
Polyester staple fibres woven fabrics, mixed mainly or solely with wool or fine animal hair	聚酯短纤机织物,主要或仅与羊毛或动物细毛混纺	5515.1300	2468
Polyester staple fibres woven fabrics, nes	聚酯短纤机织物,其他	5515.1900	2468
Polyester staple fibres yam, nes	聚酯短纤纱线,其他	5509.5900	68
Polyester staple fibres yarn, mixed mainly or solely with artificial staple fibres	聚酯短纤纱线,主要或仅与人造纤维短纤混纺	5509.5100	68
Polyester staple fibres yarn, mixed mainly or solely with cotton	聚酯短纤纱线,主要或仅与棉混纺	5509.5300	68
Polyester staple fibres yarn, mixed mainly or solely with wool or fine animal hair	聚酯短纤纱线,主要或仅与羊毛或动物细毛混纺	5509.5200	68
Polyester woven fabrics, containing 85% or more by weight of filaments, nes	聚酯机织物,按重量计长丝含量在85%及以上,其他	5407.6900	2468
Polyester woven fabrics, containing 85% or more by weight of non-textured polyester filaments	聚酯机织物,按重量计聚酯非变形长丝含量在85%及以上	5407.6100	2468

Article Description	商品名称	Tariff Code	D. R.
Polyester woven fabrics, containing 85% or more by weight of textured filaments, dyed	聚酯机织物，按重量计变形长丝含量在85%及以上，染色	5407.5200	2468
Polyester woven fabrics, containing 85% or more by weight of textured filaments, of yarns of different colours	聚酯机织物，按重量计变形长丝含量在85%及以上，色织	5407.5300	2468
Polyester woven fabrics, containing 85% or more by weight of textured filaments, printed	聚酯机织物，按重量计变形长丝含量在85%及以上，印花	5407.5400	2468
Polyester woven fabrics, containing 85% or more by weight of textured filaments, unbleached or bleached	聚酯机织物，按重量计变形长丝含量在85%及以上，未漂白或漂白	5407.5100	2468
Polyesters elastic filament, not put up for retail sale	聚酯弹力丝，非供零售用	5402.3310	3468
Polyesters filament tow	聚酯长丝丝束	5501.2000	68
Polyesters high tenacity yarn woven fabrics	聚酯高强力纱纺制的机织物	5407.1020	2468
Polyesters high tenacity yarn, not put up for retail sale	聚酯高强力纱，非供零售用	5402.2000	3468
Polyesters multiple or cabled yarn, not put up for retail sale	聚酯多股纱线或缆线，非供零售用	5402.6200	3468
Polyesters single yarn, partially oriented, untwisted or with a twist not exceeding 50 turns per metre, not put up for retail sale	聚酯单纱，部分定向的，未加捻或捻度每米不超过50转，非供零售用	5402.4600	3468
Polyesters single yarn, untwisted or with a twist not exceeding 50 turns per metre, not put up for retail sale	聚酯单纱，未加捻或捻度每米不超过50转，非供零售用	5402.4700	3468
Polyesters single yarn, with a twist exceeding 50 turns per metre, not put up for retail sale	聚酯单纱，捻度每米超过50转，非供零售用	5402.5200	3468
Polyesters staple fibres, carded, combed or otherwise processed for spinning	聚酯短纤，已梳或经其他纺前加工	5506.2000	68
Polyesters staple fibres, not carded, combed or otherwise processed for spinning	聚酯短纤，未梳或未经其他纺前加工	5503.2000	68
Polyesters textured yarn, not put up for retail sale, nes	聚酯变形纱线，非供零售用，其他	5402.3390	3468
Polyesters, in primary forms, nes	聚酯，初级形状的，其他	3907.9990	1256
Polyesters, unsaturated, in primary forms, nes	聚酯，不饱和，初级形状的，其他	3907.9100	1256
Polyethers, in primary forms, nes	聚醚，初级形状的，其他	3907.2090	1256
Polyethylene having a specific gravity of 0.94 or more, in primary forms	聚乙烯，比重在0.94及以上，初级形状的	3901.2000	1256
Polyethylene having a specific gravity of less than 0.94, in primary forms	聚乙烯，比重小于0.94，初级形状的	3901.1000	1256
Polyethylene (including polymers of ethylene) waste, parings and scrap	聚乙烯（含乙烯聚合物）的废碎料及下脚料	3915.1000	146
Polyethylene, linearity low density, in primary forms	聚乙烯，线型低密度，初级形状的	3901.9020	1256
Polyhydric alcohols, nes	多元醇，其他	2905.4990	36
Polyisobutylene	聚异丁烯	3902.2000	1256
Polyoxymethylene (POM), in primary forms	聚甲醛，初级形状的	3907.1010	1256

Article Description	商品名称	Tariff Code	D. R.
Polypeptide hormones, their derivatives and structural analogues	多肽激素及其衍生物和结构类似物	2937. 1900	36
Polypeptides, chain modified, used pri-marily as hormones	链多肽,改性的,主要用作激素的	2937. 9000	36
Polyphenols, nes	多元酚,其他	2907. 2990	36
Polyphosphates, nes, inorganic	多磷酸盐,其他,无机的	2835. 3990	3
Polyphosphoric acids, nes	多磷酸,其他	2809. 2090	6
Polypropylene	聚丙烯	3902. 1000	1256
Polypropylene filament tow	聚丙烯长丝丝束	5501. 4000	68
Polypropylene monofilament of 67 decitex or more and of which no cross-sectional dimension exceeding 1mm	聚丙烯单丝,截面尺寸不超过 1 毫米,细度在 67 分特及以上	5404. 1200	568
Polypropylene multiple or cabled yarn, not put up for retail sale	聚丙烯多股纱线或缆线,非供零售用	5402. 6910	3468
Polypropylene single yarn, with a twist exceeding 50 turns per metre, not put up for retail sale	聚丙烯单纱,捻度每米超过 50 转,非供零售用	5402. 5910	3468
Polypropylene staple fibres, not carded, combed or otherwise processed for spinning	聚丙烯短纤,未梳或未经其他纺前加工	5503. 4000	68
Polypropylene textured yarn, not put up for retail sale	聚丙烯变形纱线,非供零售用	5402. 3400	3468
Polypropylenes single yarn, untwisted or with a twist not exceeding 50 turns per metre, not put up for retail sale	聚丙烯单纱,未加捻或捻度每米不超过 50 转,非供零售用	5402. 4800	3468
Polystyrene (including polymers of styrene) waste, parings and scrap	聚苯乙烯(含苯乙烯聚合物)的废碎料及下脚料	3915. 2000	146
Polystyrene, expansible, in primary forms	聚苯乙烯,可发性的,初级形状的	3903. 1100	1256
Polystyrene, in primary forms, nes	聚苯乙烯,初级形状的,其他	3903. 1990	1256
Polystyrene, modified, in primary forms	聚苯乙烯,改性的,初级形状的	3903. 1910	1256
Polysulphides, in primary forms	多硫化物,初级形状的	3911. 9000	16
Polysulphides, nes, whether or not chemically defined	多硫化物,其他,无论是否已有化学定义	2830. 9090	
Polysulphones, in primary forms	聚砜,初级形状的	3911. 9000	16
Polyterpenes, in primary forms	多萜树脂,初级形状的	3911. 1000	16
Polytetrafluoroethylene, in primary forms	聚四氟乙烯,初级形状的	3904. 6100	1256
Polytetramethylene ether glycol (PTMEG)	聚四亚甲基醚二醇	3907. 2010	1256
Polyurethane elastomeric single yarn, untwisted or with a twist not exceeding 50 turns per metre, not put up for retail sale	氨纶弹性单纱,未加捻或捻度每米不超过 50 转,非供零售用	5402. 4410	3468
Polyurethane multiple or cabled yarn, not put up for retail sale	氨纶多股纱线或缆线,非供零售用	5402. 6920	3468
Polyurethanes	聚氨基甲酸酯	3909. 5000	1256
Pomelos	柚	0805. 4000	14
Poppy seeds	罂粟籽	1207. 9100	3

Article Description	商品名称	Tariff Code	D. R.
Poppy straw	罂粟秆	1211.4000	34
Poppy straw concentrates and salts	罂粟秆浓缩物及盐	2939.1100	34
Popsicle sticks and the like, nes	冰果棒及类似一次性制品,其他	4421.9029	56
Popsicle sticks and the like, of bamboo	冰果棒及类似一次性制品,竹制	4421.9022	56
Popsicle sticks and the like, of wood	冰果棒及类似一次性制品,木制	4421.9021	56
Porcelain articles, nes	瓷制品,其他	6914.1000	36
Porcelain wares for laboratory, chemical or other technical uses	瓷器,实验室、化学或其他专门技术用途的	6909.1100	5
Poria	茯苓	1211.9029	34
Porous-tipped pens	渗水式笔	9608.2000	
Porphyry	斑岩	2516.9000	148
Porpoises (mammals of the order cetacea)	鼠海豚(鲸目哺乳动物)	0106.1200	
Portable electric lamps parts, designed to function by their own source of energy, nes	手提式电灯零件,自供能源的,其他	8513.9090	3
Portable electric lamps, designed to function by their own source of energy, nes	手提式电灯,自供能源的,其他	8513.1090	5
Portable electric torches parts, designed to function by dry batteries	手电筒用零件,自供能源的	8513.9010	3
Portable electric torches, designed to function by dry batteries	手电筒,自供能源的	8513.1010	5
Portable forges	轻便锻炉	8205.8000	256
Portal cranes	门座式起重机	8426.3000	7
Portland cement, nes	硅酸盐水泥,其他	2523.2900	3
Positive displacement pumps, reciprocating, electric	排液泵,往复式,电动式	8413.5020	23
Positive displacement pumps, reciprocating, hydraulic, nes	排液泵,往复式,液压式,其他	8413.5039	23
Positive displacement pumps, reciprocating, nes	排液泵,往复式,其他	8413.5090	23
Positive displacement pumps, reciprocating, plunger pumps	排液泵,往复式,柱塞泵	8413.5031	23
Positive displacement pumps, reciprocating, pneumatic	排液泵,往复式,气动式	8413.5010	23
Positive displacement pumps, rotary, axial plunger pump	排液泵,回转式,轴向柱塞泵	8413.6060	27
Positive displacement pumps, rotary, gear, electric	排液泵,回转式,齿轮的,电动式	8413.6021	27
Positive displacement pumps, rotary, gear, hydraulic	排液泵,回转式,齿轮的,液压式	8413.6022	27
Positive displacement pumps, rotary, gear, nes	排液泵,回转式,齿轮的,其他	8413.6029	27
Positive displacement pumps, rotary, nes	排液泵,回转式,其他	8413.6090	27
Positive displacement pumps, rotary, radial plunger pump	排液泵,回转式,径向柱塞泵	8413.6050	27
Positive displacement pumps, rotary, screw pump	排液泵,回转式,螺杆泵	8413.6040	27
Positive displacement pumps, rotary, vane, electric	排液泵,回转式,叶片的,电动式	8413.6031	27
Positive displacement pumps, rotary, vane, hydraulic	排液泵,回转式,叶片的,液压式	8413.6032	27

Article Description	商品名称	Tariff Code	D. R.
Positive displacement pumps, rotary, vane, nes	排液泵,回转式,叶片的,其他	8413. 6039	27
Post offices sorting machines used in	邮政用分拣设备	8479. 8940	7
Postage	邮票	9704. 0010	
Postage franking machines	邮资盖戳机	8470. 9000	
Postage, unused	邮票,未经使用的	4907. 0010	1
Postal stationery	邮政信笺	9704. 0090	5
Postcards of paper or paperboard, plain	明信片,纸或纸板制的,素色的	4817. 2000	6
Postcards, printed or illustrated	明信片,印刷或有图画的	4909. 0010	4
Posts and beams, of wood	柱和梁, 木制的	4418. 6000	58
Pot scourers and the like	擦锅器及类似品	7323. 1000	24
Pot scourers and the like, of aluminium	擦锅器及类似品,铝制	7615. 1100	36
Pot scourers and the like, of copper	擦锅器及类似品,铜制	7418. 1100	56
Potash lye	钾碱液	2815. 2000	136
Potassium aluminum sulfate	钾铝矾	2833. 3010	
Potassium amide	氨基钾	2853. 0090	
Potassium bromides	溴化钾	2827. 5100	
Potassium carbonates	碳酸钾	2836. 4000	
Potassium chlorate	氯酸钾(洋硝)	2829. 1910	
Potassium chloride, analytically pure	氯化钾,分析纯的	3104. 2010	68
Potassium chloride, nes	氯化钾,其他	3104. 2090	68
Potassium cyanide	氰化钾	2837. 1910	6
Potassium hydroxide	氢氧化钾	2815. 2000	136
Potassium nitrate, for use as fertilizer	硝酸钾,肥料用	2834. 2110	
Potassium nitrate, nes	硝酸钾,其他	2834. 2190	3
Potassium permanganate	高锰酸钾	2841. 6100	1
Potassium peroxides	过氧化钾	2815. 3000	136
Potassium phosphates	钾的磷酸盐	2835. 2400	
Potassium sulphate	硫酸钾	3104. 3000	68
Potatoes, flakes, granules and pellets	马铃薯,粉片、颗粒及团粒	1105. 2000	4
Potatoes, flour, meal and powder	马铃薯,细粉、粗粉及粉末	1105. 1000	4
Potatoes, frozen	马铃薯,冷冻的	0710. 1000	1
Potatoes, nes, fresh or chilled	马铃薯,其他,鲜或冷藏的	0701. 9000	13
Potatoes, prepared or preserved otherwise than by vinegar or acetic acid, frozen	马铃薯,用醋或醋酸以外的其他方法制作或保藏的,冷冻的	2004. 1000	48
Potatoes, prepared or preserved otherwise than by vinegar or acetic acid, not frozen	马铃薯,用醋或醋酸以外的其他方法制作或保藏的,未冷冻	2005. 2000	48
Potatoes, seeds	马铃薯,种用	0701. 1000	13
Potentiometers, wirewound variable, for a power handling capacity not exceeding 20W	电位器,线绕可变,额定功率不超过20瓦	8533. 3100	58
Potentiometers, wirewound variable, nes	电位器,线绕可变,其他	8533. 3900	58
Pottery articles, nes	陶制品,其他	6914. 9000	36

Article Description	商品名称	Tariff Code	D. R.
Pottery wares for laboratory, chemical or other technical uses, having a hardness equivalent to 9 or more on the Mohs scale	陶器,实验室、化学或其他专门技术用途的,莫氏硬度为9或以上的物品	6909.1200	5
Pottery wares for laboratory, chemical or other technical uses, nes	陶器,实验室、化学或其他专门技术用途的,其他	6909.1900	5
Pouches of paper or paperboard, containing an assortment of paper stationery	纸袋子,内装各种纸制文具	4817.3000	6
Pouffes, nes	座垫,其他	9404.9090	6
Pouffes, stuffed with animal hair	座垫,兽毛填充的	9404.9020	6
Pouffes, stuffed with feathers or down	座垫,羽毛或羽绒填充的	9404.9010	6
Pouffes, stuffed with man-made fibres	座垫,化纤棉填充的	9404.9040	6
Pouffes, stuffed with silk wadding	座垫,丝棉填充的	9404.9030	6
Poultices, medical, surgical, dental or veterinary purposes	泥罨剂,供医疗、外科、牙科或兽医用	3005.9090	1346
Poultry fat, not rendered or otherwise extracted, fresh, chilled, frozen, salted, in brine, dried or smoked	家禽脂肪,未炼制或用其他方法提取的不带瘦肉的,鲜、冷、冻、干、熏、盐腌或盐渍的	0209.0000	14
Poultry fat, other than that of heading No. 02.09 or 15.03	家禽脂肪,但税号02.09及15.03的货品除外	1501.0000	
Poultry incubators and brooders	家禽孵卵器及育雏器	8436.2100	
Poultry incubators and brooders parts	家禽孵卵器及育雏器的零件	8436.9100	
Poultry Live, nes, weighing not more than 185g	家禽,其他,重量不超过185克	0105.1990	48
Poultry preparation machinery	家禽加工机器	8438.5000	
Poultry preparation machinery parts	家禽加工机器的零件	8438.9000	3
Poultry shears and similar one-handed pruners and shears	家禽剪及类似的单手操作剪刀	8201.5000	256
Poultry-keeping machinery	家禽饲养用的机器	8436.2900	
Poultry-keeping machinery parts	家禽饲养用机器的零件	8436.9100	
Pouring stoppers, of base metal	倒水塞,贱金属制	8309.9000	256
Powder and waste, coral and similar materials	粉末及废料,珊瑚及类似品,	0508.0010	14
Powder and waste, cuttlebone	粉末及废料,墨鱼骨	0508.0010	14
Powder and waste, shells of crustaceans	粉末及废料,甲壳动物壳	0508.0010	14
Powder and waste, shells of echinoderms	粉末及废料,棘皮动物壳	0508.0010	14
Powder and waste, shells of molluscs	粉末及废料,软体动物壳	0508.0010	14
Powder of titanium	粉末,钛的	8108.2030	16
Powder puffs and pads for the application of cosmetics or toilet preparations	粉扑及粉拍,施敷脂粉或化妆品用	9616.2000	16
Powders and flakes of tin	粉及片状粉末,锡制	8007.0030	16
Powders and flakes, of lead	粉末及片状粉末,铅制	7804.2000	16
Powders and flakes, of nickel alloys	粉及片状粉末,合金镍的	7504.0020	
Powders and flakes, of nickel, not alloyed	粉及片状粉末,非合金镍的	7504.0010	46
Powders and flakes, of zinc, nes	粉及片状粉末,锌的,其他	7903.9000	16

P

Article Description	商品名称	Tariff Code	D. R.
Powders of alloy steel, nes	粉末,合金钢的,其他	7205. 2100	6
Powders of antimony	粉末,锑的	8110. 1020	16
Powders of beryllium	粉末,铍的	8112. 1200	16
Powders of cadmium	粉末,镉的	8107. 2000	16
Powders of chromium	粉末,铬的	8112. 2100	16
Powders of cobalt	粉末,钴的	8105. 2090	16
Powders of gallium	粉末,镓的	8112. 9290	16
Powders of germanium	粉末,锗的	8112. 9210	16
Powders of hafnium	粉末,铪的	8112. 9290	16
Powders of indium	粉末,铟的	8112. 9230	16
Powders of lamellar structure; flakes, of aluminium	片状粉末,铝的	7603. 2000	6
Powders of magnesium	粉末,镁的	8104. 3000	16
Powders of manganese	锰粉末	8111. 0010	16
Powders of manganese	粉末,锰的	8111. 0010	16
Powders of molybdenum	粉末,钼的	8102. 1000	16
Powders of niobium	粉末,铌的	8112. 9240	16
Powders of non-lamellar structure, of aluminium	非片状粉末,铝的	7603. 1000	6
Powders of rhenium	粉末,铼的	8112. 9290	16
Powders of tantalum, loose density less than 2. 2g/cm^3	钽粉,松装密度小于2. 2克/立方厘米的	8103. 2011	16
Powders of tantalum, nes	粉末,钽的,其他	8103. 2019	16
Powders of tantalum, nes	钽粉,其他	8103. 2019	16
Powders of thallium	粉末,铊的	8112. 5100	16
Powders of tungsten (wolfram)	粉末,钨的	8101. 1000	16
Powders of vanadium	粉末,钒的	8112. 9220	16
Powders of zirconium	粉末,锆的	8109. 2000	16
Powders, Nd-Fe-B magnetic powder	粉末,钕铁硼磁粉	7202. 9912	6
Powders, of bismuth	粉末,铋的	8106. 0010	16
Powders, of magnesium	镁粉末	8104. 3000	16
Powders, of pig iron, spiegeleisen, iron or steel, nes	粉末,生铁、镜铁及钢铁的,其他	7205. 2900	6
Powder-boxes, with outer surface of leather, of composition leather or of patent leather	粉盒,以皮革、再生皮革或漆皮作面	4202. 3100	256
Powder-boxes, with outer surface of plastic sheeting or of textile materials	粉盒,以塑料片或纺织材料作面	4202. 3200	256
Power looms, for weaving fabrics of width exceeding 30cm, shuttle type, nes	动力织机,所织织物宽度超过30厘米的梭织机,其他	8446. 2190	7
Power measuring or checking instruments and apparatus, with a recording device	功率检测仪器及装置,带记录装置	9030. 3900	7
Power measuring or checking instruments and apparatus, without a recording device	功率检测仪器及装置,不带记录装置	9030. 3390	7
Pozzolana earth	火山灰	2530. 9099	13456
Prawns, for cultivation	对虾种苗	0306. 2310	3

P

Article Description	商品名称	Tariff Code	D. R.
Prawns, fresh or chilled	对虾,鲜或冷的	0306. 2391	1
Prawns, frozen, nes	对虾,冻的,其他	0306. 1329	18
Prawns, not frozen, nes	对虾,未冻的,其他	0306. 2399	14
Prazepam (INN); salts thereof	普拉西泮(INN),以及盐	2933. 9100	36
Precious metal articles or articles of metal clad with precious metal for technical or laboratory use	贵金属或包贵金属制品,工业或实验室用	7115. 9010	46
Precious metal articles or articles of metal clad with precious metal, nes	贵金属或包贵金属制品,其他	7115. 9090	46
Precious metal clad watch cases	包贵金属表壳	9111. 1000	6
Precious metal or precious metal compounds ash, nes	贵金属或金属化合物的灰,其他	7112. 3090	46
Precious metal ores and concentrates, nes	贵金属矿砂及其精矿,其他	2616. 9000	146
Precious metal watch cases	贵金属表壳	9111. 1000	6
Precious metals amalgams	贵金属,汞齐	2843. 9000	
Precious metals compounds, nes	贵金属化合物,其他	2843. 9000	
Precious metals, colloidal	贵金属,胶态的	2843. 1000	
Precious or semiprecious stones, synthetic or reconstructed, for technical use, nes	宝石或半宝石,合成或再造的,工业用,其他	7104. 9019	145
Precious or semiprecious stones, synthetic or reconstructed, nes	宝石或半宝石,合成或再造的,其他	7104. 9099	145
Precious or semiprecious stones, synthetic or reconstructed, unworked or simply sawn or roughly shaped, nes	宝石或半宝石,合成或再造的,未加工或经简单锯开或粗制成形,其他	7104. 2090	145
Precious or semi-precious stones dust and powder, natural or synthetic, nes	宝石或半宝石的粉末,天然或合成的其他	7105. 9000	145
Precious stones (other than diamonds) and semi-precious stones, unworked or simply sawn or roughly shaped	宝石(钻石除外)或半宝石,未加工或经简单锯开或粗制成形	7103. 1000	145
Precious stones (other than diamonds) and semi-precious stones, worked, nes	宝石(钻石除外)或半宝石,加工的,其他	7103. 9990	145
Precipitated copper	泥铜	7401. 0000	46
Precoated sensitized plate, unexposed	PS 版,未曝光的	3701. 3022	12368
Prednisolone (dehydrohydrocortisone)	脱氢皮质醇	2937. 2100	36
Prednisone (dehydrocortisone)	脱氢可的松	2937. 2100	36
Prefabricated buildings	活动房屋	9406. 0000	
Prefabricated structural components for building or civil engineering, nes	预制结构件,建筑或土木工程用的,其他	6810. 9190	56
Preformed bars for drawing optical fibre	光导纤维预制棒	7002. 2010	238
Preparations for infant use, put up for retail sale	婴幼儿食品,零售包装的	1901. 1000	2368
Preparations of a kind used as cores or coatings for welding electrodes or rods	做焊条芯子或焊条涂料用的制品	3810. 9000	36
Preparations of a kind used in animal feeding, nes	动物饲料,配制的,其他	2309. 9090	2468
Preparations of seaweeds and other algar, nes	海草及其他藻类制品,其他	2008. 9939	248

Article Description	商品名称	Tariff Code	D. R.
Prepared foods obtained by the roasting of cereals or cereal products	烘炒食品,谷物或谷物产品的	1904. 1000	48
Prepared foods obtained by the swelling of cereals or cereal products	膨化食品,谷物或谷物产品的	1904. 1000	48
Prepared foods obtained from mixtures of unroasted cereal flakes and roasted cereal flakes or swelled cereals	混合食品,未烘炒的谷物片与烘炒的谷物片或膨化的谷物混合而成	1904. 2000	48
Prepared foods obtained from unroasted cereal flakes	未烘炒食品,谷物片制成的	1904. 2000	48
Preparing machines for textile fibres, nes	预处理机器,纺织纤维的,其他	8445. 1900	7
Preserved jujubes by sugar (drained, glace or crystallized)	蜜枣,糖渍的	2006. 0010	48
Preserved litchi, dried	荔枝干	0813. 4040	34
Preserved olives by sugar (drained, glace or crystallized)	橄榄,糖渍的	2006. 0020	48
Press filters, for liquids	压滤机,液体用	8421. 2910	7
Presses for radioactive waste material	压实机,放射性废物用	8479. 8950	7
Presses for working metal or metal carbides, nes	压力机,加工金属或硬质合金用,其他	8462. 9990	7
Presses machinery parts, used in the manufacture of wine, cider, fruit juices or similar beverages	压榨机零件,制酒、制果或制类似饮料用	8435. 9000	3
Presses machinery parts, used in the manufacture of wine, cider, fruit juices or similar beverages	榨汁机零件,制酒、制果或制类似饮料用	8435. 9000	3
Presses machinery used in the manufacture of wine, cider, fruit juices or similar beverages	压榨机,制酒、制果汁或制类似饮料用	8435. 1000	
Presses machinery, used in the manufacture of wine, cider, fruit juices or similar beverages	压榨机,制酒、制果汁或制类似饮料用	8435. 1000	
Presses machinery, used in the manufacture of wine, cider, fruit juices or similar beverages	榨汁机,制酒、制果或制类似饮料用	8435. 1000	
Presses machines parts, for textile yarns, fabrics or made up textile articles	挤压机零件,纱线、织物及纺织制品用	8451. 9000	
Presses machines, for textile yarns, fabrics or made up textile articles	挤压机,纱线、织物及纺织制品用	8451. 3000	
Presses of hydraulic, for working metal or metal carbides, nes	压力机,液压的,加工金属或硬质合金用,其他	8462. 9190	7
Presses of mechanical, for working metal or metal carbides	压力机,机械的,加工金属或硬质合金用	8462. 9910	7
Pressing, stamping or punching tools, interchangeable	锻压或冲压用工具,可互换	8207. 3000	256
Pressure measuring or checking instruments and apparatus, nes	压力测量、检验仪器及装置,其他	9026. 2090	7
Pressure/differential pressure transmitters	压力/差压变送器	9026. 2010	7
Pressure-reducing valves	减压阀	8481. 1000	
Press-fasteners, snap-fasteners and press-studs and parts thereof	揿扣及其零件	9606. 1000	5

P

Article Description	商品名称	Tariff Code	D. R.
Prestressed concrete tubes, pipes, rods, plates, piles and similar articles	预应力混凝土管、杆、板、桩等	6810. 9110	56
Pretzels	椒盐卷饼	1905. 9000	28
Pre-shave, shaving or after-shave preparations	剃须用制剂	3307. 1000	23
Primary batteries, spent	原电池组,废的	8548. 1000	3
Primary cells and primary batteries parts, manganese dioxide	原电池及原电池组零件,二氧化锰的	8506. 9010	3
Primary cells and primary batteries parts, nes	原电池及原电池组零件,其他	8506. 9090	3
Primary cells and primary batteries, air-zinc	原电池及原电池组,锌空气的	8506. 6000	68
Primary cells and primary batteries, alkaline zinc-manganese dioxide, nes	原电池及原电池组,碱性锌锰的,其他	8506. 1019	68
Primary cells and primary batteries, lithium	原电池及原电池组,锂的	8506. 5000	68
Primary cells and primary batteries, manganese dioxide, nes	原电池及原电池组,二氧化锰的,其他	8506. 1090	68
Primary cells and primary batteries, mercuric oxide	原电池及原电池组,氧化汞的	8506. 3000	68
Primary cells and primary batteries, nes	原电池及原电池组,其他	8506. 8000	68
Primary cells and primary batteries, silver oxide	原电池及原电池组,氧化银的	8506. 4000	68
Primary cells, spent	原电池,废的	8548. 1000	3
Primates, ex. pure-bred breeding	灵长目,改良种用除外	0106. 1190	
Primates, pure-bred breeding	灵长目,改良种用	0106. 1110	3
Printed books, brochures	书籍、小册子	4901. 9900	15
Printed cards bearing personal greetings, messages or announcements	卡片,印有个人问候、祝贺、通告的	4909. 0090	4
Printed circuits, nes	印刷电路,其他	8534. 0090	5
Printed circuits, of more than 4 layers	印刷电路,4 层以上的	8534. 0010	5
Printed matter, nes	印刷品,其他	4911. 9900	346
Printers of stylus, of a kind solely used for automatic data processing machine	打印机,针式,专用于自动数据处理设备的	8443. 3211	57
Printers, capable of connecting to a network	打印机,可与网络连接的	8443. 3290	57
Printers, ink-jet, of a kind solely used for automatic data processing machine	打印机,喷墨的,专用于自动数据处理设备的	8443. 3213	57
Printers, laser, of a kind solely used for automatic data processing machine	打印机,激光的,专用于自动数据处理设备的	8443. 3212	57
Printers, of a kind solely used for automatic data processing machine, nes	打印机,专用于自动数据处理设备的,其他	8443. 3219	57
Printers, thermal, of a kind solely used for automatic data processing machine	打印机,热敏的,专用于自动数据处理设备的	8443. 3214	57
Printing ancillary machines, digital	印刷用辅助机器,数字式	8443. 9910	3
Printing ancillary machines, nes	印刷用辅助机器,其他	8443. 9110	3
Printing components making machinery parts	印刷部件制造机器零件	8442. 4000	3
Printing components preparing or making machinery, nes	印刷部件的制造机器、器具及设备,其他	8442. 3090	

P

Article Description	商品名称	Tariff Code	D. R.
Printing components, nes	印刷部件,其他	8442. 5000	
Printing ink, black	印刷油墨,黑色	3215. 1100	3
Printing ink, nes	印刷油墨,其他	3215. 1900	3
Printing lithographic stones	印刷用石板	8442. 5000	
Printing machinery of cylinder screen	印刷机,圆网的	8443. 1921	57
Printing machinery of flexographic	印刷机,苯胺的	8443. 1600	57
Printing machinery of gravure	印刷机,凹版的	8443. 1700	57
Printing machinery of letterpress, other than reel fed, excluding flexographic printing	印刷机,凸版的,除卷取进料式以外的,但不包括苯胺印刷机	8443. 1500	57
Printing machinery of letterpress, reel fed, excluding flexographic printing	印刷机,凸版的,卷取进料式,但不包括苯胺印刷机	8443. 1400	57
Printing machinery of platen screen	印刷机,平网的	8443. 1922	57
Printing machinery of screen, nes	印刷机,网式的,其他	8443. 1929	57
Printing machinery parts and accessories, nes	印刷机器零件及附件,其他	8443. 9190	3
Printing machinery, used for printing by means of plates, cylinders and other printing components, nes	印刷机器,用印刷用版(片)、滚筒及其他印刷部件进行的,其他	8443. 1980	57
Printing machines (laser printing machines), electrostatic photographic, digital	印刷机,静电照相(激光印刷机),数字式	8443. 3222	57
Printing machines parts, digital, nes	印刷设备的零件,数字式,其他	8443. 9929	3
Printing machines, digital, capelle of connecting to an APP machine or to a network, nes	印刷设备,数字式,可与自动数据处理设备或网络连接的,其他	8443. 3229	57
Printing machines, ink-jet, digital	印刷机,喷墨数字式	8443. 3221	57
Printing machines, laser, digital	印刷机,激光数字式	8443. 3222	57
Prints, original	印制画的原本	9702. 0000	
Prisms, of any material, mounted, being parts of or fittings for instruments or apparatus	棱镜,已装配的各种材料制,作为仪器或装置的零件、配件	9002. 9090	3
Prisms, of any material, mounted, for cameras	棱镜,已装配的各种材料制,照相机用	9002. 9010	3
Prisms, of any material, unmounted	棱镜,未装配的各种材料制	9001. 9090	5
Procaine	普鲁卡因	2922. 4991	36
Processing machines for the distributed control system, presented in the form of systems	分散型工业过程控制设备,以系统形式进口或出口的	8471. 4991	26
Processors, electronic integrated circuits, whether or not combined with memories, converters, logic circuits, amplifiers, clock and timing circuits, or other circuits	处理器,集成电路,不论是否带有存储器、转换器、逻辑电路、放大器、时钟及时序电路或其他电路	8542. 3100	37
Producer gas	炉煤气	2705. 0000	4
Production counters	产量计数器	9029. 1090	7
Production counters parts and accessories	产量计数器零件、附件	9029. 9000	3
Products consisting of natural milk constituents, whether or not containing added sugar or other sweetening matter, nes	含天然乳的产品,其他税号未列名的,不论是否加糖或其他甜物质	0404. 9000	6

Article Description	商品名称	Tariff Code	D. R.
Products of animal origin, edible, nes	动物产品,食用,其他税号未列名的	0410. 0090	34
Products of fish or crustaceans, molluscs or other aquatic invertebrates, nes	甲壳动物、软体动物、其他水生无脊椎动物的产品	0511. 9190	34
Products of fish, nes	鱼的产品,其他	0511. 9119	34
Products, of animal, used in the preparation of pharmaceutical products, fresh, chilled, frozen or otherwise provisionally preserved	动物产品,其他,供配制药用的,鲜、冷、冻或用其他方法暂时保藏的	0510. 0090	14
Profile projectors	轮廓投影仪	9031. 4910	
Profiles of aluminium, not alloyed	型材及异型材,非合金铝制	7604. 1090	16
Profiles, of aluminium alloys, nes	型材及异型材,铝合金制,其他	7604. 2990	16
Profiles, plates, sheets, strip and foil, of tungsten	型材及异型材,板、片、带、箔,钨的	8101. 9910	16
Profiles, plates, sheets, strip and foil, of molybdenum	型材及异型材、板、片、带、箔,钼的	8102. 9500	16
Progestogens	孕激素	2937. 2300	36
Programmable logic controller (PLC), for a voltage not exceeding 1000V, equipped with two or more switching or protecting or connecting apparatus	可编程序控制器,用于电压不超过1000伏的线路,装有两个或多个开关、保护或连接用的电器装置	8537. 1011	78
Projection screens	银幕及其他投影屏幕	9010. 6000	7
Projectors for images, nes	投影仪,其他	9008. 3090	
Projectors of a kind solely or principally used in an automatic data processing system of heading No. 84. 71	投影机,专用于或主要用于税号84. 71的自动数据处理系统的	8528. 6100	135
Projectors parts and accessories	放映机用零件、附件	9007. 9200	3
Projectors parts and accessories	投影仪零件、附件	9008. 9090	3
Projectors, black and white or other monochrome, nes	投影机,黑白或其他单色的,其他	8528. 6990	135
Projectors, colour, nes	投影机,彩色的,其他	8528. 6910	135
Projectors, digital	放映机,数字式	9007. 2010	8
Projectors, nes	放映机,其他	9007. 2090	8
Projectors, orthographical	投影仪,正射的	9008. 3010	
Propane, liquefied	丙烷,液化的	2711. 1200	1468
Propan-1-ol(propyl alcohol)	丙醇	2905. 1210	36
Propan-2-ol(isopropyl alcohol)	异丙醇	2905. 1220	36
Propellent powders	发射药	3601. 0000	6
Propellers and parts thereof, of aircraft	推进器及其零件,航空器用	8803. 1000	3
Propellers for ships or boats	推进器,船用	8487. 1000	3
Propelling pencils	活动铅笔	9608. 4000	
Propene(propylene)	丙烯	2901. 2200	368
Propionic acid	丙酸	2915. 5010	36
Propionic acid salts and esters	丙酸盐和酯	2915. 5090	36
Propiophenone	苯丙酮	2914. 3100	36
Propiram (INN); salts thereof	哌丙吡胺(INN)以及盐	2933. 3300	36
Proporating scales	配料秤	8423. 3030	

P

Article Description	商品名称	Tariff Code	D. R.
Propylene copolymers, nes	丙烯共聚物,其他	3902. 3090	1256
Propylene glycol (propane-1,2-diol)	1,2-丙二醇	2905. 3200	36
Propylene or of other olefins polymers, in primary forms, nes	丙烯或其他烯烃聚合物,初级形状的,其他	3902. 9000	1256
Propylene oxide	氧化丙烯	2910. 2000	36
Propylene, liquefied	丙烯,液化的	2711. 1400	1468
Prostaglandins, their derivatives and structural analogues	前列腺素及其衍生物和结构类似物	2937. 5000	36
Protecting electrical circuits apparatus, for a voltage not exceeding 1000V	电路保护装置,用于电压不超过1000伏的线路,其他	8536. 3000	8
Protein concentrates	蛋白质,浓缩的	2106. 1000	268
Protein hormones, their derivatives and structural analogues, nes	蛋白激素及其衍生物和结构类似物,其他	2937. 1900	36
Protein substances and their derivatives	蛋白质及其衍生物	3504. 0090	1346
Protein substances, textured	蛋白质,人组织化的	2106. 1000	268
Protractors	分度规	9017. 8000	7
Proustite	淡红银矿	2616. 1000	146
Prunes, dried	西梅,干的	0813. 2000	34
Pseudoephedrine (INN) and its salts	假麻黄碱及其盐	2939. 4200	34
Psilomelane	硬锰矿	2602. 0000	1346
Psittaciformes, ex. pure-bred breeding	鹦鹉,改良种用除外	0106. 3290	
Psittaciformes, pure-bred breeding	鹦鹉,改良种用	0106. 3210	3
Psophometers, specially designed for telecommunications	噪声计,通讯专用的	9030. 4090	7
Psychological aptitudetesting apparatus	心理功能测验装置	9019. 1090	7
Psychrometers	干湿球温度计	9025. 8000	3
Psychrometers parts and accessories	干湿球温度计零件、附件	9025. 9000	7
Pta (purified terephthalic acid)	精对苯二甲酸	2917. 3611	36
Public telephonic switching apparatus	局用电话交换机	8517. 6211	
Public works or building machinery, nes	公共工程用机器,其他	8479. 1090	7
Puer tea, in immediate packings of a content not exceeding 3kg	普洱茶,内包装每件净重不超过3千克	0902. 3020	248
Puer tea, nes	普洱茶,其他	0902. 4020	248
Puffer fish, fresh or chilled	鲀,鲜或冷的	0302. 6950	18
Puffer fish, living	鲀,活的	0301. 9992	15
Puffs and pads for the application powder of cosmetics or toilet preparations	粉扑及粉拍,施敷脂粉或化妆品用	9616. 2000	
Pulley tackle and hoists other than skip hoists or hoists of a kind used for raising vehicles, nes	滑车及提升机,倒卸式提升机及提升车辆用的提升机除外,其他	8425. 1900	78
Pulley tackle and hoists powered by electric motor, other than skip hoists or hoists of a kind used for raising vehicles	滑车及提升机,电动的,倒卸式提升机及提升车辆用的提升机除外	8425. 1100	78

P

Article Description	商品名称	Tariff Code	D. R.
Pulley tackle parts	滑车的零件	8431. 1000	3
Pulleys parts	滑轮零件	8483. 9000	3
Pulleys, including pulley blocks	滑轮,包括滑轮组	8483. 5000	3
Pullovers, knitted or crocheted, nes	套头衫,针织或钩编的,其他	6110. 9090	2456
Pullovers, knitted or crocheted, of cotton	套头衫,针织或钩编的,棉制	6110. 2000	2456
Pullovers, knitted or crocheted, of kashmir (cashmere) fine goats hair	套头衫,针织或钩编的,喀什米尔山羊细毛制	6110. 1200	2456
Pullovers, knitted or crocheted, of man-made fibres	套头衫,针织或钩编的,化学纤维制	6110. 3000	2456
Pullovers, knitted or crocheted, of other fine animal hair	套头衫,针织或钩编的,其他动物细毛制	6110. 1990	2456
Pullovers, knitted or crocheted, of other fine goats hair	套头衫,针织或钩编的,其他山羊细毛制	6110. 1910	2456
Pullovers, knitted or crocheted, of rabbit and hare	套头衫,针织或钩编的,兔毛制	6110. 1920	2456
Pullovers, knitted or crocheted, of silk or silk waste	套头衫,针织或钩编的,丝及绢丝制	6110. 9010	2456
Pullovers, knitted or crocheted, of wool	套头衫,针织或钩编的,毛制	6110. 1100	2456
Pulp making machinery of fibrous cellulosic material	纸浆制造机器,纤维素材料用	8439. 1000	
Pulp making machinery parts, of fibrous cellulosic material	纸浆制造机器的零件,纤维素材料用	8439. 9100	3
Pulp, of bamboo, derived from recovered (waste and scrap) paper or paperboard	竹浆,从回收(废碎)纸或纸板提取的	4706. 3000	4
Pulps of fibres derived from recovered (waste and scrap) paper or paperboard	纤维浆,从回收(废碎)纸或纸板提取的	4706. 2000	4
Pulse code modulation equipments	脉冲编码调制设备(PCM)	8517. 6221	7
Pulse code modulation equipments parts	脉冲编码调制设备(PCM)用零件	8517. 7020	3
Pumice stone	浮石	2513. 1000	14
Pump espresso makers, electro-thermic	泵压式咖啡机,电热的	8516. 7130	7
Pumpkin seeds	瓜子,白的	1212. 9993	134
Pumps fitted or designed to be fitted with a measuring device, nes	泵,装有或可装计量装置的,其他	8413. 1900	23
Pumps for concrete	泵,混凝土用	8413. 4000	23
Pumps for cooling medium	泵,冷却剂用	8413. 3090	23
Pumps for dispensing fuel or lubricants, of the type used in filling-stations or in garages	泵,分装燃料或润滑油的,用于加油站或车库	8413. 1100	23
Pumps for fuel, for engines of an output of 132. 39kW (180hp) or more	泵,燃油用,输出功率在 132. 39 千瓦(180 马力)及以上的发动机用	8413. 3021	23
Pumps for fuel, nes	泵,燃油用,其他	8413. 3029	23
Pumps for hand, other than those of subheading No. 8413. 11 or 8413. 19	泵,手用,但子目号 8413. 11 或 8413. 19 的货品除外	8413. 2000	23
Pumps for lubricating oil	泵,润滑油用	8413. 3030	23
Pumps of centrifugal, electric submersible oil pumps and electric submersible pumps	泵,离心式,电动潜油泵及潜水电泵	8413. 7091	27
Pumps of centrifugal, nes	泵,离心式,其他	8413. 7099	27

Article Description	商品名称	Tariff Code	D. R.
Pumps of centrifugal, rotational speed no less than 10000r/min	泵,离心式,转速在10000转/分及以上	8413.7010	27
Pumps parts	泵用零件	8413.9100	27
Pumps, for positive displacement, rotary, gear, electric	泵,排液回转式,齿轮的,电动式	8413.6021	27
Pumps, for positive displacement, rotary, axial plunger	泵,排液回转式,轴向柱塞泵	8413.6060	27
Pumps, for positive displacement, rotary, gear, hydraulic	泵,排液回转式,齿轮的,液压式	8413.6022	27
Pumps, for positive displacement, rotary, gear, nes	泵,排液回转式,齿轮的,其他	8413.6029	27
Pumps, for positive displacement, rotary, helicoida	泵,排液回转式,螺杆泵	8413.6040	27
Pumps, for positive displacement, rotary, nes	泵,排液回转式,其他	8413.6090	27
Pumps, for positive displacement, rotary, radial plunger	泵,排液回转式,径向柱塞泵	8413.6050	27
Pumps, for positive displacement, rotary, vane, electric	泵,排液回转式,叶片的,电动式	8413.6031	27
Pumps, for positive displacement, rotary, vane, hydraulic	泵,排液回转式,叶片的,液压式	8413.6032	27
Pumps, for positive displacement, rotary, vane, nes	泵,排液回转式,叶片的,其他	8413.6039	27
Pumps, nes	泵,其他	8413.8100	27
Pumps, positive displacement pumps, reciprocating, electric	泵,排液泵,往复式,电动式	8413.5020	23
Pumps, positive displacement pumps, reciprocating, hydraulic, nes	泵,排液泵,往复式,液压式,其他	8413.5039	23
Pumps, positive displacement pumps, reciprocating, nes	泵,排液泵,往复式,其他	8413.5090	23
Pumps, positive displacement pumps, reciprocating, plunger pumps	泵,排液泵,往复式,柱塞泵	8413.5031	23
Pumps, positive displacement pumps, reciprocating, pneumatic	泵,排液泵,往复式,气动式	8413.5010	23
Punch press, cnc automatic tool change, numerically controlled, for working metal	压力机,自动模式数控步冲的,加工金属用	8462.4111	7
Punch press, for working metal, nes	冲床,加工金属用,其他	8462.4900	7
Punch press, numerically controlled, for working metal	冲床,数控的,加工金属用,其他	8462.4119	7
Punching and shearing combined machines, for working metal	冲剪两用机,加工金属用	8462.4900	7
Punching and shearing combined machines, numerically controlled, for working metal	冲剪两用机,数控的,加工金属用	8462.4190	7
Pure royal jelley	鲜蜂王浆	0410.0041	12
Pure royal jelley, in powder	鲜蜂王浆粉	0410.0042	12
Puree, being cooked preparations, nes	果泥,烹煮的,其他	2007.9990	248
Puree, citrus fruit, being cooked preparations	果泥,烹煮的,柑橘属水果的	2007.9100	248
Puree, citrus fruit, being cooked preparations, in airtight containers	果泥,烹煮的,柑橘属水果的,罐头	2007.9910	248

P

Article Description	商品名称	Tariff Code	D. R.
Purifying apparatus for exhaust air, for internal combustion engines	净化装置,内燃发动机排气用	8421. 3930	7
Purifying apparatus for gases, nes	净化装置,气体用,其他	8421. 3990	7
Purifying machinery and apparatus, for filtering or purifying beverages other than water	净化机器及装置,过滤或净化饮料(水除外)用	8421. 2200	7
Purifying machinery and apparatus, for filtering or purifying water, nes	净化机器及装置,过滤或净化水用,其他	8421. 2190	7
Purifying machinery and apparatus, for liquids, nes	净化机器及装置,液体用,其他	8421. 2990	7
Purifying machinery and apparatus, of the household type, for filtering or purifying water	净化机器及装置,家用型,过滤或净化水用	8421. 2110	7
Purifying machinery and apparatus, of the household type, for gases	净化机器及装置,家用型,气体用	8421. 3910	7
Purifying machines parts, nes	净化装置用零件,其他	8421. 9990	3
Purifying machines parts, of household-type	净化装置用零件,家用型	8421. 9910	3
Pusher craft	顶推船	8904. 0000	7
Pyrargyrite	深红银矿	2616. 1000	146
Pyrazole ring compounds, containing an unfused imidazole ring, unfused in the structure, whether or not hydrogenated, nes	吡唑环化合物,结构上含有一个非稠合咪唑环,非稠合的,不论是否氢化,其他	2933. 1990	36
Pyrethrum	除虫菊	1211. 9091	34
Pyridine and its salts	吡啶及其盐	2933. 3100	36
Pyridine ring compounds, containing a quinoline or isoquinoline ring-systern, unfused in the structure, whether or not hydrogenated, nes	吡啶环化合物,结构上含有一个喹啉或异喹啉体系,非稠合,不论是否氢化,其他	2933. 3990	36
Pyrimidine ring compounds, in the structure, whether or not hydrogenated, nes	嘧啶环化合物,结构上含有,不论是否氢化,其他	2933. 5990	36
Pyromorphite	磷绿铅矿	2607. 0000	146
Pyronine (as synthetic organic colouring matter)	焦宁,派若宁(一种染料)	3204. 9090	345
Pyrophoric alloys, nes	引火合金,其他	3606. 9019	13
Pyrophoric alloys, nes, cut to shape, for immediate use	引火合金,其他,已切成形可直接使用	3606. 9011	13
Pyrophosphoric acid	焦磷酸	2809. 2019	6
Pyrotechnic articles other	烟火制品其他	3604. 9000	7
Pyrovalerone(INN); salts thereof	吡咯戊酮(INN)以及盐	2933. 9100	36
Pyrrhotite, nickeliferous	磁黄铁矿,含镍	2604. 0000	146
P-acetaminophenol	对乙酰氨基酚	2924. 2920	36
P-chlorobenzyl cyanide	对氯氰苄	2926. 9010	36
P-chlorophenol	对氯苯酚	2908. 1910	36
P-chlorotoluene	对氯甲苯	2903. 6910	36
P-dichlorobenzene:	对二氯苯	2903. 6190	36
P-dihydroxybenzene salts	对苯二酚盐	2907. 2290	36
P-isopropyl-aniline	对异丙基苯胺	2921. 4910	36
P-nitrochlorobenzene	对硝基氯化苯	2904. 9013	36

Article Description	商品名称	Tariff Code	D. R.
P-nitrophenol	对硝基酚	2908. 9910	36
P-tert-butyl-α-methyl-oxocinn amaldehyde	对叔丁基-α-甲基-氧化肉桂醛	2912. 2910	36
P-xylene	对二甲苯	2902. 4300	6

Q

Article Description	商品名称	Tariff Code	D. R.
Quail, for human consumption	鹌鹑,食用	0106.3929	34
Quail, pure-bred breeding	鹌鹑,改良种用	0106.3910	34
Quartz	石英	2506.1000	14
Quartz sands	石英砂	2505.1000	34
Quartz tubes for optical fibres use, waveguide grade	石英玻璃管,光导纤维用,波导级	7002.3110	238
Quartz, piezo-electric, synthetic or reconstructed	石英,压电,合成或再造的	7104.1000	145
Quartzite	石英岩	2506.2000	14
Quaternary ammonium hydroxides, whether or not chemically defined	季铵碱,无论是否已有化学定义	2923.9000	36
Quaternary ammonium salts, whether or not chemically defined	季铵盐,无论是否已有化学定义	2923.9000	36
Quebracho extract	坚木浸膏	3201.1000	34
Quiche	乳蛋饼	1905.9000	28
Quicklime	生石灰	2522.1000	
Quilted textile products in the piece, nes	被褥块状纺织品,其他	5811.0090	
Quilted textile products in the piece, of cotton	被褥块状纺织品,棉制	5811.0030	
Quilted textile products in the piece, of man-made fibres	被褥块状纺织品,化学纤维制	5811.0040	
Quilted textile products in the piece, of silk or silk waste	被褥块状纺织品,丝及绢丝制	5811.0010	
Quilted textile products in the piece, of wool or fine animal hair	被褥块状纺织品,羊毛或动物细毛制	5811.0020	
Quilts, nes	被子,其他	9404.9090	6
Quilts, stuffed with animal hair	被子,兽毛填充的	9404.9020	6
Quilts, stuffed with feathers or down, nes	被子,羽毛或羽绒填充的,其他	9404.9010	6
Quilts, stuffed with man-made fibres	被子,化纤棉填充的	9404.9040	6
Quilts, stuffed with silk wadding	被子,丝棉填充的	9404.9030	6
Quinces, fresh	榅桲,鲜的	0808.2020	1
Quinine or its salts medicaments, consisting of two or more constituents which have been mixed together, not put up in measured doses or in forms or packings for retail sale	含有奎宁或其盐药品,两种或两种以上成分混合而成的,未配定剂量或制成零售包装	3003.4010	368
Quinine or its salts medicaments, mixed or unmixed, put up in measured doses or in forms or packings for retail sale	含有奎宁或其盐药品,混合或未混合的,配定剂量或制成零售包装	3004.4010	368
Quinizarin	醌茜	2914.6900	36
Quinoline ring-system compounds, not further fused in the structure, whether or not hydrogenated, nes	喹啉环系化合物,结构上含有,未经进一步稠合的, 不论是否氢化,其他	2933.4990	36

Article Description	商品名称	Tariff Code	D. R.
Quinones, halogenated, sulphonated, nitrated or nitrosated derivatives of	醌,卤化、磺化、硝化或亚硝化衍生物	2914. 7000	36
Quinones, nes	醌,其他	2914. 6900	36
Quinuclidine-3-ol	奎宁环-3-醇	2933. 3920	36

Q

R

Article Description	商品名称	Tariff Code	D. R.
Ractopamine and ractopamine hydrochloride	莱克多巴胺和盐酸莱克多巴胺	2922. 1110	36
Radar apparatus parts	雷达设备用零件	8529. 9050	3
Radar apparatus, for navigational aid	雷达设备,导航用	8526. 1010	
Radar apparatus, nes	雷达设备,其他	8526. 1090	
Radar display tubes parts	雷达显示管用零件	8540. 9120	3
Radar display tubes, cathode-ray tubes	雷达显示管,阴极射线管	8540. 6010	35
Radial plunger pump, for positive displacement, rotary	径向柱塞泵,排液回转式	8413. 6050	27
Radiations apparatus, for medical, surgical, dental or veterinary uses	射线应用设备,医疗、外科、牙科或兽医用	9022. 2100	
Radiators for central heating and parts thereof, of iron or steel, not electrically heated, nes	散热器及其零件,钢铁制,非电热的,集中供暖用,其他	7322. 1900	7
Radiators for central heating and parts thereof, of cast iron, not electrically heated	散热器及其零件,铸铁制,非电热的,集中供暖用	7322. 1100	7
Radiators parts and accessories, nes	机动车辆用散热器零件、附件,其他	8708. 9190	3
Radio apparatus parts, nes	无线电设备零件,其他	8529. 9090	3
Radio communication vans	无线电通信车	8705. 9010	7
Radio navigational aid apparatus parts	无线电导航设备用零件	8529. 9050	3
Radio navigational aid apparatus, for motor vehicles	无线电导航设备,机动车辆用	8526. 9110	
Radio navigational aid apparatus, nes	无线电导航设备,其他	8526. 9190	
Radio remote control apparatus	无线电遥控设备	8526. 9200	
Radioactive waste material presses	放射性废物用压实机	8479. 8950	7
Radiography apparatus parts and accessories	射线照相设备的零件、附件	9022. 9090	3
Radiotherapy apparatus parts and accessories	射线治疗设备的零件、附件	9022. 9090	3
Radio-broadcast receivers and their combinations parts	无线电收音机及其组合机用零件	8529. 9060	3
Radio-broadcast receivers capable of operating without an external source of power, combined with sound recording or reproducing apparatus	无线电收音机,不需外接电源的,收录(放)音组合机	8527. 1300	5
Radio-broadcast receivers capable of operating without an external source of power, nes	无线电收音机,不需外接电源的,其他	8527. 1900	5
Radio-broadcast receivers not capable of operating without an external source of power, of a kind used in motor vehicles, combined with sound recording or reproducing apparatus	无线电收音机,需外接电源的,汽车用,收录(放)音组合机	8527. 2100	5
Radio-broadcast receivers not capable of operating without an external source of power, of a kind used in motor vehicles, nes	无线电收音机,需外接电源的,汽车用,其他	8527. 2900	5
Radio-broadcasting reception apparatus, combined with sound recording or reproducing apparatus	无线电广播接收设备,收录(放)音组合机	8527. 9100	5

Article Description	商品名称	Tariff Code	D. R.
Radio-broadcasting reception apparatus, nes	无线电广播接收设备,其他	8527.9900	5
Radio-broadcasting reception apparatus, not combined with sound recording or reproducing apparatus but combined with a clock	无线电广播接收设备,带时钟的收音机	8527.9200	5
Radishes, fresh or chilled	小萝卜,鲜或冷藏的	0706.9000	1
Radium and its salts	镭及镭盐,放射性的	2844.4010	
Radix angelicae sinensis	当归	1211.9011	34
Radix astragali	黄芪	1211.9023	34
Radix codonopsitis	党参	1211.9013	34
Radix paeoniae lactifiorae	白芍	1211.9021	34
Radix pseudoginseng	田七	1211.9012	34
Radix rehmanniae	地黄	1211.9026	34
Raffia	酒椰叶	1401.9090	3
Rafts, inflatable	充气筏	8907.1000	5
Rags and their articles, of textile materials, used or new, nes	碎织物及其制品，纺织材料的，新的或旧的,其他	6310.9000	146
Rags and their articles, of textile materials, used or new, sorted	碎织物及其制品，纺织材料的，新的或旧的,经分拣的	6310.1000	146
Rail automatic axle counting equipments	轨道自动计轴设备	8608.0010	3
Rail clips, bedplates, ties and other material specialized for jointing or fixing rails	钢轨夹、底板、固定板及其他专门用于连接或加固路轨的材料	7302.9090	6
Rail diesel-electric locomotives, controled by microprocessings	铁道柴油电力机车,微型机控制的	8602.1010	37
Rail diesel-electric locomotives, nes	铁道柴油电力机车,其他	8602.1090	37
Rail locomotives, controlled by microprocess-ings, drived by DC motors	铁道电力机车,微型机控制的,直流电机驱动的	8601.1011	37
Rail locomotives, drived by AC motors	铁道电力机车,交流电机驱动的	8601.1020	37
Rail locomotives, drived by DC motors, nes	铁道电力机车,直流电机驱动的,其他	8601.1019	37
Rail locomotives, nes	铁道机车,其他	8602.9000	37
Rail locomotives, powered by electric accumulators	铁道电力机车,由蓄电池驱动	8601.2000	37
Rail locomotives, powered from an external source of electricity, nes	铁道电力机车,由外部电力驱动,其他	8601.1090	37
Rails	钢轨	7302.1000	6
Railway or tramway coaches, self-propelled, nes	铁道及电车道用的自驱动客车,其他	8603.9000	37
Railway or tramway coaches, self-propelled, powered frow an external source of electricity	铁道及电车道用的自驱动客车,由外部电力驱动	8603.1000	37
Railway or tramway locomotives or rolling-stock parts, nes	铁道及电车道机车或其他车辆的零件,其他	8607.9900	3
Railway or tramway maintenance or service vehicles, nes	铁道及电车道用的维修或服务车,其他	8604.0099	37
Railway or tramway track fixtures and fittings, nes	铁道及电车道轨道固定装置及附件,其他	8608.0090	3

R

Article Description	商品名称	Tariff Code	D. R.
Railway or tramway trucks, self-propelled, nes	铁道及电车道用的自驱动敞车,其他	8603.9000	37
Railway or tramway trucks, self-propelled, powered frow an external source of electricity	铁道及电车道用的自驱动敞车,由外部电力驱动	8603.1000	37
Railway or tramway vans, self-propelled, nes	铁道及电车道用的自驱动货车,其他	8603.9000	37
Railway or tramway vans, self-propelled, powered frow an external source of electricity	铁道及电车道用的自驱动货车,由外部电力驱动	8603.1000	37
Railway passenger coaches	铁道客车	8605.0010	37
Railway sleepers of concrete	铁道用水泥枕	6810.9910	56
Railway wagon handing equipment	铁道货车搬运装置	8428.9010	
Rain rockets, nes	降雨火箭及其他	3604.9000	
Raincoats, not knitted or crocheted, for men or boys, of cotton	雨衣,非针织或钩编的,男式,棉制	6201.1290	2456
Raincoats, not knitted or crocheted, for men or boys, of man-made fibres	雨衣,非针织或钩编的,男式	6201.1390	2456
Raincoats, not knitted or crocheted, for men or boys, of other textile materials	雨衣,非针织或钩编的,男式,其他纺织材料制	6201.1900	2456
Raincoats, not knitted or crocheted, for men or boys, of wool or fine animal hair	雨衣,非针织或钩编的,男式,羊毛或动物细毛制	6201.1100	2456
Raincoats, not knitted or crocheted, for women or girls, of cotton	雨衣,非针织或钩编的,女式,棉制	6202.1290	2456
Raincoats, not knitted or crocheted, for women or girls, of man-made fibres	雨衣,非针织或钩编的,女式,化学纤维制	6202.1390	2456
Raincoats, not knitted or crocheted, for women or girls, of other textile materials	雨衣,非针织或钩编的,女式,其他纺织材料制	6202.1900	2456
Raincoats, not knitted or crocheted, for women or girls, of wool or fine animal hair	雨衣,非针织或钩编的,女式,羊毛或动物细毛制	6202.1100	2456
Rakes	耙	8201.3000	256
Rambutan, fresh	红毛丹,鲜的	0810.9040	1
Ramie woven fabrics, containing 85% or more by weight of ramie, nes	苎麻机织物,按重量计苎麻含量在85%及以上的,其他	5311.0013	2468
Ramie woven fabrics, containing 85% or more by weight of ramie, unbleached	苎麻机织物,按重量计苎麻含量在85%及以上的,未漂白	5311.0012	2468
Ramie woven fabrics, containing less than 85% by weight of ramie, nes	苎麻机织物,按重量计苎麻含量在85%以下的,其他	5311.0015	2468
Ramie woven fabrics, containing less than 85% by weight of ramie, unbleached	苎麻机织物,按重量计苎麻含量在85%以下的,未漂白	5311.0014	2468
Ramie yarn, containing 85% or more by weight of ramie, coloured yarn	苎麻纱线,按重量计苎麻含量在85%及以上的色纱线	5308.9012	568
Ramie yarn, containing 85% or more by weight of ramie, unbleached or bleached yarn	苎麻纱线,按重量计苎麻含量在85%及以上的未漂白或漂白纱线	5308.9011	568
Ramie yarn, containing less than 85% by weight of coloured yarn	苎麻纱线,按重量计苎麻含量在85%以下的色纱线	5308.9014	568

Article Description	商品名称	Tariff Code	D. R.
Ramie yarn, containing less than 85% by weight of ramie, unbleached or bleached yarn	苎麻纱线,按重量计苎麻含量在85%以下的未漂白或漂白纱线	5308.9013	568
Range hoods, hoods having a maximum horizontal side not exceeding 120cm	抽油烟机,罩的平面最大边长不超过120厘米	8414.6010	23
Rangefinders	测距仪	9015.1000	
Rape oil and fractions thereof, nes	菜子油及其分离品,其他	1514.9900	4
Rape oil and its fractions, low erucic acid, crude oil	菜子油及其分离品,低芥子酸的,初榨的	1514.1100	46
Rape oil and its fractions, low erucic acid, nes	菜子油及其分离品,低芥子酸的,其他	1514.1900	46
Rape oil, nes, crude	菜子油,其他,初榨的	1514.9110	4
Rape, nes	油菜籽,其他	1205.9090	3
Rape, nes, low erucic acid	油菜籽,其他,低芥子酸的	1205.1090	36
Rape, seed	油菜籽,种用	1205.9010	3
Rape, seed, low erucic acid	油菜籽,种用,低芥子酸的	1205.1010	36
Rapier looms, for weaving fabrics of a with exceeding 30cm, shuttleless type	剑杆织机,所织织物宽度超过30厘米的无梭织机	8446.3020	7
Rare gases, nes	稀有气体,其他	2804.2900	
Rareearth chlorides, nes	氯化稀土,其他	2846.9029	6
Rareearth fluorides	氟化稀土	2846.9030	6
Rare-earth carbonate, nes	碳酸稀土,其他	2846.9049	6
Rare-earth metals permanent magnets	稀土永磁体	8505.1110	46
Rare-earth metals, nes, not intermixed or interalloyed	稀土金属,其他,未相互混合或相互熔合	2805.3019	56
Rare-earth metals, scandium, yttrium, intermixed or interalloyed, battery grade	稀土金属、钪及钇,相互混合或相互熔合,电池级	2805.3021	56
Rare-earth metals, scandium, yttrium, intermixed or interalloyed, nes	稀土金属、钪及钇,相互混合或相互熔合,其他	2805.3029	56
Rare-earth oxides, nes	氧化稀土,其他	2846.9019	
Rashel machines	拉舍尔经编机	8447.2012	7
Raspberries, fresh	木莓,鲜的	0810.2000	1
Raspberries, frozen	木莓,冷冻的	0811.2000	1
Raspberry ketone	覆盆子酮	2914.5011	36
Raspings, turnings and granules, graded according to size, of magnesium	锉屑、车屑及颗粒,已按规格分级的,镁的	8104.3000	16
Rasps and similar tools	木锉及类似工具	8203.1000	256
Ratafias	果酒	2208.7000	2468
Rationed packing scales	定量包装秤	8423.3010	
Rationed sorting scales	定量分选秤	8423.3020	
Rattan Basketwork	藤制篮筐	4602.1200	6
Rattan Furniture	藤制家具	9403.8100	6
Rattan Mats	藤制席子	4601.2200	6
Rattan Seats	藤制坐具	9401.5100	6

R

Article Description	商品名称	Tariff Code	D. R.
Rattans	藤	1401. 2000	3456
Ravioli, whether or not cooked or otherwise prepared	馄饨,不论是否烹煮或经其他方法制作	1902. 2000	46
Ravioli, whether or not cooked or otherwise prepared	饺子,不论是否烹煮或经其他方法制作	1902. 2000	46
Raw furskins of fox, whole, with or without head, tail or paws	狐皮,整张的,不论是否带头、尾或爪	4301. 6000	15
Raw furskins of lamb (astrakhan, broadtail, caracul, persian and similar lamb, indian, chinese, mongolian or tibetan lamb, whole, with or without head, tail or paws)	羔羊毛皮,整张的,不论是否带头、尾或爪(阿斯特拉罕、喀拉科尔、波斯羔羊及类似羔羊、印度、中国或蒙古羔羊)	4301. 3000	15
Raw furskins of mink, whole, with or without head, tail or paws	水貂皮,整张的,不论是否带头、尾或爪	4301. 1000	15
Raw furskins of rabbit or hare, whole, with or without head, tail or paws	兔皮,整张的,不论是否带头、尾或爪	4301. 8010	15
Raw furskins, heads, tails, paws and pieces or cuttings, suitable for furriers use, nes	毛皮,适合加工皮货用的头、尾、爪及块、片,其他	4301. 9090	15
Raw furskins, whole, with or without head, tall or paws, nes	毛皮,整张的,其他不论是否带头、尾或爪	4301. 8090	15
Raw hides and skins of goats kids, have undergone a reversible tanning process	生皮,小山羊皮,经逆鞣处理的	4103. 9021	1458
Raw hides and skins of goats kids, nes	生皮,小山羊皮,其他	4103. 9029	1458
Raw hides and skins of goats, have undergone a reversible tanning process	生皮,山羊板皮,经逆鞣处理的	4103. 9011	1458
Raw hides and skins of goats, nes	生皮,山羊板皮,其他	4103. 9019	1458
Raw hides and skins of reptiles	生皮,爬行动物的	4103. 2000	1458
Raw hides and skins of swine	生皮,猪的	4103. 3000	1458
Raw hides and skins, nes	生皮,其他	4103. 9090	1458
Raw hides and skins, of bovine animals, whole, of a weight per skin not exceeding 8kg when simply dried, 10kg when dry-salted, or 16kg when fresh, wet-salted or otherwise preserved, have undergone a reversible tanning process	生皮,牛的,整张的,完全干燥的每张重量不超过 8 千克,干盐腌的不超过 10 千克,鲜的、湿盐腌的或以其他方法保藏的不超过 16 千克,经逆鞣处理的	4101. 2011	1458
Raw hides and skins, of bovine animals, whole, of a weight per skin not exceeding 8kg when simply dried, 10kg when dry-salted, or 16kg when fresh, wet-salted or otherwise preserved, nes	生皮,牛的,整张的,完全干燥的每张重量不超过 8 千克,干盐腌的不超过 10 千克,鲜的、湿盐腌的或以其他方法保藏的不超过 16 千克,其他	4101. 2019	1458
Raw hides and skins, of bovine animals, have undergone a reversible tanning process	生皮,牛的,经逆鞣处理的	4101. 9011	1458
Raw hides and skins, of bovine animals, nes	生皮,牛的,其他	4101. 9019	1458
Raw hides and skins, of equine animals, nes	生皮,马的,其他	4101. 9020	1458
Raw hides and skins, of equine animals, of a weight exceeding 16kg	生皮,马的,整张的,重量超过 16 千克	4101. 5020	1458

Article Description	商品名称	Tariff Code	D. R.
Raw hides and skins, of equine animals, whole, of a weight per skin not exceeding 8kg when simply dried, 10kg when dry-salted, or 16kg when fresh, wet-salted or otherwise preserved	生皮,马的,整张的,完全干燥的每张重量不超过 8 千克,干盐腌的不超过 10 千克,鲜的、湿盐腌的或以其他方法保藏的不超过 16 千克	4101. 2020	1458
Raw hides and skins, whole, of a weight exceeding 16kg, have undergone a reversible tanning process	生皮,牛的,整张的,重量超过 16 千克,经逆鞣处理的	4101. 5011	1458
Raw hides and skins, whole, of a weight exceeding 16kg, nes	生皮,牛的,整张的,重量超过 16 千克其他	4101. 5019	1458
Raw silk, nes	生丝,其他	5002. 0090	45
Raw skins of sheep or lambs with wool on	生皮,绵羊或羔羊的,带毛	4102. 1000	1458
Raw skins of sheep or lambs without wool on, have undergone a reversible tanning process	生皮,绵羊或羔羊的,不带毛的,经逆鞣处理的	4102. 2910	1458
Raw skins of sheep or lambs without wool on, nes	生皮,绵羊或羔羊的,不带毛的,其他	4102. 2990	1458
Raw skins of sheep or lambs without wool on, pickled, have undergone a reversible tanning process	生皮,绵羊或羔羊的,不带毛浸酸的,经逆鞣处理的	4102. 2110	1458
Raw skins of sheep or lambs without wool on, pickled, nes	生皮,绵羊或羔羊的,不带毛浸酸的,其他	4102. 2190	1458
Raw vegetable materials of a kind used primarily in dyeing or tanning	植物原料,主要供染料、鞣料用的	1404. 9010	3
Razor blades, including razor blade blanks in strips	剃刀刀片,包括未分开的刀片条	8212. 2000	256
Razors	剃刀	8212. 1000	256
Razors parts, nes	剃刀零件,其他	8212. 9000	256
Reaction accelerators, nes	反应促进剂,其他	3815. 9000	36
Reaction initiators, nes	反应引发剂,其他	3815. 9000	36
Rear appearance of bodies, of the motor vehicles	后围,机动车辆的	8708. 2956	3
Rear compartment covers (or rear door), of the motor vehicles	行李箱盖(或背门),机动车辆的	8708. 2955	3
Rear-view mirrors for vehicles	车辆后视镜	7009. 1000	4
Receipt books, of paper or paperboard	收据本,纸或纸板制的	4820. 1000	
Receiver valves and tubes	接收管	8540. 8100	35
Reciprocating piston engines of a kind used for the propulsion of vehicles, of a cylinder capacity exceeding 250cc but not exceeding 1000cc	往复式活塞发动机,车辆用,气缸容量(排气量)超过 250 毫升,但不超过 1000 毫升	8407. 3300	123
Reciprocating piston engines of a kind used for the propulsion of vehicles, of a cylinder capacity exceeding 3000cc	往复式活塞发动机,车辆用,气缸容量(排气量)超过 3000 毫升	8407. 3420	123
Reciprocating piston engines of a kind used for the propulsion of vehicles, of a cylinder capacity exceeding 50cc but not exceeding 250cc	往复式活塞发动机,车辆用,气缸容量(排气量)超过 50 毫升,但不超过 250 毫升	8407. 3200	123
Reciprocating piston engines of a kind used for the propulsion of vehicles, of a cylinder capacity exceeding1000cc but not exceeding 3000cc	往复式活塞发动机,车辆用,气缸容量(排气量) 超过 1000 毫升,但不超过 3000 毫升	8407. 3410	123

Article Description	商品名称	Tariff Code	D. R.
Reciprocating piston engines of a kind used for the propulsion of vehicles, of a cylinder capacity not exceeding 50cc	往复式活塞发动机,车辆用,气缸容量(排气量)不超过50毫升	8407.3100	123
Reclaimed rubber in primary forms or in plates, sheets or strip	再生橡胶,初级形状或板、片、带	4003.0000	14
Reconstituted tobacco	再造烟草	2403.9100	
Record sleeves, of paper, paperboard, nes	唱片套,纸制的,其他	4819.5000	68
Record-players, not incorporating a sound recording device, with or without loudspeakers, nes	唱机,不带录制装置的,不论是否带有扬声器,其他	8519.8910	5
Recovered (waste and scrap) paper or paperboard, including unsorted waste and scrap, nes	回收(废碎)纸或纸板,包括未分选的废碎品,其他	4707.9000	125
Rectifying towers	精馏塔	8419.4020	57
Red bean paste, in airtight containers	赤豆馅罐头	2005.5111	148
Red bean paste, prepared or preserved otherwise than by vinegar or acetic acid, not frozen, nes	赤豆馅,用醋或醋酸以外的其他方法制作或保藏的,未冷冻,其他	2005.5191	148
Red haematite, agglomerated	赤铁矿,已烧结	2601.1200	1346
Red jujubes, dried	红枣,干的	0813.4030	34
Red lead	铅丹	2824.9010	
Red watermelon seeds	瓜子,红的	1212.9992	134
Reeds	芦苇	1401.9020	3
Reeds for looms	筘,织机用	8448.4200	3
Reeling machines for textile fabrics	卷绕机器,纺织物的	8451.5000	
Reeling machines parts for textile fabrics	卷绕机器零件,纺织物的	8451.9000	
Refined borax, anhydrous	精炼硼砂,无水的	2840.1100	
Refined borax, nes	精炼硼砂,其他	2840.1900	
Refractory bricks, blocks, tiles and similar refractory ceramic constructional goods, containing by weight more than 50% of alumina (Al_2O_3), of silica (SiO_2) or of a mixture or compound of these products	耐火砖、块、瓦及类似耐火陶瓷建材制品,含有按重量计超过50%的三氧化二铝、二氧化硅或其混合物或化合物	6902.2000	6
Refractory bricks, blocks, tiles and similar refractory ceramic constructional goods, containing by weight, singly or together, more than 50% of the elements Mg, Ca or Cr, expressed as MgO, CaO or Ca_2O_3	耐火砖、块、瓦及类似耐火陶瓷建材制品,单独或同时含有按重量计超过50%的镁、钙或铬(分别以氧化镁、氧化钙及三氧化二铬的含量计)	6902.1000	6
Refractory bricks, blocks, tiles and similar refractory ceramic constructional goods, nes	耐火砖、块、瓦及类似耐火陶瓷建材制品,其他	6902.9000	6
Refractory ceramic goods, containing by weight more than 50% of alumina (Al_2O_3) or of a mixture of compound of alumina and of silica (SiO_2)	耐火陶瓷制品,含有按重量计超过50%的三氧化二铝或三氧化二铝和二氧化硅的混合物或化合物	6903.2000	6
Refractory ceramic goods, containing by weight more than 50% of graphite or other carbon or of a mixture of these pro-ducts	耐火陶瓷制品,含有按重量计超过50%的石墨、其他碳或其混合物	6903.1000	6

R

Article Description	商品名称	Tariff Code	D. R.
Refractory ceramic goods, nes	耐火陶瓷制品,其他	6903.9000	6
Refrigerated vessels, other than tanker ships	冷藏船,液货船除外	8901.3000	8
Refrigerating or freezing equipment parts, nes	制冷设备零件,其他	8418.9999	3
Refrigerating or freezing equipment parts, of a refrigerating temperature higher than −40℃ and a capacity exceeding 500L	制冷温度在−40℃以上,但容积超过500升的冷藏或冷冻设备用零件	8418.9992	3
Refrigerating or freezing equipment, nes	制冷设备,其他	8418.6990	57
Refrigerating units	制冷机组	8418.6920	57
Refrigerating units and heat pumps parts	制冷机组及热泵用零件	8418.9910	3
Refrigerators, household type, absorption-type, electrical	冷藏箱,家用型,电气吸收式	8418.2920	57
Refrigerators, household type, compression-type, of a capacity exceeding 150L	冷藏箱,家用型,压缩式,容积超过150升	8418.2110	57
Refrigerators, household type, compression-type, of a capacity exceeding 50L, not exceeding 150L	冷藏箱,家用型,压缩式,容积超过50升,但不超过150升	8418.2120	57
Refrigerators, household type, compression-type, of a capacity not exceeding 50L	冷藏箱,家用型,压缩式,容积不超过50升	8418.2130	57
Refrigerators, household type, nes	冷藏箱,家用型,其他	8418.2990	57
Refrigerators, household type, semiconductor freezing type	冷藏箱,家用型,半导体制冷式	8418.2910	57
Refrigerator-freezers, combined, fitted with separate external doors, of a capacity exceeding 200L, not exceeding 500L	冷藏-冷冻组合机,各自装有单独外门的,容积超过200升,但不超过500升	8418.1020	57
Refrigerator-freezers, combined, fitted with separate external doors, of a capacity exceeding 500L	冷藏-冷冻组合机,各自装有单独外门的,容积超过500升	8418.1010	57
Refrigerator-freezers, combined, fitted with separate external doors, of a capacity not exceeding 200L	冷藏-冷冻组合机,各自装有单独外门的,容积不超过200升	8418.1030	57
Registers, of paper or paperboard	登记本,纸或纸板制的	4820.1000	
Reinforced concrete, pipes, rods, plates, piles and similar articles, reinforced by steel	钢筋混凝土管、杆、板、桩等	6810.9110	56
Relays, for a voltage not exceeding 1000V, nes	继电器,用于电压不超过1000伏的线路,其他	8536.4900	8
Relays, for a voltage not exceeding 60V	继电器,用于电压不超过60伏的线路	8536.4100	8
Relief valves	溢流阀	8481.4000	
Remie, nes	苎麻,其他	5305.0019	4
Remie, processed but not spun	苎麻,经加工但未纺制的	5305.0012	4
Remie, raw	苎麻,生的	5305.0011	4
Remie, tow and waste	苎麻,短纤及废料	5305.0013	4
Removable in-soles, heel cushions and similar articles, of other materials	活动式鞋内底、跟垫及类似品,其他材料制	6406.9900	6
Removable in-soles, heel cushions and similar articles, of wood	活动式鞋内底、跟垫及类似品,木制	6406.9100	6

R

Article Description	商品名称	Tariff Code	D. R.
Removing machine-tools, for metal or cermets, nes	切削机床,切削金属或金属陶瓷用,其他	8461. 9090	7
Rennet and concentrates thereof	凝乳酶及其浓缩物,粗制	3507. 1000	35
Rennet bags	皱胃膜	0504. 0090	14
Repeating front louver fan, with a self-contained electric motor of an output not exceeding 125W	百叶窗扇,包括风机,本身装有一个输出功率不超过 125 瓦的电动机	8414. 5130	23
Repeating front louver fan, with a self-contained electric motor of an output not exceeding 125W	具有旋转导风轮的风扇,包括风机,本身装有一个输出功率不超过 125 瓦的电动机	8414. 5130	23
Reptiles (including snakes and turtles), for human consumption	爬行动物(包括蛇及龟鳖),食用	0106. 2020	48
Reptiles (including snakes and turtles), nes	爬行动物(包括蛇及龟鳖),其他	0106. 2090	4
Reptiles (including snakes and turtles), pure-bred breeding, nes	爬行动物(包括蛇及龟鳖),改良种用,其他	0106. 2019	3
Reservoirs, of plastics, of a capacity exceeding 300L, for builders	囤及类似容器,容积超过 300 升,建筑用	3925. 1000	23
Reservoirs, tanks, vats and similar containers for any material, of iron or steel, of a capacity exceeding 300L, whether or not lined or heat-insulated, but not fitted with mechanical or thermal equipment (other than compressed or liquefied gas)	囤、柜、罐、桶及类似容器,钢铁的,容积超过 300 升,不论是否衬里或隔热,但无机械或热力装置,盛装物料用的(装压缩气体或液化气体的除外)	7309. 0000	36
Reservoirs, tanks, vats and similar containersfor any material, of aluminium, of a capacity exceeding 300L, whether or not lined or heat-insulated, but not fitted with mechanical or thermal equipment (other than compressed or liquefied gas)	囤、柜、罐、桶及类似容器,铝制,容积超过 300 升,不论是否衬里或隔热,但无机械可热力装置,盛装物料用的(装压缩气体或液化气体的除外)	7611. 0000	68
Reservoirs, tanks, vats and similar containersfor any material, of aluminium, of a capacity not exceeding 300L, whether or not lined or heat-insulated, but not fitted with mechanical or thermal equipment (other than compressed or liquefied gas), nes	囤、柜、罐、桶及类似容器,铝制,容积超过 300 升,不论是否衬里或隔热,但无机械可热力装置,盛装物料用的(装压缩气体或液化气体的除外),其他	7612. 9090	368
Residual lyes from the manufacture of wood pulp, whether or not concentrated, desugared or chemically treated	木浆残余碱液,不论是否浓缩、脱糖或经化学处理	3804. 0000	
Residual products of the chemical or allied industries, nes	化学工业及其相关工业的副产品,其他	3825. 9000	34
Residues of starch manufacture and similar residues	制造淀粉过程中的残渣及类似的残渣	2303. 1000	56
Residues resulting from the treatment of fatty substances of animal or vegetable waxes	残渣,加工处理油脂物质及动植物蜡所剩的	1522. 0000	4
Residues, nes, of petroleum oils or of oils obtained from bituminous minerals	残渣,其他,石油或从沥青矿物提取的油类的	2713. 9000	134
Resin acides	树脂酸	3806. 1020	4
Resin acids	树脂酸盐	3806. 2010	4
Resin cements	树脂胶泥	3214. 1090	3

R

Article Description	商品名称	Tariff Code	D. R.
Resinoids, nes	香膏,其他	3301. 3090	34
Resins	树脂	1301. 9090	
Resistance measuring instruments, with a recording device	电阻测试仪,带记录装置	9030. 3900	7
Resistance measuring instruments, without a recording device	电阻测试仪,不带记录装置	9030. 3320	
Resistance welding of metals machines and apparatus	电阻焊接机器及装置零件	8515. 9000	3
Resistance welding of metals machines and apparatus, fully or partly automatic, nes	电阻焊接机器及装置,全自动或半自动的,其他	8515. 2190	
Resistance welding of metals machines and apparatus, nes	电阻焊接机器及装置,其他	8515. 2900	
Resisters, wirewound variable, nes	电阻器,线绕可变,其他	8533. 3900	58
Resistors parts	电阻器零件	8533. 9000	3
Resistors, fixed carbon, composition or film types	电阻器,固定碳质,合成或薄膜式	8533. 1000	56
Resistors, fixed, for a power handling capacity not exceeding 20W, laminate	电阻器,固定,额定功率不超过20瓦,片式	8533. 2110	5
Resistors, fixed, for a power handling capacity not exceeding 20W, nes	电阻器,固定,额定功率不超过20瓦,其他	8533. 2190	5
Resistors, fixed, nes	电阻器,固定,其他	8533. 2900	5
Resistors, variable, including rheostats and potentiometers	电阻器,可变的,包括变阻器及电位器	8533. 4000	58
Resistors, wirewourd variable, for a power handling capacity not exceeding 20W	电阻器,线绕可变,额定功率不超过20瓦	8533. 3100	58
Reticles manufacture or repair apparatus	投影掩膜版制作和修复装置	8486. 4010	7
Reticles manufacture or repair apparatus parts and accessories	投影掩膜版制作和修复装置零件及附件	8486. 9090	3
Retort carbon	甑炭	2704. 0090	34
Retorts, containing by weight more than 50% of alumina(Al_2O_3) or of a mixture of compound of alumina and of silica(SiO_2)	甑,含有按重量计超过50%的三氧化二铝或三氧化二铝和二氧化硅的混合物或化合物	6903. 2000	6
Retorts, containing by weight more than 50% of graphite or other carbon or of a mixture of these pro-ducts	甑,含有按重量计超过50%的石墨、其他碳或其混合物	6903. 1000	6
Revenue stamps	印花税票	9704. 0090	5
Revenue stamps, unused	印花税票,未经使用的	4907. 0090	5
Revolution counters	转数计	9029. 1010	
Revolution counters parts and accessories	转数计零件、附件	9029. 9000	3
Revolvers	左轮手枪	9302. 0000	
Revolvers parts and accessories	左轮手枪用零件、附件	9305. 1000	3
Rhamnose	鼠李糖	2940. 0000	6
Rhenium articles, nes	铼制品	8112. 9990	16
Rhenium powders	铼粉末	8112. 9290	16

R

Article Description	商品名称	Tariff Code	D. R.
Rhenium, unwrought	铼,未锻轧	8112.9290	16
Rheostats and potentiometers, variable	变阻器,可变的	8533.4000	58
Rheostats and potentiometers, variable	电位器,可变的	8533.4000	58
Rheostats, wirewound variable, for a power handling capacity not exceeding 20W	变阻器,线绕可变,额定功率不超过20瓦	8533.3100	58
Rheostats, wirewound variable, nes	变阻器,线绕可变,其他	8533.3900	58
Rhizoma atractylodis macrocephalae	白术	1211.9025	34
Rhizoma coptidis	黄连	1211.9014	34
Rhizoma gastrodiae	天麻	1211.9022	34
Rhizoma ligustici	川芎	1211.9018	34
Rhizoma pinelliae	半夏	1211.9019	34
Rhizomes, in growth or in flower	根茎,生长或开花的	0601.2000	
Rhizomes, nes, dormant	根茎,其他,休眠的	0601.1099	135
Rhizomes, seed, dormant	根茎,种用,休眠的	0601.1091	135
Rhodium, nes	铑,其他	7110.3990	46
Rhodium, plates and sheets	铑,板、片	7110.3910	46
Rhodium, unwrought or in powder form	铑,未锻造或粉末状	7110.3100	46
Rhododendrons and azaleas, grafted or not, nes	杜鹃(植),不论是否嫁接,其他	0602.3090	
Rhododendrons and azaleas, grafted or not, seedlings	杜鹃(植),不论是否嫁接,种用	0602.3010	3
Rhubarb	大黄	1211.9024	34
Rhubarb	籽黄	1211.9024	34
Ribbons, inked	色带, 已上油着色的	9612.1000	
Rice in husk (paddy or rough), nes	稻谷,其他	1006.1099	35
Rice in husk (paddy or rough), nes, seed	稻谷,其他,种用	1006.1019	35
Rice paper	糯米纸	1905.9000	280
Rice vermicelli, cooked	米粉干	1902.3010	46
Ricitoxin	蓖麻毒素	3002.9020	34
Ricotta	乳清干酪	0406.1000	24
Ridingcrops and the like	马鞭及类似品	6602.0000	
Rifampicin (RFP) and its derivatives; salts thereof	利福平及其衍生物以及它们的盐	2941.9030	
Rifles	步枪	9303.3000	
Rifles parts and accessories	步枪用零件、附件	9305.2900	3
Rigid disk drivers	硬盘驱动器	8471.7010	
Ring spinning frames, nes	环锭细纱机,其他	8445.2049	7
Ring travellers	钢丝圈	8448.3390	3
Ritonavir and their salts	利托那韦及盐	2934.9940	36
Rivets, of aluminium	铆钉,铝制	7616.1000	36
Rivets, of iron or steel	铆钉,钢铁制的	7318.2300	268
Road rollers parts	压路机零件	8431.4990	3
Road rollers, self-propelled, of a deadweight of 18t or more, vibration type	压路机,机动的,机重18吨及以上的,振动式	8429.4011	57

R

Article Description	商品名称	Tariff Code	D. R.
Road rollers, self-propelled, nes	压路机,机动的,其他	8429.4019	57
Road tractors for semi-trailers	公路牵引车,半挂车用的	8701.2000	
Road wheels and parts and accessories of cross-country cars(4WD)	车轮及其零件、附件,越野车(4轮驱动)用	8708.7050	3
Road wheels and parts and accessories of dumpers	车轮及其零件、附件,自卸车用	8708.7030	3
Road wheels and parts and accessories of motor vehicles with 30 seats or more	车轮及其零件、附件,30座及以上客运机动车辆用	8708.7020	3
Road wheels and parts and accessories of motor vehicles with special purpose	车轮及其零件、附件,特种车辆用	8708.7060	3
Road wheels and parts and accessories of motor vehicles, nes	车轮及其零件、附件,其他	8708.7090	3
Road wheels and parts and accessories of saloon cars	车轮及其零件、附件,小轿车用	8708.7040	3
Road wheels and parts and accessories of tractors	车轮及其零件、附件,拖拉机的	8708.7010	3
Roasted iron pyrites	焙烧黄铁矿	2601.2000	1346
Rock cutters parts	凿岩机零件	8431.4990	3
Rock cutters, nes	凿岩机,其他	8430.3900	5
Rock cutters, self-propelled	凿岩机,自推进的	8430.3100	5
Rock drilling or earth boring tools, interchangeable, nes	凿岩或钻探工具,可互换,其他	8207.1990	256
Rock drilling or earth boring tools, with working part of cermets, interchangeable	凿岩或钻探工具,带有金属陶瓷制的工作部件,可互换	8207.1300	256
Rock drilling or earth boring tools, with working part of natural or synthetic diamonds or cubic boron nitride, interchangeable	凿岩或钻探工具,带有天然或合成金刚石、立方氮化硼制的工作部件,可互换	8207.1910	256
Rock lobster and other sea crawfish (Palinurus spp., Panulirus spp., Jasus spp.), for cultivation,	龙虾种苗	0306.2110	3
Rock lobster and other sea crawfish (Palinurus spp., Panulirus spp., Jasus spp.), frozen	龙虾,冻的	0306.1100	1
Rock lobster and other sea crawfish (Palinurus spp., Panulirus spp., Jasus spp.), nes, not frozen	龙虾,其他,未冻的	0306.2190	14
Rocket launchers	火箭发射装置	9301.2000	
Rodenticides, nes	杀鼠剂,其他	3808.9990	36
Rodenticides, put up for retail sale	杀鼠剂,零售包装	3808.9910	36
Rods and profile shapes of cellular rubber	杆或型材及异型材,海绵橡胶制	4008.1900	18
Rods and profile shapes of non-cellular rubber	杆或型材及异型材,非海绵橡胶制	4008.2900	18
Rods, coated with flux material, of base metal, for soldering, brazing or welding by flame	条,贱金属制,以焊剂涂面或以焊剂为芯,钎焊或气焊用	8311.3000	56
Rods, of metal carbides, coated or cored with flux material, of a kind used for soldering, brazing, welding or deposition of metal or of metal carbides	条,硬质合金制,以焊剂涂面或以焊剂为芯,用于焊接或沉积金属、硬质合金	8311.9000	56
Roes of fish, dried, smoked, salted or in brine	鱼卵,干、熏、盐腌或盐渍的	0305.2000	4
Rolled-steel section mills	型钢轧机	8455.2120	7

R

Article Description	商品名称	Tariff Code	D. R.
Roller chain, of iron or steel, for bicycles	滚子链,钢铁的,自行车用	7315.1110	36
Roller chain, of iron or steel, for motorcycles	滚子链,钢铁的,摩托车用	7315.1120	36
Roller chain, of iron or steel, nes	滚子链,钢铁的,其他	7315.1190	36
Roller screws	滚子螺杆传动装置	8483.4010	7
Roller skates and articles	旱冰鞋及用品	9506.7020	
Rollers bearings parts	滚柱轴承零件	8482.9100	3
Rolling forming machines, for agglomerating, shaping or moulding solid mineral fuels, ceramic paste, unhardened cements, plastering materials or other mineral products in powder or paste form	辊压成型机,固体矿物燃料、陶瓷坯泥、未硬化水泥、石膏材料或其他粉状、浆状矿产品的粘聚或成形用	8474.8010	7
Rolling machines cylinders	滚压机滚筒	8420.9100	3
Rolling machines parts, nes	滚压机零件,其他	8420.9900	3
Rolling machines, other than for metals or glass	滚压机器,加工金属或玻璃用的除外	8420.1000	
Rolling mills parts, cold-rolled	冷轧机零件	8455.9000	3
Rolling mills parts, hot-rolled	热轧机零件	8455.9000	3
Rolling mills rolls	轧机用轧辊	8455.3000	3
Rolling mills, cold-rolled, nes	冷轧机,其他	8455.2290	7
Rolling mills, combination hot and cold-rolled	冷热联合轧机	8455.2190	7
Rolling mills, hot-rolled, nes	热轧机,其他	8455.2190	7
Rolls, sheets and dials, printed for self-recording apparatus	打印纸卷、纸张及纸盘,已印制的,自动记录器用	4823.4000	68
Roofing tiles, of ceramic	屋顶瓦,陶瓷制	6905.1000	5
Roofs, roofing frameworks, of aluminium	屋顶框架,铝制	7610.9000	56
Roots, edible, nes, fresh or chilled	根茎,食用,其他,鲜或冷藏的	0706.9000	1
Rope making machines	绳的制造机器	8479.4000	7
Roquefort cheese	羊乳干酪	0406.4000	2468
Roscoelite	钒云母	2615.9090	146
Roses, fresh, suitable for bouquets or for ornamental purposes	玫瑰,鲜的,制花束或装饰用的	0603.1100	34
Roses, grafted or not, nes	玫瑰,不论是否嫁接,其他	0602.4090	
Roses, grafted or not, seedlings	玫瑰,不论是否嫁接,种用	0602.4010	3
Rosin	松香	3806.1010	4
Rosin oils	松香油	3806.9000	4
Rosin or resin acids derivatives	松香或树脂酸衍生物的盐	3806.2090	4
Rosin salts	松香盐	3806.2010	4
Rosin spirit	松香精	3806.9000	4
Rotating shuttles, nes	旋梭,其他缝纫机用	8452.9091	3
Rotating shuttles, of the household type	旋梭,家用型缝纫机用	8452.9011	3
Rotochutes, parts and accessories	旋翼降落伞及其零件、附件	8804.0000	3
Rotor spinning machine	转杯纺纱机	8445.2031	7
Rotors and parts thereof, of aircraft	水平旋翼及其零件,航空器用	8803.1000	3

Article Description	商品名称	Tariff Code	D. R.
Rough movements, of watches	表芯,不完整的,未组装	9110. 1900	1
Roundabouts	旋转木马	9508. 9000	5
Routers, telecommunication apparatus for digital line system	路由器,有线数字通信设备	8517. 6236	7
Roving frames, for cotton	粗纱机,棉纺的	8445. 1321	7
Roving machines, for worsted	粗纱机,毛纺的	8445. 1322	7
Roving machines, nes	粗纱机,其他	8445. 1329	7
Rowing boats, inflatable	划艇,充气的	8903. 1000	58
Rowing boats, nes	划艇,其他	8903. 9900	58
Royal jelly, put up as tonic essences	蜂王浆制剂	2106. 9030	268
Ro-Ro ships, motor powered, loading more than 20000t	滚装船,机动的,载重量在2万吨以上	8901. 9032	8
Ro-Ro ships, motor powered, loading with 20000t or less	滚装船,机动的,载重量在2万吨及以下	8901. 9031	8
Rubber accelerators, prepared	橡胶促进剂,配制的	3812. 1000	36
Rubber antioxidants	橡胶防老剂	3812. 3010	36
Rubber articles, unvulcanized	橡胶制品,未硫化	4006. 9020	13
Rubber or plastics products working machinery, nes	橡胶或塑料产品用加工机器,其他	8477. 8000	7
Rubber or plastics working machinery parts	橡胶或塑料加工机器的零件	8477. 9000	7
Rubber or plastics working machinery, nes	橡胶或塑料加工机器,其他	8477. 8000	7
Rubber solvent	橡胶溶剂油	2710. 1130	6
Rubber solvent, paint solvent, extractive solvent	抽提溶剂油	2710. 1130	6
Rubber thread and cord, textile covered	橡胶线及绳,用纺织材料包覆的	5604. 1000	46
Rubber thread and cord, vulcanized	橡胶线及绳,硫化的	4007. 0000	18
Rubber, unvulcanized, in other forms	未硫化橡胶,其他形状的	4006. 9010	13
Rubies dust and powder	红宝石的粉末	7105. 9000	145
Rubies, unworked	红宝石,未加工	7103. 1000	145
Rubies, worked	红宝石,加工的	7103. 9100	145
Rugs, schumacks and similar handwoven	地毯,“苏麦克”及类似手织的	5702. 1000	468
Rum and other spirits obtained by distilling fermented sugar-caneproducts	朗姆酒及蒸馏已发酵甘蔗产品制得的其他烈性酒	2208. 4000	2468
Run gums	再熔胶	3806. 9000	4
Running-boards, of the motor vehicles	翼子板(或叶子板),机动车辆的	8708. 2957	3
Rusks	面包干	1905. 4000	28
Ruthenium, nes	钌,其他	7110. 4990	46
Ruthenium, plates and sheets	钌,板、片	7110. 4910	46
Ruthenium, unwrought or in powder form	钌,未锻造或粉末状	7110. 4100	46
Rutile	金红石	2614. 0000	146
Rutoside (rutin) and its derivatives	芸香苷及其衍生物	2938. 1000	34
Rye ergot alkaloids and their derivatives; salts thereof, nes	麦角生物碱及其衍生物以及它们的盐,其他	2939. 6900	34

Article Description	商品名称	Tariff Code	D. R.
Rye grass (lolium multiflorum lam., lolium perenne L.) Seed, forage plants	黑麦草种子,饲料植物用的	1209.2500	358
Rye, nes	黑麦,其他	1002.0090	3
Rye, seed	黑麦,种用	1002.0010	3

R

S

Article Description	商品名称	Tariff Code	D. R.
Saccharin and its salts	糖精及其盐	2925. 1100	36
Sack kraft paper, creped or crinkled, whether or not embossed or perforated	袋用牛皮纸,起皱的,不论是否压花或穿孔	4808. 2000	58
Sack kraft paper, uncoated, nes	袋用牛皮纸,未经涂布的,其他	4804. 2900	24568
Sack kraft paper, uncoated, unbleached	袋用牛皮纸,未经涂布的,未漂白	4804. 2100	24568
Sacks and bags (including cones), of other plastics	袋及包(包括锥形的),其他塑料制	3923. 2900	23
Sacks and bags (including cones), of polymers of ethylene	袋及包(包括锥形的),乙烯聚合物制	3923. 2100	23
Sacks and bags, of paper, paperboard, nes	纸袋,其他	4819. 4000	68
Sacks and bags, for packing, of cotton	包装袋,棉制	6305. 2000	346
Sacks and bags, for packing, of jute or of other textile bast fibres	包装袋,黄麻或其他韧皮纺织纤维制	6305. 1000	346
Sacks and bags, for packing, of man-made textile materials, nes	包装袋,其他化学纤维材料制	6305. 3900	346
Sacks and bags, for packing, of other textile materials	包装袋,其他纺织材料制	6305. 9000	346
Sacks and bags, for packing, of polyethylene or polypropylene strip or the like	包装袋,其他,聚乙烯、聚丙烯扁条或类似材料制	6305. 3300	346
Sacks and hags, having a base of a width of 40cm or more, of paper, paperboard	纸袋,底宽 40 厘米及以上的	4819. 3000	68
Saddle bags for any animal, of any material	马褡裢,适合各种动物用	4201. 0000	1458
Saddle cloths for any animal, of any material	鞍褥,适合各种动物用	4201. 0000	1458
Saddlery for any animal, of any material	鞍具,适合各种动物用,各种材料制成的	4201. 0000	1458
Saddles, of bicycles and other cycles	鞍座,自行车及脚踏车	8714. 9500	3
Saddles, of motorcycles (including mopeds)	鞍座,摩托车(包括机器脚踏两用车)用	8714. 1100	3
Safe deposit lockers for cash boxes and the like, of base metal	储存保管箱,带锁,贱金属制	8303. 0000	256
Safe deposit lockers for deed boxes and the like, of base metal	契约保管箱及类似品,带锁,贱金属制	8303. 0000	256
Safe deposit lockers for strong rooms, of base metal	保管箱,保险库用,带锁,贱金属制	8303. 0000	256
Safes, armoured or reinforced, of base metal	保险箱,装甲或加强的,贱金属制	8303. 0000	256
Safety airbags with inflater system; parts thereof	带充气系统的安全气囊及其零件	8708. 9500	3
Safety electrical equipment for airfields	安全设备,电气的,机场的	8530. 8000	
Safety electrical equipment for inland waterways	安全设备,电气的,内河航道的	8530. 8000	
Safety electrical equipment for parking facilities	安全设备,电气的,停车场的	8530. 8000	
Safety electrical equipment for port installations	安全设备,电气的,港口的	8530. 8000	
Safety electrical equipment for railways	安全设备,电气的,铁道的	8530. 1000	
Safety electrical equipment for roads	安全设备,电气的,道路的	8530. 8000	

Article Description	商品名称	Tariff Code	D. R.
Safety electrical equipment for tramways	安全设备,电气的,电车道的	8530. 1000	
Safety electrical equipment parts	安全设备的零件	8530. 9000	3
Safety equipment and parts, for airfields	安全设备及其零件,机械的,机场用	8608. 0090	3
Safety equipment and parts, for inland water-ways	安全设备及其零件,机械的,内河航道用	8608. 0090	3
Safety equipment and parts, for parking facilities	安全设备及其零件,机械的,停车场用	8608. 0090	3
Safety equipment and parts, for port installations	安全设备及其零件,机械的,港口用	8608. 0090	3
Safety equipment and parts, for railways	安全设备及其零件,机械的,铁道用	8608. 0090	3
Safety equipment and parts, for roads	安全设备及其零件,机械的,道路用	8608. 0090	3
Safety equipment and parts, for tramways	安全设备及其零件,机械的,电车道用	8608. 0090	3
Safety fuses	安全导火索	3603. 0000	
Safety headgear	安全帽	6506. 1000	26
Safety pins, of iron or steel	安全别针,钢铁制的	7319. 2000	
Safety razor blades, including razor blade blanks in strips	安全刀片,包括未分开的刀片条	8212. 2000	256
Safety seat belts	座椅安全带	8708. 2100	3
Safety valves	安全阀	8481. 4000	
Safflower oil and fractions thereof, crude oil	红花油及其分离品,初榨的	1512. 1100	4
Safflower oil and fractions thereof, nes	红花油及其分离品,其他	1512. 1900	4
Safflower seeds	红花籽	1207. 9994	3
Saffron	番红花	0910. 2000	
Safranal	藏花醛	2912. 2990	36
Safrole	黄樟脑	2932. 9400	36
Safrole	4-烯丙基-1,2-亚甲二氧基苯	2932. 9400	36
Sago	西米	1903. 0000	18
Sago pith	西谷茎髓	0714. 9090	34
Sago powder	西米粉	1106. 2000	4
Sailboards	帆板	9506. 2100	
Sailboats, with or without auxiliary motor for pleasure or sports	帆船,不论是否装有辅助发动机,娱乐或运动用	8903. 9100	58
Sails, of other textile materials	风帆,其他纺织材料制	6306. 3090	346
Sails, of synthetic fibres	风帆,合成纤维制	6306. 3010	346
Sainfoin seeds	驴喜草子	1209. 2990	358
Sainfoin, forage products	驴喜豆,饲料用	1214. 9000	
Salad beetroot, fresh or chilled	色拉甜菜根,鲜或冷藏的	0706. 9000	1
Salad dressings	色拉调味料	2103. 9090	268
Salanganes' nests	燕窝	0410. 0010	3
Salep	兰科植物块茎	0714. 9090	34
Salicylic acid	水杨酸	2918. 2110	36
Salicylic acid salts, nes	水杨酸盐,其他	2918. 2190	36
Salicylic alcohol	水杨醇	2907. 1990	36

S

Article Description	商品名称	Tariff Code	D. R.
Salmonidae, nes, fresh or chilled	鲑鱼,其他,鲜或冷的,	0302. 1900	18
Salmonidae, nes, frozen	鲑鱼,其他,冻的	0303. 2900	18
Saloon cars parts and accessories, nes	小轿车用零件、附件,其他	8708. 9949	3
Saloon cars, of a cylinder capacity exceeding 1000cc but not exceeding 1500cc, with compression-ignition internal combustion piston engine	小轿车,气缸容量(排气量)超过1000毫升,但不超过1500毫升,装有压燃式活塞内燃发动机的	8703. 3121	58
Saloon cars, of a cylinder capacity exceeding 1000cc but not exceeding 1500cc, with spark-ignition internal combustion reciprocating piston	小轿车,气缸容量(排气量)超过1000毫升,但不超过1500毫升,装有点燃往复式活塞内燃发动机的	8703. 2230	58
Saloon cars, of a cylinder capacity exceeding 1500cc but not exceeding 2000cc, with compression-ignition internal combustion piston engine	小轿车,气缸容量(排气量)超过1500毫升,但不超过2000毫升,装有压燃式活塞内燃发动机的	8703. 3211	58
Saloon cars, of a cylinder capacity exceeding 1500cc but not exceeding 2000cc, with spark-ignition internal combustion reciprocating piston	小轿车,气缸容量(排气量)超过1500毫升,但不超过2000毫升,装有点燃往复式活塞内燃发动机的	8703. 2341	58
Saloon cars, of a cylinder capacity exceeding 2000cc but not exceeding 2500cc, with compression-ignition internal combustion piston engine	小轿车,气缸容量(排气量)超过2000毫升,但不超过2500毫升,装有压燃式活塞内燃发动机的	8703. 3221	58
Saloon cars, of a cylinder capacity exceeding 2000cc but not exceeding 2500cc, with spark-ignition internal combustion reciprocating piston	小轿车,气缸容量(排气量)超过2000毫升,但不超过2500毫升,装有点燃往复式活塞内燃发动机的	8703. 2351	58
Saloon cars, of a cylinder capacity exceeding 2500cc but not exceeding 3000cc, with spark-ignition internal combustion reciprocating piston	小轿车,气缸容量(排气量)超过2500毫升,但不超过3000毫升,装有点燃往复式活塞内燃发动机的	8703. 2361	58
Saloon cars, of a cylinder capacity exceeding 2500cc, but not exceeding 3000cc, with compression-ignition internal combustion piston engine	小轿车,气缸容量(排气量)超过2500毫升,但不超过3000毫升,装有压燃式活塞内燃发动机的	8703. 3311	58
Saloon cars, of a cylinder capacity exceeding 3000cc, but not exceeding 4000cc, with compression-ignition internal combustion piston engine	小轿车,气缸容量(排气量)超过3000毫升,但不超过4000毫升,装有压燃式活塞内燃发动机的	8703. 3321	58
Saloon cars, of a cylinder capacity exceeding 3000cc, but not exceeding 4000cc, with spark-ignition internal combustion reciprocating piston	小轿车,气缸容量(排气量)超过3000毫升,但不超过4000毫升,装有点燃往复式活塞内燃发动机的	8703. 2411	58
Saloon cars, of a cylinder capacity exceeding 4000cc, with compression-ignition internal combustion piston engine	小轿车,气缸容量(排气量)超过4000毫升,装有压燃式活塞内燃发动机的	8703. 3361	58
Saloon cars, of a cylinder capacity exceeding 4000cc, with spark-ignition internal combustion reciprocating piston	小轿车,气缸容量(排气量)超过4000毫升,装有点燃往复式活塞内燃发动机的	8703. 2421	58
Saloon cars, of a cylinder capacity not exceeding 1000cc, with compression-ignition internal combustion piston engine	小轿车,气缸容量(排气量)不超过1000毫升,装有压燃式活塞内燃发动机的	8703. 3111	58

Article Description	商品名称	Tariff Code	D. R.
Saloon cars, of a cylinder capacity not exceeding 1000cc, with spark-ignition internal combustion reciprocating piston engine	小轿车,气缸容量(排气量)不超过1000毫升,装有点燃往复式活塞内燃发动机的	8703. 2130	58
Salsify, fresh or chilled	婆罗门参,鲜或冷藏的	0706. 9000	1
Salt, edible	食用盐	2501. 0011	1368
Salt, nes, of sodium chloride	盐,其他,氯化钠的	2501. 0019	1368
Salt, of sodium chloride, nes	氯化钠的盐,其他	2501. 0019	1368
Salts and esters of citric acid	柠檬酸盐及柠檬酸酯	2918. 1500	36
Salts and esters of tartaric acid	酒石酸盐及酒石酸酯	2918. 1300	36
Salts of formic acid	甲酸盐	2915. 1200	36
Salts of inorganic acids or peroxoacids, nes	无机酸盐及过氧酸盐,其他	2842. 9090	
Salts of triethanolamine	三乙醇胺盐	2922. 1320	36
Sand blasting machines and similar jet projecting machines	喷砂机及类似的喷射机器	8424. 3000	7
Sanding machines, for working wood, cork, bone, hard rubber, hard plastics or similar hard materials	砂磨机器,加工木材、软木、骨、硬质橡胶、硬质塑料或类似硬质材料的	8465. 9300	7
Sanding vehicles for on-line rails, for railway or tramway maintenance or service	钢轨在线打磨列车,铁道及电车道用	8604. 0012	37
Sandstone	砂岩	2516. 2000	148
Sanitary towels and tampons and similar sanitary articles, of paper pulp, paper, cellulose wadding or webs of cellulose fibres	卫生巾及止血塞及类似的卫生用品,纸浆、纸、纤维素絮纸或纤维素纤维网纸制的	4818. 4000	568
Sanitary towels and tampons, napkins and napkin liners for babies and similar sanitary articles, of wadding	卫生巾及止血塞、婴儿尿布或尿布垫及类似卫生用品,絮胎制	5601. 1000	6
Sanitary ware and parts thereof, of copper	卫生器具及其零件,铜制	7418. 2000	56
Sanitary ware and parts thereof, of iron or steel, nes	卫生器具及其零件,钢铁制,其他	7324. 9000	24
Sanitary ware and parts thereof, of aluminium	卫生器具及其零件,铝制	7615. 2000	36
Sanitary ware, of plastics, nes	卫生洁具,塑料的,其他	3922. 9000	236
Santalol	檀香脑	2906. 1990	36
Sapphires dust and powder	蓝宝石的粉末	7105. 9000	145
Sapphires, unworked	蓝宝石,未加工	7103. 1000	145
Sapphires, worked	蓝宝石,加工的	7103. 9100	145
Sarcosine	肌氨酸	2922. 4910	36
Sardinella and Brisling or Sprats, prepared or preserved, whole or in pieces, but not minced	黍鲱鱼,制作或保藏的,整条或切块,但未绞碎	1604. 1300	48
Sardines and brisling or sprats, prepared or preserved, whole or in pieces, but not minced	沙丁鱼,制作或保藏的,整条或切块,但未绞碎	1604. 1300	48
Sardines (Sardina pilchardus, Sardinops spp.), fresh or chilled	沙丁鱼,鲜或冷的	0302. 6100	18
Sardines (Sardina pilchardus, Sardinops spp.), frozen	沙丁鱼,冻的	0303. 7100	18

S

Article Description	商品名称	Tariff Code	D. R.
Satellite earth station, for radio-broadcasting or television, incorporating reception apparatus	卫星地面站设备,无线电广播、电视用,装有接收装置的	8525.6010	7
Satellite television ground receiving and relaying apparatus parts	卫星电视地面接收转播设备用零件	8529.9010	3
Satellite television receivers, colour	卫星电视接收机,彩色的	8528.7110	135
Satellites and suborbital and spacecraft launch vehicles	卫星及其运载工具、亚轨道运载工具	8802.6000	
Satellites suborbital launch vehicles	卫星亚轨道运载工具	8802.6000	
Saturated acyclic monocarboxylic acids and their anhydrides, halides, peroxides and peroxyacids; their halogenated, sulphonated, nitrated or nitrosated derivatives, nes	饱和无环一元羧酸及其酸酐、酰卤化物、过氧化物和过氧酸以及它们的卤化、磺化、硝化或亚硝化衍生物,其他	2915.9000	36
Saturated chlorinated derivatives of acyclic hydrocarbons, nes	无环烃的饱和氯化衍生物,其他	2903.1990	36
Saturated monohydric alcohols, nes	饱和一元醇,其他	2905.1990	36
Sauces and preparations therefor	调味汁及其制品	2103.9090	268
Sausages and similar products, nes	香肠及类似产品,其他	1601.0020	48
Sausages and similar products, with a natural casing	香肠及类似产品,用天然肠衣做外包装的	1601.0010	348
Sausages food preparations and similar products	香肠制成的食品及类似产品	1601.0030	48
Saveloys, with a natural casing	干腊肠,有天然肠衣	1601.0010	348
Savory, dried	香薄荷,干的	0712.9090	4
Savory, french savory	香薄荷	0910.9900	6
Savory, fresh or chilled	香薄荷,鲜或冷藏的	0709.9090	1
Savory, frozen	香薄荷,冷冻的	0710.8090	1
Saw blades for sawing machines	锯片,机械锯用	8202.9910	256
Saw blades, straight, for working metal, nes	直锯片,加工金属用,其他	8202.9190	256
Saw blades, band	锯片,带状	8202.2000	256
Saw blades, chain	锯片,链状	8202.4000	256
Saw blades, circular, including parts, nes	锯片,圆状,包括部件,其他	8202.3900	256
Saw blades, circular, with working part of steel	锯片,圆状,带有钢制工作部件	8202.3100	256
Saw blades, nes	锯片,其他	8202.9990	256
Saw blades, straight, for working metal, nes	锯片,直的,加工金属用,其他	8202.9190	256
Sawdust, whether or not agglomerated in logs, briquettes, pellets or similar forms	锯末,不论是否粘结成圆木段、块、片或类似形状	4401.3000	15
Sawing machines for working stone, ceramics, concrete, asbestos-cement or like mineral materials, nes	锯床,加工石料、陶瓷、混凝土、石棉水泥或类似矿物材料的,其他	8464.1090	7
Sawing machines of disk saw, for working stone, ceramics, concrete, asbestos-cement or like mineral materials	锯床,圆盘的,加工石料、陶瓷、混凝土、石棉水泥或类似矿物材料的	8464.1010	7

Article Description	商品名称	Tariff Code	D. R.
Sawing machines of scroll saw, for working stone, ceramics, concrete, asbestos-cement or like mineral materials	锯床,钢丝的,加工石料、陶瓷、混凝土、石棉水泥或类似矿物材料的	8464.1020	7
Sawing machines, boules or wafers manufacture machines and apparatus	切割设备,单晶硅柱或硅晶片的制造机器及装置	8486.1030	7
Sawing machines, for removing metal or cermets	锯床,切削金属或金属陶瓷用	8461.5000	7
Sawing machines, for working wood, cork, bone, hard rubber, hard plastics or similar hard materials	锯床,加工木材、软木、骨、硬质橡胶、硬质塑料或类似硬质材料的	8465.9100	7
Saxitoxin	石房蛤毒素	3002.9010	34
SBR latex	丁苯橡胶(SBR)胶乳,	4002.1190	12
SBR, in primary forms	羧基丁苯橡胶,初级形状的	4002.1919	1346
SBR, in primary forms, nes	丁苯橡胶,其他,初级形状的	4002.1919	1346
SBR, nes	丁苯橡胶(SBR),其他	4002.1990	1346
SBR, not worked	丁苯橡胶,未经任何加工的	4002.1911	1346
SBR, oil-filled	丁苯橡胶,充油的	4002.1912	1346
SBR, oil-filled and thermo-plasticated	丁苯橡胶,充油热塑的	4002.1914	1346
SBR, thermo-plasticated	丁苯橡胶,热塑的	4002.1913	1346
Scabbards and parts	刀鞘	9307.0000	
Scabber fish (trichurius), fresh or chilled	带鱼,鲜或冷的	0302.6910	18
Scabber fish (trichurius), frozen	带鱼,冻的	0303.7910	18
Scabber fish (trichurius), or in brine	带鱼,盐腌及盐渍的	0305.6910	4
Scales for continuous weighing of goods on conveyors, nes	秤,输送带上连续称货的,其他	8423.2090	
Scalings from the manufacture of iron or steel	氧化皮,冶炼钢铁所产生的	2619.0000	134
Scallion, salted, prepared or preserved otherwise than by vinegar or acetic acid, not frozen	咸藠头,用醋或醋酸以外的其他方法制作或保藏的,未冷冻	2005.9960	148
Scallion, fresh or chilled	大葱,鲜或冷藏的	0703.9020	1
Scallops, including queen scallops, of the genera pecten, chlamys or placopecte, for cultivation	扇贝,包括海扇,种苗	0307.2110	3
Scallops, including queen scallops, of the genera pecten, chlamys or placopecte, frozen, dried, salted or in brine	扇贝,包括海扇,冻、干、盐腌或盐渍的	0307.2900	14
Scallops, including queen scallops, of the genera pecten, chlamys or placopecte, nes, live, fresh or chilled	扇贝,包括海扇,其他,活或鲜或冷的	0307.2190	1
Scandium	钪	2805.3019	56
Scandium, inuermixed or interalloyed with rare-earth metals, battery grade	钪,与稀土相互混合或相互熔合,电池级	2805.3021	56
Scandium, inuermixed or interalloyed with rare-earth metals, nes	钪,与稀土相互混合或相互熔合,其他	2805.3029	56
Scanner	扫描仪	8471.6050	

S

Article Description	商品名称	Tariff Code	D. R.
Scarifiers, for agricultural, horticultural or forestry use, nes	松土机,农业、园艺及林业用,其他	8432. 2900	
Scarves, knitted or crocheted, nes	领巾,针织或钩编的,其他	6117. 1090	2456
Scarves, knitted or crocheted, of fine animal hair, nes	领巾,针织或钩编的,其他动物细毛制	6117. 1019	2456
Scarves, knitted or crocheted, of goats fine animal hair	领巾,针织或钩编的,山羊绒制	6117. 1011	2456
Scarves, knitted or crocheted, of wool	领巾,针织或钩编的,羊毛制	6117. 1020	2456
Scarves, not knitted or crocheted, of artificial fibres	领巾,非针织或钩编的,人造纤维制	6214. 4000	2456
Scarves, not knitted or crocheted, of goats fine animal hair	领巾,非针织或钩编的,山羊绒制	6214. 2020	2456
Scarves, not knitted or crocheted, of other fine animal hair	领巾,非针织或钩编的,其他动物细毛制	6214. 2090	2456
Scarves, not knitted or crocheted, of other textile materials	领巾,非针织或钩编的,其他纺织材料制	6214. 9000	2456
Scarves, not knitted or crocheted, of silk or silk waste	领巾,非针织或钩编的,丝或绢丝制	6214. 1000	2456
Scarves, not knitted or crocheted, of synthetic fibres	领巾,非针织或钩编的,合成纤维制	6214. 3000	2456
Scarves, not knitted or crocheted, of wool	领巾,非针织或钩编的,羊毛制	6214. 2010	2456
Scent sprays and similar, and mounts and heads thereof	香水喷雾器及其座架、喷头	9616. 1000	
Scheelite	白钨矿	2611. 0000	146
School satchels and similar containers, with outer surface of leather, of composition leather or patent leather	书包及类似容器,以皮革、再生皮革或漆皮作面	4202. 1190	1458
School satchels and similar containers, with outer surface of plastics or textile materials	书包及类似容器,以塑料或纺织材料作面	4202. 1290	256
Schumacks and similar handwoven rugs	苏麦克及类似的手织地毯	5702. 1000	468
Scintigraphic apparatus, used in medical, surgical, dental or veterinary sciences	闪烁扫描装置,医疗、外科、牙科或兽医用	9018. 1400	
Scissors and similar shears, and blades thereof	剪刀及类似品、刀片	8213. 0000	256
Scooters and similar wheeled toys	踏板车及类似的带轮玩具	9503. 0010	
Scouring or polishing pads, gloves and the like	洗刷擦光用的块垫、手套及类似品	7323. 1000	24
Scouring or polishing pads, gloves and the like, of copper	洗刷、擦光用的块垫、手套及类似品,铜制	7418. 1100	56
Scouring or polishing pads, gloves and the like, of aluminium	洗刷、擦光用的块垫、手套及类似品,铝制	7615. 1100	36
Scouring pastes and other scouring preparations	擦洗膏及类似制品	3405. 4000	36
Scouring powders and other scouring preparations	去污粉及类似制品	3405. 4000	36
Scrap ingots, for remelting	碎料钢铁锭,供再熔的	7204. 5000	46
Scrap twine, cordage, rope and cables and worn out articles thereof, nes	废线、绳、索、缆及其制品,纺织材料的,其他	6310. 9000	146
Scrap twine, cordage, rope and cables and worn out articles thereof, sorted	废线、绳、索、缆及其制品,纺织材料的,经分拣的	6310. 1000	146
Scrapers parts	铲运机零件	8431. 4990	3

S

Article Description	商品名称	Tariff Code	D. R.
Scrapers, having a capacity of shovel exceeding $10m^3$	铲运机,斗容量超过10立方米的	8429.3010	57
Scrapers, nes	铲运机,其他	8429.3090	57
Scrapers, not self-propelled	铲运机,非自推进的	8430.6920	5
Scraping machinery, for earth, minerals or ores, not self-propelled, nes	铲运机械,对泥土、矿物或矿石的,非自推进的,其他	8430.6990	5
Scraping machinery, for earth, minerals or ores, self-propelled, nes	铲运机械,对泥土、矿物或矿石的,自推进的,其他	8430.5090	5
Screen printing machinery, nes	网式印刷机,其他	8443.1929	57
Screening machines, for earth, stone, ores or other mineral substances	筛选机器,泥土、石料、矿石或其他固体矿物质的	8474.1000	
Screening machines, nes	筛选机,其他	8479.8200	7
Screens of reeds	苇帘	4601.2921	6
Screw caps, of base metal	螺口盖,贱金属制	8309.9000	256
Screw hooks, of aluminium	钩头螺钉,铝制	7616.1000	36
Screw hooks, of iron of steel	钩头螺钉,钢铁制的	7318.1300	268
Screw rings, of iron or steel	环头螺钉,钢铁制的	7318.1300	268
Screwdrivers	螺丝刀	8205.4000	256
Screws for wood, of copper	木螺钉,铜制	7415.3310	56
Screws, of aluminium	螺钉,铝制	7616.1000	36
Screws, of copper, nes	螺钉,铜制,其他	7415.3390	56
Screws, whether or not with their nuts or washers, of iron of steel, nes	螺钉,不论是否带有螺母或垫圈,钢铁制的,其他	7318.1500	268
Scroll sawing machines, for working stone, ceramics, concrete, asbestos-cement or like mineral materials	钢丝锯,加工石料、陶瓷、混凝土、石棉水泥或类似矿物材料的	8464.1020	7
Sculptures and statuary, in any material, original	雕塑品原件,各种材料制的	9703.0000	
Scythes	镰刀	8201.9000	256
Sea bass (Dicentrarchus labrax, Dicentrarchus punctatus), frozen	尖吻鲈鱼,冻的	0303.7700	18
Sea cucumbers (bechesdemer), frozen, dried, salted or in brine	海参,冻、干、盐腌或盐渍的	0307.9920	14
Sea salt	海盐	2501.0020	1368
Sea tangle	海带	1212.2010	14
Sea tangle, salted	海带,盐腌的	2008.9932	248
Sea water	海水	2501.0030	1368
Sealed beam lamp units	封闭式聚光灯	8539.1000	35
Sealed or vacuum insulating glass	中空或真空隔温、隔音玻璃	7008.0010	234
Sealing machines, for bottles, cans, boxes, bags or other containers	封口机器,瓶、罐、箱、袋或其他容器的	8422.3090	
Sealing or affixing mail machines	粘贴邮票机	8472.3090	
Sealing stamps, designed for operating in the hand	封缄戳,手用	9611.0000	
Sealing wafers	封碱	1905.9000	28
Seals and other packing accessories, of base metal	封志及其他包装用附件,贱金属制	8309.9000	256

S

Article Description	商品名称	Tariff Code	D. R.
Search lights	探照灯	9405. 4010	5
Seasonings, mixed	混合调味品	2103. 9090	268
Seat angle regulating devices, of the motor vehicles	座椅调角器,机动车辆用	9401. 9011	3
Seats of a kind used for aircraft	坐具,飞机用	9401. 1000	
Seats of a kind used for motor vehicles, nes	坐具,机动车辆用,其他	9401. 2090	6
Seats of a kind used for motor vehicles, with outer surface of leather or composition leather	坐具,机动车辆用,皮革或再生皮革面的	9401. 2010	6
Seats of bamboo or rattan	坐具,竹制或藤制的	9401. 5100	6
Seats of osier or similar materials	坐具,柳条及类似材料制	9401. 5900	6
Seats of stone	坐具,石制的	9401. 8010	6
Seats other than garden seats or camping equipment, convertible into beds, nes	两用椅,能做床用的,庭园坐具或野营设备除外,其他	9401. 4090	6
Seats other than garden seats or camping equipment, convertible into beds, with outer surface of leather or composition leather	两用椅,能做床用的,庭园坐具或野营设备除外,皮革或再生皮革面的	9401. 4010	6
Seats parts, nes	坐具零件,其他	9401. 9090	3
Seats parts, of the motor vehicles, nes	坐具零件,机动车辆用,其他	9401. 9019	3
Seats with variable height adjustment, swivel	坐具,可调高度的,转动的	9401. 3000	6
Seats, with metal frames upholstered, nes	坐具,金属框架的,装软垫的,其他	9401. 7190	6
Seats, with metal frames upholstered, with outer surface of leather or composition leather	坐具,金属框架的,装软垫的,皮革或再生皮革面的	9401. 7110	6
Seats, with metal frames, nes	坐具,金属框架的,其他	9401. 7900	6
Seats, with wooden frames upholstered, nes	坐具,木框架的,装软垫的,其他	9401. 6190	6
Seats, with wooden frames upholstered, with outer surface of leather or composition leather	坐具,木框架的,装软垫的,皮革或再生皮革面的	9401. 6110	6
Seats, with wooden frames, nes	坐具,木框架的,其他	9401. 6900	6
Seats, nes	坐具,其他	9401. 8090	6
Seat-sticks	带座手杖	6602. 0000	
Seaweed ash(kelp)	海藻灰(海草灰)	2621. 9000	134
Seaweeds and other algae	海草及其他藻类	1212. 2090	14
Sebacic acid, its salts and esters	癸二酸及其盐和酯	2917. 1310	36
Secateurs and similar one- handed pruners and shears	修枝剪及类似的单手操作剪刀	8201. 5000	256
Secateurs, one-handed pruners and shears	剪刀,修枝剪,单手操作的	8201. 5000	256
Secbutabarbital (INN); salts thereof	仲丁巴比妥 (INN)以及盐	2933. 5300	36
Secbutanol	仲丁醇	2905. 1420	36
Secobarbital(INN); salts thereof	司可巴比妥 (INN)以及盐	2933. 5300	36
Seeders, for agricultural, horticultural or forestry use	播种机,农业、园艺及林业用	8432. 3000	
Seedlings, nes	种用苗木,其他	0602. 9091	3
Seeds of anise	茴芹子	0909. 1090	
Seeds of badian	八角茴香	0909. 1010	
Seeds of caraway	香菜子	0909. 4000	

S

Article Description	商品名称	Tariff Code	D. R.
Seeds of coriander	芫荽子	0909. 2000	
Seeds of cumin	枯茗子	0909. 3000	
Seeds of fennel	小茴香子	0909. 5000	
Seeds of herbaceous plants cultivated principally for their flowers	草本花卉植物种子	1209. 3000	358
Seeds of melons	甜瓜子,种用	1209. 9920	358
Seeds of watermelons	西瓜子,种植用的	1209. 9910	358
Seeds, fruit and spores, nes, of a kind used for sowing	种子、果实及孢子,其他,种植用的	1209. 9990	358
Seeds, fruit and spores, nes, of forage plants	种子、果实及孢子,其他,饲料植物用的	1209. 2990	358
Selenium crystals doped for use in electronics, in the form of cylinders or rods	硒,经掺杂用于电子工业的晶体棒	2804. 9010	346
Selenium, nes	硒,其他	2804. 9090	346
Self-aligning ball bearings	调心球轴承	8482. 1010	5
Self-copy paper, in rolls or sheets, of a width exceeding 36cm or in roll or one side exceeding 36cm and other side exceeding 15cm in rectangular sheets	自印复写纸,成卷或成张的,卷宽度超过 36 厘米,或长超过 36 厘米且宽超过 15 厘米	4809. 2000	458
Self-copy paper, nes	自印复写纸,其他	4816. 2000	58
Self-discharging wans and wagons, other than those of subheading 8606. 1000	自卸货车,子目 8606. 1000 的货品除外	8606. 3000	37
Self-opening dieheads	自启板牙切头	8466. 1000	3
Self-propelled trucks, fitted with lifting or handing equipment, nes	自推进机动车,装有升降或搬运装置的,其他	8427. 2090	7
Self-propelled trucks, fitted with lifting or handing equipment, powered by an electric motor, nes	自推进机动车,装有升降或搬运装置的电动的,其他	8427. 1090	7
Self-tapping screws, of iron of steel	自攻螺钉,钢铁制的	7318. 1400	268
Semen, of bovine	牛的精液	0511. 1000	4
Semicarbazide	氨基脲	2928. 0000	36
Semiconductor devices or of electronic integrated circuits manufacture machines and apparatus, nes	制造半导体器件或集成电路的机器及装置,其他	8486. 2090	7
Semiconductor devices parts	半导体器件零件	8541. 9000	3
Semiconductor devices, nes	半导体器件,其他	8541. 5000	5
Semiconductor media, recorded, nes	半导体媒体,已录制,其他	8523. 5920	37
Semiconductor media, unrecorded, nes	半导体媒体,未录制,其他	8523. 5910	37
Semiconductor modules with converting function	半导体模块,具有变流功能的	8504. 4091	
Semiconductor wafers or devices measuring or checking instruments and apparatus	半导体晶片或器件用测试或检验仪器及装置	9030. 8200	
Semimilled or wholly milled rice, nes	半精米或精米,其他	1006. 3090	35
Semi-chemical pulp, derived from recovered (waste and scrap) paper or paperboard	半化学浆,从回收(废碎)纸或纸板提取的	4706. 9300	46

S

Article Description	商品名称	Tariff Code	D. R.
Senarmontite	方锑矿	2617.1090	146
Sensitizing chemical preparations, for use in photocopying apparatus	感光用化学制剂,复印机用	3707.9020	36
Sensitizing emulsions	感光乳液	3707.1000	36
Separating machines, for earth, stone, ores or other mineral substances	分离机器,泥土、石料、矿石或其他固体矿物质的	8474.1000	
Serine	丝氨酸	2922.5000	36
Serum globulins	血清球蛋白	3002.1000	34
Serviettes, of paper pulp, paper, cellulose wadding or webs of cellulose fibres	餐巾纸,纸浆、纸、纤维素絮纸或纤维素纤维网纸制的	4818.3000	568
Sesame oil and its fractions	芝麻油及其分离品	1515.5000	4
Sesame, otherwise prepared, or preserved	芝麻,用其他方法制作或保藏的	2008.1992	248
Sesamum seeds for cultivation	芝麻,种用	1207.4010	3
Sesamum seeds, nes	芝麻,其他	1207.4090	3
Sets consisting of woven fabric and yarn, whether or not with accessories, for making up into rugs, tapestries, embroidered table cloths or serviettes, or similar textile articles, put up in packings for retail sale	成套物品,由机织物及纱线构成的,不论是否带附件,用以制作小地毯、装饰毯、绣花台布、餐巾或类似的纺织物品,零售包装	6308.0000	3
Sets for personal travel toilet, sewing or shoe or clothes cleaning	成套旅行用具,个人梳妆、缝纫或清洁鞋靴、衣服用	9605.0000	6
Sets of assorted kitchenware articles, nes	成套厨房用具,其他	8215.2000	256
Sets of assorted knives with cutting blades, serrated or not (including pruning knives), other than knives of heading No. 82.08, and blades therefor	成套刀及刀片,不论是否有锯齿(包括整枝刀),税号 82.08 的刀除外	8211.1000	256
Sets of assorted tableware articles, nes	成套餐桌用具,其他	8215.2000	256
Sets of christmas trees lighting	成套灯具,圣诞树用	9405.3000	5
Sets of colours	成套颜料	3213.1000	3
Sets of gaskets	成套物品,密封垫的	8484.9000	56
Sets of tools, of two or more of other subheadings of hand tools	成套工具,由两个或多个子目所列手工工具组成的	8205.9000	256
Sets of tools, of two or more of the headings No. 82.02 to 82.05, put up for retail sale	成套工具,由税号 82.02 至 82.05 中两个或多个税号所列组成的,零售包装	8206.0000	256
Sets of toys, of constructional toys	成套玩具,缩小(按比例缩小)的建筑的	9503.0040	5
Sets of two or more pens	成套的笔,由上述两个或多个组成的	9608.5000	
Sets or outfits of toys, nes	成套或全套的组装玩具,其他	9503.0081	5
Setts, of natural stone (except slate)	长方砌石,天然石料(不包括板岩)制的	6801.0000	46
Sewage sludge	下水道淤泥	3825.2000	34
Sewing binders for book	锁线机,订书用	8440.1010	
Sewing binders parts, for book	锁线机零件,订书用	8440.9000	3

S

Article Description	商品名称	Tariff Code	D. R.
Sewing machine needles	缝纫机针	8452. 3000	
Sewing machines bases and parts thereof	缝纫机专用的特制底座及其零件	8452. 4000	3
Sewing machines covers and parts thereof	缝纫机专用的特制罩盖及其零件	8452. 4000	3
Sewing machines furniture and parts thereof	缝纫机专用的特制家具及其零件	8452. 4000	3
Sewing machines of household type, hand operated	缝纫机,家用型,手动式	8452. 1091	
Sewing machines of household type, multifunctional	缝纫机,家用型,多功能	8452. 1010	
Sewing machines of household type, nes	缝纫机,家用型,其他	8452. 1099	
Sewing machines parts, nes	缝纫机零件,其他	8452. 9099	3
Sewing machines parts, of the household type sewing machines, nes	缝纫机零件,家用型缝纫机用,其他	8452. 9019	3
Sewing machines, automatic units, nes	缝纫机,自动的,其他	8452. 2190	
Sewing machines, flat seam	缝纫机,平缝机	8452. 2110	
Sewing machines, nes	缝纫机,其他	8452. 2900	
Sewing needles, for use in the hand, of iron or steel	缝针,钢铁制的,手工用	7319. 9000	
Sewing thread of artificial filaments, not put up for retail sale	缝纫线,人造纤维长丝纺制,非供零售用	5401. 2010	3468
Sewing thread of artificial filaments, put up for retail sale	缝纫线,人造纤维长丝纺制,供零售用	5401. 2020	3468
Sewing thread of synthetic filaments, not put up for retail sale	缝纫线,合成纤维长丝纺制,非供零售用	5401. 1010	3468
Sewing thread of synthetic filaments, put up for retail sale	缝纫线,合成纤维长丝纺制,供零售用	5401. 1020	3468
Sewing thread reels and the like, of wood	线轴及类似品,缝纫用,木制	4421. 9010	56
Shaft couplings	联轴器	8483. 6000	
Shaft couplings parts	联轴器零件	8483. 9000	3
Shallots, fresh or chilled	青葱,鲜或冷藏的	0703. 1020	1
Shampoos	香波	3305. 1000	23
Sharks, nes, fresh or chilled	鲨鱼,其他,鲜或冷的	0302. 6500	18
Sharks, nes, frozen	鲨鱼,其他,冻的	0303. 7500	18
Shark's fin, dried	鱼翅,干的	0305. 5920	4
Shark's fin, in airtight containers	罐头,鱼翅的	1604. 2011	48
Shark's fin, nes, prepared or preserved	鱼翅,制作或保藏的,其他	1604. 2091	48
Sharpening machines, for metal or cermets, nes	刃磨机床,加工金属或金属陶瓷用,其他	8460. 3900	7
Sharpening machines, numerically controlled, for metal or cermets	刃磨机床,数控的,加工金属或金属陶瓷用	8460. 3100	7
Sharpening stones, hand used, nes	磨石,手用,其他	6804. 3090	36
Shavers parts, with self-contained electric motor	剃须刀零件,电动的	8510. 9000	3
Shaving brushes	剃须刷	9603. 2900	
Shawls, knitted or crocheted, nes	披巾,针织或钩编的,其他	6117. 1090	2456
Shawls, knitted or crocheted, of goats fine animal hair	披巾,针织或钩编的,山羊绒制	6117. 1011	2456

Article Description	商品名称	Tariff Code	D. R.
Shawls, knitted or crocheted, of other fine animal hair, nes	披巾,针织或钩编的,其他动物细毛制	6117.1019	2456
Shawls, knitted or crocheted, of wool	披巾,针织或钩编的,羊毛制	6117.1020	2456
Shawls, not knitted or crocheted, of artificial fibres	披巾,非针织或钩编的,人造纤维制	6214.4000	2456
Shawls, not knitted or crocheted, of goats fine animal hair	披巾,非针织或钩编的,山羊绒制	6214.2020	2456
Shawls, not knitted or crocheted, of other fine animal hair	披巾,非针织或钩编的,其他动物细毛制	6214.2090	2456
Shawls, not knitted or crocheted, of other synthetic fibres	披巾,非针织或钩编的,合成纤维制	6214.3000	2456
Shawls, not knitted or crocheted, of other textile materials	披巾,非针织或钩编的,其他纺织材料制	6214.9000	2456
Shawls, not knitted or crocheted, of silk or silk waste	披巾,非针织或钩编的,丝或绢丝制	6214.1000	2456
Shawls, not knitted or crocheted, of wool	披巾,非针织或钩编的,羊毛制	6214.2010	2456
Shea nuts	牛油树果	1207.9991	3
Shearing lengthwise, for working metal, nes	板带纵剪机,加工金属用,其他	8462.3910	7
Shearing lengthwise, numerically controlled, for working metal	板带纵剪机,数控的,加工金属用	8462.3110	7
Shearing machines, for working metal, nes	剪切机床,加工金属用,其他	8462.3990	7
Shearing machines, numerically controlled, for working metal, nes	剪切机床,数控的,加工金属用,其他	8462.3190	7
Shearing transverse, for working metal, nes	板带横剪机,加工金属用,其他	8462.3920	7
Shearing transverse, numerically controlled, for working metal	板带横剪机,数控的,加工金属用	8462.3120	7
Shears for cutting metal, hand tools	剪刀,白铁剪	8203.3000	256
Shears for one-handed pruning	剪刀,单手操作的	8201.5000	256
Shears for poultry	剪刀,家禽剪,单手操作的	8201.5000	256
Shears for two-handed pruning	剪刀,双手操作的	8201.6000	256
Sheath contraceptives	避孕套	4014.1000	23
Sheaths and parts	剑鞘	9307.0000	3
Sheep casings, salted	盐渍绵羊肠衣	0504.0012	14
Sheep, live, ex. pure-bred breeding	绵羊,改良种用除外	0104.1090	3
Sheep, live, pure-bred breeding	绵羊,改良种用	0104.1010	3
Sheet mills, cold-rolled	板材冷轧机	8455.2210	7
Sheet mills, hot-rolled	板材热轧机	8455.2110	7
Sheet piling of iron or steel	钢铁板桩	7301.1000	6
Sheets, film, foil, tape, strip and other flat shapes, of plastics, in rolls, self-adhesive plates, of a width not exceeding 20cm, based on acrylic resin	塑料板、片、膜、箔、带、扁条及其他扁平形状材料,成卷,自粘的,宽度不超过20厘米,丙烯酸树脂类为基本成分	3919.1010	16

S

Article Description	商品名称	Tariff Code	D. R.
Sheets, film, foil, tape, strip and other flat shapes, of plastics, in rolls, self-adhesive plates, of a width not exceeding 20cm, nes	塑料板、片、膜，箔、带、扁条及其他扁平形状材料，成卷，自粘的，宽度不超过 20 厘米，其他	3919. 1099	16
Sheets, film, foil, tape, strip and other flat shapes, of plastics, whether or not in rolls, self-adhesive plates, nes	塑料板、片、膜，箔、带、扁条及其他扁平形状材料，不论是否成卷，自粘的，其他	3919. 9090	16
Sheets, strip and foil of a thickness (excluding any backing) not exceeding 0. 2mm, of lead	片、带及厚度(衬背除外)不超过 0. 2 毫米的箔，铅制	7804. 1100	16
Shelled, of freshwater crawfish	虾仁，淡水小龙虾的	0306. 1911	1
Shelled, of prawns, frozen	虾仁，冻的	0306. 1321	18
Shelled, of shrimps, frozen	虾仁，冻的	0306. 1311	18
Shells of crustaceans	甲壳动物壳	0508. 0090	14
Shells of molluscs	软体动物壳	0508. 0090	14
Sherry wine	雪利酒	2204. 2900	24568
Shiitake, dried	香菇，干的	0712. 3910	4
Shiitake, fresh or chilled	香菇，鲜或冷藏的	0709. 5920	1
Shingle, whether or not bead-treated	鹅卵石，不论是否热处理	2517. 1000	13
Shingles and shakes, of wood	瓦及盖屋板，木制的	4418. 5000	58
Ship loading cranes	装船机	8426. 1910	7
Ship unloading cranes, grab	卸船机，抓斗式	8426. 1921	7
Ship unloading cranes, nes	卸船机，其他	8426. 1929	7
Ships or boats blades	船桨叶	8487. 1000	3
Ships or boats propellers and blades therefor	船用推进器及桨叶	8487. 1000	3
Shirts and shirtblouses, not knitted or crocheted, for women or girls, of cotton	衬衫，非针织或钩编的，女式，棉制	6206. 3000	2456
Shirts and shirtblouses, not knitted or crocheted, for women or girls, of man-made fibres	衬衫，非针织或钩编的，女式，化学纤维制	6206. 4000	2456
Shirts and shirtblouses, not knitted or crocheted, for women or girls, of other textile materials	衬衫，非针织或钩编的，女式，其他纺织材料制	6206. 9000	2456
Shirts and shirtblouses, not knitted or crocheted, for women or girls, of silk or silk waste	衬衫，非针织或钩编的，女式，丝及绢丝制	6206. 1000	2456
Shirts and shirtblouses, not knitted or crocheted, for women or girls, of wool or fine animal hair	衬衫，非针织或钩编的，女式，羊毛或动物细毛制	6206. 2000	2456
Shirts, knitted or crocheted, for men or boys, for man-made fibres	衬衫，针织或钩编的，男式，化学纤维制	6105. 2000	2456
Shirts, knitted or crocheted, for men or boys, of cotton	衬衫，针织或钩编的，男式，棉制	6105. 1000	2456
Shirts, knitted or crocheted, for men or boys, of other textile materials	衬衫，针织或钩编的，男式，其他纺织材料制	6105. 9000	2456
Shirts, knitted or crocheted, for women or girls, of cotton	衬衫，针织或钩编的，女式，棉制	6106. 1000	2456
Shirts, knitted or crocheted, for women or girls, of man-made fibres	衬衫，针织或钩编的，女式，化学纤维制	6106. 2000	2456

Article Description	商品名称	Tariff Code	D. R.
Shirts, knitted or crocheted, for women or girls, of other textile materials	衬衫,针织或钩编的,女式,其他纺织材料制	6106. 9000	2456
Shirts, not knitted or crocheted, for men or boys, nes	衬衫,非针织或钩编的,男式,其他	6205. 9090	2456
Shirts, not knitted or crocheted, for men or boys, of cotton	衬衫,非针织或钩编的,男式,棉制	6205. 2000	2456
Shirts, not knitted or crocheted, for men or boys, of man-made fibres	衬衫,非针织或钩编的,男式,化学纤维制	6205. 3000	2456
Shirts, not knitted or crocheted, for men or boys, of silk or silk waste	衬衫,非针织或钩编的,男式,丝及绢丝制	6205. 9010	2456
Shirts, not knitted or crocheted, for men or boys, of wool or fine animal hair	衬衫,非针织或钩编的,男式,羊毛或动物细毛制	6205. 9020	2456
Shooting galleries	射击用靶	9508. 9000	5
Shopping-bags, nes	购物袋,其他	4202. 9900	256
Shopping-bags, with outer surface of leather, of composition leather or of patent leather	购物袋,以皮革、再生皮革或漆皮作面	4202. 9100	256
Shopping-bags, with outer surface of plastic sheeting or of textile materials	购物袋,以塑料片或纺织材料作面	4202. 9200	256
Shortening oil	起酥油	1517. 9010	246
Shorts, knitted or crocheted, for men or boys, of cotton	短裤,针织或钩编的,男式,棉制	6103. 4200	2456
Shorts, knitted or crocheted, for men or boys, of other textile materials	短裤,针织或钩编的,男式,其他纺织材料制	6103. 4900	2456
Shorts, knitted or crocheted, for men or boys, of synthetic fibres	短裤,针织或钩编的,男式,合成纤维制	6103. 4300	2456
Shorts, knitted or crocheted, for men or boys, of wool or fine animal hair	短裤,针织或钩编的,男式,羊毛或动物细毛制	6103. 4100	2456
Shorts, knitted or crocheted, for women or girls, of cotton	短裤,针织或钩编的,女式,棉制	6104. 6200	2456
Shorts, knitted or crocheted, for women or girls, of other textile materials	短裤,针织或钩编的,女式,其他纺织材料制	6104. 6900	2456
Shorts, knitted or crocheted, for women or girls, of synthetic fibres	短裤,针织或钩编的,女式,合成纤维制	6104. 6300	2456
Shorts, knitted or crocheted, for women or girls, of wool or fine animal hair	短裤,针织或钩编的,女式,羊毛或动物细毛制	6104. 6100	2456
Shorts, not knitted or crocheted, for men or boys, of cotton	短裤,非针织或钩编的,男式,棉制	6203. 4290	2456
Shorts, not knitted or crocheted, for men or boys, of other textile material	短裤,非针织或钩编的,男式,其他纺织材料制	6203. 4990	2456
Shorts, not knitted or crocheted, for men or boys, of synthetic fibres	短裤,非针织或钩编的,男式,合成纤维制	6203. 4390	2456
Shorts, not knitted or crocheted, for men or boys, of wool or fine animal hair	短裤,非针织或钩编的,男式,羊毛或动物细毛制	6203. 4100	2456
Shorts, not knitted or crocheted, for women or girls, of cotton	短裤,非针织或钩编的,女式,棉制	6204. 6200	2456

Article Description	商品名称	Tariff Code	D. R.
Shorts, not knitted or crocheted, for women or girls, of other textile materials	短裤,非针织或钩编的,女式,其他纺织材料制	6204. 6900	2456
Shorts, not knitted or crocheted, for women or girls, of synthetic fibres	短裤,非针织或钩编的,女式,合成纤维制	6204. 6300	2456
Shorts, not knitted or crocheted, for women or girls, of wool or fine animal hair	短裤,非针织或钩编的,女式,羊毛或动物细毛制	6204. 6100	2456
Shotgun barrels	猎枪筒	9305. 2100	3
Shotgun cartridges	猎枪子弹	9306. 2100	
Shotgun cartridges parts	猎枪子弹零件	9306. 2900	3
Shotguns	猎枪	9303. 2000	
Shotguns parts and accessories	猎枪用零件、附件	9305. 2900	3
Shoulders and cuts thereof, of swine, prepared or preserved	前腿及其肉块,猪的,制作或保藏的	1602. 4200	48
Shoulders and cuts thereof, with bone in, of swine, fresh or chilled	前腿及其肉块,猪的,鲜或冷的,带骨	0203. 1200	14
Shoulders and cuts thereof, with bone in, of swine, frozen	前腿及其肉块,猪的,冻的,带骨	0203. 2200	14
Shovel loaders	机铲装载机	8429. 5900	57
Shovels	铲子	8201. 1000	256
Shovels, parts of bulldozer or cranes	铲斗,推土机或起重机零件	8431. 4100	3
Shower-baths, of plastics	淋浴盘,塑料的	3922. 1000	236
Shrimps and prawns, prepared or preserved	小虾及对虾,制作或保藏的	1605. 2000	48
Shrimps, for cultivation	小虾种苗	0306. 2310	3
Shrimps, nes, frozen	小虾,其他,冻的	0306. 1319	18
Shrimps, nes, not frozen	小虾,其他,未冻的	0306. 2399	14
Shutter units for cameras	快门组件,照相机用	9006. 9192	3
Shuttering for concrete constructional work, of wood	模板,水泥构件用的,木制的	4418. 4000	58
Shutters and similar articles and parts thereof, of plastics	窗板或类似制品及其零件,塑料的	3925. 3000	23
Shuttle changing mechanisms, weaving auxiliary machines	换梭装置,织机的辅助机器	8448. 1900	3
Shuttles for looms	梭子,织机用	8448. 4930	3
Side appearance of bodies, of the motor vehicles	侧围,机动车辆的	8708. 2951	3
Siderite, agglomerated	菱铁矿,已烧结	2601. 1200	1346
Signal flares project devices	信号弹的发射装置	9303. 9000	
Signal generators parts, nes	信号发生器用零件,其他	8543. 9029	3
Signal generators parts, with a frequency range of less than 1500MHz	信号发生器用零件,输出信号频率在1500 兆赫兹以下的通用信号发生器用	8543. 9021	3
Signal generators, nes	信号发生器,其他	8543. 2090	37
Signal generators, universal signal generators, with a frequency range of less than 1500MHz	信号发生器,输出信号频率在 1500 兆赫兹以下的通用信号发生器	8543. 2010	37

S

Article Description	商品名称	Tariff Code	D. R.
Signalling electrical equipment for airfields	信号设备,电气的,机场的	8530. 8000	
Signalling electrical equipment for inland waterways	信号设备,电气的,内河航道的	8530. 8000	
Signalling electrical equipment for parking facilities	信号设备,电气的,停车场的	8530. 8000	
Signalling electrical equipment for port installations	信号设备,电气的,港口的	8530. 8000	
Signalling electrical equipment for railways	信号设备,电气的,铁道的	8530. 1000	
Signalling electrical equipment for roads	信号设备,电气的,道路的	8530. 8000	
Signalling electrical equipment for tramways	信号设备,电气的,电车道的	8530. 1000	
Signalling electrical equipment parts	信号设备的零件	8530. 9000	3
Signalling equipment and parts, for airfields	信号设备及其零件,机械的,机场用	8608. 0090	3
Signalling equipment and parts, for inland waterways	信号设备及其零件,机械的,内河航道用	8608. 0090	3
Signalling equipment and parts, for parking facilities	信号设备及其零件,机械的,停车场用	8608. 0090	3
Signalling equipment and parts, for port installations	信号设备及其零件,机械的,港口用	8608. 0090	3
Signalling equipment and parts, for railways	信号设备及其零件,机械的,铁道用	8608. 0090	3
Signalling equipment and parts, for roads	信号设备及其零件,机械的,道路用	8608. 0090	3
Signalling equipment and parts, for tramways	信号设备及其零件,机械的,电车道用	8608. 0090	3
Signalling flares	信号弹	3604. 9000	
Signalling glassware, not optically worked	信号玻璃器,未经光学加工的	7014. 0090	345
Signalling instruments, mouth-blown sound	信号器,口吹音响的	9208. 9000	5
Sign-plates, of base metal, excluding those of heading No. 94. 05	标志牌,贱金属制,税号 94. 05 的货品除外	8310. 0000	256
Silencers (mufflers), exhaust pipes and parts, of motor vehicles	消声器(消音器)、排气管及其零件,机动车辆用	8708. 9200	3
Silica sands	硅砂	2505. 1000	34
Silicates, complex	硅酸络盐	2842. 1000	
Silicates, double	硅酸复盐	2842. 1000	
Silicates, nes	硅酸盐,其他	2839. 9000	
Siliceous earths	硅质土	2512. 0090	1234568
Siliceous earths bricks, blocks, tiles and other ceramic goods	硅土制的砖、块、瓦及其他陶瓷制品	6901. 0000	6
Siliceous fossil meals bricks, blocks, tiles and other ceramic goods	硅质化石粉制的砖、块、瓦及其他陶瓷制品	6901. 0000	6
Siliceous fossil meals, nes	硅质化粗粉,其他	2512. 0090	1234568
Silicides, whether or not chemically defined but other than the carbon compounds classified to 28. 49	硅化物,不论是否已有化学定义,但可归入税号 28. 49 的碳化物除外	2850. 0000	
Silicon carbides	碳化硅	2849. 2000	
Silicon dioxide	二氧化硅	2811. 2200	1346
Silicon, containing by weight not less than 99. 99%, nes	硅,按重量计含硅量不少于 99. 99%,其他	2804. 6190	1346
Silicon, nes	硅,其他	2804. 6900	346
Silicones in primary forms	聚硅氧烷,初级形状的	3910. 0000	136

Article Description	商品名称	Tariff Code	D. R.
Silk or of silk waste fabrics, containing 85% or more by weight of silk or of silk waste other than noil silk, nes	丝或绢丝机织物,按重量计丝或绢丝含量在85%及以上,其他	5007.2090	4568
Silk or of silk waste fabrics, unbleached or bleached	丝或绢丝机织物,未漂白或漂白	5007.9010	4568
Silk or of silk waste fabrics, nes	丝或绢丝机织物,其他	5007.9090	4568
Silk waste fabrics, containing 85% or more by weight of silk or of silk waste, nes	绢丝机织物,按重量计丝或绢丝含量在85%及以上,其他	5007.2039	4568
Silk waste fabrics, unbleached or bleached, containing 85% or more by weight of silk or of silk waste	绢丝机织物,按重量计丝或绢丝含量在85%及以上,未漂白或漂白	5007.2031	4568
Silk waste, cocoon outer floss, not carded or combed	废丝,茧衣,未梳	5003.0010	145
Silk waste, garnetted stock, not carded or combed	废丝,回收纤维,未梳	5003.0010	145
Silk waste, nes	废丝,其他	5003.0099	145
Silk waste, not carded or combed	废丝,未梳	5003.0010	145
Silk waste, silk top, nes	废丝,锦球,其他	5003.0091	145
Silk yarn, put up for retail sale	丝纱线,供零售用	5006.0000	356
Silk yarn, not put up for retail sale	丝纱线,非供零售用	5004.0000	3
Silkworm eggs	蚕蛹	0511.9930	
Silkworm graine	蚕种	0511.9930	
Silk-worm cocoons, mulberry feeding	桑蚕茧,适于缫丝的	5001.0010	45
Silk-worm cocoons, suitable for reeling, nes	蚕茧,适于缫丝的,其他	5001.0090	45
Silk-worm gut	蚕胶丝	5006.0000	356
Sillimanite	硅线石	2508.5000	134
Silver clothing base metals, not further worked than semi-manufactured	银,以贱金属为底的,未加工成半成品的	7107.0000	46
Silver compounds, nes	银化合物,其他	2843.2900	
Silver nitrate	硝酸银	2843.2100	
Silver or silver compounds ash	银或银化合物的灰	7112.3010	46
Silver ores and concentrates	银矿砂及其精矿	2616.1000	146
Silver powder, flake, average diameter less than 10μm	银粉,片状,平均粒径小于10微米	7106.1021	145
Silver powder, flake, nes	银粉,片状,其他	7106.1029	145
Silver powder, not flake, average diameter less than 3μm	银粉,非片状,平均粒径小于3微米	7106.1011	145
Silver powder, not flake, nes	银粉,非片状,其他	7106.1019	145
Silver (including silver plated with gold or platinum), unwrought, nes	银(包括镀金、镀铂的银),未锻造,其他	7106.9190	145
Silver (including silver plated with gold or platinum), unwrought, of a purity of 99.99% or more	银(包括镀金、镀铂的银),未锻造,纯度达99.99%及以上	7106.9110	145
Silver (including silver plated with gold or platinum), semi-manufactured, nes	银(包括镀金、镀铂的银),半制成,其他	7106.9290	145

S

Article Description	商品名称	Tariff Code	D. R.
Silver (including silver plated with gold or platinum), semi-manufactured, of a purity of 99. 99% or more	银(包括镀金、镀铂的银),半制成,纯度达 99. 99% 及以上	7106. 9210	145
Single flat wire, barbed or not, of a kind used for fencing, of iron or steel	单股扁丝,不论是否带刺,钢铁的,围篱用的	7313. 0000	36
Single station construction machines, for working metal	组合机床,单工位的,加工金属的	8457. 2000	7
Single yarn, untwisted or with a twist not exceeding 50 turns per metre, not put up for retail sale, nes	单纱,未加捻或捻度每米不超过 50 转,非供零售用,其他	5402. 4900	3468
Single yarn, with a twist exceeding 50 turns per metre, not put up for retail sale, nes	单纱,捻度每米超过 50 转,非供零售用,其他	5402. 5990	3468
Singlets and other vests, not knitted or crocheted, for men or boys, nes	背心及其他内衣,非针织或钩编的,男式,其他	6207. 9990	2456
Singlets and other vests, not knitted or crocheted, for men or boys, of cotton	背心及其他内衣,非针织或钩编的,男式,棉制	6207. 9100	2456
Singlets and other vests, not knitted or crocheted, for men or boys, of man-made fibres	背心及其他内衣,非针织或钩编的,男式,化学纤维制	6207. 9920	2456
Singlets and other vests, not knitted or crocheted, for men or boys, of silk or silk waste	背心及其他内衣,非针织或钩编的,男式,丝及绢丝制	6207. 9910	2456
Singlets and other vests, not knitted or crocheted, for women or girls, nes	背心及其他内衣,非针织或钩编的,女式,其他	6208. 9990	2456
Singlets and other vests, not knitted or crocheted, for women or girls, of cotton	背心及其他内衣,非针织或钩编的,女式,棉制	6208. 9100	2456
Singlets and other vests, not knitted or crocheted, for women or girls, of man-made fibres	背心及其他内衣,非针织或钩编的,女式,化学纤维制	6208. 9200	2456
Singlets and other vests, not knitted or crocheted, for women or girls, of silk or silk waste	背心及其他内衣,非针织或钩编的,女式,丝及绢丝制	6208. 9910	2456
Singlets, knitted or crocheted, nes	汗衫,针织或钩编的,其他	6109. 9090	2456
Singlets, knitted or crocheted, of cotton	汗衫,针织或钩编的,棉制	6109. 1000	2456
Singlets, knitted or crocheted, of silk or silk waste	汗衫,针织或钩编的,丝及绢丝制	6109. 9010	2456
Single-cell microorganisms, dead, nes	单细胞微生物,已死的,其他	2102. 2000	28
Sinkers for knitting machines	沉降片,针织机的	8448. 5190	3
Sinks and wash basins, of stainless steel	洗涤槽及脸盆,不锈钢制	7324. 1000	24
Sinks, of porcelain or china	洗涤槽,瓷制	6910. 1000	268
Sinks, of pottery	洗涤槽,陶制	6910. 9000	268
Sinks, of plastics	洗涤槽, 塑料的	3922. 1000	236
Sirens parts, electric	电笛零件,电气的	8531. 9090	3
Sirens, electric	电笛,电气的	8531. 8090	3
Sisal and other textile fibres of the genus agave, raw	西沙尔麻及其他纺织用龙舌兰类纤维	5305. 0091	4
Sizing machines	浆纱机	8445. 9020	7
Sizing machines auxiliary	浆纱机的辅助机器	8448. 1900	3
Skateboards	滑板	9506. 9120	

S

Article Description	商品名称	Tariff Code	D. R.
Ski suits, knitted or crocheted, nes	滑雪服,针织或钩编的,其他	6112. 2090	2456
Ski suits, knitted or crocheted, of cotton	滑雪服,针织或钩编的,棉制	6112. 2010	2456
Ski suits, not knitted or crocheted, of cotton	滑雪服,非针织或钩编的,棉制	6211. 2010	2456
Ski suits, not knitted or crocheted, of other textile materials	滑雪服,非针织或钩编的,其他纺织材料制	6211. 2090	2456
Skid chain, of iron or steel	防滑链,钢铁的	7315. 2000	36
Skimmers, other than plated with precious metal	漏勺,非镀贵金属的	8215. 9900	256
Skimmers, plated with precious metal	漏勺,镀贵金属的	8215. 9100	256
Skin care preparations, in powders, whether or not compressed	护肤品,粉状,不论是否压紧	3304. 9100	23
Skin care preparations, nes	护肤品,其他	3304. 9900	23
Skins of birds, with their feathers or down	鸟皮,带有羽毛或羽绒的	0505. 9090	34
Skins of sheep or lambs, tanned or crust, without wool on, in the dry state	皮及其坯革,绵羊或者羔羊的,鞣制的不带毛,干革	4105. 3000	1458
Skins of sheep or lambs, tanned or crust, without wool on, in the wet state, nes	皮及其坯革,绵羊或者羔羊的,鞣制的不带毛,湿革,其他	4105. 1090	1458
Skins of sheep or lambs, tanned or crust, without wool on, wet -blue	皮及其坯革,绵羊或者羔羊的,鞣制的不带毛,蓝湿的	4105. 1010	1458
Skins or leather preparing machinery	生皮、皮革的处理机器	8453. 1000	
Skins or leather repairing machinery	生皮、皮革的修理机器	8453. 8000	
Skins or leather tanning machinery	生皮、皮革的鞣制机器	8453. 1000	
Skins or leather tanning machinery parts	皮革鞣制机器零件	8453. 9000	3
Skins or leather working machinery	生皮、皮革的加工机器	8453. 1000	
Skins or leather working machinery parts	皮革加工机器零件	8453. 9000	3
Skip hoists parts	倒卸式起重机的零件	8431. 3100	3
Skip hoists parts	起重机的零件,倒卸式的	8431. 3100	3
Skipjack and bonito (Sarda spp.), prepared or preserved, whole or in pieces, but not minced	鲣鱼,制作或保藏的,整条或切块,但未绞碎	1604. 1400	48
Skipjack or stripebellied bonito, frozen	鲣鱼,冻的	0303. 4300	18
Skipjack or stripe-bellied bonito [Euthynnus (Katsuwonus) pelamis], fresh or chilled	鲣鱼,鲜或冷的	0302. 3300	18
Skirts and divided skirts, knitted or crocheted, for women or girls, of cotton	裙子及裙裤,针织或钩编的,女式,棉制	6104. 5200	2456
Skirts and divided skirts, knitted or crocheted, for women or girls, of other textile materials	裙子及裙裤,针织或钩编的,女式,其他纺织材料制	6104. 5900	2456
Skirts and divided skirts, knitted or crocheted, for women or girls, of synthetic fibres	裙子及裙裤,针织或钩编的,女式,合成纤维制	6104. 5300	2456
Skirts and divided skirts, knitted or crocheted, for women or girls, of wool or fine animal hair	裙子及裙裤,针织或钩编的,女式,羊毛或动物细毛制	6104. 5100	2456
Skirts and divided skirts, not knitted or crocheted, for women or girls, nes	裙子及裙裤,非针织或钩编的,女式,其他	6204. 5990	2456

Article Description	商品名称	Tariff Code	D. R.
Skirts and divided skirts, not knitted or crocheted, for women or girls, of cotton	裙子及裙裤,非针织或钩编的,女式,棉制	6204. 5200	2456
Skirts and divided skirts, not knitted or crocheted, for women or girls, of silk or silk waste	裙子及裙裤,非针织或钩编的,女式,丝及绢丝制	6204. 5910	2456
Skirts and divided skirts, not knitted or crocheted, for women or girls, of synthetic fibres	裙子及裙裤,非针织或钩编的,女式,合成纤维制	6204. 5300	2456
Skirts and divided skirts, not knitted or crocheted, for women or girls, of wool or fine animal hair	裙子及裙裤,非针织或钩编的,女式,羊毛或动物细毛制	6204. 5100	2456
Skis	滑雪屐	9506. 1100	
Ski-boots, with outer soles and uppers of rubber or plastics	滑雪靴,橡胶或塑料制外底及鞋面的	6402. 1200	26
Ski-boots, with outer soles of rubber, plastics, leather or composition leather and upers of leather	滑雪靴,橡胶、塑料、皮革或再生皮革制外底,皮革制鞋面的	6403. 1200	26
Ski-draglines, nes	滑雪拉索,其他	8428. 6090	
Ski-fastenings (ski-bindings)	滑雪屐扣件(滑雪屐带)	9506. 1200	
Slack wax	疏松石蜡	2712. 9090	6
Slag and ash, nes	矿渣及矿灰,其他	2621. 9000	134
Slag cement	矿渣水泥	2523. 9000	3
Slag sand, nes, from the manufacture of iron or steel	熔渣砂,其他,冶炼钢铁所产生的	2618. 0090	146
Slag wool, rock wool and similar mineral wools (including intermixtures thereof), in bulk, sheets or rolls	矿渣棉、岩石棉及类似的矿质棉(包括其相互混合物),块状、成片或成卷	6806. 1000	68
Slag, other than granulated slag, from the manufacture of iron or steel	熔渣(粒状熔渣除外),冶炼钢铁所产生的	2619. 0000	134
Slag, ash and residues (other than from the manufacture of iron or steel) containing antimony, beryllinm, cadmium, chromium or their mixtures	矿渣、矿灰及残渣(冶炼钢铁所产生的灰、渣除外),含锑、铍、镉、铬及其混合物	2620. 9100	134
Slag, ash and residues (other than from the manufacture of iron or steel) containing arsenic, mercury, thallium or their mixtures, of a kind used for the extraction of arsenic or those metals or for the manufacture of their chemical compounds	矿渣、矿灰及残渣(冶炼钢铁所产生的灰、渣除外),含砷、汞、铊及其混合物,用于提取或生产砷、汞、铊及其化合物	2620. 6000	134
Slag, ash and residues (other than from the manufacture of iron or steel) containing mainly aluminium	矿渣、矿灰及残渣(冶炼钢铁所产生的灰、渣除外),主要含铝	2620. 4000	134
Slag, ash and residues (other than from the manufacture of iron or steel) containing mainly copper	矿渣、矿灰及残渣(冶炼钢铁所产生的灰、渣除外),主要含铜	2620. 3000	134
Slag, ash and residues (other than from the manufacture of iron or steel) containing mainly lead, nes	矿渣、矿灰及残渣(冶炼钢铁所产生的灰、渣除外),主要含铅,其他	2620. 2900	134
Slag, ash and residues (other than from the manufacture of iron or steel) containing mainly tungsten	矿渣、矿灰及残渣(冶炼钢铁所产生的灰、渣除外),主要含钨	2620. 9910	134

Article Description	商品名称	Tariff Code	D. R.
Slag, ash and residues (other than from the manufacture of iron or steel) containing mainly zinc, nes	矿渣、矿灰及残渣(冶炼钢铁所产生的灰、渣除外),主要含锌,其他	2620. 1900	134
Slag, ash and residues (other than from the manufacture of iron or steel) containing metals or their compounds, nes	矿渣、矿灰及残渣(冶炼钢铁所产生的灰、渣除外),含有金属及其化合物的,其他	2620. 9990	134
Slag, ash and residues (other than from the manufacture of iron or steel) containing hard zinc spelter	矿渣、矿灰及残渣(冶炼钢铁所产生的灰、渣除外),含硬锌	2620. 1100	134
Slaked lime	熟石灰	2522. 2000	
Slate	板岩	2514. 0000	
Slate articles	板岩的制品	6803. 0010	4
Slate articles, agglomerated	板岩的制品,粘聚的	6803. 0090	4
Slate, worked	已加工的板岩	6803. 0010	4
Slates, with writing or drawing surfaces	石板,具有书写或绘画面的	9610. 0000	
Sleepers (crossties) of wood, for railway or tramway, nes	枕木,铁道及电车道,其他	4406. 9000	4
Sleepers (crossties) of wood, for railway or tramway, not impregnated	枕木,铁道及电车道,未浸渍	4406. 1000	4
Sleepers (cross-ties), for railway or tramway track construction, of iron or steel	轨枕,钢铁制,铁道用	7302. 9010	6
Sleeping bags, nes	睡袋,其他	9404. 3090	6
Sleeping bags, stuffed with feathers or down	睡袋,羽毛或羽绒填充的	9404. 3010	6
Slice pop-up toasters	片式烤面包机(多士炉)	8516. 7220	7
Slicing machines, for working wood, cork, bone, hard rubber, hard plastics or similar hard materials	切片机器,加工木材、软木、骨、硬质橡胶、硬质塑料或类似硬质材料的	8465. 9600	7
Slide fasteners, fitted with chain scoops of base metal	拉链,装有贱金属制咪牙齿的	9607. 1100	5
Slide fasteners, nes	拉链,其他	9607. 1900	5
Slide fasteners, parts	拉链,零件	9607. 2000	3
Slide projectors	幻灯机	9008. 1000	
Slide projectors parts and accessories	幻灯机零件、附件	9008. 9090	3
Sliding pencils	活动铅笔	9608. 4000	
Slips and petticoats, knitted or crocheted, for women or girls, nes	长衬裙及衬裙,针织或钩编的,女式,其他	6108. 1990	2456
Slips and petticoats, knitted or crocheted, for women or girls, of cotton	长衬裙及衬裙,针织或钩编的,女式,棉制	6108. 1910	2456
Slips and petticoats, knitted or crocheted, for women or girls, of man-made fibres	长衬裙及衬裙,针织或钩编的,女式,化学纤维制	6108. 1100	2456
Slips and petticoats, knitted or crocheted, for women or girls, of silk or silk waste	长衬裙及衬裙,针织或钩编的,女式,丝及绢丝制	6108. 1920	2456
Slips and petticoats, not knitted or crocheted, for women or girls, nes	长衬裙及衬裙,非针织或钩编的,女式,其他	6208. 1990	2456

Article Description	商品名称	Tariff Code	D. R.
Slips and petticoats, not knitted or crocheted, for women or girls, of cotton	长衬裙及衬裙,非针织或钩编的,女式,棉制	6208.1920	2456
Slips and petticoats, not knitted or crocheted, for women or girls, of man-made fibres	长衬裙及衬裙,非针织或钩编的,女式,化学纤维制	6208.1100	2456
Slips and petticoats, not knitted or crocheted, for women or girls, of silk or silk waste	长衬裙及衬裙,非针织或钩编的,女式,丝及绢丝制	6208.1910	2456
Slips and similar preparations, of a kind used in the ceramic, enamelling or glass industry	泥釉及类似制品,陶瓷、搪瓷及玻璃工业用	3207.2000	13
Slips, for live plants	接穗,活植物的	0602.1000	3
Sloes, fresh	李,鲜的	0809.4000	1
Slotting machines, for removing metal or cermets	插床,切削金属或金属陶瓷用	8461.2020	7
Small red (Adzuki) beans (Phaseolus or Vigna angularis), frozen	红小豆,冷冻的	0710.2210	1
Small red (adzuki) beans (phaseolus or vigna angularis), nes, shelled, dried	赤豆,其他,脱荚的,干的	0713.3290	34
Small red (adzuki) beans (phaseolus or vigna angularis), seed, nes, shelled, dried	赤豆,种用,其他,脱荚的,干的	0713.3219	34
Small red (Adzuri) beans, seed, shelled, dried	红小豆,种用,脱荚的,干的	0713.3211	34
Small white agaric, in airtight containers	罐头,小白蘑菇	2003.1011	248
Smart cards, nes	智能卡,其他	8523.5290	37
Smart cards, unrecorded	智能卡,未录制	8523.5210	37
Smithsonite	菱锌矿	2608.0000	146
Smoke analysis apparatus	烟雾分析仪	9027.1000	
Smoked fish, including fillet, atlantic salmon	熏鱼,包括鱼片,大西洋鲑鱼	0305.4110	4
Smoked fish, including fillet, danube salmon	熏鱼,包括鱼片,多瑙哲罗鱼	0305.4120	4
Smoked fish, including fillet, herrings (clupea harengus, clupea pallasii)	熏鱼,包括鱼片,鲱鱼(大西洋鲱鱼、太平洋鲱鱼)	0305.4200	4
Smoked fish, including fillet, nes	熏鱼,包括鱼片,其他	0305.4900	4
Smoked fish, including fillet, pacific salmon	熏鱼,包括鱼片,大马哈鱼	0305.4120	4
Smoked sheets	烟胶片	4001.2100	12
Smoking pipes and pipe bowls	烟斗及烟斗头	9614.0010	
Smoking pipes parts	烟斗零件	9614.0090	5
Smoking tobacco, whether or not containing tobacco substitutes in any proportion	烟草,供吸用的,不论是否含有任何比例的烟草代用品	2403.1000	3
Snails, other than sea snails, for cultivation	螺,种苗	0307.6010	8
Snails, other than sea snails, for cultivation	蜗牛,种苗	0307.6010	8
Snails, other than sea snails, nes	蜗牛及螺,其他	0307.6090	148
Snow	雪	2201.9090	248
Snow skis	滑雪屐	9506.1100	
Snow ski-fastenings (ski-bindings)	滑雪屐扣件(滑雪屐带)	9506.1200	
Snow sweep vehicles for cleansing streets or airfield runways	扫雪车	8705.9070	7

S

Article Description	商品名称	Tariff Code	D. R.
Snow travelling vehicles	雪地行走专用车	8703.1090	58
Snowboard boots, with outer soles and uppers of rubber or plastics	滑雪板靴,橡胶或塑料制外底及鞋面的	6402.1200	26
Snowboard boots, with outer soles of rubber, plastics, leather or composition leather and upers of leather	滑雪板靴,橡胶、塑料、皮革或再生皮革制外底,皮革制鞋面的	6403.1200	26
Snow-blowers	吹雪机	8430.2000	5
Snow-blowers parts	吹雪机零件	8431.4990	3
Snow-ploughs	扫雪机	8430.2000	5
Snow-ploughs parts	扫雪机零件	8431.4990	3
Snow-ski equipmen, nes	滑雪用具,其他	9506.1900	5
Soap and organic surface-active products and preparations, nes	肥皂及有机表面活性产品,其他	3401.1990	123
Soap for laundry	肥皂,洗衣用	3401.1910	123
Soap impregnated (coated or covered) paper (wadding, felt and Non-wovens), for toilet use	肥皂浸渍、涂面或包覆的纸、絮胎、毡呢及无纺织物,盥洗用	3401.1100	123
Soap in other form	肥皂,其他形状的	3401.2000	123
Soap, in the form of bars, cakes, moulded pieces or shapes, for toilet use	肥皂,条状、块状或模制形状的,盥洗用	3401.1100	123
Soapstone, crushed or powdered	皂石,破碎或研粉	2526.2010	4
Soapstone, not crushed, not powdered	皂石,未破碎及未研粉	2526.1010	4
Sockeye salmon (red salmon) (on corhynchus nerka), frozen	红大马哈鱼,冻的	0303.1100	18
Soda lye	氢氧化钠浓溶液	2815.1200	136
Soda water	苏打水	2201.1020	28
Soda, liquid	烧碱,液体	2815.1200	136
Sodamide	氨基钠	2853.0090	
Sodium	钠	2805.1100	
Sodium acetate	乙酸钠	2915.2910	36
Sodium bicarbonate	小苏打	2836.3000	
Sodium bromides	溴化钠	2827.5100	
Sodium chlorates	氯酸钠	2829.1100	
Sodium chloride, pure	氯化钠,纯的	2501.0020	1368
Sodium cyanide	氰化钠	2837.1110	6
Sodium cyanide oxide	氧氰化钠	2837.1120	6
Sodium cyclamate	环已基氨基磺酸钠	2929.9010	36
Sodium cyclamate	甜蜜素	2929.9010	36
Sodium dichromate	重铬酸钠	2841.3000	1
Sodium dithionites	钠的连二亚硫酸盐	2831.1010	
Sodium fluorides	氟化钠	2826.1920	
Sodium glutamate	谷氨酸钠	2922.4220	36
Sodium hexafluoroaluminate	六氟铝酸钠	2826.3000	
Sodium hexametaphosphate, food grade	六偏磷酸钠,食品级的	2835.3911	

S

Article Description	商品名称	Tariff Code	D. R.
Sodium hexametaphosphate, nes	六偏磷酸钠,其他	2835. 3919	3
Sodium hydrogencarbonate	碳酸氢钠	2836. 3000	
Sodium hydroxide, in aqueous solution	氢氧化钠,水溶液	2815. 1200	136
Sodium hydroxide, solid	氢氧化钠,固体	2815. 1100	136
Sodium metasilicates	偏硅酸钠	2839. 1100	
Sodium nitrate	硝酸钠	3102. 5000	68
Sodium peroxides	过氧化钠	2815. 3000	136
Sodium p-nitro-phenolate	对硝基酚钠	2908. 9910	36
Sodium salicylate	水杨酸钠	2918. 2110	36
Sodium silicates	钠的硅酸盐,其他	2839. 1900	
Sodium sulphates, nes	钠的硫酸盐,其他	2833. 1900	
Sodium sulphide	硫化钠	2830. 1010	
Sodium sulphides, nes	钠的硫化物,其他	2830. 1090	
Sodium sulphites	钠的亚硫酸盐	2832. 1000	
Sodium sulphoxylates	钠的次硫酸盐	2831. 1020	
Sodium triphosphate, food grade	三磷酸钠,食品级的	2835. 3110	
Sodium triphosphate, nes	三磷酸钠,其他	2835. 3190	3
Sodium tripolyphosphate, food grade	三聚磷酸钠,食品级的	2835. 3110	
Sodium tripolyphosphate, nes	三聚磷酸钠,其他	2835. 3190	3
Sodium tungstate	钨酸钠	2841. 8020	1
Sodium vapour lamps	钠蒸汽灯	8539. 3230	35
Solar cells	太阳能电池	8541. 4020	5
Solder, containing by weight less than 0. 1% of lead	焊锡,按重量计含铅量在 0. 1% 以下的	8001. 2021	16
Soldering guns	焊枪	8515. 1100	
Soldering irons	烙铁	8515. 1100	
Soldering, brazing or welding fluxes and other auxiliary preparations, nes	焊接用辅助剂,其他	3810. 9000	36
Soldering, brazing or welding pastes consisting of metal and other materials	焊粉,金属及其他材料制成的	3810. 1000	36
Soldering, brazing or welding powders consisting of metal and other materials	焊膏,金属及其他材料制成的	3810. 1000	36
Soldering, brazing or welding preparations, nes	焊剂,其他	3810. 9000	36
Sole (Solea spp.), fresh or chilled	鳎鱼,鲜或冷的	0302. 2300	18
Sole (Solea spp.), frozen	鳎鱼,冻的	0303. 3300	18
Solid cylinders, including discs, of agglomerated cork	实心圆柱体,包括圆片,压制软木制	4504. 1000	16
Solid fuels manufactured from coal, nes	煤制成的固体燃料,其他	2701. 2000	156
Solid or cushion tyres, nes	实心或半实心橡胶轮胎,其他	4012. 9090	234
Solid or cushion tyres, of a kind used on aircraft	实心或半实心橡胶轮胎,航空器用	4012. 9010	234
Solid or cushion tyres, of a kind used on motor cars, buses or lorries	实心或半实心橡胶轮胎,汽车用	4012. 9020	234

Article Description	商品名称	Tariff Code	D. R.
Solid residues, resulting from the extraction of groundnut oil	固体残渣,其他,提炼花生油所得的	2305.0000	46
Solid residues, resulting from the extraction of soyabean oil	固体残渣,其他,提炼豆油所得的	2304.0090	46
Solid-liquor separators, centrifuges	固液分离机,离心式	8421.1920	7
Somatotropin, its derivatives and structural analogues	生长激素及其衍生物和结构类似物	2937.1100	36
Soot removers, auxiliary plant for use with central heating boilers	除灰器,集中供暖用的热水锅炉的辅助设备	8404.1020	3
Soot removers, auxiliary plant for use with steam or other vapour generating watertube boilers	除灰器,蒸汽锅炉的辅助设备	8404.1010	3
Soot removers, auxiliary plant for use with super-heated water boilers	除灰器,过热水锅炉的辅助设备	8404.1010	3
Sorbitol, nes	山梨醇,其他	3824.6000	1346
Sorting machines for eggs, fruit or other agricultural produce	分选机器,对蛋类、水果或其他农产品的	8433.6000	
Sorting machines for seed, grain or dried leguminous vegetables	分选机器,种子、谷物或干豆用	8437.1090	3
Sorting machines parts for eggs, fruits or other agricuture products	分选机器零件,对蛋类、水果或其他农产品的	8433.9090	
Sorting machines parts, for seed, grain or dried leguminous vegetables	分选机器零件,种子、谷物或干豆用	8437.9000	3
Sorting machines with color, for seed, grain or dried leguminous vegetables	色选机器,种子、谷物或干豆用	8437.1010	3
Sorting machines, for earth, stone, ores or other mineral substances	分类机器,泥土、石料、矿石或其他固体矿物质的	8474.1000	
Sorting machines, used in post offices	分拣设备,邮政用	8479.8940	7
Sorting or banding mail machines	分拣及封装信件设备,邮政用	8472.3010	
Sorting, counting or wrapping machines, for coin	分类、计数及包装机,硬币的	8472.9090	
Sound absorbing mineral materials, mixtures and articles	吸音性能的矿物材料的混合物及制品,其他	6806.9000	68
Sound insula-ting mineral materials, mixtures and articles, nes	隔音的矿物材料的混合物及制品,其他	6806.9000	68
Sound or visual signalling apparatus, electric, nes	音响或视觉信号装置,电气的,其他	8531.8090	3
Sound recorders, flash memory type, incorporating sound reproducing apparatus	声音录制设备,装有声音重放装置的,闪速存储器型	8519.8131	5
Sound recording or reproducing apparatus parts and accessories, nes	声音录制或重放设备用零件、附件,其他	8522.9099	3
Sound recording or reproducing apparatus, nes	声音录制或重放设备,其他	8519.8990	5
Sound recording or reproducing apparatus, operated by coins, banknotes, bank cards, tokens or by other means of payment	声音录制或重放设备,用硬币、钞票、银行卡、代币或其他支付方式使其工作的设备	8519.2000	5
Sound recording or reproducing apparatus, using magnetic media, nes	声音录制或重放设备,使用磁性媒体的,其他	8519.8119	5

S

Article Description	商品名称	Tariff Code	D. R.
Sound recording or reproducing apparatus, using optical media, nes	声音录制或重放设备,使用光学媒体的,其他	8519.8129	5
Sound recording or reproducing apparatus, using semiconductor media, nes	声音录制或重放设备,使用半导体媒体的,其他	8519.8139	5
Sound reproducing apparatus, cassette-type, not incorporating a sound recording device, other than transcribing machines	声音重放装置,未装有声音录制装置的,盒带型,编辑节目用放声机除外	8519.8111	5
Sound signalling equipment for bicycles	音响信号装置,自行车用	8512.3090	7
Sound signalling equipment for motor vehicles, nes	音响信号装置,机动车辆用,其他	8512.3019	7
Sound signalling equipment parts for cycles or motor vehicles	音响信号装置零件,自行车或机动车辆用	8512.9000	3
Sound signalling instruments, mouth-blown	音响信号器,口吹的	9208.9000	5
Soups and broths and preparations therefor	汤料及其制品	2104.1000	28
Southern bluefin tunas (Thunnus maccoyii), fresh or chilled	南金枪鱼,鲜或冷的	0302.3600	18
Southern bluefin tunas (Thunnus maccoyii), frozen	南金枪鱼(南方蓝鳍金枪鱼),冻的	0303.4600	18
Southern bluefin tunas, nes, living	南方蓝鳍金枪鱼,其他	0301.9590	15
Southernwood	青蒿	1211.9035	34
Soya beans, black	大豆,黑色	1201.0092	3
Soya beans, green	大豆,青色	1201.0093	3
Soya beans, nes	大豆,其他	1201.0099	3
Soya beans, seed	大豆,种用	1201.0010	3
Soya beans, yellow	大豆,黄色	1201.0091	3
Soya sauce	酱油	2103.1000	268
Soyabean oil and its fractions, crude oil, whether or not degummed	豆油及其分离品,初榨的,不论是否脱胶	1507.1000	4
Soyabean oil and its fractions, nes	豆油及其分离品,其他	1507.9000	4
Space heating apparatus, electric, radiant	电加热器,辐射式	8516.2920	7
Space heating apparatus, electric convection, fan type	电加热器,对流式,风扇式	8516.2931	7
Space heating apparatus, electric convection, nes	电加热器,对流式,其他	8516.2939	7
Space heating apparatus, oil-filled types, electric convection	电加热器,对流式,充液式	8516.2932	7
Spacecraft (including satellites) and suborbital and spacecraft launch vehicles	航天器(包括卫星)及其运载工具、亚轨道运载工具	8802.6000	
Spades	锹	8201.1000	256
Spaghetti manufacture machinery	面条生产机器	8438.1000	
Spaghetti manufacture machinery parts	面条生产机器的零件	8438.9000	3
Spaghetti, uncooked, containing eggs	意大利面条,生的,含蛋的	1902.1100	46
Spaghetti, uncooked, nes	意大利面条,生的,其他	1902.1900	46
Spangles, of base metal	亮晶片,贱金属制	8308.9000	256
Spanner sockets, interchangeable, with or without handles, hand tools	扳手套筒,可互换的,不论是否带手柄	8204.2000	256

S

Article Description	商品名称	Tariff Code	D. R.
Spanners and wrenches, hand-operated, adjustable	扳手及扳钳,手动,可调的	8204.1200	256
Spanners and wrenches, hand-operated, non-adjustable	扳手及扳钳,手动,固定的	8204.1100	256
Sparking plugs, for electrical ignition or starting equipment	火花塞,点燃式或压燃式内燃发动机用的	8511.1000	
Spatula and the like, nes	压舌片及类似一次性制品,其他	4421.9029	56
Spatula and the like, of bamboo	压舌片及类似一次性制品,竹制	4421.9022	56
Spatula and the like, of wood	压舌片及类似一次性制品,木制	4421.9021	56
Special purpose railway or tramway coaches, not self-propelled, nes	铁道及电车道用的非机动特殊用途车辆,其他	8605.0090	37
Spectacle cases, toilet bags, wallets, purses, cigarette-cases, tobacco-pouches, powder-boxes, nes	眼镜盒、化妆包、钱夹、钱包、烟盒、烟袋、粉盒,其他	4202.3900	256
Spectacle cases, with outer surface of leather, of composition leather or of patent leather	眼镜盒,以皮革、再生皮革或漆皮作面	4202.3100	256
Spectacle cases, with outer surface of plastic sheeting or of textile materials	眼镜盒,以塑料片或纺织材料作面	4202.3200	256
Spectacle lenses of glass, nes	眼镜片,玻璃制,其他	9001.4099	5
Spectacle lenses of other materials	眼镜片,其他材料制,其他	9001.5099	
Spectacles frames and mountings of other materials	眼镜架,其他材料制	9003.1900	3
Spectacles frames and mountings of plastics	眼镜架,塑料制	9003.1100	3
Spectacles frames and mountings parts	眼镜架零件	9003.9000	3
Spectacles, corrective	眼镜,矫正视力用	9004.9090	5
Spectrographs parts and accessories	摄谱仪零件、附件	9027.9000	3
Spectrographs, using optical radiations (UV, visible, IR)	摄谱仪,使用光学射线(紫外线、可见光、红外线)的	9027.3000	
Spectrometers parts and accessories	分光仪零件、附件	9027.9000	3
Spectrometers, using optical radiations (UV, visible, IR)	分光仪,使用光学射线(紫外线、可见光、红外线)的	9027.3000	
Spectrophotometers parts and accessories	分光光度计零件、附件	9027.9000	3
Spectrophotometers, using optical radiations (UV, visible, IR)	分光光度计,使用光学射线(紫外线、可见光、红外线)的	9027.3000	
Speed indicators for motor vehicles	速度计,车辆用	9029.2010	
Speed indicators parts and accessories	速度计零件、附件	9029.9000	3
Speed indicators, nes	速度计,其他	9029.2090	7
Spent (irradiated) fuel elements (cartridges) of nuclear reactors	核反应堆已耗尽(已辐照)的燃料元件(释热元件)	2844.5000	
Spermaceti	鲸蜡	1521.9090	
Spherical roller bearings	鼓形滚子轴承	8482.3000	5
Sphygmomanometers and appliances	血压测量仪器及器具	9018.9020	
Spiegeleisen	镜铁	7201.5000	6

S

Article Description	商品名称	Tariff Code	D. R.
Spinach, New Zealand spinach and orache spinach (garden spinach), fresh or chilled	菠菜,鲜或冷藏的	0709.7000	1
Spinach, New Zealand spinach and orache spinach (garden spinach), frozen	菠菜,冷冻的	0710.3000	1
Spinner machine auxiliary	纺纱机的辅助机器	8448.1900	3
Spinner machine or of their auxiliary machines' parts and accessories, nes	纺纱机及其辅助机器的零件、附件,其他	8448.3990	3
Spinner machine, jet	纺纱机,喷气式	8445.2032	7
Spinner machine, open-end, nes	纺纱机,自由端的,其他	8445.2039	7
Spinning frame, for cotton ring	细纱机,棉的	8445.2041	7
Spinning frame, for worsted ring	细纱机,毛的	8445.2042	7
Spinning frames, for ring, nes	细纱机,环锭式,其他	8445.2049	7
Spinning jets auxiliary, for artificial fibres	纺丝机的辅助机器,人造纤维的	8448.1900	3
Spinning jets for artificial fibres	纺丝机,人造纤维的	8444.0030	
Spinning jets for synthetic filaments	纺丝机,合成纤维长丝的	8444.0010	
Spinning jets for synthetic staple fibres	纺丝机,合成纤维短纤的	8444.0020	
Spinning jets machines or of their auxiliary machines's parts and accessories, nes	纺丝机及其辅助机器的零件、附件,其他	8448.2090	3
Spinning machine, rotor	纺纱机,转杯式	8445.2031	7
Spinning rings	纺丝环	8448.3390	3
Spiralling tube welding machines, fully or partly automatic	螺旋焊管机,全自动或半自动的	8515.3110	
Spirits obtained by distilling grape wine or grape marc	烈性酒,蒸馏葡萄酒制得的	2208.2000	2468
Spirits, chinese distilled	白酒	2208.9020	2468
Split poles, coniferous	木劈条,针叶木的	4404.1000	15
Split poles, non-coniferous	木劈条,非针叶木的	4404.2000	15
Splitting machines, for working wood, cork, bone, hard rubber, hard plastics or similar hard materials	剖开机器,加工木材、软木、骨、硬质橡胶、硬质塑料或类似硬质材料的	8465.9600	7
Sponge iron rotary kiln parts	海绵铁回转窑用零件	8417.9010	3
Sponges of animal origin, natural	动物质海绵,天然的	0511.9990	34
Sponges of animal origin, natural	海绵,天然的,动物质	0511.9990	34
Sponges of vegetable origin, natural	植物质海绵,天然的	1404.9090	
Sponges of vegetable origin, natural	海绵,天然的,植物质	1404.9090	
Spongy ferrous products, in lumps, pellets or similar forms, nes	海绵铁产品,块、团、团粒及类似形状,其他	7203.9000	6
Spools and the like, of wood	卷轴及类似品,木制	4421.9010	56
Spools, cops, bobbins and similar supports, of plastics	卷轴、纡子、筒管及类似品,塑料的	3923.4000	23
Spoons, other than plated with precious metal	餐匙,非镀贵金属的	8215.9900	256
Spoons, other than plated with precious metal	餐匙,非镀贵金属的	8215.9900	256
Spoons, plated with precious metal	餐匙,镀贵金属的	8215.9100	256
Sporting rifles, nes	运动用步枪,其他	9303.3000	

S

Article Description	商品名称	Tariff Code	D. R.
Sporting shotguns, including combination shotgun rifles	运动用猎枪,包括组合式滑膛来复枪	9303. 2000	
Sports footwear, tennis shoes, basketball shoes, gym shoes, training shoes and the like	运动鞋靴;网球鞋、篮球鞋、体操鞋、训练鞋及类似鞋,橡胶或塑料制外底的鞋靴,纺织材料制鞋面的	6404. 1100	26
Sports footwear, with outer soles and uppers of rubber or plastics, nes	运动鞋靴,橡胶或塑料制外底及鞋面的,其他	6402. 1900	26
Sports footwear, with outer soles of rubber, plastics, leather or composition leather and upers of leather, nes	运动鞋靴,橡胶、塑料、皮革或再生皮革制外底,皮革制鞋面的,其他	6403. 1900	26
Spot lights	聚光灯	9405. 4020	5
Spray guns and similar appliances	喷枪及类似器具	8424. 2000	7
Spraying lorries	喷洒车	8705. 9090	7
Spraying mechanical appliances parts, nes	喷雾喷射机械器具零件,其他	8424. 9090	
Spraying mechanical appliances parts, of the household type	喷雾喷射机械器具零件,家用型	8424. 9020	
Spraying mechanical appliances, agricultural or horticultural	喷雾喷射机械器具,农业或园艺用	8424. 8100	7
Spraying mechanical appliances, nes	喷雾喷射机械器具,其他	8424. 8999	7
Spraying mechanical appliances, of the household type	喷雾喷射机械器具,家用型	8424. 8910	7
Spreading machines for stabilizer	摊铺机,稳定土用	8479. 1022	7
Spreading machines, for spreading bituminous concrete	摊铺机,沥青混凝土用	8479. 1021	7
Spreading machines, nes	摊铺机,其他	8479. 1029	7
Spring balances, having a maximum weighing capacity not exceeding 30kg	弹簧秤,最大称量不超过 30 千克	8423. 8120	
Spring guns	弹簧枪	9304. 0000	
Spring washers, of iron or steel	弹簧垫圈,钢铁制的	7318. 2100	268
Springs and leaves for springs, of iron or steel, for railway locomotives and rollingstock	弹簧及弹簧片,钢铁制,铁道车辆用	7320. 9010	36
Springs and leaves for springs, of iron or steel, nes	弹簧及弹簧片,钢铁制,其他	7320. 9090	36
Springs of copper	弹簧,铜制	7419. 9920	4
Springs, including hairsprings, of clock or watch	发条,包括游丝,钟、表的	9114. 1000	6
Sprocket wheels, of bicycles and other cycles	链轮,自行车及脚踏车的	8714. 9390	3
Spun from noil	细丝纱线	5005. 0010	356
Spunlaced equipment, for the manufacture of felt or non-wovens	水刺设备,毡呢或无纺织物制造用	8449. 0020	7
Squabs	乳鸽	0106. 3921	3
Squeegees	橡皮扫帚	9603. 9090	3
Squid flour, unfit for human consumption	鱿鱼粉,不适合食用	2301. 2090	136
Squid for bait	鱿鱼制作的饵料	0511. 9190	34

S

Article Description	商品名称	Tariff Code	D. R.
Squid meal, fit for human consumption	鱿鱼粉,食用	0307. 9990	14
Squid(Ommastrephes spp. ,Loligo spp. , Nototodarus spp. ,Sepioteuthis spp.),live,fresh or chilled	鱿鱼,其他,活、鲜或冷的	0307. 4190	18
Squid(Ommastrephes spp. ,Loligo spp. ,Nototodarus spp. ,Sepioteuthis spp.),for cultivation	鱿鱼,种苗	0307. 4110	3
Squid(Ommastrephes spp. ,Loligo spp. ,Nototodarus spp. ,Sepioteuthis spp.),frozen,dried,salted or in brine	鱿鱼,其他,冻、干、盐腌或盐渍的	0307. 4900	148
Squid,preserved	鱿鱼,制作的	1605. 9090	48
Stabilizer spreading machines	稳定土摊铺机	8479. 1022	7
Stackers of track alleyway, powered by an electric motor	堆垛机,有轨的,电动的	8427. 1010	7
Stackers of trackless alleyway,powered by an electric motor	堆垛机,无轨的,电动的	8427. 1020	7
Stackers parts	堆垛机的零件	8431. 2000	3
Stainless steel ingots and other primary forms	不锈钢,锭状及其他初级形状	7218. 1000	468
Stainless steel of rectangular (other than square) crosssection	不锈钢,矩形(正方形除外)截面的	7218. 9100	468
Stainless steel semi-finished products,nes	不锈钢半制成品,其他	7218. 9900	468
Stainless steel wire	不锈钢丝	7223. 0000	468
Stamping foils	压印箔	3212. 1000	136
Stamps for printing or embossing, designed for operating in the hand,nes	印戳,手用,其他	9611. 0000	
Stamp-impressed paper	印有邮票或印花税票的纸品	4907. 0090	5
Stamp-post-marks	邮戳盖销印	9704. 0090	5
Stapler	订书机,装订用	8472. 9022	
Staples and similar articles, of copper or of iron or steel with heads of copper	U 形钉及类似品,铜制或钢铁制带铜头的	7415. 1000	56
Staples in strips	订书钉,成条的	8305. 2000	256
Staples of aluminium	U 形钉,铝制	7616. 1000	36
Staples,of iron or steel	U 形钉,钢铁制的	7317. 0000	36
Stapling machines,nes	装订用机器,其他	8472. 9029	
Starch of manioc (cassava)	淀粉,木薯的	1108. 1400	
Starch of potato	淀粉,马铃薯的	1108. 1300	
Starch of wheat	小麦的	1108. 1100	
Starch,of maize(corn)	淀粉,玉米的	1108. 1200	
Starche glues	淀粉胶	3505. 2000	36
Starches,esterified	淀粉,酯化的	3505. 1000	36
Starches,modified,nes	改性淀粉,其他	3505. 1000	36
Starches,nes	淀粉,其他	1108. 1900	
Starches,pregelatinized	淀粉,预凝化的	3505. 1000	36

S

Article Description	商品名称	Tariff Code	D. R.
Starter motors for engines of an output of 132.39kW (180hp) or more, for electrical ignition or starting equipment	发动机用启动电机,输出功率在132.39千瓦(180马力)及以上的,点燃式或压燃式内燃发动机用的	8511.4091	7
Starter motors, for electrical ignition or starting equipment, nes	起动电机,点燃式或压燃式内燃发动机用的,其他	8511.4099	7
Starter motors, for locomotives, aircraft or ships, for electrical ignition or starting equipment	起动电机,机车、航空器及船舶用,点燃式或压燃式内燃发动机用的	8511.4010	7
Static converters parts	静止式变流器零件	8504.9090	3
Static converters, nes	静止式变流器,其他	8504.4099	
Station wagons (with 9 seats or less), of a cylinder capacity exceeding 1500cc but not exceeding 2000cc, with spark-ignition internal combustion reciprocating piston	小客车,9座及以下的,气缸容量(排气量)超过1500毫升,但不超过2000毫升,装有点燃往复式活塞内燃发动机的	8703.2343	58
Station wagons (with 9 seats or less), of a cylinder capacity exceeding 2000cc but not exceeding 2500cc, with spark-ignition internal combustion reciprocating piston	小客车,9座及以下的,气缸容量(排气量)超过2000毫升,但不超过2500毫升,装有点燃往复式活塞内燃发动机的	8703.2353	58
Station wagons (with 9 seats or less), of a cylinder capacity exceeding 2500cc but not exceeding 3000cc, with spark-ignition internal combustion reciprocating piston	小客车,9座及以下的,气缸容量(排气量)超过2500毫升,但不超过3000毫升,装有点燃往复式活塞内燃发动机的	8703.2363	58
Station wagons (with 9 seats or less), of a cylinder capacity exceeding 3000cc, but not exceeding 4000cc, with spark-ignition internal combustion reciprocating piston	小客车,9座及以下的,气缸容量(排气量)超过3000毫升,但不超过4000毫升,装有点燃往复式活塞内燃发动机的	8703.2413	58
Station wagons (with 9 seats or less), of a cylinder capacity exceeding 4000cc, with spark-ignition internal combustion reciprocating piston	小客车,9座及以下的,气缸容量(排气量)超过4000毫升,装有点燃往复式活塞内燃发动机的	8703.2423	58
Station wagons (with 9 seats or less), of a cylinder capacity exceeding 1000cc but not exceeding 1500cc, with compression-ignition internal combustion piston engine	小客车,9座及以下的,气缸容量(排气量)超过1000毫升,但不超过1500毫升,装有压燃式活塞内燃发动机的	8703.3123	58
Station wagons (with 9 seats or less), of a cylinder capacity exceeding 1000cc but not exceeding 1500cc, with spark-ignition internal combustion reciprocating piston	小客车,9座及以下的,气缸容量(排气量)超过1000毫升,但不超过1500毫升,装有点燃往复式活塞内燃发动机的	8703.2250	58
Station wagons (with 9 seats or less), of a cylinder capacity exceeding 1500cc but not exceeding 2000cc, with compression-ignition internal combustion piston engine	小客车,9座及以下的,气缸容量(排气量)超过1500毫升,但不超过2000毫升,装有压燃式活塞内燃发动机的	8703.3213	58
Station wagons (with 9 seats or less), of a cylinder capacity exceeding 2000cc but not exceeding 2500cc, with compression-ignition internal combustion piston engine	小客车,9座及以下的,气缸容量(排气量)超过2000毫升,但不超过2500毫升,装有压燃式活塞内燃发动机的	8703.3223	58

Article Description	商品名称	Tariff Code	D. R.
Station wagons (with 9 seats or less), of a cylinder capacity exceeding 2500cc, but not exceeding 3000cc, with compression-ignition internal combustion piston engine	小客车,9座及以下的,气缸容量(排气量)超过2500毫升,但不超过3000毫升,装有压燃式活塞内燃发动机的	8703.3313	58
Station wagons (with 9 seats or less), of a cylinder capacity exceeding 3000cc, but not exceeding 4000cc, with compression-ignition internal combustion piston engine	小客车,9座及以下的,气缸容量(排气量)超过3000毫升,但不超过4000毫升,装有压燃式活塞内燃发动机的	8703.3323	58
Station wagons (with 9 seats or less), of a cylinder capacity exceeding 4000cc, with compression-ignition internal combustion piston engine	小客车,9座及以下的,气缸容量(排气量)超过4000毫升,装有压燃式活塞内燃发动机的	8703.3363	58
Station wagons (with 9 seats or less), of a cylinder capacity not exceeding 1000cc, with spark-ignition internal combustion reciprocating piston engine	小客车,9座及以下的,气缸容量(排气量)不超过1000毫升,装有点燃往复式活塞内燃发动机的	8703.2150	58
Statuettes and ornaments, of wood, nes	雕像及装饰品,木制,其他	4420.1090	56
Statuettes and other ornamental articles, of plastics	小雕塑品及其他装饰品,塑料的	3926.4000	236
Statuettes and other ornaments of base metal, cloisonne	雕塑像及其他装饰品,贱金属制,景泰蓝的	8306.2910	256
Statuettes and other ornaments of base metal, nes	雕塑像及其他装饰品,贱金属制,其他	8306.2990	256
Statuettes and other ornaments of base metal, plated with precious metal	雕塑像及其他装饰品,贱金属制,镀贵金属的	8306.2100	256
Statuettes and other ornaments of lampworked glass, other than imitation jewellery	玻璃塑像,灯工方法制作的,以及其他玻璃装饰品,但仿首饰除外	7018.9000	3458
Stavudine and their salts	司他夫定及它们的盐	2938.9010	34
Steam blasting machines and similar jet projecting machines	喷汽机及类似的喷射机器	8424.3000	7
Steam espresso makers, electro-thermic	蒸馏渗滤式咖啡机,电热的	8516.7120	7
Steam or other vapour generating boilers parts	蒸汽锅炉零件	8402.9000	27
Steam or other vapour generating boilers, including hybrid boilers, nes	蒸汽锅炉,包括混合式锅炉,其他	8402.1900	27
Steam or other vapour generating watertube boilers auxiliary plant	蒸汽锅炉的辅助设备	8404.1010	3
Steam or other vapour generating watertube boilers auxiliary plant parts	蒸汽锅炉的辅助设备的零件	8404.9090	3
Steam or other vapour generating watertube boilers, with a steam production 900t or more per hour, for generating electricity	蒸汽锅炉,蒸发量在900吨/时及以上的发电用水管锅炉	8402.1110	27
Steam or other vapour generating watertube boilers, with a steam production exceeding 45t per hour, nes	蒸汽锅炉,蒸发量超过45吨/时的水管锅炉,其他	8402.1190	27
Steam or other vapour generating watertube boilers, with a steam production not exceeding 45t per hour	蒸汽锅炉,蒸发量不超过45吨/时的水管锅炉	8402.1200	27
Steam or vapour turbines for marine propulsion	汽轮机,船舶动力用	8406.1000	3

S

Article Description	商品名称	Tariff Code	D. R.
Steam or vapour turbines parts	汽轮机零件	8406. 9000	3
Steam or vapour turbines, of an output exceeding 100 MW but not exceeding 350 MW	汽轮机,输出功率超过 100 兆瓦,但不超过 350 兆瓦的	8406. 8120	3
Steam or vapour turbines, of an output exceeding 350 MW	汽轮机,输出功率超过 350 兆瓦的	8406. 8130	3
Steam or vapour turbines, of an output exceeding 40 MW but not exceeding 100MW	汽轮机,输出功率超过 40 兆瓦,但不超过 100 兆瓦的	8406. 8110	3
Steam or vapour turbines, of an output not exceeding 40 MW	汽轮机,输出功率不超过 40 兆瓦的	8406. 8200	3
Stearic acid	硬脂酸	2915. 7010	36
Stearic acid salts and esters	硬脂酸盐和酯	2915. 7090	36
Stearic acid, industrial use	硬脂酸,工业用	3823. 1100	6
Steel making electric furnaces parts	炼钢电炉用零件	8514. 9010	3
Steering and rudder equipment for ships	舵机,船舶用	8479. 8910	7
Steering and rudder equipment parts, for ships	舵机零件,船舶用	8479. 9010	3
Steering wheels, steering columns, steering boxes and parts of cross-country cars(4WD)	转向盘、转向柱、转向器及其零件,越野车(4 轮驱动)用	8708. 9450	3
Steering wheels, steering columns, steering boxes and parts of dumpers	转向盘、转向柱、转向器及其零件,自卸车用	8708. 9430	3
Steering wheels, steering columns, steering boxes and parts of motor vehicles with 30 seats or more	转向盘、转向柱、转向器及其零件,30 座及以上客运机动车辆用	8708. 9420	3
Steering wheels, steering columns, steering boxes and parts of motor vehicles with special purpose	转向盘、转向柱、转向器及其零件,特种车辆用	8708. 9460	3
Steering wheels, steering columns, steering boxes and parts of saloon cars	转向盘、转向柱、转向器及其零件,小轿车用	8708. 9440	3
Steering wheels, steering columns, steering boxes and parts of tractors	转向盘、转向柱、转向器及其零件,拖拉机的	8708. 9410	3
Steering wheels, steering columns, steering boxes and parts, nes	转向盘、转向柱、转向器及其零件,其他	8708. 9490	3
Stemware drinking glasses, other than of glass-ceramics, nes	高脚杯,但玻璃陶瓷制的除外,其他	7013. 2800	356
Stemware drinking glasses, other than of glass-ceramics, of lead crystal	高脚杯,但玻璃陶瓷制的除外,铅晶质玻璃制	7013. 2200	356
Stencil correctors and the like	蜡纸改正液及类似品	3824. 9020	36
Stencil duplicating machines	油印机	8472. 1000	
Step and repeat alignersw parts and accessories, semiconductor devices or of electronic integrated circuits or flat panel displays manufacture machines and apparatus	步进光刻机零件及附件,制造半导体器件、集成电路、平板显示器的机器及装置	8486. 9090	3
Step and repeat alignersw parts and accessories, semiconductor devices or of electronic integrated circuits or flat panel displays manufacture machines and apparatus	分步重复光刻机(步进光刻机)零件及附件,制造半导体器件、集成电路、平板显示器的机器及装置	8486. 9090	3

S

Article Description	商品名称	Tariff Code	D. R.
Step and repeat alignersw, flat panel displays manufacture machines and apparatus	分步重复光刻机,平板显示器的制造机器及装置	8486. 3031	7
Step and repeat alignersw, semiconductor devices or of electronic integrated circuits manufacture machines and apparatus	步进光刻机,制造半导体器件或集成电路的机器及装置	8486. 2031	7
Step and repeat alignersw, semiconductor devices or of electronic integrated circuits manufacture machines and apparatus	分步重复光刻机(步进光刻机),制造半导体器件或集成电路的机器及装置	8486. 2031	7
Stephanite	脆银矿	2616. 1000	146
Stereoscopic microscopes, optical	立体显微镜,光学的	9011. 1000	
Sterilizers, with a process involving a change of temperature, for medical, surgical or laboratory use	消毒器具,利用温度变化处理,医用或实验室用	8419. 2000	57
Steroidal hormones, their derivatives and structural analogues, nes	甾族激素及其衍生物和结构类似物,其他	2937. 2900	36
Sterol	固醇	2906. 1310	36
Stethoscopes	听诊器	9018. 9010	
Stibnite	辉锑矿	2617. 1090	146
Stigma croci corms, dormant	番红花球茎,休眠的	0601. 1010	135
Still image video cameras parts, camera modules without special purposes	静像视频摄像机用零件,非特种用途的取像模块	8529. 9042	3
Still image video cameras parts, nes	静像视频摄像机用零件,其他	8529. 9049	3
Still image video cameras parts, of special purposes	静像视频摄像机用零件,特种用途的	8529. 9041	3
Stitch machinery, for the manufacture of felt or non-wovens	针刺机,毡呢或无纺织物制造用	8449. 0010	7
Stitches forming articles for knitting machines	成圈机件,针织机的	8448. 5190	3
Stitch-bonded fibre fabrics	纤维缝编织物	5602. 1000	46
Stitch-bonding machines	缝编机	8447. 2030	7
Stitch-bonding machines auxiliary	缝编机的辅助机器	8448. 1900	3
Stock, share or bond certificates and similar documents of title	股票、债券及类似所有权凭证	4907. 0030	5
Stocking, socks and socketes, not knitted or crocheted	袜子及袜套,非针织或钩编的	6217. 1010	2456
Stockings, socks and other hosiery, knitted or crocheted, of cotton	丝袜、短袜及其他袜类,针织或钩编的,棉制	6115. 9500	2456
Stockings, socks and other hosiery, knitted or crocheted, of cotton	袜,丝袜、短袜及其他袜类,针织或钩编的,棉制	6115. 9500	2456
Stockings, socks and other hosiery, knitted or crocheted, of other textile materials	丝袜、短袜及其他袜类,针织或钩编的,其他纺织材料制	6115. 9900	2456
Stockings, socks and other hosiery, knitted or crocheted, of other textile materials	袜,丝袜、短袜及其他袜类,针织或钩编的,其他纺织材料制	6115. 9900	2456
Stockings, socks and other hosiery, knitted or crocheted, of synthetic fibres	丝袜、短袜及其他袜类,针织或钩编的,合成纤维制	6115. 9600	2456
Stockings, socks and other hosiery, knitted or crocheted, of synthetic fibres	袜,丝袜、短袜及其他袜类,针织或钩编的,合成纤维制	6115. 9600	2456

Article Description	商品名称	Tariff Code	D. R.
Stockings, socks and other hosiery, knitted or crocheted, of wool or fine animal hair	丝袜、短袜及其他袜类,针织或钩编的,羊毛或动物细毛制	6115.9400	2456
Stockings, socks and other hosiery, knitted or crocheted, of wool or fine animal hair	袜,丝袜、短袜及其他袜类,针织或钩编的,羊毛或动物细毛制	6115.9400	2456
Stomachs of animals (other than fish)	胃,动物的(鱼除外)	0504.0029	14
Stone or of other mineral articles, containing magnesite, dolomite or chromite	石制品及矿物制品含有,菱镁矿、白云石或铬铁矿的	6815.9100	6
Stone or of other mineral articles, nes	石制品及矿物制品,其他	6815.9990	6
Stones and kernels, apricot, peach (including nectarine) or plum, nes	核及核仁,杏、桃(包括油桃)、梅或李的,其他	1212.9919	134
Stoppers of natural corks	塞子,天然软木制	4503.1000	568
Stoppers, of base metal	塞子,贱金属制	8309.9000	256
Stoppers, lids and other similiar closures, of glass	塞子、盖及类似的封口器,玻璃制	7010.2000	8
Stoppers, lids, caps and other similiar closures, of plastics	塞子、盖子及类似品,塑料的	3923.5000	23
Stop-watches, electrically operated, nes	秒表,电力驱动的,其他	9102.9100	56
Stop-watches, electrically operated, with case of precious metal or of metal clad with precious metal	秒表,电力驱动的,表壳用贵金属或包贵金属制成的	9101.9100	56
Stop-watches, nes	秒表,其他	9102.9900	56
Stop-watches, with case of precious metal or of metal clad with precious metal, nes	秒表,表壳用贵金属或包贵金属制成的,其他	9101.9900	56
Storage boxes and similar articles, of a kind used in offices, shops or the like, of paper, paperboard,	存储盒及类似品,办公室、商店及类似场所使用的,纸制的	4819.6000	68
Storage heating radiators, electric	电散热器,储存式	8516.2100	7
Straight saw blades, for sawing machines	锯片,直的,机械锯用	8202.9110	256
Straight saw blades, for sawing machines	直锯片,机械锯用	8202.9110	256
Straightening machines, for working metal, nes	矫直或矫平机,加工金属用,其他	8462.2910	7
Straightening or flattening machines, numerically controlled, for working metal	矫直或矫平机,数控的,加工金属用	8462.2110	7
Straining cloth of a kind used in oil presses or the like, including that of human hair	滤布,用于榨油机器或类似机器的,包括人发制滤布	5911.4000	
Stranded wire, cables plaited bands and the like, of copper, not electrically insulated	绞股线、缆、编带及类似品,非绝缘的铜丝	7413.0000	6
Stranded wire, cables, plaited bands and the like, of aluminium, not electrically insulated, nes	绞股线、缆、编带及类似品,铝制,非绝缘的,其他	7614.9000	6
Stranded wire, cables, plaited bands and the like, of aluminium, not electrically insulated, with steel core	绞股线、缆、编带及类似品,铝制,非绝缘的,带钢芯的	7614.1000	6
Stranded wire, ropes and cables, of iron or steel, not electrically insulated	绞股线、绳、缆,非绝缘钢铁的	7312.1000	36
Straw or fodder balers parts	草料打包机零件	8433.9090	
Straw or fodder balers, including pickup balers	草料打包机,包括收集打包机	8433.4000	
Strawberries, fresh	草莓,鲜的	0810.1000	1

S

Article Description	商品名称	Tariff Code	D. R.
Strawberries, frozen	草莓,冷冻的	0811. 1000	1
Strawberries, otherwise prepared or preserved	草莓,用其他方法制作或保藏的	2008. 8000	248
Streptomycins and their derivatives; salts thereof	链霉素及其衍生物以及它们的盐	2941. 2000	
String musical instruments, keyboard, nes	弦乐器,键盘的,其他	9201. 9000	5
String musical instruments, nes	弦乐器,其他	9202. 9000	5
String musical instruments, played with a bow	弦乐器,用弓演奏的	9202. 1000	5
Strings for musical instruments	弦,乐器用的	9209. 3000	
Strip and the like of artificial textile materials of an apparent width not exceeding 5mm	扁条及类似品,表观宽度不超过5毫米,人造纤维纺织材料制	5405. 0000	568
Strip and the like of synthetic textile materials of an apparent width not exceeding 5mm	扁条及类似品,表观宽度不超过5毫米,合成纤维纺织材料制	5404. 9000	568
Strip or the like woven fabrics	扁条及类似品的机织物	5407. 2000	2468
Stripping apparatus, flat panel displays manufacture machines and apparatus, nes	剥离装置,平板显示器的制造机器及装置,其他	8486. 3049	7
Stripping towers	提净塔,蒸馏或精馏设备	8419. 4010	57
Stroboscopes	频闪观测仪	9029. 2090	7
Stroboscopes parts and accessories	频闪观测仪零件、附件	9029. 9000	3
Strong boxes doors, of base metal	保险库的门,贱金属制	8303. 0000	256
Strong boxes, armoured or reinforced, of base metal	保险柜,装甲或加强的,贱金属制	8303. 0000	256
Strontium carbonate	锶的碳酸盐	2836. 9200	
Strontium oxides, hydroxides and peroxides	锶的氧化物、氢氧化物及过氧化物	2816. 4000	
Structures and parts of structures, of iron or steel, nes	结构体及其部件,钢铁的,其他	7308. 9000	6
Strychnine and its salts	番木鳖碱及其盐	2939. 9920	34
Strychnine and its salts	士的年及其盐	2939. 9920	34
Studs, imitation jewellery, of base metal, whether or not plated with precious metal	饰扣,仿首饰,贱金属制,不论是否镀贵金属	7117. 1100	46
Stud-link, of iron or steel	日字环节链,钢铁的	7315. 8100	36
Stylus printers, of a kind solely used for automatic data processing machine	针式打印机,专用于自动数据处理设备的	8443. 3211	57
Styrene	苯乙烯	2902. 5000	6
Styrene polymers, in primary forms, nes	苯乙烯聚合物,初级形状的,其他	3903. 9000	1256
Styrene-acrylonitrile (SAN) copolymers, in primary forms	苯乙烯-丙烯腈(SAN)共聚物,初级形状的	3903. 2000	1256
Submersible drilling or production platforms	潜水式钻探或生产平台	8905. 2000	
Substitutes for vinegar, obtained from acetic acid	醋代用品,用醋酸制得的	2209. 0000	268
Succinimide	琥珀酰亚胺	2925. 1900	36
Sucking pig	乳猪	0203. 2110	14
Sucking pig, fresh or chilled, carcasses and half-carcasses	乳猪,鲜或冷的,整头及半头	0203. 1110	14
Sucrose, chemically pure	糖,蔗糖,化学纯	1701. 9910	
Sufentanil(INN); salts thereof	舒芬太尼(INN)及盐	2934. 9100	36

S

Article Description	商品名称	Tariff Code	D. R.
Sugar acetals, and their salts, other than products of heading No. 29. 37, 29. 38 or 29. 39	糖缩醛及其盐,但不包括税号 29. 37、29. 38 及 29. 39 的产品	2940. 0000	6
Sugar apple, fresh	番荔枝,鲜的	0810. 9050	1
Sugar beet	甜菜	1212. 9100	14
Sugar beet seed	糖甜菜子,饲料植物用的	1209. 1000	358
Sugar cane	甘蔗	1212. 9995	134
Sugar confectionery, nes, not containing cocoa	糖食,不含可可的,其他	1704. 9000	258
Sugar esters, and their salts, other than products of heading No. 29. 37, 29. 38 or 29. 39	糖酯及其盐,但不包括税号 29. 37、29. 38 及 29. 39 的产品	2940. 0000	6
Sugar ethers, and their salts, other than products of heading No. 29. 37, 29. 38 or 29. 39	糖醚及其盐,但不包括税号 29. 37、29. 38 及 29. 39 的产品	2940. 0000	6
Sugar manufacture machinery	制糖机器	8438. 3000	
Sugar manufacture machinery parts	制糖机器的零件	8438. 9000	3
Sugar tongs, other than plated with precious metal	糖块夹,非镀贵金属的	8215. 9900	256
Sugar tongs, plated with precious metal	糖块夹,镀贵金属的	8215. 9100	256
Sugar, beet sugar, raw	糖,甜菜原糖	1701. 1200	46
Sugar, cane sugar, raw	糖,甘蔗原糖	1701. 1100	46
Sugar, containing added flavouring or colouring matter	糖,加有香料或着色剂	1701. 9100	4
Sugar, granulated	糖,砂糖	1701. 9910	
Sugar, nes	糖,其他	1701. 9910	
Sugar, superfine	糖,绵白糖	1701. 9920	
Sugars, chemically pure, other than sucrose, lactose, maltose, glucose and fructose	化学纯糖,但蔗糖、乳糖、麦芽糖、葡萄糖及果糖除外	2940. 0000	6
Suits, not knitted or crocheted, for men or boys, nes	西服套装,非针织或钩编的,男式,其他	6203. 1990	2456
Suits, not knitted or crocheted, for men or boys, of silk or silk waste	西服套装,非针织或钩编的,男式,丝及绢丝制	6203. 1910	2456
Suits, not knitted or crocheted, for men or boys, of synthetic fibres	西服套装,非针织或钩编的,男式,合成纤维制	6203. 1200	2456
Suits, not knitted or crocheted, for men or boys, of wool or fine animal hair	西服套装,非针织或钩编的,男式,羊毛或动物细毛制	6203. 1100	2456
Suits, knitted or crocheted, for men or boys, of other textile materials	西服套装,针织或钩编的,男式,其他纺织材料制	6103. 1090	2456
Suits, knitted or crocheted, for men or boys, of synthetic fibres	西服套装,针织或钩编的,男式,合成纤维制	6103. 1020	2456
Suits, knitted or crocheted, for men or boys, of wool or fine animal hair	西服套装,针织或钩编的,男式,羊毛或动物细毛制	6103. 1010	2456
Suits, knitted or crocheted, for women or girls, nes	西服套装,针织或钩编的,女式,其他	6104. 1990	2456
Suits, knitted or crocheted, for women or girls, of cotton	西服套装,针织或钩编的,女式,棉制	6104. 1920	2456
Suits, knitted or crocheted, for women or girls, of synthetic fibres	西服套装,针织或钩编的,女式,合成纤维制	6104. 1300	2456

Article Description	商品名称	Tariff Code	D. R.
Suits, knitted or crocheted, for women or girls, of wool or fine animal hair	西服套装,针织或钩编的,女式,羊毛或动物细毛制	6104. 1910	2456
Suits, not knitted or crocheted, for women or girls, nes	西服套装,非针织或钩编的,女式,其他	6204. 1990	2456
Suits, not knitted or crocheted, for women or girls, of cotton	西服套装,非针织或钩编的,女式,棉制	6204. 1200	2456
Suits, not knitted or crocheted, for women or girls, of silk or silk waste	西服套装,非针织或钩编的,女式,丝及绢丝制	6204. 1910	2456
Suits, not knitted or crocheted, for women or girls, of synthetic fibres	西服套装,非针织或钩编的,女式,合成纤维制	6204. 1300	2456
Suits, not knitted or crocheted, for women or girls, of wool or fine animal hair	西服套装,非针织或钩编的,女式,羊毛或动物细毛制	6204. 1100	2456
Suit-cases, with outer surface of leather, of composition leather or of patent leather	提箱,以皮革、再生皮革或漆皮作面	4202. 1190	1458
Suit-cases, with outer surface of plastics or of textile materials	提箱,以塑料或纺织材料作面	4202. 1290	256
Sulfa drugs medicaments, consisting of two or more constituents which have been mixed together, not put up in measured doses or in forms or packings for retail sale	磺胺类药品,两种或两种以上成分混合而成的,未配定剂量或制成零售包装	3003. 9010	368
Sulfa drugs medicaments, mixed or unmixed, put up in measured doses or in forms or packings for retail sale	磺胺类药品,混合或未混合的,配定剂量或制成零售包装	3004. 9010	368
Sulfadimidine	磺胺双甲基嘧啶	2935. 0020	36
Sulfamethoxazole	磺胺甲口恶唑	2935. 0030	36
Sulfobenzylpenicillin	磺苄青霉素	2941. 1095	
Sulfur dichloride	二氯化硫	2812. 1042	
Sulfur monochloride	一氯化硫(氯化硫)	2812. 1041	
Sulphadiazine	磺胺嘧啶	2935. 0010	36
Sulphate turpentine oils	硫酸盐松节油	3805. 1000	36
Sulphates, nes, inorganic	硫酸盐,其他,无机的	2833. 2990	
Sulphides of non-metals, nes	非金属硫化物,其他	2813. 9000	
Sulphides, nes, whether or not chemically defined	硫化物,其他,无论是否已有化学定义	2830. 9090	
Sulphite turpentine and other crude paracymene	亚硫酸盐松节油及其他粗制对异丙基苯甲烷;	3805. 9090	36
Sulphites, nes, inorganic	亚硫酸盐,其他,无机的	2832. 2000	
Sulphonamides, nes	磺(酰)胺,其他	2935. 0090	36
Sulphonated, nitrated or nitrosated derivatives of hydrocarbons, whether or not halogenated, nes	烃的磺化、硝化或亚硝化衍生物,不论是否卤化,其他	2904. 9090	36
Sulphonitric acids	磺硝酸	2808. 0000	6
Sulphoxide chloride	氯化亚砜	2812. 1010	
Sulphoxylates, nes, inorganic	次硫酸盐,其他,无机的	2831. 9000	

S

Article Description	商品名称	Tariff Code	D. R.
Sulphur black and preparations based thereon	硫化黑(硫化青)及以其为基本成分的制品	3204. 1911	345
Sulphur of all kinds, other than sublimed sulphur, precipitated sulphur and colloidal sulphur	硫磺,但升华硫磺、沉淀硫磺及胶态硫磺除外	2503. 0000	1468
Sulphur, sublimed	升华硫磺	2802. 0000	
Sulphur, of colloidal	硫磺,胶态的	2802. 0000	
Sulphur, precipitated	沉淀硫磺	2802. 0000	
Sulphur, precipitated	硫磺,沉淀的	2802. 0000	
Sulphur, sublimed	硫磺,升华的	2802. 0000	
Sulphuric acid	硫酸	2807. 0000	346
Sultams	磺内酰胺	2934. 9910	36
Sultones	磺内酯	2934. 9910	36
Sun tan preparations	晒黑油	3304. 9900	23
Sunblinds, nes	遮阳篷,其他	6306. 1990	346
Sunblinds, of bast fibres	遮阳篷,麻制	6306. 1910	346
Sunblinds, of cotton	遮阳篷,棉制	6306. 1920	346
Sunblinds, of synthetic fibres	遮阳篷,合成纤维制	6306. 1200	346
Sunflower seed, nes	葵花籽,其他	1206. 0090	3
Sunflower seed, seedlings	葵花籽,种用	1206. 0010	3
Sunflowerseed oil and fractions thereof, crude oil	葵花油及其分离品,初榨的	1512. 1100	4
Sunflowerseed or safflower oil and fractions thereof, nes	葵花油及其分离品,其他	1512. 1900	4
Sunglasses	太阳镜	9004. 1000	
Sunglasses spectacle lenses, of glass	太阳镜片,玻璃制	9001. 4091	
Sunglasses spectacle lenses, of other materials	太阳镜片,其他材料制	9001. 5091	
Sungmo, frozen	松茸,冷冻的	0710. 8010	1
Sungmo, fresh or chilled	松茸,鲜或冷藏的	0709. 5910	1
Sungmo, in brine, provisionally preserved, but unsuitable in that state for immediate consumption	松茸,盐水的,暂时保藏,但不适合直接使用的	0711. 5911	34
Sunroofs, electric	天窗,电动的	8708. 2941	3
Sunroofs, hand-operated	天窗,手动的	8708. 2942	3
Sunscreen preparations	防晒油	3304. 9900	23
Superchargers for engines	增压器,发动机用	8414. 8030	23
Supercomputer	巨型机(计算机)	8471. 4110	26
Supercomputer, mainframes, mid-sized computer machine, mini-computers and their processing units's parts and accessories	巨型机、大型机、中型机及小型机及其处理部件的零件、附件	8473. 3010	3
Supercomputer, presented in the form of systems	巨型机(计算机),以系统形式进口或出口的	8471. 4910	26
Supercomputer, processing units	巨型机处理部件	8471. 5010	26
Superphosphates, nes	过磷酸钙,其他	3103. 1090	68
Supersulphate cement	富硫酸盐水泥	2523. 9000	3

S

Article Description	商品名称	Tariff Code	D. R.
Super-heated water boilers	过热水锅炉	8402. 2000	27
Super-heated water boilers auxiliary plant	过热水锅炉的辅助设备	8404. 1010	3
Super-heated water boilers auxiliary plant parts	过热水锅炉的辅助设备的零件	8404. 9090	3
Super-heated water boilers parts	过热水锅炉零件	8402. 9000	27
Super-heaters, auxiliary plant for use with boilers	过热器,过热水锅炉的辅助设备	8404. 1010	3
Super-heaters, auxiliary plant for use with central heating boilers	过热器,集中供暖用的热水锅炉的辅助设备	8404. 1020	3
Super-heaters, auxiliary plant for use with steam or other vapour generating watertube boilers	过热器,蒸汽锅炉的辅助设备	8404. 1010	3
Supported catalysts, nes	载体催化剂,其他	3815. 1900	36
Supported catalysts, with nickel or nickel compounds as the active substance	载体催化剂,以镍及其化合物为活性物的	3815. 1100	36
Supported catalysts, with precious metal or precious metal compounds as the active substance	载体催化剂,以贵金属及其化合物为活性物的	3815. 1200	36
Surface tempering machines and appliances, gas-operated	表面回火机器及装置,气体推动的	8468. 2000	57
Surf-boards	冲浪板	9506. 2900	5
Surge suppressors, for a voltage exceeding 1000V	电涌抑制器,用于电压超过 1000 伏的线路	8535. 4000	8
Surgical instruments and appliances, nes	外科用仪器及器具,其他	9018. 9090	7
Surveying instruments and appliances for photogrammetrical	测量仪器及装置,摄影用	9015. 4000	
Surveying instruments and appliances parts and accessories	测量仪器及装置的零件、附件	9015. 9000	3
Surveying instruments and appliances, hydrological, nes	测量仪器及装置,水文的,其他	9015. 8000	7
Surveying instruments and appliances, meteorological, nes	测量仪器及装置,气象的,其他	9015. 8000	7
Surveying instruments and appliances, nes	测量仪器及装置,其他	9015. 8000	7
Surveying instruments and appliances, oceanographic, nes	测量仪器及装置,海洋的,其他	9015. 8000	7
Suspenders, of man-made fibres	吊袜带,化学纤维制	6212. 9010	2456
Suspenders, of other textile materials	吊袜带,其他纺织材料制	6212. 9090	2456
Suspension systems and parts thereof (including shock-absorbers), nes	悬挂系统及其零件(包括减震器),其他	8708. 8090	3
Suture materials, sterile	缝合材料,无菌	3006. 1000	3
Swedes, forage products	芜菁甘蓝,饲料用	1214. 9000	
Sweet apricot kernels	甜杏仁	1212. 9912	134
Sweet biscuits	甜饼干	1905. 3100	28
Sweet corn (Zea mays var. Saccharata), prepared or preserved otherwise than by vinegar or acetic acid, not frozen	甜玉米,用醋或醋酸以外的其他方法制作或保藏的,未冷冻	2005. 8000	148

S

Article Description	商品名称	Tariff Code	D. R.
Sweet corn, frozen	甜玉米,冷冻的	0710. 4000	1
Sweet potatoes, chilled or frozen	甘薯,冷或冻的	0714. 2030	34
Sweet potatoes, dried	甘薯,干的	0714. 2020	34
Sweet potatoes, for cultivation, fresh	甘薯,种用,鲜的	0714. 2011	34
Sweet potatoes, nes, fresh	甘薯,其他,鲜的	0714. 2019	34
Sweetmeats	蜜饯	1704. 9000	258
Sweetsops, in airtight containers	番荔枝,罐头	2008. 9990	248
Swimming crab, frozen	梭子蟹,冻的	0306. 1410	1
Swimming crab, not frozen	梭子蟹,未冻的	0306. 2492	14
Swimming pools	游泳池	9506. 9900	5
Swimwear, not knitted or crocheted, for men or boys	游泳服,非针织或钩编的,男式	6211. 1100	2456
Swimwear, not knitted or crocheted, for women or girls	游泳服,非针织或钩编的,女式	6211. 1200	2456
Swimwear, knitted or crocheted, for men or boys, of other textile materials	游泳服,针织或钩编的,男式,其他纺织材料制	6112. 3900	2456
Swimwear, knitted or crocheted, for men or boys, of synthetic fibres	游泳服,针织或钩编的,男式,合成纤维制	6112. 3100	2456
Swimwear, knitted or crocheted, for women or girls, of other textile materials	游泳服,针织或钩编的,女式,其他纺织材料制	6112. 4900	2456
Swimwear, knitted or crocheted, for women or girls, of synthetic fibres	游泳服,针织或钩编的,女式,合成纤维制	6112. 4100	2456
Swine, live, pure-bred breeding	猪,改良种用	0103. 1000	34
Swine, live, weighing 10kg or more, but less than 50kg	猪,重量在 10 千克及以上,但在 50 千克以下	0103. 9120	48
Swine, live, weighing 50kg or more	猪,重量在 50 千克及以上	0103. 9200	48
Swine, live, weighing less than 10kg	猪,重量在 10 千克以下	0103. 9110	48
Swings	秋千	9508. 9000	5
Switch blades, crossing frogs, point rods and other crossing pieces	道岔尖轨、辙叉、尖轨拉杆及其他叉道段体	7302. 3000	6
Switches and the like, of animal hair or textile materials, nes	假辫子及类似品,动物毛或纺织材料制的,其他	6704. 9000	4
Switches and the like, of human hair	假辫子及类似品,人发制	6704. 2000	4
Switches and the like, of synthetic textile materials, nes	假辫子及类似品,合成纤维纺织材料制,其他	6704. 1900	4
Switches, for a voltage not exceeding 1000V, nes	开关,用于电压不超过 1000 伏的线路,其他	8536. 5000	8
Switching apparatus for public telephonic	交换机,局用电话的	8517. 6211	
Switching apparatus for telegraphic	交换机,电报的	8517. 6211	
Switching apparatus for toll telephonic	交换机,长途电话的	8517. 6211	
Switching apparatus, telegraphic, digital program-controlled, nes	交换机,数字式程控电话用,其他	8517. 6219	
Switching system for mobile communication	交换机,移动通信的	8517. 6212	

S

Article Description	商品名称	Tariff Code	D. R.
Swivel seats with variable height adjustment	转动坐具,可调高度的	9401. 3000	6
Swordfish (Xiphias gladius), fresh or chilled	剑鱼,鲜或冷的	0302. 6700	18
Swordfish (Xiphias gladius), frozen	剑鱼,冻的	0303. 6100	18
Swords and parts	剑及其零件	9307. 0000	
Sygar and sugar syrup, nes	糖及糖浆,其他	1702. 9000	
Sylvite	钾盐	3104. 9010	68
Synthetic cryolite	人造冰晶石	2826. 3000	
Synthetic fibres waste	合成纤维的废料	5505. 1000	68
Synthetic filament tow, nes	合成纤维长丝丝束,其他	5501. 9000	68
Synthetic filament yarn woven fabrics, dyed, nes	合成纤维长丝机织物,染色,其他	5407. 9200	2468
Synthetic filament yarn woven fabrics, of yarns of different colours, nes	合成纤维长丝机织物,色织,其他	5407. 9300	2468
Synthetic filament yarn woven fabrics, printed, nes	合成纤维长丝机织物,印花,其他	5407. 9400	2468
Synthetic filament yarn woven fabrics, unbleached or bleached, nes	合成纤维长丝机织物,未漂白或漂白,其他	5407. 9100	2468
Synthetic filament yarn, put up for retail sale	合成纤维长丝纱线,供零售用	5406. 0010	
Synthetic filaments woven fabrics, containing 85% or more by weight, dyed	合成纤维机织物,按重量计长丝含量在85%及以上,染色	5407. 7200	2468
Synthetic filaments woven fabrics, containing 85% or more by weight, of yarns of different colours	合成纤维机织物,按重量计长丝含量在85%及以上,色织	5407. 7300	2468
Synthetic filaments woven fabrics, containing 85% or more by weight, printed	合成纤维机织物,按重量计长丝含量在85%及以上,印花	5407. 7400	2468
Synthetic filaments woven fabrics, containing 85% or more by weight, unbleached or bleached	合成纤维机织物,按重量计长丝含量在85%及以上,未漂白或漂白	5407. 7100	2468
Synthetic filaments woven fabrics, containing less than 85% by weight, mixed mainly or solely with cotton, dyed	合成纤维机织物,按重量计长丝含量在85%以下,主要或仅与棉混纺,染色	5407. 8200	2468
Synthetic filaments woven fabrics, containing less than 85% by weight, mixed mainly or solely with cotton, of yarns of different colours	合成纤维机织物,按重量计长丝含量在85%以下,主要或仅与棉混纺,色织	5407. 8300	2468
Synthetic filaments woven fabrics, containing less than 85% by weight, mixed mainly or solely with cotton, printed	合成纤维机织物,按重量计长丝含量在85%以下,主要或仅与棉混纺,印花	5407. 8400	2468
Synthetic filaments woven fabrics, containing less than 85% by weight, mixed mainly or solely with cotton, unbleached or bleached	合成纤维机织物,按重量计长丝含量在85%以下,主要或仅与棉混纺,未漂白或漂白	5407. 8100	2468
Synthetic monofilament of 67 decitex or more and of which no cross-sectional dimension exceeding 1mm, nes	合成纤维单丝,截面尺寸不超过1毫米,细度在67分特及以上,其他	5404. 1900	568
Synthetic rubber latex, nes	合成橡胶胶乳,其他	4002. 9100	136
Synthetic rubber (including latex) mixtures with natural rubber (including latex)	合成橡胶(含胶乳)与天然橡胶(含胶乳)的混合物	4002. 8000	136
Synthetic rubber, in primary forms, nes	合成橡胶,初级形状的,其他	4002. 9911	136

S

Article Description	商品名称	Tariff Code	D. R.
Synthetic rubber, nes	合成橡胶,其他	4002. 9919	136
Synthetic staple fibres multiple or cabled yarn, containing 85% or more by weight of acrylic or modacrylic staple fibres	多股纱线或缆线,按重量计聚丙烯腈或变性聚丙烯腈短纤含量在85%及以上	5509. 3200	68
Synthetic staple fibres multiple or cabled yarn, containing 85% or more by weight of polyester staple fibres	合成纤维短纤多股纱线或缆线,按重量计聚酯短纤含量在85%及以上	5509. 2200	68
Synthetic staple fibres multiple or cabled yarn, containing 85% or more by weight of staple fibres of nylon or other polyamides	合成纤维短纤多股纱线或缆线,按重量计尼龙或其他聚酰胺短纤含量在85%及以上	5509. 1200	68
Synthetic staple fibres multiple or cabled yarn, containing 85% or more by weight of synthetic staple fibres, nes	合成纤维短纤多股纱线或缆线,按重量计合成纤维短纤含量在85%及以上,其他	5509. 4200	68
Synthetic staple fibres sewing thread, whether or not put up for retail sale	合成纤维短纤缝纫线,不论是否供零售用	5508. 1000	68
Synthetic staple fibres single yarn, containing 85% or more by weight of acrylic or modacrylic staple fibres	合成纤维短纤单纱,按重量计聚丙烯腈或变性聚丙烯腈短纤含量在85%及以上	5509. 3100	68
Synthetic staple fibres single yarn, containing 85% or more by weight of polyester staple fibres	合成纤维短纤单纱,按重量计聚酯短纤含量在85%及以上	5509. 2100	68
Synthetic staple fibres single yarn, containing 85% or more by weight of staple fibres of nylon or other polyamides	合成纤维短纤单纱,按重量计尼龙或其他聚酰胺短纤含量在85%及以上	5509. 1100	68
Synthetic staple fibres single yarn, containing 85% or more by weight of synthetic staple fibres, nes	合成纤维短纤单纱,按重量计合成纤维短纤含量在85%及以上,其他	5509. 4100	68
Synthetic staple fibres woven fabrics, containing 85% or more by weight of acrylic or modacrylic staple fibres, nes	合成纤维短纤机织物,按重量计聚丙烯腈或变性聚丙烯腈短纤含量在85%及以上,其他	5512. 2900	2468
Synthetic staple fibres woven fabrics, containing 85% or more by weight of acrylic or modacrylic staple fibres, unbleached or bleached	合成纤维短纤机织物,按重量计聚丙烯腈或变性聚丙烯腈短纤含量在85%及以上,未漂白或漂白	5512. 2100	2468
Synthetic staple fibres woven fabrics, containing 85% or more by weight of polyester staple fibres, nes	合成纤维短纤机织物,按重量计聚酯短纤含量在85%及以上,其他	5512. 1900	2468
Synthetic staple fibres woven fabrics, containing 85% or more by weight of polyester staple fibres, unbleached or bleached	合成纤维短纤机织物,按重量计聚酯短纤含量在85%及以上,未漂白或漂白	5512. 1100	2468
Synthetic staple fibres woven fabrics, containing 85% or more by weight of synthetic staple fibres, nes	合成纤维短纤机织物,按重量计合成纤维短纤含量在85%以上,其他	5512. 9900	2468
Synthetic staple fibres woven fabrics, containing less than 85% by weight of such fibres, mixed mainly or solely with cotton, of a weight exceeding 170g/m², dyed, nes	合成纤维短纤机织物,按重量计合成纤维短纤含量在85%以下,主要或仅与棉混纺,每平方米重量超过170克,染色,其他	5514. 2900	2468

Article Description	商品名称	Tariff Code	D. R.
Synthetic staple fibres woven fabrics, containing less than 85% by weight of such fibres, mixed mainly or solely with cotton, of a weight exceeding 170g/m^2, of yarns of different colours, nes	合成纤维短纤机织物,按重量计合成纤维短纤含量在85%以下,主要或仅与棉混纺,每平方米重量超过170克,色织,其他	5514.3090	2468
Synthetic staple fibres woven fabrics, containing less than 85% by weight of such fibres, mixed mainly or solely with cotton, of a weight exceeding 170g/m^2, printed, nes	合成纤维短纤机织物,按重量计合成纤维短纤含量在85%以下,主要或仅与棉混纺,每平方米重量超过170克,印花,其他	5514.4900	2468
Synthetic staple fibres woven fabrics, containing less than 85% by weight of such fibres, mixed mainly or solely with cotton, of a weight exceeding 170g/m^2, unbleached or bleached, nes	合成纤维短纤机织物,按重量计合成纤维短纤含量在85%以下,主要或仅与棉混纺,每平方米重量超过170克,未漂白或漂白,其他	5514.1990	2468
Synthetic staple fibres woven fabrics, containing less than 85% by weight of such fibres, mixed mainly or solely with cotton, of a weight not exceeding 170g/m^2, dyed, nes	合成纤维短纤机织物,按重量计合成纤维短纤含量在85%以下,主要或仅与棉混纺,每平方米重量不超过170克,染色,其他	5513.2900	2468
Synthetic staple fibres woven fabrics, containing less than 85% by weight of such fibres, mixed mainly or solely with cotton, of a weight not exceeding 170g/m^2, of yarns of different colours, nes	合成纤维短纤机织物,按重量计合成纤维短纤含量在85%以下,主要或仅与棉混纺,每平方米重量不超过170克,色织,其他	5513.3990	2468
Synthetic staple fibres woven fabrics, containing less than 85% by weight of such fibres, mixed mainly or solely with cotton, of a weight not exceeding 170g/m^2, printed, nes	合成纤维短纤机织物,按重量计合成纤维短纤含量在85%以下,主要或仅与棉混纺,每平方米重量不超过170克,印花,其他	5513.4990	2468
Synthetic staple fibres woven fabrics, containing less than 85% by weight of such fibres, mixed mainly or solely with cotton, of a weight not exceeding 170g/m^2, unbleached or bleached, nes	合成纤维短纤机织物,按重量计合成纤维短纤含量在85%以下,主要或仅与棉混纺,每平方米重量不超过170克,未漂白或漂白的,其他	5513.1900	2468
Synthetic staple fibres woven fabrics, mixed mainly or solely with man-made filaments, nes	合成纤维短纤机织物,主要或仅与化学纤维长丝混纺,其他	5515.9100	2468
Synthetic staple fibres woven fabrics, nes	合成纤维短纤机织物,其他	5515.9900	2468
Synthetic staple fibres woven fabrics, unbleached or bleached	合成纤维短纤机织物,未漂白或漂白	5512.9100	2468
Synthetic staple fibres yarn, containing 85% or more by weight of such fibres, put up for retail sale	合成纤维短纤纱线,按重量计合成纤维短纤含量在85%及以上,供零售用	5511.1000	68
Synthetic staple fibres yarn, containing less than 85% by weight of such fibres, put up for retail sale	合成纤维短纤纱线,按重量计合成纤维短纤含量在85%以下,供零售用	5511.2000	68
Synthetic staple fibres yarn, mixed mainly or solely with cotton	合成纤维短纤纱线,主要或仅与棉混纺	5509.9200	68
Synthetic staple fibres yarn, mixed mainly or solely with wool or fine animal hair	合成纤维短纤纱线,主要或仅与羊毛或动物细毛混纺	5509.9100	68
Synthetic staple fibres yarn, nes	合成纤维短纤纱线,其他	5509.9900	68

S

Article Description	商品名称	Tariff Code	D. R.
Synthetic staple fibres, carded, combed or otherwise processed for spinning, nes	合成纤维短纤,已梳或经其他纺前加工,其他	5506. 9000	68
Synthetic staple fibres, not carded, combed or otherwise processed for spinning, nes	合成纤维短纤,未梳或未经其他纺前加工,其他	5503. 9000	68
Syringes, with or without needles	注射器,不论是否装有针头	9018. 3100	

S

T

Article Description	商品名称	Tariff Code	D. R.
T sections, not further worked than hot-rolled, hot-drawn or extruded, of a height of 80mm or more	丁字钢,除热轧、热拉拔或热挤压外未经进一步加工,截面高度在 80 毫米及以上	7216. 4020	468
T sections, not further worked than hot-rolled, hot-drawn or extruded, of a height of less than 80mm	丁字钢,除热轧、热拉拔或热挤压外未经进一步加工,截面高度低于 80 毫米	7216. 2200	468
Table fans, with a self-contained electric motor of an output not exceeding 125W	台扇,包括风机,本身装有一个输出功率不超过 125 瓦的电动机	8414. 5191	23
Table knives having fixed blades	餐刀,刃面固定的	8211. 9100	256
Table linen, embroidered, of cotton	餐桌用织物制品,刺绣的,棉制	6302. 5110	346
Table linen, embroidered, of flax	餐桌用织物制品,刺绣的,亚麻制	6302. 5911	346
Table linen, embroidered, of man-made fibres	餐桌用织物制品,刺绣的,化学纤维制	6302. 5310	346
Table linen, knitted or crocheted, hand-worked	餐桌用织物制品,针织或钩编的,手工制	6302. 4010	346
Table linen, knitted or crocheted, nes	餐桌用织物制品,针织或钩编的,其他	6302. 4090	346
Table linen, of cotton, nes	餐桌用织物制品,棉制,其他	6302. 5190	346
Table linen, of flax, nes	餐桌用织物制品,亚麻制,其他	6302. 5919	346
Table linen, of man-made fibres, nes	餐桌用织物制品,化学纤维制,其他	6302. 5390	346
Table linen, of other textile materials	餐桌用织物制品,其他纺织材料制	6302. 5990	346
Table or desk lamps, electric	台灯,电气的	9405. 2000	5
Table, kitchen or household articles and parts thereof, of aluminium, nes	餐桌、厨房家用器具及其零件,铝制,其他	7615. 1900	36
Table, kitchen or other household articles and parts theref, for household, Of cast iron, enamelled	餐桌、厨房器具及其零件,铸铁制,家用,已搪瓷	7323. 9200	24
Table, kitchen or other household articles and parts theref, for household, Of cast iron, not enamelled	餐桌、厨房器具及其零件,铸铁制,家用,未搪瓷	7323. 9100	24
Table, kitchen or other household articles and parts theref, for household, Of stainless steel	餐桌、厨房器具及其零件,家用,不锈钢制	7323. 9300	24
Table, kitchen or other household articles and parts thereof, for household, of iron or steel, nes	餐桌、厨房器具及其零件,钢铁制,家用,其他	7323. 9900	24
Table, kitchen or other household articles and parts thereof, of copper, nes	餐桌、厨房或家用器具及其零件,铜制,其他	7418. 1990	56
Table, kitchen or other household articles and parts thereof, of iron or steel, for household, enamelled, nes	餐桌、厨房器具及其零件,钢铁制,家用,已搪瓷,其他	7323. 9490	24
Tablecloths, of paper pulp, paper, cellulose wadding or webs of cellulose fibres	台布纸,纸浆、纸、纤维素絮纸或纤维素纤维网纸制的	4818. 3000	568
Tableware and kitchenware, of bamboo, nes	餐具及厨房用具,竹制,其他	4419. 0091	6
Tableware and kitchenware, of other wood	餐具及厨房用具,其他木制	4419. 0099	6

Article Description	商品名称	Tariff Code	D. R.
Tableware, in sets of assorted articles containing at least one article plated with precious metal	餐桌用具,成套货品,至少其中一件物品是镀贵金属的	8215.1000	256
Tableware, in sets of assorted articles, nes	餐桌用具,成套货品,其他	8215.2000	256
Tableware, nes	餐桌用具,其他	8215.9900	256
Tableware, of plastics	餐具,塑料的	3924.1000	23
Tableware, of porcelain	餐具,瓷制	6911.1010	268
Tableware, of pottery	餐具,陶制	6912.0010	268
Tableware, plated with precious metal	餐桌用具,镀贵金属的	8215.9100	256
Table-tennis articles and equipment, nes	乒乓球运动用品及器械,其他	9506.4090	5
Table-tennis balls	乒乓球	9506.4010	
Tachometers	转速表	9029.2090	7
Tachometers parts and accessories	转速表零件、附件	9029.9000	3
Tachymeters (tacheometers)	视距仪	9015.2000	
Tacks and similar articles, of copper or of iron or steel with heads of copper	平头钉及类似品,铜制或钢铁制带铜头的	7415.1000	56
Tacks, of aluminium	平头钉,铝制	7616.1000	36
Tacks, of iron or steel	平头钉,钢铁制的	7317.0000	36
Tadpole and young frogs	蛙苗	0106.9011	3
Tahitian pearls, natural, nes	黑珍珠,天然的,其他	7101.1091	145
Tahitian pearls, natural, ungraded	黑珍珠,天然的,未分级	7101.1011	145
Tailors chalks	裁缝划粉	9609.9000	3
Tailors dummies and other lay figures	人体模型及其他人体活动模型,裁缝用	9618.0000	
Tailors shears and similar shears, and blades therefor	裁缝剪刀及类似品、剪刀片	8213.0000	256
Talc, crushed or powdered	滑石,已破碎或已研粉	2526.2020	4
Talc, not crushed, not powdered	滑石,未破碎及未研粉	2526.1020	4
Tall oil fatty acids, industrial use	妥尔油脂肪酸,工业用	3823.1300	6
Tall oil, whether or not refined	妥尔油,不论是否精炼	3803.0000	3
Tallow oil, not emulsified or mixed or otherwise prepared	非食用脂油,未经乳化、混合或其他方法制作	1503.0000	4
Tamping machinery, for earth, minerals or ores, self-propelled, nes	捣固机械,对泥土、矿物或矿石的,自推进的,其他	8430.5090	5
Tamping machinery, not self-propelled	捣固机械,非自推进的	8430.6100	5
Tamping machines parts	捣固机零件	8431.4990	3
Tamping machines, nes	捣固机械,其他	8429.4090	57
Tank wagons and the like	油罐货车及类似车	8606.1000	37
Tanker ships, nes	液货船,其他	8901.2090	8
Tanker trailers and tanker semi-trailer, nes	罐式挂车及半挂车,货运,其他	8716.3190	
Tanks parts and accessories	坦克的零件和附件	8710.0090	3
Tanks, assembled	坦克整车	8710.0010	

T

Article Description	商品名称	Tariff Code	D. R.
Tanks, casks, drums, cans, boxes and similar containers, for any material, of iron or steel, of a capacity of 50L or more, whether or not lined or heat-insulated, but not fitted with mechanical or thermal equipment (other than compressed or liquefied gas)	柜、桶、罐、听、盒及类似容器,钢铁的,盛装物料用,容积在50升及以上,不论是否衬里或隔热,但无机械或热力装置(装压缩气体或液化气体的除外)	7310.1000	36
Tanks, casks, drums, cans, boxes and similar containers, for any material, of iron or steel, Of a capacity of less than 50L, whether or not lined or heat-insulated, but not fitted with mechanical or thermal equipment (other than compressed or liquefied gas), nes	柜、桶、罐、听、盒及类似容器,钢铁的,盛装物料用,容积在50升以下,不论是否衬里或隔热,但无机械或热力装置(装压缩气体或液化气体的除外),其他	7310.2900	36
Tanks, of plastics, of a capacity exceeding 300L, for builders	柜及类似容器,容积超过300升,建筑用	3925.1000	23
Tanned or dressed furskins of grey squirrel, ermine, other marten, fox, otter, marmot and lynx, whole skins and pieces or cuttings thereof, assembled	已鞣毛皮,灰鼠、白鼬、貂、狐、水獭、旱獭及猞猁的整张毛皮及其块、片,已缝制的	4302.3010	15
Tanned or dressed furskins of grey squirrel, ermine, other marten, fox, otter, marmot and lynx, whole skins, with or without head, tail or paws, not assembled	已鞣毛皮,灰鼠皮、白鼬皮、其他貂皮、狐皮、水獭皮、旱獭皮及猞猁皮,未缝制的整张毛皮,不论是否带头、尾或爪	4302.1910	15
Tanned or dressed furskins of lamb, (astrakhan, broadtail, caracul, persian and similar lamb, indian, chinese, mongolian or tibetan lamb), whole skins, with or without head, tail or paws, not assembled	已鞣毛皮,羔羊的(阿斯特拉罕、喀拉科尔、波斯羔羊及类似羔羊、印度、中国或蒙古羔羊),未缝制的整张毛皮,不论是否带头、尾或爪	4302.1930	15
Tanned or dressed furskins of rabbit or hare, whole skins, with or without head, tail or paws, not assembled	已鞣毛皮,兔皮,未缝制的整张毛皮,不论是否带头、尾或爪	4302.1920	15
Tanned or dressed furskins whole skins, with or without head, tail or paws, not assembled	已鞣毛皮,水貂的,未缝制的整张毛皮,不论是否带头、尾或爪	4302.1100	15
Tanned or dressed furskins, heads, tails, paws and other pieces or cuttings, not assembled	已鞣毛皮,未缝制的头、尾、爪及其他块、片	4302.2000	15
Tanned or dressed furskins, whole skins and pieces or cuttings thereof, assembled, nes	已鞣毛皮,整张的,已缝制的,其他	4302.3090	15
Tanned or dressed furskins, whole skins, with or without head, tail or paws, not assembled, nes	已鞣毛皮,未缝制的整张毛皮,不论是否带头、尾或爪,其他	4302.1990	15
Tanning extracts, nes	鞣料浸膏,其他	3201.9010	34
Tanning preparations, whether or not containing natural tanning substances	鞣料制剂,不论是否含有天然鞣料	3202.9000	68
Tanning substances, inorganic	鞣料,无机的	3202.9000	68
Tanning substances, synthetic organic	鞣料,有机合成的	3202.1000	68

Article Description	商品名称	Tariff Code	D. R.
Tannins and their salts, ethers, esters and other derivatives	鞣酸及其盐、醚、酯和其他衍生物	3201.9090	34
Tantalite	钽铁矿	2615.9090	146
Tantalum articles, nes	钽制品,其他	8103.9090	16
Tantalum ores and concentrates	钽矿砂及其精矿	2615.9010	146
Tantalum wire, nes	丝,钽的,其他	8103.9019	16
Tantalum, unwrought, including bars and rods obtained simply by sintering	钽,未锻轧,包括简单烧结而成的条、杆	8103.2090	16
Tapered roller bearings, including cone and tapered roller assemblies	锥形滚子轴承,包括锥形滚子组件	8482.2000	5
Tapers and the like	蜡烛,细长的	3406.0000	
Tapestries, Aubusson type hand-woven and the like	装饰毯,"奥步生"及类似式样的手织装饰毯	5805.0090	468
Tapioca and substitutes therefor prepared from starch, in the form of flakes, grains, pearls, siftings or in similar forms	珍粉及淀粉制成的珍粉代用品,片、粒、珠、粉或类似形状的	1903.0000	18
Taps parts	龙头用零件	8481.9090	3
Taps, for pipes, boiler shells, tanks, vats or the like	龙头,用于管道、锅炉、罐、桶或类似品的	8481.8090	
Tar distilled from coal, from lignite or from peat, and other mineral tars, whether or not dehydrated or partially distilled	焦油及其他矿物焦油,从煤、褐煤或泥煤蒸馏所得的,不论是否脱水或部分蒸馏	2706.0000	146
Tar sands	焦油砂	2714.1000	1346
Target shooting rifles, nes	打靶用步枪,其他	9303.3000	
Target shooting shotguns, including combination shotgun rifles	打靶用猎枪,包括组合式滑膛来复枪	9303.2000	
Taroes(Colocasia esculenta)	芋头	0714.9030	34
Taros	芋头	0714.9030	34
Tarpaulins, nes	油苫布,其他	6306.1990	346
Tarpaulins, of bast fibres	油苫布,麻制	6306.1910	346
Tarpaulins, of cotton	油苫布,棉制	6306.1920	346
Tarpaulins, of synthetic fibres	油苫布,合成纤维制	6306.1200	346
Tarred macadam	沥青碎石	2517.3000	13
Tarred paper and paperboard	焦油纸及纸板	4811.1000	458
Tars, reconstituted	焦油,再造的	2706.0000	146
Tartaric acid	酒石酸	2918.1200	36
Tassels, pompons and similar articles	流苏、绒球及类似品	5808.9000	468
Tatuettesa and other ornamental ceramic articles, of porcelain or china	塑像及其他装饰用品,瓷制	6913.1000	36
Tatuettesa and other ornamental ceramic articles, of pottery	塑像及其他装饰用品,陶制	6913.9000	36
Taximeters	车费计	9029.1020	

Article Description	商品名称	Tariff Code	D. R.
Taximeters parts and accessories	车费计零件、附件	9029. 9000	3
Tea extracts, essences and concentrates, including tea or maté extracts, essences and concentrates	茶浓缩精汁,包括马黛茶浓缩精汁	2101. 2000	268
Tea makers, electro-thermic	茶壶,电热的	8516. 7190	7
Tea preparations with a basis of extracts, essences and concentrates, including maté preparations with a basis of extracts, essences and concentrates	茶浓缩精汁为基本成分的制品,包括马黛茶浓缩精汁为基本成分的制品	2101. 2000	268
Tea preparations with abasis of tea, including tea preparations with abasis of maté	茶为基本成分的制品,包括马黛茶为基本成分的制品	2101. 2000	268
Teals	野鸭	0106. 3923	34
Tear tab ends and bodies thereof	易拉罐及罐体	7612. 9010	368
Teats	奶嘴	4014. 9000	23
Telecommunication apparatus for digital line system, nes	有线数字通信设备,其他	8517. 6239	7
Teleferics parts	缆车零件	8431. 3900	3
Teleferics, nes	缆车,其他	8428. 6090	
Telegraphic switching apparatus	电报交换机	8517. 6211	
Telegraphic switching apparatus parts	电报交换机用零件	8517. 7010	3
Telegraphic switching apparatus, digital program-controlled, nes	电话交换机,数字式程控,其他	8517. 6219	
Telephone answering machines	电话应答机	8519. 5000	
Telephone sets, nes	电话机,其他	8517. 1800	
Telephones for cellular networks or for other wireless networks, nes	电话机,用于蜂窝网络或其他无线网络的,其他	8517. 1290	
Telephonic apparatus parts, digital program-controlled	电话设备用零件,数字式程控的	8517. 7010	3
Telescopes designed to form parts of machines, appliances, instruments or apparatus	望远镜,作为机器、设备、仪器或器具部件的	9013. 1000	
Telescopic sights for fitting to arms	望远镜瞄准具,武器用	9013. 1000	
Telescopic sights parts and accessories, for fitting to arms	望远镜瞄准具的零件、附件,武器用	9013. 9010	3
Television camera tubes	电视摄像管	8540. 2010	35
Television camera tubes parts	电视摄像管用零件	8540. 9910	3
Television cameras parts, camera modules without special purposes	电视摄像机用零件,非特种用途的取像模块	8529. 9042	3
Television cameras parts, nes	电视摄像机用零件,其他	8529. 9049	3
Television cameras parts, of special purposes	电视摄像机用零件,特种用途的	8529. 9041	3
Television cameras, broadcast quality, not for special purposes	视摄像机,非特种用途的广播级	8525. 8012	7
Television cameras, for special purposes	视摄像机,特种用途的	8525. 8011	7
Television cameras, not for special purposes	视摄像机,非特种用途的其他类型	8525. 8013	7
Television picture tubes parts	电视显像管用零件	8540. 9110	3

T

Article Description	商品名称	Tariff Code	D. R.
Television receivers parts, plasma display modules and part thereof	电视接收机用零件,等离子显像组件及其零件	8529. 9082	3
Television receivers parts, nes	电视接收机用零件,其他	8529. 9089	3
Television receivers parts, of colour television receivers (other than plasma display modules or parts thereof)	电视接收机用零件(等离子显像组件及其零件除外)彩色的	8529. 9081	3
Television reception apparatus, colour, analogue	电视接收装置,彩色的,模拟的	8528. 7291	135
Television reception apparatus, colour, digital	电视接收装置,彩色的,数字的	8528. 7292	135
Television reception apparatus, colour, nes	电视接收装置,彩色的,其他	8528. 7299	135
Television reception apparatus, colour, of CRT, analogue	电视接收装置,彩色的,阴极射线显像管的,模拟的	8528. 7211	135
Television reception apparatus, colour, of CRT, digital	电视接收装置,彩色的,阴极射线显像管的,数字的	8528. 7212	135
Television reception apparatus, colour, of CRT, nes	电视接收装置,彩色的,阴极射线显像管的,其他	8528. 7219	135
Television reception apparatus, colour, of LCD, analogue, nes	电视接收装置,彩色的,液晶显示器的,模拟的,其他	8528. 7221	135
Television reception apparatus, colour, of LCD, digital	电视接收装置,彩色的,液晶显示器的,数字的,其他	8528. 7222	135
Television reception apparatus, colour, of LCD, nes	电视接收装置,彩色的,液晶显示器的,其他	8528. 7229	135
Television reception apparatus, colour, of plasma, analogue	电视接收装置,彩色的等离子显示器的,模拟的	8528. 7231	135
Television reception apparatus, colour, of plasma, digital	电视接收装置,彩色的等离子显示器的,数字的	8528. 7232	135
Television reception apparatus, colour, of plasma, nes	电视接收装置,彩色的等离子显示器的,其他	8528. 7239	135
Television reception apparatus, black and white or other monochrome, nes	电视接收装置,其他黑白或单色的	8528. 7300	135
Television reception apparatus, not designed to incorporate a video display or screen, black and white or other monochrome	电视接收装置,在设计上不带有视频显示器或屏幕的,黑白的或其他单色的	8528. 7190	135
Television reception apparatus, not designed to incorporate a video display or screen, colour, nes	电视接收装置,在设计上不带有视频显示器或屏幕的,彩色的,其他	8528. 7180	135
Television transmission or translation apparatus parts	电视发送、差转设备用零件	8529. 9010	3
Tellurium	碲	2804. 5000	
Temazepam (INN); salts thereof	替马西泮(INN)以及盐	2933. 9100	36
Tennis balls, nes	网球,其他	9506. 6900	5
Tennis rackets, nes	网球拍,其他	9506. 5900	5
Tenorite	黑铜矿	2603. 0000	146
Tents, nes	帐篷,其他	6306. 2990	346
Tents, of cotton	帐篷,棉制	6306. 2910	346
Tents, of synthetic fibres	帐篷,合成纤维制	6306. 2200	346

Article Description	商品名称	Tariff Code	D. R.
Tequila, mezcal	龙舌兰酒	2208.9010	2468
Terbium	铽	2805.3013	56
Terbium carbonate	碳酸铽	2846.9042	6
Terbium chloride	氯化铽	2846.9021	
Terbium oxide	氧化铽	2846.9016	
Terephthalic acid, nes	对苯二甲酸,其他	2917.3619	36
Terephthalie acid salts	对苯二甲酸盐	2917.3690	36
Terminal registers for market	销售点终端出纳机	8470.5010	
Terminating machines for the huge computers, mainframes and minicomputers	终端,巨型机、大型机、中型机及小型机用	8471.6040	
Terpenic byproducts of the deterpenation of essential oils of citrus fruit	萜烯副产品,柑橘属果实精油脱萜所得的	3301.9020	34
Terpenic byproducts of the deterpenation of essential oils, nes	萜烯副产品,精油脱萜时所得的,其他	3301.9090	34
Terpenic oils produced by the distillation or other treatment of coniferous woods	萜烯油,用蒸馏或其他方法从针叶木制得	3805.9010	36
Terphenyls	三联苯	2902.9090	6
Terpineols	萜品醇	2906.1910	36
Terry towelling and terry fabrics, nes	毛巾及毛圈织物,狭幅织物除外,其他	5802.2090	468
Terry towelling and terry fabrics, of cotton, nes	毛巾及毛圈织物,狭幅织物除外,棉制,其他	5802.1900	468
Terry towelling and terry fabrics, of cotton, unbleached	毛巾及毛圈织物,狭幅织物除外,棉制,未漂白	5802.1100	468
Terry towelling and terry fabrics, of man-made fibres	毛巾及毛圈织物,狭幅织物除外,化学纤维制	5802.2030	468
Terry towelling and terry fabrics, of silk or silk waste	毛巾及毛圈织物,狭幅织物除外,丝及绢丝制	5802.2010	468
Terry towelling and terry fabrics, of wool or fine animal hair	毛巾及毛圈织物,狭幅织物除外,羊毛或动物细毛制	5802.2020	468
Tertiary butanol	叔丁醇	2905.1430	36
Test benches	试验台	9031.2000	
Testing coaches and track inspection vehicles, for railway or tramway maintenance or service, nes	检验车及查道车,铁道及电车道用,其他	8604.0019	37
Testliner (recycled liner board), uncoated, weighing 150g/m^2 or less	强韧箱纸板(再生挂面纸板),未经涂布的,每平方米重量在150克及以下	4805.2400	
Testliner (recycled liner board), uncoated, weighing more than 150g/m^2	强韧箱纸板(再生挂面纸板),未经涂布的,每平方米重量超过150克	4805.2500	
Tetrachlorodifluoroethane	四氯二氟乙烷	2903.4530	36
Tetrachloroethylene	四氯乙烯	2903.2300	36
Tetrachlorotetrafluoropropane	四氯四氟丙烷	2903.4570	36
Tetracyclines	四环素	2941.3011	

T

Article Description	商品名称	Tariff Code	D. R.
Tetracyclines derivatives and their salts	四环素衍生物及其盐	2941. 3020	
Tetracyclines salts	四环素盐	2941. 3012	
Tetrahedrite	黝铜矿	2603. 0000	146
Tetrahydrobenzoic anhydride	四氢苯酐	2917. 2010	36
Tetrahydrocannabinols(all is omers)	四氢大麻酚(所有的异构体)	2932. 9500	36
Tetrahydrofuran	四氢呋喃	2932. 1100	36
Tetrahydronaphthalene(tetralin)	四氢萘	2902. 9010	6
Tetrazepam (INN) and triazdam(INN); salts thereof	四氢西泮(INN)和三唑仑(INN)以及盐	2933. 9100	36
Textile bast fibres (excluding flax, true hemp and ramie), raw or retted	纺织用韧皮纤维(不包括亚麻、大麻及苎麻),生的或经沤制的	5303. 1000	4
Textile doubling machines	并线机	8445. 3000	7
Textile doubling machines auxiliary	并线机的辅助机器	8448. 1900	3
Textile fabrics and felts, endless or fitted with linking devices, of a kind used in paper-making or similar machines, weighing 650g/m^2 or more	纺织物及毡呢,环状或装有连接装置的,用于造纸机器或类似机器,每平方米重量在650克及以上	5911. 3200	
Textile fabrics and felts, endless or fitted with linking devices, of a kind used in paper-making or similar machines, weighing less than 650g/m^2	纺织物及毡呢,环状或装有连接装置的,用于造纸机器或类似机器,每平方米重量在650克以下	5911. 3100	
Textile fabrics coated with gum or amylaceous substances, of a kind used for the outer covers of books or the like, nes	纺织物,用胶或淀粉物质涂布的,作书籍封面及类似用途的,其他	5901. 1090	
Textile fabrics coated with gum or amylaceous substances, of a kind used for the outer covers of books or the like, of cotton or bast fibres	纺织物,用胶或淀粉物质涂布的,作书籍封面及类似用途的,棉或麻制	5901. 1010	
Textile fabrics coated with gum or amylaceous substances, of a kind used for the outer covers of books or the like, of man-made fibres	纺织物,用胶或淀粉物质涂布的,作书籍封面及类似用途的,化学纤维制	5901. 1020	
Textile fabrics, felt and felt-lined woven fabrics, coated, covered or laminated with rubber, leather or other material, of a kind used for card clothing, and similar fabrics of a kind used for other technical purposes, nes	纺织物、毡呢及毡呢衬里机织物,用橡胶、皮革或其他材料涂布、包覆或层压的,作针布用以及作专门技术用途的类似织物,其他	5911. 1090	
Textile fabrics, impregnated, coated or covered, nes	纺织物,浸渍、涂布或包覆的,其他	5907. 0090	4
Textile fabrics, impregnated, coated, covered or laminated with plastics, nes	纺织物,用塑料浸渍、涂布、包覆或层压的,其他	5903. 9090	
Textile fabrics, impregnated, coated, covered or laminated with poly(vinyl chloride), nes	纺织物,用聚氯乙烯浸渍、涂布包覆或层压的,其他	5903. 1090	
Textile fabrics, impregnated, coated, covered or laminated with polyurethane, nes	纺织物,用聚氨基甲酸酯浸渍、涂布、包覆或层压的,其他	5903. 2090	
Textile fabrics, knitted or crocheted, rubberized	纺织物,针织或钩编的,用橡胶处理的	5906. 9100	48
Textile fabrics, rubberized, nes	纺织物,用橡胶处理的,其他	5906. 9990	48

Article Description	商品名称	Tariff Code	D. R.
Textile fibres preparing auxiliary machines's parts and accessories, nes	纺织纤维预处理机器的零件、附件,其他	8448.3200	3
Textile flock and dust and mill neps, not exceeding 5mm in length	纤维屑、纤维粉末及球结,长度不超过5毫米	5601.3000	6
Textile products and articles, for technical uses, nes	纺织产品及制品,作专门技术用途的,其他	5911.9000	
Textile reeling machines	摇纱机	8445.4090	7
Textile reeling machines auxiliary	摇纱机的辅助机器	8448.1900	3
Textile spinning machines, nes	纺纱机,其他	8445.2090	7
Textile twisting machines	加捻机	8445.3000	7
Textile twisting machines auxiliary	加捻机的辅助机器	8448.1900	3
Textile wall coverings	糊墙织物	5905.0000	8
Textile winding machines auxiliary	络纱机的辅助机器	8448.1900	3
Textile winding machines, nes	络纱机,其他	8445.4090	7
Textile yarn, and strip and the like, impregnated, coated, covered or sheathed with rubber or plastics	纺织纱线、扁条及类似品,用橡胶或塑料浸渍、涂布、包覆或套裹的	5604.9000	46
Textiles articles, made up, nes	纺织制成品,其他	6307.9000	346
Textured yarn, not put up for retail sale, nes	变形纱线,非供零售用,其他	5402.3900	3468
Texturing machinery for man-made textile materials	组织化处理机,化学纺织纤维的	8444.0090	
Thallium articles, nes	铊制品,其他	8112.5900	16
Thallium powders	铊粉末	8112.5100	16
Thallium, unwrought	铊,未锻轧	8112.5100	16
Thebacon (INN) and salts	醋氢可酮(INN)及盐	2939.1100	34
Thebaine and salts	蒂巴因及盐	2939.1100	34
Theodolites	经纬仪	9015.2000	
Theophylline and their derivatives; salts thereof, nes	茶碱及其衍生物以及它们的盐,其他	2939.5900	34
Therapeutic respiration apparatus, nes	呼吸器具,治疗用,其他	9019.2000	
Thermal print heads	热敏打印头	8443.9921	3
Thermal printers, of a kind solely used for automatic data processing machine	热敏打印机,专用于自动数据处理设备的	8443.3214	57
Thermionic valves and tubes parts, nes	热电子管零件,其他	8540.9990	3
Thermocopying apparatus	热敏复印设备	8443.3923	57
Thermometers and pyrometers, not combined with other instruments, nes	温度计及高温计,未与其他仪器组合,其他	9025.1990	7
Thermometers and pyrometers, for technical use, not combined with other instruments	温度计及高温计,工业用,未与其他仪器组合	9025.1910	7
Thermometers and pyrometers, liquid-filled, for direct reading, not combined with other instruments	温度计及高温计,液体的,可直接读数,未与其他仪器组合	9025.1100	
Thermometers or pyrometers parts and accessories	温度计及高温计零件、附件	9025.9000	7
Thermostatically controlled valves	恒温控制阀	8481.8040	
Thermostats	恒温器	9032.1000	
Thermo-sublime copying apparatus	热升华复印设备	8443.3924	57

T

Article Description	商品名称	Tariff Code	D. R.
Thiamin (Vitamin B_1)	硫胺	2936. 2200	36
Thiazole ring compounds, unfused in the structure, whether or not hydrogenated	噻唑环化合物,结构上含有,非稠合的,不论是否氢化	2934. 1000	36
Thin sheets, of glass fibres	薄片,玻璃纤维制	7019. 3200	56
Thiocarbamates	硫代氨基甲酸盐(或酯)	2930. 2000	36
Thiocyanates	硫氰酸盐	2842. 9010	
Thiols	硫醇	2930. 9090	36
Thiophosgene	硫光气	2853. 0090	
Thiophosphoric esters (phosphorothioates) and their salts; their halogenated, sulphonated, nitrated or nitrosated derivatives, nes	硫代磷酸酯及其盐以及它们的卤化、磺化、硝化或亚硝化衍生物,其他	2920. 1900	36
Thiosulphates, inorganic	硫代硫酸盐,无机的	2832. 3000	
Thiourea resins, in primary forms	硫尿树脂,初级形状的	3909. 1000	1256
Thiuram disulphide	二硫化二烃氨基硫羰	2930. 3000	36
Thiuram monosulphide	一硫化二烃氨基硫羰	2930. 3000	36
Thiuram tetrasulphide	四硫化二烃氨基硫羰	2930. 3000	36
Thorite	硅酸钍矿	2612. 2000	146
Thorium and its compounds	钍及其化合物	2844. 3000	
Thorium ores and concentrates	钍矿砂及其精矿	2612. 2000	146
Thread rolling machines, for working metal or cermets, without removing material	螺纹滚轧机,金属或金属陶瓷用,非切削	8463. 2000	7
Threaded articles, of iron of steel, nes	螺纹制品,钢铁制的,其他	7318. 1900	268
Threaded bungs, of base metal	螺口塞	8309. 9000	256
Threaded elbows, bends and sleeves, of iron or steel, nes	螺纹肘管、弯管及管套,钢铁的,其他	7307. 9200	6
Threaded elbows, bends and sleeves, of stainless steel	螺纹肘管、弯管及管套,不锈钢制	7307. 2200	6
Threading or tapping machines, for removing metal, nes	攻丝机床,切削金属的,其他	8459. 7000	7
Threading or tapping tools, hand tools	攻丝工具	8205. 1000	256
Threading or tapping tools, interchangeable	攻丝工具,可互换	8207. 4000	256
Threshing machinery	脱粒机	8433. 5200	
Threshing machinery parts	脱粒机零件	8433. 9090	
Thromboxanes, their derivatives and structural analogues	血栓烷及其衍生物和结构类似物	2937. 5000	36
Throwing shuttle boxes for looms	投梭箱,织机用	8448. 4910	3
Thrust ball bearings	推力球轴承	8482. 1040	5
Thunnus maccoyii, nes, living	南方蓝鳍金枪鱼,其他	0301. 9590	15
Thunnus thynnus, nes, living	蓝鳍金枪鱼,其他	0301. 9490	15
Thyme	麝香草	0910. 9900	6
Thymol	百里香酚	2907. 1990	36
Thymol blue	百里酚蓝	2934. 9910	36
Thyristors, other than photosensitive devices	半导体开关元件,但光敏器件除外	8541. 3000	5

Article Description	商品名称	Tariff Code	D. R.
Tichlorotrifluoroethanes	三氯三氟乙烷	2903. 4300	36
Ticket issuing machines	售票机	8470. 9000	
Ties, bow ties and cravats knitted or crocheted	领带及领结,针织或钩编的	6117. 8010	2456
Ties, bow ties and cravats, not knitted or crocheted, of man-made fibres	领带及领结,非针织或钩编的,化学纤维制	6215. 2000	2456
Ties, bow ties and cravats, not knitted or crocheted, of other textile materials	领带及领结,非针织或钩编的,其他纺织材料制	6215. 9000	2456
Ties, bow ties and cravats, not knitted or crocheted, of silk or silk waste	领带及领结,非针织或钩编的,丝或绢丝制	6215. 1000	2456
Tilapia, fresh or chilled	罗非鱼,鲜或冷的	0302. 6940	18
Tilapia, frozen	罗非鱼,冻的	0303. 7940	18
Tilapia, living	罗非鱼	0301. 9991	15
Tilapia, prepared or preserved, whole or in pieces, but not minced	罗非鱼,制作或保藏的,整条或切块,但未绞碎	1604. 1920	48
Tilapia, salted or in brine	罗非鱼,盐腌及盐渍的	0305. 6940	4
Tiles and similar articles of vegetable fibre, of straw or of shavings, chips, particles, sawdust or other waste, of wood, agglomerated with cement, plaster or other mineral binders	瓦及类似品,用水泥、石膏及其他矿物粘合材料粘合植物纤维、稻草、刨花、木片屑、木粉、锯末或木废料制成	6808. 0000	456
Tilidine(INN) and its salts	替利定(INN)及其盐	2922. 4400	36
Timber wedges	楔子,伐木用	8201. 9000	256
Timber wedges	伐木楔子	8201. 9000	256
Time intervals indicating apparatus, with clock or watch movement or with synchronous motor	时间间隔指示装置,装有钟、表机芯或同步电动机的	9106. 9000	5
Time of day recording apparatus, with clock or watch movement or with synchronous motor	时间记录器,装有钟、表机芯或同步电动机的	9106. 9000	5
Time switches with clock or watch movement or with synchronous motor	定时开关,装有钟、表机芯或同步电动机的	9107. 0000	5
Time-recorders	时刻记录器	9106. 1000	5
Time-registers	考勤钟	9106. 1000	5
Tin alloys, nes	锡合金,其他	8001. 2029	16
Tin articles, nes	锡制品,其他	8007. 0090	16
Tin foil (whether or not printed or backed with paper, paperboard, plastics or similar backing materials), of a thickness (excluding any backing) not exceeding 0. 2mm	锡箔(不论是否印花或用纸、纸板、塑料或类似材料衬背),厚度(衬背除外)不超过0. 2毫米	8007. 0030	16
Tin ores and concentrates	锡矿砂及其精矿	2609. 0000	146
Tin, not alloyed	锡,非合金	8001. 1000	16
Tin, unwrought, nes	锡,未锻轧,其他	8001. 2090	16
Tissue adhesives for surgical wound closure, sterile	粘合胶布,外伤创口闭合用的,无菌	3006. 1000	3
Titanic anhydride	二氧化钛	2823. 0000	4
Titanium articles, nes	钛制品,其他	8108. 9090	16

T

Article Description	商品名称	Tariff Code	D. R.
Titanium ores and concentrates	钛矿砂及其精矿	2614. 0000	146
Titanium oxides	钛的氧化物	2823. 0000	4
Titanium powder	钛粉末	8108. 2030	16
Titanium sponge	海绵钛	8108. 2021	16
Titanium white	钛白粉	3206. 1110	2368
Titanium, unwrought, nes	钛,未锻轧,其他	8108. 2029	16
Toasted bread	吐司烤面包	1905. 4000	28
Toasters, nes	烤面包器,其他	8516. 7290	7
Toasters, slice pop-up	多士炉	8516. 7220	7
Toasters, slice pop-up	片式烤面包机(多士炉)	8516. 7220	7
Tobacco extracts and essences	烟草精汁	2403. 9900	
Tobacco preparing or making machinery	烟草加工及制作机器	8478. 1000	7
Tobacco preparing or making machinery parts	烟草加工及制作机器的零件	8478. 9000	7
Tobacco refuse	烟草废料	2401. 3000	
Tobacco, not stemmed/stripped, flue-cured	烤烟,未去梗的	2401. 1010	4
Tobacco, not stemmed/stripped, nes	烟草,其他,未去梗的	2401. 1090	4
Tobacco, partly or wholly stemmed/stripped, flue-cured	烤烟,部分或全部去梗的	2401. 2010	4
Tobacco, partly or wholly stemmed/stripped, nes	烟草,其他,部分或全部去梗的	2401. 2090	4
Toilet articles, of plastics	盥洗用具,塑料的	3924. 9000	23
Toilet bags, with outer surface of leather, of composition leather or of patent leather	化妆包,以皮革、再生皮革或漆皮作面	4202. 3100	256
Toilet bags, with outer surface of plastic sheeting or of textile materials	化妆包,以塑料片或纺织材料作面	4202. 3200	256
Toilet brushes for use on the person, nes	化妆用刷,其他	9603. 2900	
Toilet linen, nes	盥洗用制品,其他	6302. 5990	346
Toilet linen, of cotton, nes	盥洗用制品,棉制,其他	6302. 9100	346
Toilet linen, of flax, nes	盥洗用制品,亚麻制,其他	6302. 9910	346
Toilet linen, of man-made fibres, nes	盥洗用制品,化学纤维制,其他	6302. 9300	346
Toilet linen, of terry towelling or similar terry fabrics, of cotton, nes	盥洗用制品,毛巾织物或类似的毛圈织物的,棉制,其他	6302. 6090	346
Toilet paper, in rolls of a width not exceeding 36cm, or cut to size or shape	卫生纸,成卷宽度不超过 36 厘米或切成一定尺寸或形状的	4818. 1000	568
Toilet sprays, and mounts and heads thereof	化妆用喷雾器及其座架、喷头	9616. 1000	
Toilet tissue stock, in rolls or sheets	卫生纸,成卷或成张的	4803. 0000	58
Toilet waters	花露水	3303. 0000	2
Toll telephonic switching apparatus	长途电话交换机	8517. 6211	
Toluene	甲苯	2902. 3000	6
Toluene diisocyanate	甲苯二异氰酸酯 TDI	2929. 1010	36
Toluene diisocyanate	2,4-和 2,6-甲苯二异氰酸酯混合物	2929. 1010	36
Toluene diisocyanate	TDI	2929. 1010	36

Article Description	商品名称	Tariff Code	D. R.
Toluidines and their derivatives;salts thereof	甲苯胺及其衍生物以及它们的盐	2921.4300	36
Toluole	粗甲苯	2707.2000	6
Tolylhydrazine	甲苯肼	2928.0000	36
Tomato juice	番茄汁	2009.5000	2468
Tomato paste, in airtight containers, weighing more than 5kg	番茄酱罐头,重量大于5kg的番茄酱罐头	2002.9019	28
Tomato paste, in airtight containers, weighing not more than 5kg	番茄酱罐头,重量不超过5kg的番茄酱罐头	2002.9011	28
Tomatoes,fresh or chilled	番茄,鲜或冷藏的	0702.0000	1
Tomatoes,nes,prepared or preserved otherwise than by vinegar or acetic acid	番茄,其他,用醋或醋酸以外的其他方法制作或保藏的	2002.9090	48
Tomatoes, whole or in pieces, nes, prepared or preserved otherwise than by vinegar or acetic acid	番茄,整个或切片,其他,用醋或醋酸以外的其他方法制作或保藏的	2002.1090	248
Tomography apparatus,X-rays computed	断层检查仪,X射线的	9022.1200	
Tone converters or transmission apparatus of a kind used for vehicles	车载音频转播器或发射器	8522.9091	3
Tongues of bovine animals,frozen,edible	牛舌,冻的	0206.2100	15
Tool bodies,of other wood	工具支架,其他木制的	4417.0090	56
Tool bodies,of radiata pine	工具支架,辐射松制的	4417.0010	56
Tool handles,of other wood	工具柄,其他木制的	4417.0090	56
Tool handles,of radiata pine	工具柄,辐射松制的	4417.0010	56
Tool holders	工具夹具	8466.1000	3
Tools sets, of two or more of other subheadings of hand tools	工具成套货品,由两个或多个子目所列手工工具组成的	8205.9000	256
Tools sets,of two or more of the headings No. 82.02 to 82.05,put up for retail sale	工具成套货品,由税号82.02至82.05中两个或多个税号所列组成的,零售包装	8206.0000	256
Tools,of other wood	工具,其他木制的	4417.0090	56
Tools,of radiata pine	工具,辐射松制的	4417.0010	56
Tooth brushes, including ventalplate brushes	牙刷,包括齿板刷	9603.2100	
Toothed wheels parts	传动元件零件	8483.9000	3
Toothed wheels, chain sprockets and other transmission elements presented separately	传动元件,单独报验的带齿的轮、链轮及其他	8483.9000	3
Toothfish (Dissostichus spp.),fresh or chilled	南极犬牙鱼(Dissostichus spp.),鲜或冷的	0302.6800	18
Toothfish (Dissostichus spp.),frozen	南极犬牙鱼(Dissostichus spp.),冻的	0303.6200	18
Toothpastes	牙膏	3306.1010	23
Topographical or similar purposes plans and drawings,being originals drawn by hand	地形或类似用途的设计图纸,手绘的	4906.0000	
Topographical plans,printed	地形图,印制的	4905.9900	1
Torpedo tubes and similar projectors	鱼雷发射管及类似发射装置自推进的	9301.2000	
Torpedoes and parts	鱼雷及其零件	9306.9000	3

T

Article Description	商品名称	Tariff Code	D. R.
Torque converters	扭矩变换器	8483. 4090	7
Tortoiseshell and powder thereof	龟壳及其粉末	0507. 9090	14
Tortoise-shell, worked	玳瑁壳,已加工的	9601. 9000	5
Toughened (tempered) safety glass, for aircraft, spacecraft or vessels	钢化安全玻璃,航空器、航天器及船舶用	7007. 1110	234
Toughened(tempered) safety glass, nes	钢化安全玻璃,其他	7007. 1900	234
Toughened(tempered) safety glass, of size and shape suitable for vehicles	钢化安全玻璃,车辆用	7007. 1190	234
Towel or napkin stock and similar paper of a kind used for household or sanitary purposes, in rolls or sheets	餐巾纸以及家庭或卫生用的类似纸,成卷或成张的	4803. 0000	58
Towelling coverlets, of cotton, nes	毛巾被,棉制,其他	6302. 3192	346
Tower cranes	塔式起重机	8426. 2000	7
Towers and lattice masts, of iron or steel	塔楼及格构杆,钢铁的	7308. 2000	6
Toxoids	类毒素	3002. 9090	34
Toy animals	玩具动物	9503. 0021	5
Toy musical instruments and apparatus	玩具乐器	9503. 0050	5
Toy of model assembly kits, reduced-size ("scale"), nes	玩具模型组件,缩小(按比例缩小)的,成套的,其他	9503. 0039	5
Toys for intelligence	智力玩具	9503. 0060	5
Toys for puzzles	玩具,智力玩具	9503. 0060	5
Toys of model assembly kits, of constructional toys	玩具,缩小(按比例缩小)的建筑,成套的	9503. 0040	5
Toys parts and accessories	玩具零件、附件	9503. 0090	5
Toys, electric trains, reduced-size model assembly kits	玩具,电动火车,缩小的成套模型组件	9503. 0031	5
Toys, incorporating a motor, nes	玩具或模型,带动力装置的,其他	9503. 0082	5
Toys, nes	玩具,其他	9503. 0089	5
Toys, pedal cars and similar, wheeled	玩具,踏板汽车及类似的,带轮的	9503. 0010	
Toys, put up in sets or outfits, nes	玩具,组装成套或全套的,其他	9503. 0081	5
Traces for any animal, of any material	缰绳,适合各种动物用	4201. 0000	1458
Tracing cloth of cotton or bast fibres	描图布,棉或麻制	5901. 9091	
Tracing cloth of man-made fibres	描图布,化学纤维制	5901. 9092	
Tracing cloth, nes	描图布,其他	5901. 9099	
Tracing papers	描图纸	4806. 3000	58
Track alleyway stackers, powered by an electric motor	有轨巷道堆垛机,电动的	8427. 1010	7
Track scales	轨道衡	8423. 8920	
Track suits, not knitted or crocheted, for men or boys, of cotton	运动服,非针织或钩编的,男式,棉制	6211. 3220	2456
Track suits, not knitted or crocheted, for men or boys, of man-made fibres	运动服,非针织或钩编的,男式,化学纤维制	6211. 3320	2456
Track suits, knitted or crocheted, of cotton	运动服,针织或钩编的,棉制	6112. 1100	2456

T

Article Description	商品名称	Tariff Code	D. R.
Track suits, knitted or crocheted, of other textile materials	运动服,针织或钩编的,其他纺织材料制	6112. 1900	2456
Track suits, knitted or crocheted, of synthetic fibres	运动服,针织或钩编的,合成纤维制	6112. 1200	2456
Track suits, not knitted or crocheted, for women or girls, of cotton, nes	运动服,非针织或钩编的,女式,棉制,其他	6211. 4210	2456
Track suits, not knitted or crocheted, for women or girls, of man-made fibres, nes	运动服,非针织或钩编的,女式,化学纤维制,其他	6211. 4310	2456
Trackless alleyway stackers, powered by an electric motor	无轨巷道堆垛机,电动的	8427. 1020	7
Trackliners, for railway or tramway maintenance or service	轨道校正车,铁道及电车道用	8604. 0099	37
Track-laying tractors	履带式牵引车、拖拉机	8701. 3000	
Traction mechanisms for funiculars, nes	索道用牵引装置,其他	8428. 6090	
Tractors parts and accessories, nes	拖拉机用零件、附件	8708. 9910	3
Tractors, electrical, not fitted with lifting or handling equipment, for short distance transport of goods	牵引车,电动的,短距离运输货物的,未装有提升或搬运设备	8709. 1110	
Tractors, nes	牵引车,其他	8701. 9090	5
Tractors, other than wheeled	拖拉机,非轮式	8701. 9019	5
Tractors, self-propelled, not fitted with lifting or handling equipment, for short distance transport of goods	牵引车,自驱动的,短距离运输货物的,未装有提升或搬运设备	8709. 1910	
Tractors, wheeled	拖拉机,轮式	8701. 9011	5
Trade advertising material, commercial catalogues and the like, nes	商业广告品、商品目录及类似印刷品,其他	4911. 1090	3
Trade advertising material, commercial catalogues and the like, no commercial value	商业广告品、商品目录及类似印刷品,无商业价值的	4911. 1010	3
Traffic control electrical equipment for airfields	交通管理设备,电气的,机场的	8530. 8000	
Traffic control electrical equipment for inland waterways	交通管理设备,电气的,内河航道的	8530. 8000	
Traffic control electrical equipment for parking facilities	交通管理设备,电气的,停车场的	8530. 8000	
Traffic control electrical equipment for port installations	交通管理设备,电气的,港口的	8530. 8000	
Traffic control electrical equipment for railways	交通管理设备,电气的,铁道的	8530. 1000	
Traffic control electrical equipment for roads	交通管理设备,电气的,道路的	8530. 8000	
Traffic control electrical equipment for tramways	交通管理设备,电气的,电车道的	8530. 1000	
Traffic control electrical equipment parts	交通管理设备的零件	8530. 9000	3
Traffic control equipment and parts, for airfields	交通管理设备及其零件,机械的,机场用	8608. 0090	3
Traffic control equipment and parts, for inland waterways	交通管理设备及其零件,机械的,内河航道用	8608. 0090	3
Traffic control equipment and parts, for parking facilities	交通管理设备及其零件,机械的,停车场用	8608. 0090	3

T

Article Description	商品名称	Tariff Code	D. R.
Traffic control equipment and parts, for port installations	交通管理设备及其零件,机械的,港口用	8608. 0090	3
Traffic control equipment and parts, for railways	交通管理设备及其零件,机械的,铁道用	8608. 0090	3
Traffic control equipment and parts, for roads	交通管理设备及其零件,机械的,道路用	8608. 0090	3
Traffic control equipment and parts, for tramways	交通管理设备及其零件,机械的,电车道用	8608. 0090	3
Trailers and semi-trailers for agricultural purposes, self-loading or self-unloading	挂车及半挂车,农用自装或自卸式	8716. 2000	
Trailers and semi-trailers for the transport of goods, nes	挂车及半挂车,货运用,其他	8716. 3990	
Trailers and semi-trailers of oil tanker	挂车及半挂车,油罐的	8716. 3110	
Trailers and semi-trailers of the caravan type, for housing or camping	挂车及半挂车,供居住或野营用厢式	8716. 1000	
Trailers and semi-trailers parts	挂车及半挂车零件	8716. 9000	3
Trailers and semi-trailers, nes	挂车及半挂车,其他	8716. 4000	
Trailers and semi-trailers, van type	挂车及半挂车,货柜的	8716. 3910	
Trailers and tanker semi-trailer of tanker, nes	挂车及半挂车,罐式货运,其他	8716. 3190	
Transcribing machines for data	转录数据的机器	8471. 9000	
Transfer papers, in rolls or sheets, of width exceeding 36cm or in roll or one side exceeding 36cm and other side exceeding 15cm in rectangular sheets	转印纸,成卷或成张的,卷宽度超过36厘米,或长超过36厘米且宽超过15厘米	4809. 9000	458
Transfers(decalcomanias), vitrifiable	釉转印贴花纸(移画印花法用图案纸)	4908. 1000	4
Transfers, nes	转印贴花纸,其他	4908. 9000	4
Transformers parts, liquid dielectric, having a power handling capacity exceeding 400MVA but less than 500MVA	变压器用零件,液体介质,额定容量在400兆伏安及以上,但小于500兆伏安	8504. 9011	3
Transformers parts, liquid dielectric, nes	变压器用零件,液体介质,其他	8504. 9011	3
Transformers parts, nes	变压器用零件,其他	8504. 9019	3
Transformers, having a power handling capacity exceeding 16kVA but not exceeding 500kVA	变压器,额定容量超过16千伏安,但不超过500千伏安	8504. 3300	78
Transformers, having a power handling capacity exceeding 1kVA but not exceeding 16kVA	变压器,额定容量超过1千伏安,但不超过16千伏安,其他	8504. 3290	78
Transformers, having a power handling capacity exceeding 500kVA	变压器,额定容量超过500千伏安	8504. 3400	78
Transformers, having a power handling capacity not exceeding 1kVA	变压器,额定容量不超过1千伏安,其他	8504. 3190	78
Transformers, liquid dielectric, having a power handing capacity exceeding 10MVA but less than 220MVA	变压器,液体介质,额定容量超过10兆伏安,但小于220兆伏安	8504. 2311	78

T

Article Description	商品名称	Tariff Code	D. R.
Transformers, liquid dielectric, having a power handling capacity exceeding 220MVA but less than 330MVA	变压器,液体介质,额定容量在220兆伏安及以上,但小于330兆伏安	8504.2312	78
Transformers, liquid dielectric, having a power handling capacity exceeding 330MVA but less than 400MVA	变压器,液体介质,额定容量在330兆伏安及以上,但小于400兆伏安	8504.2313	78
Transformers, liquid dielectric, having a power handling capacity exceeding 400MVA but less than 500MVA	变压器,液体介质,额定容量在400兆伏安及以上,但小于500兆伏安	8504.2321	78
Transformers, liquid dielectric, having a power handling capacity exceeding 650kVA but not exceeding 10MVA	变压器,液体介质,额定容量超过650千伏安,但不超过10兆伏安	8504.2200	78
Transformers, liquid dielectric, having a power handling capacity not exceeding 650kVA	变压器,液体介质,额定容量不超过650千伏安	8504.2100	78
Transformers, liquid dielectric, nes	变压器,液体介质,其他	8504.2329	78
Transistors, other than photosensitive transistors, nes	晶体管,但光敏晶体管除外,其他	8541.2900	5
Transistors, other than photosensitive transistors, with a dissipation rate of less than 1W	晶体管,但光敏晶体管除外,耗散功率小于1瓦的	8541.2100	5
Transmission apparatus for radio-broadcasting or television	发送设备,无线电广播、电视用	8525.5000	7
Transmission apparatus for radio-broadcasting or television, incorporating reception apparatus, nes	发送设备,无线电广播、电视用,装有接收装置的,其他	8525.6090	7
Transmission belts or belting, of vulcanized rubber, nes	传动带及带料,硫化橡胶制的,其他	4010.3900	1368
Transmission or conveyor belts or belting, of textile material, whether or not impregnated, coated, covered or laminated with plastics, or reinforced with metal or other material	传动带或输送带及带料,纺织材料制的,不论是否用塑料浸渍、涂布、包覆或压层,也不论是否用金属或其他材料加强	5910.0000	
Transmission shafts parts	传动轴零件	8483.9000	3
Transmission shafts, for ships, nes	传动轴,船舶用,其他	8483.1010	
Transmission shafts, nes	传动轴,其他	8483.1090	
Transmission shafts, of motor vehicles, nes	传动轴,机动车辆用,其他	8709.9992	3
Transmissions valves, for oleohydraulic	传动阀,油压的	8481.2010	
Transmissions valves, for pneumatic	传动阀,气压的	8481.2020	
Transplanters, for agricultural, horticultural or forestry use	移植机,农业、园艺及林业用	8432.3000	
Transport mechanisms, whether or not incorporating a magnetic head, of cassette magnetic tape recorders or reproducers	走带机构(机芯),不论是否装有磁头,盒式磁带录音机或放声机用	8522.9021	3
Transporter cranes	桁架桥式起重机	8426.1990	7
Trass earth	火山土	2530.9099	13456
Travel sets for personal toilet, sewing or shoe or clothes cleaning	旅行用具,成套的,个人梳妆、缝纫或清洁鞋靴、衣服用	9605.0000	6

T

Article Description	商品名称	Tariff Code	D. R.
Travelling circuses	流动马戏团	9508. 1000	
Travelling menageries	流动动物园	9508. 1000	
Travelling theatres	流动剧团	9508. 9000	5
Travelling wave tubes	行波管	8540. 7900	35
Travelling-bags, ruck-sacks, tool bags, sports bags, insulated food or beverages bags, nes	旅行包、帆布包、工具包、运动包、食品或饮料保温包,其他	4202. 9900	256
Travelling-bags, ruck-sacks, tool bags, sports bags, insulated food or beverages bags, with outer surface of leather, of composition leather or of patent leather	旅行包、帆布包、工具包、运动包、食品或饮料保温包,以皮革、再生皮革或漆皮作面	4202. 9100	256
Travelling-bags, ruck-sacks, tool bags, sports bags, insulated food or beverages bags, with outer surface of plastic sheeting or of textile materials	旅行包、帆布包、工具包、运动包、食品或饮料保温包,以塑料片或纺织材料作面	4202. 9200	256
Travertine and articles thereof, worked, nes	石灰华及其制品,已加工的,其他	6802. 9190	3468
Travertine carvings	石灰华石刻	6802. 9110	3468
Travertine monumental or building stone and articles thereof, simply cut or sawn, with a flat or even surface	石灰华碑石或建筑用石及其制品,简单切削或锯开并具有一个平面的	6802. 2120	3468
Travertine, crude or roughly trimmed	石灰华,原状或粗加修整	2515. 1100	148
Travertine, merely cut, by sawing or otherwise, into blocks or slabs of a rectangular (including square) shape	石灰华,用锯或其他方法切割成矩形,包括正方形	2515. 1200	148
Trays, dishes, plates, cups and the like, of bamboo	盘、碟、盆、杯及类似品,竹浆纸制	4823. 6100	68
Trays, dishes, plates, cups and the like, of paper or paperboard, nes	盘、碟、盆、杯及类似品,纸或纸板制的,其他	4823. 6900	68
Trees, shrubs and bushes, grafted or not, of kinds which bear edible fruit or nuts, nes	食用水果或食用坚果的树、灌木,不论是否嫁接,其他	0602. 2090	
Trees, shrubs and bushes, grafted or not, of kinds which bear edible fruit or nuts, seedlings	苗木,种用的,食用水果或食用坚果的树、灌木,不论是否嫁接	0602. 2010	3
Trehalose	海藻糖,茧蜜糖	2940. 0000	6
Triacs, other than photosensitive devices	三端双向可控硅开关元件,但光敏器件除外	8541. 3000	5
Triazine ring compounds, unfused in the structure, whether or not hydrogenated, nes	三嗪环化合物,结构上含有,非稠合的,不论是否氢化,其他	2933. 6990	36
Triazolam (INN); salts thereof	三唑仑(INN)以及盐	2933. 9100	36
Trichloroethylene	三氯乙烯	2903. 2200	36
Trichlorofluoromethane	三氯氟甲烷	2903. 4100	36
Trichloroisocyanurate acid	三氯异氰脲酸	2933. 6922	36
Trichloronitromethane (chloropicrin, nitrochloroform)	氯化苦	2904. 9030	36
Trichloronitromethane (chloropicrin, nitrochloroform)	三氯硝基甲烷	2904. 9030	36
Trichloronitromethane (chloropicrin, nitrochloroform)	硝基氯仿	2904. 9030	36
Trichloropentafluoropropane	三氯五氟丙烷	2903. 4580	36

T

Article Description	商品名称	Tariff Code	D. R.
Tricholoma mongolicum imai, dried	口蘑,干的	0712.3940	4
Tricholoma mongolicum imai, fresh or chilled	口蘑,鲜或冷藏的	0709.5950	1
Tricot machines	特里科经编机	8447.2011	7
Tricycles and similar wheeled toys	三轮车及类似的带轮玩具	9503.0010	
Tricycles for delivery	三轮脚踏车,运货用	8712.0090	8
Triethanolamine	三乙醇胺	2922.1310	36
Trimeperidine (INN); salts thereof	三甲利定(INN)以及盐	2933.3300	36
Trimethyl phosphite	亚磷酸三甲酯	2920.9011	36
Trimethyl phosphite	亚磷酸三乙酯	2920.9012	36
Trimethylamine and their salts	三甲胺及其盐	2921.1100	36
Trimmings making machines	装饰带机	8447.9090	7
Trinitrotoluene (TNT)	三硝基甲苯(TNT)	2904.2040	36
Tripe	牛肚	0504.0029	14
Tripe, in airtight container	牛肚,罐头	1602.5010	248
Triple superphosphates	重过磷酸钙	3103.1010	68
Tris (2,3-dibromopropyl) phosphate	三(2,3-二溴丙基)磷酸酯	2919.1000	36
Trisodium phosphate	磷酸三钠	2835.2910	
Tri-(2-chloroethyl) amine	三(2-氯乙基)胺	2921.1950	36
Tri-chloroacetic acids, their salts and esters	三氯乙酸及其盐和酯	2915.4000	36
Trousers, knitted or crocheted, for men or boys, of synthetic fibres	长裤,针织或钩编的,男式,合成纤维制	6103.4300	2456
Trousers, knitted or crocheted, for men or boys, of cotton	长裤,针织或钩编的,男式,棉制	6103.4200	2456
Trousers, knitted or crocheted, for men or boys, of other textile materials	长裤,针织或钩编的,男式,其他纺织材料制	6103.4900	2456
Trousers, knitted or crocheted, for men or boys, of wool or fine animal hair	长裤,针织或钩编的,男式,羊毛或动物细毛制	6103.4100	2456
Trousers, knitted or crocheted, for women for girls, of cotton	长裤,针织或钩编的,女式,棉制	6104.6200	2456
Trousers, knitted or crocheted, for women or girls, of other textile materials	长裤,针织或钩编的,女式,其他纺织材料制	6104.6900	2456
Trousers, knitted or crocheted, for women or girls, of synthetic fibres	长裤,针织或钩编的,女式,合成纤维制	6104.6300	2456
Trousers, knitted or crocheted, for women or girls, of wool or fine animal hair	长裤,针织或钩编的,女式,羊毛或动物细毛制	6104.6100	2456
Trousers, not knitted or crocheted, for men or boys, of cotton	长裤,非针织或钩编的,男式,棉制	6203.4290	2456
Trousers, not knitted or crocheted, for men or boys, of other textile material	长裤,非针织或钩编的,男式,其他纺织材料制	6203.4990	2456
Trousers, not knitted or crocheted, for men or boys, of synthetic fibres	长裤,非针织或钩编的,男式,合成纤维制	6203.4390	2456

T

Article Description	商品名称	Tariff Code	D. R.
Trousers, not knitted or crocheted, for men or boys, of wool or fine animal hair	长裤,非针织或钩编的,男式,羊毛或动物细毛制	6203. 4100	2456
Trousers, not knitted or crocheted, for women or girls, of cotton	长裤,非针织或钩编的,女式,棉制	6204. 6200	2456
Trousers, not knitted or crocheted, for women or girls, of fine animal hair	长裤,非针织或钩编的,女式,羊毛或动物细毛制	6204. 6100	2456
Trousers, not knitted or crocheted, for women or girls, of other textile materials	长裤,非针织或钩编的,女式,其他纺织材料制	6204. 6900	2456
Trousers, not knitted or crocheted, for women or girls, of synthetic fibres	长裤,非针织或钩编的,女式,合成纤维制	6204. 6300	2456
Trout (Salmo trutta, Oncorhynchus my kiss, Oncorhynchus clarki, Oncorhynchus aguabonita, Oncorhynchus gilae, Oncorhynchus apache and Oncohynchus chrysogaster), fresh or chilled	鳟鱼,鲜或冷的	0302. 1100	18
Trout (Salmo trutta, Oncorhynchus mykiss, Oncorhynchus clarki, Oncorhynchus aguabonita, Oncorhynchus gilae, Oncorhynchus apache and Oncorhynchus chrysogaster), frozen	鳟鱼,冻的	0303. 2100	18
Trout, nes, living	鳟鱼,其他,活的	0301. 9190	15
True hemp tow	大麻短纤	5302. 9000	4
True hemp waste	大麻废麻	5302. 9000	4
True hemp woven fabrics	大麻机织物	5311. 0030	2468
True hemp yarn	大麻纱线	5308. 2000	568
True hemp, raw or retted	大麻,生的或经沤制的	5302. 1000	4
Truffle, fresh or chilled	块菌,鲜或冷藏的	0709. 5960	1
Truffles	块菌	2003. 2000	248
Trumpets	小号	9205. 1000	5
Truncheons	警棍	9304. 0000	
Trunks and suit-cases, with outer surface of plastics or of textile materials	衣箱,以塑料或纺织材料作面	4202. 1210	256
Trunks, suit-cases, vanity-cases, executive-cases, briefcases, school satchels and similar containers, nes	衣箱、提箱、小手袋、公文箱、公文包、书包及类似容器,其他	4202. 1900	256
Trunks, with outer surface of leather, of composition leather or of patent leather	衣箱,以皮革、再生皮革或漆皮作面	4202. 1110	1458
Tube mills for cold-rolled	冷轧管机	8455. 1020	7
Tube mills for cold-rolled	轧管机,冷轧的	8455. 1020	7
Tube mills parts	轧管机零件	8455. 9000	3
Tube mills, for hot-rolled	热轧管机	8455. 1010	7
Tube mills, for hot-rolled	轧管机,热轧的	8455. 1010	7
Tube mills, fixed and reduced	轧管机,定减径的	8455. 1030	7
Tube mills, nes	轧管机,其他	8455. 1090	7

T

Article Description	商品名称	Tariff Code	D. R.
Tube or pipe fittings of nickel	管子附件,镍制	7507. 2000	6
Tube or pipe fittings, of copper-nickel base alloys (cupronickel)	管子附件,铜镍合金(白铜)制	7412. 2010	6
Tube or pipe fittings, of copper-nickel-zinc base alloys (nickel silver)	管子附件,铜镍锌合金(德银)制	7412. 2010	6
Tube or pipe fittings, of aluminium	管子附件,铝制	7609. 0000	6
Tube or pipe fittings, of copper alloys, nes	管子附件,铜合金制,其他	7412. 2090	6
Tube or pipe fittings, of iron or steel, cast fittings, nes	管子附件,钢铁铸件,其他	7307. 1900	6
Tube or pipe fittings, of iron or steel, nes	管子附件,钢铁的,其他	7307. 9900	6
Tube or pipe fittings, of non-malleable cast iron	管子附件,无可锻性铸铁制	7307. 1100	6
Tube or pipe fittings, of refined copper	管子附件,精炼铜制	7412. 1000	6
Tube or pipe fittings, of stainless steel, nes	管子附件,不锈钢制,其他	7307. 2900	6
Tuberous roots, in growth or in flower	块根,生长或开花的	0601. 2000	
Tuberous roots, nes, dormant	块根,其他,休眠的	0601. 1099	135
Tuberous roots, seed, dormant	块根,种用,休眠的	0601. 1091	135
Tubers, in growth or in flower	块茎,生长或开花的	0601. 2000	
Tubers, nes, dormant	块茎,其他,休眠的	0601. 1099	135
Tubers, seed, dormant	块茎,种用,休眠的	0601. 1091	135
Tubes and pipes of circular cross-section, of the internal diameter of 500mm or more	管及空心异型材,铸铁的,内径在500毫米及以上的圆形截面管	7303. 0010	6
Tubes and pipes of copper alloys, nes	管,铜合金制,其他	7411. 2900	6
Tubes and pipes of copper-nickel base alloys (cupronickel)	管,铜镍合金(白铜)制	7411. 2200	6
Tubes and pipes of copper-nickel-zinc base alloys (nickel silver)	管,铜镍锌合金(德银)制	7411. 2200	6
Tubes and pipes of copper-zinc base alloys (brass), in coils	管,铜锌合金(黄铜)制,盘卷的	7411. 2110	6
Tubes and pipes of copper-zinc base alloys (brass), nes	管,铜锌合金(黄铜)制,其他	7411. 2190	6
Tubes and pipes of nickel alloys	管,镍合金制	7507. 1200	6
Tubes and pipes of nickel, not alloyed	管,非合金镍制	7507. 1100	6
Tubes and pipes of refined copper, having an outside diameter exceeding 70mm	管,精炼铜制,外径超过70毫米的	7411. 1020	6
Tubes and pipes of refined copper, having an outside diameter not exceeding 25mm, nes	管,精炼铜制,外径不超过25毫米的,其他	7411. 1019	6
Tubes and pipes of refined copper, having an outside diameter not exceeding 25mm, threaded or with fins	管,精炼铜制,外径不超过25毫米的,带有螺纹或翅片的	7411. 1011	6
Tubes and pipes of refined copper, nes	管,精炼铜制,其他	7411. 1090	6
Tubes and pipes, of aluminium alloys, having a wall thickness not exceeding 25mm	管,铝合金制,壁厚不超过25毫米	7608. 2091	68

T

Article Description	商品名称	Tariff Code	D. R.
Tubes and pipes, of aluminium alloys, having an outside diameter not exceeding 10cm	管,铝合金制,外径不超过10厘米的	7608.2010	68
Tubes and pipes, of aluminium alloys, nes	管,铝合金制,其他	7608.2099	68
Tubes and pipes, of aluminium, not alloyed	管,非合金铝制	7608.1000	68
Tubes and pipes, of iron or steel, having circular cross-sections, longitudinally welded, the external diameter of which exceeds 406.4mm	管,钢铁的,圆形截面的,纵向焊接的,外径超过406.4毫米	7305.3100	6
Tubes and pipes, of iron or steel, having circular cross-sections, the external diameter of which exceeds 406.4mm, nes	管,钢铁的,圆形截面的,外径超过406.4毫米,其他	7305.9000	6
Tubes and pipes, of iron or steel, having circular cross-sections, the external diameter of which exceeds 406.4mm, welded, nes	管,钢铁的,圆形截面的,焊接的,外径超过406.4毫米,其他	7305.3900	6
Tubes or pipes, of titanium	管,钛的	8108.9040	16
Tubes, of metal carbides, coated or cored with flux material, of a kind used for soldering, brazing, welding or deposition of metal or of metal carbides	管,硬质合金制,以焊剂涂面或以焊剂为芯,用于焊接或沉积金属、硬质合金	8311.9000	56
Tubes, pipes and hollow profiles, nes	管及空心异型材,其他	7306.9000	6
Tubes, pipes and hollow profiles, of alloy steel, of circular cross-section, welded, nes	管及空心异型材,合金钢的圆形截面,焊接的,其他	7306.5000	6
Tubes, pipes and hollow profiles, of cast iron, nes	管及空心异型材,铸铁的,其他	7303.0090	6
Tubes, pipes and hollow profiles, of iron or non-alloy steel, of circular cross-section, welded, having an outside diameter not exceeding 10mm, and having a wall thickness of 0.7mm or less	管及空心异型材,铁或非合金钢的,圆形截面,焊接的,外径不超过10毫米的,壁厚在0.7毫米及以下	7306.3011	6
Tubes, pipes and hollow profiles, of iron or non-alloy steel, of circular cross-section, welded, having an outside diameter not exceeding 10mm, nes	管及空心异型材,铁或非合金钢的,圆形截面,焊接的,外径不超过10毫米的,其他	7306.3019	6
Tubes, pipes and hollow profiles, of iron or non-alloy steel, of circular cross-section, welded, nes	管及空心异型材,铁或非合金钢的,圆形截面,焊接的,其他	7306.3090	6
Tubes, pipes and hollow profiles, of other non-circular cross-section, welded	管及空心异型材,其他非圆形截面的,焊接的	7306.6900	6
Tubes, pipes and hollow profiles, of square or rectangular cross-section, welded	管及空心异型材,矩形或正方形截面的,焊接的	7306.6100	6
Tubes, pipes and hollow profiles, of stainless steel, of circular cross-section, welded, nes	管及空心异型材,不锈钢的,圆形截面,焊接的,其他	7306.4000	6
Tubes, pipes and hollow profiles, seamless, of alloy steel, of circular cross-section, cold-drawn or cold-rolled, nes	管及空心异型材,无缝的,合金钢的,圆形截面管,冷拔或冷轧的,其他	7304.5190	6
Tubes, pipes and hollow profiles, seamless, of alloy steel, of circular cross-section, nes	管及空心异型材,无缝的,合金钢的,圆形截面管,其他	7304.5990	6
Tubes, pipes and hollow profiles, seamless, of circular cross-section, of stainless steel, nes	管及空心异型材,无缝的,不锈钢的,圆形截面,其他	7304.4990	6

T

Article Description	商品名称	Tariff Code	D. R.
Tubes, pipes and hollow profiles, seamless, of iron or non-alloysteel, of circular cross-section, cold-drawn or cold-rolled, nes	管及空心异型材,无缝的,铁或非合金钢的,圆形截面,冷拔或冷轧的,其他	7304. 3190	6
Tubes, pipes and hollow profiles, seamless, of iron or non-alloysteel, of circular cross-section, nes	管及空心异型材,无缝的,铁或非合金钢的,圆形截面,其他	7304. 3990	6
Tubes, pipes and hollow profiles, seamless, of iron or steel, nes	管及空心异型材,无缝的,钢铁的,其他	7304. 9000	6
Tubes, pipes and hollow profiles, seamless, of stainless steel, of circular cross-section, cold-drawn or cold-rolled, nes	管及空心异型材,无缝的,不锈钢的,圆形截面,冷拔或冷轧的,其他	7304. 4190	6
Tubes, pipes and hoses, flexible, of plastics, having a minimum burst pressure of 27. 6 MPa	软管,塑料制的,爆破压力不低于27. 6兆帕斯卡	3917. 3100	36
Tubes, pipes and hoses, of plastics, nes	塑料管,其他	3917. 3900	36
Tubes, pipes and hoses, of plastics, not reinforced or otherwise combined with other materials, with fittings	塑料管子,装有附件的,未经加强也未与其他材料合制	3917. 3300	36
Tubes, pipes and hoses, of plastics, not reinforced or otherwise combined with other materials, without fittings	塑料管,未装有附件的,未经加强也未与其他材料合制	3917. 3200	36
Tubes, pipes and hoses, of vulcanized rubber other than hard rubber, not reinforced or otherwise combined with other materials, with fittings	管子,硫化橡胶(硬质橡胶除外)制的,未经加强或未与其他材料合制,装有附件	4009. 1200	136
Tubes, pipes and hoses, of vulcanized rubber other than hard rubber, not reinforced or otherwise combined with other materials, without fittings	管子,硫化橡胶(硬质橡胶除外)制的,未经加强或未与其他材料合制,未装有附件	4009. 1100	136
Tubes, pipes and hoses, of vulcanized rubber other than hard rubber, reinforced or otherwise combined only with metal, with fittings	管子,硫化橡胶(硬质橡胶除外)制的,用金属加强或只与金属合制,装有附件	4009. 2200	136
Tubes, pipes and hoses, of vulcanized rubber other than hard rubber, reinforced or otherwise combined only with metal, without fittings	管子,硫化橡胶(硬质橡胶除外)制的,用金属加强或只与金属合制,未装有附件	4009. 2100	136
Tubes, pipes and hoses, of vulcanized rubber other than hard rubber, reinforced or otherwise combined only with textile materials, with fittings	管子,硫化橡胶(硬质橡胶除外)制的,用纺织材料加强或只与纺织材料合制,装有附件	4009. 3200	136
Tubes, pipes and hoses, of vulcanized rubber other than hard rubber, reinforced or otherwise combined only with textile materials, without fittings	管子,硫化橡胶(硬质橡胶除外)制的,用纺织材料加强或只与纺织材料合制,未装有附件	4009. 3100	136
Tubes, pipes and hoses, of vulcanized rubber other than hard rubber, reinforced or otherwise combined with other materials, with fittings	管子,硫化橡胶(硬质橡胶除外)制的,用其他材料加强或与其他材料合制,装有附件	4009. 4200	136
Tubes, pipes and hoses, of vulcanized rubber other than hard rubber, reinforced or otherwise combined with other materials, without fittings	管子,硫化橡胶(硬质橡胶除外)制的,用其他材料加强或与其他材料合制,未装有附件	4009. 4100	136

Article Description	商品名称	Tariff Code	D. R.
Tubes, pipes and hoses, rigid, of other plastics	硬管,其他塑料制	3917.2900	36
Tubes, pipes and hoses, rigid, of polymers of ethylene	硬管,乙烯聚合物制	3917.2100	36
Tubes, pipes and hoses, rigid, of polymers of propylene	硬管,丙烯聚合物制	3917.2200	36
Tubes, pipes and hoses, rigid, of polymers of vinyl chloride	硬管,氯乙烯聚合物制	3917.2300	36
Tubes, pipes and tube or pipe fittings (for example couplings, elbows, sleeves) of zinc	管及管子附件(例如,接头、肘管、管套),锌制	7907.0020	16
Tubes, pipes and tube or pipe fittings (for example, couplings, elbows, sleeves) of tin	管及管子附件(例如,接头、肘管、管套),锡制	8007.0040	16
Tubs and other coopers products and parts thereof, of wood, including staves, of other wood	箍桶及其零件,包括桶板,其他木制的	4416.0090	56
Tubs and other coopers products and parts thereof, of wood, including staves, of radiata pine	箍桶及其零件,包括桶板,辐射松制的	4416.0010	56
Tubular metal needles, used in medical, surgical, dental or veterinary sciences	管状金属针头,医疗、外科、牙科或兽医用	9018.3210	
Tubular rivets, of base metal	管形铆钉,贱金属制,	8308.2000	256
Tufted textile fabrics of cotton or bast fibres	簇绒织物,棉或麻制	5802.3030	468
Tufted textile fabrics of man-made fibres	簇绒织物,化学纤维制	5802.3040	468
Tufted textile fabrics of silk or silk waste	簇绒织物,丝及绢丝制	5802.3010	468
Tufted textile fabrics of textile materials, nes	簇绒织物,纺织材料制,其他	5802.3090	468
Tufted textile fabrics of wool or fine animal hair	簇绒织物,羊毛或动物细毛制	5802.3020	468
Tufting machines auxiliary, for making carpets or rugs	簇绒机的辅助机器	8448.1900	3
Tufting machines, for making carpets or rugs	簇绒机,地毯织机	8447.9011	7
Tufting machines, nes	簇绒机,其他	8447.9019	7
Tugs craft	拖轮	8904.0000	
Tulle lace making machines	花边薄纱机	8447.9090	7
Tulles and other net fabrics, of cotton	网眼薄纱及其他网眼织物,棉制	5804.1020	468
Tulles and other net fabrics, of man-made fibres	网眼薄纱及其他网眼织物,化学纤维制	5804.1030	468
Tulles and other net fabrics, of silk or silk waste	网眼薄纱及其他网眼织物,丝及绢丝制	5804.1010	468
Tulles and other net fabrics, of textile materials, nes	网眼薄纱及其他网眼织物,纺织材料制,其他	5804.1090	468
Tunas, nes, fresh or chilled	金枪鱼,其他,鲜或冷的	0302.3900	18
Tunas, nes, frozen	金枪鱼,其他,冻的	0303.4900	18
Tunas, prepared or preserved, whole or in pieces, but not minced	金枪鱼,制作或保藏的,整条或切块,但未绞碎	1604.1400	48
Tung nuts (oleococca seeds)	油桐子	1207.9999	3
Tung oil and its fractions	桐油及其分离品	1515.9030	
Tungstates (wolframates), nes	钨酸盐,其他	2841.8090	1
Tungsten (wolfram) articles, nes	钨制品,其他	8101.9990	16

T

Article Description	商品名称	Tariff Code	D. R.
Tungsten (wolfram) powders	钨粉末	8101. 1000	16
Tungsten carbides	碳化钨	2849. 9020	
Tungsten halogen, for locomotives and rolling-stock, aircraft or ships	卤钨灯,火车、航空器及船舶用	8539. 2120	35
Tungsten halogen, for motor vehicles	卤钨灯,机动车辆用	8539. 2130	35
Tungsten halogen, for scientific or medical uses only	卤钨灯,科研、医疗专用	8539. 2110	35
Tungsten halogen, other	卤钨灯,其他	8539. 2190	35
Tungsten ores and concentrates	钨矿砂及其精矿	2611. 0000	146
Tungsten oxides and hydroxides, nes	钨的氧化物及氢氧化物,其他	2825. 9019	
Tungsten wire	钨丝	8101. 9600	16
Tungsten, unwrought, including bars and rods obtained simply by sintering	钨,未锻轧,包括简单烧结而成的条、杆	8101. 9400	16
Tungstic acid	钨酸	2825. 9011	
Tungstic oxide	三氧化钨	2825. 9012	
Tuning forks	音叉	9209. 9910	3
Tunnelling machinery parts	隧道掘进机零件	8431. 4990	3
Tunnelling machinery, nes	隧道掘进机,其他	8430. 3900	5
Tunnelling machinery, self-propelle	隧道掘进机,自推进的	8430. 3100	5
Turbines for marine propulsion	汽轮机,船舶动力用	8406. 1000	3
Turbines parts	汽轮机零件	8406. 9000	3
Turbines, of an output exceeding 100 MW but not exceeding 350 MW	汽轮机,输出功率超过 100 兆瓦,但不超过 350 兆瓦的	8406. 8120	3
Turbines, of an output exceeding 350 MW	汽轮机,输出功率超过 350 兆瓦的	8406. 8130	3
Turbines, of an output exceeding 40 MW but not exceeding 100 MW	汽轮机,输出功率超过 40 兆瓦,但不超过 100 兆瓦的	8406. 8110	3
Turbines, of an output not exceeding 40 MW	汽轮机,输出功率不超过 40 兆瓦的	8406. 8200	3
Turbo fan engines, of a thrust exceeding 25kN	涡轮风扇发动机,推力超过 25 千牛顿	8411. 1210	27
Turbo fan engines, of a thrust not exceeding 25kN	涡轮风扇发动机,推力不超过 25 千牛顿	8411. 1110	27
Turboshaft engines parts	涡轮轴发动机用零件	8411. 9910	27
Turbo-jets parts	涡轮喷气发动机用零件	8411. 9100	27
Turbo-jets, of a thrust not exceeding 25kN, nes	涡轮喷气发动机,推力不超过 25 千牛顿,其他	8411. 1190	27
Turbo-propellers parts	涡轮螺桨发动机用零件	8411. 9100	27
Turbo-propellers, of a power exceeding 1100kW but not exceeding 2238kW	涡轮螺桨发动机,功率超过 1100 千瓦,但不超过 2238 千瓦	8411. 2210	27
Turbo-propellers, of a power exceeding 2238kW but not exceeding 3730kW	涡轮螺桨发动机,功率超过 2238 千瓦,但不超过 3730 千瓦	8411. 2220	27
Turbo-propellers, of a power exceeding 3730kW	涡轮螺桨发动机,功率超过 3730 千瓦	8411. 2230	27
Turbo-propellers, of a power not exceeding 1100kW	涡轮螺桨发动机,功率不超过 1100 千瓦	8411. 2100	27
Turkeys, prepared or preserved	火鸡,制作或保藏的	1602. 3100	48

Article Description	商品名称	Tariff Code	D. R.
Turkeys, ex. pure-bred breeding, weighing more than 185g	火鸡,改良种用除外,重量超过185克	0105. 9994	48
Turkeys, ex. pure-bred breeding, weighing not more than 185g	火鸡,改良种用除外,重量不超过185克	0105. 1290	48
Turkeys, not cut in pieces, frozen	整只火鸡,冻的	0207. 2500	1
Turkeys, not cut in pieces, fresh or chilled	整只火鸡,鲜或冷的	0207. 2400	1
Turkeys, pure-bred breeding, weighing more than 185g	火鸡,改良种用,重量超过185克	0105. 9910	48
Turkeys, pure-bred breeding, weighing not more than 185g	火鸡,改良种用,重量不超过185克	0105. 1210	48
Turmric (curcuma)	姜黄	0910. 3000	
Turning centres, for removing metal, nes	车削中心,切削金属的,其他	8458. 9900	7
Turning centres, horizontal, for removing metal, nes	车削中心,卧式,切削金属的,其他	8458. 1900	7
Turning centres, horizontal, numerically controlled, for removing metal	车削中心,卧式,数控的,切削金属的	8458. 1100	7
Turning centres, numerically controlled, for removing metal, nes	车削中心,数控的,切削金属的,其他	8458. 9100	7
Turning tools, interchangeable, nes	车削用工具,可互换,其他	8207. 8090	256
Turning tools, interchangeable, with working part of diamonds etc.	车削用工具,可互换,带有金刚石等工作部件的	8207. 8010	256
Turnips, fresh or chilled	萝卜,鲜或冷藏的	0706. 1000	1
Turntables (record-decks)	转盘(唱机唱盘)	8519. 3000	
Turntables (record-decks) or record-players parts and accessories	转盘或唱机用零件、附件	8522. 9010	3
Turtles' eggs	海龟蛋	0410. 0090	34
Tussah silk	柞蚕丝	5002. 0020	45
Tussah silk fabrics, containing 85% or more by weight of silk or of silk waste, nes	柞蚕丝机织物,按重量计丝或绢丝含量在85%及以上,其他	5007. 2029	4568
Tussah silk fabrics, unbleached or bleached, containing 85% or more by weight of silk or of silk waste	柞蚕丝机织物,未漂白或漂白,按重量计丝或绢丝含量在85%及以上	5007. 2021	4568
Tweezers and similar tools	镊子及类似工具	8203. 2000	256
Twine, cordage, rope sand cables, of polyethylene or polypropylene, nes	线、绳、索、缆,聚乙烯或聚丙烯制,其他	5607. 4900	368
Twine, cordage, rope sand cables, nes	线、绳、索、缆,其他	5607. 9090	368
Twine, cordage, rope sand cables, of abaca or other hard fibres	线、绳、索、缆,蕉麻或其他硬质纤维纺制	5607. 9010	368
Twine, cordage, rope sand cables, of sisal or other texile fibres of the genus Agave, nes	线、绳、索、缆,西沙尔麻或其他纺织用龙舌兰类纤维制,其他	5607. 2900	368
Twine, cordage, rope sand cables, of synthetic fibres, nes	线、绳、索、缆,合成纤维制,其他	5607. 5000	368
Twisted hoop, barbed or not, of a kind used for fencing, of iron or steel	绞带,不论是否带刺,钢铁的,围篱用的	7313. 0000	36

T

Article Description	商品名称	Tariff Code	D. R.
Two-handed pruning shears and similar two-handed shears	双手修枝剪及类似的双手操作剪刀	8201.6000	256
Type casters	铸字机	8442.3010	
Typesetting machinery, apparatus and equipment, nes	制版机器、器具及设备,其他	8442.3029	
Typewriters, automatic	打字机,自动的	8469.0012	
Typewriters, electric, nes	打字机,电动的,其他	8469.0020	
Typewriters, non-electric, nes	打字机,非电动,其他	8469.0030	
Tyre cord fabric of high tenacity yarn of nylon or polyamides, nes	帘子布,尼龙或聚酰胺制高强力纱,其他	5902.1090	
Tyre cord fabric of high tenacity yarn of nylon-6	帘子布,尼龙-6 高强力纱制	5902.1010	
Tyre cord fabric of high tenacity yarn of nylon-6,6	帘子布,尼龙-6,6 高强力纱制	5902.1020	
Tyre cord fabric of high tenacity yarn of polyesters	帘子布,聚酯高强力纱制	5902.2000	
Tyre cord fabric of high tenacity yarn of viscose rayon	帘子布,粘胶纤维高强力纱制	5902.9000	
Tyre flaps, of rubber	橡胶轮胎衬带	4012.9090	234
Tyre treads, of rubber	橡胶胎面	4012.9090	234
Tyrosine	酪氨酸	2922.5000	36
T-shirts, knitted or crocheted, nes	T 恤衫,针织或钩编的,其他	6109.9090	2456
T-shirts, knitted or crocheted, of cotton	T 恤衫,针织或钩编的,棉制	6109.1000	2456
T-shirts, knitted or crocheted, of silk or silk waste	T 恤衫,针织或钩编的,及绢丝制	6109.9010	2456

U

Article Description	商品名称	Tariff Code	D. R.
U sections, not further worked than hot-rolled, hot-drawn or extruded, of a height of 80mm or more	槽钢,除热轧、热拉拔或热挤压外未经进一步加工,截面高度在 80 毫米及以上	7216. 3100	468
U sections, not further worked than hot-rolled, hot-drawn or extruded, of a height of less than 80mm	槽钢,除热轧、热拉拔或热挤压外未经进一步加工,截面高度低于 80 毫米	7216. 1090	468
Ultramarine and preparations based thereon	群青及以其为基本成分的制品	3206. 4100	2368
Ultrasonic apparatus for cleaning, flat panel displays manufacture machines and apparatus	超声波清洗装置,平板显示器的制造机器及装置	8486. 3041	7
Ultrasonic apparatus parts and accessories for cleaning, flat panel displays manufacture machines and apparatus	超声波清洗装置零件及附件,平板显示器的制造机器及装置	8486. 9090	3
Ultrasonic diagnostic equipment, B-type	超声波诊断仪,B 型	9018. 1210	
Ultrasonic diagnostic equipment, chromoscope	超声波诊断仪,彩色	9018. 1291	
Ultrasonic examinations apparatus	超声波探伤检测仪	9031. 8031	
Ultrasonic scanning apparatus, nes	超声波扫描装置,其他	9018. 1299	7
Ultra-violet lamps	紫外线灯	8539. 4900	35
Ultra-violet ray apparatus, used in medical, surgical, dental or veterinary sciences	紫外线装置,医疗、外科、牙科或兽医用	9018. 2000	
Umbrella frames, including frames mounted on shafts (sticks)	伞骨,包括装在伞柄上的伞骨	6603. 2000	
Umbrellas and sun umbrellas, having a telescopic shaft	雨伞及阳伞,折叠	6601. 9100	
Umbrellas and sun umbrellas, having a telescopic shaft	折叠伞	6601. 9100	
Umbrellas and sun umbrellas, nes	雨伞及阳伞,其他	6601. 9900	
Umbrellas parts, nes	伞的零件,其他	6603. 9000	
Umbrellas, for garden or similar usage	伞及类似伞,庭园用	6601. 1000	
Underpants and briefs, knitted or crocheted, for men or boys, nes	内裤及三角裤,针织或钩编的男式,其他	6107. 1990	2456
Underpants and briefs, knitted or crocheted, for men or boys, of cotton	内裤及三角裤,针织或钩编的男式,棉制	6107. 1100	2456
Underpants and briefs, knitted or crocheted, for men or boys, of man-made fibres	内裤及三角裤,针织或钩编的男式,化学纤维制	6107. 1200	2456
Underpants and briefs, knitted or crocheted, for men or boys, of silk or silk waste	内裤及三角裤,针织或钩编的男式,丝及绢丝制	6107. 1910	2456
Underpants and briefs, not knitted or crocheted, for men or boys, nes	内裤及三角裤,非针织或钩编的,男式,其他	6207. 1990	2456
Underpants and briefs, not knitted or crocheted, for men or boys, of cotton	内裤及三角裤,非针织或钩编的,男式,棉制	6207. 1100	2456

Article Description	商品名称	Tariff Code	D. R.
Underpants and briefs, not knitted or crocheted, for men or boys, of man-made fibres	内裤及三角裤,非针织或钩编的,男式,化学纤维制	6207.1920	2456
Underpants and briefs, not knitted or crocheted, for men or boys, of silk or silk waste	内裤及三角裤,非针织或钩编的,男式,丝及绢丝制	6207.1910	2456
Under-carriages and parts thereof, of aircraft	起落架及其零件	8803.2000	3
Uninterrupted power suppliers	不间断供电电源	8504.4020	8
Uninterrupted power suppliers parts	不间断供电电源用零件	8504.9020	3
Unit construction machines (single station), for working metal	单工位组合机床,加工金属的	8457.2000	7
Units of automatic data processing machines, nes	自动数据处理设备的其他部件	8471.8000	
Universal joints	万向节	8483.6000	
Universal joints parts	万向节零件	8483.9000	3
Unreeling machines for textile fabrics	退绕机器,纺织物的	8451.5000	
Unreeling machines parts for textile fabrics	退绕机器零件,纺织物的	8451.9000	
Unrooted cuttings	无根插枝	0602.1000	3
Unsaturated acyclic monocarboxylic acids, their anhydrides, halides, peroxides, peroxyacids and their derivatives, nes	不饱和无环一元羧酸及其酸酐、酰卤化物、过氧化物和过氧酸以及它们的衍生物,其他	2916.1900	36
Unsaturated chlorinated derivatives of acyclic hydrocarbons, nes	无环烃的不饱和氯化衍生物,其他	2903.2990	36
Unsaturated monohydric alcohols, nes	不饱和一元醇,其他	2905.2900	36
Upright pianos	竖式钢琴	9201.1000	5
Uranium and its compounds, natural	铀及其化合物,天然的	2844.1000	
Uranium depleted in U235 and its compounds	U235 贫化铀及其化合物	2844.3000	
Uranium enriched in U235 and its compounds	U235 浓缩铀及其化合物	2844.2000	
Uranium ores and concentrates	铀矿砂及其精矿	2612.1000	146
Uranothorianite	方铀钍石	2612.1000	146
Urbo-jets, of a thrust exceeding 25kN, nes	涡轮喷气发动机,推力超过 25 千牛顿,其他	8411.1290	27
Urea resins, in primary forms	尿素树脂,初级形状的	3909.1000	1256
Urea, whether or not in aqueous solution	尿素,不论是否水溶液	3102.1000	68
Ureides and their derivatives; salts thereof	酰脲及其衍生物以及它们的盐	2924.2100	36
Urinals and similar sanitary fixtures, of porcelain or china	小便池及类似的固定卫生设备,瓷制	6910.1000	268
Urinals and similar sanitary fixtures, of pottery	小便池及类似的固定卫生设备,陶制	6910.9000	268
Uspension systems and parts thereof (including shock-absorbers), of motor vehicles with seats less than 10	悬挂系统及其零件(包括减震器),10座以下客车用	8708.8010	3
UV spectrometers, spectrophotometers and spectrographs	紫外线分光仪、分光光度计及摄谱仪	9027.3000	

V

Article Description	商品名称	Tariff Code	D. R.
Vaccines for human medicine	人用疫苗	3002. 2000	34
Vaccines for veterinary medicine	兽用疫苗	3002. 3000	34
Vacuum cleaners parts, nes	真空吸尘器零件,其他	8508. 7090	3
Vacuum cleaners parts, of vacuum cleaners which having self-contained electric motor, of a power not exceeding 1500W and having a dust bag or other receptacle capacity not exceeding 20L, of the cleaners of subheading 8508. 1100	真空吸尘器零件,电动吸尘器的,功率不超过 1500 瓦,且带有容积不超过 20 升的集尘袋或其他集尘容器,子目 8508. 1100 所列吸尘器用	8508. 7010	3
Vacuum cleaners, nes	真空吸尘器,其他	8508. 6000	78
Vacuum cleaners, with self-contained electric motor, nes	真空吸尘器,电动的,其他	8508. 1900	78
Vacuum cleaners, with self-contained electric motor, of a power not exceeding 1500W and having a dust bag or other receptacle capacity not exceeding 20L	真空吸尘器,电动的,功率不超过 1500 瓦,且带有容积不超过 20 升的集尘袋或其他集尘容器	8508. 1100	78
Vacuum flasks, complete with case	保温瓶,带壳的	9617. 0010	
Vacuum moulding machines, for working rubber or plastics or for the manufacture of products from these materials, nes	真空模塑机器,加工橡胶或塑料及其产品用,其他	8477. 4090	7
Vacuum pumps	真空泵	8414. 1000	27
Vacuum pumps parts	真空泵零件	8414. 9090	23
Vacuum vessels and parts thereof, other than glass inners	真空容器及其零件,玻璃瓶胆除外	9617. 0090	5
Valentinite	锑华	2617. 1090	146
Valine	缬氨酸	2922. 4910	36
Valves and tubes, nes	灯管,其他	8540. 8900	35
Valves parts	阀门用零件	8481. 9010	3
Valves, nes	阀门,其他	8481. 8040	
Van trailers and semi-trailers	货柜挂车及半挂车	8716. 3910	
Vanadinite	钒铅矿	2615. 9090	146
Vanadium articles	钒制品	8112. 9920	16
Vanadium ores and concentrates	钒矿砂及其精矿	2615. 9090	146
Vanadium oxides and hydroxides, nes	钒的氧化物及氢氧化物,其他	2825. 3090	
Vanadium powders	钒粉末	8112. 9220	16
Vanadium, unwrought	钒,未锻轧	8112. 9220	16
Vanilla	香子兰豆	0905. 0000	
Vanillin	香草醛	2912. 4100	36
Vanity-cases, with outer surface of leather, of composition leather or of patent leather	小手袋,以皮革、再生皮革或漆皮作面	4202. 1190	1458

Article Description	商品名称	Tariff Code	D. R.
Vanity-cases, with outer surface of plastics or of textile materials	小手袋,以塑料或纺织材料作面	4202. 1290	256
Vats, of other wood	盆,其他木制的	4416. 0090	56
Vats, of plastics, of a capacity exceeding 300L, for builders	罐及类似容器,容积超过300升,建筑用	3925. 1000	23
Vats, of radiata pine	盆,辐射松制的	4416. 0010	56
Vegetable fats and oil and fractions thereof, partly or wholly hydrogenated, interesterified, reesterified or elaidinized, whether or not refined, but not further prepared	植物油脂及其分离品,全部或部分氢化,相互酯化,再酯化或反油酸化,不论是否精制,但未经进一步加工	1516. 2000	
Vegetable fats and oils and fractions thereof, nes	植物油脂及其分离品,其他	1518. 0000	46
Vegetable juice extractors, electro-mechanical domestic appliances	蔬菜榨汁机,家用电动器具	8509. 4010	
Vegetable juice, of any other single vegetable	蔬菜汁,其他单一蔬菜的	2009. 8020	2468
Vegetable materials and veget-able waste, vegetable residues and by-products, whether or not in the form of pellets, of a kind used in animal feeding, not elsewhere specified or included	动物饲料用的其他税号未列名的植物原料、废料、残渣及副产品,不论是否制成团粒	2308. 0000	36
Vegetable materials, primarily for plaiting	植物材料,主要作编结用的	1401. 9090	3
Vegetable materials, rushes	植物材料,灯心草属的	1401. 9039	3
Vegetable parchment	植物羊皮纸	4806. 1000	58
Vegetable pitch	植物沥青	3807. 0000	3
Vegetable products, nes	植物产品,其他	1404. 9090	
Vegetable saps and extracts, azadirachtin	液汁及浸膏,印楝素	1302. 1920	14
Vegetable saps and extracts, crude lacquer	液汁及浸膏,生漆的	1302. 1910	14
Vegetable saps and extracts, nes	液汁及浸膏,其他	1302. 1990	
Vegetable saps and extracts, of hops	液汁及浸膏,啤酒花的	1302. 1300	146
Vegetable saps and extracts, of liquorice	液汁及浸膏,甘草的	1302. 1200	14
Vegetable saps and extracts, of pyrethrum or of the roots of plants containing rotenone	液汁及浸膏,除虫菊的或含鱼藤酮植物根茎的	1302. 1930	14
Vegetable saps and extracts, opium	液汁及浸膏,鸦片的	1302. 1100	14
Vegetable seeds	蔬菜种子,种植用的	1209. 9100	358
Vegetable textile fibres yarn, nes	植物纺织纤维纱线,其他	5308. 9099	568
Vegetable textile fibres yarn, nes	植物纤维机织物,纺织用,其他	5311. 0090	2468
Vegetable textile fibres, tow, noils and waste of these fibres, nes	植物纤维及其短纤、落麻及废料,纺织用,其他	5305. 0099	4
Vegetable waxes	植物蜡	1521. 1000	6
Vegetables and mixtures of vegetables, in airtight containers	罐头,其他,蔬菜及什锦蔬菜	2005. 9991	148
Vegetables and mixtures of vegetables, nes	蔬菜及什锦蔬菜,其他	2005. 9999	148
Vegetables preparation machinery	蔬菜加工机器	8438. 6000	
Vegetables preparation machinery parts	蔬菜加工机器的零件	8438. 9000	3

V

Article Description	商品名称	Tariff Code	D. R.
Vegetables, nes, dried	蔬菜,其他,干的	0712.9090	4
Vegetables, nes, fresh or chilled	蔬菜,其他,鲜或冷藏的	0709.9090	1
Vegetables, nes, frozen	蔬菜,其他,冷冻的	0710.8090	1
Vegetables, nes, in brine, provisionally preserved, but unsuitable in that state for immediate consumption	蔬菜,其他,盐水的,暂时保藏,但不适合直接使用的	0711.9039	34
Vegetables, nes, prepared or preserved otherwise than by vinegar or acetic acid	蔬菜,其他,用醋或醋酸以外的其他方法制作或保藏的	2004.9000	48
Vegetables, nes, provisionally preserved, but unsuitable in that state for immediate consumption	蔬菜,其他,暂时保藏,但不适合直接使用的	0711.9090	34
Vehicles parts, not mechanically propelled	非机械驱动车辆零件	8716.9000	3
Vehicles specially designed for travelling on snow	雪地行走专用车	8703.1090	58
Vehicles, not mechanically propelled, nes	非机械驱动车辆,其他	8716.8000	
Veils and the like, knitted or crocheted, nes	面纱及类似品,针织或钩编的,其他	6117.1090	2456
Veils and the like, knitted or crocheted, of fine animal hair, nes	面纱及类似品,针织或钩编的,其他动物细毛制	6117.1019	2456
Veils and the like, knitted or crocheted, of goats fine animal hair	面纱及类似品,针织或钩编的,山羊绒制	6117.1011	2456
Veils and the like, knitted or crocheted, of wool	面纱及类似品,针织或钩编的,羊毛制	6117.1020	2456
Veils and the like, not knitted or crocheted, of artificial fibres	面纱及类似品,非针织或钩编的,人造纤维制	6214.4000	2456
Veils and the like, not knitted or crocheted, of goats fine animal hair	面纱及类似品,非针织或钩编的,山羊绒制	6214.2020	2456
Veils and the like, not knitted or crocheted, of other fine animal hair	面纱及类似品,非针织或钩编的,其他动物细毛制	6214.2090	2456
Veils and the like, not knitted or crocheted, of other textile materials	面纱及类似品,非针织或钩编的,其他纺织材料制	6214.9000	2456
Veils and the like, not knitted or crocheted, of silk or silk waste	面纱及类似品,非针织或钩编的,丝或绢丝制	6214.1000	2456
Veils and the like, not knitted or crocheted, of synthetic fibres	面纱及类似品,非针织或钩编的,合成纤维制	6214.3000	2456
Veils and the like, not knitted or crocheted, of wool	面纱及类似品,非针织或钩编的,羊毛制	6214.2010	2456
Veneer sheets, of a thickness not exceeding 6mm, coniferous, for plywood	单板,厚度不超过6毫米,针叶木,制胶合板用	4408.1020	458
Veneer sheets, of a thickness not exceeding 6mm, coniferous, nes	单板,厚度不超过6毫米,针叶木,制类似多层板用,其他	4408.1090	458
Veneer sheets, of a thickness not exceeding 6mm, coniferous, nes	单板,厚度不超过6毫米,针叶木的,其他	4408.1019	458
Veneer sheets, of a thickness not exceeding 6mm, coniferous, of laminated plywood	单板,厚度不超过6毫米,针叶木的,用多层板制的	4408.1011	458
Veneer sheets, of a thickness not exceeding 6mm, nes	单板,厚度不超过6毫米,其他	4408.9019	458
Veneer sheets, of a thickness not exceeding 6mm, nes	单板,厚度不超过6毫米,其他	4408.9099	458

V

Article Description	商品名称	Tariff Code	D. R.
Veneer sheets, of a thickness not exceeding 6mm, of laminated plywood, nes	单板,厚度不超过6毫米,用多层板制的,其他	4408. 9011	458
Veneer sheets, of a thickness not exceeding 6mm, of laminated plywood, nes	单板,厚度不超过6毫米,制胶合板用,其他	4408. 9029	458
Veneer sheets, of a thickness not exceeding 6mm, of meranti (Dark Red, Light Red and Bakau), for plywood	单板,厚度不超过6毫米,红柳桉木,制胶合板用	4408. 3120	458
Veneer sheets, of a thickness not exceeding 6mm, of meranti (Dark Red, Light Red and Bakau), nes	单板,厚度不超过6毫米,红柳桉木的,其他	4408. 3119	458
Veneer sheets, of a thickness not exceeding 6mm, of meranti (Dark Red, Light Red and Bakau), nes	单板,厚度不超过6毫米,红柳桉木的,其他	4408. 3190	458
Veneer sheets, of a thickness not exceeding 6mm, of meranti (Dark Red, Light Red and Bakau), of laminated plywood	单板,厚度不超过6毫米,红柳桉木的,用多层板制的	4408. 3111	458
Veneer sheets, of a thickness not exceeding 6mm, of temperate non-coniferous wood, nes	单板,厚度不超过6毫米,温带非针叶木制,其他	4408. 9091	458
Veneer sheets, of a thickness not exceeding 6mm, of temperate non-coniferous wood, of laminated plywood	单板,厚度不超过6毫米,温带非针叶木制,制胶合板用	4408. 9021	458
Veneer sheets, of a thickness not exceeding 6mm, of temperate non-coniferous wood, of laminated plywood	单板,厚度不超过6毫米,温带非针叶木制,用多层板制的	4408. 9012	458
Veneer sheets, of a thickness not exceeding 6mm, of tropical wood, for plywood	单板,厚度不超过6毫米,热带木,制胶合板用	4408. 3920	458
Veneer sheets, of a thickness not exceeding 6mm, of tropical wood, nes	单板,厚度不超过6毫米,红柳桉木,其他	4408. 3990	458
Veneer sheets, of a thickness not exceeding 6mm, of tropical wood, nes	单板,厚度不超过6毫米,热带木的,其他	4408. 3919	458
Veneer sheets, of a thickness not exceeding 6mm, of tropical wood, of laminated plywood	单板,厚度不超过6毫米,热带木的,用多层板制的	4408. 3911	458
Ventilating or recycling hoods, hoods having a maximum horizontal side not exceeding 120cm, nes	通风罩或循环气罩,罩的平面最大边长不超过120厘米的,其他	8414. 6090	23
Vermiculite, unexpanded	蛭石,未膨胀的	2530. 1020	13456
Vermouth, in containers holding 2L or less	味美思酒罐装,少于2升	2205. 1000	248
Vermouth, nes	味美思酒,其他	2205. 1000	248
Very pistols	维利式信号枪	9303. 9000	
Very pistols	信号枪,维利式	9303. 9000	
Vessels for the transport of persons, motor vessels	客运船舶,机动船舶	8901. 1010	5
Vessels for the transport of persons, not-motorized vessels	客运船舶,非机动船舶	8901. 1090	5
Vessels segments	船舶分段	8906. 9030	5
Vessels, the navigability of which is subsidiary to their main function, nes	船舶,不以航行为主要功能,其他	8905. 9090	37

V

Article Description	商品名称	Tariff Code	D. R.
Vessels, with non-motor, nes	船舶,非机动的,其他	8901.9090	8
Vessels, for breaking up	船舶,供拆卸的	8908.0000	5
Vessels, for pleasure or sports, nes	船舶,娱乐或运动用,其他	8903.9900	58
Vessels, motor powered, multi-purposes	船舶,机动的,多用途的	8901.9050	8
Vessels, motor powered, nes	船舶,机动的,其他	8901.9080	8
Vessels, unfinished or incomplete	船舶,未制成或不完整的	8906.9030	5
Vests, knitted or crocheted, nes	背心,针织或钩编的,其他	6109.9090	2456
Vests, knitted or crocheted, of cotton	背心,针织或钩编的,棉制	6109.1000	2456
Vests, knitted or crocheted, of silk or silk waste	背心,针织或钩编的,丝及绢丝制	6109.9010	2456
Vetches, forage products	巢菜,饲料用	1214.9000	
Veterinary sciences instruments and appliances, nes	兽医用仪器及器具,其他	9018.9090	7
Vibrating devices, for ingot continuous casting machines	振动装置,钢坯连铸机用	8454.9022	3
Vices and the like	台钳及类似品	8205.7000	256
Video camera recorders parts, camera modules without special purposes	视频摄录一体机用零件,非特种用途的取像模块	8529.9042	3
Video camera recorders parts, nes	视频摄录一体机用零件,其他	8529.9049	3
Video camera recorders parts, of special purposes	视频摄录一体机用零件,特种用途的	8529.9041	3
Video camera recorders, broadcast quality, not for special purposes	视频摄录一体机,非特种用途的广播极	8525.8032	7
Video camera recorders, for special purposes	视频摄录一体机,特种用途的	8525.8031	7
Video camera recorders, household-type, not for special purposes	视频摄录一体机,非特种用途的家用型	8525.8033	7
Video camera recorders, not for special purposes	视频摄录一体机,非特种用途的其他类型	8525.8039	7
Video compact disc player	视频高密光盘(VCD)播放机	8521.9011	5
Video compact disc player	VCD 播放机	8521.9011	5
Video games of a kind used with a television receiver	游戏机,与电视接收机配套使用的	9504.1000	5
Video games, operated by coins, bank notes, bank cards, tokens or by other means of payment	游戏机,用硬币、钞票、银行卡、代币或其他支付方式使其工作的	9504.3010	5
Video games, nes	游戏机,其他	9504.9010	5
Video recording or reproducing apparatus parts and accessories, nes	视频信号录制或重放设备用零件、附件,其他	8522.9039	3
Video recording or reproducing apparatus, whether or not incorporating a video tuner, nes	视频信号录制或重放设备,不论是否装有高频调谐器,其他	8521.9090	5
Video tape recorders, magnetic tape-type, broadcast quality	录像机,磁带型,广播级	8521.1011	5
Video tape recorders, magnetic tape-type, nes	录像机,磁带型,其他	8521.1019	5
Video tape reproducers, magnetic tape-type	放像机,磁带型	8521.1020	5
Vinegar	醋	2209.0000	268
Vinyl acetate	乙酸乙烯酯	2915.3200	36

V

Article Description	商品名称	Tariff Code	D. R.
Vinyl acetate copolymers, in aqueous dispersion, in primary forms	乙酸乙烯酯共聚物,水分散体,初级形状的	3905.2100	1256
Vinyl acetate copolymers, in primary forms, nes	乙酸乙烯酯共聚物,初级形状的,其他	3905.2900	1256
Vinyl acetate or of other vinyl esters copolymers, in primary forms	乙酸乙烯酯或其他乙烯酯聚合物的共聚物,初级形状的	3905.9100	1256
Vinyl acetate or of other vinyl esters polymers, in primary forms, nes	乙酸乙烯酯或其他乙烯酯聚合物,初级形状的,其他	3905.9900	1256
Vinyl chloride copolymers, in primary forms, nes	氯乙烯共聚物,初级形状的,其他	3904.4000	1256
Vinyl chloride (chloroethylene)	氯乙烯	2903.2100	36
Vinyl chloride-vinyl acetate copolymers, in primary forms	氯乙烯-乙酸乙烯酯共聚物,初级形状的	3904.3000	1256
Vinyl copolymers, in primary forms	乙烯基聚合物的共聚物,初级形状的	3905.9100	1256
Vinyl polymers in primary forms, nes	乙烯基聚合物,其他	3905.9900	1256
Vinylbital (INN); salts thereof	乙烯比妥(INN)以及盐	2933.5300	36
Vinylidene chloride polymers, in primary forms	偏二氯乙烯聚合物,初级形状的	3904.5000	1256
Violins	小提琴	9202.1000	5
Violins parts and accessories	小提琴的零件、附件	9209.9200	3
Viscose rayon high tenacity yarn woven fabrics	粘胶纤维高强力纱的机织物	5408.1000	2468
Viscose rayon high tenacity yarn, not put up for retail sale	粘胶纤维高强力纱,非供零售用	5403.1000	3468
Viscose rayon multiple or cabled yarn	粘胶纤维多股纱线或缆线	5403.4100	3468
Viscose rayon single yarn, not put up for retail sale, nes	醋酸纤维单纱,非供零售用,其他	5403.3390	3468
Viscose rayon single yarn, untwisted or with a twist not exceeding 120 turns per metre, not put up for retail sale, nes	粘胶纤维单纱,未加捻或捻度每米不超过120转,非供零售用,其他	5403.3190	3468
Viscose rayon single yarn, with a twist exceeding 120 turns per rnette, not put up for retail sale, nes	粘胶纤维单纱,捻度每米超过120转,非供零售用,其他	5403.3290	3468
Viscose rayon staple fibres, not carded, combed or otherwise processed for spinning, nes	粘胶纤维短纤,未梳或未经其他纺前加工,其他	5504.1090	68
Viscose rayon woven fabrics, containing 85% or more by weight of artificial filament or strip or the like, dyed	粘胶纤维制机织物,按重量计人造纤维长丝、扁条或类似品含量在85%及以上,染色	5408.2210	2468
Viscose rayon woven fabrics, containing 85% or more by weight of artificial filament or strip or the like, of yarns of different colours	粘胶纤维制机织物,按重量计人造纤维长丝、扁条或类似品含量在85%及以上,色织	5408.2310	2468
Viscose rayon woven fabrics, containing 85% or more by weight of artificial filament or strip or the like, printed	粘胶纤维制机织物,按重量计人造纤维长丝、扁条或类似品含量在85%及以上,印花	5408.2410	2468
Viscose rayon woven fabrics, containing 85% or more by weight of artificial filament or strip or the like, unbleached or bleached	粘胶纤维制机织物,按重量计人造纤维长丝、扁条或类似品含量在85%及以上,未漂白或漂白	5408.2110	2468
Viscosity improvers, for mineral oils and alike	粘度改良剂,用于矿物油及类似液体	3811.9000	236

Article Description	商品名称	Tariff Code	D. R.
Visible spectrometers, spectrophotometers and spectrographs	可见光分光仪、分光光度计及摄谱仪	9027. 3000	
Visual signalling equipment of a kind used for motor vehicles	视觉信号装置,机动车辆用	8512. 2090	7
Visual signalling equipment of a kind used on bicycles	视觉信号装置,自行车用	8512. 1000	7
Visual signalling equipment parts for cycles or motor vehicles	视觉信号装置,自行车或机动车辆用	8512. 9000	3
Vitamin B_1 and its derivatives	维生素 B_1 及其衍生物	2936. 2200	36
Vitamin B_{12} and its derivatives	维生素 B_{12} 及其衍生物	2936. 2600	36
Vitamin B_2 and its derivatives	维生素 B_2 及其衍生物	2936. 2300	36
Vitamin B_3 and its derivatives	维生素 B_3 及其衍生物	2936. 2400	36
Vitamin B_5 and its derivatives	维生素 B_5 及其衍生物	2936. 2400	36
Vitamin B_6 and its derivatives	维生素 B_6 及其衍生物	2936. 2500	36
Vitamin C and its derivatives	维生素 C 及其衍生物	2936. 2700	36
Vitamin E and its derivatives	维生素 E 及其衍生物	2936. 2800	36
Vitamins A and their derivatives	维生素 A 及其衍生物	2936. 2100	36
Vitamins and their derivatives, mixed	维生素及其衍生物,混合的	2936. 9000	36
Vitamins and their derivatives, unmixed, nes	维生素及其衍生物,未混合的,其他	2936. 2900	36
Vitamins medicaments, mixed or unmixed, put up in measured doses or in forms of packings for retail sale or other products of heading No. 29. 36	维生素类药品,混合或未混合的,配定剂量或制成零售包装,不包括税号 29. 36 的其他产品	3004. 5000	368
Vitamins, natural concentrates	维生素,天然浓缩物	2936. 9000	36
Vodka	伏特加酒	2208. 6000	2468
Voiles, of glass fibres	巴厘纱,玻璃纤维制	7019. 3200	56
Volleyballs	排球	9506. 6210	
Voltage limiters, for a voltage exceeding 1000V	电压限幅器,用于电压超过 1000 伏的线路	8535. 4000	8
Voltage-stabilized suppliers parts	稳压电源用零件	8504. 9020	3
Voltage-stabilized suppliers, nes	稳压电源,其他	8504. 4019	78
Voltage-stabilized suppliers, of the machines of heading No. 84. 71	稳压电源,税号 84. 71 所列机器用	8504. 4013	78
Voltmeters, without a recording device, nes	电压表,不带记录装置,其他	9030. 3390	
Voltmeters, of measuring range of 5. 5 or less, digital, without a recording device	电压表,量程在五位半及以下的,数字的,不带记录装置	9030. 3310	
Voltmeters, with a recording device	电压表,带记录装置	9030. 3900	
Vulcanized rubber thread and cord	硫化橡胶线及绳	4007. 0000	18

V

W

Article Description	商品名称	Tariff Code	D. R.
Wadding and articles of cotton	絮胎及制品，棉制	5601.2100	6
Wadding and articles, nes	絮胎及制品，其他	5601.2900	6
Wadding and articles, of man-made fibres	絮胎及制品，化学纤维制	5601.2290	6
Waferboard of wood	华夫板	4410.1900	6
Wafers	圣餐饼	1905.3200	28
Waffles	华夫饼	1905.3200	28
Wagon tippers	货车倾卸装置	8428.9010	
Waistcoats and similar articles, knitted or crocheted, nes	背心及类似品，针织或钩编的，其他	6110.9090	2456
Waistcoats and similar articles, knitted or crocheted, of cotton	背心及类似品，针织或钩编的，棉制	6110.2000	2456
Waistcoats and similar articles, knitted or crocheted, of fine animal hair	背心及类似品，针织或钩编的，其他动物细毛制	6110.1990	2456
Waistcoats and similar articles, knitted or crocheted, of kashmir (cashmere) goats	背心及类似品，针织或钩编的，喀什米尔山羊细毛制	6110.1200	2456
Waistcoats and similar articles, knitted or crocheted, of man-made fibres	背心及类似品，针织或钩编的，化学纤维制	6110.3000	2456
Waistcoats and similar articles, knitted or crocheted, of other goats	背心及类似品，针织或钩编的，其他山羊细毛制	6110.1910	2456
Waistcoats and similar articles, knitted or crocheted, of rabbit and hare	背心及类似品，针织或钩编的，兔毛制	6110.1920	2456
Waistcoats and similar articles, knitted or crocheted, of silk or silk waste	背心及类似品，针织或钩编的，丝及绢丝制	6110.9010	2456
Waistcoats and similar articles, knitted or crocheted, of wool	背心及类似品，针织或钩编的，毛制	6110.1100	2456
Walkie-talkie	对讲机	8517.1220	
Walkie-talkie parts, other than aerials	对讲机用零件(天线除外)	8517.7040	3
Walking-sticks	手杖	6602.0000	
Walking-sticks parts	手杖的零件	6603.9000	
Wall clocks, electrically operated	挂钟，电力驱动的	9105.2100	5
Wall clocks, nes	挂钟，其他	9105.2900	5
Wall fans, with a self-contained electric motor of an output not exceeding 125W	壁扇，包括风机，本身装有一个输出功率不超过125瓦的电动机	8414.5193	23
Wall or ceiling coverings, of other plastics	糊墙品，其他塑料制	3918.9010	36
Wall or ceiling coverings, of polymers of vinyl chloride	糊墙品，氯乙烯聚合物制	3918.1010	36
Wallets of paper or paperboard, containing an assortment of paper stationery	纸夹子，内装各种纸制文具	4817.3000	6

W

Article Description	商品名称	Tariff Code	D. R.
Wallets, purses, with outer surface of leather, of composition leather or of patent leather	钱包、钱夹,以皮革、再生皮革或漆皮作面	4202.3100	256
Wallets, purses, with outer surface of plastic sheeting or of textile materials	钱包、钱夹,以塑料片或纺织材料作面	4202.3200	256
Wallpaper and similar wall coverings, consisting of paper coated or covered, on the face side, with a grained, embossed, coloured, design-printed or otherwise decorated layer of plastics	壁纸及类似品,用塑料涂面或盖面的,起纹、压花、着色、印刷图案或经其他装饰	4814.2000	4
Wallpaper base	壁纸原纸	4802.4000	3458
Wallpaper of "ingrain"	壁纸,用木粒或草粒等饰面的	4814.1000	4
Walnut meats, in airtight containers	核桃仁,罐头	2008.1910	248
Walnuts, in shell	核桃,未去壳	0802.3100	134
Walnuts, shelled	核桃,去壳	0802.3200	134
Warp knit fabrics, nes	经编织物,其他	6005.9090	46
Warp knit fabrics, of artificial fibres, dyed	经编织物,人造纤维制,染色	6005.4200	46
Warp knit fabrics, of artificial fibres, of yarns of different colours	经编织物,人造纤维制,色织	6005.4300	46
Warp knit fabrics, of artificial fibres, printed	经编织物,人造纤维制,印花	6005.4400	46
Warp knit fabrics, of artificial fibres, unbleached or bleached	经编织物,人造纤维制,未漂白或漂白	6005.4100	46
Warp knit fabrics, of cotton, dyed	经编织物,棉制,染色	6005.2200	46
Warp knit fabrics, of cotton, of yarns of different colours	经编织物,棉制,色织	6005.2300	46
Warp knit fabrics, of cotton, printed	经编织物,棉制,印花	6005.2400	46
Warp knit fabrics, of cotton, unbleached or bleached	经编织物,棉制,未漂白或漂白	6005.2100	46
Warp knit fabrics, of synthetic fibres, dyed	经编织物,合成纤维制,染色	6005.3200	46
Warp knit fabrics, of synthetic fibres, of yarns of different colours	经编织物,合成纤维制,色织	6005.3300	46
Warp knit fabrics, of synthetic fibres, printed	经编织物,合成纤维制,印花	6005.3400	46
Warp knit fabrics, of synthetic fibres, unbleached or bleached	经编织物,合成纤维制,未漂白或漂白	6005.3100	46
Warp knit fabrics, of wool or fine animal hair	经编织物,羊毛或动物细毛制,其他	6005.9010	46
Warp knitting machines auxiliary	经编机的辅助机器	8448.1900	3
Warp knitting machines, nes	经编机,其他	8447.2019	7
Warp knitting machines, rashel machines	经编机,拉舍尔式	8447.2012	7
Warp knitting machines, tricot machines	经编机,特里科式	8447.2011	7
Warping machines	整经机	8445.9010	7
Warping machines auxiliary	整经机的辅助机器	8448.1900	3
Warships	军舰	8906.1000	
Wash basin pedestals, of porcelain or china	脸盆座,瓷制	6910.1000	268
Wash basin pedestals, of pottery	脸盆座,陶制	6910.9000	268
Wash basins, of porcelain	脸盆,瓷制	6910.1000	268

W

Article Description	商品名称	Tariff Code	D. R.
Wash basins, of pottery	脸盆,陶制	6910. 9000	268
Washers (including spring washers), of copper	垫圈(包括弹簧垫圈),铜制	7415. 2100	56
Washers and similar articles, of aluminium	垫圈及类似品,铝制	7616. 1000	36
Washers, of iron or steel, nes	垫圈,钢铁制的,其他	7318. 2200	268
Washing machines parts, each of a dry linen capacity exceeding 10kg, household or laundry type	洗衣机用零件,干衣量超过 10 千克的,家用或洗衣房用	8450. 9090	3
Washing machines parts, each of a dry linen capacity not exceeding 10kg, household or laundry type	洗衣机用零件,干衣量不超过 10 千克的,家用或洗衣房用	8450. 9010	3
Washing machines parts, for textile yarns, fabrics or made up textile articles, nes	洗涤机器零件,纱线、织物及纺织制品用	8451. 9000	
Washing machines, each of a dry linen capacity not exceeding 10kg, nes, household or laundry type	洗衣机,干衣量不超过 10 千克的洗衣机,其他,家用或洗衣房用	8450. 1900	7
Washing machines, for earth, stone, ores or other mineral substances	洗涤机器,泥土、石料、矿石或其他固体矿物质的	8474. 1000	
Washing machines, with built-in centrifugal drier, each of a dry linen capacity not exceeding 10kg, household or laundry type	洗衣机,装有离心甩干机,干衣量不超过 10 千克的洗衣机,家用或洗衣房用	8450. 1200	7
Washing machines, each of a dry linen capacity exceeding 10kg, household or laundry type	洗衣机,干衣量超过 10 千克的,家用或洗衣房用	8450. 2000	7
Washing machines, for textile yarns, fabrics or made up textile articles, nes	洗涤机器,纱线、织物及纺织制品用	8451. 4000	
Washing machines, fully-automatic machines, each of a dry linen capacity not exceeding 10kg, household or laundry type, nes	洗衣机,全自动的,干衣量不超过 10 千克的洗衣机,家用或洗衣房用,其他	8450. 1190	7
Washing machines, fully-automatic machines, of the continuously rotating impeller, each of a dry linen capacity not exceeding 10kg, household or laundry type	洗衣机,全自动的,波轮式,干衣量不超过 10 千克的洗衣机,家用或洗衣房用	8450. 1110	7
Washing machines, fully-automatic machines, of the drum type, each of a dry linen capacity not exceeding 10kg, household or laundry type	洗衣机,全自动的,滚筒式,干衣量不超过 10 千克的洗衣机,家用或洗衣房用	8450. 1120	7
Wash-basins, of plastics	盥洗盆,塑料的	3922. 1000	236
Waste and scrap of alloy steel, nes	废碎料,合金钢的,其他	7204. 2900	46
Waste and scrap of aluminium	废碎料,铝的	7602. 0000	46
Waste and scrap of antimony	废碎料,锑的	8110. 2000	16
Waste and scrap of beryllium	废碎料,铍的	8112. 1300	16
Waste and scrap of bismuth	废碎料,铋的	8106. 0010	16
Waste and scrap of cadmium	废碎料,镉的	8107. 3000	16
Waste and scrap of cast iron	废碎料,铸铁的	7204. 1000	46
Waste and scrap of cermets and articles thereof	废碎料,金属陶瓷及其制品的	8113. 0090	16
Waste and scrap of chromium	废碎料,铬的	8112. 2200	16
Waste and scrap of cobalt	废碎料,钴的	8105. 3000	16

Article Description	商品名称	Tariff Code	D. R.
Waste and scrap of copper	废碎料，铜的	7404. 0000	46
Waste and scrap of gallium	废碎料，镓的	8112. 9290	16
Waste and scrap of germanium	废碎料，锗的	8112. 9210	16
Waste and scrap of glass	废玻璃	7001. 0000	13
Waste and scrap of gold or gold compounds, including metal clad with gold but excluding swee-pings containing other precious metals	废碎料，金及包金的，但含有其他贵金属的除外	7112. 9110	46
Waste and scrap of hafnium	废碎料，铪的	8112. 9290	16
Waste and scrap of indium	废碎料，铟的	8112. 9230	16
Waste and scrap of lead	废碎料，铅的	7802. 0000	46
Waste and scrap of magnesium	废碎料，镁的	8104. 2000	16
Waste and scrap of manganese	废碎料，锰的	8111. 0010	16
Waste and scrap of nickel	废碎料，镍的	7503. 0000	46
Waste and scrap of niobium	废碎料，铌的	8112. 9240	16
Waste and scrap of platinum, including metal clad with platinum but excluding sweepings containing other precious metals	废碎料，铂及包铂的，但含有其他贵金属的除外	7112. 9210	46
Waste and scrap of primary cells, primary batteries and electric accumulators	废碎料，原电池、原电池组及蓄电池的	8548. 1000	3
Waste and scrap of rhenium	废碎料，铼的	8112. 9290	16
Waste and scrap of stainless steel	废碎料，不锈钢的	7204. 2100	46
Waste and scrap of tantalum	废碎料，钽的	8103. 3000	16
Waste and scrap of thallium	废碎料，铊的	8112. 5200	16
Waste and scrap of tin	废碎料，锡的	8002. 0000	16
Waste and scrap of tinned iron or steel	废碎料，镀锡钢铁的	7204. 3000	46
Waste and scrap of tungsten	废碎料，钨的	8101. 9700	16
Waste and scrap of vanadium	废碎料，钒的	8112. 9220	16
Waste and scrap of zirconium	废碎料，锆的	8109. 3000	16
Waste and scrap with gold or gold compounds	废碎料，含有金或金化合物的	7112. 9120	46
Waste and scrap with other precious metals, nes	含有其他贵金属或贵金属化合物的废碎料，其他	7112. 9990	46
Waste and scrap with other precious metals, of a kind used principally for the recoverey of precious metal	含有其他贵金属或贵金属化合物的废碎料，主要用于回收贵金属	7112. 9920	46
Waste and scrap with silver or silver compounds	含有银或银化合物的废碎料	7112. 9910	46
Waste and scrap, ferrous, nes	废碎料，钢铁的，其他	7204. 4900	46
Waste and scrap, of molybdenum	废碎料，钼的	8102. 9700	16
Waste and scrap, of titanium	废碎料，钛的	8108. 9090	16
Waste of bristles or hair, for making brush, nes	废料，兽毛，制刷用，其他	0502. 9020	3
Waste of coarse animal hair	动物粗毛废料	5103. 3000	5
Waste of fine animal hair	动物细毛废料	5103. 2090	5
Waste of pigs' bristles	废料，猪鬃的	0502. 1030	
Waste of pigs' hair	废料，猪毛的	0502. 1030	

W

Article Description	商品名称	Tariff Code	D. R.
Waste of wool	羊毛废料	5103. 2010	5
Waste oils, containing poly chlorinated biphenyls (PCBs), polychlorinated terphenyls (PCTs) or polybrominated biphenyls(PBBs)	废油,含多氯联苯(PCBs)、多氯三联(PCTs)或多溴联苯(PBBs)的	2710. 9100	4
Waste oils, nes	废油,其他	2710. 9900	4
Waste organic solvents, halogenated	废有机溶剂,卤化物的	3825. 4100	34
Waste organic solvents, nes	废有机溶剂,其他	3825. 4900	34
Waste pharmaceuticals	废药物	3006. 9200	3
Waste, ferrous, from turnings, shavings, chips, milling sawdust, filings, trimmings and stampings, whether or not in bundles	废料,钢铁的,车、刨、铣、磨、锯、锉、剪、冲加工过程中产生的不论是否成捆	7204. 4100	46
Waste, parings and scrap of rubber (other than hard rubber) and powders and granules obtained therefrom	废碎料、下脚料及其粉、粒,橡胶(硬质橡胶的除外)的	4004. 0000	146
Wasted and scrap with platinum, but excluding sweepings containing other precious metals	废碎料,含有铂或铂化合物的,但含有其他贵金属的除外	7112. 9220	46
Wastes from chemical or allied industries, mainly containing organic constituents	废物,化学工业及相关工业的,主要含有有机成分的	3825. 6100	34
Wastes from chemical or allied industries, nes	废物,化学工业及相关工业的,其他	3825. 6900	34
Wastes of antifreeze fluids	废的防冻液	3825. 5000	34
Wastes of brake fluids	废的制动油	3825. 5000	34
Wastes of hydraulic fluids	废的液压油	3825. 5000	34
Wastes of metal pickling liquors	废的金属酸液	3825. 5000	34
Watch cases parts	表壳零件	9111. 9000	6
Watch cases, nes	表壳,其他	9111. 8000	6
Watch cases, of base metal, whether or not gold-plated or silver-plated	表壳,贱金属的,不论是否镀金或镀银	9111. 2000	6
Watch cases, of precious metal or of metal clad with precious metal	表壳,贵金属或包贵金属的	9111. 1000	6
Watch movements, complete and assembled, automatic winding	表芯,已组装完整的,自动上弦的	9108. 2000	58
Watch movements, complete and assembled, electrically operated, nes	表芯,已组装完整的,电力驱动的,其他	9108. 1900	58
Watch movements, complete and assembled, electrically operated, with mechanical display only or with a device to which a mechanical display can be incorporated	表芯,已组装完整的,电力驱动的,仅有机械指示器或有可装机械指示器的装置的	9108. 1100	58
Watch movements, complete and assembled, electrically operated, with optoelectronic display only	表芯,已组装完整的,电力驱动的,仅有光电显示器的	9108. 1200	58
Watch movements, complete and assembled, measuring 33. 8mm or less	表芯,已组装完整的,表面尺寸在33. 8毫米及以下	9108. 9010	58
Watch movements, complete and assembled, nes	表芯,已组装完整的,其他	9108. 9090	58

Article Description	商品名称	Tariff Code	D. R.
Watch movements, complete, unassembled or partly assembled (movement sets)	表芯,完整的,未组装或部分组装(机芯套装件)	9110. 1100	1
Watch movements, incomplete, assembled	表芯,不完整的,已组装	9110. 1200	1
Watch movements, incomplete, unassembled	表芯,不完整的,未组装	9110. 1900	1
Watch straps, watch bands and watch bracelets, and parts thereof, nes	表带及其零件,其他	9113. 9000	6
Watch straps, watch bands and watch bracelets, and parts thereof, of base metal, whether or not gold-plated or silver-plated	表带及其零件,贱金属制,不论是否镀金或镀银	9113. 2000	6
Watch straps, watch bands and watch bracelets, and parts thereof, of precious metal or of metal clad with precious metal	表带及其零件,贵金属或包贵金属制	9113. 1000	
Watches, electrically operated, nes	表,电力驱动的,其他	9102. 9100	56
Watches, electrically operated, with case of precious metal or of metal clad with precious metal, nes	表,电力驱动的,表壳用贵金属或包贵金属制成的,其他	9101. 9100	56
Watches, nes	表,其他	9102. 9900	56
Watches, with case of precious metal or of metal clad with precious metal, nes	表,表壳用贵金属或包贵金属制成的,其他	9101. 9900	56
Water chestnut	荸荠	0714. 9010	34
Water chestnut (trapa natas)	菱角	0802. 9090	134
Water chestnut, in airtight containers, prepared or preserved otherwise than by vinegar or acetic acid, not frozen	清水马蹄罐头,用醋或醋酸以外的其他方法制作或保藏的,未冷冻	2005. 9910	1248
Water closet pans, of porcelain or china	抽水马桶,瓷制	6910. 1000	268
Water closet pans, of pottery	抽水马桶,陶制	6910. 9000	268
Water dispensers, electro-thermic	饮水机,电热的	8516. 7910	7
Water gas	水煤气	2705. 0000	4
Water gas generators parts	水煤气发生器的零件	8405. 9000	3
Water gas generators, with or without their purifiers	水煤气发生器,不论有无净化器	8405. 1000	3
Water heaters parts	热水器用零件	8419. 9010	3
Water heaters, non-electric, instantaneous, nes	热水器,非电热的,速热的,其他	8419. 1990	57
Water heaters, non-electric, instantaneous, storage type, nes	热水器,非电热的,贮备式,其他	8419. 1990	57
Water heaters, non-electric, instantaneous, gas type	热水器,非电热的,燃气速热的	8419. 1100	57
Water heaters, of solar enegy	热水器,太阳能的	8419. 1910	57
Water jet looms, for weaving fabrics of a with exceeding 30cm, shuttleless type	喷水织机,所织织物宽度超过 30 厘米的无梭织机	8446. 3040	7
Water meters	水表	9028. 2010	
Water meters parts and accessories, for industrial use	水表零件、附件,工业用	9028. 9010	3
Water meters parts and accessories, nes	水表零件、附件,其他	9028. 9090	3
Water process gas generators parts	水解气体发生器的零件	8405. 9000	3

Article Description	商品名称	Tariff Code	D. R.
Water process gas generators, with or without their purifiers	水解气体发生器,不论有无净化器	8405. 1000	3
Water tank radiators, of motor vehicles	水箱散热器,机动车辆用	8708. 9110	3
Waterheaters heaters, immersion, electric	电热水器,浸入式	8516. 1090	7
Waterheaters heaters, immersion, electric	热水器,电的,浸入式	8516. 1090	7
Waterheaters, electric instantaneous	热水器,电的,即热式	8516. 1020	7
Waterheaters, instantaneous, electric	电热水器,即热式	8516. 1020	7
Waterheaters, storage, electric	电热水器,储存式	8516. 1010	7
Waterheaters, storage, electric	热水器,电的,储存式	8516. 1010	7
Watermelons, fresh	西瓜,鲜的	0807. 1100	12
Waterproof footwear, incorporating a protective metal toe-cap, the uppers of which are neither fixed to the sole nor assembled by stitching, riveting, nailing, screwing, plugging or similar processes, with outer soles of rubber or of plastics and uppers of rubber	防水鞋靴,装有金属防护鞋头,其鞋面不是用缝、铆、钉、旋、塞或类似方法固定在鞋底上的,橡胶或塑料制外底,橡胶制鞋面的	6401. 1010	26
Waterproof footwear, incorporating a protective metal toe-cap, the uppers of which are neither fixed to the sole nor assembled by stitching, riveting, nailing, screwing, plugging or similar processes, with outer soles of rubber or of plastics and uppers of rubber and uppers of plastics	防水鞋靴,装有金属防护鞋头,其鞋面不是用缝、铆、钉、旋、塞或类似方法固定在鞋底上的,橡胶或塑料制外底,塑料制鞋面的	6401. 1090	26
Waterproof footwear, the uppers of which are neither fixed to the sole nor assembled by stitching, riveting, nailing, screwing, plugging or similar processes, with outer soles and uppers of rubber or of plastics, nes	防水鞋靴,其鞋面不是用缝、铆、钉、旋、塞或类似方法固定在鞋底上的,橡胶或塑料制外底及鞋面的,其他	6401. 9900	26
Waterproof footwear, the uppers of which are neither fixed to the sole nor assembled by stitching, riveting, nailing, screwing, plugging or similar processes, with outer soles of rubber or of plastics and uppers of plastics, covering the ankle but not covering the knee	防水鞋靴,其鞋面不是用缝、铆、钉、旋、塞或类似方法固定在鞋底上的,橡胶或塑料制外底,塑料制鞋面的,中、短统靴(过踝但未到膝)	6401. 9290	26
Waterproof footwear, the uppers of which are neither fixed to the sole nor assembled by stitching, riveting, nailing, screwing, plugging or similar processes, with outer soles of rubber or of plastics and uppers of rubber, covering the ankle but not covering the knee	防水鞋靴,其鞋面不是用缝、铆、钉、旋、塞或类似方法固定在鞋底上的,橡胶或塑料制外底,橡胶制鞋面的,中、短统靴(过踝但未到膝)	6401. 9210	26
Waters, containing added sugar or other sweetening matter or flavoured	水,加味、加糖或其他甜物质的	2202. 1000	248
Water-skis	滑水板	9506. 2900	5
Water-sport equipment, nes	水上运动用具,其他	9506. 2900	5

Article Description	商品名称	Tariff Code	D. R.
Wattle extract	荆树皮浸膏	3201. 2000	34
Watt-hour meter parts and accessories, for industrial use	电度表零件、附件,工业用	9028. 9010	3
Watt-hour meter parts and accessories, nes	电度表零件、附件,其他	9028. 9090	3
Watt-hour meter, nes	电度表,其他	9028. 3019	7
Watt-hour meter, single-phase electronic types (static)	电度表,单相电子式(静止式)	9028. 3013	
Watt-hour meter, single-phase induction types	电度表,单相感应式	9028. 3011	
Watt-hour meter, three-phase electronic types (static)	电度表,三相电子式(静止式)	9028. 3014	
Watt-hour meter, three-phase induction types	电度表,三相感应式	9028. 3012	
Wax apple, fresh	莲雾,鲜的	0810. 9070	1
Wax of poly-ethyleneglycol	蜡,聚乙二醇制	3404. 2000	136
Wax of poly-oxyethylene	蜡,聚氧乙烯制	3404. 2000	136
Waxes, artificial and prepared, nes	蜡,人造及调制的,其他	3404. 9000	136
Weasel tail hair	黄鼠狼尾毛	0502. 9012	3
Weasel tails	黄鼠狼尾	4301. 9010	15
Weaving machines or of their auxiliary machinery's parts and accessories, nes	织机及其辅助机器的零件、附件,其他	8448. 4990	3
Weaving machines (looms) auxiliary	织机的辅助机器	8448. 1900	3
Weaving machines (looms), for making carpets or rugs, powered, for weaving fabrics of a width exceeding 30cm, shuttle type	织机,地毯用,动力的,所织织物宽度超过 30 厘米的梭织机	8446. 2110	7
Weaving machines (looms), for weaving fabrics of a width exceeding 30cm, shuttle type, nes	织机,所织织物宽度超过 30 厘米的梭织机,其他	8446. 2900	7
Weaving machines (looms), for weaving fabrics of a width exceeding 30cm, shuttleless type, nes	织机,所织织物宽度超过 30 厘米的无梭织机,其他	8446. 3090	7
Weaving machines (looms), for weaving fabrics of a width not exceeding 30cm	织机,所织织物宽度不超过 30 厘米的织机	8446. 1000	7
Weaving machines (looms), powered, for weaving fabrics of a width exceeding 30cm, shuttle type, nes	织机,动力的,所织织物宽度超过 30 厘米的梭织机,其他	8446. 2190	7
Web feeder	领纸机	8443. 9111	3
Webs of cellulose fibres	纤维素纤维网	4811. 9000	458
Webs of cellulose fibres, in rolls or sheets	和纤维素纤维网纸,成卷或成张的	4803. 0000	58
Weeders, for agricultural, horticultural or forestry use, nes	除草机,农业、园艺及林业用,其他	8432. 2900	
Weft insertion for looms	引纬装置,织机用	8448. 4920	3
Weft knitting machines auxiliary	纬编机的辅助机器	8448. 1900	3
Weft knitting machines, flat	纬编机,平型的	8447. 2020	7
Weft-winding machines	卷纬机	8445. 4090	7
Weft-winding machines auxiliary	卷纬机的辅助机器	8448. 1900	3
Weigh bridges, having a maximum weighing capacity exceeding 30kg but not exceeding 5000kg	地中衡,最大称量超过 30 千克,但不超过 5000 千克	8423. 8210	

W

Article Description	商品名称	Tariff Code	D. R.
Weigh bridges, nes	地中衡，其他	8423. 8910	
Weighing machine weights of all kinds	衡器用的各种砝码、秤砣	8423. 9000	
Weighing machine weights of all kinds, for weighing machine	秤砣，衡器用	8423. 9000	
Weighing machine weights of all kinds, for weighing machine	砝码，衡器用	8423. 9000	
Weighing machinery parts	衡器的零件	8423. 9000	
Weighing machinery, having a maximum weighing capacity exceeding 30kg but not exceeding 5000kg, nes	衡器，最大称量超过 30 千克，但不超过 5000 千克，其他	8423. 8290	
Weighing machinery, having a maximum weighing capacity not exceeding 30kg, nes	衡器，最大称量不超过 30 千克，其他	8423. 8190	
Weighing machinery, nes	衡器，其他	8423. 8990	
Welded link, of iron or steel, nes	焊接链，钢铁的，其他	7315. 8200	36
Welding machines and apparatus of metals, with arc, nes	焊接机器及装置，电弧的	8515. 3900	
Welding machinery and apparatus parts	焊接机器及装置的零件	8468. 9000	3
Welding machinery and apparatus, gas-operated	焊接机器及装置，气体推动的	8468. 2000	57
Welding machinery and apparatus, nes	焊接机器及装置，其他	8468. 8000	57
Welding of metals machines and apparatus, fully or partly automatic, nes	焊接机器及装置，全自动或半自动的，其他	8515. 3190	
Whale oil	鲸油	1504. 3000	4
Whalebone and powder thereof	鲸须及其粉末	0507. 9090	14
Whalebone hair and powder thereof	鲸须毛及其粉末	0507. 9090	14
Whales	鲸	0106. 1200	
Wheat gluten, whether or not dried	面筋，不论是否干制	1109. 0000	
Wheat, nes	小麦，其他	1001. 9090	356
Wheat, nes, seed	小麦，其他，种用	1001. 9010	356
Wheel mounted cranes, self-propelled	轮胎式起重机，自推进的	8426. 4110	7
Wheel rims and spokes, of bicycles and other cycles	轮圈及辐条，自行车及脚踏车的	8714. 9200	3
Wheels, of railway or tramway locomotives or rolling-stock	轮，铁道及电车道机车或其他车辆的	8607. 1990	3
Wheel-sander, hand tools with self-contained electric motor	砂轮机，手提式，本身装有电动动力装置的	8467. 2910	57
Whey cheese	乳清乳酪	0406. 1000	24
Whey, modified, whether or not concentrated or containing added sugar or other sweetening matter	改性乳清，不论是否浓缩、加糖或其他甜物质	0404. 1000	248
Whey, whether or not concentrated or containing added sugar or other sweetening matter	乳清，不论是否浓缩、加糖或其他甜物质	0404. 1000	248
Whips	鞭子	6602. 0000	
Whips parts	鞭子的零件	6603. 9000	
Whiskies	威士忌酒	2208. 3000	2468

Article Description	商品名称	Tariff Code	D. R.
Whistles	哨子	9208.9000	5
White cement, whether or not artificially coloured	白水泥,不论是否人工着色	2523.2100	3
White chocolate	白巧克力	1704.9000	258
White mushroom, in brine, provisionally preserved, but unsuitable in that state for immediate consumption	白蘑菇,盐水的,暂时保藏,但不适合直接使用的	0711.5112	34
White puddings, with a natural casing	白香肠,有天然肠衣	1601.0010	348
Wickerwork and other articles, made directly to shape from plaiting materials or made up from goods	柳条编结品及其他制品,用编结材料直接编成	4602.1930	6
Wicks and candles, put up for retail sale	杀虫灯芯、蜡烛,零售包装	3808.9910	36
Wicks, of woven textile, plaited or knitted, for candles or the like	烛芯或类似品,用纺织材料机织、编结或针织而成的	5908.0000	
Wicks, of woven textile, plaited or knitted, for lighters or the like	打火机芯或类似品,用纺织材料机织、编结或针织而成的	5908.0000	
Wicks, of woven textile, plaited or knitted, for stoves or the like;	灯芯或类似品,用纺织材料机织、编结或针织而成的	5908.0000	
Wide anticorrosive photographic plate for printed circuit processing, unexposed, without perforations, of a width exceeding 610mm and of a length exceeding 200 m	印刷电路板制造用光致抗蚀干膜,未曝光的,无齿孔的,宽度超过610毫米,长度超过200米	3702.4221	12368
Wigs and the like, of animal hair or textile materials, nes	假发及类似品,动物毛或纺织材料制的,其他	6704.9000	4
Wigs and the like, of human hair	假发及类似品,人发制	6704.2000	4
Wigs and the like, of synthetic textile materials, nes	假发及类似品,合成纤维纺织材料制,其他	6704.1900	4
Wigs, complete, of synthetic textile materials	整头假发,合成纤维纺织材料制	6704.1100	4
Wild brake, dried	蕨菜,干的	0712.9040	4
Wild ginseng (other than american ginseng)	野山参(西洋参除外)	1211.2020	34
Winches specially designed for use underground, nes	卷扬机,专为井下使用设计的	8425.3910	78
Winches, nes	卷扬机,其他	8425.3990	78
Winches, powered by electric motor, specially designed for use underground	卷扬机,电动的,专为井下使用设计的	8425.3110	78
Winches, powered by electric motor, nes	卷扬机,电动的,其他	8425.3190	78
Winding spindle	络筒锭	8448.3310	3
Winding spindle flyers	络筒锭壳	8448.3390	3
Winding wire, nes	绕组电线,其他	8544.1900	35
Winding wire, of copper	绕组电线,铜制	8544.1100	35
Window fans, nes	换气扇,其他	8414.5920	23
Window fans, with a self-contained electric motor of an output not exceeding 125W	换气扇,包括风机,本身装有一个输出功率不超过125瓦的电动机	8414.5120	23
Window transparencies of paper	窗用透明纸	4814.9000	4
Windowpane raiser	车窗玻璃升降器	8708.2930	3

W

Article Description	商品名称	Tariff Code	D. R.
Windows and their frames, of plastics	窗及其框架,塑料的	3925. 2000	23
Windows, French-windows and their frames, of radiata pine	窗、法兰西式(落地)窗及其框架,辐射松制的	4418. 1010	58
Windows, French-windows and their frames, of radiata pine, of other wood	窗、法兰西式(落地)窗及其框架,辐射松制的,其他木制的	4418. 1090	58
Windscreen wipers for bicycles	风挡刮水器,自行车用	8512. 4000	7
Windscreen wipers for motor vehicles	风挡刮水器,机动车辆用	8512. 4000	7
Wind-cheaters and similar articles, knitted or crocheted, for women or girls, of other textile materials	风衣及类似品,针织或钩编的,女式,其他纺织材料制	6102. 9000	2456
Wind-cheaters and similar articles, knitted or crocheted, for men or boys, of cotton	风衣及类似品,针织或钩编的,男式,棉制	6101. 2000	2456
Wind-cheaters and similar articles, knitted or crocheted, for men or boys, of man-made fibres	风衣及类似品,针织或钩编的,男式,化学纤维制	6101. 3000	2456
Wind-cheaters and similar articles, knitted or crocheted, for men or boys, of other texitile materials	风衣及类似品,针织或钩编的,男式,其他纺织材料制	6101. 9090	2456
Wind-cheaters and similar articles, knitted or crocheted, for men or boys, of wool or fine animal hair	风衣及类似品,针织或钩编的,男式,羊毛或动物细毛制	6101. 9010	2456
Wind-cheaters and similar articles, knitted or crocheted, for women or girls, of cotton	风衣及类似品,针织或钩编的,女式,棉制	6102. 2000	2456
Wind-cheaters and similar articles, knitted or crocheted, for women or girls, of man-made fibres	风衣及类似品,针织或钩编的,女式,化学纤维制	6102. 3000	2456
Wind-cheaters and similar articles, knitted or crocheted, for women or girls, of wool or fine animal hair	风衣及类似品,针织或钩编的,女式,羊毛或动物细毛制	6102. 1000	2456
Wind-cheaters, not knitted or crocheted, for men or boys, for man-made fibres	防风衣,非针织或钩编的,男式,化学纤维制	6201. 9390	2456
Wind-cheaters, not knitted or crocheted, for men or boys, of cotton	防风衣,非针织或钩编的,男式,棉制	6201. 9290	2456
Wind-cheaters, not knitted or crocheted, for men or boys, of other textile materials	防风衣,非针织或钩编的,男式,其他纺织材料制	6201. 9900	2456
Wind-cheaters, not knitted or crocheted, for men or boys, of wool or fine animal hair	防风衣,非针织或钩编的,男式,羊毛或动物细毛制	6201. 9100	2456
Wind-cheaters, not knitted or crocheted, for women or girls, of cotton	防风衣,非针织或钩编的,女式,棉制	6202. 9290	2456
Wind-cheaters, not knitted or crocheted, for women or girls, of man-made fibres	防风衣,非针织或钩编的,女式,化学纤维制	6202. 9390	2456
Wind-cheaters, not knitted or crocheted, for women or girls, of other textile materials	防风衣,非针织或钩编的,女式,其他纺织材料制	6202. 9900	2456
Wind-cheaters, not knitted or crocheted, for women or girls, of wool or fine animal hair	防风衣,非针织或钩编的,女式,羊毛或动物细毛制	6202. 9100	2456

Article Description	商品名称	Tariff Code	D. R.
Wind-jackets and similar articles, knitted or crocheted, for men or boys, of cotton	防风短上衣及类似品,针织或钩编的,男式,棉制	6101. 2000	2456
Wind-jackets and similar articles, knitted or crocheted, for men or boys, of man-made fibres	防风短上衣及类似品,针织或钩编的,男式,化学纤维制	6101. 3000	2456
Wind-jackets and similar articles, knitted or crocheted, for men or boys, of other textile materials, nes	防风短上衣及类似品,针织或钩编的,男式,其他	6101. 9090	2456
Wind-jackets and similar articles, knitted or crocheted, for men or boys, of wool or fine animal hair	防风短上衣及类似品,针织或钩编的,男式,羊毛或动物细毛制	6101. 9010	2456
Wind-jackets and similar articles, knitted or crocheted, for women or girls, of cotton	防风短上衣及类似品,针织或钩编的,女式,棉制	6102. 2000	2456
Wind-jackets and similar articles, knitted or crocheted, for women or girls, of man-made fibres	防风短上衣及类似品,针织或钩编的,女式,化学纤维制	6102. 3000	2456
Wind-jackets and similar articles, knitted or crocheted, for women or girls, of other textile materials, nes	防风短上衣及类似品,针织或钩编的,男式,其他	6102. 9000	2456
Wind-jackets and similar articles, knitted or crocheted, for women or girls, of wool or fine animal hair	防风短上衣及类似品,针织或钩编的,女式,羊毛或动物细毛制	6102. 1000	2456
Wind-jackets and similar articles, not knitted or crocheted, for men or boys, of cotton	防风短上衣及类似品,非针织或钩编的,男式,棉制	6201. 9290	2456
Wind-jackets and similar articles, not knitted or crocheted, for men or boys, of man-made fibres	防风短上衣及类似品,非针织或钩编的,男式,化学纤维制	6201. 9390	2456
Wind-jackets and similar articles, not knitted or crocheted, for men or boys, of other textile materials	防风短上衣及类似品,非针织或钩编的,男式,其他纺织材料制	6201. 9900	2456
Wind-jackets and similar articles, not knitted or crocheted, for men or boys, of wool or fine animal hair	防风短上衣及类似品,非针织或钩编的,男式,羊毛或动物细毛制	6201. 9100	2456
Wind-jackets and similar articles, not knitted or crocheted, for women or girls, of cotton	防风短上衣及类似品,非针织或钩编的,女式,棉制	6202. 9290	2456
Wind-jackets and similar articles, not knitted or crocheted, for women or girls, of man-made fibres	防风短上衣及类似品,非针织或钩编的,女式,化学纤维制	6202. 9390	2456
Wind-jackets and similar articles, not knitted or crocheted, for women or girls, of other textile materials	防风短上衣及类似品,非针织或钩编的,女式,其他纺织材料制	6202. 9900	2456
Wind-jackets and similar articles, not knitted or crocheted, for women or girls, of wool or fine animal hair	防风短上衣及类似品,非针织或钩编的,女式,羊毛或动物细毛制	6202. 9100	2456
Wine lees	葡萄酒渣	2307. 0000	
Wine of fresh grapes, in containers holding 2L or less, flavoured with plants or aromatic substances	葡萄酒,鲜葡萄酿造的,装入2升及以下容器的,加植物或香料的	2205. 1000	248

W

Article Description	商品名称	Tariff Code	D. R.
Wine of fresh grapes, nes	葡萄酒,鲜葡萄酿造的,其他	2204.2900	24568
Wine of fresh grapes, nes, flavoured with plants or aromatic substances	葡萄酒,鲜葡萄酿造的,其他,加植物或香料的	2205.9000	248
Wine of fresh grapes, nes, in containers holding 2L or less	葡萄酒,鲜葡萄酿造的,装入2升及以下容器的	2204.2100	24568
Wine of fresh grapes, sparkling	汽酒	2204.1000	24568
Wire and rods, of agglomerated basemetal powder, used for metal spraying	丝或条,贱金属粉粘聚而成的,供金属喷镀用	8311.9000	56
Wire bonders parts and accessories, solely or principally of a kind used for assembling or encapsulating semiconductor devices	引线键合装置用零件及附件,主要用于或专用于装配与封装半导体器件或集成电路	8486.9020	3
Wire bonders, solely or principally of a kind used for assembling or encapsulating semiconductor devices	引线键合装置,主要用于或专用于装配与封装半导体器件或集成电路	8486.4022	7
Wire drawing machines, for working metal or cermets, without removing material	拔丝机,金属或金属陶瓷用,非切削	8463.1020	7
Wire mills	线材轧机	8455.2130	7
Wire of high speed steel	丝,高速钢制	7229.9010	6
Wire of iron or non-alloy steel, nes	铁丝或非合金钢丝,其他	7217.9000	468
Wire of iron or non-alloy steel, not plated or coated, whether or not polished	铁丝或非合金钢丝,未经镀或涂层,不论是否抛光	7217.1000	468
Wire of iron or non-alloy steel, plated or coated with base metals, nes	铁丝或非合金钢丝,镀或涂贱金属的,其他	7217.3090	468
Wire of iron or non-alloy steel, plated or coated with copper	铁丝或非合金钢丝,镀或涂铜的	7217.3010	468
Wire of iron or non-alloy steel, plated or coated with zinc	铁丝或非合金钢丝,镀或涂锌的	7217.2000	468
Wire of iron or steel, barbed	钢铁丝,带刺的	7313.0000	36
Wire of other alloy steel, nes	丝,合金钢的,其他	7229.9090	6
Wire of silico-manganese steel	丝,硅锰钢制	7229.2000	6
Wire of tantalum, less than 0.5mm in diameter	钽丝,直径小于0.5毫米	8103.9011	16
Wire of tantalum, nes	钽丝,其他	8103.9019	16
Wire of titanium	丝,钛的	8108.9020	16
Wire of tungsten	丝,钨的	8101.9600	16
Wire working machines, for working metal or cermets, without removing material	金属丝加工机,非切削	8463.3000	7
Wire, coated with flux material, of base metal, for soldering, brazing or welding by flame	丝,贱金属制,以焊剂涂面或以焊剂为芯,钎焊或气焊用	8311.3000	56
Wire, of aluminium alloys, nes	丝,铝合金制,其他	7605.2900	16
Wire, of aluminium alloys, of which the maximum cross-sectional dimension exceeding 7mm	丝,铝合金制,最大截面尺寸超过7毫米	7605.2100	16
Wire, of aluminium, not alloyed, nes	丝,非合金铝制,其他	7605.1900	16

Article Description	商品名称	Tariff Code	D. R.
Wire, of aluminium, not alloyed, of which the maximum cross-sectional dimension exceeding 7mm	丝,非合金铝制,最大截面尺寸超过7毫米	7605. 1100	16
Wire, of metal carbides, coated or cored with flux material, of a kind used for soldering, brazing, welding or deposition of metal or of metal carbides	丝,硬质合金制,以焊剂涂面或以焊剂为芯,用于焊接或沉积金属、硬质合金	8311. 9000	56
Wire, of molybdenum	丝,钼的	8102. 9600	16
Wire, of nickel alloys	丝,镍合金制	7505. 2200	46
Wire, of nickel, not alloyed	丝,非合金镍制	7505. 2100	46
Wire, of refined copper, nes	丝,精炼铜制,其他	7408. 1900	16
Wire, of refined copper, of which the maximum cross-sectional dimension exceeding 6mm	丝,精炼铜制,最大截面尺寸超过6毫米	7408. 1100	16
Wire, of stainless steel	丝,不锈钢的	7223. 0000	468
Wired network equipments, nes	有线设备,其他	8517. 6990	
Wired network interface cards, telecommunication apparatus for digital line system	有线网络接口卡,有线数字通信设备	8517. 6237	7
Wireless digital telecommunication apparatus, nes	无线数字通信设备,其他	8517. 6299	7
Wireless network equipments, nes	无线设备,其他	8517. 6910	
Wireless network interface cards	无线网络接口卡	8517. 6292	7
Wireless telephone handsets (including installed in the vehicle)	无线电话机,手持(包括车载)式	8517. 1210	
Wireless telephone parts, other than aerials	无线电话机用(天线除外)零件,手持式	8517. 7030	3
Wiring sets, for motor vehicles ignition	布线组,机动车辆点火用	8544. 3020	35
Wiring sets, for motor vehicles, nes	布线组,机动车辆用,其他	8544. 3020	35
Wiring sets, nes	布线组,其他	8544. 3090	35
Witherite	毒重石	2511. 2000	4
Witloof chicory (cichoriym intybus var. foliosum), fresh or chilled	维特罗夫菊苣,鲜或冷藏的	0705. 2100	1
Wolframite	钨锰铁矿	2611. 0000	146
Wollastonite	硅灰石	2530. 9091	13456
Wood artificial staple fibres, not carded, combed or otherwise processed for spinning	木制人造纤维短纤,未梳或未经其他纺前加工	5504. 1020	
Wood carvings	木刻	4420. 1011	56
Wood continuously shaped along any of its edges, ends or faces, coniferous, nes	木材,任何一边端或面制成连续形状的,针叶木,其他	4409. 1090	158
Wood continuously shaped along any of its edges, ends or faces, non-coniferous	木材,任何一边端或面制成连续形状的,非针叶木,其他	4409. 2990	158
Wood continuously shaped along any of its edges, ends or faces, of bamboo	木材,任何一边端或面制成连续形状的,竹的,其他	4409. 2190	158
Wood creosote	木杂酚油	3807. 0000	3
Wood ears (Auricularia spp.), dried	木耳,干的	0712. 3200	4

W

Article Description	商品名称	Tariff Code	D. R.
Wood flour	木粉	4405. 0000	
Wood in chips or particles, coniferous	木片或木粒,针叶木	4401. 2100	15
Wood in chips or particles, non-coniferous	木片或木粒,非针叶木	4401. 2200	15
Wood in the rough, Anisopter spp.	原木,异翅香木	4403. 4970	458
Wood in the rough, ash	原木,水曲柳	4403. 9950	458
Wood in the rough, coniferous, nes	原木,针叶木,其他	4403. 2090	458
Wood in the rough, Dipterocarpus spp. Keruing	原木,龙脑香木(克隆)	4403. 4930	458
Wood in the rough, Intsia spp. (Mengaris)	原木,印加木(波罗格)	4403. 4950	458
Wood in the rough, Kapur (Dryobalanops spp.)	原木,山樟(香木)	4403. 4940	458
Wood in the rough, Koompassia spp. (Mengaris or Kempas)	原木,大干巴豆(门格里斯或康派斯)	4403. 4960	458
Wood in the rough, korean pine and Mongolian scotch pine	原木,红松和樟子松	4403. 2010	458
Wood in the rough, larch	原木,落叶松	4403. 2040	458
Wood in the rough, Meranti (Dark Red Meranti, Light Red Metanti and Meranti Bakau)	原木,柳桉木(深红、浅红、巴栲红)	4403. 4100	458
Wood in the rough, nes	原木,其他	4403. 9990	458
Wood in the rough, north american hard wood (including cherry, walnut, and maple)	原木,北美硬阔叶木(包括樱桃木、黑胡桃木、枫木)	4403. 9960	458
Wood in the rough, of beech (Fagus spp.)	原木,山毛榉木	4403. 9200	458
Wood in the rough, of camphor wood	原木,樟木	4403. 9920	458
Wood in the rough, of Kiri (Paulownia)	原木,泡桐木	4403. 9940	458
Wood in the rough, of nan mu (Phoebe)	原木,楠木	4403. 9910	458
Wood in the rough, of oak (Quercus spp.)	原木,栎木(橡木)	4403. 9100	458
Wood in the rough, of rosewood	原木,红木	4403. 9930	458
Wood in the rough, okoume (Aukoumed Klaineana)	原木,奥克曼(奥克榄)	4403. 4920	458
Wood in the rough, radiata pine	原木,辐射松	4403. 2030	458
Wood in the rough, teak	原木,柚木	4403. 4910	458
Wood in the rough, temperate non-coniferous, nes	原木,温带非针叶木,其他	4403. 9980	458
Wood in the rough, treated with paint, stains, creosote or other preservatives	原木,用油漆、着色剂、杂酚油或其他防腐剂处理	4403. 1000	458
Wood in the rough, tropical non-coniferous, nes	原木,热带非针叶木,其他	4403. 4990	458
Wood in the rough, white pine (spruce and fir)	原木,白松(云杉和冷杉)	4403. 2020	458
Wood marquetry and inlaid wood	镶嵌木	4420. 9010	56
Wood naphtha	粗木精	3807. 0000	3
Wood pulp obtained by a combination of mechanical and chemical pulping processes	木浆,用机械与化学联合制浆法制得的	4705. 0000	46
Wood sawn or chipped lengthwise, sliced or peeled, of a thickness exceeding 6mm, Acajou	木材,经纵锯、纵切、刨切或旋切的,厚度超过6毫米,非洲桃花心木	4407. 2920	458
Wood sawn or chipped lengthwise, sliced or peeled, of a thickness exceeding 6mm, Balsa	木材,经纵锯、纵切、刨切或旋切的,厚度超过6毫米,美洲轻木	4407. 2200	458

W

Article Description	商品名称	Tariff Code	D. R.
Wood sawn or chipped lengthwise, sliced or peeled, of a thickness exceeding 6mm, coniferous, nes	木材,经纵锯、纵切、刨切或旋切的,厚度超过6毫米,针叶木,其他	4407.1090	458
Wood sawn or chipped lengthwise, sliced or peeled, of a thickness exceeding 6mm, Imbuia	木材,经纵锯、纵切、刨切或旋切的,厚度超过6毫米,巴西胡桃木	4407.2200	458
Wood sawn or chipped lengthwise, sliced or peeled, of a thickness exceeding 6mm, Iroko	木材,经纵锯、纵切、刨切或旋切的,厚度超过6毫米,伊罗科木	4407.2800	458
Wood sawn or chipped lengthwise, sliced or peeled, of a thickness exceeding 6mm, mahogany (Swietenia spp.)	木材,经纵锯、纵切、刨切或旋切的,厚度超过6毫米,美洲桃花心木	4407.2100	458
Wood sawn or chipped lengthwise, sliced or peeled, of a thickness exceeding 6mm, meranti (Dark Red Meranti, Light Red Metanti and Meranti Bakau)	木材,经纵锯、纵切、刨切或旋切的,厚度超过6毫米,柳安木(深红、浅红、巴栲红)	4407.2500	458
Wood sawn or chipped lengthwise, sliced or peeled, of a thickness exceeding 6mm, Merban	木材,经纵锯、纵切、刨切或旋切的,厚度超过6毫米,波罗格	4407.2930	458
Wood sawn or chipped lengthwise, sliced or peeled, of a thickness exceeding 6mm, nes	木材,经纵锯、纵切、刨切或旋切的,厚度超过6毫米,其他	4407.9990	458
Wood sawn or chipped lengthwise, sliced or peeled, of a thickness exceeding 6mm, north american hard wood (including walnut)	木材,经纵锯、纵切、刨切或旋切的,厚度超过6毫米,北美硬阔叶材(含黑胡桃木)	4407.9930	458
Wood sawn or chipped lengthwise, sliced or peeled, of a thickness exceeding 6mm, of ash (Fraxinus spp.)	木材,经纵锯、纵切、刨切或旋切的,厚度超过6毫米,白蜡木	4407.9500	458
Wood sawn or chipped lengthwise, sliced or peeled, of a thickness exceeding 6mm, of beech (Fagus spp.)	木材,经纵锯、纵切、刨切或旋切的,厚度超过6毫米,山毛榉木	4407.9200	458
Wood sawn or chipped lengthwise, sliced or peeled, of a thickness exceeding 6mm, of camphor-wood	木材,经纵锯、纵切、刨切或旋切的,厚度超过6毫米,樟木	4407.9910	458
Wood sawn or chipped lengthwise, sliced or peeled, of a thickness exceeding 6mm, of cherry (Prunus spp.)	木材,经纵锯、纵切、刨切或旋切的,厚度超过6毫米,樱桃木	4407.9400	458
Wood sawn or chipped lengthwise, sliced or peeled, of a thickness exceeding 6mm, of douglas fir	木材,经纵锯、纵切、刨切或旋切的,厚度超过6毫米,花旗松	4407.1040	458
Wood sawn or chipped lengthwise, sliced or peeled, of a thickness exceeding 6mm, of korean pine and mongolian scotch pine	木材,经纵锯、纵切、刨切或旋切的,厚度超过6毫米,红松和樟子松	4407.1010	458
Wood sawn or chipped lengthwise, sliced or peeled, of a thickness exceeding 6mm, of maple (Acer spp.)	木材,经纵锯、纵切、刨切或旋切的,厚度超过6毫米,枫木	4407.9300	458
Wood sawn or chipped lengthwise, sliced or peeled, of a thickness exceeding 6mm, of nanmu	木材,经纵锯、纵切、刨切或旋切的,厚度超过6毫米,楠木	4407.9910	458
Wood sawn or chipped lengthwise, sliced or peeled, of a thickness exceeding 6mm, of oak (Ouercus spp.)	木材,经纵锯、纵切、刨切或旋切的,厚度超过6毫米,栎木(橡木)	4407.9100	458
Wood sawn or chipped lengthwise, sliced or peeled, of a thickness exceeding 6mm, of Paulownia	木材,经纵锯、纵切、刨切或旋切的,厚度超过6毫米,泡桐木	4407.9920	458
Wood sawn or chipped lengthwise, sliced or peeled, of a thickness exceeding 6mm, of rediata pine	木材,经纵锯、纵切、刨切或旋切的,厚度超过6毫米,辐射松	4407.1030	458

Article Description	商品名称	Tariff Code	D. R.
Wood sawn or chipped lengthwise, sliced or peeled, of a thickness exceeding 6mm, of rosewood	木材,经纵锯、纵切、刨切或旋切的,厚度超过6毫米,红木	4407.9910	458
Wood sawn or chipped lengthwise, sliced or peeled, of a thickness exceeding 6mm, of tropical wood, nes	木材,经纵锯、纵切、刨切或旋切的,厚度超过6毫米,热带木,其他	4407.2990	458
Wood sawn or chipped lengthwise, sliced or peeled, of a thickness exceeding 6mm, Sapelli	木材,经纵锯、纵切、刨切或旋切的,厚度超过6毫米,沙比利	4407.2700	458
Wood sawn or chipped lengthwise, sliced or peeled, of a thickness exceeding 6mm, teak	木材,经纵锯、纵切、刨切或旋切的,厚度超过6毫米,柚木	4407.2910	458
Wood sawn or chipped lengthwise, sliced or peeled, of a thickness exceeding 6mm, temperate non-coniferous wood, nes	木材,经纵锯、纵切、刨切或旋切的,厚度超过6毫米,温带非针叶材,其他	4407.9980	458
Wood sawn or chipped lengthwise, sliced or peeled, of a thickness exceeding 6mm, Virola	木材,经纵锯、纵切、刨切或旋切的,厚度超过6毫米,苏里南肉豆蔻木	4407.2200	458
Wood sawn or chipped lengthwise, sliced or peeled, of a thickness exceeding 6mm, White Lauan, White Meranti, White Seraya, Yellow Meranti and Alan	木材,经纵锯、纵切、刨切或旋切的,厚度超过6毫米,白柳安木、白色红柳桉木、白色柳安木、黄色红柳桉木及阿兰木	4407.2600	458
Wood sawn or chipped lengthwise, sliced or peeled, of a thickness exceeding 6mm, white pine (spruce and fir)	木材,经纵锯、纵切、刨切或旋切的,厚度超过6毫米,白松(云杉和冷杉)	4407.1020	458
Wood screws, of iron or steel, nes	木螺钉,钢铁制的,其他	7318.1200	268
Wood tar	木焦油	3807.0000	3
Wood tar oils	精制木焦油	3807.0000	3
Wood treating machinery	木材处理机	8479.3000	7
Wood turpentine oils	木松节油	3805.1000	36
Wood waste and scrap, whether or not agglomerated in logs, briquettes, pellets or similar forms	木废料及碎片,不论是否粘结成圆木段、块、片或类似形状	4401.3000	15
Wood wool	木丝	4405.0000	
Wooden fans	木扇	4420.1020	56
Wooden sticks, suitable for the manufacture of walking-sticks, umbrellas, tool handles or the like, coniferous	木棒,适合制手杖、伞柄、工具把柄及类似品,针叶木的	4404.1000	15
Wooden sticks, suitable for the manufacture of walking-sticks, umbrellas, tool handles or the like, non-coniferous	木棒,适合制手杖、伞柄、工具把柄及类似品,非针叶木的	4404.2000	15
Wool grease	羊毛脂	1505.0000	
Wool or other animal hair or other textile materials, prepared for use in making wigs or the like	羊毛、其他动物毛或其他纺织材料,作假发及类似品用的	6703.0000	4
Wool tops	羊毛条	5105.2900	5
Wool, not carded or combed, carbonized	羊毛,碳化的	5101.3000	48
Wool, not carded or combed, degreased, not carbonized, nes	羊毛,未梳的,脱脂的,未碳化,其他	5101.2900	48

W

Article Description	商品名称	Tariff Code	D. R.
Wool, not carded or combed, degreased, not carbonized, shorn wool	羊毛,未梳的,脱脂的,未碳化,剪羊毛	5101.2100	48
Wool, not carded or combed, greasy, nes	羊毛,未梳的,含脂的,其他	5101.1900	48
Wool, not carded or combed, greasy, shorn wool	羊毛,未梳的,含脂的,剪羊毛	5101.1100	48
Wool, carded	羊毛,粗梳的	5105.1000	5
Wool, combed in fragments	羊毛,精梳的,片毛	5105.2100	5
Wool, combed, nes	羊毛,精梳的,其他	5105.2900	5
Word-processing machines	文字处理机	8469.0011	
Work holders	工件夹具	8466.2000	3
Working machinery of cereals or dried leguminous vegetables, other than farm-type machinery	加工机器,谷物、干豆用,农业用机器除外	8437.8000	3
Working machinery parts, of cereals or dried leguminous vegetables, other than farm-type machinery	加工机器零件,谷物、干豆用,农业用机器除外	8437.9000	3
Works trucks fitted with lifting or handing equipment, nes	工作车,装有升降或搬运装置的,其他	8427.9000	7
Works trucks parts, of self-propelled works trucks, not fitted with lifting or handling equipment, for short distance transport of goods	工作车零件,自驱动工作车的,短距离运输货物的,未装有提升或搬运设备	8709.9000	3
Works trucks, electrical, not fitted with lifting or handling equipment, for short distance transport of goods, nes	工作车,电动的,短距离运输货物的,未装有提升或搬运设备,其他	8709.1190	
Works trucks, self-propelled, not fitted with lifting or handling equipment, for short distance transport of goods, nes	工作车,自驱动的,短距离运输货物的,未装有提升或搬运设备,其他	8709.1990	
Workshops, for railway or tramway maintenance or service	工场车,铁道及电车道用	8604.0099	37
Worn appliances, to compensate for a defect or disability	穿戴器具,弥补生理缺陷或残疾的	9021.9000	3
Worn clothing and other worn articles	旧衣物	6309.0000	1
Worsted comber	毛精梳机	8445.1220	7
Worsted ring spinning frame	毛细纱机	8445.2042	7
Worsted roving machines	毛纺粗纱机	8445.1322	7
Woven cloth, of iron or steel wire, nes	机织品,钢铁丝制,其他	7314.1900	36
Woven cloth, of stainless steel wire, nes	机织品,不锈钢丝制,其他	7314.1400	36
Woven fabrics of a width exceeding 30cm, plain weave, weighing less than $250g/m^2$, of filaments measuring per single yarn not more than 136 tex, of glass fibres	机织物,宽度超过30厘米的长丝平纹织物,每平方米重量不超过250克,单根纱线细度不超过136特克斯,玻璃纤维制	7019.5200	468
Woven fabrics of a width not exceeding 30cm, of glass fibres	机织物,宽度不超过30厘米的,玻璃纤维制	7019.5100	468

W

Article Description	商品名称	Tariff Code	D. R.
Woven fabrics of carded fine animal hair, containing 85% or more by weight of wool or of fine animal hair, of a weight not exceeding $300g/m^2$, of fine animal hair, nes	动物细毛的机织物,粗梳的,按重量计羊毛或动物细毛含量在85%及以上,每平方米重量不超过300克,其他动物细毛的	5111.1119	4568
Woven fabrics of carded fine animal hair, containing 85% or more by weight of wool or of fine animal hair, of a weight not exceeding $300g/m^2$, of goats	动物细毛的机织物,粗梳的,按重量计羊毛或动物细毛含量在85%及以上,每平方米重量不超过300克,山羊绒的	5111.1111	4568
Woven fabrics of carded fine animal hair, containing 85% or more by weight of wool or of fine animal hair, of fine animal hair	动物细毛的机织物,粗梳的,按重量计羊毛或动物细毛含量在85%及以上,其他动物细毛的	5111.1919	4568
Woven fabrics of carded fine animal hair, containing 85% or more by weight of wool or of fine animal hair, of goats	动物细毛的机织物,粗梳的,按重量计羊毛或动物细毛含量在85%及以上,山羊绒的	5111.1911	4568
Woven fabrics of carded fine animal hair, mixed mainly or solely with man-made filaments	动物细毛的机织物,粗梳的,主要或仅与化学纤维长丝混纺	5111.2000	4568
Woven fabrics of carded fine animal hair, mixed mainly or solely with man-made staple fibres	动物细毛的机织物,粗梳的,主要或仅与化学纤维短纤混纺	5111.3000	4568
Woven fabrics of carded fine animal hair, nes	动物细毛的机织物,粗梳的,其他	5111.9000	4568
Woven fabrics of carded wool, mixed mainly or solely with man-made staple fibres	羊毛的机织物,粗梳的,主要或仅与化学纤维短纤混纺	5111.3000	4568
Woven fabrics of carded wool, containing 85% or more by weight of wool or of fine animal hair	羊毛的机织物,粗梳的,按重量计羊毛或动物细毛含量在85%及以上	5111.1990	4568
Woven fabrics of carded wool, containing 85% or more by weight of wool or of fine animal hair, of a weight not exceeding $300g/m^2$	羊毛的机织物,粗梳的,按重量计羊毛或动物细毛含量在85%及以上,每平方米重量不超过300克	5111.1190	4568
Woven fabrics of carded wool, mixed mainly or solely with man-made filaments	羊毛的机织物,粗梳的,主要或仅与化学纤维长丝混纺	5111.2000	4568
Woven fabrics of carded wool, nes	羊毛的机织物,粗梳的,其他	5111.9000	4568
Woven fabrics of coarse animal hair	动物粗毛的机织物	5113.0000	4568
Woven fabrics of combed fine animal hair, containing 85% or more by weight of wool or of fine animal hair, nes	动物细毛的机织物,精梳的,按重量计羊毛或动物细毛含量在85%及以上,其他	5112.1900	4568
Woven fabrics of combed fine animal hair, containing 85% or more by weight of wool or of fine animal hair, of a weight not exceeding $200g/m^2$	动物细毛的机织物,精梳的按重量计羊毛或动物细毛含量在85%及以上,每平方米重量不超过200克	5112.1100	4568
Woven fabrics of combed fine animal hair, mixed mainly or solely with man-made filaments	动物细毛的机织物,精梳的,主要或仅与化学纤维长丝混纺	5112.2000	4568
Woven fabrics of combed fine animal hair, mixed mainly or solely with man-made staple fibres	动物细毛的机织物,精梳的,主要或仅与化学纤维短纤混纺	5112.3000	4568
Woven fabrics of combed fine animal hair, nes	动物细毛的机织物,精梳的,其他	5112.9000	4568
Woven fabrics of combed wool, mixed mainly or solely with man-made filaments	羊毛的机织物,精梳的,主要或仅与化学纤维长丝混纺	5112.2000	4568

W

Article Description	商品名称	Tariff Code	D. R.
Woven fabrics of combed wool, mixed mainly or solely with man-made staple fibres	羊毛的机织物,精梳的,主要或仅与化学纤维短纤混纺	5112. 3000	4568
Woven fabrics of combed wool, containing 85% or more by weight of wool or of fine animal hair, nes	羊毛的机织物,精梳的,按重量计羊毛或动物细毛含量在85%及以上,其他	5112. 1900	4568
Woven fabrics of combed wool, containing 85% or more by weight of wool or of fine animal hair, of a weight not exceeding 200g/m^2	羊毛的机织物,精梳的,按重量计羊毛或动物细毛含量在85%及以上,每平方米重量不超过200克	5112. 1100	4568
Woven fabrics of combed wool, nes	羊毛的机织物,精梳的,其他	5112. 9000	4568
Woven fabrics of cotton, containing 85% or more by weight of cotton, weighing more than 200g/m^2, bleached, 3-thread or 4-thread twill, including cross twill	棉机织物,按重量计含棉量在85%及以上,每平方米重量超过200克,漂白,三线或四线斜纹机织物,包括双面斜纹机织物	5209. 2200	468
Woven fabrics of cotton, containing 85% or more by weight of cotton, weighing more than 200g/m^2, bleached, other fabrics	棉机织物,按重量计含棉量在85%及以上,每平方米重量超过200克,漂白,其他机织物	5209. 2900	468
Woven fabrics of cotton, containing 85% or more by weight of cotton, weighing more than 200g/m^2, bleached, plain weave	棉机织物,按重量计含棉量在85%及以上,每平方米重量超过200克,漂白,平纹机织物	5209. 2100	468
Woven fabrics of cotton, containing 85% or more by weight of cotton, weighing more than 200g/m^2, dyed, 3-thread or 4-thread twill, including cross twill	棉机织物,按重量计含棉量在85%及以上,每平方米重量超过200克,染色,三线或四线斜纹机织物,包括双面斜纹机织物	5209. 3200	468
Woven fabrics of cotton, containing 85% or more by weight of cotton, weighing more than 200g/m^2, dyed, other fabrics	棉机织物,按重量计含棉量在85%及以上,每平方米重量超过200克,染色,其他机织物	5209. 3900	468
Woven fabrics of cotton, containing 85% or more by weight of cotton, weighing more than 200g/m^2, dyed, plain weave	棉机织物,按重量计含棉量在85%及以上,每平方米重量超过200克,染色,平纹机织物	5209. 3100	468
Woven fabrics of cotton, containing 85% or more by weight of cotton, weighing more than 200g/m^2, of yarns of different colours, denim	棉机织物,按重量计含棉量在85%及以上,每平方米重量超过200克,色织,粗斜纹布	5209. 4200	468
Woven fabrics of cotton, containing 85% or more by weight of cotton, weighing more than 200g/m^2, of yarns of different colours, other fabrics	棉机织物,按重量计含棉量在85%及以上,每平方米重量超过200克,色织,其他机织物	5209. 4900	468
Woven fabrics of cotton, containing 85% or more by weight of cotton, weighing more than 200g/m^2, of yarns of different colours, other fabrics of 3-thread or 4-thread twill, including cross twill	棉机织物,按重量计含棉量在85%及以上,每平方米重量超过200克,色织,三线或四线斜纹机织物,包括双面斜纹机织物	5209. 4300	468
Woven fabrics of cotton, containing 85% or more by weight of cotton, weighing more than 200g/m^2, of yarns of different colours, plain weave	棉机织物,按重量计含棉量在85%及以上,每平方米重量超过200克,色织,平纹机织物	5209. 4100	468

Article Description	商品名称	Tariff Code	D. R.
Woven fabrics of cotton, containing 85% or more by weight of cotton, weighing more than 200g/m², printed, 3-thread or 4-thread twill, including cross twill	棉机织物,按重量计含棉量在85%及以上,每平方米重量超过200克,印花,三线或四线斜纹机织物,包括双面斜纹机织物	5209.5200	468
Woven fabrics of cotton, containing 85% or more by weight of cotton, weighing more than 200g/m², printed, other fabrics	棉机织物,按重量计含棉量在85%及以上,每平方米重量超过200克,印花,其他机织物	5209.5900	468
Woven fabrics of cotton, containing 85% or more by weight of cotton, weighing more than 200g/m², printed, plain weave	棉机织物,按重量计含棉量在85%及以上,每平方米重量超过200克,印花,平纹机织物	5209.5100	468
Woven fabrics of cotton, containing 85% or more by weight of cotton, weighing more than 200g/m², unbleached, 3-thread or 4-thread twill, including cross twill	棉机织物,按重量计含棉量在85%及以上,每平方米重量超过200克,未漂白,三线或四线斜纹机织物,包括双面斜纹机织物	5209.1200	468
Woven fabrics of cotton, containing 85% or more by weight of cotton, weighing more than 200g/m², unbleached, other fabrics	棉机织物,按重量计含棉量在85%及以上,每平方米重量超过200克,未漂白,其他机织物	5209.1900	468
Woven fabrics of cotton, containing 85% or more by weight of cotton, weighing more than 200g/m², unbleached, plain weave	棉机织物,按重量计含棉量在85%及以上,每平方米重量超过200克,未漂白,平纹机织物	5209.1100	468
Woven fabrics of cotton, containing 85% or more by weight of cotton, weighing not more than 200g/m², bleached, 3-thread or 4-thread twill, inluding cross twill	棉机织物,按重量计含棉量在85%及以上,每平方米重量不超过200克,漂白,三线或四线斜纹机织物,包括双面斜纹机织物	5208.2300	468
Woven fabrics of cotton, containing 85% or more by weight of cotton, weighing not more than 200g/m², bleached, other fabrics	棉机织物,按重量计含棉量在85%及以上,每平方米重量不超过200克,漂白,其他机织物	5208.2900	468
Woven fabrics of cotton, containing 85% or more by weight of cotton, weighing not more than 200g/m², bleached, plain weave, weighing more than 100g/m²	棉机织物,按重量计含棉量在85%及以上,每平方米重量不超过200克,漂白,平纹机织物,每平方米重量超过100克	5208.2200	468
Woven fabrics of cotton, containing 85% or more by weight of cotton, weighing not more than 200g/m², bleached, plain weave, weighing not more than 100g/m²	棉机织物,按重量计含棉量在85%及以上,每平方米重量不超过200克,漂白,平纹机织物,每平方米重量不超过100克	5208.2100	468
Woven fabrics of cotton, containing 85% or more by weight of cotton, weighing not more than 200g/m², dyed, 3-thread or 4-thread twill, including cross twill	棉机织物,按重量计含棉量在85%及以上,每平方米重量不超过200克,染色,三线或四线斜纹机织物,包括双面斜纹机织物	5208.3300	468
Woven fabrics of cotton, containing 85% or more by weight of cotton, weighing not more than 200g/m², dyed, other fabrics	棉机织物,按重量计含棉量在85%及以上,每平方米重量不超过200克,染色,其他机织物	5208.3900	468

Article Description	商品名称	Tariff Code	D. R.
Woven fabrics of cotton, containing 85% or more by weight of cotton, weighing not more than $200g/m^2$, dyed, plain weave, weighing more than $100g/m^2$	棉机织物,按重量计含棉量在85%及以上,每平方米重量不超过200克,染色,平纹机织物,每平方米重量超过100克	5208.3200	468
Woven fabrics of cotton, containing 85% or more by weight of cotton, weighing not more than $200g/m^2$, dyed, plain weave, weighing not more than $100g/m^2$	棉机织物,按重量计含棉量在85%及以上,每平方米重量不超过200克,染色,平纹机织物,每平方米重量不超过100克	5208.3100	468
Woven fabrics of cotton, containing 85% or more by weight of cotton, weighing not more than $200g/m^2$, of yarns of different colours, 3-thread or 4-thread twill, including cross twill	棉机织物,按重量计含棉量在85%及以上,每平方米重量不超过200克,色织,三线或四线斜纹机织物,包括双面斜纹机织物	5208.4300	468
Woven fabrics of cotton, containing 85% or more by weight of cotton, weighing not more than $200g/m^2$, of yarns of different colours, other fabrics	棉机织物,按重量计含棉量在85%及以上,每平方米重量不超过200克,色织,其他机织物	5208.4900	468
Woven fabrics of cotton, containing 85% or more by weight of cotton, weighing not more than $200g/m^2$, of yarns of different colours, plain weave, weighing more than $100g/m^2$	棉机织物,按重量计含棉量在85%及以上,每平方米重量不超过200克,色织,平纹机织物,每平方米重量超过100克	5208.4200	468
Woven fabrics of cotton, containing 85% or more by weight of cotton, weighing not more than $200g/m^2$, of yarns of different colours, plain weave, weighing not more than $100g/m^2$	棉机织物,按重量计含棉量在85%及以上,每平方米重量不超过200克,色织,平纹机织物,每平方米重量不超过100克	5208.4100	468
Woven fabrics of cotton, containing 85% or more by weight of cotton, weighing not more than $200g/m^2$, printed, 3-thread or 4-thread twill, including cross twill	棉机织物,按重量计含棉量在85%及以上,每平方米重量不超过200克,印花,三线或四线斜纹机织物,包括双面斜纹机织物	5208.5910	468
Woven fabrics of cotton, containing 85% or more by weight of cotton, weighing not more than $200g/m^2$, printed, other fabrics	棉机织物,按重量计含棉量在85%及以上,每平方米重量不超过200克,印花,其他机织物	5208.5990	468
Woven fabrics of cotton, containing 85% or more by weight of cotton, weighing not more than $200g/m^2$, printed, plain weave, weighing more than $100g/m^2$	棉机织物,按重量计含棉量在85%及以上,每平方米重量不超过200克,印花,平纹机织物,每平方米重量超过100克	5208.5200	468
Woven fabrics of cotton, containing 85% or more by weight of cotton, weighing not more than $200g/m^2$, printed, plain weave, weighing not more than $100g/m^2$	棉机织物,按重量计含棉量在85%及以上,每平方米重量不超过200克,印花,平纹机织物,每平方米重量不超过100克	5208.5100	468
Woven fabrics of cotton, containing 85% or more by weight of cotton, weighing not more than $200g/m^2$, unbleached, 3-thread or 4-thread twill, including cross twill	棉机织物,按重量计含棉量在85%及以上,每平方米重量不超过200克,未漂白,三线或四线斜纹机织物,包括双面斜纹机织物	5208.1300	468

Article Description	商品名称	Tariff Code	D. R.
Woven fabrics of cotton, containing 85% or more by weight of cotton, weighing not more than $200g/m^2$, unbleached, other fabrics	棉机织物,按重量计含棉量在85%及以上,每平方米重量不超过200克,未漂白,其他机织物	5208.1900	468
Woven fabrics of cotton, containing 85% or more by weight of cotton, weighing not more than $200g/m^2$, unbleached, plain weave, weighing more than $100g/m^2$	棉机织物,按重量计含棉量在85%及以上,每平方米重量不超过200克,未漂白,平纹机织物,每平方米重量超过100克	5208.1200	468
Woven fabrics of cotton, containing 85% or more by weight of cotton, weighing not more than $200g/m^2$, unbleached, plain weave, weighing not more than $100g/m^2$	棉机织物,按重量计含棉量在85%及以上,每平方米重量不超过200克,未漂白,平纹机织物,每平方米重量不超过100克	5208.1100	468
Woven fabrics of cotton, containing less than 85% by weight of cotton, mixed mainly or solely with man-made fibres, weighing more than $200g/m^2$, bleached	棉机织物,按重量计含棉量在85%以下,主要或仅与化学纤维混纺,每平方米重量超过200克,漂白	5211.2000	468
Woven fabrics of cotton, containing less than 85% by weight of cotton, mixed mainly or solely with man-made fibres, weighing more than $200g/m^2$, dyed, 3-thread or 4-thread twill, including cross twill	棉机织物,按重量计含棉量在85%以下,主要或仅与化学纤维混纺,每平方米重量超过200克,染色,三线或四线斜纹机织物,包括双面斜纹机织物	5211.3200	468
Woven fabrics of cotton, containing less than 85% by weight of cotton, mixed mainly or solely with man-made fibres, weighing more than $200g/m^2$, dyed, other fabrics	棉机织物,按重量计含棉量在85%以下,主要或仅与化学纤维混纺,每平方米重量超过200克,染色,其他机织物	5211.3900	468
Woven fabrics of cotton, containing less than 85% by weight of cotton, mixed mainly or solely with man-made fibres, weighing more than $200g/m^2$, dyed, plain weave	棉机织物,按重量计含棉量在85%以下,主要或仅与化学纤维混纺,每平方米重量超过200克,染色,平纹机织物	5211.3100	468
Woven fabrics of cotton, containing less than 85% by weight of cotton, mixed mainly or solely with man-made fibres, weighing more than $200g/m^2$, of yarns of different colours, denim	棉机织物,按重量计含棉量在85%以下,主要或仅与化学纤维混纺,每平方米重量超过200克,色织,粗斜纹布	5211.4200	468
Woven fabrics of cotton, containing less than 85% by weight of cotton, mixed mainly or solely with man-made fibres, weighing more than $200g/m^2$, of yarns of different colours, other fabrics	棉机织物,按重量计含棉量在85%以下,主要或仅与化学纤维混纺,每平方米重量超过200克,色织,其他机织物	5211.4900	468
Woven fabrics of cotton, containing less than 85% by weight of cotton, mixed mainly or solely with man-made fibres, weighing more than $200g/m^2$, of yarns of different colours, other fabrics of 3-thread or 4-thread twill, including cross twill	棉机织物,按重量计含棉量在85%以下,主要或仅与化学纤维混纺,每平方米重量超过200克,色织,三线或四线斜纹机织物,包括双面斜纹机织物	5211.4300	468

Article Description	商品名称	Tariff Code	D. R.
Woven fabrics of cotton, containing less than 85% by weight of cotton, mixed mainly or solely with man-made fibres, weighing more than 200g/m², of yarns of different colours, plainweave	棉机织物,按重量计含棉量在85%以下,主要或仅与化学纤维混纺,每平方米重量超过200克,色织,平纹机织物	5211.4100	468
Woven fabrics of cotton, containing less than 85% by weight of cotton, mixed mainly or solely with man-made fibres, weighing more than 200g/m², printed, 3-thread or 4-thread twill, including cross twill	棉机织物,按重量计含棉量在85%以下,主要或仅与化学纤维混纺,每平方米重量超过200克,印花,三线或四线斜纹机织物,包括双面斜纹机织物	5211.5200	468
Woven fabrics of cotton, containing less than 85% by weight of cotton, mixed mainly or solely with man-made fibres, weighing more than 200g/m², printed, other fabrics	棉机织物,按重量计含棉量在85%以下,主要或仅与化学纤维混纺,每平方米重量超过200克,印花,其他机织物	5211.5900	468
Woven fabrics of cotton, containing less than 85% by weight of cotton, mixed mainly or solely with man-made fibres, weighing more than 200g/m², printed, plain weave	棉机织物,按重量计含棉量在85%以下,主要或仅与化学纤维混纺,每平方米重量超过200克,印花,平纹机织物	5211.5100	468
Woven fabrics of cotton, containing less than 85% by weight of cotton, mixed mainly or solely with man-made fibres, weighing more than 200g/m², unbleached, 3-thread or 4-thread twill, including cross twill	棉机织物,按重量计含棉量在85%以下,主要或仅与化学纤维混纺,每平方米重量超过200克,未漂白,三线或四线斜纹机织物,包括双面斜纹机织物	5211.1200	468
Woven fabrics of cotton, containing less than 85% by weight of cotton, mixed mainly or solely with man-made fibres, weighing more than 200g/m², unbleached, other fabrics	棉机织物,按重量计含棉量在85%以下,主要或仅与化学纤维混纺,每平方米重量超过200克,未漂白,其他机织物	5211.1900	468
Woven fabrics of cotton, containing less than 85% by weight of cotton, mixed mainly or solely with man-made fibres, weighing more than 200g/m², unbleached, plain weave	棉机织物,按重量计含棉量在85%以下,主要或仅与化学纤维混纺,每平方米重量超过200克,未漂白,平纹机织物	5211.1100	468
Woven fabrics of cotton, containing less than 85% by weight of cotton, mixed mainly or solely with man-made fibres, weighing not more than 200g/m², bleached, 3-thread or 4-thread twill, including cross twill	棉机织物,按重量计含棉量在85%以下,主要或仅与化学纤维混纺,每平方米重量不超过200克,漂白,三线或四线斜纹机织物,包括双面斜纹机织物	5210.2910	468
Woven fabrics of cotton, containing less than 85% by weight of cotton, mixed mainly or solely with man-made fibres, weighing not more than 200g/m², bleached, other fabrics	棉机织物,按重量计含棉量在85%以下,主要或仅与化学纤维混纺,每平方米重量不超过200克,漂白,其他机织物	5210.2990	468
Woven fabrics of cotton, containing less than 85% by weight of cotton, mixed mainly or solely with man-made fibres, weighing not more than 200g/m², bleached, plain weave	棉机织物,按重量计含棉量在85%以下,主要或仅与化学纤维混纺,每平方米重量不超过200克,漂白,平纹机织物	5210.2100	468

Article Description	商品名称	Tariff Code	D. R.
Woven fabrics of cotton, containing less than 85% by weight of cotton, mixed mainly or solely with man-made fibres, weighing not more than 200g/m², dyed, 3-thread or 4-thread twill, including cross twill	棉机织物,按重量计含棉量在85%以下,主要或仅与化学纤维混纺,每平方米重量不超过200克,染色,三线或四线斜纹机织物,包括双面斜纹机织物	5210.3200	468
Woven fabrics of cotton, containing less than 85% by weight of cotton, mixed mainly or solely with man-made fibres, weighing not more than 200g/m², dyed, other fabrics	棉机织物,按重量计含棉量在85%以下,主要或仅与化学纤维混纺,每平方米重量不超过200克,染色,其他机织物	5210.3900	468
Woven fabrics of cotton, containing less than 85% by weight of cotton, mixed mainly or solely with man-made fibres, weighing not more than 200g/m², dyed, plain weave	棉机织物,按重量计含棉量在85%以下,主要或仅与化学纤维混纺,每平方米重量不超过200克,染色,平纹机织物	5210.3100	468
Woven fabrics of cotton, containing less than 85% by weight of cotton, mixed mainly or solely with man-made fibres, weighing not more than 200g/m², of yarns of different colours, 3-thread or 4-thread twill, including cross twill	棉机织物,按重量计含棉量在85%以下,主要或仅与化学纤维混纺,每平方米重量不超过200克,色织,三线或四线斜纹机织物,包括双面斜纹机织物	5210.4910	468
Woven fabrics of cotton, containing less than 85% by weight of cotton, mixed mainly or solely with man-made fibres, weighing not more than 200g/m², of yarns of different colours, other fabrics	棉机织物,按重量计含棉量在85%以下,主要或仅与化学纤维混纺,每平方米重量不超过200克,色织,其他	5210.4990	468
Woven fabrics of cotton, containing less than 85% by weight of cotton, mixed mainly or solely with man-made fibres, weighing not more than 200g/m², of yarns of different colours, plain weave	棉机织物,按重量计含棉量在85%以下,主要或仅与化学纤维混纺,每平方米重量不超过200克,色织,平纹机织物	5210.4100	468
Woven fabrics of cotton, containing less than 85% by weight of cotton, mixed mainly or solely with man-made fibres, weighing not more than 200g/m², printed, 3-thread or 4-thread twill, including cross twill	棉机织物,按重量计含棉量在85%以下,主要或仅与化学纤维混纺,每平方米重量不超过200克,印花,三线或四线斜纹机织物,包括双面斜纹机织物	5210.5910	468
Woven fabrics of cotton, containing less than 85% by weight of cotton, mixed mainly or solely with man-made fibres, weighing not more than 200g/m², printed, other fabrics	棉机织物,按重量计含棉量在85%以下,主要或仅与化学纤维混纺,每平方米重量不超过200克,印花,其他机织物	5210.5990	468
Woven fabrics of cotton, containing less than 85% by weight of cotton, mixed mainly or solely with man-made fibres, weighing not more than 200g/m², printed, plain weave	棉机织物,按重量计含棉量在85%以下,主要或仅与化学纤维混纺,每平方米重量不超过200克,印花,平纹机织物	5210.5100	468
Woven fabrics of cotton, containing less than 85% by weight of cotton, mixed mainly or solely with man-made fibres, weighing not more than 200g/m², unbleached, 3-thread or 4-thread twill, including cross twill	棉机织物,按重量计含棉量在85%以下,主要或仅与化学纤维混纺,每平方米重量不超过200克,未漂白,三线或四线斜纹机织物,包括双面斜纹机织物	5210.1910	468

W

Article Description	商品名称	Tariff Code	D. R.
Woven fabrics of cotton, containing less than 85% by weight of cotton, mixed mainly or solely with man-made fibres, weighing not more than 200g/m², unbleached, other fabrics	棉机织物,按重量计含棉量在85%以下,主要或仅与化学纤维混纺,每平方米重量不超过200克,未漂白,其他机织物	5210.1990	468
Woven fabrics of cotton, containing less than 85% by weight of cotton, mixed mainly or solely with man-made fibres, weighing not more than 200g/m², unbleached, plain weave	棉机织物,按重量计含棉量在85%以下,主要或仅与化学纤维混纺,每平方米重量不超过200克,未漂白,平纹机织物	5210.1100	468
Woven fabrics of cotton, weighing more than 200g/m², bleached, nes	棉机织物,每平方米重量超过200克,漂白,其他	5212.2200	468
Woven fabrics of cotton, weighing more than 200g/m², dyed, nes	棉机织物,每平方米重量超过200克,染色,其他	5212.2300	468
Woven fabrics of cotton, weighing more than 200g/m², of yarns of different colours, nes	棉机织物,每平方米重量超过200克,色织,其他	5212.2400	468
Woven fabrics of cotton, weighing more than 200g/m², printed, nes	棉机织物,每平方米重量超过200克,印花,其他	5212.2500	468
Woven fabrics of cotton, weighing more than 200g/m², unbleached, nes	棉机织物,每平方米重量超过200克,未漂白,其他	5212.2100	468
Woven fabrics of cotton, weighing not more than 200g/m², bleached, nes	棉机织物,每平方米重量不超过200克,漂白,其他	5212.1200	468
Woven fabrics of cotton, weighing not more than 200g/m², dyed, nes	棉机织物,每平方米重量不超过200克,染色,其他	5212.1300	468
Woven fabrics of cotton, weighing not more than 200g/m², of yarns of different colours, nes	棉机织物,每平方米重量不超过200克,色织,其他	5212.1400	468
Woven fabrics of cotton, weighing not more than 200g/m², printed, nes	棉机织物,每平方米重量不超过200克,印花,其他	5212.1500	468
Woven fabrics of cotton, weighing not more than 200g/m², unbleached, nes	棉机织物,每平方米重量不超过200克,未漂白,其他	5212.1100	468
Woven fabrics of horsehair	马毛的机织物	5113.0000	4568
Woven fabrics of Metal thread, combined with man-made fibres, of a kind used in apparel, as furnishing fabrics or for similar purposes	金属纱线的机织物,与化学纤维混制,用于衣着、装饰及类似用途	5809.0020	468
Woven fabrics of metal thread, combined with cotton, of a kind used in apparel, as furnishing fabrics or for similar purposes	金属纱线的机织物,与棉混制,用于衣着、装饰及类似用途	5809.0010	468
Woven fabrics of metal thread, of a kind used in apparel, as furnishing fabrics or for similar purposes, nes	金属纱线的机织物,用于衣着、装饰及类似用途,其他	5809.0090	468
Woven fabrics of rovings, of glass fibres	粗纱机织物,玻璃纤维制	7019.4000	46
Woven fabrics, of glass fibres, nes	机织物,玻璃纤维制,其他	7019.5900	468
Wrapping paper, sulphite, uncoated	包装纸,亚硫酸盐浆的,未经涂布的	4805.3000	458
Wrist-watches, electrically operated whether or not incorporating a stop-watch facility, nes	手表,电力驱动的,不论是否附有秒表装置,其他	9102.1900	56

Article Description	商品名称	Tariff Code	D. R.
Wrist-watches, electrically operated whether or not incorporating a stop-watch facility, with case of precious metal or of metal clad with precious metal, nes	手表,电力驱动的,不论是否附有秒表装置,表壳用贵金属或包贵金属制成的,其他	9101. 1990	56
Wrist-watches, electrically operated whether or not incorporating a stop-watch facility, with mechanical display only, nes	手表,电力驱动的,不论是否附有秒表装置,仅有机械指示器的,其他	9102. 1100	56
Wrist-watches, electrically operated whether or not incorporating a stop-watch facility, with mechanical display only, with case of precious metal or of metal clad with precious metal	手表,电力驱动的,不论是否附有秒表装置,仅有机械指示器的,表壳用贵金属或包贵金属制成的	9101. 1100	56
Wrist-watches, electrically operated whether or not incorporating a stop-watch facility, with optoelectronic display only, nes	手表,电力驱动的,不论是否附有秒表装置,仅有光电显示器的,其他	9102. 1200	56
Wrist-watches, electrically operated whether or not incorporating a stop-watch facility, with optoelectronic display only, with case of precious metal or of metal clad with precious metal	手表,电力驱动的,不论是否附有秒表装置,仅有光电显示器的,表壳用贵金属或包贵金属制成的	9101. 1910	56
Wrist-watches, whether or not incorporating a stop-watch facility, automatic winding, nes	手表,不论是否附有秒表装置,自动上弦的,其他	9102. 2100	56
Wrist-watches, whether or not incorporating a stop-watch facility, automatic winding, with case of precious metal or of metal clad with precious metal	手表,不论是否附有秒表装置,自动上弦的,表壳用贵金属或包贵金属制成的	9101. 2100	56
Wrist-watches, whether or not incorporating a stop-watch facility, nes	手表,不论是否附有秒表装置,其他	9102. 2900	56
Wrist-watches, whether or not incorporating a stop-watch facility, with case of precious metal or of metal clad with precious metal, nes	手表,不论是否附有秒表装置,表壳用贵金属或包贵金属制成的、其他	9101. 2900	56
Writing brushes	毛笔	9603. 3020	
Writing compendiums of paper or paperboard, containing an assortment of paper stationery	书写册子,内装各种纸制文具	4817. 3000	6
Wulfenite, roasted	钼铅矿,已焙烧	2613. 1000	146

W

X

Article Description	商品名称	Tariff Code	D. R.
Xanthates	黄原酸酯(或盐)	2930. 9020	36
Xanthophyll	叶黄素,胡萝卜醇	3203. 0019	34
Xenotime	磷钇矿	2530. 9020	13456
Xiang pears, fresh	香梨,鲜的	0808. 2013	1
XSBR latex	羧基丁苯橡胶胶乳	4002. 1110	12
XSBR, nes	羧基丁苯橡胶(XSBR),其他	4002. 1990	1346
Xuan paper	宣纸	4802. 1010	3458
Xylitol	木糖醇	2905. 4910	36
Xylole	粗二甲苯	2707. 3000	6
Xylophones	木琴	9206. 0000	5
X-ray intensifiers	X 射线影像增强器	9022. 9010	
X-ray measuring or detecting instruments and apparatus	X 射线的测量或检验仪器及装置	9030. 1000	
X-ray security inspecting equipment, low dosage	X 射线安全检查设备,低剂量	9022. 1910	
X-ray tubes	X 射线管	9022. 3000	
X-rays apparatus, for dental uses, nes	X 射线的应用设备,牙科用,其他	9022. 1300	3
X-rays apparatus, for medical, surgical or veterinary uses, nes	X 射线的应用设备,医疗、外科或兽医用,其他	9022. 1400	3
X-rays apparatus, nes	X 射线的应用设备,其他	9022. 1990	3
X-rays computed tomography apparatus	X 射线断层检查仪	9022. 1200	

Y

Article Description	商品名称	Tariff Code	D. R.
Ya pears, fresh	鸭梨,鲜的	0808. 2012	1
Yachts, inflatable, for pleasure or sports	快艇,充气的,娱乐或运动用	8903. 1000	58
Yarn of carded wool, not put up for retail sale, containing 85% or more by weight of wool	羊毛纱线,粗梳的,非供零售用,按重量计羊毛含量在85%及以上	5106. 1000	346
Yarn of carded wool, not put up for retail sale, containing less than 85% by weight of wool	羊毛纱线,粗梳的,非供零售用,按重量计羊毛含量在85%以下	5106. 2000	346
Yarn of coarse animal hair, whether or not put up for retail sale	动物粗毛纱线,不论是否供零售用	5110. 0000	56
Yarn of combed wool, not put up for retail sale, containing 85% or more by weight of wool	羊毛纱线,精梳的,非供零售用,按重量计羊毛含量在85%及以上	5107. 1000	346
Yarn of combed wool, not put up for retail sale, containing less than 85% by weight of wool	羊毛纱线,精梳的,非供零售用,按重量计羊毛含量在85%以下	5107. 2000	346
Yarn of fine animal hair, combed, not put up for retail sale, containing 85% or more by weight of fine animal hair, of goats	动物细毛纱线,精梳的,非供零售用,按重量计动物细毛含量在85%及以上的,山羊绒的	5108. 2011	346
Yarn of fine animal hair, carded, not put up for retail sale, containing 85% or more by weight of fine animal hair, nes	动物细毛纱线,粗梳的,非供零售用,按重量计动物细毛含量在85%及以上的,其他	5108. 1019	346
Yarn of fine animal hair, carded, not put up for retail sale, containing 85% or more by weight of fine animal hair, of goats	动物细毛纱线,粗梳的,非供零售用,按重量计动物细毛含量在85%及以上的,山羊绒的	5108. 1011	346
Yarn of fine animal hair, carded, not put up for retail sale, nes	动物细毛纱线,粗梳的,非供零售用,其他	5108. 1090	346
Yarn of fine animal hair, combed, not put up for retail sale, containing 85% or more by weight of fine animal hair, nes	动物细毛纱线,精梳的,非供零售用,按重量计动物细毛含量在85%及以上的,其他	5108. 2019	346
Yarn of fine animal hair, combed, not put up for retail sale, nes	动物细毛纱线,精梳的,非供零售用,其他	5108. 2090	346
Yarn of fine animal hair, put up for retail sale, containing 85% or more by weight of wool or of fine animal hair, of fine animal hair, nes	动物细毛纱线,供零售用,按重量计羊毛或动物细毛含量在85%及以上,其他动物细毛的	5109. 1019	346
Yarn of fine animal hair, put up for retail sale, containing 85% or more by weight of wool or of fine animal hair, of goats	动物细毛纱线,供零售用,按重量计羊毛或动物细毛含量在85%及以上,山羊绒的	5109. 1011	346
Yarn of fine animal hair, put up for retail sale, nes	动物细毛纱线,供零售用,其他	5109. 1090	346
Yarn of fine animal hair, put up for retail sale, of fine animal hair, nes	动物细毛纱线,供零售用,其他动物细毛的	5109. 9019	346
Yarn of fine animal hair, put up for retail sale, of goats	动物细毛纱线,供零售用,山羊绒的	5109. 9011	346

Y

Y

Article Description	商品名称	Tariff Code	D. R.
Yarn of horse hair, whether or not put up for retail sale	马毛纱线,不论是否供零售用	5110. 0000	56
Yarn of wool, put up for retail sale	羊毛纱线,供零售用	5109. 9090	346
Yarn spun from silk waste, not put up for retail sale, nes	绢纺纱线,非供零售用,其他	5005. 0090	356
Yarn spun from silk waste, put up for retail sale	丝纱钱及绢纺纱线,供零售用	5006. 0000	356
Yellow croaker(pseudosicaena), fresh or chilled	黄鱼,鲜或冷的	0302. 6920	18
Yellow croaker(pseudosicaena), frozen	黄鱼,冻的	0303. 7920	18
Yellow croaker(pseudosicaena), salted or in brine	黄鱼,盐腌及盐渍的	0305. 6920	4
Yellow rice wine	黄酒	2206. 0010	248
Yellowfin tunas(thunnus albacares), fresh or chilled	黄鳍金枪鱼,鲜或冷的	0302. 3200	18
Yellowfin tunas(thunnus albacares), frozen	黄鳍金枪鱼,冻的	0303. 4200	18
Yogurt	酸乳	0403. 1000	
Yttrium	钇	2805. 3019	56
Yttrium oxide	氧化钇	2846. 9011	
Yttrium, intermixed or interalloyed with rare-earth metals, battery grade	钇,与稀土相互混合或相互熔合,电池级	2805. 3021	56
Yttrium, intermixed or interalloyed with rare-earth metals, nes	钇,与稀土相互混合或相互熔合,其他	2805. 3029	56

Z

Article Description	商品名称	Tariff Code	D. R.
Z sections, not further worked than hot-rolled, hot-drawn or extruded	乙字钢,除热轧、热拉拔或热挤压外未经进一步加工	7216. 5010	468
Zein	玉米蛋白	3504. 0090	1346
Zidovudine and their salts	齐多夫定及它们的盐	2938. 9010	34
Zinc alloys	锌合金	7901. 2000	16
Zinc articles, nes	锌制品,其他	7907. 0090	16
Zinc biscuits	电池壳体坯料,锌制	7907. 0030	16
Zinc dust	锌末	7903. 1000	16
Zinc ores and concentrates	锌矿砂及其精矿	2608. 0000	146
Zinc oxide	氧化锌	2817. 0010	34
Zinc peroxide	过氧化锌	2817. 0090	34
Zinc waste and scrap	锌废碎料	7902. 0000	16
Zinc white (zinc oxide)	锌白	2817. 0010	34
Zinc, containing by weight 99. 99% or more of zinc, but less than 99. 995%	锌,按重量计含锌量在 99. 99% 及以上,但少于 99. 995%	7901. 1190	16
Zinc, containing by weight 99. 995% or more of zinc	锌,按重量计含锌量在 99. 995% 及以上	7901. 1110	16
Zinc, containing by weight less than 99. 99% of zinc	锌,按重量计含锌量低于 99. 99%	7901. 1200	16
Zincite	红锌矿	2608. 0000	146
Zine sulphate	硫酸锌	2833. 2930	
Zipeprol (INN); salts thereof	齐培丙醇(INN)以及盐	2933. 5500	36
Zircon sands	锆英石	2615. 1000	1346
Zirconium articles, nes	锆制品,其他	8109. 9000	16
Zirconium carbonate	碳酸锆	2836. 9950	
Zirconium chloride oxides and chloride hydroxides	锆的氯氧化物及氢氧基氯化物	2827. 4910	
Zirconium dioxide	二氧化锆	2825. 6000	
Zirconium ores and concentrates	锆矿砂及其精矿	2615. 1000	1346
Zirconium powders	锆粉末	8109. 2000	16
Zirconium, unwrought	锆,未锻轧	8109. 2000	16

Else

Article Description	商品名称	Tariff Code	D. R.
1,1,1-trichloroethane(methylchloro form)	1,1,1-三氯乙烷(甲基氯仿)	2903.1910	36
1,1,1-trichloro-2,2-bis(p-chlorophenyl)ethane	1,1,1-三氯-2,2-双(4-氯苯基)乙烷	2903.6200	36
1,1,3,3,3-pentafluro-2-trifluromethyl-1-propene	1,1,3,3,3-五氟-2 三氟甲基-1-丙烯	2903.3910	36
1,2,3,4,5,6-hexachlorocyclohexane	1,2,3,4,5,6-六氯环已烷	2903.5100	36
1,2-dichloroethane(ethylene dichloride)	1,2-二氯乙烷	2903.1500	36
1-(1,3-benzodioxol-5-yl) propan-2-one	1-(1,3-苯并二茂-5 基)丙烷-2 酮	2932.9200	36
1-butene	1-丁烯	2901.2310	368
1-chloro-2,3-epoxypropane	1-氯-2,3-环氧丙烷	2910.3000	36
1-cyanoguanidine	1-氰基胍	2926.2000	36
1-naphthylamine (α-naphthy lamine) and their derivatives;salts thereof	1-萘胺(α-萘胺)及其衍生物以及它们的盐	2921.4500	36
2,2-diphenyl-2-hydroxyacetic acid	2,2-二苯基-2-羟基乙酸	2918.1910	36
2,2'-oxydiethanol	2,2'-氧联二乙醇	2909.4100	36
2,4,5-T(ISO), its salts and esters	2,4,5-涕(ISO)及其盐或酯	2918.9100	36
2, 4, 5-trichlorophenoxyacetic acid, its salts and esters	2,4,5-三氯苯氧基乙酸及其盐或酯	2918.9100	36
2,5-dimethyl hexandiol	2,5-二甲基已二醇	2905.3910	36
2,6-diethylaniline	2,6-二乙基苯胺	2921.4940	36
2,6-methyl ethyl aniline	2,6-甲基乙基苯胺	2921.4930	36
2-acetamidobenzoic acid and its salts	2-乙酰氨基苯甲酸及其盐	2924.2300	36
2-butene	2-丁烯	2901.2320	368
2-ethyl-2-(hydroxymethyl) propane-1, 3-diol (trimethylolpropane)	2-乙基-2-(羟甲基)丙烷-1,3-二醇(三羟甲基丙烷)	2905.4100	36
2-furaldehyde(furfuraldehyde)	2-糠醛	2932.1200	36
2-hydroxy-4-methoxydibenzophenone	2-羟基-4-甲氧基二苯甲酮	2914.5020	36
2-methylpropylene	2-甲基丙烯	2901.2330	368
2-naphthols	2-萘酚	2907.1510	36
2-naphthylamine (β-naphthylamine) and their derivatives;salts thereof	2-萘胺(β-萘胺)及其衍生物以及它们的盐	2921.4500	36
2-phenylethyl alcohol	2-苯基乙醇	2906.2910	36
3,3-dimethyl-2-butanol(pinacolyl alcohol)	3,3-二甲基丁-2-醇(频哪基醇)	2905.1910	36
3,4-dichlorotrifluoride toluene	3,4-二氯三氟甲苯	2903.6920	36
3-chloro-1-propene	3-氯-1-丙烯	2903.2910	36
3-ethoxy-4-hydroxyben-zaldehyde	3-乙氧基-4-羟基苯甲醛	2912.4200	36
4,4-isopropylidenediphenol and its salts	4,4'-异亚丙基联苯酚及其盐	2907.2300	36
4-(4'-alkylcyclohexyl) cyclohexyl ethylene	4-(4'-烷基环已基)环已基乙烯	2902.9040	6
4-(4'-alkylphenyl)-1-(4'-alkylphenyl)-2-fluorobenzene	4-(4'-烷基苯基)-1-(4'-烷基苯基)-2-氟苯	2903.6930	36

Article Description	商品名称	Tariff Code	D. R.
4-cyano-2-dimethylamino-4,4-diphenylbutane	4-氰基-2-二甲氨基-4,4-二苯基丁烷	2926. 3000	36
4-hydroxy-3-methoxybenzaldehyde	3-甲氧基-4-羟基苯甲醛	2912. 4100	36
4-methl1-2-pentanone	4-甲基-2-戊酮	2914. 1300	36
6-aminopenicillanic acid	6-氨基青霉烷酸(6APA)	2941. 1093	
6-hexanolactam (epsilon-caprolactam)	6-己内酰胺	2933. 7100	36
7-aminocephalosporianic acid	7-氨基头孢烷酸	2941. 9051	
7-aminodeacetoxycefanoic acid	7-氨基脱乙酰氧基头孢烷酸	2941. 9051	
β-naphthol	β-萘酚	2907. 1510	36
Γ- carotene	胡萝卜素,天然 γ 型	3203. 0019	34